# COST ACCOUNTING

SECOND EDITION

# COST ACCOUNTING

**SHANE MORIARITY**
*University of Oklahoma*

**CARL P. ALLEN**

*1817*

HARPER & ROW, PUBLISHERS, New York
Cambridge, Philadelphia, San Francisco, Washington,
London, Mexico City, São Paulo, Singapore, Sydney

*To our students:*
*Past, present, and future*

Material from the Certified Internal Auditor Examinations by The Institute of Internal Auditors, Inc. Copyright 1978–1981 by the Institute of Internal Auditors, Inc., 249 Maitland Avenue, Altamonte Springs, Florida 32701. Reprinted with permission.

Material reprinted, with permission, from the CICA Uniform Final Examinations, 1975–1980, published by the Canadian Institute of Chartered Accountants, Toronto, Canada.

Material from the Certificate in Management Accounting Examinations, copyright © 1972, 1973, 1974, 1975, 1976, 1977, 1978, 1979, 1980, 1981, 1982, 1983, 1984 by the National Association of Accountants, is reprinted and/or adapted with permission.

Material from Uniform CPA Examination Questions and Unofficial Answers, copyright © 1958, 1963, 1971, 1972, 1973, 1974, 1975, 1976, 1977, 1980, 1981, 1982, 1983, 1984, 1985 by the American Institute of Certified Public Accountants, Inc., is reprinted or adapted with permission.

Material from the Society of Management Accountants of Canada Examinations, January 1978 through May 1985, reprinted or adapted with permission.

*Sponsoring Editor: Peter Coveney*
*Development Editor: Jonathan Haber*
*Project Editor: Donna DeBenedictis*
*Text and Cover Design: Edward A. Butler*
*Text Art: Vantage Art, Inc.*
*Production Manager: Jeanie Berke*
*Production Assistant: Paula Roppolo*
*Compositor: Waldman Graphics, Inc.*
*Printer and Binder: R. R. Donnelley & Sons Company*
*Cover Printer: Lehigh Press*

**Cost Accounting, Second Edition**


**Library of Congress Cataloging-in-Publication Data**
Moriarity, Shane, 1944–
Cost accounting.

Includes bibliographies and index.
1. Cost accounting. I. Allen, Carl P. II. Title.
HF5686.C8M673 1987 657′.42 86-22761
ISBN 0-06-044601-3

86 87 88 89 9 8 7 6 5 4 3 2 1

# CONTENTS

# PREFACE

In the second edition of *Cost Accounting* we again attempt to convey the dynamic nature of cost accounting and the important role accountants play as part of the management team. We are pleased with the warm reception accorded the first edition and the many kind comments we have received. While we have made significant changes and improvements, our focus remains the same for the second edition.

## MAJOR FEATURES OF THE TEXT

### Organization

We continue to base our presentation on a logical but flexible structure. The text again proceeds from planning and budgeting to cost accumulation, performance evaluation, and governmental regulation—the actual order in which issues should be addressed in setting up a new firm or product line. We believe that this approach improves the students' ability to integrate the planning, control, and evaluation cycles in the management accounting system. Moreover, we have structured Part Two, Planning and Budgeting, and Part Three, Product Costing, as independent units, to accommodate those instructors who prefer to cover budgeting later in the course. The extensive introductory chapters now fully prepare students for the early study of cost accumulation.

The chapters, taken alone, provide the foundation for a thorough first course in cost accounting. They include sufficient material for a basic one-term course. The chapters are supplemented by appendixes, located where they naturally fit. The appendixes provide a choice of extensions appropriate for a two-term cost accounting sequence, a second cost course, or a course with greater emphasis on the use of quantitative techniques.

### Assignment Material

As in the first edition, examples and problems make liberal use of actual accounting situations, appropriately disguised so that we can use fairly complete data. The abundant problems range from single-issue exercises to clearly labeled cases that integrate material from several chapters. They frequently relate to services and not-for-profit entities, and many raise substantive international issues. Several more problems have been added that use the computer as a tool; these problems tend to focus on data requirements and the accounting interpretation of results.

Users of the first edition unanimously praised the problems for their diversity and comprehensiveness. Instructors familiar with the NAA–AAA Management Accounting Symposia Series will see that in this edition we have drawn ideas from that source and have included several problems addressing issues of current concern to practicing management accountants. In addition, we again include material from recent U.S. and Canadian certification examinations. However, the vast majority of problems are questions that we have developed and class tested to highlight important issues.

We have continued to avoid the temptation to be encyclopedic in the numerical examples within the text, but extensive variations on concepts and procedures appear in the problems and cases. We believe that if students thoroughly understand the basic principles covered in each chapter, they should be able to think through new situations and perform the necessary analysis. Substituting new numbers into a similar example given in the text may improve student confidence, but we doubt that it provides preparation for a meaningful career.

### Learning Aids in the Text

A number of other features integrate and reinforce the diverse topics that constitute cost accounting:

*Three comprehensive cases* integrate the material covered in each major part of the text. The cases, which build on a single set of data, tie the entire cost accounting system together. For instructors wishing to have students work through the entire cost accounting system, we have provided alternative data for the comprehensive cases in the Instructor's Manual. In essence, the use of the alternative data amounts to assigning a practice set.

*Demonstration problems* review and integrate the key topics in each chapter. To ensure that students read and fully understand these problems, a question is usually included in the chapter's assignment material that asks readers to redo the demonstration problem with new data.

*Chapter summaries* provide a broad overview of the topics and their importance in management accounting, not just a rehash of the chapters' details.

Lists of *key terms and concepts* in each chapter are a resource for quick reference. Students can determine when further review is needed.

*Further readings,* listed at the end of every chapter, offer an excellent starting point for undergraduate term papers. The articles we have selected should be understandable to the average student, and most have appeared in widely available journals.[1]

A *glossary* at the end of the text gives definitions for the cost accounting terms used in the text. Common alternative terminology is also defined.

### Computer Use with the Text

As in the first edition, we are providing a diskette containing several general-purpose computer programs for use with the text. Our emphasis is on the use of computers to aid in the understanding of cost accounting, not as an end in itself. To meet this objective, we have devoted considerable effort to the development of interesting problem material that makes nontrivial use of the computer and yet concentrates on accounting issues. Problems for which a computer is required or strongly recommended are identified in the problem title and called to the reader's attention by a diskette symbol in the text margin. Although a computer could be used with many of our other problems, we believe students should manually solve those problems that can be worked more quickly by hand.

The second edition's accompanying diskette includes several new programs, and we have modified some of the previous programs. One new program is intended for use with Chapter 2, "Introduction to Cost Accounting," in classes whose students have little or no prior experience with computers. This program, titled CGMAS, prepares a simple statement of cost of goods manufactured and sold. The program provides the instructor with a vehicle for a quick introduction to the use of computers. Other new programs make it possible for students to calculate the present value of the tax shield for cost recovery, to fit learning curves to data, to determine an optimal order for allocating service department costs with the step method, and to use an integrated payroll program. The changes made to prior programs include more error traps for common mistakes. We have also made it possible to print output running more than a few lines as hard copy, and we have made the display of detailed instructions optional.

[1]Advanced students in search of relevant academic papers will be better served by the list of references in Robert Magee's *Advanced Managerial Accounting* (Harper & Row, Publishers, Inc., 1986).

We have not modified the programs to "do everything," however. Students must still enter as data those figures that require a knowledge of cost accounting concepts. We also are still providing the programs in source code so that you can easily make alterations if you wish to do so (for example, changing DIMENSION statements to solve larger problems). Most of the programs run quickly in source code, but you may wish to compile the simulation programs if you desire faster results.

In addition, Gerald M. Myers of Pacific Lutheran University has prepared a LOTUS 1-2-3 supplement to *Cost Accounting.* The LOTUS 1-2-3 supplement is tied directly to the text. Professor Myers has identified 50 problems (marked in the text margin with a document symbol) for spreadsheet application. In many cases he has extended the requirements of a problem to make significant use of the capabilities of the spreadsheet program while ensuring that the emphasis remains on understanding the managerial accounting issues involved. Instructors who do not make use of spreadsheet programs should still consider assigning the problems marked with the document symbol. They can be solved manually, and they are among our most interesting problems.

## MAJOR CHANGES IN THE SECOND EDITION

For this edition we have added over 200 new problems and cases, bringing the total to over 1000. We have also deleted or revised a few ambiguous or troublesome problems. In addition, we have made several significant changes to improve the logical structure, flexibility, and comprehensiveness of the text.

**1.** To better assist instructors wishing to cover cost accumulation before budgeting, we have expanded Part One to four chapters. Cost behavior and the contribution margin concept now appear within this introductory part of the text. We have also moved the coverage of establishing standards from Chapter 6 to Chapter 3, "Estimating Cost Behavior."

**2.** To provide greater flexibility in level of coverage, we have extended capital budgeting to two chapters. Chapter 8 now introduces the basics, and Chapter 9 covers the effects of taxes and capital rationing. These two chapters, together with Chapter 10 on PERT/Cost, are self-contained topics within Part Two. They may be included in the study of planning and budgeting, where we believe they logically belong, or deferred to the end of the course.

**3.** This time we devote an entire chapter to inventory planning and control. Chapter 7 discusses material requirements planning, just-in-time, EOQ, and some less formal systems. We take care to contrast the systems and explain the conditions under which each should be used. The implications of a just-in-time system are also raised in other chapters where appropriate.

**4.** Appendix 3A now includes a discussion of multiple and nonlinear regression. We have also added a new appendix to Chapter 5 that extends the concept of the cost of a prediction error to the determination of the expected value of perfect information.

**5.** The service sector of the economy is becoming increasingly important. Recognizing this fact, we have added a section to Chapter 3 on how to set labor standards for service personnel. This coverage is reinforced throughout the text with many problems concerning organizations that perform service functions.

**6.** We have added more emphasis on behavioral aspects of accounting throughout the text. Further, when more than one accounting technique is acceptable for a particular topic, we explain when and why each approach should be used.

**7.** Several users of the text suggested two other changes that we have incorporated. In the columnar approach to variance calculations, the left-hand column now represents actual costs and the right-hand column, budgeted costs. In the same chapter we have deleted coverage of what we had termed the output adjustment variance. This had been intended as a bridge to the topic of reconciling actual income earned to the master budget. Our experience, as well as that of several others, has been that the section was a source more of confusion than of enlightenment.

## SUPPLEMENTS

We are again providing a complete set of supplements. With the addition of several new items, the second edition of *Cost Accounting* is more than ever a pedagogically sound package.

### Study Guide

The *Study Guide,* prepared by William F. Bentz, director of the School of Accounting at the University of Oklahoma, summarizes the major points to be learned from each chapter, provides alternative explanations of difficult points, and includes many solved exercises and problems. Self-tests allow students to identify subjects requiring further study.

### Spreadsheets to Accompany *Cost Accounting*

The LOTUS 1-2-3 supplements prepared by Gerald M. Myers of Pacific Lutheran University consist of two manuals with diskettes. One manual offers the student a brief introduction to LOTUS and a guide to its use with the problems in the text. An accompanying diskette has both completed and partially completed templates to help students get started using the spreadsheet to solve problems. The *Instructor's Manual* (free to adopters) contains complete printed solutions, notes and tips, and two diskettes with the complete solutions to the student templates.

### Instructor's Manual

The *Instructor's Manual* has been revised by Dick D. Wasson of Central Washington University. It provides a wealth of information not only for first-time adopters, but also for seasoned users. The manual includes a list of check figures for the problems; learning objectives for each chapter; breakdowns of the assignment material by learning objective, length, and conceptual difficulty; two sets of lecture outlines, one for a first course in cost accounting and another for an intermediate-level course; comments on topics students tend to find difficult; suggestions for extending the text material; hints on alternative topic sequences; examples that can serve as the basis for lectures; and lecture transparency masters.

### Solutions Manual

A separate *Solutions Manual* supplies complete solutions to every question, exercise, problem, and case in the text. Every problem has been solved by us and at least one outside reviewer as a check on our calculations. We have been more complete in our solutions, with more step-by-step explanations than before.

### Test Bank

The *Test Bank* has been revised by Duane Milano of East Texas State University. For each chapter, it contains objective questions and short problems that range from straightforward to challenging.

### BASIC Programs

A diskette containing programs written in BASIC is again free to adopters. The programs are self-contained, including instructions for their use. A short manual explains the diskette to those new to the personal computer. The diskette is available in both IBM and Apple versions from Shane Moriarity, School of Accounting, University of Oklahoma, Norman, Oklahoma 73019.

### Transparencies

A set of transparencies for the solutions to the longer problems in the text is also available to adopters.

## ACKNOWLEDGMENTS

Several readers have complimented us on the lack of errors in the first edition. We are pleased to receive these comments, but much of the credit should go to the conscientious efforts of the reviewers of the first edition and to a student who checked all of our calculations.

For this edition we again have had all calculations recomputed in proof. We express our thanks to Paul Dierks of the University of Texas at Arlington, Kung H. Chen of the University of Nebraska-Lincoln, and Sun-kook Kwon of the University of Oklahoma for their efforts and attention to detail. In both this and the first edition we were also fortunate to have the assistance of Ruth Sanchez-Figueras, CPA, who reviewed both galley and page proof for the entire text and more than once saved us from embarrassment.

Most of the improvements in this edition resulted from suggestions from reviewers and users of the text. We wish to thank the following individuals for their helpful insights:

William T. Anderson, *James Madison University*
Roy E. Baker, *University of Missouri–Kansas City*
S. C. Beiner, *Concordia University*
Richard J. Campbell, *State University of New York, College at Fredonia*
Norman Cannon, *University of Minnesota at Duluth*
Jay H. Coats, *West Virginia University*
William M. Cready, *The University of North Carolina at Chapel Hill*
Mohamed H. El-Badawi, *Texas A&M University*
Paul Sheldon Foote, *New York University*
Alan H. Friedberg, *Louisiana State University*
Horace R. Givens, *University of Maine at Orono*
Grace M. Goodrich, *California State University–San Bernardino*
Robert E. Hansen, *The University of Toledo*
Cynthia D. Heagy, *The University of Georgia*
Robert J. Hehre, *Northeastern University*
Fred A. Jacobs, *Georgia State University*
Harold L. Jones, *University of Idaho*
Leonore K. Ken, *California State University–Stanislaus*
Cristi Lindblom, *University of Connecticut*
Donald R. Loster, *University of California–Santa Barbara*

Chris Luneski, *University of Oregon*
George O. Machlan, *Susquehanna University*
Patrick B. McKenzie, *Arizona State University*
Frank A. Mayne, *University of Texas at El Paso*
Gerald M. Myers, *Pacific Lutheran University*
Susan Ormsby, *Stephen F. Austin State University*
Lawrence Allen Roman, *Cuyahoga Community College*
Grant Russell, *University of Waterloo*
Marlene K. Sanderson, *Moorhead State University*
F. W. Schaeberle, *Western Michigan University*
Lawrence J. Syck, *University of Minnesota at Duluth*
Lakshmi U. Tatikonda, *University of Wisconsin–Oshkosh*
Marvin W. Tucker, *Southern Illinois University*
Dick D. Wasson, *Central Washington University*
Richard A. Young, *University of Texas at Austin*

Reviewers of the first edition included Frank M. Barton, Philip B. Hartley, Gordon B. Harwood, Song K. Kim, Robert W. Koehler, Ronald M. Marshall, Elzy V. McCollough, Pekin Ogan, John H. Salter, Lee L. Schmidt, Ghouse A. Shareef, Gary Siegel, and James D. Suver.

We also express our appreciation to the following organizations for allowing us to use and adapt material from their professional examinations (the abbreviations in parentheses are used in the text to identify the source of each problem): The Institute for Management Accounting of the National Association of Accountants (CMA), The American Institute of Certified Public Accountants (CPA), The Society of Management Accountants of Canada (SMA), The Canadian Institute of Chartered Accountants (CICA), and The Institute of Internal Auditors (CIA).

Our stated objective in the first edition was to provide a well-written, accurate, comprehensive treatment of basic cost accounting. The people and organizations that have provided comments and suggestions have greatly assisted us in meeting that objective. We sincerely appreciate their efforts. If you have suggestions for further improvements, we would be most grateful to hear from you.

***Shane Moriarity***

***Carl P. Allen***

# PART ONE

# INTRODUCTION

CHAPTER

1

# THE COST ACCOUNTING ENVIRONMENT

The development of cost accounting as a specialty within the field of accounting coincided with the increased complexity of business enterprises. In simpler times, when goods and services were provided by individual artisans, elaborate accounting records were unnecessary. An individual producer could simply compare cash receipts to cash disbursements to evaluate the viability of the operation.

The use of credit and the acquisition of long-lived assets complicated matters. The purchase and use of long-lived assets made the comparison of cash receipts and disbursements for a particular period an unreliable measure of the entrepreneur's increased "well-offness" during a period. Credit transactions cast further doubt on the usefulness of cash receipts and disbursements information as a measure of earnings. Credit also led to the need for a formal memory for the operation. The producer needed to know the amounts owed to suppliers and the amounts due from customers not only for income measurement but also to ensure that all proper amounts were paid and received.

## THE EVOLUTION OF COST ACCOUNTING

The rise of multiply owned enterprises produced the need for the development of objective and equitable procedures (financial accounting) for the determination of net income so that owners could determine their fair share of the proceeds from the enterprise. But it was the rise of the large firm producing numerous products and services that created the need for cost accounting. Firmwide net income no longer provided sufficient information for making operating decisions. The use of common labor and facilities to produce a wide range of products made it extremely difficult to determine the profitability of each of the products. In turn, decisions concerning the expansion or contraction of product lines became difficult.

Traditional cost accountants concerned themselves with developing reporting systems that would yield costs so that the profitability of individual product lines could be evaluated. Unfortunately, in too many cases the study of procedures became an end in itself. Accountants frequently lost sight of the objectives for the procedures. "Acceptable" techniques were applied whether they were appropriate to a particular situation or not. This, in turn, led to criticism of cost accounting as a discipline that provided a great deal of largely irrelevant data to management.

Fortunately the discipline is changing, and cost accountants are becoming much more concerned with providing information that will help management meet the firm's goals. In this text we hope to continue this movement toward emphasis on the objectives of internal accounting. By concentrating on the end uses to be made of our accounting information we expect that you, the reader, will develop an understanding of the strengths and weaknesses of alternative techniques that will enable you to implement the most relevant technique when needed in practice.

In financial (external) accounting, fairness and objectivity play an almost equal role with relevance in the determination of the most appropriate accounting procedures. The Financial Accounting Standards Board (FASB), the Securities and Exchange Commission (SEC), and committees of the American Institute of Certified Public Accountants (AICPA) all specify accounting and reporting practices that must be followed. In some cases the opinions of these groups are backed only by the accepted stature of the promulgating organization, whereas in others the imposed requirements carry the weight of law behind them. In nearly every case the intent of the suggested or required practice is to promote fairness in the reports to be used by a diverse audience of financial statement readers.

Cost accounting[1] is not as constrained as financial accounting. Cost accountants face only one general class of user for internal accounting reports: management. We are thus free to provide any information, using whatever techniques we feel are appropriate, to help management make the necessary decisions to operate the firm. Of course, some cost account-

[1]We use the terms *cost accounting* and *managerial accounting* interchangeably. Some view cost accounting solely as the practice of accumulating individual product costs, whereas managerial accounting is used more broadly for all internal reports and information systems needed to aid management.

ing information may be used both for internal and external reporting, such as inventory costing. In these cases we may choose to use an approach internally that will also be acceptable for external reporting in order to minimize the cost of providing information. However, this is a choice. There is no requirement that we prepare the same reports for internal use as those that are required for external reporting.

## BASIC CONCEPTS

The *managerial accounting system* is defined as the formal system of accumulating and reporting data useful for the achievement of management objectives. Whether we are concerned with a profit-seeking firm, a governmental unit, a not-for-profit philanthropic institution, or any other organization, there are general characteristics that the management accounting system must possess. Several of these are discussed in the following sections.

### Efficiency and Effectiveness

Whatever its mission, an organization will have a set of objectives (usually including the delivery of products or services). Management of the entity will require information for planning how to achieve these objectives and also information on whether objectives are actually being achieved. This latter aspect focuses on two factors: (1) whether the goals were met—that is, **effectiveness;** and (2) whether we were able to provide the product or service with a minimal expenditure of resources—that is, **efficiency.** In general, the purpose in measuring effectiveness and efficiency is to help management control the activities of the firm.

Effectiveness and efficiency may be illustrated with a simple example. Assume that a firm's public relations department has been charged with informing the purchasers of one of the firm's products that the product is being recalled. Management has determined that 300,000 units of the affected product were sold. Management has set as its goal having 90% of the units returned (some items will have been retired from service, others are in the hands of people whom it would be nearly impossible to contact—for example, persons who live in isolated places and those who have moved outside the country). Assume further that management has budgeted $2 per returned unit as the cost of informing customers of the recall. Thus management expects to incur a total cost of $540,000 for the return of 90% of the 300,000 units sold.

Now assume that the public relations department spends $510,000 for advertising, store displays, and press releases. The program results in the return of 250,000 units. We now ask whether the department has been effective and efficient.

The goal of the program was to have 90% of 300,000 units, or 270,000 units, returned. Because only 250,000 units were returned, the department was not effective in achieving its goal. In contrast, we might think that the department was efficient since they spent only $510,000 out of the allocated budget of $540,000. But this is not so. Efficiency is measured relative to the level of effectiveness achieved. For the 250,000 returned units the firm should have spent $2 per unit or $500,000, not $510,000. Thus the public relations department spent $10,000 more than it should have for the return of 250,000 units.

Consider the analysis if 280,000 units were returned and the public relations department incurred costs of $550,000. The department would have been effective, getting a higher number of units returned than budgeted. The department would also have been efficient, even though it spent $550,000 instead of the $540,000 budgeted. For the budget of $2 per returned unit allowed for a cost of $560,000 when 280,000 units were returned, but for that level of effectiveness they spent only $550,000.

### Responsibility Accounting

Each individual with decision-making authority in an organization has responsibility for some aspect of achieving the entity's objective. Management accountants recognize this through the development of a responsibility accounting system. That is, the focus of the internal accounting system is on responsibility centers. A **responsibility center** is an activity or collection of activities supervised by a single individual. In the planning process, objectives are proposed for each responsibility center. The responsibility centers then become the focal point for control.

Responsibility centers are classified by the authority of the person in charge. A center is a **cost center** if the manager has authority only over the level of costs incurred. In some cases this may mean all costs, including fixed costs of capacity. This situation occurs when a manager has the authority to acquire and dispose of all facilities needed to provide the center's product or service. Many service centers fit this situation. For example, the manager of a firm's computer services department may have broad authority to acquire equipment that will best meet the firm's demand for computer services. In such a case the manager would be held responsible for all costs incurred, including equipment depreciation.

More commonly, cost center managers have authority only over a subset of costs. A line supervisor, for example, is generally responsible only for the efficient use of labor and materials. Generally, a line supervisor has little or no authority over wage rates, materials prices, or capacity costs such as depreciation. In preparing internal accounting reports for this type of center, we will try to be careful to hold the supervisors responsible only for those costs over which they can actually exert authority.

At some level in the firm's hierarchy someone will always have authority for all costs. But often this is at a level at which the manager also has responsibility for generating revenues. When an individual is responsible for both revenues and costs, we call the responsibility center a **profit center.** In a profit center we measure the performance of the unit by comparing its net income to budgeted income.

Another type of center is the investment center. An **investment center** is a responsibility center in which a manager has responsibility for net income and also has authority over the amount of investment committed to the center. In single-plant firms, or centralized firms, an investment center may be defined only at the overall firm level. In these cases the persons responsible for the investment center's performance are the firm's board of directors. The board is responsible to the stockholders for utilizing the shareholders' investment in the owners' best interest. In decentralized firms, investment centers may also exist on a divisional or company level. For example, if several companies are each a part of a conglomerate, and individual company officials may control the amount of investment devoted to each company, the individual companies can then be considered investment centers.

### Segment Performance versus Managerial Performance

In measuring and evaluating performance, a distinction is made between the performance of a responsibility center (a segment of the firm) and the performance of its manager. For decisions concerning whether the organization should continue to provide a product or service, all the costs incurred for a responsibility center are accumulated. This practice allows management to make such decisions as whether the firm should continue to process its own payroll or contract it out to a service bureau.

In contrast, only a subset of the costs incurred by a responsibility center are ordinarily used for measuring the performance of its manager. That is, a managerial performance report usually contains only those costs that the manager has the authority to affect. The manager is then evaluated, in part, by comparing the level of controllable costs incurred to a budget. In this way a manager may be judged to have performed efficiently given the task, but the responsibility center itself might be considered an inefficient means of accomplishing a particular task. For example, even though the payroll manager may be doing an excellent job of managing the payroll department, a service bureau might be able to take advantage of positive returns to scale and provide the service more cheaply than the firm can.

### Behavioral Aspects of Responsibility Accounting

Although it may appear that accounting deals solely with numbers, cost accounting deals primarily with people. A major task for internal accounting systems is to help motivate an entity's personnel to work toward the organization's goals. This means that the accounting system must accurately represent goals and should foster cooperation among personnel, provide help in identifying and correcting problem areas, encourage good performance, and discourage nonproductive activities. Unfortunately, as we will see, a poorly designed system often has the opposite effect. A system that sets unrealistically high goals and emphasizes penalties, as opposed to rewards, frequently leads personnel to rebel against the organization or even to engage in minor sabotage. Less dramatic, but equally costly reactions can occur when people strive to meet an objective that is incorrectly represented in the accounting system. For example, the accounting system may encourage salespeople to maximize sales dollars rather than profits. Salespeople can increase dollar sales by cutting prices (and profit margins) and by pushing products with low margins. The firm's objective, of course, is usually to try to increase profitability, not just sales dollars. Thus as we design our internal systems, we must constantly be aware of how people will react to forms, reports, or data requests.

### The Cost versus the Benefit of Information

In meeting our accounting objectives, we must be concerned with balancing the cost of obtaining, processing, and reporting accounting information with the benefits that the information will provide for management. For providing accounting information at a cost in excess of its benefits drains resources from the firm just as surely as selling products at a price less than the cost to obtain them.

This concern has increased with the ready accessibility of computers. It is now relatively inexpensive to acquire highly sophisticated accounting subsystems through the purchase of commercial software. However, the cost of operating these systems can be very expensive. Someone must gather the needed data and the data must be input into the computerized system. A large automobile assembly plant can probably justify the installation of an accounting system that monitors individual and departmental absenteeism. This will allow managers who may be physically removed from operations to determine whether a particular department is having absentee problems (possibly due to an unpopular supervisor). Further, such a system will provide the documentation required by the union if a particular employee is going to be dismissed.

In contrast, an independent pharmacist with one or two employees is unlikely to be able to justify the cost of such a system. The pharmacist will know through day-to-day observation whether an employee is absent excessively. In addition, it is unlikely that the pharmacist needs to document specific absences formally to a third party. Thus, in contemplating the introduction of an accounting system, we must weigh the cost of installing and operating the system against its benefits. The critical question is whether the value of the information to be obtained exceeds the cost of providing the information.

**Cost-benefit analysis** has received a great deal of bad press recently, particularly in regard to governmental programs. Governmental agencies frequently use cost-benefit analysis to justify projects such as the construction of dams and to justify actions such as the imposition of regulations mandating safety equipment on cars and lawn mowers. But it should be noted that the complaints most commonly lodged against such government analyses are usually directed not to the wisdom of comparing costs to benefits but to the actual measurement of the costs and benefits. Thus politicians and journalists often question the dollar value of projected flood-control benefits or question the assumed value of a human life. These same measurement issues will also plague the use of cost-benefit analysis for determining the need for accounting accuracy. We will find that costs can usually be measured fairly accurately, but the benefits resulting from extremely accurate versus reasonably accurate accounting information are hard to document. When we use well-defined decision models, we will be able to use some analyses developed in the field of information economics to estimate the value of more accurate information. For the most part, however, we must rely on common sense to tell us when we are spending more to acquire data than the data are worth.

## THE ACCOUNTANT IN THE MANAGERIAL HIERARCHY

The role of the managerial accountant has changed dramatically from the days when the accountant simply calculated product costs and prepared financial statements. Management accountants are now largely responsible for preparing detailed financial plans for future operations, are asked to help in measuring the effectiveness of operations and suggesting improvements, are involved in identifying and proposing solutions to emerging problems, and are primarily responsible for designing the firm's information systems, developing procedures to safeguard assets, and assuring compliance with government reporting requirements.

In light of the expanding duties involved, the importance of the accounting function is usually recognized in firms' organization charts by having the controller (the chief management accountant) report directly to the president. Figure 1-1 is an example of a fairly common organization chart, highlighting the controller's department.

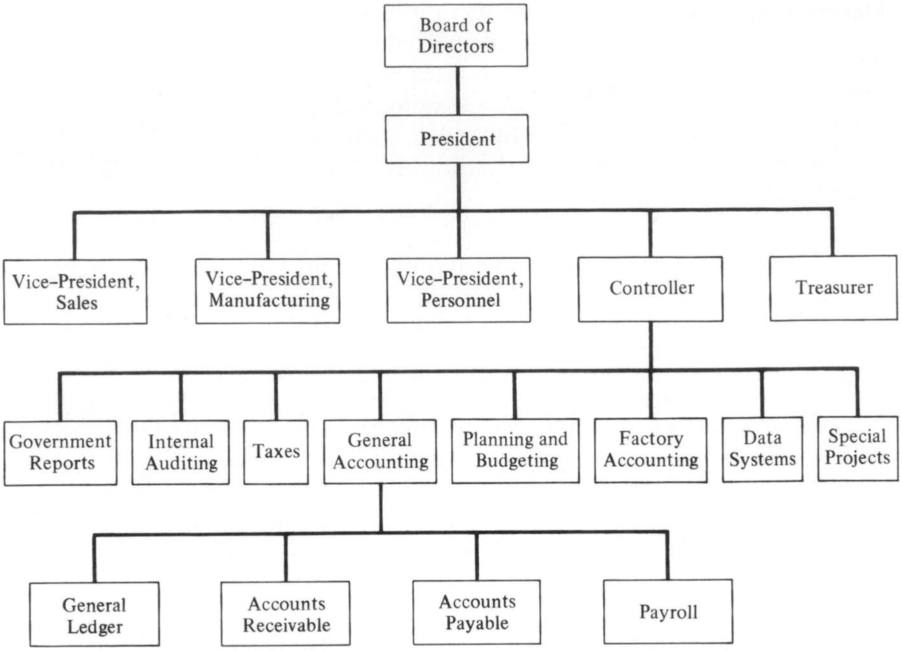


**FIGURE 1-1 Organization chart for a manufacturing company.**

Although Figure 1-1 includes many of the activities performed by the controller's department, space limitations prevent us from illustrating all of the tasks coming under the controller's direction. Each of the responsibility centers reporting to the controller is generally responsible for overseeing the activities of a number of other responsibility centers (this relationship is shown only for General Accounting in Figure 1-1). But even with this limited organization chart, the wide range of responsibilities of an organization's accounting department becomes apparent. The controller is responsible for financial planning for future operations, routine record keeping for governmental and external financial reports, and designing and implementing reporting and performance evaluation systems.

Just as we cannot illustrate all of the controller's functions in the organization chart, neither can we describe in this text all the activities and procedures performed by the controller's department. This text concentrates on the functions performed to assist managers in making operating decisions, planning for future operations, and evaluating and controlling current operations. Occasionally we relate these functions to the firm's external reporting systems or to government requirements, but for a detailed examination of these other accounting functions, the reader should study financial accounting, taxation, and auditing texts.

### Career Opportunities

The opportunities for management accountants are excellent. A large number of the chief executive officers (CEOs) of major firms began their careers as management accountants. However, the path to the top is highly varied. There is no lockstep career path that management accountants follow. Even the types of entry level positions for management accountants vary. Many larger firms offer formal financial management training programs. These firms rotate entry level management accountants through three to five very different job assignments during the employee's first 18 to 24 months. At the conclusion of the program, the employee then selects the job preferred. Such programs give the new employee a broad exposure to the nature of the firm's business.

Other firms hire entry level management accountants as internal auditors for their first two to three years. This approach gives the new employee exposure to all facets of the firm's business. Still other firms hire new accountants to fill specific operating positions: revenue accountant, general staff accountant, staff analyst, assistant plant controller, and so forth.

In all cases, after your first position, advancement is a matter of hard work and taking advantage of opportunities. A person who quickly learns a job and excels at it is likely to be offered many promotion opportunities. In order to select which opportunities you should accept, you should undertake, even in your first job, to learn the nature of the responsibilities of the people you work with and which of these positions are of interest to you. Accepting positions that you find fun and challenging will be personally rewarding and you will be more likely to excel. Success at each level should then lead to opportunities at higher levels with more responsibility.

Reading about the career paths of management accountants is fascinating because of their diversity. The National Association of Accountants (NAA) frequently publishes stories about individuals' career paths in its monthly magazine, *Management Accounting*. In addition, the NAA has collected several of these stories into a booklet, *From Management Accountant to CEO*. If your instructor doesn't have a copy, contact your nearest chapter of the NAA. As you do, look into the opportunity of becoming a student member. As a member, you will have the opportunity to meet a large number of practicing management accountants and you will likely learn of many exciting job prospects available upon graduation.

## THE ORGANIZATION OF THE TEXT

Part One of the text provides an overview of the objectives of cost accounting, an introduction to basic terminology, cost and profit behavior, and a general description of the flow of product cost information through the general ledger. Part Two concentrates on the problem-solving role of the management accountant and examines what activities the firm should undertake and how it should go about these activities. Most of the coverage is devoted to planning for what will be routine operations for the firm, but some nonroutine "special problems" are also examined.

Part Three concentrates on the score-keeping role of the accountant—the routine accumulation of data indicating the status of operations. In this section the actual results for each of the responsibility centers are compiled, from which the financial statements eventually can be prepared.

Part Four focuses on the attention-directing role of accounting. Here performance is evaluated by comparing actual results to plans. Effectiveness and efficiency are examined for the purpose of directing management's attention to those problem areas needing further analysis or corrective action.

Part Five focuses on the problems that surface when firms contract to provide goods and services to the government. It examines the requirements that government contractors must meet to conform with mandated government accounting standards.

## COST ACCOUNTING AND PROFESSIONAL EXAMS

In the United States the Certificate in Management Accounting (CMA) is awarded by the Institute of Certified Management Accountants of the National Association of Accountants and is valued by many progressive firms as an indication of professional competence and educational attainment in the field of management accounting. The five-part exam is offered twice a year (generally in December and June) at many sites across the country. The five parts of the exam cover

1. Economics and Business Finance
2. Organization and Behavior, including Ethical Considerations
3. Public Reporting Standards, Auditing, and Taxes
4. Periodic Reporting for Internal and External Purposes
5. Decision Analysis, including Modeling and Information Systems

Specific information concerning the timing of future exams and admission requirements to take the exam can be obtained from The Institute of Certified Management Accountants, 10 Paragon Drive, Montvale, New Jersey 07645-1760.

Of course, the CPA (Certified Public Accountant) certificate is also recognized as a symbol of accounting competence. Although it is generally more concerned with auditing and external reporting, the CPA exam also tests the candidate's knowledge of managerial accounting topics.

In Canada, three professional groups offer certificate exams that include coverage of cost accounting topics: The Canadian Institute of Chartered Accountants, 250 Bloor Street East, Toronto, Ontario M4W 1G5; The Society of Management Accountants of Canada, 154 Main Street East, Hamilton, Ontario L8N 3C3; and The Canadian Certified General Accountants' Association, 740-1176 West Georgia Street, Vancouver, British Columbia V6E 4A2.

Throughout this text we include in the problem sections questions from most of these professional exams to give you practice in solving the types of questions asked. Further, in selecting subjects for the text we have tried to cover all the cost accounting topics that have been commonly included in the professional exams, as well as other topics likely to be added in the near future. If you thoroughly review this text we believe that you will find the coverage more than adequate for the cost accounting sections of these exams.

## SUMMARY

Cost-managerial accounting has evolved into a discipline concerned with providing internal information that will help managers achieve an organization's goals. Once objectives have been established, internal accounting systems are designed to help evaluate the effectiveness and efficiency with which these objectives have been met. At the same time, the choice of the accounting systems and procedures must also be evaluated for effectiveness and efficiency.

## DEMONSTRATION PROBLEM

At the end of each chapter a demonstration problem or case illustrates the application of each chapter's major points to an actual problem. The first case involves the Greater Chicago Service Club, an organization formed to provide an opportunity for new members of the professional community to work together. Typically, the club forms committees to provide support to the children's hospital, entertainment for orphans, hot holiday meals to the elderly, and other specific services to needy people. While providing direct assistance to underprivileged citizens, the club also gives its members—who are generally young attorneys, accountants, company managers, and banking personnel—the opportunity to establish friendships and contacts that are likely to prove valuable in the members' later careers.

The club derives its revenue from membership dues and fund-raising events sponsored by each committee to support its specific projects. To get started, at the beginning of the year the club treasury allocates funds to each activity committee. At the end of the year the committees return excess funds to the club's treasurer. After covering any deficits incurred by committees, paying bills incurred for club administration, and making a small contribution to a reserve fund, the organization donates any excess treasury cash to the United Way campaign.

It is now year-end. The executive committee of the club is analyzing the performance of its activity committees to determine how well each committee performed, whether specific activities should be continued, and whether the chairperson of each committee should be given a more responsible position next year, left in the current position, or "promoted" to membership (but not given the leadership) of a different committee.

The club's controller-treasurer prepared a reporting form, which each committee leader completed. At the executive committee meeting the controller provided summaries from two of the committee reports. The first report indicated that Hylbak, the new assistant controller at Wilson Brothers, headed up a committee of 12 members that prepared income tax returns for the elderly. The executive committee provided them with $5,000 for the project. Hylbak reported that they spent $2,000 on advertising, $500 on postage and supplies, and $1,700 on meals. Hylbak explained the $1,700 on meals by noting that the committee met eight times. After each meeting (returns were actually prepared at the last seven meetings), the members went out for dinner and drinks. The attendance at each meeting was 12, 11, 12, 10, 9, 11, 11, and 10 members, respectively (or nearly $20 each for dinner and drinks).

The committee prepared returns for 812 elderly people. Hylbak noted that this year the committee provided the tax service in a suburb one night (past years' committees always stayed in the inner city). It cost $500 to advertise the availability of the suburban service, and only 20 people took advantage of the service. Hylbak suggested that cost-benefit analysis leads to the conclusion that in the future the committee should offer the service only in the city itself: "Valuing our tax service at $15 per return, it cost us $500 to provide only $300 (20 × $15) of service at the suburban location."

To offset expenses, the committee held a charity auction. Committee members contacted local businesses to donate merchandise or services, which were then auctioned. A highlight, which made the Chicago papers, was the mayor's offer to take two people out to dinner. That one item sold for $250. Total proceeds from the auction came to $2,400. At the end of the year the committee returned $3,200 to the treasury.

The second report indicates that Jackson, the new attorney with the First National Bank, headed a committee of 20 members to send inner-city youths to summer camp. The executive committee provided $10,000 to Jackson. Jackson's group coordinated the youths' fund-raising efforts, which resulted in net income of $3,000 from car washes and $6,000 from candy sales. The committee's expenses consisted of $600 in publicity costs for the fund raising, $450 for lunches for committee members, and $12,000 to send 60 youths to two weeks of summer camp. The committee met five times (at lunch), with attendance of 18, 14, 10, 9, and 9 members for an average lunch cost of $7.50. At the end of the year Jackson returned $5,950 to the treasury.

The controller-treasurer noted, "Last year the tax preparation committee prepared 900 returns at a net cost to the treasury of $3,150. Last year's summer camp program, on the other hand, sent only 50 kids to camp at a net cost of $1,800 to the treasury."

**Required**

Assuming you are a member of the executive committee, which program leader, Hylbak or Jackson, did a better job?

**Solution**

Several aspects of performance can be considered in this case. Let us begin by looking at the financial results. From the description in the case we can prepare the following statements of cash receipts and disbursements for the two committees.

| | Tax Return Committee | | Summer Camp Committee | |
|---|---|---|---|---|
| Receipts | | | | |
| Initial contribution from the club treasury | $5,000 | | $10,000 | |
| Fund-raising proceeds | 2,400 | | 9,000 | |
| Total receipts | | $7,400 | | $19,000 |
| Disbursements | | | | |
| Publicity | $2,000 | | $ 600 | |
| Meals | 1,700 | | 450 | |
| Supplies | 500 | | — | |
| Camp fees | — | | 12,000 | |
| Total disbursements | | 4,200 | | 13,050 |
| Funds returned to treasury | | $3,200 | | $ 5,950 |
| Net cost of activity to the club (initial contribution less returned funds) | | $1,800 | | $ 4,050 |

In analyzing the financial performance we might note that the camp committee returned more funds to the treasury than the tax committee. However, simple comparison of the dollar amounts ignores the club's initial contribution to each committee. We might then look at the proportion of each committee's costs for which the committee was able to raise its own funds. The tax committee raised $2,400 toward its costs of $4,200, or 57%. The camp committee raised $9,000 toward its costs of $13,050, or 69%. The tax committee returned $3,200 of $5,000, or 64%, whereas the camp committee returned $5,950 out of $10,000, or 59%. On the other hand, a committee that did nothing could return 100% of the initial funds. Our analysis so far has ignored the activity levels of the committees.

A better means to evaluate financial performance is to evaluate the *efficiency* with which each committee operated. The tax committee served 812 clients at a net cost to the club of $1,800, for an average cost of $2.22 per client. This compares with the previous year's results of serving 900 people at a cost of $3,150 or $3.50 per client. Relative to the previous year, the tax committee was more efficient in financial terms. In contrast, the camp committee served 60 youths at the net cost of $4,050, or an average cost of $67.50 per client. Last year the camp committee served 50 clients at a cost of $1,800, or $36.00 per youth. Relative to last year, the camp committee was less efficient.

Although cost efficiency should not be ignored, it probably should not be a major concern for the service club. In neither case are the amounts of money involved particularly large. Another criterion might be the *effectiveness* of each committee. This year the tax committee served 812 clients as compared to 900 the previous year. Relative to last year the tax committee was less effective this year (probably explained by the session held in the suburbs). On the other hand, the camp committee sent 60 youngsters to camp this year, compared with 50 the previous year. Thus the camp committee was more effective this year than last. This increased effectiveness in turn may explain the committee's poorer performance on efficiency. The committee no doubt set its goal for the number of youths at the beginning of the project (and then recruited that number of youths to participate in the fund-raising projects). It would appear that although they were able to send a larger number of youths to camp, they were unable to raise the same amount of funds per youth as in the previous year.

Rather than concentrating on the costs incurred by each committee, we might look instead at the benefits each committee provided to the community. One means to quantify the benefits provided would be to look at the market value of the services each committee provided. Assuming that the prevailing rate for preparing a simple tax return is $15, the tax committee provided $15 × 812, or $12,180 in services. Similarly, it appears that the cost to attend summer camp is $200, so for the 60 children who were sent the camp committee provided $12,000 worth of services. Note that this again is a measure of effectiveness, but it is now expressed in terms of the market value of services.

As before, we might want to look at the efficiency with which each committee provided its benefits. The tax committee delivered its $12,180 worth of services at a net cost of $1,800; that is, it provided $6.77 of service for each dollar expended. The camp committee delivered $12,000 worth of services at a net cost of $4,050, or $2.96 per dollar of cost. This analysis seems to suggest that the tax committee was substantially more efficient than the camp committee. But care needs to be taken with this type of analysis. We are presuming that the market value of services accurately measures the real worth of the services provided to the community. However, it is not at all clear that preparing 13 tax returns (13 × $15 = $195) is really equivalent to the benefits to society of sending one youngster to summer camp for two weeks ($200). The effect on an inner-city youth's future life (attitude and motivation) arising from the summer camp experience and the fund-raising activities may substantially exceed the fee for attending summer camp, whereas the future benefits from preparing an elderly person's tax return are likely minimal. As mentioned in the chapter, the measurement of benefits in cost-benefit analysis is often very difficult, and the reliance on an easily available measure (such as the market value of services in this case) can be very misleading.

We have looked at several potential measures of performance. Now, which committee performed better? To answer this question we must examine the goals of the organization. That is, appropriate performance measures are those indicators that measure progress in meeting the objectives of the club. If a major goal of the club is to grow and expand its financial base so that it can provide increasing services to the community, then a measure that reflects financial growth would be appropriate. In this case the proportion of funds returned to the treasury relative to the club's initial contribution would make sense. (By the way, if growth is the primary objective, then these proportions should exceed 100%.) Inasmuch as the club donates its excess funds to the United Way each year, it seems apparent that growth is not a goal of *this* organization (though it is typically a major goal for profit-oriented organizations).

Another possible goal for the club is to maximize the benefits the club can provide to the community given its limited resources. In this case the measures of efficiency and effectiveness relating to the value of the services provided would be appropriate. However, it is again not likely that this is the primary goal of the organization. For if the club wanted to maximize the benefits to society from its activities, it could probably do so by donating all its resources to larger, established charities (e.g., United Way). These charities with their higher returns to scale can most likely provide community services much more efficiently than the civic club.

What, then, is the club's objective? We believe that the primary goal of the club, as stated in the case description, is to provide new members of the professional community with the opportunity of working together to develop friendships and contacts that are likely to prove valuable in the members' later careers. Our financial performance numbers do not measure progress toward this goal. Instead, we will have to look to other factors that reflect the primary goal. One such measure is attendance at committee meetings and functions. Note that the tax committee met eight times and that attendance averaged 10.75 members per meeting. Thus an average of 10.75 ÷ 12, or 90%, of the committee members participated in the committee's activities. In contrast, the camp committee met only five times, with an average attendance of 12 of its 20 members, for a 60% participation rate. If members are going to establish friendships and contacts, it is important for them to get together. The tax committee seems to have been much more effective in this matter. Further evidence supporting this conclusion is seen in the trend of participation. Participation in the tax committee's activities was relatively constant, whereas the camp committee's participation declined substantially over time.

Although we can measure participation quantitatively as an indicator of meeting our objective, qualitative evaluation in this case is even more valuable. There are two substantial differences in the activities of these two committees that seem to indicate that the tax committee better met the club's goals. The camp committee apparently held its meetings at lunchtime. Given the limited time most people have available in the middle of the day, these meetings were likely to be primarily devoted to the committee's task of raising money to send children to camp. It is not likely that there was much time for socializing. In contrast, the tax committee held its meetings and then retired to dinner and drinks. This latter approach provided an excellent opportunity for relaxed social interaction (the development of friendships and contacts).

The second difference relates to the manner in which the committees raised funds for their activities. The camp committee supervised the youths in activities that would not have gotten the members involved with the professional community (car washes and candy sales). Although the camp committee did raise a lot of money and did provide a service to the youths by getting them involved in goal-directed behavior, this is not the primary goal of the club. In contrast, the auction held by the tax committee, which required its members to contact other members of the business community, obviously resulted in making new business contacts and even some contacts with the local politicians in the mayor's office. This type of activity is precisely the sort of thing that the organizers of the club seem to have had in mind.

The qualitative performance evaluation makes it clear that the tax committee was the better performer. Note that for the *primary* goal, traditional accounting measures played no role. But even for this club, financial measures would play a role. The club would not want to ignore totally measures of financial efficiency and effectiveness. The charitable activities of the club form the vehicle by which the club meets its major objective. We would still establish financial and activity-related goals to provide a challenge to the committee members: to motivate them to work together toward a common end. But the executive committee must be careful not to allow these subgoals to become so important that the committees devote all their energy to meeting financial and operating goals to the exclusion of having a good time and making friends.

This case was designed to show that accounting measures are not always of overriding importance. Throughout this text we will, of course, be concentrating almost exclusively on accounting performance measures. For most organizations the formal quantitative measures of performance are extremely important, but as managers we should also consider the qualitative aspects of performance.

## KEY TERMS AND CONCEPTS

Effectiveness
Efficiency
Responsibility center
Cost center
Profit center
Investment center
Cost-benefit analysis

## FURTHER READING

Alleman, Raymond H. "Controllership at ITT," *Management Accounting* (May 1985), p. 24.

Croll, David B. "Cost Accounting in the CPA Examination—Revisited," *The Accounting Review* (April 1982), p. 420.

Hartman, Bart P., Vincent C. Brenner, Richard A. Lydecker, and Jeffrey M. Wilkinson. "Mission Control Starts in the Controller's Department," *Management Accounting* (September 1981), p. 27.

Janell, Paul A., and Raymond M. Kinnunen. "Portrait of the Divisional Controller," *Management Accounting* (June 1980), p. 15.

Johnson, H. Thomas. "Toward a New Understanding of Nineteenth-Century Cost Accounting," *The Accounting Review* (July 1981), p. 510.

Kaplan, Robert S. "The Evolution of Management Accounting," *The Accounting Review* (July 1984), p. 390.

Parker, L. D. "Management Accounting and the Corporate Environment," *Management Accounting* (February 1978), p. 15.

Skousen, Clifford R. "A Profile and Index of the CMA Examination—An Update," *The Accounting Review* (July 1981), p. 659.

Williams, Kathy, and Robert L. Shultis. "Nabisco Brands' Schaeberle: From Management Accountant to Industry Spokesman," *Management Accounting* (January 1984), p. 21.

## QUESTIONS AND EXERCISES

**1-1** "Our primary responsibility is to our stockholders, and our accounting system should be designed with this in mind. Accordingly, the only accounts required are those needed for the primary financial statements—namely, the income statement, the balance sheet, and the statement of changes in financial position." Comment.

**1-2** The manager of a department has been given a budget for the year with the stipulation that the manager will receive a bonus equal to 10% of the amount by which the department's actual costs come in under budget. Comment.

**1-3** Refer to the demonstration problem at the end of the chapter. As the respected senior member of the Greater Chicago Service Club, you have been assigned the task of designing a "point system" to assist in the evaluation process. What elements would you include, and how would you weight them?

**1-4** For each of the following responsibility centers, (a) the cafeteria in the student union, (b) the College (School, Department) of Business in your university, (c) the bursar's office in the university, (d) the local Sears store, (e) the local post office, (f) the local chamber of commerce, identify whether it is a cost center, profit center, or investment center for purposes of performance evaluation. Also, indicate what you feel each center's primary objective ought to be.

**1-5** DNF, Inc., is a customer-oriented company. The company's sales force spends about a quarter of its time with the people in production going over such things as adaptations in existing products to meet specific customer needs, suggestions for new products, and so on. The manager of the marketing department thinks that the cost of sales time spent in this manner should be charged to the production department. The head of the production department disagrees, of course. They turn to you, the firm's controller, to resolve the disagreement. What do you recommend?

**1-6** Wink, Inc., has quarterly objectives of producing 1,000 units at a total cost of $150,000 and selling them for $250 each. Data for the past year are as follows:

| Quarter | Units Produced | Total Production Cost | Units Sold |
|---|---|---|---|
| First | 900 | $135,000 | 1,000 |
| Second | 1,100 | 154,000 | 900 |
| Third | 1,200 | 150,000 | 1,250 |
| Fourth | 800 | 124,000 | 900 |
| Totals | 4,000 | $563,000 | 4,050 |

Regarding production and sales, in which quarter or quarters was Wink (a) efficient and (b) effective? (c) How would you assess performance for the year as a profit center?

**1-7** The credit manager of a regional chain has been budgeted $3,000 per month for credit checks on applicants for the chain's charge card. The manager would like to use the money in such a way as to maximize the number of reports for the dollars spent. The alternatives being considered are as follows:

Use a national service, which will cost $1,000 per month plus $10 per report.
Use a regional service, which will cost $1,200 per month plus $8 per report.
Use the in-house department to generate the information.

Given the alternatives, what is the minimum number of reports to be generated monthly if the in-house department does the work?

**1-8** A particular department has a product reject rate of 200 units per month. These units are reworked at a cost of approximately $50 each. The supervisor thinks that if units were inspected halfway through the process, 75% of the mistakes could be corrected, at an average cost of $20 each. All units, however, would still have to be inspected at the final stage. What is the most the supervisor would be willing to spend monthly to improve the operations of this department?

## PROBLEMS AND CASES

**1-9** **Efficiency/Effectiveness.**
Sgord had planned on producing 1,000 units of product at a cost of $33 per unit and selling them at $50 each. In fact, it produced 1,100 at a cost of $31 per unit and sold 900 at $50 each.

**Required**

**a.** What was planned profit?
**b.** What was actual profit?
**c.** How much of the difference between planned and actual profit is due to (1) effectiveness and (2) efficiency?

**1-10 Cost-benefit analysis.**
A firm has acquired a computer. It is now deciding what type of software to acquire. The alternatives are:

Type A Requires five weeks to learn but an employee can do twice the work as with B.
Type B Requires one week to learn.

There is no place for employees who learn these skills to advance within the firm; consequently, employees are expected to turn over every three months on the average.

**Required**
**a.** Which software package should be acquired?
**b.** What might the firm do to reduce employee turnover?

**1-11 Cost-benefit analysis of information.**
In reaction to a recent softening in the market for the Parker Company's products, central management directed all departmental supervisors to reduce expenses by 10%. The manager of the credit department decided that the easiest savings could be achieved by reducing the use of office supplies. In the manager's opinion, office supplies worth $40 to $50 are taken home by employees or prematurely thrown away each month.

To reduce the use of office supplies, each of the department's 10 employees is now required to prepare a daily inventory of pencils, pens, notepads, envelopes, letterhead, paper clips, and rubber bands. The inventory is taken at the end of the day. Each employee must record the beginning balance of each type of supply, add the amount of supplies requisitioned (the requisition form must be approved by the credit manager), and then account for the use of supplies, which, when subtracted from the supplies available, yields the ending balance for each type of supply. On a random basis, the credit department manager audits employees' supply records.

**Required**
Comment on the credit manager's approach to reducing costs.

**1-12 Segment performance versus manager's performance.**
The Erie Division of the Johnson Company has been losing money for several years. The division's net losses for the past 5 years were as follows:

| | |
|---|---|
| 19X4 | $(150,000) |
| 19X5 | $(225,000) |
| 19X6 | $(216,000) |
| 19X7 | $(312,000) |
| 19X8 | $(195,000) |

The Erie Division was one of the first plants established by the Johnson Company nearly 50 years ago. For many years it had been very profitable, but in recent years its outdated plant and equipment has seemingly made it impossible for the division to produce its products at a competitive cost. In addition, the plant has a strong union with which management has had poor relations.

Early in 19X8, John Platt took over as plant manager. Platt transferred to the position from the Buffalo Division (Johnson's most profitable division in recent years), where he had also been plant manager. Platt quickly set about to mend relations with the union, with the most important result being to relax some extremely restrictive work rules that had been established in the mid-1950s. In addition, Platt replaced some relatively inexpensive equipment that had previously severely hampered production. Production bottlenecks are no longer a major problem.

For the present year, 19X9, Platt projects the Erie Division will lose $25,000 to $50,000. The year after, the division could make a small profit, but he indicates that major new investment in plant and equipment will be required before central management can expect the Erie Division to make a viable profit. However, he suggests that such an investment probably cannot be justified under current conditions in the market for Erie's product.

**Required**

**a.** Evaluate the performance of the Erie Division.

**b.** Evaluate Platt's performance.

**1-13 The influence of information on management.**

On Wednesday a vital piece of equipment broke down. Management asked an accounting clerk to quickly determine the least expensive means to repair the equipment. The clerk considered four alternatives: (1) fix the equipment with the firm's own personnel, (2) have it repaired by Ace Engineering, (3) have it repaired by City Mechanical, Inc. (owned by the clerk's brother-in-law), (4) have it repaired by The Ohlson Company.

The clerk determined that it would take the firm's personnel at least a week to repair the equipment. Each of the outside vendors promised they could have the machine repaired in one day. Ace Equipment submitted a bid of $3,800 for the job. City Mechanical's bid was $3,500, while the Ohlson bid was for $3,400.

The clerk sent the following memo to the manager:

*The plant manager estimates that our personnel could fix the equipment, but it would take at least a week to acquire the appropriate parts, plans, and tools. Although it is difficult to estimate the losses that we would incur from such downtime, I estimate that it could easily be in the range of $5,000 per day. Thus I feel this alternative is unacceptable.*

*Outside vendors have the appropriate experience and tooling to complete the repairs in just one day. Ace Equipment has bid $3,800 to perform the job. City Mechanical has bid $3,500. Each company promises to begin the work this afternoon and be done by tomorrow. Both are local companies that have been in business for more than 10 years. They each have fine reputations for performing timely, quality work.*

**Required**

What do you expect the manager will do? Discuss the consequences and implications raised in this case.

CHAPTER

2

# INTRODUCTION TO COST ACCOUNTING: THE BASICS

In this chapter we introduce some basic terminology and trace the cost accumulation process through the general ledger. This material provides a foundation and a framework for the rest of the text.

## COST TERMINOLOGY

As with any field of study, cost accounting has its own vocabulary that must be mastered. This section summarizes some of the more pervasive terms. There is a complete glossary at the end of the book.

### Cost Object

Throughout the text we will refer to cost objects. A **cost object** can be any function, process, organizational unit, or physical item of interest to management for which a separate measurement of cost is desired. It is a general term referring to the thing for which we account. It is a basic term, equivalent to the entity concept in financial accounting. If we are asked to determine the cost to produce a unit of product, the unit of product is the cost object. If we want to know the cost of maintaining an in-house engineering department, the department is the cost object. Other cost objects might be the cost of a safety program, the cost of operating a particular production line, the firm's total energy cost, or the cost of an advertising campaign.

### Costs and Expenses

As we shall see, costs are classified in many ways: (1) by what was acquired, (2) by how the cost object was used, or (3) by the functional form that relates the cost to some other variable. In all cases, however, the following definition of cost will hold: A **cost** is the value of assets given up, or to be given up, to acquire other assets. Cost is distinguished from **expense,** which is the value of assets given up to generate revenue.

Clearly, most costs eventually become expenses. In fact, some become an expense virtually at the same time as the cost is incurred. When this is true, we often use the terms cost and expense interchangeably. For example, if a firm buys supplies for salespeople only as the supplies are needed and the supplies are used immediately to help generate sales, we usually call the outlay for supplies an expense. But in fact there was both a cost and an expense involved. The distinction can be seen more clearly if we change the example slightly. Consider a firm that buys sales supplies in bulk and uses them over time. Now the cost of supplies is the value of the assets given up to acquire the inventory of supplies. The expense for supplies will be the value of the assets (supplies) that are given up (used) during a particular period to generate revenue.

Classifying an item directly as an expense without first recognizing the cost of an acquired asset is a convenience. On the other hand, it does lead to confusion of the terms *cost* and *expense,* which can be bothersome in situations where the distinction between them is important. In service organizations and retail organizations, for example, most labor services are used directly to generate revenues. In these cases there is no harm in referring to the expenditures for labor as labor expense. In many situations, however, labor services are not used directly to generate revenue; instead, they are used to produce a product. In these cases the cost of labor services becomes part of the cost of the product produced. We use cash to acquire labor services, and the labor services are used to acquire completed units of product. The labor will become an expense only when the associated product is finally used to generate revenue (i.e., when the product is sold). Hence, in a manufacturing organization, the labor to construct a product becomes part of the cost of the product. Similarly, for a firm that supplies computer software, the labor to write a computer program becomes part of the cost of the program. These costs become expenses in the first case when the product is sold and, in the second case, over time as the computer program is leased to customers. Note that when products are sold, accountants by convention refer to the *cost of goods sold.* The cost of goods sold is the accumulated cost of the products given up to generate revenues. Because the transaction relates to revenue production, a more appropriate term might be *expense for goods sold.*

We mentioned that most costs eventually become expenses. There is an exception when assets are given up for nothing in return. In these cases the value of the assets given up becomes a **loss.** Thus, if some sales supplies are carelessly destroyed, the firm will have incurred a loss from destroyed supplies. Figure 2-1 portrays the relationship of costs, expenses, and losses.

## TYPES OF COSTS

The primary concern of a cost accountant is, of course, costs. How we categorize and accumulate costs depends upon the use to be made of the data. Accordingly, accountants make a distinction among several different types of costs.

### Fixed and Variable Costs

A common management question is, "What will happen to costs if we change our level of activity?" For questions of this kind, a distinction between fixed and variable costs is useful. **Fixed costs** are those costs that in

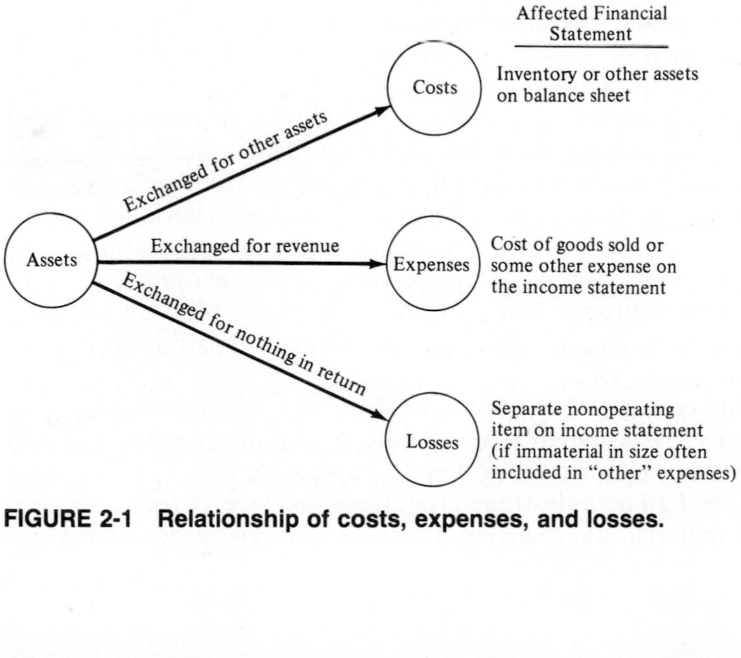


**FIGURE 2-1 Relationship of costs, expenses, and losses.**

total will not change as a function of the proposed change in activity level. Clearly, if a sufficiently large change is proposed, say increasing output 100-fold, all costs are likely to change. Fixed costs, then, can be fixed only over a restricted range of possible levels of activity. Another term, the **relevant range,** refers to that range of activity in which management expects the firm to be operating in the next planning period.

The potential range in which a firm might operate in the next period is likely to be quite large. Its product may become a fad, in which case sales will be much higher than management actually expects. At the other extreme, a labor strike or a natural disaster may hold sales to far less than what management expects. The relevant range is not the firm's total potential range of activity, but instead encompasses only the range that management expects to experience with a high degree of probability. It is the relatively narrow range of activity levels on which management plans are predicated. With this in mind, costs are classified as fixed if they are fixed within the firm's relevant range.

In most cases the change in the level of activity is measured in terms of the number of units of product to be manufactured. For that activity base, a fixed cost is one that does not change in total as we adjust the number of units of output. Thus, property taxes on a building are likely to be fixed in relation to the number of units produced. However, note that if we calculate the average fixed cost per unit of product manufactured, the fixed cost per unit will decrease as we increase production. If rent is $500 per month and we produce 2 units of product, the average fixed cost is $250 per unit. But if we produce 10 units, the average fixed cost is $50 per unit.

Fixed costs are often further divided into committed costs and discretionary costs. **Committed fixed costs** are those costs necessary to have the capacity to provide goods and services. They include such costs as depreciation on plant and equipment, property taxes, rent of necessary facilities, and many administrative salaries. In contrast, **discretionary fixed costs** are costs that management has chosen to incur and that could be discontinued without a major short-term impact on the firm's ability to maintain operations. Discretionary fixed costs include charitable contributions, the cost of a factory safety program, and many advertising costs. Once the decision has been made to operate or continue operating, management has little short-run control over the level of spending for committed costs, but the level of discretionary costs can be adjusted if management wishes to do so.

**Variable costs** are those that in total will change proportionately as levels of activity are changed. If every unit of product requires 1 pound of a material, then that material cost will be a variable cost. If we produce 10 units, we need 10 pounds of material; if we produce 15 units, we need 15 pounds of material. Alternatively, a variable cost can be viewed as a cost

**EXHIBIT 2-1 Cost Behavior in Relation to Changes in Activity**

| Type of Cost | Total Cost | Per-Unit Cost |
|---|---|---|
| Fixed | Constant | Inversely related to activity |
| Variable | Directly related to activity | Constant |

that is constant on a *per-unit* basis no matter what our level of output. If labor costs us \$2,500 when we produce 500 units and \$3,500 when we produce 700 units, then labor is a variable cost because labor cost is \$5 per unit at both levels of output. Exhibit 2-1 and Figure 2-2 contrast the behavior of fixed and variable costs both in total and on a per-unit basis.

We have used the term *activity level* in our definition of fixed and variable costs to highlight that the categorization of costs as fixed or variable depends on the question being asked by management. It may well be that costs that are variable for changes in level of output may be fixed in relation to other questions. For example, consider a student who is planning to obtain a degree that requires 130 credit hours at \$50 per credit hour. If the student is trying to decide whether to complete the degree in four years versus five years, variable costs will include living costs, but total

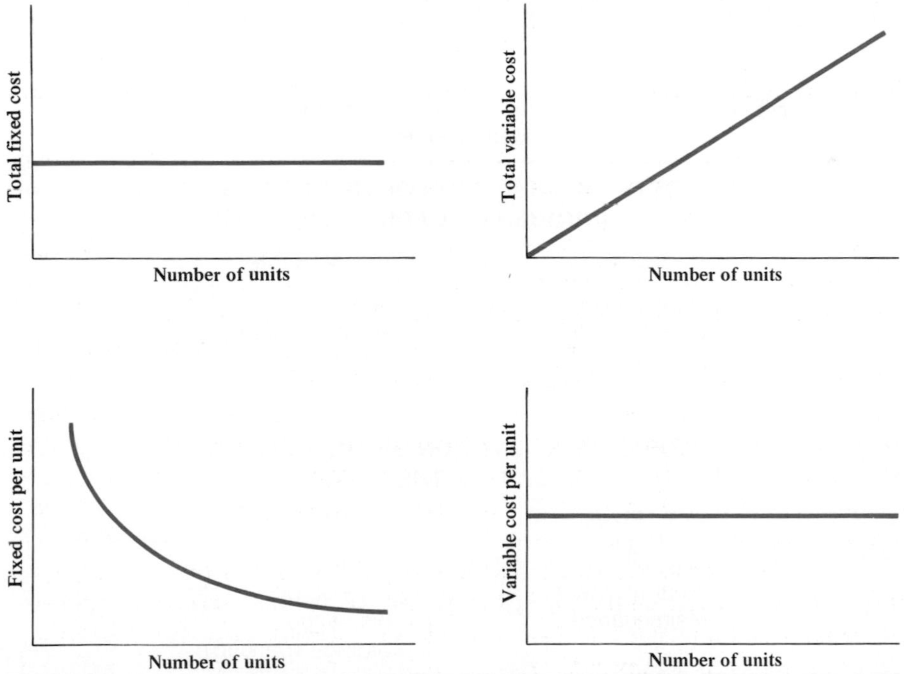


**FIGURE 2-2 Graphic representation of fixed and variable costs.**

tuition costs will be fixed. That is, if the cost object is the *total cost of obtaining the degree,* tuition costs are fixed at 130 × $50 = $6,500 by the degree requirements. However, for a particular semester the student's living costs will be fairly fixed, but relative to the cost object, *cost for the semester,* the tuition cost will be variable depending on the number of credit hours taken during the term. Another example of how the fixed and variable distinction depends on the measurement base is given in Exhibit 2-2. For simplicity, when the terms *fixed* and *variable costs* are used in this text, we will presume that the distinction is being made on the basis of changes in the level of production. When the terms relate to some other activity measure, an appropriate modifier will be used.

### Direct and Indirect Costs

Another common classification of costs is based on the ease with which costs may be traced to a cost object. A **direct cost** is a cost that is easily traced to a cost object, whereas an **indirect cost** is one that is not easily traceable to a cost object. Traceability refers to the existence of a clear cause-and-effect relationship between the cost object and the incurrence of a cost, while the modifier "easily" limits direct costs to those items for which we can justify the record-keeping costs to accurately trace them to the cost object. An example should clarify the distinction.

**EXHIBIT 2-2 Fixed and Variable Costs for a Motor Pool Relative to Basis of Measurement**

| COSTS AS A FUNCTION OF MILES DRIVEN (NUMBER OF CARS FIXED) | |
|---|---|
| **Fixed** | **Variable** |
| Depreciation | Gas, oil |
| License plates | Wear and tear |
| Insurance | Maintenance |
| Storage (parking) | |
| **COSTS AS A FUNCTION OF THE NUMBER OF CARS IN THE POOL[a]** | |
| **Fixed** | **Variable** |
| Gas, oil | Depreciation |
| Wear and tear | License plates |
| Maintenance | Insurance |
| | Storage (parking) |

[a]Assuming that the total mileage is unaffected by the number of cars.

If the cost object of concern is a particular department, then the cost of labor for people who work solely in that department is a traceable cost. If labor costs are a significant cost of operating the department, the labor costs would be treated as a direct cost. The electricity consumed by the department is also capable of being traced to the department if appropriate meters are installed. But if electricity costs are relatively minor, management may trade off the value of having more accurate data on the cost of operating the department against the cost of installing the meters. If the meters cannot be justified on a cost-benefit basis, the cost of electricity will be treated as an indirect cost and charged to the department based upon an estimate.

The most common use of the terms direct and indirect costs are in reference to the products or services produced by a firm. For a firm that manufactures calculators, direct costs would include the cost of the major components of the calculator and the labor cost needed to assemble the product. In this case the cost object is an individual calculator. The direct costs are those for which the associated assets are clearly incorporated into the resulting calculator. The indirect product costs are those costs necessary for the production of the product but not easily traced to an individual product. For example, the costs of minor supplies, such as glue and rivets, are often classified as indirect costs. Although it is possible to trace these costs to the product, the cost of the record keeping exceeds the benefit of having precise figures. Note, however, that the classification of a particular cost as direct or indirect can change over time. When energy costs were relatively low, it was common to treat them as indirect costs. Now that energy costs can be quite significant, many firms find it worthwhile to go to the trouble of classifying them as direct costs. As shown in subsequent chapters, direct costs are subject to greater planning and management control. It is the significance of costs—and hence the need for the control of particular costs—that determines the classification of traceable costs as direct or indirect.

Exhibit 2-3 indicates that a particular cost may be a direct cost for some cost objects but an indirect cost for others. Again, for simplicity, throughout the text we will presume that the direct cost reference is to units of product. An appropriate modifying term will be used when the distinction is being made on some other basis.

### Manufacturing and Nonmanufacturing Costs

The distinction between **manufacturing** and **nonmanufacturing costs** depends on whether the costs are considered direct costs in relation to the firm's manufacturing activities taken as a whole. Thus, although the costs of operating a factory personnel department are not direct *product* costs (the cost cannot easily be traced to an individual unit of product), they are

**EXHIBIT 2-3 Direct and Indirect Costs Relative to Several Cost Objects**

| | Cost Object | | | | |
|---|---|---|---|---|---|
| | | Product Line | | Individual Unit of Product | |
| **Cost Item** | **Assembly Department** | **A** | **B** | **A** | **B** |
| Direct laborers: Assembly department | Direct | Direct | Direct | Direct | Direct |
| Line foreman: Product B | Direct | — | Direct | — | Indirect |
| Assembly department manager | Direct | Indirect | Indirect | Indirect | Indirect |
| Major subassemblies | Direct | Direct | Direct | Direct | Direct |
| Miscellaneous supplies | Direct | Indirect | Indirect | Indirect | Indirect |
| Plantwide heating and cooling | Indirect | Indirect | Indirect | Indirect | Indirect |

direct to the entire manufacturing process and are manufacturing costs. In contrast, marketing costs are costs involved in disposing of the products, not in producing them. Thus selling costs are nonmanufacturing costs. Administrative costs fall in between. Many firms treat administrative costs as nonmanufacturing costs; however, we are aware that some firms, particularly defense contractors, allocate a portion of administrative costs to manufacturing. This practice is, of course, inconsistent with the definition that manufacturing costs are direct costs to the production process. Unless noted otherwise, we will treat administrative costs as nonmanufacturing costs in this text.

### Inventoriable and Period Costs

**Inventoriable costs** are those costs that are included as part of the cost of the product produced by a firm. If the product is not immediately sold, these costs will be assigned to the firm's inventory, and thus the term. For most firms, inventoriable costs are all the costs identified as manufacturing costs. Some firms, however, choose to exclude fixed manufacturing costs from inventoriable costs for internal reports. In this case, fixed manufacturing costs are not **product costs**[1] (another term for inventoriable costs) but instead are considered period costs. For external purposes, however,

[1]The term *product cost* is the more traditional term, but we consider it too narrow. Many firms are engaged to some degree in services, and such firms may properly "inventory" costs associated with contracts in progress. For example, magazines will "inventory" stories in progress and public accounting firms "inventory" audits in process.

generally accepted accounting principles (and the Internal Revenue Code) require fixed manufacturing costs to be included as product costs.

**Period costs** are those costs that are expensed in the period in which the associated services have been acquired. It is assumed that period costs have helped generate revenues in the period incurred and that they will not affect the revenues of future periods. Although this is not always strictly true, it is usually very difficult to estimate the future benefits that will arise from cost items identified as period costs. For example, most selling and administrative costs are considered period costs. Exceptions include items such as administrative supplies, in which there exists a measurable amount of inventory supplies on hand at the end of the period. In contrast, although some accountants have argued that a portion of advertising costs should be postponed to the subsequent periods benefiting from the expenditure, most accountants treat advertising costs as a period cost because of the difficulty of determining how much should be deferred.

### Other Terminology

The last bit of terminology consists of a separation of manufacturing costs into three classifications: direct materials, direct labor, and overhead. **Direct materials** and **direct labor** are the materials and labor that can be easily traced to individual units of product. Those inputs traced directly to the product are often called the **prime costs;** that is, prime costs are the sum of direct labor and direct materials costs. All other manufacturing costs, including indirect materials and indirect labor, are **overhead** (sometimes called **factory burden**). The individual direct costs are generally subject to close managerial control, whereas overhead costs tend to be controlled as a group. In addition, direct materials and direct labor are clearly identified with the product and these costs are easily assigned to the product. Overhead, on the other hand, must usually be assigned to the product somewhat arbitrarily.

Later we will see that determining how to assign the overhead costs to units of product is a significant problem for cost accountants. Typically, firms produce a number of heterogeneous products and services. Rather than attempt to trace overhead directly to the products and services, accountants in these situations often trace overhead to a measure of an input that is common to the products or services. Since labor is usually a common input and one for which we generally have fairly detailed records anyway (for payroll purposes), labor is often the basis for applying overhead to products. When this occurs, it is convenient to have a term that refers to both labor and overhead costs. **Conversion costs** or **processing costs** are the sum of direct labor and overhead costs. We can think of these as the costs to convert raw materials into finished products.

The interrelationships of the terms we have defined in their most common usage are given in Exhibit 2-4. Because costs are such an important concern for management planning and control, you are going to see many other classifications of costs as we proceed through this text. We will introduce new terms as they are needed. But you should keep in mind that with all these distinctions, even though the definitions may seem precise, in practice the distinctions frequently become very fuzzy. The exercises at the end of this chapter should prove that observation.

## COST FLOWS

The flow of *nonmanufacturing* costs through the accounting system is straightforward. Typically these costs are assigned as incurred to a responsibility center (the department or organizational unit with the most control over the cost incurred) by function. Thus, a cost might be classified as Controller's Department: Salaries, another as Controller's Department: Supplies, and another as Sales Department: Salaries. In this way the manager of each responsibility center can be informed of both the total costs incurred and the types of assets and services acquired. When it is time to

**EXHIBIT 2-4 Relationship of Cost Terms for a Typical Manufacturer Where Both the Direct and Variable Distinctions Are Based on Units of Product[a]**

**MANUFACTURING COSTS**

| | | | |
|---|---|---|---|
| | Direct costs | | Always inventoriable (product) costs. They become expenses only when the associated product is sold. |
| Prime costs (Direct materials, Direct labor) | Direct materials | Variable costs | |
| Conversion costs (Direct labor, Indirect costs) | Direct labor | | |
| | Indirect costs | | |
| | Variable overhead | | |
| | Fixed overhead | Fixed costs | Inventoriable cost for some purposes, period costs for other purposes |

**NONMANUFACTURING COSTS**

| | |
|---|---|
| Selling costs<br>Variable<br>Fixed<br><br>Administrative costs<br>Variable<br>Fixed | With a very few exceptions, period costs. They become expenses in the same period that they are incurred. |

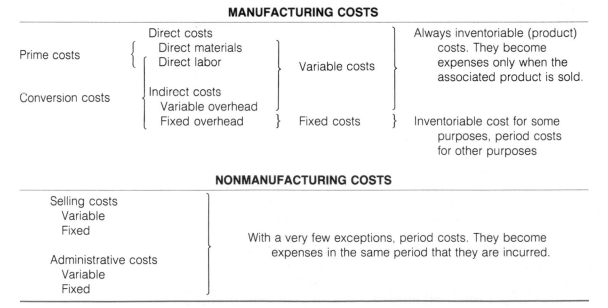

[a]As discussed in the text, the direct-indirect and fixed-variable distinctions can be made on several other bases.

prepare financial statements, these costs are accumulated across departments. After any appropriate adjusting entries, the nonmanufacturing cost accounts should be ready for incorporation into external financial statements.

The flow of *manufacturing* costs through the accounting system is not so straightforward. In fact, in a large multidepartmental firm the cost flows can be quite complex. Since it is our intent to introduce only the basic cost flows at this point, let us consider a simplified firm that records actual costs and has just two departments related to manufacturing the firm's product: assembly and factory housekeeping. The assembly department is a **production department;** that is, it works directly on the product being manufactured. The factory housekeeping department is a **service department.** It does not work on the product; rather, it provides janitorial service to the assembly department.

As materials are *purchased,* they are added to the Raw Materials Inventory account. As materials are *used,* they are removed from the inventory account and assigned to the appropriate department by function. To keep direct costs and overhead costs separate, a distinction is maintained in the assembly department between direct materials and indirect materials.[2] Similarly, labor costs when incurred are classified by department and function; again, a distinction is maintained between direct and indirect labor in the assembly department. Finally, all other indirect costs are recorded by department and function. By recording costs in this manner each department will have a complete list of the costs it has incurred, by function, for control purposes. That is, each department is charged for all the costs it incurs directly so that the departmental manager can be held responsible for total departmental costs incurred. The amount of detail and the number of different functions—such as heat, electricity, and supplies—maintained for each department will depend on the importance of controlling the individual costs.

At the end of the accounting period the total costs accumulated by the factory housekeeping department are transferred to the assembly department via a journal entry and become an overhead item for that department. In this way all manufacturing costs have been accumulated in the production department. Next, the manufacturing costs are assigned to the products that were produced. The costs assigned to units completed are then transferred out of the assembly department as **cost of goods completed** or **cost of goods manufactured** to the finished goods inventory. The costs attached to units not completed remain in the department and constitute the work-in-process inventory at the end of the period for fi-

[2]Some firms maintain a distinction between direct and indirect materials at the time of acquisition. For these firms only direct materials are recorded in the Raw Materials account. Indirect materials are recorded in an account called Supplies.

nancial statement presentation. Finally the cost of any units sold is removed from the Finished Goods Inventory and transferred to the expense account, Cost of Goods Sold.

## THE BASIC INVENTORY MODEL

In a manufacturing environment there are three types of inventory accounts: raw materials, work-in-process, and finished goods. No matter which inventory account we are concerned with, the basic accounting model for it is the same. In every case we can say that the beginning inventory balance plus additions to it, less transfers out, must equal the ending inventory balance. It can be stated equivalently that the beginning balance plus additions must equal the ending balance plus transfers out. This latter form indicates that the total of the beginning balance and additions must be accounted for as either being in ending inventory or having been transferred out. Exhibit 2-5 illustrates the relationship between the inventory accounts from this perspective and notes the varying terms that we use to refer to additions and transfers for the individual accounts.

The foregoing discussion was a broad description of how costs flow through an accounting system. The description was greatly simplified, and some sticky problems have been ignored. The actual process for recording cost flows is sufficiently complex that we devote Chapters 11–17 to the topic. At this point we want to make it clear that costs are accumulated by department for control purposes and that there are three separate inventory accounts for manufacturing costs:

Raw Materials, which reflects the costs of materials that we have available for production

**EXHIBIT 2-5 The Relationship of the Inventory Accounts in a Simplified Situation[a]**

| | | Materials | Work-in-Process | Finished Goods |
|---|---|---|---|---|
| Cost accumulation | Beginning balance | Beginning | Beginning | Beginning |
| | + Additions | Purchases | Materials used | Goods completed |
| | | | Labor used | |
| | | | Overhead | |
| | To be accounted for | Available | Available | Available |
| Cost distribution | − Ending balance | Ending | Ending | Ending |
| | = Transfers | Uses | Goods completed | Goods sold |

[a]For any department the beginning balance plus additions represent the costs *accumulated* by that department and the total costs to be accounted for. The total costs to be accounted for are, in turn, *distributed* between the ending inventory for that department and transfers out.

Work-in-Process, which includes the inventoriable costs attached to partially completed production that is still in the production departments
Finished Goods, which represents the inventoriable costs attached to goods that are complete but not yet sold

Another way of viewing the inventory accounts is to observe that raw materials constitute an inventory of items on which no work has been done, finished goods are those items on which we have completed our manufacturing effort, and work-in-process is everything in between.

Let us now demonstrate the inventory cost flows with a simple example. We are dealing with a new firm, so we begin our accounting period with no inventories. During the period we purchase $20,000 of raw materials and put $17,000 of them into production. Labor costs incurred during the period are $22,000, and manufacturing overhead costs amount to $35,000. At the end of the period we note that we have $4,000 of partially completed units still in production, and the cost of the units in ending finished goods inventory amounts to $9,000.

Exhibit 2-6 portrays the relationship of costs in T-account form, and Exhibit 2-7 summarizes the numerical information for our example in T-account form. The account for Raw Materials indicates that we began with no inventory, added $20,000 in purchases, and used $17,000 for production, resulting in an ending balance in materials inventory of $3,000.

The $17,000 of materials used are transferred to Work-in-Process Inventory, where they are added to the beginning balance of zero. In addition, the direct labor and overhead costs are also added to Work-in-Process. The total manufacturing costs sum to $74,000, but the example stated that we ended the period with $4,000 of goods still in process; therefore, $70,000 worth of products must have been completed.

The cost of completed products is then transferred to the Finished Goods Inventory. Because there was no beginning inventory, only the $70,000 of completed units were available for sale. The example indicates that we ended the period with $9,000 of product in ending finished goods; hence $61,000 worth of product must have been sold.

**EXHIBIT 2-6 Flow of Costs through Inventory Accounts**

| Raw Materials Inventory | | Work-in-Process Inventory | | Finished Goods Inventory | |
|---|---|---|---|---|---|
| Beginning balance<br>+ Purchases | Raw materials used | Beginning balance<br>+ Materials<br>+ Direct labor<br>+ Overhead | Cost of goods completed | Beginning balance<br>+ Cost of goods completed | Cost of goods sold |
| Ending balance | | Ending balance | | Ending balance | |

**EXHIBIT 2-7 An Illustration of Inventory Cost Flows**

**Raw Materials Inventory**

| | |
|---|---|
| — | |
| 20,000 | 17,000 → |
| 3,000 | |

**Work-in-Process Inventory**

| | | |
|---|---|---|
| | — | |
| | → 17,000 | 70,000 → |
| Labor | 22,000 | |
| Overhead | 35,000 | |
| | 4,000 | |

**Finished Goods Inventory**

| | |
|---|---|
| — | |
| → 70,000 | 61,000 |
| 9,000 | |

The movement of costs through the general ledger is accomplished with journal entries. The entries which summarize the major events for the prior example are as follows:

| | | |
|---|---|---|
| Raw Materials Inventory | 20,000 | |
| Cash (or Accounts Payable) | | 20,000 |
| To record the purchase of materials | | |
| Work-in-Process Inventory | 17,000 | |
| Raw Materials Inventory | | 17,000 |
| To record the cost of materials placed into production | | |
| Work-in-Process Inventory | 22,000 | |
| Wages Payable | | 22,000 |
| To record labor costs incurred for production | | |
| Work-in-Process Inventory | 35,000 | |
| Overhead | | 35,000 |
| To transfer the accumulated overhead costs to production | | |
| Finished Goods Inventory | 70,000 | |
| Work-in-Process Inventory | | 70,000 |
| To record and transfer the cost of goods manufactured (completed) | | |
| Cost of Goods Sold | 61,000 | |
| Finished Goods Inventory | | 61,000 |
| To record the cost of the goods that were sold | | |

## STATEMENT OF COST OF GOODS MANUFACTURED

The T-account representation of cost flows makes it easy to see what is happening with manufacturing costs. For reports to management, however, we usually prepare a more formal presentation, called a *statement of*

**EXHIBIT 2-8 Statement of Cost of Goods Manufactured (and Sold) Format**

| | | |
|---|---|---|
| [Beginning balance: Raw materials inventory | XX | |
| Plus raw materials purchased | XX | |
| Equals raw materials available for use | XXX | |
| Less ending balance: Raw materials inventory | XX | |
| Equals raw materials used | | XX |
| Plus beginning balance: Work-in-process inventory | | XX |
| Plus direct labor costs incurred | | XX |
| Plus overhead costs incurred | | XX |
| Equals total costs in work-in-process | | XXX |
| Less ending balance: Work-in-process inventory | | XX |
| Equals cost of goods manufactured] | | XXX |
| (Plus beginning balance: Finished goods inventory | | XX |
| Equals cost of goods available for sale | | XXX |
| Less ending balance: Finished goods inventory | | XX |
| Equals cost of goods sold) | | XXX |

[ ] Statement of Cost of Goods Manufactured
( ) Statement of Cost of Goods Sold

*cost of goods manufactured.* The statement provides the same information as that represented in the T-accounts but also provides several important subtotals. A typical format is given in Exhibit 2-8. The statement of cost of goods manufactured (indicated in square brackets) ends, of course, with the determination of cost of goods manufactured. If we add to the statement an analysis of the Finished Goods Inventory (in round brackets), we transform it into a *statement of cost of goods manufactured and sold.*

Exhibit 2-8 illustrates just one of several possible formats. Recall that in management accounting we are concerned solely with presenting information to management in a form that we believe will best enable management to comprehend it. We are not constrained by rules imposed by outside third parties. Exhibit 2-9 presents an alternative statement of cost of goods manufactured and sold, this time incorporating the data from the example used to illustrate the flow of costs through T-accounts. Still another format is provided in Exhibit 14-6.

## SUMMARY

Management may request that costs be accumulated for any of a large number of cost objects. This variety of potential cost objects led to the development of a number of classifications for costs, such as direct or indirect and fixed or variable. It is the purpose to which the cost information is going to be put that determines the most appropriate classification of costs.

**EXHIBIT 2-9 An Alternate Format for the Statement of Cost of Goods Manufactured and Sold**

| | | | | |
|---|---|---|---|---|
| Beginning finished goods inventory | | | | |
| Beginning work-in-process inventory | | | — | |
| Beginning raw materials inventory | — | | | |
| Plus raw materials purchased | $20,000 | | | |
| Equals raw materials available for use | $20,000 | | | |
| Less ending raw materials inventory | 3,000 | | | |
| Equals raw materials used | | $17,000 | | |
| Plus direct labor costs incurred | | 22,000 | | |
| Plus overhead costs incurred | | 35,000 | | |
| Equals current period manufacturing cost | | | $74,000 | |
| Total costs in work-in-process | | | $74,000 | |
| Less ending work-in-process inventory | | | 4,000 | |
| Equals cost of goods manufactured | | | | $70,000 |
| Cost of goods available for sale | | | | $70,000 |
| Less ending finished goods inventory | | | | 9,000 |
| Equals cost of goods sold | | | | $61,000 |

Manufacturing firms typically maintain three separate inventory accounts: Raw Materials, Work-in-Process, and Finished Goods. Raw Materials consists of material inputs awaiting processing, whereas Finished Goods consists of the outputs awaiting sale. During the operating period the three types of manufacturing costs—direct materials, direct labor, and overhead—are accumulated to determine product costs. Costs attached to partially completed units at the end of the period are reported as the cost of ending work-in-process.

## DEMONSTRATION PROBLEM

Hadley Industries began the current period with raw materials costing $5,000, partially completed products costing $1,000, and completed products costing $10,000. During the period the firm purchased $40,000 of raw materials. From the raw materials inventory, direct materials costing $25,000 were used by the assembly department. An additional $7,000 of indirect materials was used by the assembly department and $3,000 of materials was used by the equipment maintenance department (a service department).

Also during the period the firm incurred labor costs of $50,000. Of this amount, $35,000 was direct labor in the assembly department, another $5,000 was indirect labor in the assembly department, and the remaining $10,000 was labor used in the equipment maintenance department. Other manufacturing costs amounted to $12,000 for the assembly department and $4,000 for the equipment maintenance department.

The cost of the units completed by the assembly department during the period was $98,000. A count of finished goods inventory at the end of the period revealed goods with a cost of $6,000 still on hand.

**Required**

**a.** Trace the flow of manufacturing costs through the inventory accounts using T-accounts.

**b.** What were the total prime costs, conversion costs, direct costs, and manufacturing costs incurred by this firm during the period?

**Solution**

**a.** The $5,000 cost of raw materials on hand at the beginning of the period would be Hadley's beginning balance in the Raw Materials Inventory account. Similarly, the $1,000 of partially completed product on hand must be the beginning balance in Work-in-Process Inventory, while the $10,000 worth of completed product is the beginning Finished Goods Inventory balance. These beginning balances have been placed in the appropriate T-accounts in Exhibit 2-10.

In addition to the beginning inventory balances, we have also included in Exhibit 2-10 the flow of materials costs. The $25,000 of materials considered direct materials are traced directly to the assembly department's Direct Materials account, while the $7,000 of indirect materials are traced to the assembly department's Overhead account (recall that indirect materials are a part of overhead). Finally we traced the materials used by equipment maintenance to that department. Since the equipment maintenance department is a service department that does not work directly on the product produced by the firm, we do

**EXHIBIT 2-10 Flow of Materials Costs**

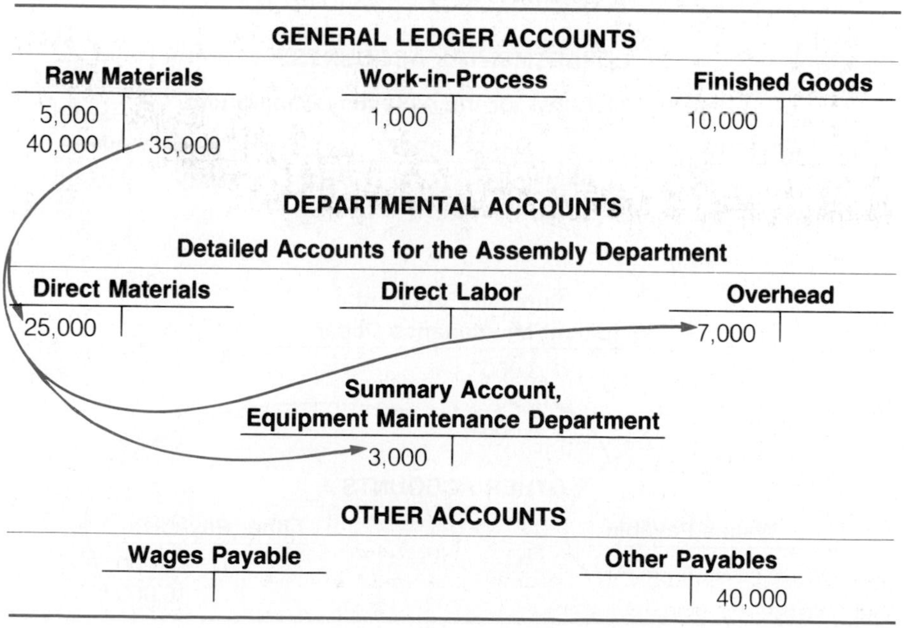

not segregate direct from indirect costs (none of this department's costs are direct product costs).

In Exhibit 2-11 we have added the labor costs to the T-accounts. We can see that the $35,000 of direct labor costs are maintained in a separate account for the assembly department. Again, the assembly department's $5,000 of indirect labor costs are added to the departmental overhead account and the $10,000 of labor costs for the equipment maintenance department are added to that department's accumulated costs. Also in Exhibit 2-11 we distribute the $16,000 of "other manufacturing costs." Since the $12,000 of these costs which are attributable to the assembly department were not specified as direct costs, they must be overhead costs, so we have added these costs to departmental overhead. Once again, we see that for the service department, equipment maintenance, we do not distinguish between direct and indirect costs, so the "other costs" are simply added to the department's accumulated costs.

Exhibit 2-12 completes the tracing of the cost flows. The first step, illustrated at the bottom of the exhibit, is to close the $17,000 balance in the Equipment Maintenance account to the assembly department's Overhead account. Let us again explain why this is done. The costs were first accumulated in the Equip-

**EXHIBIT 2-11 Flow of Labor and Overhead Costs**

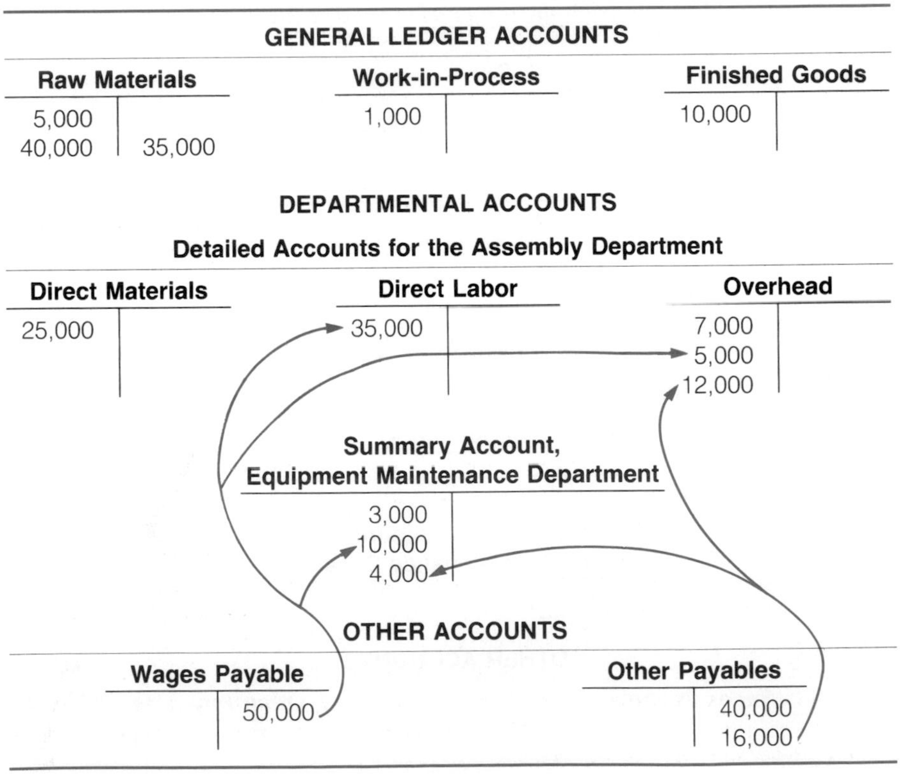

**EXHIBIT 2-12 Flow of Costs through Work-in-Process and Finished Goods**

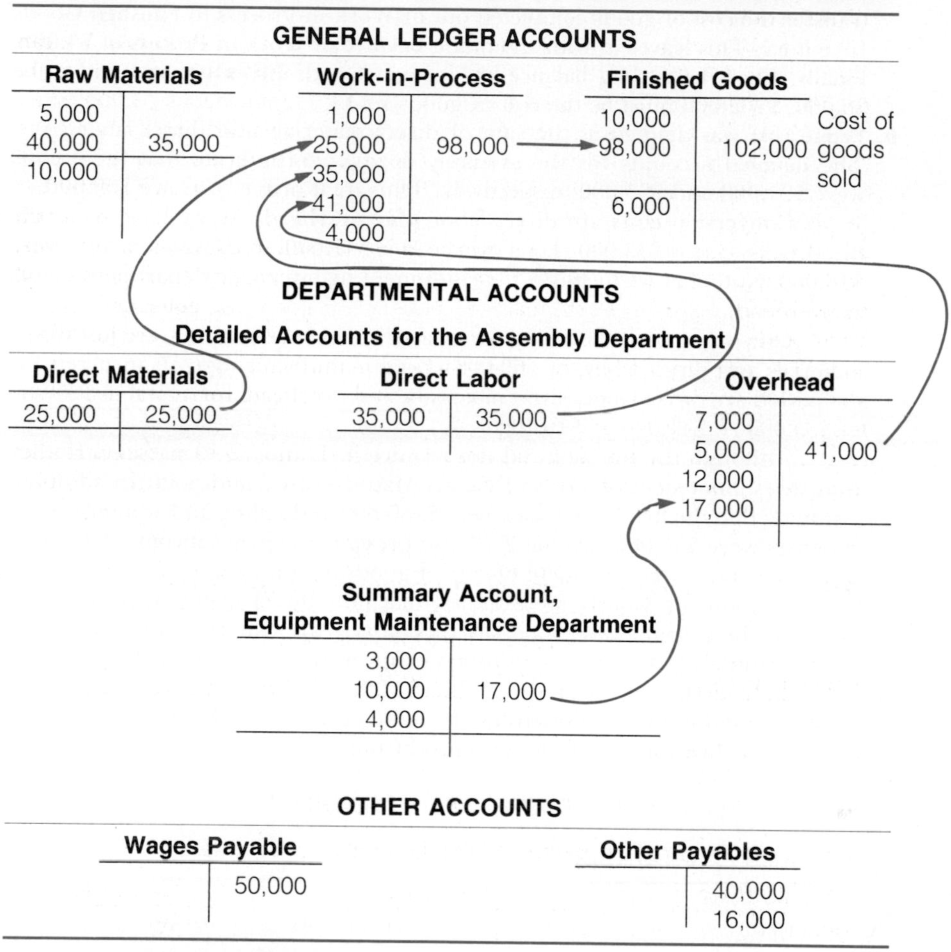
GENERAL LEDGER ACCOUNTS
Raw Materials
5,000
40,000
35,000
10,000
Work-in-Process
1,000
25,000
35,000
41,000
98,000
4,000
Finished Goods
10,000
98,000
102,000
Cost of goods sold
6,000
DEPARTMENTAL ACCOUNTS
Detailed Accounts for the Assembly Department
Direct Materials
25,000
25,000
Direct Labor
35,000
35,000
Overhead
7,000
5,000
12,000
17,000
41,000
Summary Account, Equipment Maintenance Department
3,000
10,000
4,000
17,000
OTHER ACCOUNTS
Wages Payable
50,000
Other Payables
40,000
16,000

ment Maintenance account so that we would know the cost of providing these services and so that the manager of the department could be held responsible for the level of costs incurred. Nonetheless, these are manufacturing costs, so they must be included in the costs assigned to production. We accomplish this by charging all manufacturing costs to production departments. That is, the costs of the equipment maintenance department were incurred for the benefit of the production department. Since these are not direct product costs, they are included as part of the assembly department's overhead costs. At this point we have all manufacturing costs accumulated in the production department. Now all manufacturing costs are assigned to the units of product produced. We represent this by transferring all the assembly department's costs to the General Ledger account Work-in-Process.

Next the problem stated that goods costing $98,000 were finished, so we transfer the cost of goods completed out of Work-in-Process to Finished Goods Inventory. This leaves us with an ending balance in Work-in-Process of $4,000. Finally, since the ending balance in Finished Goods Inventory was said to be $6,000, $102,000 must be the cost of goods sold.

**b.** Prime cost was defined as the sum of direct materials and direct labor costs. The detailed accounts for the assembly department indicate that these costs were $25,000 and $35,000, respectively. Thus total prime costs are $60,000.

Conversion costs are direct labor plus overhead. As we have seen, the direct labor cost is $35,000. Total overhead is $41,000, so conversion costs were $76,000. Note that we included the equipment maintenance department's costs as overhead.

Our direct costs, assuming we mean direct to the product, are just direct materials and direct labor, or $60,000. Total manufacturing costs incurred for the period are direct labor, direct materials, and overhead, for a total of $25,000 + $35,000 + $41,000 = $101,000.

Although the problem did not require it, Exhibit 2-13 presents Hadley Industries' Statement of Costs of Goods Manufactured and Sold. In addition, assuming that the firm's total sales were $180,000 and selling and administration expenses were $50,000, Exhibit 2-13 also presents the firm's income statement. Note a change in the statement of cost of goods manufactured from that given in the chapter. Previously, we assumed that only direct materials were inventoried in the account Raw Materials Inventory. Any materials used had to be direct materials put into work-in-process. But in this problem, both direct and indirect materials were included in Raw Materials Inventory. Thus the total materials used must be adjusted for the indirect materials charged to overhead to yield the direct materials put into production.

## KEY TERMS AND CONCEPTS

Cost object
Cost
Expense
Loss
Fixed cost
Relevant range
Committed fixed costs
Discretionary fixed costs
Variable cost
Direct costs
Indirect costs
Manufacturing costs
Nonmanufacturing costs
[Inventoriable costs
[Product costs
Period costs
Direct materials
Direct labor
Prime costs
[Overhead
[Factory burden
[Conversion costs
[Processing costs
Production department
Service department
[Cost of goods completed
[Cost of goods manufactured

[ Bracketed terms are equivalent in meaning.

**EXHIBIT 2-13 Two Financial Statements for Hadley Industries**

**STATEMENT OF COSTS OF GOODS MANUFACTURED AND SOLD**

| | | |
|---|---|---|
| Beginning balance: Raw materials inventory | $ 5,000 | |
| Plus raw materials purchased | 40,000 | |
| Equals raw materials available for use | $45,000 | |
| Less ending balance: Raw materials inventory | 10,000 | |
| Equals total raw materials used | $35,000 | |
| Less indirect materials used | 10,000 | |
| Equals direct materials put into work-in-process | | $ 25,000 |
| Plus beginning balance: Work-in-process inventory | | 1,000 |
| Plus direct labor costs incurred | | 35,000 |
| Plus overhead costs incurred | | 41,000 |
| Equals total costs in work-in-process | | $102,000 |
| Less ending balance: Work-in-process inventory | | 4,000 |
| Equals cost of goods manufactured | | $ 98,000 |
| Plus beginning balance: Finished goods inventory | | 10,000 |
| Equals cost of goods available for sale | | $108,000 |
| Less ending balance: Finished goods inventory | | 6,000 |
| Equals cost of goods sold | | $102,000 |

**INCOME STATEMENT**

| | |
|---|---|
| Sales | $180,000 |
| Cost of goods sold | 102,000 |
| Gross margin | $ 78,000 |
| Selling and administration expenses | 50,000 |
| Net income | $ 28,000 |

## FURTHER READING


Accountants International Study Group. *Comparative Glossary of Accounting Terms in Canada, the United Kingdom and the United States*. New York: AICPA and others, 1975.

Estes, Ralph. *Dictionary of Accounting*. Cambridge, Mass.: The MIT Press, 1981.

Haseman, Wilbur C. "An Interpretive Framework for Cost," *The Accounting Review* (October 1968), p. 738.

Kohler, Eric L. *A Dictionary for Accountants*, 5th ed. Englewood Cliffs, N.J.: Prentice-Hall, 1975.

Lang, Theodore. "Concepts of Cost, Past and Present," *NACA Bulletin* (July 15, 1947), p. 1377.

Mepham, M. J. "Concepts of Cost," *The Accountant* (January 18, 1964), p. 61.

Price Waterhouse & Co. *Thesaurus of Accounting and Auditing Terminology*. New York: Price Waterhouse & Co., 1974.

Wiener, Julius. "Separation of Fixed and Variable Costs," *The Accounting Review* (October 1960), p. 686.

## QUESTIONS AND EXERCISES

**2-1** When does a product cost become a period cost?

**2-2** What is similar and what is different between the terms *prime cost* and *conversion cost*?

**2-3** How does a statement of cost of goods manufactured differ from a statement of cost of goods manufactured and sold?

**2-4** Cost of goods manufactured has been overstated. The firm employs periodic inventory methods. How will this affect net income for the period, if at all?

**2-5** Illustrate the difference between direct material and indirect material.

**2-6** What is the significance of the concept of "relevant range" to the accounting process?

**2-7** "Direct costs are all variable and indirect costs are all fixed." Comment.

**2-8** "Fixed costs do not require periodic cash outlays." Comment.

**2-9** Distinguish between a direct cost and an indirect cost. What determines the accounting classification?

**2-10** This chapter has indicated, among other things, that a particular cost may be classified differently depending upon the purpose. Using insurance as an example, illustrate when this may be properly classified as direct, indirect, fixed, and variable.

**2-11** A firm customarily purchases a part at a cost of $1,600 and pays transportation and handling of $100. Owing to a rush order, the firm acquired the part from a nonconventional source for $1,500 plus $300 air freight charges; it cost the firm an additional $50 to pick up the part at the airport. At what cost should the part be recorded in inventory?

**2-12** Beginning and ending work-in-process inventories are equal. For the period, prime costs were $300, conversion costs were $270, and total manufacturing costs incurred were $390. What was the cost of direct labor, direct material, and overhead?

**2-13** Production costs incurred during the period totaled $880. Work-in-process decreased $30 and finished goods increased $80. Determine the cost of goods manufactured and the cost of goods sold.

**2-14** Philips Chips incurred total manufacturing costs of $58,000 in April. Direct materials costs amounted to $12,000 and direct labor costs were three times the amount of overhead. What were the totals for direct labor and overhead, respectively?

**2-15** The local Community Services Board solicits donations of used appliances. The group hires handicapped individuals to repair the appliances, which are then sold through the organization's Red Badge Store. At the end of the current period the repair facility had an ending work-in-process inventory of $300 and an ending finished goods inventory of $200. Cost of goods for which repairs were completed was $630 and cost of goods sold was $540. Costs incurred for making repairs during the period were $620. What were the beginning costs for Work-in-Process Inventory and Finished Goods Inventory?

**2-16** The following salaries and wages have been accrued for T. H., Inc., for the month.

| | |
|---|---|
| Direct labor: Plant | $210,000 |
| Indirect labor: Plant | 85,000 |
| Supervision: Plant | 32,000 |
| Sales commissions | 40,000 |
| Sales salaries | 18,000 |
| | $385,000 |

Of the total, how much would be properly classified as (a) product cost and period cost and (b) fixed cost and variable cost?

**2-17** The following accounts and balances pertain to raw materials.

| | |
|---|---|
| Raw materials, September 1 | $110 |
| Purchases (at invoice cost) | 405 |
| Transportation-in | 20 |
| Insurance | 10 |
| Purchase discounts taken | 8 |
| Purchase returns | 15 |
| Purchase allowances | 5 |
| Raw materials, September 30 | 130 |

What is the cost of raw materials placed into production?

**2-18** Given the following data for the period, find (a) the cost of goods completed and (b) the cost of goods sold.

Direct materials purchases were $48,000 and the direct materials inventory decreased by $3,000.
Direct labor earned $200,000 and was paid $198,000.
Indirect costs assigned to production amounted to $94,000.
The ending work-in-process inventory was $10,000 higher than the beginning inventory.
The ending finished goods inventory was $2,000 less than the beginning inventory.

**2-19** Interco ships components to its subsidiary in the German protectorate of the Island of Isle. On Isle, the components are assembled and then shipped out as completed units. The only costs on Isle are labor and supervision, expressed here in Deutsche marks (DM). Inventories for the third quarter were as follows:

| | **Beginning** | **Ending** |
|---|---|---|
| Raw materials | 120,000 DM | 140,000 DM |
| Work-in-process | 180,000 | 170,000 |
| Finished goods | 260,000 | 290,000 |

Wages and salaries for the third quarter amounted to 150,000 DM. Materials with a cost of 130,000 DM were received during the quarter. What were the cost of goods manufactured and cost of goods shipped?

## PROBLEMS AND CASES

**2-20 Review of introductory accounting and Chapter 2.**
The following selected accounts and balances are taken from the general ledger of Selbac, Inc. (000s omitted).

| | April 1 | April 30 |
|---|---|---|
| Cash | $ 56 | $ 42 |
| Accounts receivable | 200 | 220 |
| Raw materials | 41 | 47 |
| Work-in-process | 120 | 116 |
| Finished goods | 105 | 110 |
| Accounts payable | 15 | 18 |
| Direct labor payable | 30 | 35 |
| Raw materials purchases | — | 53 |
| Direct labor | — | 140 |
| Indirect production costs | — | 93 |
| Selling expenses | — | 85 |
| Administrative expenses | — | 90 |
| Sales | — | 510 |

**Required**

**a.** Prepare a statement of cost of goods manufactured.
**b.** Prepare an income statement.
**c.** How much was paid to suppliers during April?
**d.** How much was paid to direct labor during April?
**e.** How much was collected from customers during April?

**2-21 Terminology.**
During 19X1, Barton Dollies incurred the following costs to manufacture the firm's line of dolls.

| | |
|---|---|
| Manufacturing direct labor | $300,000 |
| Sales and administrative salaries | 200,000 |
| Administrative supplies | 40,000 |
| Sales taxes | 30,000 |
| Fixed manufacturing overhead | 150,000 |
| Manufacturing direct materials | 260,000 |
| Sales commissions | 90,000 |
| Variable manufacturing overhead | 120,000 |

**Required**

Determine the following costs for 19X1.
**a.** Conversion costs
**b.** Inventoriable costs
**c.** Manufacturing costs
**d.** Variable manufacturing costs
**e.** Total fixed costs

**f.** Prime costs
**g.** Direct costs
**h.** Total variable costs
**i.** Total product costs

**2-22 Cost definitions.**
This month's income statement for Fergus, Inc., is as follows (000s omitted).

| | | |
|---|---|---|
| Sales | | $112 |
| Less variable expenses | | |
| Direct labor | $14 | |
| Direct materials | 12 | |
| Indirect manufacturing | 8 | |
| Selling | 16 | |
| Administration | 4 | 54 |
| | | $ 58 |
| Less fixed expenses | | |
| Indirect manufacturing | $13 | |
| Selling | 9 | |
| Administration | 20 | 42 |
| Income before taxes | | $ 16 |

**Required**
**a.** From the income statement, what dollar amount was initially recorded as "product cost"?
**b.** From the income statement, what were "prime costs"?
**c.** From the income statement, what were "conversion (or processing) costs"?
**d.** From the income statement, what total would have been identified as "period costs" when they were incurred or accrued, rather than when they expired?
**e.** What is gross margin or gross profit for the month?

**2-23 Cost flow: General ledger.**
You are given the following information:

| Raw Materials | | |
|---|---|---|
| Beginning | 15,000 | |
| Purchases | 35,000 | |
| End | 10,000 | |

| Work-in-Process | | |
|---|---|---|
| Beginning | 22,000 | |
| End | 2,000 | |

| Finished Goods | | |
|---|---|---|
| Beginning | 10,000 | |
| End | 15,000 | |

| | |
|---|---|
| Sales | $200,000 |
| Cost of goods sold | ? |
| Gross margin | $ 60,000 |

One dollar of overhead is incurred for each dollar of direct labor.

**Required**
Determine raw material used, direct labor incurred, overhead incurred, cost of goods manufactured, and cost of goods sold.

**2-24 Cost flows: Manufacturing.**

| | Case X | Case Y |
|---|---|---|
| Raw materials inventory, beginning of year | $ 6,000 | $ ? |
| Work-in-process inventory, beginning of year | ? | 12,000 |
| Finished goods inventory, beginning of year | 5,000 | 24,000 |
| Raw materials purchased | 42,000 | 230,000 |
| Raw materials used | 40,000 | 227,000 |
| Manufacturing labor costs | 15,000 | 100,000 |
| Total manufacturing overhead | 9,000 | ? |
| Cost of goods manufactured (completed) | 65,000 | ? |
| Cost of goods sold | ? | ? |
| Raw materials inventory, end of year | ? | 19,000 |
| Work-in-process inventory, end of year | 3,000 | 4,000 |
| Finished goods inventory, end of year | 7,000 | 28,000 |
| Sales | 100,000 | 420,000 |
| Selling and administration costs | ? | 40,000 |
| Net income | 17,000 | ? |
| Owners' equity, beginning of year | ? | 170,000 |
| Owners' equity, end of year | 70,000 | 188,000 |
| Dividends | 10,000 | 6,000 |

**Required**

**a.** Determine the amounts to be substituted for each of the question marks.
**b.** For each case, prepare a statement of cost of goods manufactured.
**c.** For each case, what would be different if you had to prepare a statement of cost of goods manufactured *and* sold?
**d.** For each case, for the year, what are the total costs assigned to production as:
  **1.** direct costs?
  **2.** prime costs?
  **3.** conversion costs?

**2-25 Statements for cost of goods manufactured and sold, and income.** Fledgling is a corporation engaged in the processing and sale of fledges. The following data for September are taken from Fledgling's general ledger.

| | September 1 | September 30 |
|---|---|---|
| Accounts receivable | $200 | $ 100 |
| Accounts payable | 30 | 40 |
| Wages and salaries payable | 60 | 50 |
| Direct materials | 80 | 60 |
| Work-in-process | 170 | 200 |
| Finished goods | 300 | 350 |
| Direct materials usage | — | 230 |
| Direct labor | — | 400 |
| Overhead | — | 600 |
| Sales | — | 3,000 |
| Selling expenses | — | 800 |
| Administrative expenses | — | 600 |
| Other expenses | — | 600 |

**Required**
Prepare a statement of cost of goods manufactured and sold and an income statement.

**2-26 Cost of goods manufactured and sold.**
Marvel Manufacturing provides you with the following summary data for the year (000s omitted).

| | Dec. 31, X1 | Dec. 31, X2 |
|---|---|---|
| Direct materials | $20 | $15 |
| Work-in-process | 14 | 11 |
| Finished goods | 25 | 29 |
| Payroll payable (direct and indirect) | 5 | 8 |
| | $64 | $63 |

Production costs incurred in 19X2 were as follows:

| | | |
|---|---|---|
| Direct materials | | $ 50 |
| Direct labor | | 100 |
| Overhead | | |
| Labor | $20 | |
| Utilities | 10 | |
| Depreciation | 25 | |
| Other | 5 | 60 |
| | | $210 |

**Required**
**a.** Prepare, in good form, a statement of cost of goods manufactured and sold.
**b.** What was the total direct and indirect labor incurred during the period?
**c.** What were total payments to direct and indirect labor during the period?

**2-27 Cost of goods manufactured and sold—computer recommended.**
Refer to the data given in 2–26.

**Required**
Determine the cost of goods sold after incorporating each change listed below. Incorporate each change cumulatively; that is, make the change in part (a) and determine cost of goods sold, then make the change in part (b), leaving the part (a) change in the data, and again determine cost of goods sold. Continue in this manner through part (e). The use of the program CGMAS is recommended.

| | |
|---|---|
| **a.** Direct labor costs: | $120 |
| **b.** Total overhead costs: | 50 |
| **c.** Ending work-in-process: | 16 |
| **d.** Beginning finished goods: | 35 |
| **e.** Ending finished goods: | 44 |

**2-28 Cost of goods manufactured and sold** (CMA adapted).
Selected data concerning the past fiscal year's operations (000s omitted) of the Televans Manufacturing Company are as follows:

| | Inventories | |
|---|---|---|
| | Beginning | Ending |
| Raw materials | $75 | $ 85 |
| Work-in-process | 80 | 30 |
| Finished goods | 90 | 110 |

Other data are as follows:

| | |
|---|---|
| Raw materials used | $326 |
| Total manufacturing costs charged to production during the year (includes raw materials, direct labor, and factory overhead equal to 60% of direct labor cost) | 686 |
| Cost of goods available for sale | 826 |
| Selling and general expenses | 25 |

**Required**
Prepare, in good form, a statement of cost of goods manufactured and sold.

**2-29 General journal entries.**
Refer to the data for Televans Manufacturing Company in 2–28.

**Required**
Journalize the transactions for the year in as much detail as the data permit.

**2-30 Statement of cost of goods manufactured and sold.**
Eskabob, Ltd., manufactures several products. Inventories and other data for the year are as follows:

| Inventories | Mar. 31, X2 | Mar. 31, X3 |
|---|---|---|
| Direct materials | $187 | $159 |
| Work-in-process | 210 | 230 |
| Finished goods | 300 | 350 |

Other data are as follows:

| | |
|---|---|
| Direct materials purchases | $ 412 |
| Direct labor | 350 |
| Overhead | 270 |
| Selling costs | 340 |
| Administrative costs | 280 |
| Sales | 1,500 |

**Required**
**a.** Prepare a statement of cost of goods manufactured and sold.
**b.** Prepare a simple income statement.

**2-31 General journal entries.**
Refer to the data for Eskabob, Ltd., in 2–30.

**Required**
Journalize the transactions for the year.

**2-32 Cost flow—direct costs.**
The following (partially completed) schedule is available to you.

**GENERAL LEDGER ACCOUNTS**

| | Direct Materials Type A | Direct Materials Type B | Direct Labor Payable | Work-in-Process | Finished Goods |
|---|---|---|---|---|---|
| June 1 | a | 4,000 | 8,000 | 5,000 | 4,000 |
| Increases | 2,000 | c | e | h | j |
| Total | 5,000 | 9,000 | f | i | k |
| June 30 | 1,000 | d | 9,000 | 5,000 | 7,000 |
| Decreases | b | 6,000 | g | 20,000 | l |

**Required**
Complete the schedule for the lettered unknowns. Do *not* concern yourself with indirect manufacturing costs (overhead) in this problem; all figures represent dollars.

**2-33 Cost flow and terminology.**
Phlamboyent, Inc., reports the following data for the month of June.

| | June 1 | June 30 |
|---|---|---|
| Direct materials | $ 40 | $ 70 |
| Work-in-progress | 120 | 160 |
| Finished goods | 200 | 210 |

The following information is available for June.

Direct materials purchases were $100.
Direct costs of production were $210.
Variable costs of production were $260.
Indirect costs of production were $150.
Selling and administrative costs were $240.
Sales amounted to $600.

**Required**
**a.** What were the total costs of production?
**b.** What was the cost of materials used?
**c.** What was the cost of direct labor?
**d.** What was the cost of variable overhead?
**e.** What was fixed manufacturing overhead?
**f.** What was cost of goods manufactured?
**g.** What was cost of goods sold?
**h.** What was gross profit?
**i.** What was net income?
**j.** What were conversion costs?
**k.** What were prime costs?

**2-34 Cost of lost inventory.**
The County Board of Corrections solicits contracts for assembly work as a means

of rehabilitation. Unfortunately, a recent fire resulted in total destruction of the building in which work took place and inventory was kept. Beginning inventories for the period were as follows:

| | |
|---|---|
| Raw materials | $12,000 |
| Work-in-process | 8,000 |
| Finished goods | — |

Conversion costs are approximately equal to materials costs. Materials costing $48,000 were received during the period. The conversion costs for the period amounted to $42,000 and goods with a cost of $80,000 were completed of which 70% were shipped.

**Required**
Determine the cost associated with the loss of each of the inventories.

**2-35 Manufacturing costs.**
The following data for Euphoria, Inc., are available.

**EUPHORIA, INC.**
**Income Statement**
**Year-End 19X1**

| | |
|---|---|
| Sales | $30,000 |
| Less cost of goods sold | 15,000 |
| Gross margin | $15,000 |
| Less selling and administrative expenses | 12,000 |
| Net income before taxes | $ 3,000 |

**INVENTORY DATA**

| | Beginning | Ending |
|---|---|---|
| Direct materials | $ 600 | $ 400 |
| Work-in-process | 1,000 | 1,000 |
| Finished goods | 1,000 | 2,000 |

**Required**
**a.** What were the total manufacturing costs actually incurred during 19X1?
**b.** What was the cost of goods manufactured during 19X1?
**c.** Total production costs have been accounted for. If work-in-process at the end of the year is overstated by $1,000, what will be the effect on cost of goods manufactured?

**2-36 Statement of cost of goods manufactured and sold and income statement.**
TGA, Inc., manufactures a single product. The following information is available for the period just ended.

Direct materials: The beginning inventory was $40, the ending inventory was $10, and the total available during the period was $130.

| | |
|---|---|
| Direct labor and overhead: | Overhead amounted to one-third of direct labor cost. |
| Conversion costs: | The conversion costs assigned to production for the period were equal in total to the amount of direct material costs incurred during the period. |
| Work-in-process: | The beginning inventory is $100 and the ending inventory is $80. |
| Finished goods: | The beginning inventory is $90 and the ending inventory is $50. |
| Income statement: | Sales for the period totaled $1,000 and net income before taxes was $100. |

**Required**
Prepare a statement of cost of goods manufactured and sold and an income statement.

2-37 **Reworking the demonstration problem.**
Refer to the demonstration problem for Hadley Industries at the end of the chapter. Assume that all costs incurred were exactly as given. However, now assume that the equipment maintenance department devotes all of its time to maintaining the firm's office equipment. With this assumption, the equipment maintenance department's costs are no longer a product cost but, instead, should be included as part of selling and administration costs.

**Required**
Prepare the statements given in Exhibit 2–13 incorporating this new assumption.

2-38 **Statement of cost of goods manufactured and sold and income statement.**
JSA Incorporated produces a single product. The following data apply to the period just ended.

| Inventories | Beginning | Ending |
|---|---|---|
| Direct materials | $100 | $ 70 |
| Work-in-progress | 140 | 150 |
| Finished goods | 200 | 300 |

The following additional information has been provided.

The total materials available for use during the period amounted to $250.
Prime costs assigned to production during the period totaled $400.
Overhead amounted to 50% of direct labor cost.
Sales for the period were $1,000, and net income before taxes was $250.

**Required**
Prepare a statement of cost of goods manufactured and sold and an income statement.

2-39 **Interpretation, journal entries, and T-accounts.**
The following is an alternate format for a schedule of cost of goods manufactured and sold (000s omitted).

**McALICE COMPANY**
**Schedule of Cost of Goods Manufactured and Sold**
**June 19XX**

| | | |
|---|---|---|
| Manufacturing costs | | |
| Direct materials, June 1 | $20 | |
| Purchases | 38 | |
| Available | $58 | |
| Direct materials, June 30 | 17 | |
| Direct materials used | | $ 41 |
| Direct labor | | 160 |
| Indirect manufacturing costs | | 92 |
| | | $293 |
| Add change in work-in-process | | |
| Inventory, June 1 | $47 | |
| Inventory, June 30 | 43 | 4 |
| | | $297 |
| Less change in finished goods | | |
| Inventory, June 1 | $61 | |
| Inventory, June 30 | 69 | (8) |
| | | $289 |

**Required**

**a.** In this schedule, what do the numbers $293, $297, and $289 represent?
**b.** Prepare general journal entries for the June transactions.
**c.** Using T-accounts, account for all of the data for June.

**2-40 Cost flows.**

Ralph Kant was an accounting clerk for the Daylight Plant of Metropolis Manufacturing. His duties were to keep the firm's inventory ledgers. One evening, Kant loaded a truck full of the firm's inventory and drove away. He has not been seen since.

The firm is now trying to determine the amount of inventory stolen and its value. From last year's balance sheet we can determine that the firm had 5,000 pounds of raw materials on hand, costing $15,000; there was no work-in-process and there were 2,000 units of finished goods inventory on hand costing $50,000. Sales records indicate the firm had sales in the current period of $600,000; its products sell for $30 per unit. After the theft, Metropolis counted its inventory. There are 4,000 pounds of raw materials on hand, there is no work-in-process, and there are only 200 units of product in finished goods (Kant evidently overlooked them). From the purchases journal we see that the firm bought 80,000 pounds of materials for $240,000. The payroll register indicates the company paid direct labor $486,000 during the period. Overhead is 60% of direct labor cost. It takes 2 pounds of materials to make 1 unit of product.

**Required**

**a.** How many units were stolen?
**b.** What was their cost, using FIFO for finished goods?

**2-41 Reconstruct statement of cost of goods manufactured and sold from incomplete records** (SMA adapted).

On January 30, a manufacturing facility of a medium-sized company was severely damaged by an earthquake followed by a fire. As a direct result, the company's direct materials, work-in-process and finished goods inventories were destroyed. The company did have access to certain incomplete accounting records which revealed the following:

**1.** Beginning inventories, January 1:
   Direct materials, $32,000
   Work-in-process, $68,000
   Finished goods, $30,000

**2.** Key ratios for this plant are:
   Gross profit = 20% of net sales
   Prime costs = 70% of manufacturing costs
   Ending work-in-process averages 10% of the monthly manufacturing costs
   Factory overhead = 40% of conversion costs

**3.** All costs are incurred uniformly in the manufacturing process.

**4.** Actual operations data for January:
   Net sales, $900,000
   Direct materials purchases, $320,000
   Direct labour incurred, $360,000

**Required**

**a.** From the above data, reconstruct a schedule of cost of goods manufactured and sold.

**b.** Calculate an estimate of the total cost of each category of inventory lost.

# CHAPTER 3

# ESTIMATING COST BEHAVIOR

In this chapter we examine how costs behave as the level of operations changes and we set standards, or targets, for costs. In the next chapter we will extend this analysis to how profits react to changes in the activity level.

## COST EQUATIONS

For budgeting, management will want to know the anticipated costs to be incurred during a period in order to ensure that the necessary resources will be available. Similarly, to evaluate the efficiency of past performance, management will need to know what levels of costs should have been incurred. To provide this information accountants must understand how the firm's costs react to changes in operations. This chapter begins with an overview of cost functions and progresses to the development of specific cost equations for each of a firm's major costs.

### Relevant Range

Economic theory tells us that a firm's cost function should be similar to the pattern of Figure 3-1a. But the cost function in Figure 3-1a anticipates

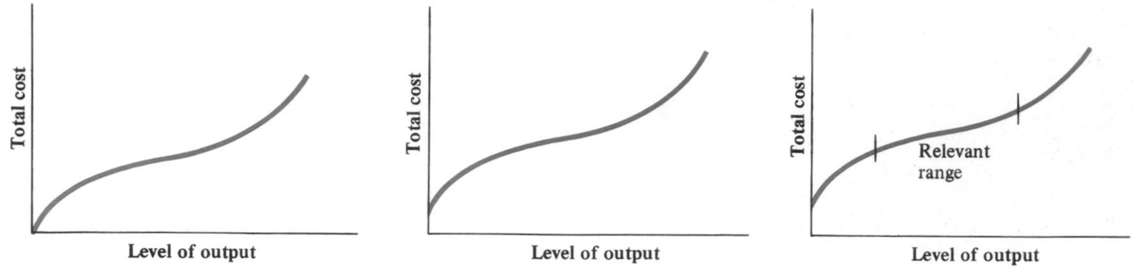


(a) Long-run cost behavior from an economist's point of view

(b) Short-run cost behavior over a particular period of time

(c) Cost behavior over a relevant range of activity

**FIGURE 3-1 Cost functions.**

production over a wide range of output and time. Inherent in the economic concept of costs is the possibility of changing technologies as output increases or falls. Although this may be true in the long run, at any point in time a firm will have a particular set of resources that will limit production in the short run. For the short run, economists usually represent a firm's cost function as in Figure 3-1b. When we restrict our attention to a particular unit of time, some costs become fixed, not subject to change. In addition, it is rare that a firm would anticipate operating over the entire range of feasible production illustrated in Figure 3-1b. Instead, for a particular period of time, the range of production in which the firm can reasonably expect to operate would be much narrower. This reasonable range of activity in which management expects to operate is the **relevant range.** Figure 3-1c illustrates a possible relevant range imposed on the economist's short-run cost curve.

### Linear Cost Equations

Within the relevant range, about the only limit we can place on the *form* of the cost equation is that it will be at least flat or steadily increasing with increased volume; that is, the *total* cost of an item seldom decreases as we increase production. This still leaves an infinite number of possibilities for the form of the cost equation, but fortunately experience shows that we can usually represent most actual cost functions quite accurately with straight lines or series of straight lines. For now, we will assume that straight-line approximations of the short-run cost equation for the relevant range are sufficiently accurate for planning purposes. Appendix 3B at the end of this chapter discusses a class of nonlinear equations that is sometimes also used to approximate the cost curve.

Although we assume that linear equations are reasonably accurate within the firm's relevant range, they are not presumed to be accurate outside this range. As Figure 3-1c indicates, short-term marginal costs will generally begin to rise rapidly as a firm reaches short-term capacity. In the discussion on estimating cost equations that follows shortly, keep in mind that the derived cost equations should not be used for making cost predictions outside the firm's normal range of operations.

The firm's overall cost function is the sum of the cost equations for each type of cost incurred. Let us now turn to the examination of the cost functions for individual costs. We assume that these cost functions can also be accurately represented by linear functions in the relevant range. Figure 3-2 illustrates the four most common types of functions used by accountants to approximate cost functions. Figure 3-2a represents a strictly **variable cost.** For a strictly variable cost item each additional unit of output requires the same amount of the cost item that each previous unit required. In the manufacture of envelopes, for example, the cost of paper is a strictly variable cost. Algebraically the cost equation can be represented by

$$y = bx$$

where $y$ = the total cost
$b$ = the cost per unit
$x$ = the measure of activity

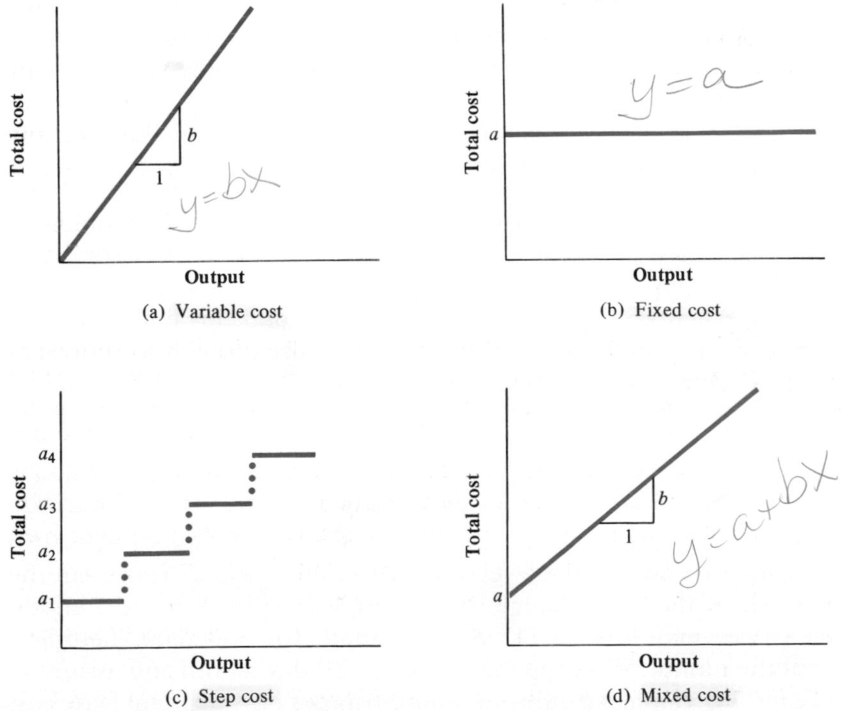

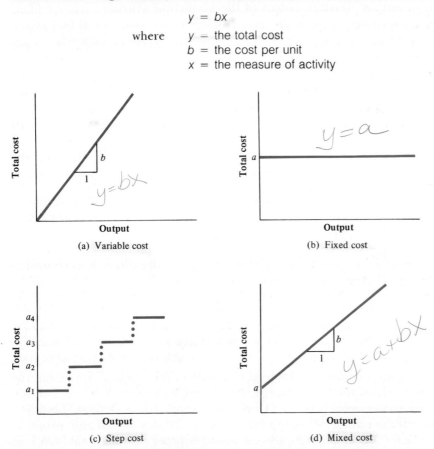

**FIGURE 3-2 Four common linear approximations for cost curves.**

Assuming that it costs \$0.01 for paper to make an envelope, then it costs \$1 to make 100 envelopes. Here $b$ = \$0.01, $x$ = 100, and $y$ = \$1.

Referring back to our usual definition of direct materials and direct labor (materials and labor that are easily traceable to a unit of product), we see that these costs must be strictly variable when the measure of activity is units of output. Of course, other manufacturing costs may also be strictly variable even if they are not considered to be direct costs. The glue used to make envelopes is strictly variable, but its cost is unlikely to be significant enough to be treated as a direct cost. In addition, certain nonmanufacturing costs, such as sales commissions, may also be strictly variable with production if inventories are kept constant.

In contrast to Figure 3-2a, Figure 3-2b represents a strictly **fixed cost.** A strictly fixed cost is one that *over the relevant range* will not change in total, regardless of the level of output achieved during the period. Fire insurance on a firm's factory is likely to be strictly fixed with regard to units of output. Similarly, many of the nonmanufacturing costs are likely to be fixed costs; for example, most administrative salaries will be fixed in relation to production output in the relevant range. Fixed costs can be represented algebraically as

$$y = a$$

where $y$ = the total cost
$a$ = the amount of the fixed cost per period

Note that $x$, the measure of activity, does not appear in the equation because the cost does not depend on activity.

Figure 3-2c represents a **step cost,** also referred to as a **semifixed cost.** A step cost is fixed over a short range of output but then suddenly jumps to a new higher level at some level of production. Supervisory costs often exhibit this type of behavior. A supervisor may be able to oversee 10 laborers, but when we expand the work force beyond this limit, an additional supervisor must be hired. Step costs are more difficult to represent algebraically. One way of representing them is

$$y = \begin{cases} a_1 & \text{if } 0 \le x \le x_1 \\ a_2 & \text{if } x_1 < x \le x_2 \\ a_3 & \text{if } x_2 < x \le x_3 \end{cases}$$

Again, $y$ is cost, $x$ is the level of activity, and $x_1, x_2, \ldots$ represent the points at which the costs change. For example, a New York to London charter service may lease a 747 by the month for \$500,000. Letting $x$ represent the number of group tours sold per 30-day month and assuming that a single 747 can make only one round trip per day, the total lease cost per month ($y$) might be

$$y = \begin{cases} \$500{,}000 & \text{if } 0 \le x \le 30 \\ \$1{,}000{,}000 & \text{if } 31 \le x \le 60 \\ \$1{,}500{,}000 & \text{if } 61 \le x \le 90 \end{cases}$$

where each step reflects the need to lease an additional 747. Note that whether this cost is treated as a fixed cost or a step cost depends on the firm's relevant range. If the firm expects to operate between 40 and 50 group tours per month, the lease cost is a fixed cost of $1,000,000. But if the firm's relevant range is 15 to 80 tours per month, the lease cost must be represented as a step cost. The relevant range determines the most appropriate cost function.

Finally, Figure 3-2d illustrates a **mixed cost,** also known as a **semivariable cost.** Mixed costs consist of both fixed and variable components. Most utility bills (electricity, phone, gas, and water) are semivariable. There is a fixed periodic charge to cover the cost of having service available, plus a variable charge for the actual use of the service. If the amount of service varies with the number of units produced, these costs would exhibit a semivariable pattern as a function of production. If, for example, it takes 10 kilowatt hours of electricity to produce an ingot of aluminum, and if electricity costs $500 per month, plus $0.10 per kwh, then it will cost $1,000 to produce 500 ingots per month and $1,500 to produce 1,000 ingots per month. Semivariable costs are represented algebraically as

$$y = a + bx$$

where $y$ = the total cost
$a$ = the fixed charge per period
$b$ = the variable cost per unit
$x$ = the measure of the level of activity

The algebraic expressions for the various types of cost functions are summarized in Exhibit 3-1.

**EXHIBIT 3-1 Equations for the Basic Cost Functions**[a]

| | |
|---|---|
| Strictly variable cost | $y = bx$ |
| Strictly fixed cost | $y = a$ |
| Step cost | $y = \begin{cases} a_1 & \text{if } 0 \le x \le x_1 \\ a_2 & \text{if } x_1 < x \le x_2 \end{cases}$ |
| Mixed cost | $y = a + bx$ |

[a]In these equations, $y$ is the total cost, $x$ is the level of activity, $b$ is the variable cost per unit of activity, and $a$ is the fixed cost per unit of time.

## ESTIMATING COST EQUATIONS

The process of estimating a cost equation for any cost item amounts to estimating the value of the *a*'s and *b*'s in the cost equations given in the previous section. Our choice of *how* we make these determinations depends on the data we have available for making the estimate, the cost we are willing to incur to make the estimate, and the amount of accuracy we require in the estimate. Some common approaches will now be described.

### Account Analysis

account analysis requires that all costs be classified as either fixed or variable

Account analysis is the easiest method and has the added advantage that it can be used when only one period's operating data are available. It can be used for new firms or for firms that experience a major change in circumstances. With this procedure we examine each type of cost being incurred by the firm and classify it as either strictly fixed or strictly variable. We know, for example, that if we are using units of output as our measure of activity, direct materials and direct labor should be strictly variable. If in a given period, direct material F-235 cost a firm $10,000 and it produced 5,000 units, then the cost function for material F-235 can be estimated with reasonable reliability as: cost = $2 per unit produced (or $y = \$2x$). Similarly, strictly fixed costs are usually easy to identify. If we rent a factory for $8,000 per period, we should have no trouble in estimating the cost function for rent as $8,000 per period ($y = \$8{,}000$).

The troublesome aspect of account analysis arises when we encounter step and semivariable costs. For these costs, the rule of thumb is to classify them as either fixed or variable depending on whether the preponderance of the amount of the cost is thought to be fixed or variable. If, for example, a water bill is $2,000 for the period and we estimate that $1,800 of it is fixed, the water bill will be classified as totally fixed. If the electricity bill is $20,000 and we estimate $3,000 of it is fixed, electricity is classified as variable. Clearly, if one could actually estimate what amount of each bill is fixed, we could separate the fixed and variable portions. Although it is not likely that we can estimate the precise portion of each account that is fixed or variable, our knowledge of our business and the types of costs charged to a particular account should generally allow us to determine what the predominant cost behavior is.

Surprisingly, for many firms, account analysis is a fairly accurate means of estimating total costs (although the estimates of some individual costs may not be very accurate). This result is obtained when the majority of costs are in fact truly fixed or truly variable (not an uncommon situation). When applying the account analysis technique, we must be careful, however, to adjust for any known inefficiencies or unusual expenditures incurred in the period from which the data were drawn. Any uncorrected errors will have a direct effect on the accuracy of our estimates.

### Engineering Approach

The engineering approach is one of the most time-consuming ways of estimating cost behavior, but it can be used without any past operating data. The engineering approach analyzes the specifications for manufacturing a product and deduces what costs will need to be incurred. Thus, if a firm manufactures an end table with a 2- by 3-foot plastic top, one of the costs that will have to be incurred for each unit is the cost of a 2- by 3-foot sheet of plastic. The engineering approach is fairly straightforward for direct materials, somewhat more difficult for direct labor, and quite difficult for many overhead items. The approach is commonly used for direct materials and is sometimes used for estimating direct labor cost on highly repetitive operations (such as the assembly of electronic components), but it is rarely used for estimating overhead items. The major advantage of the engineering approach is that it tells management what amount of costs *should be* incurred for a particular item or operation, whereas the other techniques describe what cost patterns *have been* incurred in the past.

### High-Low Approach

The high-low approach requires two or more observations of past operating results. From the records available on cost and output we select the period with the highest output and the period with the lowest output for an item. From these two data points we can then derive the linear equation that passes through these two points. For example, if we observe that the cost of electricity was $3,000 in a period when the firm produced 1,500 units and was $5,800 in a period when 5,000 units were produced, we can derive the cost equation as follows.

First we note that since we are fitting a straight line to these points, the basic equation will be

$$y = a + bx$$

or $$\text{total cost} = \text{fixed cost} + \text{variable cost}$$

where

$y$ = the total cost of electricity
$a$ = the fixed charge for electricity per period
$b$ = the cost of electricity per unit manufactured
$x$ = the number of units manufactured

Under the assumption that the cost equation is a straight line, Figure 3-3 illustrates that the change in cost between the two levels of output *must* be due to variable costs. The problem then is to determine the rate of change of cost (or, geometrically, the slope of the cost equation), which on a per-unit basis must be the variable cost per unit of activity. Letting sub-

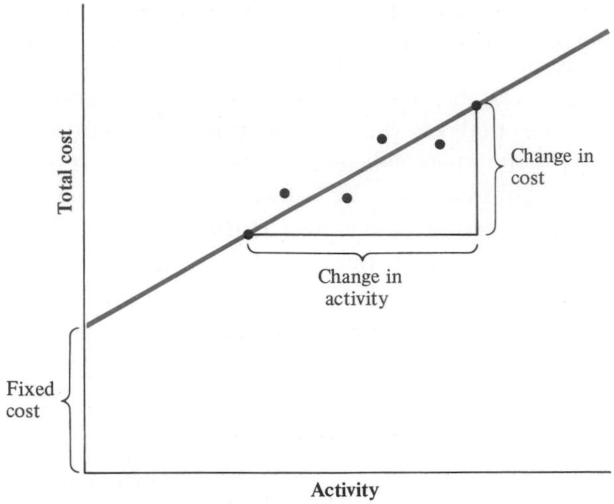


**FIGURE 3-3 Graphic illustration of the high-low technique.**

scripts denote the appropriate values for the two data points we have available, we can then determine variable cost from the relationship

$$b = \frac{y_1 - y_2}{x_1 - x_2}$$

$$= \frac{\text{change in total cost}}{\text{change in activity}}$$

Substituting the actual values from our example, we get

$$b = \frac{\$5{,}800 - \$3{,}000}{5{,}000 - 1{,}500}$$

$$= \frac{\$2{,}800}{3{,}500}$$

$$= \$0.80 \text{ per unit}$$

Once we have the variable cost per unit we can then substitute the value into one of the relationships of cost and output and solve for the fixed cost *a*. That is, we can solve either of the following two relationships.

| | | |
|---|---|---|
| $\$5{,}800 = a + 5{,}000(\$0.80)$ | | $\$3{,}000 = a + 1{,}500(\$0.80)$ |
| $\$5{,}800 = a + \$4{,}000$ | or | $\$3{,}000 = a + \$1{,}200$ |
| $\$1{,}800 = a$ | | $\$1{,}800 = a$ |

To check for arithmetic errors we should also substitute the value of $b$ into the second cost-output relationship to ensure that we get the same result.

Figure 3-4 illustrates the major drawback of the high-low approach. The line joining the highest cost point observed and the lowest observed may not be representative of the firm's cost function. One way around this problem is to plot the data points we have available. We can then visually fit a line that seems to fit the data most closely, measure the distances on the graph for two points at either end of the fitted line to yield cost numbers and output volume numbers, and solve as before. Of course, the numbers representing cost and volume will be only as accurate as our measurements of the distances on the graph we have drawn. This approach is frequently called the *scattergraph technique.* An alternative to this graphic approach is to pick two actual cost/volume points that seem *representative* of the other data points and use these two points to derive the cost equation. The *representative high-low* approach is often used to estimate cost equations. The strict high-low approach is rarely used in practice, but frequently appears in accounting examinations (including professional certification exams).

### Linear Regression

A mathematical technique known as linear regression can also be used to determine a cost equation. Regression requires several data points. The

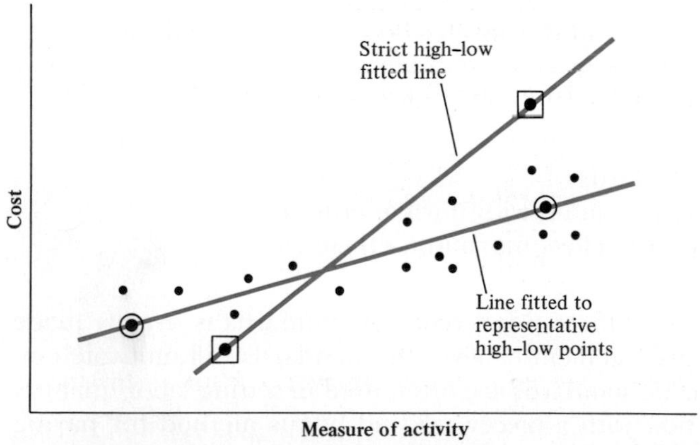


**FIGURE 3-4 Strict high-low versus representative high-low approach.** The use of the highest and lowest cost points to fit a line to cost data may not represent the majority of data well. A better approach is to pick two representative data points—one with a relatively high cost and the other with a low cost—that when joined produce a line close to the majority of data points.

technique then derives the cost equation that minimizes the sum of the squared values between the vertical distances of every data point and the fitted line. Regression is a very powerful and useful technique for estimating cost functions. However, a thorough discussion of regression requires a substantial digression into computational details. Such a discussion is included as Appendix 3A at the end of this chapter.

## STANDARD COSTS

Now that we have introduced the general techniques used to estimate costs, let us apply the techniques to develop standard costs for the inputs used by the firm. **Standard costs** are per-unit estimates of direct materials costs, direct labor costs, and overhead costs. These standards represent the firm's goals for resource usage and costs. The standards are used both for budget preparation and for the evaluation of actual performance.

In developing standard costs we will determine two measures for each type of cost: the **standard quantity** of each resource (input) allowed for each unit of product (output) and the **standard price** for each unit of resource (input). The ease with which we can make these estimates depends on the type of cost with which we are dealing.

### Types of Standards

In setting standard costs we must consider how tight the standards should be. That is, there are three levels of standards that have been advocated for use by different firms.

1. Easily attainable standards
2. Standards we expect to attain with normal efficiency
3. Ideal standards, which reflect maximum efficiency

The choice among these three types of standards is usually made on the basis of how management believes the standards will motivate employees. Easily attainable standards are often used in setting labor quantity standards in connection with a piecework and bonus method for paying employees. The intent is that employees will be able to earn their base pay level relatively easily, and additional productivity will be encouraged by paying a bonus for output in excess of "standard." In effect, this type of system requires a certain minimal level of output and then encourages additional efficiency through the bonus. For example, if a firm establishes a standard of 20 minutes of labor for each unit of output, then the firm is asking for 3 units per hour or 24 units per 8-hour day. If, in fact, it takes an average of 15 minutes per unit at normal efficiency, we would expect people to be able to turn out 4 units per hour or 32 units per 8-hour day. But if we pay a bonus for every unit produced beyond 24, our employees may be motivated to work harder, at more than normal efficiency, so that the actual average production may turn out to be more than 32 units per day. At the same time, we have the minimum standard of 24 units per day. If an employee consistently fails to meet this lower standard, the employee will probably be invited to search for employment elsewhere. Although the rationale for easily attainable standards sounds logical, there is some question whether the method actually encourages greater than normal efficiency in the long run. In fact, if the base wage is fairly high, employees may place a relatively low value on earning extra income, and long-run production may average just over 24 units per day.

The justification for using ideal standards also rests on the assumed motivational effects of such a standard. Proponents of ideal standards argue that employees will strive to achieve whatever goal is set. If standards are set at the best possible level of operations, then employees will strive for that goal. This argument claims that even when the goal is not met, we still will achieve the best effort that was possible under the circumstances. Thus, in the previous example we may have found that if an employee never leaves an assigned work station, if all materials are ready and easily available when needed, and all other support services are operating efficiently, then an employee should need only 12 minutes per unit. Under these ideal conditions an employee could turn out 5 units per hour or 40 units per day. Proponents of ideal standards argue that a standard of 12 minutes per unit will yield an average level of production closer to the 40 units per day than will a normal standard of 15 minutes per unit (32 units per day). Once again, there is some question whether ideal standards will actually result in greater than normal efficiency in the long run. It may be that continual failure to meet the standard will lead to frustration, which in turn may lead to a lack of effort on the part of employees to attempt to achieve any particular level of output.

If either easily attainable or ideal standards are used for motivation, two sets of standards will be required: (1) a set for establishing reported goals and for preparing the measures of employee efficiency to be reported to employees, and (2) a set that incorporates management's actual expectations. This latter set will be required so that management can budget for the actual resources that it expects will have to be acquired. A major advantage of using a standard that reflects normal anticipated efficiency is that the same standard can be used for reporting to employees and for budgeting. In our remaining discussion we will restrict ourselves to standards that are attainable with normal efficiency.

### Direct Materials Standards

Determining standard costs for the three major types of manufacturing costs—direct materials, direct labor, and overhead—gets progressively more difficult. We begin with the easiest: direct materials. Selecting the standard price for each direct material should be fairly straightforward. We can simply ask suppliers to give us a quote as to the prices we will have to pay for materials given the anticipated quantities and quality we will be buying. In fact, there would normally be only two problems that need attention in establishing direct materials price standards. The first is to make sure that the standard price reflects all the costs necessary to obtain the materials and have them ready for their intended use. This cost not only will be the seller's invoice price, but also should include sales tax, shipping and handling charges, and so forth.

The second problem is what to do about possible price increases. We will be able to get quotes on current prices, but if we intend to use the standard for a long period, such as a year, we will want to estimate the average price to be incurred over the year. Unfortunately, even government economists have a poor record in making inflation predictions. So management must use its past experience with particular goods, knowledge of anticipated factors that will affect supplies, and suppliers' estimates, if available, of what will happen to future prices. Fortunately, accountants do not normally get directly involved in these forecasts. Most firms will either have a purchasing agent or a manager whose duties include purchasing. This person is likely to have the experience and expertise to judge fairly accurately what will happen to resource prices during the next period.

Determining the standard quantity of each direct material to be used for each unit of product should also be straightforward. An engineering approach can be used since, by definition, direct materials are those that are easily traced to the finished product. That is, a study of the manufacturing specifications should reveal materials requirements. For example, if we are manufacturing a chair with 24-inch legs, it is fairly obvious we need enough material to make four 24-inch legs. However, that is an ideal standard. If the legs are made of wood, it is likely that we cut the legs from larger pieces of wood. In this case we must make an allowance for any necessary scrap. If we buy wood in 50-inch lengths, we can get two 24-inch legs plus 2 inches of scrap. In most situations, our standard cost for a chair leg would be the cost of the 50-inch piece of wood divided by 2, not 24/50 of the cost. Similarly, we should make an allowance for anticipated spoilage. In an ideal setting we would always cut the 50-inch piece of wood into two perfect chair legs. But with normal efficiency we should anticipate that every once in a while the wood will be cut incorrectly, yielding a $24\frac{1}{2}$-inch leg, a $23\frac{1}{2}$-inch spoiled leg, and 2 inches of scrap. Similarly, every now and then the wood will splinter as we cut it, ruining the entire piece. If we are establishing normally attainable standards, allowances for expected problems should be incorporated. One approach for doing so is to determine the average amount of materials required per unit of output in those past periods that we believe represented normal efficiency.

### Direct Labor Standards

The determination of a standard labor rate and the quantity of direct labor required per unit of output is a bit more difficult. Although basic labor rates are likely to be set either by management fiat or a labor union contract, there are still two problems. Persons earning different wages may well perform the same task from time to time. Thus in order to determine the standard rate for a particular labor operation, we may have to estimate the proportion of time the operation is performed by persons earning different rates and then calculate a weighted-average rate. The second problem involves fringe benefits and payroll taxes. We know that these costs are necessary to obtain labor services and therefore are part of the labor costs. Those taxes and benefits that vary directly with the number of hours an employee works are no problem. If we pay \$0.20 per hour into a retirement fund for every employee, we simply increase the stated earnings rate by \$0.20 to get our labor cost per hour. But many labor-related costs do not vary directly with hours worked. States require employers to pay an unemployment insurance premium for each employee, but often on only the first \$3,000 or \$4,000 of earnings per year per employee. Similarly, there is a limit to total earnings on which FICA taxes are paid. Firms also usually pay an overtime premium if an employee works more than 40 hours in a given week or works on holidays. That is, firms generally pay overtime at a rate of $1\frac{1}{2}$ times the normal rate. If our basic wage is \$6 per hour, an employee will earn \$9 per hour on hours in excess of 40 hours per week. The first \$6 per hour of the \$9 rate is the normal wage rate that we pay for straight time. But there is a \$3-per-hour premium for the overtime hours worked.

How do we build the overtime premium, taxes, and fringe benefits into our direct labor rate? One solution is to estimate the total amount of payroll taxes, benefits, and overtime premium that will be incurred in the next budgeting period. We can then also estimate the total number of labor hours that will be used and determine an estimated average cost per direct labor hour. Unfortunately, if we do this, we know that there will be errors in our standard direct labor rate.[1] To keep the standard direct labor rate

[1]Early in the period when taxes and benefits are being paid, actual costs will exceed standard. Later in the period, when some taxes and benefits are no longer being paid, actual costs will be less than standard costs. Some firms set up a deferred charge account for the fringe benefits to even out the actual costs, but this adds to the cost of bookkeeping.

as free from error as possible, most firms will classify labor-related costs that do not vary directly with hours worked as overhead. As we will see later, there are already enough problems with overhead that the inclusion of labor-related costs in overhead will have little effect on the accuracy of our standard cost for overhead.

Direct labor, like direct materials, is also easily traced to the final product and should be amenable to an engineering approach. However, unlike direct materials, it is not quite as easy to specify how much labor is required to perform a specific task. One problem is that we must make allowances for normal set-up time and idle time. At the beginning and end of each shift it is likely that equipment must be powered up and settings checked or the equipment stopped. When we begin work on a different product, settings may need to be changed and new materials substituted for the materials used in the previous product. Similarly, some idle labor time is probably unavoidable. There are machine breakdowns or delays in materials handling that will prevent employees from being 100% efficient in the use of their time.

We can handle idle and set-up time in one of two ways. The first is to include an allowance in our labor quantity standard for expected idle and set-up time. If we believe that employees can turn out 4 units of product per hour of productive time, but that 1 hour per day is lost to normal idle and set-up time, then we can calculate the labor quantity standard as follows:

Productive time: 7 hours
Units per hour, productive time: 4
Total units per day: 28
Total time per day (7 hours of productive time, 1 hour of idle and set-up time): 8
Standard hours per unit: 8 hours ÷ 28 = 0.2857 hours per unit

When this approach is used, the existence of more or less than normal idle time will show up in our performance reports as a deviation from standard time. That is, if operations are especially efficient in a given week, we may turn out 1,550 units of product using 400 direct labor hours. The labor quantity standard would have allowed 0.2857 × 1,550 units = 442.9 hours for this level of output. The comparison of the 400 hours actually used to the 442.9 standard hours allowed for the output shows that we operated more efficiently than anticipated by the standards.

A second approach is to have employees keep a detailed daily record of how they spend their time. That is, set-up time and idle time will be specifically recorded. Using this approach we can monitor directly the amount of idle and set-up time being incurred in each period. Further, the standard amount of labor time per unit of product would reflect only productive time. Thus in the previous example the standard amount of productive labor time would be 0.25 hours per unit (we had assumed we could produce 4 units per productive hour).

When comparing actual performance to standard we would now compare actual *productive* hours to the productive hours allowed for the output achieved. If we produced 1,550 units of product, the standard hours allowed would be $0.25 \times 1{,}550 = 387.5$. But assume that out of the 400 hours actually worked during the period, 390 hours were productive and only 10 hours were idle. We can then determine that the work rate was slightly below standard. That is, we used 390 productive hours but were only allowed 387.5 for the units produced. On the other hand, if we compare the number of idle hours, 10, to the historical average, we see that we were very effective in holding idle time to a minimum. (Presuming that 1 hour out of 8 is normally idle time, we would expect an average of 50 idle hours for 400 hours worked.)

This latter approach allows us to monitor nonproductive time more closely, as well as employee productivity during productive time. However, it does impose the record-keeping requirement of recording actual nonproductive time for employees. Clearly, some firms believe the benefits are worth the cost, as evidenced by some very sophisticated computer monitoring systems in which an employee inserts an identification card and pushes a few buttons each time there is a switch from productive to nonproductive time.

The determination of the amount of productive labor time required per unit is usually made by industrial engineers, who have developed several approaches for calculating standard times. In repetitive assembly operations every required hand movement can be determined, each movement assigned a standard time, and then the standard time for the entire task is determined by adding the times for individual movements. This very detailed approach is known as **methods time measurement.** Less detailed approaches include timing an individual who we believe works at an appropriate level of efficiency. Alternatively, for products that we have produced for a while, we could analyze past production records to determine the average amount of labor time it has taken in the past to produce our product.

Because time standards will be used to judge the efficiency of employees, and sometimes compensation is tied to labor standards, time standards are of great interest to employees and their unions. In many cases the time standards become a matter of negotiation in a labor contract. Although management may not like the level of a negotiated time standard, the existence of a standard in the labor contract should make budgeting easier. For, if the standard is of sufficient interest to have become a bargaining point, employees are not likely to work much more, or less, efficiently than the agreed standard.

### Labor Standards for Services

Our discussion so far has concentrated on standards in manufacturing situations. Labor time standards for repetitive nonmanufacturing tasks, such as data entry by clerks in a computerized billing department or mail sorting in a post office, require no change in our discussion. However, in many nonmanufacturing situations people perform a variety of tasks. A bank teller takes deposits, cashes checks, sells traveler's checks, transfers funds between accounts, and so on. Similarly, a nurse will administer drugs, monitor patients' vital signs, supervise aides, and prepare reports.

In such cases it is usually necessary to identify the actual tasks performed and also to estimate the average time required per task. One approach for doing so is called **work sampling.** With work sampling, random observations are made of an employee. For each observation a record is made of what the employee is doing. After a large number of observations, we can prepare a fairly accurate list of the tasks performed, the proportion of time spent on each task, and the proportion of time that the employee is idle. If we also have a record of the tasks accomplished during the work sampling period (for a bank teller this is readily available from each teller's record of transactions), we can convert the proportions to standard times per task.

Exhibit 3-2 illustrates how time standards would be calculated for a bank teller. On the first line we see that in 350 of the 2,000 work samples the teller was cashing a check. This implies that 17.5% of the teller's time during the study was spent cashing checks. Assuming that the study took place over a 40-hour period, this translates into 7 hours. If the records show that the teller cashed 168 checks during the study period, then 0.0417 hours (or $2\frac{1}{2}$ minutes) was the average time required to cash a check.

One drawback of work sampling is that it reveals the actual time an

**EXHIBIT 3-2 Time Standards for a Bank Teller Derived from Work Sampling**

| Task | Number of Observations | Proportion | Hours[a] | Transactions Completed | Hours per Transaction |
|---|---|---|---|---|---|
| Cash check | 350 | 0.175 | 7 | 168 | 0.0417 |
| Receive deposit | 1,100 | 0.55 | 22 | 440 | 0.05 |
| Sell traveler's checks | 200 | 0.10 | 4 | 24 | 0.1667 |
| Prepare cashier's check | 100 | 0.05 | 2 | 15 | 0.1333 |
| Customer relations[b] | 150 | 0.075 | 3 | — | — |
| Idle | 100 | 0.05 | 2 | — | — |
| | 2,000 | 1.000 | 40 | | |

[a]The observations were made randomly over a five-day period representing 40 working hours. The hours spent on each task are estimated as the proportion of time spent on each task multiplied by 40 hours.

[b]Chatting with customers.

individual spent on each task, not the amount of time that should have been spent. Thus, to obtain normally attainable standards, one should use as the subject for the work sample an individual believed to be working at normal efficiency.

### Overhead Standards

Overhead standards are the least accurate of the standard costs. Overhead includes many items that are not incurred uniformly over time, such as the taxes on labor costs (FICA and unemployment insurance). In addition, overhead items are seldom accorded the precise accrual accounting that we give to direct labor and direct materials. Instead, we typically charge all miscellaneous supplies to overhead in the period in which the bill is paid. We seldom worry about whether all the supplies were actually used in that period. Because overhead consists of a wide variety of different types of costs, it is also difficult to conceptualize what constitutes the quantity of overhead or its price per unit of resource. In fact, we make no attempt to set a standard cost for each type of overhead item. If an individual overhead item is sufficiently important to deserve individual attention, it is advisable to go to the trouble of defining it as a direct cost and relating the cost specifically to units of product.

Because we can seldom relate overhead directly to the various products being manufactured, we first relate overhead to some common denominator, such as direct labor hours, direct materials costs, or machine hours used. The choice of which basis to use should be made by determining the base that best explains changes in overhead. As illustrated in Figure 3-5, the scattergraph technique may be useful for depicting the degree of association between overhead and the alternative bases. Whatever base is chosen becomes the quantity measure of overhead. If, for example, we relate overhead to direct labor hours, then the quantity of

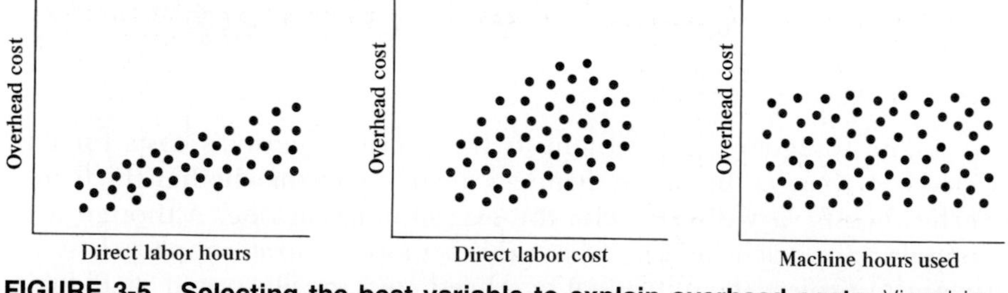


**FIGURE 3-5 Selecting the best variable to explain overhead costs.** Visual inspection of these graphs suggests that the best predictor of overhead costs is direct labor hours. A more scientific approach than the visual fit is presented in Appendix 3A.

overhead resources used will be measured in terms of the number of direct labor hours used.

Traditionally, direct labor hours has been the most common base for applying overhead. It is a cost-effective choice because detailed labor records are already available for payroll purposes. In addition, labor is generally a common input to all products in a multiproduct firm. It therefore represents a homogeneous base for charging overhead to all products. However in recent years the move to automation has caused many firms to question whether labor hours properly reflect the differential effort devoted to products. Many automated firms are now basing overhead charges on the number of machine hours used to produce each product.

If a firm has records for several periods' actual overhead costs and actual labor hours, it can use the representative high-low, scattergraph, or regression technique to derive an overhead cost function. Two other approaches rely only on the firm's most recent experience. An easy approach is simply to take last period's actual overhead costs and add an adjustment for inflation. For example, assume that the most recent period's fixed overhead amounted to \$75,000 and variable overhead was \$90,000. In addition, the firm relates variable overhead to machine hours, and 30,000 standard machine hours were used last period. If management anticipates a general inflation rate of 8% next period and expects to use 32,000 standard machine hours, overhead could be estimated as follows:

$$\begin{aligned}\text{fixed overhead} &= \$75{,}000 \times 1.08 \\ &= \$81{,}000 \\ \text{variable overhead rate} &= \frac{\$90{,}000}{30{,}000} \times 1.08 \\ &= \$3.24/\text{hr}\end{aligned}$$

The total expected standard overhead for the next period would be

$$\begin{aligned}\text{total overhead} &= \$81{,}000 + \$3.24 \times 32{,}000 \\ &= \$184{,}680\end{aligned}$$

The foregoing method adjusts the previous period's costs for expected cost changes, but it is dependent in large part on whether the firm's overhead costs vary directly with the overall inflation rate. Although it is a popular approach because it is easy, a more accurate approach is to attempt to project the individual overhead costs, as illustrated in Exhibit 3-3. Beginning with the actual overhead costs incurred in the previous period, anticipated individual adjustments are made to cost items to reflect management's best estimates of the cost to be incurred for the next period.

**EXHIBIT 3-3 Departmental Overhead Standard Cost Worksheet**

| Fixed Overhead Costs | Last Period | Adjustments and Explanation | | Next Period |
|---|---|---|---|---|
| Building depreciation | $ 76,000 | — | | $ 76,000 |
| Equipment depreciation | 53,400 | −$1,850 | Anticipated disposals | |
| | | +3,490 | Anticipated acquisitions | 55,040 |
| Property tax | 2,200 | +220 | 10% tax increase | 2,420 |
| Insurance | 1,400 | — | | 1,400 |
| Supervision | 38,000 | +3,040 | 8% salary increase | 41,040 |
| Total fixed overhead | $171,000 | | | $175,900 |

| Variable Overhead Costs | Rate per Machine Hour: Last Period | Adjustments and Explanation | | Next Period |
|---|---|---|---|---|
| Fringe benefits | $1.60 | +$0.160 | 10% wage increase | $1.760 |
| Electricity | 0.70 | −0.035 | Expected effect from conservation program | 0.665 |
| Idle time | 0.20 | +0.020 | 10% wage increase | |
| | | −0.040 | Improved scheduling | 0.180 |
| Spoilage and scrap | 0.12 | — | | 0.120 |
| Training costs | 0.35 | +0.155 | Effect of new equipment | 0.505 |
| Supplies | 0.40 | +0.020 | 5% price increase | 0.420 |
| Total variable overhead rate | $3.37 | | | $3.650 |

Next period's standard overhead cost equation will be

$$\text{total overhead} = \$175{,}900 + \$3.65 \text{ per standard machine hour}$$

In most of our examples and problem material, we assume for simplicity that a department has only one overhead account. However many departments will utilize more than one overhead cost pool. In this case an attempt is made to group overhead costs into relatively homogeneous cost pools. For example, all labor-related overhead costs such as payroll taxes, fringe benefits, and indirect labor might be placed in one pool, whereas all overhead costs related to the operation of machinery, such as repairs and maintenance, utilities, and miscellaneous supplies, might be accumulated in a second cost pool. In the first case labor-related overhead costs will likely be associated with direct labor hours as the overhead base, but for the second overhead pool the number of machine hours used is probably a better measure of overhead quantity.

Once the standard cost equation for overhead has been determined, the standards for all manufacturing costs can be combined to yield a standard cost for each of the firm's products. The standard variable per-unit costs might then be reported as follows:

| | |
|---|---|
| Direct materials ($1\frac{1}{2}$ lb per unit × \$3 per lb) | \$ 4.50 |
| Direct labor ($\frac{1}{2}$ hr per unit × \$7 per hr) | 3.50 |
| Variable overhead ($\frac{1}{2}$ hr per unit × \$4 per hr) | 2.00 |
| Total variable cost | \$10.00 |

Note that the quantity standards are stated in terms of the units of resources required per unit of output, whereas the standard prices are stated in terms of the price per unit of the resource. The product of the standard quantity and standard price gives the standard cost per unit of output. Because fixed overhead costs are not supposed to vary with output, standard fixed costs should simply be stated as a single total number.

## DATA REQUIREMENTS

Accountants would not have to get involved in the cost behavior estimation, or standard-setting process if the only problem were to fit an equation to a number of data points. An engineer can do that. The fundamental problem in cost estimation is obtaining the data. As accountants, we tend to know what problems are inherent in the routine data accumulated by the accounting system, and as such are in the best position to make the appropriate adjustments to the existing data to meet our needs. The following paragraphs summarize some of the considerations that will affect the data we gather.

1. *Proper Matching of Data.* The routine data available concerning the number of units produced during a particular period are probably correct. But costs recognized in a particular period often do not relate solely to that period. For example, labor costs are usually recorded at the time a payroll is prepared. However, the amount paid to labor on a particular payday may well reflect the cost of services used in a period prior to the period in which the wages are paid. Utilities are almost invariably paid for in a period that follows the period of use. Similarly, the total amount for supplies may be charged as a cost in the period in which the invoice is paid, yet the supplies may be used in periods both prior and subsequent to the period in which payment occurs. Thus a major effort must be made to adjust the cost figures available in the accounting system so that we match the actual costs *incurred* in a period (whether paid or not in that period) to the production of that period. This, of course, amounts to nothing more than making accrual adjustments for each period of interest just as we normally do when it is time to prepare financial statements.

2. *Eliminate the Effect of Changing Prices.* The objective when estimating cost behavior is to predict what future costs will be. Therefore, if

there have been some changes in the prices of inputs, these price changes must be incorporated. When we are dealing with observations from several different accounting periods, an attempt should be made to adjust all previous prices to a common level. A reasonable approach is to adjust all prices to those expected to be incurred in the period for which we are making the estimate.

3. *Ensure Constant Technology.* Over time most firms make adjustments in their manufacturing techniques. It is unreasonable to expect that we can adjust for every change; but if there has been a significant change in technology, then the cost data for periods prior to the change should not be used in developing our cost estimates. Similarly, the cumulative effect of several small changes may eventually make old cost data inaccurate as a predictor for the future. Depending on the rate of technological change in the firm, the accountant should be wary of data more than a few years old.

4. *Eliminate Clerical Errors.* No matter how good the accounting system, clerical errors occur. Numbers are added wrong, a cost that should be charged to Department A gets charged to Department B, an item is charged as a cost of operations when it should have been capitalized as an asset, and some items are capitalized that should be expensed. The accountant, in gathering cost and production data, should scan the data, searching for any obvious clerical errors.

5. *Eliminate Unrepresentative Periods.* A new business or a business introducing new products will initially incur many unnecessary costs as personnel learn to cope with unanticipated problems. Rarely are the costs incurred by a firm in these first few operating periods indicative of future cost levels. Therefore, the data from these periods should not be used in making future cost estimates. Similarly, an event may have occurred during a period that resulted in the firm's operating outside its normal relevant range. For example, a strike or fire that closes the plant for several weeks during a particular month is likely to result in that month's cost and production data being unrepresentative of the level of costs to be incurred during normal operations. Recall that although our linear approximations of costs may be fairly accurate in the relevant range, the costs may behave quite differently outside this range. Therefore, the data from those rare periods when the firm operates outside its normal relevant range should not be expected to be indicative of normal levels of cost.

6. *Balance the Cost and Benefit of More Accurate Information.* The cost to ensure *total* precision in the data for cost estimation is likely prohibitive. Total precision would require as a minimum the examination of every transaction recorded by the firm during a period. In determining the amount of accuracy for which we should strive, we must take into consideration the relevant costs and benefits. We must ask ourselves: What are the estimates going to be used for? How sensitive are management decisions (how

will decisions change) to errors in the estimates? How costly will incorrect decisions be? From the answers to these questions we should be able to determine how much cost, and hence accuracy, will be required in gathering that data.

## SUMMARY

Management must understand how costs react as activities change—both to project future operating costs and to evaluate prior performance. Four common linear equations are frequently used to approximate a firm's costs in the relevant range of activity. These equations correspond to strictly variable costs, strictly fixed costs, step costs, and mixed costs.

Standard costs are detailed per-unit estimates of the costs that should be incurred. These standards represent management's expectations for both resource usage and the prices to be experienced in the next operating period. Subsequent chapters will illustrate that standard cost systems provide the opportunity for excellent cost control.

The accuracy of the data from which cost equations are derived is as important as the choice of the method by which cost equations are deduced. No method of deriving a cost function from a set of data can overcome errors present in the data.

## DEMONSTRATION PROBLEM

The management of the Sandpiper Companies has asked for a new cost study to improve next year's budget forecasts. The data set that follows was taken from the records of costs and activity levels for the shipping department. The data represent daily activity for the past 2 weeks. The shipping department does not have its own delivery trucks. Instead, the firm contracts for the use of trucks and drivers as needed on a daily basis from a delivery service. Shipping supplies include the cost of several items such as boxes, tape, excelsior, labels, and shipping forms.

| Day | Units Shipped | Delivery Service Cost | Shipping Supplies |
|---|---|---|---|
| 1 | 100 | $310 | $125 |
| 2 | 2,400 | 930 | 226 |
| 3 | 1,500 | 622 | 195 |
| 4 | 2,050 | 928 | 228 |
| 5 | 900 | 309 | 150 |
| 6 | 1,200 | 615 | 190 |
| 7 | 800 | 306 | 170 |
| 8 | 2,860 | 935 | 263 |
| 9 | 250 | 315 | 130 |
| 10 | 1,800 | 620 | 201 |

**Required**

**a.** Plot delivery service costs as a function of units shipped. Plot shipping supplies costs against units shipped. Estimate the two cost functions relating cost to activity level.

**b.** What level of costs should the firm expect if it ships 1,500 units in a day? 2,500 units? 3,500 units?

**Solution**

**a.** The two required graphs are presented in Figures 3-6 and 3-7. From Figure 3-6 it would appear that delivery costs are a step function. This also seems consistent with the description of how the firm acquires delivery services. Apparently the shipping department contracts each day for the number of trucks and drivers needed during the day. Each truck has a fixed capacity, and once that capacity is exceeded by the number of orders to be shipped, an additional truck must be hired.

The average cost for deliveries when between 100 and 1,000 units are shipped is (\$310 + \$309 + \$306 + \$315) ÷ 4 = \$310. The average cost for deliveries of 1,001 to 2,000 units is \$619 and the average cost for delivery of 2,001 to 3,000 units is \$931. Thus it appears that each step adds approximately \$310 in delivery costs. Using \$310 as the step cost, the cost function becomes

$$\text{delivery cost} = \begin{cases} \$310 & \text{if } 1 \text{ to } 1{,}000 \text{ units are shipped} \\ \$620 & \text{if } 1{,}001 \text{ to } 2{,}000 \text{ units are shipped} \\ \$930 & \text{if } 2{,}001 \text{ to } 3{,}000 \text{ units are shipped} \end{cases}$$

Figure 3-7 plots shipping supplies against units shipped. The graph suggests that shipping supplies are a mixed cost. In this case it appears that a line connecting the high cost point and the low cost point results in a line representative of the remaining cost data. Hence the use of the high-low method can be justified for determining the cost equation for supplies. The high point rep-

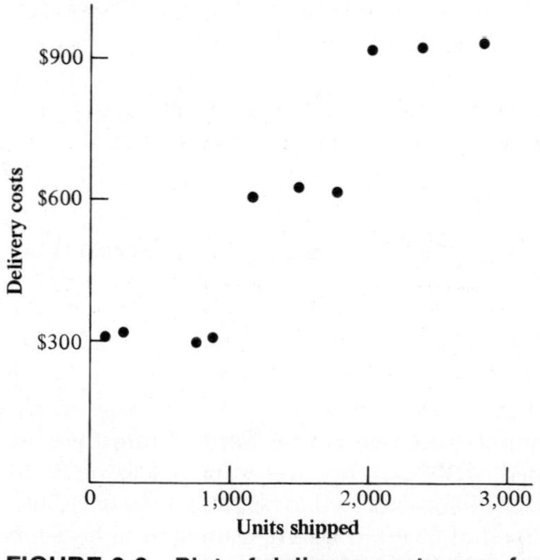


**FIGURE 3-6 Plot of delivery costs as a function of units shipped.**

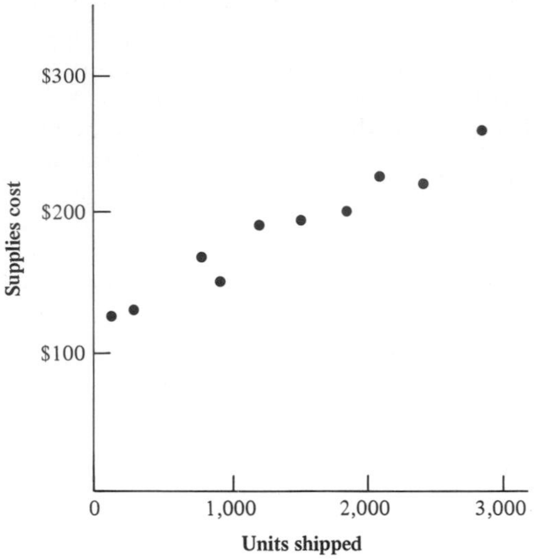


**FIGURE 3-7 Plot of supplies cost as a function of units shipped.**

resents total costs of $263 when 2,860 units were shipped, whereas the low point indicates that costs were $125 when 100 units were shipped. The variable cost can then be determined by dividing the change in cost by the change in units shipped as follows:

$$\text{variable supplies cost} = \frac{\$263 - \$125}{2{,}860 - 100 \text{ units}}$$
$$= \$0.05 \text{ per unit}$$

The fixed portion of supplies cost is found by substituting the variable cost into one of the known relationships between cost and units shipped:

$$\$263 = \text{fixed supplies cost} + \$0.05(2{,}860)$$
$$\$263 = \text{fixed supplies cost} + \$143$$
$$\$120 = \text{fixed supplies cost}$$

Combining the fixed and variable cost information yields the supplies cost function:

$$\text{supplies cost} = \$120 \text{ per day} + \$0.05 \text{ per unit}$$

**b.** To predict the costs to be incurred at various activity levels, it is now a simple matter to substitute the expected number of units to be shipped into the cost functions. If 1,500 units are shipped, delivery costs are estimated to be $620 (the second step), and the supplies costs can be expected to be $120 + $0.05(1,500) = $195. When 2,500 units are shipped, delivery costs are estimated to be $930 and supplies costs are predicted to be $120 + $0.05(2,500) = $245.

Similar calculations can be made under the assumption that 3,500 units are to be shipped. We must be very careful in using these predictions, however, because the 3,500-unit activity level lies outside our range of experience. Management cannot be assured that the same cost relationships will continue to hold once activity exceeds 3,000 units. For example, the delivery service that the firm uses may not have enough trucks. If more trucks are needed, the cost of acquiring the services of another delivery truck could be substantially different from that of the current service. Similarly, if shipping activity increases substantially, the shipping department may have to add new personnel. New personnel may not be as efficient in the use of shipping supplies as experienced workers. Thus, although we can calculate estimated costs from the cost functions for an activity level of 3,500 units, it is not appropriate to do so without additional information.

## KEY TERMS AND CONCEPTS

Relevant range
Variable cost
Fixed cost
[ Step cost
[ Semifixed cost
[ Mixed cost
[ Semivariable cost

Standard costs
Standard quantity
Standard price
Methods time measurement
Work sampling

[ Bracketed terms are equivalent in meaning.

## FURTHER READING

Baloff, Nicholas, and John W. Kennelly. "Accounting Implications of Product and Process Start-Ups," *Journal of Accounting Research* (Autumn 1967), p. 131.

Bartenstein, Edwin. "Different Costs for Different Purposes," *Management Accounting* (August 1978), p. 42.

Bryant, Murray J., and Mary Claire Mahaney. "The Politics of Standard Setting," *Management Accounting* (March 1981), p. 26.

Chow, Chee W. "The Effects of Job Standard Tightness and Compensation Scheme on Performance: An Exploration of Linkages," *The Accounting Review* (October 1983), p. 667.

Clayton, Henry L. "Setting Standards and Evaluating Performance," *Cost and Management* (May 1965), p. 195.

Dean, Joel. *Statistical Cost Estimation.* Bloomington: Indiana University Press, 1976.

Demski, Joel S., and Gerald A. Feltham. *Cost Determination: A Conceptual Approach.* Ames: Iowa State University Press, 1976.

Hakala, Gregory. "Measuring Costs with Machine Hours," *Management Accounting* (October 1985), p. 57.

Harris, Le Brone C., and William L. Stephens. "The Learning Curve: A Case Study," *Management Accounting* (February 1978), p. 47.
Imhoff, Eugene A., Jr. "The Learning Curve and Its Applications," *Management Accounting* (February 1978), p. 44.
Kravitz, Bernard J. "The Standard Cost Review," *Management Controls* (November 1968), p. 253.
Nurnberg, Hugo. "An Unrecognized Ambiguity of the High-Low Method," *Journal of Business Finance and Accounting* (Winter 1977), p. 427.
Piper, Roswell M. "Engineering Standards and Standard Costs," *Management Accounting* (September 1976), p. 44.
Singh, Prem S., and Gordon L. Chapman. "Is Linear Approximation Good Enough?" *Management Accounting* (January 1978), p. 53.

## QUESTIONS AND EXERCISES

**3-1** An automobile assembly plant closes every August to retool for the next year's model. How should August's cost data be used in estimating overhead rates?

**3-2** At two levels of activity within the relevant range, a firm observes that average costs are $192 and $188, respectively. Assuming the cost function is linear, what can be said about the existence of fixed and variable costs?

**3-3** You have been asked to provide the president with an approximate cost function for the firm's activities. This has to be done by this afternoon. Which approach should you take to cost estimation? Why?

**3-4** One common problem in estimating cost functions has to do with the proper matching of data. Would using a strictly cash basis accounting system (matching receipts with disbursements) solve this problem?

**3-5** As volume increases, total cost increases and unit cost decreases. What type of linear cost function does this describe?

**3-6** What are the primary advantages to the use of standard costs?

**3-7** Why are unit standards rather than past actual costs preferred for evaluating performance?

**3-8** Management has established unrealistically tight standards for direct labor. What might be expected as a result?

**3-9** Spencer and Church is a CPA firm engaged in local practice. Some selected items from its chart of accounts are listed. For each account, you are to indicate whether the account represents a fixed, variable, or mixed cost. If mixed, indicate whether it is predominantly fixed or variable. The accounts are (a) Wages: Staff, (b) Wages: Clerical, (c) Rent, (d) Telephone and Telegraph, (e) Licenses, (f) Insurance, (g) Office Supplies, (h) Postage, (i) Professional Dues, (j) Professional Subscriptions, (k) FICA Taxes, (l) Property Taxes, (m) Depreciation: Autos, (n) Depreciation: Fixtures, and (o) Promotional Expenses.

**3-10** Among the expense accounts for Biff's Auto Supply are those listed here. For each, you are to indicate whether it is fixed or variable. If it is a mixed cost, indicate whether it is predominantly fixed or variable. The selected accounts are (a) Cost of Parts Sales, (b) Cost of Labor Sales, (c) Payroll: Supervision, (d) Payroll: Office, (e) Payroll: Sales, (f) Payroll: Casual, (g) Advertising, (h) Bad Debt Expense, (i) Dues and Publications, (j) Uniform Rentals, and (k) Bookkeeping Expense.

**3-11** The assembly department of Toyco has the following costs over its relevant range of output for a month.

| Output | Fixed Costs | Variable Costs | Total Costs |
|---|---|---|---|
| 3,000 | $94,500 | $ 75,000 | $169,500 |
| 3,500 | 94,500 | 87,500 | 182,000 |
| 4,000 | 94,500 | 100,000 | 194,500 |
| 4,500 | 94,500 | 112,500 | 207,000 |
| 5,000 | 94,500 | 125,000 | 219,500 |

(a) Draw (freehand) the total and unit cost curves for fixed costs. (b) Draw (freehand) the total and unit cost curves for variable costs. (c) Draw (freehand) the total and unit cost curves for fixed and variable costs combined (total costs).

**3-12** The manager of a department provides you with the following information.

| | March | April |
|---|---|---|
| Hours worked | 2,000 | 3,000 |
| Average cost per hour | $8.10 | $7.40 |

It is thought that the departmental cost function is approximately linear. You are to estimate the monthly fixed costs and the variable cost per hour.

**3-13** Hinds Optical Company seeks your assistance in developing a budget for indirect costs. These costs are thought to be linearly related to the number of prescriptions filled. You are provided with the following data.

| | Indirect Costs | Prescriptions Filled |
|---|---|---|
| March | $114,400 | 9,300 |
| April | 104,800 | 8,100 |

You are to determine (a) the average variable cost per unit; (b) the fixed costs per month; (c) the expected total indirect costs if 8,800 prescriptions are filled; and (d) the average indirect cost if 8,100, 8,800, and 9,300 prescriptions are filled.

**3-14** When 800 units are produced, the average cost is $33; when 1,100 units are produced, the average cost is $30. Assuming a linear cost function, what will the average cost be if 1,000 units are produced?

**3-15** From the data that follow, you are to use high-low methods to determine (a) the fixed costs per quarter and (b) the variable costs per unit of activity.

| | Second Quarter | Third Quarter |
|---|---|---|
| Total cost | $31,200 | $29,400 |
| Unit cost | 39.00 | 42.00 |

**3-16** The general ledger accounts for McKim are set up on a functional, rather than a cost behavior, basis. The data are to be used to estimate fixed and variable costs.

| | March | April |
|---|---|---|
| Sales | $280,000 | $320,000 |
| Gas | 3,200 | 3,600 |
| Water | 5,800 | 6,600 |
| Electric | 8,700 | 9,600 |
| Sewage | 2,700 | 2,700 |
| Telephone | 12,600 | 13,800 |

Assuming that sales represent an appropriate measure of activity, use the high-low method to determine the fixed and variable components of each cost.

**3-17** A particular direct material costs $10 per kilogram. The material loses 40% of its weight through normal processing; no other material is added. The final product weighs 57.6 kilograms. What is the direct material cost per unit of finished product?

**3-18** A particular type of plastic foam is employed in an injection-molding process. For every pound of plastic placed into the process, it is expected that 20% will be recovered for reuse and 10% will be lost. The raw material costs $12 per pound. The final product weighs 24.5 pounds. You are to determine (a) how much material must be placed initially into the process to obtain one finished unit and (b) the direct materials cost of one finished unit.

**3-19** Refer to the demonstration problem data for Sandpiper Companies in the text. You have determined that the extreme values for units shipped should not be used with the high-low method. If these values are ignored, what are the new estimated fixed and variable costs for shipping supplies using the high-low method?

**3-20** Standards under different conditions for the material used to produce one finished unit of product are as follows:

| | Easy | Normal | Ideal |
|---|---|---|---|
| Price per unit of material | $11 | $10 | $10 |
| Quantity required | 3.7 | 3.5 | 3.4 |

During the period, 3,000 units costing $10.20 per unit were used to produce 840 finished units. What is the material cost per unit of finished product if the firm elects to use standards that are (a) easy, (b) normal, and (c) ideal? (d) What is the actual unit cost of production?

**3-21** Barbara Green is sole owner of a consulting firm that has one employee. This employee is paid by the hour (travel time is included). Clients are billed only for productive time. This employee spends approximately 20% of the time traveling and is only 70% productive on the job. If the owner would like to bill a client for 30 hours per week, approximately how many hours will have to be budgeted for the employee's time?

**3-22** Boyd's work study engineer determined that employees produced 4 units of product per hour. The engineer estimated that employees were working at 90% of standard efficiency. If Boyd's wishes to establish standard labor times based upon normal expectations, what is the standard labor time to produce *1 unit?*

**3-23** A department has five employees who work as a team. During productive time the team produces 20 units per hour. The employees are paid for an 8-hour day, which includes 1 hour for breaks and clean-up time. A product rejection rate of 10% is considered normal. The employees are paid as follows:

| Number of Employees | Pay per Hour |
|---|---|
| 1 | $14 |
| 1 | 10 |
| 2 | 8 |
| 1 | 6 |

(a) What is the direct labor cost of producing one (good) finished unit? (b) An employee is not paid for absences. During any absences a temporary employee is used to complete the crew at a cost of $20 per hour. How should this cost be treated?

**3-24** Windrose Enterprises is planning a new venture. The engineering and architectural consultants to the firm have designed a facility that ideally will produce 1,200 units per month at a cost of $300,000 plus $160 per unit. The relevant range is from 1,000 to 1,300 units monthly. If normal capacity is 90% of ideal capacity, what is the unit cost of production.

**3-25** Whoso, Inc., has estimated production costs of $200,000 plus $46 per unit. Its marketing and administration costs are estimated at $150,000 plus $6 per unit. Ideal capacity is 1,000 units. (a) What is the average product cost per unit at ideal capacity? (b) If normal capacity is 85% of ideal capacity, what is the average product cost at this level of activity?

## PROBLEMS AND CASES

**3-26 Cost estimation and account analysis.**
Ben's Pizza Parlor recently opened for business. The owner wishes to make a rough approximation of the firm's cost function. The manager feels that last month's results are fairly representative of the monthly costs that can be expected to be incurred in the future. Last month the parlor sold 600 pizzas. From the following information, use account analysis to approximate the firm's cost equation as a function of the number of pizzas sold.

| | |
|---|---|
| Wages: Part-time help | $1,210 |
| Pizza toppings | 180 |
| Pizza dough | 120 |
| Store rent | 400 |
| Depreciation on furniture and ovens | 80 |
| Napkins, paper plates, cups | 75 |
| Liability insurance | 100 |
| Advertising | 60 |
| Cleaning supplies | 15 |
| Manager's salary | 900 |
| Utilities (electricity, telephone) | 110 |
| Soft drink purchases | 375 |

**Required**
Using the cost equation you just developed, estimate the total costs to be incurred if 700 pizzas are sold next month.

**3-27 Cost estimation: Engineering approach.**
A machinist is paid for 8 hours per day, although only 7 hours are spent productively. The rate of pay is $20 per hour. It is expected that 10 parts will be machined per productive hour and that 20% of this output will be rejected and scrapped.

**Required**
If the total labor cost is assigned to the good units produced, what will be the unit cost?

**3-28 Cost estimation: Engineering approach.**
Julie Long, the manager of the Hamburger Haven, has been told that to earn a respectable profit she should price her hamburgers at 300% of the cost of ingredients. Ms. Long has gathered the following data on the cost of ingredients used to make a hamburger.

1. Preformed frozen hamburger patties are purchased from a distributor. There are seven patties per pound. The distributor charges $1.69 per pound.
2. Hamburger buns are purchased for $1.29 per dozen.
3. Dill pickle slices are purchased by the gallon. A gallon costs $8.95 and contains roughly 2,000 pickle slices. Four slices are placed on each hamburger.
4. Large, ripe tomatoes currently sell for $0.69 each. A tomato yields eight slices, and one slice is placed on each hamburger.
5. A $0.59 head of lettuce provides enough lettuce for 40 hamburgers.
6. Mayonnaise is purchased in 16-ounce jars for $1.49. One-quarter ounce of mayonnaise is placed on a hamburger.
7. A $0.79 jar of mustard provides enough mustard for 150 hamburgers.
8. A $0.99 jar of catsup is sufficient for 50 hamburgers.
9. A pound of cheese yields 16 slices. The cheese costs $2.59 per pound, and each cheeseburger receives one slice.
10. Onions cost $0.15 each and yield enough chopped onions for 45 hamburgers.

**Required**
**a.** What is the cost of ingredients for a plain hamburger (meat and bun only)?
**b.** What is the cost of materials and suggested selling price for a cheeseburger with "everything"?
**c.** People are willing to pay only $0.25 extra for cheese. What price should Ms. Long charge for a hamburger with everything except cheese if she wants the price of a cheeseburger with everything to be 300% of the cost of ingredients?

**3-29 Cost behavior: Graphs.**
The accompanying graphs describe the behavior of various types of costs. The vertical axes represent the total cost of the item in question and the horizontal axes represent the number of units of output. The axes intersect at zero.

**Required**
For each of the following items, select the graph that best describes the behavior of the cost.
**a.** The firm has a long-term purchase agreement for a particular part. A minimum

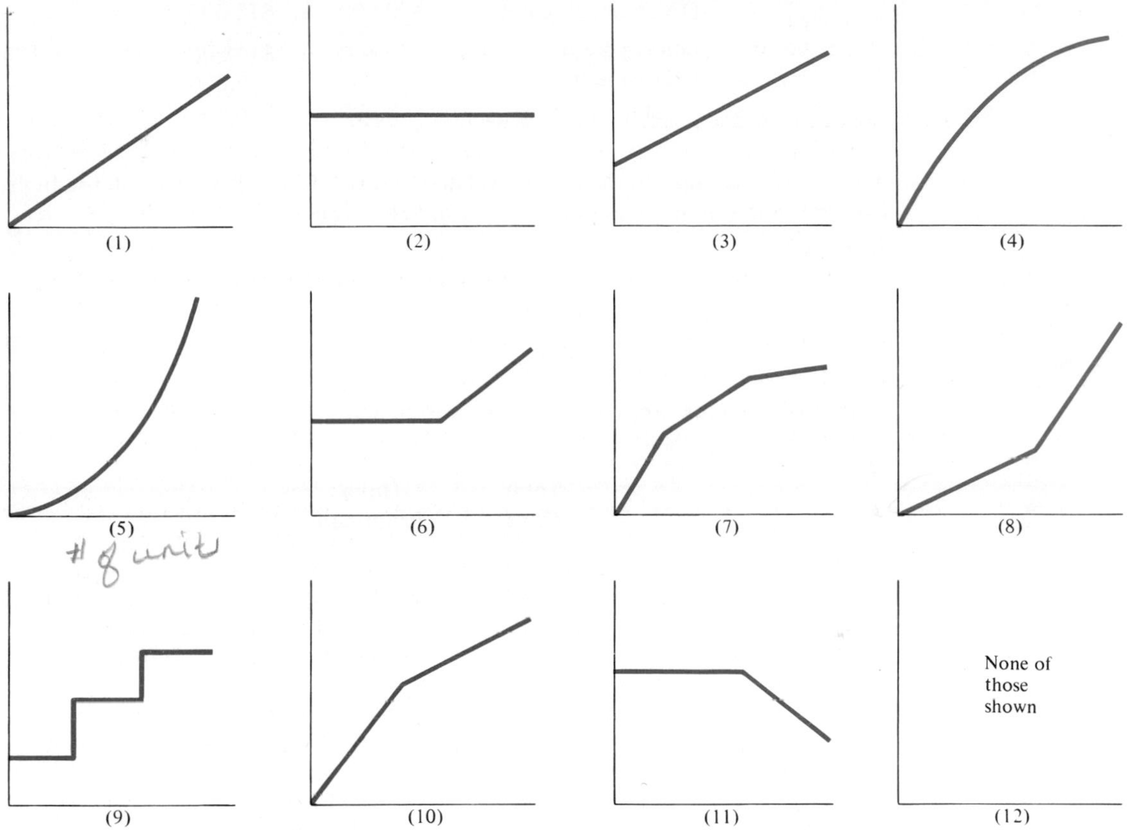


quantity will be purchased at a set price; any additional parts require a 10% premium.

**b.** Straight-line depreciation on buildings.

**c.** Units produced (or output) method of depreciation on specialized machinery.

**d.** Utilities requiring a flat rate up to a certain point of utilization, with a variable rate beyond this point.

**e.** Supervisory costs, given that the firm adds additional shifts as output expands.

**f.** A supplier grants a discount on cumulative purchases for the year (i.e., each unit purchased costs less than the last unit) to a certain point, beyond which a minimum charge is incurred.

**g.** A maintenance contract, costing $500 per month, which guarantees service within 2 hours. The firm is also billed for parts and labor. Such service is directly related to the usage of this equipment.

**h.** Plant security requires one guard per 100 workers.

**3-30 High-low cost estimation.**

The following indirect cost data for labor and material consist of cost totals taken from two representative periods.

| | | |
|---|---|---|
| Direct labor payroll | $12,000 | $15,000 |
| Indirect labor | $10,600 | $11,500 |
| Indirect materials | 4,400 | 5,000 |
| Total | $15,000 | $16,500 |

The costs are assumed to be linearly related to direct labor. The firm will use high-low techniques in order to budget these indirect costs.

**Required**

**a.** What are the unit variable costs for these two indirect items combined?
**b.** What are the fixed costs per period?
**c.** If the direct labor payroll is $13,200, how much would be allowed for indirect labor and indirect materials, individually?

**3-31 High-low methods: Representative versus strict.**
Plot the following data.

| Total Cost | Units Produced |
|---|---|
| $12,550 | 300 |
| 17,525 | 500 |
| 7,000 | 150 |
| 11,300 | 250 |
| 22,500 | 700 |
| 14,950 | 400 |
| 18,700 | 550 |
| 30,000 | 800 |
| 19,980 | 600 |
| 10,000 | 200 |

**Required**

**a.** Determine the cost equation using the strict high-low method.
**b.** Determine the cost equation using the representative high-low method.
**c.** Which equation better fits the data?

**3-32 Selecting the best cost equation.**
The Deli City Sandwich Shop is attempting to estimate a cost function to help future planning. The manager has suggested two potential bases for the cost function: (a) number of customers served and (b) total sales revenue. The manager has gathered the following data for the past 6 months.

| Month | Total Cost | Number of Customers | Total Sales |
|---|---|---|---|
| March | $ 9,985 | 5,156 | $14,250 |
| April | 10,750 | 5,067 | 15,300 |
| May | 10,645 | 5,097 | 15,350 |
| June | 10,945 | 5,446 | 15,890 |
| July | 10,360 | 5,206 | 14,600 |
| August | 9,890 | 4,693 | 13,780 |

**Required**

**a.** Using the high-low approach, determine a cost equation based on the number of customers and another equation based on total sales.

**b.** Plot the cost data against both total customers and total sales. Plot the equations developed in (a). Which is the better explanatory variable?

**3-33 Relevant range and cost estimation.**

W. Matson has acquired a franchise for Dairy Delight soft ice cream. The franchisor has provided Matson with the following cost data developed from its experience with several hundred stores. Matson expects daily demand to average 700 cones per day, plus or minus 20%.

| Daily Demand (cones) | Total Cost |
|---|---|
| 300 | $ 80 |
| 350 | 87 |
| 400 | 105 |
| 450 | 122 |
| 500 | 150 |
| 550 | 157 |
| 600 | 163 |
| 650 | 172 |
| 700 | 180 |
| 750 | 188 |
| 800 | 197 |
| 850 | 202 |
| 900 | 230 |
| 950 | 257 |
| 1,000 | 300 |

**Required**

**a.** What is Matson's relevant range for daily demand?

**b.** In the relevant range, estimate Matson's total cost as a function of daily demand.

**c.** Use the equation in (b) to predict total costs if demand on a day is 1,000 cones. Compare this figure to the franchisor's predicted cost. Why are these two figures so different?

**3-34 Cost estimation: Step costs.**

Local State University uses graduate teaching assistants to teach principles of accounting. Teaching assistants are paid $1,800 per course taught per term. University policy prohibits any class from exceeding 40 students. A class must consist of at least 10 students or the section will be dropped (for example, if 48 students desire to enroll, there will be one class of 40 students and the other 8 students will be told to take a different course).

**Required**

**a.** Assuming that the university registrar can force students into classes at the convenience of the university, determine the cost for graduate teaching assistant salaries for each of the following levels of desired student enrollment.

| Number of Students Desiring to Enroll in Principles of Accounting | Graduate Teaching Assistant Salaries |
|---|---|
| 100 | ? |
| 115 | |
| 135 | |
| 150 | |
| 160 | |
| 165 | |
| 185 | |
| 190 | |
| 200 | |

**b.** Graph graduate teaching assistant salaries as a function of enrollment demand over the range of 0 to 200 students.

**3-35 Relevant range.**
The corrugated paper industry (which makes cardboard boxes) is characterized by a large number of fairly small manufacturers. Although there are some returns to scale from expansion, transportation and handling costs grow quickly, making it generally uneconomic for a firm to become very large.

Assume that the Corrugated Paper Manufacturers' Association has gathered the following information on the average total costs incurred by its membership. The production data represent daily production of corrugated fabric (cardboard) in thousands of square feet.

| Production | Cost |
|---|---|
| 1 | $ 810 |
| 2 | 1,590 |
| 3 | 2,180 |
| 4 | 2,800 |
| 5 | 3,410 |
| 6 | 3,980 |
| 7 | 4,340 |
| 8 | 4,700 |
| 9 | 5,060 |
| 10 | 5,400 |
| 11 | 5,760 |
| 12 | 6,110 |
| 13 | 6,600 |
| 14 | 7,320 |
| 15 | 8,180 |

**Required**

**a.** Graph industry average costs as a function of daily fabric production.

**b.** City Paper and Packaging estimates its cost function for producing corrugated fabric as $1,900 per day + $350 per thousand square feet. What is the apparent relevant range that City Paper must be anticipating?

**c.** The local office of Acme Moving is contemplating producing its own cardboard boxes. If they do, they expect costs to be \$400 per day + \$600 per thousand square feet. What is Acme's projected relevant range?

**3-36 Direct labor standards.**

Bantam Manufacturing is trying to determine the standard cost for direct labor per unit of product. A time study revealed that an employee working at full efficiency could turn out 4 units per hour. However, an employee cannot work at full efficiency all day long. In a typical 8-hour day an employee must spend 30 minutes each morning setting up equipment and 30 minutes each afternoon putting things away; there are 15-minute breaks in both the morning and afternoon, and another 30 minutes per day are usually devoted to bringing in raw materials and carrying out finished product.

Each employee is paid \$240 for a 40-hour week. The firm uses a 52-week fiscal year for budgeting. Employees get 2 weeks of paid vacation per year (10 working days). The firm recognizes five holidays for which employees are paid. Other company fringe benefits of a normal recurring nature amount to 20% of gross pay.

**Required**

Determine the standard labor cost per unit of output to the nearest penny.

**3-37 Standard direct labor cost.**

A clerk for Weston Machine Tools has gathered the information necessary to determine the standard cost per direct labor hour in the firm's grinding department. All employees in the department earn \$8 per hour. FICA taxes for next year will be 6% on the first \$39,000 of earned income (note that the employee pays 6% and the employer pays another 6%). Unemployment taxes, paid by the firm, are 3.2% on the first \$4,500 of income per employee. Workmen's compensation insurance is 1.2% of gross earnings. The firm recognizes 11 paid holidays each year. In addition, each employee receives 2 weeks (10 working days) of paid vacation each year. The firm pays \$24 per month for major medical insurance for each employee and contributes 5% of gross wages to a pension fund. Employees work a normal 8-hour day, 5 days a week. Coffee breaks, cleanup time, and so on, use an average of 45 minutes per day.

**Required**

**a.** What is the standard cost per direct labor hour in the grinding department? If you left some of the items just mentioned out of the rate, indicate why and to what account you would charge the items.

**b.** In February, Weston's 10 employees worked 1,600 hours. There were no holidays and no one took vacation time in February. Prepare the journal entry to recognize direct labor costs and establish the appropriate liabilities. (Ignore withholding for income taxes.)

**3-38 Developing materials standards: Metric** (CMA).

Danson Company manufactures chemicals for industrial users. The company plans to introduce a new chemical solution and needs to develop a standard product cost for it.

The new chemical solution is made by combining a chemical compound (nyclyn) and a solution (salex), boiling the mixture, adding a second compound (protet), and bottling the resulting solution in 10-liter containers. The initial mix, which is 10 liters in volume, consists of 12 kilograms of nyclyn and 9.6 liters of salex. A 20% reduction in volume occurs during the boiling process. The solution is then cooled slightly before 5 kilograms of protet are added; the addition of protet does not affect the total liquid volume.

The purchase prices of the raw materials used in the manufacture of this new chemical solution are as follows:

| | |
|---|---|
| Nyclyn | $1.30 per kilogram |
| Salex | 1.80 per liter |
| Protet | 2.40 per kilogram |

**Required**
Determine the standard quantity for each of the raw materials needed to produce a 10-liter container of Danson Company's new chemical solution and the standard materials cost of a 10-liter container of the new product.

**3-39 Work sampling time standards.**
Work sampling was used to study the tasks performed by a telephone operator. The study was performed over a 2-week period representing 80 working hours. The study produced the following data.

| Task | Observations | Transactions |
|---|---|---|
| Place person-to-person call | 700 | 560 |
| Place collect call | 400 | 160 |
| Place credit card call | 500 | 800 |
| Repair service call back | 800 | 426 |
| Installation call back | 400 | 80 |
| Idle | 200 | — |
| | 3,000 | |

**Required**
From the information presented, calculate the average hours spent on each task.

**3-40 Evaluating efficiency of a customer service department.**
Customer service representatives at a local utility engage in several activities. A recent work sampling study provided the following standard times for each task. The study also revealed that employees were idle, on average, 5% of the time.

| Task | Standard Time |
|---|---|
| New service order | 10 minutes |
| Service disconnect | 6 minutes |
| Billing inquiry | 5 minutes |
| Repair order | 8 minutes |
| Line location inquiry | 15 minutes |

In the month just ended the employees in the customer service department worked 800 hours. During the month they handled 2,560 new service orders, 1,800 service disconnects, 1,020 billing inquiries, 420 repair orders, and 145 line location requests.

**Required**

Were the employees more or less efficient than called for by the standards?

**3-41 Determining unit cost.**

The authors of this text mail a large number of computer disks to people. The disks are enclosed in a rigid mailer for protection. Such mailers are commercially available for prices in the range of $0.50 to $1.25 each. Being unwilling to pay those prices, we produced our own.

We have a part-time employee who works on an as-needed basis. The employee earns $6.00 per hour and is paid through a university account. We pay the university $7.20 per hour to cover the wages and fringe benefits.

The employee went to the student union bookstore and purchased six sheets of cardboard measuring 40 by 60 inches. The bookstore allowed the employee the free use of a large paper cutter. The cardboard sheets were cut into rectangles measuring 11 inches by $5\frac{3}{4}$ inches. It took the employee one hour to cut the rectangles. The cardboard sheets cost $2.00 per sheet plus 6% sales tax.

Next, the rectangles were scored with a knife. That is, a cut was made halfway through the cardboard along the center of each rectangle. The rectangle could then be folded to yield a $5\frac{1}{2}$- by $5\frac{3}{4}$-inch disk mailer. It took the employee 3 hours to score the cardboard.

**Required**

How many units were produced and what was the cost per mailer?

**3-42 Ideal unit costs and actual unit costs.**

There is a manual for using the computer programs that accompany this text. It is sent to instructors. The following description chronicles our actual experience in producing the manual for our first edition.

The front and back covers of the text are sheets of green paper. The back cover is plain, while the front cover has the title copied onto it. The body of the manual consists of five pages of two-sided copy. A ream of green paper was purchased for $12.76. We paid $0.025 per page to copy the title onto 150 pages of the green paper.

We have a part-time secretary who earns $6.00 per hour. She is paid through a university account. We pay the university $7.20 per hour to cover wages and fringe benefits. She works on an as-needed basis.

The secretary brought the body of the manual to a copy shop and had 150 collated sets made. It took one hour of her time to go to the shop, wait for the order, and return. The bill from the copy shop was $55.65.

Upon her return, the secretary began to assemble the manuals. A plain sheet of green paper is put on the back of a set, a title sheet on the front, and the manual is stapled together. After preparing five completed manuals, she realized that the sets from the copy shop were in error. The second side of each paper had been copied in reverse order. Thus the page numbers were 1, 10, 3, 8, 5, 6, 7, 4, 9, 2 instead of being in numerical order. It turned out that the copying had been done in batches of 50. The first 50 were correct, but the last 100 were incorrect. The five completed manuals were thrown away.

The secretary returned the defective sets to the copy shop and they produced 100 corrected sets. There was no additional charge, but it took the secretary an hour to identify the extent of the error, return to the copy shop, wait for the order, and return.

This time, when the secretary returned, she was able to assemble and staple the manuals in 4 hours.

**Required**

Ignoring the cost of the staples and the author's time to buy the green paper and have the front cover copied, determine

**a.** What the cost per manual should have been under ideal circumstances.

**b.** The actual cost per manual.

**3-43 Unit standards for direct costs.**

The fitting department of the Flander's Flange Factory has four employees. Workers in this department custom-fit flanges to precision axles. The finished product is sold to manufacturers of medical equipment. Quality control is extremely important, so each unit is assembled by hand. The employees must grind the axles and/or flange to get a perfect fit. An industrial engineer has determined that under optimal conditions, an employee should use one axle (at a cost of $23.48) and one flange (cost, $1.83) for each completed unit. The engineer also estimates that an employee should be able to produce 5 units per hour.

Employees A and B have been with the firm for more than 10 years. They earn $8 per hour. Employees C and D are new; they earn $6.80 per hour. Employees A and B receive 3 weeks of paid vacation and C and D receive 2 weeks of paid vacation per year. All four employees also receive six additional paid holidays.

All employees work a 40-hour week. Assume that the FICA tax is 6% of the first $39,000 of earnings (6% is paid by the employer and an additional 6% by the employee). State and federal unemployment taxes total 2.7% of the first $4,200 in earnings and workmen's compensation insurance is 1.2% of total earnings. The firm pays 2% of gross earnings into a pension fund and pays $40 per month per employee for medical insurance.

The following table summarizes some production data for the past 5 months.

| Month | Number of Axles | Number of Flanges | Number of Regular Hours | Number of Overtime Hours | Units Completed |
|---|---|---|---|---|---|
| January | 3,334 | 3,396 | 672 | 8 | 3,278 |
| February | 3,133 | 3,164 | 640 | 0 | 3,072 |
| March | 3,603 | 3,607 | 736 | 4 | 3,522 |
| April | 3,063 | 3,102 | 600 | 20 | 3,006 |
| May | 3,221 | 3,243 | 656 | 4 | 3,155 |

**Required**

Determine the standard materials and standard labor cost for 1 unit of output. Express the standards both in terms of costs and quantities. The firm includes in its standard wage rate only those costs that vary directly with the total hours worked. The standards you develop should be based on normal efficiency as reflected by past performance.

# APPENDIX 3A

# LINEAR REGRESSION

In the chapter we suggested that if a firm had several observations of costs and volume, we might plot the data and visually fit the best line to the data. Although we may be satisfied with the line we fit in this manner, we cannot be certain that we have the best fitting line. If, however, we can define what constitutes the best fit, we can mathematically derive the best equation.

The most widely accepted criterion for the line that best fits a set of data is the line that minimizes the sum of the squared vertical distances of all points from the line. We can derive the line that meets this criterion through simple linear regression (also known as ordinary least-squares analysis).

## THE MECHANICS

Now this is an accounting text, not a statistics or an operations research text. Hence, in our discussion of regression that follows (and the discussion of other mathematical techniques in later chapters) we are not going to prove that the technique works. Proofs are available in introductory statistics books. Our concern is solely with the use of the technique in an accounting context. We will get into the details of the mathematics only to the extent required for making appropriate applications of the technique. As accountants we will generally have access to a computer or an electronic calculator. We will only need to supply the data, and the machine will provide the result. In this context we need only be concerned with a knowledge of what we are seeking, what the data requirements are, and how we should interpret the results.

## LINEAR REGRESSION

**EXHIBIT 3-4 Hypothetical Cost and Production Data**

| Observation Number ($i$) | Actual Costs ($y_i$) | Units of Production ($x_i$) |
|---|---|---|
| 1 | $6,705 | 1,550 |
| 2 | 5,916 | 1,210 |
| 3 | 7,500 | 1,870 |
| 4 | 6,900 | 1,630 |

### A Manual Regression Calculation

Recall that the basic linear cost equation can be represented as $y = a + bx$. If we have several observations of actual cost and production data as in Exhibit 3-4, our task is to find values of the coefficients $a$ and $b$ that provide us with a line that best fits the data. Let us call the actual costs $y_i$, where the $i$ is a counter from 1 to $n$ indicating to which data observation we are referring and $n$ is the total number of observations. Similarly, let us call the actual level of production $x_i$. For small data sets such as that in Exhibit 3-4 we can determine the best values for $a$ and $b$ directly from the following equations:

$$a = \frac{(\Sigma y_i)(\Sigma x_i^2) - (\Sigma x_i)(\Sigma x_i y_i)}{n(\Sigma x_i^2) - (\Sigma x_i)^2}$$

$$b = \frac{n(\Sigma x_i y_i) - (\Sigma x_i)(\Sigma y_i)}{n(\Sigma x_i^2) - (\Sigma x_i)^2}$$

Exhibit 3-5 presents the required summations for our example. Substituting the values from Exhibit 3-5 into the equations yields

$$a = \frac{(27{,}021)(10{,}020{,}400) - (6{,}260)(42{,}823{,}110)}{4(10{,}020{,}400) - (6{,}260)(6{,}260)}$$

$$= \frac{2{,}688{,}559{,}800}{894{,}000}$$

$$= 3{,}007.34$$

and

$$b = \frac{4(42{,}823{,}110) - (6{,}260)(27{,}021)}{4(10{,}020{,}400) - (6{,}260)(6{,}260)}$$

$$= \frac{2{,}140{,}980}{894{,}000}$$

$$= 2.395$$

**EXHIBIT 3-5 Calculations Needed for Simple Regression**

| $i$ | $y_i$ | $x_i$ | $x_i^2$ | $x_i y_i$ |
|---|---|---|---|---|
| 1 | 6,705 | 1,550 | 2,402,500 | 10,392,750 |
| 2 | 5,916 | 1,210 | 1,464,100 | 7,158,360 |
| 3 | 7,500 | 1,870 | 3,496,900 | 14,025,000 |
| 4 | 6,900 | 1,630 | 2,656,900 | 11,247,000 |
| Sum | $\Sigma y_i$ = 27,021 | $\Sigma x_i$ = 6,260 | $\Sigma x_i^2$ = 10,020,400 | $\Sigma x_i y_i$ = 42,823,110 |

Having calculated both coefficients we obtain, as our cost prediction equation,

$$\text{total cost} = \$3{,}007.34 + \$2.395 \text{ per unit}$$

With this simple example, which has only four data points, you can already appreciate why we would not want to fit regression lines by hand to realistic data sets containing 20 or more observations. The calculations become too cumbersome. In fact, prior to the ready accessibility of computers, it was rare for any firm to go to the trouble of using regression. But recently two developments have occurred that have greatly expanded the use of regression. First, computers are now relatively inexpensive and readily available. Second, even moderately priced hand calculators have built-in regression programs. With this technology available, computational difficulty is no longer a justification for not using regression. With either a computer or a calculator we need only to enter the cost and production data, push a button, and read the results.

## ACCOUNTING APPLICATIONS

Given the ready availability of computational technology, our problem then reduces to an understanding of when regression can be useful to the accountant, of how to interpret the regression results, and what the limitations are. There are two uses that we will make of regression: (1) estimating the relationship between variables and (2) selecting the variable that best seems to explain changes in another variable.

### Estimating the Relationship between Variables

Estimating the relationship between total cost and measures of activity was addressed briefly in the chapter. There we mentioned several approaches for estimating linear cost functions. As we have just seen, we can also use regression to estimate the relationship of cost to production output. Regression can also be used to estimate other relationships, such as sales in a city as a function of the population of that city or a department's overhead costs as a function of the direct labor hours used by the department.

### Selecting the Variable That Best Explains Changes in Another Variable

In many cases there are several candidate variables that might be able to explain changes in a variable of interest. Regression can help us select the variable that seems to do the best job. Assume, for example, that a firm wishes to estimate the overhead costs incurred by a department. Also assume that management considers overhead to be either a function of the number of machine hours used in the department, the number of labor hours, or the amount of labor cost. Our task is to determine which variable will give us the best estimate. Regression programs frequently provide measures of fit to help with this task.

## MEASURES OF FIT

Recall that regression fits a line to a set of data points such that the sum of the squares of the vertical deviations of the data points from the fitted line is minimized. This was our definition of the best fit for a pair of variables. An obvious criterion for selecting the variable with the best fit, then, is to choose the variable having the smaller sum of squared deviations about the fitted line. But that would be too simple, so most computer programs generate a ratio that embodies the same information: the coefficient of determination, $R^2$.

### The Coefficient of Determination

The coefficient of determination is a measure of the reduction in the sum of squared deviations from using the regression equation rather than a simple average prediction. If our only information about a cost—say, overhead—was the level of cost incurred in several periods, how would we predict a level for the next period? Without any further information, our best estimate is the average of the previous values. A measure of the accuracy of this estimate can be found by adding together the squared deviations of each previously observed cost from the average value. This sum is referred to as the *total variation* in the data, and can be represented algebraically as $\Sigma(y_i - \bar{y})^2$.

If overhead costs are related to another variable, such as units produced, we would expect an estimate of overhead based on this relationship to be more accurate than simply estimating overhead as the average of past observations. That is, if we measured the distance of actual cost observations from our cost estimates based on the level of activity, we would expect this distance to be smaller than the difference of each actual cost from the average cost (see Figure 3-8). If we represent the predicted cost from our cost function for each level of activity as $y'_i$, we can calculate a measure of the accuracy of our estimated cost function as $\Sigma(y_i - y'_i)^2$. This latter measure is the amount of variation in the data that we were still unable to explain even when we considered the level of activity as part of our prediction. If we divide this *unexplained variation* by the total variation, we get the *proportion* of the total variation still not explained by our equation. Looking at the positive side, if we subtract the unexplained proportion of the variation from one, then we are left with the proportion of variation that we were able to explain; that is,

$$R^2 = 1 - \frac{\Sigma(y_i - y'_i)^2}{\Sigma(y_i - \bar{y})^2}$$

is the proportion of the total variation in the original data that our cost equation was able to explain. This number, referred to as $R^2$, is the coefficient of determination. If our cost equation perfectly predicted costs (an unlikely situation), then there would be no unexplained variation left in the data and the value of $R^2$ would be 1. Readers familiar with statistics

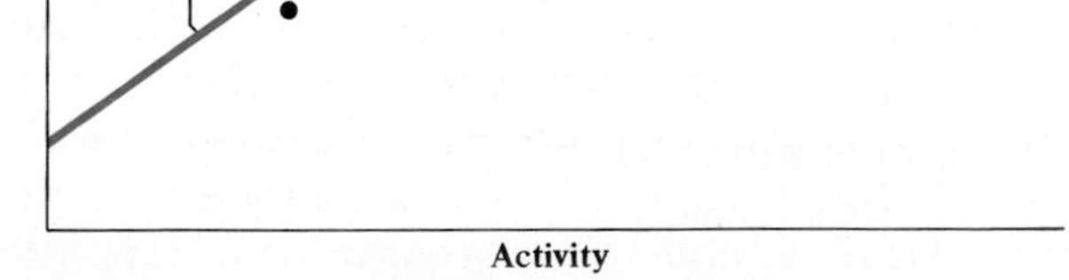

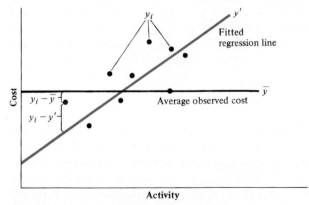


**FIGURE 3-8 Illustration of $y_i$, $y'$, and $\bar{y}$.** The individual data points $y_i$ are the actual costs, $\bar{y}$ is the average actual cost, and $y'$ is the cost predicted by the fitted cost equation.

will notice that the square root of the coefficient of determination, or simply $R$, is the correlation coefficient for the data. The correlation coefficient has important applications in statistics, but it will not be of concern to us in this text. Exhibit 3-6 illustrates the manual calculation of the total variation in the data and the coefficient of determination for our previous example. Calculator and computer programs routinely yield $R^2$ for regression equations.

We can now use the coefficient of determination to help us select the variable that best explains changes in costs. For example, assume that

**EXHIBIT 3-6 Manual Calculation of $R^2$**

| Observation Number, $i$ | Actual Cost, $y_i$ | Level of Production, $x_i$ | Predicted Cost, $y'_i = 2.395x + 3{,}007.34$ |
|---|---|---|---|
| 1 | 6,705 | 1,550 | 6,719.6 |
| 2 | 5,916 | 1,210 | 5,905.3 |
| 3 | 7,500 | 1,870 | 7,486.0 |
| 4 | 6,900 | 1,630 | 6,911.2 |
| | 27,021 | | |

$$\text{Average value of } y\text{: } \bar{y} = \frac{27{,}021}{4} = 6{,}755.25$$

$$\text{Total variation around } \bar{y}\text{: } \sum_{i=1}^{4} (y_i - \bar{y})^2$$

$$\begin{aligned} (6{,}705 - 6{,}755.25)^2 &= 2{,}525 \\ (5{,}916 - 6{,}755.25)^2 &= 704{,}341 \\ (7{,}500 - 6{,}755.25)^2 &= 554{,}653 \\ (6{,}900 - 6{,}755.25)^2 &= 20{,}953 \\ \text{Total variation} &= 1{,}282{,}472 \end{aligned}$$

$$\text{Variation not explained by regression equation } \sum_{i=1}^{4} (y_i - y'_i)^2$$

$$\begin{aligned} (6{,}705 - 6{,}719.6)^2 &= 213 \\ (5{,}916 - 5{,}905.3)^2 &= 114 \\ (7{,}500 - 7{,}486.0)^2 &= 196 \\ (6{,}900 - 6{,}911.2)^2 &= 125 \\ &\phantom{=} 648 \end{aligned}$$

$$R^2 = 1 - \frac{\text{unexplained variation}}{\text{total variation}} = 1 - \frac{648}{1{,}282{,}472} = 0.9995$$

The $R^2$ of .9995 implies that we have explained 99.95% of the variation in the cost data. This means our estimated cost function fits the observed data extremely well.

based on the same set of cost data we derived three equations that predict overhead costs. The equations were based on (1) direct labor hours, (2) direct labor cost, and (3) machine hours. If the equations had coefficients of determination of 0.75, 0.70, and 0.83, respectively, then we could say that machine hours best predicted overhead. That is, of the total variation in the overhead cost data, machine hours as a measure of activity was able to explain more of the variation than the other measures of activity. Keep in mind that this does not necessarily mean that machine hours is *the* best measure of activity. There may be some other better measure, but machine hours is the best of those alternatives that we considered.

### Other Measures of Accuracy

One of the advantages of using regression is that most computer programs routinely provide other statistics that also help us determine the accuracy of our estimated cost equations. For simple regression, three measures are usually provided: the standard error of the estimate, the standard error of the $a$ coefficient, and the standard error of the $b$ coefficient.

The *standard error of the estimate* is a measure of how far the actual cost figures deviate from our estimate of cost. We know that we will not be able to predict perfectly the level of cost at each level of activity. The standard error of the estimate gives us a means for estimating the amount of error that we can reasonably expect around our best estimate of the dependent variable. Using our previous notation, the standard error of the estimate $S_e$ is

$$S_e = \sqrt{\frac{\Sigma(y_i - y')^2}{n - 2}}$$

where $n$ is the number of data points that were used in determining the regression line. If we have two or more cost equations with roughly equal $R^2$ values, we would generally prefer the equation with the smaller standard error of the estimate.

The standard error of the estimates for the coefficients $a$ and $b$ tells us the amount of variation we can expect in our estimates of the value of each of these coefficients. Intuitively, if we calculated the slope of every line between every possible pair of data points we would have a distribution of possible values of $b$. Similarly, if we calculated the $y$ intercept (the value of $a$) for every one of these lines, we would have a distribution of $a$ values. Again intuitively, but not precisely accurately, the mean of each of these distributions becomes the value of $a$ and $b$, and the standard errors of $a$ and $b$ are the standard deviations of the distributions. The actual formulas for calculating the standard error of the estimate of the $a$ coefficient, $S_a$, and the $b$ coefficient, $S_b$, are

$$S_a = S_e \sqrt{\frac{1}{n} + \frac{\bar{x}^2}{\Sigma(x_i - \bar{x})^2}} \qquad S_b = \frac{S_e}{\sqrt{\Sigma(x_i - \bar{x})^2}}$$

How we use these measures of accuracy is the subject of the next section.

## USING REGRESSION RESULTS

When the standard error of the estimate is available, and when the regression line meets some assumptions that we will list later, we are able to construct *confidence intervals* about our estimates and to make probabilistic statements about the likelihood of certain events. Intuitively, a confidence interval is the range in which we would expect the actual cost to fall with a stated level of probability.[1] An example will illustrate its calculation.

Assume that we have estimated the relationship between a department's overhead cost and the number of direct labor hours used in that department. Further assume that our estimate is based on a regression equation derived from 20 observations of the relationship and that the resulting equation turned out to be as follows:

$$\text{overhead} = \$3 \text{ per direct labor hour} + \$5{,}000 \text{ per month}$$

Last, assume that the standard error of the estimate is $175. If for the next month management expects to use 1,500 hours of direct labor, what range of overhead costs can this department expect to incur with 95% confidence? To answer this question we first calculate our best estimate of overhead as

$$\begin{aligned} \text{overhead} &= \$3(1{,}500) + \$5{,}000 \\ &= \$9{,}500 \end{aligned}$$

If the assumptions of regression are met, the actual costs will be distributed about our estimated equation following a known distribution. This distribution is the $t$-distribution with $n - 2$ degrees of freedom.[2]

[1]Strictly speaking, the probability or level of confidence relates to how likely it is for the procedure we used to construct the confidence interval to contain the true cost value. In our applications this distinction is not likely to be important.

[2]The degrees of freedom refers to the number of data points we have available independent of the data points needed to estimate our equation. Two data points were "used up" to estimate the equation, leaving us with $n - 2$ additional data points to measure the variance around the equation.

Fortunately, one of the things we know about the *t*-distribution is the probability (or percentage) of observations falling in any given range. These probabilities are tabulated in Exhibit 3-7. From these values and the *t*-distribution we can determine the range of cost to be expected 95% of the time. This is done in two steps. First we determine the number of standard errors that we must move away from the mean to capture 95% of the possible observations in the confidence interval. This is equivalent to finding the number of standard errors we must move and leave a total of 5% of the observations in the tails of the distribution outside of our confidence interval (see Figure 3-9). Exhibit 3-7 tells us the number of standard errors that we must move from the mean to leave various percentages in one tail of the distribution. To calculate our 95% range we look in the table under the column $p_{.025}$ ($2\frac{1}{2}$% of the area in each tail) and the row for 18 (that is, $n - 2$) degrees of freedom to see that we must move 2.101 standard errors from our best estimate.[3] In the second step we multiply the number of standard errors needed for our desired level of confidence by the *value* of each standard error as determined by our regression results.[4] Since the value of the standard error for our example was assumed to be \$175, the 95% confidence interval becomes

$$\begin{aligned}&\text{mean value} \pm \text{number of standard errors for 95\% confidence}\\ &\quad \times \text{value of a standard error} = \$9{,}500 \pm 2.101 \times \$175\\ &\quad = \$9{,}500 \pm \$367.68\end{aligned}$$

We interpret this to mean that we can expect overhead to fall in the range of \$9,132.32 to \$9,867.68 with 95% confidence.

In addition to knowing the possible range of cost we might experience, we often want to know how likely it is that cost will exceed a specific amount. Assume, for example, that we have contracted to devote next month to a task requiring 1,500 hours of direct labor and we built into the contract an allowance of \$9,815 for overhead. How likely is it that the actual overhead will turn out to be more than \$9,815? The approach to

[3]How do you know whether to be concerned with one tail of the distribution or both tails? If a question asks for the probability that cost is more than a stated amount, then we are concerned with a limit on only one side of the distribution and should allow all the probability in a single tail. The same is true if the question asks for the probability that cost is less than some amount. However, if the question asks for a range of costs, we are concerned with both an upper and lower limit on costs. In this case the probability must be split between both tails of the distribution.

[4]The discussion here is not precisely correct. When making predictions, the standard error must be adjusted using the following correction factor.

$$\text{adjusted standard error: } S_e\left[1 + \frac{1}{n} + \frac{(x_0 - \bar{x})^2}{\Sigma\,(x_i - \bar{x})^2}\right]$$

We ignore the correction factor in order to concentrate on the managerial uses of the information rather than statistical precision.

## EXHIBIT 3-7 *t*-Distribution

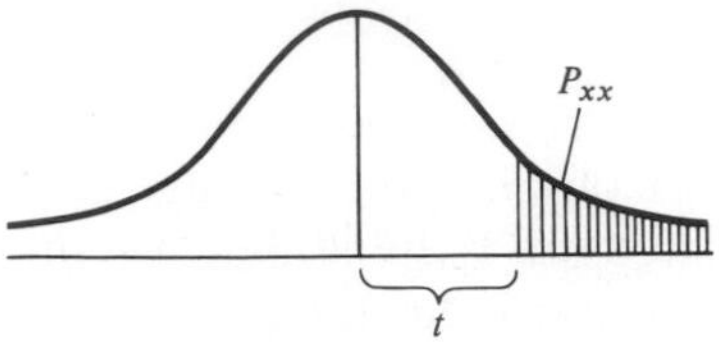


| df | $p_{.15}$ | $p_{.10}$ | $p_{.05}$ | $p_{.025}$ | $p_{.005}$ | $p_{.0005}$ |
|---|---|---|---|---|---|---|
| 1 | 1.963 | 3.078 | 6.314 | 12.706 | 63.657 | 636.619 |
| 2 | 1.386 | 1.886 | 2.920 | 4.303 | 9.925 | 31.598 |
| 3 | 1.250 | 1.638 | 2.353 | 3.182 | 5.841 | 12.941 |
| 4 | 1.190 | 1.533 | 2.132 | 2.776 | 4.604 | 8.610 |
| 5 | 1.156 | 1.476 | 2.015 | 2.571 | 4.032 | 6.859 |
| 6 | 1.134 | 1.440 | 1.943 | 2.447 | 3.707 | 5.959 |
| 7 | 1.119 | 1.415 | 1.895 | 2.365 | 3.499 | 5.405 |
| 8 | 1.108 | 1.397 | 1.860 | 2.306 | 3.355 | 5.041 |
| 9 | 1.100 | 1.383 | 1.833 | 2.262 | 3.250 | 4.781 |
| 10 | 1.093 | 1.372 | 1.812 | 2.228 | 3.169 | 4.587 |
| 11 | 1.088 | 1.363 | 1.796 | 2.201 | 3.106 | 4.437 |
| 12 | 1.083 | 1.356 | 1.782 | 2.179 | 3.055 | 4.318 |
| 13 | 1.079 | 1.350 | 1.771 | 2.160 | 3.012 | 4.221 |
| 14 | 1.076 | 1.345 | 1.761 | 2.145 | 2.977 | 4.140 |
| 15 | 1.074 | 1.341 | 1.753 | 2.131 | 2.947 | 4.073 |
| 16 | 1.071 | 1.337 | 1.746 | 2.120 | 2.921 | 4.015 |
| 17 | 1.069 | 1.333 | 1.740 | 2.110 | 2.898 | 3.965 |
| 18 | 1.067 | 1.330 | 1.734 | 2.101 | 2.878 | 3.922 |
| 19 | 1.066 | 1.328 | 1.729 | 2.093 | 2.861 | 3.883 |
| 20 | 1.064 | 1.325 | 1.725 | 2.086 | 2.845 | 3.850 |
| 21 | 1.063 | 1.323 | 1.721 | 2.080 | 2.831 | 3.819 |
| 22 | 1.061 | 1.321 | 1.717 | 2.074 | 2.819 | 3.792 |
| 23 | 1.060 | 1.319 | 1.714 | 2.069 | 2.807 | 3.767 |
| 24 | 1.059 | 1.318 | 1.711 | 2.064 | 2.797 | 3.745 |
| 25 | 1.058 | 1.316 | 1.708 | 2.060 | 2.787 | 3.725 |
| 26 | 1.058 | 1.315 | 1.706 | 2.056 | 2.779 | 3.707 |
| 27 | 1.057 | 1.314 | 1.703 | 2.052 | 2.771 | 3.690 |
| 28 | 1.056 | 1.313 | 1.701 | 2.048 | 2.763 | 3.674 |
| 29 | 1.055 | 1.311 | 1.699 | 2.045 | 2.756 | 3.659 |
| 30 | 1.055 | 1.310 | 1.697 | 2.042 | 2.750 | 3.646 |
| 35 | 1.052 | 1.306 | 1.690 | 2.030 | 2.724 | 3.591 |
| 40 | 1.050 | 1.303 | 1.684 | 2.021 | 2.704 | 3.551 |
| 45 | 1.048 | 1.301 | 1.680 | 2.014 | 2.690 | 3.520 |
| 50 | 1.047 | 1.299 | 1.676 | 2.008 | 2.678 | 3.496 |
| 55 | 1.047 | 1.297 | 1.673 | 2.004 | 2.669 | 3.476 |
| ∞ | 1.036 | 1.282 | 1.645 | 1.960 | 2.576 | 3.290 |

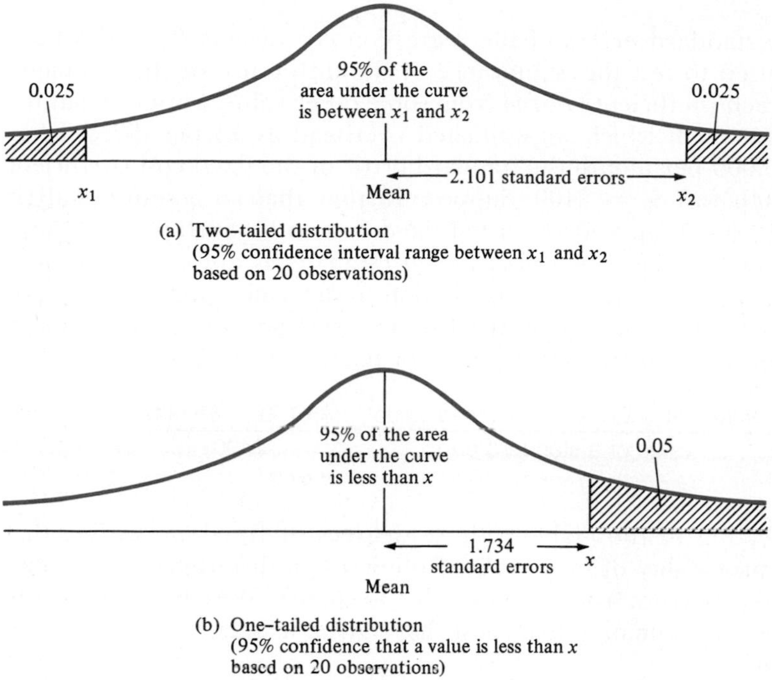


**FIGURE 3-9 Graphic representation of the difference between a two-tailed and a one-tailed distribution.**

answering this question is just the reverse of calculating a confidence interval. This time we calculate the number of standard errors that the amount under question is away from our best estimate. To do this we determine the difference between the questioned amount ($9,815) and the best estimate of the cost ($9,500, which equals $3 per labor hour + $5,000 for the month) and divide this difference by the value of a standard error ($175):

$$\frac{\$9,815 - \$9,500}{\$175} = 1.8 \text{ standard errors}$$

Thus $9,815 is 1.8 standard errors away from our best estimate of overhead cost for this project. We now look to the *t*-table to see how likely it is for a cost to be 1.8 or more standard errors from the mean. We look across the row for 18 degrees of freedom for the value 1.8. Noting that the value lies between $p_{.05}$ (1.734) and $p_{.025}$ (2.101) and also noting that we are interested in only the probability that the cost *exceeds* 1.8 standard errors from the mean (that is, we are only interested in the area under the curve in one tail of the distribution), we can conclude that the probability is slightly less than 5% that the actual overhead cost will exceed $9,815.

The standard errors of the regression coefficients ($S_a$ and $S_b$) are generally used to test the significance of the difference of the estimated value for each coefficient (*a* or *b*) from some other value. Suppose that for the department in which we estimated overhead as \$3 per direct labor hour + \$5,000 per month the standard error of the fixed cost coefficient ($a$ = \$5,000) was $S_a$ = \$400. Suppose further that an account analysis method of estimation had predicted fixed cost to be \$6,150 per month. We might ask whether the difference in estimates is due to chance or is significant. Again we use the *t*-distribution to determine the likelihood of observing a difference this great. We determine that \$6,150 is 2.875 standard errors from the estimated mean value for fixed cost of \$5,000; that is,

$$\frac{\text{alternative value} - \text{observed value}}{\text{value of a standard error}} = \frac{\$6{,}150 - \$5{,}000}{\$400} = 2.875$$

Referring to the *t*-table with 18 degrees of freedom, we see that there is a probability of only 0.5% of observing a difference larger than 2.875 standard errors from the mean due to chance. We conclude that the two methods of estimating fixed costs have given us statistically significant different answers.

A very common question concerning the value of the regression parameters is: What is the probability that the estimated values of the parameters are significantly different from zero? Note that if the value of *b* is zero, or not significantly different from zero, we may be dealing with a fixed cost. If *a* is zero, or not significantly different from zero, we may be dealing with a variable cost. If neither *a* nor *b* is significantly different from zero, the independent and dependent variables are not linearly related; either some other functional form is required or we should look for another explanatory variable. Continuing our previous example, suppose that the standard error of the estimate of *b* is \$1. Can we conclude that the variable cost portion of the cost estimate is significantly different from zero? To answer the question we compare the observed mean value of \$3 for *b* to the alternative value, zero, to see how many standard errors the alternative value is away from the observed value. We find that zero is 3 standard errors from the mean.

$$\frac{\text{alternative value} - \text{observed value}}{\text{value of a standard error}} = \frac{0-3}{1} = -3.0$$

Referring to the *t*-table we see that the probability of seeing an observation more than 3 standard errors from the mean is less than 0.5% (that is, 0.005) and conclude that the variable cost component is significantly different from zero. The test of whether regression parameters are significantly different from zero is so common that computer regression programs often include the calculation of the *t*-value (number of standard errors that zero is from the mean) for each parameter.

## EXTENSIONS TO ORDINARY LEAST-SQUARES REGRESSION

The simple linear regression model that we have presented derives a straight-line relationship between one dependent variable and one independent variable. Many extensions and refinements to the simple model have been made, two of which are discussed here: (1) multiple regression, which includes more than one independent variable, and (2) nonlinear regression, in which the relationship between the variables is a curve.

### Multiple Regression

In many applications a single explanatory or independent variable is insufficient for making accurate cost estimates. Consider, for example, a firm that imprints company names on ballpoint pens. If the firm wishes to estimate the costs to be incurred in a period, the number of pens printed will be one factor to be considered, but in addition it is likely that the number of different orders processed will also affect costs. Presumably, for each order a new company name or message will have to be inserted into the printing press. Consequently, producing 1,000 pens for each of 10 customers will be more costly than producing 10,000 pens for one customer. In this case the cost estimation formula would be of the form

$$\text{total cost} = \text{fixed cost} + b_1 \times \text{number of pens} + b_2 \times \text{number of orders}$$

where $b_1$ and $b_2$ represent the marginal effect on cost for increasing the total number of units or from increasing the number of orders, respectively.

The procedure for using multiple regression is similar to that for simple regression. Data must be gathered on total costs and the values of each of the independent variables. The calculations necessary to derive the values of the coefficients, however, quickly become too laborious to be done by hand. Consequently, we do not present the appropriate equations. The calculations have been programmed for computers and a program is provided on the disk that accompanies the text. Our interest is in knowing how to interpret the results provided by the program.

Exhibit 3-8 presents hypothetical data for a firm that imprints pens. The program accompanying the text was used to provide the solution

**EXHIBIT 3-8 Multiple Regression Example**

| Month | Total Units | Total Orders | Total Cost |
|---|---|---|---|
| January | 25,000 | 18 | 9,100 |
| February | 32,000 | 20 | 11,300 |
| March | 27,000 | 22 | 10,500 |
| April | 39,000 | 30 | 13,750 |
| May | 18,000 | 7 | 5,000 |
| June | 24,000 | 16 | 8,400 |
| July | 41,000 | 31 | 14,000 |
| August | 36,000 | 28 | 12,900 |
| September | 35,000 | 30 | 14,200 |
| October | 56,000 | 42 | 18,750 |
| November | 52,000 | 40 | 17,800 |
| December | 28,000 | 21 | 10,000 |

**Computer Output**

| | |
|---|---|
| Constant | 1797.5536 |
| Variable (1) | .0761 |
| Variable (2) | 304.0021 |
| Coefficient of determination ($R^2$) | .9897 |
| Multiple correlation coefficient | .9949 |
| Standard error of estimate | 438.8752 |

given in the exhibit. From the computer output, the cost function would be estimated as

$$\text{total cost} = \$1{,}797.55 \text{ per month} + \$0.0761 \text{ per pen} + \$304 \text{ per order}$$

The equation has an unrealistically high $R^2$ of 0.9897, implying a very good fit. The correlation coefficient is again the square root of the coefficient of determination. The standard error of the estimate for total cost is a relatively low \$438.87, again indicating that the cost function fits the data quite well.

### Nonlinear Regression

If a cost function is known to be nonlinear, and if the form of the cost function is known, then regression can be used to estimate nonlinear functions. For example, assume that a manufacturer of ball bearings wishes to estimate the cost to produce a standard run of 10,000 ball bearings. Management knows that there is a setup cost for each production run and that the major production cost is the cost of the steel used to make the bearings.

However, the amount of steel required depends on the size of the bearing. Assume management has gathered the data presented in Exhibit 3-9. From the description given by management and the knowledge that the volume of a sphere is given by the equation

$$\text{volume} = 0.5236\ (\text{diameter})^3$$

the form of the cost equation is expected to be

$$\text{cost} = a + b\ (\text{diameter})^3$$

where $a$ represents the set-up cost and $b$ represents variable (material) costs. The easiest way to estimate $a$ and $b$ using regression is to cube the values of the diameters by hand (done in column 4 in Exhibit 3-9) and use these as the values of the independent variable in a regression program. Using the linear regression program accompanying the text yielded the output given in the bottom portion of Exhibit 3-9. From this information the cost to produce an order of 10,000 ball bearings is estimated as:

$$\text{cost} = \$347.85 + \$4{,}983.43d^3$$

where $d$ is the diameter of the ball bearing requested by a customer. The remaining computer output once again indicates that there is an extraordinarily close fit between the cost function and the data.

**EXHIBIT 3-9 Nonlinear Regression Example**

| Order | Total Cost | Diameter | Diameter$^3$ |
|---|---|---|---|
| 110 | $ 800 | 0.45 | 0.091125 |
| 111 | 1,000 | 0.50 | 0.125 |
| 112 | 550 | 0.35 | 0.042875 |
| 113 | 1,400 | 0.60 | 0.216 |
| 114 | 1,200 | 0.55 | 0.166375 |
| 115 | 825 | 0.45 | 0.091125 |
| 116 | 650 | 0.40 | 0.064 |
| 117 | 950 | 0.50 | 0.125 |

**Computer Output**

```
The value of the intercept is               347.8460
The value of the slope is                  4983.4329
The value of R-square is                       .9939
The standard error of the estimate is        23.6436
The standard error of the b coefficient is  159.4662
```

It is also possible to use regression to estimate the coefficients $a$ and $b$ in a function of the form

$$\text{cost} = a(\text{output})^b$$

Such an approach is illustrated in Appendix 3B.

## ASSUMPTIONS OF REGRESSION

The validity of the statistical tests and statements that we made in the previous section rests on some assumptions that must be met. If these assumptions are not met, the tests will be inaccurate. The major assumptions are as follows:

1. The error terms—that is, the $(y - y')$ terms—have a constant variance over the range of observations. If this is not true, the standard errors will change depending on the level of activity. The most common problem in an accounting context is illustrated in Figure 3-10a, wherein the variance of the data increases at higher levels of activity.

2. The error terms are independent. If not (that is, if they follow a pattern), they are said to be serially correlated. If serial correlation is present, the standard errors of the coefficients will be understated. In an accounting context, serial correlation is likely to arise when we fit a linear cost curve to nonlinear data. Figure 3-10b illustrates this situation.

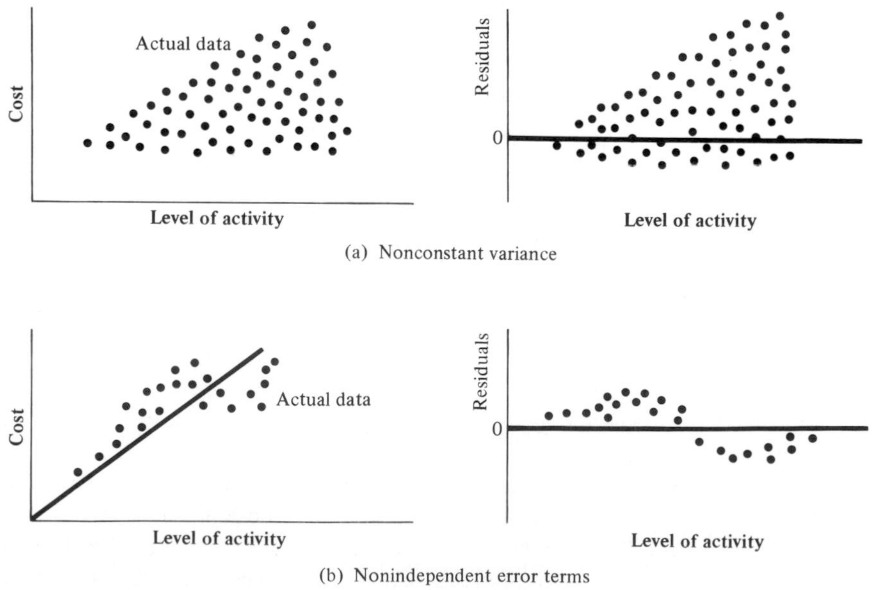


**FIGURE 3-10 Possible problems with regression.**

3. The error terms are normally distributed about a mean of zero. Our use of the *t*-table assumes that the errors are normally distributed. If not, the confidence intervals we calculate will be incorrect.

4. In multiple regression, the various independent variables are not highly correlated. If the independent variables are highly correlated, the derived coefficients for the independent variables are likely to be inaccurate.

Each of these assumptions is routinely tested in the more sophisticated computer packages. The testing of the assumptions is called residual analysis. If these tests are not available, one can plot the error terms (the residuals) to determine visually whether the residuals appear to meet the needed assumptions.

### Other Factors to Consider

In addition to the foregoing assumptions, there are a number of other factors that the user must consider when using regression.

1. The regression line will be no more accurate than the data used. In fact, for typical accounting uses of regression, the integrity of the data is probably more important than the regression assumptions. As mentioned in the chapter, the major data problems that we should be alert for are as follows:

The proper matching of cost and activity data to the appropriate period
Ensuring that cost data are measured in terms of constant prices
Ensuring that data reflect constant technology
Ensuring that the data are free of clerical errors
Ensuring that data from nonrepresentative periods are eliminated

2. Regression will fit a line to any set of data, even if there is no relationship between the variables. If there is no relationship between the variables, an analysis of the significance of the parameters should indicate that they are not significantly different from zero. But chance relationships can appear. A means for preventing this result is to refrain from running a regression unless there is some logical basis for believing that a relationship should exist between the variables. A plot of the variables will also often be useful for seeing whether there appears to be a relationship and, if so, whether the relationship is linear.

3. The estimated relationship is valid only for the range of observations actually used to derive the regression line. This is an extension of the relevant range concept introduced in the chapter. A linear equation may adequately describe the relationship of variables over the relevant range; however, predictions of cost outside the relevant range are at best

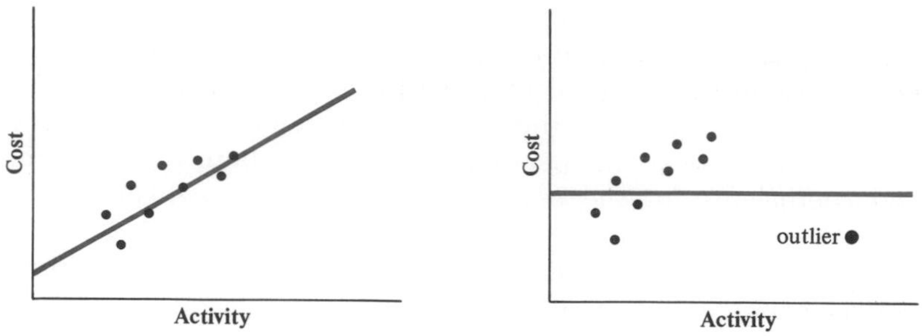


(a) Fitted equation without outlier

(b) Fitted equation with outlier

**FIGURE 3-11 The effect of an outlier on a regression fitted equation.**

tenuous, for outside this range the relationship may be significantly nonlinear.

4. The regression criterion of minimizing squared deviations implies that large prediction errors are more important than small errors. This has two effects. First an "outlier," a data point quite different from all others, will have a substantial effect on the fitted line, as can be seen in Figure 3-11. The user should analyze outliers to ensure that they are accurate representations of relationships that can be expected to continue into the future. Second, if large deviations are no more important than small deviations, in a cost-benefit sense, an alternate method such as minimizing the absolute value of errors, or a representative high-low approach, may be better.

5. Finally, just because we get a good fit for a relationship between two variables does not imply that we have the best fit. We may find, for example, that we get a high $R^2$ and a low standard error of the estimate when we fit overhead as a function of direct labor cost. However, it may turn out to be true that a fit of overhead to direct labor hours might provide an even more accurate estimate of overhead costs.

## DEMONSTRATION PROBLEM: REGRESSION

Our firm is preparing to submit a bid for a government contract that will fully utilize our capacity for a month. Management is quite concerned about the amount of overhead it will incur for the contract. We have been asked to provide an estimate of the overhead costs likely to be incurred.

Using monthly cost and production data for the past 30 months, we have determined two potential overhead cost prediction equations by regression. The first equation was based on direct labor hours as the explanatory variable, whereas

**EXHIBIT 3-10 Computer Output for Regression Equation**

| Variable | Coefficient | Standard Error | *t*-Value | $R^2$ |
|---|---|---|---|---|
| Dependent | — | 175 | — | 0.92 |
| Intercept | 250 | 100 | 2.5 | |
| Independent | 3.2 | 0.8 | 4.0 | |
| $n = 30$ | | | | |

Plot of residuals

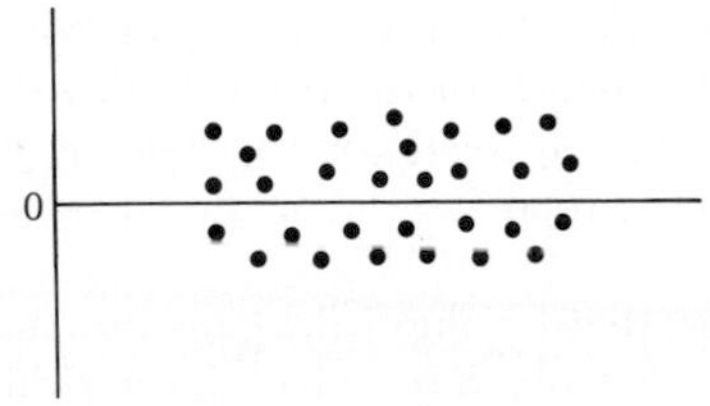


the second used machine hours as the activity measure. Exhibits 3-10 and 3-11 present the computer output for each equation.

**Required**

**a.** Assuming that the contract will require 3,000 direct labor hours and 4,500 machine hours and will be concluded in 1 month, determine the best estimate of overhead that will be incurred for this contract.

**b.** What is the 90% confidence interval for total overhead cost?

**c.** We can be 90% confident that total overhead will be less than what amount?

**EXHIBIT 3-11 Computer Output for Regression Equation Based on Machine Hours**

| Variable | Coefficient | Standard Error | *t*-Value | $R^2$ |
|---|---|---|---|---|
| Dependent | — | 245 | — | 0.80 |
| Intercept | 800 | 150 | 5.3 | |
| Independent | 2.0 | 1.2 | 1.7 | |
| $n = 30$ | | | | |

Plot of residuals

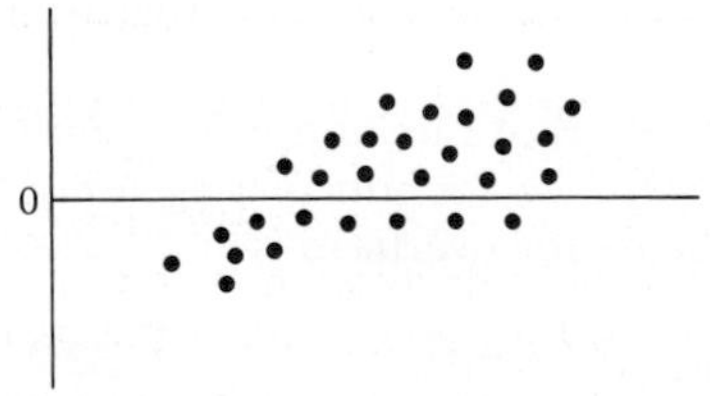

**Solution**

**a.** Our first problem is to determine which regression equation better predicts overhead. The computer output in Exhibit 3-10 tells us that overhead (the dependent variable) is predicted to be \$250 per month (the intercept value is the fixed portion of overhead) plus \$3.20 per direct labor hour (direct labor is the independent variable in Exhibit 3-10). Similarly, Exhibit 3-11 tells us that our second regression equation is

$$\text{overhead} = \$800 \text{ per month} + \$2 \text{ per machine hour}$$

The column headed Standard Error in both exhibits gives, first, the standard error of the estimate for the predicted overhead. The second number is the standard error of the fixed cost parameter (\$100 in Exhibit 3-10) and the last number is the standard error of the variable cost parameter (\$0.80 in Exhibit 3-10).

The column headed *t*-Value calculates how many standard errors each parameter value is away from zero. That is, the *t*-value is the coefficient value divided by its associated standard error. The last column gives us the $R^2$ for the equation.

This particular computer output also provides us with a plot of the individual error terms (residuals) around the predicted equation. With this explanation of the computer output we should now be able to determine which equation better predicts overhead.

We start by examining the $R^2$ for each equation. Note that for direct labor the $R^2$ is 0.92, whereas for machine hours it is 0.80. On this basis, direct labor appears to be the better equation. Further analysis confirms this choice. We should also note that the standard error of the estimate is smaller for the labor-based equation than the machine hours equation, implying more accurate cost predictions. Further, the *t*-values for the labor-based equation coefficients are fairly high, implying that each is significantly different from zero. For the machine hours equation the *t*-value for the fixed cost term is very high, and the *t*-value for the variable cost term is 1.7. Referring to Exhibit 3-7 for 28 degrees of freedom we see that the variable cost term is significantly different from zero with 95% confidence. Although this level of confidence is usually acceptable, it is not as high as that for the labor-based equation.

Finally, the analysis of residuals seems to indicate that the error terms for the labor-based equation are independent, have constant variance, and are normally distributed. In contrast, there appears to be an increasing pattern to the residuals for the machine hour equation (they are not independent) and the variance does not seem to be constant; that is, it increases with increased activity.

Based on our analysis of the output we choose the labor-based equation to predict overhead. Since we are anticipating using 3,000 labor hours for the contract, our best estimate for overhead is

$$\begin{aligned}\text{predicted overhead} &= \$250 + \$3.2 \times 3{,}000 \\ &= \$9{,}850\end{aligned}$$

**b.** A 90% confidence interval implies that we can allow 5% of the possible observations to be higher than our interval and 5% to be lower. Thus we need to know how many standard errors we must move from the mean to capture all but 5% of the observations. Looking at Exhibit 3-7 under $p_{.05}$ for 28 degrees of freedom we see we must move 1.701 standard errors. Exhibit 3-10 tells us that the value of each standard error of the estimate is \$175. Thus our 90% confidence interval becomes

$$\text{confidence interval} = \$9{,}850 \pm 1.701 \times \$175$$
$$= \$9{,}552.33 \text{ to } \$10{,}147.68$$

**c.** If we wish to be 90% confident that overhead will be less than a particular amount, we are saying that 10% of all possible observations can be higher than our specified limit. Thus we need to determine how many standard errors we must move to capture all but 10% of the observations in one tail of the distribution. Exhibit 3-7 for $p_{.10}$ and 28 degrees of freedom says we must move 1.313 standard errors. Again, using the \$175 value of a standard error, we are 90% confident that total overhead will be less than \$10,079.77; that is,

$$\text{upper limit} = \$9{,}850 + 1.313 \times \$175$$
$$= \$10{,}079.78$$

## QUESTIONS AND EXERCISES: APPENDIX 3A

**3-44** Refer to the demonstration problem at the end of the chapter (Sandpiper Companies). Use linear regression to determine the fixed and variable components of shipping supplies in relation to the number of units shipped; also, calculate the coefficient of determination. (The use of a computer is recommended.) How do these results compare with those obtained by using the high-low technique?

**3-45** Phoxco is considering purchasing a cafeteria in a small shopping center. In order to estimate daily receipts, the company made observations over the past 4 days as follows:

| Number of Customers | Total Receipts |
|---|---|
| 320 | \$1,500 |
| 280 | 1,400 |
| 400 | 1,800 |
| 360 | 1,700 |

You are to (a) plot these relationships on a graph, (b) compute the fixed and variable receipts using least-squares analysis, and (c) using the least-squares formula, estimate daily receipts assuming an average of 380 customers.

3-46 City College is interested in determining whether there is a relationship between class size and the cost of duplicating materials for a class. Five classes from last semester were sampled, with observations as follows:

| Class Size | Cost of Duplication |
|---|---|
| 30 | $200 |
| 40 | 250 |
| 20 | 180 |
| 50 | 400 |
| 40 | 260 |

You are to (a) plot these relationships on a graph, (b) determine fixed and variable costs using simple regression, and (c) comment on the results.

## PROBLEMS AND CASES: APPENDIX 3A

**3-47 Regression interpretation.**
The cost to produce a product is estimated as follows:

$$\text{cost} = \$4{,}000 + \$6x$$

where $x$ is the number of direct labor hours used. The standard error of this estimate of total cost is $400.

**Required**
If a product is estimated to require 500 labor hours, what is the 95% confidence interval for total expected cost (the appropriate $t$-value is 1.96)?

**3-48 Using simple regression.**
Docking Publishing has determined that the cost of publishing a text is linearly related to the number of pages. The marginal cost per page is estimated at $0.0050, and the fixed cost per book title is $1,500. This relationship was determined by fitting a regression line to data on cost and number of pages for its last 25 books.

**Required**
**a.** If the correlation coefficient for this regression line was 0.81, what is the coefficient of determination?
**b.** If the standard error of the estimate for this equation is $20, determine the 95% confidence interval for the cost of publishing 1,000 copies of a book 500 pages long.
**c.** If the standard error of the marginal cost is $0.002, what is the probability that there is no relationship between the cost of a book and the number of pages in that book?

**3-49 Evaluating regression alternatives.**
GHI is attempting to determine an equation to predict overhead costs. Regression has been used to determine the following three possible relationships.

Overhead = \$4,000 + \$2.50 per direct labor hour
Number of observations: 36
$R^2 = 0.72$
Standard error of the estimate: \$180

Overhead = \$5,000 + \$4.75 per machine hour
Number of observations: 48
$R^2 = 0.73$
Standard error of the estimate: \$850

Overhead = \$8,000 + \$0.50 per direct material dollar
Number of observations: 40
$R^2 = 0.51$
Standard error of the estimate: \$625

**Required**
Which equation would you use? Why?

**3-50 Evaluating and using simple regression results.**
Dalton Manufacturing has constructed two equations to predict overhead costs. Both equations were based upon 100 observations and were determined using regression. The fitted equations are as follows:

**1.** Overhead = \$5,000 + \$1.50 (direct labor hours)

$$S_e = \$400 \qquad S_a = \$3{,}000 \qquad S_b = \$0.10$$

**2.** Overhead = \$2,000 + \$2.00 (machine hours)

$$S_e = \$900 \qquad S_a = \$500 \qquad S_b = \$0.50$$

The data used to estimate Eq. (1) included observations in which direct labor hours ranged from 1,500 to 3,000 hours. The data for Eq. (2) included observations in which machine hours ranged from 4,000 to 5,000 hours.

**Required**
**a.** Which equation is a better fit? Why?
**b.** If the firm anticipates using 2,000 labor hours next period, what is the range of overhead costs the firm can expect with 95% confidence?
**c.** What is the anticipated range of expected overhead costs (with 90% confidence) if the firm anticipates using 3,000 machine hours?

**3-51 Linear regression: Interpretation** (SMA).
The accountant in a firm that produces a special electrical gauge wishes to determine the relationship or relationships between overhead costs and number of gauges produced. He has the following data from the last 5 months of operations.

| Month | Gauges Produced | Overhead Costs |
|---|---|---|
| January | 0 | \$295 |
| February | 150 | 410 |
| March | 125 | 348 |
| April | 110 | 334 |
| May | 175 | 440 |

By considering number of gauges as the independent variable $x$, and overhead as the dependent variable $y$, the accountant presumes a linear relationship of the type $y = a + bx$. Various statistical calculations produce the following data:

$a = 115$
$b = 1.9$
$r^2 = .9727$ = correlation (sample) squared
Standard error of estimate, $S_e = 11.21$
Standard error of coefficient, $S_b = .1835$
The $t$-value for 3 degrees of freedom for a one-tail test probability of .025 is
$t_{.025} = 3.182$
The formula for the $t$-test is

$$\frac{\text{coefficient}}{\text{standard error of the coefficient}}$$

**Required**

**a.** Is the accountant's assumption of a linear relationship justified? Give two reasons to substantiate it.
**b.** Given that the accountant is correct in his assumption, calculate a 95% confidence interval for the variable overhead per gauge.
**c.** The actual overhead costs incurred would fall within what range of values?
**d.** Predict the value of variable overhead if the number of gauges produced is 180.

**3-52 Interpreting regression** (SMA).
Small, Limited, produces two products, A and B, and uses simple regression techniques to determine overhead costs. Both products have to go through two departments: the machining department, where basic raw materials are blended to form major components, and the assembly department, where subcomponents are added on to the major ones. Each unit of A requires 6 direct labour hours in assembly and 0.6 machine hours. Each unit of B requires 9 direct labour hours in assembly and 0.8 machine hours. The financial and production records in the month of November for the assembly department yield the following information.

| Independent Variable | Coefficient | Standard Error | $t$-Value | Coefficient of Determination |
|---|---|---|---|---|
| Intercept | 10,000 | 400 | 25 | |
| Direct labour hours | 8 | 1 | 8 | .967 |
| Intercept | 6,500 | 812 | 8 | |
| Machine hours | 15 | 5 | 3 | .884 |

**Required**

**a.** Which independent variable should the accountant at Small, Limited, use to predict overhead for the assembly department? Give two reasons for your choice.
**b.** November is a normal production month. Predict the total annual overhead if the master budget calls for 10,000 units of A and 12,000 units of B.

**3-53 Regression: Not-for-profit organization.**
The Compliance Division of the Regional Social Security Administration Office audits recipients of social security to ensure that correct benefits are being paid. Field representatives meet with clients in their homes, ask questions, and calculate correct benefits.

PROBLEMS AND CASES: APPENDIX 3A

As part of the Regional Office's budgetary process, we have estimated the total compliance audit costs as a function of the number of clients interviewed. From the previous 12 months of data we ran a regression that revealed the following cost equation:

$$\text{total compliance audit costs} = \$25{,}000 \text{ per month} + \$120 \text{ per interviewee}$$
$$R^2 = 0.55$$
$$\text{standard error} = \$10{,}000$$

**Required**

**a.** Next month the Compliance Division will interview a random sample of 75 recipients. What is the best estimate of the total compliance audit costs to be incurred next month?

**b.** The regional supervisor can be 90% confident that total compliance audit costs will be less than what amount?

**c.** Why would regression not provide a very accurate cost equation in this situation? (Use common sense in your answer.)

**3-54 Cost estimation using simple regression** (CICA adapted).
Gibbs Plastic Ltd. was engaged in its budgeting program for the coming year. Division 2 had special problems and has sought your assistance in your capacity as controller of the company. Their problem is as follows:

Division 2 produces one product, M. The management of the division has plotted a scatter diagram and has found that a linear relationship exists between mixed (fixed and variable) cost and the number of machine hours. Management has asked you to do the following:

1. Develop the equation for the budget formula ($y = a + bx$) using the simple regression line (least-squares) method.
2. State the budgeted fixed and variable costs for a batch run 32 machine hours long.

The following observations have been provided.

| (1) Machine Hours | (2) Fixed and Variable Costs | $(1)^2$ | $(2)^2$ | (1)(2) |
|---|---|---|---|---|
| 23 | $ 25 | 529 | 625 | 575 |
| 21 | 20 | 441 | 400 | 420 |
| 27 | 30 | 729 | 900 | 810 |
| 29 | 32 | 841 | 1,024 | 928 |
| 29 | 33 | 841 | 1,089 | 957 |
| 26 | 31 | 676 | 961 | 806 |
| 19 | 32 | 361 | 1,024 | 608 |
| 20 | 24 | 400 | 576 | 480 |
| 21 | 24 | 441 | 576 | 504 |
| 27 | 34 | 729 | 1,156 | 918 |
| 19 | 26 | 361 | 676 | 494 |
| 30 | 38 | 900 | 1,444 | 1,140 |
| 291 | $349 | 7,249 | 10,451 | 8,640 |

Note the following formulae:

$$\Sigma Y = na + b(\Sigma X)$$
$$\Sigma XY = a(\Sigma X) + b(\Sigma X^2)$$

**Required**
As controller of the company, present your solution to the problem of Division 2.

3-55 **Adjusting data for regression.**
Snotop is the last existing manufacturer of non-frost-free refrigerators. It makes two models—regular and deluxe. In Department 25 automatic ice makers are installed. It takes 2 hours to install an ice maker in the regular unit and 3 hours to install an ice maker in the deluxe unit.

We are preparing to run a regression to explain the department's overhead as a function of the direct labor hours used in a week. Laborers are paid on Tuesday for wages earned in the previous week (through Friday). The labor expense is recognized at the time payroll is issued.

Your supervisor has gathered the appropriate data for many weeks, but has asked you to put together the data for the most recent 3 weeks. Departmental records reveal the following.

| | | Units of Production | | |
|---|---|---|---|---|
| Overhead Costs | | Regular | Deluxe | Straight-Time Wages Paid |
| Week 1 | | | | |
| Overtime premium | $ 350 | 160 | 110 | $4,900 |
| Monthly rent | 520 | | | |
| Supplies | 1,215 | | | |
| Depreciation | 600 | | | |
| Administration cost | 950 | | | |
| | $3,685 | | | |
| Week 2 | | | | |
| Overtime premium | $ 400 | 115 | 130 | 4,550 |
| Supplies | 1,050 | | | |
| Depreciation | 610 | | | |
| Semiannual insurance premium | 1,300 | | | |
| Administration cost | 925 | | | |
| | $3,895 | | | |
| Week 3 | | | | |
| Overtime premium | $ 100 | 150 | 135 | 4,340 |
| Supplies | 1,400 | | | |
| Regular ice makers (150 units) | 2,500 | | | |
| Depreciation | 605 | | | |
| Administration cost | 975 | | | |
| | $6,580 | | | |

**Required**
Determine the three proper values of the dependent variable and the three proper values of the independent variable assuming that we wish to run a regression relating overhead costs to direct labor hours. The overtime premium recorded in week 4 was $1,100.

**3-56 Adjusting data for use with regression—computer recommended.** Smeyer Industries is a very large firm with over 40 departments, each employing between 35 and 100 persons. Recent experience suggests that the equation being used to predict overhead in Department IP-14 is no longer appropriate. The current formula was developed 3 years ago. Since then, there have been a number of changes in the facilities and processes used in Department IP-14. The changes occurred one at a time. Each time the cost accountant felt the change was not major enough to justify calculating a new overhead formula. Now it is clear that the cumulative effect of the several changes has been large. Recent actual overhead costs have been quite different from those predicted by the equation.

You have been assigned the task to develop a new formula for overhead in Department IP-14. Corporate policy indicates that "direct labor hours" is to be used as the overhead base. Departmental records are available for 9 months. The records reveal the following information.

| Month | Actual Overhead | Direct Labor Hours |
|---|---|---|
| March | $68,200 | 8,812 |
| April | 71,250 | 8,538 |
| May | 68,150 | 8,740 |
| June | 73,500 | 9,176 |
| July | 38,310 | 2,123 |
| August | 60,790 | 9,218 |
| September | 80,350 | 8,943 |
| October | 68,750 | 8,821 |
| November | 68,200 | 8,794 |

An assistant has analyzed the data for March through July and made the appropriate adjustments except for the following items (for which the assistant was unsure of the proper treatment).

**a.** The semiannual property tax bill for Department IP-14 was paid on June 30. The entire amount, $3,000, was charged to overhead for June.

**b.** The costs to install a new piece of equipment with a life of 10 years in the department were charged to overhead in April. The installation costs were $4,300.

**c.** Factory depreciation is allocated to Department IP-14 every month. The department's share, $8,000, is included in overhead.

**d.** A strike closed the plant for three weeks in July. Several nonunion employees were kept on payroll during the strike. Their duties for the most part were general housekeeping and "busy work." These costs were charged to overhead.

You also have the details for the overhead account for the months of August and September. They are reproduced in the following table. You were hired on October 1 and have been keeping the departmental accounts since then. Therefore you know that the data for October and November are correct, except for the adjustments needed for items (a) through (d).

**DEPARTMENT IP-14**
**Overhead Control**
**August**

| Date | Explanation | Amount |
|---|---|---|
| Aug. 4 | Miscellaneous supplies | $10,450 |
| Aug. 5 | Payroll for indirect labor | 5,500 |
| Aug. 15 | Power costs: Department IP-14 | 12,250 |
| Aug. 19 | Payroll for indirect labor | 6,000 |
| Aug. 19 | Overtime premium | 890 |
| Aug. 24 | Factory depreciation | 8,000 |
| Aug. 26 | Miscellaneous supplies | 27,700 |
| | Total for August | $60,790 |

**DEPARTMENT IP-14**
**Overhead Control**
**September**

| Date | Explanation | Amount |
|---|---|---|
| Sept. 2 | Payroll for indirect labor | $ 6,000 |
| Sept. 7 | Miscellaneous supplies | 12,100 |
| Sept. 15 | Power costs: Department IP-14 | 11,100 |
| Sept. 15 | Power costs: Department IB-4 | 10,850 |
| Sept. 16 | Payroll for indirect labor | 6,500 |
| Sept. 16 | Overtime premium | 950 |
| Sept. 21 | Miscellaneous supplies | 19,350 |
| Sept. 28 | Factory depreciation | 8,000 |
| Sept. 30 | Payroll for indirect labor | 5,500 |
| | Total for September | $80,350 |

AUGUST

| S | M | T | W | T | F | S |
|---|---|---|---|---|---|---|
| | 1 | 2 | 3 | 4 | 5 | 6 |
| 7 | 8 | 9 | 10 | 11 | 12 | 13 |
| 14 | 15 | 16 | 17 | 18 | 19 | 20 |
| 21 | 22 | 23 | 24 | 25 | 26 | 27 |
| 28 | 29 | 30 | 31 | | | |

SEPTEMBER

| S | M | T | W | T | F | S |
|---|---|---|---|---|---|---|
| | | | | 1 | 2 | 3 |
| 4 | 5 | 6 | 7 | 8 | 9 | 10 |
| 11 | 12 | 13 | 14 | 15 | 16 | 17 |
| 18 | 19 | 20 | 21 | 22 | 23 | 24 |
| 25 | 26 | 27 | 28 | 29 | 30 | |

**Required**

Determine the best equation to relate overhead costs in Department IP-14 to direct labor hours. The use of the program REGR is recommended.

## PROBLEMS AND CASES: APPENDIX 3A

**3-57 Linear regression—computer recommended.**
Drogs, Inc., would like to determine the behavior of administrative costs. The data shown are to be used for this purpose.

| | Admin. Costs | Units Produced | Units Sold | Hours Worked | Grievances Filed |
|---|---|---|---|---|---|
| March | 21,000 | 100 | 110 | 1,100 | 10 |
| April | 19,000 | 80 | 100 | 900 | 7 |
| May | 24,000 | 120 | 90 | 1,100 | 15 |
| June | 20,000 | 105 | 95 | 1,050 | 6 |
| July | 26,000 | 130 | 120 | 1,200 | 20 |

**Required**

**a.** Which independent variable appears to be the best predictor of administrative costs? Why?

**b.** What is the cost equation if units produced are used to predict?

**c.** If the firm uses units sold to predict, what are administrative costs expected to be if 100 units are sold?

**3-58 Regression: Estimating international sales—computer recommended.**
The management of the Fuji Motor Car Company is contemplating exporting its successful high-performance sports car. We are aware that the total number of cars purchased in a country is a function of that society's disposable income. Management has requested that we develop a model that will predict total market demand in a country as a function of disposable income.

A recent United Nations report reveals the following statistics for last year.

| Country | New Car Sales (millions of cars) | Estimated Total Disposable Net Income (billions) | Exchange Rate to U.S. Dollars |
|---|---|---|---|
| United States | 9.4 | 550.4 $ | 1.000 |
| Great Britain | 2.9 | 82.2 £ | 2.130 |
| West Germany | 3.4 | 470.6 DM | 0.425 |
| Canada | 1.7 | 114.0 Can.$ | 0.877 |
| Mexico | 2.2 | 1,445.7 Mex.$ | 0.081 |
| Japan | 4.3 | 83,300 Y | 0.003 |
| Italy | 2.1 | 31,250 Lit | 0.004 |
| Norway | 0.4 | 121.9 N Kr | 0.205 |
| Sweden | 0.5 | 98.6 S Kr | 0.254 |
| Australia | 1.3 | 56.3 Aust.$ | 1.331 |

Next year we estimate that Saudi Arabia's disposable income will be 212 billion riyals (exchange rate: 1 riyal = $0.33).

**Required**

**a.** Estimate total new car sales for Saudi Arabia next period.

**b.** What is the 90% confidence interval for total sales to Saudi Arabia?

**3-59 Overhead estimation: Regression—computer recommended.**
Barbara Hinsen, the auto service department manager at the local H-Mart Department Store, has asked your help in preparing a new overhead estimation equation. Ms. Hinsen has suggested three possible bases that might explain changes in overhead costs: (a) the number of service orders (customers), (b) the number of direct labor hours used, and (c) the cost of direct materials used.

Ms. Hinsen has made the following information available to you from her records for the last year.

| Month | Overhead | Number of Service Orders | Direct Labor Hours Used | Direct Materials Costs |
|---|---|---|---|---|
| 1 | $2,400 | 42 | 330 | $4,500 |
| 2 | 2,450 | 36 | 345 | 2,900 |
| 3 | 2,100 | 39 | 290 | 3,600 |
| 4 | 2,200 | 45 | 300 | 3,200 |
| 5 | 2,600 | 47 | 360 | 4,100 |
| 6 | 2,250 | 41 | 310 | 3,750 |
| 7 | 2,350 | 39 | 325 | 4,100 |
| 8 | 2,100 | 37 | 285 | 4,400 |
| 9 | 2,800 | 31 | 370 | 2,800 |
| 10 | 2,550 | 40 | 365 | 3,500 |
| 11 | 2,700 | 44 | 380 | 3,900 |
| 12 | 2,350 | 38 | 330 | 3,250 |

**Required**
If Ms. Hinsen plans on working on 40 service orders, requiring 300 direct labor hours and $3,200 in materials next month, what level of overhead should she expect to incur?

**3-60 Determining rental fees using regression—computer recommended.**
The City of Tucson operates a motor pool. The motor pool is responsible for purchasing, servicing, and maintaining all passenger cars owned by the city (trucks are purchased by individual departments). The motor pool "rents" the autos to each of the other city departments. The rental fee is established so that the motor pool will just cover all of its costs; the motor pool is not expected to operate at a profit. Currently, the fee is established by estimating the motor pool's total annual costs and dividing this total by the estimated total mileage that will be put on all cars in the fleet. For example, last year the department anticipated incurring total costs of $600,000 and expected its fleet to log 3 million miles. Thus the rental fee was set at $0.20 per mile.

The police commissioner has noted that auto rental charges have become a significant part of the Police Department's budget. The commissioner has asked for a cost study to justify the rental fee and/or to find a better fee structure. The city auditor's department has prepared the following weekly data from the motor pool's records.

PROBLEMS AND CASES: APPENDIX 3A

| Week | Servicing Costs | Maintenance Costs | Overhead Costs | Fleet Miles |
|---|---|---|---|---|
| 1 | $4,500 | $1,300 | $1,875 | 65,000 |
| 2 | 4,800 | 1,350 | 1,925 | 68,000 |
| 3 | 5,000 | 1,400 | 2,000 | 71,000 |
| 4 | 5,200 | 1,500 | 2,050 | 74,000 |
| 5 | 4,800 | 1,400 | 1,950 | 69,000 |
| 6 | 4,700 | 1,350 | 1,925 | 67,500 |
| 7 | 5,300 | 1,500 | 2,075 | 75,000 |
| 8 | 5,000 | 1,450 | 2,000 | 72,000 |
| 9 | 5,000 | 1,400 | 1,975 | 70,000 |
| 10 | 5,100 | 1,450 | 2,025 | 73,000 |
| 11 | 5,000 | 1,400 | 2,000 | 70,500 |
| 12 | 4,700 | 1,350 | 1,900 | 66,500 |

The servicing costs reflect only the cost of gas and oil used; similarly, maintenance costs reflect only the costs of parts and materials used for maintenance. All labor costs and miscellaneous costs are included in overhead. Depreciation costs are not included in any of the preceding figures (depreciation is recorded only on an annual basis). The city has a policy of trading in its cars when they are 2 years old. The difference between the purchase price and the selling price of cars has been quite stable recently at $4,000 per car. That is, a car purchased new for $9,000 can usually be sold for $5,000 after 2 years. Finally, during the 12-week study, the fleet size remained unchanged at 120 cars.

The projected mileage for the cars used by each city department for the current year is as follows:

| Department | Number of Cars | Average Mileage per Car per Year | Total Mileage for Each Department |
|---|---|---|---|
| Parks and Recreation | 15 | 3,000 | 45,000 |
| Police | 55 | 60,000 | 3,300,000 |
| Public Works | 20 | 10,000 | 200,000 |
| Other | 30 | 5,000 | 150,000 |

**Required**

**a.** Based on the 12-week study and the additional information, project the anticipated total annual cost to be incurred by the motor pool.

**b.** Using the motor pool's current procedure for determining a rental fee per car, determine the expected total annual rental charges to be billed to each of the four city departments.

**c.** Develop a better fee structure for car rentals. Determine the projected total annual rental fee for each city department using your new rental rate.

**d.** The police commissioner should be happy with your new rate (assuming you have done it right), but the mayor's office (included in the category "other" in the table immediately preceding) is not likely to be happy. Explain to the mayor's aide why your fee structure is more fair.

**3-61 Multiple regression analysis** (CMA adapted).
Brown Company employs 20 salespeople to market its products in well-defined sales territories. The company has analyzed the weekly sales order-getting costs for the past year using regression analysis. The following relationship was derived from the regression analysis.

$$C = \$6{,}000 + \$0.50M + \$6.00S$$

where $C$ = weekly sales order-getting costs
$M$ = number of miles driven per week by the sales force
$S$ = number of sales calls completed per week

Standard error of the estimate for $C$ given the values for $M$ and $S$ = 400

**Required**

**a.** The sales department has estimated that the sales force will drive 10,000 miles and make 500 calls during the first week in July. Calculate the estimated sales order-getting costs for the week.

**b.** What does the value of 400 for the standard error of the estimate for $C$ mean, and how might it be used in cost estimation?

**3-62 Interpreting multiple regression** (CIA).
The internal auditing staff of Green Lake, Inc., uses regression analysis to review analytically each period's sales expense. Based on data collected over a long period of time, the following statistical regression equation was developed.

sales expense ($ thousands) = $34.5 + 0.04 company sales ($ thousands)
+ 0.2 shipping costs ($ thousands)
+ 0.01 industry sales ($ millions)

The following statistical report was generated by a standard computer program.

| | Coefficient | Standard Error | *t*-Statistic |
|---|---|---|---|
| Constant | 34.5 | 0.61 | 56.6 |
| Company sales | 0.04 | 0.0026 | 15.4 |
| Shipping costs | 0.2 | 0.015 | 13.3 |
| Industry sales | 0.01 | 0.25 | 0.04 |
| Standard error of regression | 10.2 | | |
| $R^2$ | 70.0 | | |

**Required**

**a.** Identify the dependent and the independent variables in the regression equation.

**b.** Assume that, for the current period, the company incurred sales expense of $400,000 and shipping costs of $800,000 to generate sales of $5 million. Industry sales for the period are estimated to be $2 billion. Based on this information, what point estimate of this period's sales expense would the regression model provide?

**c.** Indicate how a 95% confidence interval for the current period's sales expense point estimate would be constructed. Assume that sales expense is normally distributed.

PROBLEMS AND CASES: APPENDIX 3A

**d.** Which variables, if any, in the equation could be eliminated without seriously reducing the explanatory power of the regression model?

**3-63 Multiple regression—computer required.**
Saneras, Inc., is attempting to determine the cost behavior of packing supplies from the data provided below.

| | Packing Supplies | Units Produced | Units Shipped | Orders Filled | Orders Taken |
|---|---|---|---|---|---|
| Aug. | $18,000 | 1,700 | 1,400 | 160 | 170 |
| Sept. | 26,000 | 2,000 | 2,100 | 250 | 230 |
| Oct. | 20,000 | 1,900 | 1,600 | 170 | 180 |
| Nov. | 28,000 | 2,100 | 1,900 | 240 | 270 |
| Dec. | 24,000 | 1,500 | 2,000 | 210 | 200 |

**Required**

**a.** Which independent variable is the best predictor of the cost of packing supplies? Why?

**b.** Using multiple regression, what is the cost equation for packing supplies if units shipped and orders filled are used as the independent variables?

**c.** What is the estimated cost of packing supplies for January if it is expected that 1,600 units will be shipped and 170 orders will be filled?

**3-64 Multiple regression—computer required.**
Refer to problem 3-57.

**Required**

**a.** What is the cost equation for administrative costs if units produced and hours worked are used as the independent variables?

**b.** What are administrative costs expected to be in August if it is estimated that 110 units will be produced and 1,150 hours will be worked?

**3-65 Multiple regression—computer required.**
The Texas Poly Corporation manufactures plastic pellets, which are approximately the size of BBs and are used as a raw material by the firm's customers for a wide variety of plastic products. The pellets are made to the specifications demanded by each customer.

In the past the firm estimated the cost to produce an order solely as a function of the total weight of the order. However, the market has become very competitive and management now wishes to be able to make more accurate estimates of the cost to produce an order.

Discussions have been held with plant personnel to determine the factors that are likely to influence the cost to produce an order. The size of the order, as measured by total weight, was unanimously selected as the major factor. In addition, most of the people involved felt that the color intensity of the pellets affected total cost—the more intense colors being more expensive. A third potential factor was the diameter of the pellets being produced. A few people thought that smaller pellets were harder to make and thus more expensive, but several people disagreed.

Based on these discussions, a careful study was undertaken to measure the actual costs incurred for several orders. For these orders the following costs and specifications were recorded.

| Order Number | Weight (pounds) | Intensity[a] | Diameter[b] | Total Cost |
|---|---|---|---|---|
| 1 | 3,300 | 80 | 2.4 | 5,904 |
| 2 | 5,000 | 30 | 1.9 | 6,795 |
| 3 | 8,700 | 80 | 1.2 | 13,633 |
| 4 | 5,800 | 10 | 2.6 | 7,417 |
| 5 | 3,400 | 50 | 2.0 | 5,341 |
| 6 | 4,300 | 80 | 1.1 | 7,048 |
| 7 | 6,200 | 60 | 1.8 | 10,162 |
| 8 | 1,900 | 20 | 1.0 | 2,686 |
| 9 | 4,500 | 70 | 1.7 | 7,169 |
| 10 | 7,100 | 70 | 3.0 | 10,374 |
| 11 | 5,900 | 30 | 2.7 | 6,028 |
| 12 | 2,000 | 50 | 1.4 | 3,530 |
| 13 | 3,200 | 40 | 1.8 | 5,838 |
| 14 | 5,000 | 50 | 2.0 | 7,325 |
| 15 | 4,300 | 90 | 2.6 | 7,291 |

[a]Measured as a percent of full color (100%).
[b]In millimeters.

**Required**

**a.** Estimate the cost function to produce an order.

**b.** Estimate the cost to produce an order for 6,500 pounds of 3.0-mm pellets at a color intensity of 75%.

# APPENDIX 3B

# LEARNING CURVES

For most firms operating in a fairly small relevant range, linear cost functions are usually sufficient for accounting applications. However, there is one exception that is encountered by a large number of firms: learning curves. This appendix addresses the issues of how to estimate learning effects and how to account for costs when learning effects are present.

## THE EFFECT OF EXPERIENCE

It has been discovered that on many repetitive projects (especially large construction projects such as the manufacture of airplanes, ships, computers, and spacecraft) that the amount of labor time required to produce succeeding units decreases substantially. The explanation for this phenomenon seems to be that as people gain experience with the particular project, they can produce each unit more efficiently than the preceding unit. Thus, for example, a worker on the first unit must consult a blueprint for virtually every part to be installed. On the second unit, the worker may at least remember what part of the blueprint to look at in order to find out how to install a part. Eventually the worker may simply remember where and how to install a particular part. Although materials costs sometimes follow the same pattern, the learning effect is most often restricted to labor costs and any costs directly related to labor.

## LEARNING CURVES

### Learning Curves

For projects of the type just described, studies have found that when the time spent on successive units is graphed, it tends to follow an exponential curve. The functional form of the curve is

$$y = ax^{-\beta}$$

where $a$ is the amount of time spent on the first unit produced, $x$ is the total number of units produced, $\beta$ is a coefficient that describes the amount of learning that takes place, and $y$ is the average time to produce all $x$ units (that is, the average per-unit time for units 1 through $x$). This equation is known as the learning curve. (Note that you may see alternative formulations of the curve; however, this is the most popular formulation at this time.)

### The Equation Approach

Let us illustrate the use of the learning curve equation with an example. In financial accounting courses, students are often asked to prepare depreciation schedules over the life of a machine using a particular depreciation method. It is not uncommon for a student to take 45 minutes to solve one of these problems the first time it is encountered. However, if a second, similar problem is solved, the solution time will usually be much less, say 27 minutes. From these two observations, we can determine the equation that describes the amount of learning as a function of the number of problems solved. The time to solve the first problem, $a$, is 45 minutes. When $x$, the total number of problems solved, is 2, then the average time to solve both of the problems, or $y$, is 36 minutes—that is, $(27 + 45)/2$. Substituting the values for $a$, $x$, and $y$, the learning curve becomes

$$36 = (45)(2)^{-\beta}$$

To solve the equation for $\beta$, first take the log[1] of both sides of the equation to get $\log(36) = \log(45) - \beta \log(2)$, or

$$\beta = \frac{\log(45) - \log(36)}{\log(2)}$$

At this point we either refer to a table of logarithms, or better, have a pocket calculator that handles logarithms. In either case we find that the value of $\beta$ is 0.3219.

[1] *Log* refers to the common (base-10) logarithm; use of the natural (base-$e$) logarithm, represented by *ln*, would yield identical results.

The general equation for the average time to solve a total of $x$ problems is $y = (45)(x)^{-0.3219}$. Once we have the general equation, we can then predict that if this student solved six problems, and if learning continued at the same rate, then the average time to solve a total of six problems would decrease to[2]

$$\begin{aligned} y &= 45(6)^{-0.3219} \\ &= 25.3 \text{ minutes} \end{aligned}$$

How long would we predict that it would take this student to solve the last (sixth) problem? We can answer this question by first calculating the average time to solve all six questions, done above. Then multiply this average time by 6 to get the total time to solve six problems. Similarly, we calculate the average time to solve five problems as

$$\begin{aligned} y &= 45(5)^{-0.3219} \\ &= 26.8 \text{ minutes} \end{aligned}$$

and multiply by 5 to get the total time to solve the first five problems. Subtracting the total times then provides us with the predicted time to solve the last (sixth) problem:

| | | |
|---|---|---|
| Total time to solve the first six problems | 6 × 25.3 = | 151.8 minutes |
| Total time to solve the first five problems | 5 × 26.8 = | 134.0 |
| Time to solve the sixth problem | | 17.8 minutes |

Therefore, if learning continues at the same rate as occurred between problems 1 and 2, then the sixth problem should be solved in 17.8 minutes.

Specific learning curves are given names (such as a 90% learning curve). The names are derived from the effect that learning has on average production time when production is doubled. For example, let $x$ equal a particular level of production and $y$ equal the average time to produce all $x$ units. When we observe a new value for $y$ (say, $y'$) after production reaches $2x$, the learning curve is named after the relationship $y'/y$. Thus if $y'$ is 80% of $y$, we say we have an 80% learning curve. For example, if it takes 10 hours to produce the first unit of product and an average of 9 hours each to produce 2 units, we say we have a 90% learning curve. Similarly, if it took an average of 40 hours per unit to build 100 units of another product, then the average time to build 200 units should be 32 hours if we experience an 80% learning effect.

[2]Raising a number to a fractional power is not a task that we recommend doing by hand. However, many inexpensive calculators have the function $y^x$, which makes short work of these calculations.

Note that the name of the learning curve is derived from this relationship. The name is not the value of β in the formula presented earlier. There is, however, a relationship between the name of the learning curve and β. This relationship is

$$\beta = -\frac{\log(\text{name})}{\log(2)}$$

Thus for an 80% learning curve we can find the value of β as follows:

$$\beta = -\frac{\log(0.80)}{\log(2)}$$
$$= \frac{0.09691}{0.30103}$$
$$= 0.3219$$

and an 80% learning curve can be represented as

$$y = ax^{-0.3219}$$

A table of β values for various learning curves is given in Exhibit 3-12.

The equation we have been using provides the average time to complete a given number of units. As we have seen, we frequently need to know the total time to complete a stated number of units. The total time to complete units 1 through $x$ can be found directly with the formula

total time to complete all units

$$t = ax^{1-\beta}$$

where $a$, $x$, and β are the same as before and $t$ is the total time required.

It is also the case that we frequently want to know the time to complete a specific unit. The most accurate approach is what we did previously. That is, calculate the total time for $x$ units, the total time for $x - 1$ units and subtract to get the marginal time to complete unit $x$. However, this calculation can be approximated directly as follows:

total time to complete a specific unit

$$m = a(1 - \beta)\,x^{-\beta}$$

where $m$ represents the marginal time required for unit $x$. Unfortunately, this equation is quite inaccurate for small values of $x$ because it is a continuous approximation of a discrete function. The equation should only be used for values of $x$ larger than 250.

### The Doubling Approach

Although the equation approach must be used in many cases to calculate average production time, a much easier approach is available if we restrict

**EXHIBIT 3-12 A Table of β Values for Various Learning Curves**

| Value of β | Name of Learning Curve | Value of β | Name of Learning Curve |
|---|---|---|---|
| 0.0144 | 99% | 0.1681 | 89% |
| 0.0291 | 98 | 0.1844 | 88 |
| 0.0439 | 97 | 0.2009 | 87 |
| 0.0589 | 96 | 0.2176 | 86 |
| 0.0740 | 95 | 0.2345 | 85 |
| 0.0893 | 94 | 0.2515 | 84 |
| 0.1047 | 93 | 0.2688 | 83 |
| 0.1203 | 92 | 0.2863 | 82 |
| 0.1361 | 91 | 0.3040 | 81 |
| 0.1520 | 90 | 0.3219 | 80 |

ourselves only to doubling of production. For in these cases we can take advantage of what we know about the relationship of average production time and the doubling of production.

For example, if it takes 500 hours to produce the first unit of production, and the product is subject to a 90% learning effect, then the average time to produce 2 units (a doubling of production) will be 450 hours (90% of 500); similarly the average time to produce 4 units (another doubling of production) will be 405 hours (90% of 450). Note that the calculation results in the *average* time to produce all units to date. Thus to find the *total* time to produce the first two units we must multiply the average time for the 2 units by 2 to yield 2 × 450 = 900 hours. Similarly, the time to produce 4 units is 4 × 405 = 1,620 hours.

If we wish to know the time to produce just the third and fourth units, we must calculate the total time to produce all 4 units and subtract the time to produce the first 2 units. In this way we get the additional time to produce the last 2 units. In the example given this would be 1,620 − 900, or the last 2 units should require only 720 hours to complete. Exhibit 3-13 summarizes these calculations.

**EXHIBIT 3-13 The Doubling Approach: 90% Learning Curve When First Unit Required 500 Hours**

| Total Number of Units Produced | Average Time to Produce All Units to Date | Total Time to Produce All Units to Date |
|---|---|---|
| 1 | 500 | 500 |
| 2 | 450 | 900 |
| 4 | 405 | 1,620 |
| 8 | 364.5 | 2,916 |
| 16 | 328.05 | 5,248.8 |

## ESTIMATING LEARNING CURVES

The coefficients of the learning curve can be estimated from past data using regression. Although the form of the equation as given, $y = ax^{-\beta}$, is not linear, we can note that if we take the logarithm of both sides, the equation will be converted to a linear equation.

$$\log y = \log a - \beta \log x$$

With this conversion, we can use historical data to estimate the *a* and *b* coefficients. To do so, we enter the log of the average time to complete *x* units and the log of the number of the units (*x*) produced into a standard regression program. We must then be careful to remember that although the solution provided will give us the value of β, it will give us the *logarithm* of the value of *a*. To reconstruct the equation we must take the antilog of the *a* value provided by the computer to get the actual *a* value. Thus, if we obtained the following result from a computer,

| Variable | Coefficient |
|---|---|
| Intercept | 2.4771213 |
| x | 0.1047 |

the learning curve equation would be $y = 300x^{-0.1047}$. The intercept value is the log of *a*, using a calculator to derive the antilog of 2.4771213 gives us the value of *a* as 300. The value of β is given in the proper form as 0.1047. Reference to Exhibit 3-12 indicates that this is a 93% learning curve.

## DEFERRED LEARNING CURVE COSTS

Costs subject to a learning effect present a problem for financial reporting and, subsequently, for the preparation of pro forma (budgeted) financial statements. For financial statement purposes, firms typically value cost of goods sold at the average cost expected to be incurred for all units in the production run. For example, consider the project in Exhibit 3-14. Assume that the firm intends to produce 10 units, but in its first operating period only produces and sells unit number 1. Further, assume that the cost to build each unit averages $1 per hour. It is felt that reporting the cost of goods sold as $100, the actual cost to produce the first unit, will understate expected earnings and distort the trend of reported earnings. If the firm produces only 1 unit per period, then taken alone, the reporting of actual production cost for each unit (which decreases over subsequent units) would result in an increasing trend of earnings. To counter this appearance, firms

**EXHIBIT 3-14 Unit, Average, and Total Times for a 90% Learning Curve**[a]

| Unit | Time to Complete Unit | Average Time, All Units | Total Time, All Units |
|---|---|---|---|
| 1 | 100 | 100 | 100 |
| 2 | 80 | 90 | 180 |
| 3 | 73.86 | 84.62 | 253.86 |
| 4 | 70.14 | 81 | 324.0 |
| 5 | 67.5 | 78.3 | 391.5 |
| 6 | 65.46 | 76.16 | 456.96 |
| 7 | 63.84 | 74.4 | 520.8 |
| 8 | 62.40 | 72.9 | 583.2 |
| 9 | 61.29 | 71.61 | 644.49 |
| 10 | 60.21 | 70.47 | 704.70 |

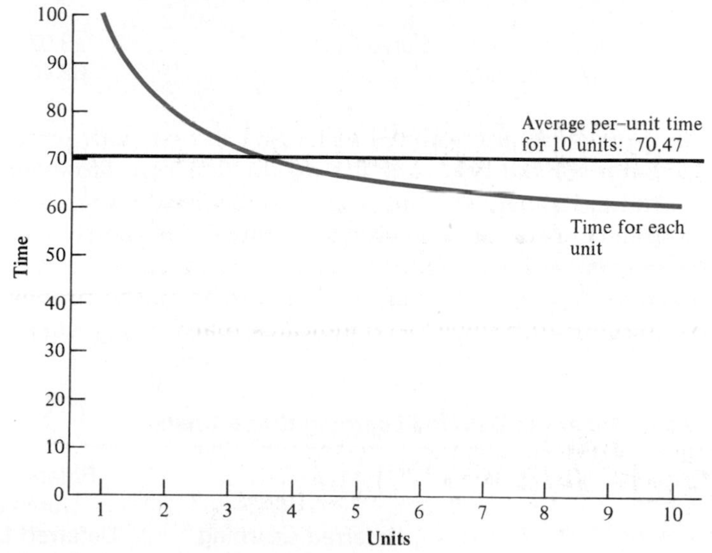


[a]90% learning curve, $\beta = 0.1520$, time for first unit = 100

will generally charge to cost of goods sold the average cost expected for all units in the production run. For the project in Exhibit 3-14, this means a cost of $70.47.

Now clearly we have a problem. If the actual cost to produce the first unit is $100 but we expense it in cost of goods sold as $70.47, what do we do with the difference? These costs will be deferred. That is, they will be set up initially in a holding account titled Deferred Learning Curve Costs. For the initial units in the production run, actual costs will exceed average cost, so the deferred account will be increased. But later in the run, actual costs will be less than the average product cost. For these latter units we will then decrease the balance in the Deferred Learning Curve Costs account. When the entire production run is sold, the balance in the Deferred Cost account will be zero. We illustrate the change in the deferred cost balance in Exhibit 3-15. The specific journal entries for the first unit in the run and the eighth unit are illustrated here. Note that the deferred costs are recognized at the time of sale, not production. The reason for this is discussed momentarily.

| | | |
|---|---|---|
| For unit 1 | | |
| Cost of Goods Sold | 70.47 | |
| Deferred Learning Curve Costs | 29.53 | |
| Finished Goods | | 100.00 |
| For unit 8 | | |
| Cost of Goods Sold | 70.47 | |
| Deferred Learning Curve Costs | | 8.07 |
| Finished Goods | | 62.40 |

The procedure just outlined will result in a smooth pattern of reported earnings for the firm over the production run. However, it does result in a rather strange account, which will be listed on the asset side of the firm's balance sheet: the Deferred Learning Curve Costs account. This "asset" will be recovered in the future only if we in fact are able to sell the entire anticipated production run. If we fail to sell all of the units in the run, this "asset" will have to be written off as a loss. Thus when deferred

**EXHIBIT 3-15 Pattern of Deferred Learning Curve Costs**

| Unit | Cost to Complete Specific Unit | Average Cost for All Units | Deferred Learning Curve Costs for the Unit | Balance in the Cumulative Deferred Learning Curve Costs Account |
|---|---|---|---|---|
| 1 | $100.00 | $70.47 | $29.53 | $29.53 |
| 2 | 80.00 | 70.47 | 9.53 | 39.06 |
| 3 | 73.86 | 70.47 | 3.39 | 42.45 |
| 4 | 70.14 | 70.47 | −0.33 | 42.12 |
| 5 | 67.50 | 70.47 | −2.97 | 39.15 |
| 6 | 65.46 | 70.47 | −5.01 | 34.14 |
| 7 | 63.84 | 70.47 | −6.63 | 27.51 |
| 8 | 62.40 | 70.47 | −8.07 | 19.44 |
| 9 | 61.29 | 70.47 | −9.18 | 10.26 |
| 10 | 60.21 | 70.47 | −10.26 | -0- |

learning curve costs are presented in a firm's financial statements, we should also inform readers of the statements (and management) of the likelihood that these deferred charges will be recovered by future operations. We do so by indicating the proportion of the remaining units in the production run for which we have specific sales orders; that is, we calculate

$$\frac{\text{proportion of deferred learning}}{\text{curve costs covered by orders}} = \frac{\text{remaining units covered by specific orders}}{\text{remaining units in the production run}}$$

Returning to the previous example, if we have produced and sold 2 units to date, then our deferred costs are \$39.06. Assume the firm has orders for 5 more units. The proportion of the remaining units in the production run covered by orders is five-eighths. There were 10 units in the run and 2 have been sold, so there are 8 remaining to be sold, and of those 8 we have orders for 5. Many firms then multiply this proportion by the balance in the deferred cost account and report that $\frac{5}{8} \times \$39.06 = \$24.41$ of the deferred costs are covered by sales orders.

The Securities and Exchange Commission's Accounting Series Release 164 requires that firms subject to SEC jurisdiction report the amount of deferred costs covered by sales orders in their 10-K report. The release specifies the computation provided in the previous paragraph. That procedure was probably selected because it is very easy. However, it overstates (often substantially) the amount of the deferred costs actually covered by sales orders. A more accurate approach would be to calculate the balance that would exist in the deferred learning account if all units for which orders have been received were sold. Subtracting this figure from the current balance for deferred learning costs would then yield the deferred costs actually covered by sales orders.

Using the data for the previous example, the more accurate computation of the deferred costs covered by sales orders is as follows:

| | |
|---|---|
| Current balance of deferred costs | \$39.06 |
| Balance in deferred costs if 5 more units are sold (refer to Exhibit 3-15 for total sales of 7 units) | 27.51 |
| Deferred costs covered by sales orders | \$11.55 |

Note that this calculation reveals that the covered deferred costs are less than half the amount reported as covered when using the SEC computation. The problem of course is that the SEC computation is a straight-line approximation of a nonlinear relationship.

When we prepare our cash and operating budgets for a particular period, we should budget for the actual costs we anticipate incurring. However, when we are preparing the pro forma financial statements and have costs subject to a learning effect, we must remember to adjust the statements for the effect of deferred learning curve costs.

The mathematics of the learning curve are somewhat more complex than working with straight-line cost equations. However, learning curves do represent a real phenomenon and are widely used in practice. The derivation and justification of the particular learning curves used in preparing bids for defense contracts have become an important aspect of the bidding process. Additional applications are illustrated in the problems for this appendix.

## DEMONSTRATION PROBLEM: LEARNING CURVES

Our firm has just succeeded in winning an army contract to build a small missile. The prototype that we constructed to win the contract cost us $30,000 in materials and $20,000 in labor. The Defense Contract Audit Agency insists that our labor costs will be subject to a 93% learning rate. Management agrees that this is a proper rate.

**Required**

**a.** Management expects to build 7 missiles during the next period. What is the budgeted amount of materials and labor costs we should expect to incur?

**b.** Assume that the initial contract was for a total of 32 missiles, but after the first 8 missiles were delivered (including the prototype), the army canceled the contract. If cost of goods sold has been valued at expected average cost for all units in the contract, what was the amount of deferred learning curve costs that had to be written off at the time the contract was canceled?

**Solution**

**a.** Because the labor costs are subject to a learning effect, the labor costs to build a unit change as production increases. We must identify specifically, then, which units we are building during the period. The prototype has already been constructed, so we are really building units numbered 2 through 8 in the next period. To determine the total budgeted labor costs for these 7 units, we determine the total cost to build all 8 units and subtract the cost for the first unit. We can use either the equation approach or the doubling approach to solve this problem. If we use the equation approach, the average labor cost for 8 units (using 0.1047 as the $\beta$ value for a 93% learning curve, from Exhibit 3-12) is as follows:

$$\begin{aligned}\text{average labor cost, 8 units} &= \$20{,}000(8)^{-0.1047}\\ &= \$16{,}087\end{aligned}$$

Using the doubling approach we get

| Units | Average Cost | Explanation |
|---|---|---|
| 1 | $20,000 | |
| 2 | 18,600 | $20,000 × 0.93 |
| 4 | 17,298 | 18,600 × 0.93 |
| 8 | 16,087 | 17,298 × 0.93 |

In either case, our total labor cost for 8 units is 8 times $16,087, or $128,696. Subtracting from this the $20,000 of labor used on the first unit gives us a total budgeted labor cost of $108,696 for the 7 missiles to be built next period.

Assuming that materials costs are not subject to a learning effect, the budget for materials is simply 7 times our first unit cost of $30,000, or $210,000. Our resulting total materials and labor budget for next period will be

| | |
|---|---|
| Materials | $210,000 |
| Labor | 108,696 |
| Total | $318,696 |

**b.** To determine the amount of deferred learning costs on the books after 8 units were sold, we first need to determine the average labor cost used in valuing cost of goods sold. The average cost used for cost of sales would be the average for all 32 units expected to be manufactured as specified in the contract. Using the equation approach, the average labor cost for 32 units would be

$$\text{average labor cost, 32 units} = \$20{,}000(32)^{-0.1047} = \$13{,}914$$

Thus, every time we sold a unit, we would have valued the labor cost portion of the unit as $13,914. Since we sold 8 units, 8 times $13,914 or $111,312 of labor costs were expensed. However, our actual costs for these early units would have been higher than the average cost. To estimate the total actual cost for the first 8 units we can determine the average cost for the first 8 units and multiply by 8. We already did this in part (a) of our solution. The actual labor cost for the first 8 units was determined to be $128,696.

The difference between our overall average cost and our actual cost for these units would have been accumulated in the Deferred Learning Curve Cost account. Therefore, at the end of the period, the balance of this account would be

| | |
|---|---|
| Total actual cost | $128,696 |
| Total average cost | 111,312 |
| Deferred costs | $ 17,384 |

so that when the contract was canceled, we would have to write off as a loss, the $17,384 in deferred costs.

## QUESTIONS AND EXERCISES: APPENDIX 3B

3-66 A department can assemble a component in 60 hours. Using the doubling approach, how long will it take to assemble a second component if (a) a 90% learning curve applies and (b) an 80% learning curve applies?

3-67 A firm has produced a component recording data to date as follows:

| Cumulative Quantity | Cumulative Total Hours |
|---|---|
| 1 | 500 |
| 2 | 700 |

The firm has an order for two additional components. Assuming the given pattern of the learning curve continues, how long will it take to produce these additional 2 units?

3-68 Home Improvement, Inc., has begun a new line of activity. It is expected that inefficiencies will occur initially, but improvement will result from successive contracts. The first contract for 5 units cost $30,000, of which 40% is not subject to the learning curve. If a 90% learning curve is in effect, what is the estimated cost of the next 5 units?

3-69 Ajax Corporation just completed building a small bridge for the county. Materials for the bridge cost $650,000. Labor cost was 20,000 labor hours at $8 per labor hour, or $160,000. The county government was so pleased with the job that it has requested Ajax to build three more identical bridges at various locations in the county. If, in fact, the bridges are identical and an 80% learning curve is applicable to labor hours, what will be the total cost for the three additional bridges?

3-70 Empirial Electric has bid on a contract requiring delivery of eight specialized generators. Revenues and matching expenses will be reported as the generators are completed and delivered. All costs are subject to an 80% learning curve. Costs and production to date are as follows:

| Total Number of Units Produced | Average Cost to Produce | Total Cost to Produce |
|---|---|---|
| 1 | $10,000 | $10,000 |
| 2 | 8,000 | 16,000 |
| 4 | 6,400 | 25,600 |
| 8 | ? | ? |

You are to determine (a) the average and total cost of producing 8 units, and (b) the deferred learning curve costs if 4 units have been completed and delivered.

3-71 A firm is going to construct seven modular units. The conversion costs of the first unit are expected to be $30,000 and are subject to a 90% learning curve; the material costs of the first unit are expected to be $20,000 and are subject to a 100% learning curve. What is the entry to the Deferred Learning Curve Costs account on delivery and sale of each of the 7 units?

## PROBLEMS AND CASES: APPENDIX 3B

**3-72 Using learning curves: Basic.**
Zeron is preparing a bid to produce some test equipment. The firm will construct 8 units. The cost to construct the first unit is estimated to be $50,000. All costs are estimated to be subject to a 90% learning effect.

**Required**
If the firm wishes to make a total profit of $80,000 on this project, what is the price per unit that Zeron should submit in its bid?

**3-73 Learning curve: Golf scores.**
Joe C. has been attempting to fit the learning curve to beginning golfers, who will play once a month without taking lessons. He has established that an 85% learning curve applies.

**Required**
What score can be expected after 8 months from a golfer who shoots 180 on the first round?

**3-74 Using learning curves: Basic.**
Morris Aviation has developed a new airplane. The cost of building the first model was $2 million. All manufacturing costs of the plane are expected to follow a 90% learning curve.

**Required**

**a.** What will be the average cost per plane if the firm manufactures 16 planes?
**b.** What is the total budgeted cost to build 32 planes?
**c.** Given that the firm has already built 32 planes, what will be the total cost to build an additional 32 planes?

**3-75 Learning curves: Working backward.**
Certainty Company has just determined that the average cost to build a new product turned out to be $63,700.99 per unit. This product is known to have been subject to a 96% learning effect.

**Required**
If the cost to build the first unit was $75,000, how many units were produced?

**3-76 Learning curves and labor standards** (CMA adapted).
Kelco plans to manufacture a product called Electrocal, which requires a substantial amount of direct labor on each unit. Based on the company's experience with other similar products, management believes there is a learning factor in the production process used to manufacture Electrocal.

Each unit of Electrocal requires material costing $1,500. The direct labor rate is $25 per direct labor hour. Variable overhead is incurred at a rate of $40 per direct labor hour. Kelco adds 30% to the variable manufacturing cost in determining an initial bid price for all products.

Data on the production of the first two lots (16 units) of Electrocal are as follows:

1. The first lot of 8 units required a total of 3,200 direct labor hours.
2. The second lot of 8 units required a total of 2,240 direct labor hours.

Based on prior production experience, Kelco anticipates that there will be no significant improvement in production time after the first 32 units. Therefore, a standard for direct labor hours will be established based on the average hours per unit for units 17–32.

**Required**

**a.** What is the basic premise of the learning curve?

**b.** Based upon the data presented for the first 16 units, what learning rate appears to be applicable to the direct labor required to produce Electrocal? Support your answer with appropriate calculations.

**c.** Calculate the standard for direct labor hours which Kelco will establish for each unit of Electrocal.

**d.** Comment on Kelco's standard for Electrocal. Is it an ideal standard, a normally attainable standard, or an easily attainable standard?

**3-77 Learning curve and pricing—equation approach required.**

Bradley Automotive custom-modifies automobiles, primarily for very wealthy individuals. A typical order involves installing a wet bar, telephones, a TV set, and a soundproof partition between the front and back seats of Cadillac limousines. Recently, the leader of a small republic requested the firm to submit a bid for making the following alterations to 12 Rolls-Royces: armor plate, bulletproof glass, automatic weapons mounted on the hood and recessed into the trunk, plus the normal internal amenities. The automobiles will be used by the leader and staff to ensure continuity of office.

Bradley estimates the security modifications on the first car will require 1,200 hours. The firm has had very little experience with these kinds of modifications, so a rather high learning effect of 80% has been estimated. The internal amenities are quite similar to those supplied in its normal business, so the firm estimates only a 95% learning effect, with the first car requiring 400 labor hours. Labor costs average $13 per hour.

By purchasing all of the Rolls-Royces at once, Bradley can obtain them for $104,000 each. Security-related materials will be $35,000 per car, and the internal materials will cost $20,000 per car. Materials costs will not be subject to learning effects. Variable overhead is estimated to cost $6 per direct labor hour. Bradley will submit a bid equal to 150% of average variable costs.

**Required**

Based on the learning curves and the other data, what will be the bid?

**3-78 Deferred learning curve costs.**

LRN, Inc., is building a product known to be subject to an 85% learning curve for labor and variable overhead. The first unit manufactured cost $40,000 for materials, $70,000 for labor, and $20,000 for variable overhead. During the production run, the firm will value cost of goods sold at the expected average cost per unit of $95,271.25.

**Required**

**a.** How many units does the firm expect to manufacture? (Note that materials are *not* subject to a learning effect.)

**b.** After the firm sells two units, what will be the balance in the Deferred Learning Curve Cost account?

## PROBLEMS AND CASES: APPENDIX 3B

**3-79 Deferred learning curve costs.**
Western Oil Equipment, Inc., has agreed to manufacture 16 drilling platforms for the Philmobilco Oil Exploration Company. Each platform requires $1.4 million of materials. The first platform required 250,000 labor hours to construct at an average wage rate of $8 per hour. The firm budgets variable overhead at $3 per labor hour. The labor and overhead for this contract will be subject to an 88% learning curve. Materials are not subject to a learning effect. The first unit was constructed in period 1. In period 2 the firm completed units 2 through 4.

**Required**
Prepare the journal entry for period 2 that records cost of goods sold at average contract cost and utilizes a Deferred Learning Curve Costs account.

**3-80 Deferred learning curve costs.**
Scientific Meteorological Predictions Incorporated has just developed a device that can accurately predict tomorrow's weather 13% of the time. This is such an improvement over existing technology that the firm expects to be able to sell eight of these machines. The first unit constructed required 2,000 labor hours. Materials costs amounted to $7,000. Labor is paid $6 per hour; overhead is applied at the rate of 80% of direct labor cost. Labor time to complete subsequent units is expected to follow an 88% learning curve. Unit 1 was constructed and sold in 19X6, unit 2 in 19X7, and units 3 and 4 in 19X8.

**Required**
**a.** Assuming that actual costs were exactly as planned, prepare the journal entry to record the cost of the units sold in 19X8.
**b.** If at the end of 19X8, units 1, 2, 3, and 4 were sold, and the firm had orders for another 3 units, what are the *total* deferred learning costs *not* covered by specific orders that would be reported on the balance sheet at the end of the year (as required by the SEC)?

**3-81 Deferred learning curve costs.**
Leer Construction has received a contract to build some duplexes. The firm anticipates building a total of 16 duplexes for the client, but the current contract is for 10 buildings. Construction began in January 19X7. During the period January through March 19X7, 2 units will be completed. Units are sold immediately upon completion. Another 2 units will be completed during April through July 19X7, and 4 more units will be completed during August through December 19X7. It is anticipated that the last 8 units will be built in 19X8. The client has tentatively set February 19X8 as the time to sign contracts for the last 6 units not currently under contract. Leer expects the first unit to cost $20,000 in materials and $30,000 in labor. Overhead is expected to be $500 per month plus $0.50 per labor dollar. Materials usage is not subject to a learning effect, but labor is expected to be subject to an 85% learning effect.

**Required**
**a.** Determine the total costs Leer can expect to incur during the period August through December 19X7.
**b.** What is the amount of deferred learning curve costs covered by specific orders that must be shown on Leer's December 31, 19X7, balance sheet according to the SEC?

c. What is the theoretically correct amount of deferred learning curve costs covered by specific orders as of December 31, 19X7?

**3-82 Learning curves with contract renegotiation—equation approach required.**
NorthAm Rockway (NAR) received a contract from the Air Force to build 20 fighter escorts. The first unit cost the firm $1,300,000 to complete. This consisted of $500,000 in materials and $800,00 in labor and overhead. Subsequent units will be subject to a 90% learning effect for labor and overhead. Materials costs will remain unchanged per unit. The contract selling price for each unit is $1,250,000.

**Required**

**a.** Prepare the journal entry to record the sale of the first unit.

**b.** After 6 units were completed and sold, the Air Force canceled the order. Renegotiations established an agreement whereby the Air Force will pay NAR enough additional funds (beyond the sales price for the first 6 units) so that NAR will make 40% of the profit that would have been made had the original contract been completed. How much in additional funds will the Air Force pay?

**3-83 Deferred learning curve costs.**
Wombat Enterprises, Inc. intends to manufacture 16 units of a product subject to a 90% learning effect. Costs of the first unit, which were subject to the learning effect, were $150,000. At the end of the first accounting period, the firm produced and sold 4 units and has committed orders for an additional 3 units.

**Required**

**a.** What is the dollar amount that the firm must report as deferred learning curve costs not covered by specific orders as of the end of period 1? Use the approach required by the SEC.

**b.** Prepare the journal entry that would be made in the second accounting period if another 4 units were sold. That is, prepare the entry to transfer the goods from finished inventory to cost of goods sold at expected average cost.

**c.** If at the end of the second period the firm has committed orders for an additional 5 units, what is the amount of deferred learning curve costs not covered by specific orders? Use the theoretically correct method.

**3-84 Learning curves and renegotiation.**
Embarka, Inc., manufactures loading ramps used by airlines to get passengers from the passenger lounge to the airplane. The ramps are constructed on site and require a significant amount of labor. During the first 3 years, 19X1 to 19X3, the firm constructed 47 ramps for East Coast civilian airports. The firm prices its work at 150% of budgeted direct costs. Direct labor was budgeted using a learning curve. The first unit had required $176,412 of labor. The firm used a learning coefficient of 0.1563, which a government report had listed as typical for this type of business.

In 19X4 and 19X5, the firm switched to full-time work installing the ramps at Air Force terminals. The firm constructed 66 ramps for the Air Force and continued to use the same learning curve. However, in early 19X6, a government auditor discovered that the learning coefficient was supposed to have been 0.1653, that is, the middle two digits had erroneously been transposed in Embarko's calculations. The government is demanding a refund of its overpayment.

## PROBLEMS AND CASES: APPENDIX 3B

**Required**

**a.** How much were the civilian customers overcharged?

**b.** How much was the government charged for labor?

**c.** The auditor has proposed that we determine the total budgeted cost for 113 ramps and subtract from this the cost charged to the civilian airports for the first 47. If this approach is used, how much will we refund to the government? Is there a more fair refund? If so, what is the amount?

**d.** The auditor has also suggested that the learning rate may have changed. Rather than try to work out the cost of both the civilian and Air Force ramps, he suggests we treat the Air Force contract as a new project. He notes that the forty-eighth unit actually cost $77,786 to construct. He suggests we use this as the cost of the first unit for the Air Force's contract of 66 units. In a magnanimous gesture he says he will allow us to use the 0.1563 learning coefficient if we agree to this. If we do, how much would we bill the Air Force for labor on the ramps? What is wrong with the auditor's latest proposal?

**3-85 Learning curves—equation approach required.**
Advanced Systems, Inc., introduced a complex piece of new oil well monitoring equipment last year. The firm anticipated being able to sell 100 of the units to the major oil-producing firms. As of October 1 of the current year they have sold 60 units. The first unit that was manufactured required materials costing $45,000 and labor costing $80,000. All labor costs are subject to a 92% learning effect (a $\beta$ value of 0.1203). There is no learning effect for materials.

**Required**

**a.** If the firm produced and sold 25 of the units last year, if the units are sold for $110,000 each, and if the firm values cost of goods sold at the average expected cost for all units in the production run, what is net income for the current year (the second year) as of October 1?

**b.** If the firm ends up selling a total of 70 units and then abandons the product, what amount of deferred learning costs will need to be written off as a loss?

**3-86 Deferred learning curve costs—equation approach required.**
Lerco has a contract to sell 30 units of a product for $12,000 each. The first unit cost the firm $15,000 to build. All costs are subject to a 92% learning effect. During the current year, the firm constructed and sold units 6 through 10.

**Required**

**a.** Determine the amount of learning costs that would be deferred during the current year assuming that cost of goods sold is valued at anticipated average cost.

**b.** Determine the current year's net income (1) if cost of goods sold are valued at anticipated average cost and (2) if cost of goods sold are recorded at the actual cost incurred for the manufacture of specific units (there are no inefficiencies).

**c.** What are the total deferred learning costs for this project at the end of the current year?

**d.** If at the end of the year the firm had orders for only 12 more units (beyond those manufactured already), what would be the amount of uncovered deferred learning costs that the firm would report using the SEC approach?

**3-87 Learning curves** (CMA adapted).

Catonic Inc. recently developed a new product that includes as a component a rather complex printed circuit board (PCB) that is purchased from an independent supplier. The first contract for 50 units of the PCB was awarded to Rexco on the basis of a competitive bid. Three additional orders for 50 units each were placed with Rexco shortly after. Each of the four orders had a unit price of $374 and a total price of $18,700.

Catonic's buyer has determined that the next order for PCBs should be for 600 units. Rexco offered to provide them at $355 per unit. The buyer has scheduled a meeting with Rexco next week and requests the assistance of the cost accounting department in evaluating the $355 unit price.

The price bid on the original contract for 50 units was estimated to be a "full cost" based price since, at that time, Catonic was not sure whether there would be future contracts for PCBs. The cost of materials included in the PCB is estimated to be $180 per unit. Cost accounting is fairly sure that Rexco assigns overhead at 100% of direct labor and employee benefit cost. The overhead is thought to be 50 percent fixed and 50% variable. Recent publicity indicates Rexco's labor costs to total $25 per hour. Work of this type is subject to a 90% learning curve effect. Rexco adds 10% to the full cost of producing a PCB to obtain its profit.

**Required**

**a.** Show how Rexco arrived at its original $374 unit price.

**b.** Prepare a schedule that may be used by the buyer during his meeting with Rexco next week. This schedule should incorporate the learning curve effect that Rexco would have experienced on the first 200 units produced and should be of use to the buyer in negotiating a contract with Rexco.

**c.** Identify factors that would tend to reduce the degree of learning that takes place in an industrial operation.

**3-88 Learning curves—computer recommended.**

Learcur Foundry has received a contract for 16 castings. Its winning bid was 60 percent above its average cost of production. The first unit will cost $29,000, and the units are subject to a 93% learning curve.

**Required**

**a.** What was the price that Learcur bid per unit?

**b.** Provide the journal entry for the production and sale of the fifth unit.

**c.** Provide the journal entry for the production and sale of the tenth unit.

**d.** Graph the cost of producing each unit.

**3-89 Learning curves: Interpreting computer output.**

E. D. Norton Industries is bidding on an order for 26 super pumps. Cost estimates indicate that the first unit should cost $200,000; engineering estimates that a 92% learning curve applies. The firm wants to make a 50% profit above the learning curve costs. The following information was obtained from running the computer program LEARN four times.

**RUN 1**

```
Enter the requirement to complete the first unit in the
batch ? 200000
```

```
Enter the number of the first unit in your batch ? 4
Enter the number of the last unit in your batch ? 4
Enter the learning percent as a decimal, i.e. 80% =
.80 ? .92
The average requirement to complete 4 units is 169280
The average requirement to complete 3 units is 175240.8
The total requirement to complete units 4 through 4 is
151397.8
```

**RUN 2**

```
Enter the requirement to complete the first unit in the
batch ? 200000
Enter the number of the first unit in your batch ? 1
Enter the number of the last unit in your batch ? 26
Enter the learning percent as a decimal, i.e. 80% =
.80 ? .92
The average requirement to complete 26 units is 135150.3
The average requirement to complete 0 units is 0
The total requirement to complete units 1 through 26 is
3513907
```

**RUN 3**

```
Enter the requirement to complete the first unit in the
batch ? 200000
Enter the number of the first unit in your batch ? 21
Enter the number of the last unit in your batch ? 21
Enter the learning percent as a decimal, i.e. 80% =
.80 ? .92
The average requirement to complete 21 units is 138667.5
The average requirement to complete 20 units is 139483.8
The total requirement to complete units 21 through 21 is
122342.5
```

**RUN 4**

```
Enter the requirement to complete the first unit in the
batch ? 200000
Enter the number of the first unit in your batch ? 1
Enter the number of the last unit in your batch ? 21
Enter the learning percent as a decimal, i.e. 80% =
.80 ? .92
The average requirement to complete 21 units is 138667.5
The average requirement to complete 0 units is 0
The total requirement to complete units 1 through 21 is
2912018
```

**Required**

**a.** What is the total and unit cost for the 26 units?
**b.** What price should be bid per unit?
**c.** What are the deferred learning curve costs for the fourth unit?
**d.** What are the deferred learning curve costs for the twenty-first unit?
**e.** Provide the general journal entry for the manufacture, completion, and sale of the twenty-first unit.
**f.** What is the expected cost of producing the last six units?

**3-90 Learning curves—computer recommended.**

Uneak has a contract to manufacture 33 large pumps for an oil pipeline being constructed over the next two years. Uneak will receive an amount equal to 125% of the average cost of production as determined by a 96% learning curve. The contract specifies that Uneak will be paid an amount equal to learning curve costs as each unit is delivered, with the balance being paid when the contract is complete. The expected cost of producing the first unit is $80,000.

**Required**

**a.** What is the average cost of producing all units?
**b.** What is the average selling price of each unit?
**c.** Provide the journal entry for completion of unit 23.
**d.** Provide the journal entry for delivery of unit 23.
**e.** How much cash does Uneak expect to receive when the last unit is delivered?

**3-91 Fit learning curve to data—computer required.**

ASI has produced for several months an automatic cannon for the army. A contract for additional units is being put out for competitive bids. ASI is confident that they will be the low bidder because of learning effects. Nonetheless, in preparing its bid, management wants an accurate estimate of the labor costs to be incurred for this contract. The contract is for 85 units and they will be produced over a three-month period.

Past production of the cannon has been in lots. The accounting records contain information only on the total labor required for each lot. There is no information available on the hours required to construct specific units. The data available are as follows:

| Lot | Lot Size | Total Labor Hours | Run Time |
|---|---|---|---|
| 1 | 20 | 3,280 | 2 months |
| 2 | 25 | 2,240 | 1 |
| 3 | 35 | 5,600 | 4 |
| 4 | 30 | 4,250 | 3 |
| 5 | 40 | 3,625 | 2 |

The labor hours include supervisory time which is thought to be fixed per month. Supervisors are paid $15 per hour. Production labor is paid $9 per hour.

**Required**

Estimate the total labor costs to produce the lot of 85 units. Use the computer program LRNFIT.

## PROBLEMS AND CASES: APPENDIX 3B

**3-92 Derive learning curve—computer required.**
Synchtech has produced several batches of a highly sophisticated power converter used in commercial aircraft. A customer has asked for a bid to produce another batch of 180 converters. The customer is quite price conscious, so management needs an accurate estimate of the labor costs to be incurred on these units when preparing the bid. Production of the units will be over a four-month period.

Past production of these units has been done in lots. The only data available in the accounting system are presented below.

| Lot | Lot Size | Months to Produce | Total Hours |
|---|---|---|---|
| 1 | 45 | 1 | 180 |
| 2 | 100 | 2 | 260 |
| 3 | 110 | 2 | 240 |
| 4 | 160 | 3 | 300 |
| 5 | 60 | 1 | 110 |

Most of the labor hours are subject to a learning effect, but management suspects there are some labor hours that are fixed per month. The average wage rate is $9.50 per hour.

**Required**
Estimate the labor cost to produce the converters. Use the program LRNFIT.

**3-93 Learning curves and uncertainty.**
Comfab Inc. has studied the learning effects on 20 of the firm's previous projects. The average value of the learning coefficient of the learning curve equation was found to be 0.1681, with a standard deviation of 0.00934.

**Required**
What is the range of the learning coefficient that can be expected with 90% confidence?

**3-94 Learning curves and uncertainty.**
Fabcom has studied the learning effects on 20 of its previous projects. The average value of the learning coefficient of the learning curve equation was found to be 0.1681, with a standard deviation of 0.01112.

**Required**
If the firm wants to be 0.995 confident that the total cost to build two units of product will be less than $81,900, how much can the first unit cost? (Assume that all costs are subject to learning.)

# CHAPTER 4

# COST-VOLUME-PROFIT ANALYSIS

This chapter concludes Part One of the text, which concentrates on broad issues affecting all of cost accounting. In this chapter we use our knowledge of cost behavior from Chapter 3 to analyze how profits react to changes in activity levels. The approach taken, called *cost-volume-profit (CVP) analysis,* will also prove helpful in making pricing decisions and in evaluating the effects of changing cost structures. Although it is somewhat imprecise, CVP analysis is a powerful planning tool.

## THE COST-VOLUME-PROFIT EQUATION

For external reporting, expenses on an income statement are traditionally listed in one of two ways. One approach categorizes expenses by the type of resources acquired. This categorization is referred to as a *natural classification*. The second—and more common—approach, called the *functional classification*, lists expenses by how the acquired resources were used. For internal planning and reporting, however, managerial accountants suggest a third approach for listing expenses: by *cost behavior*. (Exhibit 4-1 illustrates each of these income statement formats.) The cost behavior classification separates all costs, both manufacturing and nonmanufacturing, by whether they are fixed or variable.

**EXHIBIT 4-1 Income Statements Using Natural, Functional, and Cost Behavior Classifications**

**INCOME STATEMENT USING THE NATURAL CLASSIFICATION OF COSTS**

| | |
|---|---|
| Sales | $100,000 |
| Wages | 27,000 |
| Materials and supplies | 30,000 |
| Depreciation | 13,000 |
| Energy | 5,000 |
| Net income | $ 25,000 |

**INCOME STATEMENT USING THE FUNCTIONAL CLASSIFICATION OF COSTS**

| | |
|---|---|
| Sales | $100,000 |
| Cost of goods sold | 60,000 |
| Gross margin | $ 40,000 |
| Selling expenses | 7,000 |
| Administration expenses | 8,000 |
| Net income | $ 25,000 |

**INCOME STATEMENT WITH COSTS CLASSIFIED BY COST BEHAVIOR**

| | |
|---|---|
| Sales | $100,000 |
| Variable manufacturing costs | 50,000 |
| Variable nonmanufacturing costs | 9,000 |
| Contribution margin | $ 41,000 |
| Fixed manufacturing costs | 10,000 |
| Fixed nonmanufacturing costs | 6,000 |
| Net income | $ 25,000 |

All three income statements can be represented as

$$\text{total revenue} - \text{total costs} = \text{net income}$$

or

$$TR - TC = NI$$

But if we assume that total costs can be reasonably approximated by a linear cost function,[1] then total cost can also be represented as

$$\text{total cost} = \text{average variable cost} \times \text{quantity} + \text{fixed cost}$$

or

$$TC = vq + fc$$

[1]In Chapter 3 we argued that a linear cost function is typically a good approximation to a firm's actual cost function in the firm's relevant range.

If we also assume that the revenue function is linear, revenue can be represented as

$$\text{total revenue} = \text{price} \times \text{quantity}$$

or

$$TR = pq$$

Hence, when we combine total revenue and total cost, the entire income statement can be represented as a simple linear equation:

$$pq - vq - fc = NI$$

This equation, called the **cost-volume-profit equation,** is one of the most useful fundamental planning tools available to management. In the next several sections we will demonstrate the wide variety of uses to which the equation has been applied.

### Terminology

Before looking at applications of the CVP equation, let us define some terms that will be used frequently. The per-unit **contribution margin** of a product is that product's selling price less its variable cost. If a product is sold for $8 and the variable cost is $5 per unit, the contribution margin is $3. If 2,000 units are sold, the total contribution margin will be $6,000. The contribution margin is also referred to as the **variable profit** because it is the amount by which profit or loss will change if one more unit of product is sold. This margin is what is available from the sale of the product to cover the firm's fixed expenses and contribute to income. The contribution margin is also frequently calculated as a percent of selling price. In the example, the **contribution margin percent** or **contribution margin ratio,** or **profit/volume ratio** (P/V ratio), is $3/$8 = 37.5%.[2] That is, each sales dollar generates $0.375 of contribution margin.

contribution margin ratio or profit/volume ratio
C M / Selling Price =

## PROFIT PLANNING

The CVP equation allows us easily and quickly to project an anticipated level of income for any level of operations when the selling price and costs are known. Thus, if a firm sells its product for $15 per unit, variable costs are $6 per unit, and fixed costs are $20,000, then we can readily find the

[2]This latter term is popular in the financial press; it presumes that volume is measured in dollar terms.

answer to the question, "What income can we expect if we sell 5,000 units next period?" That is,

$$pq - vq - fc = NI$$

or

$$\$15(5{,}000) - \$6(5{,}000) - \$20{,}000 = \$25{,}000$$

However, management seldom knows precisely how many units will be sold in a future period. Therefore, a more common question is: "How many units must be sold to meet a particular income objective?" To solve these problems we work backward. Assuming the same cost and selling price figures as in the previous example, we can determine the number of units that must be sold for the firm to earn $7,000 by substituting $7,000 into the equation for net income, and solving for the required value of *q* as follows:

$$\begin{aligned} \$15q - \$6q - \$20{,}000 &= \$7{,}000 \\ \$9q &= \$27{,}000 \\ q &= 3{,}000 \text{ units} \end{aligned}$$

### The Breakeven Point

One particular level of income is of sufficient widespread interest that it is given a name. The level of operations at which the firm earns zero income (i.e., total revenue is exactly equal to total costs) is called the **breakeven point.** In the above example the breakeven point is calculated as follows:

$$\begin{aligned} \$15q - \$6q - \$20{,}000 &= 0 \\ \$9q &= \$20{,}000 \\ q &= 2{,}222 \text{ units} \end{aligned}$$

At any level of operations below 2,222 units the firm will incur a loss, and at any level above 2,222 units the firm will earn a profit.

In evaluating the sales potential of the firm, the breakeven point is critical. If the firm cannot anticipate average sales per period in excess of the breakeven point, it will not be able to survive in the long run. In the short run the firm may be able to generate positive amounts of cash even when it is operating below breakeven because some expenses, such as depreciation, do not require cash payments. However, a firm that is operating below breakeven should not replace its fixed assets and should expect to go out of business eventually. In fact, if the firm cannot earn a profit amounting to a reasonable return on its investment, it should cease to exist even if operating slightly above breakeven.

### Margin of Safety

If a firm has projected its expected sales for a period, the difference between expected unit sales and breakeven unit sales is called the **margin of safety.** If projected sales are 3,000 units and breakeven sales are 2,222 units, then the firm has a margin of safety of 778 units. In other words, sales could drop 778 units below management's predicted value before the firm would incur a loss. The margin of safety can also be expressed in dollar amounts by multiplying the margin of safety by the sales price per unit (in this case, 778 × \$15 = \$11,670). With this approach, we can report the amount by which sales, in dollars, can drop from our predicted level before we reach the breakeven point.

### Graphical Approach to Cost-Volume-Profit Analysis

Because we have assumed that the cost and revenue functions are linear, the CVP relationships are easily graphed. Figure 4-1 illustrates the facts used in our example. With such a graph, management can estimate quickly what level of income can be expected at each level of activity. Similarly, we can prepare an income graph, which eliminates the details of the cost and revenue functions as in Figure 4-2. This graph, called a **profit graph,** or **profit/volume chart,** is particularly useful for calling to management's

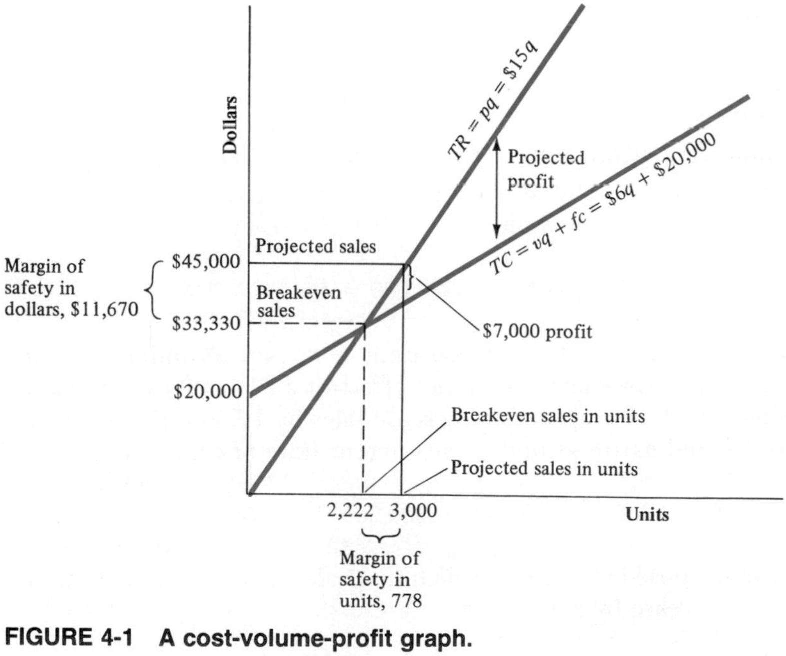


**FIGURE 4-1 A cost-volume-profit graph.**

Be able to label & make these graphs

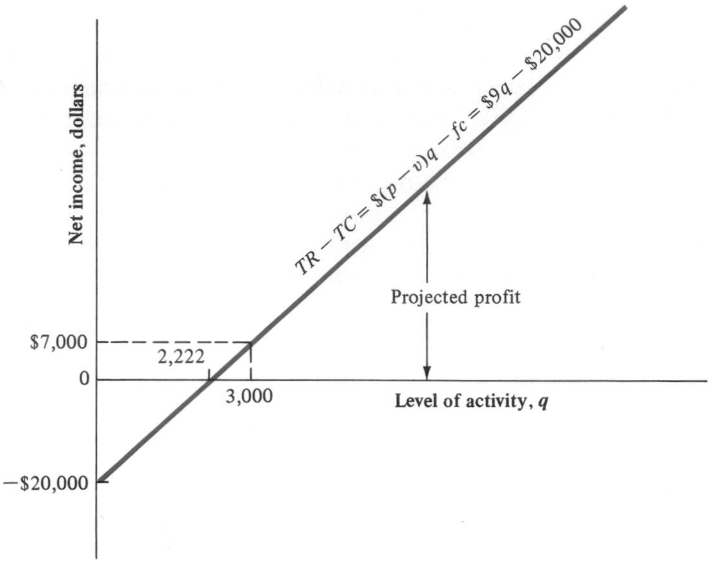


**FIGURE 4-2 A profit graph.**

attention the direct effect of volume on income. It directly graphs net income as a function of volume. For example, the graph shows a net loss for any level of operations below 2,222 units and a profit of $7,000 when 3,000 units are sold.

### Evaluating Cost Changes

For more complex questions the use of equation analysis is required. But the equation approach is still an easy means for analyzing the effects of changes on earnings. For example, if our CVP equation is

$$\$15q - \$6q - \$20{,}000 = NI$$

and we are projecting sales to be 5,000 units next period under present conditions, we can easily calculate the net effect of a $10,000 expenditure on advertising, which is projected to increase sales by 1,500 units. We first solve for anticipated earnings under the current state of affairs as

$$\$15(5{,}000) - \$6(5{,}000) - \$20{,}000 = \$25{,}000$$

and under the proposed change (in which unit sales increase by 1,500 and fixed expenses increase by $10,000) as

$$\$15(6{,}500) - \$6(6{,}500) - \$30{,}000 = \$28{,}500$$

We see then that the net effect of the change would be an increase in net income of \$28,500 − \$25,000 = \$3,500. Alternatively, we can also analyze the effect of the proposed change by examining the **differential revenues and costs**—that is, the revenues and costs that change when we move from one strategy to another.

For our example, sales will increase by 1,500 units times the sales price per unit of \$15, or \$22,500; variable costs will increase by 1,500 units times the variable cost per unit of \$6, or \$9,000, and fixed costs will increase by \$10,000. Total income then increases by \$3,500, as follows:

| | |
|---|---|
| Increase in sales (1,500 × \$15) | \$22,500 |
| Increase in variable costs (1,500 × \$6) | (9,000) |
| Increase in fixed costs (\$10,000) | (10,000) |
| Increase in income | \$ 3,500 |

An even easier approach is to notice that our contribution margin will increase by 1,500 units multiplied by the contribution margin per unit of \$15 − \$6 = \$9, or \$9 × 1,500 = \$13,500, while fixed costs increase by \$10,000. Again, the change turns out to be an increase in income of \$3,500:

| | |
|---|---|
| Increase in contribution margin | \$13,500 |
| Increase in fixed costs | (10,000) |
| Increase in income | \$ 3,500 |

We can also ask what the effect on income will be if we increase the quality of our product by using more expensive materials. Assume that this change will raise our variable cost to \$7 per unit, and the increased quality will increase sales by 1,000 units. The net effect of the change can then be calculated by solving for the new level of income:

$$\$15(6{,}000) - \$7(6{,}000) - \$20{,}000 = \$28{,}000$$

Subtracting the previous level of income reveals that this proposed change would increase income by \$28,000 − \$25,000 = \$3,000. This time directly analyzing the differential effects is more difficult. Sales increase by 1,000 units times the per-unit sales price of \$15, or \$15,000. Variable costs, on the other hand, increase by the new variable cost of \$7 per unit times the 1,000 new units (\$7,000) *plus* the increase of \$1 per unit for the 5,000 units (\$5,000) we initially expected to sell. The net effect on income is still \$3,000, as follows:

| | |
|---|---|
| Increase in sales (\$15 × 1,000 units) | \$15,000 |
| Increase in variable costs (\$7 × 1,000 + \$1 × 5,000) | (12,000) |
| Increase in income | \$ 3,000 |

## LIMITATIONS OF COST-VOLUME-PROFIT ANALYSIS

Although we have said that CVP analysis is a powerful tool, it does have limitations. The limitations arise because the analysis is a *short-run approximation* of actual CVP relationships.

The analysis is limited to the short run because we have assumed that we can reliably split costs into fixed and variable components. Costs are fixed, of course, only in the short run. Further, CVP analysis is based on constant technology and efficiency. Thus the relationships we depict are appropriate only as long as our existing technology and efficiency continue. Finally, the analysis assumes that our selling prices and the prices we pay for resources will be constant. This again is likely to be true only in the relatively short run.

CVP analysis is also limited because it is only an approximation of the true underlying relationships. As we saw when we were estimating cost behavior, cost equations do not perfectly represent actual cost behavior. Any error in the cost equation will translate directly into errors in profit estimates. Typically we represent cost equations by straight lines, but we know that this approximation is usually accurate only in a relatively small relevant range. Further, the straight-line approximation presumes that there are no significant step costs to be encountered in the relevant range. Finally, the most common use of CVP analysis assumes that there will be no significant changes in inventory levels during our planning period. That is, the quantity of units sold will be the same as the quantity of units produced.

## REFINEMENTS OF THE COST-VOLUME-PROFIT MODEL

Although the limitations with respect to the *short-run* nature of the CVP model are largely unavoidable, we can adjust the analysis for the errors due to *approximations*. More resources can be devoted to determining cost equations more accurately. Step costs could be explicitly recognized, and it is possible to adjust CVP analysis for changes in inventory levels. Whether we should do so is, of course, a question of cost versus benefit. Apparently the widespread use of simple, linear CVP analysis suggests that many firms do not consider the additional accuracy of sufficient value to justify the costs of preparing more accurate CVP models. However, there are several common adjustments to the simple model that are routinely made. Let us look at a few of them.

### Cost-Volume-Profit Analysis and Taxes

Because income taxes depend on net income they are typically not well represented by linear cost functions. Thus we can usually improve our cost-volume-profit analysis by treating taxes separately and incorporating their actual cost behavior. For very large firms the necessary adjustment to our analysis is relatively easy. For large firms the firm's marginal and average income tax rates will be approximately equal and stable in the firm's anticipated relevant range of activity. For example, assume that the current tax rates for corporations are 20% on the first $25,000 of income and 45% on annual income in excess of $25,000.[3] Further assume that a firm's relevant range of activity as measured in pretax earnings is $2 million to $3 million. When pretax earnings are $2 million, the total tax bill will be computed as

| | |
|---|---|
| 20% × $25,000 | $ 5,000 |
| 45% × $1,975,000 | 888,750 |
| Total tax | $893,750 |

which is 44.7% of pretax earnings. If pretax earnings are $3,000,000, the total tax bill is

| | |
|---|---|
| 20% × $25,000 | $ 5,000 |
| 45% × $2,975,000 | 1,338,750 |
| Total tax | $1,343,750 |

which is 44.8% of pretax earnings. For this firm, in its anticipated relevant range, the use of the firm's 45% marginal tax rate in CVP analysis will result in a relatively negligible error.

For large firms, then, we can incorporate the income tax effect into our analysis by including the marginal tax rate times pretax net income as a separate cost. Letting $m$ represent the firm's marginal rate, the tax expense is

$$\text{tax expense} = m(pq - vq - fc)$$

and the firm's after-tax net income can be represented as

$$\begin{aligned} NI &= pq - vq - fc - m(pq - vq - fc) \\ &= (1 - m)(pq - vq - fc) \end{aligned}$$

We will illustrate the use of this relationship to answer typical questions.

Assume that a firm faces a marginal tax rate of 45%. In the company's anticipated relevant range, the average tax rate is nearly equal to the marginal tax rate. The firm's product sells for $25, variable costs are

[3]Tax rates seem to change almost annually. For that reason we have not made an attempt to use "current" tax rates. Current tax rates are likely to change between the time we write this and publication, and again between the time of publication and the time you read the book.

\$10 per unit, and annual fixed costs are \$500,000. What after-tax income can this firm expect if it sells 200,000 units?

This question simply requires us to plug our known numbers into the income equation. Anticipated net income will be

$$\begin{aligned} NI &= (1 - 0.45)(\$25 \times 200{,}000 - \$10 \times 200{,}000 - \$500{,}000) \\ &= (0.55)(\$5{,}000{,}000 - \$2{,}000{,}000 - \$500{,}000) \\ &= (0.55)(\$2{,}500{,}000) \\ &= \$1{,}375{,}000 \end{aligned}$$

A more difficult problem is to determine how many units the firm must sell in order to earn \$1,500,000 after tax. Again, we substitute our known figures into the equation, but now the algebra requires a little extra effort:

$$\begin{aligned} \$1{,}500{,}000 &= (1 - 0.45)(\$25q - \$10q - \$500{,}000) \\ \$1{,}500{,}000 &= 0.55(\$15q - \$500{,}000) \\ \$1{,}500{,}000 &= \$8.25q - \$275{,}000 \\ \$1{,}775{,}000 &= \$8.25q \\ 215{,}152 &= q \end{aligned}$$

If we sell 215,152 units of product, the firm will earn approximately \$1,500,000 after tax. We know that this answer is not precisely correct because we acted as if the firm's tax rate was 45%, when we know that the average tax rate is slightly different from 45%.

Although large firms can ignore changing marginal tax rates, the errors from estimating an average tax rate for small firms can be quite significant. Unfortunately, when we have to deal with the actual marginal rates, the required CVP analysis is something of a bother. The problem develops because there is a kink in the cost curve representing tax expense. For example, if there are just two marginal tax rates, $M_1$ in force up to pretax earnings of \$25,000 and $M_2$ for income in excess of \$25,000, the tax expense can be represented graphically as in Figure 4-3 or in equation form as

$$\text{tax expense} = \begin{cases} (pq - vq - fc)M_1 & \text{if } pq - vq - fc \leq \$25{,}000 \\ \$25{,}000M_1 + (pq - vq - fc - \$25{,}000)M_2 & \text{if } pq - vq - fc > \$25{,}000 \end{cases}$$

The easiest approach for predicting income levels for a firm subject to multiple tax rates is to use simple CVP to determine *pretax* income and

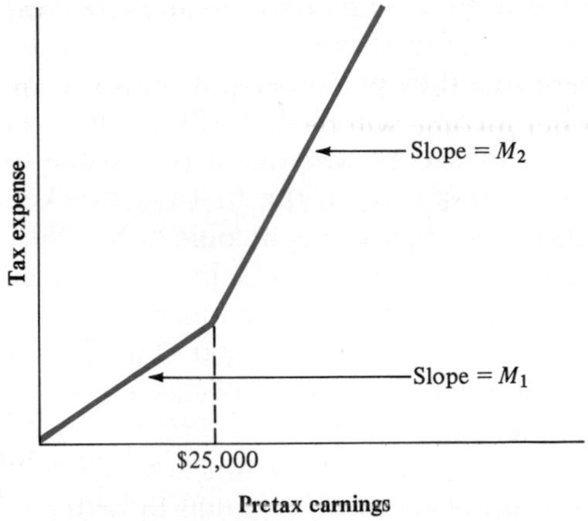


**FIGURE 4-3 Graph of tax expenses with two marginal tax rates.**

then calculate the tax expense separately. For example, assume that a firm sells its product for $25 per unit, variable costs are $10 per unit, and fixed costs are $500,000 per year. The firm must pay a 20% tax on all income up to $25,000 and a 45% tax on income in excess of $25,000. If this firm expects to sell 40,000 units of product, what level of after-tax income can it expect?

Ignoring the tax aspect, we can calculate pretax income as follows:

$$\begin{aligned}\text{pretax income} &= \$25 \times 40{,}000 - \$10 \times 40{,}000 - \$500{,}000 \\ &= \$1{,}000{,}000 - \$400{,}000 - \$500{,}000 \\ &= \$100{,}000\end{aligned}$$

We can now separately determine the tax on $100,000 of pretax income. The first $25,000 of income is taxed at 20% for a tax of $5,000. The 45% tax rate then applies to the income in *excess* of $25,000. This means that $75,000 in income is taxed at the 45% rate for a tax of $33,750 on the higher bracket income. The total tax then is

| | |
|---|---:|
| 20% × $25,000 | $ 5,000 |
| 45% × $75,000 | 33,750 |
| Total | $38,750 |

so the after-tax income when selling 40,000 units is $100,000 − $38,750 = $61,250.

Answering questions concerning how many units must be sold in order to earn a specific after-tax dollar amount is also more difficult when there is more than one relevant marginal tax rate. Using the data from our previous example let us now determine how many units must be sold to earn $50,000 after tax. Again, when there is more than one tax rate, the CVP analysis is most easily accomplished by performing it in two steps.

First we calculate the necessary pretax income that will result in an after-tax income of $50,000. We start by seeing whether it is possible to have an after-tax income of $50,000 and still be in the first tax bracket. Obviously, since the first bracket cuts off at a before-tax income of $25,000, it is not possible. Then we calculate how much after-tax income can be generated in the first tax bracket. If there is $25,000 or more in pretax earnings, the tax will be 20% of the first $25,000 or $5,000. Thus, after tax we get $20,000 in earnings from the first $25,000 of pretax earnings. The remaining $30,000 in after-tax earnings ($50,000 − $20,000) must come from earnings subject to the tax in the second tax bracket. We then ask how much pretax earnings there must be above $25,000 in order to leave $30,000 in after-tax earnings. Since earnings at this level are taxed at a 45% rate, only 55% of the pretax earnings will remain in the firm. Hence, to obtain $30,000 in after-tax earnings the following relationship must be true:

$$0.55(\text{second-bracket pretax earnings}) = \$30{,}000$$

Dividing both sides by 0.55 indicates that we need an additional $54,545 of earnings to yield the desired $30,000 after tax. The total pretax earnings needed to provide $50,000 in income after tax can then be determined by adding the required pretax earnings from each bracket:

| Tax Bracket | Pretax Earnings | Tax | After-Tax Earnings |
|---|---|---|---|
| 20% | $25,000 | $ 5,000 | $20,000 |
| 45% | 54,545 | 24,545 | 30,000 |
| Totals | $79,545 | $29,545 | $50,000 |

This analysis reveals that we need $79,545 in pretax earnings to earn $50,000. To determine the sales quantity necessary to generate this pretax earnings, we can now use the simple CVP analysis (which ignores taxes) to get

$$\begin{aligned}
\$79{,}545 &= \$25q - \$10q - \$500{,}000 \\
\$79{,}545 &= \$15q - \$500{,}000 \\
\$579{,}545 &= \$15q \\
38{,}636 &= q
\end{aligned}$$

Finally, we have the solution. In order for our firm to earn $50,000 after tax, we will have to sell 38,636 units of product.

With more than two applicable marginal tax rates the computations become more onerous, but the procedure is the same.

### Cost-Volume-Profit Analysis with Bonuses

The existence of income-related executive bonuses is another common situation that can be incorporated into our CVP analysis. To motivate management performance, firms will frequently set aside a percentage of the firm's profit to be distributed as a management bonus.[4] Since it is based on income, this type of bonus is analogous to an income tax. If the bonus is a flat percentage rate, we can use an approach similar to the one we used when we had a single tax rate. Assume again that the company sells its product for \$25 per unit, variable costs are \$10 per unit, and fixed costs are \$500,000. If we pay management a bonus of 5% of pretax net income how many units must be sold to earn a before-tax, but after-bonus, net income of \$40,000?

Since the bonus can be represented as

$$\text{bonus} = 0.05(pq - vq - fc)$$

the net income after the bonus can be represented as

$$NI = (1 - 0.05)(pq - vq - fc)$$

or

$$\$40{,}000 = (1 - 0.05)(\$25q - \$10q - \$500{,}000)$$
$$\$40{,}000 = (0.95)(\$15q - \$500{,}000)$$
$$\$40{,}000 = \$14.25q - \$475{,}000$$
$$\$515{,}000 = \$14.25q$$
$$36{,}140 = q$$

That is, 36,140 units must be sold to earn a pretax, after-bonus net income of \$40,000.

If bonus rates change depending on the level of net income (e.g., one rate for the first \$100,000 of net income and another rate for income in excess of \$100,000), then the analysis would parallel the analysis used for firms that pay taxes in two or more tax brackets. Since it is so similar, we will not repeat it here. However, an additional complicating factor is the existence of both bonuses and taxes. Again, let us assume that we sell our product for \$25 and that variable costs are \$10 and fixed costs are \$500,000. Now assume that management is given a 5% bonus of *after-tax*

[4]The study of optimal management incentive plans and the interface with the choice of accounting systems has recently gained considerable attention in the accounting literature. This topic, broadly referred to as **agency theory,** is reviewed in the article by Baiman cited in the Further Reading section at the end of the chapter.

income and the firm faces an average tax rate of 45% in its expected relevant range. If the firm sells 200,000 units of product, what net income can it expect?

This is a difficult problem because the bonus is after tax, and the tax will be after the bonus (the bonus is deductible for tax purposes).[5] First we set up the equations for the amount of the bonus and the amount of the tax. Let $B$ represent the total amount of the bonus, $T$ the total amount of the tax, $b$ the bonus-set-aside percentage, and $m$ the marginal tax rate; then

$$B = b(pq - vq - fc - T)$$
$$\text{and} \quad T = m(pq - vq - fc - B)$$

Now note that by substituting our known values into these equations, we can perform some, but not all, of the arithmetic. The equation for the bonus becomes

$$\begin{aligned} B &= 0.05(\$25 \times 200{,}000 - \$10 \times 200{,}000 - \$500{,}000 - T) \\ &= 0.05(\$5{,}000{,}000 - \$2{,}000{,}000 - \$500{,}000 - T) \\ &= 0.05(\$2{,}500{,}000 - T) \\ &= \$125{,}000 - 0.05T \end{aligned}$$

The equation for taxes becomes

$$\begin{aligned} T &= 0.45(\$25 \times 200{,}000 - \$10 \times 200{,}000 - \$500{,}000 - B) \\ &= 0.45(\$5{,}000{,}000 - \$2{,}000{,}000 - \$500{,}000 - B) \\ &= 0.45(\$2{,}500{,}000 - B) \\ &= \$1{,}125{,}000 - 0.45B \end{aligned}$$

At this point, we have two equations and two unknowns:

$$B = \$125{,}000 - 0.05T$$
$$T = \$1{,}125{,}000 - 0.45B$$

We can now solve for one variable by substituting the value of the other variable into one of the equations. Let us substitute the equation for the bonus into the equation for taxes.

[5]Our analysis presumes that the bonus is a percent of the income earned after tax but before deducting the bonus. If the bonus were a percent of the "bottom line" after both taxes and the bonus have been deducted, the analysis would be considerably easier.

$$T = \$1{,}125{,}000 - 0.45(\$125{,}000 - 0.05T)$$
$$T = \$1{,}125{,}000 - \$56{,}250 + 0.0225T$$
$$0.9775T = \$1{,}068{,}750$$
$$T = \$1{,}093{,}350$$

Now substituting the value for taxes into the bonus equation, we get

$$B = \$125{,}000 - 0.05(\$1{,}093{,}350)$$
$$= \$125{,}000 - \$54{,}667$$
$$= \$70{,}333$$

Finally we are in a position to determine anticipated income if we sell 200,000 units. The after-tax income will be

$$NI = pq - vq - fc - T - B$$
$$= \$25 \times 200{,}000 - \$10 \times 200{,}000 - \$500{,}000 - \$1{,}093{,}350 - \$70{,}333$$
$$= \$1{,}336{,}317$$

The resulting projected income statement is given in Exhibit 4-2. Note that the tax is, in fact, 45% of pretax earnings, and the bonus is 5% of income after tax but before the bonus.

Let us now solve for the number of units we must sell to earn $2,000,000 after tax and after bonus. This is actually a slightly easier cal-

**EXHIBIT 4-2 Income Statement with Bonus and Taxes**

| | |
|---|---|
| Sales ($25 × 200,000) | $5,000,000 |
| Variable costs ($10 × 200,000) | 2,000,000 |
| Fixed costs | 500,000 |
| Net income before bonus and tax | $2,500,000 |
| Bonus | 70,333 |
| Net income before tax | $2,429,667 |
| Income tax | 1,093,350 |
| Net income | $1,336,317 |

$$\frac{\text{income tax}}{\text{net income before tax}} = \frac{\$1{,}093{,}350}{\$2{,}429{,}667} = 45\%$$

$$\frac{\text{bonus}}{\text{net income before bonus, after tax}} = \frac{\$70{,}333}{\$1{,}336{,}317 + \$70{,}333} = 5\%$$

culation than the preceding one. If after-tax income is to be \$2,000,000, then pretax income must be

$$\begin{aligned} \text{pretax income} &= \$2{,}000{,}000 + 0.45(\text{pretax income}) \\ 0.55(\text{pretax income}) &= \$2{,}000{,}000 \\ \text{pretax income} &= \$3{,}636{,}363 \end{aligned}$$

We also know that the bonus is 5% of net income after tax but before the bonus, so the bonus $B$ must be as follows:

$$\begin{aligned} B &= 0.05(\$2{,}000{,}000 + B) \\ B &= \$100{,}000 + 0.05B \\ 0.95B &= \$100{,}000 \\ B &= \$105{,}263 \end{aligned}$$

Thus the net income before the bonus and before the tax must be

| | |
|---|---|
| Pretax income | \$3,636,363 |
| Plus bonus | 105,263 |
| Net income before tax and bonus | \$3,741,626 |

We can now use simple CVP analysis to determine how many units must be sold to earn \$3,741,626 before taxes and bonus:

$$\begin{aligned} \$25q - \$10q - \$500{,}000 &= \$3{,}741{,}626 \\ \$15q &= \$4{,}241{,}626 \\ q &= 282{,}775 \text{ units} \end{aligned}$$

**EXHIBIT 4-3 Income Statement for Example in Which the Goal Is to Earn \$2,000,000 after Tax and Bonus**

| | |
|---|---|
| Sales (\$25 × 282,775) | \$7,069,375 |
| Variable costs (\$10 × 282,775) | 2,827,750 |
| Fixed costs | 500,000 |
| Net income before bonus and tax | \$3,741,625 |
| Bonus | 105,263 |
| Net income before tax | \$3,636,362 |
| Tax | 1,636,363 |
| Net income | \$1,999,999 |

$$\frac{\text{income tax}}{\text{net income before tax}} = \frac{\$1{,}636{,}363}{\$3{,}636{,}362} = 45\%$$

$$\frac{\text{bonus}}{\text{net income before bonus, after tax}} = \frac{\$105{,}263}{\$1{,}999{,}999 + \$105{,}263} = 5\%$$

In other words, we must sell 282,775 units if we wish to earn \$2,000,000 after tax and bonus. The resulting projected income statement for the sale of 282,775 units is presented in Exhibit 4-3. Note there is a slight rounding error, resulting in \$1 less of income than desired.

### Another Approach to Cost-Volume-Profit Analysis with Bonuses

The preceding analysis required the solution of two simultaneous equations. The simultaneous equations can be avoided if the bonus and taxes are expressed in terms of their relationship to net income after tax.

Let us return to the example in which a firm wishes to determine net income when 200,000 units are sold, the selling price is \$25 per unit, variable costs are \$10 per unit, fixed costs are \$500,000, the tax rate is 45%, and the bonus is 5% of net income after tax but before the bonus. The alternative analysis starts by noting that net income before tax and before the bonus will be \$25(200,000) − \$10(200,000) − \$500,000 = \$2,500,000.

Let us now represent net income before the tax and bonus by *NIBB*, let *B* represent the bonus, *T* the tax, *NIBT* net income before tax but after the bonus, and finally *NIAT* net income after tax and after the bonus. Then the relationship of these variables is

$$\begin{array}{r} NIBB \\ -B \\ \hline NIBT \\ -T \\ \hline NIAT \end{array}$$

From the definition of how the bonus was calculated, we know

$$\begin{aligned} B &= 0.05(NIAT + B) \\ B &= 0.05NIAT + 0.05B \\ 0.95B &= 0.05NIAT \\ B &= \frac{5}{95}NIAT \end{aligned}$$

We also know that

$$T = 0.45NIBT$$

and given the relationship of the variables, it must be the case that

$$NIAT = 0.55NIBT$$

Dividing both sides by 0.55 yields

$$NIBT = \frac{NIAT}{0.55}$$

Substituting this relationship into the equation for tax yields

$$T = 0.45\,\frac{NIAT}{0.55}$$

$$T = \frac{45}{55}NIAT$$

With both the tax and the bonus now expressed as a function of *NIAT*, we can solve directly for *NIAT*:

$$\begin{aligned} NIBB - B - T &= NIAT \\ \$2{,}500{,}000 - \frac{5}{95}NIAT - \frac{45}{55}NIAT &= NIAT \\ \$2{,}500{,}000 &= 1.8708134NIAT \\ NIAT &= \$1{,}336{,}317 \end{aligned}$$

The calculations for the bonus and tax are

$$\begin{aligned} B &= \frac{5}{95}(\$1{,}336{,}317) \\ &= \$70{,}333 \\ T &= \frac{45}{55}(\$1{,}336{,}317) \\ &= \$1{,}093{,}350 \end{aligned}$$

Of course, this alternative analysis provides the same answer as the previous approach. Which method of analysis you choose to use should be determined by which approach you find easier to understand.

## SUMMARY

Cost-volume-profit analysis is a powerful tool that allows managers to answer "what if" questions quickly and easily. The approximate effects on income of major changes in alternative pricing strategies are easily discernible once cost-volume-profit relationships have been determined. In addition, managers can study the effect of making trade-offs such as substituting fixed for variable costs. Although cost-volume-profit analysis is limited by its short-run nature and does not purport to capture all changes that will occur in a period (such as inventory changes), it is nonetheless a very useful technique for establishing initial plans.

## DEMONSTRATION PROBLEM

A food processing firm recently introduced a new product: processed and formed potato chips. The chips are sold in 1-pound canisters, but they are packed in cases of 50 canisters. A case is therefore considered the basic sales unit. Although management had made detailed estimates of cost and volume prior to undertaking this venture, new projections based on our actual cost experience are now desired.

Income statements for the last two quarters are each thought to be representative of the costs and productive efficiency we can expect in the next few quarters. There were virtually no inventories on hand at the end of either quarter. These income statements reveal the following.

| | First Quarter | | Second Quarter |
|---|---|---|---|
| Sales (50,000 @ \$24) | \$1,200,000 | (70,000 @ \$24) | \$1,680,000 |
| Cost of goods sold | 700,000 | | 880,000 |
| Gross margin | \$ 500,000 | | \$ 800,000 |
| Selling and administration | 650,000 | | 690,000 |
| Net income before tax | \$ (150,000) | | \$ 110,000 |
| Tax | (60,000) | | 44,000 |
| Net income | \$ (90,000) | | \$ 66,000 |

The earnings and losses incurred by this product line are, so far, negligible in relation to the firm's overall earnings. The firm's overall marginal and average income tax rate is 40%. This 40% figure has been used to estimate the tax liability arising from the potato chip operation.

**Required**

**a.** Management would like to know the breakeven point in terms of quarterly case sales for the chips.

**b.** Management estimates that there is an investment of \$3,000,000 in this product line. What quarterly case sales and total revenue are required each quarter to earn an after-tax return of 20% on investment?

**c.** The firm's marketing people predict that if the selling price is reduced by \$1.50 per case (\$0.03 off per canister) and a \$150,000 advertising campaign is mounted to call consumers' attention to the new reduced price, sales will increase by 20% over second-quarter sales. Should the plan be implemented?

**Solution**

**a.** Our first problem is to estimate the fixed and variable costs associated with the potato chips. Using the two-point method for estimating cost equations discussed in Chapter 3, we can note that cost of goods sold was \$700,000 when 50,000 units were sold, and \$880,000 when 70,000 units were sold. Our variable manufacturing cost per unit then must be

$$\frac{\text{change in cost}}{\text{change in activity}} = \frac{\$880{,}000 - \$700{,}000}{70{,}000 - 50{,}000} = \frac{\$180{,}000}{20{,}000} = \$9 \text{ per unit}$$

Fixed costs can be determined as follows:

$$\begin{aligned}\text{cost of goods sold} &= \text{fixed manufacturing cost} + \text{variable manufacturing cost}\\ \$700{,}000 &= \text{fixed manufacturing cost} + \$9 \times 50{,}000 \text{ units}\\ \$250{,}000 &= \text{fixed manufacturing cost}\end{aligned}$$

The nonmanufacturing, or selling and administration (S&A) fixed and variable costs can be found in the same manner.

$$\text{variable S\&A costs} = \frac{\$690{,}000 - \$650{,}000}{70{,}000 - 50{,}000} = \frac{\$40{,}000}{20{,}000} = \$2 \text{ per unit}$$

$$\begin{aligned}\text{total S\&A costs} &= \text{fixed S\&A costs} + \text{variable S\&A costs}\\ \$650{,}000 &= \text{fixed S\&A costs} + \$2 \times 50{,}000\\ \$550{,}000 &= \text{fixed S\&A costs}\end{aligned}$$

Combining the manufacturing and nonmanufacturing costs gives us the total cost equation:

$$\begin{aligned}\text{manufacturing costs} &= \$250{,}000 \text{ per quarter} + \$\ 9 \text{ per unit}\\ \text{nonmanufacturing costs} &= \$550{,}000 \text{ per quarter} + \$\ 2 \text{ per unit}\\ \hline \text{total costs} &= \$800{,}000 \text{ per quarter} + \$11 \text{ per unit}\end{aligned}$$

Both income statements indicate a selling price per unit of \$24. Combining the cost equation with the unit selling price gives the cost-volume-profit equation:

$$\$24q - \$11q - \$800{,}000 = NI \text{ per quarter}$$

To find breakeven in terms of units, we solve for zero net income. Note that at zero net income there are no taxes, so we can ignore taxes for the moment.

$$\begin{aligned} \$24q - \$11q - \$800{,}000 &= 0 \\ \$13q &= \$800{,}000 \\ q &= 61{,}538 \text{ units} \end{aligned}$$

So quarterly breakeven sales are 61,538 cases.

**b.** If we want a 20% return on $3,000,000 we desire annual net income of $600,000. This translates to quarterly after-tax net income of $150,000. Since the tax rate is 40%, pretax income can be found as follows:

$$\begin{aligned} \text{pretax income} - 40\% \times \text{pretax income} &= \$150{,}000 \\ \text{pretax income} &= \$250{,}000 \end{aligned}$$

Thus unit sales must be

$$\begin{aligned} \$24q - \$11q - \$800{,}000 &= \$250{,}000 \\ \$13q &= \$1{,}050{,}000 \\ q &= 80{,}769 \end{aligned}$$

In terms of sales dollars we can multiply the 80,769 by the selling price of $24 per unit to get the total desired revenue of $1,938,456.

**c.** The proposal from the marketing department will reduce the selling price from $24 per case to $22.50 per case. In addition, the advertising outlay will increase the fixed costs from $800,000 to $950,000. Thus the new CVP equation after these changes would be

$$\$22.50q - \$11q - \$950{,}000 = NI$$

A 20% increase over last quarter's sales would increase sales from 70,000 units to 84,000 units. At 84,000 units, with the adjusted CVP relationship, the expected earnings before tax would be

$$\begin{aligned} \$22.50 \times 84{,}000 - \$11 \times 84{,}000 - \$950{,}000 &= NI \\ \$16{,}000 &= NI \end{aligned}$$

After subtracting the 40% tax, net income would be projected to be $9,600.

Inasmuch as we earned $66,000 before the change, the suggested change does not appear to be advisable. However, this evaluation is based only on the short-run profit consequences. We should note that management's intent in reducing the price may be to increase consumer exposure to the product in the hope that in the long run we might increase unit sales even when we return to our previous pricing policy. In an actual application we would know the true motives, but nonetheless the type of analysis we have just performed would still be useful for estimating the short-run effect on profits of our marketing actions.

## KEY TERMS AND CONCEPTS

| | |
|---|---|
| Cost-volume-profit (CVP) equation | Margin of safety |
| [ Contribution margin | [ Profit graph |
| [ Variable profit | [ Profit/volume chart |
| [ Contribution margin percent | Differential revenues and costs |
| [ Contribution margin ratio | Agency theory |
| [ Profit/volume ratio | |
| Breakeven point | |

[ Bracketed terms are equivalent in meaning.

## FURTHER READING


Adar, Zvi, Amir Barnea, and Baruch Lev. "A Comprehensive Cost-Volume-Profit Analysis under Uncertainty," *The Accounting Review* (January 1977), p. 137.

Baiman, Stanley. "Agency Research in Managerial Accounting: A Survey," *Journal of Accounting Literature* (Spring 1982), p. 154.

Driscoll, Donna A., W. Thomas Lin, and Paul R. Watkins. "Cost-Volume-Profit Analysis under Uncertainty: A Synthesis and Framework for Evaluation," *Journal of Accounting Literature* (Spring 1984), p. 85.

Hilliard, Jimmy E., and Robert A. Leitch. "Breakeven Analysis of Alternatives Under Uncertainty," *Management Accounting* (March 1977), p. 53.

Jaedicke, Robert K., and Alexander A. Robichek. "Cost-Volume-Profit Analysis Under Conditions of Uncertainty," *The Accounting Review* (October 1964), p. 917.

Khoury, E. N., and H. Wayne Nelson. "Simulation in Financial Planning," *Management Services* (March/April 1965), p. 13.

Kottas, John F., and Hon-Shiang Lau. "Direct Simulation in Stochastic CVP Analysis," *The Accounting Review* (July 1978), p. 698.

Martin, Howard. "Breaking through the Breakeven Barriers," *Management Accounting* (May 1985), p. 31.

Morse, Wayne J., and Imogene A. Posey. "Income Taxes Do Make a Difference in C-V-P Analysis," *Management Accounting* (December 1979), p. 20.

Nash, John F. "A Note on Cost-Volume-Profit Analysis and Price Elasticity," *The Accounting Review* (April 1975), p. 384.

Wood, Edwin A., and Robert G. Murdick. "A Practical Solution to Forecasting Problems," *Management Accounting* (May 1980), p. 45.


## QUESTIONS AND EXERCISES

**4-1** If a firm has a conventional mixed cost function, a 10% increase in volume should increase income by more than 10%. Briefly explain.

**4-2** Can the "margin of safety" ever be negative? Explain.

**4-3** A firm experiences a 20% increase in net income when dollar sales increase 20%. Assuming linearity, what can be said about the firm's cost function?

**4-4** What do contribution margin and gross margin have in common and how do they differ?

**4-5** What is the effect on a firm's breakeven point if the income tax rate is lowered?

**4-6** For which types of organizations is it, perhaps, appropriate to focus on and emphasize breakeven?

**4-7** In the term *cost-volume-profit,* where do sales fit in?

**4-8** Why is *cost-volume-profit* a more appropriate term than *breakeven analysis?*

**4-9** In response to a 10% increase in direct labor cost, a firm increases its selling price 10%. What is the effect on the number of units and the total revenues required to break even?

**4-10** Briefly, how does a differential cost approach differ from a total cost approach?

**4-11** Refer to the demonstration problem at the end of the chapter. Marketing is considering a "cents-off" campaign for the third quarter. The objective is to gain market penetration by selling 20% more potato chips in the third quarter, while maintaining net income at $66,000 after taxes. By how much could the selling price be cut per case?

**4-12** A firm sells its product for $13 per unit. Direct materials cost $3 per unit and direct labor costs $2 per unit. Overhead costs are $20,000 per period plus $4 per unit. How many units must this firm sell to break even?

**4-13** Restaurants typically price their meals at 150% of variable costs (food plus labor). If a restaurant has fixed costs of $1,600 per month, what total sales per month are required to break even?

**4-14** A firm sells its product for $10 per unit. Variable costs are $7 per unit and fixed costs are $65,000 per period. How many units must this firm sell so that its profit will be 10% of total costs?

**4-15** When Jay Products sold 4,000 units of product, total costs were $21,200. When the firm sold 6,200 units, total costs were $26,700. If the selling price per unit is $5.25, how many units must the firm sell to earn $5,025?

**4-16** Last year a firm earned $10,000 on total sales of $100,000. Variable costs were 60% of sales. This year the selling price per unit was doubled. This price increase reduced total sales to $80,000. How much did the firm earn?

**4-17** A firm expects to be able to sell its product for $10 per unit. If 5,000 units are sold, the following costs are anticipated.

| | |
|---|---|
| Rent | $ 4,000 F |
| Direct materials | 10,000 V |
| Property taxes | 3,000 F |
| Administrative salaries | 7,000 F |
| Direct labor | 7,500 V |
| Variable overhead | 12,500 V |

How many units must be sold to earn $12,000?

**4-18** Last year's sales were $400,000, fixed expenses were 40% of sales, and income before taxes was 20% of sales. If these CVP relationships can be projected to next year when sales are expected to increase by 25%, what is the expected income?

**4-19** A firm's P/V ratio is 4/9 and breakeven sales are $54,000. What is projected net income for sales of $67,500? $45,000?

**4-20** Fixed costs are $60,000 and breakeven sales are $200,000. If sales are projected as $240,000, what is net income?

**4-21** When sales are $200,000, net income is $40,000. Variable costs are 30% of sales. What is the margin of safety in sales dollars? What is the expected income if sales are $180,000?

**4-22** Total revenue for February was $400,000 and total costs were $320,000; total revenue for March was $480,000 and total costs were $380,000. Given these CVP relationships (a) what is the breakeven point in sales and (b) what is income if sales are $460,000?

**4-23** Goode Company manufactures a single product. Normally Goode projects production *and* sales of 500 units per month and projects costs as follows:

| | Manufacturing | Nonmanufacturing |
|---|---|---|
| Variable | $10,000 | $5,000 |
| Nonvariable | 12,500 | 7,500 |

The product sells for $110. (a) What is Goode's contribution margin per unit? (b) What is the profit/volume ratio or contribution margin percentage? (c) What volume, in terms of units, must Goode sell to break even? (d) If the company desires a net income of 22% on sales after taxes of 28%, what is the equivalent before-tax return on sales?

**4-24** A firm provides janitorial services. Its costs are as follows:

| | Fixed, per Period | Variable, per Hour |
|---|---|---|
| Direct costs | $1,000 | $5 |
| Indirect costs | 5,000 | 3 |

(a) The firm charges $10 per hour. How many hours must be worked per period to break even? (b) If the firm works 4,000 hours per period, what hourly rate should be charged to earn $1,000?

**4-25** A firm has fixed costs of $20,000 per period and variable costs equal to 60% of sales. What sales volume is necessary (a) to break even, (b) to earn $8,000 per period, (c) to earn 15% on sales, and (d) to earn an amount equal to 20% of total costs?

**4-26** Given the accompanying graph, (a) what happened to fixed costs from January to February? (b) what happened to the contribution margin? Briefly explain.

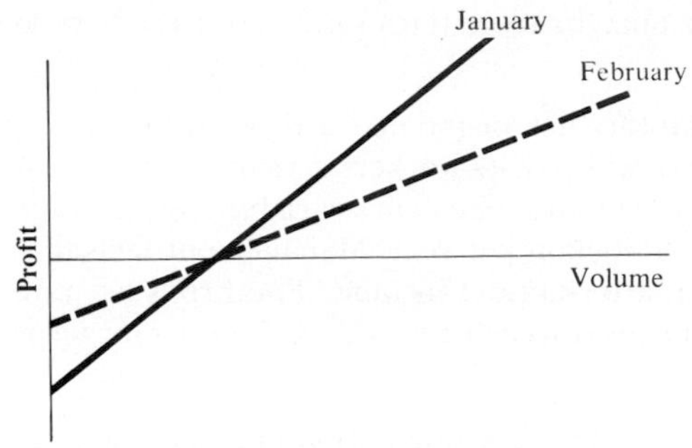


**4-27** Aptitude, Inc., provides various types of testing services. The college division estimates its costs as $1,200 each time an exam is administered plus $2 per candidate, in addition to annual fixed costs of $200,000. Candidates pay $30 each to take the exam. The division projects that an average of 50 will take an exam each time it is given. How many times a year must exams be given if the division is to break even?

**4-28** Division A has a profit/volume ratio of 26% and fixed expenses of $42,000; Division B has a profit/volume ratio of 34% and fixed expenses of $58,000. You are to determine (a) breakeven for each division, (b) the sales level at which the two divisions will have the same income, and (c) the profit/volume graph for each division (put both on the same graph).

**4-29** A firm has fixed costs of $20,000 per period and variable costs equal to 60% of sales. Taxes on income average 40%. What sales volume is necessary (a) to break even, (b) to earn $8,000 per period after taxes, (c) to earn 15% on sales after taxes, and (d) to earn an amount equal to 20% of total costs after taxes? (Do not include taxes in total costs.)

**4-30** Millstone Industries established a bonus plan for selected employees who are to receive a bonus of $50 per unit for every unit sold in excess of 2,000. The contribution per unit is $100, and fixed costs are $100,000. How many units must be sold for management to distribute $50,000 in bonuses this period?

**4-31** The board of directors has established that management will receive a bonus equal to 25% of pretax and prebonus profits if pretax and prebonus profits are at least $100,000. The firm's contribution margin is $20 and fixed costs are $150,000. Determine the minimum number of units to be sold (a) if the bonus is to take effect and (b) if management targets a minimum bonus of $40,000.

**4-32** A consultant has a contract with a firm that grants her a fee equal to all net income in excess of $100,000 after taxes. Taxes are 20% and her fee is deductible for tax purposes. If there is $200,000 before fees and taxes, what is the amount of her fee?

**4-33** Ajax pays its employees a bonus of 10% of net income before tax and before the bonus. The firm's variable costs (not counting the bonus or taxes) average 60% of sales. Fixed costs are $200,000 per year. The firm's tax rate is 30% of the first $50,000 of income and 45% on income above $50,000. (a) If sales total $800,000, what will be the firm's net income after tax? (b) What must sales be for the firm to earn net income after tax of $100,000?

**4-34** The employees' union of Mammoth Motors has negotiated a new profit-sharing scheme with the firm. Mammoth Motors will pay its workers a year-end bonus of 7% of its earnings after tax, but before the bonus. The firm's variable costs average 80% of sales and fixed costs are about $25 billion per year. Management feels that shareholders will demand a $1.5 billion after-tax net income. The firm's tax rate is 45%. What level of sales will the firm need to achieve? (*Hint:* Ignore the zeros and just deal in billions.)

**4-35** Stoh, Inc., has given its newly acquired president a compensation plan that includes a bonus equal to 10% of net income before the bonus but after taxes of 40%. The bonus is deductible to Stoh for tax purposes. Stoh's accountant projects net income of $100,000 before bonus and taxes. (a) What is the projected bonus? (b) What is Stoh's projected income after taxes?

**4-36** Net income before tax and bonus is $600,000. The bonus agreement is $15,000 plus 20% of net income after tax and after bonus. The tax rate is 30%. What is the total amount of the bonus?

## PROBLEMS AND CASES

**4-37 CVP analysis.**

General View, Inc., owns 100 popcorn stands; around each popcorn stand a theater has been constructed. The theaters draw an average of 2,000 patrons a week at a price of $3.00 each. Management rents films for showing at 50% of gross ticket sales. All other costs, including the cost to make popcorn, are 30% of gross ticket sales plus fixed costs of $2,000 per week.

**Required**

**a.** If 60% of the patrons buy popcorn, how much should it be sold for if GV desires a weekly profit before taxes of $1,000?

**b.** Refer to (a). How much should a box of popcorn sell for if GV desires a weekly profit of $1,000 after taxes of 40%?

**4-38 CVP analysis.**

Barron Brothers produces backup buzzers for bicycles. Last month it sold 4,000 units at $25 per unit and had a loss of $2,000. This month it sold 5,000 units and showed a profit of $3,000. It is assumed that the cost and revenue functions are linear.

**Required**

**a.** What is the contribution margin per unit?

**b.** What is the variable cost per unit?

**c.** What are monthly fixed costs?

**d.** How many units must be sold to break even?

**4-39 CVP.**

BAP, Inc., manufactures insecticide. It can break even on a volume of 15,000 cases; a case sells for $20 and the profit/volume ratio is 1/4.

**Required**

**a.** What is the average variable cost per case?
**b.** What are the total fixed costs?
**c.** How many cases would have to be sold to earn 20% on sales before taxes of 20%?
**d.** How many cases would have to be sold to earn 20% on sales after taxes of 20%?
**e.** If BAP sells 18,000 cases, what is the margin of safety?

**4-40 Profit/volume graph.**
The graph shown is the profit/volume chart for Juice Resources, Inc., which markets concentrated orange juice in 1-gallon cans. The customer adds an equal amount of water to obtain 2 gallons.

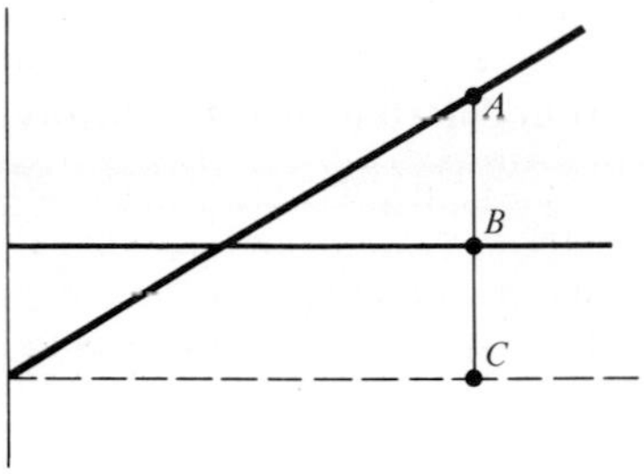


**Required**

**a.** What does the line segment *AB* represent?
**b.** What does the line segment *BC* represent?
**c.** What does the line segment *AC* represent?

**4-41 CVP graph.**
You are given the CVP or breakeven chart shown. Of interest is the level of activity shown as *D*. At this level, point *A* totals $50,000; point *B* totals $45,000; and point *C* totals $10,000.

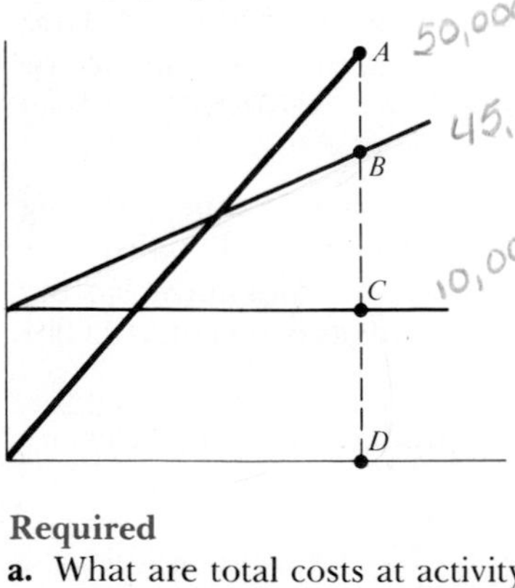


**Required**

**a.** What are total costs at activity *D*?
**b.** What are total variable costs at activity *D*?
**c.** What is total contribution margin at activity *D*?
**d.** From the data given, what are breakeven sales?
**e.** From the data given, what is the margin of safety in terms of sales dollars?

**4-42 CVP with pretax bonus.**
Tedium, Inc., has established a profit-sharing plan for its employees. They are to receive 40% of all pretax profits in excess of $100,000. The firm's product sells for $10 and has variable costs of $4. Fixed costs are $200,000.

**Required**
How many units must be sold if management targets $50,000 as the minimally desired amount to be distributed to employees?

**4-43 Obtaining fixed costs from CVP data.**
Traxton Manufacturing earned $30,000 last year on sales of 200,000 units of product. This year, the firm reduced its fixed costs to $100,000, lowered its selling price to $7 per unit, kept the same variable cost per unit, and earned $50,000 on the sale of 250,000 units.

**Required**
If last year's variable costs were 80% of the selling price, determine the fixed costs incurred last year.

**4-44 Cost estimation and CVP.**
The Swingline Company has performed a study of the costs incurred for making its only product. The costs incurred from the past three accounting periods were as follows:

| | Activity Level | | |
|---|---|---|---|
| **Costs** | **13,300** | **14,000** | **14,400** |
| Raw materials | $ 4,788 | $ 5,040 | $ 5,184 |
| Labor | 34,250 | 36,000 | 37,000 |
| Electricity | 1,680 | 1,750 | 1,790 |
| Other | 22,610 | 23,450 | 23,930 |

In the next accounting period, rent is expected to be increased from $1,200 per period to $1,600. The electric company charges a fixed amount per period plus a charge per kilowatt-hour used by the customer. Due to heavy advertising costs incurred by the electric company to fight a local annexation issue, the electric company will increase its charges per kilowatt-hour by 50%.

**Required**
**a.** What are the expected costs to be incurred by the Swingline Company during the next accounting period if the anticipated activity level is 15,200 units?
**b.** If Swingline sells its product for $5 per unit, how many units must be sold during the next accounting period to earn a 15% return on its equity of $10,000?

**4-45 Basic CVP with taxes.**
Burton Limited's selling price is $4 per unit for its product. Variable costs are $2.50 per unit and fixed costs are $225,000 per year.

**Required**
**a.** How many units must be sold per year to break even?
**b.** How many units must be sold to earn $30,000 per year?
**c.** How many units must be sold to earn $40,000 per year if the firm pays an income tax of 45% of net income?

**d.** How many units must the firm sell to earn a net profit of 5% of sales if the firm faces a 30% income tax?

**4-46 Effects of changes on breakeven volume.**
The following is a list of changes, each of which is independent of the others.

**Required**
You are to state whether, as the result of each of these changes, the new breakeven volume *in dollars* is higher, unchanged, lower, or indeterminate.

**a.** The government imposes an excess profits tax on your industry.
**b.** The product mix changes. Customers are buying more of your product with the highest contribution margin percentage and less of your product with the higher contribution per unit.
**c.** Variable costs and selling prices increase by the same percentage.
**d.** Variable costs and selling prices increase by the same dollar amount.

**4-47 Conflict between marketing and production.**
Spinoff is a wholly owned division producing and selling a single product. The production department has sufficient capacity to triple volume to 3,000 units per month; doing so would cut costs from $500 to $350 (the production cost curve is linear). The marketing department is against the proposal on the grounds that existing outlets cannot absorb the increase in production. New channels of distribution would have to be opened, with the result that the selling price of the product would have to be dropped from the present $800 to $500 for all units sold. Marketing expenses are 10% of sales, and other expenses are $100,000 per month.

**Required**
Should the division expand? Explain.

**4-48 CVP, demand, and pricing** (CMA adapted).
Hollis Company manufactures and markets a regulator that is used to maintain high levels of accuracy in timing clocks. The market for these regulators is limited and highly dependent upon the selling price.

Based upon past relationships between the selling price and the resultant demand, as well as an informal survey of customers, management has derived the following demand function, which is highly representative of the actual relationships.

$$D = 1{,}000 - 2P$$

where $D$ = annual demand in units
$P$ = price per unit

The estimated manufacturing and selling costs for the coming year are as follows:

| | |
|---|---|
| Variable costs | |
| Manufacturing | $75 per unit |
| Selling | $25 per unit |
| Fixed costs | |
| Manufacturing | $24,000 per year |
| Selling | $ 6,000 per year |

**Required**
Determine the number of regulators Hollis Company should produce and the selling price it should charge per regulator in order to maximize the company's profits from the regulator product line for the coming year.

**4-49 CVP.**
Ersatz, Inc., manufactures a single product. The following is an income statement for two different levels of activity, which are assumed to be within Ersatz's relevant range.

**ERSATZ, INC.**
**Income Statement**

| | Activity Level | |
|---|---|---|
| | **1,000 Units** | **1,500 Units** |
| Sales @ $100 | $100,000 | $150,000 |
| Less variable expenses | | |
| Manufacturing @ $40 | 40,000 | 60,000 |
| Selling @ $10 | 10,000 | 15,000 |
| Administration @ $6 | 6,000 | 9,000 |
| Contribution margin | $ 44,000 | $ 66,000 |
| Less fixed expenses | | |
| Manufacturing | 10,000 | 10,000 |
| Selling | 11,000 | 11,000 |
| Administration | 20,000 | 20,000 |
| Net income | $ 3,000 | $ 25,000 |

**Required**
**a.** At an activity level of 1,000 units, what is Ersatz's gross margin?
**b.** What is Ersatz's breakeven point?
**c.** If Ersatz plans to sell 1,300 units, what will net income be?
**d.** Your boss has asked you to draft an explanation for Ersatz's major stockholder, who wants to know why net income increases by more than 800% when sales increase by just 50%. Both your boss and the stockholder are busy people and expect very short answers.
**e.** Management expects that variable costs and selling prices will rise by 3%, but fixed costs will not change. What will the new breakeven point be? What is the explanation for the result?
**f.** Management is considering changing the structure of selling costs. At present, the costs are $11,000 + $10 per unit. It will replace this formula with a simple $20-per-unit cost. At what level of sales will it make no difference which cost function is used?
**g.** Refer to (f). Which of the two cost functions will minimize selling expenses above the level of sales at which it makes no difference?

**4-50 CVP and price** (SMA).
The Martell Company has recently established operations in a very competitive market. Management has been aggressive in its attempt to establish a market share.

The price of the product was set at $5 per unit, well below that of the company's major competitors. Variable costs were $4.50 per unit, and total fixed costs were $600,000 during the first year.

**Required**

**a.** Assume that the firm was able to sell 1 million units in the first year. What was the profit (loss) for the year?

**b.** Assume that the variable per-unit and total fixed costs do not increase in the second year. Management has been successful in establishing its position in the market. What price must be set to achieve a profit of $25,000? Assume that the output cannot be increased over the first-year level.

**4-51 CVP relationships.**

Vend-a-Sand, Inc., produces sandwiches, which it sells in bulk to vending machine operators. Only one type of meat is used, but because of the extensive list of condiments employed, a wide variety of sandwiches has been created. Sandwiches are made in batches of 1,000, with variable costs per batch as follows:

| | |
|---|---|
| Meat | $ 80 |
| Labor | 220 |
| Other | 100 |

Fixed production costs are $20,000 per month. Sandwiches are sold to vendors for $0.60 each.

**Required**

**a.** What is the monthly breakeven?

**b.** What is the monthly income if 200,000 sandwiches are sold?

**c.** At a monthly volume of 200,000, the owners think that net income should be at least $25,000. By how much would the contribution margin have to change in order to attain this?

**d.** If fixed costs could be changed, what change would be necessary to earn $25,000 on a monthly volume of 200,000 sandwiches?

**e.** Competitive pressures have depressed selling prices to $0.50 each. Management is willing to sustain a short-term loss of $5,000 per month. What volume is necessary under these conditions?

**4-52 CVP.**

As a part-time activity, you are engaged in the sale of gazebos. The manner in which a sale is made is as follows: You take a different route to school, church, work, and so on, each day. Each time you pass a house without a gazebo, you write down the address. Later, the address is checked against a reverse directory to obtain the phone number. Between classes, you borrow a faculty member's phone to call your prospects. The costs involved in this procedure are minimal at most. The terms of the sale are $1,700 cash. There is only one model available. You provide the materials by calling a supplier, who has the complete list of specifications called for by one gazebo; the supplier delivers the materials to the site at a total cash cost of $450. Any shortages in materials are to be paid for by the customer; in this manner, the customer becomes totally responsible for the security of materials.

You treat your only employee as an independent contractor, paying her $20 per hour. She is responsible for furnishing her own tools and transportation.

**Required**

**a.** What determines whether you make any money on a particular project?
**b.** What is breakeven on a particular project?
**c.** Draw the cost-volume-profit and profit/volume graphs for a particular project. How are these interpreted?
**d.** What is the difference between this situation and the conventional situations as discussed in the text?

**4-53 CVP and pricing.**

You are in charge of your organization's annual picnic. The charge given to you by the officers is to price the tickets in such a way as to cover all costs and leave a surplus of $600 for next year. You have $800 carried forward from last year to work with. The costs this year are $300 to rent the facility and the caterer charges $5 for each person in attendance.

**Required**

**a.** What price should be charged if 400 people are expected to attend?
**b.** Draw, freehand, the graph that describes these CVP relationships.
**c.** If only 385 tickets are sold, how much will you have to put in personally if you are to meet your goals?

**4-54 Effects of changes on breakeven.**

The following income statement is projected for Yo-Yo, Inc., for the next year:

| | | |
|---|---|---|
| Sales | | $8,000,000 |
| Less variable expenses | | |
| Cost of goods sold | $3,000,000 | |
| Selling and administration | 1,000,000 | 4,000,000 |
| Contribution margin | | $4,000,000 |
| Less fixed expenses | | |
| Cost of goods sold | $1,500,000 | |
| Selling and administration | 2,000,000 | 3,500,000 |
| Net income | | $ 500,000 |

For the questions (a) through (f) relating to Yo-Yo, you are to use the following key.

1. Higher
2. Unchanged
3. Lower
4. Cannot be determined without knowledge of units, unit prices, or unit costs
5. Cannot be determined for other reasons

Each of the questions is independent of the others. In other words, for each question you are to go back to the original data.

**Required**

**a.** What is the effect on the number of *units* required to break even if selling prices and variable costs both increase 10%? Lower
**b.** What is the effect on the number of sales *dollars* required to break even if selling prices and variable costs both increase 10%? unchanged

**c.** What is the effect on the number of *units* required to break even if physical production and sales are 5% higher than projected?

**d.** What is the effect on the number of *units* required to break even if selling prices and fixed costs both increase 10%?

**e.** What is the effect on the number of sales *dollars* required to break even if selling prices and total costs both increase 10%?

**f.** What is the effect on the number of *units* required to break even if a "praise" campaign by supervisors results in increasing the productivity of hourly direct laborers?

**4-55 CVP with income taxes** (CMA adapted).

Mr. Calderone started a pizza restaurant in 19X1. For this purpose a building was rented for $400 per month. Two people were hired to work full time at the restaurant and six college students were hired to work 30 hours per week delivering pizza. An outside accountant was hired for tax and bookkeeping purposes. For this service, Calderone Company pays $300 per month. The necessary restaurant equipment and delivery cars were purchased with cash. Expenses for utilities and supplies have been relatively constant.

Business increased between 19X1 and 19X4, and profits more than doubled during this period. Mr. Calderone does not understand why profits have increased faster than volume.

A projected income statement for 19X5 has been prepared by the accountant and is as follows:

**CALDERONE COMPANY**
**Projected Income Statement**
**For the Year Ended December 31, 19X5**

| | | |
|---|---|---|
| Sales | | $95,000 |
| Cost of food sold | $28,500 | |
| Wages and fringe benefits: restaurant help | 8,150 | |
| Wages and fringe benefits: delivery personnel | 17,300 | |
| Rent | 4,800 | |
| Accounting services | 3,600 | |
| Depreciation: delivery equipment | 5,000 | |
| Depreciation: restaurant equipment | 3,000 | |
| Utilities | 2,325 | |
| Supplies (soap, floor wax, and so on) | 1,200 | 73,875 |
| Net income before taxes | | $21,125 |
| Income taxes (at 30%) | | 6,338 |
| Net income | | $14,787 |

Assume that the average pizza sells for $2.50 and that the income tax rate is 30%.

**Required**

**a.** What is the breakeven point in number of pizzas that must be sold?

**b.** What is the cash flow breakeven point in number of pizzas that must be sold?

In other words, how many pizzas must be sold such that cash receipts will equal cash disbursements?

**c.** If Mr. Calderone withdraws $4,800 for personal use, how much cash will be left from the 19X5 income-producing activities?

**d.** Mr. Calderone would like an after-tax net income of $20,000. What volume must be reached in number of pizzas sold to obtain the desired income?

**e.** Briefly explain why profits have increased at a faster rate than sales.

**f.** Briefly explain why the cash flow for 19X5 will exceed profits.

**4-56 CVP with taxes and cost-price changes** (CMA adapted).

All-Day Candy Company is a wholesale distributor of candy. The company services grocery, convenience, and drug stores in a large metropolitan area.

Small but steady growth in sales has been achieved by the All-Day Candy Company over the past few years, but candy prices also have been increasing. The company is formulating its plans for the coming fiscal year. The following data were used to project the current year's after-tax net income of $110,400.

| | |
|---|---|
| Average selling price | $4.00 per box |
| Average variable costs | |
| Cost of candy | $2.00 per box |
| Selling expenses | 0.40 per box |
| Total | $2.40 per box |
| Annual fixed costs | |
| Selling | $160,000 |
| Administrative | 280,000 |
| Total | $440,000 |

Expected annual sales volume (390,000 boxes): $1,560,000
Tax rate: 40%

Manufacturers of candy have announced that they will increase prices of their products an average of 15% in the coming year because of increases in raw material (sugar, cocoa, peanuts, and so on) and labor costs. All-Day Candy Company expects that all other costs will remain at the same rates or levels as during the current year.

**Required**

**a.** What is All-Day Candy Company's breakeven point in boxes of candy for the current year?

**b.** What selling price per box must All-Day Candy Company charge to cover the 15% increase in the variable cost of candy and still maintain the current contribution margin ratio?

**c.** What volume of sales in dollars must the All-Day Candy Company achieve in the coming year to maintain the same net income after taxes as projected for the current year if the selling price of candy remains at $4 per box and the cost of candy increases 15%?

**4-57 CVP and taxes** (CMA adapted).

Laraby Company produces a single product. It sold 25,000 units last year with the following results.

| | | |
|---|---|---|
| Sales | | $625,000 |
| Variable costs | $375,000 | |
| Fixed costs | 150,000 | 525,000 |
| Net income before taxes | | $100,000 |
| Income taxes (45%) | | 45,000 |
| Net income | | $ 55,000 |

In an attempt to improve its product, Laraby is considering replacing a component part in its product that has a cost of $2.50 with a new and better part costing $4.50 per unit during the coming year. A new machine would also be needed to increase plant capacity. The machine would cost $18,000, with a useful life of 6 years and no salvage value. The company uses straight-line depreciation on all plant assets.

**Required**

**a.** What was Laraby Company's breakeven point in number of units last year?

**b.** How many units of product would Laraby Company have had to sell in the past year to earn $77,000 in net income after taxes?

**c.** If Laraby Company holds the sales price constant and makes the suggested changes, how many units of product must be sold in the coming year to break even?

**d.** If Laraby Company holds the sales price constant and makes the suggested changes, how many units of product will the company have to sell to make the same net income after taxes as last year?

**e.** If Laraby Company wishes to maintain the same contribution margin ratio, what selling price per unit of product must it charge next year to cover the increased materials costs?

**4-58 Bonus with fixed and variable components and taxes.**

The management of Rooth, Inc., has established a bonus pool for employees amounting to $12,000 plus 10 percent of income. Taxes are 30 percent; the bonus is deductible for tax purposes; and income before bonus and tax is $300,000.

**Required**

**a.** What is the total bonus if the variable component is based on income before bonus and tax?

**b.** What is the total bonus if the variable component is based on income before taxes?

**c.** What is the total bonus if the variable component is based on income after taxes?

**d.** What is the total bonus if the variable component is based on income after taxes but before any bonus?

**4-59 CVP with bonus and taxes.**

The management team of Bruxton Industries has been awarded a 5% bonus of after-tax, after-bonus, net income provided that net income after tax and after bonus exceeds $100,000 for the period. The firm sells a variety of products, but uses a constant markup of 100% of variable cost. The firm's fixed costs per period are $250,000. The firm's federal, state, and local income taxes total 45% of pretax income.

**Required**

**a.** What dollar amount of sales is necessary for the management bonus to amount to $50,000?

**b.** If total sales are $6,000,000, what is the expected amount of the bonus?

**c.** What is the maximum dollar amount of sales that the firm can enjoy and yet not pay the management bonus? Note this is a more difficult question than it may appear because if the after-tax but *before*-bonus net income is $100,100, the effect of the bonus would be to bring after-tax, *after*-bonus net income below $100,000, so the bonus would not be paid.

**4-60 CVP and foreign exchange rates.**

Borg Controls has a net investment in its West German subsidiary of $2.68 million. The firm attempts to earn a 15% return on its investment in terms of dollars.

Variable costs for the German subsidiary are 60% of sales. Annual fixed costs are 857,000 DM. For the current year, the manager of the German subsidiary anticipates sales of 4.5 million Deutsche marks. The exchange rate is expected to be 3.2 DM = $1.

**Required**

**a.** If operations meet expectations, what is the rate of return that Borg Controls will earn from its West German subsidiary?

**b.** What level of sales in Deutsche marks would be required of the subsidiary in order for the parent to earn exactly a 15% rate of return in dollars? (Assume that the exchange rate remains as expected.)

**c.** Earnings in dollars will be directly affected by changes in the exchange rate. If the subsidiary's sales are 4.5 million DM, what exchange rate is required for earnings to translate into a 15% return on investment for Borg Controls?

**4-61 Case study involving operating alternatives.**

Two recent graduates opened a restaurant in a small strip mall located in the midst of a residential area. The site was chosen because there are no other restaurants or commercial developments within a one-mile radius of the mall. Furthermore, zoning laws will prevent any new commercial developments in the area for the foreseeable future.

The partners named the restaurant The Huntsman and prepared a menu that emphasized plain, but hearty, sandwiches. The decor was modeled after an exclusive English hunting club. The owners also obtained a class A liquor license.

A class A liquor license is restricted to businesses that are primarily restaurants (defined by local law as a business that derives 50% or more of its gross revenue from the sale of food). A class B liquor license is for businesses that primarily sell alcoholic beverages. A class B license is subject to special zoning, prohibits minors on the premises, and requires more restricted operating hours.

From the day it opened, The Huntsman has done a fair lunch business. But, initially, the late afternoon and early evening business was quite poor. But after a few months The Huntsman became known as a very comfortable place to relax and have a drink. Now the evening cocktail business is quite brisk and very profitable. In talking with customers, the owners have found that virtually all of their customers are young professionals who live within 8 to 10 blocks of The Huntsman. For the most part they are married and have young children. Although they like to eat out at restaurants, most are still very budget conscious. Because The Huntsman is viewed by most of its customers as a drinking establishment (albeit a very nice one), they don't consider it as a place to bring the family for dinner.

When the partners opened the business, they had each hoped to earn about $30,000 per year. Recent results have been much better than that. In fact, the following income statement for the most recent month is quite typical of normal operations.

| | Food | Beverage | Total |
|---|---|---|---|
| Sales | $25,000 | $40,000 | $65,000 |
| Direct costs | 12,000 | 8,000 | 20,000 |
| Margin | $13,000 | $32,000 | $45,000 |
| Labor costs | | | 22,000 |
| Occupancy costs | | | 3,000 |
| Net income | | | $20,000 |

Although the owners are very pleased with these financial results, they have a significant problem. Food sales are substantially below 50% of gross revenues. The owners are quite concerned that they will not be able to renew their class A liquor license. They have already approached the city zoning commission asking for a variance to allow them to have a class B license on the premises, but have been turned down. There are several people in the neighborhood who object to having a drinking establishment in their midst. They fought the request for the zoning exemption and are expected to raise objections when it is time to renew the class A license. The owners are convinced that food sales must constitute 50% or more of gross sales in the future if they are to retain their class A license.

An analysis of the firm's operations revealed that the costs classified as direct costs are nearly totally variable. Occupancy costs are mostly fixed and, because the business is fairly stable, labor costs also appear to be fixed. During lunchtime, from Monday through Friday, The Huntsman operates at about 60% of capacity. Labor costs would not change if the Monday through Friday lunch business increased to 100% of capacity. The Huntsman is closed until 5 P.M. on Saturday and Sunday. From about 4 P.M. to 7 P.M. Monday through Friday, The Huntsman operates at nearly 100% of capacity. On Saturday The Huntsman operates at about 70% of capacity from 5 P.M. to 9 P.M. On Sunday, from 5 P.M. to 8 P.M., The Huntsman operates at 40% of capacity. Throughout the week only an insignificant proportion of the sales during the late afternoon and evening are due to food sales. Nearly all of the revenues are from the sale of beverages.

With this background, the owners are now considering several alternatives.

1. We can do nothing and lose the liquor license. We can expect food sales to increase by 20% due to increased evening food sales. Labor costs will be cut in half.
2. We can reduce the price of drinks sufficiently to bring total beverage sales down to 50% of total sales. Because we are at capacity already, it is unlikely that this action will increase the volume of sales.
3. We can try to increase food prices to bring total revenue up to 50% of sales. What increase would be needed? Is this really feasible?

4. If we decrease our food prices by 20% and spend about $20,000 per month in advertising, we ought to be able to get total food revenues up to $40,000.
5. We could open for brunch on Saturday and Sunday from 10 A.M. to 2 P.M. This would require additional labor costs of $3,000 per month. If we set our price low, say $5 per person, and offer fabulous food, we could generate the 3,000 customers a month needed. But how much could we afford to spend per serving to make this a viable alternative?

**Required**

**a.** Evaluate the various alternatives being considered.

**b.** After reviewing the alternatives, the owners instituted the weekend brunch idea. They charge $5 for brunch and spend $7.50 per meal in direct variable costs. This is such a good bargain that the brunch has become very popular. Monthly sales from the brunch alone are now $25,000. Prepare a new monthly income statement.

**c.** If The Huntsman institutes a policy of brunch by "reservation only," they can turn down sufficient reservations to assure that revenues from brunch sales total only $15,000. What net income will they earn under this policy?

# APPENDIX 4

# COST-VOLUME-PROFIT ANALYSIS AND UNCERTAINTY

In Appendix 3A we used regression analysis to estimate cost functions. One of the advantages of using regression was that it enabled us to construct confidence intervals concerning expected costs. We now incorporate this uncertainty into cost-volume-profit analysis. We continue to make simplifying assumptions to avoid getting bogged down in a mass of calculations. At the same time we believe that the calculations we do propose are practical and will give managers a useful feel for the approximate effects of uncertainty on our accounting projections. The reader is cautioned, however, that our intent is merely to introduce the topic of uncertainty and CVP analysis. The literature on this topic is extensive and complex. Readers who require more accurate estimates of the effect of uncertainty are referred to the literature in the major academic journals.

## ANALYTIC MODELS

One approach to incorporating uncertainty into the cost-volume-profit model is to derive the distribution of net income mathematically, given our knowledge of the uncertainty inherent in the variables. If, for example, we know the form of the distribution of total cost, we can derive the effect that the stochastic cost function will have on the distribution of expected earnings. This is called an analytic approach to incorporating uncertainty into the CVP model. Though accurate, the analytic approach can quickly become very complicated.

### When Sales Are Known

The easiest situation that incorporates uncertainty into CVP analysis arises when we have a known selling price and a known quantity of goods to be sold. This situation can arise when a firm deals with only one customer, and the terms are spelled out in a contract. Although these arrangements do occur occasionally in the private sector, such as in long-term purchase contracts, the most common instance is when the customer is a government agency. When prices and quantities are set by contract, the only uncertainty that should affect the firm's net income is the uncertainty inherent in the firm's estimate of total cost. Total cost will be a random variable, but sales will be a known constant. Subtracting a random variable from a constant provides a result with precisely the same distribution as the random variable. In other words, the distribution of the firm's income around the best estimate of income will be precisely the same as the distribution of total cost around the best estimate of total cost.

As is usually the case, an example should clarify the point. Assume that a firm has a contract to sell 50,000 units of product next period at a price of \$4 per unit. Also assume that the firm's cost function has been estimated using regression based on 23 previous observations of cost and output on similar contracts. The regression equation obtained was

$$\text{total cost} = \$2.50 \text{ per unit} + \$70{,}000 \text{ per period}$$

The standard error of the estimate is \$1,500 and the assumptions of regression have been met. With that information available, management would like to know what range of income can be expected with 95% confidence.

We start first by calculating the best estimate of income. Since we already know the sales quantity, we estimate total costs to be

$$\begin{aligned}\text{total cost} &= \$2.50 \times 50{,}000 + \$70{,}000 \\ &= \$195{,}000\end{aligned}$$

Total revenue is set by the contract as $\$4 \times 50{,}000 = \$200{,}000$. Subtracting our best estimate of cost from the known value for sales yields a best estimate of income of $\$200{,}000 - \$195{,}000 = \$5{,}000$. Because total cost has a standard error of \$1,500 and because there is no variability in the sales figure, the resulting net income figure must also have a standard error of the estimate of \$1,500 (see Figure 4-4). With that knowledge we can calculate the 95% confidence interval of net income.

First we notice that we are searching for a two-sided confidence interval. Because we assume that the distribution of actual costs, and therefore income, is normally distributed around our best estimate, the distribution will be symmetric. Therefore we can say that there should be only a 2½% chance that actual income will be higher than (or lower than) the

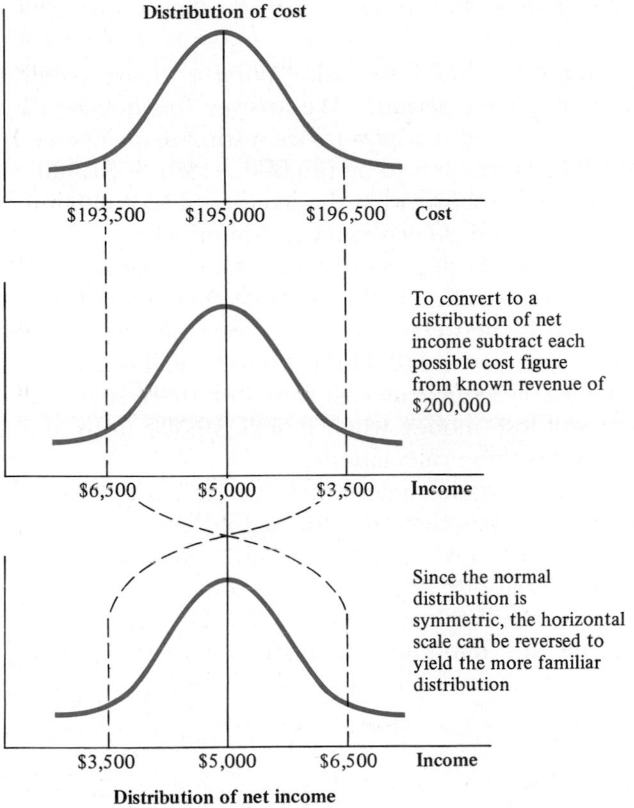
Distribution of cost
$193,500
$195,000
$196,500
Cost
To convert to a distribution of net income subtract each possible cost figure from known revenue of $200,000
$6,500
$5,000
$3,500
Income
Since the normal distribution is symmetric, the horizontal scale can be reversed to yield the more familiar distribution
$3,500
$5,000
$6,500
Income
Distribution of net income

**FIGURE 4-4 Distribution of net income when sales are certain but costs are uncertain.**

largest (smallest) income figure in our confidence interval. We can then refer to Exhibit 3-7 in Appendix 3A to see how many standard errors we must move away from the best estimate to capture all but 2½% of the likely observations.

We obtain this figure from the row for 21 degrees of freedom (two less than the number of data points used for determining the regression equation) under the column for 2½% of observations beyond the confidence interval. The table tells us that we must move 2.080 standard errors to capture all but 2½% of the observations. Multiplying this factor by the actual value of a standard error ($1,500) for our income estimate, we find that the width of our confidence interval will be 2.080 × $1,500 = $3,120. The 95% confidence interval for net income will be our best estimate of income plus and minus the width of the confidence interval. Therefore, we can anticipate with 95% confidence that net income will be in the range of \$5,000 ± \$3,120 or \$1,880 to \$8,120 when we sell 50,000 units at \$4 per unit.

For this same example, we could also ask, "What is the probability that this firm will lose money next period?" We answer this question by first calculating how many standard errors our best estimate of income is away from zero income. That turns out to be (\$5,000 − \$0) ÷ \$1,500 = 3.333. We now refer to the *t*-table to see what the likelihood is of obtaining an observation 3.333 or more standard errors away from the best estimate. In Exhibit 3-7, along the row for 21 degrees of freedom, we see that 3.333 standard errors is not in the table. Therefore, we cannot say precisely what the probability is, but it will be between one-half of one percent (0.005) and five one-hundredths of one percent (0.0005). Therefore, if our regression equation accurately describes our true cost function, there is virtually no chance that the firm will lose money when it sells 50,000 units at \$4 per unit. Figure 4-5 illustrates these calculations.

Another variant of this situation might arise when it is time to negotiate the size of a contract. Assuming that the selling price is already settled at \$4 per unit and we are now haggling over the quantity of units to be sold, we might want to tell our negotiator that there is a minimum quantity below which the firm will refuse to undertake the contract. Suppose management says that the minimum quantity per period must be large enough so that we are 95% confident of at least breaking even. How

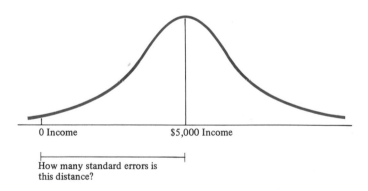

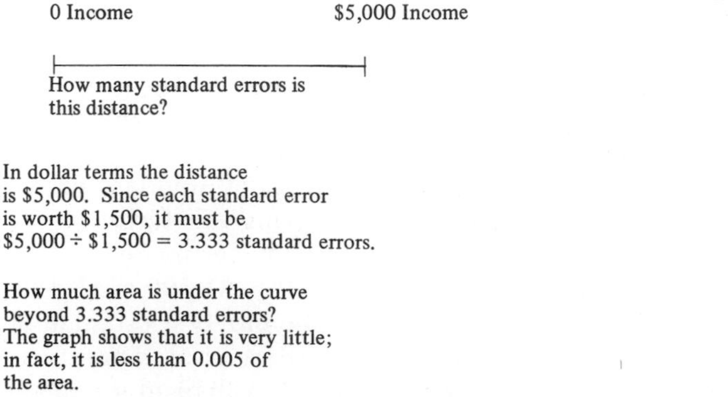
0 Income
\$5,000 Income
How many standard errors is this distance?
In dollar terms the distance is \$5,000. Since each standard error is worth \$1,500, it must be \$5,000 ÷ \$1,500 = 3.333 standard errors.
How much area is under the curve beyond 3.333 standard errors? The graph shows that it is very little; in fact, it is less than 0.005 of the area.

**FIGURE 4-5 Probability of losing money.**

do we calculate that quantity? We start by setting up the CVP equation for breakeven as follows:

$$\$4q - \$2.50q - \$70{,}000 = 0$$

We do not want the best estimate of breakeven sales, however. Instead we want the level of sales that will result in breakeven, even if costs are at their worst in our 95% confidence interval. So we add to the breakeven equation a factor that adjusts total cost to reflect a worst-case situation. We are interested in only one side of the distribution, so Exhibit 3-7 shows that with 95% confidence, costs will be less than 1.721 standard errors from the mean ($t_{.05}$ with 21 degrees of freedom). Since each standard error is \$1,500, costs could be as much as 1.721 × \$1,500 = \$2,582 higher than the best estimate. Thus our adjusted CVP equation is

$$\$4q - \$2.50q - \$70{,}000 - \$2{,}582 = 0$$
$$\$1.5q = \$72{,}582$$
$$q = 48{,}388 \text{ units}$$

That is, if we set the number of units sold under the contract to be 48,388 units per period we will be 95% confident of at least breaking even.

### When Sales Quantity Is Uncertain

In Chapter 3 we noted that regression might also be used to predict sales volume on the basis of population, gross national product, disposable income, or some other variable. If a firm has used regression to predict sales, we can also construct confidence intervals on net income due to the variability in sales volume.

First, consider the case where costs and selling price per unit are known with certainty. Examples of this situation are a bit unusual, but a beverage vendor at a ball game might meet the conditions. The vendor pays a fixed fee to have the right to sell at the game, the product is purchased from the franchisee for ball park concessions with return privileges, and prices are set by management. Let us assume that studies have shown that the number of bottles sold in a seating section is a function of the number of fans seated in the section. A regression equation was estimated on the basis of 28 observations and revealed the following prediction of sales.

$$\text{sales units} = 1.3(\text{number of fans}) + 200 \text{ per game}$$

The standard error of the estimate was 48. The vendor sells the product for \$0.75 per unit, the cost per unit is \$0.25, and the vendor pays \$250 per game for the right to sell in one section at the park. If on a given day the vendor is assigned a section in which 800 fans are seated, what range of income can the vendor expect with 90% confidence?

The vendor's CVP equation is

$$\$0.75q - \$0.25q - \$250 = NI$$

In this situation the only random variable is sales units, so we start by determining the range of units that might be sold. For 800 fans, the best estimate of unit sales is $1.3 \times 800 + 200 = 1{,}240$. Then the 90% confidence interval for sales is $1{,}240 \pm 1.706 \times 48$ (the $t$ value that leaves 0.05 of the area under the distribution in each tail with 26 degrees of freedom is 1.706, and each standard error has a value of 48). Thus the range of expected sales, illustrated in Figure 4-6, is 1,158 to 1,322 units. We can now calculate the level of income at each of these levels of sales by substituting the upper and lower limits of anticipated sales into the CVP equation. This yields a lower limit of

$$\$0.75(1{,}158) - \$0.25(1{,}158) - \$250 = \$329$$

and the highest estimate is

$$\$0.75(1{,}322) - \$0.25(1{,}322) - \$250 = \$411$$

Therefore, with 800 fans in a section the vendor can expect to earn between \$329 and \$411 with 90% confidence.

If the vendor wants to be 90% confident of at least breaking even, what is the minimum number of fans that must be present in a section to satisfy the vendor's objective? In effect, the vendor is insisting on a certain

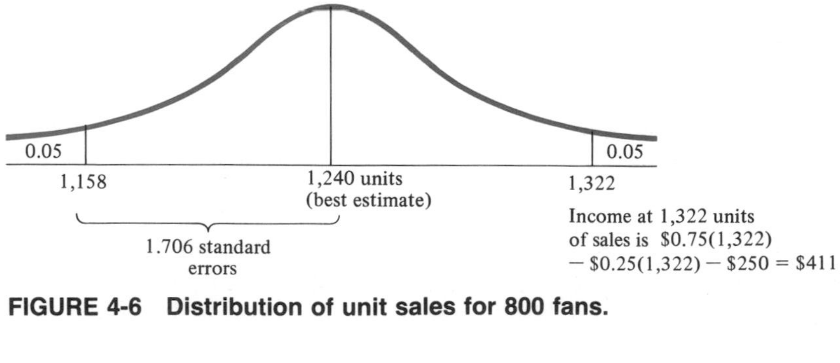


**FIGURE 4-6 Distribution of unit sales for 800 fans.**

minimum number of fans in a section before paying the $250 fee. We start by determining how many units must be sold to break even, as follows:

$$\begin{aligned} \$0.75q - \$0.25q - \$250 &= 0 \\ \$0.5q &= 250 \\ q &= 500 \text{ units} \end{aligned}$$

The best estimate of the number of fans that must be present in order to sell 500 units is

$$\begin{aligned} 500 &= 1.3(\text{number of fans}) + 200 \\ \text{number of fans} &= 231 \end{aligned}$$

However, if there were 231 fans, the mean of the income distribution would be zero (breakeven), resulting in a 50% chance of losing money. Recall that we wanted to be 90% confident of breaking even. To do so we must adjust for the variation inherent in the regression equation that predicts sales. We do this by first asking what is the mean level of sales that is implied when the sale of 500 units is at the lower end of a one-sided 90% confidence interval? Exhibit 3-7 indicates that for 26 degrees of freedom the end point is 1.315 standard errors from the unknown mean (this is illustrated in Figure 4-7). Therefore the mean sales must be 500 + 1.315(48) = 563 units to be 90% confident of selling at least 500 units. The number of fans required to yield mean sales of 563 units can then be derived as

$$\begin{aligned} 563 &= 1.3(\text{number of fans}) + 200 \\ \text{number of fans} &= 279 \end{aligned}$$

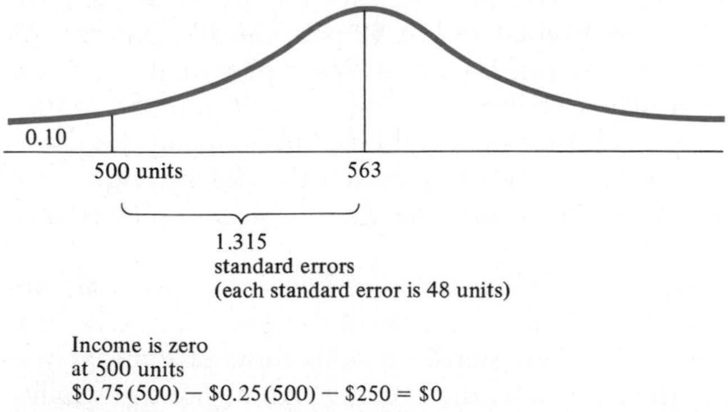


**FIGURE 4-7 With sales of 563 units there is a 90% confidence of at least breaking even.**

### More Complex Situations

So far we have considered uncertainty in only one variable at a time. In actual applications there frequently will be uncertainty in all of the variables simultaneously. Furthermore, there are likely to be interdependencies between some of the variables. For example, the distribution of the number of units sold is likely to depend on the actual selling price attained for the product. There have been several attempts to derive analytically the distribution of net income that could be expected under these types of situations. However, the mathematics quickly become far too complex for coverage in this text.

Keep in mind that the objective of our examination of uncertainty in CVP analysis is to provide management with an *approximation* of the results that might be experienced in various circumstances. The errors likely to exist in our estimates of the distribution of variables will most likely be much larger than the errors that may be introduced by simplifying our description of the environment. With this in mind, we suggest a simple, inexpensive approach to examining complex situations: the simulation approach.

## SIMULATION

Simulation is basically a sampling process in which we first model or describe a probabilistic process. We then generate information inputs for the model a large number of times to estimate the distribution of possible results from the model. For example, assume you have been asked to set up a simple gambling game for a charity fund-raising party. You are considering charging players $8 to throw two dice, and you will pay the player $1 for the sum of the dots on the upper face of the dice. Thus the most the charity will win is $6 (the original $8 less $2 paid out if a player rolls two ones). The most the charity can lose on a single play of the game is $4 (by rolling two sixes a player receives $12 but has paid only $8 to play the game). Before deciding whether we should use this game at the party, the organizers would like to know how much money the charity might earn or lose from the game. We estimate that the game would be played 200 times during the evening.

If you had recently had a statistics course you could probably determine analytically what the anticipated results of the game would be. But if you felt uncomfortable with your statistical skills, how else might you estimate the outcome of the game over the evening? An obvious possibility is to play the game yourself 200 times and record the results. But this of course is just one possible result for the evening. So you might play 200 sets of the game several times to estimate the overall outcome. Unfortunately, this would be a very time-consuming process. But if you had a computer available, you could have the computer simulate the game a large number of times rather quickly. We would proceed as follows.

First we develop a model of the game. The model in this case is a simple equation that gives our earnings per trial of the game as

$$\text{earnings} = \$8 - x$$

where $x$ is the sum of the total points on two dice. One estimate of the total earnings from the game over the evening is the sum of the earnings for 200 plays of the game. Our next step is to model the process that determines the value for $x$ for each trial of the game. To do so, we can program the computer to generate two random digits between 1 and 6 for each trial. These random digits will correspond to the possible outcomes of rolling the dice. We can then set $x$ equal to the sum of these two digits. The tricky part of the simulation is generally the modeling of the probabilistic process. In this example we need to program the computer so that the digits 1, 2, 3, 4, 5 and 6 are each equally likely to appear when a random digit is generated (to model the fact that a 1, 2, 3, 4, 5, or 6 is equally likely to show up on a fair die). Fortunately, most common computer languages have a function that will generate equally likely digits.[1]

We have now described the simulation of our gambling game. We can now program the simulation on a computer (Exhibit 4-4 lists an annotated program, written in the programming language BASIC, which will perform the simulation). By running the program many times, we can estimate the distribution of possible outcomes from using the game at our fundraising event. Exhibit 4-5 presents the results when the program in Exhibit 4-4 was run 100 times (or a total of 20,000 plays of the game).

With our simulation results we can now make the same types of statements that we made using analytic results for CVP and uncertainty. For example, what range of income can we expect to earn with 90% confidence? To answer this, we let 5% of the observations lie above the highest projected income and 5% lie below the lowest projected income. Because

[1]Discrete distributions for outcomes that are not equally likely are also fairly easily simulated. If we have an event A that occurs 10% of the time, an event B that occurs 20% of the time, and an event C that occurs 70% of the time, we can simulate these outcomes as follows. We first ask the computer to generate a digit between 1 and 10, with each digit being equally likely. We then check the value of the digit generated. If a 1 is produced, we say outcome A has occurred. If a 2 or a 3 is generated, then we say event B has occurred. Finally if the digit is a 4, 5, 6, 7, 8, 9, or a 10, the outcome is said to be event C. This process in the long run will result in event A occurring 10% of the time, B occurring 20% of the time, and C occurring 70% of the time. Slightly more complex transformations are required to model continuous distributions, but the transformations are readily available in many operations research texts.

**EXHIBIT 4-4 A Computer Program to Simulate a Simple Dice Game (written in BASIC)**

| Program | Explanatory Comments: What the Program Statement Is Doing |
|---|---|
| 10 FOR I = 1 to 200 | Play the game 200 times |
| 20 A = RND (6) | Roll the first die[a] |
| 30 B = RND (6) | Roll the second die |
| 40 X = A + B | Sum the two dice |
| 50 E = 8 − X | Determine earnings on this game |
| 60 TE = TE + E | Accumulate total earnings |
| 70 NEXT I | Play the game again |
| 80 PRINT TE | Print total earnings for all 200 plays of the game |

[a]RND (6) is a command that generates a digit equally likely to be a 1, 2, 3, 4, 5, or 6.

we have a total of 100 observations, 5% of the observations is 5. Referring to Exhibit 4-5, we can then simply count the first observations and note that 5% of the outcomes lie below a projected net income of $157. Similarly, we can count off the five highest projected net incomes and conclude that 5% of the observations lie above a projected net income of $267. Thus, we can estimate that there is a 90% chance that income will fall between $157 and $267 if we play this game 200 times.

To solve problems such as finding the probability that we will earn $200 or more, we simply count the number of simulation results that produced an income of $200 or more and take that number as a percent of the total observations. Referring to Exhibit 4-5, there are 53 simulated income figures out of the total of 100 figures that are $200 or more. We can estimate then that there is a 53% chance of earning more than $200.

### The Accountant's Role in Simulation

The particular example we used to explain simulation is not very indicative of the type of use to which a business firm would put it. The demonstration problem that follows provides a more realistic application; even so it is limited to a simple CVP situation in which we estimate earnings. Simulation can also be used to project balance sheets, cash budgets, and production levels. In cases in which we are simulating a potential financial characteristic for the firm (such as an ending cash balance for a period), the accountant will generally become heavily involved in the modeling process. That is, we will be called upon to help specify what factors affect the figure being simulated (collections of accounts receivable, bad debts, and cash

**EXHIBIT 4-5 Distribution of Total Earnings from Playing a Simple Dice Game 200 Times[a]**

| Net Income | Frequency | Net Income | Frequency | Net Income | Frequency |
|---|---|---|---|---|---|
| $ 96 | 1 | $186 | 2 | $216 | 1 |
| 125 | 1 | 187 | 1 | 217 | 3 |
| 138 | 1 | 188 | 3 | 218 | 1 |
| 145 | 1 | 189 | 1 | 219 | 2 |
| 152 | 1 | 191 | 1 | 220 | 1 |
| 157 | 1 | 193 | 3 | 223 | 1 |
| 158 | 1 | 194 | 1 | 229 | 1 |
| 160 | 2 | 195 | 2 | 230 | 2 |
| 161 | 1 | 196 | 2 | 231 | 3 |
| 163 | 1 | 198 | 1 | 234 | 1 |
| 164 | 1 | 200 | 4 | 236 | 2 |
| 169 | 2 | 201 | 2 | 237 | 1 |
| 170 | 3 | 205 | 2 | 238 | 1 |
| 171 | 1 | 207 | 1 | 244 | 1 |
| 172 | 2 | 208 | 1 | 251 | 1 |
| 173 | 2 | 209 | 2 | 261 | 1 |
| 176 | 1 | 210 | 3 | 263 | 1 |
| 178 | 1 | 211 | 1 | 267 | 1 |
| 181 | 1 | 212 | 1 | 272 | 2 |
| 182 | 1 | 213 | 2 | 273 | 1 |
| 183 | 3 | 214 | 2 | 281 | 1 |
| 184 | 1 | 215 | 2 | 317 | 1 |

[a]The simulation program in Exhibit 4-4 was run to provide an entry in this table. Then the program was run an additional time to provide a second entry. This process was repeated 100 times to yield the 100 entries in this table.

discounts will all affect a projected cash balance). Further, we will probably be asked to estimate the ranges of values that variables may take on and possibly the probabilities associated with specific figures. Our accounting records of past experience will often be good sources for estimating average collection time of receivables, the range of collection times, the proportion of people who take discounts, and so forth. As the people who prepare and maintain these records, we are generally in the best position to find and interpret the relevant information.

Having played an essential part in developing the simulation data, we are also likely to get involved in interpreting the output. Our experience with the organization should provide an excellent basis for evaluating the reasonableness of the output. And we may be asked to make probabilistic statements from simulation output. On the other hand, it is not likely that we would actually have to write a computer program to do simulations.

### Limitations of Simulation

The historic problem with simulation has been the cost of computer time to perform the simulations. To have a reasonable level of confidence that the output of a simulation accurately describes the true distribution of possible outcomes, simulations generally need to be run several thousand times. With the computers available as recently as a decade ago, the cost to run a realistic simulation several thousand times was prohibitive. But once again, the advance of technology has significantly eliminated this problem. The cost of computer time has declined so substantially that the cost to run a simulation is now usually nominal ($10 or less for several thousand trials).

The major existing problem with simulation is its dependence on the skill of the person who models the system of interest. Any error in describing the process will, of course, directly affect the results of the simulation. This makes it necessary for us to check and recheck our model description carefully to ensure that we have not forgotten to include relevant factors and that our description of relationships between variables is correct.

## DEMONSTRATION PROBLEM: SIMULATION

The Campus Film Committee has $20,000 in its bank account from last term's earnings. At the beginning of each term the committee is required to give any excess funds above its projected needs to the general fund of the Student Government Association. It is now time to make the payment, so the committee must project its likely earnings or losses for next term.

Unfortunately, there are several important undecided factors that will have a direct impact on the committee's earnings potential. For example, the committee has not yet set its ticket price for next term. Tickets are sold only in groups of five (allowing buyers to attend any five films of their choice). Last term the price was $12.50 for a book of five tickets, but arguments have been made both to raise and lower the ticket price. Although the current price of $12.50 is the most likely price for next term, we estimate that the following prices are possible, and have indicated our best guess as to the probability of each.

| Selling Price | Probability | Cumulative Probability |
|---|---|---|
| $12.00 | 0.1 | 0.1 |
| 12.35 | 0.2 | 0.3 |
| 12.50 | 0.4 | 0.7 |
| 12.65 | 0.2 | 0.9 |
| 13.00 | 0.1 | 1.0 |

The club acquires all of its films from a regional distributor. Rather than rent each film for a flat fee, the committee has agreed to pay the distributor $7.60 for each book of five tickets sold. The distributor has indicated that next term a higher fee will be required. Based on our knowledge of the fees the distributor has charged other college film clubs, we anticipate the following film rental fees and probabilities per book of five tickets.

| Rental Fee | Probability | Cumulative Probability |
|---|---|---|
| $7.60 | 0.05 | 0.05 |
| 7.90 | 0.3 | 0.35 |
| 8.00 | 0.3 | 0.65 |
| 8.10 | 0.3 | 0.95 |
| 8.40 | 0.05 | 1.00 |

The club also rents an auditorium from the college to display the films. Last term the rent was $78,000, but the administration has indicated an intent to raise the fee to $82,000 for the next term. The club intends to fight the increase but, being realistic, suspects that there will be a compromise fee. The likely charges and probabilities are

| Auditorium Rent | Probability | Cumulative Probability |
|---|---|---|
| $78,000 | 0.25 | 0.25 |
| 80,000 | 0.50 | 0.75 |
| 82,000 | 0.25 | 1.00 |

Finally, the club has had to estimate the number of ticket books that will be sold. The low prices (relative to commercial theaters) and high quality of the films shown has resulted in very strong sales, both to college students and members of the community. Further, the quantity of ticket books sold has remained quite stable. We estimate that next term's sales will be as follows:

| Ticket Books Sold | Probability | Cumulative Probability |
|---|---|---|
| 19,000 | 0.3 | 0.3 |
| 19,400 | 0.4 | 0.7 |
| 19,800 | 0.3 | 1.0 |

**Required**
Prepare an analysis of how much of the film club's current balance of $20,000 can safely be turned over to the Student Government Association's General Fund.

**Solution**
Our objective in this problem is to estimate the distribution of earnings that the club can expect. We will incorporate the uncertainty about price, quantity, and cost

information using simulation. The appropriate model for projecting earnings in this case is a CVP model. We have information on ticket selling prices and possible quantities of sales. The film rental fee is a strictly variable cost with respect to ticket sales and the auditorium rent is a strictly fixed cost with respect to ticket sales. Our model of earnings then is

$$pq - vq - fc = NI$$

where $p$ = the selling price of a booklet of tickets
$q$ = the number of booklets sold
$v$ = the film rental cost
$fc$ = the auditorium rental fee
$NI$ = projected net income

A computer was programmed to generate price, quantity, and cost data consistent with the probability distributions for each variable.[2] Exhibit 4-6 summarizes the results for 5,000 simulations of net income for the conditions listed. Let us now interpret the results.

The particular program used provides us first with the average income for all the simulation runs performed. For the 5,000 simulations, our average (best estimate) net income is $7,326. In addition, the program presents an approximation of the distribution of net income based on the facts in the simulation. The distribution is approximated by tallying the number of times net income fell into each of 20 income ranges. Thus Exhibit 4-6 indicates that of the 5,000 trials net income fell between −$15,000 and −$12,750 only once, but 1,167 of the 5,000 simulations resulted in net income falling between $5,250 and $7,500.

Using the information in Exhibit 4-6 we can now estimate the probability that net income will fall in specific ranges. For example, we can estimate that there is a 20% chance that net income will be greater than $12,000. We determine this by noting that 3,996 of the 5,000 simulations resulted in net income less than $12,000. Therefore 5,000 − 3,996 = 1,004 trials produced a net income higher than $12,000 for a relative frequency (and estimate of the probability) of 1,004 ÷ 5,000 ≈ 20% that income will exceed $12,000.

For our specific problem we might ask about the probability that the club will break even or better. This requires some interpolation of the information in Exhibit 4-6 to estimate what portion of the 228 observations in the range −$1,500 to $750 is greater than zero. Presuming that the observations are evenly spread over that range, we can estimate that 750 ÷ 2,250 of the observations are greater than zero. That is, the width of the interval is 750 minus a negative 1,500 = 2,250, and the range from zero to 750 represents the income figures greater than zero. Our estimate then is that

$$\frac{750}{2{,}250} \times 228 = 76$$

[2]This program, called DCVPSIM, is available on the disk that accompanies the text.

**EXHIBIT 4-6 Illustration of a CVP Simulation with Uncertainty Using Discrete Distributions**

| Selling Price per Unit | Probability |
|---|---|
| $12.00 | 0.1 |
| 12.35 | 0.2 |
| 12.50 | 0.4 |
| 12.65 | 0.2 |
| 13.00 | 0.1 |

| Sales Quantity, Total Units | Probability |
|---|---|
| 19,000 | 0.3 |
| 19,400 | 0.4 |
| 19,800 | 0.3 |

| Variable Cost per Unit | Probability |
|---|---|
| $7.60 | 0.05 |
| 7.90 | 0.3 |
| 8.00 | 0.3 |
| 8.10 | 0.3 |
| 8.40 | 0.05 |

| Fixed Cost per Period | Probability |
|---|---|
| $78,000 | 0.25 |
| 80,000 | 0.5 |
| 82,000 | 0.25 |

The average net income based on 5,000 iterations is $7,326.14.

| Range of Income | Frequency | Cumulative Frequency |
|---|---|---|
| -$15,000 to -12,750 | 1 | 1 |
| -12,750 to -10,500 | 8 | 9 |
| -10,500 to -8,250 | 13 | 22 |
| -8,250 to -6,000 | 39 | 61 |
| -6,000 to -3,750 | 168 | 229 |
| -3,750 to -1,500 | 167 | 396 |
| -1,500 to 750 | 228 | 624 |
| 750 to 3,000 | 385 | 1,009 |
| 3,000 to 5,250 | 503 | 1,512 |
| 5,250 to 7,500 | 1,167 | 2,679 |
| 7,500 to 9,750 | 808 | 3,487 |
| 9,750 to 12,000 | 509 | 3,996 |
| 12,000 to 14,250 | 445 | 4,441 |
| 14,250 to 16,500 | 183 | 4,624 |
| 16,500 to 18,750 | 166 | 4,790 |
| 18,750 to 21,000 | 159 | 4,949 |
| 21,000 to 23,250 | 31 | 4,980 |
| 23,250 to 25,500 | 10 | 4,990 |
| 25,500 to 27,750 | 8 | 4,998 |
| 27,750 to 30,000 | 2 | 5,000 |

of the trials from the range which included breakeven represent net income at breakeven or better. Adding this to the 5,000 − 624 = 4,376 observations greater than $750 in income yields an estimate that the probability of breaking even or better is

$$\frac{4{,}452}{5{,}000} = 89\%$$

Thus there is an 89% chance that the club will not need any cash reserves to cover losses next term. Conversely, there is an 11% chance that the club will need some cash reserves.

Assume that the club wants to be 95% certain that it will have enough cash on hand to meet any losses. How much cash should they keep? We can answer this by finding the income level for which there is a 5% chance that actual net income will be less than the target amount. We do so by searching for the approximate net income figure that leaves 5% of the observations in the lower tail of the distribution. For the simulation based on 5,000 trials this means leaving 250 observations in the lower tail of the distribution. In Exhibit 4-6 we see that 229 of the observations are less than −$3,750 but 396 are less than −$1,500. Interpolating once again, we estimate that the cutoff value for net income that leaves 5% of the observations below it is

$$-\$3{,}750 + \frac{21}{167} \times \$2{,}250 = -\$3{,}750 + \$283$$
$$= -\$3{,}467$$

Again, the width of the interval is $2,250 and the particular interval from −$3,750 to −$1,500 contains 167 observations. A total of 229 observations are below −$3,750, so we need 21 more observations to get to our total of 250. Assuming that the 167 net income figures are evenly distributed over the income range, we must move 21/167 of the way through the range to get the appropriate cutoff point. This analysis suggests that if the club keeps a reserve of $3,467, it can be 95% certain of having enough cash to get through the next term.

The actual amount of cash the club should keep depends on the committee's attitude toward risk. Should it be 99% certain of having enough cash, or 85% certain? This in turn would depend on the willingness of the Student Government Association to return funds to the film committee if necessary. In any case, our simulation provides us with the information needed to quantify risk so that an informed decision can be made.

### Extension to Continuous Distributions

The possible values for the variables in this problem were stated in terms of discrete distributions (only specific values were possible). Let us now solve the problem again using continuous distributions.

**EXHIBIT 4-7 Illustration of CVP with Uncertainty and Continuous Distributions**

The average net income on 5,000 simulations is $7,323.56.

| Income Range | Number of Observations |
|---|---|
| -$10,460.8 to -8,782.45 | 1 |
| -8,782.45 to -7,104.12 | 4 |
| -7,104.12 to -5,425.79 | 16 |
| -5,425.79 to -3,747.47 | 46 |
| -3,747.47 to -2,069.14 | 127 |
| -2,069.14 to -390.81 | 202 |
| -390.81 to 1,287.52 | 321 |
| 1,287.52 to 2,965.85 | 440 |
| 2,965.85 to 4,644.18 | 459 |
| 4,644.10 to 6,322.51 | 574 |
| 6,322.51 to 8,000.84 | 524 |
| 8,000.84 to 9,679.17 | 545 |
| 9,679.17 to 11,357.5 | 493 |
| 11,357.5 to 13,035.8 | 462 |
| 13,035.8 to 14,714.2 | 370 |
| 14,714.2 to 16,392.5 | 200 |
| 16,392.5 to 18,070.8 | 131 |
| 18,070.8 to 19,749.1 | 56 |
| 19,749.1 to 21,427.5 | 23 |
| 21,427.5 to 23,105.8 | 6 |

Frequency Distribution Graph for Net Income

| | |
|---|---|
| -$10,460.8 to -8,782.45 | |
| -8,782.45 to -7,104.12 | |
| -7,104.12 to -5,425.79 | * |
| -5,425.79 to -3,747.47 | **** |
| -3,747.47 to -2,069.14 | *********** |
| -2,069.14 to -390.81 | ****************** |
| -390.81 to 1,287.52 | **************************** |
| 1,287.52 to 2,965.85 | ************************************** |
| 2,965.85 to 4,644.18 | **************************************** |
| 4,644.18 to 6,322.51 | ************************************************** |
| 6,322.51 to 8,000.84 | ********************************************** |
| 8,000.84 to 9,679.17 | *********************************************** |
| 9,679.17 to 11,357.5 | ******************************************* |
| 11,357.5 to 13,035.8 | **************************************** |
| 13,035.8 to 14,714.2 | ******************************** |
| 14,714.2 to 16,392.5 | ***************** |
| 16,392.5 to 18,070.8 | *********** |
| 18,070.8 to 19,749.1 | ***** |
| 19,749.1 to 21,427.5 | ** |
| 21,427.5 to 23,105.8 | * |

Now assume that the club officers estimate that the possible selling price for the tickets is normally distributed with a mean of $12.50 and a standard deviation of $0.15. Any rental fee between $7.60 and $8.40 is considered equally likely; thus the distribution is modeled as a uniform distribution with a minimum value of $7.60 and a maximum value of $8.40. This time assume the auditorium rent has been contracted for $80,000. Thus the rent is a constant. Finally, the tickets to be sold are also thought to follow a normal distribution with a mean of 19,400 and a standard deviation of 200.

Again, a computer program was used to simulate net income, this time with continuous distributions.[3] Running the simulation 5,000 times yielded the distribution given in Exhibit 4-7 on page 205. Note that exactly the same types of questions that were answered with the discrete distribution program can be answered with the continuous program.

## PROBLEMS AND CASES: APPENDIX 4

**4-62 Interpret simulation output: Demonstration problem.**
Refer to the computer output provided in Exhibit 4-7. Based on that output, answer the following questions.

**Required**

**a.** What is the best estimate of earnings?
**b.** What is the probability that the club will lose money next term?
**c.** What is the probability that the club will earn more than $12,000?
**d.** Estimate the 90% confidence interval for earnings for next term.

**4-63 CVP and uncertainty.**
Ghent Merchandisers had determined with certainty that materials costs are $3 per unit, and labor costs are $2 per unit. Based on 20 observations, the firm ran a regression that projected overhead as

overhead = $1,200 per period + 150% of direct labor cost

The regression line had an $R^2$ of 0.9 and a standard error of the estimate of $225.

**Required**

**a.** If the firm's marketing department projects sales of 3,000 units at $9 per unit, what is the *range* of income this firm can expect with 90% confidence?
**b.** If the firm expects to sell 2,400 units at $8.50 per unit, what is the probability that the firm will lose money?
**c.** If the selling price is set at $10 per unit, how many units must be sold to be 90% certain of earning at least $1,000?

**4-64 CVP and uncertainty.**
Business Text Publishers, Ltd., has developed the following estimate for the cost to publish an accounting text.

total cost = $120,000 + $2.50 per book

[3] The program, called CCVPSIM, is available on the disk that accompanies the text.

The equation was derived by fitting a regression line to the costs incurred for the firm's 15 most recent texts. The fitted line produced an $R^2$ of 0.915 and a standard error of the estimate of $2,000.

The firm is considering publishing a new cost accounting text. The retail price of the text will be $36. The publisher sells the texts to bookstores at a 25% discount from retail price. The author will receive a royalty of 15% of the publisher's sales for the texts sold.

**Required**

**a.** Determine the best estimate of the number of copies that must be sold for the publisher to break even.

**b.** If 9,000 copies of the text are sold, the firm can be 90% confident of earning more than what amount?

**c.** What is the range of income that the publisher can expect with 95% confidence if 8,000 copies of the text are sold?

**4-65 CVP and uncertainty.**

Small Business Consultants, Inc., has just estimated a client's cost function. The equation was determined by fitting a regression line to the client's monthly sales and monthly total cost figures. The 12 pairs of data were taken directly from the client's general ledger. The fitted equation was

$$\text{cost} = \$2{,}100 + 0.76 \times \text{sales}$$

The standard error of the estimate is $450, the $R^2$ is 0.61.

**Required**

**a.** What is the best estimate of the client's breakeven level of sales?

**b.** What level of sales must the client reach to be 90% certain of earning at least $300 per month?

**c.** Determine the 95% confidence interval on earnings if monthly sales are $9,500.

**d.** From knowledge of the client's business, the consultant expected a much higher $R^2$. What factors or potential errors may have led to the rather moderate $R^2$ of 0.61? List four items.

**4-66 CVP and simple regression** (SMA).

The David Company has carried out a simple regression on its monthly costs for the past 24 months. The results of the regression are

$$y = \$168{,}338 + \$38.47x$$

where $y$ = total costs

$x$ = number of units

standard error of intercept = $515

standard error of coefficient = $3.15

$R^2 = 0.873$

Monthly sales (and production) in the past 2 years varied between 500 units and 15,000 units. The selling price is $55.

**Required**

**a.** Using the expected fixed costs implied by the regression results, compute the breakeven point in unit sales.

**b.** If the income tax rate is 40%, calculate the unit sales required for an after-tax net income of $24,000.

**4-67 CVP and uncertainty.**

Based on 27 observations, Caplan Manufacturing estimates that the variable cost of producing 1 unit of its product is $4. The standard error of this estimate is $0.25. Fixed costs are known with certainty to be $4,000 per month. Caplan estimates that if it sets its selling price at $9 per unit, it can sell 1,000 units per month. If the selling price is set at $10 per unit, Caplan can sell 950 units.

**Required**

**a.** If the price is set at $9, the firm can expect to earn more than what amount with 90% confidence?

**b.** If the price is set at $10, determine the range of earnings that the firm can expect to experience with 90% confidence.

**c.** Which price should the firm set? Why?

**4-68 CVP and uncertainty.**

JKL used regression, based on 18 observations, to determine the following equation for the cost to produce its sole product.

$$\text{total cost} = \$3{,}000 + \$4 \text{ per unit}$$

The $R^2$ was 0.85 and the standard error of the estimate was $300. The data used to determine the cost equation covered a demand range from 1,000 to 7,000 units per period.

**Required**

**a.** If the firm sells its products for $6 per unit and expects to sell 1,500 units, what is the range of income the firm can expect with 90% confidence?

**b.** How many units must this firm sell in order to earn at least $2,000 with 90% confidence when the selling price is $6 per unit?

**c.** If the firm is guaranteed that it can sell 5,000 units, what selling price must it set to earn at least $8,000 with 95% confidence?

**d.** If the firm sells its product for $5 per unit and can sell 15,000 units per period, how confident can management be that the firm will earn more than $12,000?

**4-69 CVP and uncertainty.**

The children's wear department of the Bigbucks Department Store tries to operate on a standard markup. They have estimated their total cost equation with regression, based on 70 observations of monthly operating results. The equation, which has a standard error of the estimate of $700 and an $R^2$ of 0.91, is

$$\text{total cost} = 0.65 \times \text{sales} + \$3{,}400$$

**Required**

**a.** In a month when sales are $10,000, what is the range of income this department can expect with 90% confidence?

**b.** How much must sales be for the department to be 97.5% confident that income will be at least $4,000?

**c.** If sales are $14,350, what is the approximate probability that this department will incur a loss?

**d.** If sales are $20,000, the firm can be 50% confident of earning more than what amount?

## PROBLEMS AND CASES: APPENDIX 4

**4-70 Interpreting results of simulation: Not-for-profit organization.** The State Turnpike Authority is contemplating changing the speed limit on a major toll road. It is thought that increasing the speed limit from 55 mph to 70 mph would increase the use of the road because it would reduce motorists' travel time relative to other routes. Currently the turnpike is logging 450 million miles of traffic per year. The toll fee is $0.03 per mile. If the speed limit is raised to 70 mph, the Turnpike Authority predicts that traffic will increase to 600 million miles per year with a probability of 60%, or to 650 million miles per year with a probability of 40%.

Variable operating costs (road repairs, emergency vehicle services, toll gate operators, and so forth) are currently $0.01 per mile of traffic. The higher speed limit is expected to increase the accident rate dramatically and therefore the cost of emergency service. In addition, higher speeds will cause more roadway damage. Variable costs could go to $0.013 per mile with a probability of 30%, to $0.015 per mile with a probability of 40%, or to $0.017 per mile with a probability of 30%.

Fixed costs for the turnpike (mostly interest on bonds) are currently $8 million per year. The interest is partially subsidized by the federal government. Although the Turnpike Authority hopes that fixed costs will not change if the speed limit is changed, there is a 25% probability that the federal government will rescind the subsidy. This would increase fixed costs by $2 million per year.

The foregoing information was fed into a simulation program and simulated 10,000 times. The resulting distribution is as follows:

| Range of Net Incomes (thousands of dollars) | Number of Observations in Range |
|---|---|
| −2,400 to −2,000 | 436 |
| −2,000 to −1,600 | 0 |
| −1,600 to −1,200 | 297 |
| −1,200 to −800 | 580 |
| −800 to −400 | 0 |
| −400 to 0 | 1,748 |
| 0 to 400 | 459 |
| 400 to 800 | 926 |
| 800 to 1,200 | 2,060 |
| 1,200 to 1,600 | 0 |
| 1,600 to 2,000 | 1,248 |
| 2,000 to 2,400 | 1,350 |
| 2,400 to 2,800 | 0 |
| 2,800 to 3,200 | 896 |

The average net income on 10,000 trials is $809,838.

**Required**

**a.** What is the current income being earned by the turnpike?

**b.** What is the minimum income that might result from the proposed change in the speed limit?

**c.** What is the maximum income that might result from the proposed change in the speed limit?

**d.** What is the best estimate of expected net income after the proposed change?
**e.** Estimate the probability that net income will increase with the speed limit change over the current net income being experienced by the turnpike.
**f.** Should the turnpike authority increase the speed limit? Your justification is more important than your yes-or-no answer.

**4-71 Cost-volume-profit simulation—computer required.**
Marble Products has decided to set the selling price for its product at $12 next period. At this price the firm estimates its demand function as:

| Units Sold | Probability |
|---|---|
| 15,000 | 0.2 |
| 16,000 | 0.2 |
| 17,000 | 0.2 |
| 18,000 | 0.2 |
| 19,000 | 0.2 |

The firm purchases the product for $8 and has a firm contract at this price for the next period. Management anticipates the following distribution for its fixed costs.

| Total Fixed Costs | Probability |
|---|---|
| $56,000 | 0.1 |
| 57,000 | 0.2 |
| 58,000 | 0.4 |
| 59,000 | 0.2 |
| 60,000 | 0.1 |

**Required**
**a.** Estimate the distribution of net income that Marble Products can expect. Use the simulation program DCVPSIM.
**b.** Management is considering spending $10,000 for advertising. It if does, the demand function is expected to change as follows:

| Units Sold | Probability |
|---|---|
| 16,000 | 0.1 |
| 18,000 | 0.1 |
| 19,000 | 0.3 |
| 20,000 | 0.3 |
| 21,000 | 0.2 |

Should the firm incur the advertising costs?

**4-72 Comprehensive CVP and uncertainty—computer required.**
Biotech Industries is considering entering a new market. The firm has developed a computer chip that gives more precise control over the exposure time for dental X-ray machines. Management is uncertain as to what price it will be able to obtain (a rumor is out that a competitor has developed a similar chip). The marketing

people have estimated the demand that they can expect at three equally likely prices (the estimates incorporate the probability that the competition enters the market). Their estimates are as follows:

| Selling Price | Probability | Demand Level | Probability |
|---|---|---|---|
| $6.00 | 0.33 | 210,000 | 0.8 |
| | | 180,000 | 0.1 |
| | | 140,000 | 0.1 |
| $6.50 | 0.34 | 200,000 | 0.4 |
| | | 170,000 | 0.4 |
| | | 130,000 | 0.2 |
| $7.00 | 0.33 | 190,000 | 0.1 |
| | | 160,000 | 0.3 |
| | | 120,000 | 0.6 |

Management's best estimate of the variable cost to produce the chip is $4.60. The distribution around the estimate is expected to be normal. The discrete distribution provided in the following table is considered to be sufficiently accurate as an approximation for planning purposes. Similarly, fixed costs are expected to be $210,000, but they may vary as follows:

| Variable Cost | Probability | Fixed Cost | Probability |
|---|---|---|---|
| $4.20 | 0.05 | $200,000 | 0.2 |
| 4.40 | 0.2 | 210,000 | 0.7 |
| 4.60 | 0.5 | 220,000 | 0.1 |
| 4.80 | 0.2 | | |
| 5.00 | 0.05 | | |

**Required**

**a.** What are the maximum and minimum expected levels of income?
**b.** Estimate the probability that the firm will lose money if it undertakes this project. Use the program DCVPSIM.
**c.** Estimate the expected value of net income.
**d.** Estimate the probability that the firm will earn between $23,000 and $187,800.
**e.** The firm can be approximately 90% confident of earning more than what amount?
**f.** There is a 50% chance that the firm will earn less than what amount?
**g.** How likely is it that the firm will earn more than $300,000?

**4-73 CVP simulation—computer required.**

Bayview Hospital charges $110 per day per bed. It has an 80-bed capacity. Bayview uses a calendar for financial reporting made up of 13 four-week "months."

In recent months the hospital has been operating at 60% of capacity (1,344 bed days per month). Variable costs have averaged $45 per bed per day, and fixed costs have averaged $80,000 per month.

Management now wishes to project the effect on operations of several possible changes. The personnel director predicts a 40% probability that wages will have to be raised next period. If wages are raised, variable costs will increase by $7 per bed per day.

The purchasing director informs management that there is a 50% chance that the city council will be increasing the charge for municipal services (water, trash, sewer, and so forth). The proposed increase would raise fixed costs by $2,000 per period.

Finally, Congress is considering liberalizing Medicare benefits. Under one proposal (given a 25% chance of being enacted), the federal government will add hospital coverage for a currently popular disease. The hospital administrator estimates that if the bill passes, occupancy will increase to 70% of capacity. A second congressional proposal (given only a 5% chance of passing) would provide coverage for unbalanced accountants. If passed, the hospital can count on operating at 100% of capacity.

The hospital is currently covered by a federal price freeze on medical fees and charges. Hence it cannot change its daily room rate. The possible changes mentioned are independent of each other. If the changes are not made, costs and demand will remain at their current levels.

**Required**

**a.** If none of the changes are made, what will next period's net income be?
**b.** What are the lowest possible earnings for the hospital, given the worst combination of events?
**c.** What is the highest possible net income, given the best possible combination of events?
**d.** Using the simulation program DCVPSIM, estimate the probability that the hospital will earn more than $10,000 next month.
**e.** What is the estimated average income this hospital will earn next period? What is the probability that the hospital will earn that dollar amount?

**4-74 CVP and uncertainty: Continuous distributions—computer required.**
Diamond D Drill Bits, Inc., is investigating the possibility of entering a new market. Based on similar products for other industries, the firm is able to make some estimates concerning the likely costs to be experienced. Management predicts that fixed costs will be between $30,000 and $40,000. They assign a uniform probability distribution to this range (i.e., all possible costs in this range are equally likely). Variable costs have been estimated using regression. The mean variable cost is $26 with a standard error of $4. (Since the assumptions of regression have been met, the probability distribution for variable costs will be normal.)

The firm hopes to sell the product for $39. However, if the firms already in the market try to force Diamond D out, the selling price could drop to as low as $34. Thus the marketing manager feels that any price in the range $34 to $39 is equally likely. The quantity sold is expected to follow a normal distribution, with a mean of 4,000 units and a standard deviation of 1,000 units.

**Required**

**a.** Use the program CCVPSIM to estimate the distribution of net income.
**b.** What is the probability that the firm will earn more than $30,000?
**c.** Should the firm enter this business?

**4-75 Interpreting simulation results.**
MGAF Specialty Products, Inc., is considering modernizing its production operations. Its management has carefully gathered appropriate marketing and cost data

PROBLEMS AND CASES: APPENDIX 4

and has run a simulation of expected operating results under both the current conditions and under the proposed change. The distributions of net income from simulating each situation 5,000 times are provided below.

| Current Situation | | After Modernization | |
|---|---|---|---|
| **Range of Income** | **Observations** | **Range of Income** | **Observations** |
| −10,000 to −5,000 | 300 | −30,000 to −20,000 | 25 |
| −5,000 to 0 | 400 | −20,000 to −10,000 | 175 |
| 0 to 5,000 | 400 | −10,000 to 0 | 300 |
| 5,000 to 10,000 | 500 | 0 to 10,000 | 300 |
| 10,000 to 15,000 | 500 | 10,000 to 20,000 | 2,100 |
| 15,000 to 20,000 | 600 | 20,000 to 30,000 | 800 |
| 20,000 to 25,000 | 1,500 | 30,000 to 40,000 | 700 |
| 25,000 to 30,000 | 500 | 40,000 to 50,000 | 300 |
| 30,000 to 35,000 | 200 | 50,000 to 60,000 | 200 |
| 35,000 to 40,000 | 100 | 60,000 to 70,000 | 100 |

**Required**

Which option (current situation or modernization) should the firm select under each of the following decision rules? Explain why.

**a.** The firm wishes to minimize the maximum potential loss.
**b.** The firm wishes to minimize the probability of operating at less than breakeven.
**c.** The firm wishes to maximize the amount of potential net income.
**d.** The firm wishes to maximize the probability of earning $20,000 or more per period.
**e.** The firm wishes to maximize the probability of earning $30,000 or more.

**4-76 CVP simulation (continuous)—computer required.**

The vice-president of International Sales has asked for a projection of earnings to be received from the firm's Brazilian plant. The plant produces ball bearings exclusively for the Brazilian market.

You have received a telex from the plant manager containing the following estimates.

1. Sales quantity for the year is expected to be between 800 and 1,200 tons. All sales volumes within this range are equally likely.
2. The target selling price in U.S. dollars is $750 per ton, but due to exchange rate fluctuations the actual selling prices in dollars will likely follow a normal distribution with a $50 standard deviation.
3. Variable manufacturing costs will also follow a normal distribution. The manager's best estimate is that variable costs will average $480 per ton with a $20 standard deviation.
4. Fixed costs are in fact fixed. The manager states categorically that they will be $150,000 for the year.

**Required**

**a.** Use the program CCVPSIM to estimate the distribution of net income for this plant (run the simulation 200 times).

**b.** The firm has a net investment in the plant of $650,000. Estimate the probability that the plant will earn a rate of return of more than 16%.
**c.** Estimate the 90% confidence interval for net income.

**4-77 CVP simulation (continuous)—computer required.**
The National Muffler Company is considering a plan to alter its marketing efforts. Currently its shops offer to install a muffler in any make of car for $79.95. Demand per shop per year is uniformly distributed over the range of 2,500 to 3,500 units. The variable cost to install a muffler is normally distributed, with a mean of $38 and a standard deviation of $10 per unit. Fixed costs per store are normally distributed, with a mean of $82,000 and a standard deviation of $6,000.

A proposal has been made to reduce the price for installing a muffler to $69.95. This will be coupled with an increase in advertising expenditures of $10,000 per year per store. Variable costs will remain unchanged, but demand per store is expected to change. The new demand per store is expected to follow a normal distribution, with a mean demand of 3,200 units per year and a standard deviation of 500 units.

**Required**
Use the CCVPSIM program to estimate the distribution of net income for a store under the firm's current policy and under the proposed policy (use 200 simulations). Which approach do you recommend, and why?

# PART TWO

## PLANNING AND BUDGETING

CHAPTER

# 5

# PROFIT PLANNING: SHORT-TERM DECISIONS, MULTIPLE PRODUCTS

In this and the next several chapters we examine operational plans and budgets in considerably more detail than in Part One. We start in this chapter by showing that a knowledge of cost behavior can help managers make many short-term decisions. It also extends the single-product cost-volume-profit model to multiple products.

## SHORT-TERM DECISIONS

People seem to like to deal in average costs. The press frequently reports the current average cost to operate an automobile, and managers show great interest in the average cost to produce a product. In part this interest in average cost is appropriate. For in the long run, a firm must sell its products at an average price in excess of its average costs if it is to be profitable. However, in the short run, a preoccupation with average costs can lead to incorrect decisions.

### Relevant Costs

Assume that the current average cost to operate an automobile is estimated to be $0.20 per mile. An employee who already owns a car is required to drive to a client's office 100 miles away. The choices offered to the employee are to use the employee's car and be reimbursed $0.15 per mile or to use a company-owned vehicle. Is the employee financially better off to use the company car? Comparing the reimbursement rate to the average cost to operate a car may make it appear that the employee would lose $0.05 per mile by using the employee's own car. However, if the actual cost function for operating an automobile is estimated to be $1,200 per year plus $0.08 per mile (the average cost was figured on an assumed 10,000 miles of driving per year), the decision changes. In the short run, since the employee already has a car, the only operating costs that will change if the car is used will be the variable costs of $0.08 per mile. At a reimbursement rate of $0.15 per mile, the employee is $0.07 better off by using the employee's car.

With a knowledge of the estimated cost function, the employee is in a position to evaluate the relevant costs for the decision. The **relevant costs** are those costs that will differ between two alternative courses of action. In this case the major relevant costs are the variable costs of operating the employee's car compared to the reimbursement rate. For most (but not all) short-run decisions, the most significant relevant costs will be the variable costs of alternative actions. However, there are usually other relevant considerations. For example, the employee just mentioned should also consider the relative risk of an accident using a familiar car (the employee's) versus an unfamiliar car (the employer's). In addition, fixed costs do sometimes change between alternatives. If they do, the fixed costs that change should also be treated as relevant costs.

## Evaluating a Special Order

Frequently firms are approached by potential customers seeking a special deal. A discount department store chain may be planning a big spring sale. They offer to make a large one-time purchase of our firm's product but want a reduced price. A foreign buyer is interested in our product and also requests a reduced selling price. In each case management must decide

**EXHIBIT 5-1 Projected Income Statement**

| | | Total | Per Unit |
|---|---|---|---|
| Expected sales (100,000 units) | | $800,000 | $8 |
| Variable costs | $250,000 | | |
| Fixed costs | 350,000 | | |
| Cost of goods sold | | 600,000 | 6 |
| Net income | | $200,000 | $2 |

**EXHIBIT 5-2 Income Statements with and without the Special Order**

| | Without Special Order | | With Special Order | |
|---|---|---|---|---|
| Sales (80,000 @ $8 or 80,000 @ $8 + 10,000 @ $4) | | $640,000 | | $680,000 |
| Variable costs (@ $2.50) | $200,000 | | $225,000 | |
| Fixed costs | 350,000 | | 350,000 | |
| Cost of goods sold | | 550,000 | | 575,000 |
| Net income | | $ 90,000 | | $105,000 |
| | | $15,000 difference | | |

whether to accept the order at a reduced selling price. Let us examine the typical costs that are relevant to such a decision.

Assume that a firm anticipates selling 100,000 units of product during the year at its normal price of $8 per unit; its fixed costs are budgeted at $350,000 and variable costs are expected to be $250,000. Based on this information, the firm has prepared the expected income statement given in Exhibit 5-1. Note that the firm's planned average cost per unit is $6.

Now assume that toward the end of the year it becomes clear that the firm will sell only 80,000 units at $8. About this time a foreign customer offers to buy 10,000 units at a price of $4. Should the order be accepted?

Based on the information in Exhibit 5-1, management might reject the order, arguing that the offered price of $4 per unit is below the cost to produce the product. But such an analysis ignores the behavior of the firm's costs. Not all of the average costs are relevant costs. The budgeted variable costs are $2.50 per unit produced. If we accept the special order, our additional costs will be $2.50 per unit. Fixed costs will remain unchanged. The offered price of $4 per unit exceeds variable costs, implying that the sale will provide a positive contribution to profits. The contribution margin earned on the foreign sale will be $1.50 per unit, so for the 10,000-unit special order, the firm should be $15,000 better off by accepting the order. This analysis is confirmed by preparing income statements with and without the special order, as in Exhibit 5-2.

### Other Costs Relevant to Special Orders

In the preceding analysis of a special order, the acceptance decision was based solely on whether the order would provide a positive contribution to the firm's profits. Although such a decision rule may be appropriate in some cases, it ignores some potentially significant relevant costs.

When deciding whether to accept a reduced selling price, management must estimate what effect, if any, the reduced price will have on

**EXHIBIT 5-3 Income Statements with and without Special Order that Exceeds Capacity**

| | Without Special Order | | With Special Order | |
|---|---|---|---|---|
| Sales (94,000 @ $8 or 90,000 @ $8 + 10,000 @ 4) | | $752,000 | | $760,000 |
| Variable costs (@ $2.50) | $235,000 | | $250,000 | |
| Fixed costs | 350,000 | | 350,000 | |
| Cost of goods sold | | 585,000 | | 600,000 |
| Net income | | $167,000 | | $160,000 |
| | | $7,000 difference | | |

selling prices to regular customers. If the special-order customer sells the product in competition with regular customers, the regular customers are likely to be quite upset and demand similar prices. In fact, if the special sale is made to an existing customer's competitor, and if there is no cost-based justification for the reduced price, the regular customer can take legal action against the firm under provisions of the **Robinson-Patman Act.** This federal law prohibits a firm from discriminating against some customers by selling the same products to competitors at reduced prices (unless there is a cost-based reason such as quantity discounts).

Management must also be assured that it has sufficient capacity to produce the special order without affecting normal sales. If it is necessary to reduce regular sales to accommodate the special order, then the contribution margin foregone on regular sales becomes a cost of accepting the special order. For instance, if the firm in the previous example anticipated normal sales of 94,000 units at $8, and if its production capacity is limited to 100,000 units, the special order of 10,000 units should not be accepted. The relevant costs to accept the special order would now be the $25,000 variable costs plus a foregone contribution margin of ($8 − $2.50) × 4,000 = $22,000 on regular sales that could not be made (only 90,000 units could be sold at the regular price if the 10,000-unit special order is accepted). The total cost of accepting the special order, $47,000, would now exceed the offered selling price of $40,000. Again, the analysis is confirmed by preparing income statements with and without the special order, as illustrated in Exhibit 5-3.

### Make-or-Buy Decisions

Another short-term decision frequently faced by management involves the choice of making or buying the components used in the manufacture of a product. Production of such basic materials as screws, nails, washers, sheet metal, and so on is not usually economical owing to specialization and returns to scale. These materials can almost always be acquired more cheaply from outside suppliers. But for many materials, such as subassemblies and special parts, it is not always clear which is the least costly means of acquisition.

Again, the appropriate means of analysis is to compare the relevant costs of the options under consideration. Typically, the relevant costs for the purchase option are quite obvious, but the relevant costs for making the part may not be. Let us examine an example.

Consider a firm that has just acquired a special casting machine. The purchase price was $80,000 and the machine will last 1 year, after which it will have no salvage value. Because of the special nature of the equipment, it can currently be sold for only $20,000. The firm anticipates producing 10,000 castings during the year. The cost of direct materials will be $3 per unit and the cost of direct labor will be $2 per unit. Variable overhead is charged to products at the rate of $0.30 per direct labor dollar and the firm's fixed factory overhead is $400,000 per year. The fixed factory overhead is assigned to products on the basis of the number of square feet of factory space required to produce each product. There are 100,000 square feet of factory space being used by the firm of which the casting operation uses 5,000 square feet. Included in the fixed factory overhead is $12,000 for the premium on a special rider to the firm's insurance policy to cover liability for accidents in the casting operation (which is considerably more dangerous than the firm's other operations).

Based on the preceding information, the firm's accountant has prepared the following analysis of the cost to manufacture the casts.

| Cost Item | Total Cost | Cost per Unit |
|---|---|---|
| Equipment depreciation | $ 80,000 | $ 8.00 |
| Direct materials | 30,000 | 3.00 |
| Direct labor | 20,000 | 2.00 |
| Variable overhead | 6,000 | .60 |
| Fixed overhead (5% of $400,000) | 20,000 | 2.00 |
| Total | $156,000 | $15.60 |

Now assume that the firm has been approached by a company that specializes in custom casting. The company offers to manufacture the castings for $10 per unit or $100,000 for a year's supply. Should management continue to produce the castings or should it purchase them?

An initial response might be to compare the $15.60 cost to make the castings with the $10 purchase price and conclude that the castings should be purchased. However, not all of the costs that have been used to determine the total cost to manufacture the castings are relevant costs for purposes of this short-term decision. For example, the $80,000 purchase price of the casting equipment is a sunk cost. A **sunk cost** is a cost that has been incurred in the past and cannot be changed. Although the purchase of the machine may or may not have been a good idea, the purchase has already been made. Being irrevocable, the purchase price should not affect future decisions. Instead, the relevant cost to the firm of using the equipment to manufacture castings is the opportunity cost of using the machine instead of selling it. An **opportunity cost** is the benefit foregone from an alternative use of a resource. In the example the equipment is said to be currently worth $20,000. If management chooses to use the equipment, it must give up the opportunity to sell it for $20,000. Thus the relevant cost for the decision is $20,000.

The direct material, direct labor, and the variable overhead costs are all costs that must be incurred to manufacture the castings but can be avoided if they are purchased. Hence they are relevant costs. Note, however, that if the firm had already purchased a year's supply of materials, and if the materials had no alternative use, they would also be sunk costs and would be irrelevant to the decision.

Most of the fixed overhead costs are not relevant costs. Whether the firm makes or buys the castings, most of the $400,000 in fixed overhead costs will have to be incurred anyway. If the fixed costs do not change between alternatives, they are irrelevant. However, it does appear that $12,000 of the fixed costs are differential costs. Apparently the insurance rider is needed only if the firm does the casting. If they discontinue the casting operation, they can drop the insurance rider and have the premium returned. Therefore, the fixed cost for the insurance rider is a relevant cost.

For purposes of making the short-term make-or-buy decision, the relevant costs are now as follows:

| Cost Item | Total Cost | Cost per Unit |
|---|---|---|
| Equipment opportunity cost | $20,000 | $2.00 |
| Direct materials | 30,000 | 3.00 |
| Direct labor | 20,000 | 2.00 |
| Variable overhead | 6,000 | .60 |
| Insurance rider | 12,000 | 1.20 |
| Total | $88,000 | $8.80 |

The correct analysis of the relevant costs indicates that in the short run the firm should continue to manufacture the castings.

Although the short-run relevant cost analysis leads to the correct decision of continuing to manufacture the castings, inappropriate reliance on short-term analysis may lead to serious operating errors. For example, if management reports to operating personnel, "After a careful analysis, we have decided that it is to the firm's advantage to manufacture castings," what is likely to happen when the "short term" expires? If operating personnel take management's announcement as a directive to continue making castings in the long run, they are likely to decide to replace the casting equipment with new equipment at year-end and continue to manufacture castings.

But, for the example, the decision to make the castings turns out to be dependent on already having the casting equipment. That is, if the firm already has the machine, the only relevant cost to the decision to continue operating is the machine's opportunity cost. But if they do not have the machine (the example stated that the machine would wear out after 1 year, so at the beginning of the second year the firm would not have the equipment), then the entire purchase price is a relevant cost. For in contrast to the sunk cost, management can now choose either to incur or avoid the entire cost. The relevant costs for year 2 are as follows:

| Cost Item | Total Cost | Cost per Unit |
|---|---|---|
| Equipment purchase price | $ 80,000 | $ 8.00 |
| Direct materials | 30,000 | 3.00 |
| Direct labor | 20,000 | 2.00 |
| Variable overhead | 6,000 | .60 |
| Insurance rider | 12,000 | 1.20 |
| Total | $148,000 | $14.80 |

Now the option to purchase the castings is a better decision. It becomes clear then that when a decision is made on short-run considerations, company personnel should be advised to be wary of incurring costs that extend the short term to the long term.

### Minimizing Short-Term Losses

Unfortunately, not all short-term decisions relate to prospects for increasing profit. Sometimes managers are faced with decisions on how to minimize short-term losses. Although the context of the question may be changed, the analysis remains unchanged. Managers must compare the relevant costs of the available actions.

For example, in the mid-1970s, when there was considerable excess capacity in the oceangoing oil tanker industry, the financial press reported that shipowners were accepting cargoes at freight rates less than variable operating costs. A shipment of oil taking 20 days to get from the Persian Gulf to the Gulf of Mexico might be accepted at a price of $490,000 even though the variable operating cost of the tanker was $25,000 per day. The explanation for this seemingly irrational behavior was that the lost contribution margin from operating the ship was less than the variable cost of putting the ship in anchorage. That is, if the variable costs to keep the ship tied up at a dock (anchorage fees, a skeleton maintenance crew, and so forth) were \$2,000 per day, the firm would be better off to accept the contract just described. The lost contribution margin from operating the ship would be \$10,000, but the lost variable costs for having the ship docked for 20 days would be \$40,000. In this case the firm could reduce its loss by \$30,000 by accepting a contract at less than variable operating costs.

### Selecting Alternative Technologies

Previously we talked about using CVP relationships in the context of a given technology for manufacturing a product. A similar approach can also be used to evaluate alternative technologies. The decision between technologies may involve major manufacturing decisions such as the type of equipment to purchase or minor day-to-day decisions such as whether to use a photocopier or mimeograph to make copies. In this type of problem one technology typically has a higher fixed, or set-up, cost than the other, but a lower variable operating cost. The question then becomes: At what volume level can we justify the higher fixed cost? Consider a firm that is contemplating two means for manufacturing a product that will sell for \$8 per unit. Technology A will require variable costs of \$4 per unit and will require fixed costs of \$10,000 per period. Technology B will lead to variable costs of \$2 per unit and fixed costs of \$25,000 per period. Which alternative should the firm select?

The answer, of course, depends on the anticipated level of sales. The approach to solving the question is to determine which alternative is preferred for every possible level of sales. We begin by graphing the two cost functions and the revenue functions as in Figure 5-1. Referring to Figure 5-1, note that for a level of sales from zero to $q_2$, technology A has the lower costs. Beyond point $q_2$, technology B is less costly. Therefore, for demand less than $q_2$ we prefer A, and for demand greater than $q_2$ we prefer B. We can solve for point $q_2$ by noting that it is the point at which the two technologies incur identical costs. Therefore, to solve for $q_2$, we set the cost of the two technologies equal to each other. (Note that since the revenues are the same at each level of sales for each alternative, revenues can be ignored in this calculation.)

$$\$4q_2 + \$10{,}000 = \$2q_2 + \$25{,}000$$
$$\$2q_2 = \$15{,}000$$
$$q_2 = 7{,}500 \text{ units}$$

Thus both technologies result in the same cost at a level of output of 7,500 units. But will technology A be preferred at all levels of demand from zero to 7,500 units? No, there is also a range of demand for which we would

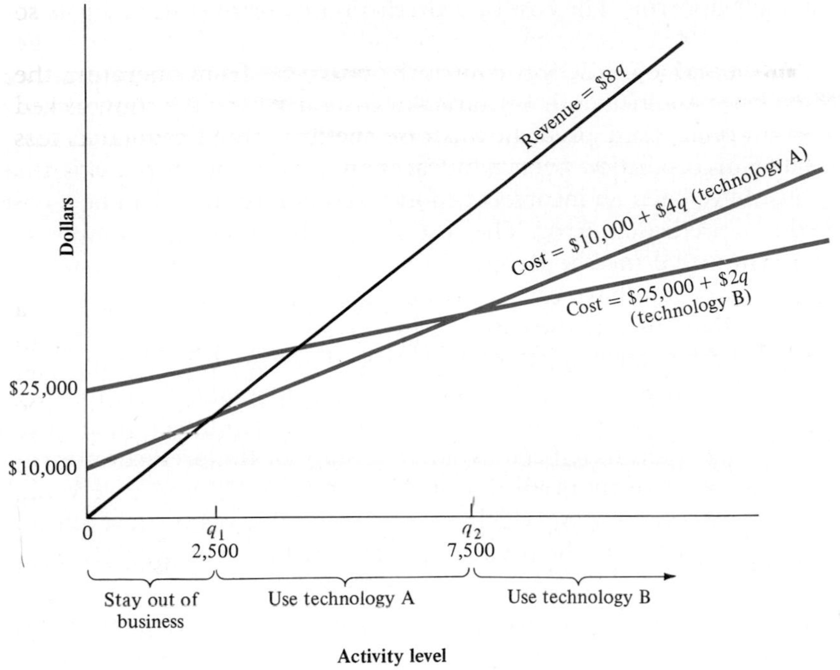


**FIGURE 5-1 Choosing between alternative technologies.**

choose neither technology—that is, when demand is less than the break-even point for technology A, point $q_1$. Thus, we can also solve for point $q_1$:

$$\$8q_1 - \$4q_1 - \$10{,}000 = 0$$
$$q_1 = 2{,}500 \text{ units}$$

Our decision rule then becomes: Stay out of this business if demand is projected to be less than 2,500 units per period, select technology A if demand is between 2,500 and 7,500 units per period, and select technology B if demand is expected to be greater than 7,500 units per period.

## COST OF PREDICTION ERRORS

The previous example allows us to demonstrate the concept of the cost of a prediction error. This concept will come up again in later chapters, but in every case the objective is the same: The degree of accuracy we should achieve in our estimates of costs or demand depends on the cost of acquiring more accurate estimates and the cost we can expect to incur if our estimates are in error. The cost of a prediction error measures this latter cost.

The **cost of a prediction error** is the foregone contribution margin, or additional costs incurred, because the firm selected an action among alternatives based on a prediction, an action that would not have been taken had our prediction been more accurate. The critical point is that there must have been an incorrect action taken before there can be a cost attached to a prediction error. The cost of a prediction error is simply the difference in actual income earned based on a chosen action versus the income that we could have earned by taking a better action.

Let us demonstrate the cost of a prediction error with our example concerning the two alternative technologies. If we predict sales of 8,000 units, then the *action* we would take based on that prediction is to select technology B. If demand turns out to be 7,000 units, we will incur additional costs that could have been avoided because of the prediction error. That is, had we correctly predicted demand to be 7,000 units, we would have selected technology A, which results in lower costs at that output. The amount of the cost of the prediction error can be calculated as follows:

Income that would have been made had we selected the correct action (A):

$$\$8 \times 7{,}000 - \$4 \times 7{,}000 - \$10{,}000 = \$18{,}000$$

Income made under the action selected (B):

$$\$8 \times 7{,}000 - \$2 \times 7{,}000 - \$25{,}000 = \underline{\$17{,}000}$$

Cost due to the prediction error: $\underline{\underline{\$\ 1{,}000}}$

Thus our income was $1,000 less than it could have been because we took the incorrect action based on our prediction of demand. The cost of the prediction error is $1,000. Note, by the way, that since revenue was the same under both actions, we could have directly calculated the extra cost incurred by choosing the wrong action as follows:

Cost that would have been incurred under action A:

$$\$4 \times 7{,}000 + \$10{,}000 = \$38{,}000$$

Cost that was incurred under action B:

$$\$2 \times 7{,}000 + \$25{,}000 = \$39{,}000$$

to yield an additional cost of \$1,000. Note also that the originally predicted sales of 8,000 units was not used in any of our calculations of the cost of the prediction error. The cost of the prediction error is the difference in actual income earned for the level of sales achieved versus the income that we could have earned at this achieved level of sales. Had we correctly predicted the actual level of sales that would be achieved, we would have taken the preferred action.

Using our previous example, if we had predicted demand to be 8,000 units, but demand turned out to be 7,800 units, what is the cost of the prediction error? If we had known that demand was going to be 7,800 units, we would still have selected technology B. So our total cost under the best action is \$2 × 7,800 + \$25,000 = \$40,600, which is exactly the same as our actual cost given our actual action of selecting technology B. Because we would not have changed the action that we took even if the prediction had been correct, there is *no cost* to the prediction error.

When we predicted demand to be 8,000 units, we also predicted income to be \$8 × 8,000 − \$2 × 8,000 − \$25,000 = \$23,000. When demand turned out to be 7,800 units, we earned \$8 × 7,800 − \$2 × 7,800 − \$25,000 = \$21,800. Should we not consider \$23,000 − \$21,800 = \$1,200 a cost due to a prediction error? No. The achievement of the \$23,000 of income was never a real possibility. It is only the amount of income we would achieve if demand were 8,000 units. But demand is not 8,000 units; it is 7,800 units. There is a cost incurred due to a prediction error only when we take an action that turns out not to be optimal after we find out the true value of the predicted variable.

## COST-VOLUME-PROFIT ANALYSIS WITH MULTIPLE PRODUCTS

To this point we have restricted our attention to a firm that sells a single product. Such firms generally exist only in the minds of textbook writers. We now examine the usefulness of the CVP technique for firms that deal in several products. In the general case the CVP equation could be represented as:

$$p_1q_1 + p_2q_2 + \cdots + p_nq_n - v_1q_1 - v_2q_2 - \cdots - v_nq_n - fc = NI$$

where $p_i$ = the selling price per unit of product $i$
$q_i$ = the number of units of $i$ produced and sold
$v_i$ = the unit variable cost for product $i$
$fc$ = the fixed costs per period
$NI$ = income

Unfortunately, the use of generalized notation will be burdensome and is usually confusing, so we will restrict our examples in this chapter to firms that deal in two products. The first thing we can notice is that for a multiproduct firm there are infinitely many ways to earn any particular level of income. For example, refer to the data in Exhibit 5-4. What is the firm's breakeven point? If the firm sells zero units of product 1, its breakeven in terms of product 2 is

$$\begin{aligned} \$5q_2 - \$20{,}000 &= \$0 \\ q_2 &= 4{,}000 \text{ units} \end{aligned}$$

Conversely, if the firm sells zero units of product 2, its breakeven in terms of product 1 is

$$\begin{aligned} \$4q_1 - \$20{,}000 &= \$0 \\ q_1 &= 5{,}000 \text{ units} \end{aligned}$$

But there are even more breakeven points. If the firm sells 1,000 units of product 1, its breakeven point is

$$\begin{aligned} \$4 \times 1{,}000 + \$5q_2 - \$20{,}000 &= \$0 \\ \$5q_2 &= \$16{,}000 \\ q_2 &= 3{,}200 \text{ units} \end{aligned}$$

In Figure 5-2 we have graphed these breakeven points and connected them. Note that all three points lie on a straight line. It turns out that any combination of values of $q_1$ and $q_2$ lying on that line results in the firm breaking even. The formula for the line describing all the combinations of $q_1$ and $q_2$ that will lead to breakeven is $\$4q_1 + \$5q_2 = \$20{,}000$. Note that this equation, in effect, says that the sum of the contribution margin from selling product 1 and the contribution margin from product 2 must equal total fixed costs. Similarly, the formula $\$4q_1 + \$5q_2 = \$30{,}000$ will describe all combinations leading to an *income* of $10,000. This time

**EXHIBIT 5-4 Data for a Two-Product Firm**

| Per-Unit Data | Product 1 | Product 2 |
|---|---|---|
| Selling price | $5 | $8 |
| Variable cost | 1 | 3 |
| Contribution margin | $4 | $5 |
| Contribution margin per sales dollar | 0.80 | 0.625 |
| Fixed costs per period | $20,000 | |

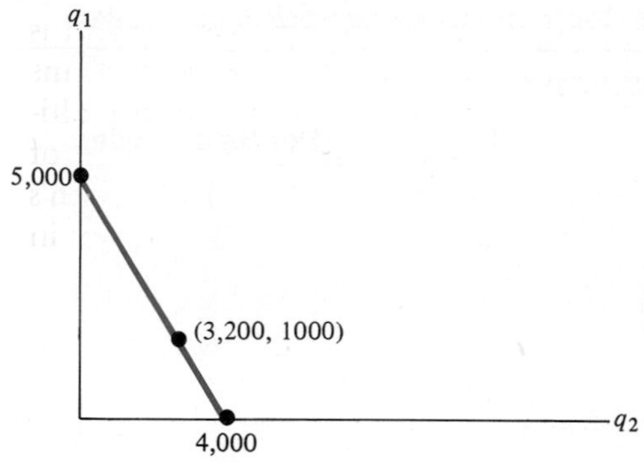


**FIGURE 5-2 Breakeven points for a two-product firm.**

the sum of the contribution margins covers fixed costs plus $10,000 of income. In fact, for any desired level of income there will be a line representing the combination of sales of $q_1$ and $q_2$ that will yield the desired income.

The preceding analysis shows that calculating breakeven volume in terms of the number of units sold is not very helpful for most multiple-product firms. Hence, instead of units, most large firms define the measure of volume to be total sales dollars. As long as the overall mix of products sold stays reasonably stable (the usual case for large firms), we can use a sales volume approach to relate profit to volume.

If product mix is stable, then the variable cost incurred per sales dollar will also be stable.[1] This, in turn, leads to a stable contribution margin per dollar (contribution margin percent).

Exhibit 5-5 presents some data for the previous two-product firm. Based upon the experience reflected in Exhibit 5-5, this firm could calculate breakeven sales as

$$\begin{aligned} \text{sales} - 0.29\ \text{sales} - \$20{,}000 &= \$0 \\ 0.71\ \text{sales} &= \$20{,}000 \\ \text{sales} &= \$28{,}169 \end{aligned}$$

If the firm wants to earn $30,000 per period, its target sales should be

$$\begin{aligned} \text{sales} - 0.29\ \text{sales} - \$20{,}000 &= \$30{,}000 \\ 0.71\ \text{sales} &= \$50{,}000 \\ \text{sales} &= \$70{,}423 \end{aligned}$$

[1]Many small firms, such as restaurants and gift shops, go a step further and use constant markups. For these firms, the variable cost per dollar of sales is a constant regardless of sales mix.

**EXHIBIT 5-5 Variable Cost and Contribution Margin per Sales Dollar**

**PERIOD 1**

| | Total | Per Sales Dollar |
|---|---|---|
| Sales (5,000 @ \$5 + 3,000 @ \$8) | \$49,000 | 1.00 |
| Variable costs (\$1 and \$3) | 14,000 | 0.29 |
| Contribution margin | \$35,000 | 0.71 |
| Fixed costs | 20,000 | NA |
| Net income | \$15,000 | NA |

**PERIOD 2**

| | Total | Per Sales Dollar |
|---|---|---|
| Sales (6,300 @ \$5 + 3,800 @ \$8) | \$61,900 | 1.00 |
| Variable costs (\$1 and \$3) | 17,700 | 0.29 |
| Contribution margin | \$44,200 | 0.71 |
| Fixed costs | 20,000 | NA |
| Net income | \$24,200 | NA |

Although the approach just described is widely used in practice, we must keep in mind that the predictions are only accurate so long as product mix stays nearly the same. But sometimes, if management places a great deal of emphasis on meeting a sales quota, salespeople will react by pushing products with low contribution margins per sales dollar because these products represent the customer's best buy per dollar and are easier to sell. Thus, while the total sales quota may be met, the change in product mix may lead to a failure to meet the profit goal. Exhibit 5-6 illustrates how meeting the \$70,423 sales quota for the example firm fails to achieve

**EXHIBIT 5-6 Meeting Sales Goal but Not Profit Goal[a]**

| | Total | Per Sales Dollar |
|---|---|---|
| Sales (2,245 @ \$5 + 7,400 @ \$8) | \$70,425 | 1.00 |
| Variable costs (\$1 and \$3) | 24,445 | 0.35 |
| Contribution margin | \$45,980 | 0.65 |
| Fixed costs | 20,000 | |
| Net income | \$25,980 | |

[a]Based on the prior sales mix, the firm had expected to earn \$30,000 on sales of \$70,423.

$$\$70{,}423 - 0.29(\$70{,}423) - \$20{,}000 = \text{net income}$$
$$\$30{,}000 = \text{net income}$$

While the sales goal was met, it was met through proportionately higher sales of product 2.

the expected $30,000 profit. The error arises because a substantially larger proportion of units of product 2 were sold than were sold in the past.

An alternative approach is to consider unit sales instead of dollar sales. This approach is useful when the proportion of the various products sold is fairly constant, such as in fast-food restaurants where the number of soft drinks sold per hamburger is rather stable. In these cases, we can define a sales unit as a batch of products. Using the data in Exhibit 5-4, if a customer typically buys 5 units of product 1 and 3 units of product 2, then the selling price of a batch is 5 × $5 + 3 × $8 = $49. Similarly, the variable cost for this batch is 5 × $1 + 3 × $3 = $14. Breakeven in terms of the number of batches is then found using the cost-volume-profit equation as

$$\begin{aligned} \$49q - \$14q - \$20{,}000 &= \$0 \\ \$35q &= \$20{,}000 \\ q &= 571 \end{aligned}$$

Thus to break even, we must make 571 sales to customers and each sale must be a typical sale. That is, these sales must translate into 5 × 571 = 2,855 units of product 1 and 3 × 571 = 1,713 units of product 2.

This approach is useful because it helps management focus on the number of sales transactions (customers) required. However, it does require that customers typically buy a common basket of products. When customer purchases are dissimilar, the approach concentrating on total sales dollars is preferred.

### Maximizing Income When There Is a Scarce Resource

The result of the change in sales mix illustrated in Exhibit 5-6 may have come as a surprise. The product mix changed in favor of the product with the higher contribution margin per unit, yet income fell below expectations. The reason for this is that we held sales dollars constant as we changed product mix. If sales are held constant, we want to sell the products with the highest contribution margin ratio, not the highest contribution margin per unit. To illustrate, assume a customer has $40 to spend. Which product, 1 or 2, would we hope to sell? If the customer spends the $40 to buy 8 units of product 1, our total contribution margin is 8 × $4 = $32, but if the customer spends the $40 to buy 5 units of product 2, we only get 5 × $5 = $25. Thus for each sales *dollar* received we earn a higher contribution margin with product 1.

If we change the constraint, however, the analysis changes. If a customer arrives who wants a unit of product 1 or a unit of product 2, but not both, we now hope to sell a unit of product 2. On a *per-unit* basis product 2 is more profitable.

Consider another example. Assume that management wants to know the effect of spending \$10,000 on specific product advertising. Which product should be advertised? Product 2 has the higher contribution margin, but the answer depends not only on the per-unit contribution but also on the response of the number of units sold to the advertising. If advertising product 1 will generate an additional 4,000 units of sales of $q_1$ and advertising product 2 will yield additional sales of 2,500 units of $q_2$, then advertising product 1 will be preferable. That is, the additional contribution margin from advertising product 1 is

$$4{,}000 \times \$4 = \$16{,}000$$

whereas the additional contribution margin from advertising product 2 is

$$2{,}500 \times \$5 = \$12{,}500$$

Another way of looking at it is that management should select the action that maximizes the **contribution margin per unit of scarce resource.** In this example, the scarce resource is advertising dollars. For every advertising dollar spent on product 1 we earn a contribution margin of \$16,000 ÷ \$10,000 = \$1.60, but for every dollar spent on product 2 we earn a contribution margin of only \$12,500 ÷ \$10,000 = \$1.25. Therefore the higher return per advertising dollar comes from product 1.

A second example should reinforce the concept. Assume that in the short run a firm has only 15,000 machine hours available to produce its two products. Product 1 requires 1 hour of machine time, whereas product 2 requires 2 hours. Assume that the contribution margins of the two products are again \$4 and \$5, respectively, and fixed costs are \$20,000 per period. Then the firm will be better off producing product 1, which yields a contribution margin per unit of scarce resource (machine hours) of \$4. On the other hand, the contribution margin for product 2 is just \$2.50 per machine hour. The reader can check that producing only product 1 will lead to a net income of \$40,000, whereas producing only product 2 will yield a net income of \$17,500.

### Linear Programming

When a firm manufactures several products and has multiple constraints, such as limited machine time on several machines, sales volume maxima, and constraints on the availability of raw materials, the analysis is similar but more complex. In these situations the use of a mathematical solution technique called linear programming becomes necessary. *Linear program-*

*ming* finds the combination of products to manufacture that maximizes the return per unit of combinations of scarce resources. Appendix 5A at the end of this chapter explains the use of linear programming in more detail.

## SUMMARY

The question of whether management should accept a special order is answered by determining whether the additional revenues generated by the order will exceed the additional costs incurred to fill the order. The largest of the additional costs are usually the variable manufacturing costs to produce the extra units of product or service. Thus a knowledge of the firm's cost function is essential to make informed decisions regarding special orders.

Similarly, a knowledge of cost functions will allow managers to select the cheapest means of providing goods and services as a function of activity levels. When the cost functions for alternative technologies are available, we can also gain valuable information on the degree of precision required in making predictions of anticipated activity levels.

When a firm deals in many products, cost-volume-profit analysis becomes more complex. The key to making optimal resource allocation decisions is to maximize the return to the firm per unit of scarce resource. For persons with the appropriate mathematical background, Appendix 5A generalizes this concept to many scarce resources.

## DEMONSTRATION PROBLEM

Metropolitan Packaging specializes in the manufacture of 1-gallon plastic bottles. The firm's customers include dairy processors, wholesalers of distilled water, bleach manufacturers, and fruit juice processors. The bottles are produced by a process called blow molding. A machine heats plastic to the melting point. A bubble of molten plastic is formed inside a mold, and a jet of hot air forced into the bubble blows the plastic into the shape of the mold. The machine releases the molded bottle, an employee trims off any flashing (excess plastic around the edge), and the bottle is complete.

The firm has four molding machines, each capable of producing 100 bottles per hour. The firm estimates that the variable cost of producing a plastic bottle is \$0.02. The bottles are sold for \$0.05 each.

Management has been approached by a local toy company that would like the firm to produce a molded plastic toy for them. The toy company is willing to pay \$0.30 per unit for the toy. The variable cost to manufacture the toy will be \$0.24. In addition, Metropolitan would incur a cost of \$2,000 to construct the needed mold. Because the toy uses more plastic and is of a more intricate shape than a bottle, a molding machine can produce only 40 units per hour. The customer wants 100,000 units. Assume that Metropolitan Packaging has a total capacity of 10,000 machine hours available during the period in which the toy company wants delivery of the toys. The firm's fixed costs, excluding the cost to construct the toy mold, during this same period will be $20,000.

**Required**

**a.** If management predicts that demand for its bottles will require the use of 7,500 machine hours or less during the period, should the special order be accepted?

**b.** If management predicts that demand for its bottles will be higher than its ability to produce bottles, should the order be accepted?

**c.** Management has located a firm that has just entered the molded plastic business. This firm has considerable excess capacity and more efficient molding machines and is willing to subcontract the toy job, or any portion of it, for $0.28 per unit. It will construct its own toy mold. Determine Metropolitan's minimum expected excess machine hour capacity needed to justify producing any portion of the order itself rather than subcontracting it entirely.

**d.** Management predicted that it would have 1,600 hours of excess machine hour capacity available during the period. Consequently, it accepted the toy order and subcontracted 36,000 units to the other plastic company. In fact, demand for bottles turned out to be 900,000 units for the period. The firm was able to produce only 840,000 units because it had to produce the toys. What was the cost of the prediction error for failure to predict demand correctly?

**Solution**

**a.** The special order requires 2,500 hours of machine time for production (100,000 units ÷ 40 units per hour). If management expects to have 2,500 hours or more of excess machine time, it should accept the order. The order will provide $30,000 in revenues while requiring $24,000 in variable costs and $2,000 in fixed costs. Acceptance of the order will increase net income by $4,000.

**b.** Since available machine time is constraining total production, we should calculate the contribution margin earned per hour of machine time for each of the products. An hour's machine time devoted to producing bottles will generate 100 units selling for $5. Variable cost for 100 bottles is $2, yielding an earned contribution margin of $3 per hour of machine time. An hour's machine time devoted to the toys will generate 40 toys selling for $12. The variable cost of 40 toys amounts to $9.60 for an earned contribution margin of $2.40 per machine hour. The firm should not accept the order because it will get a higher return from manufacturing bottles. Another way of analyzing this question is to note that if the order is accepted, the firm will earn $4,000 from the sale of the toys, as stated in (a). But using 2,500 hours of machine time for the toys means that the firm gives up the opportunity to produce and sell 250,000 bottles (2,500 hours times 100 bottles per hour). The earnings from selling 250,000 bottles at a markup of $0.03 would be $7,500.

**c.** In essence this question asks at what point the firm is indifferent between producing the toys and subcontracting them. If the firm has excess production time available, its cost function will be $2,000 + $0.24 per unit. The cost function for subcontracting the units is just $0.28 per unit. The firm is indifferent between the alternative strategies when the costs are equal. Letting $X$ represent the number of units produced, we can solve for the indifference point as follows:

$$\$2{,}000 + \$0.24X = \$0.28X$$
$$\$2{,}000 = \$0.04X$$
$$X = 50{,}000 \text{ units}$$

As long as Metropolitan has the free time available to produce 50,000 or more units, it is cheaper to do so than to buy them from the subcontractor. But the firm is better off to avoid the fixed charge of $2,000 for the mold by subcontracting the entire order if it has time to produce only 50,000 units or less. In terms of number of hours of expected idle machine time, the firm must expect to have 50,000 units ÷ 40 units per hour = 1,250 hours available before it can justify producing any of the toys.

**d.** Based on anticipated demand the firm chose to produce 64,000 of the toys and subcontract 36,000 units. This choice limited actual bottle production to 840,000 units. The firm's actual net income based on this action was $7,760.

| | Bottle Sales (840,000 units) | Toy Sales: Produced (64,000 units) | Toy Sales: Subcontracted (36,000 units) | Total |
|---|---|---|---|---|
| Sales (@ $0.05 and $0.30) | $42,000 | $19,200 | $10,800 | $72,000 |
| Variable costs (@ $0.02, $0.24, and $0.28) | 16,800 | 15,360 | 10,080 | 42,240 |
| Contribution margin | $25,200 | $ 3,840 | $ 720 | $29,760 |
| Fixed costs | 20,000 | 2,000 | — | 22,000 |
| Net income | $ 5,200 | $ 1,840 | $ 720 | $ 7,760 |

Had it been known that demand for bottles was going to be for 900,000 units, management would have realized that there would only be 1,000 hours of excess machine time. The analysis in (c) has shown that in this case the firm should have subcontracted the entire special order. Having done so, the firm would have earned $9,000.

| | Bottle Sales (900,000 units) | Subcontracted Toys (100,000 units) | Total |
|---|---|---|---|
| Sales (@ $0.05 and $0.30) | $45,000 | $30,000 | $75,000 |
| Variable costs (@ $0.02 and $0.28) | 18,000 | 28,000 | 46,000 |
| Contribution margin | $27,000 | $ 2,000 | $29,000 |
| Fixed costs | 20,000 | — | 20,000 |
| Net income | $ 7,000 | $ 2,000 | $ 9,000 |

Thus the cost of the prediction error is $1,240, computed as follows:

| | |
|---|---|
| Net income: Optimal action | $9,000 |
| Net income: Actual action | 7,760 |
| Cost of prediction error | $1,240 |

## KEY TERMS AND CONCEPTS

Relevant costs
Robinson-Patman Act
Sunk cost
Opportunity cost
Cost of a prediction error
Contribution margin per unit of scarce resource

## FURTHER READING

Dillon, Ray D., and John F. Nash. "The True Relevance of Relevant Costs," *The Accounting Review* (January 1978), p. 11.

El Sheshai, Kamal M., Gorden B. Harwood, and Roger H. Hermanson. "Cost-Volume-Profit Analysis with Integer Goal Programming," *Management Accounting* (October 1977), p. 43.

Hassan, Nabil, R. Penny Marquette, and Joseph M. McKeon, Jr. "Sensitivity Analysis: An Accounting Tool for Decision Making," *Management Accounting* (April 1978), p. 43.

Leininger, Wayne E. "Opportunity Costs: Some Definitions and Examples," *The Accounting Review* (January 1977), p. 248.

Sharav, Itzhak. "Cost Justification Under the Robinson-Patman Act," *Management Accounting* (July 1978), p. 15.

Whiting, Herbert G. "Cost Justification of Price Differences," *Management Services* (July/August 1966), p. 30.

## QUESTIONS AND EXERCISES

**5-1** Are all future costs relevant? Explain.

**5-2** Define the cost of a prediction error.

**5-3** Define contribution margin percentage. When would this be useful to CVP decisions?

**5-4** "We lose money on every unit we sell, but we sell so many that we make a profit." How might this be explained?

**5-5** Publishers of academic and trade journals frequently offer subscriptions to students at a substantial discount. Why do you suppose such a decision is made?

**5-6** A firm is operating at capacity. Should it accept a request for a special order based on variable cost plus 40%?

**5-7** A decision by the management of a theater to present matinees at reduced prices may be viewed as a special-order situation. Explain briefly.

5-8 A firm is considering two alternative technologies for the introduction of a new product. One alternative is capital intensive and the other is labor intensive. Given changes in volume, which of the two alternatives will display the widest fluctuations in net income?

5-9 A firm sells two products. Product A has a contribution margin percentage of 25% and product B's is 30%. What is the effect on the breakeven point in terms of total revenue if the sales mix is changed to emphasize product B?

5-10 A firm sells two products. For the period, total planned dollar sales equaled actual dollar sales; however, dollar sales of the product with the higher contribution margin percentage were greater than expected. What is the effect on income?

5-11 Refer to the demonstration problem at the end of the chapter. How would the answers change if Metropolitan Packaging could convince the toy company to provide the necessary mold?

5-12 Cheap Car Rental charges its customers $10 per day plus $0.10 per mile. Its competition rents cars for $12 per day and $0.08 per mile. The cars of both companies have a junkyard appearance. How many miles would have to be driven on a 4-day weekend so that the cost of the two alternatives would be the same?

5-13 A firm finds that it has some discretion in combining inputs in order to produce. The alternatives and their costs are as follows:

| Alternative | Fixed Costs | Average Variable Cost per Unit Produced |
|---|---|---|
| A | $20,000 | $1.00 |
| B | 30,000 | 0.80 |
| C | 40,000 | 0.70 |

Indicate, for management, the range of output over which each alternative is best.

5-14 A firm is trying to decide which of two machines it should purchase. Machine A will result in fixed costs of $26,000 per period and variable costs of $0.05 per unit. Machine B will require fixed costs of $17,000 per period and variable costs of $0.07 per unit produced. Assuming that the firm sells its product for $0.10 per unit, determine the range of demand per period for which the firm should (a) not operate at all, (b) use machine A, and (c) use machine B.

5-15 Snokold, Inc., produces portable refrigerators for export to Antarctica. It is their only product. The 19X9 operations showed:

| | |
|---|---|
| Units sales | 9,000 |
| Sales price | $8.00 |
| Average cost (variable cost, $3.00) | $5.00 |

The marketing department estimates that 12,000 could be sold at the reduced price of $7.00. The production department estimates variable costs of $3.00 and fixed costs of $1.50 per unit at this volume. Should they sell these units at that price?

**5-16** The Pick Corporation will purchase one of two machines. Machine A will incur variable costs of $1.70 per unit plus fixed costs of $50,000 per month. Machine B will incur total costs of $57,000 per month if 10,000 units are produced and $68,000 per month if 15,000 units are produced each month. The product sells for $4.20 per unit. (a) What is the breakeven point in units for each of the two machines? (b) At what monthly demand level would you be indifferent between the two alternatives? (c) Over what range of output is each machine most profitable?

**5-17** Ariel Mann, Inc., can sell its product for $5 per unit. The firm is considering two alternative methods for manufacturing its product. Process 1 requires annual fixed costs of $45,000 and a variable cost of $3.50 per unit. The second approach would require annual fixed costs of $150,000 and a variable cost of $2.25 per unit. If these are the only costs to be incurred, determine the range of annual demand for which the firm (a) should not be in business, (b) should use process 1, and (c) should use process 2.

**5-18** One-Drawer-Full, Inc., sells two products. Left sells for $10 and has variable costs per unit of $5; right sells for $9 and has variable costs per unit of $5. Two lefts are sold for every right. Fixed costs total $1,000 and cannot be traced uniquely to either product. Given the proportions in which they are sold: (a) how many lefts are sold at breakeven, and (b) how many lefts *and* rights must be sold to earn $1,500?

**5-19** Triplets, Inc., sells three products:

| Product | Price | Variable Cost | Mix |
|---|---|---|---|
| X | $15 | $10 | 20% |
| Y | 25 | 17 | 50 |
| Z | 30 | 20 | 30 |

Fixed costs are $1,200 per period. Given the sales mix, determine (a) how many units of each will be sold at breakeven, and (b) what sales dollars for each are required in order to earn $400 before taxes.

**5-20** A firm sells two products with profit/volume ratios of 1/4 and 1/3, respectively. Actual *total* dollar sales were as planned, although sales of the product with a P/V ratio of 1/4 were greater than planned. As a result of this, how will planned income compare with actual income?

**5-21** Delphi Corp. sells 3 units of product X to 2 units of service. Product X contributes $10 per unit and service contributes $20 per unit. Fixed costs are $164,000 per period. How many units of product and service must be sold to earn $42,000 after taxes of 30%?

**5-22** The manager of the men's shirt department of a local department store must order the shirts to be sold in the fall season earlier in the year. Typically, if fall weather is normal, the department sells 3,000 short-sleeved shirts and 5,000 long-sleeved shirts. If fall weather is hot, 4,000 short-sleeved shirts and 3,000 long-sleeved shirts will be sold. If the fall is cold, 1,000 short-sleeved shirts and 8,000 long-sleeved shirts will be sold. The shirts sell for $12 each and cost $5. Any unsold shirts at the end of the season are sold in a closeout sale for half price. The manager predicted that this would be a hot fall and ordered appropriately. The fall weather turned out to be "normal." Estimate the cost of the prediction error.

## PROBLEMS AND CASES

**5-23 Make or buy.**

Read, Inc., is presently purchasing 5,000 parts monthly at a cost of $13 each. It takes one-half hour to make a part, and the direct costs amount to $8 per unit. The firm is presently operating at 80% of capacity, at which indirect costs are $220,000. If the part is made, the firm will be operating at 90% of capacity and indirect costs are expected to be $235,000.

**Required**

Prepare a brief report indicating whether the part should be made or purchased. Also, what is the monthly capacity?

**5-24 Alternate technologies.**

Ambivalent, Inc., can produce one of its products on either of two machines. The first machine requires 6 hours to set up and can produce 10 units per hour. The second machine requires 4 hours to set up and can produce 5 units per hour. The costs per hour of set-up time and operating time are the same regardless of which machine is used.

**Required**

**a.** At what level of production will the cost of using the first machine equal the cost of using the second machine?

**b.** Assume that the second machine is already set up. How large an order would it take to justify setting up the first machine rather than to continue running the second machine?

**5-25 Make or buy: Alternative costs.**

Makurby, Inc., is currently purchasing part MB for $13 but is considering making the part itself. The plant engineer has two alternatives: The first alternative involves fixed costs of $12,000 per period and variable costs of $9 per part, whereas the second alternative involves costs of $20,000 and $7, respectively.

**Required**

**a.** What level of volume is necessary to justify making the part?

**b.** Over what relevant ranges of volume is each alternative optimal?

**c.** At a level of output of 3,500 units, which alternative is more profitable?

**d.** How can (c) be answered without knowing what the product sells for or what other costs are?

**5-26 CVP: Alternative technologies and prediction error** (CMA adapted).

Candice Company had decided to introduce a new product. The new product can be manufactured by either a capital-intensive method or a labor-intensive method. The manufacturing method will not affect the quality of the product. If the capital-intensive method is used, the contribution margin will be $14 per unit and fixed manufacturing costs will increase by $2,440,000. If the labor-intensive method is used, the contribution margin will be $10.40 per unit and fixed manufacturing costs will increase by $1,320,000. Fixed selling expenses will increase by $500,000 regardless of which method of manufacture is chosen.

**Required**

**a.** Calculate the estimated breakeven point in annual unit sales for each method of manufacture.

**b.** Determine the annual unit sales volume at which the firm would be indifferent between the two methods.

**c.** The firm projected annual sales of 300,000 units and invested accordingly. If annual sales, in fact, turn out to be 350,000, what, if any, is the cost of the prediction error?

5-27 **CVP and planned loss.**

Last year a firm earned $50,000 on sales of $200,000. Variable costs were 60% of sales. For tax purposes, the firm wishes to lose money this year. It will hold sales volume constant and reduce the selling price of its product to 90% of last year's selling price. The firm will also make a contribution to a local charity in an amount to show a net loss of $10,000.

**Required**

How large a contribution will be necessary?

5-28 **Set-up and operating time.**

Indart is a small machine shop producing custom orders. One of the parts it makes can be produced on either of two pieces of equipment. Machine A takes 3 hours to set up and can produce 15 parts per hour. Machine B takes 5 hours to set up and can produce 20 parts per hour. Hourly set-up costs are approximately the same as hourly operating costs. Take-down time is nominal for both machines.

**Required**

**a.** At what level of output will the cost of using machine A be the same as the cost of using machine B?

**b.** Over what range of output is each machine best suited?

**c.** If machine A is already set up, how large an order will be required to justify setting up machine B?

**d.** If set-up time costs $20 per hour and operating time costs $10 per hour, what will be the effect on your answers to (a), (b), and (c)?

5-29 **CVP: Alternate modes.**

Carl's Catalina Cruises has two vessels that can be used to make identical trips. During the peak tourist season, both ships are used. However, during the off-season, daily decisions must be made as to whether to use the smaller one (*S.S. Lilliputian*) or the larger one (*S.S. Gigantuan*). The operating costs are as follows:

*S.S. Lilliputian:* $1,000 per day plus $3 per passenger per day
*S.S. Gigantuan:* $2,000 per day plus $2 per passenger per day

Ticket prices are the same on both ships. The *S.S. Gigantuan* averages an additional $1 contribution per passenger per day due to its extensive galley service. Because of Coast Guard regulations, capacity cannot be exceeded on either ship.

**Required**
How many passengers are required for net income to be the same on both vessels? Which vessel should be used if expectations are below this capacity? Why?

**5-30 Alternate processes and prediction error.**
Warrior Products had the option to buy one of two machines. Machine A had fixed costs of $10,000 per period plus $2 per unit produced. Machine B had fixed costs of $4,000 per period plus $4 per unit produced. The firm anticipated selling 4,000 units per period at $10 each, so it chose machine A. Demand, however, turned out to be 2,500 units per period.

**Required**
What is the cost of the prediction error per period?

**5-31 Alternate technologies and prediction error.**
A firm had the option to purchase one of two machines. Machine A had fixed costs of $20,000 per period and variable costs of $5 per unit produced. Machine B required fixed costs of $44,000 per period and variable costs of $3 per unit produced. The firm predicted that it could sell 14,000 units of product, so it purchased the machine that resulted in lower costs at that level of output. However, demand for the product turned out to be only 10,000 units per period.

**Required**
If the selling price per unit is $9, what was the cost of the prediction error?

**5-32 Alternative technologies and prediction error.**
Altech, Inc., has a particular part that is made outside the firm. One manufacturer charges $4,000 plus $12 per part, and another charges $7,000 plus $10 per part. Altech estimates its needs for the next month and then places the order in such a way as to minimize cost.

**Required**
**a.** Over what range of sales should each supplier be used?
**b.** Graph the relationships obtained in (a).
**c.** If Altech expected sales of 1,700 units but actually sold only 1,400 units (it called the supplier and asked to have the order held to 1,400 units), what is the cost of the prediction error?
**d.** If Altech places an order for 1,400 units and during production discovers it needs 300 more units, what is the cost of the prediction error?

**5-33 Alternative technologies, prediction error, and graphs.**
A firm can make a part one way at a cost of $3,600 plus $70 each or another at a cost of $5,400 plus $50 each. It bases its decision each week on projected demand. This week they projected that 110 units would be produced and sold when, in fact, only 80 units were produced and sold.

**Required**
**a.** What is the cost of the prediction error?
**b.** What are the fixed and variable components of the error?
**c.** Graph the alternative cost functions and show how the cost of the prediction error is obtained from the graph.

**5-34 Alternate technologies and prediction error.**

Alteco considered the acquisition of one of three presses, each of which has operating costs as follows:

1st: $10,000/period + $18/unit
2nd: $18,000/period + $13/unit
3rd: $15,000/period + $16/unit

**Required**

**a.** Over what range of volume is each of the presses most efficient? Graph these relationships.

**b.** Alteco made its decision based on a forecast of 1,500 units per period and selected the appropriate press. In fact, demand turned out to be stable at 1,800 units per period. What is the cost of the prediction error per period?

**5-35 Special order with capacity constraint.**

The A-1 Copy Shop provides copying services to the general public. Their equipment is capable of making 1,800 copies per hour. Due to set up time and time to resupply paper and toner, the practical capacity of the equipment is 7 hours per day.

Customers expect quick service. If copies cannot be made within an hour (for whatever reason), the customer will go to a competitor. Because of its excellent location, the business has a fairly steady demand of 10,000 copies per day (approximately 80% of capacity). The firm charges $0.05 a copy, and total variable costs are $0.02 per copy.

**Required**

**a.** One morning, at 8:00 A.M., a customer brings in 5,000 pages to be copied. The customer must have the copies by closing time. For this one-time order, the customer will only pay $0.04 per copy. Should the order be accepted?

**b.** What is the largest order from this customer that the shop could accept at $0.04 per copy and still break even?

**5-36 CVP: Two products.**

A firm manufactures two products, ferns and duffs. Information for the next period is expected to be as follows:

| | Ferns (5,000 units) | | Duffs (1,000 units) |
|---|---|---|---|
| Revenue from sales | $500,000 | | $200,000 |
| Variable expenses | 400,000 | | 100,000 |
| Contribution margin | $100,000 | | $100,000 |
| Fixed expenses[a] | | $100,000 | |
| Net income | | $100,000 | |

[a]All fixed expenses are common to both ferns and duffs, and no attempt is made, nor should it be made, to allocate them between the products.

Management is considering changing the product mix from 5,000 and 1,000 to 4,000 and 2,000, respectively. It plans to do this through advertising. However, there is a limit to how much should be spent.

**Required**
How much could be spent on advertising to obtain the new product mix without making the firm any worse off as a result?

**5-37 CVP: Multiple products.**
Twinc sells two products. Product A has a contribution margin of $5 per unit and a profit/volume ratio of 25%. Product B has a contribution margin of $4 per unit and a profit/volume ratio of 40%. Total fixed costs per period amount to $35,200. The income tax rate is 40%.

**Required**
**a.** What is the unit selling price for product A?
**b.** If a consumer buys either product A or product B, but not both, which product would the firm prefer to sell? Why?
**c.** If the firm sells 2 units of A for every 3 units of B, how many total units (A plus B) must be sold to break even?
**d.** With respect to the previous question, what proportion (fraction or decimal) of the total units sold at breakeven will consist of units of product A?

**5-38 Sales mix, CM%, and services.**
A large regional CPA firm has a sales mix in terms of dollars as follows:

| | Mix | CM% |
|---|---|---|
| Audit | 60% | 40% |
| Tax | 30 | 50 |
| Other | 10 | 60 |

Fixed costs are $500,000 and the partners wish to share $400,000, quarterly.

**Required**
**a.** How much must quarterly billings (revenues) be to meet the objective?
**b.** How much of the billings and contribution will be provided by each of the three areas?
**c.** The firm can change its mix of services to 50-30-20, but only if it lowers its billing rate for "Other." How low can the CM% for "Other" be without affecting the volume of billings obtained in (a)?

**5-39 Sales mix, taxes, and bonus.**
Your firm sells two products. Product A has a contribution margin of $4 and product B has a contribution margin of $7. Two A's are sold for every 3 B's. Fixed expenses are $9,000. The firm desires a net income of $1,500 after taxes of 40%. Your bonus is 20% of net income before tax and before the bonus.

**Required**
How many units of A and B must be sold to achieve the minimum objective?

**5-40 Sales mix, taxes, and bonus.**
A firm sells three products in the ratio of 3-2-6 and each contributes, respectively, $10, $25 and $30. Fixed expenses are $120,000 per year.

**Required**
**a.** How many of each product must be sold to earn $18,000 per month?
**b.** How many of each product must be sold to earn $18,000 per month after taxes of 40%?

**c.** How many of each product must be sold to earn $18,000 per month after taxes of 40% if management gets a bonus equal to 20% of net income after taxes but before the bonus?

**5-41 Multiple products: With constraints.**
Cyclops, Inc., has the capacity to produce a variety of products. These are all readily marketable at set prices provided that the quantities made available for sale do not exceed the levels detailed in the following table. The plant has a limited capacity of 110 hours per period.

| | Product | | | |
|---|---|---|---|---|
| | A | B | C | D |
| Selling price per unit | $22 | $14 | $36 | $10 |
| Variable cost per unit | $16 | $ 6 | $32 | $ 3 |
| Hours required to produce 10 units | 6 | 6 | 4 | 2 |
| Maximum number of units that can be sold at the fixed selling price | 600 | 200 | 600 | 100 |

**Required**
Determine which products should be produced and how many of each.

**5-42 Scheduling with constraints.**
Phlange, Inc., can produce four different products interchangeably on three machines. Information on these products is as follows:

| | W | X | Y | Z |
|---|---|---|---|---|
| Contribution margin per unit | $10 | $ 8 | $ 8 | $12 |
| Units produced per hour | 10 | 12 | 14 | 10 |
| Marketing requirements | | | | |
| Minimum quantity | 100 | none | 200 | 150 |
| Maximum quantity | 200 | 200 | none | 300 |

The total machine hours available are 70.

**Required**
How many units of each product should be produced?

**5-43 Multiple objectives and sales mix.**
A firm sells two products. Product A has a selling price of $20 and a contribution of $10; product B has a selling price of $25 and a contribution of $20. Management has set a target of $10,000 for sales and $6,000 for contribution margin.

**Required**
**a.** How many units of each must be sold in order to meet both objectives?
**b.** Graph the given relationships.

**5-44 Maximizing per unit of scarce resource.**
A firm can produce three products by using different combinations of direct labor, direct materials, and machine time as reflected by variable overhead.

| | A | B | C |
|---|---|---|---|
| Contribution margin ($) | 100 | 70 | 110 |
| Direct labor (hours) | 30 | 25 | 35 |
| Direct materials (units) | 25 | 10 | 20 |
| Variable overhead (hours) | 15 | 15 | 25 |

**Required**

**a.** What is the preferred order of production if direct labor is in short supply?
**b.** What is the preferred order of production if direct material is in short supply?
**c.** What is the preferred order of production if variable overhead (machine time) is in short supply?

**5-45 CVP: Product mix—difficult** (CMA).
Helene's, a high-fashion women's dress manufacturer, is planning to market a new cocktail dress for the coming season. Helene's supplies retailers in New England and the mid-Atlantic states.

Four yards of material are required to lay out the dress pattern. After cutting, some material remains that can be sold as remnants. The leftover material could also be used to manufacture a matching cape and handbag. However, if the leftover material is to be used for the cape and handbag, more care will be required in the cutting, and therefore the cutting costs will increase.

The company expects to sell 1,250 dresses if a matching cape and handbag are not available. Helene's market research reveals, however, that dress sales will be 20% higher if a matching cape and handbag are available. The market research indicates that the cape and/or handbag will not be sold individually but only as accessories with the dress. The various combinations of dresses, capes, and handbags that are expected to be sold by retailers are as follows:

| | |
|---|---|
| Complete sets of dress, cape, and handbag | 70% |
| Dress and cape | 6 |
| Dress and handbag | 15 |
| Dress only | 9 |
| Total | 100% |

The material used in the dress costs $12.50 a yard, or $50.00 for each dress. The cost of cutting the dress if the cape and handbag are not manufactured is estimated at $20.00 a dress, and the resulting remnants can be sold for $5.00 for each dress cut out. If the cape and handbag are to be manufactured, the cutting costs will be increased by $9.00 per dress. There will be no salable remnants if the capes and handbags are manufactured in the quantities estimated.

The selling prices and the costs to complete the three items once they are cut are as follows:

| | Selling Price per Unit | Unit Cost to Complete[a] |
|---|---|---|
| Dress | $200.00 | $80.00 |
| Cape | 27.50 | 19.50 |
| Handbag | 9.50 | 6.50 |

[a]Excludes cost of material and cutting operation.

**Required**

**a.** Calculate Helene's incremental (differential) profit or loss from manufacturing the capes and handbags in conjunction with the dresses.

**b.** Identify any nonquantitative factors that could influence the company's decision to manufacture the capes and handbags that match the dress.

**5-46 Add or drop a product** (SMA adapted).
The Straus Company operates a small factory in which it manufactures two products, A and B. Production and sales results for last year were as follows:

| | A | B |
|---|---|---|
| Units sold | 8,000 | 20,000 |
| Selling price per unit | $95 | $78 |
| Variable costs per unit | 50 | 45 |
| Fixed costs per unit | 22 | 22 |

For purposes of simplicity, the firm averages total fixed costs over the total number of units of A and B produced and sold.

The research department has developed a new product (C) as a replacement to product B. Market studies show that Straus Company could sell 11,000 units of C next year at a price of $120; the variable costs per unit of C are $42. The introduction of product C will lead to a 10% increase in demand for product A and discontinuation of product B. If the company does not introduce the new product, the firm expects next year's results to be the same as last year's.

**Required**

Should the Straus Company introduce product C next year? Show calculations to support your decision.

**5-47 Special order** (CMA).
George Jackson operates a small machine shop. He manufactures one standard product available from many other similar businesses, and he also manufactures custom-ordered products. His accountant prepared the following annual income statement.

| | Custom Sales | Standard Sales | Total |
|---|---|---|---|
| Sales | $50,000 | $25,000 | $75,000 |
| Costs | | | |
| Material | $10,000 | $ 8,000 | $18,000 |
| Labor | 20,000 | 9,000 | 29,000 |
| Depreciation | 6,300 | 3,600 | 9,900 |
| Power | 700 | 400 | 1,100 |
| Rent | 6,000 | 1,000 | 7,000 |
| Heat and light | 600 | 100 | 700 |
| Other | 400 | 900 | 1,300 |
| Total costs | $44,000 | $23,000 | $67,000 |
| Net income | $ 6,000 | $ 2,000 | $ 8,000 |

The depreciation charges are for machines used in the respective product lines. The power charge is apportioned on an estimate of power consumed. The rent is for the building space, which has been leased for 10 years at $7,000 per year. The rent and the heat and light are apportioned to the product lines based on the amount of floor space occupied. All other costs are current expenses identified with the product line causing them.

A valued custom-parts customer has asked Jackson if he would manufacture 5,000 special units for him. Jackson is working at capacity and would have to give up some other business in order to take this business. He cannot renege on custom orders already agreed to, but he would have to reduce the output of his standard product by about one-half for a year while producing the specially requested custom part. The customer is willing to pay $7.00 for each part. The material cost will be about $2.00 per unit and the labor will be $3.60 per unit. Jackson will have to spend $2,000 for a special device that will be discarded when the job is done.

**Required**

**a.** Calculate and present the following costs related to the 5,000-unit custom order.
  **1.** The incremental cost of the order
  **2.** The full cost of the order
  **3.** The opportunity cost of taking the order
  **4.** The sunk costs related to the order

**b.** Should Mr. Jackson take the order? Explain your answer.

**5-48 Make or buy** (CMA).

The Vernom Corporation, which produces and sells to wholesalers a highly successful line of summer lotions and insect repellents, has decided to diversify in order to stabilize sales throughout the year. A natural area for the company to consider is the production of winter lotions and creams to prevent dry and chapped skin.

After considerable research, a winter products line has been developed. However, because of the conservative nature of company management, Vernom's president has decided to introduce only one of the new products for this coming winter. If the product is a success, further expansion in future years will be initiated.

The product selected is a lip balm that will be sold in a lipstick-type tube. The product will be sold to wholesalers in boxes of 24 tubes for $8.00 per box. Because of available capacity, no additional fixed charges will be incurred to produce the product. However, a $100,000 fixed charge will be absorbed by the product to allocate a fair share of the company's present fixed costs to the new product.

Using the estimated sales and production of 100,000 boxes of lip balm as the standard volume, the accounting department has developed the following costs per box of 24 tubes.

| | |
|---|---|
| Direct labor | $2.00 |
| Direct materials | 3.00 |
| Total overhead | 1.50 |
| Total | $6.50 |

Vernom has approached a cosmetics manufacturer to discuss the possibility of purchasing the tubes for the new product. The purchase price of the empty tubes from the cosmetics manufacturer would be $0.90 per 24 tubes. If the Vernom Corporation accepts the purchase proposal, it is estimated that direct labor and variable overhead costs would be reduced by 10% and direct materials costs would be reduced by 20%.

**Required**

**a.** Should the Vernom Corporation make or buy the tubes? Show calculations to support your answer.

**b.** What would be the maximum purchase price acceptable to the Vernom Corporation for the tubes? Support your answer with an appropriate explanation.

**c.** Instead of sales of 100,000 boxes, revised estimates show sales volume at 125,000 boxes. At this new volume, additional equipment, at an annual rental of $10,000, must be acquired to manufacture the tubes. However, this incremental cost would be the only additional fixed cost required, even if sales increased to 300,000 boxes. (The 300,000 level is the goal for the third year of production.) Under these circumstances should the Vernom Corporation make or buy the tubes? Show calculations to support your answer.

**d.** The company has the option of making and buying at the same time. What would be your answer to (c) if this alternative was considered? Show calculations to support your answer.

**e.** What nonquantifiable factors should the Vernom Corporation consider in determining whether they should make or buy the lipstick tubes?

**5-49 Special order: Contribution pricing** (CMA).

E. Berg and Sons builds custom-made pleasure boats, which range in price from $10,000 to $250,000. For the past 30 years Ed Berg, Sr., has determined the selling price of each boat by estimating the costs of materials, labor, a prorated portion of overhead, and adding 20% to these estimated costs. For example, a recent price quotation was determined as follows:

| | |
|---|---|
| Direct materials | $ 5,000 |
| Direct labor | 8,000 |
| Overhead | 2,000 |
| | $15,000 |
| Plus 20% | 3,000 |
| Selling price | $18,000 |

The overhead figure was determined by estimating total overhead costs for the year and allocating them at 25% of direct labor.

If a customer rejected the price and business was slack, Ed Berg, Sr., would often be willing to reduce his markup to as little as 5% over estimated costs. Thus, average markup for the year is estimated at 15%.

Ed Berg, Jr., has just completed a course on pricing and believes the firm could use some of the techniques discussed in the course. The course emphasized the contribution margin approach to pricing and he believes that such an approach would be helpful in determining the selling prices of their custom-made pleasure boats.

Total overhead, which includes selling and administrative expenses for the year, has been estimated at $150,000, of which $90,000 is fixed and the remainder is variable in direct proportion to direct labor.

**Required**

**a.** Assume that the customer in the example rejected the $18,000 quotation and also rejected a $15,750 quotation (5% markup) during a slack period. The customer countered with a $15,000 offer.

  **1.** What is the difference in net income for the year between accepting or rejecting the customer's offer?

  **2.** What is the minimum selling price that could have been quoted without reducing or increasing net income?

**b.** What advantages does the contribution margin approach to pricing have over the approach used by Ed Berg, Sr.?

**c.** What pitfalls are there, if any, to contribution margin pricing?

**5-50 Cost of prediction error and exchange rate hedging.**
General Robotics, Inc., has received an order from an English firm to produce ten robots that will perform welding tasks on the customer's assembly line. Management of General Robotics estimates that it will take 4 months to produce and deliver the robots. The total variable costs to produce the robots will be $600,000. The selling price to the customer is £64,000. Typically, payment is made at the time of delivery.

Currently the exchange rate between the British pound and the U.S. dollar is £1 = $1.25. Management is concerned that there may be an adverse change in the exchange rate between now and 4 months from now. Three alternatives for dealing with this potential problem have been proposed:

**1.** Do nothing and hope for the best.

**2.** Offer the customer a $10,000 price reduction if the customer will pay one-half of the selling price now with the remainder due on delivery.

**3.** Buy a 4-month option that gives the firm the right to sell £640,000 for $800,000. The cost of the option would be $30,000.

**Required**

**a.** Prepare a schedule that shows the best action for every exchange rate that might occur 4 months from now (ignore any interest on the money).

**b.** Assume that the firm chose option 3 and the actual exchange rate turned out to be $1.35 to a pound. What is the cost of the prediction error?

**5-51 Cost of prediction error** (SMA adapted).
A company sets the price for its product at $300 per unit. Predicted variable costs are $175 per unit, and fixed costs are expected to be $600,000 per year. Sales for the year are expected to be 8,000 units.

The company has the capacity to produce 10,000 units per year. Expansion of capacity is not feasible at present. Assume that the beginning inventory was zero.

**Required**

**a.** Determine the cost of the prediction error if actual variable costs were $190 per unit. All other predictions were correct.

**b.** Assume that all predictions were correct, except that 11,000 units could have been sold at the $300 price if enough had been available. However, only 8,000 units were produced, and consequently sales were limited to 8,000 units. Determine the cost of the prediction error.

**5-52 Pricing options and prediction error.**

Sigma Rho Omega is planning its major Spring Dance. The dance is the group's primary source of funds for its other social activities. The band that the group wants has offered three alternative means of being compensated: (1) \$6 per person who attends, (2) \$1,500 plus \$2 per person who attends, or (3) a flat fee of \$3,500. Tickets for the dance will be sold for \$8 per person.

**Required**

**a.** If the group opts for paying \$1,500 plus \$2 per head to the band, how many tickets must be sold to break even?

**b.** If the group opts for paying \$1,500 plus \$2 per head to the band, how many tickets must be sold to earn a profit of \$3,000 from the dance?

**c.** Determine the range for the number of tickets sold such that (1) payment option 1 is the best for the group, (2) option 2 is the best, and finally (3) the range for which option 3 is the best.

**d.** The group predicted that 800 tickets would be sold and acted accordingly. In fact, the dance was a huge success and 1,200 tickets were sold. Determine the cost of the prediction error.

**5-53 CVP, alternative technologies, and uncertainty, comprehensive—requires prior study of Appendix 3A.**

Sede, Inc., has two alternative means of manufacturing its product. Process 1 has fixed costs of \$20,000 per period and a variable cost of \$6 per unit produced. Process 2 requires fixed costs of \$45,000 per period plus a variable cost of \$4 per unit produced. The product sells for \$8 per unit. The firm has forecast sales to be as follows:

$$\text{sales} = 8{,}000 \text{ units per period} + 0.0002 \times \text{disposable income}$$

The equation was determined by fitting a regression line to 25 pairs of data relating sales to the disposable income of residents in various marketing areas. The standard error of the estimate is 700 units. The firm estimates that the disposable income of residents in a new marketing area is \$25,000,000.

**Required**

**a.** If the firm uses process 2 in this new area, what is the probability of losing money?

**b.** What is the range of sales the firm can expect in the new area with confidence of 90%?

**c.** What is the probability that sales in this area will exceed 14,964 units per period?

**d.** At what level of sales will the firm be indifferent between the two alternative processes for manufacturing the product?

**e.** If the firm predicts sales to be 15,000 units and therefore chooses to use process 2, what is the cost of the prediction error if demand turns out to be 11,000 units?

**5-54 CVP, uncertainty, and prediction error—requires prior study of Appendix 3A.**

Lyceum General operates a fine arts theater in a medium-sized college town. The firm specializes in films that are unlikely ever to appear on prime-time network television. Admission price is \$5 per ticket. Film rental terms in this industry are not firmly established. The distributor is willing to lease films to the theater on one of two options. The first option calls for a payment of $100 plus $2 per person who attends the showing. Alternatively, the distributor will lease a film for $1,060 plus $0.80 per viewer.

The theater owner has estimated a demand function for viewership based on the number of students enrolled in accounting courses at the local college. The regression equation, based on 15 observations, is

$$\text{number of viewers} = 50 + 0.6 \times \text{number of accounting enrollees}$$

The equation has a standard error of the estimate of 42, and its $R^2$ is 0.85. During the current term there are 1,100 students enrolled in accounting courses.

**Required**

**a.** Which lease option should the theater owner choose?

**b.** If demand turns out to be 750 viewers, what is the cost of the prediction error?

**c.** Estimate the probability that the firm will make a prediction error.

**5-55 Relevant costs for production expansion.**

The Waterloo Manufacturing Company rents its manufacturing facility at a cost of $6 per square foot per month. The firm has a 5-year lease on a 100,000-square-foot building. Currently, the space in the building is fully utilized and there is no economic means for expansion.

The product manager for one of the firm's products, the EZ Use Wrench, wants to expand production. To do so will require the firm to subcontract the production of its Thumb Thumper Hammer to another manufacturer at a cost of $4 per hammer. The hammers sell for $5 each.

The manager has prepared the following analysis of costs for the hammers.

| | |
|---|---|
| Variable costs | $420,000 |
| Supervisors' salaries (3 people) | 90,000 |
| Rent | 300,000 |
| Total annual costs | $810,000 |

The manager added, "This analysis is for our normal production of 200,000 hammers, implying an average cost of $4.05 each. This is more than the subcontractor will charge. In addition, the supervisors would be dismissed if production were subcontracted." Production of the hammers uses 5,000 square feet of manufacturing space.

If the production of wrenches is expanded, the manager noted that the following costs would be incurred.

| | |
|---|---|
| Variable costs | $200,000 |
| Supervisor's salary (1 person) | 30,000 |
| Rent | 240,000 |
| Total | $470,000 |

These costs are for the production of an additional 100,000 wrenches that sell for $5.00 each. Expanding production requires hiring the additional supervisor indicated in the costs. The expanded operation would require only 4,000 square feet of space. The additional 1,000 square feet of space would remain idle. The manager points out that the firm will save $0.05 per unit on the hammers and earn $0.30 per unit on the wrenches by making the change.

**Required**
Should the firm expand the production of wrenches?

**5-56 Expansion and marginal cost analysis.**
State University's summer-session classes are self-supporting; that is, the legislature does not appropriate any funds to help support these classes. Consequently, only classes that will generate large enrollments (and tuition fees) are offered during the summer.

During the past several years the university has offered 60 summer-session classes. The university has used an arbitrary rule that only classes with an initial enrollment of 40 students would be held. Last year's budget is reproduced below.

**19X7 Summer Session Budget[a]**

| | |
|---|---|
| Tuition revenue[b] | $264,600 |
| Instructional salaries[c] | $168,000 |
| Salaries—registrar | 20,800 |
| Salaries—computer center | 2,000 |
| Supplies | 5,000 |
| Building maintenance[d] | 50,000 |
| Total costs | $245,800 |
| Addition to the general fund | $ 18,800 |

[a]All revenues and costs are incremental costs incurred solely due to the offering of summer classes.

[b]Sixty classes averaging 42 students per class.

[c]Sixty instructors at $2,800.

[d]Includes additional janitors, repairs, air conditioning, and so forth required to keep the two classroom buildings open during the summer.

Prior to the current summer session, a member of the English department, noting last year's surplus, made a study of costs. The professor discovered that all administrative salaries were covered by annual appropriations and did not come out of the summer budget. To save money, all summer classes were housed in two buildings. There are sufficient classrooms to offer 85 classes. The cost of supplies per student is minimal and is estimated as $2 per student. The cost of operating the computer center was mostly the cost of having someone keep the center open from 10:00 A.M. to 3:00 P.M. The registrar's office has to add one part-time employee for every 100 students enrolled. Last year's enrollment of 2,520 students required 26 employees. These employees could handle an additional 80 students. The part-time employees earn $800 for the summer session. Each class offered carries 3 credit hours and the tuition is $35 per credit hour. Finally, the average English instructor earns $2,100 per summer-session class taught.

Based on this analysis, the professor calculated the following breakeven point for the number of students needed to justify offering a course.

Tuition per student (net of supplies cost): $35 × 3 − $2 = $103
Incremental cost to offer a course: $2,100
Enrollment needed: $2,100/$103 = 21

The instructor went to the administration and argued that the university could offer more classes and still break even if the minimum class size was reduced to 21 for the English department.

Based on this analysis, the English department was allowed to offer any course enrolling 21 or more students. Upon hearing of this, the philosophy department noted that the only difference between philosophy and English was the cost of the instructional salaries. The philosophy department's average summer-session salary is $2,000, yielding a breakeven point at 20 students. Next, the engineering department did the same calculations on the basis of an average salary of $3,200, resulting in a breakeven at 32 students. In each case the administration acquiesced to the new lower limits in class size required to offer a course.

The change had a dramatic effect on course offerings. During the summer 90 classes were held. There were, of course, some difficulties encountered due to the large increase. It was necessary to increase the hours that the computer center was open from 5 hours to 8 hours per day. In addition, a third classroom building was used.

When the summer session ended, the administration prepared a summary of the session's financial results (provided below). Needless to say, the administration was quite disappointed.

**19X8 Summer Session Budget**

| | |
|---|---|
| Tuition revenue[a] | $340,200 |
| Instructional salaries[b] | $243,000 |
| Salaries—registrar | 26,400 |
| Salaries—computer center | 3,200 |
| Supplies | 6,500 |
| Building maintenance | 74,000 |
| Total costs | $353,100 |
| Deficit | $ 12,900 |

[a]Ninety classes averaging 36 students per class.
[b]Ninety instructors averaging $2,700.

**Required**
Analyze the 19X8 results. What went wrong? Was the English professor's marginal analysis of costs incorrect?

**5-57 Foreign versus domestic production and comparative advantage.**
Scott Mills was originally a producer of fabrics, but several years ago intense foreign competition led management to restructure the firm as a vertically integrated cotton garment manufacturer. They purchased spinning firms that produce raw yarn and fabricators that produce the final garment. The firm has both domestic and international operations.

The domestic spinning and knitting operations are highly automated, using the latest technology. The domestic operations are able to produce cotton fabric for $0.76 per pound. The domestic fabricating operations are located exclusively in rural areas. This keeps total average labor costs to $8.20 per hour (including fringe benefits). The cost to ship products to the firm's distribution center are $0.05 per pound.

The firm's foreign subsidiary is a fabricating operation located in the Maldives (a group of islands near India). The average wage rate there is \$0.35 per hour. The subsidiary purchases cotton fabric locally for \$0.80 per pound. The finished products are shipped to Scott Mills' distribution center in New Orleans at a cost of \$1,800 per ton. Both the domestic and foreign subsidiary use the same amount of fabric per product.

Scott Mills has been producing three products for the private label market: sweatshirts, dress shirts, and lightweight jackets. In the past the firm processed a new order at whichever fabricating plant had the next available capacity. However, projections for the next few years indicate that orders will far exceed capacity. Management wants each plant to specialize in one of the products.

The plants are constrained by the amount of sewing time available in each. The domestic plant has 8,000 hours of sewing machine time available per week, while the foreign subsidiary has 10,000 hours available per week. The domestic plant's variable overhead is charged to products at \$2 per machine hour, while the subsidiary's variable overhead averages \$0.50 per machine hour.

The sweatshirts require one pound of cotton fabric to produce, the dress shirts use four ounces of fabric, and the jackets require one pound of fabric. The domestic plant has special-purpose equipment that allows workers to sew a sweatshirt in 6 minutes, a shirt in 15 minutes, and a jacket in 1 hour. The foreign plant's equipment constrains production to 5 sweatshirts per hour, 3 dress shirts per hour, or 2 jackets per hour. The wholesale prices are \$4.38 each for the sweatshirts, \$3.75 for the dress shirts, and \$18.50 for the jackets.

**Required**

**a.** Due to the tremendous difference in wage rates, should the firm close its domestic operations and expand the foreign subsidiary?

**b.** If demand for each product exceeds capacity, in which product should each plant specialize?

**c.** Management insists on making all three products in order to maintain their good customer relations. If demand for each product exceeds capacity, each plant would prefer to specialize according to your answer to part (b). At which plant should management produce the third product?

# APPENDIX 5A

# LINEAR PROGRAMMING

This appendix discusses a linear-programming approach to maximizing income. A **linear-programming** problem involves finding the optimal value of a linear objective function subject to linear constraints. If you are already familiar with linear programming, you need only skim the text and concentrate on the demonstration problem at the end of the appendix, which gives detailed guidance on the proper interpretation of a linear-programming solution. If you are not familiar with linear programming you should study the text carefully before proceeding to the demonstration problem.

## OUTPUT CONSTRAINTS

If management wants to maximize income, our previous formulation of the CVP equation would suggest that management maximize sales. But if there is no upper limit to sales, it would seem that management could make an infinite amount of income through infinite sales (see Figure 5-3). We rarely see firms making an infinite income, so apparently as a maximization problem, something is missing from the CVP equation. What is missing, of course, is some limit (constraint) to production or sales.

For most firms the constraining factor limiting the level of operations is the maximum number of units that customers will buy at a given price. Less frequently there are firms for which the available production facilities may limit the maximum number of units that can be produced. If we add a production or sales constraint to the CVP equation and include the objective of maximizing net income, we can convert the CVP analysis to an optimization technique.

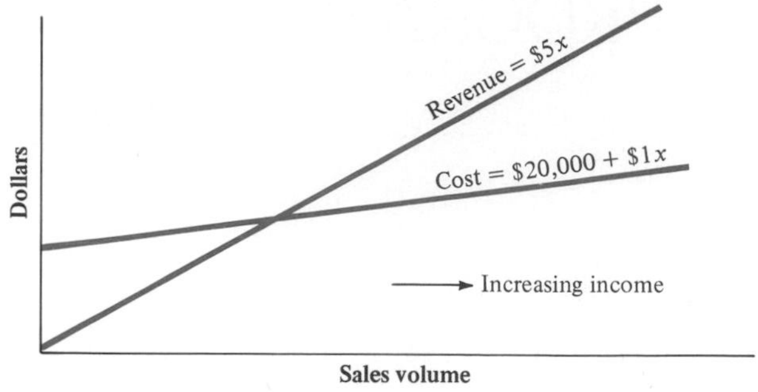


**FIGURE 5-3 Simple cost-volume-profit graph.** Although the CVP graph illustrates the effect of volume on profit, it says nothing about maximizing profit.

### The Single-Product, Single-Constraint Case

Assume that a firm manufactures a single product, which we will call product 1. The product is sold for $5 per unit, variable costs are $1 per unit, and fixed costs are $20,000 per period. Assume further that each unit requires 2 hours of machine time to construct and that the firm has a maximum of 14,000 hours of machine time available. What is the maximum income this firm can earn? We can formulate the problem as

$$\text{maximize: } 5x_1 - 1x_1 - 20{,}000 = NI$$
$$\text{subject to: } 2x_1 \leq 14{,}000 \text{ hours}$$

where $x_1$ is the number of units of product 1.

The first equation is just the CVP equation, with the indication that our objective is to maximize income. In optimization problems it is referred to as the **objective function.** The second item, the inequality, represents the **constraint** due to the limited number of machine hours that are available. Each unit of product 1 that we manufacture will use 2 hours of machine time, and the total number of machine hours used must be less than 14,000. This problem is depicted graphically in Figure 5-4. Note that with one variable and one constraint the solution to the problem is straightforward. The largest income is earned when we produce 7,000 units. That is, the machine-hours constraint limits our production to 7,000 units, but income increases steadily as we increase production, so we produce as many units as possible.

In Figure 5-5 we have redrawn the problem to indicate that maximizing the firm's contribution margin $\$5x_1 - \$1x_1 = \$4x_1$ will yield exactly

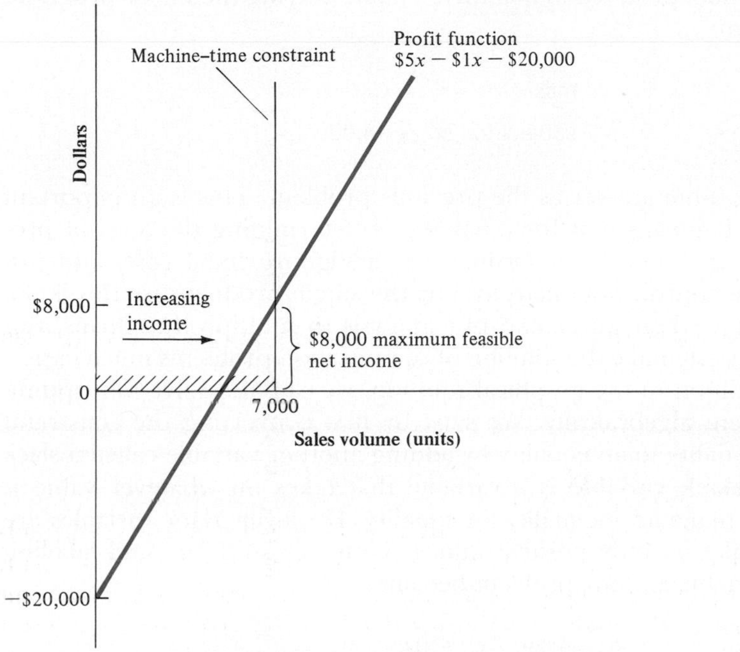


**FIGURE 5-4 Profit graph with production constraint.** The shaded portion of the volume axis represents feasible production.

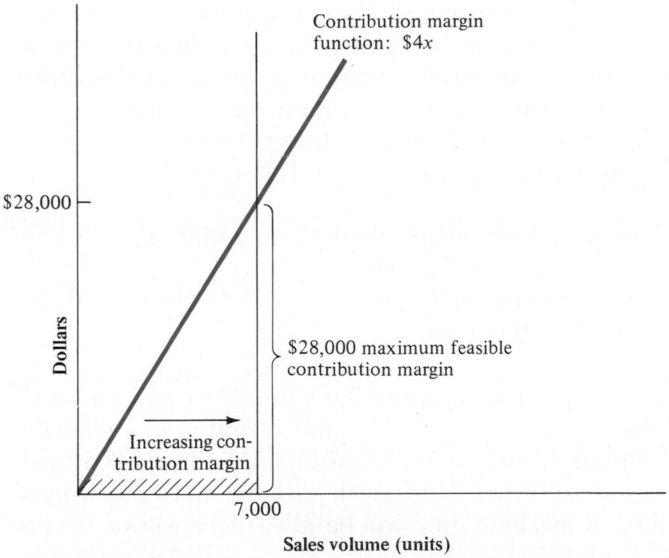


**FIGURE 5-5 Maximum contribution margin with single constraint.** The shaded portion of the volume axis represents feasible production.

the same optimal production quantity. That is, solving the linear-programming problem

$$\text{maximize: } 4x_1 = CM$$
$$\text{subject to: } 2x_1 \leq 14{,}000$$

will yield the same answer as the previous problem. This is an important observation. It means that for purposes of determining the level of production that maximizes net income we can ignore fixed costs and just maximize the contribution margin. For the single-product case this is not important, but when we extend our analysis to multiproduct firms, this simplification will make the solution of optimization problems much easier.

In addition to the graphical solution, we can also solve our optimization problem algebraically. We start by first converting the constraint from an inequality to an equality by adding another variable called a slack variable. A **slack variable** is a variable that takes on whatever value is necessary to make an inequality an equality. However, slack variables are allowed to take on only positive values. With this addition, and labeling our slack variable $x_{s1}$, our problem becomes[1]

$$\text{maximize: } 4x_1 + 0x_{s1}$$
$$\text{subject to: } 2x_1 + x_{s1} = 14{,}000$$

We now determine the possible solutions to the constraints that result when each variable takes on its highest permissible value. We then pick the solution that yields the highest contribution margin as our **optimal solution.** Note that we have one equation and two unknowns, so there are two possible solutions. The solutions and the resulting values of the objective function (amount of contribution margin) are as follows:

**a.** If we let $x_1$ take its maximum value, then $x_1 = 7{,}000$, $x_{s1} = 0$, and $CM = \$4 \times 7{,}000 + \$0 \times 0 = \$28{,}000$.
**b.** If we let $x_{s1}$ take its maximum value, then $x_{s1} = 14{,}000$, $x_1 = 0$, and $CM = \$4 \times 0 + \$0 \times 7{,}000 = \$0$.

The first solution tells us that if we produce 7,000 units, we will use all the machine time available, leaving no slack time and resulting in a contribution margin of $28,000 (or income of $8,000 after subtracting fixed costs). The second solution indicates that if the slack variable takes on its maximum value of 14,000, all machine time will be idle, there will be no pro-

[1]Note that having slack resources available contributes nothing to profitability, so the contribution margin coefficient on $x_{s1}$ in the objective function is zero.

duction, and we will earn a contribution margin of zero (or income of minus \$20,000 after deducting fixed costs). Solution (a) gives us the highest contribution margin, so it is the optimal solution.

One of the benefits of using linear programming is that we can also determine the marginal value of having resources available. This marginal value is called the **shadow price,** or **dual price,** of a resource. In our example, we can determine the value to the firm of having an additional hour of machine time available. If we had 14,001 hours of machine time available, we could produce 7,000.5 units of product and earn \$8,002 (we could complete the unit in the next period and sell it to yield a \$4 contribution margin, but we were still able to produce half a unit more this period than previously, and so we recognize that we are \$2 better off). In this case the shadow price for machine time indicates that we would be willing to pay up to \$2 to acquire another hour of machine time.

### The Single-Product, Two-Constraint Case

Let us now complicate the example by adding a second constraint. Assume that two machines are needed to build the product. In addition to the processing on the previous machine, each unit of product also requires $\frac{1}{2}$ hour on machine 2. There are 4,000 hours of machine-2 time available per period. The problem now becomes

$$\begin{aligned} \text{maximize: } & 4x_1 + 0x_{s1} + 0x_{s2} \\ \text{subject to: } & 2x_1 + x_{s1} = 14{,}000 \quad \text{(machine 1)} \\ & \tfrac{1}{2}x_1 + x_{s2} = 4{,}000 \quad \text{(machine 2)} \end{aligned}$$

where $x_{s2}$ is the slack variable needed for the second machine to produce equality. We can graph this problem as in Figure 5-6. Note that only one constraint, the first, is binding. A **binding constraint** is one that actually limits our production. Looking only at the second constraint, it would limit production to 8,000 units (4,000 ÷ $\frac{1}{2}$), but production was already limited to 7,000 units by the first constraint, so the second constraint will not be active. If we calculate the shadow price of time on machine 2, we get a value of zero. That is, with 4,000 hours of time available on machine 2 we can produce 7,000 units; however, with 4,001 hours available we could still only produce 7,000 units. There is no change in production and no change in total income, and therefore there is no marginal value to having another unit of machine-2 time available.

Note, however, that the shadow price of machine 1's time is still \$2. If we add another hour of machine-1 time, we will increase earnings by \$2. However, this will not hold indefinitely because as we increase the amount of machine-1 time available beyond 16,000 hours (allowing the

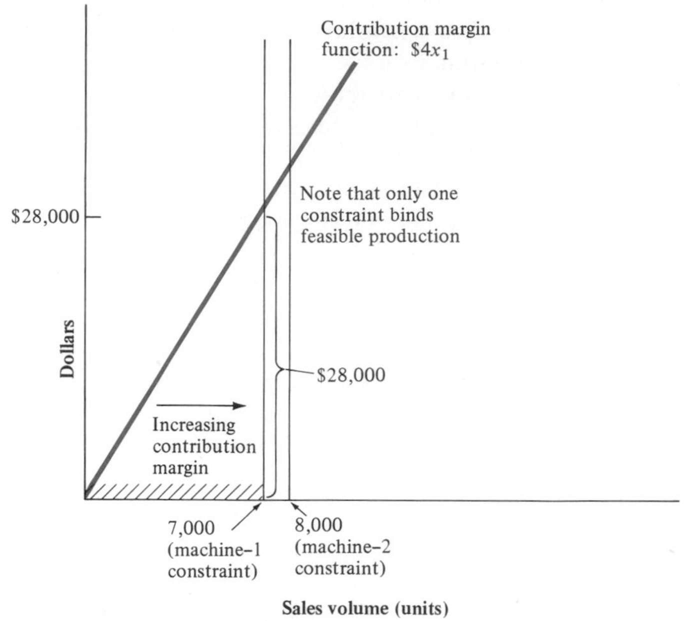


**FIGURE 5-6 Maximum contribution margin with two constraints.** The shaded portion of the volume axis represents feasible production.

production of 8,000 units), the second constraint becomes binding. So for increases beyond 16,000 hours the shadow price of machine 1 becomes zero. If for some reason we had more than 16,000 hours of machine 1 available, then the shadow price of machine-2 time would be \$8. That is, for each hour of machine-2 time made available we could now produce 2 units of product, each earning a contribution margin of \$4. Again, the shadow price of machine-2 time, however, would be accurate only for increases up to the point at which the revised machine-1 constraint becomes binding. Thus a general rule can be observed. A constraint will have a positive shadow price only so long as the constraint is a binding constraint. The shadow price for a nonbinding constraint is zero.

The algebraic solution to our one-product, two-constraint problem would proceed as follows:

**a.** If $x_1$ takes its highest possible value, then $x_1 = 7{,}000$, $x_{s1} = 0$, $x_{s2} = 500$, and $CM = \$28{,}000$.
**b.** If $x_{s1}$ takes its highest possible value, then $x_1 = 0$, $x_{s1} = 14{,}000$, $x_{s2} = 4{,}000$, and $CM = \$0$.
**c.** If $x_{s2}$ takes its highest possible value, then $x_1 = 0$, $x_{s1} = 14{,}000$, $x_{s2} = 4{,}000$, and $CM = \$0$.

We note that the solutions that allow for the highest value of $x_{s1}$ and $x_{s2}$ are exactly the same, but we include both for completeness. Again, the algebraic solution indicates that the optimal production is 7,000 units of $x_1$, and produces a contribution margin of \$28,000.

### Two Products and Two Constraints

Let us now add a second product. Assume that product 2 sells for \$8 per unit and requires variable costs of \$3 per unit. The firm's fixed costs remain at \$20,000. Our objective function now becomes to maximize $\$4x_1 + \$5x_2$. Let us also assume that product 2 requires machine time on both machines 1 and 2. Each unit of product 2 requires 1 hour of time on machine 1 and $\frac{2}{3}$ hour on machine 2. Adding slack variables, our entire problem becomes:

$$\begin{aligned} \text{maximize: } & 4x_1 + 5x_2 + 0x_{s1} + 0x_{s2} \\ \text{subject to: } & 2x_1 + 1x_2 + x_{s1} = 14{,}000 \quad \text{(machine 1)} \\ & \tfrac{1}{2}x_1 + \tfrac{2}{3}x_2 + x_{s2} = 4{,}000 \quad \text{(machine 2)} \end{aligned}$$

We can depict this problem graphically as in Figure 5-7. Now we have had to use both axes of the graph in order to represent units of sales for each product. The constraints are represented by the line segments that indicate the maximum *combination* of products allowable by each constraint separately. For example, constraint 1 allows for the production of 7,000 units of product 1 and no product 2, or 14,000 units of product 2 and no units of product 1, or 6,000 units of product 1 and 2,000 units of product 2, and so forth. The line in the graph representing the constraint joins all these possibilities. The shaded area in Figure 5-7 represents the production possibilities that meet both constraints.

To solve the problem graphically we superimpose lines representing the combinations of the level of production of units of products 1 and 2 that yield an equal amount of contribution margin. For example, producing 5,000 units of product 1 and no units of product 2 provides \$20,000 in contribution margin, as does producing no product 1 and 4,000 units of product 2 or 2,500 units of product 1 and 2,000 units of product 2. These combinations are joined by a dashed line in Figure 5-7. The choice of \$20,000 as the total contribution margin is arbitrary; all we are doing at this point is determining the slope of the equal contribution margin (objective function) lines. Having drawn this line we can note that equal contribution margin lines are parallel to each other, with higher contribution margins represented by lines farther from the origin. The maximum solution is determined by finding the highest contribution margin line that is just tangent to a point still in the area of feasible production

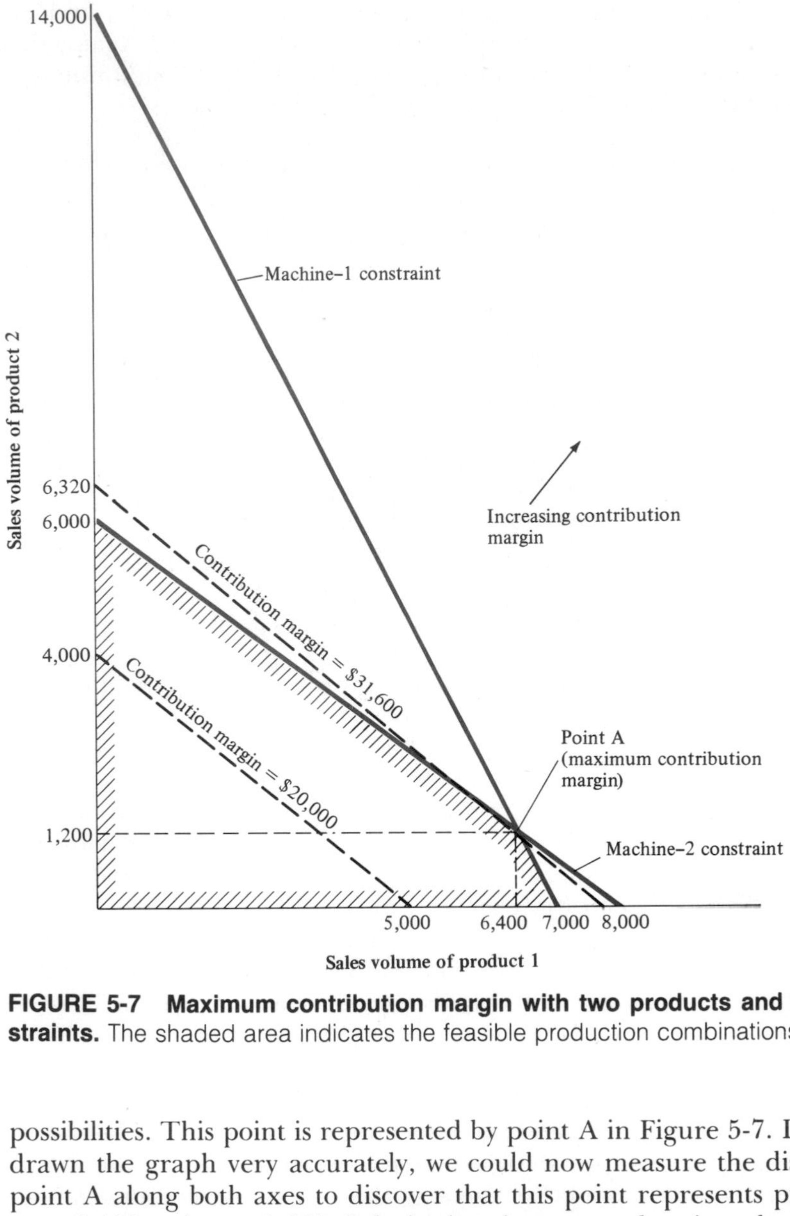


**FIGURE 5-7 Maximum contribution margin with two products and two constraints.** The shaded area indicates the feasible production combinations.

possibilities. This point is represented by point A in Figure 5-7. If we had drawn the graph very accurately, we could now measure the distance of point A along both axes to discover that this point represents producing $x_1$ = 6,400 and $x_2$ = 1,200. Substituting these two values into the objective function, we would see that the firm would earn a contribution margin of $31,600 at this level of production. However, we could also solve the problem algebraically.

As before, we can algebraically solve the system of equations for the highest permissible values for each variable. But now we have two equations and four unknowns. To solve the two-constraint problem, we must simultaneously solve the constraint equations for every *pair* of variables and choose the solution with the highest contribution margin. Exhibit 5-7 shows the necessary computations. Solutions 2 and 5 in Exhibit 5-7 result in negative slack variables. A negative slack variable means we are using more hours of machine time than we have available; in other words, we are violating the associated machine-hour constraint. Therefore these solutions are discarded as infeasible. From the remaining feasible solutions, we see that solution 1 has the highest contribution margin. Once again, the optimal solution is to produce 6,400 units of product 1 and 1,200 units of product 2. This solution results in a contribution margin of $31,600 or, after subtracting fixed costs, a net income of $11,600.

**EXHIBIT 5-7 Calculations for Two-Product, Two-Constraint Linear-Programming Problem**

| Pair of Variables Taking on Maximum Value and the Problem to Solve | Solution | Resulting Contribution Margin |
|---|---|---|
| 1. For $x_1$ and $x_2$, | | |
| $2x_1 + 1x_2 = 14{,}000$ | $x_1 = 6{,}400$ | $CM - \$4 \times 6{,}400 + \$5 \times 1{,}200$ |
| $\frac{1}{2}x_1 + \frac{2}{3}x_2 = 4{,}000$ | $x_2 = 1{,}200$ | $= \$31{,}600$ |
| 2. For $x_1$ and $x_{s1}$, | | |
| $2x_1 + x_{s1} = 14{,}000$ | $x_1 = 8{,}000$ | Not a feasible solution[a] |
| $\frac{1}{2}x_1 = 4{,}000$ | $x_{s1} = -2{,}000$ | |
| 3. For $x_1$ and $x_{s2}$, | | |
| $2x_1 = 14{,}000$ | $x_1 = 7{,}000$ | $CM = \$4 \times 7{,}000 + \$0 \times 500$ |
| $\frac{1}{2}x_1 + x_{s2} = 4{,}000$ | $x_{s2} = 500$ | $= \$28{,}000$ |
| 4. For $x_2$ and $x_{s1}$, | | |
| $1x_2 + x_{s1} = 14{,}000$ | $x_2 = 6{,}000$ | $CM = \$5 \times 6{,}000 + \$0 \times 8{,}000$ |
| $\frac{2}{3}x_2 = 4{,}000$ | $x_{s1} = 8{,}000$ | $= \$30{,}000$ |
| 5. For $x_2$ and $x_{s2}$, | | |
| $1x_2 = 14{,}000$ | $x_2 = 14{,}000$ | Not a feasible solution[a] |
| $\frac{2}{3}x_2 + x_{s2} = 4{,}000$ | $x_{s2} = -5{,}333.33$ | |
| 6. For $x_{s1}$ and $x_{s2}$, | | |
| $x_{s1} = 14{,}000$ | $x_{s1} = 14{,}000$ | $CM = \$0 \times 14{,}000 + \$0 \times 4{,}000$[a] |
| $x_{s2} = 4{,}000$ | $x_{s2} = 4{,}000$ | $= \$0$ |

[a]If we had already graphed the solution as in Figure 5-8, we know that these points would not be serious candidates for the optimal solution and we could have avoided these calculations. Without the graph, however, it is necessary to check all possible combinations of variables.

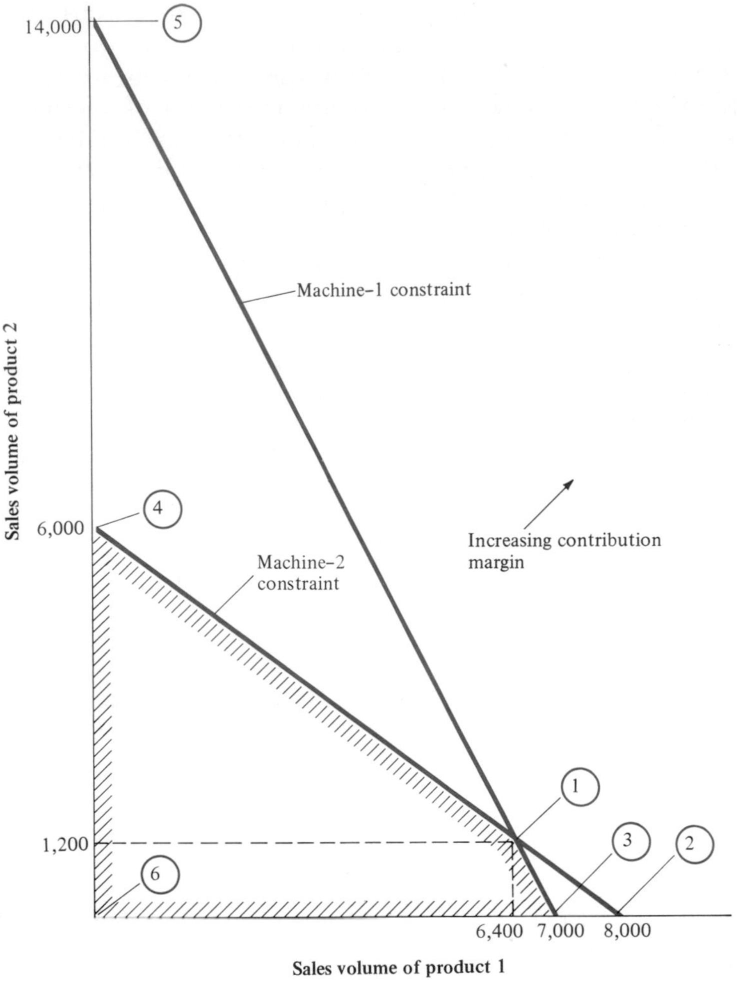


**FIGURE 5-8 The points corresponding to the calculations in Exhibit 5-7.** The shaded area indicates the feasible production combinations.

We could now solve the problem again, first with 14,001 hours of machine-1 time available and then with 4,001 hours of machine-2 time available, to get the shadow prices of the two resources. Those solutions, not reproduced here, result in a shadow price of $0.20 for machine 1 and $7.20 for machine 2. Thus if someone offered to rent us machine time on equivalent machines for $3 per hour, we would not want to rent the equivalent of machine 1, because we would only earn an additional $0.20 (which is less than the additional cost, or rent, of $3). Conversely, we should rent machine-2 time since we would earn \$7.20, which is more than the rental charge.

The approaches we have taken are completely generalizable to any number of products and any number of constraints. However, as a practical matter, graphical solutions cannot be used for more than two products since graphs of three or more dimensions are quite tricky to draw. Similarly, the algebraic method we used gets impractical as either the number of products or the number of constraints increases. For example, with three products and three constraints, the approach we used would require us to solve all possible sets of three equations and six unknowns. Fortunately, there is available an easier algebraic technique, called the simplex method. Unfortunately, although the simplex method is easier, it is still very laborious; even with the simplex method the solution of a problem of a realistic size by hand is impractical. With the use of computers, practical-sized linear-programming problems can be solved relatively quickly. Although the particular solution format will vary depending on the program used, Exhibit 5-8 presents an annotated example of a typical solution format for our two-product, two-constraint problem. A solution with even more information is illustrated in the demonstration problem following this appendix.

**EXHIBIT 5-8 Annotated Computer Solution to a Linear-Programming Problem**

| | |
|---|---|
| VALUE OF OBJECTIVE<br>FUNCTION: 31,600 | The total contribution margin earned by the optimal solution. |
| SOLUTION VARIABLES<br>x1 = 6,400<br>x2 = 1,200<br>s1 = 0<br>s2 = 0 | These figures give the number of units of each product that should be made and the number of units of excess resources (if any) available for each constraint. |
| SHADOW PRICES<br>x1 = 0<br>x2 = 0<br>s1 = 0.2<br>s2 = 7.2 | The shadow prices for slack variables give the marginal value of having an additional unit of the associated resource available. If a product variable has a shadow price, the shadow price indicates the marginal amount of contribution margin the firm will lose if the product is manufactured (only products not included in the optimal solution will have shadow prices). |
| RESOURCE RANGE<br>s1: 6,000 to 16,000<br>s2: 3,500 to 9,333 | These are the ranges of the amount of resources available (the amount of a constraint) over which the shadow prices are relevant. These ranges are valid only when each resource is considered singly (not when simultaneous changes are made in more than one constraint). |

## THE ACCOUNTANT'S ROLE IN LINEAR PROGRAMMING

We have discussed linear programming only in the context of maximizing income subject to capacity constraints. Linear-programming techniques also have many applications in areas in which a firm wishes to accomplish a task at minimum cost—for example, how to assign auditors to a variety of clients in a particular time period or to determine the optimal geographic location for a firm's distribution facilities. Although these other applications are also important and accountants are likely to get involved in supplying data for them, we believe that all of the important concepts with which accountants must be familiar have been raised in our application of linear programming to short-run profit maximization.

In most applications the accountant will not be responsible for actually setting up and solving a linear-programming problem (the audit staff assignment problem being an obvious exception). Rather, the accountant's role will usually be limited to providing relevant data to the engineer assigned to solve the problem, and interpreting the solution to a linear-programming problem in order to incorporate its implications into our plans.

### Data Requirements

Broadly, three types of information are required to solve a linear-programming problem:

1. Product contribution margins for the objective function
2. The technical coefficients (e.g., the amount of machine time it takes to produce a particular product)
3. The amount of resources available for each constraining resource (the total amount of machine time available in our example problem)

This last item will generally be estimated by an engineer, but accountants will get involved in the determination of the first two items.

The determination of the unit contribution margins requires the same type of information that we needed for cost-volume-profit analysis. We must estimate expected selling prices for each product and the total variable costs for each product. Accountants are generally in a better position than engineers to sort out the irrelevant costs such as unitized fixed costs that will not change with volume. Also, accountants should be more aware of the shortcomings of historical cost records as predictors of future costs. In any planning model we want to predict relevant future costs and revenues. Certain accounting techniques, such as FIFO inventory costing, will often make historical records poor predictors of future costs. Accountants are presumably more likely to know when readily available records should be ignored in the search for estimates of relevant future costs.

In Chapter 3 we developed procedures for estimating the standard quantities of materials and labor required per unit of product. We can use these same procedures for developing the technical coefficients for a linear-programming problem.

### Interpreting an LP Solution

The solution to a linear-programming problem will provide considerable information that will be useful in preparing budgets. Once production quantities have been determined, predictions can be developed for the amounts of labor, materials, and other resources required during the period. In addition, shadow prices for each of the constraining resources will allow us to decide whether additional units of resources should be acquired at prevailing market rates. Finally, the more sophisticated LP solutions will provide us with information that will allow us to determine the sensitivity of the solution to errors in the estimates of the contribution margins. Each of these points is discussed more thoroughly in the demonstration problem at the end of this appendix.

## LIMITATIONS OF LINEAR PROGRAMMING

The limitations of linear programming are very similar to those of CVP analysis. Linear programming is a short-run planning tool. The selling prices and costs incorporated in the analysis are not likely to stay static for any lengthy period of time. Further, the firm's manufacturing technology and available manufacturing resources are subject to change. As in CVP analysis, this may result in changing product contribution margins. But further, unlike CVP analysis, linear programming requires estimates of resource constraints for each period of time. Changing technology, more productive equipment, and equipment with less downtime can also change these resource constraints.

Linear programming also assumes that our basic cost and revenue functions are linear with production. As with CVP analysis, this assumption may be met in the firm's relevant range, but we must be careful of any plans outside that range. Linear programming does provide us extra information such as shadow prices, but we must be careful to realize that these figures are meaningful only when we speak of altering one resource.

In spite of its limitations, linear programming is a powerful and useful technique for short-term planning purposes. Although linear programming is not used as widely in practice as cost-volume-profit analysis, it is used extensively by many large firms. Again, as computers become cheaper and more widely available, we anticipate that LP applications will become even more common.

## DEMONSTRATION PROBLEM: LINEAR PROGRAMMING

Now that we have covered the objectives and terminology for linear programming, let us examine an illustration that reflects the type of data that accountants must supply to solve a typical LP problem. We will then examine the solution to the problem to illustrate the kinds of valuable information such a solution can supply.

Consider Irvine, Inc., a firm that sells four products (referred to simply as products A, B, C, and D). Let us assume that the firm faces a short-run constraint on work-in-process storage (the products must age for a time), a constraint on the amount of a critical material that will be available, and also constraints on the amount of machine time that can be used on each of two machines required to produce the products. Our first problem then is to estimate the capacity limits of each constraining resource and the amount of each resource that each product requires per unit of output.

For the storage constraint we can simply measure the volume of space we have available multiplied by the number of days in our planning period to provide the cubic foot days (cfd) of space available. However, we must remember to allow space for handling the products (putting them into and taking them out of storage). For the material constraint we can simply ask our supplier to estimate how much of the material will be made available during our planning period. Machine time most likely will be measured in terms of the number of hours of processing time available on each type of machine. This will depend, of course, on how many shifts we intend to operate and whether we will work overtime and on weekends. In making these estimates we must take care to remember to allow time for routine maintenance and machine set-up time.

The procedure for estimating the amount of each resource required by each product will be very similar to estimating the standard amounts of materials and labor required for each product (discussed in Chapter 3). In general, our knowledge of the product should allow us to measure fairly accurately the number of cubic foot days (cfd) of storage each product requires as well as the amount of the critical material and processing time needed on each of the machines.

Let us assume that we have determined that we will have 8,000 cfd of storage available during our planning period. Further, we anticipate that only 6,000 pounds of the critical material will be available and that we will have 9,000 hours of time available on machine 1 and 6,000 hours on machine 2. The resource requirements for each of the products is given in Exhibit 5-9.

From this information we can now construct our constraint functions. Since each unit of product A requires 3 cfd of storage, then the total storage requirements for producing $X_1$ units of product A will be $3X_1$. Similarly, the total storage

**EXHIBIT 5-9 Resource Requirements per Unit of Each Product**

| | Product | | | |
|---|---|---|---|---|
| **Resource** | **A** | **B** | **C** | **D** |
| Storage | 3 cfd | 2 cfd | 6 cfd | 1 cfd |
| Materials | ½ lb | 1 lb | 2 lb | 3 lb |
| Machine 1 | 2 hr | 2 hr | 1 hr | 2 hr |
| Machine 2 | 1 hr | 3 hr | 2 hr | 1 hr |

required by producing $X_2$ units of product B will be $2X_2$ because each unit requires 2 cfd of storage. In turn, we will need $6X_3$ and $1X_4$ units of storage to produce $X_3$ and $X_4$ units of products C and D. Because we only have 8,000 cfd of storage available, the total production of products A through D will be constrained by the relationship

$$3X_1 + 2X_2 + 6X_3 + 1X_4 \leq 8{,}000$$

We derive the remaining constraints in a similar manner.

Our next task is to estimate the amount of contribution margin per unit that each product sold will provide to the firm. This requires precisely the same information that we needed to solve CVP problems. For each product we subtract from the product's anticipated selling price the total variable cost to produce and sell the product (direct materials, direct labor, variable overhead, and variable selling and administrative costs). Let us assume that the contribution margins are \$5, \$3.50, \$1, and \$2 for products A, B, C, and D, respectively. Then we can represent the objective function (total contribution margin) that we will earn by selling $X_1$, $X_2$, $X_3$, and $X_4$ units of our four products as

$$\$5X_1 + \$3.5X_2 + \$1X_3 + \$2X_4$$

We now wish to solve the LP problem to determine the number of units of each product that we should produce and sell to maximize the amount of contribution margin that we will earn. The problem is as follows:

$$\begin{aligned}
\text{maximize: } & 5X_1 + 3.5X_2 + 1X_3 + 2X_4 & \\
\text{subject to: } & 3X_1 + 2X_2 + 6X_3 + 1X_4 \leq 8{,}000 & \text{(storage constraint)} \\
& \tfrac{1}{2}X_1 + 1X_2 + 2X_3 + 3X_4 \leq 6{,}000 & \text{(materials constraint)} \\
& 2X_1 + 2X_2 + 1X_3 + 2X_4 \leq 9{,}000 & \text{(machine-1 constraint)} \\
& 1X_1 + 3X_2 + 2X_3 + 1X_4 \leq 6{,}000 & \text{(machine-2 constraint)}
\end{aligned}$$

Recall that our solution procedure really solves a set of equations, not inequalities. To convert the inequalities to equalities we add slack variables to each constraint. By convention we number the slack variables sequentially, associating the first slack with the first constraint, the second slack with the second constraint, and so on. As we will see in a moment, this convention is very important for helping us quickly interpret the solution to the LP problem. With the slack variables added, our complete problem becomes:

$$\begin{aligned}
\text{maximize: } & 5X_1 + 3.5X_2 + 1X_3 + 2X_4 + 0S_1 + 0S_2 + 0S_3 + 0S_4 \\
\text{subject to: } & 3X_1 + 2X_2 + 6X_3 + 1X_4 + 1S_1 + 0S_2 + 0S_3 + 0S_4 = 8{,}000 \\
& \tfrac{1}{2}X_1 + 1X_2 + 2X_3 + 3X_4 + 0S_1 + 1S_2 + 0S_3 + 0S_4 = 6{,}000 \\
& 2X_1 + 2X_2 + 1X_3 + 2X_4 + 0S_1 + 0S_2 + 1S_3 + 0S_4 = 9{,}000 \\
& 1X_1 + 3X_2 + 2X_3 + 1X_4 + 0S_1 + 0S_2 + 0S_3 + 1S_4 = 6{,}000
\end{aligned}$$

Note that variables $X_1$ through $X_4$ represent the products we produce (they are the real, or primary, variables) and variables $S_1$ through $S_4$ are our slack variables. The problem is now ready to be solved.

Our interest is not in the solution procedure, but rather in the interpretation of the solution. Hence we now skip directly to the solution. Exhibit 5-10 gives the solution that is available from the computer program LINPRO that accompanies the text. Let us now examine it to see what it tells us.

The first part of the solution indicates the number of units to produce in order to optimize net income, as well as the values for the slack variables. Recall that the first four variables are real variables. Thus the solution tells us that we should produce 1,513 units of product A, 1,027 units of product B, no units of product C and 1,405 units of product D. The remaining variables, labeled X(5) through X(8) are the slack variables. The solution tells us that all of the storage capacity is used [that is, the first slack variable, X(5), has a value of zero, meaning there is no slack]. Similarly, all the materials will be used. But X(7) has a value of 1,108, which means that there are 1,108 excess hours of time available on machine 1. Finally, all of the time on machine 2 will be fully utilized. Note that the only way we know which slack variable is associated with which constraint is by the convention that we used in numbering them: The first slack variable is for the first constraint, the second slack variable is for the second constraint, and so on.

The program provides shadow prices only for those variables that are not in the optimal solution (conventionally, the term *basis* is used to refer to the set of variables in the solution, so nonbasic variables are those not in the solution). The shadow prices for variables in the solution are zero, and are not printed. According to the optimal solution, product C is not worth producing. The shadow price for this real variable tells us that the total contribution margin would decrease by $9.11 if one unit of product C was produced. Now this doesn't mean we lose money on product C per se. Product C has a positive contribution margin of $1. If we produce a unit of product C, we will earn that $1 contribution margin. But by using resources to produce product C, we will have to reduce the number of units of products A, B, and D that are produced. These are more profitable products, and the net effect of producing product C and reducing the production of the alternative products will be a reduction in total contribution margin of $9.11. We gain $1 from product C and lose $10.11 from the alternate products we would otherwise have produced, for a net reduction of $9.11.

**EXHIBIT 5-10 A Linear-Programming Solution**

| OPTIMAL SOLUTION | | SHADOW PRICES FOR NON-BASIC VARIABLES |
|---|---|---|
| x( 1) = | 1513.51 | |
| x( 2) = | 1027.03 | |
| x( 3) = | 0.00 | 9.11 |
| x( 4) = | 1405.41 | |
| x( 5) = | 0.00 | 1.64 |
| x( 6) = | 0.00 | 0.11 |
| x( 7) = | 1108.11 | |
| x( 8) = | 0.00 | 0.04 |

Objective function = 13972.97

| Current values for constraints | | Right-hand side ranges Lower limit | Upper limit |
|---|---|---|---|
| y( 1) = | 8000.00 | 4500.00 | 10050.00 |
| y( 2) = | 6000.00 | 2285.71 | 8562.50 |
| y( 3) = | 9000.00 | 7891.89 | UNBOUNDED |
| y( 4) = | 6000.00 | 3764.71 | 11600.00 |

Objective Function Coefficient Ranges

| Variable | Current value | Lower limit | Upper limit |
|---|---|---|---|
| x( 1 ) | 5 | 1.21875 | 5.15 |
| x( 2 ) | 3.5 | 3.411765 | 4.5 |
| x( 3 ) | 1 | UNBOUNDED | 10.10811 |
| x( 4 ) | 2 | 1.714286 | 2.374999 |

This shadow price information allows us to make a rational decision as to whether we want to produce a full product line; that is, customers may have come to expect us to be able to sell them product C. If we do not have it available, we may lose some customer goodwill. Our solution tells us that if we value this potential goodwill at more than \$9.10 per unit, we should go ahead and produce the product. Otherwise, we should not produce product C.

The remaining shadow prices are for the slack variables for each resource. As mentioned earlier, if we can obtain an additional unit of a binding resource, we will be able to increase our total contribution margin. The solution tells us that an additional cubic foot day of storage space will generate \$1.64 of additional contribution margin. Similarly, another pound of raw material is worth \$0.11, and an hour of machine-2 time will yield \$0.04 in additional contribution margin. The shadow price of machine-1 time is zero. This, of course, agrees with common sense. Since we already have excess (idle) time available on machine 1, acquiring another hour's worth of time will not increase our earnings. The shadow prices are important for planning. We can use them to determine whether we should attempt to acquire more resources. If we can rent additional storage space for less than

\$1.64 per cubic foot day, we should do so, but if the cost is greater than \$1.64, it will not be worth it for us to rent the space.

The next line gives us the optimal value of the objective function. Producing and selling the units called for in the optimal solution will provide the firm with a contribution margin of \$13,972.97.

The next set of data in the solution tells us how much each capacity constraint can change without changing the mix of which products we are producing. Recall that we said a unit of storage was worth \$1.64 to us. Will this hold true for all increases? No. If we continue to add storage space, eventually some other constraint will become binding and storage space will no longer be worth \$1.64 per unit to us. In fact, the solution tells us that when we acquire a total of 10,050 units of storage, the shadow price of storage space will change. Similarly, if we decrease storage space to 4,500 units, the value of storage space will also change (increase). In contrast, the solution tells us that there is no upper limit to the amount of machine-1 time ($y_3$) that we can have available (we have idle time already). If, however, we reduce the number of machine-1 hours by 1,108.1, to 7,891.9, machine 1 will become a binding constraint.

This set of information is used in combination with the shadow prices for planning purposes. The two pieces of data tell us how much more of a particular resource we can acquire at a set price without having to re-solve the problem. If we want to acquire more than 10,050 units of storage capacity, we must solve the problem again to find the impact on earnings.

The last set of data tells us how much the contribution margins per unit for each product can change without changing the optimal product mix (without changing which products we should produce). Recall that we solved the problem to determine the product mix that will maximize the total contribution margin. It makes sense that if we greatly increase (or decrease) the contribution margin per unit for a particular product, we may want to produce more of (or drop) the particular product. The solution tells us that the optimal product mix will not change as long as the contribution margin for product A stays in the range \$1.22 to \$5.15. Similarly, the specific products produced will not change if the contribution margin of product B stays in the range \$3.41 to \$4.50. In contrast, product C will enter the solution if its contribution margin rises above \$10.11, but the solution will not change for *any* contribution margin below \$10.11. This information is useful for **sensitivity analysis.**

If the solution is not sensitive (will not change) for a fairly wide range of values, we need not be concerned with getting more precise estimates of variable costs (used to calculate the contribution margins). If these ranges are very tight, however, we may wish to attempt to obtain more accurate cost estimates. Under such circumstances we would say that the solution is sensitive to minor fluctuations in the values of the contribution margins.

Note, by the way, that all of the foregoing discussion presumes that we are making only one change at a time in the problem. That is, if we want to add capacity to two or more resources simultaneously, the shadow prices will not provide the joint effect of both changes on our earned contribution margin. Similarly, we cannot determine the effect of changing two or more unit contribution margins simultaneously. The only way to find the effect of a change in more than one variable at a time is to solve the problem again with revised data.

## QUESTIONS AND EXERCISES: APPENDIX 5A

**5-58** (CPA). Johnson, Inc., manufactures product X and product Y, which are processed as follows:

| | Machine | |
|---|---|---|
| | **Type A** | **Type B** |
| Product X | 6 hours | 4 hours |
| Product Y | 9 hours | 5 hours |

The contribution margin is $12 for product X and $7 for product Y. The available time daily for processing the two products is 120 hours for machine type A and 80 hours for machine type B. How would the restriction (constraint) for machine type B be expressed?

**5-59** (CPA). Quepea Company manufactures two products, Q and P, in a small building with limited capacity. The selling price, cost data, and production time are as follows:

| | **Product Q** | **Product P** |
|---|---|---|
| Selling price per unit | $20 | $17 |
| Variable costs of producing and selling a unit | $12 | $13 |
| Hours to produce a unit | 3 | 1 |

Based on this information, what is the profit maximization objective function?

**5-60** (CPA). Patsy, Inc., manufactures two products, X and Y. Each product must be processed in each of three departments: machining, assembling, and finishing. The hours needed to produce 1 unit of product per department and the maximum possible hours per department follow:

| | Production Hours per Unit | | |
|---|---|---|---|
| **Department** | **X** | **Y** | **Maximum Capacity in Hours** |
| Machining | 2 | 1 | 420 |
| Assembling | 2 | 2 | 500 |
| Finishing | 2 | 3 | 600 |

Other restrictions follow:

$$X \geqslant 50$$
$$Y \geqslant 50$$

where $X$ and $Y$ are the number of units of products X and Y, respectively. The objective function is to maximize profits, where profit = $\$5X + \$2Y$. Given the objective and constraints, what is the most profitable number of units of X and Y, respectively, to manufacture?

**5-61** (CPA). Williamson Manufacturing intends to produce two products, X and Y. Product X requires 6 hours of time on machine 1 and 12 hours of time on machine 2. Product Y requires 4 hours of time on machine 1 and no time on machine 2. Both machines are available for 24 hours. Assuming that the objective function of the total contribution margin is $\$2X + \$1Y$, what product mix will produce the maximum profit?

**5-62** (CPA). Watch Corporation manufactures products A, B, and C. The daily production requirements are as follows:

| | | Hours Required per Unit per Department | | |
|---|---|---|---|---|
| Product | Profit per Unit | Machining | Plating | Polishing |
| A | $10 | 1 | 1 | 1 |
| B | 20 | 3 | 1 | 2 |
| C | 30 | 2 | 3 | 2 |
| Total hours per day per department | | 16 | 12 | 6 |

Set up the linear-programming problem that would be used to determine the daily production of each unit.

## PROBLEMS AND CASES: APPENDIX 5A

**5-63** **Linear programming: Equations and solution** (SMA adapted).
The controller of the Rustler Company recently attended a seminar on linear programming and feels that some of the concepts may be useful in planning operations for the coming year. The company produces two models (Standard and Deluxe) of its basic product. The company operates in a competitive market and, hence, can sell as many of each unit as it can produce.

The controller has prepared the following estimates of prices and costs per unit for the coming year.

| | Standard | Deluxe |
|---|---|---|
| Selling price | $112.00 | $152.00 |
| Direct material A | 54.00 | 108.00 |
| Direct material B | 18.75 | 18.75 |
| Direct labor | 18.00 | 9.00 |
| Variable overhead | 6.25 | 6.25 |

Direct material A costs $9 per kilogram and the company can purchase up to 60,000 kilograms from its supplier. Direct material B is in short supply and the company can only acquire 90,000 liters at a price of $1.25 per liter. Direct labor is paid $4.50 per hour and the capacity of the factory is 20,000 direct labor hours.

When the solution is graphed, the following possibilities (in units) are shown

| Standard | Deluxe |
|---|---|
| 0 | 5,000 |
| 2,000 | 4,000 |
| 4,000 | 2,000 |
| 5,000 | 0 |

**Required**

**a.** Formulate the equations for this problem.
**b.** Show, graphically, how the combinations were obtained.
**c.** Which combination maximizes contribution and, hence, income?

**5-64 Two products, two constraints.**

Dynamic Duo produces two products. The manufacture of these products is partially automated. Total available machine hours are 400, and total available finishing hours (labor) are 600.

Time requirements and contribution per unit for each product are as follows:

| | Product A | Product B |
|---|---|---|
| Machine hours per unit | 2 | 3 |
| Finishing hours per unit | 4 | 2 |
| Contribution per unit | $5 | $4 |

**Required**

**a.** What is the equation to be maximized?
**b.** What are the constraints?
**c.** What are the equations that express the constraints?
**d.** What is the greatest number of units of A that can be produced, given the constraints? Of B?
**e.** What is the optimal solution to the problem?
**f.** Graph the solution.

**5-65 Two products, two constraints.**

Natural Products, Inc., a foreign subsidiary of a U.S. corporation, produces two products, X and Y. The contribution margins are $3 and $2, respectively. The basic inputs are raw material (available locally) and foreign exchange (used to pay the workers). Product X requires three units of material and $2 of foreign exchange; product Y requires 1 unit of material and $2 of foreign exchange. On an average daily basis, 10 units of material and $12 of foreign exchange are available.

**Required**

**a.** What is the expression to be maximized?
**b.** What are the equations that express the constraints?
**c.** What is the greatest number of X or Y that could be produced daily?
**d.** What is the optimal daily mix of products X and Y?
**e.** Graph the solution.

**5-66 CVP with constraints** (CICA adapted).

Gibbs Plastic Ltd. was engaged in its budgeting program for the coming year. Division 1 had special problems and had sought your assistance in your capacity as controller of the company. Their problem is as follows: Division 1 can sell all the units of its two products, C and D, that can be produced. Each of the products must pass through both machines R and S before being completed. The division management wishes you to advise them how much of each product should be produced to maximize the division's contribution margin. The following details are provided.

| | Product C | | Product D |
|---|---|---|---|
| Contribution margin per unit | $500 | | $300 |
| Machine hours needed to produce | | | |
| One unit on machine R | 10 | | 8 |
| One unit on machine S | 12 | | 6 |
| Machine hours available | | | |
| On machine R | | 2,000 | |
| On machine S | | 1,800 | |

**Required**

As controller, present your solution.

**5-67 Linear programming: Two products, multiple constraints, but straightforward** (CMA).

Leastan Company manufactures a line of carpeting that includes a commercial carpet and a residential carpet. Two grades of fiber—heavy-duty and regular—are used in manufacturing both types of carpeting. The mix of the two grades of fiber differ in each type of carpeting, with the commercial grade using a greater amount of heavy-duty fiber.

Leastan will introduce a new line of carpeting after next month to replace the current line. The present fiber in stock will not be used in the new line. Management wants to exhaust the present stock of regular and heavy-duty fiber during the last month of production.

Data regarding the current line of commercial and residential carpeting are as follows:

| | Commercial | Residential |
|---|---|---|
| Selling price per roll | $1,000 | $800 |
| Production specifications per roll of carpet | | |
| Heavy-duty fiber | 80 lb | 40 lb |
| Regular fiber | 20 lb | 40 lb |
| Direct labor hours | 15 | 15 |
| Standard cost per roll of carpet | | |
| Heavy-duty fiber ($3 per lb) | $240 | $120 |
| Regular fiber ($2 per lb) | 40 | 80 |
| Direct labor ($10 per DLH) | 150 | 150 |
| Variable manufacturing overhead (60% of direct labor cost) | 90 | 90 |
| Fixed manufacturing overhead (120% of direct labor cost) | 180 | 180 |
| Total standard cost per roll | $700 | $620 |

Leastan has 42,000 pounds of heavy-duty fiber and 24,000 pounds of regular fiber in stock. All fiber not used in the manufacture of the present types of carpeting during the last month of production can be sold as scrap at $0.25 a pound.

A maximum of 10,500 direct labor hours are available during the month. The labor force can work on either type of carpeting.

Sufficient demand exists for the present line of carpeting so that all quantities produced can be sold.

**Required**

**a.** Calculate the number of rolls of commercial carpet and residential carpet Leastan Company must manufacture during the last month of production to exhaust completely the heavy-duty and regular fiber still in stock.

**b.** Can Leastan Company manufacture these quantities of commercial and residential carpeting during the last month of production? Explain your answer.

**c.** A member of Leastan Company's cost accounting staff has stated that linear programming should be used to determine the number of rolls of commercial and residential carpeting to manufacture during the last month of production.

   **1.** Explain why linear programming should be used in this application.

   **2.** Formulate the objective and constraint functions so that this application can be solved by linear programming.

**5-68 Linear programming: Data requirements for two products, three constraints.**

The following information summarizes production and cost data for Brenden Manufacturing's two products. An engineering study has shown that product A should require 6 pounds of materials and product B should require 8 pounds. A recent study revealed that 2 units of A were built with 1 hour of direct labor. In contrast, it took 3 hours to build 1 unit of B. Product A requires 3 hours of machine time and product B requires 2 hours of machine time.

Materials cost $10 per pound; labor is paid $5 per hour. Experience shows that when the firm uses 200 machine hours, factory overhead is $1,600. When the firm uses 300 machine hours, overhead is $1,900. Product A sells for $90 per unit, and B sells for $120 per unit. Management expects that the firm can acquire 400 pounds of materials, 150 hours of direct labor, and 200 hours of machine time next period.

**Required**

Set up (but do not solve) the appropriate linear-programming problem (objective function and constraints) that would aid Brenden in determining how much of each product should be produced.

**5-69 Linear programming: Data requirements for three products and two constraints—comprehensive; requires prior study of Appendix 3A.**

GHI can manufacture three products: 1, 2, and 3. The products sell for $25, $25, and $50 each, respectively. Recent records relate the number of labor hours required to produce varying amounts of each of these products:

| | Product 1 | | Product 2 | | Product 3 | |
|---|---|---|---|---|---|---|
| Week | Units | Hours | Units | Hours | Units | Hours |
| 1 | 899 | 450 | 452 | 900 | 216 | 650 |
| 2 | 1,205 | 600 | 430 | 876 | 180 | 525 |
| 3 | 1,145 | 575 | 404 | 800 | 205 | 625 |
| 4 | 1,251 | 625 | 442 | 880 | 164 | 495 |

Labor is paid $4.50 per hour.

The firm can make 2 units of product 1 out of 3 pounds of material, 3 units of product 2 out of a pound of material, and 1 unit of product 3 out of 2 pounds of material. Material costs $6 per pound.

The firm tried two approaches to estimating overhead using regression. The first yielded

$$\text{overhead} = \$15{,}000 + \$2 \text{ per labor hour}$$

This equation has an $R^2$ of 0.80 and a standard error of $2,000. The second approach yielded

$$\text{overhead} = \$10{,}000 + 50\% \text{ of material costs}$$

This equation has an $R^2$ of 0.75 and a standard error of $3,000.

The firm has only 2,000 labor hours available per period and can obtain only 1,900 pounds of material per period.

**Required**

Set up (do not solve) the appropriate linear-programming problem to determine which products and amounts this firm should produce.

**5-70 Setting up constraints for tax audits.**

The state treasurer wants to determine how many of each of various types of income tax returns should be selected for audit. A computer categorizes all tax returns received into one of three categories: probable fraud, probable honest error, probable no error. Past averages indicate that the state will get additional taxes of $25,000 from audits of the fraud returns, $8,000 from audits of honest-error returns and $50 from the probable no-error returns. On the average it costs $12,000 to audit a fraudulent return (this includes the cost of providing room and board for guilty filers), $2,000 to audit an honest-error return, and $45 to audit a probable no-error return.

All audits are conducted by two types of auditors (reviewers and investigators). A reviewer does relatively little with a probable fraud return and can process three fraud returns per hour, but it takes a reviewer an average of 8 hours to process an honest-error return. A reviewer spends one hour on a probable no-error return if it is selected for audit. Investigators do the bulk of the work on the probable fraud returns and spend an average of 100 hours on each. Investigators average 4 hours on the probable honest-error returns and 15 minutes on probable no-error returns. The treasurer has a staff who can provide 20,000 hours of review time and 16,000 hours of investigative time. The treasurer insists on auditing a minimum of 100 probable no-error returns in order to be able to establish statistical relationships for the computer selection process.

**Required**
Set up the appropriate linear-programming problem.

**5-71 Linear-programming equations: Difficult** (SMA adapted).
Raymond Company manufactures three products known as A, B, and C. There is no upper ceiling on demand in the market for these products since they are all well accepted. Data concerning the three products are as follows:

| | A | B | C |
|---|---|---|---|
| Selling price | $15 | $19 | $24 |
| Material costs | 5 | 10 | 13 |
| Other variable costs (paid when incurred) | 6 | 4 | 7 |
| Portion of revenue collected in month of sale | $\frac{1}{3}$ | 0 | 0 |

Each product requires 1 unit of its own special raw material and these materials are not interchangeable. The raw materials at the beginning of the month are

200 units of material for A
120 units of material for B
50 units of material for C

Additional quantities can be bought immediately when required and are paid for in cash at the prices shown.

The products pass through two departments. The maximum machine time during the month is 400 hours in Department 1 and 800 hours in Department 2. Machine time for processing a unit in each department is as follows:

| | Hours Required by One Unit of | | |
|---|---|---|---|
| **Department** | **A** | **B** | **C** |
| 1 | 0.5 | 1 | 0.25 |
| 2 | 1 | 1 | 4.5 |

Fixed costs will be $900 during the month for both departments; this amount includes $200 for depreciation. The balance of fixed cost is paid in cash. The beginning cash balance is expected to be $6,660, and the ending balance cannot be less than $3,000. The company will have no accounts receivable outstanding at the beginning of the month.

**Required**

**a.** Formulate an objective function to maximize profits.

**b.** Identify and formulate all constraints applicable to this function. Do not solve the problem.

**c.** Which product should the firm produce if the *only* constraint is machine time in Department 1?

**5-72 Interpreting linear-programming solutions.**
Triton Industries is considering several marketing strategies for the next period. To help management make the correct decision, the following information on each of our products has been gathered.

| | Products | | | |
|---|---|---|---|---|
| | A | B | C | D |
| Selling price | $11 | $40 | $15 | $20 |
| Variable cost | 5 | 34 | 12 | 11 |
| Contribution margin | $ 6 | $ 6 | $ 3 | $ 9 |

In addition, the firm experiences fixed costs of $30,000 per period. Production is constrained by several resources. We have considered these constraints and set up and solved the appropriate linear-programming problems given on the following pages.

**Required**

**a.** If management's desire is to maximize income, how many units of each product should be produced?

**b.** If management decides to maximize market penetration (maximize total unit sales), what will be the firm's decreased contribution margin as compared with its optimal contribution margin?

**c.** What *net income* will the firm earn if it chooses to maximize sales revenue?

**d.** If the firm chooses to maximize income, what is the allowable range for the contribution margin for product A such that the solution will not change?

**Solution 1**

```
10 DATA 5,0,0,4
20 DATA 1,2,2,0
30 DATA 3,.5,1,.5
40 DATA 2,0,3,4
50 DATA 1,0,6,0
60 DATA 0,2,0,1
70 DATA 6,6,3,9
80 DATA 12000,20000,40000,8000,7000
RUN

An optimal solution has been found after 3 iterations.

                                SHADOW PRICES FOR
 OPTIMAL SOLUTION              NON-BASIC VARIABLES
x( 1) =     5357.14
x( 2) =        0.00                 7.71
x( 3) =      428.57
x( 4) =     7000.00
x( 5) =     5785.71
x( 6) =        0.00                 1.71
x( 7) =        0.00                 0.43
x( 8) =       71.43
x( 9) =        0.00                 6.43
```

```
Objective function = 96428.57
Current values for              Right-hand side ranges
   constraints                 Lower limit      Upper limit
y( 1) =    12000.00              6214.29         UNBOUNDED
y( 2) =    20000.00             19944.45          21500.00
y( 3) =    40000.00             39000.00          40029.41
y( 4) =     8000.00              7928.57         UNBOUNDED
y( 5) =     7000.00              6992.13           7272.73
    Objective Function Coefficient Ranges
             Current        Lower           Upper
Variable      value         limit           limit
 x( 1 )         6          2               8.999999
 x( 2 )         6         UNBOUNDED        13.71429
 x( 3 )         3          2               5.347827
 x( 4 )         9          5.142857        UNBOUNDED
```

**Solution 2**

```
10 DATA 5,0,0,4
20 DATA 1,2,2,0
30 DATA 3,.5,1,.5
40 DATA 2,0,3,4
50 DATA 1,0,6,0
60 DATA 0,2,0,1
70 DATA 11,40,15,20
80 DATA 12000,20000,40000,8000,7000
RUN
An optimal solution has been found after 4 iterations.
                              SHADOW PRICES FOR
 OPTIMAL SOLUTION            NON-BASIC VARIABLES
x( 1) =     5833.33
x( 2) =     2722.22
x( 3) =      361.11
x( 4) =     1555.56
x( 5) =        0.00                  0.71
x( 6) =        0.00                  2.83
x( 7) =    21027.78
x( 8) =        0.00                  1.79
x( 9) =        0.00                 18.58
Objective function = 209583.3
Current values for              Right-hand side ranges
   constraints                 Lower limit      Upper limit
y( 1) =    12000.00              6243.35          13647.06
y( 2) =    20000.00             13000.00          26500.00
y( 3) =    40000.00             18972.22         UNBOUNDED
y( 4) =     8000.00              6000.00          22149.53
y( 5) =     7000.00              5250.00          13361.35
```

```
      Objective Function Coefficient Ranges
                Current        Lower            Upper
Variable         value         limit            limit
 x( 1 )           11          2.500007         32.5
 x( 2 )           40          38.5             52.9
 x( 3 )           15          5.076923         66
 x( 4 )           20          13.55            20.75
```

**Solution 3**

```
10 DATA 5,0,0,4
20 DATA 1,2,2,0
30 DATA 3,.5,1,.5
40 DATA 2,0,3,4
50 DATA 1,0,6,0
60 DATA 0,2,0,1
70 DATA 1,1,1,1
80 DATA 12000,20000,40000,8000,7000
RUN
An optimal solution has been found after 5 iterations.
                                 SHADOW PRICES FOR
 OPTIMAL SOLUTION              NON-BASIC VARIABLES
x( 1) =     5353.61
x( 2) =        3.80
x( 3) =      441.06
x( 4) =     6992.40
x( 5) =     5756.65
x( 6) =        0.00                   0.24
x( 7) =        0.00                   0.11
x( 8) =        0.00                   0.07
x( 9) =        0.00                   0.44
Objective function = 12790.87
Current values for               Right-hand side ranges
   constraints                 Lower limit    Upper limit
y( 1) =    12000.00              6243.35      UNBOUNDED
y( 2) =    20000.00             19944.45       27250.00
y( 3) =    40000.00             18972.22       40029.41
y( 4) =     8000.00              7928.57       22149.53
y( 5) =     7000.00              6992.13       13361.35
      Objective Function Coefficient Ranges
                Current        Lower            Upper
Variable         value         limit            limit
 x( 1 )           1         .3541667          2.461539
 x( 2 )           1         8.661409E-02      1.852941
 x( 3 )           1         .5869564          4.875
 x( 4 )           1         .5735295          1.678572
```

## PROBLEMS AND CASES: APPENDIX 5A

**5-73 Solving linear-programming problems—computer required.**
Bartle Products is faced with a pleasant problem. They have more orders for their products for the next 3 months than they can produce. Because they view this situation as temporary, the firm is unwilling to purchase additional machinery or hire additional labor. Production records reveal the following relationships (per unit):

| | | | Machine Time Required (hours) | | | |
|---|---|---|---|---|---|---|
| **Product** | **Direct Labor Hours** | **Direct Materials Cost** | **A** | **B** | **C** | **Selling Price** |
| 1 | 2 | $10 | 1 | 2 | 2 | $55 |
| 2 | 3 | 12 | 3 | 1 | 1 | 72 |
| 3 | 1 | 7 | 5 | 0 | 2 | 37 |
| 4 | 4 | 5 | 4 | 1 | 3 | 83 |
| 5 | 3 | 8 | 2 | 4 | 0 | 60 |

If product 1 is not produced, then fixed costs are reduced by $5,000. If product 2 is not produced, fixed costs are reduced by $3,000. If products 3, 4, or 5 are not produced, there is no appreciable effect on fixed costs.

Labor is paid $6 per hour. When 500 hours of labor were used, overhead was $22,000; when 750 hours were used, overhead totaled $23,000. The firm has only 2,000 hours of machine time available on machine A, 2,000 on machine B, and 2,500 on machine C. A maximum of 5,000 labor hours are available per period.

**Required**

**a.** Set up and solve the linear-programming problems necessary to determine what products this firm should produce. Are there any other considerations that management should think about?

**b.** What will be the effect on product mix and profitability if the firm decides it must produce a minimum of 30 units of product 3?

**5-74 Interpreting a linear-programming solution.**
LKJ set up the following linear-programming problem to determine which of its products—$X_1$, $X_2$, or $X_3$—to produce (fixed costs are $5,000 per period):

$$\text{maximize: } 45X_1 + 89X_2 + 62X_3$$

$$\begin{aligned} \text{subject to: } \quad 3X_1 + 4X_2 + 5X_3 &\leq 2{,}000 \quad \text{(machine A)} \\ 8X_1 + 2X_2 + 5X_3 &\leq 6{,}000 \quad \text{(machine B)} \\ 8X_1 + 5X_2 + 2X_3 &\leq 1{,}000 \quad \text{(labor)} \end{aligned}$$

A computer provided the following solution.

**Solution to LKJ**

| OPTIMAL SOLUTION | | SHADOW PRICES FOR NON-BASIC VARIABLES |
|---|---|---|
| x( 1) = | 0.00 | 71.00 |
| x( 2) = | 58.82 | |
| x( 3) = | 352.94 | |
| x( 4) = | 0.00 | 7.76 |
| x( 5) = | 4117.65 | |
| x( 6) = | 0.00 | 11.59 |

Objective function = 27117.65

| Current values for constraints | | Right-hand side ranges Lower limit | Upper limit |
|---|---|---|---|
| y( 1) = | 2000.00 | 800.00 | 2500.00 |
| y( 2) = | 6000.00 | 1882.35 | UNBOUNDED |
| y( 3) = | 1000.00 | 800.00 | 2500.00 |

Objective Function Coefficient Ranges

| Variable | Current value | Lower limit | Upper limit |
|---|---|---|---|
| x( 1 ) | 45 | UNBOUNDED | 116 |
| x( 2 ) | 89 | 53.5 | 155 |
| x( 3 ) | 62 | 35.6 | 111.25 |

**Required**

**a.** What products are being produced?

**b.** What net income will the firm earn if it follows the solution?

**c.** If the firm can obtain another unit of machine-A time for $8, should the firm acquire the time? Why?

**d.** If the firm can obtain another unit of machine-B time for $5, should the firm acquire the time? Why?

**e.** If the firm can obtain another hour of labor for $8.50 per hour, should the firm acquire the labor? Why?

**f.** If the firm decided to produce at least one unit of each product, what would the firm's net income be next period?

**g.** What is the minimum amount of each resource that the firm must have next period to earn the net income implied by the above solution?

**5-75 Interpreting a linear-programming solution.**

J. K. Lester Enterprises can produce three different products with its facilities. The firm solved the following linear-programming problem as the basis for its budget for the next operating period. Lester's fixed costs are $2 per period.

maximize: $0.42X_1 + 0.3X_2 + 0.23X_3$

subject to:

$6.7X_1 + 5.0X_2 + 3.5X_3 \leq 150$ (machine hours)

$1.0X_1 + 1.0X_2 + 1.0X_3 \leq 30$ (storage capacity)

$1.666X_1 + 1.333X_2 + 1.0X_3 \leq 40$ (labor hours)

PROBLEMS AND CASES: APPENDIX 5A

**Solution to J. K. Lester**

| OPTIMAL SOLUTION | | SHADOW PRICES FOR NON-BASIC VARIABLES |
|---|---|---|
| x( 1) = | 14.06 | |
| x( 2) = | 0.00 | 0.02 |
| x( 3) = | 15.94 | |
| x( 4) = | 0.00 | 0.06 |
| x( 5) = | 0.00 | 0.02 |
| x( 6) = | 0.63 | |

Objective function = 9.571874

| Current values for constraints | | Right-hand side ranges Lower limit | Upper limit |
|---|---|---|---|
| y( 1) = | 150.00 | 105.00 | 153.05 |
| y( 2) = | 30.00 | 22.39 | 32.34 |
| y( 3) = | 40.00 | 39.37 | UNBOUNDED |

Objective Function Coefficient Ranges

| Variable | Current value | Lower limit | Upper limit |
|---|---|---|---|
| x( 1 ) | .42 | .3793334 | .4402857 |
| x( 2 ) | .3 | UNBOUNDED | .3190625 |
| x( 3 ) | .23 | .219403 | .42 |

**Required**

**a.** What products are being produced?

**b.** What net income will the firm earn if it follows the solution?

**c.** If the firm can obtain another unit of storage capacity for \$0.02, should it acquire the capacity? Why?

**d.** If the firm can obtain another unit of labor for \$0.05, should it acquire the labor? Why?

**e.** If the firm can obtain another machine hour for \$0.07, should it acquire the machine time? Why?

**f.** If the firm decided to produce at least 1 unit of each product, what would its net income be next period?

**g.** What is the minimum amount of each resource that the firm must have next period to earn the net income implied by the given solution?

**5-76 Interpreting a linear-programming solution.**

Merryweather Manufacturing is capable of producing three products (called 1, 2, and 3 for convenience). The firm's operations are constrained by four factors (two machines, a maximum limit on the number of items that can be sent through the company's cramped shipping facilities, and a limit on intermediate storage space). To find the optimal production plan, management set up the following linear program.

$$\text{maximize: } 4X_1 + 8X_2 + 12X_3$$

$$\begin{aligned} \text{subject to: } 0.5X_1 + 1X_2 + 0.25X_3 &\le 1{,}000 \text{ hours} && \text{(machine 1)} \\ 2X_1 + 0.2X_2 + 1X_3 &\le 5{,}700 \text{ hours} && \text{(machine 2)} \\ 3X_1 + 2X_2 + 0.75X_3 &\le 5{,}000 \text{ units} && \text{(shipping capacity)} \\ 0X_1 + 1X_2 + 1X_3 &\le 2{,}000 \text{ cubic feet} && \text{(storage capacity)} \end{aligned}$$

The solution to this problem is as follows:

**Solution to Merryweather**

| OPTIMAL SOLUTION | | SHADOW PRICES FOR NON-BASIC VARIABLES |
|---|---|---|
| x( 1) = | 1000.00 | |
| x( 2) = | 0.00 | 10.00 |
| x( 3) = | 2000.00 | |
| x( 4) = | 0.00 | 8.00 |
| x( 5) = | 1700.00 | |
| x( 6) = | 500.00 | |
| x( 7) = | 0.00 | 10.00 |

Objective function = 28000

| Current values for constraints | | Right-hand side ranges Lower limit | Upper limit |
|---|---|---|---|
| y( 1) = | 1000.00 | 500.00 | 1083.33 |
| y( 2) = | 5700.00 | 4000.00 | UNBOUNDED |
| y( 3) = | 5000.00 | 4500.00 | UNBOUNDED |
| y( 4) = | 2000.00 | 1333.33 | 4000.00 |

Objective Function Coefficient Ranges

| Variable | Current value | Lower limit | Upper limit |
|---|---|---|---|
| x( 1 ) | 4 | UNBOUNDED | 24 |
| x( 2 ) | 8 | UNBOUNDED | 18 |
| x( 3 ) | 12 | 2 | UNBOUNDED |

**Required**

**a.** What contribution margin can this firm expect to earn with optimal production?

**b.** What products should be produced for optimal results?

**c.** What is the amount of excess capacity for each resource?

**d.** The firm next door offers to rent Merryweather some storage space for $9 per cubic foot. Should the company accept the offer?

**e.** What will be the effect on contribution margin if Merryweather produces one more unit of $X_2$?

**f.** What will be the effect on contribution margin if Merryweather acquires one more hour of time on machine 1?
**g.** What will be the effect on contribution margin if Merryweather acquires one more hour of time on machine 2?
**h.** What is the maximum amount of shipping capacity that Merryweather can have available before the solution changes?
**i.** If Merryweather's storage capacity drops to 1,200 cubic feet, what will be the effect on contribution margin?
**j.** If Merryweather's storage capacity drops to 1,500 cubic feet, what will be the effect on contribution margin?

**5-77 Interpreting a linear-programming solution** (CMA adapted).
Jenlock Mill Company produces two grades of interior plywood from fir and pine lumber. The fir and pine lumber can be sold as saw lumber or used in the plywood.

To produce the plywood, thin layers of wood must be peeled, glued, and dried. The peeler can produce 300,000 sheets of plywood in a month; the dryer has a capacity of 1,200,000 minutes for the month. The amount of lumber used and the drying time required for each sheet of plywood by grade is shown below.

| | Grade A Plywood Sheets | Grade B Plywood Sheets |
|---|---|---|
| Fir (in board feet) | 18 | 15 |
| Pine (in board feet) | 12 | 15 |
| Drying time (in minutes) | 4 | 6 |

The only restriction on the production of fir and pine lumber is the capacity of the mill saws to cut the logs into boards. These saws have a capacity of 500,000 board feet per month regardless of species.

Jenlock has the following quantities of lumber available for July production.

| | |
|---|---|
| Fir | 2,700,000 board feet |
| Pine | 3,000,000 board feet |

The contribution margins for each type of output are as follows:

| | |
|---|---|
| Fir lumber | $0.20 per board foot |
| Pine lumber | $0.10 per board foot |
| Grade A plywood | $2.25 per sheet |
| Grade B plywood | $1.80 per sheet |

The demand in July for plywood is expected to be a maximum of 80,000 sheets for grade A and a maximum of 100,000 sheets for grade B. There are no demand restrictions on pine and fir lumber.

The firm used a linear-programming model to determine the production quantities of each product. The correct formulation of the problem is presented below and a summary of the solution follows.

**FORMULATION**

F = board feet of fir lumber to be sold
P = board feet of pine lumber to be sold
A = number of sheets of grade A plywood to be sold
B = number of sheets of grade B plywood to be sold

maximize: $0.20F + 0.10P + 2.25A + 1.80B$

subject to:

| | | | | | | |
|---|---|---|---|---|---|---|
| Amount of fir available | F | + | 18A + | 15B | ≤ | 2,700,000 |
| Amount of pine available | | P + | 12A + | 15B | ≤ | 3,000,000 |
| Peeler capacity | | | A + | B | ≤ | 300,000 |
| Dryer capacity | | | 4A + | 6B | ≤ | 1,200,000 |
| Saw capacity | F + | P | | | ≤ | 500,000 |
| Maximum demand: | | | | | | |
| Grade A plywood | | | A | | ≤ | 80,000 |
| Grade B plywood | | | | B | ≤ | 100,000 |

**SUMMARY OF SOLUTION**

**Summary of the Primal Problem**

| Solution Variables | Solution Values |
|---|---|
| Pine lumber to be sold | 500,000 board feet |
| Grade A plywood to be sold | 80,000 sheets |
| Grade B plywood to be sold | 84,000 sheets |
| Slack items: | |
| Pine available | 280,000 board feet |
| Peeler capacity | 136,000 sheets |
| Dryer capacity | 376,000 minutes |
| Demand for grade B plywood | 16,000 sheets |
| **Nonsolution Variables** | **Opportunity Costs** |
| Fir lumber to be sold | \$0.02 |
| Constraining items: | |
| Fir available | \$0.12 |
| Saw capacity | \$0.10 |
| Demand for grade A plywood | \$0.09 |

**Ranges of the Restraining Values of the Constraints (000 omitted)**

| Constraints | Initial Constraint Value | Lower Limit | Upper Limit |
|---|---|---|---|
| Amount of fir available | 2,700 | 1,440 | 2,940 |
| Amount of pine available | 3,000 | 2,720 | Infinity |
| Peeler capacity | 300 | 164 | Infinity |
| Dryer capacity | 1,200 | 824 | Infinity |
| Saw capacity | 500 | –0– | 780 |
| Demand for plywood | | | |
| Grade A | 80 | 67 | 150 |
| Grade B | 100 | 84 | Infinity |

**Ranges of Objective Function Coefficients**

| Objective Coefficient | Initial Value | Lower Bound | Upper Bound |
|---|---|---|---|
| Fir lumber | \$0.20 | Negative infinity | \$0.22 |
| Pine lumber | \$0.10 | \$0.08 | Positive infinity |
| Grade A plywood | \$2.25 | \$2.16 | Positive infinity |
| Grade B plywood | \$1.80 | \$1.50 | \$1.875 |

**Required**

**a.** How much of each product should be produced and what is the total contribution of this mix?

**b.** Will all resources be used to capacity during July if the firm follows the solution derived? Explain.

**c.** Two items regarding fir lumber appear under nonsolution variables. Explain what each means.

**d.** Assuming no change in price, should they attempt to acquire any more fir for use during July, and if so, how much? Explain your answer.

**e.** The firm has been approached by a competitor asking to sell it some drying time. How much, if any, drying time should it sell? Explain your answer.

**f.** Additional mill saw capacity can be acquired at the rate of \$1,800 for an 8-hour day. The additional capacity can process 20,000 board feet of lumber in an 8-hour day. Should they acquire this extra capacity, and if so, how much time should they acquire? Explain.

**g.** What is the range within which the contribution of the grade B plywood can fluctuate before the optimal solution changes?

**5-78 Linear programming: Data requirements for multiple products and constraints.** MNO is equipped to produce four dolls: Andy, Bonnie, Christy, and Denny. The basic bodies for all the dolls are the same and are molded from plastic. The plastic costs $1.50 per doll. The molding machine can produce a total of 4,500 doll bodies per month. The major differences in the dolls are the heads and clothing. Heads for Andy and Denny are produced by one machine. This machine can turn out 2,500 heads per month. A different molding machine produces heads for Bonnie and Christy. This machine can produce 2,200 heads per month. The Andy and Denny heads cost $0.50 each for materials; the Bonnie and Christy heads cost $0.70 each. The clothing for Andy and Bonnie costs $0.80 per doll; the clothes for the "top-of-the-line" models, Christy and Denny, cost $0.95 each. The only direct labor in the production process is for packaging the dolls. Andy and Bonnie can be packed at the rate of 10 per hour, while Christy and Denny are packed 6 in an hour. Labor is paid $3 per hour. Management refuses to hire more laborers, so total available labor hours are limited to 500 per month. Overhead is estimated to be $7,000 per month plus $8.10 per direct labor hour. Andy and Bonnie sell for $10 each; Christy and Denny sell for $16.50 each.

**Required**

**a.** Set up the linear-programming problem that will determine the firm's optimal production quantities.
**b.** What does it mean for a slack variable to be in the optimal LP solution?
**c.** What is the economic interpretation of a shadow price for a primary variable; for a slack variable?
**d.** If a computer is available, solve the problem set up in (a).

**5-79 Linear programming: Data requirements for multiple products and constraints.** Berry Industries manufactures plastic kitchen utensils. The firm makes three products: a dish drainer, a cutting board, and a spatula. The suggested retail prices are $2.29 for the drainer, $1.49 for the cutting board, and $0.79 for the spatula. The products are sold through manufacturer's representatives. The representatives buy the products from Berry at a discount of 60% from the suggested retail price.

All three products are made from the same type of plastic. The firm currently has 800 pounds of plastic (less than a week's supply) in inventory, at a cost of $35 per hundred pounds. Suppliers have informed the firm that subsequent deliveries of plastic will cost $40 per hundredweight.

The molds for making the drainer and the spatula cost $20,000 each. The cutting board mold cost $5,000. The molds were all acquired 2 years ago and are being depreciated over a 15-year life, although their useful life is estimated to be 25 years.

The products are all made on the same machine (the appropriate mold is inserted for each product). The machine can produce 50 drainers per hour, 120 spatulas per hour, or 150 cutting boards per hour. The machine can be operated only 40 hours per week. Once the products are molded, the flashing (the excess plastic on the edges) must be trimmed by hand. An employee can trim 25 units per hour (all the products can be trimmed in the same amount of time). There are five employees, each of whom is paid $4 per hour. There is no additional work space available in the plant, so more trimmers cannot be hired. Each employee works 40 hours per week.

Once trimming is completed, a floral design is printed on the cutting board and the spatula. The printing press can print 125 cutting boards per hour or 150 spatulas per hour. The ink costs \$0.005 per unit for the spatulas and \$0.02 for each cutting board. The press can be operated for 40 hours per week.

Overhead has been found to vary closely with the cost of raw materials (ink and plastic) used. A regression analysis of overhead resulted in the following equation (the equation has been adjusted to reflect anticipated price changes).

$$\text{overhead (exclusive of depreciation)} = \$0.30 \text{ per dollar of raw materials} + \$700 \text{ per week}$$

The dish drainer requires 1 pound of plastic per unit, the cutting board requires 8 ounces, and the spatula requires 2 ounces.

**Required**

**a.** Set up the appropriate linear-programming problem to determine the quantity of each product that Berry should manufacture and sell.

**b.** If a computer is available, solve the problem set up in (a).

**5-80 Linear programming: Comprehensive—computer required.**

Retley Manufacturing makes three products: A, B, and C. The products sell for \$25, \$45, and \$50, respectively. The firm's salesman is paid \$400 per month plus a sales commission of 10% of the value of the products sold. Each product requires processing on each of two machines. The grinding machine is operated 8 hours a day for 25 days a month. Product A requires 2 hours of grinding, B requires 3 hours, and C requires 6 hours. The finishing machine can theoretically be operated 8 hours a day for 25 days, but in fact the firm usually loses 25% of this time due to breakdowns. Product A uses 2 hours of finishing time, B uses 4 hours, and C uses 2 hours.

Final assembly of the products is done by hand. Four units of A can be assembled by a laborer per hour, while it takes 2 hours to put together a unit of B, and 30 minutes to assemble a unit of C. All three products use the same raw material. Product A needs 3 pounds, B needs 5 pounds, and C needs 8 pounds.

Labor is paid \$7 per hour and raw materials cost \$3 per pound. The firm uses the following equation to predict overhead.

$$\text{overhead} = \$100 + \$3 \text{ per direct labor hour}$$

**Required**

**a.** Determine the optimal product mix if management's goal is to maximize net income.

**b.** Assume that management wishes to maximize market penetration. What products and quantities should it sell to maximize sales? What is the cost to Retley of increasing market share instead of maximizing income?

**c.** Assume that Retley is a subsidiary of a large corporation. If Retley's management is given a bonus as a percentage of dollar sales, what will management produce in order to maximize the bonus? What will be the net income?

**d.** Assume that Retley's marketing division insists on the company producing and selling at least 10 units of each product. What is the optimal production? What is the opportunity cost of this action?

**5-81 Formulation for linear-programming equations—computer required.** (CMA adapted).

SmyCo manufactures two types of display boards; one is a marking board and the other is a tack board. Both boards pass through two manufacturing departments. All of the raw materials—board base, board covering, and aluminum frames—are cut to size in the Cutting Department. Both types of boards are the same size and use the same frames. They are assembled in one of two departments—the Automated Assembly Department or the Labor Assembly Department.

Automated is a capital-intensive operation that has been in operation for 18 months and was intended to replace labor. However, the business expanded so rapidly that both assembly operations are needed and used. The final results of the two assembly operations are identical. The only difference between the two is the proportion of machine time versus direct labor in each department and, thus, different costs. However, workers have been trained for both operations so that they can be switched between the two operations.

Data regarding the two products and their manufacture are presented in the following schedules.

**SALES DATA**

| | Marking Board | Tack Board |
|---|---|---|
| Selling price per unit | $60.00 | $45.00 |
| Variable selling expenses per unit | $3.00 | $3.00 |
| Annual fixed selling and administrative expenses (allocated equally between the two products) | $900,000 | $900,000 |

**UNIT VARIABLE MANUFACTURING COSTS**

| | Cutting Department | | | |
|---|---|---|---|---|
| | Marking Board | Tack Board | Labor Assembly Department[a] | Automated Assembly Department[a] |
| Raw materials | | | | |
| Base | $ 6.00 | $6.00 | $ — | $ — |
| Covering | 14.50 | 7.75 | — | — |
| Frame | 8.25 | 8.25 | — | — |
| Direct labor | | | | |
| (@ $10/DLH) | 2.00 | 2.00 | — | — |
| (@ $12/DLH) | — | — | 3.00 | 0.60 |
| Manufacturing overhead | | | | |
| Supplies | 1.25 | 1.25 | 1.50 | 1.50 |
| Power | 1.20 | 1.20 | 0.75 | 1.80 |

[a]The unit costs for the marking board and the tack board are the same within each of the two assembly departments.

**MACHINE HOUR DATA**

| | Cutting Department | Labor Assembly Department | Automated Assembly Department |
|---|---|---|---|
| Machine hours required per board | 0.15 | 0.02 | 0.05 |
| Monthly machine hours available | 25,000 | 1,500 | 5,000 |
| Annual machine hours available | 300,000 | 18,000 | 60,000 |

SmyCo produced and sold 600,000 marking boards and 900,000 tack boards last year. Management estimates that total unit sales for the coming year could increase 20% if the units can be produced. It has contracts to produce and sell 30,000 units of each board each month.

Sales, production, and cost incurrence are uniform throughout the year. There is a monthly maximum labor capacity of 30,000 hours in the Cutting Department and a total of 40,000 hours in the two assembly departments.

**Required**

**a.** Formulate and label the objective function and the constraint functions. Be sure to define your variables.

**b.** Solve the problem using a computer.

# APPENDIX 5B

# THE EXPECTED VALUE OF PERFECT INFORMATION

In the chapter we mentioned that calculating the cost of a prediction error is a useful means for determining whether we should spend resources to get more accurate accounting data. This appendix expands that discussion. If we can make some simplifying assumptions about what outcomes are likely, we can calculate the expected value of the benefits that should accrue if we obtained perfect information. Because it is doubtful that we can ever get perfect information, this expected value is a useful maximum limit for the amount we should be willing to spend to get better data.

Assume that management is choosing which of two processes to use to acquire a product. The relevant costs are:

Process A: $ 40,000 per period + $9 per unit
Process B: $100,000 per period + $4 per unit

The product sells for $15 per unit.

The appropriate choice of processes, of course, depends upon the anticipated level of operations. Setting the cost of the two processes equal to each other and solving for the indifference level of volume yields

$$\begin{aligned} \$40{,}000 + \$9x &= \$100{,}000 + \$4x \\ \$5x &= \$60{,}000 \\ x &= 12{,}000 \end{aligned}$$

That is, process A will be preferred at demand levels below 12,000 units and process B is preferred at demand levels greater than 12,000 units per period. Further, calculating the breakeven point for process A yields

$$\begin{aligned} \$15x - \$9x - \$40{,}000 &= \$0 \\ \$6x &= \$40{,}000 \\ x &= 6{,}666.67 \end{aligned}$$

These calculations provide the following decision rule. The firm should stay out of this business if average demand is less than 6,666.67 units per period, should use process A if demand is between 6,666.67 and 12,000 units per period, and should use process B if periodic demand is expected, on the average, to exceed 12,000 units. This relationship is depicted graphically in Figure 5-9.

As in the chapter, we can calculate the cost of a prediction error under specific assumptions. For example, assume that management made a prediction that demand would be 11,000 units per period, but demand turned out to be 13,000 units. The cost of the prediction error is computed by comparing the costs incurred by taking the action that, based upon the prediction, seemed best with the cost of the optimal action given the true demand for the product. In this case the cost would be:

| | |
|---|---|
| Cost of actual action | |
| (use of process A): $ 40,000 + $9(13,000) = | $157,000 |
| Cost of optimal action | |
| (use of process B): $100,000 + $4(13,000) = | 152,000 |
| Opportunity cost (cost of the prediction error) | $ 5,000 |

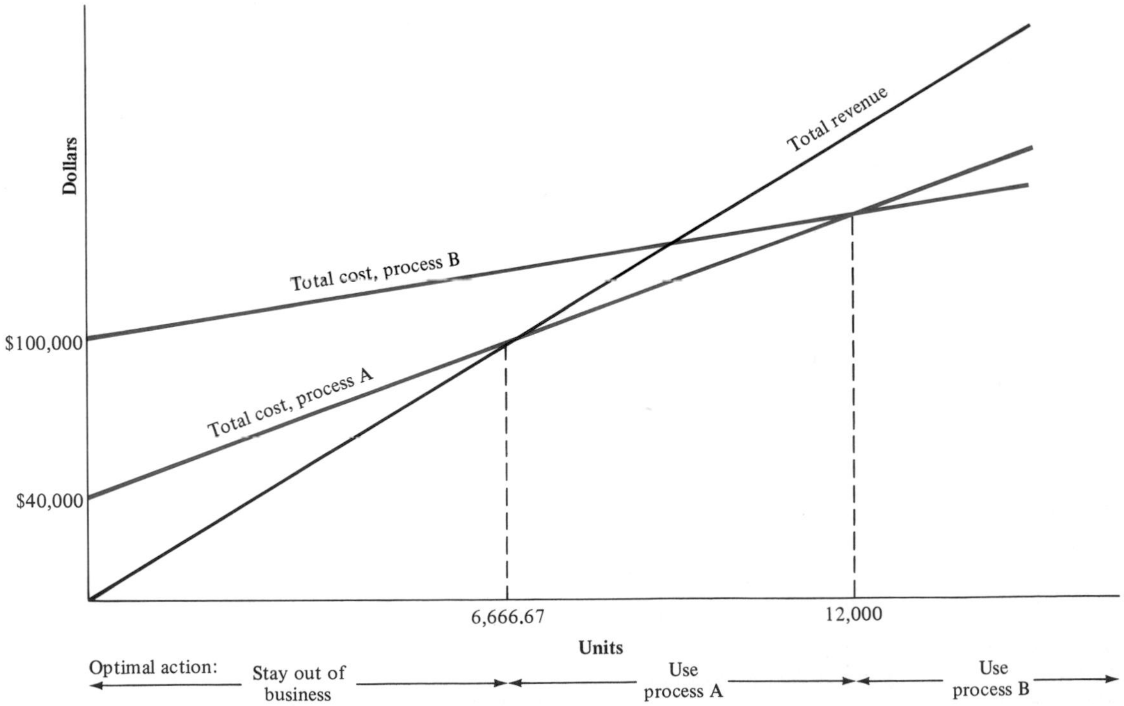


**FIGURE 5-9 Graphic solution to the decision problem.**

Note again that if a prediction error does not lead to an action different from the optimal action, there is no cost due to the prediction error. That is, if management predicted demand to be 11,000 units but demand turned out to be 10,500 units, there would be no cost due to the prediction error because both the actual action and the optimal action would be to use process A. Thus, on the high side, a prediction error only occurs if demand exceeds 12,000 units.

The preceding calculations for the cost of a prediction error are the same as those shown in the chapter. Although the computations are useful for showing the effect that specific prediction errors may have, the approach does not provide an estimate of what is actually likely to happen. This latter value can be estimated by calculating the expected value for the prediction error.

## DISCRETE DEMAND

If only a few levels of discrete demand are possible it is a relatively easy task to compute the cost of the prediction error for each level of demand, multiply by the probability that demand would be equal to that level, and sum to get the expected cost of the prediction error. For example, assume that management feels that only five levels of demand are possible. The possible levels of demand and the estimate of the probability that demand will be equal to each level are:

| Demand | Probability |
|---|---|
| 8,000 | 0.1 |
| 9,500 | 0.2 |
| 11,000 | 0.4 |
| 12,500 | 0.2 |
| 14,000 | 0.1 |

If management chooses process A, the computations in Exhibit 5-11 reveal that the expected cost of the prediction error is $1,500. Thus, using expected values as a criterion, $1,500 is the most that management should be willing to pay to obtain perfect information as to what demand will be.

## CONTINUOUS DEMAND

Discrete distributions are easy to work with, but they tend to be unrealistic. In the example, demand is much more likely to follow a continuous dis-

**EXHIBIT 5-11 Expected Cost of Prediction Error—Discrete Demand**

| Demand | Probability | Cost of Prediction Error | Expected Cost |
|---|---|---|---|
| 8,000 | 0.1 | $ 0 | $ 0 |
| 9,500 | 0.2 | 0 | 0 |
| 11,000 | 0.4 | 0 | 0 |
| 12,500 | 0.2 | 2,500[a] | 500 |
| 14,000 | 0.1 | 10,000[b] | 1,000 |
| Total expected cost | | | $1,500 |

[a][$40,000 + $9(12,500)] − [$100,000 + $4(12,500)] = $ 2,500
[b][$40,000 + $9(14,000)] − [$100,000 + $4(14,000)] = $10,000

tribution. Fortunately, if anticipated demand can be represented by a well-behaved continuous distribution, the expected cost of the prediction error can still be easily calculated. We discuss two such distributions in the next sections.

### Demand Uniformly Distributed

If demand is thought to follow a uniform distribution (that is, management estimates that all levels of demand in a given interval are equally likely), then the calculation of the expected cost of a prediction error is quite straightforward. Returning to the previous example, assume that management represents potential demand as being uniformly distributed over the range of 9,000 to 13,000 units per period. Thus the mean demand is still 11,000 units and management again chooses to use process A.

As indicated before, there is a cost due to a prediction error only if demand turns out to be greater than 12,000 units. If demand turns out to be 12,001 units, the cost of the prediction error is:

$$\$40{,}000 + \$9(12{,}001) - \$100{,}000 - \$4(12{,}001) = \$5$$

Similar calculations would show that the cost of the prediction error for an actual demand level of 12,002 is $10 and for demand of 12,003 the cost is $15. The pattern is quite clear: The cost of the prediction error can be represented as a linear function of the amount by which actual demand exceeds 12,000 units. The variable opportunity cost per unit of the excess demand is $5. Letting $d$ represent actual demand, the function can be represented as:

$$\text{Opportunity cost} = \begin{cases} \$0 & \text{for } d \leq 12{,}000 \\ \$5(d - 12{,}000) & \text{for } d > 12{,}000 \end{cases}$$

Because the cost function is linear, and the probability density function for a uniform distribution is also linear, the expected cost of the prediction error is a simple average. It is only necessary to calculate the amount of the probability associated with demand being between 12,000 and 13,000 units and multiply this result by the average cost of the prediction error in this demand interval.

Because one-fourth of the probability density over the range 9,000 to 13,000 units is associated with the range of 12,000 to 13,000 units, there is a 25% chance that a prediction error will occur; that is,

$$\frac{13{,}000 - 12{,}000}{13{,}000 - 9{,}000} = 0.25$$

The average cost of a prediction error in this range is (\$5,000 + \$0)/2 = \$2,500.[1] Hence the expected cost of the prediction error turns out to be \$2,500 (0.25) = \$625.

### Demand Normally Distributed

The case in which potential demand is normally distributed is almost as easy as the previous illustration. Assume that management's prediction of potential demand is best represented by a normal distribution with a mean of 11,000 units and a standard deviation of 1,500 units. Such a distribution may have been obtained from the use of regression to estimate the demand function for similar products or in similar markets. An intuitive approach to solving the problem is to estimate the probability that demand will equal 12,001 units (plus or minus half a unit), multiply this probability by the cost of the prediction error for a demand of 12,001 units and add this amount to the result from similar calculations for demands of 12,002 units, 12,003, and so on. Although this would be an onerous task, it is not a conceptually difficult one.

Fortunately, these calculations[2] have already been made for the standard normal distribution, with a linear loss function, incorporating a variable cost per unit of deviation of \$1. These calculations have been tabulated in the Linear Normal Loss Integral, a portion of which is reproduced in Exhibit 5-12. Because all normal distributions have the same area beyond a stated number of standard deviations from the mean, one need only determine how far the critical point (the point at which a loss begins to occur: 12,000 in the example) is from the mean. Then the tabulated

[1]The cost of the prediction error is zero if demand is 12,000 units, and \$5(13,000 − 12,000) = \$5,000 if demand is 13,000 units.

[2]The actual calculations were made using calculus, not the intuitive approach described.

figures from the Linear Normal Loss Integral can be used to calculate the expected cost if the variable cost per unit is $1. Then, because the loss function is linear, the expected cost for a variable cost other than $1 can be obtained by multiplying the figure from Exhibit 5-12 by the actual variable cost per unit of deviation. The last adjustment needed is to convert the standard deviation of the tabulated figures from a distribution with a standard deviation of 1 to the actual standard deviation. This is also accomplished by simply multiplying by the actual value of the standard deviation. Thus letting $L$ represent the appropriate factor from Exhibit 5-12, letting $S$ be the standard deviation of the predicted demand distribution, and letting $V$ be the variable cost per unit for the prediction error, the expected cost of the prediction error is simply:

$$\text{expected cost} = V \times S \times L$$

The calculations are illustrated with the example problem. The first step is to determine the appropriate factor from the table for the loss

**EXHIBIT 5-12 Table of the Linear Normal Loss Integral**

| z | L | z | L | z | L |
|---|---|---|---|---|---|
| .00 | .3989 | 1.00 | .0833 | 2.00 | .0085 |
| .05 | .3744 | 1.05 | .0757 | 2.05 | .0074 |
| .10 | .3509 | 1.10 | .0686 | 2.10 | .0065 |
| .15 | .3284 | 1.15 | .0621 | 2.15 | .0056 |
| .20 | .3069 | 1.20 | .0561 | 2.20 | .0049 |
| .25 | .2863 | 1.25 | .0506 | 2.25 | .0042 |
| .30 | .2668 | 1.30 | .0455 | 2.30 | .0037 |
| .35 | .2481 | 1.35 | .0409 | 2.35 | .0032 |
| .40 | .2304 | 1.40 | .0367 | 2.40 | .0027 |
| .45 | .2137 | 1.45 | .0328 | 2.45 | .0023 |
| .50 | .1978 | 1.50 | .0293 | 2.50 | .0020 |
| .55 | .1828 | 1.55 | .0261 | 2.55 | .0017 |
| .60 | .1687 | 1.60 | .0232 | 2.60 | .0015 |
| .65 | .1554 | 1.65 | .0206 | 2.65 | .0012 |
| .70 | .1429 | 1.70 | .0183 | 2.70 | .0011 |
| .75 | .1312 | 1.75 | .0162 | 2.75 | .0009 |
| .80 | .1202 | 1.80 | .0143 | 2.80 | .0008 |
| .85 | .1100 | 1.85 | .0126 | 2.85 | .0006 |
| .90 | .1004 | 1.90 | .0111 | 2.90 | .0005 |
| .95 | .0916 | 1.95 | .0097 | 2.95 | .0005 |

$z$ is the number of standard deviations from the mean at which the linear loss begins.
$L$ is the expected cost for a $1 per unit loss given the standard normal distribution.

integral. This requires knowledge of how many standard deviations the critical value (the point at which the loss begins to occur) is from the mean of the demand distribution. This distance is $(12{,}000 - 11{,}000)/1{,}500 \approx 0.70$ standard deviations. For a critical value 0.7 standard deviations from the mean, Exhibit 5-12 reveals that the loss factor is 0.1429. Since the variable cost is \$5 per unit of error, and the standard deviation of the demand distribution is 1,500 units, the expected cost of the prediction error is \$5(1,500)(0.1429) = \$1,072.

### A More Complicated Example

In the previous example the possibility that demand could turn out to be less than 6,666.67 units (the point at which the firm should choose not to operate) was ignored. Because that critical value was quite far away from the mean demand, the cost of a prediction error for demands less than 6,666.67 units would be very small, and could be safely ignored. The next example incorporates this possibility. Assume that management characterizes potential demand as a normal distribution with a mean of 11,000 units and a standard deviation of 5,500 units. Based upon this prediction, management again chose process A. In calculating the expected cost of the prediction error, it is now necessary to incorporate the possibility that demand will be less than 6,666.67 units as well as the possibility that demand will exceed 12,000 units. That is, the optimal action is to select process A if demand is between 6,666.67 and 12,000 units, but the optimal action if demand is below 6,666.67 units is to stay out of the business. A second issue involves what to do with the portion of the demand function related to demand levels of less than zero. The range of the normal distribution is infinite; yet, as a practical matter, demand is never negative.

The first problem can be handled as follows: The variable cost of a prediction error as a function of demand is \$5 per unit for demand in excess of 12,000 units. The expected cost of the prediction error is again calculated by first determining the expected cost for demand in excess of 12,000 units. The loss factor for $(12{,}000 - 11{,}000)/5{,}500 \approx 0.20$ is 0.3069, yielding an expected cost of \$5(5,500)(0.3069) = \$8,440.

A similar set of calculations is also necessary to determine the expected cost of the prediction error for demand less than 6,666.67 units. For demand less than 6,666.67 units, the firm's optimal action is to stay out of the business. Thus if demand is 6,666 units, the cost of the prediction error is:

| | | |
|---|---|---|
| Optimal action | (stay out of the business) | \$0 |
| Actual action | \$15(6,666) − \$9(6,666) − \$40,000 = | (4) |
| Cost of the prediction error | | \$4 |

But that is the cost for an error of just 0.67 units, so we will do some more calculations. If demand is 6,665 units, the cost of the prediction error would be \$10, and for a demand of 6,664 the cost is \$16. Now we can see that for demand less than 6,666.67 units, the loss function can be expressed as \$6(6,666.67 − $d$). As before, the linear normal loss integral is used to determine the expected cost of the prediction error. The loss factor for (11,000 − 6,666.67)/5,500 ≈ 0.80 is 0.1202. Multiplication yields the expected cost as \$6(5,500)(0.1202) = \$3,967. But this calculation includes the possibility that demand is less than zero.

Negative demand might imply that people are attempting to sell the product to the firm. On the reasonable assumption that management would not purchase the product, it would appear that the firm's maximum loss would be the fixed costs incurred during the period. In the example, these fixed costs amount to \$40,000 per period for process A. To correct the previous calculation for the expected cost for demand less than 6,666.67 units, it is necessary to subtract out the additional opportunity cost of \$6 per unit for demand levels below zero. Note that the expected value of the fixed loss of \$40,000 has been properly included in that calculation. Thus the only correction needed involves looking up the linear normal loss factor for (11,000 − 0)/5,500 = 2.00, finding that the factor is 0.0085 and multiplying to get the expected value of the variable cost for demand less than zero as \$6(5,500)(0.0085) = \$280. Subtracting this figure from the previous calculation gives the expected cost of the prediction error for demand less than 6,666.67 units as \$3,967 − \$280 = \$3,687. Finally, combining this last figure with the expected cost of the prediction error for demand greater than 12,000 units provides the total expected cost of the prediction error as \$8,440 + \$3,687 = \$12,127.

## THE VALUE OF INFORMATION

The expected cost of a prediction error is the average of all possible prediction errors (including many with a value of zero) weighted by their probability of occurrence. In information theory, this is called the **expected value of perfect information.** That is, it is the value of receiving every possible error-free information signal weighted by the prior probability of receiving each signal. This in turn sets the maximum limit on the amount that one should be willing to pay to obtain more accurate information.

The computations shown here have been extended to calculate the expected value of imperfect information. For these latter computations we need to be able to estimate the effect that imperfect information will have on the distribution of anticipated demand levels. Although the ensuing computations are similar to those we have demonstrated, they go beyond the intended level of this text.

## PROBLEMS AND CASES: APPENDIX 5B

**5-82 Expected cost of prediction error: Capacity constraint.**
A firm has the capacity to produce 10,000 units of a made-to-order product per day. Typical daily demand is normally distributed with a mean of 6,000 units and a standard error of 1,000 units. (Note that capacity is 4 standard deviations from average demand, so it is highly unlikely that demand would ever exceed capacity.)

Customers insist on same-day service. If such service is not available they will go elsewhere. The product sells for $3 per unit and costs $0.75 in variable costs to produce.

One morning a customer from outside the normal marketing area places a special order for 3,000 units at $2 per unit. Management assumes that the day's demand from regular customers will still have a mean of 6,000 units.

**Required**
Assuming that management accepts the order, what is the expected opportunity cost from lost regular sales? (*Hint:* This is a very slight variation on the expected cost of a prediction error.)

**5-83 Expected value of perfect information: Normal distribution.**
ALA Associates has landed a military contract to produce an expensive, but seldom used, spare part. The fee is sufficiently high that the firm will make a profit even if only one unit is produced, but management doesn't know how many units will be ordered. Management's best guess is that 20 units will be ordered, but potential demand is thought to be normally distributed, with a standard deviation of 4 units.

There are two ways to build this part. The first requires a set-up cost of $100,000 and a variable cost of $4,000 per unit. The second approach requires a set-up cost of $118,000 and a variable cost of $3,000.

**Required**
If management acts on its best guess, what is the expected cost of the prediction error?

**5-84 Expected value of perfect information: Uniform distribution.**
Lederman Products is evaluating two alternative embossing machines for acquisition. The machine selected will be used to manufacture a single product for sale during the coming summer. At the end of the summer the machine will be scrapped. The first machine costs $12,000 and will make the product at a variable cost of $15 per unit. The second machine costs $48,000 but manufactures the product for $9 per unit. The product sells for $18 per unit.

Management's best guess is that 5,000 units will be sold during the summer. However, potential demand is thought to be equally likely over the range of 3,000 to 7,000 units. A marketing firm has offered to do a survey at a cost of $500. They promise that the survey will be able to predict demand exactly.

**Required**
Should the firm hire the marketing firm to do the survey?

**5-85 Expected cost of perfect information: Discrete distribution.**
City College uses one of two means for producing examinations: an offset printer or a xerographic copier. The copier produces copies from typed material on plain

paper at a cost of \$0.08 per page. The offset printer requires that the original be typed onto a special mat that costs \$3 a sheet; however, the copies are then produced at a cost of \$0.03 per page.

On a Friday a professor brought a one-page quiz to be typed by the departmental secretary. The professor will come back on Saturday to reproduce the quiz. Unfortunately, the professor did not tell the secretary how many copies will be produced.

The secretary is aware that the professor has three sections of the class for which the quiz was produced. Each class has 20 students. The secretary estimates that there is a 60% probability that the quiz will be used for all three sections, a 30% probability it will be used in two sections, and a 10% chance it will be used in only one section.

The secretary decides to type the quiz on an offset mat, but before doing so, asks you whether it would be wise to call the professor for instructions. The professor lives out of town so there will be a \$0.75 toll charge for the call.

**Required**

On an expected-value basis, should the secretary call the professor to determine how many copies will be made?

**5-86 Expected cost of perfect information—comprehensive.**

Trimble Industries has been purchasing a steel roller pin for several years. The pin sells for \$0.65, and variable manufacturing costs have been stable at \$0.34 per unit for quite some time. The firm has been producing at its capacity of 1 million units per period, and could expect to do so in the future.

An engineer has suggested that the firm convert to manufacturing a titanium roller. The firm could produce 600,000 of these units at capacity. There is tremendous demand for the product. At a selling price of \$3.00 per unit the firm would have more orders than it could fill.

Management has decided to produce the titanium rollers. However, there is uncertainty as to the variable cost per unit to produce them.

**Required**

**a.** Determine the expected cost of the prediction error if management predicts that the distribution of possible unit variable costs is as follows:

| Cost per Unit | Probability |
|---|---|
| \$2.35 | 0.15 |
| 2.40 | 0.20 |
| 2.45 | 0.30 |
| 2.50 | 0.20 |
| 2.55 | 0.15 |

**b.** What is the expected cost of the prediction error if management estimates that the variable cost per unit is uniformly distributed over \$2.20 to \$2.75?

**c.** What is the expected cost of the prediction error if management estimates that the distribution of potential variable cost values is normal, with a mean of \$2.40 and a standard deviation of \$0.1666?

**d.** A detailed engineering study could be performed prior to the conversion to the new product. This study would cost \$15,000, but would determine actual variable cost with certainty. Should the study be undertaken?

# CHAPTER 6

# PREPARATION OF THE MASTER BUDGET

Using the techniques developed in Chapters 4 and 5, management will have developed an operating plan for the firm. We now take this overall plan and combine it with the detailed standards developed in Chapter 3 to produce the firm's master budget. The **master budget** is a budget prepared prior to the beginning of the accounting period that details plans for the amount of sales and the level of costs anticipated for all segments of the firm. As such, the master budget is really a collection of **pro forma** (projected) **financial statements** for the next period. Included are an expected statement of cost of goods manufactured, a pro forma income statement, a budget detailing the anticipated acquisition of resources, and a statement of estimated cash flows.

## THE USEFULNESS OF BUDGETS

Many managers, particularly those unfamiliar with accounting, criticize budgets as being a waste of effort. They often complain that there are too many estimates in the budget, making the budgeted projections too uncertain to be useful. However, every major firm prepares budgets. Why?

Formal budgets serve several useful purposes; they

1. Force advance planning.
2. Provide lead time to solve problems.

3. Communicate management's expectations.
4. Communicate management's priorities.
5. Grant spending authority.
6. Establish prices for internal services.
7. Form the basis for performance evaluations.

Among the most important purposes served by budgets is that they force managers to think about the future, project trends, and develop appropriate strategies. Although this sounds trite, most of us get so involved with managing day-to-day problems that unless there is an externally imposed requirement to sit down and prepare plans, the planning function will lose out to what at the moment seem to be higher-priority tasks. Yet if we do not consider where we are going and how we are going to adjust to changes in the marketplace, our current operations will soon become obsolete. A formal budgeting system will assure us that we have given at least *some* consideration to the future.

Budgets also provide us with lead time to solve problems. For example, if our budget shows that we are going to be $200,000 short of cash during the fourth quarter of the year, we are far better off knowing it in January than in October. In January we will have several months to arrange the best line of credit. If the cash squeeze comes as a surprise in October, we may have to accept the first source of credit that becomes available (or, far worse, find that none is available). Similarly, if we project very large increases (or decreases) in demand for our product, we can start to obtain the necessary capacity so that it will be available when needed (alternatively, we can search for other uses of capacity if demand is expected to decrease).

Budgets also prove to be excellent communication devices. The budget will incorporate all of management's financial and operating goals for the period. Thus the budget serves to tell middle and first-line managers what upper management's expectations are. In this way subordinates can monitor their own progress to try to ensure that they are meeting their superior's expectations (thereby gaining promotion and salary increases).

In the same vein, budgets serve to communicate management priorities. The budget may emphasize the traditional "bottom line" (profits), market share, company image (pushing prestige products), employee relations, or whatever factors management feels are important for the next period.

Budgets also are a means for formally granting authority to managers. Particularly in not-for-profit organizations, but also for profit-oriented firms, many budget figures become the authorization for a manager to spend funds. Budgets for office supplies, charitable contributions, and computer time are, in effect, limits up to which managers are free to make expenditures that they feel are necessary or useful. This dispenses with the need for a manager to get approval for decisions involving routine operating costs.

At the same time, budgets establish prices for internally generated services. For example, we can estimate the total operating cost for our central computer (say, \$292,500), and the total number of hours it will be used (say, 4,500 hours), and calculate a budgeted cost per hour (\$292,500 ÷ 4,500 = \$65). This budgeted cost per hour then becomes the price that users will pay whenever they use the computer. Users then will know in advance what costs to expect when they utilize the service.

Finally, budgets serve as the basis for performance evaluation. We cannot tell how well we have done unless we know what was possible. Measuring actual performance against a budget will allow us to determine whether we were effective (Did we accomplish what was planned?) and whether we were efficient (Did we do what we did using the minimum resources?).

Although many people will complain about the budget and the budgeting process, budgets are indispensable in large modern organizations. Virtually every major U.S corporation has a budgeting department located in the corporate headquarters office. The major duty of such a department is to prepare and keep current the operating and long-range planning budgets.

## PREPARING THE MASTER BUDGET

As we will see next, the actual preparation of the budget is a rather mechanical process. In spite of the relative ease with which the numbers can be manipulated, we should not be lulled into thinking we can be careless in its preparation. Given the large number of people in the organization who will be using the budget as a guide to their activities, any errors, even small ones, may have a significant impact on our operations.

### Forecasting Limited Resources

The budgeting process begins with a projection of the factor that constrains the size of operations. For most firms this means projecting anticipated sales. That is, production plans will depend on the level of sales orders we believe can be achieved. However, there are organizations for which some other factor may limit the scope of operations. For farmers the amount of available land may be the primary constraint around which the budget is prepared. For many nonprofit agencies the budgeting process may begin with a projection of the grants and donations they will receive. In each case we project the availability of our scarce resource, set a goal for the level of operations to be achieved given our projection, and then plan for how to achieve that goal efficiently.

### Sales Forecasting

Since the amount of product or services that a firm can sell is by far the most common factor limiting the size of operations, we should be aware of the more common sales forecasting approaches. Sales forecasts may be made very informally or may utilize sophisticated marketing techniques. For new firms, or for new product lines, the forecasts will necessarily be somewhat subjective. Management may look at sales in similar markets, sales of firms already in the industry, or use test markets. In the first two cases the first step is to estimate the size of the market in the intended distribution area and then predict what market share the firm will be able to capture. The estimate of market share will likely be based on the experience of other new entrants to the industry and the firm's own experience in entering similar new markets.

A large firm, anticipating a nationwide market, may consider test marketing the new product. This is particularly useful for innovative products for which there is little experience with similar products. The firm either may pick a few market areas that it believes are representative of the nation or may choose a range of marketing areas differing by such factors as rural versus urban setting or disposable income. In the first case, if the test markets are truly representative of the nationwide market, the firm may be able to make direct projections from the test markets to the entire market. The second approach, on the other hand, may also provide information as to the segments of the market on which the firm should concentrate its sales effort. For example, if the product does well only in urban markets, there is no need for heavily promoting it in rural areas.

For established firms, sales forecasts may be as simple as projecting the firm's past sales growth to the future. Unfortunately, few firms enjoy smooth, continuous growth. In the more common case, management will need to project future economic or environmental conditions that will affect the firm's sales. For many firms seasonal factors are extremely important. For example, the sales of air conditioners (summer), colognes (Christmas), toys (Christmas), food coloring (Easter), and electric blankets (winter) all experience sharp seasonal effects. However, even for these firms sales will also likely be affected by economic events, in particular the overall level of consumer disposable income.

Especially for large industries, firms may have to predict national trends. Home building and auto sales seem to respond rather directly to national income and interest rates. In turn, the home building industry has secondary effects on the sales of appliances, carpeting, and construction services. Firms in these latter industries closely monitor the number of new housing starts. In addition, some firms may have to predict the mood and spending inclinations of Congress. Research and development firms and military contractors are very dependent on congressional spending patterns.

### Mechanics of Master Budget Preparation

Let us now illustrate the preparation of a master budget for a simple, single-product firm.[1] The firm in this example manufactures a vitreous china product considered indispensable in the modern home. There is virtually no replacement market for this product, so management forecasts sales as a function of the number of new housing starts in the firm's marketing area. Management anticipates capturing 35% of the market next year.

The first step for preparing the budget is to project sales for each budget period. Although it would be more realistic to prepare monthly budgets, we will prepare quarterly budgets to conserve space. Assume that Exhibit 6-1 represents the forecasted number of new housing starts for the firm's marketing area as projected by the economic staff of the regional Federal Reserve Bank. Based on this information, our expected market share, and an anticipated selling price of $65 per unit, we can then estimate our quarterly sales as in Exhibit 6-2.

In Exhibit 6-2 we have combined the quarterly projected housing starts with the results of a marketing study that indicates the average number of products which have historically been included in new homes. Multiplying these figures gives us an estimate of the total market for our type of product. Multiplying the total market by the anticipated market share yields the anticipated unit sales. Finally, multiplying by the expected unit sales price yields the projected quarterly dollar sales.

Combining budgeted unit sales with desired inventory levels, we can next derive a production budget. Assume that the firm expects to begin

**EXHIBIT 6-1 Projected New Housing Starts in Marketing Area**

| Quarter | Housing Starts | |
|---|---|---|
| First | 3,000 | $68,250 |
| Second | 12,000 | 273,000 |
| Third | 6,000 | 136,500 |
| Fourth | 2,000 | 45,500 |

[1]A more complex demonstration is presented in Comprehensive Case 1: Budgeting, which follows this chapter.

**EXHIBIT 6-2 Converting New Housing Starts to Sales Budget**

| Quarter[a] | Housing Starts | Average Units of Product per Home | Total Product Market | Market Share | Projected Sales (units) | Projected Sales Dollars (@ $65 each) |
|---|---|---|---|---|---|---|
| First | 3,000 | 2.0 | 6,000 | 35% | 2,100 | $136,500 |
| Second | 12,000 | 1.9 | 22,800 | 35 | 7,980 | 518,700 |
| Third | 6,000 | 2.0 | 12,000 | 35 | 4,200 | 273,000 |
| Fourth | 2,000 | 2.1 | 4,200 | 35 | 1,470 | 95,550 |

[a]It would not be unusual for there to be a delay between the start of building a home and the installation of the product. Thus a more realistic approach might be to project sales partly as a function of the current and past quarter's housing starts. For simplicity we ignore that minor complication.

the year with 200 units costing $6,230 in finished goods inventory. Management informs us that they would like to end each quarter with 10% of the following quarter's sales in ending inventory. Production requirements are derived by reversing the normal process of determining an ending inventory balance. That is, we typically determine an ending balance by adding acquisitions to the beginning balance to get the goods available for use. Subtracting the goods used from those available yields the ending balance. Reversing this process, we can see that the ending balance plus the goods used must also equal the goods available for use; subtracting the beginning balance from the goods needed to be available yields the goods that must be acquired. These calculations are summarized in Exhibit 6-3.

Once our production requirements have been determined we are able to prepare a schedule of resource needs—that is, raw materials, direct labor, and overhead requirements. Using approaches such as those discussed in Chapter 3, management has determined that we need 40 pounds of raw material (clay) for each finished unit of product. In addition, each unit requires 3 hours of direct labor time. Once we have these estimates,

**EXHIBIT 6-3 Production Budget (units)**

| | Quarter | | | |
|---|---|---|---|---|
| | First | Second | Third | Fourth |
| Desired ending inventory[a] | 798 | 420 | 147 | 210[b] |
| Sales (from Exhibit 6-2) | 2,100 | 7,980 | 4,200 | 1,470 |
| Total units required to be available | 2,898 | 8,400 | 4,347 | 1,680 |
| Beginning inventory | (200) | (798) | (420) | (147) |
| Required production | 2,698 | 7,602 | 3,927 | 1,533 |

[a]10% of next quarter's sales.

[b]Using this year's first-quarter sales to project next year's first-quarter sales.

**EXHIBIT 6-4 Manufacturing Resource Requirements**

| Quarter | Units of Production (from Exhibit 6-3) | Pounds of Material per Unit | Total Materials Requirements (pounds) | Hours of Labor per Unit | Total Labor Requirements (hours) |
|---|---|---|---|---|---|
| First | 2,698 | 40 | 107,920 | 3 | 8,094 |
| Second | 7,602 | 40 | 304,080 | 3 | 22,806 |
| Third | 3,927 | 40 | 157,080 | 3 | 11,781 |
| Fourth | 1,533 | 40 | 61,320 | 3 | 4,599 |

it is a simple matter to multiply them by the number of units we intend to produce to yield total material and labor needs (see Exhibit 6-4).

The materials needed for production are then adjusted for the amount of raw materials inventory on hand at the beginning of the period and the desired level of ending raw materials inventory. The result of these adjustments yields the materials acquisition budget presented in Exhibit 6-5. In Exhibit 6-5 we assume that there will be 10,000 pounds of materials on hand at the beginning of the year.

The materials acquisition budget in Exhibit 6-5 is stated in terms of the pounds of materials needed, and the labor requirements derived in Exhibit 6-4 are in hours. To convert these budgets into dollar terms, we need to estimate the average purchase price for raw materials and the estimated prevailing wage rate for labor. Assuming that our suppliers predict that materials will cost $0.25 per pound, and our union contract specifies a labor rate of $6 per hour, Exhibit 6-6 presents our budgeted costs for materials and labor.

The budgeting for our prime costs has been relatively logical and straightforward. But as we have seen in Chapter 3, the budgeting for overhead costs is more circuitous. Generally we do not attempt to relate

**EXHIBIT 6-5 Materials Acquisition Budget (pounds)**

| | Quarter | | | |
|---|---|---|---|---|
| | First | Second | Third | Fourth |
| Desired ending inventory[a] | 30,408 | 15,708 | 6,132 | 10,792 |
| Production needs | 107,920 | 304,080 | 157,080 | 61,320 |
| Total requirements | 138,328 | 319,788 | 163,212 | 72,112 |
| Beginning inventory | (10,000) | (30,408) | (15,708) | (6,132) |
| Required acquisitions | 128,328 | 289,380 | 147,504 | 65,980 |

[a]Assumed to be 10% of the following quarter's production requirements. Needs for the first quarter of next year are assumed to be the same as the current year's first quarter.

**EXHIBIT 6-6 Budgeted Materials and Labor Costs**

| Quarter | Materials Acquisitions (Exhibit 6-5) | Materials Cost ($0.25 per Pound) | Labor Requirements (Exhibit 6-4) | Labor Cost ($6 per Hour) | Total Costs (DM + DL) |
|---|---|---|---|---|---|
| First | 128,328 | $ 32,082 | 8,094 | $ 48,564 | $ 80,646 |
| Second | 289,380 | 72,345 | 22,806 | 136,836 | 209,181 |
| Third | 147,504 | 36,876 | 11,781 | 70,686 | 107,562 |
| Fourth | 65,980 | 16,495 | 4,599 | 27,594 | 44,089 |
| Totals | 631,192 | $157,798 | 47,280 | $283,680 | $441,478 |

overhead costs directly to our level of production but rather to other measures of activity that we believe more closely capture a cause-and-effect relationship for the amount of overhead costs incurred.

Assume that our firm is organized into just two departments: (1) production and (2) sales and administration. In the production department our accounting system records four types of overhead costs: indirect labor, supplies, depreciation, and "other" (everything else). We start by using account analysis to determine whether some of the costs are obviously fixed or variable costs. Depreciation is a likely candidate for being a purely fixed cost. Checking our records we note that we use straight-line depreciation and that depreciation charged to the production department has been $4,500 per quarter for some time. Since management does not anticipate acquiring any additional fixed assets next year, we will continue to budget depreciation at $4,500 per quarter.

The cost behavior of indirect labor, supplies, and "other" is not intuitively obvious. For these costs we have examined our past records to determine a relationship between their level and several possible variables; our study revealed that they seem to vary most closely with the amount of direct labor hours that we use. Based on these studies we estimate the following relationships.

| | | |
|---|---|---|
| Indirect labor cost | $0.30 | per direct labor hour |
| Supplies cost | 0.26667 | per direct labor hour |
| Other costs | 0.10 | per direct labor hour |
| Total | $0.66667 | per direct labor hour |

Although these are not exact relationships, we feel they are close enough to establish reasonably accurate budget estimates for the costs. Thus in the first quarter when we anticipate using 8,094 direct labor hours (see Exhibit 6-6), we will budget $2,428 for indirect labor, $2,158 for supplies, and $809 for "other" (see Exhibit 6-7).

**EXHIBIT 6-7 Budgeted Departmental Overhead**

| | Quarter | | | | |
|---|---|---|---|---|---|
| | First | Second | Third | Fourth | Total |
| Production department | | | | | |
| Variable costs | | | | | |
| Indirect labor | $2,428 | $ 6,842 | $ 3,534 | $1,380 | $14,184 |
| Supplies | 2,158 | 6,082 | 3,142 | 1,226 | 12,608 |
| Other | 809 | 2,280 | 1,178 | 460 | 4,727 |
| Total variable costs | $5,395 | $15,204 | $ 7,854 | $3,066 | $31,519 |
| Fixed costs | | | | | |
| Depreciation | $4,500 | $ 4,500 | $ 4,500 | $4,500 | $18,000 |
| Total fixed costs | $4,500 | $ 4,500 | $ 4,500 | $4,500 | $18,000 |
| Grand total | $9,895 | $19,704 | $12,354 | $7,566 | $49,519 |
| Sales and administrative | | | | | |
| Variable costs | | | | | |
| Commissions | $13,650 | $51,870 | $27,300 | $ 9,555 | $102,375 |
| Total variable costs | $13,650 | $51,870 | $27,300 | $ 9,555 | $102,375 |
| Fixed costs | | | | | |
| Salaries | $11,000 | $11,000 | $11,000 | $11,000 | $ 44,000 |
| Depreciation | 1,200 | 1,200 | 1,200 | 1,200 | 4,800 |
| Other | 650 | 700 | 675 | 550 | 2,575 |
| Total fixed costs | $12,850 | $12,900 | $12,875 | $12,750 | $ 51,375 |
| Grand total | $26,500 | $64,770 | $40,175 | $22,305 | $153,750 |

For the sales and administration department we also record costs in four categories: salaries, sales commissions, depreciation, and all other. This time, account analysis again reveals that depreciation is a fixed cost, which we will budget at $1,200 per quarter. Account analysis also suggests that salaries are likely to be a fixed cost and that commissions will vary directly with sales. The intended salary schedule budgets salaries at $11,000 per quarter, and company policy is to pay a 10% commission to sales representatives. Commissions then are budgeted simply as 10% of the budgeted quarterly sales (provided in Exhibit 6-2). Finally, for the other costs we are unable to determine a relationship between them and any other item, so we simply budget them to be equal to last year's actual costs plus an adjustment for inflation. The bottom half of Exhibit 6-7 completes the budget for overhead.

Once we have the budgeted overhead costs, we can prepare the budgeted statement of cost of goods manufactured and sold. Earlier the cost of the beginning finished goods inventory was stated to be $6,230. With that information, the assumption that there are no goods in process,

**EXHIBIT 6-8 Budgeted Statement of Cost of Goods Manufactured and Sold**

| | Quarter | | | | |
|---|---|---|---|---|---|
| | First | Second | Third | Fourth | Total |
| Beginning materials | $ 2,500 | $ 7,602 | $ 3,927 | $ 1,533 | $ 2,500 |
| Plus purchases | 32,082 | 72,345 | 36,876 | 16,495 | 157,798 |
| Less ending materials | 7,602 | 3,927 | 1,533 | 2,698 | 2,698 |
| Cost of materials used | $26,980 | $ 76,020 | $ 39,270 | $15,330 | $157,600 |
| Plus beginning work-in-process | — | — | — | — | — |
| Cost of direct labor used | 48,564 | 136,836 | 70,686 | 27,594 | 283,680 |
| Cost of overhead | 9,895 | 19,704 | 12,354 | 7,566 | 49,519 |
| Less ending work-in-process | — | — | — | — | — |
| Cost of goods manufactured | $85,439 | $232,560 | $122,310 | $50,490 | $490,799 |
| Beginning finished goods | 6,230 | 25,271 | 12,849 | 4,578 | 6,230 |
| Goods available for sale | $91,669 | $257,831 | $135,159 | $55,068 | $497,029 |
| Less ending finished goods[a] | 25,271 | 12,849 | 4,578 | 6,916 | 6,916 |
| Cost of goods sold | $66,398 | $244,982 | $130,581 | $48,152 | $490,113 |

[a]Ending units (from Exhibit 6-3) times current cost of goods manufactured divided by units manufactured in the current period. For the first quarter the computation is 798($85,439/2,698) = $25,271.

and the assumption that the firm uses a first-in, first-out inventory flow assumption (ending inventories are valued at current period production costs), Exhibit 6-8 provides the budgeted statement of cost of goods manufactured and sold.

In Exhibit 6-8 the figures for purchases and labor are taken from Exhibit 6-6, and the overhead costs are from Exhibit 6-7. The calculation of the cost of ending finished goods inventory requires knowledge of the number of units produced in each quarter and each quarter's ending finished goods inventory in units. These figures are found in Exhibit 6-3.

Next the budgeted income statement is prepared. This statement, provided in Exhibit 6-9, uses budgeted sales from Exhibit 6-2, cost of goods

**EXHIBIT 6-9 Budgeted (Pro Forma) Income Statement**

| | Quarter | | | | |
|---|---|---|---|---|---|
| | First | Second | Third | Fourth | Total |
| Sales | $136,500 | $518,700 | $273,000 | $95,550 | $1,023,750 |
| Cost of goods sold | 66,398 | 244,982 | 130,581 | 48,152 | 490,113 |
| Gross margin | $ 70,102 | $273,718 | $142,419 | $47,398 | $ 533,637 |
| Selling and administration | 26,500 | 64,770 | 40,175 | 22,305 | 153,750 |
| Net income | $ 43,602 | $208,948 | $102,244 | $25,093 | $ 379,887 |

sold from Exhibit 6-8, and budgeted selling and administration costs from Exhibit 6-7.

Our next step is to prepare a statement of budgeted cash receipts and disbursements. While the budgeted income statement shows that we expect to be quite profitable, there is no guarantee that there will be a positive cash flow.

To prepare the cash receipts and disbursements report we need to know how the timing of cash flows relates to actual sales and expenses. Let us assume that customers pay in the month following sale. In that case we receive two-thirds of each quarter's sales in cash during the quarter and one-third in the quarter following. Multiplying these proportions by the sales quantity figures given in Exhibit 6-2 provides the receipts listed in Exhibit 6-10.

We also assume that we pay for material purchases in the month following purchase. Finally, all other costs—labor, supplies, commissions and so forth—are paid in the month in which the costs are incurred. Most of these latter figures are given in Exhibit 6-7. With these assumptions and

**EXHIBIT 6-10 Budgeted Cash Receipts and Disbursements**

| | Quarter | | | | |
|---|---|---|---|---|---|
| | First | Second | Third | Fourth | Total |
| Receipts | | | | | |
| From current quarter's sales | $ 91,000 | $345,800 | $182,000 | $ 63,700 | $ 682,500 |
| From prior quarter's sales | 31,000 | 45,500 | 172,900 | 91,000 | 340,400 |
| Total receipts | $122,000 | $391,300 | $354,900 | $154,700 | $1,022,900 |
| Disbursements | | | | | |
| For current quarter's purchases | $ 21,388 | $ 48,230 | $ 24,584 | $ 10,997 | $ 105,199 |
| For prior quarter's purchases | 5,500 | 10,694 | 24,115 | 12,292 | 52,601 |
| Direct labor costs | 48,564 | 136,836 | 70,686 | 27,594 | 283,680 |
| Indirect labor | 2,428 | 6,842 | 3,534 | 1,380 | 14,184 |
| Supplies | 2,158 | 6,082 | 3,142 | 1,226 | 12,608 |
| Salaries | 11,000 | 11,000 | 11,000 | 11,000 | 44,000 |
| Commissions | 13,650 | 51,870 | 27,300 | 9,555 | 102,375 |
| Other | 1,459 | 2,980 | 1,853 | 1,010 | 7,302 |
| Dividends | — | — | — | 375,000 | 375,000 |
| Total disbursements | $106,147 | $274,534 | $166,214 | $450,054 | $ 996,949 |
| Beginning cash balance | $ 9,250 | $ 25,103 | $141,869 | $330,555 | $ 9,250 |
| Plus receipts | 122,000 | 391,300 | 354,900 | 154,700 | 1,022,900 |
| Less disbursements | 106,147 | 274,534 | 166,214 | 450,054 | 996,949 |
| Ending cash balance | $ 25,103 | $141,869 | $330,555 | $ 35,201 | $ 35,201 |

knowledge of the beginning cash balance (assumed to be $9,250), the current balance for accounts receivable from last month's sales (assumed to be $31,000), and the current balance for payables for material purchases (assumed to be $5,500), we can prepare the cash receipts and disbursements budget in Exhibit 6-10. We have included in disbursements an anticipated fourth-quarter dividend of $0.50 per share for an assumed 750,000 shares outstanding. Also note that depreciation does not show up in the schedule since it has no effect on the cash balance.

Exhibit 6-10 indicates that the firm will have adequate cash resources to finance planned production. In fact, it appears that there will be considerable excess cash available during the third and fourth quarters (until the dividend is paid). Management should consider placing these excess funds in short-term investments. The effect of short-term investments or borrowing on the cash budget is developed in detail in the demonstration problem at the end of this chapter.

The very last step in preparing the master budget is the preparation of the pro forma balance sheet. Because the balance sheets require quite

**EXHIBIT 6-11 Pro Forma Balance Sheet and Statement of Retained Earnings**

**PRO FORMA BALANCE SHEET**

| | Beginning of Year | | End of Year | | |
|---|---|---|---|---|---|
| Assets | | | | | |
| Cash | | $ 9,250 | | $ 35,201 | (Exhibit 6-10) |
| Raw materials inventory | | 2,500 | | 2,698 | (Exhibit 6-8) |
| Finished goods inventory | | 6,230 | | 6,916 | (Exhibit 6-8) |
| Accounts receivable | | 31,000 | | 31,850 | ($\frac{1}{3}$ of 4th-quarter sales) |
| Total current assets | | $ 48,980 | | $ 76,665 | |
| Building and equipment | $912,000 | | $912,000 | | (Assumed) |
| Accumulated depreciation | (114,000) | 798,000 | (136,800) | 775,200 | (Exhibit 6-7) |
| Total assets | | $846,980 | | $851,865 | |
| Equities | | | | | |
| Accounts payable (purchases) | | $ 5,500 | | $ 5,498 | ($\frac{1}{3}$ of 4th-quarter purchases) |
| Common stock | | 750,000 | | 750,000 | (Assumed) |
| Retained earnings | | 91,480 | | 96,367 | (Below) |
| Total equities | | $846,980 | | $851,865 | |

**STATEMENT OF RETAINED EARNINGS**

| | |
|---|---|
| Beginning balance (above) | $ 91,480 |
| Plus net income (Exhibit 6-9) | 379,887 |
| Less dividends (Exhibit 6-10) | 375,000 |
| Ending balance | $ 96,367 |

a bit of space, we will simply present beginning-of-year and end-of-year statements. Exhibit 6-11 summarizes our previous assumptions concerning beginning account balances and adds assumed initial balances for buildings and equipment, accumulated depreciation, and retained earnings. All of the other transactions are incorporated into the ending balances, which are cross-referenced to the previous exhibits. Finally, at the bottom of Exhibit 6-11 we have also included a budgeted statement of retained earnings.

## THE FLEXIBLE BUDGET

The master budget is the budget reflecting our best estimate of the level of operations we expect to achieve. While useful for planning, it will not be very useful for performance evaluation. The reason is that the actual level of operations achieved will most likely differ from that planned in the master budget. Thus, for performance evaluation we will need another budget that reflects the actual level of operations achieved. The **flexible budget,** or **variable budget,** is a set of cost relationships that can be used to determine the level of costs which should be incurred for any level of output within the relevant range. At the end of the accounting period, the actual level of operations attained will be substituted into the flexible budget to obtain a standard against which actual costs incurred can be compared.

The flexible budget uses the same per-unit variable cost data as the master budget, while fixed costs are budgeted as a lump sum. For example, the flexible budget for manufacturing costs for the example used to illustrate the preparation of the master budget would be as follows:

| | |
|---|---|
| Direct materials costs | $0.25 × 40 pounds per unit |
| Direct labor costs | $6 × 3 hours per unit |
| Variable overhead costs | $0.67 × 3 hours per unit |
| Fixed overhead costs | $18,000 per year |

Once we have the flexible budget cost relationships, it is a simple matter to calculate the budgeted cost allowances for any level of production. If during the year we produce 16,000 units of product, the flexible budget for costs would be

| | | |
|---|---|---|
| Direct materials | $0.25 × 40 × 16,000 | $160,000 |
| Direct labor | $6 × 3 × 16,000 | 288,000 |
| Variable overhead | $0.67 × 3 × 16,000 | 32,160 |
| Fixed overhead | | 18,000 |
| Total | | $498,160 |

If we produce 18,000 units, the flexible budget allowance for costs is

| | | |
|---|---|---|
| Direct materials | $0.25 × 40 × 18,000 | $180,000 |
| Direct labor | $6 × 3 × 18,000 | 324,000 |
| Variable overhead | $0.67 × 3 × 18,000 | 36,180 |
| Fixed overhead | | 18,000 |
| Total | | $558,180 |

Notice that the "flex" in the flexible budget comes solely from the adjustment of variable costs to reflect the costs budgeted for a particular level of activity. The budgeted fixed costs will not change as we adjust the level of production. In addition, we assume that the cost functions are linear in the firm's relevant range. Therefore the variable *per-unit* costs for the resources will remain unchanged.

The flexible budget is a valuable tool for performance evaluation. It allows us to easily compare the actual costs incurred with those which should have been incurred. For example, the master budget for our illustration called for the production of 15,760 units of product (the total production in Exhibit 6-3) and total manufacturing costs of $490,799 (see total cost of goods manufactured in Exhibit 6-8). Assume that we actually produced 16,500 units at a total cost of $510,000. If we compare actual performance to the master budget, it would appear that we operated inefficiently (the actual costs have been assumed).

| | Master Budget | Actual Cost | Over (under) Budget |
|---|---|---|---|
| Direct materials | $157,600 | $163,500 | $ 5,900 |
| Direct labor | 283,680 | 294,600 | 10,920 |
| Variable overhead | 31,519 | 34,300 | 2,781 |
| Fixed overhead | 18,000 | 17,600 | (400) |
| Total | $490,799 | $510,000 | $19,201 |

But the comparison ignores the fact that 16,500 units were produced instead of the 15,760 called for in the master budget. To reflect the efficiency with which we produced the actual output, we should compare the actual costs to a flexible budget for the 16,500 units produced:

| | Flexible Budget (16,500 units) | Actual Costs | Over (under) Budget |
|---|---|---|---|
| Direct materials | $165,000 | $163,500 | $(1,500) |
| Direct labor | 297,000 | 294,600 | (2,400) |
| Variable overhead | 33,165 | 34,300 | 1,135 |
| Fixed overhead | 18,000 | 17,600 | (400) |
| Total | $513,165 | $510,000 | $(3,165) |

This latter comparison reveals that on an overall basis, for the output attained, the firm was efficient. While more was spent for variable overhead items than was budgeted, this was more than offset by savings in materials, labor, and fixed overhead costs. Thus the total costs incurred were less than those anticipated in the flexible budget.

## PARTICIPATION IN THE BUDGETING PROCESS

Both in our setting of unit standards in Chapter 3, and in the preparation of the master budget in this chapter we have assumed that we could unambiguously determine the proper budget amounts. Of course, our figures are actually goals. If central management specifies these goals without consulting line managers and production workers, the budget is called an *imposed* budget. Although management may feel it has the necessary information to prepare the budget, imposed budgets are often viewed by subordinates with suspicion. In some cases employees may feel that managers are trying to squeeze out extra production by overworking the employees. If these feelings develop, it is unlikely that employees will accept the budget goals and be motivated to achieve the budgeted results.

To overcome the possible problems with imposed budgets, many managers advocate **participative budgeting,** wherein appropriate employees and line managers are asked to assist in the budgeting process. For example, we can ask our salespeople to assist in the preparation of sales forecasts and our production employees to assist in the standard-setting process. In addition, departmental managers should help in the estimation of departmental overhead costs and the scheduling of production. It is believed that if all employees play a role in the development of the budget, they are much more likely to accept the final product as a statement of realistic goals. In turn, they are more likely to make a concerted effort to attain the budgeted results.

Unfortunately, participative budgeting can lead to **budgetary slack,** which results when understated revenues or overstated costs are included in the budget. These misstatements provide employees with a cushion to make the attainment of budgetary goals easier to achieve. Obviously, the inclusion of budgetary slack means that the budget no longer represents the standard for efficient performance.

## DYSFUNCTIONAL EFFECTS OF BUDGETS

Although budgets are indispensable in most large organizations, they are also blamed for encouraging behavior not in the best interests of the firm.

For example, if budgetary allowances for discretionary spending are based on an adjustment to the previous period's spending, managers are encouraged to spend all funds by year-end. By exhausting discretionary funds the managers expect to preclude the possibility of reduced future funding. **Zero-based budgeting,** which requires a manager to justify all funds requested (not just an increase over the previous year), is an attempt to solve this problem.

If too much emphasis is placed on meeting the budget, the budget may be met at the expense of not meeting other firm objectives. Concentrating only on meeting short-term financial results may result in ignoring long-term results. Short-term sales goals may be met by turning out shoddy, hastily assembled products, but such an action may have disastrous long-term results for the firm. Similarly, deferral of maintenance and repair costs may lead to significant breakdowns and expenses in future periods.

Possibly the worst effect of an overemphasis on meeting the budget occurs when employees take actions that misrepresent actual results. One such common practice is to ship goods that were not ordered to customers at year-end. The sales, and income, are booked in the year of shipment. The entries are then reversed when the goods are returned, but this occurs in the next year. Perpetrators of such a scheme hope to be able to make up for the returned goods during the ensuing year. When such practices occur, upper management is misled about both the demand for the firm's products and the profitability of the firm. For example, a recent story in the financial press reported that a large manufacturer of computer equipment had been expanding manufacturing capacity on the basis of constantly increasing sales. However, an audit revealed that the firm's largest division had been overstating sales for several years by making year-end shipments of unordered products. In the year the discrepancy was found, the division's sales had been overstated by 25%. Further analysis showed that while the firm was expanding capacity, legitimate sales were actually flat. The firm ended up in bankruptcy.

### Environmental and Behavioral Influences

An extensive and often contradictory literature exists regarding how people react to budgets and budgetary pressure. The findings to date indicate that strict adherence to tight budgets are preferable in some environments, whereas in other environments budgets should only be used as a general guide for operations. Unfortunately, the appropriate choice in this range of alternatives is made difficult because there appears to be a very large number of relevant variables affecting the optimal choice. For example, it appears that the stability of the environment has an effect. A strong emphasis on budgets tends to be more effective in environments with little technological change, where relationships between inputs and outputs are fairly constant. But in environments where the relationships assumed in the budget quickly become out-of-date, a strong emphasis on meeting budget goals may be counterproductive.

Personalities also play a role. Some people are more comfortable with precise, detailed goals, whereas others prefer a more general statement of objectives. Additional factors found to have an influence are the nature of the firm's compensation plan, the size of the work groups in the firm, the leadership ability of first-line supervisors, and a host of others. Because there are so many variables involved, it is not surprising that little concrete advice can be given for choosing the most appropriate emphasis on budgets for a particular firm. Nonetheless, the budgets themselves are essential for most firms.

## SUMMARY

The master budget represents management's expectations for a period. It establishes the goal for the level of operations to be achieved and communicates to each responsibility center what that center's role will be in helping to achieve that goal. By being prepared in advance the master budget provides managers with lead time to solve anticipated problems. The budget also establishes internal prices, such as the cost of providing internal services, thereby allowing managers to adjust demand for services accordingly. The flexible budget is a set of cost equations that can be used to calculate budget allowances for the level of activity attained. The efficiency of actual performance is measured relative to the flexible budget.

## DEMONSTRATION PROBLEM

Giant Greens, Inc., processes and wholesales frozen green peas. Its balance sheet reveals the following as of January 1, 19X5.

| Assets | | Equities | |
|---|---|---|---|
| Cash | $ 15,000 | Commissions payable | $ 20,000 |
| Marketable securities | 30,000 | Common stock | 600,000 |
| Inventory | 210,000 | Retained earnings | 135,000 |
| Office building (net) | 500,000 | | |
| Total assets | $755,000 | Total equities | $755,000 |

During 19X5 management anticipates selling ~~10,000~~ 11,000 cases of peas per month at $10 per case. The beginning inventory consists of 70,000 cases costing $3 per case

**EXHIBIT 6-12 Monthly Cash Budget**

| 1 | 2 | 3 | 4 | 5 | 6 |
|---|---|---|---|---|---|
| Month | Beginning Balance | Cash from Operations | Dividends | Projected Balance | Investing |
| January | $15,000 | $ 45,000 | — | $ 60,000 | $ 40,000 |
| February | 20,240 | 45,000 | — | 65,240 | 40,000 |
| March | 25,800 | 45,000 | $ 30,000 | 40,800 | 20,000 |
| April | 21,680 | 45,000 | — | 66,680 | 40,000 |
| May | 27,720 | 45,000 | — | 72,720 | — |
| June | 74,080 | (327,000) | 30,000 | (282,920) | (170,000) |
| July | 27,080 | 45,000 | — | 72,080 | — |
| August | 20,330 | 45,000 | — | 65,330 | — |
| September | 23,580 | 45,000 | 30,000 | 38,580 | — |
| October | 27,455 | 45,000 | — | 72,455 | 10,000 |
| November | 21,830 | 45,000 | — | 66,830 | 40,000 |
| December | 26,410 | 45,000 | 30,000 | 41,410 | 20,000 |
| Selected totals and balances | | | $120,000 | | $ 20,000 |

on a FIFO basis. In June the firm will purchase enough peas to prepare 120,000 cases of product. The peas will cost $240,000, and processing costs will amount to $132,000. Both amounts will be paid in June.

The firm pays its salespeople a commission of $2 per case in the month following sale. General administrative expenses requiring cash payments are $35,000 per month. In addition, the office building is depreciated at $5,000 per month. The firm's customers must pay cash on delivery. The firm pays dividends of $30,000 in March, June, September, and December.

During the year the firm wishes to maintain a minimum cash balance of $20,000 on the first of each month. Excess cash in multiples of $10,000 can be invested, on the last day of the month, in marketable securities earning 0.8% interest per month. The interest is paid to the firm in cash on the last day of the month. If the firm anticipates being short of cash, it can borrow on the first of the month in multiples of $10,000. The interest is 1.25% per month and must be paid on the first day of the subsequent month. Principal repayments are made on the last day of a month.

**Required**
Prepare a monthly cash budget for the year. Also prepare a pro forma income statement for the year and the pro forma year-end balance sheet.

**Solution**
Exhibit 6-12 presents the condensed cash budget. In column 3, only the net cash from operations has been reported. This figure for every month but June is determined by subtracting cash expenses from sales, as follows:

| 7<br>Current Period's Investment | 8<br>Interest Income | 9<br>Borrowing | 10<br>Loan Balance | 11<br>Interest Expense | 12<br>Ending Balance |
|---|---|---|---|---|---|
| $ 30,000 | $ 240 | — | — | — | $20,240 |
| 70,000 | 560 | — | — | — | 25,800 |
| 110,000 | 880 | — | — | — | 21,680 |
| 130,000 | 1,040 | — | — | — | 27,720 |
| 170,000 | 1,360 | — | — | — | 74,080 |
| — | — | $140,000 | $140,000 | — | 27,080 |
| — | — | (50,000) | 90,000 | $1,750 | 20,330 |
| — | — | (40,000) | 50,000 | 1,750 | 23,580 |
| — | — | (10,000) | 40,000 | 1,125 | 27,455 |
| — | — | (40,000) | — | 625 | 21,830 |
| 10,000 | 80 | — | — | 500 | 26,410 |
| 50,000 | 400 | — | — | — | 21,810 |
| $ 50,000 | $4,560 | | | $5,750 | $21,810 |

| | |
|---|---|
| Sales | $100,000 |
| Commissions | 20,000 |
| General administration | 35,000 |
| Cash from operations | $ 45,000 |

Note that although sales commissions are paid one month late, the amount is a constant $20,000 each month; also, depreciation expense has been left out because it does not require the payment of cash. For June the cash from operations recognizes that the firm must pay $240,000 for materials and $132,000 for processing; that is, $(327,000) = $45,000 − $240,000 − $132,000.

Column 4 reflects dividend payments and column 5 gives each month's projected ending cash balance before financing and investing activities. Column 6 is the amount of excess funds that the firm can invest on the last day of the month. For January the firm is projecting a cash balance at the end of the month of $60,000. Since the firm needs only $20,000 in cash at the start of February, it can invest $40,000 on January 31. Column 7 reports the amount of invested funds on which the firm earns interest for the current month. Since the beginning balance sheet shows that $30,000 was invested on January 1, the firm will earn $240 in interest during January. The interest income is shown in column 8.

Column 9 records any borrowing necessary during the month. Column 10 reflects the loan balance outstanding at the end of the month. The interest payment is recorded in column 11 and reflects the interest rate of 1.25% multiplied by the previous month's loan balance (recall that interest payments are paid on the first day of the month following the month in which the interest is accrued). Finally, column 12 reflects the ending cash balance after reflecting anticipated financing and investing activities.

Most of the entries in Exhibit 6-12 follow the pattern just explained. However, the June entries need some explanation. The firm begins June with a balance of $74,080. Because the firm will run short of cash during June, it will not invest its cash in excess of $20,000 on May 31. The net effect of the beginning cash balance of $74,080, the $327,000 cash operating deficit and the $30,000 dividend payment yields the projected deficit at month-end of $282,920. The firm can cover part of this shortfall by selling its marketable securities on June 1 resulting in an inflow of $170,000. This still leaves a projected shortage of $112,920, and, when combined with the $20,000 minimum desired cash balance, means that the firm

**EXHIBIT 6-13 Pro Forma Financial Statements**

**INCOME STATEMENT**

| | | |
|---|---|---|
| Sales | | $1,200,000 |
| Cost of goods sold | | |
| Beginning inventory | $ 210,000 | |
| Cost of goods manufactured | 372,000 | |
| Ending inventory | (217,000) | 365,000 |
| Gross margin | | $ 835,000 |
| Sales commissions | | 240,000 |
| General administration | | 420,000 |
| Office depreciation | | 60,000 |
| Net income from operations | | $ 115,000 |
| Interest income | | 4,560 |
| Interest expense | | 5,750 |
| Net income | | $ 113,810 |

**STATEMENT OF RETAINED EARNINGS**

| | |
|---|---|
| Beginning retained earnings | $ 135,000 |
| Plus net income | 113,810 |
| Less dividends | 120,000 |
| Ending retained earnings | $ 128,810 |

**BALANCE SHEET**

| Assets | | Equities | |
|---|---|---|---|
| Cash | $ 21,810 | Commissions payable | $ 20,000 |
| Marketable securities | 70,000 | Common stock | 600,000 |
| Inventory | 217,000 | Retained earnings | 128,810 |
| Office building (net) | 440,000 | Total equities | $748,810 |
| Total assets | $748,810 | | |

needs to borrow at least $132,920. Since borrowing is restricted to multiples of $10,000, the firm will need to borrow $140,000 on June 1. Although interest will accrue on the loan during June, the interest payment does not need to be made until July 1. Hence the ending cash balance for June is $27,080.

Exhibit 6-13 presents the firm's pro forma income statement for 19X5 and its balance sheet as of December 31, 19X5. Most of the information needed for the financial statements was also required to prepare Exhibit 6-12. However, there are a couple of differences. For both the income statement and balance sheet, we need the value of ending inventory. The firm started the year with 70,000 cases in inventory, plans to sell 120,000 cases, and plans to produce 120,000 cases. Therefore, in units, ending inventory should consist of 70,000 cases. Since the firm uses FIFO costing, these units must be valued at 19X5 production cost. The cost of goods manufactured during 19X5 amounted to $372,000 for 120,000 cases, or $3.10 per case. Multiplying the ending inventory units by $3.10 gives the cost of $217,000 reflected in Exhibit 6-13.

The other difference in Exhibit 6-13 is our need to recognize depreciation expense in the income statement. This figure was given as $5,000 per month, which yields $60,000 for the year. We must, of course, also remember to adjust the net book value of the office building on the balance sheet for this same $60,000. These adjustments plus the previously derived information should explain all the figures provided in Exhibit 6-13.

## KEY TERMS AND CONCEPTS

Master budget
Pro forma financial statement
[ Flexible budget
[ Variable budget
Participative budgeting
Budgetary slack
Zero-based budgeting

[ Bracketed terms are equivalent in meaning.

## FURTHER READING

Brownell, Peter. "Participation in Budgeting, Locus of Control and Organizational Effectiveness," *The Accounting Review* (October 1981), p. 844.

Brownell, Peter. "Participation in the Budgeting Process—When It Works and When It Doesn't," *Journal of Accounting Literature* (Spring 1982), p. 124.

Carruth, Paul J., and Thurrel O. McClendon. "How Supervisors React to 'Meeting the Budget' Pressure," *Management Accounting* (November 1984), p. 50.

Chandler, John S., and Thomas N. Trone. " 'Bottom Up' Budgeting and Control," *Management Accounting* (February 1982), p. 37.

Geurts, Michael D., and Thomas A. Buchman. "Accounting for 'Shocks' in Forecasts," *Management Accounting* (April 1981), p. 21.

Kenis, Izzettin. "Effects of Budgetary Goal Characteristics on Managerial Attitudes and Performance," *The Accounting Review* (October 1979), p. 707.

Leitch, Robert A., John B. Barrack, and Sue H. McKinley. "Controlling Your Cash Resources," *Management Accounting* (October 1980), p. 58.

Merchant, Kenneth A. "The Design of the Corporate Budgeting System: Influences on Managerial Behavior and Performance," *The Accounting Review* (October 1981), p. 813.

Shen, Paul. "Cash Flow Budgeting for the Importer," *Management Accounting* (September 1980), p. 33.

Trapani, Cosmo S. "Six Critical Areas in the Budgeting Process," *Management Accounting* (November 1982), p. 52.

## QUESTIONS AND EXERCISES

**6-1** What is the usual relationship among the sales budget, the production budget, and the materials acquisition budget?

**6-2** How can budgeting assist an organization in its use of human resources?

**6-3** The budgeting process facilitates "management by exception." Explain.

**6-4** Budgeting has been proposed as a partial solution to the problem of "management by crisis." Explain.

**6-5** What are the objectives of participatory budgeting?

**6-6** What is the distinguishing characteristic of zero-based budgeting?

**6-7** How are the master budget and the flexible budget related?

**6-8** The master budget is employed both before the period begins and after the period ends. Explain.

**6-9** How do unit standards relate to the master budgeting process?

**6-10** Although a university includes in each department's budget a dollar amount for computer usage, the department is not given any cash for computer usage nor is cash transferred to the computer center when a department uses the computer. What is the purpose of this budget?

**6-11** (CPA adapted). Stevens Corporation began operations in 19X0. For the year ended December 31, 19X0, Stevens made available the following information.

| | |
|---|---|
| Total merchandise purchases for the year | $350,000 |
| Merchandise inventory at December 31, 19X0 | 70,000 |
| Collections from customers | 200,000 |

All merchandise was marked to sell at 40% above cost. Assuming that all sales are on a credit basis and all receivables are collectible, what should be the balance in accounts receivable at December 31, 19X0?

**6-12** (CPA adapted). Mapes Corporation has estimated its activity for January. Selected data from these estimated amounts are as follows:

| | |
|---|---|
| Sales | $1,400,000 |
| Gross profit (based on sales) | 30% |
| Increase in trade accounts receivable during month (gross) | $ 40,000 |
| Change in accounts payable during month | $ 0 |
| Increase in inventory during month | $ 20,000 |

Variable selling, general, and administrative (S, G, & A) expenses include a charge for uncollectible accounts of 1% of sales. No receivables are expected to be written off in January.

Total S, G, & A expenses are $142,000 per month plus 15% of sales. Depreciation expense of $80,000 per month is included in fixed S, G, & A expenses.

What are the estimated cash receipts and cash disbursements for January?

**6-13** (CPA adapted). Fields Corporation projects the following transactions for its first year of operations.

| | |
|---|---|
| Proceeds from issuance of common stock | $1,000,000 |
| Sales on account | 2,200,000 |
| Collections of accounts receivable | 1,800,000 |
| Cost of goods sold | 1,400,000 |
| Disbursements for purchases of merchandise and expenses | 1,200,000 |
| Disbursements for income taxes | 250,000 |
| Disbursements for purchase of fixed assets | 800,000 |
| Depreciation on fixed assets | 150,000 |
| Proceeds from borrowings | 700,000 |
| Payments on borrowings | 80,000 |

What is the projected cash balance for the end of the year?

**6-14** Bynsel, Inc., projects the following unit purchases and sales for the first 4 months of the year.

| Month | Purchases | Sales |
|---|---|---|
| 1 | 300 | 200 |
| 2 | 400 | 300 |
| 3 | 300 | 400 |
| 4 | 400 | 300 |

The cost of 1 unit is $100, of which two-thirds is paid in the month of purchase and one-third is paid in the month following. A discount of 3% is granted on payments made within the same month as purchase.

The goods are sold for $200 each. Sales are 60% for cash and the remainder with credit cards. The bank charges a 5% fee on all credit card purchases, and credits Bynsel's account immediately upon receipt of the charge slip.

What are cash receipts and disbursements for the third month?

**6-15** (CPA adapted). Davis Company has budgeted its activity for April. Selected data from estimated amounts are as follows:

| | |
|---|---|
| Net income | $120,000 |
| Increase in gross amount of trade accounts receivable during month | 35,000 |
| Decrease in accounts payable during month | 25,000 |
| Depreciation expense | 65,000 |
| Provision for income taxes | 80,000 |

On the basis of the foregoing data, what is the cash increase for the month budgeted by Davis?

**6-16** (CPA). Total production costs for Gallop Inc., are budgeted at $230,000 for 50,000 units of budgeted output and at $280,000 for 60,000 units of budgeted output. Because of the need for additional facilities, budgeted fixed costs for 60,000 units are 25% more than budgeted fixed costs for 50,000 units. Determine the fixed costs for each level of output and the budgeted variable cost per unit of output.

**6-17** The flexible budget and actual operating data for the county coroner's office are as follows:

| | Flexible Budget | | Actual |
|---|---|---|---|
| Cases | 1,200 | 1,500 | 1,300 |
| Wages and salaries | $26,000 | $29,000 | $27,500 |
| Materials | $60,000 | $75,000 | $64,600 |
| Overhead | $48,000 | $49,500 | $49,100 |

Determine what the flexible budget allowances are for the actual caseload and whether the office is over or under budget for each item.

**6-18** The typing and duplicating department for a trade school has budgeted its costs at $28,000 per month plus $4.20 per student. Normally, 450 students are enrolled. During January there were 420 students (which is within the relevant range), fixed costs were $29,000, and variable costs were $1,800. Determine (a) the flexible budget allowances for January and (b) departures from the budget.

**6-19** J. Brown sells insect repellant during the evening at a local beach. On clear evenings, Brown averages sales of 10 aerosol cans per night; on overcast evenings sales plummet to an average of 1 can per night. On partly cloudy evenings, many people come to the beach to view the sunset, and sales average 30 cans per night.

Brown has gathered the following historical data from the local weather bureau.

| | Percentage of Days That Are | | | |
|---|---|---|---|---|
| | Clear | Overcast | Partly Cloudy | Total Days |
| July | 80.2 | 6.1 | 13.7 | 31 |
| August | 75.4 | 11.4 | 13.2 | 31 |
| September | 60.1 | 12.7 | 27.2 | 30 |

Estimate the monthly sales in units for July through September.

6-20 Martique, N.K.V., operates a subsidiary in the Deshtaki People's Republic. The People's Republic has imposed centrally planned currency controls. Persons or firms wishing to purchase goods from outside the country must apply for the necessary foreign currency from the central bank.

Martique will begin the first quarter of 19X1 with 12,000 pounds of a critical raw material in inventory valued at 48,000 TLZ (TLZ is Deshtaki's local currency). The firm wishes to end the quarter with a minimum of 5,000 pounds of raw material on hand. For the quarter, Martique has permission to spend 20,000 Deutsche marks to acquire 70,000 pounds of the material.

It takes $2\frac{1}{2}$ pounds of the material to manufacture one unit of product. The official exchange rate is 14.285 TLZ = 1 DM. How many units of product will Martique be able to produce in the first quarter, and what is the total cost of the units produced in terms of the local currency? (Use FIFO costing.)

6-21 HiTimes Records sells "The Best of" records for popular singers currently out of popularity. The firm uses television and magazine advertisements and direct mail to sell the records. Management has discovered that it can very accurately predict the results from its ads. Four viewers per thousand persons who see a TV commercial will send in an order within 2 weeks after airing. No one will respond after 2 weeks. Direct mail is always sent to arrive close to the end of the month (when people pay bills). Research shows that 0.5% of the ads mailed will result in a purchase during the month the ad is sent. Another 0.75% of the persons receiving the ads will send in an order in the month following the mailing. Magazine ads will generate 25 responses per 10,000 subscribers in the month the magazine is published, 6 responses per 10,000 subscribers in the month after publication, and 1 response per 10,000 in the second month following publication.

HiTimes has set up a marketing campaign for the rock group "The Gratefully Still Alive." The firm will place ads in February magazines having total subscribers of 4,500,000. They will also send out 200,000 pieces of direct mail to arrive in February. In addition, they will run 20 late-night TV commercials during the first 2 weeks in February. These commercials will reach a total of 18 million viewers.

Determine anticipated unit sales per month for February through April.

## PROBLEMS AND CASES

6-22 **Physical budget for materials.**

Budgot, Inc., must budget a particular direct material very carefully because of its scarcity and its cost. One unit of this material is used to produce one unit of finished product. Physical beginning inventory data are as follows:

| | |
|---|---|
| Direct materials | 1,200 |
| Materials-in-process | 400 |
| Finished goods | 2,000 |

The firm would like to double inventories by the end of the period. It also plans on selling 10,000 units during the period.

**Required**

**a.** How many units must be completed to achieve these goals?
**b.** How many units must be placed into production to achieve these goals?
**c.** How many units must be purchased to achieve these goals?
**d.** Assume that Budgot's purchasing agent is very sure that no more than 10,000 units of this material can be acquired next period. If the firm holds to its expectations as to ending inventories, how many units can be sold?

**6-23 Budgeting cash receipts** (CPA adapted).

Reid Company is developing a forecast of March cash receipts from credit sales. Credit sales for March are estimated to be $320,000. The Accounts Receivable balance at February 29 is $300,000, one-quarter representing January credit sales and the remainder from February credit sales. All accounts receivable from months prior to January have been collected or written off. Reid's history of accounts receivable collections is as follows:

| | |
|---|---|
| In the month of sale | 20% |
| In the first month after month of sale | 50% |
| In the second month after month of sale | 25% |
| Written off as uncollectible at the end of the second month after sale | 5% |

**Required**

Forecast all March cash receipts from credit sales.

**6-24 Budgeting cash receipts and disbursements.**

Boleys, Inc., made sales of $147,000 in January and $110,000 in February. The firm purchases its product as needed. The firm sets its selling price equal to 150% of the purchase price of its product. Collections from customers are generally 50% in the month of sale and 45% in the month following sale. On the average, 5% of sales are never collected. The firm pays its suppliers 60% in the month of purchase and 40% in the month following purchase. Salespersons are paid a commission of 4% of selling price. Commissions are paid in the month following sale. Administrative costs are $8,000 per month (including $2,000 of depreciation). The administrative costs are paid as incurred. The firm has a cash balance of $12,000 on February 1.

**Required**

What is the anticipated cash balance on February 28?

**6-25 Cash receipts budget.**

The bookkeeper for Redinc has prepared an aging schedule for accounts receivable as of February 1:

| Days Outstanding | Amount |
|---|---|
| 1–30 | $200,000 |
| 31–60 | 100,000 |
| 61–90 | 50,000 |
| 91– | 10,000 |
| | $360,000 |

The pattern of collections experienced is 50% in the month of sale, 30% one month later, 15% two months later, and 20% of the remaining balance three months later. A 5% discount is granted if payment is received in the month of sale and a 2% discount is given in the month following.

**Required**

If February sales are projected to be $400,000, what are the total projected cash receipts from customers in February?

**6-26 Cash receipts and disbursements.**

A college student, Cy Lentz, plans to acquire some wealth during the fall term by selling cordless phones by mail order. He buys them for $32 and sells them for $50.

He will grant a 10% discount if payment accompanies the order (estimated to be 40% of sales) and a 5% discount on telephoned-in orders accompanied by a valid credit card number (30% of sales). The remaining collections are estimated to be:

| | |
|---|---|
| One month following | 15% |
| Two months following | 6 |
| Three months following | 4 |
| Uncollectible | 5 |

The sales forecast is as follows:

| | |
|---|---|
| September | 12,000 units |
| October | 22,000 units |
| November | 32,000 units |
| December | 40,000 units |
| January | out of the business |

He plans to pay his supplier 50% in the month of purchase and 50% in the month following. A 6% discount is granted on payments made in the month of purchase; however, he will not be able to take any discounts on September purchases owing to constraints on his cash flow. That is, all September purchases will be paid for in October.

There are 5,000 cordless phones on hand (purchased in August and to be paid for in September), and it is planned to maintain a sufficient end-of-the-month inventory to meet 70% of the next month's sales. Receivables and payables are carried at gross.

**Required**

**a.** Prepare schedules for monthly cash receipts and cash disbursements for the life of this venture.

**b.** Cy had planned simply to write off the uncollectibles. However, his accounting professor suggested he turn them over to a collection agency. How much could Cy let the collection agency keep so that he would be no worse off?

**6-27 Budgeting inventory and cash receipts** (CPA adapted).
The Zel Company operates at local flea markets. It has budgeted the following sales for the indicated months.

| | June | July | August |
|---|---|---|---|
| Sales on account | $1,500,000 | $1,600,000 | $1,700,000 |
| Cash sales | 200,000 | 210,000 | 220,000 |
| Total sales | $1,700,000 | $1,810,000 | $1,920,000 |

Zel's success in this specialty market is due in large part to the extension of credit terms and the budgeting techniques implemented by the firm's owner, Barbara Zel. Ms. Zel is a recycler; that is, she collects her merchandise daily at neighborhood garage sales and sells the merchandise weekly at regional flea markets. All merchandise is marked up to sell at its invoice cost (as purchased at garage sales) plus 25%. Stated differently, cost is 80% of selling price. Merchandise inventories at the beginning of each month are 30% of that month's projected cost of goods sold. With respect to sales on account, 40% of receivables are collected in the month of sale, 50% are collected in the month following, and 10% are never collected.

**Required**

**a.** What is the anticipated cost of goods sold for June?
**b.** What is the beginning inventory for July expected to be?
**c.** What are July purchases expected to be?
**d.** What are the projected July cash collections?

**6-28 Budgeting unit sales, given constraints.**
Aussie Enterprises manufactures boomerangs. Each boomerang must go through three separate, but sequential, processes. Process 1 begins by shaping 1 unit of material A. Process 2 covers the product with 1 unit of material B (a Teflon-like material that decreases wind resistance). Process 3 colors the boomerang red.

At the start of the budget period, there are no work-in-process inventories; there are 150 units of material A on hand, 100 units of material B, and a lifetime supply of red paint. The demand for Aussie's product is such that it can sell all it produces. However, materials A and B are in short supply; during the upcoming period, no more than 500 units of A and 400 units of B can be obtained. Furthermore, given the intricacies of processing, the most that process 1 can produce during the period is 600 units; process 2 can produce at most 550 units; and process 3 can produce no more than 700 units.

**Required**

If Aussie Enterprises goes all out, how many units can (in fact) be sold during the period?

**6-29 Physical budgets: Materials.**
Sea Products, Inc., is a locally based firm that processes various types of marine life. The operation is quite flexible, ranging from gourmet items to cat food and fertilizer.

Management prefers keeping the operations as close to capacity as possible. The main bottleneck to capacity is insufficient supply of materials; it is frequently necessary to supplement local supplies by purchasing from Brazil, Japan, Iceland, and other countries.

There are three separate processing operations. Although materials may pass through all three processes, it is not uncommon to sell a product after it is finished at one stage. In other words, process 1 may sell some of its output as is and pass the rest to process 2; process 2, in turn, may sell some of its output and pass the rest to process 3. Process 3 delivers all of its output to the firm's finished product warehouse.

The accounting department assists management by forecasting monthly input requirements 4 months ahead; that is, it is now February and the accounting department is budgeting for June requirements.

Accounting is working with the following data for June.

**1.** Inventories

| | Estimated Physical Inventories June (tons) | |
|---|---|---|
| | **Beginning** | **Ending** |
| Process 1 | 150 | 180 |
| Process 2 | 220 | 210 |
| Process 3 | 200 | 220 |
| Finished product | 700 | 800 |

**2.** Sales

| | |
|---|---|
| Process 1 | One-half of its finished product will be transferred to process 2, and the other one-half will be sold |
| Process 2 | Four-fifths of its finished product will be transferred to process 3, and the other one-fifth will be sold |
| Finished product | 5,000 tons will be sold |

**Required**

Use T-accounts to trace the product flows for the month. Be sure to show how many tons must be started in process 1.

**6-30 Production and direct labor budgets** (CMA adapted).

Roletter Company makes and sells artistic frames for pictures. The controller is responsible for preparing the master budget and has accumulated the information below for 19X5.

| | **January** | **February** | **March** | **April** | **May** |
|---|---|---|---|---|---|
| Estimated unit sales | 10,000 | 12,000 | 8,000 | 9,000 | 9,000 |
| Sales price per unit | $50.00 | $47.50 | $47.50 | $47.50 | $47.50 |
| Direct labor hours per unit | 2.0 | 2.0 | 1.5 | 1.5 | 1.5 |
| Wage per direct labor hour | $8.00 | $8.00 | $8.00 | $9.00 | $9.00 |

Labor-related costs include pension contributions of $0.25 per hour, workers' compensation insurance of $0.10 per hour, employee medical insurance of

$0.40 per hour, and social security taxes. Assume that as of January 1 the base figure for computing social security taxes is $37,800 and that the rates are 7% for employers and 6.7% for employees. The cost of employee benefits paid by Roletter is treated as a direct labor cost.

Roletter has a labor contract that calls for a wage increase to $9.00 per hour on April 1. New labor saving machinery has been installed and will be fully operational by March 1.

Roletter expects to begin the year with 16,000 frames on hand and has a policy of carrying an end-of-month inventory of 100% of the following month's sales plus 50% of the second following month's sales.

**Required**

**a.** Prepare a production budget and a direct labor budget for Roletter by month and for the first quarter of the year. The direct labor budget should include direct labor hours and show the detail for each direct labor cost category.

**b.** For each item used in Roletter's production budget and its direct labor budget, identify the other component(s) of the master budget (budget package) that would also use these data.

**6-31 Production, acquisition, receipts budgets.**

Seer, Inc., has projected sales of its product for the next 6 months as follows:

| | |
|---|---|
| January | 40 units |
| February | 90 units |
| March | 100 units |
| April | 80 units |
| May | 30 units |
| June | 70 units |

The product sells for $100, variable expenses are $70 per unit, and fixed expenses are $1,500 per month.

The finished product requires 3 units of raw material and 10 hours of direct labor. The company tries to maintain an ending inventory of finished goods equal to the next 2 months of sales and an ending inventory of raw materials equal to half of the current month's usage.

All sales are on account with collections as follows:

50% in month of sale (2% discount)
25% in month following (2% disount)
25% during the 2 months following (no discount)

**Required**

**a.** Prepare a production budget for February, March, and April.

**b.** Prepare a materials acquisition budget for February, March, and April.

**c.** Prepare a labor requirements budget for February, March, and April.

**d.** Prepare a cash receipts budget for February, March, and April (this is a new product that will be introduced in January).

**6-32 Physical and cash budgets.**

Hades, Inc., produces heat-resistant materials. One of its products is a kiln-fired conductor. The firm operates only 9 months a year (January through September) and always begins the year without inventories, payables, or receivables. The plant supervisor provides the following data.

| | Planned | |
|---|---|---|
| | Units Sold | Units Produced |
| January | 800 | 1,000 |
| February | 700 | 1,200 |
| March | 1,000 | 1,100 |
| April | 1,200 | 1,200 |
| May | 1,000 | 900 |

*Inventory requirements:* The ending inventory of a particular material each month should be an amount sufficient to meet half of the following month's production requirements. It takes 1 unit of material to produce 1 unit of finished product; a unit of this material costs $10.

*Accounts payable:* All purchases are on account. Normally, half a month's purchases are paid for in the month of purchase and half in the month following. A cash discount of 2% is taken on all purchases.

*Accounts receivable:* The finished product sells for $100. A 2% discount is granted if payment accompanies the order. The pattern of collections is as follows:

50% in month of sale with payment accompanying the order
40% one month following
9% two months following
1% never collected

**Required**

**a.** What are the material purchase requirements for January, February, March, and April?
**b.** What are the production requirements for January, February, March, and April?
**c.** Show cash disbursements for purchases to suppliers in January, February, March, and April.
**d.** Show cash receipts from customers in January, February, March, and April.

**6-33 Flexible budget analysis.**

Cardinal Products hired a new marketing manager early this year. After an informal consumer survey, the marketing manager decided to lower the firm's selling price by 10% and increase television advertising.

The operating results at year-end were disappointing. The marketing manager prepared the following analysis for the president.

| | Master Budget (100,000 units) | Actual (115,000 units) | Deviation |
|---|---|---|---|
| Sales | $600,000 | $621,000 | $ 21,000 |
| Direct materials | 200,000 | 227,700 | (27,700) |
| Direct labor | 125,000 | 138,000 | (13,000) |
| Variable overhead | 50,000 | 57,000 | (7,000) |
| Fixed overhead | 75,000 | 75,200 | (200) |
| Advertising | 20,000 | 40,000 | (20,000) |
| Net income | $130,000 | $ 83,100 | $(46,900) |

"As you can see," the marketing manager reported, "the major problem is due to inefficiencies in production. My plan would have worked if production had kept its costs in line."

**Required**
Prepare a more accurate analysis of operations. What is the real source of the disappointing results?

**6-34 Cash budgets** (SMA).
The Big Boy Company is in a seasonal business and prepares quarterly budgets. Its fiscal year runs from July 1 through June 30. Production occurs only in the first quarter (July to September), but sales take place throughout the year. The forecast for the coming year shows sales as:

| | |
|---|---|
| First quarter | $390,000 |
| Second quarter | 750,000 |
| Third quarter | 390,000 |
| Fourth quarter | 390,000 |

There are no cash sales, and the beginning balance of receivables is expected to be collected in the first quarter. Subsequent collections are two-thirds in the quarter in which sales take place and one-third in the quarter following.

Material purchases valued at $360,000 are made in the first quarter and none in the last three quarters. Payment is made when materials are purchased.

Direct labor of $350,000 is incurred and paid only in the first quarter. Factory overhead of $430,000 is also incurred and paid in the first quarter. Factory overhead is at a standby level of $100,000 during the other three quarters. Selling and administrative expenses are paid at $50,000 per quarter throughout the year. Big Boy maintains an operating line of credit with its bank at an interest rate of 6% per annum. The company plans to maintain at least $8,000 at all times, and it will borrow and repay in multiples of $5,000. All borrowings are made at the beginning of a quarter, and all payments are made at the end of a quarter. Interest is paid only on that portion of the loan repaid in a quarter.

The company plans to purchase equipment in the second and fourth quarters in the amounts of $150,000 and $50,000, respectively. Cash balance on July 1 is $23,000 and accounts receivable is $130,000.

**Required**
Prepare a cash budget for the year showing receipts, disbursements, ending cash balance before borrowing, amounts borrowed, repaid, interest payments, and ending cash balance.

**6-35 Cash budget** (CIA adapted).
The treasurer of a medium-size retail organization is preparing a cash budget for the last quarter of 19X9 and has asked you for guidance in its preparation. The accounting department provided the following information.

Store fixtures purchased in March 19X9 were financed by a term loan. The loan is being repaid to a bank in monthly installments of $35,000.

Salaries and wages represent about 10% of sales each month.

The average markup on all merchandise is 40% of the selling price. Purchases during a month are based on sales projected for the following month (for example, budgeted purchases for October would be $4,200,000). Payment terms of all purchases are net 30.

Dividends totaling $420,000 are expected to be declared on November 1, payable to shareholders on December 15, 19X9.

Monthly store rent, due December 1, will increase from $90,000 to $95,000.
Interest of $50,000 on outstanding bonds is payable on November 15.
Miscellaneous operating expenses, including sales and advertising, are approximately $110,000 per month.
Bad-debt expense in 19X8 was 3% of sales. No percentage change is expected in 19X9.
Two trucks will be purchased for cash in November 19X9 for an estimated $28,000 less a total trade-in value of $8,000.

A regression model indicates that sales and credit collections for each month of the last quarter of 19X9 will be as follows:

| | October | November | December |
|---|---|---|---|
| Cash sales | $2,500,000 | $3,000,000 | $4,000,000 |
| Credit sales | 2,500,000 | 4,000,000 | 4,500,000 |
| Credit collections | 1,500,000 | 2,500,000 | 2,000,000 |

**Required**
Prepare a cash budget for November 19X9 showing components of projected receipts and disbursements and the net cash gain (loss) for the month. Ignore any cash balance carried forward from October.

**6-36 Budgeting cash receipts and cash disbursements** (SMA adapted).
You have recently been hired as the assistant controller of the I. M. Rich Company and are eager to display your skills in managerial accounting. The controller has asked you to prepare a cash budget for the month of June.

To aid you in forecasting cash collections, the sales manager has furnished the following information.

| | Sales |
|---|---|
| May | $650,000 |
| April | 610,000 |
| March | 595,000 |

Traditionally, 50% of all sales are cash sales, 30% of sales are collected in the month following sale, 17% of sales are collected 2 months after sale, and on the average, 3% of all sales are uncollectible.

Additional data for the month of June (all expenses are paid in the month incurred unless otherwise stated) are as follows:

| | |
|---|---|
| Sales | $710,000 |
| Merchandise purchases | 285,000 |
| Utilities | 10,000 |
| Depreciation | 25,000 |
| General administration | 20,000 |
| Supervisory salaries | 17,500 |
| Rent | 12,000 |
| Advertising | 150,000 |
| Cash balance, June 1 | 32,250 |
| Bank loan (received on May 1) | 200,000 |

The company follows a policy of paying for merchandise purchases in the month following purchase. Purchases for May were $300,000. The company pays a commission of 5% of sales to its salespeople. The commission is paid in the month of the sale. The company incurred advertising expenses of $125,000 in the month of May. The bank loan calls for annual interest of 15%, and the interest is paid at the end of each month.

**Required**
Prepare a cash receipts and disbursements budget for the month of June.

**6-37 Budgeting cash receipts, cash disbursements, acquisitions** (SMA adapted).
The following information concerning Stayley Limited has been made available for the development of cash and other budget information for the months of July, August, and September.

Balances at July 1 are expected to be as follows:

| | |
|---|---|
| Cash | $ 5,500 |
| Accounts receivable | 416,100 |
| Inventories | 309,400 |
| Accounts payable | 133,055 |

The budget is to be based on the following assumptions:

Each month's sales are billed on the last day of the month.
Customers are allowed a 3% discount if payment is made within 10 days after the billing date. Receivables are booked at gross.
Sixty percent of the billings are collected within the discount period, 25% are collected by the end of the month after the date of sale, 9% are collected by the end of the second month after the date of sale, and 6% prove uncollectible.
Fifty-four percent of all purchases of material and selling, general, and administrative expenses are paid in the month purchased. The remainder is paid in the following month.
Each month's units of ending inventory are equal to 130% of the next month's units of sales.
The cost of each unit of inventory is $20.
Selling, general, and administrative expenses, of which $2,000 is depreciation, are equal to 15% of the current month's sales.

Actual and projected sales are as follows:

| Month | Sales | Units |
|---|---|---|
| May | $354,000 | 11,800 |
| June | 363,000 | 12,100 |
| July | 357,000 | 11,900 |
| August | 342,000 | 11,400 |
| September | 360,000 | 12,000 |
| October | 366,000 | 12,200 |

**Required**
**a.** What are the budgeted cash disbursements during the month of August?
**b.** What are the budgeted cash collections during the month of July?
**c.** What is the budgeted number of units of inventory to be purchased during the month of September?

**6-38 Various budgeting** (CPA adapted).
The Dilly Company marks up all merchandise at 25% of gross purchase price. All purchases are made on account with terms of 1/10, net/60. Purchase discounts,

which are recorded as miscellaneous income, are always taken. Normally, 60% of each month's purchases are paid for in the month of purchase, whereas the other 40% are paid during the first 10 days of the first month after purchase. Inventories of merchandise at the end of each month are kept at 30% of the next month's projected cost of goods sold.

Terms for sales on account are 2/10, net/30. Cash sales are not subject to discount. Fifty percent of each month's sales on account are collected during the month of sale, 45% are collected in the succeeding month, and the remainder are usually uncollectible. Seventy percent of the collections in the month of sale are subject to discount, and 10% of the collections in the succeeding month are subject to discount.

Projected sales data and cost of sales for selected months are as follows:

| | Sales on Account: Gross | Cash Sales | Cost of Goods Sold |
|---|---|---|---|
| December | $1,900,000 | $400,000 | $1,840,000 |
| January | 1,500,000 | 250,000 | 1,400,000 |
| February | 1,700,000 | 350,000 | 1,640,000 |
| March | 1,600,000 | 300,000 | 1,520,000 |

**Required**

Choose the correct answer to each of the following questions.

**a.** Projected gross purchases for January are
(a) $1,400,000 (b) $1,470,000 (c) $1,472,000 (d) $1,248,000 (e) something else

**b.** Projected inventory at the end of December is
(a) $420,000 (b) $441,600 (c) $552,000 (d) $395,750 (e) something else

**c.** Projected sales discounts to be taken by customers making remittances during February are
(a) $5,250 (b) $15,925 (c) $30,500 (d)$11,900 (e) something else

**d.** Projected total collections from customers during February are
(a) $1,875,000 (b) $1,861,750 (c) $1,511,750 (d) $1,188,100 (e) something else

**6-39 Master budgeting.**

Johnson Inks requests your assistance in preparing the master budget for October. The following balance sheet is available.

| | October 1 (Actual) | October 31 (Planned) |
|---|---|---|
| Cash | $ 23,000 | $ ? |
| Accounts receivable (at gross) | 40,000 | ? |
| Raw material X ($3 per unit) | 12,000 | 18,000 |
| Raw material Y ($2 per unit) | 5,000 | 8,000 |
| Finished goods ($20 per unit) | 40,000 | 60,000 |
| Total assets | $120,000 | $ ? |
| Accounts payable (at gross) | $ 38,000 | $ ? |
| Owners' equity | 82,000 | ? |
| Total equities | $120,000 | $ ? |

Additional information is as follows:

1. August sales were $90,000 and September sales were $80,000.
2. All sales are on account. Half is collected within the month of sale and a 3% discount is granted; the other half is collected in the month following without the discount.
3. August purchases were $32,000 and September purchases were $40,000.
4. All purchases are on account, with payments as follows:
   a. One-quarter in the month of purchase, taking a 2% discount.
   b. One-quarter in the month following, taking a 2% discount.
   c. One-quarter in the month following, taking no discount.
   d. One-quarter two months following, taking no discount.
5. Selling and administrative costs are $5 per unit variable and $60,000 per month fixed. The firm has no depreciable assets of any kind.
6. Projected sales for October are 4,000 units at $50 per unit.
7. Each finished unit requires two units of material X and one of material Y.

**Required**

a. How many units must be produced to meet the goals?
b. How many units of material X must be purchased to meet the goals?
c. How many units of material Y must be purchased to meet the goals?
d. How much cash (in total) will be disbursed to materials suppliers during the month?
e. What will collections from customers in October total?
f. What is the projected net income for October?

**6-40 Master budgeting: Cash and income.**

Sarg Idram set himself up in a mirror-making business upon retirement. The business has since grown to the point at which he thinks a system of budgetary controls is desirable. Budgeted data for the next 4 months follow.

| | Sales | Purchases | Expenses Other Than Cost of Goods Sold |
|---|---|---|---|
| April | $80,000 | $50,000 | $20,000 |
| May | 40,000 | 10,000 | 18,000 |
| June | 60,000 | 40,000 | 24,000 |
| July | 60,000 | 30,000 | 26,000 |

*Sales:* Half of all sales are made to retail customers for cash and half of all sales are made to commercial customers on credit. Half of all credit sales are collected in the month of sale; a 10% discount is allowed on these collections. The other half of commercial sales is collected in the month following; no discount is allowed. Retail customers are not given a discount.

*Purchases:* All purchases are made on account. The company pays half in the month of purchase, and half in the month following. A 5% discount is allowed for payments made in the month of purchase; nothing is allowed in the month following.

*Cost of Goods Sold:* Cost of goods sold is 50% of gross selling price.

*Expenses Other than Cost of Goods Sold:* Other expenses include monthly depreciation of $1,800 and prepaid insurance of $200 which expires monthly. The balance is for salaries, which are paid in the month they are earned.

**Required**
**a.** Prepare a cash receipts and disbursements budget for June.
**b.** Prepare a pro forma income statement for June.

**6-41 Rework demonstration problem.**
Refer to the demonstration problem at the end of the chapter. Prepare a new monthly cash budget, income statement, and balance sheet assuming that the firm sells 11,000 cases of peas per month.

**6-42 Pro forma financial statements** (CMA adapted).
Kelco is a retail sporting goods store that uses accrual accounting for its records. Facts regarding Kelco's operations are as follows:

1. Sales are budgeted at $220,000 for December and $200,000 for January.
2. Collections are expected to be 60% in the month of sale and 38% in the month following the sale. Two percent of sales are expected to be uncollectible.
3. Gross margin is 25 percent of sales.
4. A total of 80% of the merchandise for resale is purchased in the month prior to the month of sale and 20% is purchased in the month of sale. Payment for merchandise is made in the month following purchase.
5. Other expected monthly expenses to be paid in cash are $22,600.
6. Annual depreciation is $216,000.

Kelco's Statement of Financial Position at the close of business on November 30 follows.

**KELCO**
**Statement of Financial Position**
**November 30**

| Assets | |
|---|---|
| Cash | $ 22,000 |
| Accounts receivable (net of $4,000 allowance for uncollectible accounts) | 76,000 |
| Inventory | 132,000 |
| Property, plant and equipment (net of $680,000 accumulated depreciation) | 870,000 |
| Total assets | $1,100,000 |

| Liabilities and Stockholders' Equity | |
|---|---|
| Accounts payable | $ 162,000 |
| Common stock | 800,000 |
| Retained earnings | 138,000 |
| Total liabilities and stockholders' equity | $1,100,000 |

**Required**
Prepare the pro forma balance sheet and income statement for December.

**6-43 Cash budget for a trust fund.**
The MFS trust was established in December 19X4 to award college scholarships to seniors from a local high school. Three brothers contributed a total of $11,100 to

the trust. The trust will award one scholarship in the amount of $1,000 to a student each June.

One of the steps necessary to gain a ruling as a tax-exempt organization is to submit to the IRS a projected cash flow statement for each of the first 3 years of the organization's life. In addition, the trustees must assure themselves that they will have cash available each June to give to the scholarship recipient.

The trust's only expenses consist of postage and copying costs. These are expected to amount to $25 per year and are paid in March and April. The founders of the trust anticipate making contributions totaling $500 each year to the trust. These contributions will be made in early December.

On December 20, 19X4, the trustees invested $11,000 in a six-month certificate of deposit earning 8% annual interest (paid as a single amount at maturity). This left $100 in a checking account to pay for expenses. CD's are purchased in multiples of $500 and the trustees have agreed to invest only in 6-month maturities. Although it is impossible to predict future interest rates accurately, the trustees have decided to use the 8% current rate in all plans. The trustees wish to start each year with a minimum of $100 in the checking account to cover minor contingencies. Investments in CD's will be made in late December and late June.

**Required**

**a.** Prepare cash flow statements for the years 19X5, 19X6, and 19X7.

**b.** The IRS also requires that tax-exempt scholarship trusts distribute at least 85% of their earnings each year. Is this trust in imminent danger of violating this rule (contributions received are not considered income)?

**6-44 Forecasting cash position** (CMA adapted).

The Barker Corporation manufactures and distributes wooden baseball bats. This is a seasonal business, with a large portion of sales occurring in late winter and early spring. The production schedule for the last quarter of the year is heavy in order to build up inventory to meet expected sales volume.

The company experiences a temporary cash strain during this heavy production period. Payroll costs rise during the last quarter because overtime is scheduled to meet the increased production needs. Collections from customers are low because the fall season produces only modest sales. This year the company's concern is intensified because of the rapid increases in prices during the current inflationary period. In addition, the sales department forecasts sales of less than 1 million bats for the first time in 3 years. This decrease in sales appears to be caused by the growing popularity of aluminum bats.

The cash account builds up during the first and second quarters as sales exceed production. The excess cash is invested in U.S. Treasury bills and other commercial paper. During the last half of the year the temporary investments are liquidated to meet the cash needs. In the early years of the company, short-term borrowing was used to supplement the funds released by selling investments, but this has not been necessary in recent years. Because costs are higher this year, the treasurer asks for a forecast for December to judge whether the $40,000 in temporary investments will be adequate to carry the company through the month with a minimum balance of $10,000. Should the $40,000 be insufficient, he wants to begin negotiations for a short-term loan.

The unit sales volume for the past 2 months and the estimate for the next 4 months are as follows:

| | |
|---|---|
| October (actual) | 70,000 |
| November (actual) | 50,000 |
| December (estimated) | 50,000 |
| January (estimated) | 90,000 |
| February (estimated) | 90,000 |
| March (estimated) | 120,000 |

The bats are sold for $3 each. All sales are made on account. Half of the accounts are collected in the month of the sale, 40% are collected in the month following the sale, and the remaining 10% in the second month following the sale. Customers who pay in the month of the sale receive a 2% cash discount.

The production schedule for the 6-month period beginning with October reflects the company's policy of maintaining a stable year-round work force by scheduling overtime to meet production schedules:

| | |
|---|---|
| October (actual) | 90,000 |
| November (actual) | 90,000 |
| December (estimated) | 90,000 |
| January (estimated) | 90,000 |
| February (estimated) | 100,000 |
| March (estimated) | 100,000 |

The bats are made from wooden blocks that cost $6 each. Ten bats can be produced from each block. The blocks are acquired 1 year in advance so that they can be properly aged. Barker pays the supplier one-twelfth of the cost of this material each month until the obligation is retired. The monthly payment is $60,000.

The plant is normally scheduled for a 40-hour, 5-day work week. During the busy production season, however, the work week may be increased to six 10-hour days. Workers can produce 7.5 bats per hour. Normal monthly output is 75,000 bats. Factory employees are paid $4 per hour (up $0.50 from last year) for regular time and $6 for overtime.

Other manufacturing costs include variable overhead of $0.30 per unit and annual fixed overhead of $280,000. Depreciation charges totaling $40,000 are included among the fixed overhead. Selling expenses include variable costs of $0.20 per unit and annual fixed costs of $60,000. Fixed administrative costs are $120,000 annually. All fixed costs are incurred uniformly throughout the year.

The controller has accumulated the following additional information:

**1.** The balances of selected accounts as of November 30, 19X4, are as follows:

| | |
|---|---|
| Cash | $ 12,000 |
| Marketable securities (cost and market are the same) | 40,000 |
| Accounts receivable | 96,000 |
| Prepaid expenses | 4,800 |
| Account payable (arising from raw material purchase) | 300,000 |
| Accrued vacation pay | 9,500 |
| Equipment note payable | 102,000 |
| Accrued income taxes payable | 50,000 |

2. Interest to be received from the company's temporary investments is estimated at $500 for December.
3. Prepaid expenses of $3,600 will expire during December, and the balance of the prepaid account is estimated at $4,200 for the end of December.
4. Barker purchased new machinery in 19X4 as part of a plant modernization program. The machinery was financed by a 24-month note of $144,000. The terms call for equal principal payments over the next 24 months with interest paid at the rate of 1% per month on the unpaid balance at the first of the month. The first payment was made May 1, 19X4.
5. Old equipment, which has a book value of $8,000, is to be sold during December for $7,500.
6. Each month the company accrues $1,700 for vacation pay by charging Vacation Pay Expense and crediting Accrued Vacation Pay. The plant closes for 2 weeks in June, when all plant employees take a vacation.
7. Quarterly dividends of $0.20 per share will be paid on December 15 to stockholders of record. Barker Corporation has authorized 10,000 shares. The company has issued 7,500 shares, and 500 of these are classified as treasury stock.
8. The quarterly income taxes payment of $50,000 is due on December 15, 19X4.

**Required**

**a.** Prepare a schedule that forecasts the cash position at December 31, 19X4. What action, if any, will be required to maintain a $10,000 cash balance?

**b.** Without prejudice to your answer in (a), assume that Barker regularly needs to arrange short-term loans during the November-to-February period. What changes might Barker consider in its method of doing business to reduce or eliminate the need for short-term borrowing?

# COMPREHENSIVE CASE 1
# BUDGETING

Norman Metals was established to manufacture two types of valve housings, known as alpha and beta. The manufacturing process involves casting the housings and then machining smooth the coupling joints.

The firm was initially capitalized with $110,000. The firm purchased equipment for $114,500 with cash of $54,500 and a note payable of $60,000 and also acquired a $210,000 building for $30,000 in cash and a $180,000 mortgage. Thus the firm's balance sheet as of the beginning of next year will be as indicated in Exhibit CC1-1. Management is now preparing the master budget for the first year of operations.

## Sales Budget

The preparation of the master budget begins with the sales budget for this firm. Management feels that the ability to generate sales will be the factor constraining the firm's level of operations. Management expects to meet established market prices for its valve housings of $18 for alpha and $31 for beta. The firm already has verbal commitments from buyers for 2,000 units of alpha and 5,000 units of beta. Further orders will depend on how well the firm performs and how aggressive the sales representative is in finding new customers. Our sales representative has estimated that total sales of alpha will amount to 3,500 units and sales of beta will be 8,500 units. Management feels that these estimates, reflected in Exhibit CC1-2, are quite conservative. But wishing to refrain from overoptimism, we will base our budget on these sales estimates.

**EXHIBIT CC1-1 Beginning Balance Sheet for Norman Metals**

| Assets | | Equities | |
|---|---|---|---|
| Cash | $ 25,500 | Notes payable | $ 60,000 |
| Equipment | 114,500 | Mortgage | 180,000 |
| Building | 210,000 | Capital stock | 110,000 |
| Total assets | $350,000 | Total equities | $350,000 |

## Production Budget

From our projected sales we can now deduce the production requirements for both products. We add to our unit sales the number of units we wish to have in ending inventory. From this total we subtract the beginning units that we already have on hand. Norman Metals expects sales to grow rapidly in the future. Therefore, management has expressed a desire to end the next accounting period with 500 units of alpha and 1,500 units of beta in finished goods inventory. Since this is a new firm, there is no beginning inventory. In Exhibit CC1-3, sales and desired ending inventory are combined to yield budgeted production for the period as 4,000 units of alpha and 10,000 units of beta.

## Materials Acquisition Budget

Having determined what the firm will produce, we can now determine what raw materials will be required. The firm will use a standard cost system, so resource requirements can be deduced from the standards. The firm's industrial engineer has prepared standards that call for 2 pounds of metal per alpha casting and 2.5 pounds per beta casting. So multiplying planned production by the materials needed per unit will give us the production needs. But in addition to acquiring enough metal for current production, management also desires to end the period with 2,000 pounds of metal in raw materials inventory. So we add this desired inventory to pro-

**EXHIBIT CC1-2 Projected Sales**

| Product | Units | Price | Total |
|---|---|---|---|
| Alpha | 3,500 | $18 | $ 63,000 |
| Beta | 8,500 | 31 | 263,500 |
| | | | $326,500 |

**EXHIBIT CC1-3 Production Budget in Units**

| | Alpha | Beta |
|---|---|---|
| Budgeted sales | 3,500 | 8,500 |
| Planned ending inventory | 500 | 1,500 |
| Less beginning inventory | — | — |
| Planned production | 4,000 | 10,000 |

duction needs to yield total acquisitions. The purchasing agent anticipates that the metal can be purchased at an average cost of $1 per pound. Incorporating the price information with the quantities needed gives the total required expenditures of $35,000 for materials, as indicated in Exhibit CC1-4.

## Direct Labor Budget

The firm's standards can also be used to determine direct labor requirements. However, since labor cannot be inventoried, we can restrict our attention to the labor needed for current production. The standards for a unit of alpha call for 0.3 hours of direct labor in casting and 0.2 hours in machining; the standards for a unit of beta call for 0.6 hours in casting and 0.4 hours in machining. Using management's anticipated average cost for labor of $6 per hour yields the labor budget in Exhibit CC1-5.

## Factory Overhead Budget

The factory overhead budget presented in Exhibit CC1-6 is really a series of budgets. Each department in the firm estimates the costs it will incur for each of its overhead items. Further, since the firm will employ a standard

**EXHIBIT CC1-4 Materials Acquisition Budget**

| | Material (pounds) | Costs ($1 per lb) |
|---|---|---|
| Alpha (4,000 units × 2 lb per unit) | 8,000 | $ 8,000 |
| Beta (10,000 units × 2.5 lb per unit) | 25,000 | 25,000 |
| Desired ending inventory | 2,000 | 2,000 |
| Total materials needed | 35,000 | $35,000 |

**EXHIBIT CC1-5 Direct Labor Budget**

| | Hours | | | |
|---|---|---|---|---|
| | Casting | Machining | Total | Cost ($6 per hr) |
| 4,000 units of alpha @ 0.3 hr and 0.2 hr | 1,200 | 800 | 2,000 | $12,000 |
| 10,000 units of beta @ 0.6 hr and 0.4 hr | 6,000 | 4,000 | 10,000 | 60,000 |
| Total hours | 7,200 | 4,800 | 12,000 | $72,000 |
| Departmental budgets | $43,200 | $28,800 | $72,000 | |

cost system, these costs should be categorized as variable or fixed. These individual departmental budgets will later be used to evaluate how well each department controlled its actual overhead costs.

In addition to being used for performance evaluation, the departmental overhead budgets also become the basis for allocating service department costs and establishing overhead application rates. Service departments do not work on the final product, but instead provide services to other departments. Nonetheless, because these service department costs are manufacturing costs, they will be charged to the production departments.

Norman Metals has two service departments. Service department 1 handles all factory personnel matters: payroll, insurance, hiring, retirement benefits, and so forth. The firm anticipates having 10 factory employees and expects the variable costs to operate the personnel department to average $750 per employee. Exhibit CC1-6 reflects the expected makeup of the $7,500 in variable costs, and allocates these costs to the other departments on the assumption that there will be two employees in the maintenance department (service department 2), three employees in casting, and five in machining. The personnel department's fixed costs are estimated to be $9,000 and will be allocated on a lump-sum basis of $1,800 to maintenance, $2,700 to casting, and $4,500 to machining.

The maintenance department is budgeted to make 120 service calls during the period, 60 calls each for the casting and machining departments. The maintenance manager estimates that it will cost an average of $100 in variable costs per service call, as illustrated in Exhibit CC1-6. The fixed costs to operate the maintenance department are thought to benefit the two production departments equally. Therefore the fixed costs of $8,400 will be allocated $4,200 each to the casting and machining departments. It is important to note that next period each production department will be charged $4,200 for fixed maintenance costs, no matter how many service

**EXHIBIT CC1-6 Factory Overhead Budget**

| | Departments | | | |
|---|---|---|---|---|
| | Personnel | Maintenance | Casting | Machining |
| Variable overhead items | | | | |
| Indirect labor | $4,500 | $ 8,500 | $ 4,000 | $12,250 |
| Supplies | 2,000 | 1,500 | 13,000 | 900 |
| Utilities (variable portion) | 1,000 | 500 | 5,710 | 1,100 |
| Total: Personnel | $7,500 | | | |
| Allocation to other departments | (7,500) | 1,500 | 2,250 | 3,750 |
| Total: Maintenance | | $12,000 | | |
| Allocation to production departments | | (12,000) | 6,000 | 6,000 |
| Total variable overhead | | | $30,960 | $24,000 |
| Budgeted labor hours | | | 7,200 | 4,800 |
| Budgeted variable overhead per direct labor hour | | | $4.30 | $5.00 |
| Fixed overhead items | | | | |
| Property taxes | $1,000 | $ 2,000 | $ 2,100 | $ 300 |
| Utilities (fixed portion) | 3,000 | 2,400 | 5,000 | 800 |
| Depreciation | 5,000 | 2,200 | 26,000 | 200 |
| Total: Personnel | $9,000 | | | |
| Allocation to other departments | (9,000) | 1,800 | 2,700 | 4,500 |
| Total: Maintenance | | $ 8,400 | | |
| Allocation to production departments | | (8,400) | 4,200 | 4,200 |
| Total fixed overhead | | | $40,000 | $10,000 |
| Fixed costs charged to production of alpha | | | $16,000 | $ 5,000 |
| Cost per unit of alpha (production 4,000 units) | | | $4.00 | $1.25 |
| Fixed costs charged to production of beta | | | $24,000 | $ 5,000 |
| Cost per unit of beta (production 10,000 units) | | | $2.40 | $0.50 |

calls they require. On the other hand, the production departments will be charged only $100 per service call in variable costs, regardless of the total variable costs incurred by the maintenance department. Thus the production departments know precisely what service will cost them, and they will not be held responsible for inefficiencies in the operation of the maintenance department.

Having budgeted the service department costs that will be incurred by the production departments, we now have the full budget for overhead for the two production departments: casting and machining. Management has decided to apply the production department's variable overhead on the basis of direct labor hours incurred. From the variable overhead budget, Exhibit CC1-6, and the budget for direct labor, Exhibit CC1-5, the standard variable overhead application rates of $30,960 ÷ 7,200 = $4.30 and $24,000 ÷ 4,800 = $5.00 per direct labor hour are calculated for the casting and machining departments.

Although fixed overhead is usually applied on the same basis as variable overhead, Norman Metals did not consider direct labor hours to be an appropriate basis for fixed overhead. Instead management noted that approximately 60% of the equipment and facilities in the casting department were devoted to the production of beta and 50% of the facilities in the machining department were devoted to beta. Thus management decided to allocate 40% of the fixed costs of casting to alpha and 60% to beta, respectively, and split the fixed machining costs evenly between the two products. The fixed overhead application rates are then determined by dividing the appropriate fixed costs by the number of units budgeted to be produced. The fixed overhead application rates are calculated in the last four lines of Exhibit CC1-6.

## Cost of Goods Sold and Ending Finished Goods Budget

Having determined the overhead application rates, we can now calculate the budgeted cost to manufacture the products. Exhibit CC1-7 calculates the cost per unit by dividing the total manufacturing cost by the number of units produced. Once the per-unit cost is known, multiplication gives us the cost of goods sold and ending finished goods inventory figures.

**EXHIBIT CC1-7 Cost of Goods Sold and Ending Finished Goods Budget**

| | Alpha | Beta | Total |
|---|---|---|---|
| Direct materials cost (from Exhibit CC1-4) | $ 8,000 | $ 25,000 | |
| Direct labor cost (from Exhibit CC1-5) | 12,000 | 60,000 | |
| Variable overhead: Casting ($4.30 per hr; Exhibits CC1-5 and CC1-6) | 5,160 | 25,800 | |
| Variable overhead: Machining ($5.00 per hr; Exhibits CC1-5 and CC1-6) | 4,000 | 20,000 | |
| Fixed overhead (Exhibit CC1-6) | 21,000 | 29,000 | |
| Total cost | $50,160 | $159,800 | $209,960 |
| Planned production (Exhibit CC1-3) | 4,000 | 10,000 | |
| Standard cost per unit | $12.54 | $15.98 | |
| Budgeted cost of goods sold (3,500 and 8,500 units) | $43,890 | $135,830 | $179,720 |
| Budgeted ending finished goods (500 and 1,500 units) | 6,270 | 23,970 | 30,240 |
| Total costs accounted for | $50,160 | $159,800 | $209,960 |

**EXHIBIT CC1-8 Budgeted Selling and Administration Expenses**

| | |
|---|---|
| Sales commissions (10% of sales) | $32,650 |
| Administration salaries | 15,000 |
| Advertising | 3,000 |
| Supplies | 1,000 |
| Interest | 16,000 |
| Total budgeted selling and administration | $67,650 |

## Budgeted Selling and Administration Costs

Exhibit CC1-8 presents management's budget for selling and administration costs. No new issues arise in this budget, so we will simply accept the figures as given.

## Pro Forma Income Statement

With all of our costs now budgeted, the information in Exhibits CC1-2, CC1-7, and CC1-8 is combined to prepare the pro forma (budgeted) income statement for the period. This statement, Exhibit CC1-9, represents management's best guess as to what the results of operations next period will be.

## Budgeted Cash Receipts and Disbursements

The pro forma income statement projects that Norman Metals will earn $79,130 next year, but there is no guarantee that the firm will have adequate cash flows to maintain its operations. Cash flow is especially critical for new firms such as this that are attempting not only to produce for current sales but also to build inventories. Exhibit CC1-10 presents man-

**EXHIBIT CC1-9 Pro Forma Income Statement**

| | |
|---|---|
| Sales (Exhibit CC1-2) | $326,500 |
| Cost of goods sold (Exhibit CC1-7) | 179,720 |
| Gross margin | $146,780 |
| Selling and administration expenses (Exhibit CC1-8) | 67,650 |
| Net income before taxes | $ 79,130 |

**EXHIBIT CC1-10 Budgeted Cash Receipts and Disbursements**

| | 1 | 2 | 3 | 4 | Total |
|---|---|---|---|---|---|
| Cash receipts | | | | | |
| From current sales (70% of sales) | $45,710 | $45,710 | $68,565 | $68,565 | $228,550 |
| Last quarter's sales (30% of previous quarter's sales) | — | 19,590 | 19,590 | 29,385 | 68,565 |
| Total receipts | $45,710 | $65,300 | $88,155 | $97,950 | $297,115 |
| Cash disbursements | | | | | |
| Materials | $ 8,750 | $ 8,750 | $ 8,750 | $ 8,750 | $ 35,000 |
| Direct labor | 18,000 | 18,000 | 18,000 | 18,000 | 72,000 |
| Indirect labor | 7,312 | 7,313 | 7,312 | 7,313 | 29,250 |
| Factory supplies | 4,350 | 4,350 | 4,350 | 4,350 | 17,400 |
| Utilities | 3,251 | 4,878 | 4,878 | 4,878 | 17,885 |
| Property tax | — | — | 2,700 | — | 2,700 |
| Sales commissions (10% of sales) | 6,530 | 6,530 | 9,795 | 9,795 | 32,650 |
| Salaries | 3,750 | 3,750 | 3,750 | 3,750 | 15,000 |
| Advertising | 750 | 750 | 750 | 750 | 3,000 |
| Supplies | 250 | 250 | 250 | 250 | 1,000 |
| Interest | 4,000 | 4,000 | 4,000 | 4,000 | 16,000 |
| Loan principal | 11,000 | 11,000 | 11,000 | 11,000 | 44,000 |
| Total disbursements | $67,943 | $69,571 | $75,535 | $72,836 | $285,885 |
| Beginning cash balance (Exhibit CC1-1) | $25,500 | $ 3,267 | $ (1,004) | $11,616 | $ 25,500 |
| Plus receipts | 45,710 | 65,300 | 88,155 | 97,950 | 297,115 |
| Less disbursements | 67,943 | 69,571 | 75,535 | 72,836 | 285,885 |
| Ending balance | $ 3,267 | $ (1,004) | $11,616 | $36,730 | $ 36,730 |

agement's cash budget on a quarterly basis (monthly would be more realistic but would require too much space here).

To prepare the quarterly budget of receipts and disbursements we need more detailed information than before. A summary of the assumptions on which Exhibit CC1-10 is based follows.

Sales are presumed to be $65,300 in each of the first two quarters and $97,950 each in the third and fourth quarters. On the average, 70% of our customers are expected to pay in the quarter in which the sale is made and 30% will pay in the quarter following the sale. Production will be spread uniformly over the year (one-fourth of all costs are incurred each quarter). The firm will pay for materials, supplies, and labor in the quarter the cost is incurred. Utilities will be paid 1 month after incurred (that is, one-third of each quarter's costs are deferred to the next quarter). Half the property tax is payable in the first and third quarters, but the first payment for a new firm is not made until the third quarter (that is, the tax bill is always paid 6 months late). Sales commissions are paid in the quarter a sale is made, but other selling and administration costs are paid and incurred uniformly. Finally, the firm makes mortgage payments of $15,000 per quarter ($11,000 in repayments of principal plus $4,000 in interest expense).

As can be seen in Exhibit CC1-10, Norman Metals is projecting a cash shortage at the end of the second quarter (and a very thin reserve at the end of the first quarter). Being forewarned, management should take action now to ensure that adequate funds will be available. Given the positive cash flow in later quarters, management should be able to convince a banker to extend a loan.

## Pro Forma Balance Sheet

The last step in the preparation of the master budget is the preparation of the pro forma balance sheet. This statement will present management's best estimate of what the firm's financial position will be at the end of the year. The necessary information for the balance sheet comes from almost all of the previous exhibits. Norman Metal's pro forma balance sheet is presented in Exhibit CC1-11. A brief discussion of each item in the balance sheet follows.

The cash balance comes from Exhibit CC1-10. The accounts receivable balance is 30% of fourth-quarter sales. The inventory balances are

**EXHIBIT CC1-11 Pro Forma Balance Sheet**

| Assets | | | Liabilities and Owners' Equity | |
|---|---|---|---|---|
| Cash | | $ 36,730 | Utilities payable | $ 1,625 |
| Accounts receivable | | 29,385 | Property taxes payable | 2,700 |
| Inventory | | | Total current liabilities | $ 4,325 |
| Raw materials | $ 2,000 | | Notes payable | 36,000 |
| Finished goods | 30,240 | 32,240 | Mortgage payable | 160,000 |
| Total current assets | | $ 98,355 | Total liabilities | $200,325 |
| Equipment | $114,500 | | Capital stock | 110,000 |
| Less accumulated depreciation | 22,900 | 91,600 | Retained earnings | 79,130 |
| Building | $210,000 | | Total liabilities and | |
| Less accumulated depreciation | 10,500 | 199,500 | owners' equity | $389,455 |
| Total assets | | $389,455 | | |

from Exhibits CC1-4 and CC1-7, respectively. The $33,400 of depreciation reflected in Exhibit CC1-6 is assumed to be split $22,900 for equipment and $10,500 for the building. The utilities payable is one-twelfth of the annual bill and property taxes are one-half of the annual bill. The $44,000 repayments of principal listed in Exhibit CC1-10 are assumed to be split $24,000 for the note payable and $20,000 for the mortgage. There is no change in capital stock, and the retained earnings balance is simply the budgeted earnings for the year since the beginning balance was zero and we have not budgeted any dividend payments.

## Departmental Budgets

Although all the budgets necessary for planning purposes have been presented, we should prepare several more budgets that will be used for performance evaluation. During the year, managers will want to know how well each department is staying within its budget. Thus we will need a budget for each of the operating departments. The budgets for the service departments in Exhibit CC1-6 are probably satisfactory for control purposes, but all the various information relating to the production departments has not been combined in one place. Therefore, Exhibits CC1-12

**EXHIBIT CC1-12 Operating Budget for the Casting Department**

| | | |
|---|---|---|
| Direct materials (33,000 lb @ $1) | | $ 33,000 |
| Direct labor (7,200 hr @ $6) | | 43,200 |
| Variable overhead costs | | |
| Indirect labor | $ 4,000 | |
| Supplies | 13,000 | |
| Utilities | 5,710 | |
| Variable personnel | 2,250 | |
| Variable maintenance | 6,000 | |
| Total variable costs (to be applied at $4.30 per DLH) | | 30,960 |
| Fixed overhead costs | | |
| Property taxes | $ 2,100 | |
| Utilities | 5,000 | |
| Depreciation | 26,000 | |
| Fixed personnel | 2,700 | |
| Fixed maintenance | 4,200 | |
| Total fixed overhead costs (to be applied at $4 per unit to alpha and $2.40 per unit to beta) | | 40,000 |
| Total budgeted costs, casting department | | $147,160 |

**EXHIBIT CC1-13 Operating Budget for the Machining Department**

| | | |
|---|---|---|
| Direct materials (transferred in from casting; see Exhibit CC1-12) | | $147,160 |
| Direct labor (4,800 hours @ $6) | | 28,800 |
| Variable overhead costs | | |
| Indirect labor | $12,250 | |
| Supplies | 900 | |
| Utilities | 1,100 | |
| Variable personnel | 3,750 | |
| Variable maintenance | 6,000 | |
| Total variable costs (to be applied at $5.00 per DLH) | | 24,000 |
| Fixed overhead costs | | |
| Property taxes | $ 300 | |
| Utilities | 800 | |
| Depreciation | 200 | |
| Fixed personnel | 4,500 | |
| Fixed maintenance | 4,200 | |
| Total fixed overhead costs (to be applied to alpha at $1.25 per unit and to beta at $0.50 per unit) | | 10,000 |
| Total budgeted costs, machining department | | $209,960 |

and CC1-13 present the overall operating budgets for the casting and machining departments. These budgets are simply department-based summaries of the information in Exhibits CC1-4, CC1-5, and CC1-6.

Although we believe that the source of the information in Exhibits CC1-12 and CC1-13 is reasonably obvious, one word of explanation is warranted. In the budget for the machining department we have $147,160 in direct materials. Yet no new materials are added to the products in the machining department. What is happening is that when the cast units are transferred from the casting department to the machining department, the costs incurred by the casting department to produce the castings are transferred with the products to the machining department. As far as the machining department is concerned, these transferred costs are the direct materials costs of acquiring the castings.

CHAPTER

7

# INVENTORY CONTROL

Once the master budget has been established, we can then derive the total resources needed. At the operating level, however, we will also need to be concerned with the specific timing for the acquisition of resources. For services, such as labor and utilities, the resources can typically be acquired on an "as-needed" basis. However, we have the choice of acquiring products, such as raw materials and supplies, early (and carrying them in inventory) or acquiring them as needed. Most firms will use both approaches.

## THE NEED FOR INVENTORIES

The overall objective when selecting a materials acquisition system is the minimization of costs. The primary costs involved are the costs of placing orders, the cost of storing inventory, the costs incurred if we fail to have a needed material, and the cost of operating the accounting system.

How we minimize costs will depend in large part on the nature of the demand for a product. At the extremes, if demand for a product is uncertain and demand must be met relatively quickly, the firm will have to maintain an inventory of the product. In contrast, if demand can be accurately predicted or if the demand need not be satisfied for a time period that exceeds the time necessary to acquire the product, an inventory of the product will not be required. However, operating without inventories requires careful planning, scheduling, and monitoring of resource usage. Systems that do this planning and monitoring are called **materials requirements planning** (MRP) **systems**.

## MRP SYSTEMS

An MRP system requires that management be able to predict or schedule demand for products. Thus MRP is used mostly in firms that can schedule the production of orders or product runs several weeks in advance. Once production is scheduled, the MRP system works backward to determine what materials are needed and when they are needed. This, in turn, requires that the firm must have a complete **bill of materials** (BOM) for each product it manufactures. The BOM is a complete listing of all parts or ingredients needed to produce a unit of product. Multiplying the number of units of product to be produced by each item in the BOM then provides a complete listing of all the materials needed for a production run. The next step in MRP is to determine when to order the materials. For this the system requires that we know the **lead time** (amount of time required between sending an order to a supplier and receipt of the materials) for each material. Subtracting the lead time from the scheduled production date then yields the date on which the purchase order for materials will be sent.

Sophisticated MRP systems will also monitor orders and production. Periodically, the system checks to see whether purchase orders have been acknowledged by the supplier and whether the supplier has agreed to the required shipment date. If problems develop, the system then provides messages to production scheduling to suggest that production of certain orders may need to be rescheduled or that the purchasing agent should attempt to expedite a shipment.

### Just in Time

The system just described is an ideal system; with reliable suppliers, no inventories would be required. When this point is reached, such a system is called a **just-in-time** or **zero-stock system**. While a just-in-time system requires excellent planning and close cooperation with suppliers, it also avoids all inventory holding costs. For example, no warehouse space needs to be rented or constructed for inventories.

### Factors Leading to Inventories in MRP Systems

Not all MRP systems are designed to yield a zero-stock situation, but an effective MRP system should result in minimal inventories. Typically, the only inventories held will be a safety stock and an inventory resulting from lot size considerations. A **safety stock** is a small inventory of materials to cover unexpected events. If we need 100 motors to produce an order, we will order 100 motors. But, if one of them turns out to be defective or if we accidentally ruin one, we would not be able to produce the required 100 units of the final product. To cover this contingency, the firm may keep two or three spare motors as a safety stock.

The other motivation for inventories is lot size considerations. At the retail level, it is considerably cheaper per unit to buy a case of motor oil than it is to buy a single can of oil. The same is true in industrial supply. Most suppliers will charge a lower unit cost if materials are purchased in some standard lot size (per case, per gross, per carload, or whatever). Thus, although a firm may have a current need for only 80 units of a material, it may purchase 100 units if that is the standard lot size, if there is a significant unit cost savings, and if the material will be used again in the future.

Although MRP systems are not conceptually difficult, they require a significant amount of record keeping and computations. Let's turn briefly to the details of a typical system.

### An MRP Illustration

For each material the firm uses, an inventory status record will be required. An example of an inventory status record is provided in Exhibit 7-1. These records provide an item description, price, names of preferred suppliers, and acquisition lead times. In addition, they provide a record of the total units currently in inventory. From this total the safety stock is subtracted, as well as any units that have been committed (allocated) to specific future production orders but have not yet been taken out of inventory. The net result is the number of remaining units available for production that has not yet been scheduled.

For each product manufactured, a bill of materials is required. An example is given in Exhibit 7-2. The BOM allows us to determine the materials needed to produce a particular order.

Next, a materials requirement planning matrix is needed for each material. This matrix summarizes the planned status of inventories for each material for several periods into the future. Assume that the firm has just scheduled a production run of 425 units of Home Computer Model V in period 6. Previously, the firm had scheduled 260 units for production in period 2. The current date is period 1. Based on these assumptions, Exhibit 7-3 summarizes the materials requirement planning matrix for cathode-ray tubes. The first row in Exhibit 7-3 indicates the total tubes needed for production for each period. In period 2, the firm will produce 260 computers; the BOM in Exhibit 7-2 indicates that one tube is needed

**EXHIBIT 7-1 Inventory Status Record**

| | | | | | |
|---|---|---|---|---|---|
| Item | | Cathode-ray tube | | | |
| Primary supplier | | Miller Electronics | | | |
| Price | $47.50 | Lead time | 3 periods | Lot size | 100 |
| Alternate supplier | | RB&S Distributors | | | |
| Price | $52.25 | Lead time | 2 periods | Lot size | 50 |

STATUS AS OF PERIOD 1

| | |
|---|---|
| Units on hand | 75 |
| Safety stock | 5 |
| Allocated | 60 |
| Available | 10 |

for each computer. Therefore, 260 tubes are needed in period 2. Similarly, 425 tubes are needed in period 6.

The second row gives the number of tubes that have been ordered previously but have not yet been received. At the time that the production for period 2 was scheduled, the system would have scheduled the release

**EXHIBIT 7-2 Bill of Materials**

**Item** Home Computer Model V

**Component/parts**

Keyboard and computer
- 1 keyboard cover
- 1 set keyboard caps
- 1 8086 computer chip
- 2 128K memory chips
- 6 RX7 parts

Monitor
- 1 cathode-ray tube
- 1 monitor housing
- 1 RS assembly kit

**EXHIBIT 7-3 Materials Requirement Planning Matrix**

**CATHODE-RAY-TUBE**

| | Period | | | | | |
|---|---|---|---|---|---|---|
| | **1** | **2** | **3** | **4** | **5** | **6** |
| Total requirement | | 260 | | | | 425 |
| Scheduled receipts | | 200 | | | | |
| Scheduled on hand | 70 | 10 | 10 | 10 | 10 | 10 |
| Amount needed | | | | | | 415 |
| Planned orders | | | | | | 500 |

of a purchase order at the appropriate time. In the exhibit we have assumed that a purchase order for 200 units was sent and that these units will be received in period 2.

The third row indicates the number of tubes available at the end of each period. For example, in period 2 the firm will receive 200 units and had 70 units on hand at the end of period 1. Thus, 270 units are available *during* period 2. Production uses 260 units, leaving 10 units available at the *end* of the period.

The fourth row shows the number of tubes that remain to be acquired. As of today (assumed to be period 1), additional tubes are not needed until period 6. In period 6, the firm will need 415 additional units. The last row indicates the number of units that must be ordered for each period. Presuming that the firm orders from its preferred supplier, it will order in lots of size 100 (see Exhibit 7-1). Thus, 500 units will need to be ordered for period 6. But the purchase order may not be sent out immediately. To minimize inventories, the firm will issue the purchase order so that the tubes will arrive in period 6. Exhibit 7-1 indicated that the lead time is three periods, so the purchase order will be sent in period 3. Of course, if the supplier would respect the firm's desired delivery date, the purchase order could be sent immediately.

If no new production requiring the tubes is scheduled, the MRP matrix in period 2 will continue to show the 500 units in period 6 as planned orders. In period 3, however, after the purchase order has been sent, the 500 units will then be shown in row 2 as scheduled receipts.

The foregoing calculations must be made for every material (probably hundreds or thousands of items) that the firm uses. Further, to be effective, all of the records must be updated frequently (possibly daily, but at least weekly). As you can imagine, this requires hundreds of thousands of calculations. Consequently, as a practical matter, an MRP system must be computerized.

## OPTIMAL INVENTORY SIZE

When demand for a product or material cannot be scheduled, the carrying of inventories becomes necessary. Most retailers cannot predict precisely when specific goods will be sold. Similarly, many firms produce goods to order and promise rapid delivery dates. In these cases the firms must maintain sufficient inventories to cover the normal fluctuations in demand. The determination of the optimal level of inventories will involve a trade-off between the costs of holding inventory and the incremental cost of placing additional orders to acquire inventory. Let us now turn to an examination of the data requirements and the factors we need to consider for choosing the best timing for the acquisition of materials for inventory.

Assume that our firm plans to produce 50,000 units of product next year. Production will be erratic and on short notice. Each unit requires 1½ pounds of a particular material, so we anticipate needing 75,000 pounds of this material. Our objective now is to determine when to buy the materials. There are two extreme solutions available: (1) buy all the materials right away and store them until they are needed, or (2) buy each day's requirements as needed. The first approach will minimize the costs to acquire the materials (costs to type purchase orders, delivery charges, and so forth), but may involve some significant costs to store the inventory (handling costs, insurance, property taxes, and so on). At the other extreme, the second approach will minimize storage costs, but at the expense of increasing acquisition costs. Our objective is to try to minimize the sum of these two costs.

Assume that management has arbitrarily chosen to order 2,000 pounds of material each time it places an order. First, let us look at what our annual inventory ordering and storage costs will be. If it costs $10 to place an order, then the total costs to place orders will be \$10 multiplied by the number of orders placed. Since we assumed that we would need 75,000 units of inventory during the year, we will have to place 37.5 orders if we order 2,000 units at a time.[1]

$$\text{number of orders} = \frac{\text{annual demand}}{\text{order size}}$$
$$= \frac{75{,}000}{2{,}000}$$
$$= 37.5$$

Thus our total costs to place orders will be \$375, calculated as follows:

$$\text{order placement costs} = \text{cost to place an order} \times \text{number of orders}$$
$$= \$10 \times 37.5$$
$$= \$375$$

Assume further that it costs \$1.50 per year to store a unit in inventory, let us now calculate our annual storage costs. To do so, we need to know the average number of units that will be held in inventory over the year. We will simplify our estimate of the average number of units in inventory by assuming that demand for these materials is uniform. That is, we use exactly the same number of units every day.[2] If demand follows this pattern, then we can time the ordering of new units so that they arrive at precisely the moment we run out of stock. This, in turn, means that the largest number of units that we will ever have on hand is 2,000. That is, at the moment a new order arrives we will have 2,000 units in inventory. The smallest number of units that we will ever have is zero, which will occur just before a new order arrives. With uniform demand, we also know that precisely halfway through the time period between orders there will be 1,000 units remaining in inventory (this is our definition of uniform demand). Therefore, we can graph the pattern of the number of units of inventory on hand as in Figure 7-1. As Figure 7-1 indicates, the average number of units in inventory when demand is uniform is one-half the size of the order that we place. Hence, in our example, our inventory will

[1]During a particular year we will place either 37 or 38 orders, but on average we will place 37.5 orders per year.

[2]This is an unrealistic assumption. If we knew daily demand exactly, we would use an MRP system.

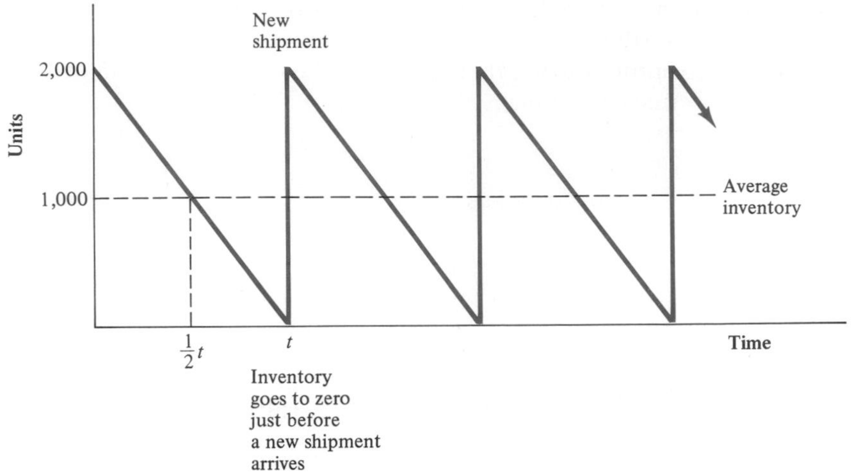


**FIGURE 7-1 Number of units in inventory over time when demand is uniform (order quantity = 2,000 units).**

average 1,000 units over the year. At a cost of \$1.50 per unit per year, our annual storage cost will be \$1,500.

$$\text{annual storage costs} = \frac{\text{storage cost per}}{\text{unit per year}} \times \frac{\text{average units}}{\text{in inventory}}$$

$$= \$1.50 \times 1{,}000$$

$$= \$1{,}500$$

Thus our total ordering and storage costs will be the sum of the ordering and storage costs, or \$375 + \$1,500 = \$1,875. That is, our arbitrary decision to order 2,000 units each time we place an order should result in total ordering and storage costs of \$1,875 per year.

### Economic Order Quantity

Our objective in inventory management and purchasing policy is to try to minimize this total cost. The costs can be minimized by finding the optimal number of units we should buy every time we place an order. This optimal order size is known as the **economic order quantity**. Let us define the following terms:

let $A$ = total annual demand for units

$C$ = the cost to place an order

$S$ = the cost to store a unit of inventory for a year

and $X$ = the number of units acquired in each order

Then we can represent the annual cost to place orders as

$$\text{annual cost to place orders} = \frac{\text{cost to place}}{\text{an order}} \times \frac{\text{number of}}{\text{orders}}$$

$$= \frac{\text{cost to place}}{\text{an order}} \times \frac{\text{annual demand}}{\text{order size}}$$

$$= C \times \frac{A}{X}$$

Assuming a uniform demand, we said that the average number of units in inventory will be one-half the size of an order, so the annual storage cost can be represented as

$$\text{annual storage cost} = \frac{\text{storage cost per}}{\text{unit per year}} \times \frac{\text{average units}}{\text{in inventory}}$$

$$= \frac{\text{storage cost per}}{\text{unit per year}} \times \frac{\text{order size}}{2}$$

$$= S \times \frac{X}{2}$$

and combining these two costs the total cost to place orders and store inventory will be

$$\text{total ordering and storage costs} = \frac{AC}{X} + \frac{SX}{2}$$

The number of units to be purchased in each order that will minimize the total ordering and storage costs is[3]

$$X = \sqrt{\frac{2AC}{S}}$$

That is, the economic order quantity (EOQ) is the square root of twice

[3]The optimal order quantity is found by differentiating

$$\frac{AC}{X} + \frac{SX}{2}$$

with respect to $X$ and setting the result equal to zero to yield

$$-\frac{AC}{X^2} + \frac{S}{2} = 0$$

and, rearranging,

$$\frac{S}{2} = \frac{AC}{X^2}$$

$$X^2S = 2AC$$

$$X^2 = \frac{2AC}{S}$$

$$X = \sqrt{\frac{2AC}{S}}$$

annual demand times the cost to place an order divided by the cost to carry a unit of inventory for a year.

Let us now calculate the EOQ for our example and see what effect the optimal order size has on our ordering and holding costs. The EOQ would be

$$\begin{aligned}\text{optimal order size} &= \sqrt{\frac{2 \times 75{,}000 \times \$10}{\$1.50}} \\ &= \sqrt{1{,}000{,}000} \\ &= 1{,}000 \text{ units}\end{aligned}$$

If we order 1,000 units each time we place an order, we will need to place 75 orders per year, and our average inventory will be 500 units. Our total ordering and storage costs then will be

$$\begin{aligned}\text{optimal ordering and storage costs} &= 75 \times \$10 + 500 \times \$1.50 \\ &= \$1{,}500\end{aligned}$$

Comparing this cost to the $1,875 we would incur if we used the arbitrary order size of 2,000 units, we can see that the optimal policy will save us approximately $375 per year.

## THE ACCOUNTANT'S ROLE IN INVENTORY MODELS

The EOQ model that we have developed is a very simple one. It assumes a known demand and uniform usage. Operations researchers have developed much more realistic and complex models that allow for uncertain demand, variable usage rates, and different ordering policies. However, our interest is not with the models themselves but with the accounting information that we must supply to them and the budgeting implications that their results have for us. In our view, this simple EOQ model will be adequate for illustrating the accounting implications of inventory models.

### Information Requirements

The data requirements needed to determine the optimal order size were

1. The total units to be used during a period
2. The cost associated with placing an order
3. The cost of holding one unit in inventory for the entire period

Let us briefly summarize how we would gather this information. We will obtain the first item, periodic demand, from our overall production plans. That is, by using the techniques described in Chapters 4 and 5 we will have estimated our total sales for the year. Adjusting total sales for desired changes in ending inventory levels will provide us with the number of units of product we must produce. For each of our materials we can then simply multiply the standard quantity of materials needed per unit of product by the number of units we expect to produce to get our total materials requirements for the period.

The second item, the cost to place an order, is more complex. We want to identify the costs that we incur because we place an order. But often it is difficult to distinguish a cost associated with placing an order from a cost we would have incurred anyway. The invoice price of materials is a good example. When we place an order for 1,000 units at an invoice price of \$2 each, is the \$2,000 a cost of placing an order? No. As long as the decision has been made to acquire 1,000 units of inventory, we are going to have to incur the \$2,000 cost whether we order them all at once or one at a time. The key to recognizing a variable ordering cost is to ask whether the total cost will change if we place two orders instead of one. In this case, we incur a total invoice cost of 1,000 units × \$2 × 1 order = \$2,000 if we place one order, or 500 units × \$2 × 2 orders = \$2,000 if we place two orders. On the other hand, if we must make a long-distance phone call to our supplier every time we place an order, then the cost of the telephone call is an order-placing cost. If the toll charge is \$3, then if we place one call our cost is \$3, but placing two orders will require two calls, increasing our cost to \$6. In other words, we are looking for variable costs where the variability is measured against the number of orders placed, not the more common basis of the number of units acquired.

Although we might try to identify each component of variable ordering cost to estimate the cost to place an order, an easier approach is available if all ordering is done by a purchasing department. If purchasing handles all orders, then we can use the techniques of Chapter 3 to estimate the purchasing department's cost equation as a function of the number of orders placed. An example is provided in Exhibit 7-4. The variable portion of such a cost function would then be a significant portion of the cost to place an order. (We still have to be careful to search for other costs that vary per order, such as a fixed transportation fee per order, but are not costs of operating the purchasing department.) Although such an approach yields an average variable cost to place an order (not the cost to place a specific order), we will see momentarily that small errors in cost estimates have an insignificant effect on inventory costs.

The **carrying cost**, or cost of carrying a unit in inventory, raises a similar problem to the cost of placing an order. This time we want to include as carrying costs those costs that vary with respect to the *average*

**EXHIBIT 7-4 The Average Variable Cost to Place an Order**

| | 19X8 | 19X9 |
|---|---|---|
| Total cost to operate purchasing department | $135,000 | $150,000 |
| Total purchase orders | 10,000 | 12,000 |

Average variable cost to place an order:

$$\frac{\$150{,}000 - \$135{,}000}{12{,}000 - 10{,}000} = \$7.50 \text{ per order}$$

Fixed cost of operating purchasing department:

$$\$150{,}000 - \$7.50(12{,}000) = \$60{,}000$$

Purchasing department cost function:

$$\$60{,}000 \text{ per year} + \$7.50 \text{ per order}$$

number of units kept in inventory (again, not those costs that vary with the total number of units acquired). This time we ask whether the cost will change if we increase the average number of units residing in inventory over the year by 1 unit. If in the past we have kept an average of 100 units in inventory and the cost of having a guard service patrol our warehouse is $3,000 per year, is the guard service a cost of carrying a unit in inventory? The guard service is clearly a cost of *having* an inventory, but if we increase our average inventory to 101 units, the cost will not change. Therefore, we do not include the cost as a cost of carrying a single unit of inventory for the year. Conversely, the cost of rotating inventory may well change as we increase the average size of inventory and would be included as a carrying cost.

For most firms, the major cost of carrying a unit in inventory is the cost of capital. If we buy a unit of inventory for $20 and let it sit in a warehouse for a year, that is the same thing as having $20 in cash sitting idle. If we borrowed the money to buy inventory, then we are paying interest on the money tied up in inventory. Even if we did not borrow the money, there is still the opportunity cost for not using the money in an alternative investment. That is, presumably we could invest the cash tied up in inventory in some other asset that would earn a return. To determine the cost of having capital tied up in inventory, we will need two things. First we need to know the total amount of costs incurred to get a unit (remember our carrying cost is on a per-unit basis) into inventory. This cost represents the investment that we have tied up in a unit of inventory.

It will include the invoice price of the unit, any variable per-unit shipping costs, and any variable handling costs incurred to get the unit into storage. The second piece of information needed is the firm's cost of capital. As readers familiar with the financial literature are aware, the actual measurement of a firm's cost of capital is fairly difficult. Many firms do not even try, but instead estimate a cost of capital or specify a desired rate of return that is "reasonable." We discuss this problem more in Chapter 9, but for now we will assume that either a cost of capital or a desired rate-of-return figure is available. Once we have the investment in each unit and the cost-of-capital figure, these figures are multiplied together to get the cost of having money tied up in inventory. This cost becomes one of the costs of carrying a unit in inventory for a year.

Let us illustrate the computation of the cost to carry a unit of inventory for a year with a simple example. Assume that the invoice cost of one of our raw materials is $7 per unit. In addition, we pay a shipping fee of $20 per shipment plus $1 per unit shipped. The insurance company bases its fire and theft insurance premiums for inventory on the average number of units kept in inventory. The insurance fee is $0.30 per unit per year for the average number of units on hand. Finally, management estimates that the cost of capital is 15% per year. Let us now determine the cost to carry a unit of inventory for a year.

In this example there are two carrying costs. First, the insurance fee depends directly on the average number of units of inventory on hand. If we keep an average inventory of 500 units on hand, the insurance bill will be $150, but if we keep an average inventory of 501 units, our insurance cost will be $150.30. Since insurance varies directly with the average number of units kept on hand, it is a carrying cost. On a per-unit basis, this cost is $0.30 per unit per year.

The other carrying cost is the cost of capital for our investment in inventory. In this example, each unit of inventory acquired will require an outlay for the $7 invoice price and a variable shipping charge of $1. That is, if we buy 10,000 units in a year we will have to pay $80,000 for the product, including variable shipping. If we buy 10,001 units, the cost will be $80,008. Thus our variable investment in each unit is $8. Note that we do not include the fixed transportation charge of $20 per shipment as part of investment in inventory. This fee does not depend on the total number of units that we acquire. Rather, it depends on how many shipments (orders) we request. If we ordered all of our inventory needs at one time, the total per-shipment fixed fee for the year would be $20, but if we acquired the total inventory in two shipments, we would have to pay $40. This per-shipment fee then is a cost of placing an order. It is not a part of the investment in a unit of inventory.

Given an investment of $8 in each unit, the cost of capital for tying up a unit in inventory for a year is $8 × 15% = $1.20 per unit per year.

Adding to this figure the carrying cost of \$0.30 per unit per year for insurance gives us a total carrying cost of \$1.50 per unit per year.

### When to Order

As we have seen, the solution to the inventory model provides the quantity of inventory that should be purchased every time we place an order. The actual timing of purchases should take into account three factors: the average daily demand for the units of inventory, the lead time to receive an order, and the desired level of safety stock. We must place an order while there is still enough inventory on hand to last until the new order is received. To determine the level of inventory on hand at which we should place an order, called the **reorder point**, we determine our average daily demand (periodic demand ÷ number of days in the period) and multiply by the lead time in days.

In an earlier example we assumed an annual demand for 75,000 units of a product. If we operate 250 days per year, our average daily demand will be 75,000 ÷ 250 = 300 units per day. If our purchasing agent estimates an average lead time of 4 business days, we should reorder inventory when our inventory drops to 1,200 units (300 units used per day times the 4 day lead time).

If demand were uniform and lead times known with precision, the reorder point calculated in the preceding paragraph would assure us that we would not run out of inventory. But in realistic settings inventories are kept because demand is variable and supply may be uncertain. In order to cover possible variations in demand, firms often increase the reorder point to include a safety stock that serves as an extra cushion of inventory to cover variations in our estimates of demand.

Previously we calculated a reorder point of 1,200 units based on average usage of 300 units per day for a 4-day lead time. However, management may very well want to have more than just average usage quantities on hand when placing an order. If maximum daily demand is estimated to be 350 units per day, we may decide on a reorder point of 350 × 4 = 1,400 units. That is, we place an order when inventory drops to 1,400 units to cover expected demand of 1,200 units during the lead time and to maintain a 200-unit safety stock in case daily demand is at the maximum.

A conservative approach to determining safety stock is to calculate the difference between the highest daily demand experienced and the average demand and then multiply this difference by the longest lead time experienced. However, more scientific approaches to the determination of the level of safety stock balance the cost of carrying additional stock with the cost incurred if we run out of inventory, known as the **stock-out cost**. Although these more complex inventory models will not be derived here, accountants are frequently asked to estimate stock-out costs, so let us take a brief look at how we might measure them.

**Stock-out Costs**

The calculation of stock-out costs depends on what management's reaction to a stock-out situation will be. One reaction might be to go to extraordinary lengths to acquire the inventory. If, for example, we see that we are running out of an item and a new shipment is not expected for some time, we might have additional units shipped in by air freight, send an employee directly to the supplier to get additional units, or buy from another supplier nearby at a higher cost. If this type of action is taken, our stock-out cost becomes the extra costs incurred to acquire the needed units. But we must be careful to include only the *extra* costs, not costs that would otherwise have been incurred if the units had been purchased in the normal course of business. Thus, additional shipping costs would be those above and beyond normal shipping costs. Similarly, if we normally buy units for \$15 from our regular supplier but cover shortages by buying units from a local supplier at \$18, the extra cost due to a stock-out is just \$3 per unit.

The other possible reaction is to suffer the consequences of a stock out. If the inventory is needed for production, it may be necessary to shut down the production line. The cost of such an action can be very large. For example, a firm's contract with a labor union may require the firm to pay employees when the shutdown is due to causes under the control of management. These losses (costs incurred for no resulting asset) would be part of the stock-out costs. In addition, if the firm is operating at or near capacity, the firm may not be able to make up in the future for the units of product that could have been produced currently. In this case the firm will also lose the contribution margin it would have earned on those units. If the inventory items are not used in production, but are instead held for direct sale to customers, the stock-out cost will be the contribution margin on lost sales. In this case we must estimate how many customers will not wait for us to replenish our supply and instead buy the product from a competitor. We must also keep in mind that a customer purchasing from a competitor may also choose to continue dealing with the competitor. So our stock-out cost is not only the contribution margin lost on a particular sale but also the lost contribution margin on lost future sales.

Consider the data given in Exhibit 7-5. If management chooses to meet every customer's demand, it must place a special order when a stock-out condition occurs. We assume that a routine order will have already been placed before the stock-out occurred, so management buys only enough units in the special order to meet a particular customer's demand. The costs for placing the special order are the same as for a routine order.

**EXHIBIT 7-5 Data for the Illustration of Stock-out Calculations**

| | |
|---|---|
| Sales price of the product | $9 per unit |
| Invoice cost | $5 per unit |
| Variable transportation-in cost | $0.40 per unit |
| Normal order size from supplier | 5,000 units |
| Normal size of a sale to a customer | 100 units |
| Cost to place an order with the supplier | $18 |

However, instead of being shipped by ground transportation, assume that the product is shipped air freight so that the customer's demand will be met that same day. Our supplier charges $15 to cover the cost of bringing the units to the airport, and the air transportation company charges $2 per unit to transport the units to the firm.

We include the cost to place an order as a stock-out charge on the assumption that by incurring this cost for a special order, we will not be reducing other ordering costs. In that case this is an extra cost caused solely by the stock-out situation. If, instead of ordering only enough units for a particular customer, we placed a routine order for 5,000 units, the order placement costs would not be a stock-out cost.

The supplier's $15 charge to bring the units to the airport is clearly an extra charge that applies only because of the stock-out situation. It therefore is properly included as a stock-out cost. We also incur the $2-per-unit air transportation charge. However, by incurring this cost we also avoid the $0.40-per-unit ground transportation charge that we normally incur. Thus the extra transportation cost due to the stock-out situation is simply the net difference, or $2.00 − $0.40 = $1.60 per unit. Finally, presuming that we want an estimate of the average stock-out cost, our calculation is based on the average customer order of 100 units of product. In this situation the stock-out costs are as follows:

| | |
|---|---|
| Cost to place the order | $ 18.00 |
| Supplier's delivery charge | 15.00 |
| Extra transportation charge | 160.00 |
| Total stock-out cost | $193.00 |

As mentioned previously, management might not choose to meet a customer's order. Instead we might simply ask a customer who arrives when we are out of stock to return in a few days when our normal order arrives. In this case we need estimates of how many customers will actually come back later and of the effect on future sales of turning the customer away. We can get an estimate of the first number (and try to maximize it) by filling out a back order sales slip when the customer arrives. A **back order** is the common term for an order for which we could not meet demand. When the goods arrive, we can then call the customer to see whether they still want the product. Not only is this good customer relations, providing us with the opportunity to consummate the sale, but in addition, the back orders that customers refuse provide us with information on the amount of sales lost due to stock-outs.

Although we can fairly easily estimate the actual direct sales that we lose, estimating the amount of lost future sales is much more difficult. We might try to look at past customer history to see whether we can identify a pattern, or we might simply add an arbitrary factor to estimate the effect on future sales.

For our example let us assume that it costs $2 to prepare a back order invoice. Moreover, our records show that 60% of back orders are normally filled. Finally, management has estimated that two additional sales are lost for each customer who buys the product elsewhere. In this case stock-out costs can be estimated as follows:

| | |
|---|---|
| Cost to prepare back order | $ 2 |
| Lost contribution margin on current sales | 144 |
| Lost contribution margin on future sales | 288 |
| Stock-out cost | $434 |

We include the cost to write up a back order as a stock-out cost on the assumption that if the order is filled we will still have to prepare a regular invoice. In that case the cost of preparing the back-order invoice is clearly an extra cost resulting from the stock-out condition.

The calculation of the lost contribution margin on a sale is more complicated. When we lose a sale, we of course lose the total revenue from the sale, but we also do not have to give up the product. Thus the actual loss to the firm is just the contribution margin on the product. In this case the $9 selling price less the $5.40 in variable costs gives us a contribution margin of $3.60 per unit. Assuming that a normal order is for 100 units, the total cost of losing an order is $360. However, when we turn away a customer, we do not necessarily lose the order. Past records suggest that we lose only 40% of such orders (60% of the customers return). Therefore, on an expected value basis, when we experience a stock-out situation our expected costs are just 40% of the $360 total possible loss, or $144. That is, 40% of the time we lose $360 but 60% of the time we lose nothing, so on the average we lose $144. Finally, since we estimate that we lose two future sales for every lost current sale, we multiply our average lost current sales by two to get the effect of lost future sales.

We have calculated stock-out costs two ways depending on management's intended reaction. In deciding which reaction is most appropriate, we should estimate stock-out costs using both approaches to determine what the least expensive action is. In our example, stock-out costs would be \$193 if we make the effort to meet demand, whereas they are \$434 if we ask customers to return. These calculations should convince management in this situation to adopt a policy of meeting demand when a stock-out occurs.

### Cost of Prediction Errors

Whenever we have formal decision models such as the inventory model, we can estimate the cost of making an error in the estimate of the values of the parameters used in the model. This in turn gives us an indication of the amount of accuracy we should strive for in determining these values.

Let us return to the example provided earlier in the chapter in which annual demand is for 75,000 units, the cost to place an order is \$10, and carrying cost was \$1.50 per unit per year. This information resulted in an optimal order quantity of 1,000 units per order and a total ordering and holding cost of \$1,500. Let us assume these figures to be right; that is, an extensive study would show that each of the foregoing costs and estimates is correct.

Now let us calculate the effect of making an error in one of these estimates. Probably the most difficult value to estimate is the cost of holding a unit in inventory for a year. Assume that we make a large error in this estimate (we used an incorrect rate for cost of capital or made a poor estimate of the cost to rotate inventory). In fact, assume we erred by 50%. Instead of estimating the carrying cost as \$1.50 per unit per year, we actually estimate the cost as \$2.25 per unit per year.

With this incorrect estimate we will actually order 816 units each time we place an order.

$$\text{order quantity} = \sqrt{\frac{2 \times 75{,}000 \times \$10}{\$2.25}} = 816$$

Our actual ordering and holding costs will then be as follows:

$$\begin{aligned}\text{actual holding and ordering costs} &= \frac{75{,}000}{816} \times \$10 + \frac{816}{2} \times \$1.50 \\ &= \$919 + \$612 \\ &= \$1{,}531\end{aligned}$$

Note that in calculating our actual costs we include the actual carrying costs at \$1.50 per unit per year because we posited this as the correct figure. Our actual costs, not our estimates, will of course be the true costs. Our calculations show that even if we erred by 50% in our estimate of the carrying costs, our actual costs (\$1,531) exceed our optimal cost (\$1,500) by only $31. This is approximately a 2% deviation from optimal cost. The implication for accountants is that in estimating these costs we need not go to great lengths to assure absolute accuracy. Reasonable estimates will get us extremely close to optimal results. This is generally true even with the more complex inventory models.

We have described the EOQ model as it is used to determine optimal order quantities. The same model can be used for determining the size of a production run when goods are produced for inventory. In such a situation the costs for holding inventory are calculated in the same way. But now the cost to place an order is replaced by the set-up cost to produce an order. If we produce a whole year's inventory in one production run, we will need to incur equipment set-up costs only once, but if we produce the products in two batches, we must incur the set-up costs twice. The set-up costs that change are the variable set-up costs to be used in the EOQ calculation.

## OTHER INVENTORY SYSTEMS

Both the MRP and EOQ systems require considerable data. For many minor items (screws, washers, and so on) we cannot justify the expense of gathering such data. For example, a detailed analysis might show that the optimal average inventory for some washers is $3 worth. But, even if we carry $6 or $10 worth, the additional carrying costs will be trivial—much smaller than the cost to make the proper analysis. For these types of items more informal systems are used.

One such system is the **tag system**. If you have a checking account, you are familiar with this system. Typically, blank checks are bound in packets of 25, and sold in lots of 200 (eight packets). On the last packet, there is a reorder form bound as the first page. When you get to the last packet, you mail in the form to get more blank checks. The reorder form is referred to as the tag in a tag system.

A slight variation on the tag system is the **two-bin system**. In this approach each inventory item is kept in two containers. When the first container becomes empty, an order is issued for more of the item. In either of these systems, no formal analysis of order size is made. Typically, the firm orders a standard lot size, or relies on production personnel to use their judgment for the appropriate order size.

### ABC Inventory Control

We started the chapter by saying most firms use several inventory control systems. The matching of which system to use for which products is an exercise in balancing the cost of operating the system against the savings from inventory control. Many firms adopt (either formally or informally) the **ABC inventory control system**. All inventoried items are classed as being an A, a B, or a C item. Category A includes the very costly items used frequently. These are monitored very closely, and formal systems are used extensively. The items in category B are intermediate; they may be given formal, but loose, treatment. Category C includes those relatively inexpensive items that are stocked using informal methods.

The savings in accounting and data gathering costs from using the ABC approach can be very significant. One large firm did a study of its inventories and found that only 8% of their items deserved A status, but these items accounted for 75% of the dollar volume of inventory, another 25% of the items were classed as B items and accounted for 20% of their inventory's dollar volume, while a whopping 67% of the items in total made up only 5% of the dollar volume of inventory. These items were treated as being in category C.

## SUMMARY

Once management has determined its planned scope of operations, it becomes possible to estimate the level of resources that will be necessary to achieve those plans. How we choose to acquire these resources involves balancing the cost of operating the accounting systems, the cost of placing orders, the cost of storing inventory, and the cost of stock-outs. In each case accountants can be expected to be called upon to provide the appropriate cost information.

## DEMONSTRATION PROBLEM

St. Regina Paper Company's production plans for 19X4 call for the manufacture of 15,000 tons of newsprint (paper). The most significant material input for paper manufacturing is wood. The wood is purchased by the cord (a cord is a stack of wood 4 feet wide, 4 feet high, and 8 feet long; a cord of wood weighs approximately $2\frac{1}{4}$ tons). The wood is stripped of its bark, and then ground into pulp to be used to manufacture the paper. Recent records for the amount of wood required to produce newsprint reveal the following:

| Period | | Cords of Wood Processed | Tons of Newsprint Produced |
|---|---|---|---|
| Third quarter | 19X2 | 1,460 | 3,120 |
| Fourth quarter | 19X2 | 1,811 | 3,850 |
| First quarter | 19X3 | 1,950 | 4,135 |
| Second quarter | 19X3 | 1,882 | 4,010 |
| Third quarter | 19X3 | 1,874 | 3,985 |

The current market price of a cord of wood delivered to the plant is $120. It costs $5.92 in telephone and clerical costs to place an order plus $3 to process the vendor's invoice. The firm estimates its cost of capital as 20% per year. It costs approximately $20 per cord of wood to forklift it from the suppliers' trucks and place it into inventory. It also costs $20 per cord to take the wood out of inventory and put it into production. The plant will be in operation 250 days next year, and the lead time to receive an order of wood after the order has been placed is one day.

**Required**

**a.** What is the quantity of wood required per ton of paper?
**b.** Determine the optimal inventory ordering policy for wood.
**c.** Find the total ordering costs and carrying costs for the year using the optimal ordering policy.
**d.** Determine the firm's reorder point for wood.

**Solution**

**a.** One might be tempted to conclude that each cord of wood should yield $2\frac{1}{4}$ tons of paper since the amount (weight) of paper produced will depend almost totally on the amount (weight) of wood put into process. After all, very little pulp is lost in the papermaking process, and the additional materials (chemicals) used in the process are negligible relative to the wood pulp. However, the wood is purchased with its bark still on. The bark is stripped before the wood is processed, so the total weight of wood purchased is not put into process. Further, the amount of stripped wood obtainable from a cord of wood will not be constant. The relative amount of bark on a 3-inch-diameter log is much higher than that on a 15-inch-diameter log. So in this case the best approach for estimating the amount of wood needed per ton of paper will be to rely on past experience. Assuming that the quarterly operating data available are representative of normal production yields, we can estimate our materials needs by calculating the average amount of wood needed per ton of paper in the past.

On the basis of the foregoing data, 8,977 cords of wood were processed over a period of five quarters. During the same period, 19,100 tons of paper were manufactured. Dividing inputs by outputs indicates that on average it took 8,977/19,100 = 0.47 cords of wood to produce a ton of paper. Hence the quantity of wood needed per ton of paper is 0.47 cords.

**b.** Now that we have an estimate of the amount of wood needed per ton of paper we can predict the amount of wood needed to produce the 15,000 tons of paper we expect to manufacture next year. Multiplying the 15,000 tons of output by the 0.47 cords of wood needed per ton reveals that approximately 7,050 cords of wood will be required next year. Let us now turn to determining the best ordering strategy for acquiring the wood.

The annual demand for wood is, of course, the 7,050 cords estimated. We also need to estimate the cost of placing an order for wood. The only costs mentioned in the problem that seem to vary by the number of orders placed are the $5.92 for telephone and clerical costs plus the $3 for processing the invoice. Thus the ordering costs appear to be $8.92 per order. In this problem the only carrying cost is the cost of capital tied up in inventory. To calculate this cost we first need to know the total cost that we have invested in each unit (cord) of inventory. The investment will include the $120 invoice cost per cord plus the \$20 handling charge for putting the wood into inventory. It does not, however, include the \$20 cost to remove the wood from inventory; that is, the investment in inventory includes only those costs necessary to get the wood *into* inventory—in this case, \$140. Multiplying the investment by the 20% cost of capital yields the cost for holding a unit of wood in inventory for a year as \$28.

We can now substitute annual demand, order costs, and carrying costs into the economic order quantity model to determine optimal order size. The model yields

$$\text{EOQ} = \sqrt{\frac{2 \times 7{,}050 \times \$8.92}{\$28}}$$
$$= 67 \text{ cords}$$

**c.** If we order 67 cords each time an order is placed, we will order 7,050 ÷ 67 = 105.2 times during the year, and our average inventory will be 67 ÷ 2 = 33.5 cords on hand. Multiplying these figures by the ordering costs and carrying costs, respectively, and adding the results gives the total anticipated ordering and carrying costs, as follows:

$$\text{total costs} = 105.2 \times \$8.92 + 33.5 \times \$28$$
$$= \$938 + \$938$$
$$= \$1{,}876$$

**d.** Since it only takes one day to receive an order of wood, our inventory reorder point is one day's anticipated usage of wood. We are predicting that we will use 7,050 cords of wood during the firm's 250 operating days, so the average usage of wood per day is 7,050 ÷ 250 = 28 cords per day. Thus we would need to reorder wood when the inventory approaches 28 cords.

## KEY TERMS AND CONCEPTS

Material requirements planning systems
Bill of materials
Lead time
[Just-in-time system
Zero-stock system
Safety stock
Economic order quantity
Carrying cost
Reorder point
Stock-out cost
Back order
Tag system
Two-bin system
ABC inventory control system

[Bracketed terms are equivalent in meaning.

## FURTHER READING

Bowers, Billy B. "Product Costing in the MRP Environment," *Management Accounting* (December 1982), p. 24.

Cohen, Morris A., and Robert Halperin. "Optimal Inventory Order Policy for a Firm Using the LIFO Inventory Costing Method," *Journal of Accounting Research* (Autumn 1980), p. 375.

Davenport, Frederick. "Financial Management through MRP," *Management Accounting* (June 1982), p. 26.

Kimes, James D. "Are You Really Managing Your Inventory?" *Management Accounting* (February 1984), p. 70.

Sadhwani, Arjan T., M.H. Sarhan, and Dayal Kiringoda. "Just-in-Time: An Inventory System Whose Time Has Come," *Management Accounting* (December 1985), p. 36.

Seglund, Ragnor, and Santiago Ibarreche. "Just-in-Time: The Accounting Implications," *Management Accounting* (August 1984), p. 43.

## QUESTIONS AND EXERCISES

**7-1** What are the major cost savings that accrue from adopting a zero-stock inventory policy?

**7-2** Given the apparent financial success of many Japanese firms that have adopted just-in-time systems, should all firms attempt to eliminate inventories?

**7-3** The widespread adoption of materials requirements planning systems has come about in the past decade. Why were such systems not popular before that time?

**7-4** A design change in one of a firm's products will replace a sleeve and cover by a single molded cap. What changes will be required in the firm's materials requirements planning system?

**7-5** For what decision regarding inventories would the depreciation on the firm's warehouse be a relevant cost?

**7-6** What is the underlying objective of economic order quantity?

**7-7** If a firm's sales per year double and if inventory levels are properly managed, will the average size of inventory double, less than double, or more than double?

**7-8** What is a back order?

**7-9** What is the purpose of safety stock?

**7-10** Of the major costs to be considered in determining economic order quantity, which is probably the most difficult to determine (measure)?

**7-11** Our firm has just received an order for 150 power transformers. Each transformer contains two transmissions. A transmission is made up of one housing and four gears. Each gear requires two washers. The firm operates on a zero-stock basis so it does not have any of these parts in inventory. How many units of each part will need to be ordered?

**7-12** The drawing below shows a small portion of the parts required to assemble a lawn mower engine. Item 47 is the head, 46 is the head gasket, items 5 and 6 are valves, items 8 and 10 are valve spring caps, items 9 are valve springs, item 49 is a carriage bolt, and item 51 is a spark plug.

Using the information in the engineering drawing, prepare a partial bill of materials for the assembly of a lawn mower engine. If the firm plans to assemble 625 lawn mowers next week, how many units of each part will be required?

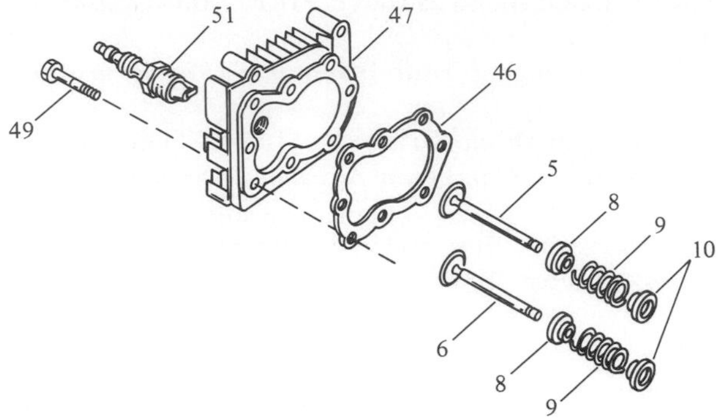


**7-13** Refer to the demonstration problem at the end of the chapter. (a) If the company desired a safety stock of 100 cords of wood and if it takes 3 days (instead of 1 day) to receive an order, what is the reorder point? (b) If the market price for wood jumps to $150, what will be the effect on the economic order quantity, if any?

**7-14** The costs and requirements of a raw material are as follows:

| | |
|---|---|
| Ordering costs | $10 per order |
| Holding costs | $4 per unit per year |
| Usage | 500 units per week |
| Safety stock | 200 units |
| Lead time | 2 weeks |

Determine (a) the economic order quantity and (b) the reorder point.

**7-15** (CPA). Reid Company is budgeting sales of 100,000 units of product R for the month of September 19X2. Production of one unit of product R requires two units of material A and three units of material B. Actual inventory units at September 1 and budgeted inventory units at September 30 are as follows:

| | Actual Inventory at September 1 | Budgeted Inventory at September 30 |
|---|---|---|
| Product R | 20,000 | 10,000 |
| Material A | 25,000 | 18,000 |
| Material B | 22,000 | 24,000 |

How many units of material B is Reid planning to purchase during September 19X2?

**7-16** Periodic usage of a raw material is 1,000 units, and the economic order quantity is 200 units. If it costs $0.50 to hold a unit of inventory one period, what must be the ordering costs?

**7-17** The cost of placing an order is $50, the economic order quantity is 100 units, and periodic usage is 300 units. What is the periodic holding cost per unit?

**7-18** (CPA). Garmar, Inc., has determined the following for a given year:

| | |
|---|---|
| Economic order quantity (standard order size) | 5,000 units |
| Total cost to place purchase orders for the year | $10,000 |
| Cost to place one purchase order | $50 |
| Cost to carry one unit for a year | $4 |

What is Garmar's estimated annual usage in units?

**7-19** (CPA). Pierce Incorporated is required to manufacture 10,000 blades for its electric lawn mower division. The blades will be used evenly throughout the year. The set-up cost every time a production run is made is $80, and the cost to carry a blade in inventory for the year is $0.40. Pierce's objective is to produce the blades at the lowest cost possible. Assuming that each production run will be for the same number of blades, how many production runs should Pierce make?

**7-20** Records show that 35% of our firm's back orders are refused by customers when the products finally arrive. It costs $1.50 to prepare a back order. What is the expected stock-out cost if a customer asks for 25 units of a product that we sell for $18, and we are out of stock? The variable costs for the product are $12 per unit.

**7-21** Salesco usually orders 20 units of a part each time it places an order. It costs $15 in clerical costs to place an order, and the units are purchased for $37 each. The normal supplier bills Salesco $65 for shipping costs to deliver the products to the firm. If the firm runs short of the part, the purchasing agent immediately telegraphs an order for 20 units to a closer supplier. The telegraph charge is $6 and the clerical costs for placing the rush order are $14. The firm then hires a truck costing $70 to pick up the parts and bring them to the firm. The nearby supplier charges $39 each for the parts. What is Salesco's cost of a stock-out for this part?

## PROBLEMS AND CASES

**7-22 Estimate savings from inventory reduction.**
The Waldon Company is considering upgrading its inventory/production planning and control system. Currently, the firm holds an average inventory of $4,500,000. Management estimates that an improved system will reduce average inventory to $1,700,000. The firm has kept records on the cost of maintaining its warehouse and the materials handling costs incurred by warehouse employees. The data, adjusted for inflation, reveals that warehousing costs were $320,000 when average inventory was $1,000,000 and $845,000 when average inventory was $4,500,000. The firm has several very large bank loans outstanding, on which it pays interest of 12%.

**Required**
Estimate the annual savings if inventory is reduced as planned.

**7-23 Decision to adopt zero-stock policy.**
The Boston Assembly Division of ADI, Inc., has been maintaining inventories of its raw materials (mostly subassemblies). The firm has been using EOQ and carries an average materials inventory costing $1,500,000. Its total cost for materials used per year is fairly steady at $10 million. Management is considering going to a just-

in-time approach. The following data have been gathered.

Suppliers are willing to make twice-daily deliveries. The total cost to acquire materials will increase by 5%. The division will be able to sell its raw materials warehouse for $3 million. In addition, five materials handlers will be terminated. These people each earn $17,000 per year. Two people will have to be added to the purchasing department to monitor purchase orders and deliveries. Each will earn $22,000 per year. Except for the salaries for these workers, there will be no change in the cost of placing orders. The firm will continue to carry a safety stock on the shop floor of critical materials. These materials will have a cost of $100,000.

The firm has a revolving credit line with the bank. Currently, the firm's bank debt is $22 million, with an 11% interest rate. Any savings generated by the change in inventory policy will be used to reduce the bank debt.

**Required**
Should the firm make the change?

**7-24 Update materials requirement planning matrix.**
The following materials requirement planning matrix was prepared in period 1. This part is ordered in a lot size of 100 units and has a lead time of one period. In period 2, production of goods requiring 275 of these parts has been scheduled for period 5.

| | Period | | | | |
|---|---|---|---|---|---|
| | 1 | 2 | 3 | 4 | 5 |
| Total requirement | | 100 | 350 | | |
| Scheduled receipts | | | | | |
| Scheduled on hand | 120 | 20 | 20 | | |
| Amount needed | | | 330 | | |
| Planned orders | | | 400 | | |

**Required**
Prepare an updated planning matrix as of period 2.

**7-25 Materials requirement planning.**
An expensive carbon steel blade is used in only one of a firm's products. The lead time to acquire the blade is three periods. Currently there are 65 of the blades in stock. A purchase order has been issued for 250 blades. They are expected to arrive in period 2. As of today, period 1, the firm has orders to produce products

requiring 300 of the blades in period 2 and 270 in period 6. The blades are ordered in a lot size of 50 units.

**Required**

**a.** Prepare a materials requirement planning matrix as of the end of period 1. When is the next purchase order expected to be sent out and for how many units will it be?

**b.** In period 2, additional production requiring 160 blades is scheduled for period 6 and production requiring 320 blades is scheduled for period 7. Prepare a revised MRP matrix as of the end of period 2. What is the new expected timing and amount for purchase orders to be issued?

**c.** No further orders requiring blades were scheduled in period 3. Prepare the revised MRP matrix as of the end of period 3.

**7-26 Materials requirements planning.**

Today is Monday, March 4. Each Monday our firm performs a materials requirement planning review for the next 3 weeks. One part of this review is the determination of the dates on which purchase orders should be sent to suppliers.

On March 20 the firm has scheduled the production of 1,000 units of product X12 and on March 21 the firm will produce 800 units of Z10. The bill of materials for each product is given below. The materials used for these products will not be required for any of the other products produced from March 4 through March 22. There are no outstanding purchase orders for any of these materials.

The relevant portion of the inventory status records follows.

| Material | Lot Size | Lead Time[a] | On Hand | Safety Stock | Allocated | Available |
|---|---|---|---|---|---|---|
| Flange A | 500 | 6 | 225 | 50 | 0 | 175 |
| Pin PR | 250 | 2 | 75 | 25 | 20 | 30 |
| Axle K2 | 0 | 4 | 40 | 10 | 0 | 30 |
| Bearing 7X2 | 100 | 7 | 550 | 100 | 0 | 450 |

[a]In business days (M–F).

**Product X12 Bill of Materials**

| Quantity | Item |
|---|---|
| 1 | Flange A |
| 3 | Bearing 7X2 |

**Product Z10 Bill of Materials**

| Quantity | Item |
|---|---|
| 2 | Flange A |
| 1 | Axle K2 |
| 4 | Bearing 7X2 |

MARCH

| S | M | T | W | T | F | S |
|---|---|---|---|---|---|---|
| | | | | | 1 | 2 |
| 3 | 4 | 5 | 6 | 7 | 8 | 9 |
| 10 | 11 | 12 | 13 | 14 | 15 | 16 |
| 17 | 18 | 19 | 20 | 21 | 22 | 23 |
| 24 | 25 | 26 | 27 | 28 | 29 | 30 |
| 31 | | | | | | |

**Required**

Determine the size of each purchase order and the date on which each should be issued. The firm's receiving dock is open only on Mondays. All receipts of materials must arrive on the Monday morning in the week needed.

**7-27 Economic order quantity.**

Stone Supply is preparing its master budget for the upcoming year. The firm uses the following simple deterministic inventory model for its purchasing decision.

$$EOQ = \sqrt{\frac{2AC}{S}}$$

Using quarterly data for the past 3 years, Stone has estimated order-placing costs as \$2,500 + \$1.75(number of orders). The invoice cost of obtaining inventory is \$30 per unit. Transportation costs are \$1 per unit. Annual warehousing costs are estimated to be \$25,000 + \$4 (average number of units in inventory). Marketing costs usually average \$3 per unit. The firm's cost of capital is 10%. Stone expects to be able to sell 30,000 units this coming year.

**Required**

**a.** Determine the optimal order size.
**b.** What are the total anticipated inventory related costs for the next year?

**7-28 Economic order quantity.**

Hilda's Hobby House is planning its inventory strategy for stocking the new Space Wars Intergalactic Transporter. The toy has a retail price of \$45. Hilda buys the items for \$27 each. Experience with similar toys leads management to believe that demand for the product will be fairly even over the year and will total 20,000 units. The cost to place an order, including the cost of a long-distance telephone call and miscellaneous supplies, averages \$8. Shipping costs paid by HHH average \$30 per order plus \$1 per unit. Customers of HHH frequently play with the items on display and occasionally damage the product. Management estimates its loss as \$3 per unit per year in average inventory. The firm's cost of capital is 15% per year. Salespeople are paid a commission of 10% of the retail price for all units sold.

**Required**

**a.** Determine the number of units HHH should order each time it places an order.
**b.** Assuming that the firm is open for business 360 days per year and that it takes 3 days for an order to arrive, what is the reorder point?

**7-29 Economic order quantity: Cost of information.**

On January 1, 19X4, Halsey Retailers made the following estimates related to inventory: cost to place an order, \$12; cost to carry 1 unit of inventory for a year, \$6; anticipated annual demand, 10,000 units. At the end of 19X4 the firm determined that the actual cost to place an order during the year was \$12 and carrying cost was \$6; however, the demand for the year was only 8,200 units. Halsey used a simple EOQ model for determining order quantities. On January 1, 19X4, Halsey could have received a report from a market researcher that was guaranteed to predict annual demand accurately. The researcher's price was \$100.

**Required**

Should Halsey have engaged the researcher's services? Support your answer with appropriate calculations.

**7-30 Economic order quantity.**

The California Computer Company plans its inventory levels on a *quarterly* basis because there is a significant seasonal effect on sales. For the next quarter the firm expects to sell 45,000 units. The cost to purchase a unit is $44. They are sold for $80 and a sales commission of 10% of sales is paid to salespeople. The costs to place an order total $15 for clerical costs. Inventory obsolescence is a major problem for the firm. To protect themselves, the firm buys obsolescence insurance which costs $5 per unit per year for the weighted average number of units on hand. When units are acquired, the transportation fee is $50 per shipment plus $1 per unit. The firm's cost of capital is 12%.

**Required**

**a.** Determine the optimal number of units the firm should order each time it places an order.

**b.** Based upon your answer in (a), what is the total ordering cost the firm should expect to incur during the next quarter?

**7-31 Economic order quantity.**

Roanoke Industries wholesales bulk California wines to private-label bottlers. For 19X7 Roanoke estimates a total sales volume of 4,000,000 gallons. Roanoke purchases the wine by railroad tank car. There is a fixed handling charge of $500 for obtaining any size or quantity of tank cars. A variable loading charge of $0.01 a gallon is also charged by the railroad. Orders for bulk wine are telegraphed to a broker in California at an average cost of $10. Labor costs to prepare and process orders average $30 each. When the wine arrives at Roanoke's tank farm there is a $100 state inspector's fee. Unloading generally costs about $0.045 per gallon in variable labor cost. Inventory, inspection, and handling costs (all labor costs) average approximately $0.02 per gallon per year for the average quantity of wine in inventory. In addition, taxes are levied on average annual inventory on hand at the rate of $0.035 per gallon. Depreciation on the storage tanks is $20,000 per year. Other overhead amounts to $60,000 per year plus $2 per labor dollar. Roanoke purchases the bulk wine for $0.80 per gallon. The firm must borrow funds to finance its inventory. Its average cost of capital is 15% per year.

**Required**

**a.** Determine the quantity of wine that Roanoke should order each time it places an order.

**b.** What are the anticipated annual costs relating to the placing of orders?

**c.** What are the anticipated annual carrying costs for inventory?

**7-32 Economic order quantity.**

Having solved the appropriate linear-programming problem, Astre Industries will produce 4,000 units of product 1 and 8,000 units of product 2 next year. Product 1 requires 3 pounds of raw material, and product 2 requires 5 pounds per unit. The invoice price of the raw material is $2.50 per pound, but the supplier offers a 2% discount if the bill is paid within 30 days. Astre always pays its bills within the discount period. The shipping company that Astre uses charges $300 plus $0.25 per pound for each shipment of raw materials. Astre leases its warehouse space. The firm is charged $2 per pound per year for units in storage. Astre determined that it costs $8 in clerical costs to place an order. Astre's cost of capital is 15%.

**Required**

**a.** Determine the amount of raw material Astre should order each time it places an order.

**b.** If the firm actually orders 5,000 units each time it places an order, what will be the annual carrying cost for inventory?

**7-33 Economic order quantity.**

Sole Product, Inc., is a retailing firm handling only one product. The firm is evaluating how well it controlled its purchases of inventory last year. A look at the financial statements reveals that the firm sold 23,400 units last year. It began the year with 360 units in inventory and finished the year with 60 units. The firm buys the product for $40 each in an unassembled state. It takes 2 hours of labor time to assemble the product before it is put on the shelf ready for sale. It costs $19.50 in postage, telephone, supplies, and so forth, to place an order. The firm pays insurance of $0.50 per unit for the average number of units on hand in inventory over the year. It is estimated that it takes 1 hour of labor time per unit per year to dust, rotate, and inspect inventory. When the firm purchases inventory, it pays a shipping charge of $300 plus $2 per unit. Sole Product's overhead is $20,000 per year plus $3 per labor hour. Labor is paid $6 per hour; sales personnel are paid a commission of $2 per unit sold. The firm's cost of capital is considered to be 8%.

**Required**

**a.** Determine what Sole Product's optimal order size should have been for last year. (Note that the firm pays a property tax based on December 31 inventory; therefore it is preferable to have no inventory on hand on December 31.)

**b.** What is the amount of insurance this firm should have paid (given optimal ordering)?

**c.** Assuming that the actual insurance bill for the year was $275, how many orders of what size did the firm place last year?

**7-34 Economic order quantity: Stock-out costs versus idle-time costs.**

The Citrus Fresh Beverage Company manufactures and cans a regional brand of soft drinks. The firm sells three flavors of soda: lemon-lime, orange, and grapefruit. Next year the firm anticipates selling 250,000 cans of lemon-lime soda, 200,000 of orange soda, and 100,000 cans of grapefruit soda. The firm operates 5 days a week for 50 weeks (250 days per year).

At the moment the firm is concerned with its inventory policy regarding aluminum cans, which are purchased from a manufacturer in another city. Each can costs $0.08. Shipping and handling costs are $800 per shipment plus $0.01 per can. A recent cost study indicates that the variable warehousing costs seem to be running about $0.112 per can for the average number of units held in inventory over the year. Clerical costs, telephone costs, and so forth are approximately $50 to place an order. The firm's cost of capital is 20%.

**Required**

**a.** Determine the number of cans that should be ordered every time the company places an order.

**b.** Assume that it takes 2 weeks (10 working days) to receive an order once it has been placed. What is the firm's reorder point?

**c.** If a stock-out occurs, the company either can wait for the next shipment to arrive (an order presumably was placed when the reorder point was reached) or it can arrange a special shipment. If it places a special order, the nonroutine nature of the order will increase the clerical costs of placing the order to $85. In addition, Citrus Fresh will have to hire its own truck to pick up the shipment. This truck will cost $1,000 plus the $0.01 per can handling cost. The firm can generally foresee a stock-out situation developing a day before it actually occurs. Thus if it places the special order, it can get the goods delivered before a stock-out is experienced. Instead of placing a special order, Citrus Fresh can simply wait until the next scheduled shipment arrives. In this case it will have to send the five canning employees home when the stock-out occurs. But the union contract requires that these employees be paid anyway (the stock-out is considered a management responsibility for which employees should not be penalized). When the cans actually arrive, the firm will then have to work overtime to make up for lost production (each day's lost production will require 8 hours of production at overtime rates). The regular wage rate for these employees is $6 per hour. The overtime rate is 150% of the normal rate. Assume that a special order will have no effect on future ordering patterns and a stock-out will negate a full day's production. Determine when Citrus Fresh should place a special order and when it should wait. That is, if an order is expected to arrive in $x$ days or more, the firm should place a special order; if the order is expected in less than $x$ days, the firm should wait for it.

**7-35 Economic order quantity: Comprehensive.**
Bob's TV Sales sells approximately 700 sets a year. The average selling price is $395 per set. Bob's invoice cost per set is $210. Sales personnel are paid a commission of $50 per set sold. Rent for the store is $250 per month. Clerical costs to place an order are $10. The units are shipped from a nearby city. The freight company charges $75 plus $5 per set. The firm's insurance company computes its premium as $3 per set for the average number of sets on hand during the year. Bob finances his inventory with an inventory loan from the local bank. The current annual percentage rate is 16%. It takes 5 days from the time an order is placed until the sets are received. Note that Bob can order only whole sets (not fractions); therefore, round your answer to the nearest whole number. The firm operates 350 days a year.

**Required**

**a.** How many sets should be ordered every time an order is placed?

**b.** What is the reorder point (when inventory gets to what level should we place another order)?

**c.** If the firm decides on an order quantity of 50 units, what excess cost will be incurred over a year?

**d.** If a customer wants a set that is temporarily out of stock, the salesperson can place an order by telephone. This must be followed up with an order in writing. The total clerical costs for a special order are estimated to be $15. For special orders Bob hires a high school student to drive to the nearby city to pick up the set and deliver it to the customer. The student is paid $20 plus $0.15 per mile. The round-trip averages 40 miles. What is the stock-out cost?

**e.** When he is out of stock, Bob is considering a new policy of telling customers to come back later. He estimates that 70% of the customers will come back later. Whether or not he meets a particular demand, Bob feels there is no effect on future sales beyond the one potential lost sale. Should Bob undertake the new policy? Why or why not?

**7-36 EOQ and expansion of storage facilities** (SMA adapted).
The Sweet Company is a multidivisional Canadian Corporation. One of its divisions processes sugar and apples into candied apples. All sugar requirements are purchased and refined in Cuba, shipped to Vancouver, and then delivered by truck to its sugar warehouse.

At present, the purchase price of sugar is $285 per ton. Because of the uncertain period of time it takes to receive sugar shipments after ordering them, Sweet maintains a 100-ton safety stock. The sugar warehouse is leased on a long-term basis at $20,000 per year with the provision that only sugar can be stored on the premises. The warehouse capacity is 150 tons of sugar.

In addition, Sweet must pay $1,000 per year for insurance on the warehouse structure and $15 per ton of average inventory per year to insure the contents of the warehouse.

The sugar-ordering system is based on an expected demand of 400 tons annually. The refinery in Cuba charges a fixed price of $400 per shipment in order to discourage uneconomic small shipments.

Once the sugar is refined, Sweet's agent in Cuba tests the sugar for purity at $100 per shipment. The sugar is then shipped to Vancouver at a cost of $12 per ton, cleared through the Vancouver port for $250 per shipment, and delivered by truck to the warehouse for an additional $3 per ton. Sweet's opportunity cost of capital is 15%.

**Required**

**a.** How many tons of sugar should the Sweet Company purchase per shipment?

**b.** In terms of tons of sugar, by how much would the Sweet Company wish to increase sugar warehouse capacity in order to operate at the optimal position? How much should Sweet be willing to pay for this increase in warehouse capacity?

**7-37 Direct labor requirements with alternative technologies and safety stocks** (CMA adapted).
Valbec Company manufactures and distributes toy doll houses. Since the toy industry is a seasonal business, a large portion of Valbec's sales occur in the late summer and fall.

The projected sales in units for 19X8 are shown in the schedule that follows. With a sales price of $10 per unit, the total sales revenue for 19X8 is projected at $1.2 million. Valbec scheduled its production in the past so that finished goods inventory at the end of each month, exclusive of a safety stock of 4,000 doll houses, would equal the next month's sales. One-half hour of direct labor time is required to produce each doll house under normal operating conditions. Using the production schedule followed in the past, the total direct labor hours by month that would be required to meet the 19X8 sales estimate are shown in the following schedule.

**VALBEC COMPANY**
**Projected Sales and Planned Production**
**For Year Ended December 31, 19X8**

| | Projected Sales (in units) | Direct Labor Hours Required[a] |
|---|---|---|
| January | 8,000 | 4,000 |
| February | 8,000 | 4,000 |
| March | 8,000 | 4,000 |
| April | 8,000 | 4,000 |
| May | 8,000 | 5,000 |
| June | 10,000 | 6,000 |
| July | 12,000 | 6,000 |
| August | 12,000 | 6,500 |
| September | 13,000 | 6,500 |
| October | 13,000 | 6,000 |
| November | 12,000 | 4,000 |
| December | 8,000 | 4,000[b] |
| Total | 120,000 | 60,000 |

[a]This schedule does not incorporate any additional direct labor hours resulting from inefficiencies.

[b]Sales for January 19X9 are projected at 8,000 units.

The production schedule followed in the past requires the scheduling of overtime hours for any production in excess of 8,000 units (4,000 direct labor hours) in one month. Although the use of overtime is feasible, the Valbec management has decided that it should consider two other possible alternatives: (1) hire temporary help from an agency during the peak months, or (2) expand its labor force and adopt a level production schedule. The use of a second shift was not considered because management believed the community would not support this alternative.

Factory employees are paid $6 per hour for regular time, and fringe benefits average 20% of regular pay. For hours worked in excess of 4,000 hours per month, employees receive time and one-half; however, fringe benefits average only 10% on these additional wages. Past experience has shown that when overtime is required, labor inefficiencies do occur during overtime at the rate of 5% of overtime hours; this 5% inefficiency is not included in the direct labor hour estimates presented in the schedule.

Rather than pay overtime to its regular labor force, Valbec can hire temporary employees when production exceeds 8,000 units per month. The temporary workers can be hired through an agency at the same labor rate of $6 per hour, but there are no fringe benefit costs. Management estimates that the temporary workers would require 25% more time than the regular employees to produce the doll houses.

If Valbec should go to a level production schedule, the labor force would be expanded, but no overtime would be required. The same labor rate of $6 per hour and fringe-benefit rate of 20% would apply.

The manufacturing facilities have the capacity to produce 18,000 doll houses per month. On-site storage facilities for completed units are adequate. The estimated annual cost of carrying inventory is $1 per unit. Valbec is subject to a 40% income tax rate.

**Required**

**a.** Prepare an analysis that compares the costs associated with each of Valbec Company's three alternatives:
   1. Schedule overtime hours
   2. Hire temporary workers
   3. Expand labor force and schedule level production

**b.** Identify and discuss briefly the noncost factors and the factors difficult to cost that Valbec Company should consider in conjunction with the cost analysis prepared in (a) before a final decision is made relative to the three alternatives.

**7-38 Cash budget and program constraints—uses EOQ and linear programming: Difficult.**

Chemical Manufacturing, Inc., is preparing its cash budget for the next several weeks. The firm has been told by suppliers that it will be able to receive only 52,000 pounds of raw material 1 and 104,000 pounds of raw material 2 this year. The firm can acquire 405 hours of skilled labor per week and has 8,000 hours of machine time available per week. Material 1 costs $2 per pound and material 2 costs $1.25 per pound. Labor is paid $4 per hour; employees are paid every Friday. There are no variable overhead costs.

The firm manufactures four products. Sales prices and variable costs to manufacture each product are as follows:

| | Product | | | |
|---|---|---|---|---|
| | 1 | 2 | 3 | 4 |
| Selling price | $6 | $10 | $5 | $12 |
| Variable costs | 4 | 5 | 2 | 4 |

The firm operates 40 hours per week, Monday through Friday. The firm's factory overhead amounts to $100,000 per year ($69,840 of which represents equipment depreciation). Administrative costs are $2,000 per week. Administrative costs and overhead costs are paid on the last day of each month.

Costs to place an order for either material 1 or 2 are $20 per order. Materials are received on the same day they are ordered. Carrying costs for material 1 are $0.40 per pound per year, and for material 2 are $0.50 per pound per year. Order costs and carrying costs are not included in the given overhead figures, but they are also paid on the last day of the month. Order costs incurred in February through the 27th of the month were $80. For budgeting purposes, it is not worth the effort to determine the actual average inventory on hand during the period. Instead, the average for each month is estimated by adding the beginning and ending balances in inventory and dividing by 2. On February 1, there were 1,740 units of material 1 and 48 units of material 2 on hand.

Production and sales may be assumed to occur uniformly over time. All sales are for cash and purchases are for cash. The firm has a cash balance of $6,000 on February 27. Production was determined by solving the following linear program.

maximize: $2X_1 + 5X_2 + 3X_3 + 8X_4$

Subject to: Material 1 ≤ 1,000 lb per week

Labor ≤ 405 hr per week

Machine time ≤ 8,000 hr per week

Material 2 ≤ 2,000 lb per week

The solution yielded $X_1 = 0$; $X_2 = 500$; $X_3 = 400$; $X_4 = 600$; $X_5 = 0$; $X_6 = 85$; $X_7 = 0$; $X_8 = 0$.

**Required**

Prepare a weekly cash budget for Chemical Manufacturing for the period from Monday, February 27, 19X8, through Friday, March 31, 19X8. The firm has 420 pounds of material 1 and 1,500 pounds of material 2 on hand as of 8:00 A.M. on February 27, 19X8.

**7-39 Comprehensive cash budget—uses EOQ and linear programming: Difficult**

MT Industries will be at the peak of its season for the next 10 to 15 weeks. During this time it will be able to sell everything that it can manufacture. The firm markets two products. Product M sells for $20 per unit, and product T sells for $25. The two products each use a common raw material, zylon, which costs $4 per pound. Labor is paid $5 per hour, and variable overhead is $2 per direct labor hour. Fixed overhead amounts to $10,000 per week. The two products are each processed on two machines. There are 2,600 hours of time available on machine 1 per week and 6,400 hours of time on machine 2. The following table presents the resource requirements to produce each product.

| | Product | |
|---|---|---|
| | M | T |
| Raw material, pounds | $\frac{1}{4}$ | 1 |
| Direct labor, hours | 1 | 1 |
| Machine-1 time, hours | 1 | 2 |
| Machine-2 time, hours | 4 | 3 |

It costs MT $50 to place an order to acquire more zylon. The firm considers its cost of capital to be 12.8%. Insurance (which is included in the overhead figures given previously) is $0.75 per unit per year of zylon held in inventory on average. There is no lead time required for ordering zylon.

MT operates 24 hours a day, 364 days a year. For planning and reporting purposes the year is split into 13 four-week periods. For the next few periods units will be sold, as produced, for cash. Four weeks (one period's worth) of variable overhead costs are paid in advance during the first week of a period. Direct labor is paid every Friday, and materials are paid in cash when delivered. Only one-fourth of the fixed overhead requires periodic payments. These payments are made at the end of each period (i.e., during the fourth week of each period). In week 3 of period 2, the firm hopes to repay a $150,000 loan taken out to tide the firm over its slow season. MT will start period 1, week 1, with $25,000 on hand and 2,100 units of zylon in inventory.

**Required**

Prepare a weekly cash budget for MT for the next two periods (8 weeks).

# CHAPTER 8

# CAPITAL BUDGETING

The planning and decision models developed to this point are primarily short-term models. By short term we mean that both the costs and the benefits from a specific course of action occur so close together in time that the time factor itself can be properly ignored in the decision process. In other words, any necessary cash outflows are quickly followed by cash inflows.

For example, assume that a study of the variable costs related to a make-or-buy decision leads a firm to the conclusion that it can make a part for $88 or buy it for $86 as needed. Each and every time the part is purchased, rather than made, the firm saves $2. Furthermore, since the part is available when needed, there does not need to be a large investment made in inventory. No analysis beyond comparing variable costs is needed to determine whether the firm should produce or purchase the part. The $2 saving occurs simultaneously with the $86 purchase.

However, assume instead that the firm requires 1,000 units of this part monthly and that the supplier requires (as a condition of the contract) that the minimum order be for 7,000 units. The firm must now make a decision as to whether to make a rather substantial investment in inventory to obtain the $2 per unit savings from buying the part rather than making it. The solution to the problem now requires that we determine whether funds should be used to carry a large inventory of the part as an investment or whether such funds can be better employed elsewhere while the firm manufactures the part in question.

To answer the type of question just asked, the models from earlier chapters may be helpful, but they are not sufficient for making the appropriate decision. In effect, we are now asking whether it is worthwhile to incur, or invest, a cash outlay in the *present* to effect savings in the *future*. In its simplest case, an investment problem is one that requires an expenditure now with corresponding benefits to be received in one or more future periods; hence we have a multiperiod problem rather than a single-period one. The answers to multiperiod questions are not always intuitively obvious. The problem is created by the time lag between making an expenditure and receiving the benefits, or vice versa.

## LONG-RUN ANALYSIS

Whenever there is a material lag between costs and/or benefits, *time*—through the interest on invested or borrowed funds—becomes an additional variable in the decision process. In this chapter and the next we analyze the capital budgeting decision: the process of evaluating long-term investments and allocating available funds among alternative investments.

### The Concept of Interest

There are several alternate ways of considering the concept of **interest.** Interest can be construed as the time value of money. That is, a dollar today has greater value than a dollar tomorrow. As an example, consider income taxes. There is nothing that prevents us from paying income taxes in advance; however, common sense suggests we should wait until they are due. In the interim the funds to be used to pay the tax can be invested in a savings account, or elsewhere, to earn some interest income. The choice is obvious: Given a choice between paying taxes today or paying taxes later (with no penalty), the prudent taxpayer chooses the latter.

Interest can also be viewed as a cost of consuming now rather than later. If funds are not available now for such purposes as buying a car, a home, or building a plant, the money may be borrowed. The cost of borrowing, the interest on the debt, is the cost that must be incurred to enjoy the consumption now rather than waiting until sufficient funds are available.

From a lender's point of view, interest can be seen as a benefit that stems from consuming later, rather than now. When excess funds are available, rather than consuming them now, we can wait until a later time.

In the meantime, the funds can be put out to loan; the money earned on such funds is interest.

### The Mathematics of Interest

The computation of compound interest is fairly straightforward, although the expressions often look imposing. Basically, the questions involving compound interest relate to one of two simple questions.

1. If a **principal,** $P$, is invested now at $i\%$ interest paid per period, what **amount,** $A$, of funds will be available in $n$ periods?
2. If we must have an amount, $A$, of funds available in $n$ periods, how much principal, $P$, must be invested now at an interest rate of $i$ to yield $A$?

In the first case, if $P$ is invested at the beginning of the first period, then at the end of the first period we will end up with the original principal plus interest on the principal: $P + iP$ or $P(1 + i)$. In the second period we will have $P(1 + i)$ invested so that at the end of the second period we end up with

$$\begin{aligned} P(1 + i) + iP(1 + i) &= P(1 + i)(1 + i) \\ &= P(1 + i)^2 \end{aligned}$$

This becomes the amount invested in the next period, and the pattern is already obvious. After $n$ periods the investment will amount to

$$A = P(1 + i)^n$$

It used to be very difficult to solve an exponential equation of this sort, but with a hand-held calculator that has an exponential function, $y^x$, available, solving this equation is trivial. If we invest \$215 at 8% interest per period for 12 periods, the investment will amount to

$$\begin{aligned} A &= \$215(1.08)^{12} \\ &= \$215(2.51817) \\ &= \$541.41 \end{aligned}$$

The second question was the reverse of the first. Knowing a desired ending amount, what must be invested now to achieve that amount? From the relationship already derived, we can rearrange the terms to answer this question.

$$\text{Since} \quad A = P(1 + i)^n$$

$$\text{then} \quad P = \frac{A}{(1 + i)^n}$$

$$= A\frac{1}{(1 + i)^n}$$

Using the data in the previous example, if we desire $541.41 at the end of 12 periods and can invest at 8% per period, we need to invest

$$P = \frac{\$541.41}{(1.08)^{12}}$$

$$= \frac{\$541.41}{2.51817}$$

$$= \$215$$

This amount is frequently called the **present value** of $541.41 for 12 periods at 8% interest. It is the present amount of principal needed to provide $541.41 in 12 periods.

Knowing the basic relationship among interest, principal, time, and amount allows us to consider other questions. For example, if we currently have $200 and want it to grow to $550 in 12 periods, what interest rate is required? Now we wish to solve the equation:

$$\$550 = \$200(1 + i)^{12}$$

$$\text{or} \quad 2.75 = (1 + i)^{12}$$

We can solve this by taking the log of the equation (assuming you have the proper calculator) to get

$$0.43933269 = 12 \log(1 + i)$$

$$0.03661106 = \log(1 + i)$$

and then the antilog: $1.08796 = 1 + i$, or $i$ must be 8.796%. Alternatively, if your calculator has both the exponential function $y^x$ and an inverse function, the problem can be solved directly by entering 2.75, pressing the inverse key, and the $y^x$ key, next entering 12, and finally the equals sign to get $1 + i = 1.08796$.

While modern calculators make very short work of solving interest problems, not everyone has such a calculator available. For those people, extensive tables have been prepared tabulating $(1 + i)^n$ and $1/(1 + i)^n$ for various values of $i$ and $n$. Such tables are provided in Exhibits 8-5 and

8-6 at the end of the chapter. Although the tables preclude the necessity of a good calculator, only problems that use values in the table can be solved exactly.

The preceding several paragraphs focus on the relationships between a single investment and the eventual amount of funds available. Another common situation involves investing or receiving a set of funds at the end of each period for several periods. This is known as an **annuity.**

The derivation of the formula relating the equal periodic annuity investments, the interest rate, the number of periods, and the eventual amount of funds accumulated is a bit more complex than that required for a single payment. However, the resulting formula is fairly similar. The total amount, $A$, of funds provided by investing $P$ at the *end* of each period for $n$ periods at an interest rate of $i$ per period is

$$A = P\left[\frac{(1 + i)^n - 1}{i}\right]$$

We could also rearrange this formula to determine the amount of each payment necessary to achieve $A$. However, a much more frequently desired number is the equivalent single payment needed now (the present value) to yield the same amount as the payments $P$ over the life of the annuity. The formula for the present value of an annuity (PVA) is

$$PVA = P\left[\frac{1 - (1 + i)^{-n}}{i}\right]$$

With these formulas, and a good calculator, we can answer such questions as: If \$50 is invested at the end of each period for 15 periods and interest is paid at the rate of 9% per period, what amount of funds will be available at the end of the fifteenth period? What is the equivalent single payment needed at the beginning of the first period (the present value) necessary to achieve the same amount of funds at the end of the fifteenth period?

For the first question we solve

$$A = \$50\left[\frac{(1.09)^{15} - 1.0}{0.09}\right]$$

to get

$$\begin{aligned} A &= \$50\left[\frac{3.642482 - 1.0}{0.09}\right] \\ &= \$50\left[\frac{2.642482}{0.09}\right] \\ &= \$50[29.3609] \\ &= \$1{,}468.05 \end{aligned}$$

The present value of the annuity is

$$\begin{aligned} PVA &= \$50\left[\frac{1-(1.09)^{-15}}{0.09}\right] \\ &= \$50\left[\frac{1-0.274538}{0.09}\right] \\ &= \$50\left[\frac{0.725462}{0.09}\right] \\ &= \$50[8.060689] \\ &= \$403.03 \end{aligned}$$

This last result can be checked by substituting the value of $403.03 into the formula for the amount of a single payment to get

$$\begin{aligned} A &= \$403.03(1.09)^{15} \\ &= \$403.03(3.642482) \\ &= \$1{,}468.03 \end{aligned}$$

Note that there is a very small rounding error.

Once again, if a good calculator is not available, the expressions in the square brackets for the annuity formulas have been tabulated for various values of $n$ and $i$. Exhibits 8-7 and 8-8 at the end of the chapter present two such tables.

By the way, the compound interest formulas are not limited in use to dollars; they can be applied to a wide range of physical events as well. For example, the U.S. Department of Forestry uses the formulas to determine by how many board feet a particular stand of timber is expected to increase in a particular year. In many cases if we are interested in the growth rate of something, the compound interest formulas may apply.

In addition, the range of problems to which present value techniques can be applied is quite large. Representative of the types of problems to which the tools apply are the following:

1. Equipment replacement decisions
2. Valuation for purposes of buying and/or selling a business
3. Renting (or leasing) versus owning assets
4. Choosing among alternative investments where (a) the investments are mutually exclusive, or (b) funds are not sufficient to permit acceptance of all minimally satisfactory proposals
5. Pricing decisions regarding new product lines
6. Determining maximum permissible purchase prices for investments
7. Determining minimum necessary cash inflows to justify a given investment

8. Minimizing the cost of doing something that does not in itself generate cash inflows
9. Showing the relative advantage of accelerated, rather than straight-line, depreciation methods

A basic distinction must be made between when it is appropriate to use the tables for amounts and when to use the tables for annuities. The tables for annuities require that several conditions be met before they can be used. There must be a series (two or more) of amounts that:

1. Are of equal size.
2. Occur at regular intervals.
3. Coincide with the interest period beginning at the end of the first period.

If any of the conditions is not met, then either adjustments have to be made to use the annuity tables; or, if adjustments cannot be made, the tables for amounts must be used.

Note also that the table for annuities is nothing more than an arithmetic sum of the entries (factors) in the table for amounts. Alternatively, the table for amounts is nothing more than the differences between corresponding entries in the tables for annuities. In other words, the two tables are related: one can always be derived from the other. Convenience determines which tables to use for a given problem.

The terminology for annuities comes from actuarial science. If an annuity begins at the start of the first period, it is referred to as an annuity due. If it begins at the end of the first period, it is referred to as an ordinary annuity. If it begins anytime after the first period, it is a deferred annuity. The tables provided for the future value of an annuity and for the present value of an annuity are for an ordinary annuity.

### Flexibility in Problem Solving

As a tool for capital budgeting, present value analysis is extremely flexible (and fun). For example, most problems can be solved by parts in any order; usually we proceed from the more straightforward aspects of a problem to the complex aspects. Moreover, to facilitate analysis you can add fictitious payments or receipts as long as you remember to take them out; or take some out as long as you remember to put them back in. (These adjustments often allow us to use annuity tables instead of the amount tables.) Also, for many applications, total receipts and disbursements can be compared at any common point in time, although we conventionally use the present period for comparative purposes.

For example, assume that we are discounting at 10% a stream of receipts to be received at the end of each year for 20 years except that there is no receipt at the end of year 11. We can put in a receipt for year 11 and then find the present value of an ordinary annuity for 20 years; from that amount we subtract the present value of the single receipt we did not receive at the end of year 11. Many of these "tricks" come with experience; the objective at this point is to become familiar with the basic models.

## ALTERNATIVE APPROACHES EMPLOYING PRESENT VALUE TECHNIQUES

The basic objective underlying capital expenditure analysis is to maximize the present value of the contribution (cash flow) from a given set of limited resources. The objective could also be stated as maximizing the contribution margin per dollar of scarce resources as a rate (interest) per unit of time. An appropriate approach to the problem gives recognition to the time value of money.

There are several acceptable alternative approaches to the problem; these are (a) the net present value approach, (b) the internal-rate-of return or time-adjusted rate-of-return approach, and (c) the profitability or present value index or ratio approach. Each of these methods will be discussed, as well as the applications, advantages, and disadvantages of each.

To facilitate the discussion we will employ the following illustrative example throughout:

*The State Employees' Retirement Fund (SERF) is considering automating one of its routine operations. The necessary equipment costs $21,000, has a life of 10 years, and will have a residual value of $1,000 at that time. It is expected that automation will save SERF approximately $3,000 per year. Since SERF is a not-for-profit organization, it has decided that an appropriate return on any such investments is an amount equal to what the money would earn if it were left in the retirement fund portfolio, which is 8%. Should SERF acquire the equipment to automate this manual function?*

### Net Present Value

This approach requires that we know the amount and timing of the costs and benefits and the minimally acceptable rate of return for investments. The **net present value** (or discounted cash flow) is defined as the present value of the benefits minus the present value of the cost of those benefits.

$$\text{net present value} = \text{present value of benefits} - \text{present value of cost}$$

The decision rule is to recommend that the investment be made if the net present value is positive or zero. If the net present value is negative, the firm will be receiving less than its required rate of return; if the net present value is zero, the firm will be receiving exactly the required rate of return; and if the net present value is positive, the firm will be receiving more than the required rate of return.

In the case of our example, the benefits are multiple. That is, SERF will be receiving (saving) $3,000 per year for each of 10 years, and also expects to receive an additional $1,000 on the disposal of the asset at the end of its 10-year useful life. The annual savings are seen as an annuity, and the residual or salvage value is seen as a single amount. There are no other benefits (savings). The present value (PV) of these benefits is calculated as follows:

$$\begin{aligned}\text{present value of benefits} &= \$3{,}000(6.710) + \$1{,}000(0.463)\\ &= \$20{,}593\end{aligned}$$

We obtain the factor 6.710 from the present value of an annuity table, Exhibit 8-8, for 10 periods at 8%, and the factor 0.463 from the present value of an amount table, Exhibit 8-6, for 10 periods at 8%.

The cost of the benefits to SERF is represented by an outlay of $21,000 now (the present) to acquire the equipment.

$$\text{present value of costs} = \$21{,}000$$

The net present value (NPV), then, is the present value of the benefits less the present value of the cost of those benefits.

$$\begin{aligned}\text{net present value} &= \$20{,}593 - \$21{,}000\\ &= -\$407\end{aligned}$$

Since the net present value is negative, we would recommend that the investment not be made since the savings are not sufficiently large. Alternatively, if the investment is to be made, it must be justified on grounds other than the dollar benefits received.

This approach is appropriate to situations where formal capital budgeting processes are in place. It requires that the minimally acceptable rate of return be known in advance. This, in turn, may be the firm's weighted-average cost to acquire capital, the firm's opportunity cost for using capital, or simply a rate mandated by management as the minimally acceptable return.

The major limitation of the net present value approach is that it does not assist in deciding among alternatives when there are more acceptable projects at hand than can be funded. For example, among alternatives, one with a larger net present value is not necessarily more desirable than one with a smaller net present value. Consider two projects with equal lives, one of which will be accepted. If one has a positive net present value of \$200 and the other has a positive net present value of \$100, which should be accepted? Would your recommendation be affected if you knew that the first required an investment of \$1 million, whereas the second required an investment of \$1,000? Fortunately, there are ways to solve this dilemma; these are discussed next.

### Present Value Index or Ratio

The **present value index** or ratio, which is also commonly referred to as a **profitability index** or ratio, utilizes the data from the net present value method in a different way. The net present value method finds the difference between the present value of the benefits and the present value of their cost. The present value index approach finds the ratio of the present value of the benefits to the present value of the cost:

$$\text{present value index} = \frac{\text{present value of the benefits}}{\text{present value of the costs}}$$

The decision rule for a solitary investment is to recommend that the investment be made if this index is equal to or greater than 1. If the ratio is less than 1, the firm will be earning less than its required rate of return; if the ratio is equal to 1, the firm will be earning exactly its required rate of return; if the ratio is greater than 1, the firm will be earning more than its required rate of return.

In the case of SERF, we have already calculated the numbers we need to use the index.[1] Accordingly,

$$\begin{aligned}\text{present value index} &= \frac{\$20{,}593}{\$21{,}000}\\ &= 0.9806\end{aligned}$$

Since the index is less than 1, we would not recommend the investment.

The NPV method and the PV index method are consistent with one another; that is, if we reject an investment using one method, we will also reject it using the other method. However, the present value index has the added advantage of indicating, simplistically, which investments give us a higher return and hence permits us to rank-order investments in terms of their relative attractiveness. Another way of phrasing it is to say that the index gives us a reading on which investments give "the biggest bang for

[1]The program NPV on the disk that accompanies the text calculates the net present value and the present value index.

a buck." For example, an index of 4.126 means that for every $1 we put into a project, we will receive the equivalent of $4.126 in terms of the present value of benefits.

As a ranking technique, the present value index can present problems if applied without judgment. However, if one keeps in mind that the objective of the organization is to maximize the present value of all funds available to it, such problems can usually be avoided. This issue will be discussed more fully in the next chapter.

### Internal Rate of Return

The **internal rate of return** (also referred to as the **time-adjusted rate of return**) is the rate of interest that equates the present value of the benefits with the present value of their costs.

present value of benefits at interest rate $i$ = present value of costs at interest rate $i$

The unknown in the equation is the interest rate. This is the rate of return generated by the investment.

The decision rule is to recommend that a solitary investment be made if the internal rate of return exceeds or equals the minimally acceptable return. In the simplest situations (involving only a simple annuity or a single amount), we obtain a number that is a factor in one of the tables. Knowing how many periods are involved, we find the factor corresponding to the periods, and then obtain the interest rate.

For SERF, let us, initially, change one fact. We will assume that there is no residual or salvage value at the end of the 10-year period; hence, there is an outlay of $21,000 now in exchange for benefits (savings) of $3,000 each year for 10 years. We then set the problem up as follows:

$$\$3{,}000(\text{annuity: } n = 10, i = ?) = \$21{,}000$$

Then, dividing each side by $3,000, we obtain

$$(\text{annuity: } n = 10, i = ?) = 7.000$$

Turning to the annuity table (Exhibit 8-8) for 10 periods, we read across until we find the factor 7.000. We observe that the factor 7.024 corresponds to 7%, whereas the factor 6.710 corresponds to 8%. Hence, the answer to the question "What is the rate of return on this investment?" is "A little above 7%." Since this return is not acceptable (SERF requires an 8% return), we would reject the investment.

The advantage of calculating the internal rate of return is that it provides us with the rate of return actually provided by a specific project.

Furthermore, it can be used as an index of desirability in selecting from a number of projects and allocating resources accordingly. Unfortunately, the disadvantage is that the method becomes very cumbersome if cash flows are uneven or include outflows as well as inflows. For example, if we go back to the original illustrative data, which includes a residual value, we cannot solve for the interest rate directly. Rather, we would be required to proceed by trial and error. That is, we would pick an initial interest rate, find the appropriate factor in each table, and then using the present value factors, we would solve the equation. We would continue with this approach until we found factors that would equate the present value of the benefits with the present value of the costs.

Using our original data, we set up the problem to find the internal rate of return as follows:

$$\$3{,}000(\text{annuity: } n = 10, i = ?) + \$1{,}000(\text{amount: } n = 10, i = ?) = \$21{,}000$$

This requires that we work with both tables simultaneously. The iterative (trial-and-error) approach selects an interest rate corresponding to the known periods, finds the factor in each table that corresponds, and solves the equation. One continues to select interest rates (and, hence, factors) until both sides of the equation are equal. By definition, when both sides of the equation are equal, we have obtained the internal or time-adjusted rate of return. Using 7%, the present value of the benefits amounts to $21,580, while the present value of the cost is $21,000. Using 8%, the present value of the benefits amounts to $20,593, while the present value of the cost is $21,000. To have the benefits equal the $21,000 cost, it would appear that an interest rate between these two is necessary (see Exhibit 8-1). Generally accepted eyeball techniques suggest that this rate would be approximately $7\frac{1}{2}$%. As before, more refined tables or better instruments will generate greater precision. Also, for any given problem it may be necessary to try several different interest rates.

Without a computer, this approach is very unwieldy for large-scale projects with many inflows and outflows and is also unwieldy if we must decide among many projects (a separate internal rate of return must be found for each and every project). However, the method is suited to those organizations that do not have a formal capital budgeting process in place or have a computer programmed to make the computations.[2] If such decisions are made infrequently, or if there is a project of special interest, it may be appropriate to employ this technique to determine what the approximate rate of return is. This approach is particularly useful to small organizations that do not make such decisions with sufficient frequency to

[2]A computer program, IRR, that will calculate the internal rate of return for uneven cash flows is included on the disk that accompanies the text.

**EXHIBIT 8-1 Finding the Internal Rate of Return for SERF by Trial and Error**[a]

| | Factors for 10 Periods | | |
|---|---|---|---|
| Interest Rate (%) | Annuity ($3,000) | Amount ($1,000) | Present Value of Benefits |
| 5 | 7.722 | 0.614 | $23,780 |
| 6 | 7.360 | 0.558 | 22,638 |
| 7 | 7.024 | 0.508 | 21,580 |
| 8 | 6.710 | 0.463 | 20,593 |
| 9 | 6.418 | 0.422 | 19,676 |

[a]Since the cost is fixed with a present value of $21,000, the objective is to find the interest rate that will make the sum of the present value of the benefits equal to $21,000. Interpolation generates an internal rate of return of 7.59%.

have a formal means for evaluating capital projects; although such organizations may not have a criterion as to a minimally acceptable rate of return, management will ordinarily be able to judge the acceptability of investments if provided with the internal rate of return.

## ALTERNATIVES TO PRESENT VALUE TECHNIQUES

Other methods of approaching the capital expenditure decision exist. These tend to be "rules of thumb" which often have an intuitively appealing basis. Such methods may be simple (e.g., one does not need to understand present value concepts to apply them), or they may satisfy an immediate pressing need (e.g., time or data may not permit a more sophisticated analysis). This, however, is unfortunate because the methods tend to ignore the very thing we are interested in, namely, the time value of money. While it may be desirable to bury or ignore such methods, we discuss them here in order to familiarize you with their shortcomings and limitations.

### Payback

The **payback period** for an investment is defined as the length of time it takes to recover the original investment. In the case of SERF the payback period is 7 years, which is the original investment of $21,000 divided by the annual savings of $3,000. If the savings are not uniform, it is then necessary to accumulate the savings year-by-year until the originally invested sum is reached.

The appeal of payback as a criterion for investment is multiple. First, risk aversion may favor short-lived investments over long-lived investments. Second, if the organization is consistently short of funds ("cash poor"), it may desire to "churn" them or turn them over more quickly with short-term investments. Third, a need for funds may be foreseeable at some definite future point in time, and, therefore, any investments in the interim should be made with regard to generating cash by that time.

Unfortunately, in and of itself, payback is deficient as a decision tool. The problem is that it disregards relative profitability. A highly profitable investment may be rejected simply because it does not meet payback requirements. Alternatively, a less profitable investment may be approved because it does.

If the payback period is of concern to management, then it should be supplemented with additional decision criteria. For example, it may be desirable to estimate the residual or disposal value of an asset year by year; this would provide a measure of the possible total cash generated to date from an investment. However, this measure, called the **bailout factor,** still does not address the question of the relative desirability of the investment from the standpoint of rate of return.

If a firm has the luxury of unlimited investment opportunities, relative to the amount of funds at hand, it may choose to combine the payback and the minimum rate of return as a means of screening proposals. For example, a firm may specify that investment proposals must satisfy a minimum payback period *and* a minimum rate of return to be considered for selection. While this does not eliminate all objections, it is clearly superior to the use of payback alone.

### Payback Reciprocal

The **payback reciprocal** is simply 1 divided by the payback period:

$$\text{payback reciprocal} = \frac{1}{\text{payback period}}$$

Using SERF's data, the payback reciprocal is 1/7 or 14.29%. This should not be interpreted as a rate of return in the sense that we used that term when calculating the time-adjusted or internal rate of return. Rather, it represents how much of the initial investment (as a percentage) is recovered each year. As such, the payback reciprocal should not be compared to the firm's minimum required rate of return. For example, doing so in this case would lead us to accept an investment that we already know should be rejected.

However, the payback reciprocal is the true rate of return in the special case in which an investment will generate a *uniform* cash flow over an *infinite* period. The mathematics of this consists of showing what happens to the formula for the present value of an annuity as $n$ becomes arbitrarily large. In the limit, the factor assumes the value of $1/i$; this factor represents the payback period. This notion has been worked with, and Exhibit 8-2 presents a table for approximating the rate of return.

To obtain reasonable approximations from the table, two conditions are necessary: (a) the annual cash flows must be uniform (or approximately so), and (b) the useful life must be at least twice the payback period. For the SERF decision, neither of the two criteria is satisfied. Nevertheless, for a useful life of 10 years and a payback period of 7 years, the rate of return in the table is shown as 8%. This would lead us to accept the proposal, which would be an incorrect decision since we have already determined that this investment yields approximately a $7\frac{1}{2}$% return. The table should not be used to make a decision or recommendation if the conditions are not satisfied. However, we can make use of the table in an attempt to cut down on the number of iterations required to find the internal rate of return. By beginning with the 8% figure from Exhibit 8-2, we should arrive at the correct rate more quickly than we would if we did not know where to start at all but had to guess.

### Average Rate of Return

The **average rate of return** (also called the **unadjusted rate of return** or, sometimes, the **accounting rate of return**) is one that relates income, rather than cash flow, to the average investment.

$$\text{average rate of return} = \frac{\text{average annual net income}}{\text{average investment}}$$

For SERF, the average annual net income will be the savings of \$3,000 reduced by annual depreciation; if we use straight-line depreciation methods, the annual straight-line depreciation will be (\$21,000 − \$1,000) ÷ 10 = \$2,000. The average investment is one-half the balance at the outset plus the residual, or $\frac{1}{2}$ × (\$21,000 + \$1,000) = \$11,000. The average rate of return for SERF is

$$\text{average rate of return} = \frac{\$1{,}000}{\$11{,}000} = 9.09\%$$

Although the average rate of return looks like an interest rate, it does not measure the rate of interest being earned. We know that the true rate of return for this project is approximately $7\frac{1}{2}$%. Using the unadjusted or average rate of return we might accept the investment, whereas using the

**EXHIBIT 8-2 Table for Approximating Rate of Return[a]**

| Number of Years Savings Will Last \ Payback Period in Years | $\frac{1}{4}$ | $\frac{1}{2}$ | $\frac{3}{4}$ | 1 | $1\frac{1}{4}$ | $1\frac{1}{2}$ | $1\frac{3}{4}$ | 2 | $2\frac{1}{4}$ | $2\frac{1}{2}$ | $2\frac{3}{4}$ | 3 | $3\frac{1}{4}$ | $3\frac{1}{2}$ | $3\frac{3}{4}$ | 4 | $4\frac{1}{4}$ | $4\frac{1}{2}$ | $4\frac{3}{4}$ | 5 | $5\frac{1}{2}$ | 6 | $6\frac{1}{2}$ | 7 | $7\frac{1}{2}$ | 8 | 9 | 10 | 12 | 14 | 16 | 18 | 20 | 30 |
|---|---|---|---|---|---|---|---|---|---|---|---|---|---|---|---|---|---|---|---|---|---|---|---|---|---|---|---|---|---|---|---|---|---|---|
| 1 | 390 | 155 | 60 | 0 | | | | | | | | | | | | | | | | | | | | | | | | | | | | | | |
| 2 | 400 | 196 | 122 | 80 | 52 | 30 | 13 | 0 | | | | | | | | | | | | | | | | | | | | | | | | | | |
| 3 | 400 | 198 | 133 | 92 | 70 | 53 | 40 | 29 | 20 | 12 | 6 | 0 | | | | | | | | | | | | | | | | | | | | | | |
| 4 | 400 | 199 | 133 | 94 | 76 | 60 | 49 | 40 | 32 | 28 | 20 | 15 | 11 | 7 | 3 | 0 | | | | | | | | | | | | | | | | | | |
| 5 | 400 | 200 | 133 | 96 | 78 | 64 | 53 | 44 | 37 | 32 | 27 | 23 | 19 | 15 | 12 | 9 | 6 | 4 | 2 | 0 | | | | | | | | | | | | | | |
| 6 | 400 | 200 | 133 | 97 | 79 | 66 | 55 | 47 | 41 | 35 | 31 | 27 | 23 | 20 | 17 | 15 | 12 | 10 | 8 | 6 | 3 | 0 | | | | | | | | | | | | |
| 7 | 400 | 200 | 133 | 97 | 80 | 67 | 56 | 48 | 42 | 37 | 33 | 29 | 26 | 23 | 20 | 18 | 15 | 13 | 11 | 10 | 7 | 4 | 2 | 0 | | | | | | | | | | |
| 8 | 400 | 200 | 133 | 98 | 80 | 67 | 57 | 49 | 43 | 38 | 34 | 30 | 27 | 25 | 22 | 20 | 18 | 16 | 14 | 13 | 10 | 8 | 5 | 3 | 1 | 0 | | | | | | | | |
| 9 | 400 | 200 | 133 | 98 | 80 | 68 | 58 | 50 | 44 | 39 | 35 | 31 | 28 | 26 | 23 | 21 | 19 | 18 | 16 | 15 | 12 | 10 | 8 | 6 | 4 | 3 | 0 | | | | | | | |
| 10 | 400 | 200 | 133 | 99 | 80 | 68 | 58 | 50 | 44 | 39 | 36 | 32 | 29 | 27 | 24 | 22 | 21 | 19 | 18 | 16 | 14 | 11 | 9 | 8 | 6 | 5 | 2 | 0 | | | | | | |
| 15 | 400 | 200 | 133 | 99 | 80 | 68 | 58 | 50 | 44 | 40 | 36 | 33 | 30 | 28 | 25 | 25 | 23 | 22 | 20 | 19 | 16 | 15 | 13 | 12 | 11 | 10 | 8 | 6 | 3 | 1 | 0 | | | |
| 20 | 400 | 200 | 133 | 99 | 80 | 68 | 58 | 50 | 44 | 40 | 36 | 33 | 30 | 28 | 26 | 25 | 23 | 22 | 20 | 19 | 18 | 16 | 15 | 13 | 12 | 11 | 10 | 8 | 6 | 4 | 2 | 1 | 0 | |
| Over 20 | 400 | 200 | 133 | 100 | 81 | 69 | 59 | 51 | 45 | 41 | 37 | 34 | 31 | 29 | 27 | 26 | 24 | 23 | 21 | 20 | 19 | 17 | 16 | 14 | 13 | 12 | 11 | 10 | 8 | 7 | 6 | 5 | 4 | 2 |

[a]Example: Project savings expected to last 12 years. Computed payback period is 4.7 years. Enter table using nearest values; that is, use 10 years for savings and $4\frac{3}{4}$ years for payback period. Table shows 18% rate of return.

SOURCE: *National Association of Accountants Research Report No. 35, Return on Capital as a Guide to Managerial Decisions,* p. 76.

adjusted rate of return we would reject the investment. The latter is the correct decision. Incidentally, if one were to calculate average cash flow in relation to investment, the result would be even more misleading: \$3,000/\$11,000 = 27.27%.

The unadjusted rate of return is frequently used in the analysis of financial statements where the data are such as to preclude the use of present value techniques. For example, in finding the return on owners' equity for the year we divide net income by average owners' equity; return on assets involves a similar computation. In these situations we are typically constrained to comparative financial statements for two periods; hence the data prevent us from employing more sophisticated analyses.

## OTHER CONSIDERATIONS

A number of other issues concerning capital budgeting should be addressed. Basic considerations are set forth in this section. Advanced topics are discussed in the following chapter.

### Cash Flows versus Income

Inasmuch as our objective is to maximize contribution per dollar invested, it is important to emphasize that our interest is in cash flows generated by investments, rather than by the income so generated. That is we invest to generate cash. The rate of return earned on an investment is dependent upon the precise timing of the cash flows, but for income measurement, revenues tend to be recognized when the right to receive cash has been earned and expenses are then matched against these revenues. For income measurement, both revenues and expenses ignore the precise timing of cash flows. Thus for capital budgeting, depreciation and similar non–cash-requiring expenses are relevant only to the extent that they affect cash flow through income taxes. The next chapter considers the effects of income taxes on cash flows.

### Total versus Incremental Approach

You may recall that when deciding among alternative courses of action, one is concerned with the relevant costs and revenues: those that will be different under different alternatives. Where an organization or individual must choose between two mutually exclusive alternative investments, the incremental approach is ordinarily the quickest. Let us consider a simple example. An operation currently being performed by Ferndale, Inc., costs \$20,000 per year for labor. The company is considering automating the operation at a cost of $50,000. It is expected that this will cut labor costs to $5,000 per year for the next 10 years. The required rate of return is 14% (we will ignore income taxes).

This is a problem in cost minimization. The objective is to employ the technology that will minimize the present value of true costs. The total approach compares the cost of the present method with the cost of the proposed method as follows:

| | |
|---|---|
| Present value of existing method: ($20,000)(5.216) | $104,320 |
| Present value of proposed method: $50,000 + ($5,000)(5.216) | 76,080 |
| Net present value | $ 28,240 |

By switching from the present to the proposed method the firm will experience cost savings with a present value of $104,320 − $76,080 or $28,240. It appears that the firm should make the investment.

If, instead, we employ the incremental approach, we can view the firm as investing $50,000 to effect savings of $15,000 per year for 10 years. At 14%, the net present value is ($15,000)(5.216) − $50,000, or $28,240. Since the net present value is positive, it appears that the firm should make the investment.

From the example, we see that the final result is the same whether we take a total approach or an incremental approach. The only difference is in the handling of the data. For simple problems the incremental approach is easier, but a word of caution: The approach becomes very unwieldy if more than two alternatives are under consideration.

## Cost of Prediction Errors

Cost-volume-profit decisions typically do not have the long-term consequences that investment decisions have. That is, if an error is made on a short-term decision, it can frequently be reversed in a following period. Accountability for such mistakes is relatively easy to establish. Prudence suggests that long-term investment decisions also be monitored or audited to determine whether or not actual results are consistent with the original estimates and plans.

In addition, any cost of a prediction error should be determined for such decisions. For example, assume that a manager makes a decision to invest $100,000 to obtain savings of $25,000 annually for 10 years. The investment has a projected internal rate of return of approximately 21%. If the firm's minimal acceptable rate of return is 20%, and if the facts and/or a revised estimate indicate that annual savings are only $20,000, what is the cost of the prediction error? Using the firm's minimum rate of return of 20%, the $20,000 annual savings are presently worth only $20,000

× 4.192 = $83,840. In other words, given the new knowledge, the investment would not be made. Thus the optimal action is to hold onto the $100,000. The actual investment of the $100,000 results in an investment with a present value of $83,840. Thus the cost of the prediction error to the firm is $100,000 − $83,840 = $16,160.

Follow-up procedures suggest that the one responsible for this decision should be held accountable and that an explanation is in order. If it can be shown that some managers are consistently optimistic (or pessimistic), this may warrant adjusting their predictions before investments are made.

### Sensitivity Analysis

In the preparation of capital expenditure proposals, a question may arise as to the accuracy of the predicted cash flows. Rather than consume a great deal of time debating the appropriateness of one or more figures, it is recommended that an initial solution be agreed upon. Once this has been done, the data can then be analyzed to determine the size of errors that would alter the final recommendation. **Sensitivity analysis** permits us to address the question: How sensitive is the decision to changes in the data?

For example, Eternal Burial (a not-for-profit cemetery) is considering investing $200,000 in equipment that should result in savings of $50,000 per year for 10 years. If the minimum rate of return is 15%, should the investment be considered? Using the capital budgeting approaches introduced earlier in the chapter, the net present value is $50,000(5.019) − $200,000 = $50,950, the present value index is 1.25, and the internal rate of return is 21.4%. All indications point toward acceptance of the proposal.

However, sensitivity analysis would permit us to address such questions as: (1) Given the cost of the investment, how low could the benefits fall for the investment to still be justified, and (2) given the benefits, what is the most that could be paid to acquire them? The answer to the first question is found by determining what the annual benefits would need to be each year for 10 years if they cost $200,000 and the interest rate is 15%. Using the present value factor for a 10-year annuity, this works out to be $200,000/5.019 = $39,849. Hence the benefits could be understated by as much as $10,151 (or 20%) annually and the investment would still be worthwhile. The second question can be addressed by considering the net present value of this investment. The NPV is a positive $50,950. Therefore the firm could expend as much as $200,000 + $50,950 = $250,950 and still earn the minimum return on its investment.

Sensitivity analysis begins with an initial solution and then analyzes the effect of any differences in estimates. Knowing the acceptable limits should permit more informed decisions.

### Amortization

A loan **amortization** schedule refers to a table showing the timing and amount of periodic payments made on a loan, the amount of interest, and the effect on the balance of the loan. That is, each loan payment consists of two parts: (a) interest for the period and (b) a reduction in the principal amount loaned or borrowed. Although such tables are typically presented and discussed from the point of view of a borrower, it is quite proper to construct a table from the investor's point of view. The amounts, flows, and changes for both would be the same, of course. The tables are used to determine the amount of income earned by a lender in each period or the amount of expense incurred by the borrower in each period.

Exhibit 8-3 provides an amortization schedule for a $5,000 loan to be repaid in five equal periodic installments at 8% per period. The size of each payment, $1,252.19, is determined by referring to the table for the present value of an annuity. For each period the interest is calculated by multiplying the loan balance at the beginning of the term by 8%. The amount of the reduction in principal is the difference between the actual payment and the interest. This difference is subtracted from the beginning loan balance to get the new loan balance for the following period.

We can observe from the exhibit that the loan balance is decreasing each period as is the interest. This is due to the fact that each payment consists, in part, of a return of principal. A simple schedule of this type can easily be constructed using a four-function calculator employing chain operations. For lengthier applications, the use of a computer is recommended. Exhibit 8-4 shows the amortization schedule as obtained using the computer program PYMTSCH, which is on the disk that accompanies the text. The difference between Exhibits 8-3 and 8-4 has to do with presentation and rounding; the ending balance of $0.54 would be added to the last payment.

**EXHIBIT 8-3 Amortization Schedule**

| | | Payment | |
|---|---|---|---|
| **Period** | **Loan Balance**[a] | **Interest**[b] | **Principal**[c] |
| 1 | $5,000.00 | $400.00 | $ 852.19 |
| 2 | 4,147.81 | 331.82 | 920.37 |
| 3 | 3,227.44 | 258.20 | 993.99 |
| 4 | 2,233.45 | 178.68 | 1,073.51 |
| 5 | 1,159.94 | 92.80 | 1,159.39 |

[a]The loan balance consists of the previous period's balance reduced by the principal repaid in the previous period.

[b]8% of the loan balance.

[c]$1,252.19 minus the interest for the period.

**EXHIBIT 8-4 Amortization Schedule Using PYMTSCH Program**

| Period | Interest Expense | Ending Balance |
|---|---|---|
| 1 | 400 | 4147.81 |
| 2 | 331.8248 | 3227.445 |
| 3 | 258.1956 | 2233.451 |
| 4 | 178.676 | 1159.937 |
| 5 | 92.79492 | 0.541504 |

## SUMMARY

We have attempted to introduce the basic ideas and methods that underlie long-range planning where costs and benefits are spread over several time periods. The best methods are those that involve the time value of money.

The basic approach can be stated simply as follows:

1. Set forth the timing and amount of each gross cash flow.
2. Apply the appropriate present value factor to each.
3. Do the arithmetic.
4. Evaluate the results.

Unfortunately, the basic approach is not always simple to apply. Difficulties can ordinarily be identified as being associated with a lack of understanding of one of the above steps or, more probably, difficulty in interpreting a problem properly. The demonstration problem that follows attempts to raise a number of such points as well as reinforcing others.

## DEMONSTRATION PROBLEM

The city council of Ladelow has instructed the park board to renovate and expand the city's only park. User fees will be charged for the new facilities, and the city will fund the deficiency, if any, with a lump sum payment for the difference between the present value of the benefits and costs as determined by the park board, subject to the council's approval. The park's current revenues are equal to current expenses. The city plans on a 10-year life cycle for renovation and expansion and a 10% rate of interest will be used.

The estimates and facts which the council and board have agreed to are as follows:

a. A concessionaire who pays $10,000 annually to the park board will have its contract terminated to make space for a new facility. The board will pay the concessionaire $5,000 to cancel this contract.

b. Because of the expanded facilities, two additional employees will be hired at an annual cost of $18,000 each. A third employee, also earning $18,000, will be added at the start of the sixth year.

**c.** User fees are expected to amount to $75,000 for the first 6 years and $100,000 for the last 4 years.
**d.** Construction costs are $400,000 during the first year and $200,000 during the second year. These amounts are paid at the end of each year.

**Required**
Given the facts, what is the amount that the city council will fund?

**Solution**
The solution consists of determining the net present value of the proposal. If it is negative, that is the amount which the city council will provide.

| | |
|---|---|
| **a.** The board must pay $5,000 now to break its contract with the concessionaire. | −$ 5,000 |
| The board will forgo annual rentals of $10,000 per year for 10 years: ($10,000)(6.145) | − 61,450 |
| **b.** The first two employees will cost (2)($18,000)(6.145). | − 221,220 |
| The third employee will cost ($18,000)(6.145 − 3.791). So that the annuity table could be used, it was assumed that the employee would work for 10 years, and then the first 5 years were subtracted. | − 42,372 |
| **c.** User fees for the first 6 years have a present value of ($75,000)(4.355). | + 326,625 |
| User fees for the last 4 years have a present value of ($100,000)(6.145 − 4.355). | + 179,000 |
| **d.** The outlay during the first year has a present value of ($400,000)(0.909). | − 363,600 |
| The outlay during the second year has a present value of ($200,000)(0.826). | − 165,200 |
| Net present value (amount to be funded) | −$353,217 |

## KEY TERMS AND CONCEPTS

- Interest
- Principal
- Amount
- Present value
- Annuity
- Net present value
- [ Present value index
- Profitability index ]
- [ Internal rate of return
- Time-adjusted rate of return ]
- Payback period
- Bailout factor
- Payback reciprocal
- [ Average rate of return
- Unadjusted rate of return
- Accounting rate of return ]
- Sensitivity analysis
- Amortization

[ Bracketed terms are equivalent in meaning.

## FURTHER READING

Bavishi, Vinod B. "Capital Budgeting Practices at Multinationals," *Management Accounting* (August 1981), p. 32.

Hendricks, James A. "Analysis of Risk in Capital Budgeting," *Management Accounting* (April 1977), p. 41.

Jablonsky, Stephen F., and Mark W. Dirsmith. "Is Financial Reporting Influencing Internal Decision Making?" *Management Accounting* (July 1979), p. 40.

Kee, Robert, and Oliver Feltus. "The Role of Abandonment Value in the Investment Decision," *Management Accounting* (August 1982), p. 34.

Kim, Suk H. "Making the Long-Term Investment Decision," *Management Accounting* (March 1979), p. 41.

Kim, Suk H., and Trevor Crick. "How Non-U.S. MNCs Practice Capital Budgeting," *Management Accounting* (January 1984), p. 28.

McCabe, George M., and George N. Sanderson. "Abandonment Value in Capital Budgeting: Another View," *Management Accounting* (January 1984), p. 32.

Spiller, Earl A., Jr. "Capital Expenditure Analysis: An Incident Process Case," *The Accounting Review* (January 1981), p. 158.

Thomsen, C. Torben. "Dangers in Discounting," *Management Accounting* (January 1984), p. 37.

van Breda, Michael F. "Capital Budgeting Using Terminal Values," *Management Accounting* (July 1981), p. 42.

*Questions and Exercises begin on page 424.*

## FUTURE VALUE—SINGLE AMOUNT

### EXHIBIT 8-5 Future Value Interest Factors for a One-Dollar Investment: $A = (1 + i)^n$

| Year | 1% | 2% | 3% | 4% | 5% | 6% | 7% | 8% | 9% | 10% |
|---|---|---|---|---|---|---|---|---|---|---|
| 1 | 1.010 | 1.020 | 1.030 | 1.040 | 1.050 | 1.060 | 1.070 | 1.080 | 1.090 | 1.100 |
| 2 | 1.020 | 1.040 | 1.061 | 1.082 | 1.102 | 1.124 | 1.145 | 1.166 | 1.188 | 1.210 |
| 3 | 1.030 | 1.061 | 1.093 | 1.125 | 1.158 | 1.191 | 1.225 | 1.260 | 1.295 | 1.331 |
| 4 | 1.041 | 1.082 | 1.126 | 1.170 | 1.216 | 1.262 | 1.311 | 1.360 | 1.412 | 1.464 |
| 5 | 1.051 | 1.104 | 1.159 | 1.217 | 1.276 | 1.338 | 1.403 | 1.469 | 1.539 | 1.611 |
| 6 | 1.062 | 1.126 | 1.194 | 1.265 | 1.340 | 1.419 | 1.501 | 1.587 | 1.677 | 1.772 |
| 7 | 1.072 | 1.149 | 1.230 | 1.316 | 1.407 | 1.504 | 1.606 | 1.714 | 1.828 | 1.949 |
| 8 | 1.083 | 1.172 | 1.267 | 1.369 | 1.477 | 1.594 | 1.718 | 1.851 | 1.993 | 2.144 |
| 9 | 1.094 | 1.195 | 1.305 | 1.423 | 1.551 | 1.689 | 1.838 | 1.999 | 2.172 | 2.358 |
| 10 | 1.105 | 1.219 | 1.344 | 1.480 | 1.629 | 1.791 | 1.967 | 2.159 | 2.367 | 2.594 |
| 11 | 1.116 | 1.243 | 1.384 | 1.539 | 1.710 | 1.898 | 2.105 | 2.332 | 2.580 | 2.853 |
| 12 | 1.127 | 1.268 | 1.426 | 1.601 | 1.796 | 2.012 | 2.252 | 2.518 | 2.813 | 3.138 |
| 13 | 1.138 | 1.294 | 1.469 | 1.665 | 1.886 | 2.133 | 2.410 | 2.720 | 3.066 | 3.452 |
| 14 | 1.149 | 1.319 | 1.513 | 1.732 | 1.980 | 2.261 | 2.579 | 2.937 | 3.342 | 3.798 |
| 15 | 1.161 | 1.346 | 1.558 | 1.801 | 2.079 | 2.397 | 2.759 | 3.172 | 3.642 | 4.177 |
| 16 | 1.173 | 1.373 | 1.605 | 1.873 | 2.183 | 2.540 | 2.952 | 3.426 | 3.970 | 4.595 |
| 17 | 1.184 | 1.400 | 1.653 | 1.948 | 2.292 | 2.693 | 3.159 | 3.700 | 4.328 | 5.054 |
| 18 | 1.196 | 1.428 | 1.702 | 2.026 | 2.407 | 2.854 | 3.380 | 3.996 | 4.717 | 5.560 |
| 19 | 1.208 | 1.457 | 1.753 | 2.107 | 2.527 | 3.026 | 3.617 | 4.316 | 5.142 | 6.116 |
| 20 | 1.220 | 1.486 | 1.806 | 2.191 | 2.653 | 3.207 | 3.870 | 4.661 | 5.604 | 6.728 |
| 21 | 1.232 | 1.516 | 1.860 | 2.279 | 2.786 | 3.400 | 4.141 | 5.034 | 6.109 | 7.400 |
| 22 | 1.245 | 1.546 | 1.916 | 2.370 | 2.925 | 3.604 | 4.430 | 5.437 | 6.659 | 8.140 |
| 23 | 1.257 | 1.577 | 1.974 | 2.465 | 3.072 | 3.820 | 4.741 | 5.871 | 7.258 | 8.954 |
| 24 | 1.270 | 1.608 | 2.033 | 2.563 | 3.225 | 4.049 | 5.072 | 6.341 | 7.911 | 9.850 |
| 25 | 1.282 | 1.641 | 2.094 | 2.666 | 3.386 | 4.292 | 5.427 | 6.848 | 8.623 | 10.835 |

# FUTURE VALUE—SINGLE AMOUNT

**EXHIBIT 8-5** *(Continued)*

| Year | 11% | 12% | 13% | 14% | 15% | 16% | 17% | 18% | 19% | 20% |
|---|---|---|---|---|---|---|---|---|---|---|
| 1 | 1.110 | 1.120 | 1.130 | 1.140 | 1.150 | 1.160 | 1.170 | 1.180 | 1.190 | 1.200 |
| 2 | 1.232 | 1.254 | 1.277 | 1.300 | 1.323 | 1.346 | 1.369 | 1.392 | 1.416 | 1.440 |
| 3 | 1.368 | 1.405 | 1.443 | 1.482 | 1.521 | 1.561 | 1.602 | 1.643 | 1.685 | 1.728 |
| 4 | 1.518 | 1.574 | 1.630 | 1.689 | 1.749 | 1.811 | 1.874 | 1.939 | 2.005 | 2.074 |
| 5 | 1.685 | 1.762 | 1.842 | 1.925 | 2.011 | 2.100 | 2.192 | 2.288 | 2.386 | 2.488 |
| 6 | 1.870 | 1.974 | 2.082 | 2.195 | 2.313 | 2.436 | 2.565 | 2.700 | 2.840 | 2.986 |
| 7 | 2.076 | 2.211 | 2.353 | 2.502 | 2.660 | 2.826 | 3.001 | 3.185 | 3.379 | 3.583 |
| 8 | 2.305 | 2.476 | 2.658 | 2.853 | 3.059 | 3.278 | 3.511 | 3.759 | 4.021 | 4.300 |
| 9 | 2.558 | 2.773 | 3.004 | 3.252 | 3.518 | 3.803 | 4.103 | 4.435 | 4.785 | 5.160 |
| 10 | 2.839 | 3.106 | 3.395 | 3.707 | 4.046 | 4.411 | 4.807 | 5.234 | 5.695 | 6.192 |
| 11 | 3.152 | 3.479 | 3.836 | 4.226 | 4.652 | 5.117 | 5.624 | 6.176 | 6.777 | 7.430 |
| 12 | 3.498 | 3.896 | 4.335 | 4.818 | 5.350 | 5.936 | 6.580 | 7.288 | 8.064 | 8.916 |
| 13 | 3.883 | 4.363 | 4.898 | 5.492 | 6.153 | 6.886 | 7.699 | 8.599 | 9.596 | 10.699 |
| 14 | 4.310 | 4.887 | 5.535 | 6.261 | 7.076 | 7.987 | 9.007 | 10.147 | 11.420 | 12.839 |
| 15 | 4.785 | 5.474 | 6.254 | 7.138 | 8.137 | 9.266 | 10.539 | 11.974 | 13.590 | 15.407 |
| 16 | 5.311 | 6.130 | 7.067 | 8.137 | 9.358 | 10.748 | 12.330 | 14.129 | 16.172 | 18.488 |
| 17 | 5.895 | 6.866 | 7.986 | 9.276 | 10.761 | 12.468 | 14.426 | 16.672 | 19.244 | 22.186 |
| 18 | 6.544 | 7.690 | 9.024 | 10.575 | 12.376 | 14.463 | 16.879 | 19.673 | 22.901 | 26.623 |
| 19 | 7.263 | 8.613 | 10.197 | 12.056 | 14.232 | 16.777 | 19.748 | 23.214 | 27.252 | 31.948 |
| 20 | 8.062 | 9.646 | 11.523 | 13.743 | 16.367 | 19.461 | 23.106 | 27.393 | 32.429 | 38.338 |
| 21 | 8.949 | 10.804 | 13.021 | 15.668 | 18.822 | 22.574 | 27.034 | 32.324 | 38.591 | 46.005 |
| 22 | 9.934 | 12.100 | 14.714 | 17.861 | 21.645 | 26.186 | 31.629 | 38.142 | 45.923 | 55.206 |
| 23 | 11.026 | 13.552 | 16.627 | 20.362 | 24.892 | 30.376 | 37.006 | 45.008 | 54.649 | 66.247 |
| 24 | 12.239 | 15.179 | 18.788 | 23.212 | 28.625 | 35.236 | 43.297 | 53.109 | 65.032 | 79.497 |
| 25 | 13.586 | 17.000 | 21.231 | 26.462 | 32.919 | 40.874 | 50.658 | 62.669 | 77.388 | 95.396 |

## PRESENT VALUE—SINGLE AMOUNT

**EXHIBIT 8-6 Present Value Factors for One Dollar: $P = \frac{1}{(1 + i)^n}$**

| Year | 1% | 2% | 3% | 4% | 5% | 6% | 7% | 8% | 9% | 10% |
|---|---|---|---|---|---|---|---|---|---|---|
| 1 | .990 | .980 | .971 | .962 | .952 | .943 | .935 | .926 | .917 | .909 |
| 2 | .980 | .961 | .943 | .925 | .907 | .890 | .873 | .857 | .842 | .826 |
| 3 | .971 | .942 | .915 | .889 | .864 | .840 | .816 | .794 | .772 | .751 |
| 4 | .961 | .924 | .888 | .855 | .823 | .792 | .763 | .735 | .708 | .683 |
| 5 | .951 | .906 | .863 | .822 | .784 | .747 | .713 | .681 | .650 | .621 |
| 6 | .942 | .888 | .837 | .790 | .746 | .705 | .666 | .630 | .596 | .564 |
| 7 | .933 | .871 | .813 | .760 | .711 | .665 | .623 | .583 | .547 | .513 |
| 8 | .923 | .853 | .789 | .731 | .677 | .627 | .582 | .540 | .502 | .467 |
| 9 | .914 | .837 | .766 | .703 | .645 | .592 | .544 | .500 | .460 | .424 |
| 10 | .905 | .820 | .744 | .676 | .614 | .558 | .508 | .463 | .422 | .386 |
| 11 | .896 | .804 | .722 | .650 | .585 | .527 | .475 | .429 | .388 | .350 |
| 12 | .887 | .788 | .701 | .625 | .557 | .497 | .444 | .397 | .356 | .319 |
| 13 | .879 | .773 | .681 | .601 | .530 | .469 | .415 | .368 | .326 | .290 |
| 14 | .870 | .758 | .661 | .577 | .505 | .442 | .388 | .340 | .299 | .263 |
| 15 | .861 | .743 | .642 | .555 | .481 | .417 | .362 | .315 | .275 | .239 |
| 16 | .853 | .728 | .623 | .534 | .458 | .394 | .339 | .292 | .252 | .218 |
| 17 | .844 | .714 | .605 | .513 | .436 | .371 | .317 | .270 | .231 | .198 |
| 18 | .836 | .700 | .587 | .494 | .416 | .350 | .296 | .250 | .212 | .180 |
| 19 | .828 | .686 | .570 | .475 | .396 | .331 | .277 | .232 | .194 | .164 |
| 20 | .820 | .673 | .554 | .456 | .377 | .312 | .258 | .215 | .178 | .149 |
| 21 | .811 | .660 | .538 | .439 | .359 | .294 | .242 | .199 | .164 | .135 |
| 22 | .803 | .647 | .522 | .422 | .342 | .278 | .226 | .184 | .150 | .123 |
| 23 | .795 | .634 | .507 | .406 | .326 | .262 | .211 | .170 | .138 | .112 |
| 24 | .788 | .622 | .492 | .390 | .310 | .247 | .197 | .158 | .126 | .102 |
| 25 | .780 | .610 | .478 | .375 | .295 | .233 | .184 | .146 | .116 | .092 |

## PRESENT VALUE—SINGLE AMOUNT

**EXHIBIT 8-6** *(Continued)*

| Year | 11% | 12% | 13% | 14% | 15% | 16% | 17% | 18% | 19% | 20% |
|---|---|---|---|---|---|---|---|---|---|---|
| 1 | .901 | .893 | .885 | .877 | .870 | .862 | .855 | .847 | .840 | .833 |
| 2 | .812 | .797 | .783 | .769 | .756 | .743 | .731 | .718 | .706 | .694 |
| 3 | .731 | .712 | .693 | .675 | .658 | .641 | .624 | .609 | .593 | .579 |
| 4 | .659 | .636 | .613 | .592 | .572 | .552 | .534 | .516 | .499 | .482 |
| 5 | .593 | .567 | .543 | .519 | .497 | .476 | .456 | .437 | .419 | .402 |
| 6 | .535 | .507 | .480 | .456 | .432 | .410 | .390 | .370 | .352 | .335 |
| 7 | .482 | .452 | .425 | .400 | .376 | .354 | .333 | .314 | .296 | .279 |
| 8 | .434 | .404 | .376 | .351 | .327 | .305 | .285 | .266 | .249 | .233 |
| 9 | .391 | .361 | .333 | .308 | .284 | .263 | .243 | .225 | .209 | .194 |
| 10 | .352 | .322 | .295 | .270 | .247 | .227 | .208 | .191 | .176 | .162 |
| 11 | .317 | .287 | .261 | .237 | .215 | .195 | .178 | .162 | .148 | .135 |
| 12 | .286 | .257 | .231 | .208 | .187 | .168 | .152 | .137 | .124 | .112 |
| 13 | .258 | .229 | .204 | .182 | .163 | .145 | .130 | .116 | .104 | .093 |
| 14 | .232 | .205 | .181 | .160 | .141 | .125 | .111 | .099 | .088 | .078 |
| 15 | .209 | .183 | .160 | .140 | .123 | .108 | .095 | .084 | .074 | .065 |
| 16 | .188 | .163 | .141 | .123 | .107 | .093 | .081 | .071 | .062 | .054 |
| 17 | .170 | .146 | .125 | .108 | .093 | .080 | .069 | .060 | .052 | .045 |
| 18 | .153 | .130 | .111 | .095 | .081 | .069 | .059 | .051 | .044 | .038 |
| 19 | .138 | .116 | .098 | .083 | .070 | .060 | .051 | .043 | .037 | .031 |
| 20 | .124 | .104 | .087 | .073 | .061 | .051 | .043 | .037 | .031 | .026 |
| 21 | .112 | .093 | .077 | .064 | .053 | .044 | .037 | .031 | .026 | .022 |
| 22 | .101 | .083 | .068 | .056 | .046 | .038 | .032 | .026 | .022 | .018 |
| 23 | .091 | .074 | .060 | .049 | .040 | .033 | .027 | .022 | .018 | .015 |
| 24 | .082 | .066 | .053 | .043 | .035 | .028 | .023 | .019 | .015 | .013 |
| 25 | .074 | .059 | .047 | .038 | .030 | .024 | .020 | .016 | .013 | .010 |

# FUTURE VALUE—ANNUITY

**EXHIBIT 8-7 Future Value Interest Factors for an Annuity of One Dollar:** $A = \left[\frac{(1+i)^n - 1}{i}\right]$

| Year | 1% | 2% | 3% | 4% | 5% | 6% | 7% | 8% | 9% | 10% |
|---|---|---|---|---|---|---|---|---|---|---|
| 1 | 1.000 | 1.000 | 1.000 | 1.000 | 1.000 | 1.000 | 1.000 | 1.000 | 1.000 | 1.000 |
| 2 | 2.010 | 2.020 | 2.030 | 2.040 | 2.050 | 2.060 | 2.070 | 2.080 | 2.090 | 2.100 |
| 3 | 3.030 | 3.060 | 3.091 | 3.122 | 3.153 | 3.184 | 3.215 | 3.246 | 3.278 | 3.310 |
| 4 | 4.060 | 4.122 | 4.184 | 4.246 | 4.310 | 4.375 | 4.440 | 4.506 | 4.573 | 4.641 |
| 5 | 5.101 | 5.204 | 5.309 | 5.416 | 5.526 | 5.637 | 5.751 | 5.867 | 5.985 | 6.105 |
| 6 | 6.152 | 6.308 | 6.468 | 6.633 | 6.802 | 6.975 | 7.153 | 7.336 | 7.523 | 7.716 |
| 7 | 7.213 | 7.434 | 7.662 | 7.898 | 8.142 | 8.394 | 8.654 | 8.923 | 9.200 | 9.487 |
| 8 | 8.286 | 8.583 | 8.892 | 9.214 | 9.549 | 9.897 | 10.260 | 10.637 | 11.028 | 11.436 |
| 9 | 9.368 | 9.755 | 10.159 | 10.583 | 11.027 | 11.491 | 11.978 | 12.488 | 13.021 | 13.580 |
| 10 | 10.462 | 10.950 | 11.464 | 12.006 | 12.578 | 13.181 | 13.817 | 14.487 | 15.193 | 15.937 |
| 11 | 11.567 | 12.169 | 12.808 | 13.486 | 14.207 | 14.972 | 15.784 | 16.646 | 17.560 | 18.531 |
| 12 | 12.682 | 13.412 | 14.192 | 15.026 | 15.917 | 16.870 | 17.889 | 18.977 | 20.141 | 21.384 |
| 13 | 13.809 | 14.680 | 15.618 | 16.627 | 17.713 | 18.882 | 20.141 | 21.495 | 22.953 | 24.523 |
| 14 | 14.947 | 15.974 | 17.086 | 18.292 | 19.599 | 21.015 | 22.551 | 24.215 | 26.019 | 27.975 |
| 15 | 16.097 | 17.294 | 18.599 | 20.024 | 21.579 | 23.276 | 25.129 | 27.152 | 29.361 | 31.773 |
| 16 | 17.258 | 18.639 | 20.157 | 21.824 | 23.658 | 25.673 | 27.888 | 30.324 | 33.003 | 35.950 |
| 17 | 18.430 | 20.012 | 21.762 | 23.697 | 25.840 | 28.213 | 30.840 | 33.750 | 36.974 | 40.545 |
| 18 | 19.615 | 21.412 | 23.414 | 25.645 | 28.132 | 30.906 | 33.999 | 37.450 | 41.301 | 45.599 |
| 19 | 20.811 | 22.841 | 25.117 | 27.671 | 30.539 | 33.760 | 37.379 | 41.446 | 46.018 | 51.159 |
| 20 | 22.019 | 24.297 | 26.870 | 29.778 | 33.066 | 36.786 | 40.996 | 45.762 | 51.160 | 57.275 |
| 21 | 23.239 | 25.783 | 28.676 | 31.969 | 35.719 | 39.993 | 44.865 | 50.423 | 56.764 | 64.003 |
| 22 | 24.471 | 27.299 | 30.537 | 34.248 | 38.505 | 43.392 | 49.006 | 55.457 | 62.873 | 71.403 |
| 23 | 25.716 | 28.845 | 32.453 | 36.618 | 41.431 | 46.996 | 53.436 | 60.893 | 69.532 | 79.543 |
| 24 | 26.973 | 30.422 | 34.426 | 39.082 | 44.502 | 50.816 | 58.177 | 66.765 | 76.790 | 88.497 |
| 25 | 28.243 | 32.030 | 36.459 | 41.646 | 47.727 | 54.865 | 63.249 | 73.106 | 84.701 | 98.347 |

## FUTURE VALUE—ANNUITY

**EXHIBIT 8-7** *(Continued)*

| Year | 11% | 12% | 13% | 14% | 15% | 16% | 17% | 18% | 19% | 20% |
|---|---|---|---|---|---|---|---|---|---|---|
| 1 | 1.000 | 1.000 | 1.000 | 1.000 | 1.000 | 1.000 | 1.000 | 1.000 | 1.000 | 1.000 |
| 2 | 2.110 | 2.120 | 2.130 | 2.140 | 2.150 | 2.160 | 2.170 | 2.180 | 2.190 | 2.200 |
| 3 | 3.342 | 3.374 | 3.407 | 3.440 | 3.473 | 3.506 | 3.539 | 3.572 | 3.606 | 3.640 |
| 4 | 4.710 | 4.779 | 4.850 | 4.921 | 4.993 | 5.066 | 5.141 | 5.215 | 5.291 | 5.368 |
| 5 | 6.228 | 6.353 | 6.480 | 6.610 | 6.742 | 6.877 | 7.014 | 7.154 | 7.297 | 7.442 |
| 6 | 7.913 | 8.115 | 8.323 | 8.536 | 8.754 | 8.977 | 9.207 | 9.442 | 9.683 | 9.930 |
| 7 | 9.783 | 10.089 | 10.405 | 10.731 | 11.067 | 11.414 | 11.772 | 12.142 | 12.523 | 12.916 |
| 8 | 11.859 | 12.300 | 12.757 | 13.233 | 13.727 | 14.240 | 14.773 | 15.327 | 15.902 | 16.499 |
| 9 | 14.164 | 14.776 | 15.416 | 16.085 | 16.786 | 17.518 | 18.285 | 19.086 | 19.923 | 20.799 |
| 10 | 16.722 | 17.549 | 18.420 | 19.337 | 20.304 | 21.321 | 22.393 | 23.521 | 24.709 | 25.959 |
| 11 | 19.561 | 20.655 | 21.814 | 23.045 | 24.349 | 25.733 | 27.200 | 28.755 | 30.404 | 32.150 |
| 12 | 22.713 | 24.133 | 25.650 | 27.271 | 29.002 | 30.850 | 32.824 | 34.931 | 37.180 | 39.581 |
| 13 | 26.212 | 28.029 | 29.985 | 32.088 | 34.352 | 36.786 | 39.404 | 42.219 | 45.245 | 48.497 |
| 14 | 30.095 | 32.393 | 34.883 | 37.581 | 40.505 | 43.672 | 47.103 | 50.818 | 54.841 | 59.196 |
| 15 | 34.405 | 37.280 | 40.417 | 43.842 | 47.580 | 51.659 | 56.110 | 60.965 | 66.261 | 72.035 |
| 16 | 39.190 | 42.753 | 46.672 | 50.980 | 55.718 | 60.925 | 66.649 | 72.939 | 79.850 | 87.442 |
| 17 | 44.501 | 48.884 | 53.739 | 59.117 | 65.075 | 71.673 | 78.979 | 87.068 | 96.022 | 105.931 |
| 18 | 50.396 | 55.750 | 61.725 | 68.394 | 75.836 | 84.141 | 93.405 | 103.740 | 115.266 | 128.117 |
| 19 | 56.940 | 63.440 | 70.749 | 78.969 | 88.212 | 98.603 | 110.284 | 123.414 | 138.166 | 154.740 |
| 20 | 64.203 | 72.052 | 80.947 | 91.025 | 102.444 | 115.379 | 130.033 | 146.628 | 165.418 | 186.688 |
| 21 | 72.265 | 81.699 | 92.470 | 104.768 | 118.810 | 134.840 | 153.138 | 174.021 | 197.848 | 225.026 |
| 22 | 81.215 | 92.502 | 105.491 | 120.436 | 137.632 | 157.414 | 180.172 | 206.345 | 236.439 | 271.031 |
| 23 | 91.148 | 104.603 | 120.204 | 138.296 | 159.276 | 183.601 | 211.801 | 244.487 | 282.362 | 326.237 |
| 24 | 102.174 | 118.155 | 136.831 | 158.658 | 184.168 | 213.977 | 248.807 | 289.495 | 337.011 | 392.484 |
| 25 | 114.414 | 133.333 | 155.619 | 181.870 | 212.793 | 249.213 | 292.104 | 342.604 | 402.043 | 471.981 |

## PRESENT VALUE—ANNUITY

**EXHIBIT 8-8 Present Value Factors for an Annuity of One Dollar:** $PVA = \left[\frac{1 - (1 + i)^{-n}}{i}\right]$

| Year | 1% | 2% | 3% | 4% | 5% | 6% | 7% | 8% | 9% | 10% |
|---|---|---|---|---|---|---|---|---|---|---|
| 1 | .990 | .980 | .971 | .962 | .952 | .943 | .935 | .926 | .917 | .909 |
| 2 | 1.970 | 1.942 | 1.913 | 1.886 | 1.859 | 1.833 | 1.808 | 1.783 | 1.759 | 1.736 |
| 3 | 2.941 | 2.884 | 2.829 | 2.775 | 2.723 | 2.673 | 2.624 | 2.577 | 2.531 | 2.487 |
| 4 | 3.902 | 3.808 | 3.717 | 3.630 | 3.546 | 3.465 | 3.387 | 3.312 | 3.240 | 3.170 |
| 5 | 4.853 | 4.713 | 4.580 | 4.452 | 4.329 | 4.212 | 4.100 | 3.993 | 3.890 | 3.791 |
| 6 | 5.795 | 5.601 | 5.417 | 5.242 | 5.076 | 4.917 | 4.767 | 4.623 | 4.486 | 4.355 |
| 7 | 6.728 | 6.472 | 6.230 | 6.002 | 5.786 | 5.582 | 5.389 | 5.206 | 5.033 | 4.868 |
| 8 | 7.652 | 7.326 | 7.020 | 6.733 | 6.463 | 6.210 | 5.971 | 5.747 | 5.535 | 5.335 |
| 9 | 8.566 | 8.162 | 7.786 | 7.435 | 7.108 | 6.802 | 6.515 | 6.247 | 5.995 | 5.759 |
| 10 | 9.471 | 8.983 | 8.530 | 8.111 | 7.722 | 7.360 | 7.024 | 6.710 | 6.418 | 6.145 |
| 11 | 10.368 | 9.787 | 9.253 | 8.760 | 8.306 | 7.887 | 7.499 | 7.139 | 6.805 | 6.495 |
| 12 | 11.255 | 10.575 | 9.954 | 9.385 | 8.863 | 8.384 | 7.943 | 7.536 | 7.161 | 6.814 |
| 13 | 12.134 | 11.348 | 10.635 | 9.986 | 9.394 | 8.853 | 8.358 | 7.904 | 7.487 | 7.103 |
| 14 | 13.004 | 12.106 | 11.296 | 10.563 | 9.899 | 9.295 | 8.745 | 8.244 | 7.786 | 7.367 |
| 15 | 13.865 | 12.849 | 11.938 | 11.118 | 10.380 | 9.712 | 9.108 | 8.559 | 8.061 | 7.606 |
| 16 | 14.718 | 13.578 | 12.561 | 11.652 | 10.838 | 10.106 | 9.447 | 8.851 | 8.313 | 7.824 |
| 17 | 15.562 | 14.292 | 13.166 | 12.166 | 11.274 | 10.477 | 9.763 | 9.122 | 8.544 | 8.022 |
| 18 | 16.398 | 14.992 | 13.754 | 12.659 | 11.690 | 10.828 | 10.059 | 9.372 | 8.756 | 8.201 |
| 19 | 17.226 | 15.679 | 14.324 | 13.134 | 12.085 | 11.158 | 10.336 | 9.604 | 8.950 | 8.365 |
| 20 | 18.045 | 16.352 | 14.878 | 13.590 | 12.462 | 11.470 | 10.594 | 9.818 | 9.129 | 8.514 |
| 21 | 18.857 | 17.011 | 15.415 | 14.029 | 12.821 | 11.764 | 10.836 | 10.017 | 9.292 | 8.649 |
| 22 | 19.660 | 17.658 | 15.937 | 14.451 | 13.163 | 12.042 | 11.061 | 10.201 | 9.442 | 8.772 |
| 23 | 20.456 | 18.292 | 16.444 | 14.857 | 13.489 | 12.303 | 11.272 | 10.371 | 9.580 | 8.883 |
| 24 | 21.243 | 18.914 | 16.936 | 15.247 | 13.799 | 12.550 | 11.469 | 10.529 | 9.707 | 8.985 |
| 25 | 22.023 | 19.524 | 17.413 | 15.622 | 14.094 | 12.783 | 11.654 | 10.675 | 9.823 | 9.077 |

## PRESENT VALUE—ANNUITY

**EXHIBIT 8-8** *(Continued)*

| Year | 11% | 12% | 13% | 14% | 15% | 16% | 17% | 18% | 19% | 20% |
|---|---|---|---|---|---|---|---|---|---|---|
| 1 | .901 | .893 | .885 | .877 | .870 | .862 | .855 | .847 | .840 | .833 |
| 2 | 1.713 | 1.690 | 1.668 | 1.647 | 1.626 | 1.605 | 1.585 | 1.566 | 1.547 | 1.528 |
| 3 | 2.444 | 2.402 | 2.361 | 2.322 | 2.283 | 2.246 | 2.210 | 2.174 | 2.140 | 2.106 |
| 4 | 3.102 | 3.037 | 2.974 | 2.914 | 2.855 | 2.798 | 2.743 | 2.690 | 2.639 | 2.589 |
| 5 | 3.696 | 3.605 | 3.517 | 3.433 | 3.352 | 3.274 | 3.199 | 3.127 | 3.058 | 2.991 |
| 6 | 4.231 | 4.111 | 3.998 | 3.889 | 3.784 | 3.685 | 3.589 | 3.498 | 3.410 | 3.326 |
| 7 | 4.712 | 4.564 | 4.423 | 4.288 | 4.160 | 4.039 | 3.922 | 3.812 | 3.706 | 3.605 |
| 8 | 5.146 | 4.968 | 4.799 | 4.639 | 4.487 | 4.344 | 4.207 | 4.078 | 3.954 | 3.837 |
| 9 | 5.537 | 5.328 | 5.132 | 4.946 | 4.772 | 4.607 | 4.451 | 4.303 | 4.163 | 4.031 |
| 10 | 5.889 | 5.650 | 5.426 | 5.216 | 5.019 | 4.833 | 4.659 | 4.494 | 4.339 | 4.192 |
| 11 | 6.207 | 5.938 | 5.687 | 5.453 | 5.234 | 5.029 | 4.836 | 4.656 | 4.487 | 4.327 |
| 12 | 6.492 | 6.194 | 5.918 | 5.660 | 5.421 | 5.197 | 4.988 | 4.793 | 4.611 | 4.439 |
| 13 | 6.750 | 6.424 | 6.122 | 5.842 | 5.583 | 5.342 | 5.118 | 4.910 | 4.715 | 4.533 |
| 14 | 6.982 | 6.628 | 6.303 | 6.002 | 5.724 | 5.468 | 5.229 | 5.008 | 4.802 | 4.611 |
| 15 | 7.191 | 6.811 | 6.462 | 6.142 | 5.847 | 5.575 | 5.324 | 5.092 | 4.876 | 4.675 |
| 16 | 7.379 | 6.974 | 6.604 | 6.265 | 5.954 | 5.669 | 5.405 | 5.162 | 4.938 | 4.730 |
| 17 | 7.549 | 7.120 | 6.729 | 6.373 | 6.047 | 5.749 | 5.475 | 5.222 | 4.990 | 4.775 |
| 18 | 7.702 | 7.250 | 6.840 | 6.467 | 6.128 | 5.818 | 5.534 | 5.273 | 5.033 | 4.812 |
| 19 | 7.839 | 7.366 | 6.938 | 6.550 | 6.198 | 5.877 | 5.584 | 5.316 | 5.070 | 4.844 |
| 20 | 7.963 | 7.469 | 7.025 | 6.623 | 6.259 | 5.929 | 5.628 | 5.353 | 5.101 | 4.870 |
| 21 | 8.075 | 7.562 | 7.102 | 6.687 | 6.312 | 5.973 | 5.665 | 5.384 | 5.127 | 4.891 |
| 22 | 8.176 | 7.645 | 7.170 | 6.743 | 6.359 | 6.011 | 5.696 | 5.410 | 5.149 | 4.909 |
| 23 | 8.266 | 7.718 | 7.230 | 6.792 | 6.399 | 6.044 | 5.723 | 5.432 | 5.167 | 4.925 |
| 24 | 8.348 | 7.784 | 7.283 | 6.835 | 6.434 | 6.073 | 5.746 | 5.451 | 5.182 | 4.937 |
| 25 | 8.422 | 7.843 | 7.330 | 6.873 | 6.464 | 6.097 | 5.766 | 5.467 | 5.195 | 4.948 |

## QUESTIONS AND EXERCISES

**8-1** For the present value of a single amount, what happens to the factor for any interest rate as *n* becomes large? What is the economic interpretation for this?

**8-2** What happens to the factor for the present value of an annuity as *n* becomes arbitrarily large? What is the explanation for this?

**8-3** What is the relationship between a table for the present value of a single amount and a table for the present value of an annuity?

**8-4** The longer-lived an asset, the more difficult it is to estimate its salvage or residual value, but the less serious are such errors on net present value. Explain.

**8-5** Why might management want to request follow-up reports on capital expenditures?

**8-6** "Follow-up audits of capital expenditures are not necessary since the investment becomes a sunk cost once the asset has been acquired and nothing can be done about it." Comment.

**8-7** For each of the following exercises determine the unknown. (a) An investment has a present value of $5,820 and will return $10,000 in 8 years. What is the annual interest rate? (b) How much will $8,000 amount to if invested at 11% for 10 years? (c) How much should be paid for an investment that will return $10,000 in 7 years if the interest rate is 9%? (d) An investment will cost $3,150 and earn 8% annually. If the proceeds from the investment will amount to $10,000, when will they be received?

**8-8** For each of the following determine the unknown. (a) $20,000 is invested now and will generate proceeds annually for 8 years at 12%. How much are the uniform annual proceeds? (b) An investment will return $3,000 per year for 12 years. If the interest rate is 6% annually, how much will be paid for this investment? (c) If $36,850 is invested now, $10,000 will be received annually for 6 years. What is the annual rate of interest? (d) An investment costing $11,070 will provide annual receipts of $2,000 yielding 9% interest. Over how many years will the $2,000 be received?

**8-9** What is the present value of an annuity of $10,000 per year for 5 years if the annuity begins at the start of the sixth year and the interest rate is 12%?

**8-10** What is the future value of an annuity of $1,000 per year for 10 years if it begins immediately and interest is 8% per year?

**8-11** An annuity costing $50,000 has been purchased. It will provide 10 equal annual payments beginning one year from the date of purchase. If the interest rate is 10%, how much is each annual payment?

**8-12** A family has just won $1 million (tax free) in a state lottery. The prize will pay the family $40,000 per year for 25 years with the first payment to be made immediately. What is the prize presently worth if interest is (a) 10% and (b) 20%?

**8-13** (CPA). Dillon, Inc., purchased a new machine for $60,000 at the beginning of the year. The machine is being depreciated on the straight-line basis over 5 years, with no salvage value. The accounting rate of return is expected to be 15% on the initial investment. Assuming a uniform cash flow from operations, how much cash is expected to be generated annually?

**8-14** (CPA). Axel Corporation is planning to buy a new machine with the expectation that this investment should earn a discounted rate of return of at least 15%. This machine, which costs $150,000, would yield an estimated net cash flow of $30,000 a year for 10 years. What is the net present value and internal rate of return on this proposal?

**8-15** (CPA). Amaro Hospital, a nonprofit institution not subject to income taxes, is considering the purchase of new equipment costing $20,000 to achieve cash savings of $5,000 per year in operating costs. The estimated useful life is 10 years, with no net residual value. Amaro's minimum expected return is 14%. (a) What is the net present value of this investment? (b) What is the internal rate of return? (c) What is the accounting rate of return based on initial investment? (d) What is the rate of return using Exhibit 8-2, the table for approximating rate of return?

**8-16** A firm purchases an investment of $80,000. It will receive $40,000 per year at the end of the first 2 years and the remainder at the end of the third year. If the rate of return on this investment is 20%, how much will be received at the end of the third year?

**8-17** A not-for-profit organization is considering investing $48,000 in equipment that will save $8,000 per year for 10 years beginning at the end of year 2. (a) What is the payback on this investment, and (b) what is the internal or time-adjusted rate of return?

**8-18** A medium-size city treats certain operations as profit centers; that is, although they are not subject to taxation, they are expected to maximize profit. One such operation is the employee cafeteria, which is currently losing $30,000 (cash) per year. A plan to automate will cost $250,000 and is expected to permit the cafeteria to break even over a 10-year period. Conventional straight-line depreciation methods are used to prepare income statements. The city requires a 20% return on projects of this type. You are to determine (a) the annual net cash inflow, (b) the payback period, (c) the payback reciprocal, (d) the average or unadjusted rate of return, (e) the approximate annual rate of return from Exhibit 8-2, (f) the internal rate of return, (g) the net present value, (h) the present value index, and (i) whether to recommend proceeding with the project.

**8-19** For each of the independent cases shown, determine the missing information indicated by the letters.

| | Case 1 | Case 2 | Case 3 |
|---|---|---|---|
| Initial investment | $30,000 | $41,920 | (e) |
| Annual cash inflow | $ 5,000 | (c) | $5,000 |
| Investment life | 10 years | (d) | 12 years |
| Payback period | (a) | 4.192 years | (f) |
| Internal rate of return | (b) | 20% | 10% |

**8-20** Foiegras, Ltd., is considering the following investment:

| | |
|---|---|
| Acquisition cost | \$100,000 |
| Working capital requirements | \$50,000 |
| Annual cash savings | \$25,000 |
| Project life | 8 years |
| Required rate of return | 16% |

Should Foiegras make the investment?

**8-21** A firm is going to invest \$400,000 and will receive \$100,000 per year. Calculate the rate of return using the approximating table (based on the payback reciprocal), assuming that the benefits last 6, 8, and 20 years.

**8-22** The Parish County government supervisors are considering the purchase of a small, used plane to save on travel costs. The plane will cost \$400,000 and can be sold in 5 years for 20% of the original cost. If 10% is the required rate of return, what must the savings in annual transportation costs be as a minimum?

**8-23** A nonprofit organization is considering buying equipment at a cost of \$120,000. The equipment will save \$40,000 per year over present methods. Although it can probably be used for 8 years, management expects to keep it for only 4 years (the life of the project on which it will be used). If 18% is the required acceptable rate of return, what is the minimum residual value necessary to justify the investment?

**8-24** The county assessor's office is considering automating certain operations at a cost of \$400,000. Annual savings of \$80,000 are expected over the next 8 years, at which time the equipment will be sold for \$50,000. The assessor's office uses its borrowing rate of 15% to evaluate capital expenditures. For reporting purposes, straight-line depreciation methods are used. Determine (a) the payback period and (b) the net present value for this proposal.

**8-25** As a second source of income, Tom Craig machines parts at home for a local corporation. He currently produces three parts per hour and sells the parts to the corporation for \$10 each. The variable indirect cost of producing the parts amounts to approximately \$1 per part; the material being machined is provided by the firm from which the work is subcontracted. Tom recently attended a trade show and saw a machine that will do the same work but will cut the variable indirect cost per part to \$0.75. The cost of the new machine is \$25,573. The existing machine has no residual or salvage value. What annual volume, over a 5-year-period, would be necessary to justify making the investment if a return of at least 20% is required? Ignore depreciaton and taxes and assume that all payments are made at the end of the year.

**8-26** Refer to the data in the chapter for SERF. Use the computer program, IRR, to calculate SERF's internal rate of return.

**8-27** Refer to the demonstration problem at the end of the chapter. By how much would user fees have to increase annually to avoid additional funding by the city council?

**8-28** Refer to the demonstration problem at the end of the chapter. If user fees are to be increased to remove the necessity for additional funding by the city council, but are to be received uniformly over the last 6 years, what will be the amount of increase per year?

**8-29** A florist has borrowed $59,380 to modernize her shop. The loan will be repaid in 11 equal annual installments at 12% per year. (a) What is the amount of the annual payment? (b) Using the computer program PYMTSCH, prepare an amortization schedule for this loan.

**8-30** A homeowner has taken a second mortgage on his home in the amount of $20,960. It will be repaid in 10 equal annual installments at an interest rate of 20%. (a) What is the amount of each payment? (b) Using the computer program PYMTSCH, prepare an amortization table for this loan.

**8-31** A college student purchased a stereo system under less than desirable circumstances. Instead of buying the equipment for $767.40 cash, he signed a note agreeing to pay $200 per month for 8 months beginning one month from the date of purchase (no money down!). Using the computer programs IRR and PYMTSCH, determine the monthly rate of interest and prepare an amortization schedule for the loan.

**8-32** (CPA). On January 1, 19X2, Robert Harrison signed an agreement to operate as a franchisee of Perfect Pizza, Inc., for an initial franchise fee of $40,000. Of this amount, $15,000 was paid when the agreement was signed and the balance is payable in five annual payments of $5,000 each, beginning January 1, 19X3. The agreement provides that the down payment is not refundable and no future services are required of the franchisor. Perfect Pizza, Inc., has used a 12% interest rate in determining the deferred payment schedule for the franchise fee. What is the acquisition cost of the franchise if Harrison pays it in full at the time of acquisition?

**8-33** Determine the internal rate of return for each of the following projects (the use of the computer program IRR on the disk that accompanies the text is suggested):

**a.** Investment at time zero: $9,000
Net returns at end of

| | |
|---|---|
| Period 1 | $ 2,000 |
| 2 | 3,000 |
| 3 | 4,000 |
| 4 | 5,000 |
| 5 | 6,000 |

**b.** Investment at time zero: $16,000
Net returns at end of

| | |
|---|---|
| Period 1 | $ 5,000 |
| 2 | (3,000) |
| 3 | 6,000 |
| 4 | 10,000 |
| 5 | (2,000) |
| 6 | 8,000 |
| 7 | 5,000 |

**c.** Investment at time zero: $6,000
Net returns at end of

| | |
|---|---|
| Period 1 | $ 4,000 |
| 2 | 7,000 |
| 3 | 12,000 |

## PROBLEMS AND CASES

**8-34 Prepare amortization table.**
Peavey, Inc., is considering an investment which will return cash flows of $2,000, $4,000, $3,000, and $5,000 for the next 4 years. Peavey requires a minimum of 10% on its investments.

**Required**
**a.** What is the maximum amount to be paid for this stream of benefits?
**b.** Using the following format and your answer to (a), complete the schedule.

| Year | Investment at Start | Interest | Receipt | Investment at End |
|---|---|---|---|---|
| 1 | | | | |
| 2 | | | | |
| 3 | | | | |
| 4 | | | | |

**8-35 Demonstration problem—computer required.**
Refer to the demonstration problem at the end of the chapter.

**Required**
**a.** What is the payback period?
**b.** Using the computer program for NPV, verify the net present value as shown in the solution.

**8-36 Loan balance.**
Douxbe, a small business, has taken out a loan of $100,000 to be repaid in seven equal semiannual installments beginning 6 months from now. The interest rate is 10% per year and the loan can be repaid in full at any time without penalty.

**Required**
If Douxbe intends to pay off the balance of the loan 2 years from now, what will be the payment at that time?

**8-37 Incremental versus total approach.**
A charitable organization is seeking to make its fund-raising operations more efficient. Present fund raising costs are $100,000 per year. If the organization acquires equipment for $70,000, it estimates that annual fund-raising costs will drop by 20%. The life of this equipment is estimated to be 8 years and the minimum required return is 16%.

**Required**
**a.** Evaluate the proposal using the total approach.
**b.** Evaluate the proposal using the incremental approach.

**8-38 Rate of return and sensitivity—computer recommended.**
A religious organization is considering acquiring a personal computer with peripherals and software for office use at a cost of $6,500. It is expected to save the organization $5,000 per year for 5 years. A member of the finance committee has agreed to purchase it for $1,000 at that time.

**Required**

**a.** What is the internal rate of return on this investment? (Use the computer program IRR.)

**b.** If the organization's desired rate of return is 20%, what are the minimum annual savings required to justify acquisition of the computer?

**8-39 Loan terms—computer recommended** (PYMTSCH).

Automobile dealers and their finance companies sometimes extend the period of a loan as a way of making higher-priced luxury cars more attractive to potential buyers. For example, a $20,000 loan at 12% results in varying payments as follows:

| Term of Loan | Monthly Payment |
|---|---|
| 36 months | $664 |
| 60 months | 445 |
| 84 months | 353 |

It has been observed that the average resale value of a luxury automobile declines by $2,500 per year.

**Required**

**a.** For each of the financing alternatives, what is the balance of the loan at the end of each year?

**b.** Given the facts, what is the danger in granting a 7-year loan?

**8-40 Equipment replacement.**

A philanthropist has established a nonprofit corporation to assist refugees. The capital acquisitions budget for the coming year includes the following proposal.

| | |
|---|---|
| Original cost of old equipment | $15,000 |
| Current salvage value of old equipment | 2,000 |
| Salvage value of old equipment in 5 years | — |
| Cost of proposed new equipment | 20,000 |
| Savings per year expected from new equipment | 6,000 |
| Salvage value of new equipment at end of life | 1,000 |
| Expected life of new equipment | 5 years |

Straight-line depreciation is used on both the old and new equipment.

**Required**

**a.** What is the incremental outlay required to acquire the new equipment? That is, how much cash will be required after disposing of the old equipment?

**b.** What is the payback period?

**c.** At a minimally desirable rate of return of 10%, what is the present value of the benefits only?

**d.** What is the net present value of this proposal at 10%?

**e.** What is the profitability index or ratio at 10%?

**f.** Approximately, what is the time-adjusted rate of return (alternatively, the internal rate of return) on this investment?

**8-41 Capital budgeting: Nonprofit.**

Protobac, Inc., is a nonprofit organization, established to do research into the effects on smokers of diminishing their environment. The organization currently uses the services of an outside lab in Tecate to perform certain tests; the cost of such tests currently runs $4,000 per year and is expected to stay at this level.

Protobac is considering purchasing special equipment so that it may perform these tests itself. The equipment will cost $21,200 delivered and installed, and is expected to last 10 years; its residual value is thought to be nominal.

Despite being a nonprofit organization, Protobac has specified a minimum desired rate of return on all investments of 15%.

**Required**

**a.** What is payback on this investment?
**b.** What is the unadjusted rate of return?
**c.** What is the payback reciprocal?
**d.** What is the net present value?
**e.** What is the present value index or ratio?
**f.** What is the internal rate of return?

**8-42 Make or buy: Disinvestment.**

Wrysun Corporation has been manufacturing a staple product. Its annual cash outlays are $400,000 plus $40 per unit. A friendly, stable third-world country has offered to enter into a 10-year contract to provide its required 20,000 parts annually at a delivered cost of $70 per part. If Wrysun accepts, it will dispose of its facilities for $1 million cash.

**Required**

If money is worth 18%, should Wrysun accept the offer?

**8-43 Not-for-profit organization: Payback with resale.**

A PTA group is considering buying a popcorn machine to make popcorn to sell at various school events. The president of the group is extremely conservative and ordinarily rejects such proposals routinely: "If this doesn't work out, we're stuck with the machine and we're out $2,900. Anyway, a payback period of $7\frac{1}{4}$ years is too long." A thorough analysis of the market for used popcorn machines shows the demand to be high—a machine that is 1 year old sells for 85% of its cost when new; a 2-year-old machine sells for 70%; a 3-year-old machine sells for 60%; and anything older sells for 50% as long as it is in working condition. It is expected that the machine will net approximately $400 per year. The association's funds are on deposit and currently earn 8% per annum.

**Required**

**a.** What is payback on this investment? (Take the resale value into consideration.)
**b.** What is the internal rate of return? (Use a life of 20 years.)
**c.** What do you recommend?

**8-44 Investment proposal—computer recommended** (CMA adapted).

Yipann Corporation is reviewing an investment proposal. The initial cost and estimates of the book value of the investment at the end of each year, the net cash flows for each year, and the net income for each year are presented in the schedule below. All cash flows are assumed to take place at the end of the year. The salvage value of the investment at the end of each year is equal to its book value. There would be no salvage value at the end of the investment's life.

**Investment Proposal**

| Year | Initial Cost and Book Value | Annual Cash Flows | Annual Net Income |
|---|---|---|---|
| 0 | $105,000 | | |
| 1 | 70,000 | $50,000 | $15,000 |
| 2 | 42,000 | 45,000 | 17,000 |
| 3 | 21,000 | 40,000 | 19,000 |
| 4 | 7,000 | 35,000 | 21,000 |
| 5 | 0 | 30,000 | 23,000 |

Yipann uses a 20% target rate of return for new investment proposals.

**Required**

**a.** What is the payback period for this proposal?
**b.** What is payback if the bailout factor is considered?
**c.** What is the accounting rate of return for the investment?
**d.** What is the net present value of this investment? (Use of the program NPV is recommended.)
**e.** What is the internal rate of return on this investment? (Use of the program IRR is recommended.)

**8-45 Equipment acquisition: Basic and comprehensive—computer recommended** (SMA adapted).

The Taylor Company Limited reported cost of goods sold of $576,000 last year when 18,000 units were produced and sold. Cost of goods sold was 35% materials, 42% direct labour, and 23% overhead.

The company is considering the purchase of a machine costing $100,000 with an expected useful life of five years and a salvage value at that time of $25,000. The machine would have a maximum capacity of 25,000 units per year and is expected to reduce direct labor costs by 25%; however, it would require an additional supervisor at a cost of $40,000 per year. The machine would be depreciated over the five years using the straight-line method of depreciation.

Production and sales for the next five years are expected to be

| | |
|---|---|
| 19X5 | 18,000 units |
| 19X6 | 18,000 units |
| 19X7 | 20,000 units |
| 19X8 | 20,000 units |
| 19X9 | 20,000 units |

**Required**

The use of the program NPV is recommended for this problem.

**a.** Should the company purchase the machine assuming the company has a minimum desired rate of return of 16%?
**b.** What is payback on this investment?
**c.** Is there a cost of prediction error if the company requires a 14% return?
**d.** At 16%, how high must the salvage value be before recommending the investment be made?

**8-46 Effect of interest rates and mortgage life on monthly payments—calculator with $y^x$ function required.**
In the 1970s, when home mortgage rates were near 8%, most people took out 30-year mortgages when purchasing a home. In the early 1980s, when interest rates were 16%, many people took out 15-year mortgages. This problem asks you to explain such behavior. Assume that the mortgage amount is $50,000.

**Required**

**a.** Determine the monthly loan payment if the interest rate is 8% and the buyer takes out (i) a 15-year mortgage and (ii) a 30-year mortgage. Calculate the percentage change in the monthly payment between the two options. Also determine the total interest paid over the life of each mortgage.
**b.** Repeat the requirement in part (a) assuming that the interest rate is 16%.
**c.** Why are the results in (a) and (b) so different?

**8-47 Value of a bond and expected value of a prize—calculator with $y^x$ function required.**
Recently, a promoter for vacation homesites offered several prizes to entice potential customers to attend a sales presentation. Postal patrons were sent letters promising the recipient that they had won either (a) a new car valued at $11,600, (b) a $1,000 government bond, or (c) a 13-inch color television receiver worth $159. To claim their prize, recipients must attend the sales presentation.

A reading of the fine print revealed that the odds of winning the car were 1 in 500,005, the odds of winning the bond were 1 in 1.000042, and for the television set the odds were 1 in 25,005. Further reading indicated that the $1,000 represented the maturity value of the bond 30 years hence.

**Required**

**a.** If the current long-term interest rate is 11.2%, what is the present value of the bond?
**b.** What is the expected value of a prize for someone attending the sales presentation?

**8-48 Net present value of services** (SMA adapted).
The owners of a newly franchised Class "A" senior hockey club are considering a deal with an older, established club whereby they can acquire the services of Pierre Leduc, a very high scorer and great gate attraction, in exchange for Robert Blain (currently receiving an annual stipend of $15,000), plus $500,000 in cash. Leduc would be Blain's replacement as the right wing on Blain's line.

The owners' accountants have assembled the following data.

| | |
|---|---|
| Estimated useful life of Leduc | 5 years |
| Estimated residual value of Leduc | $20,000 |
| Estimated useful life of Blain | 5 years |
| Estimated residual value of Blain | None |
| Current cash offer for Blain received from another Class "A" club | $50,000 |
| Applicable desired rate of return | 10% |

Other information:

| Year | Leduc's Salary | Additional Gate Receipts Because of Leduc | Additional Expenses of Handling Higher Volume |
|---|---|---|---|
| 1 | $60,000 | $330,000 | $33,000 |
| 2 | 70,000 | 300,000 | 30,000 |
| 3 | 80,000 | 200,000 | 20,000 |
| 4 | 80,000 | 100,000 | 10,000 |
| 5 | 72,000 | 40,000 | 4,000 |

**Required**

**a.** Based upon your analysis of the quantitative data given, recommend whether or not the club should acquire the services of Leduc. (Ignore income taxes.)

**b.** List and explain the other factors that should be considered before making the decision.

**8-49 Acquiring alternative services** (SMA adapted).

Camevad Limited has decided to inaugurate an express bus service between a large Canadian city and a nearby subway (one-way fare: $1.00). The company is considering the purchase of either 32- or 52-passenger buses for which pertinent estimates are as follows:

| | | |
|---|---|---|
| Number of passengers | 32 | 52 |
| Number of each to be purchased | 6 | 4 |
| Useful life | 8 years | 8 years |
| Purchase price: Paid on delivery, per bus | $80,000 | $110,000 |
| Mileage per gallon | 10 | $7\frac{1}{2}$ |
| Salvage value, per bus | $6,000 | $7,000 |
| Drivers' hourly wage rate | $7.00 | $8.40 |
| Price per gallon of fuel | $0.90 | $0.90 |
| Other annual cash expenses | $4,000 | $3,000 |

During the four daily rush hours all buses would be in service and are expected to operate at full capacity (provincial law prohibits standees) in both directions of the route, each bus covering the route 12 times (six round trips) during the period. During the remainder of the 16-hour day, 500 passengers would be carried, and Camevad would operate only four buses on the route. Part-time drivers would be employed to drive the extra hours during the rush hours. A bus traveling the route all day would go 480 miles, and one traveling only during rush hours would go 120 miles a day during the 260-day year.

**Required**

**a.** Prepare a schedule showing the computation of estimated annual revenues for both alternatives.

**b.** Prepare a schedule showing the computation of estimated annual drivers' wages for both alternatives.

**c.** Prepare a schedule showing the computation of annual cost of fuel for both alternatives.

**d.** Assume that your computations in (a), (b), and (c) are as follows:

| | 32-Passenger Bus | 52-Passenger Bus |
|---|---|---|
| Estimated revenues | $730,000 | $980,000 |
| Estimated drivers' wages | $134,000 | $136,000 |
| Estimated cost of fuel | $ 48,000 | $ 54,000 |

Assuming that a minimum rate of return of 12% before provision for income taxes is desired, and that all annual cash flows occur at the end of the year, prepare a schedule showing the present values of net cash flows for the 8-year period. Include in your answer the cost of buses and the proceeds from their disposition under both alternatives, but disregard the effect of income taxes.

CHAPTER

9

# CAPITAL BUDGETING: ADDITIONAL CONSIDERATIONS

The preceding chapter introduced the basic approaches to capital budgeting. The present chapter considers some of the problems and complications associated with capital budgeting, including the rationing of limited funds among competing proposals, the treatment of risk and inflation, and the effect of income taxes on cash flows for those entities subject to taxation.

## COMPLICATIONS IN CAPITAL BUDGETING

Several problems in capital budgeting decisions stem from a common source—namely, the selection of appropriate criteria for making the final decision. These problems include limited funds available for investment, mutually exclusive projects, and projects with unequal lives. The question concerning the appropriate present value criterion is whether we should use total net present value, the present value index, or the internal rate of return to select which projects should be undertaken.

To facilitate this discussion, consider a firm with seven investment alternatives available to it, all of which are acceptable at a required rate of return of 10%. The investments, cash flows, net present values, present value indices, and internal rates of return are summarized in Exhibit 9-1. Verification of the computations is left to the reader.

### Limitations on Available Funds

Consider yourself to be a member of the firm's capital budgeting committee. The firm has $550,000 of investment funds available to it and the committee must decide which projects to accept and which to reject or postpone. Department heads were solicited for their proposals, and the seven proposals shown in Exhibit 9-1 were found to be acceptable. There is a problem, however, in that these proposals total $1,400,000, which is far in excess of the funds available. Thus the committee is faced with a capital rationing problem—allocating the funds to the most profitable projects.

One approach to allocating the funds is to rank-order each proposal according to various criteria. Exhibit 9-2 presents the project rankings based on net present value, the present value index, and the internal rate of return.

Since the committee has only $550,000 available for capital expenditures, which criterion should be employed for purposes of making the decision? If net present value is used for project selection, proposals C and F will be selected ($150,000 + $400,000). If the present value index is employed, projects A, B, C, and D will be chosen ($100,000 + $200,000 + $150,000 + $100,000). Finally, if the internal rate of return is used, projects A, B, C, and D will again be approved ($100,000 + $200,000 + $150,000 + $100,000) but for a different reason. Unfortunately, each criterion produces a different ranking, making selection difficult.

The dilemma can be resolved if the problem is redefined as one in which we are considering investing $550,000 in the cash flows generated by C-F or A-B-C-D. In other words, we consider a single investment fol-

**EXHIBIT 9-1 Alternative Investment Opportunities: Schedule of Cash Flows**

| | Investment | | | | | | |
|---|---|---|---|---|---|---|---|
| Year | A | B | C | D | E | F | G |
| 0 | $(100,000) | $(200,000) | $(150,000) | $(100,000) | $(250,000) | $(400,000) | $(200,000) |
| 1 | 40,000 | 60,000 | 50,000 | 30,000 | 60,000 | 0 | 0 |
| 2 | 40,000 | 60,000 | 50,000 | 30,000 | 60,000 | 0 | 0 |
| 3 | 40,000 | 60,000 | 50,000 | 30,000 | 60,000 | 0 | 300,000 |
| 4 | 40,000 | 60,000 | 50,000 | 30,000 | 60,000 | 0 | |
| 5 | | 60,000 | 50,000 | 30,000 | 60,000 | 0 | |
| 6 | | | | 30,000 | 60,000 | 800,000 | |
| NPV | $26,800 | $27,460 | $39,550 | $30,650 | $11,300 | $51,200 | $25,300 |
| PV Index | 1.268 | 1.137 | 1.264 | 1.307 | 1.045 | 1.128 | 1.126 |
| IRR | 21.86 | 15.24 | 19.86 | 19.91 | 11.53 | 12.25 | 14.47 |

**EXHIBIT 9-2 Rankings of the Available Proposals**

| | Ranking According to | | |
|---|---|---|---|
| **Proposal** | **NPV** | **PV Index** | **IRR** |
| A | 5 | 2 | 1 |
| B | 4 | 4 | 4 |
| C | 2 | 3 | 3 |
| D | 3 | 1 | 2 |
| E | 7 | 7 | 7 |
| F | 1 | 5 | 6 |
| G | 6 | 6 | 5 |

lowed by the cash flows generated by the combination of projects selected. Exhibit 9-3 summarizes these results.

Evaluation of the analysis in Exhibit 9-3 indicates that the combination of projects A-B-C-D is superior to the other combination with respect to all three criteria. By viewing the scarce available funds as a single investment, the preferred recommendation is arrived at by considering the stream of benefits that will simultaneously maximize the net present value, the present value index, and the internal rate of return for this package.

A word of caution is in order. In the preceding example, each group of investments fully utilized the available funds and each group taken together had equal lives. One may ask whether the approach taken will always produce the optimal result as it did above. Just as individual investments may rank differently depending on the criteria used, groups of

**EXHIBIT 9-3 Maximizing Benefits from a Single Outlay**

| | Project Combination | |
|---|---|---|
| **Year** | **C-F** | **A-B-C-D** |
| 0 | $(550,000) | $(550,000) |
| 1 | 50,000 | 180,000 |
| 2 | 50,000 | 180,000 |
| 3 | 50,000 | 180,000 |
| 4 | 50,000 | 180,000 |
| 5 | 50,000 | 140,000 |
| 6 | 800,000 | 30,000 |
| NPV | $90,750 | $124,460 |
| PV Index | 1.165 | 1.226 |
| IRR | 13.415 | 18.524 |

investments may rank differently as well. The next section discusses why this may be the case.

### Evaluation of Investment Criteria

As Exhibit 9-2 shows, different criteria can result in different preference orderings among alternatives. The reasons for this are due to unequal lives and assumptions, explicit or implicit, about the return obtained from reinvested funds.

Consider the possibility that the firm has only $100,000 available for investment in long-lived assets and must, therefore, choose between projects A and D. Project A has a higher internal rate of return, while project D has a higher net present value and a higher present value index. Which of the two should be selected?

Although in this case both projects require the same dollar investment, usually the investment amounts are different. When investment amounts differ, the total net present value cannot be used since the total present value partially depends on the total amount invested.

Projects with unequal lives present difficulties because when the IRR is used as the criterion for project selection, the method favors short-lived projects with higher IRRs over longer-lived projects with lower IRRs. But when the life of the shorter-lived project is over, what will happen to the funds generated by the project? The use of IRR as the selection criterion assumes that the funds will be invested at the same IRR as that generated by the project. This suggests that, if the choice is between A and D, the firm should select A.

However, if it is thought that reinvested funds will earn the minimum required rate of return, then the present value index should be employed. This suggests selecting project D. Unless it can be demonstrated that funds generated in the future will earn more than the required rate of return, the present value index is to be preferred for project selection. Such problems arise whenever all acceptable projects cannot be selected because they are either mutually exclusive or funds are limited.

### Indivisibilities

The previous discussion also resulted in the utilization of all available funds. If we now increase the available investment funds to $600,000, how should the selection take place? Previously, when $550,000 was available, projects A, B, C, and D were selected. But, clearly, another proposal cannot be added to the selected group since there is no proposal costing $50,000. However, the committee might consider dropping proposal B and adding E as a way of utilizing the entire $600,000.

This problem is approached in much the same way as the original problem. There is, however, one difference; this has to do with the treatment of the $50,000 if it is not invested in one of these projects. It is frequently convenient to assume that the uninvested funds will earn the minimum required rate of return. In other words, the approach would be the same; the difference would be that unused funds are assumed to earn 10%. The question is then: Which alternative package generates the larger net present value (or index or internal rate of return)?

Another possibility is to acquire only a percentage interest in an asset when the asset is not divisible. This is very unlikely except in industries representing special cases as, for example, oil exploration and real estate. Entering into a partnership agreement is not a very common form of investment for organizations (although it may be very common for individuals).

## ADDITIONAL CONSIDERATIONS

Capital budgeting decisions are further complicated by other matters such as investing versus financing, determining the cost of capital, handling risk and inflation, and leasing. These are discussed in turn.

### Investing versus Financing

The distinction between investing and financing (borrowing) has to do with whether funds are initially paid out or received and with the cash flows that follow. A pure investment decision involves an initial cash outlay (amount invested) followed by one or more cash inflows (amounts received). A pure financing decision involves an initial cash inflow (amount borrowed) followed by one or more cash outflows (amounts repaid). The determination of an internal rate of return or interest rate in either case is straightforward (though not necessarily simple) and unique; that is, there is only one rate of interest.

However, if a decision involves both inflows and outflows that are mixed over time, both investing and financing are involved. Such situations are not always clear-cut, and judgment may have to be exercised to determine whether it is primarily an investment decision or a financing decision. In any event, it is possible in such cases that two or more internal rates of return will exist. For example, consider an investment that costs $1,000 today. It will earn a positive return at the end of the first year of $2,228.17, but also requires disposal costs of $1,241.41 at the end of the second year.

This project appears to have an internal rate of return of *both* 10% and 15% as illustrated by the following calculations.

| | | Present Value at 10% | | Present Value at 15% | |
|---|---|---|---|---|---|
| Time | Cash Flow | Factor | Amount | Factor | Amount |
| 0 | $(1,000.00) | 1.000 | $(1,000.00) | 1.000 | $(1,000.00) |
| 1 | 2,228.17 | 0.909 | 2,025.40 | 0.870 | 1,938.50 |
| 2 | (1,241.41) | 0.826 | (1,025.40) | 0.756 | (938.50) |
| NPV | | | $ 0.00 | | $ 0.00 |

These cases must be analyzed carefully. However, this is an advanced topic that is not pursued here other than to give a cautionary warning.

### Determination of the Cost of Capital

As cost accountants, we probably will work with a cost of capital or minimally acceptable rate of return provided by the firm's finance department. However, some familiarity with how such rates are obtained is appropriate.

The cost of capital represents the weighted-average cost to the firm of all funds from all sources and includes both debt and equity. The cost of obtaining funds, whether through borrowing or selling securities, is presumed to be determined by the market. The market, in effect, determines the interest rate by what it is willing to pay for various securities. The cost of debt to a firm is the interest rate paid, adjusted for income tax effects. The cost of common or preferred stock is usually determined by dividing the dividend payments by the market price of the stock without regard to taxes. This is because interest is a tax-deductible expense, whereas dividends are not.

To illustrate how the cost of capital is obtained, consider a firm with equities as follows:

| | Amount | Percentage of Total Equities | Before-Tax Cost | After-Tax Cost[a] |
|---|---|---|---|---|
| Long-term debt | $ 400,000 | 40% | 10% | 6% |
| Preferred stock | 100,000 | 10 | 10 | 10 |
| Common stock | 500,000 | 50 | 16 | 16 |
| Total equities | $1,000,000 | 100% | | |

[a]Assuming a 40% tax rate, each dollar paid in interest reduces taxes that must be paid by $0.40; thus the after-tax cost is 60% of the before-tax cost.

The **cost of capital** in this case is a composite or weighted-average of long-term debt, preferred stock, and common stock. It is determined as follows

$$(0.4)(0.06) + (0.1)(0.10) + (0.5)(0.16) = 11.4\%$$

Any investment that earns less than the weighted-average cost of capital decreases the overall return to the firm. This effect will be felt most directly by the common stockholders since they receive what has not been distributed to the other providers of capital.

Another approach is to consider the opportunity cost of capital. For example, we are aware of a large nonprofit clinic in the Midwest that has a substantial investment portfolio. Management requires that any funds to be invested in equipment or projects must earn at least the amount earned by the portfolio. If this is not the case, the clinic considers itself to be better off by leaving the funds in the portfolio. That is, the opportunity costs of the funds are their earning potential in the investment portfolio. Again, a weighted-average approach is employed. For example, if the portfolio has the following composition and returns

| | Composition | Return |
|---|---|---|
| Notes | 25% | 12% |
| Bonds | 30 | 8 |
| Stocks | 45 | 16 |
| | 100% | |

the weighted-average opportunity cost of capital is determined as

$$(0.25)(0.12) + (0.30)(0.08) + (0.45)(0.16) = 12.6\%$$

A final observation is in order. If funds are to be borrowed to invest in a particular project, the temptation is to include the cost of the funds as part of the cost of the project. However, any interest to be paid should not be considered as a cost of the project since this would be double-counting. The foregoing discussion has demonstrated that the cost of funds has already been incorporated into the cost of capital, or discount rate, to be used. If such funds or their cost are sufficiently material to change the cost of capital, then a new interest rate should be calculated.

### Risk or Uncertainty

The existence of risk or uncertainty should be apparent in capital budgeting situations. Most of the data used are estimates of future cash flows. Furthermore, it is easier to estimate cash flows for some projects than for others. Risk is viewed as fluctuations or variability in the cash flows associated with a project. In other words, the greater the potential variability in cash flows, the greater the attendant risk.

There are several approaches to dealing with risk. The most straightforward approach is to employ sensitivity analysis using both optimistic and pessimistic estimates to determine their effect on a particular decision. A second approach is to employ simulation. A third is to require a higher rate of return from high risk projects. Such projects might be grouped in a separate pool for consideration, employing a different set of criteria for selection or rejection.

### Inflation

To this point we have assumed that price levels will remain stable. If price levels are not expected to remain reasonably stable over time, it is appropriate to consider their effects on the data used for capital budgeting decisions. Several approaches may be employed to adjust for inflation (or deflation, for that matter).

Under the first approach, management may make the assumption that any inflationary increases in costs will be met with corresponding increases in selling prices. If, for example, variable costs and selling prices both increase by 10%, then contribution margin will also increase by 10%. In many cases no harm will result from this approach. It should be noted, however, that the tax consequences of inflation must be considered; many costs used to determine taxable income are based on nonadjusted historical cost figures (e.g., depreciation).

A second approach for incorporating inflation into the analysis is to adjust the rate of interest used to discount cash flows. The cost of capital, for example, can be viewed as having three components: a risk-free return, plus an adjustment for risk, plus an adjustment for inflation. If the rate of inflation can be projected, it is possible to adjust the discount rate for this. For example, if a firm requires a 15% return before considering inflation, and inflation is projected as 6%, then the required rate of return adjusted for inflation can be calculated as

$$(1.15)(1.06) = 1.219$$

Subtracting 1 from the result yields a required rate of return, adjusted for inflation, of 21.9 percent. The term $(1 + 0.219)$ would then be used, as appropriate, in the various present and future value formulas.

Note that some writers suggest simply adding the inflation rate to the interest rate to get the inflation-adjusted rate of return. That is, for the example they suggest adding the 6% inflation rate to the 15% desired return to get a required return of 21%. The determination of which approach is more appropriate depends on whether the firm desires a nominal return of 15% or a real return of 15%. Let us illustrate this point with some calculations.

If we invest $1,000 today for one year and the inflation rate is 6%, then the principal returned in 1 year must be $1,060 to maintain the purchasing power of the principal. If we earned the inflation-adjusted rate of 21% we would receive $1,210 at year end. Subtracting the adjusted principal of $1,060 leaves us with earnings of $150, which is $150/$1,000 = 15%, or a nominal 15% return on the original principal. But the purchasing power of $150 at year end is not the same as the purchasing power of $150 at the beginning of the year. If we desire a real return of 15% (in terms of the beginning of the year purchasing power), we need to earn 21.9%. For then we receive $1,219 at year end. Subtracting the adjusted principal of $1,060 leaves interest of $159; deflating this amount by 6% gives us a real return of $159/1.06 = $150 in terms of the beginning of the year purchasing power.

A third approach is to deflate the data, assuming that the cash flow projections include an allowance for inflation. However, since the rate of inflation must be determined in order to do this, it is simpler to adjust the interest rate as previously discussed.

An observation is in order, namely, that if inflation is expected, this suggests that management strongly consider investing available funds in producing assets that are nonmonetary—e.g., land. Monetary assets such as cash or receivables typically provide no return, whereas monetary assets such as notes and bonds provide a contractual return. Investments in either type of monetary asset are penalized in times of inflation. In short, inflation should not ordinarily be a deterrent to investing in long-lived producing assets.

### Leasing versus Buying

The popularity of leasing as a way of acquiring the services of assets has led to misconceptions with respect to the capital expenditure decision. Leasing is a form of financing and, as such, should be preceded by the more basic consideration of whether the asset should be acquired in the first place. In other words, the first question to be asked has to do with whether the firm desires the services of a particular asset at all (the capital budgeting question). If so, then the question of how best to acquire the asset can be addressed (the financing question). The alternatives for acquiring services are typically purchasing (with the firm's own funds or with borrowed funds), renting, or obtaining a financial lease.

Previously, we saw that the cost of borrowing is built into the firm's cost of capital. In the lease-versus-buying case, we make an exception and explicitly consider the cost of financing. If a capital expenditure has been determined to be desirable, the objective becomes that of minimizing the cost of obtaining those benefits. The form of financing that carries the smallest cost (interest rate) is preferred, assuming it does not disrupt the desired balance between debt and equity.

To illustrate, the Morall Company is considering acquiring state-of-the-art word processing equipment. The equipment costs $400,000 and is expected to reduce the cost of manuscript preparation and duplication by $150,000 a year over a 5-year period. Morall's cost of capital is 16%. This proposal has a positive net present value of $91,100, a present value index of 1.228, and an internal rate of return of approximately 25%. Consequently, the firm has decided that the equipment should be acquired. The financing question must now be addressed.

A finance company has offered to lease the equipment to Morall for $100,000 a year for 5 years, with the first payment due immediately. The interest rate implied in the lease is approximately 13 percent, determined as follows:

$$\$400{,}000 = \$100{,}000 + \$100{,}000(\text{annuity: } n = 4,\ i = ?)$$

$$(\text{annuity: } n = 4,\ i = ?) = \frac{\$300{,}000}{\$100{,}000} = 3.0$$

For an annuity factor of 3.0 and a period of 4 years, the interest rate is approximately 13%.

Since 13% is below the cost of capital, Morall should consider leasing unless it can borrow for less. Another advantage of leasing is that it gives Morall the flexibility to consider upgrading to state-of-the-art word processing equipment again 5 years hence. On the other hand, if Morall wants to keep the equipment longer than 5 years, borrowing now to buy the equipment means the firm will not have to negotiate for its purchase or renegotiate the lease contract at the end of the 5-year period. However, debt financing has the effect of increasing risk to stockholders. In the absence of these considerations and the absence of income taxes, desirable resources should be acquired at the least cost.

We observe that there may be situations where the financing and the investing decisions are not independent, as they were in the above example. For instance, the owner of property in which the firm is interested may have no interest in selling but would consider leasing. In such cases, there may be no alternative way of acquiring the services in question.

## INCOME TAXES

In Chapter 8, the various decision models were introduced using a not-for-profit organization. This permitted us to look at the alternatives with minimal distraction. For those organizations that are not subject to income taxes, the determination of cash flows is relatively straightforward. For such organizations it is entirely appropriate to exclude many of the routine accounting accruals such as depreciation and book gains or losses on disposal of assets.

In the case of organizations subject to taxation, however, it is necessary to take into account the tax effects of both cash and noncash transactions. It should be emphasized, however, that this has absolutely no effect on the manner in which the capital budgeting models developed earlier are constructed or used. Rather, the effects of taxation relate only to the computations of cash inflows and outflows. In other words, we are not altering any of the previous models; we are only altering the data employed in such models because of the effects of taxation.

The complexities of taxes are well known. It is not our intent to teach taxes here; rather, the intent is to illustrate the effect that taxation has on several simple, but common, situations. Alternate approaches may be employed when analyzing cash flows to determine their amounts after taxes. Which approach is appropriate depends on the nature of the data provided and/or the specific question or questions asked. Familiarity with each alternative is encouraged.

To illustrate the effects of taxes, let us assume that the Acronomic Construction Equipment Company (ACE) is considering investing in some materials handling equipment. The equipment costs $105,000 and has a useful life of 6 years, with no expected salvage or residual value. It is expected that using such equipment will save the firm $35,000 per year before taxes. The firm employs straight-line depreciation methods for decisions of this type. ACE is subject to average income taxes of 40% from all sources (local, state, and federal). What is ACE's expected annual cash flow from this investment after taxes?

As a first step, we construct a partial income statement that reflects the effects of this investment:

| | |
|---|---|
| Before-tax cash savings | $35,000 |
| Less depreciation (straight-line) | 17,500 |
| Taxable savings | $17,500 |
| Less income taxes at 40% | 7,000 |
| Increase in net income after taxes | $10,500 |

One approach to determining cash flow after taxes is to proceed in a manner similar to that when determining "funds from operations" for a statement of changes in financial position. That is, we begin with net income after taxes and add all noncash expenses and deduct all noncash revenues from this figure. For ACE the result is

$$\text{annual cash flow after taxes} = \$10{,}500 + \$17{,}500$$
$$= \$28{,}000$$

Alternatively, we could take a top-down approach to the income statement. This involves consideration of only those items that have a direct effect on cash—namely, the before-tax cash savings and taxes. For our data the result would be

$$\begin{aligned}\text{annual cash flow after taxes} &= \$35{,}000 - \$7{,}000\\ &= \$28{,}000\end{aligned}$$

Finally, we can consider each element of revenue and expense on a net-of-tax basis. ACE will not be permitted to keep the entire $35,000 cash savings because, in and of itself, this will increase income by a like amount and that income will be taxed at the appropriate rate. In this case, ACE will keep 60% (1 minus the tax rate) of such savings. However, ACE does get to deduct depreciation. While this is a noncash expense, it does serve to reduce taxable income; every $1 of depreciation will save 40¢ (the tax rate) in taxes. The effect of depreciation, which is a noncash expense, is to reduce taxable income, thereby reducing taxes, which do require cash disbursements. This is referred to as the **depreciation tax shield** since revenues are "shielded" from taxes to the extent of the depreciation deduction. The after-tax effects result in a tax savings equal to the amount of depreciation taken times the tax rate. The calculation in this format would be as follows:

$$\begin{aligned}\text{annual cash flow after taxes} &= (\$35{,}000)(0.60) + (\$17{,}500)(0.40)\\ &= \$28{,}000\end{aligned}$$

For problems involving the net-of-tax approach, a question that is troublesome is when to use the tax rate and when to use one minus the tax rate. The rules are simple:

1. Use the tax rate for all noncash revenues and expenses.
2. Use one minus the tax rate for all cash revenues and expenses.

As we have shown, each of the three approaches to determining cash flow after taxes results in the same figure, $28,000. Which approach is easiest for a given problem generally depends on the manner in which facts for the problem are presented.

Once we have calculated the after-tax cash flows and once we know ACE's investment objectives, we can analyze the data and make a recommendation. Let us assume that ACE requires a 10% return after taxes. Should this investment be seriously considered?

Using the earlier models that employ present value techniques, the answer to the question is yes. The net present value of this investment is

$$\begin{aligned}\text{net present value} &= (\$28{,}000 \times 4.355) - \$105{,}000\\ &= \$16{,}940\end{aligned}$$

The profitability index or ratio is 1.16+ and the internal or time-adjusted rate of return is slightly over 15%. You are invited to check the accuracy of the latter two figures.

### Accelerated Cost Recovery Systems

In most situations, a firm would prefer to take its deductions as soon as possible for tax purposes and to defer its revenues as long as possible. This has the effect of legally deferring tax payments at no cost to the firm. Prior to 1982, accelerated methods of depreciation (sum-of-the-years'-digits and declining-balance) were preferred to the straight-line method for tax purposes. These methods gave recognition to residual or salvage value and to useful life when calculating depreciation.

The Economic Recovery Tax Act of 1981, however, made these methods obsolete for tax purposes in the United States. The act specifically eliminates all depreciation methods expressed in terms of time for depreciable assets acquired in 1981 and later years. Indeed, depreciable assets are now referred to as **recovery property** and depreciation is now referred to as *cost recovery*. Actually, the term **accelerated cost recovery system (ACRS)** is used because the percentages in the tables for recovery are derived from declining-balance methods.

As we go to press, all depreciable assets are classified for tax purposes as one of five types. The original cost of an asset can be recovered over 3, 5, 10, 15, or 18 years. These property classes are given in Exhibit 9-4.

**EXHIBIT 9-4 Recovery Property Class Lives under ACRS**

| Class Life | Type of Recovery Property |
|---|---|
| 3-year | Automobiles, light trucks, machinery and equipment used for research and development, and other short-lived tangible personal property (which formerly had a life of 4 years or less) |
| 5-year | All other tangible personal property not included in the other personal property recovery classes; includes most machinery and equipment and public utility property with a useful life of 4 to 18 years |
| 10-year | Public utility personal property with a life of more than 18 but not more than 25 years, theme and amusement park property, residential manufactured homes, railroad tank cars, and certain coal utilization properties |
| 15-year public utility | All public utility personal property with a life in excess of 25 years |
| 18-year real property | All depreciable real property other than that included in the 10-year class |

**EXHIBIT 9-5 Recovery Percentages of Personal Property**

| | Property Class | | | |
|---|---|---|---|---|
| Recovery Year | 3-Year | 5-Year | 10-Year | 15-Year Public Utility |
| 1 | 25% | 15% | 8% | 5% |
| 2 | 38 | 22 | 14 | 10 |
| 3 | 37 | 21 | 12 | 9 |
| 4 | | 21 | 10 | 8 |
| 5 | | 21 | 10 | 7 |
| 6 | | | 10 | 7 |
| 7 | | | 9 | 6 |
| 8 | | | 9 | 6 |
| 9 | | | 9 | 6 |
| 10 | | | 9 | 6 |
| 11 | | | | 6 |
| 12 | | | | 6 |
| 13 | | | | 6 |
| 14 | | | | 6 |
| 15 | | | | 6 |

Each class of property has a predetermined schedule for cost recovery (depreciation). This schedule is to be followed except for certain situations to be discussed later. We present the cost recovery percentages allowable for tax purposes in two tables. Exhibit 9-5 gives the recovery percentages for personal property with 3-, 5-, or 10-year lives and 15-year public utility property. The table is based on 150% declining-balance depreciation with salvage value ignored and using the half-year convention. That is, the recovery for the year of acquisition is one-half the normal 150% declining-balance depreciation regardless of when the asset is acquired during the year. There is a change to the straight-line method when this maximizes the deduction.

The ACRS table for 18-year (nonpublic-utility) real property appears as Exhibit 9-6. This table differs from the preceding table in that the cost recovery percentages for this class of assets are based on 175% declining balance with an automatic change to straight-line when it is advantageous to do so. The half-year convention does not apply; instead, the cost recovery for each year depends on the month in which the asset was placed in service.

### Using the ACRS Tables

To demonstrate how the ACRS tables are used, we continue with the data for ACE Company. The firm is acquiring equipment with a useful life of

**EXHIBIT 9-6 ACRS Recovery Percentages for 18-Year Real Property**

| Recovery Year | Month Asset Is Placed in Service | | | | | | | | | | | |
|---|---|---|---|---|---|---|---|---|---|---|---|---|
| | Jan. | Feb. | Mar. | Apr. | May | June | July | Aug. | Sept. | Oct. | Nov. | Dec. |
| 1 | 9 | 9 | 8 | 7 | 6 | 5 | 4 | 4 | 3 | 2 | 1 | 0.4 |
| 2 | 9 | 9 | 9 | 9 | 9 | 9 | 9 | 9 | 9 | 10 | 10 | 10.0 |
| 3 | 8 | 8 | 8 | 8 | 8 | 8 | 8 | 8 | 9 | 9 | 9 | 9.0 |
| 4 | 7 | 7 | 7 | 7 | 7 | 8 | 8 | 8 | 8 | 8 | 8 | 8.0 |
| 5 | 7 | 7 | 7 | 7 | 7 | 7 | 7 | 7 | 7 | 7 | 7 | 7.0 |
| 6 | 6 | 6 | 6 | 6 | 6 | 6 | 6 | 6 | 6 | 6 | 6 | 6.0 |
| 7 | 5 | 5 | 5 | 5 | 6 | 6 | 6 | 6 | 6 | 6 | 6 | 6.0 |
| 8 | 5 | 5 | 5 | 5 | 5 | 5 | 5 | 5 | 5 | 5 | 5 | 5.0 |
| 9 | 5 | 5 | 5 | 5 | 5 | 5 | 5 | 5 | 5 | 5 | 5 | 5.0 |
| 10 | 5 | 5 | 5 | 5 | 5 | 5 | 5 | 5 | 5 | 5 | 5 | 5.0 |
| 11 | 5 | 5 | 5 | 5 | 5 | 5 | 5 | 5 | 5 | 5 | 5 | 5.0 |
| 12 | 5 | 5 | 5 | 5 | 5 | 5 | 5 | 5 | 5 | 5 | 5 | 5.0 |
| 13 | 4 | 4 | 4 | 5 | 4 | 4 | 5 | 4 | 4 | 4 | 5 | 5.0 |
| 14 | 4 | 4 | 4 | 4 | 4 | 4 | 4 | 4 | 4 | 4 | 4 | 4.0 |
| 15 | 4 | 4 | 4 | 4 | 4 | 4 | 4 | 4 | 4 | 4 | 4 | 4.0 |
| 16 | 4 | 4 | 4 | 4 | 4 | 4 | 4 | 4 | 4 | 4 | 4 | 4.0 |
| 17 | 4 | 4 | 4 | 4 | 4 | 4 | 4 | 4 | 4 | 4 | 4 | 4.0 |
| 18 | 4 | 3 | 4 | 4 | 4 | 4 | 4 | 4 | 4 | 4 | 4 | 4.0 |
| 19 | — | 1 | 1 | 1 | 2 | 2 | 2 | 3 | 3 | 3 | 3 | 3.6 |

6 years; according to the 1981 act, this equipment is classified as 5-year property for cost recovery purposes. The year-by-year cash savings from the cost recovery (depreciation) tax shield are shown in Exhibit 9-7, and the present value of these savings is shown to be $31,484.04.

It is cumbersome to calculate the effects of ACRS on the present value of cash flows since an annuity is not involved. This can, perhaps, be

**EXHIBIT 9-7 Tax Effects of ACRS**

| Year | ACRS Percentage | Cost to Be Recovered | Annual Cost Recovery | Tax Rate | Annual Tax Benefit from Cost Recovery | 10% Present Value Factor | Present Value of Tax Benefits |
|---|---|---|---|---|---|---|---|
| 1 | 15% | $105,000 | $15,750 | 40% | $6,300 | 0.909 | $ 5,726.70 |
| 2 | 22 | 105,000 | 23,100 | 40 | 9,240 | 0.826 | 7,632.24 |
| 3 | 21 | 105,000 | 22,050 | 40 | 8,820 | 0.751 | 6,623.82 |
| 4 | 21 | 105,000 | 22,050 | 40 | 8,820 | 0.683 | 6,024.06 |
| 5 | 21 | 105,000 | 22,050 | 40 | 8,820 | 0.621 | 5,477.22 |
| | Present value of the cash savings in income taxes from the use of ACRS | | | | | | $31,484.04 |

**EXHIBIT 9-8 Present Value of 5-Year ACRS Percentage Discounted at 10%**

| Year | ACRS Percentage | 10% Present Value Factor | Present Value |
|---|---|---|---|
| 1 | 15% | 0.909 | 0.13635 |
| 2 | 22 | 0.826 | 0.18172 |
| 3 | 21 | 0.751 | 0.15771 |
| 4 | 21 | 0.683 | 0.14343 |
| 5 | 21 | 0.621 | 0.13041 |
| | Present value of 5-year ACRS class at 10% | | 0.74962 |

more appreciated if one envisions an examination problem involving an asset in the 10-year class. Fortunately, the computations can be simplified and tabled for repeated use. Notice in Exhibit 9-7 that regardless of the cost of the asset or the firm's effective tax rate (a) the percentages for a class life of 5 years are the same and (b) the present value factors for 10% are the same. In effect, we can find the present value (at any rate of interest) of the cost recovery percentages (for any class life) by multiplying the two factors together. ACE's interest rate is 10% and the asset is in the 5-year class; the computations to obtain the present value of this particular combination of factors appear in Exhibit 9-8.

To obtain the present value of the after-tax cash savings resulting from the ACRS tax shield for ACE's asset, it is necessary only to multiply the cost of the asset by ACE's tax rate and by the factor shown in Exhibit 9-8. Hence,

present value of cash savings
from the use of 5-year ACRS discounted at 10% = (\$105,000)(0.40)(0.74962)
= \$31,484.04

We can observe that this is *exactly* the same result as was obtained in Exhibit 9-7. For your computational convenience, the present value factors for various interest rates and different ACRS class life percentages have been computed and are tabled (rounded to three places) in Exhibit 9-9.[1]

To obtain the net present value of ACE's proposal, it is necessary only to add the present value of the net-of-tax benefits from the operating savings to the present value of the savings from cost recovery (depreciation) and subtract the cost of the investment. The asset has a useful life of 6 years to ACE; hence the operating savings are expected to last this long regardless of the fact that its ACRS class life is only 5 years. (Recall that

[1]The computer program PVACRS on the disk that accompanies the text calculates these factors for all classes and interest rates.

**EXHIBIT 9-9 Present Value of Recovery Allowance**

| | Class of Investment | | |
|---|---|---|---|
| **Discount Rate** | **3-Year** | **5-Year** | **10-Year** |
| 5% | 0.902 | 0.861 | 0.780 |
| 6 | 0.885 | 0.837 | 0.745 |
| 7 | 0.867 | 0.814 | 0.712 |
| 8 | 0.851 | 0.792 | 0.682 |
| 9 | 0.835 | 0.770 | 0.653 |
| 10 | 0.819 | 0.750 | 0.626 |
| 12 | 0.790 | 0.711 | 0.578 |
| 15 | 0.748 | 0.659 | 0.516 |
| 20 | 0.686 | 0.585 | 0.433 |
| 25 | 0.633 | 0.523 | 0.371 |
| 30 | 0.586 | 0.471 | 0.322 |

one consequence of the 1981 act is that there is no longer a necessary relationship between the class life of an asset and its useful life.) The net present value of this investment is summarized as follows:

| | |
|---|---|
| PV of operating savings, after taxes | \$ 91,455[a] |
| PV of ACRS, after taxes | 31,484[b] |
| PV of benefits | \$122,939 |
| PV of cost | 105,000 |
| Net present value | \$ 17,939 |

[a](\$35,000)(1 − 0.40)(4.355)

[b](\$105,000)(0.40)(0.74962)

## Alternatives to ACRS

The 1981 act provides that those methods of depreciation based on use, rather than time, may continue to be employed. In addition, there is a provision for the use of an optional straight-line method. However, the period over which straight-line cost recovery may be used is predetermined and bears no relation to the actual useful life. The options available for each class of recovery property are as follows:

| Property Class | Optional Recovery Periods Using Straight-Line |
|---|---|
| 3-year | 3, 5, or 12 years |
| 5-year | 5, 12, or 25 years |
| 10-year | 10, 25, or 35 years |
| 15-year public utility | 15, 35, or 45 years |
| 18-year real property | 18, 35, or 45 years |

If the optional straight-line method of cost recovery is chosen, the **half-year convention** must be strictly followed. For example, if 5 years is chosen as the recovery period, then 10% (or one-half of a year's allowance) would be allowed in years 1 and 6, and 20% would be allowed for years 2 through 5. The effect is that the actual recovery period will always be one more year than that elected from the table. Also, the full cost of the asset will be recovered; salvage value, if any, is ignored.

If the minimum 18-year life is used for real property in the 18-year class, a table based on the month an asset is placed in service must be used. Exhibit 9-10 provides the cost recovery table for real property in the 18-year class using the optional straight-line method.

Using the data for the ACE Company, let us assume that the firm elects to use the optional straight-line recovery method over a 5-year period. Exhibit 9-11 provides the calculation of the cash benefits from the optional straight-line recovery method.

We can compare the ACRS result with the optional straight-line result. The difference in this case does not appear to be material ($31,484

**EXHIBIT 9-10 Optional Straight-Line Recovery Percentages for 18-Year Real Property Using an 18-Year Life**

| | Month Asset Is Placed in Service | | | | | |
|---|---|---|---|---|---|---|
| Recovery Year | 1–2 | 3–4 | 5–7 | 8–9 | 10–11 | 12 |
| 1 | 5 | 4 | 3 | 2 | 1 | 0.2 |
| 2 | 6 | 6 | 6 | 6 | 6 | 6 |
| 3 | 6 | 6 | 6 | 6 | 6 | 6 |
| 4 | 6 | 6 | 6 | 6 | 6 | 6 |
| 5 | 6 | 6 | 6 | 6 | 6 | 6 |
| 6 | 6 | 6 | 6 | 6 | 6 | 6 |
| 7 | 6 | 6 | 6 | 6 | 6 | 6 |
| 8 | 6 | 6 | 6 | 6 | 6 | 6 |
| 9 | 6 | 6 | 6 | 6 | 6 | 6 |
| 10 | 6 | 6 | 6 | 6 | 6 | 6 |
| 11 | 5 | 5 | 5 | 5 | 5 | 5.8 |
| 12 | 5 | 5 | 5 | 5 | 5 | 5 |
| 13 | 5 | 5 | 5 | 5 | 5 | 5 |
| 14 | 5 | 5 | 5 | 5 | 5 | 5 |
| 15 | 5 | 5 | 5 | 5 | 5 | 5 |
| 16 | 5 | 5 | 5 | 5 | 5 | 5 |
| 17 | 5 | 5 | 5 | 5 | 5 | 5 |
| 18 | 5 | 5 | 5 | 5 | 5 | 5 |
| 19 | 1 | 2 | 3 | 4 | 5 | 5 |

**EXHIBIT 9-11 Tax Effects of Optional Straight-Line Recovery Method**

| Year | Straight-Line Percentage | Cost to Be Recovered | Annual Cost Recovery | Tax Rate | Annual Tax Benefit from Cost Recovery | 10% Present Value Factor | Present Value of Tax Benefits |
|---|---|---|---|---|---|---|---|
| 1 | 10% | $105,000 | $10,500 | 40% | $4,200 | 0.909 | $ 3,817.80 |
| 2 | 20 | 105,000 | 21,000 | 40 | 8,400 | 0.826 | 6,938.40 |
| 3 | 20 | 105,000 | 21,000 | 40 | 8,400 | 0.751 | 6,308.40 |
| 4 | 20 | 105,000 | 21,000 | 40 | 8,400 | 0.683 | 5,737.20 |
| 5 | 20 | 105,000 | 21,000 | 40 | 8,400 | 0.621 | 5,216.40 |
| 6 | 10 | 105,000 | 10,500 | 40 | 4,200 | 0.564 | 2,368.80 |
| Present value of the cash savings in income taxes from the use of the optional cost recovery | | | | | | | $30,387.00 |

versus $30,387). However, the difference increases as the cost increases, as the tax rate increases, as the interest or discount rate increases, and as the class life increases.

### Investment Tax Credit

The Tax Code also provides for an **investment tax credit.** At the time that this is being written the credit is 6% of the cost of assets in the 3-year class and 10% of the cost of assets in the 5-, 10-, and 15-year public utility class. There is no investment tax credit for ordinary 18-year real property.[2] The investment tax credit is a direct dollar-for-dollar reduction in income taxes in the year the acquisition was made, but the cost of the asset must be reduced by one-half of the credit to determine the cost of the asset subject to ACRS.

In the example concerning the ACE Company we previously ignored the investment tax credit. Assuming the asset qualifies, the investment tax credit would be 10% of $105,000, or $10,500. The amount of the ITC would be shown as a cash inflow for the first year of the project's life. The cost to be recovered over the 5-year class life would then be $99,750, and the present value of the savings from cost recovery would be $99,750 × 0.4 × 0.74962 = $29,909.84.

[2]*Note:* The investment tax credit has a way of coming or going, depending on the mood of Congress. By the time you read this, the rates may have changed, or the credit may have been eliminated. Nonetheless, you should be aware of the theoretical treatment because, even if the credit does not currently exist, there is a good chance it will come back again later.

### Salvage or Residual Value

From an economic point of view, salvage or residual value is the amount expected to be recovered on disposition of an asset. Accordingly, this is considered when depreciation allowances are established for accounting purposes. However, under ACRS, the full acquisition cost of the asset, less one-half of the investment tax credit, is recovered without regard for salvage. Any salvage, then, would be a gain for purposes of income taxation. This gain will be taxed at the same rate as ordinary income. Complexities are involved if the asset is disposed of prior to the end of its ACRS class life or if the asset is traded for a similar asset. For tax purposes, the half of the ITC that is not recovered is simply ignored and is not considered in the determination of gain or loss on disposition.

### A Word of Caution

The intent of this section has been to demonstrate the relevance of income taxes to the capital budgeting decision. We have attempted to address those elements that bear most directly on capital budgeting. However, the tax law is constantly changing, so new elements may be added or old ones dropped between the time this is written and you are studying this chapter; in addition, there are many exceptions and fine points that have not been touched on here. For example, we have assumed throughout that an acquired asset will be held at least to the end of its class life; this serves to eliminate many complexities. Also, the assignment material will ordinarily make clear what the appropriate class life is for the asset in question.

### Before- and After-Tax Rates of Return

In cost-volume-profit analysis it is frequently desirable to convert an after-tax profit objective into a before-tax profit objective before proceeding further. For example, if a firm requires an income of $42,000 per period after taxes of 30%, what is the equivalent before-tax income? The answer, as we saw before, is as follows:

$$X - 0.3X = \$42,000$$

or

$$X = \$60,000$$

One may raise the question of whether an after-tax rate of return can be converted into a before-tax rate of return so that taxes can be ignored in present value analysis. For example, if the firm requires a 12%

return after taxes and taxes average 20%, why not use a 15% before-tax return and ignore the tax effects altogether?

We introduce the question because, on the surface, it has a certain intuitive appeal. Without proving our statement, we assert that the approach is not acceptable for two reasons. First, the law permits us to shift the amount and timing of taxes; hence, it matters when payments occur since we are interested in the time value of money. Second, the present value factors are not linear multiples of one another (e.g., the factors for 10% are not twice those for 20%) by virtue of the exponents in the formulas.

### Leasing versus Buying and Income Taxes

The tax consequences of leasing versus buying are important enough to warrant consideration. If the firm leases, rather than buys, the services of assets, the firm forgoes the benefits of the investment tax credit and accelerated cost recovery. These benefits belong to the lessor.

Let us return to the Morall Company discussed earlier in this chapter. They were considering buying a $400,000 word processor. Let us now add that the company is taxed at an average rate of 30%, the equipment is in a 5-year class, and the investment tax credit applies.

Using an incremental approach, the $150,000 annual savings can be ignored since they are obtained whether the equipment is purchased or leased. The differences in cash flows have to do with the benefits from the tax effects. If Morall buys the equipment, it receives the investment tax credit and cost recovery benefits. If it leases, these benefits remain with the lessor; Morall can deduct only the lease payments on its tax return. Using Morall's cost of capital, 16%, Exhibit 9-12 shows the cost of leasing

**EXHIBIT 9-12 After-Tax Cost of Buying versus Leasing**

Cost of leasing: ($100,000)(0.7) + ($100,000)(0.7)(2.798) = $265,860

Cost of buying: $400,000 − $40,000(0.862) − $73,330[a] = $292,190

[a]This is the present value of the ACRS benefits. Because the investment tax credit applies, the net investment subject to recovery is $400,000 − 0.5(40,000) = $380,000. Using the recovery percentages from Exhibit 9-5 and the present value factors for a 16% cost of capital yields:

($380,000)(0.3)(0.15)(0.862) + ($380,000)(0.3)(0.22)(0.743)
+ ($380,000)(0.3)(0.21)(0.641) + ($380,000)(0.3)(0.21)(0.552)
+ ($380,000)(0.3)(0.21)(0.476) = $73,330

versus the cost of buying. The lease payments are discounted on an after-tax basis. The cost of buying is reduced by the present value of the benefits from the investment tax credit and accelerated cost recovery. In this case, leasing is less expensive than buying the asset. A further consideration, however, has to do with the fact that the leasing company keeps the equipment upon expiration of the lease. Morall's management should consider this in its decision.

Morall's management is considering taking a loan from a bank at 10% with five equal annual payments. Is this preferable to leasing? First, an amortization schedule must be prepared. Each payment consists of principal, which is not tax deductible, and interest, which is deductible. The amortization schedule is shown in Exhibit 9-13. The annual payments are $105,519. The schedule shows the loan balance at the beginning of the year, the amount of each payment that goes to interest and principal, and the loan balance at the end of the year.

Borrowing to purchase the equipment differs from Morall's purchase without borrowing (Exhibit 9-12) in that the $400,000 loan proceeds (positive) are offset by the $400,000 purchase (negative). However, the 16% cost of capital is still used to discount the interest (after consideration of taxes) and the principal repayments. This is combined with the investment tax credit and cost recovery benefits in Exhibit 9-14.

Comparing Exhibits 9-12 and 9-14, the cost of borrowing to acquire the equipment is less than the cost of leasing by approximately $55,000. In addition, Morall will get to keep the equipment for continued use or disposal as it sees fit. Taking the facts as given, then, Morall should borrow the funds and buy the equipment.

Leasing is usually more complex than discussed here. For example, there may be room to negotiate on a lease since the lessor gets tax benefits in addition to the imputed interest on the lease. For this reason, it is not uncommon to find a lessor willing to charge less than the apparent going

**EXHIBIT 9-13 Amortization Schedule**

| Year | Beginning Balance | Interest | Principal | Ending Balance |
|---|---|---|---|---|
| 1 | $400,000 | $40,000 | $65,519 | $334,481 |
| 2 | 334,481 | 33,448 | 72,071 | 262,410 |
| 3 | 262,410 | 26,241 | 79,278 | 183,132 |
| 4 | 183,132 | 18,313 | 87,206 | 95,926 |
| 5 | 95,926 | 9,593 | 95,926 | 0 |

**EXHIBIT 9-14 Borrowing to Purchase Equipment**

| Year | | |
|---|---|---|
| 1 | (\$40,000)(0.7)(0.862) + (\$65,519)(0.862) = | \$ 80,613 |
| 2 | (\$33,448)(0.7)(0.743) + (\$72,071)(0.743) = | 70,945 |
| 3 | (\$26,241)(0.7)(0.641) + (\$79,278)(0.641) = | 62,592 |
| 4 | (\$18,313)(0.7)(0.552) + (\$87,206)(0.552) = | 55,214 |
| 5 | (\$ 9,593)(0.7)(0.476) + (\$95,926)(0.476) = | 48,857 |
| | Cost of borrowing | \$318,221 |
| | Less: | |
| | Present value of investment tax credit (\$40,000)(0.862) | − 34,480 |
| | Present value of ACRS (from Exhibit 9-12) | − 73,330 |
| | Cost of borrowing to buy | \$210,411 |

rate of interest; the difference is made up through the tax benefits of ownership by the lessor.

## SUMMARY

In this chapter we have discussed some of the complications that arise when making capital budgeting decisions. We saw that the ranking of investment opportunities can be difficult if investments have different lives, are mutually exclusive, or involve indivisibilities. Most of these problems would go away if the firm had unlimited investment funds, but as a practical matter this is rarely the case.

The chapter also briefly discussed the measurement of the cost of capital and the adjustments needed in the basic discounted cash flow analysis for risk and inflation. Finally we discussed the effects of income taxes on capital budgeting decisions. Although taxes do not change the basic analysis, they can have a significant effect on the amount and timing of cash flows.

## DEMONSTRATION PROBLEM

Jones Health Club, Inc., is looking to expand and modernize (automate) its facilities. Owing to the competitiveness of the industry, such improvements are thought to have an ACRS life of only 5 years (the IRS agrees). Income taxes are 30% and the firm requires a 20% rate of return after taxes. The following items are thought by the firm's president to be relevant to the decision as to whether to proceed or not.

**a.** The firm owns its building, which has a book value of $100,000 and a market value of $350,000. It is being depreciated on a straight-line basis and has a remaining life of 10 years. The firm does not intend to dispose of the property in the foreseeable future.
**b.** A portion of the building is being rented to a tenant at $60,000 per year, payable in full at the start of the year. However, the tenant will abandon the premises at any time on receipt of $20,000 plus a refund of any prepaid rent. The lease has 3 years to run, at which time it is expected that the tenant will relocate. If Jones takes over, it will do so at the beginning of the 3-year period.
**c.** A consulting firm has been paid $20,000 to do the market research concerning the proposed expansion and modernization.
**d.** Promotion costs to advertise the expansion will be $100,000 immediately and $50,000 at the end of each of the next 4 years.
**e.** If expansion takes place, working capital of $50,000 will be needed at the outset. This will be recovered at the end of the 5-year period.
**f.** Direct and indirect labor costs are expected to be $200,000 less per year as a result of automation (machines will replace massagers and videotapes will replace counselors).
**g.** Increased revenues each year are expected to be as follows: $300,000; $400,000; $500,000; $350,000; $200,000. These are all contract receivables that the firm sells to a finance company at 80% of face value.
**h.** If expansion takes place, it will cost $650,000 now to acquire equipment. The time required is minimal because of the availability and portability of the equipment sought. The equipment falls in the ACRS 5-year property class, and the investment tax credit applies.

**Required**

The president of the firm requests that you prepare a formal analysis of the proposal under consideration for purposes of assisting in the decision of whether the firm should expand.

**Solution**

The solution that follows is in two parts. First, Exhibit 9-15 determines the timing and amount of cash flows on an after-tax basis for each of the items (a) through (h) just listed. Second, Exhibit 9-16 combines this information with the appropriate present value factors to determine the net present value of the investment. (*Note:* The solution that follows employs a format that is very useful for organizing data where complex capital budgeting problems are involved, whether in real life or in the classroom.) Observe that the format employed permits solving the problem either by rows, using both the amount and annuity tables, or by columns, using the amount table only. For purposes of illustration, this problem has been solved both ways. In both cases the conclusion is the same: The firm should undertake the investment because it has a positive net present value in excess of $217,000.

**EXHIBIT 9-15 Determining Net Cash Flows after Taxes**

**a.** This item is irrelevant since it will not be affected by the decision. The firm does not intend to dispose of the property (it is a sunk cost).

**b.** (1) If Jones expands, the rentals will be lost (this is an opportunity cost). The after-tax cash loss is $42,000 beginning immediately. The first rental has a present value factor of 1.000 and the remaining two constitute an ordinary annuity. (2) Additionally, on a net-of-tax basis, the cost of breaking the lease is $14,000 = $20,000(1 − 0.30).

**c.** This is irrelevant to the decision since the cost has already been incurred (sunk cost) and is deductible whether or not expansion ensues.

**d.** The after-tax costs of promotion are (1) $70,000 now and (2) $35,000 for the next 4 years.

**e.** This is not an expense on either the income statement or the tax return; it is a commitment of current assets. (1) The outlay is $50,000 now and (2) it will be returned in 5 years.

**f.** The net-of-tax savings are $140,000 each year since this is a tax-deductible item.

**g.** The firm receives 80% of the face value of the contracts. However, given taxes, the firm gets to keep only 70% of this amount. The after-tax cash flow each year is as follows:

| Year | Key | Amount |
|---|---|---|
| 1 | g(1) | $300,000 × 0.8 × 0.7 = $168,000 |
| 2 | g(2) | 400,000 × 0.8 × 0.7 = 224,000 |
| 3 | g(3) | 500,000 × 0.8 × 0.7 = 280,000 |
| 4 | g(4) | 350,000 × 0.8 × 0.7 = 196,000 |
| 5 | g(5) | 200,000 × 0.8 × 0.7 = 112,000 |

**h.** (1) There is an immediate outlay, of course, of $650,000. (2) The investment tax credit amounting to $65,000 is treated as an inflow in year 1. The cost to be recovered is $650,000 less one-half the investment tax credit, or $617,500.

Each year's tax savings from cost recovery is as follows:

| Year | Key | Amount |
|---|---|---|
| 1 | h(3) | $617,500 × 0.15 × 0.3 = $27,787.50 |
| 2 | h(4) | 617,500 × 0.22 × 0.3 = 40,755.00 |
| 3 | h(5) | 617,500 × 0.21 × 0.3 = 38,902.50 |
| 4 | h(6) | 617,500 × 0.21 × 0.3 = 38,902.50 |
| 5 | h(7) | 617,500 × 0.21 × 0.3 = 38,902.50 |

**EXHIBIT 9-16 Determining Net Present Value**

| | Amount and Timing of After-Tax Cash Flows | | | | | | | |
|---|---|---|---|---|---|---|---|---|
| Key | 0 | 1 | 2 | 3 | 4 | 5 | Present Value Factor | Present Value |
| b(1) | − 42,000 | − 42,000 | − 42,000 | | | | 2.528 | −106,176 |
| b(2) | − 14,000 | | | | | | 1.000 | − 14,000 |
| d(1) | − 70,000 | | | | | | 1.000 | − 70,000 |
| d(2) | | − 35,000 | − 35,000 | − 35,000 | − 35,000 | | 2.589 | − 90,615 |
| e(1) | − 50,000 | | | | | | 1.000 | − 50,000 |
| e(2) | | | | | | + 50,000 | 0.402 | + 20,100 |
| f | | +140,000 | +140,000 | +140,000 | +140,000 | +140,000 | 2.991 | +418,740 |
| g(1) | | +168,000 | | | | | 0.833 | +139,944 |
| g(2) | | | +224,000 | | | | 0.694 | +155,456 |
| g(3) | | | | +280,000 | | | 0.579 | +162,120 |
| g(4) | | | | | +196,000 | | 0.482 | + 94,472 |
| g(5) | | | | | | +112,000 | 0.402 | + 45,024 |
| h(1) | −650,000 | | | | | | 1.000 | −650,000 |
| h(2) | | + 65,000 | | | | | 0.833 | + 54,145 |
| h(3) | | + 27,787.5 | | | | | 0.833 | + 23,147 |
| h(4) | | | + 40,755 | | | | 0.694 | + 28,284 |
| h(5) | | | | + 38,902.5 | | | 0.579 | + 22,525 |
| h(6) | | | | | + 38,902.5 | | 0.482 | + 18,751 |
| h(7) | | | | | | + 38,902.5 | 0.402 | + 15,639 |
| | | | | | | | | +217,556 |
| Cash flow by year | −826,000 | +323,787.5 | +327,755 | +423,902.5 | +339,902.5 | +340,902.5 | | |
| × present value factor | 1.000 | 0.833 | 0.694 | 0.579 | 0.482 | 0.402 | | |
| Present value | −826,000 | +269,715 | +227,462 | +245,440 | +163,833 | +137,043 | Total = | +217,493 |

CONCLUSION: Solving the problem by rows yields a positive net present value of $217,556; by columns, the net present value is positive $217,493. The difference is due to rounding of present value factors in the table.

## KEY TERMS AND CONCEPTS

Cost of capital
Depreciation tax shield
Recovery property
Accelerated cost recovery system
Half-year convention
Investment tax credit

## FURTHER READING


Bartley, Jon W. "A NPV Model Modified for Inflation," *Management Accounting* (December 1980), p. 49.

Duncan, Ian D. "The Leasing Issue—Some Important Considerations," *Cost and Management* (March–April 1980), p. 21.

Glahn, Gerald L., Kent T. Fields, and Jerry E. Trapnell. "How to Evaluate Mixed Risk Capital Projects," *Management Accounting* (December 1980), p. 34.

Hendricks, James A. "Capital Budgeting Decisions: NPV or IRR?" *Cost and Management* (March–April 1980), p. 16.

Rege, Udayan, and George C. Baxter. "Weighted Average Cost of Capital: A Tool for Decision Making," *Cost and Management* (May–June 1982), p. 36.

Sale, J. Timothy, and Robert W. Scapens. "The Control of Capital Investment in Divisionalized Companies," *Management Accounting* (October 1982), p. 24.

Sangeladji, Mohammad A. "True Rate of Return for Evaluating Capital Investments," *Management Accounting* (February 1979), p. 24.

Singhvi, Surendra, and Robert J. Lambrix. "Investment Versus Financing Decisions," *Management Accounting* (March 1984), p. 54.


## QUESTIONS AND EXERCISES

**9-1** How might inflation influence a decision to acquire an asset now rather than later?

**9-2** If a firm has access to unlimited funds, what criterion should be used to determine which projects to invest in?

**9-3** A publisher sells subscriptions in advance to a quarterly newsletter for $400 per year. Income is recognized in the quarter the magazine is mailed. If taxes are 20% and are paid quarterly, what are the quarterly cash flows associated with subscriptions?

**9-4** Equipment is sold. It was held for its class life. What cash flows are associated with this transaction?

**9-5** An existing piece of equipment is sold at a loss. What two inflows will be associated with its disposition?

**9-6** A firm employs a discount rate of 10% for all investments with a life of 10 years or less. It adds 1% to the discount rate for each year of life beyond 10 years (e.g., for an asset with an 18-year life, the firm uses 18%). The explanation given is: "This is our way of handling uncertainty. The longer-lived the investment, the greater the uncertainty concerning the cash inflows; we cope with uncertainty by increasing the required rate of return." Comment.

**9-7** An international firm requires a rate of return of 15% domestically and in developed countries, but 25% in less developed countries. How would you explain this in a manner that does not lead to the conclusion that the firm is exploiting LDCs?

**9-8** A firm that uses accrual accounting receives cash from a customer this period but will not recognize it as revenue until next period. How would this be handled in the context of a capital budgeting problem employing a net-of-tax approach?

**9-9** A well-known clinic in the Midwest is a nonprofit organization. Typical capital expenditure decisions involve acquiring equipment that will perform medical tests beyond those currently possible at the clinic (hence, adding revenues) and/or perform tests more efficiently than currently (hence, decreasing expenses). To evaluate such expenditures, the clinic uses an interest rate equal to the return on its investment trust portfolio. Briefly, explain why they do so.

**9-10** An earlier chapter demonstrated that for CVP decisions involving taxes, it is sometimes convenient to convert an after-tax income objective to an equivalent before-tax income figure. Why is it not appropriate to convert an after-tax required rate of return to a before-tax rate of return in capital budgeting? (For example, if the firm requires a 10% return after taxes of 50%, why not use a 20% return before taxes and ignore the specific tax effects?)

**9-11** Refer to the demonstration problem at the end of the chapter to respond to each of the independent situations that follow. Calculate the effect on net present value if: (a) the optional straight-line method for 5 years was used instead of ACRS; (b) only 80% of the invested working capital was recovered at the end of 5 years; and (c) the equipment was sold for approximately $100,000 at the end of 5 years.

**9-12** Use the computer program IRR to determine the internal rate of return for the demonstration problem at the end of the chapter.

**9-13** Answer the following: (a) A firm is considering contracting with a motivation specialist to lead certain seminars. The cost to the firm is $40,000 per year. If the firm is taxed at a 32% rate, what is the annual after-tax cost? (b) A local grocery has installed video games in previously unused space. The games bring in $2,000 per week and the store gets 60% of this. If its tax rate is 38%, what is the weekly after-tax cash flow? (c) A firm acquires equipment costing $80,000, which is in a 5-year ACRS class. The firm requires a 10% return after taxes of 40%. What is the present value of the cash savings from cost recovery? (d) Refer to (c). If the property is in a 10-year ACRS class, what is the present value of the cash savings from cost recovery? (e) Refer to (c). If the property is in a 5-year class and the 5-year optional straight-line method is used, what is the present value of the cash savings from cost recovery? (f) How do you reconcile the differences in your answers to (c), (d), and (e)?

**9-14** A firm invests $200,000 in equipment that will generate operating savings of $50,000 (before cost recovery and taxes) per year for 10 years. The firm has elected to use the optional straight-line method and is in a 30% tax bracket. For simplicity, use a 10-year life and ignore the half-year convention. You are to determine on an after-tax basis (a) the annual net cash flow, (b) the payback period, and (c) the internal or time-adjusted rate of return.

**9-15** Equipment with a cost of $60,000 will, if acquired, generate annual savings of $30,000 for 6 years, at which time it will have no further use or value. For cost recovery purposes, the asset is in the 5-year class. The investment credit applies. The firm is taxed at a composite (state and federal) rate of 40% and requires a 10% return after taxes. Find (a) the after-tax cash flow for each year, (b) the net present value of this investment, and (c) the payback period.

**9-16** A firm has acquired an asset at a cost of $100,000. It has a 10-year class life. The firm requires a 20% return and is subject to a 30% tax rate. Management is undecided as to whether to use the ACRS tables or to use the optional straight-line method. Which of the two will maximize the present value of the benefits from cost recovery, and by how much?

**9-17** Use the computer programs NPV and IRR to verify the results for each of the seven proposals shown in Exhibit 9-1.

**9-18** Use the computer program PYMTSCH to verify the amortization schedule in Exhibit 9-13 and the program IRR to verify the interest rate.

**9-19** A firm requires a real rate of return of 22%. One of its subsidiaries operates in a country that has an inflation rate of 28%. What is the inflation-adjusted rate of return to be required of this subsidiary?

**9-20** Donquis Corporation is considering acquiring equipment for use in research and development. The equipment costs $80,000 and is expected to have a useful life of 13 years; however, Donquis expects to sell the equipment to a foreign country for $30,000 in 5 years. The investment tax credit applies. Determine the present value of the benefits associated with this equipment, assuming a 15% required rate of return and a tax rate of 30%.

**9-21** A firm has $40,000 to invest and will select from one of three projects, as follows:

| | Project A | Project B | Project C |
|---|---|---|---|
| Equipment outlay[a] | $40,000 | $30,000 | $10,000 |
| Working capital | — | 10,000 | 30,000 |
| Annual after-tax savings[a] | 15,000 | 12,000 | 10,000 |

[a]The tax effects have already been considered.

Each alternative has a 5-year life. If the firm requires a 20% return after taxes, which project should be selected?

**9-22** Jackson Industries has $50,000 available to invest in new equipment. Management is considering four different equipment investments, each of which requires $50,000. The expected after-tax cash flow for each project has been estimated as

| | Year | | | | | |
|---|---|---|---|---|---|---|
| | 1 | 2 | 3 | 4 | 5 | 6 |
| Project 1 | $10,000 | $12,000 | $14,000 | $16,000 | $16,000 | $16,000 |
| Project 2 | 40,000 | 5,000 | (3,000) | 40,000 | 5,000 | 1,000 |
| Project 3 | 18,000 | (16,000) | 50,000 | 50,000 | 3,000 | 3,000 |
| Project 4 | 30,000 | — | — | 30,000 | 30,000 | 30,000 |

Rank-order the projects in terms of desirability using the internal rate of return for each project as the criterion. The use of the computer program IRR for calculating internal rates of return is suggested. Are there other factors that should be considered in actually making the decision of which investment to choose?

**9-23** Phinco's capital structure and the cost of each component is as follows:

| | Proportion of Equity | Current Yield |
|---|---|---|
| Common stock | 60% | 15% dividend |
| Preferred stock | 10% | 10% dividend |
| Bonds | 30% | 12% interest |

What is Phinco's weighted average cost of capital if the effective tax rate on its income is 20%?

**9-24** The financial structure of Kadok Corporation follows.

| | | |
|---|---|---|
| Notes | $ 200,000 | (14% interest) |
| Bonds | 300,000 | (10% interest) |
| Stock | 1,000,000 | (15% return) |

The firm is in a 30% tax bracket. (a) What is the after-tax cost of capital? (b) What is the after-tax cost of capital if bonds are issued at 10% to repay the notes?

**9-25** Weeknight Enterprises is considering one of three investments, each of which requires $100,000. The first will return $50,000 at the end of each of three years; the second will return $70,000 at the end of each of two years; and the third will return $175,000 at the end of three years. If Weeknight's cost of capital is 15%, which alternative should be recommended?

**9-26** A firm has offered $2 million for a small parcel of prime commercial real estate. The owner refuses to sell but is willing to lease the property for 25 years. The firm's cost of capital is 12% after taxes of 30%. Had the firm been able to purchase the property, it expected to sell it in 25 years for $5 million. What amount should the firm be willing to pay annually to lease the property?

**9-27** An insurance company promises to pay a real interest rate (net of inflation) of 3%. The long-term inflation rate is expected to average 6% per year for the next 50 years. On your twentieth birthday you wish to invest an amount of money with the insurance company sufficient to return the equivalent of $1 million in today's purchasing power, on your seventieth birthday. (a) What is the nominal amount of dollars that you will receive at age 70 (i.e., dollars with a substantially reduced purchasing power)? (b) How much must be invested at age 20 to receive the equivalent of $1 million in today's terms, at age 70? (c) If the insurance company actually earns a real rate of return (net of inflation) of 4% and defers its recognition of profit until it pays you off on your seventieth birthday, what will the insurance company's profit be in nominal dollars? (d) If the insurance company will earn a real rate of return of 4%, how much of your investment can the insurance company consume immediately and still be able to pay you off from the proceeds of the investment of the remainder of your payment?

## PROBLEMS AND CASES

**9-28 Capital budgeting: Two criteria.**
Palmer, Inc., has sufficient opportunities available that it requires a payback of 6 years and a rate of return of 20% (after taxes of 35%). It is considering acquiring equipment costing $80,000 that will result in annual labor savings of $14,000 and material savings of $5,000 over present methods. The salvage value of the equipment after 10 years is approximately equal to its removal costs, $5,000. The asset has a 5-year ACRS class life and the investment tax credit applies.

**Required**
Should the investment be made? Explain your answer.

**9-29 Investment in inventory.**
Foster, Inc., has been purchasing a particular part from a supplier for $100 each. It typically receives 1,000 units at the beginning of the month and makes payment at the end of the month. The supplier has offered to cut the price to $90 if Foster will purchase a 6-month supply at a time and make payment at the time of delivery. Ordering costs, storage costs, and so forth are nominal and can be ignored. Foster requires a monthly return of 2% after taxes of 30%.

**Required**
Should the firm invest in inventory? Explain your answer.

**9-30 Determination of cost, given taxes.**
A firm is considering an investment in new equipment that will be used for research and development. The equipment will generate savings before cost recovery and taxes of $40,000 per year for 8 years, at which time it will have only nominal salvage value. The firm requires a return of 15% after taxes and is subject to a tax rate of 30%. The investment tax credit applies.

**Required**
What is the maximum amount it should pay for the equipment?

**9-31 Various approaches to capital budgeting** (CMA adapted).
Hazman Company plans to replace an old piece of equipment that is obsolete and is expected to be unreliable under the stress of daily operations. The equipment is fully depreciated, and no salvage value can be realized upon its disposal.

One piece of new equipment being considered would provide annual cash savings of $7,000 before income taxes. The equipment would cost $18,000 and have an estimated useful life of 5 years. No salvage value would be used for depreciation purposes because the equipment is expected to have no value at the end of 5 years.

Hazman uses the straight-line depreciation method on all equipment for both book and tax purposes. The firm will use a 5-year life, will ignore the half-year convention, and cannot take an investment tax credit on this equipment. The company is subject to a 40% tax rate. Hazman has an after-tax cost of capital of 14%.

**Required**

**a.** For Hazman Company's proposed investment in new equipment, calculate the after-tax

**1.** Payback period.
**2.** Average rate of return.
**3.** Net present value.
**4.** Profitability (present value) index.
**5.** Internal rate of return.

Assume that all operating revenues and expenses occur at the end of the year.

**b.** Identify and discuss the issues Hazman Company should consider when deciding which of the five decision models identified in (a) it should employ to compare and evaluate alternative capital investment projects.

**9-32 Real property—computer recommended.**

In the fifth month of its fiscal year, a firm acquired a new building at a cost of $15.3 million. The building is in an 18-year class life. The firm is taxed at a rate of 35% and requires a 22% return on its investments after taxes.

**Required**

Calculate the present value of the after-tax cost recovery benefits under both ACRS and the optional straight-line method for 18 years.

**9-33 Capital rationing and project selection—computer recommended.**

Eloco, Inc., has a pleasant problem in that it has more investment opportunities than it can accept. It has $200 (000s omitted) available and its cost of capital is 11%. The projects and their cash flows are as follows:

| | Projects | | | | | |
|---|---|---|---|---|---|---|
| **Year** | **A** | **B** | **C** | **D** | **E** | **F** |
| 0 | $(50) | $(25) | $(50) | $(100) | $(25) | $(50) |
| 1 | 15 | 10 | 0 | 20 | 0 | 10 |
| 2 | 15 | 10 | 0 | 20 | 0 | 20 |
| 3 | 15 | 10 | 20 | 20 | 0 | 40 |
| 4 | 15 | 10 | 20 | 20 | 30 | |
| 5 | 15 | | 40 | 20 | 30 | |
| 6 | 15 | | | 50 | | |

**Required**

Which projects should Eloco fund?

**9-34 Net present value** (CPA adapted).
On January 15, Studley Company purchased a new machine for $100,000 with an estimated useful life of 5 years and a $1,000 salvage value. For tax purposes the asset has a 5-year class life and its cost will be recovered using the 5-year optional straight-line method. The annual cash flow from operations will increase by $40,000 before taxes. Studley's minimum rate of return is 12% after taxes of 40%.

**Required**
What is the net present value of the machine?

**9-35 Internal rate of return—computer recommended.**
For Problem 9-34, use the computer program IRR to determine the internal rate of return.

**9-36 Alternative technologies and capital budgeting.**
Lymbo, Inc., must install safety devices throughout its plant or it will lose its insurance coverage. Two alternatives are acceptable to the insurer. The first costs $100,000 to install and $20,000 to maintain annually. The second costs $150,000 to install and $10,000 to maintain annually. Both are in a 5-year class life and are expected to have useful lives of 15 years. The ITC applies. Lymbo's cost of capital is 12% after taxes of 30%.

**Required**
**a.** Which system should be installed? Why?
**b.** If Lymbo were a not-for-profit organization, which system would be installed?

**9-37 Determining before-tax savings.**
Astech Shoppes is considering whether to computerize its billing and collection procedures. The firm is willing to spend as much as $150,000 to acquire the necessary equipment with related peripherals and software. The investment tax credit would be taken. The equipment would have a 5-year useful life as well as class life. Astech requires a 10% return after taxes of 40%.

**Required**
What must be the minimum annual savings before taxes to justify spending $150,000 for this purpose?

**9-38 Cost of capital and taxes.**
The balance sheet of Tudor Auto Imports shows the following equities.

| | | Cost |
|---|---|---|
| Short-term debt | $300,000 | 16% |
| Bonds payable | 400,000 | 13% |
| Leases | 200,000 | 14% |
| Preferred stock | 500,000 | 8% |
| Common stock | 900,000 | 20% |

The short-term debt represents revolving credit, which is periodically renewed. Income taxes from all sources average 25%.

**Required**
What is Tudor's weighted-average cost of capital?

**9-39 Cost of capital with taxes and inflation.**
The equity section of the balance sheet for Marrsco appears below.

| | Proportion | Cost |
|---|---|---|
| Current liabilities | 20% | [a] |
| Noncurrent liabilities | 25% | 12% |
| Preferred stock | 15% | 8% |
| Common stock | 40% | 16% |

[a] A 2% discount is received if payment is made within 30 days of purchase.

**Required**

**a.** What is the weighted average cost of capital if taxes average 30%?
**b.** If inflation is projected at 6% annually, what is the inflation-adjusted cost of capital?

**9-40 Equipment replacement: Net present value and sum-of-the-years'-digits** (CMA adapted).
The WRL Company makes cookies for its chain of snack food stores. On January 2, 19X1, WRL Company purchased a special cookie-cutting machine; this machine has been used for 3 years. The firm is considering the purchase of a newer, more efficient machine. If purchased, the new machine would be acquired on January 2, 19X4. WRL Company expects to sell 300,000 dozen cookies in each of the next 4 years. The selling price of the cookies is expected to average $0.50 per dozen.

WRL Company has two options: (1) continue to operate the old machine, or (2) sell the old machine and purchase the new machine. No trade-in was offered by the seller of the new machine. The following information has been assembled to help decide which option is more desirable.

| | Old Machine | New Machine |
|---|---|---|
| Original cost of machine at acquisition | $80,000 | $120,000 |
| Salvage value at the end of useful life for depreciation purposes | $10,000 | $ 20,000 |
| Useful life from date of acquisition | 7 years | 4 years |
| Expected annual cash operating expenses | | |
| Variable cost per dozen | $0.20 | $0.14 |
| Total fixed costs | $15,000 | $ 14,000 |
| Depreciation method used for tax purposes | Straight-line | Sum-of-the-years'-digits |
| Estimated cash value of machines | | |
| January 2, 19X4 | $40,000 | $120,000 |
| December 31, 19X7 | $ 7,000 | $ 20,000 |

WRL Company is subject to an overall income tax rate of 40%. Assume that all operating revenues and expenses occur at the end of the year. Assume that any gain or loss on the sale of machinery is treated as an ordinary tax item and will affect the taxes paid by the company at the end of the year in which it occurred. Ignore the half-year convention, ACRS, and the investment tax credit.

**Required**

**a.** Use the net present value method to determine whether WRL Company should retain the old machine or acquire the new machine. WRL requires an after-tax return of 16%.

**b.** Without prejudice to your answer to (a), assume that the quantitative differences are so slight between the two alternatives that WRL Company is indifferent to the two proposals. Identify and discuss the important nonquantitative factors that the company should consider.

**c.** Identify and discuss the advantages and disadvantages of using the discounted cash flow techniques (e.g., the net present value method) for capital investment decisions.

**9-41 Capital investment with labor savings and taxes.**
Two friends formed a commercial fishing partnership. They are considering a proposal whereby an improved automated trawl, costing $30,000, will permit them to eliminate two employees whose combined gross annual earnings are $8,000. In other words, if they make the investment, it will reduce cash outflows from operations annually by $8,000 *before* cost recovery and taxes.

Salvage value is expected to be nil. The trawl, a new and improved type, is expected to last 10 years and falls in the 5-year ACRS class. The investment tax credit applies. They are taxed at an effective rate (state plus federal) of 40%.

**Required**

At 20% after taxes, what is the net present value of this proposal?

**9-42 Equipment replacement, with taxes.**
Graffiti, Inc., produces and sells wallpaper. It is considering an equipment replacement proposal. The following data are available.

| Existing Equipment | | Proposed Equipment | |
|---|---|---|---|
| Undepreciated cost | $5,000 | Invoice cost | $10,000 |
| Annual operating costs[a] | $8,000 | Annual operating costs[a] | $ 6,000 |
| Remaining life | 5 years | Expected life (also class life) | 5 years |
| Annual depreciation (straight-line) | $1,000 | Annual depreciation (straight-line) | $ 1,900 |
| Residual at end of life | — | Residual at end of life | — |
| Salvage now | $1,000 | | |

[a]These are the cash costs concerned with operating the equipment.

All of the foregoing data are on a before-tax basis. Graffiti, Inc., requires a 10% return after taxes. The firm is subject to taxes of 30% on income, including gains or losses; gains or losses are recognized immediately for tax purposes. The 10% investment tax credit applies and will be taken immediately. Ignore the half-year convention.

**Required**

**a.** What is the net cash outlay required to acquire the new machine?

**b.** Using the incremental approach, what is the present value of the after-tax cash flow advantage from cost recovery to the new equipment? (Use the optional straight-line method for 5 years and ignore the half-year convention.)

**c.** Using the incremental approach, what is the present value of the after-tax cash flow advantage from operating savings to the new equipment?

**d.** What is the net present value of this proposal?

**e.** What is the approximate internal rate of return (or time-adjusted rate of return) on this project?

**9-43 Real property.**

Methla, Inc., has acquired property at a cost of $63 million in the seventh month of its fiscal year. Ninety percent of the cost has been allocated to the building and the remaining 10% has been allocated to the land. The building is expected to have a useful life of 25 years, at which time it and the land can be sold for approximately what it cost (due to inflation). Methla is subject to an average tax rate of 33% and requires an 18% rate of return after taxes.

**Required**

**a.** What is the amount of the investment tax credit to which Methla is entitled?

**b.** What is the present value of the proceeds to be obtained when the building and land are sold, given the assumption that the tax rate and required rate of return continue?

**c.** Using the minimum class life permissible, calculate the after-tax present value of cost recovery using ACRS and the optional straight-line method.

**9-44 Capital expenditure, with income taxes.**

The management of Maize Products, Inc., is considering the purchase of special equipment that will permit Maize to manufacture a part it now purchases from an outside supplier.

The equipment will cost $55,000 installed, has no residual or scrap value, and will last approximately 10 years. Its cost will be recovered using the optional straight-line method (ignore the half-year convention and assume a 10-year period).

The predicted annual operating savings from manufacturing (without considering cost recovery) as opposed to buying are $12,000. The firm's minimum desired rate of return is *10% after taxes*; income taxes average 40% for Maize.

**Required**

**a.** By how much will cost recovery decrease the outlay of cash for income taxes annually?

**b.** What is the net after-tax annual cash flow?

**c.** What is the net present value of this investment?

**d.** What is the internal rate of return?

**e.** What is the profitability index?

**f.** If ACRS had been used employing a 5-year class life, what would be the effect on each of your answers above? You do not have to calculate.

**9-45 Conventional straight-line depreciation.**

A U.S. corporation has a subsidiary in the country of Cunfoo. For purposes of taxation, Cunfoo requires that depreciation be based on useful life and the conventional straight-line method of depreciation is mandatory. The subsidiary is considering production of a new product that will increase cash flow (before taxes) by 200,000 yen per year. The life of the product is expected to be 10 years. The required equipment has a cost of 500,000 yen and no expected salvage value. Income taxes in Cunfoo are 10%. The subsidiary is required to earn the firm's worldwide rate of 20%.

**Required**

**a.** Annual cash flow
**b.** Net present value
**c.** Internal rate of return using the approximating table (Exhibit 8-2)
**d.** Present value index or ratio
**e.** Payback
**f.** Payback reciprocal
**g.** Unadjusted rate of return

**9-46 Equipment replacement.**
Capend Company is considering replacing a durable, but antiquated, piece of equipment that it has had for 20 years. Cost and operating data concerning the existing and proposed equipment are as follows:

| Existing Equipment | | Proposed Equipment | |
|---|---|---|---|
| Book value | $12,000 | Invoice cost | $20,000 |
| Annual operating costs | $24,000 | Annual operating costs | $18,000 |
| Useful life | 6 years | Useful life | 6 years |
| Residual value | $ 2,000 now; zero in 6 years | Residual value | $ 2,000 |

Income taxes average 25% and the firm requires a 20% rate of return after taxes. Gains or losses on disposition of equipment are taken for tax purposes. The optional straight-line method is used for cost recovery purposes (use a 5-year class life). The investment tax credit applies. The old equipment is being depreciated $2,000 per year using conventional straight-line depreciation.

**Required**

Using the net present value approach, determine whether Capend should make the investment.

**9-47 Acquisition of equipment** (CMA adapted).
Wyle Company is considering a proposal to acquire new manufacturing equipment. The new equipment has the same capacity as the current equipment but will provide operating efficiencies in direct and indirect labor, direct material usage, indirect supplies, and power. Consequently, the savings in operating costs are estimated at $150,000 annually.

The new equipment will cost $300,000 and will be purchased at the beginning of the year when the project is started. The equipment dealer is certain that the equipment will be operational during the second quarter of the year it is installed. Therefore, 60% of the estimated annual savings can be obtained in the first year. Wyle will incur a one-time expense of $30,000 to transfer the production activities from the old equipment to the new equipment (these costs are not eligible for the investment tax credit but are eligible for ACRS). No loss of sales will occur, however, because the plant is large enough to install the new equipment without interfering with the operations of the current equipment. The equipment dealer states that most companies use a 5-year life when depreciating this equipment.

The current equipment has been fully depreciated and is carried in the accounts at zero book value. Management has reviewed the condition of the current equipment and has concluded that it can be used an additional 5 years. Wyle Company would receive $5,000 net of removal costs if it elected to buy the new equipment and dispose of its current equipment at this time.

Wyle currently leases its manufacturing plant. The annual lease payments are $60,000. The lease, which will have 4 years remaining when the equipment installation would begin, is not renewable. Wyle Company would be required to remove any equipment in the plant at the end of the lease. The cost of equipment removal is expected to equal the salvage value of either the old or new equipment at the time of removal. The equipment is in the 5-year cost-recovery class.

The company is subject to a 40% income tax rate and requires an after-tax return of at least 12% on any investment.

**Required**

**a.** Calculate the annual incremental after-tax cash flows for Wyle Company's proposal to acquire the new manufacturing equipment.

**b.** Calculate the net present value of Wyle Company's proposal to acquire the new manufacturing equipment using the cash flows calculated in (a) and indicate what action Wyle Company's management should take. For ease in calculation, assume that all recurring cash flows take place at the end of the year.

**9-48 Equipment acquisition** (CMA adapted).

The Baxter Company manufactures toys and other short-lived fad-type items. The research and development department came up with an item that would make a good promotional gift for office equipment dealers. Aggressive and effective effort by Baxter's sales personnel has resulted in almost firm commitments for this product for the next 3 years. It is expected that the product's value will be exhausted by that time.

In order to produce the quantity demanded, Baxter will need to buy additional machinery and rent some additional space. It appears that about 25,000 square feet will be needed; currently available are 12,500 square feet of presently unused, but leased, space. (Baxter's present lease, with 10 years to run, costs $3.00 a foot.) There is another 12,500 square feet adjoining the Baxter facility that Baxter will rent for 3 years at $4.00 per square foot per year if it decides to make this product.

The equipment will be purchased for about $900,000. It will require $30,000 in modifications, $60,000 for installation, and $90,000 for testing; all of these activities will be handled by a firm of engineers hired by Baxter. All of the expenditures will be paid for on January 1, 19X3. Ignore the investment tax credit.

The equipment should have a salvage value of about $180,000 at the end of the third year. No additional general overhead costs are expected to be incurred.

The following estimates of revenues and expenses as they would be reported on the firm's external financial statements for this product for the 3 years have been developed.

| | 19X3 | 19X4 | 19X5 |
|---|---|---|---|
| Sales | $1,000,000 | $1,600,000 | $800,000 |
| Material, labor, and incurred overhead | 400,000 | 750,000 | 350,000 |
| Assigned general overhead | 40,000 | 75,000 | 35,000 |
| Rent | 87,500 | 87,500 | 87,500 |
| Depreciation | 450,000 | 300,000 | 150,000 |
| | $ 977,500 | $1,212,500 | $622,500 |
| Income before tax | $ 22,500 | $ 387,500 | $177,500 |
| Income tax (40%) | 9,000 | 155,000 | 71,000 |
| Net income | $ 13,500 | $ 232,500 | $106,500 |

**Required**

**a.** Prepare a schedule that shows the incremental, after-tax cash flows for this project.

**b.** If the company requires a 2-year payback period for its investment, would it undertake this project? Show your supporting calculations clearly.

**c.** Calculate the after-tax accounting rate of return for the project.

**d.** A newly hired business school graduate recommends that the company consider the use of the net present value analysis to study this project. If the company sets a required rate of return of 20% after taxes, will this project be accepted? Show your supporting calculations clearly. (Assume that all operating revenues and expenses occur at the end of the year.)

**9-49 Internal rate of return and different depreciation policies.**

The Federal Auto Leasing Company leases luxury cars to executives. A typical car costs the firm $30,000 and is leased to a customer for 3 years at an annual rate of $12,000 payable at year-end. At the end of the third year, the cars are sold for $9,000. The firm's tax rate is 40%. The customer pays all license, taxes, and maintenance costs.

**Required**

Determine the internal rate of return for a car under each of the following assumptions (in each case the firm has sufficient profits that any loss shown for tax purposes will reduce the firm's tax liability in the year the loss is shown).

**a.** The car is depreciated using traditional straight-line depreciation.

**b.** The estimated total depreciable cost is expensed in the year of acquisition.

**c.** The total investment is expensed in the year of acquisition and any salvage value at disposition is recognized as income.

**9-50 Buy versus lease, residual value: Not-for-profit.**

A local trade school, Disco Tech, is considering leasing rather than owning the vehicles it requires. It can purchase vehicles at $20,000 each or lease them for 3 years at 12% per year. If the school buys them, it will borrow the money at 14%. Lease and loan payments occur at the end of the year. Maintenance contracts and insurance costs of $1,000 per vehicle per year will be paid by the college whether it leases or buys.

**Required**

**a.** What are the annual lease payments and bank payments per vehicle?

**b.** If the school leases, it forgoes any resale value the vehicles might have at the end of 3 years. What would the resale value have to be (as a minimum) for the school to be indifferent between leasing or buying?

**c.** What do you recommend?

**9-51 Plant disposal or lease: Expected value and taxes** (CMA adapted). Kravelcorp is a diversified manufacturing company with several plants. Its Dayton plant has been supplying parts to truck manufacturers for over 30 years; the last shipment will be made in December. Management is currently studying two alternatives relating to its soon-to-be-idle plant and equipment in Dayton.

It can sell the plant to Wasson Industries on January 1 for $3 million cash.

Harr Enterprises has offered to lease the facilities for four years beginning on January 1. Harr's annual lease payments would be $500,000 plus 10% of the gross dollar sales of all items produced there. Probabilities of Harr's annual gross dollar sales are estimated as follows:

| Annual Gross Dollar Sales | Estimated Probability |
|---|---|
| $2,000,000 | 0.1 |
| 4,000,000 | 0.4 |
| 6,000,000 | 0.3 |
| 8,000,000 | 0.2 |

The book value of the Dayton plant at the end of December will be $4,200,000. Kravel has used straight-line depreciation for all capital assets at the Dayton Plant. If the Dayton Plant is not sold, the annual straight-line depreciation charge for the plant and equipment will be $900,000 each year for the next 4 years. The market value of the plant and equipment at the end of the lease period is estimated to be $600,000.

Kravel requires an after-tax rate of return of 15% for capital investment decisions and is subject to corporate income tax rates of 40% on operating income.

**Required**

**a.** Calculate the present value at the end of December for each of the alternatives.

**b.** Discuss the additional factors, both quantitative and qualitative, Kravel should consider before a decision is made.

**9-52 Leasing versus borrowing to buy: Income taxes** (CMA adapted). LeToy Company produces a wide variety of children's toys, most of which are manufactured from stamped parts. The Production Department recommended that a new stamping machine be acquired for the next 5 years. Top management has concurred with the recommendation and has assigned you to supervise the acquisition and to analyze the alternative financing available.

You have narrowed the financing of the project to two alternatives. The first alternative is a lease agreement with the manufacturer calling for annual payments of $62,000 at the beginning of each year. The manufacturer retains the title to the machine and there is no purchase option at the end of 5 years.

The second alternative is to purchase the equipment for $240,000. LeToy can claim the tax credit and use a 5-year class life for cost recovery. Preliminary discussions with LeToy's bank indicate that the firm would be able to finance the asset acquisition with a 15% loan. The salvage value of $20,000 is approximately equal to the removal costs.

All maintenance, taxes, and insurance are the same under both alternatives and are paid by LeToy. LeToy requires an after-tax cutoff return of 18% for investment decisions and is subject to a 40% corporate income tax rate.

**Required**

Should LeToy lease or purchase the machine?

**9-53 Lease versus borrowing to buy: Not-for-profit** (CMA adapted).

Middleton University is a state-supported, tax-exempt institution. The university has decided to replace the computer that is being used for financial and administrative applications. The current computer is more than 8 years old and can no longer serve the university's needs adequately.

An analysis was submitted to the Board of Regents indicating that a new computer would provide the university with annual cost savings of $400,000, including the computer's maintenance and insurance. The proposed computer would cost $1 million and have an economic life of 5 years. The vendor has assured them that the computer could be sold for $100,000 after 5 years. The annual maintenance and insurance costs are estimated to be $50,000.

The Board of Regents is convinced that the proposed computer is justified. How to finance the computer acquisition is the only decision left to be made on this project; the alternatives are to borrow for the purchase or to lease.

Commerce Bank would give Middleton a 5-year $1-million loan at an annual interest rate of 15%. The bank would require the interest to be paid annually at the end of each year with the principal amount due at maturity.

DataBit, a computer leasing company, would lease the proposed computer to Middleton under a 5-year operating lease arrangement. The lease calls for rental payments at the beginning of each year starting with $340,000 at the beginning of the first year and decreasing by $40,000 in each of the subsequent 4 years.

The university's risk-free interest rate is thought to be 12%. Both Commerce Bank and DataBit are subject to a 40% income tax rate. In addition, DataBit can claim the investment tax credit and cost recovery on the computer it leases to the university.

**Required**

**a.** Prepare an analysis that shows which financing arrangement will be better for the university.

**b.** Identify factors other than the cost of financing that the university should consider when making the lease-versus-borrow decision.

**9-54 Extension of the preceding problem—computer recommended.**

Refer to the preceding problem concerning Middleton University.

**Required**

**a.** Use the computer program IRR to determine the rate of interest implied in the lease.

**b.** What might DataBit do to become more competitive with Commerce Bank?

**9-55 Site selection: Financing and depreciation alternatives—computer recommended.**

Tristan Valve Company is seeking a location for a plant to serve its oil and gas clients in the Mideast. The firm is considering a location in Kuwait and another in Pakistan.

The Kuwait site offers an environment with an income tax of only 10% but high wages. Further, shipping costs will be low and the government will provide financing at 11% interest. Only straight-line depreciation is allowable.

Pakistan offers low wages but a 60% income tax. The government will waive income taxes for the first two years of the plant's operations. To encourage development, the United Nation's Economic Development Council will finance projects in Pakistan at a 6% interest rate.

The cost of building the plant will be $8 million in either country. Tristan must invest $4 million and only the balance will be financed. The plant is expected to have a useful life of 6 years, after which it will be abandoned. For tax purposes, Pakistan allows the use of either straight-line or sum-of-the-years'-digits depreciation (depreciation must be taken in the first two years for the plant even though taxes are waived).

The schedule below summarizes the annual cash revenues and costs expected to be incurred by each plant. These figures do not include financing costs. In both countries the loan to pay off the cost of the plant will be amortized over the 6-year life of the plant. Tristan requires a minimum rate of return of 19.5%.

| | Kuwait | Pakistan |
|---|---|---|
| Sales | $4,800,000 | $4,800,000 |
| Materials | 900,000 | 1,000,000 |
| Labor | 1,000,000 | 600,000 |
| Overhead | 300,000 | 200,000 |
| Shipping | 400,000 | 600,000 |
| Net | $2,200,000 | $2,400,000 |

**Required**

In which country should the plant be built? (*Hint:* You must examine two alternatives for Pakistan.) Loan payments are made at year-end. You will find the programs PYMTSCH and NPV useful.

**9-56 Site selection, international—computer recommended.**

Blanton Industries has determined that the company needs a new manufacturing plant to serve its European customers. The capital investment is anticipated to be $2,500,000. The firm has narrowed its choice for a plant site to three cities: Amsterdam, Nice, or Hamburg.

Annual sales from this plant are expected to be $4.5 million no matter which city the plant is located in. However, production costs, income tax rates, and allowable depreciation tax policies vary in each country. In the Netherlands the firm is allowed to expense the entire cost of the plant in the year it is opened. Further, it can carry forward any tax loss for a maximum of 5 years. In France the plant must be depreciated using straight-line depreciation and a 10-year life. West Germany will allow 20% of the cost of the plant to be depreciated in the first year, 30% in the second year, and 50% in the third year. Tax losses can be carried forward for only 1 year. Salvage values may be ignored in all three countries.

The cash costs and tax rates for each country are expected to be as follows:

| | Netherlands | France | West Germany |
|---|---|---|---|
| Materials | $2,200,000 | $1,500,000 | $2,000,000 |
| Labor | 700,000 | 800,000 | 1,000,000 |
| Overhead | 500,000 | 500,000 | 200,000 |
| Transportation | 100,000 | 200,000 | 100,000 |
| Total | $3,500,000 | $3,000,000 | $3,300,000 |
| Tax rate | 52% | 62% | 55% |

The plant is expected to last for 10 years, after which its salvage value will be equal to disposal costs.

**Required**

**a.** Assuming Blanton's cost of capital is 10%, in which country should the plant be located?

**b.** If Blanton's cost of capital is 20%, in which country should the plant be located?

**c.** Why are the answers in parts (a) and (b) different?

**9-57 Learning curves and capital budgeting—computer required.**

McDonald-Hughes is a very large defense contractor. Management has been concerned with the wide swings in business activity and employment from the unpredictable winning of contracts as well as the fluctuating mood of Congress when establishing the military budget. Fearing that Congress would be cutting back on defense spending over the next several years, management established a task force to investigate possible nondefense markets that the firm could diversify into. This case concerns the task force's recommendation to build a medium-range commercial jet for the airline industry. The jet's code name is Centauri.

Research, development, and design of the Centauri will take 3 years and cost $1.2 billion. Approximately 40% of these costs will be incurred in the first year, 20% in the second year, and 40% in the third year. RD&D costs will not be amortized until production and sales of the Centauri begin.

Production will begin in year 4 at the rate of three aircraft per month. The total production costs exclusive of amortization of RD&D expenses will be $100 million for the first jet. Subsequent production costs are expected to follow the industry average learning rate of 77%, but the production rate will remain at three aircraft per month.

The total market for intermediate-range jets for the next several years is expected to be 700 units. The management of McDonald-Hughes expects to be able to capture 30.9% of the market (or 216 units). Based on this assumption, the firm calculated the average cost per jet to be

$$\begin{aligned} y &= ax^{-\beta} \\ &= \$100{,}000{,}000(216)^{-0.37707} \\ &= \$13{,}175{,}000 \end{aligned}$$

The firm anticipates being able to sell the aircraft for $22,175,000, yielding the following breakeven calculation.

$$\$22{,}175{,}000x - \$13{,}175{,}000x - \$1{,}200{,}000{,}000 = 0$$
$$x = 133 \text{ units}$$

On the basis of the same figures, the following pro forma income statements were prepared for years 4 through 9.

| | | |
|---|---|---|
| Sales | 36 × $22,175,000 | $798,300,000 |
| Production costs | 36 × $13,175,000 | 474,300,000 |
| RD&D amortization | 1,200,000,000/6 | 200,000,000 |
| Income before tax | | $124,000,000 |
| Tax (45%) | | 55,800,000 |
| Net income | | $ 68,200,000 |

This will yield an average return on investment of

$$\$68{,}200{,}000/(\$1{,}200{,}000{,}000 \times 0.5) = 11.4\%$$

which, the task force pointed out, exceeds the firm's 10% cost of capital.

**Required**

For each of the following questions, assume that all cash flows occur at the end of the year.

**a.** If the firm sells 133 aircraft, will it break even (ignoring the cost of capital)?

**b.** What is the firm's actual breakeven point (ignoring the cost of capital)?

**c.** Using the 10% cost-of-capital figure, what is the net present value of this investment at time zero?

**d.** At the beginning of year 3, management realized that its profitability analysis was incorrect. Management has asked you whether the project should be continued or abandoned.

**e.** Based on the original estimate, how many units must be sold for the net present value of the project to be zero? (Note that the firm can only produce 3 units a month, so additional production will require additional time, which changes the amount of RD&D costs to be amortized each year.)

# CHAPTER 10

# PERT/COST BUDGETING

In this chapter we look at a budgeting technique for nonroutine activities, PERT/Cost.[1] This technique is particularly useful for the planning and control of large complex projects requiring the performance of a number of separately identifiable activities. Such projects as the construction of a new manufacturing facility, undertaking a major research project, developing a new product, or instituting a major new marketing campaign can all potentially benefit from the use of PERT/Cost budgeting.

We begin with a discussion of network analysis. Then the discussion shifts to an examination of PERT/Cost—a refinement of network analysis that has accounting implications.

## COORDINATING A PROJECT'S ACTIVITIES

The first step in planning a large-scale project is to identify the necessary activities that must be accomplished to complete the project. The activities should then be arranged in the order in which they must be completed. For example, in constructing a house the building foundation needs to be

[1]For most organizations PERT/Cost would be used for nonroutine activities. After completing this chapter, the reader is likely to be able to name a variety of types of firms for which PERT/Cost would be a routine budgeting technique.

poured before framing is begun. No doubt we have all seen the results when activities have not been completed in their proper order: Walls in a new building must be damaged to put in phone lines, and it seems endemic that streets are paved first, then dug up to put in underground utilities. This failure in properly planning the ordering of activities generally leads to much higher costs for subsequent activities. Thus the proper planning of the order in which activities should be completed can yield substantial savings.

### Networks

One means of depicting the necessary ordering of activities is through the construction of a network. A **network** is simply a graphic representation of the interrelationship between activities. It quickly allows us to see any necessary relationships between activities and it also allows us to follow the progress of the project when work is under way. A simple network is represented in Figure 10-1. The network represents a few of the activities necessary to build a house. In this figure, each activity is represented by an arrow, with each arrow beginning and ending at numbered circles. This approach allows us to refer to each of the activities by the numbers at the tail and head of the activity (such as activity 1–2). The circles at each end of the arrow represent the activity's starting and ending points. An alternative approach is to represent each activity by a circle and to use the

| Activity | Predecessor Activity |
|---|---|
| Framing | None |
| External walls | Framing |
| Internal walls | External walls |
| Roof | Framing |
| Appliances | Roof, internal walls |
| Guttering | Roof |

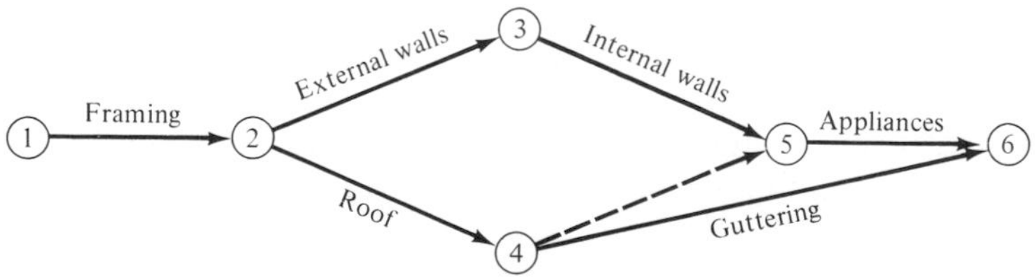

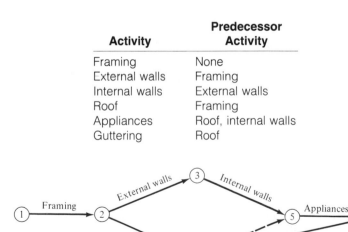

**FIGURE 10-1 A simple network, with arrows representing activities.**

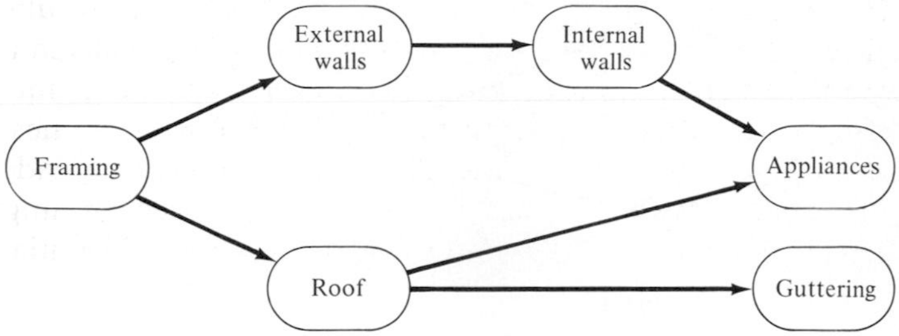


**FIGURE 10-2 A simple network, with nodes representing activities.**

arrows to represent the necessary temporal relationship between the activities. Figure 10-2 recasts the project in Figure 10-1 in these terms. The two approaches are completely interchangeable. The authors are more familiar with the use of arrows as activities, so throughout this chapter we will use that method.

We cannot suggest a mechanical approach for drawing the networks so that they look nice. It seems to be a trial-and-error process. But in preparing a network, you should try to avoid crossing lines, or the network gets to be difficult to understand. One technique to help represent difficult dependencies is to introduce dummy activities. A **dummy activity** is one that represents a necessary dependency (relationship between activities) but entails no work itself. In Figure 10-1, activity 4–5 is a dummy activity. It depicts the requirement that for the project represented, the roof must be completed before we install appliances. Yet there is no separate activity that takes place between completing the roof and installing the appliances.

### The Critical Path

The next step in the budgeting process is to obtain an estimate of the time that management expects each activity will require for completion. With these estimates, we can now plan how long it will take to complete the project, and precisely when we should arrange to have the various subcontractors available to perform their tasks. For the example in Figure 10-1, assume that management estimates that it will take 5 days for framing, 4 days for the external walls, 7 days for the roof, 6 days for the internal walls, 3 days for appliance installation, and 2 days for the completion of guttering. Superimposing these estimates on the network, as in Figure 10-3, makes it a trivial task to determine the amount of time required to complete each path in the network. A **path** is simply a string of connected activities that must be completed sequentially from the beginning of the

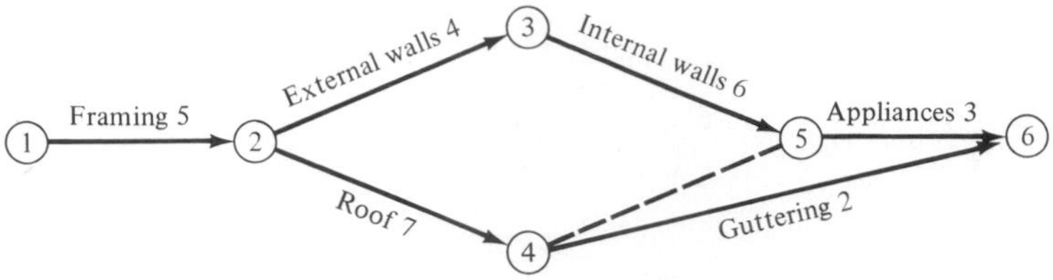


**PATH 1**

| Activity | Completion Time (days) |
|---|---|
| 1–2 framing | 5 |
| 2–3 external walls | 4 |
| 3–5 internal walls | 6 |
| 5–6 appliances | 3 |
| Total 1–2–3–5–6 | 18 |

**PATH 2**

| Activity | Completion Time (days) |
|---|---|
| 1–2 framing | 5 |
| 2–4 roof | 7 |
| 4–5 dummy | 0 |
| 5–6 appliances | 3 |
| Total 1–2–4–5–6 | 15 |

**PATH 3**

| Activity | Completion Time (days) |
|---|---|
| 1–2 framing | 5 |
| 2–4 roof | 7 |
| 4–6 guttering | 2 |
| Total 1–2–4–6 | 14 |

**FIGURE 10-3 An example of a network.**

project to the end. For our example there are three possible paths through the network, as follows:

| Path | Time to Complete |
|---|---|
| 1–2–3–5–6 | 18 days |
| 1–2–4–5–6 | 15 days |
| 1–2–4–6 | 14 days |

Adding the required times needed to complete each activity on a path gives us the needed time to complete that path. The longest path, 1–2–3–5–6, is called the critical path. The **critical path** is the sequence of activities that constrains the total completion time for the project. That is, the entire project cannot be completed until all of the activities on the longest path are completed. Thus, although the activities on path 1–2–4–6 can be completed in 14 days, the project will not be completed in 14 days. The first path indicates that it will take 18 days from the start of the project to the completion of activity 5–6.

You may ask why we calculated the time to complete all paths if only one path constrains the project completion time. Basically the answer is that until you do the calculations you do not know which path is the critical path. For this simple problem, we might be able to "eyeball" the critical path, but for more realistic networks, the critical path may not be at all obvious. In addition, the calculations for the other paths allow us to identify slack time.

### Slack Time

The critical path requires 18 days to complete, whereas the third path requires only 14. There exists then a maximum of 4 days of slack time on the third path. **Slack time** is the amount of time by which we can delay an activity without affecting the completion time of the project. Assuming that activities 1–2 and 2–4 were completed as budgeted, then we could delay the start of activity 4–6 by 4 days and still complete activity 4–6 by the eighteenth day of the project. For activity 4–6 then, the maximum slack time is 4 days. But beware, this is based on the assumption that activities 1–2 and 2–4 were completed on time. If 2–4 was delayed by 1 day, then the remaining slack time for 4–6 would be only 3 days.

The slack time of an activity depends on that activity's relationship to all subsequent activities in the network. For example, although activity 1–2 is on the third path and the third path has a maximum slack time of 4 days, the slack time for activity 1–2 is zero. This occurs because activity 1–2 is also on the critical path. Any delay in activity 1–2 will directly affect the time to complete the critical path, and therefore the project. By the definition of the critical path, any activity on the critical path has zero slack time.

In between these extremes, we can see that the slack time for activity 2–4 is only 3 days. That is, if we delay activity 2–4 by 3 days, the third path will require 17 days to completion, still leaving a day of slack. However, the second path will require 18 days if activity 2–4 is delayed 3 days. If we extend activity 2–4 by another day, the second path will delay the completion of the project to 19 days. Thus the second path restricts the slack time for activity 2–4 to 3 days.

It should be apparent that network analysis is a valuable tool for budgeting and controlling complex projects.[2] We can plan ahead for when activities must be undertaken, and we can quickly evaluate the effect that a delay in completion time of an activity will have on the project. If the delay is on a critical path, we should attempt to make up the delay elsewhere; however, short delays on noncritical activities may not require any corrective action if they do not create a new critical path.

Although useful as is, there have been two major refinements made to network analysis. The first, generally referred to as PERT (Program Evaluation and Review Technique) adds probabilistic estimates to the basic network analysis. PERT recognizes that there is some uncertainty as to precisely when activities will be completed. From estimates of the distribution of the amount of time that will be required to complete each activity, we can make probabilistic statements regarding the completion time of the entire project. Similarly, if activities are delayed, we can analyze the probable effect on project completion time. Although it is of great interest to engineers and managers, PERT itself has no unique accounting implications, so we will not discuss it further.

## THE MECHANICS OF PERT/COST

The second refinement to network analysis, known as **PERT/Cost,** is concerned with trading off the costs involved in shortening the completion times of activities versus the benefits of more quickly completing the project. That is, we try to determine the optimal time to complete a project by minimizing overall project costs. Many accounting estimates are required for implementing PERT/Cost, so we consider it a proper subject for coverage.

### Cost as a Function of Time

With PERT/Cost we determine the cost to complete an activity for each of several completion times. That is, we estimate the cost to complete an activity as a function of its completion time. This cost function will generally be **U**-shaped. Presumably by incurring extra costs, such as authorizing overtime and hiring additional laborers, we can accelerate the completion of an activity. Similarly, beyond some least-cost completion time, if

[2] If you have studied Chapter 7, you should also be able to see that network analysis is valuable in working with MRP inventory systems.

it takes longer to complete an activity, costs will also rise (additional equipment rental charges, insurance, and so forth).

### The Optimal Budget

For our previous example, assume that management has estimated the cost and completion times for each activity as presented in Exhibit 10-1. Our objective is to minimize the total cost of completing the project. To

**EXHIBIT 10-1 Cost to Complete Each Activity as a Function of Time**

| Completion Time | Cost | Change in Cost | Completion Time | Cost | Change in Cost |
|---|---|---|---|---|---|
| **ACTIVITY 1–2** | | | **ACTIVITY 2–3** | | |
| 3 days | $ 825 | | 2 days | $1,000 | |
| | | $(175) | | | $(200) |
| 4 days | 650 | | 3 days | 800 | |
| | | (150) | | | (100) |
| 5 days[a] | 500 | | 4 days[a] | 700 | |
| | | 100 | | | 50 |
| 6 days | 600 | | 5 days | 750 | |
| **ACTIVITY 2–4** | | | **ACTIVITY 3–5** | | |
| 4 days | $3,000 | | 4 days | $1,025 | |
| | | $(500) | | | $(325) |
| 5 days | 2,500 | | 5 days | 700 | |
| | | (250) | | | (300) |
| 6 days | 2,250 | | 6 days[a] | 400 | |
| | | (150) | | | 200 |
| 7 days[a] | 2,100 | | 7 days | 600 | |
| | | 100 | | | |
| 8 days | 2,200 | | | | |
| **ACTIVITY 5–6** | | | **ACTIVITY 4–6** | | |
| 1 day | $ 950 | | 1 day | $ 150 | |
| | | $(400) | | | $ (50) |
| 2 days | 550 | | 2 days[a] | 100 | |
| | | (350) | | | 25 |
| 3 days[a] | 200 | | 3 days | 125 | |
| | | 75 | | | |
| 4 days | 275 | | | | |

[a]These are the times for which an *activity's* costs are minimized. PERT/Cost searches for the times that will minimize the total costs for the *project*.

start with, we choose the least cost time to complete each *activity* (marked with an [a] in Exhibit 10-1). Using these completion times we determine the times to complete each path through the network just as before, and identify the critical path. For example, we once again get

| Path | Completion Time |
|---|---|
| 1–2–3–5–6 | 18 days |
| 1–2–4–5–6 | 15 days |
| 1–2–4–6 | 14 days |

Our next step is to estimate the benefits accruing to the firm if the *project* is completed in less than the time indicated by the initial critical path. That is, we may have agreed to a penalty if the project runs over 12 days, or we may be incurring large interest charges on the investment in the project. For the example, assume that the firm has agreed to a penalty of $500 per day for every day over 12 that the project takes for completion. If we can shorten the project from 18 days to 17 days, then the firm will save $500. Should we do it? We answer that question by checking to see whether we can shorten an activity on the critical path for less than $500. Note that we need check *only* the activities on the critical path because shortening an activity that is not on the critical path will have no effect on the completion time for the project. From Exhibit 10–1 we can see that activity 1–2 can be shortened by 1 day (from 5 days to 4 days) at a cost of $150; 2–3 can be shortened at a cost of $100; 3–5 at a cost of $300; and 5–6 at a cost of $350. Hence, the cheapest means of shortening the critical path by 1 day entails speeding up activity 2–3 at a cost of $100. The cost to shorten the project ($100) is less than the benefit received from shortening the project ($500), so it pays to speed up the activity.

We can now calculate the new times to complete each path through the network. They are as follows:

| | |
|---|---|
| 1–2–3–5–6 | 17 days |
| 1–2–4–5–6 | 15 |
| 1–2–4–6 | 14 |

We are still incurring a $500 per day penalty for exceeding the target completion date, so we check to see whether the project time can be further shortened. The costs to shorten each activity on the critical path are now

| | |
|---|---|
| 1–2 | $150 |
| 2–3 | 200 (we have already shortened 2–3 to 3 days) |
| 3–5 | 300 |
| 5–6 | 350 |

Now the cheapest way to shorten the project completion time is $150 by shortening activity 1–2. Again, the cost is less than the savings from shortening the project, so we do so. The new completion times for each path are (note that the times for *all* paths are changed because activity 1–2 is on every path):

| | |
|---|---|
| 1–2–3–5–6 | 16 days |
| 1–2–4–5–6 | 14 |
| 1–2–4–6 | 13 |

And we continue. The costs now to shorten activities on the critical path by one day are

| | |
|---|---|
| 1–2 | $175 |
| 2–3 | 200 |
| 3–5 | 300 |
| 5–6 | 350 |

Again the best way to shorten the project is by accelerating activity 1–2 by another day. The new path completion times are

| | |
|---|---|
| 1–2–3–5–6 | 15 days |
| 1–2–4–5–6 | 13 |
| 1–2–4–6 | 12 |

The $500 penalty is still with us, so once again we look at thc costs to shorten the critical path. Note now that since 1-2 has been shortened its maximum amount, it is no longer a candidate.

| | |
|---|---|
| 1–2 | — |
| 2–3 | $200 |
| 3–5 | 300 |
| 5–6 | 350 |

This time we shorten 2–3 to get

| | |
|---|---|
| 1–2–3–5–6 | 14 days |
| 1–2–4–5–6 | 13 |
| 1–2–4–6 | 12 |

The costs to shorten activities further are

| | |
|---|---|
| 1–2 | — |
| 2–3 | — |
| 3–5 | $300 |
| 5–6 | 350 |

The cost to shorten activity 3–5 is still less than the savings from shortening the project so we get

| | |
|---|---|
| 1–2–3–5–6 | 13 days |
| 1–2–4–5–6 | 13 |
| 1–2–4–6 | 12 |

Now look what has happened. We have two critical paths. Both the first and second paths restrict the project completion time to 13 days. To shorten the project further we must shorten *both* critical paths. Thus to check whether we should further accelerate the project, we must find the cheapest means to shorten both. The possibilities are

shorten 2–4 @ $150 and 3–5 @ $325, for a total cost of $475.
shorten 5–6, which is on both paths, at a cost of $350.

Thus we can still shorten the project time at a cost less than the penalty by choosing to shorten 5–6, so we do so. The path completion times become

| | |
|---|---|
| 1–2–3–5–6 | 12 days |
| 1–2–4–5–6 | 12 |
| 1–2–4–6 | 12 |

All paths are now critical, but each completion time also allows us to meet the target completion time of 12 days. There is no further benefit to accelerating the project further, so we now have our optimal PERT/Cost

**EXHIBIT 10-2 Original and Optimal Budget for the Example**

| | Project Budget Based On Least-Cost Time for Each Activity | | Optimal Project Budget | |
|---|---|---|---|---|
| **Activity** | **Time** | **Cost** | **Time** | **Cost** |
| 1–2 | 5 days | $ 500 | 3 days | $ 825 |
| 2–3 | 4 | 700 | 2 | 1,000 |
| 2–4 | 7 | 2,100 | 7 | 2,100 |
| 3–5 | 6 | 400 | 5 | 700 |
| 5–6 | 3 | 200 | 2 | 550 |
| 4–6 | 2 | 100 | 2 | 100 |
| Fine: 6 days @ $500 | | 3,000 | | — |
| Total budget | | $7,000 | Total budget | $5,275 |
| Project completion time: 18 days | | | Project completion time: 12 days | |

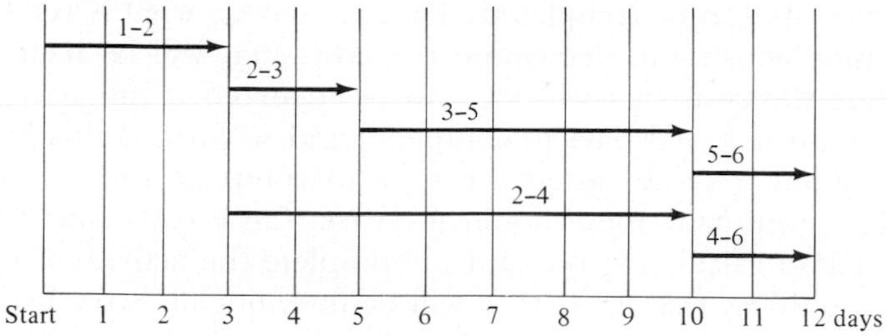


| | | | | | | | | | | | | |
|---|---|---|---|---|---|---|---|---|---|---|---|---|
| | $275 | 275 | 275 | 500 | 500 | 140 | 140 | 140 | 140 | 140 | 275 | 375 |
| | | | | 300 | 300 | 300 | 300 | 300 | 300 | 300 | 50 | 50 |
| Daily budget | $275 | 275 | 275 | 800 | 800 | 440 | 440 | 440 | 440 | 440 | 325 | 325 |

**FIGURE 10-4 Gantt chart for the optimal solution of the example.**

budget. Exhibit 10-2 presents the total cost that we should expect to incur for this budget and compares the optimal budget to the cost we would have incurred had we finished the project in 18 days. Note that the **least-cost project time** is 12 days, whereas 18 days are required if each activity is completed in the **least-cost activity time.** The object of PERT/Cost is to balance project and activity costs to yield the optimal project cost.

Having determined the optimal budget, we can now prepare a **Gantt chart,** a simple plot that displays the specific time periods in which activities will be undertaken. Figure 10-4 depicts the Gantt chart for our example. Having plotted the Gantt chart, if we further know when activity costs will be incurred, we can prepare a daily cost budget. Assume, for example, that activity costs (the costs of materials, labor, and so on) are uniformly incurred. That is, since activity 1–2 takes 3 days to complete at a total cost of $825, let us assume that one-third of the cost, or $275, is incurred each day. Then the daily budget for the project is as given at the bottom of Figure 10-4. Having the budget restated on a daily basis allows us to incorporate the cash flows from this project into the firm's cash budget (see Chapter 6).

## THE ACCOUNTANT'S ROLE IN PERT/COST BUDGETING

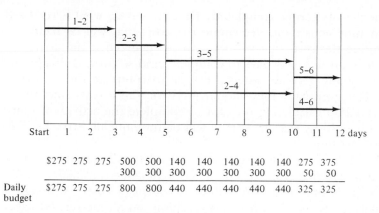

As with the other budgeting techniques we have examined, the accountant's major task in PERT/Cost budgeting is to estimate the cost figures needed in the solution technique. The major difficulty is determining the cost for each activity as a function of the time to complete the activity. An approach for gathering this information is to start by asking how we can complete an activity in *x* days, where *x* is an estimate of the fastest reasonable time the activity can be completed. Then, based on what is required to meet that time constraint, determine the costs that will be incurred. Next, determine the costs that will have to be incurred if the activity is lengthened to require $x + 1$ days to complete, and so forth. Initially, the activity costs should decrease when the time to complete the activity is lengthened. But eventually they should increase. Once costs start to increase you can stop calculating the cost to complete the activity in more days, since it is unlikely that an activity will be intentionally stretched beyond its least-cost time.

In determining the cost to complete an activity, we should be careful to include only costs that really do change as we change completion times. The major troublesome items are allocated overhead costs. Although a firm may allocate overhead such as depreciation, on a time-related basis, it may well be that the actual level of costs incurred will have no relation to the completion time of an activity. On the other hand, to the extent that these costs represent opportunity costs (say an activity requires a large amount of supervision time that could be used elsewhere) these should be reflected in the cost to complete an activity.

While we believe that all of the demonstration problems in this text are valuable, you should definitely read the one for this chapter. It illustrates a quicker technique for solving PERT/Cost problems than that used in the chapter.

## SUMMARY

PERT/Cost is a useful budgeting tool for complex projects. Although as accountants we may never be required to solve a PERT/Cost problem, we should be familiar with the technique so that we can supply the needed cost figures. In addition, a basic knowledge of the technique is also required so that we can provide meaningful reports to management concerning the progress of actual operations. This latter aspect will be dealt with in Chapter 19.

## DEMONSTRATION PROBLEM

The example we used to explain the derivation of a PERT/Cost budget was fairly simple, but it used nonlinear functions for the cost to complete an activity as a function of time. In this demonstration problem we illustrate a simpler solution technique that can be used if the cost functions are linear.

In many situations the cost to shorten an activity from its least-cost time is approximated as a constant amount per unit of time. Thus if it costs \$200 to shorten an activity by one day, it costs $400 to shorten it two days, and $600 to shorten it by three days ($200 per day). With this type of problem, the PERT/Cost solution can be accomplished with fewer calculations and a lot less writing than our previous procedure. Let us now examine the following, more typical, problem.

Figure 10-5 presents a network of activities for a project subject to a $1,000-per-day fine for every day over 13 that it takes to complete. The least cost, the least-cost time, the cost to reduce the activity time by one day, and the fastest possible time to complete each activity are also given below the network. Our task is to find the optimal budget for the project, using PERT/Cost.

*Step 1.* To solve this problem quickly and easily, first copy all of the completion time information and costs to shorten activities onto the network. In Figure 10-6, we represent the least-cost completion time by the small number above each activity line. The adjacent numbers in parentheses are the fastest possible completion times. Finally, the cost to accelerate the completion time of each activity is placed just below each activity arrow. Next list all the paths through the project and determine the time to complete each path (this can now be easily read off the network). Identify the critical path and shade it on the network.

*Step 2.* The next step is to search the activities on the critical path to find the one which can be shortened at the least additional cost. As can now be easily seen in Figure 10-6, activity 3–6 can most cheaply be accelerated at a cost of $450. Compare this cost to the benefit of shortening the project ($1,000); since the cost is less than the benefit, shorten 3–6 by 1 day. We record this change by drawing

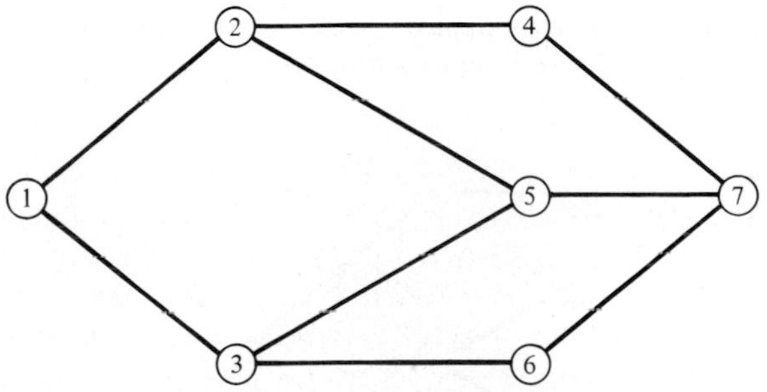


| Activity | Least Cost | Least-Cost Time | Cost to Reduce Activity by 1 Day | Fastest Possible Completion Time |
|---|---|---|---|---|
| 1–2 | $175 | 4 | $250 | 2 |
| 1–3 | 230 | 7 | 800 | 6 |
| 2–4 | 475 | 5 | 125 | 4 |
| 2–5 | 190 | 3 | 360 | 1 |
| 3–5 | 50 | 4 | 100 | 3 |
| 3–6 | 380 | 6 | 450 | 3 |
| 4–7 | 210 | 3 | 400 | 2 |
| 5–7 | 335 | 5 | 700 | 2 |
| 6–7 | 600 | 4 | 600 | 3 |

**FIGURE 10-5 A typical PERT/Cost problem.**

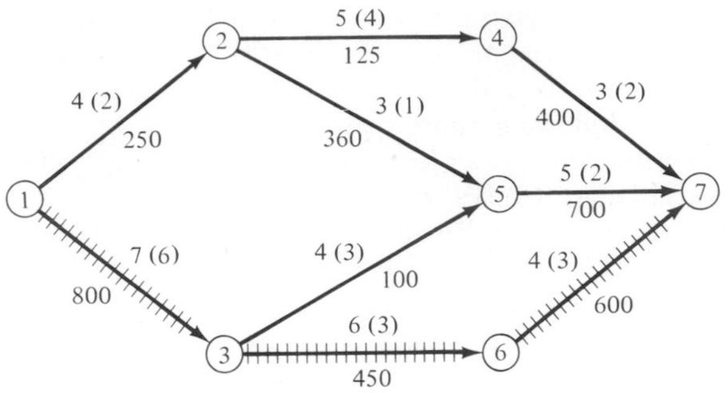


| Paths | Length |
|---|---|
| 1–2–4–7 | 12 |
| 1–2–5–7 | 12 |
| 1–3–5–7 | 16 |
| 1–3–6–7 | 17 (critical path) |

**FIGURE 10-6 Step 1 of the solution to the PERT/Cost problem.**

a slash through the completion time for activity 3–6 in the network and writing in the new time of 5 days (see Figure 10-7). We then adjust the completion times for each path by adding a column next to the least-cost completion time for each path (the times for the reduced paths are listed in Figure 10-7). There is no need to copy all of this information over again; you can simply add onto your original list. We have gone to a new figure only to highlight the change.

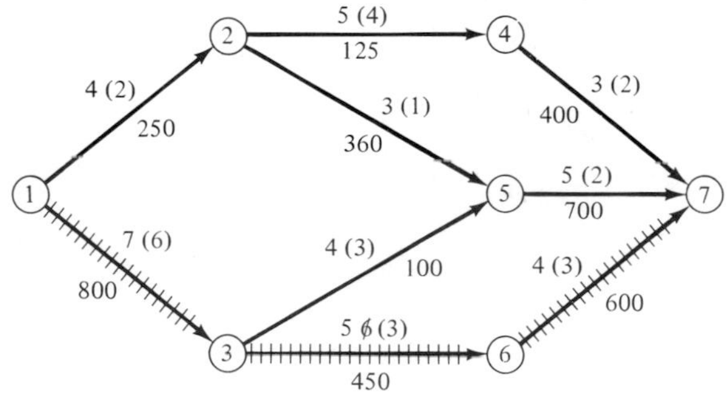


| Paths | Length | Step 2 | |
|---|---|---|---|
| 1–2–4–7 | 12 | 12 | |
| 1–2–5–7 | 12 | 12 | |
| 1–3–5–7 | 16 | 16 | both |
| 1–3–6–7 | 17 | 16 | critical |
| Shorten activity | | 3–6 | |
| Cost to shorten | | $450 | |

**FIGURE 10-7 Step 2 of the solution to the PERT/Cost problem.**

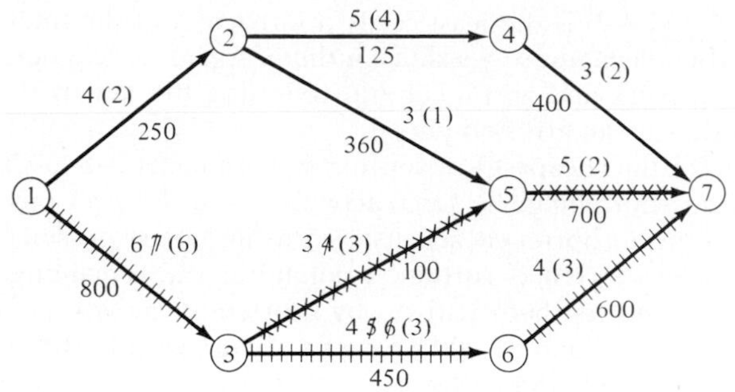


| Paths | Length | Step 2 | Step 3 | Step 4 | Step 5 |
|---|---|---|---|---|---|
| 1–2–4–7 | 12 | 12 | 12 | 12 | |
| 1–2–5–7 | 12 | 12 | 12 | 12 | — |
| 1–3–5–7 | 16 | 16 | 15 | 14 | Stop |
| 1–3–6–7 | 17 | 16 | 15 | 14 | — |
| Shorten activity | | 3–6 | 3–5 and 3–6 | 1–3 | |
| Cost to shorten | | $450 | $550 | $800 | |

**GANTT CHART FOR OPTIMAL SOLUTION**

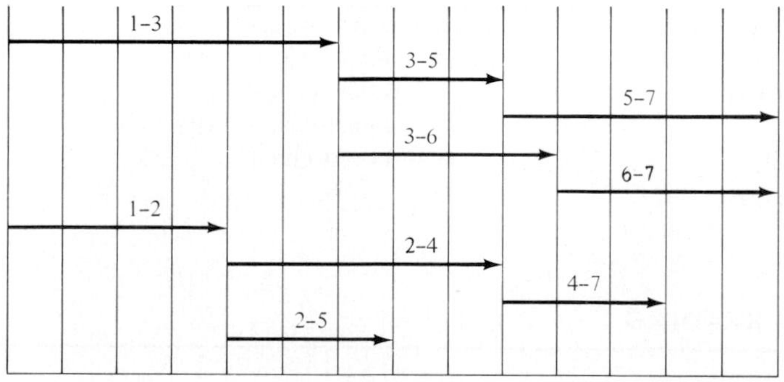


**FIGURE 10-8 Steps 3 through 5 of the solution to the PERT/Cost problem.**

*Step 3*. Note that path 1–3–5–7 has now also become critical. Shade in that path also in the network (done with x's in Figure 10-8). We must now shorten both critical paths, so determine all possible ways to shorten both paths simultaneously. The possibilities and their costs are as follows:

| Shorten | Cost |
|---|---|
| 1–3 | $ 800 |
| 3–5 and 3–6 | 550 |
| 3–5 and 6–7 | 700 |
| 5–7 and 3–6 | 1,150 |
| 5–7 and 6–7 | 1,300 |

Shortening both activities 3–5 and 3–6 is the least costly approach, and the total cost of $550 is less than the $1,000 benefit, so we shorten them. Again, we change the completion times on the network and add a column reflecting the new path completion times (be sure to shorten all affected paths).

*Step 4.* Again we search for the cheapest way to shorten both paths 1–3–5–7 and 1–3–6–7. Often this means shortening the same activities as in the previous step. Notice, however, that we have shortened activity 3–5 to its fastest possible completion time, so it cannot be shortened further. Looking at the remaining alternatives, the cheapest way to shorten both paths is by shortening activity 1–3 at a cost of $800. Since this cost is less than $1,000 we do so. Again, we adjust the completion times in the network and for the paths.

*Step 5.* Now activity 1–3 has also been shortened to its fastest possible completion time. So now the only remaining possibilities for shortening both critical paths are to shorten activities 5–7 and 3–6 at a total cost of $1,150 or to shorten 5–7 and 6–7 at a total cost of $1,300. However, both alternatives require incurring a cost in excess of the project savings if the project is shortened by 1 day, so we should not shorten the project further. Hence our optimal budget will call for the completion of the project in 14 days. Even though our budget calls for the incurrence of a fine of $1,000 for failure to finish the project in 13 days, we do so because the fine is less expensive than the minimum cost to accelerate the project.

## KEY TERMS AND CONCEPTS

Network
Dummy activity
Path
Critical path
Slack time
PERT/Cost
Least-cost project time
Least-cost activity time
Gantt chart

## FURTHER READING

Bailey, F. A. "A Note on PERT/Cost Resource Allocation," *The Accounting Review* (April 1967), p. 361.

DeCoster, Don T. "PERT/Cost—The Challenge," *Management Services* (May–June 1964), p. 13.

Elikai, Fara, and Shane Moriarity. "Variance Analysis with PERT/Cost," *The Accounting Review* (January 1982), p. 161.

Krogstad, Jack L., Gary Grundnitski, and David W. Bryant. "PERT and PERT/Cost for Audit Planning and Control," *Journal of Accountancy* (November 1977), p. 82.

Ross, W. R. "PERT/Cost Resource Allocation Procedure," *The Accounting Review* (July 1966), p. 464.

Ross, W. R. "Evaluating the Cost of PERT/Cost," *Management Services* (September–October 1966), p. 43.

## QUESTIONS AND EXERCISES

**10-1** What is the critical path?

**10-2** What is meant by the term *slack*?

**10-3** Can the critical path have slack?

**10-4** What is the purpose of the Gantt chart if one already has drawn a network?

**10-5** Distinguish between the terms *project* and *activity* as used in this chapter.

**10-6** It is 5:00 P.M. and you expect to serve dinner to your guests at 6:00 P.M. You have chosen to serve stir-fried shrimp and vegetables over rice.

The rice must be soaked for 40 minutes, then brought to a boil (5 minutes), and finally covered and steamed for 15 minutes. It will take 10 minutes to chop the vegetables and 15 minutes to shell and clean the shrimp. The shrimp will be stir-fried first (5 minutes), and then the vegetables will be fried (5 minutes). When the shrimp and vegetables are cooked, they will be combined with a sauce and immediately served over the cooked rice.

The sauce is made up of soy sauce, cornstarch, ginger, and chicken broth (it will take 2 minutes to find and mix the ingredients). When mixed, the sauce is heated over low heat for 16 minutes. You plan to refresh your guests' drinks from 5:25 to 5:40.

Prepare a Gantt chart for the period 5:00 to 6:00 showing precisely when each activity must occur to have dinner ready at 6:00 P.M. The time required to turn on the stove, transfer ingredients, and so forth is negligible and can be ignored.

**10-7** The annual Accounting Club Awards Banquet for City University is just 6 weeks away. It is anticipated that it will take 2 weeks to locate and engage a "well-known" speaker. Only after a speaker is chosen can tickets be printed for the event. Also, once the name of the speaker is known, posters can be prepared and displayed at the university. It will take 1 week to print the tickets and 2 weeks to prepare the posters. The tickets will be delivered on Monday, and immediately thereafter a large number of them will be mailed to public and industrial accountants. It will take 10 days to mail the tickets and have checks returned from the accountants for payment for the tickets. It is expected that 100 tickets at $15 will be sold to these accounting practitioners. Once the posters are displayed, student tickets at $10 each will be placed on sale. It is expected that 200 student tickets will be sold, the sales occurring evenly over the period commencing with the posting of the posters and ending with the period in which the banquet is held.

A $200 fee must be paid immediately to reserve and rent the banquet hall. The speaker will not be paid a fee. The printer must be paid $100 during the week in which the tickets are printed. The posters will require supplies costing $50. These latter costs must be incurred during the first week the posters are being prepared. It will cost another $50 to mail the tickets to the accountants. Payment of $3,000 to the caterer for the banquet must be made just prior to the banquet.

Schedule the timing of the activities leading up to the banquet and prepare a schedule of cash inflows and outflows for weeks 1 through 6. Assume that today is Monday of week 1 and the banquet will be held Saturday of week 6.

**10-8** Alpho Oil Exploration Company wishes to have seismic readings taken at a potential drilling site. The necessary equipment can be rented for $200 per day. The firm can hire enough people to operate the equipment for 24 hours and get the readings in 1 day. However to do so would require salaries and transportation costs of $1,600. Salaries and transportation costs can be reduced if fewer people are hired, but it will take a longer time to obtain the readings. The necessary salary and transportation costs and the time to get the readings with a reduced work force are summarized as follows:

| Days Needed | Salary and Transportation Costs |
|---|---|
| 2 | $1,100 |
| 3 | 750 |
| 4 | 500 |
| 5 | 400 |
| 6 | 350 |

Determine the cost to obtain the seismic readings as a function of time over the range of 1 to 6 days. What is the least-cost time to get the readings?

**10-9** The Taggard Company wishes to raze a building to make way for a new parking lot. As long as the building, or any part of it, is standing, the firm must pay property taxes of $500 per month to the city. Once the building is leveled and cleared, property taxes will drop to $100 per month.

One option for razing the building is to hire a demolition crew that uses explosives. This company promises that they can have the building down and the lot cleared in 2 months. Their charge is $5,000. The Lo-Bid Destruction Company promises that they can have the building down and cleared in 3 months, using conventional means, at a cost of $3,000. Professional Wrecking Contractors, Inc., has bid $3,500 for the job. They indicate that they can have the building down and the lot cleared in 4 months. But in addition, they will be more careful and deliberate in the process, thereby yielding salvaged materials that can be sold for $1,000.

The last option under consideration is to allow local university students to use the building for unsupervised parties. After one semester ($4\frac{1}{2}$ months) the building would be completely destroyed. The rubble could be hauled off in half a month for a cost of $1,500. Under this last option, Taggard estimates that they will incur fines for "disturbing the peace" and "maintaining a public nuisance" in the amount of $1,000.

Determine the cost to raze the building and clear the lot as a function of the number of months to completion. What is the lowest-cost time to complete this activity?

**10-10** Assume that you are a volunteer in charge of civil defense planning in a small community. You have been asked to help formulate a disaster reaction plan. If a major accident occurs on the nearby interstate highway, the local police can be at the scene within 10 minutes after the sheriff's dispatcher has been notified (say by a passerby). The community ambulance is operated by two volunteer residents: a young attorney and the local undertaker. When a call reporting an accident comes to the sheriff's dispatcher, the two volunteers are notified. On average it takes the volunteers 15 minutes to get to the ambulance and another 10 minutes to get to the scene of the accident. Injured persons can be transported to the local hospital within 10 minutes of the arrival of the ambulance at the accident. When the police arrive at the scene, they determine whether anyone is injured. If so, they immediately radio the sheriff's dispatcher, who in turn calls the local medical doctor and tells the doctor to go to the hospital. It takes the doctor 20 minutes to get to the hospital.

If a person is injured in an automobile accident on the interstate, how much time will elapse between notification of the accident to the sheriff's dispatcher and initial treatment by the doctor at the hospital?

**10-11** The new county courthouse is nearly completed. The only remaining activities of consequence are to finish the plumbing, install a sprinkler system for fire protection, and complete the internal wiring for electricity. The main water line is ready to be installed now and can be completed in 2 weeks. Installation of the main power line can also be started now and will take 3 weeks. Once the main power line is installed, the internal wiring can be completed. Internal wiring will take another 3 weeks.

After the water line is in, work can begin on connecting the sprinkler system. Connecting the sprinkler system will take 5 weeks. Also, once the main water line is in, work can begin on connecting showers, sinks, and so forth. This will require 3 weeks.

The general contractor for the building need not be paid until all construction is complete and all inspections have been passed. There will be a county inspection of the electrical work, the plumbing work, and the fire sprinkler system. Normally each inspection (performed by separate individuals) would be completed in 1 week, but if told to do so, an inspector can stretch an inspection to 2 weeks. The funds to pay for the building are in an interest-bearing bank account. As county commissioner, which inspector would you tell to do a particularly thorough job (i.e., delay the time to complete the inspection) in order to maximize the county's interest income?

**10-12** Your company's director of international operations has called to say that a subsidiary in Senegal is in urgent need of help with its cost accounting system. You have been selected to go to the subsidiary and straighten matters out. Unfortunately, you do not have a currently valid passport.

It will take 4 weeks to obtain a new passport. In addition you will need to get a visa from the consulate for Senegal. You must send in your passport to the consulate when you apply for a visa. It will take 1 week for your application to reach the consulate. The subsidiary will have to obtain an entry permit for you from local authorities. This will take 1 week. The entry permit will then have to be sent to the consulate for Senegal in the U.S. This will take 2 weeks. The consulate will issue your visa only after it receives both the entry permit and your passport and visa application. It will take 1 week for you to receive the visa after the consulate receives the appropriate paperwork.

Airline and hotel reservations can be made at any time. When is the earliest that you will be able to go to Senegal?

**10-13** Refer to the demonstration problem at the end of the chapter. For the optimal solution identify the maximum amount of slack time that would exist for each of the nine activities if all other activities were finished on time.

## PROBLEMS AND CASES

**10-14 Network: Time and cost budget.**
Austere Enterprises, Inc., has provided you with the network shown. The figures above the paths are the anticipated number of days to complete each activity.

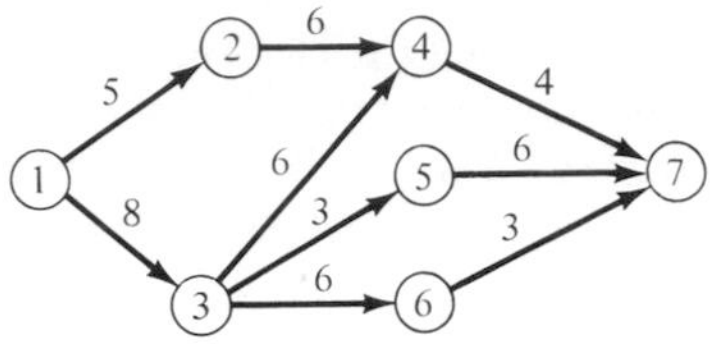


You are given the following information.

| Activity | Cost to Shorten Activity by 1 Day | Activity May Not Be Shortened to Less Than |
|---|---|---|
| 1–2 | $ 100 | 2 days |
| 1–3 | 1,200 | 6 |
| 2–4 | 200 | 5 |
| 3–4 | 500 | 4 |
| 3–5 | 400 | 1 |
| 3–6 | 200 | 2 |
| 4–7 | 300 | 2 |
| 5–7 | 300 | 4 |
| 6–7 | 400 | 2 |

The firm can save $1,001 per day for each day it shortens the completion time of this project.

**Required**

**a.** Identify the critical path on the network of activities.

**b.** Determine the least-cost time to complete this project.

**10-15 Determining the cost to complete an activity as a function of time.**
Activity 3–6 for Boa Construction is the assembly of equipment on site. The work will begin on a Monday. The various pieces of equipment cost $40,000. The pieces will arrive in two boxcars at Boa's railroad siding early Monday morning. A minimum crew of four people will have to be available at all times to handle the equipment during assembly. The firm estimates that it will take 192 labor hours to complete the job. Labor is paid $7 per hour. Total labor hour requirements will be the same no matter how many people are hired. More than six people is not

considered feasible because the employees would get in each other's way. Labor laws prevent the firm from allowing workers to work more than 12 hours per day. Overtime (more than 8 hours in any day or work on weekends) will be paid double time, plus a $10 meal allowance for work over 8 hours in one day. It costs $200 (insurance, agency fees, paperwork) to hire an employee. The railroad charges $20 per boxcar for each day or partial day held. The boxcars can be returned only after the equipment is fully assembled.

**Required**
Determine the cost to complete this activity as a function of time.

**10-16 Identify critical path and completion time** (CMA adapted).
Crespi Company will soon begin work on a bank building. Work on the building was started by another construction firm that has gone out of business. Crespi has agreed to complete the project. Crespi's schedule of activities and related expected completion times are shown below.

| Activity | Description of Activity | Predecessor Activity | Estimated Time Required (in weeks) |
|---|---|---|---|
| A | Obtain on-site work permit | — | 1 |
| B | Repair damage done by vandals | A | 4 |
| C | Inspect construction materials left on site | A | 1 |
| D | Order and receive additional construction materials | C | 2 |
| E | Apply for waiver to add new materials | C | 1 |
| F | Obtain waiver to add new materials | E | 1 |
| G | Perform electrical work | B, D, F | 4 |
| H | Complete interior partitions | G | 2 |

**Required**

**a.** Identify the critical path by letters and determine the expected time in weeks for the project.

**b.** Explain the effect on the critical path and expected time for the project if Crespi had not been required to apply and obtain the waiver to add new materials.

**10-17 Identify critical path and completion time** (CMA adapted).
The Dryfus Company specializes in large construction projects. The company management regularly employs the Program Evaluation and Review Technique (PERT) in planning and coordinating its construction projects. The following schedule of separable activities and their expected completion times has been developed for an office building to be constructed by Dryfus Company.

| Activity Description | Predecessor Activity | Expected Activity Completion Time (in weeks) |
|---|---|---|
| a. Excavation | — | 2 |
| b. Foundation | a | 3 |
| c. Underground utilities | a | 7 |
| d. Rough plumbing | b | 4 |
| e. Framing | b | 5 |
| f. Roofing | e | 3 |
| g. Electrical work | f | 3 |
| h. Interior walls | d, g | 4 |
| i. Finish plumbing | h | 2 |
| j. Exterior finishing | f | 6 |
| k. Landscaping | c, i, j | 2 |

**Required**
Identify the critical path for this project and determine the expected project completion time in weeks.

**10-18 Network and critical path** (CMA adapted).
Creighton Construction uses critical path analysis in scheduling its projects. The following list of activities and the network diagram presented below were prepared by Creighton for an apartment project prior to the start of work on the project.

| Activity | Description of Activity | Estimated Time Required (weeks) |
|---|---|---|
| A | Site selection and land purchase | 6 |
| B | Survey | 1 |
| C | Excavation | 3 |
| D | Foundation | 4 |
| E | City water and sewage lines | 8 |
| F | Rough plumbing | 8 |
| G | Framing and roofing | 6 |
| H | Wiring | 4 |
| I | Interior walls | 3 |
| J | Plumbing fixtures | 3 |
| K | Exterior siding and painting | 9 |
| L | Landscaping | 2 |

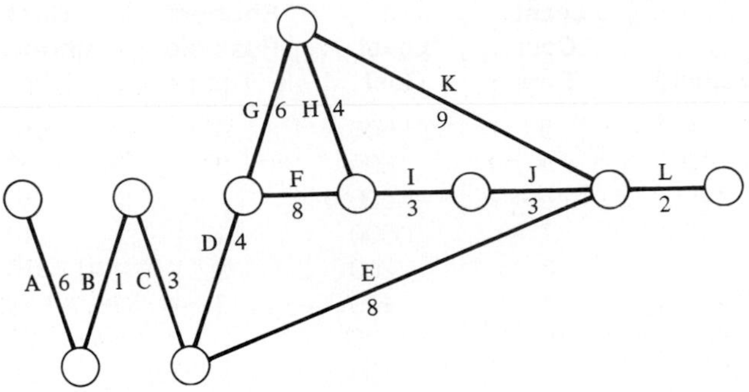


The apartment project is now in progress. An interim progress report indicates that the city water and sewage lines, rough plumbing, and wiring are all one-half complete and that the exterior siding and painting have not yet begun.

**Required**

**a.** Identify the critical path by letters and determine the expected completion time in weeks as estimated prior to the start of the project.

**b.** Using the interim progress report, identify the critical path by letters and determine the expected number of weeks for the remainder of the project.

**10-19 Cost to complete an activity as a function of time.**

Activity 5–8 of the Allied Construction Company involves the assembly of some equipment on a large construction site. It will take 160 labor hours to complete the assembly. The company has a crew of five persons available. Each member of the crew is paid $7 per hour. If a crew member shows up for any part of the day, that person must be paid for an entire 8-hour day. There is no cost if a person is not called in for a day. Up to three additional laborers may be obtained from Manpower for $150 per person for each day or portion of a day worked. Manpower employees will work only 8 hours per day; Allied's own employees can work for up to 12 hours per day, but hours over 8 are paid at the rate of 150% of straight time. Allied must rent equipment used in the assembly process for $30 per day. It pays the union a flat $10 for each of its employees who is called to the site for this activity (whether a person works for 1 day or 5, the charge is $10; the company can avoid the charge only by never calling a particular crew member to the site). Work begins on Monday.

**Required**

**a.** What is the minimum *time* required to complete this activity?

**b.** What is the dollar cost to complete this activity in 2, 3, 4, and 5 days?

**10-20 PERT/Cost: Time and cost budget.**

Cando, Inc., has set forth the following data in connection with a large-scale construction project in which it is participating as a subcontractor.

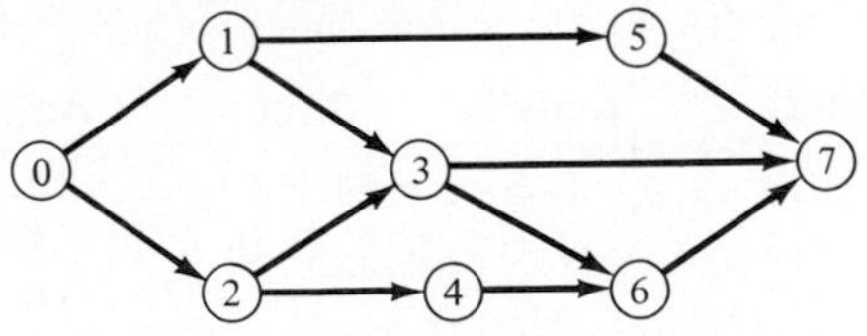

| Activity | Least-Cost Time | Least Cost | Shortest Possible Time | Cost to Shorten by 1 Period |
|---|---|---|---|---|
| 0–1 | 5 | $ 500 | 3 | $600 |
| 0–2 | 4 | 600 | 3 | 225 |
| 1–5 | 6 | 1,000 | 4 | 300 |
| 1–3 | 7 | 1,500 | 4 | 400 |
| 2–3 | 3 | 200 | 2 | 200 |
| 2–4 | 4 | 400 | 3 | 500 |
| 5–7 | 5 | 600 | 3 | 325 |
| 3–7 | 8 | 1,200 | 4 | 250 |
| 3–6 | 2 | 400 | 1 | 275 |
| 4–6 | 4 | 500 | 3 | 100 |
| 6–7 | 5 | 700 | 3 | 350 |

There is a $700 fine for each period in excess of 10.

**Required**

**a.** What is the optimal time to complete this project?

**b.** What is the optimal project (least) cost?

**10-21 PERT/Cost: Budget.**

A firm has contracted to construct a special piece of equipment. The customer wants the job to be completed within 10 days. If the job is not completed within the allotted time, there will be a $2,000-per-day fine for each day in excess of 10. An analysis of the blueprints reveals the following interrelationships between necessary activities. Activities 1–2 and 1–3 can both be started at the same time; 1–2 must be completed before 2–4 or 2–5 can be started; 2–4 must be completed before 4–7; 3–6 can start as soon as 1–3 is complete; when 3–6 is completed, work can begin on activity 6–7; and 5–7 can start after 2–5 is complete. The project is complete when milestone 7 is accomplished.

If the cost of each activity were minimized, it would take the following time to complete each activity.

| Activity | Time | Activity | Time | Activity | Time |
|---|---|---|---|---|---|
| 1–2 | 5 | 2–5 | 3 | 4–7 | 3 |
| 1–3 | 3 | 3–6 | 6 | 5–7 | 5 |
| 2–4 | 4 | | | 6–7 | 2 |

The activities can be shortened, however, by incurring extra costs (each activity can be shortened by at most one day). The costs to shorten each activity are as follows:

| Activity | Cost | Activity | Cost | Activity | Cost |
|---|---|---|---|---|---|
| 1–2 | $1,800 | 2–5 | $1,200 | 4–7 | $ 600 |
| 1–3 | 400 | 3–6 | 300 | 5–7 | 1,000 |
| 2–4 | 500 | | | 6–7 | 500 |

The minimum cost for each activity is as follows:

| Activity | Cost | Activity | Cost | Activity | Cost |
|---|---|---|---|---|---|
| 1–2 | $3,000 | 2–5 | $2,200 | 4–7 | $ 800 |
| 1–3 | 900 | 3–6 | 3,000 | 5–7 | 1,200 |
| 2–4 | 1,200 | | | 6–7 | 1,400 |

**Required**

**a.** Determine the least-cost time to complete this project.

**b.** If 40% of an activity's costs are incurred during the first day of the activity and the remainder of the costs are incurred in the last day of the activity, prepare the daily budget for this project.

**10-22 Critical path: Time and cost estimates.**

Apex Construction has prepared the following network diagram, which shows the interrelationships of several activities that must be completed to finish a project under contract. The contract calls for a penalty to be imposed on Apex in the amount of $1,000 per day for each day in excess of 15 that it takes to complete the project.

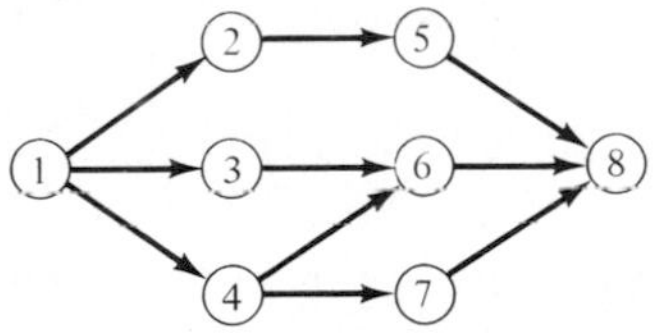


The firm has also prepared the following cost and time data.

| Activity | Least Cost to Complete | Least-Cost Time | Cost to Shorten by 1 Day | Shortest Possible Time |
|---|---|---|---|---|
| 1–2 | $2,000 | 5 | $300 | 2 |
| 1–3 | 6,000 | 3 | 500 | 2 |
| 1–4 | 5,000 | 10 | 800 | 7 |
| 2–5 | 1,000 | 7 | 400 | 6 |
| 3–6 | 4,000 | 8 | 900 | 6 |
| 4–6 | 6,000 | 7 | 600 | 4 |
| 4–7 | 3,000 | 4 | 500 | 3 |
| 5–8 | 7,000 | 6 | 700 | 5 |
| 6–8 | 8,000 | 5 | 700 | 3 |
| 7–8 | 2,000 | 6 | 600 | 4 |

**Required**

**a.** Determine the critical path.

**b.** What is the optimal time to complete this project?

**c.** What will be the total cost to complete the project?

**10-23 PERT/Cost: Budget.**
Phlowthru, Inc.'s, engineers have prepared the following diagram to represent the relationships among the activities necessary to complete a project.

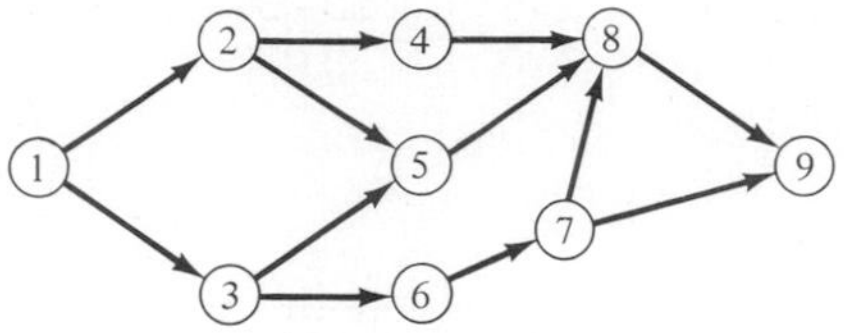


| Activity | Lowest Cost | Time Required Lowest Cost | Cost to Shorten by 1 Week | Shortest Time for Completion |
|---|---|---|---|---|
| 1–2 | $ 900 | 3 weeks | $300 | 2 weeks |
| 1–3 | 2,200 | 5 | 500 | 2 |
| 2–4 | 3,000 | 6 | 400 | 4 |
| 2–5 | 700 | 4 | 200 | 3 |
| 3–5 | 3,500 | 8 | 400 | 4 |
| 3–6 | 1,200 | 2 | 700 | 2 |
| 4–8 | 2,600 | 4 | 600 | 2 |
| 5–8 | 3,500 | 5 | 700 | 3 |
| 6–7 | 1,400 | 5 | 300 | 4 |
| 7–8 | 1,900 | 4 | 500 | 2 |
| 7–9 | 3,100 | 5 | 600 | 3 |
| 8–9 | 300 | 2 | 200 | 1 |

In order to prevent this project from holding up a bigger project, there is a penalty schedule as follows:

| Time Required | Weekly Penalty |
|---|---|
| 10 weeks or less | — |
| More than 10 weeks | $ 400 |
| More than 15 weeks | 900 |
| More than 17 weeks | 1,200 |
| More than 22 weeks | 1,500 |

**Required**
Prepare the budget for this project after costs have been optimized. Mark the activities in the budget which are on the critical path.

**10-24 Network: Time and cost budget.**
Bujit, Inc., provides the following information about a project.

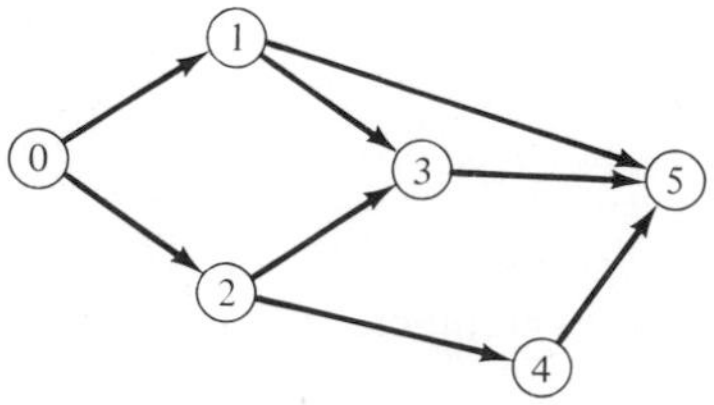

| Activity | Least Cost | Least-Cost Time | Cost to Shorten by 1 Period | Fastest Possible Completion Time |
|---|---|---|---|---|
| 0–1 | $ 800 | 4 | $200 | 1 |
| 0–2 | 1,700 | 3 | 600 | 3 |
| 1–3 | 2,000 | 5 | 700 | 3 |
| 2–3 | 2,100 | 3 | 600 | 2 |
| 2–4 | 1,900 | 4 | 800 | 3 |
| 1–5 | 1,400 | 3 | 700 | 2 |
| 3–5 | 1,100 | 4 | 500 | 2 |
| 4–5 | 1,300 | 5 | 300 | 2 |

The firm faces the following schedule of fines.

| Completion in Period | Incremental Fine | Total Fine |
|---|---|---|
| 0–7 | — | — |
| 8 | $ 500 | $ 500 |
| 9 | 500 | 1,000 |
| 10 | 1,000 | 2,000 |
| 11 | 1,000 | 3,000 |
| 12 | 2,500 | 5,500 |
| 13 | 2,500 | 8,000 |
| 14 | 4,000 | 12,000 |

**Required**

**a.** Determine the critical path.

**b.** Determine the least-cost budget for this firm.

**10-25 PERT/Cost: Draw network, determine fee, and minimize cost** (SMA adapted). Speedy Scientific Incorporated has a government contract to design and develop an air pollution control device. A study of the design problems likely to be encountered gives rise to the following schedule of times and costs.

| | Estimated Time (months) | | Estimated Costs | |
|---|---|---|---|---|
| Task | Earliest | Expected | Expected Cost for Expected Time | Cost to Reduce Task Time per Month |
| 0–1 | 6 | 8 | $ 1,000,000 | $ 50,000 |
| 0–2 | 3 | 5 | 2,000,000 | 20,000 |
| 0–4 | 6 | 10 | 4,000,000 | 10,000 |
| 1–3 | 10 | 12 | 1,500,000 | 30,000 |
| 1–4 | 12 | 16 | 5,000,000 | 100,000 |
| 2–4 | 6 | 7 | 1,800,000 | 25,000 |
| 2–5 | 6 | 9 | 3,000,000 | 40,000 |
| 3–6 | 2 | 2 | 3,500,000 | 15,000 |
| 4–6 | 3 | 4 | 2,500,000 | 10,000 |
| 4–7 | 6 | 8 | 2,000,000 | 30,000 |
| 5–7 | 2 | 3 | 500,000 | 35,000 |
| 6–8 | 7 | 9 | 1,500,000 | 20,000 |
| 7–8 | 10 | 11 | 4,500,000 | 50,000 |
| | | | $32,800,000 | |

The contract calls for a fee based on the foregoing cost estimate plus a fixed amount of $3 million. The contract provides for completion in 36 months with a penalty of $200,000 for each month late.

**Required**

**a.** Present a schedule showing eight different paths leading to completion and the time in months taken for each path. Identify the critical path. A diagram may help.

**b.** If the expected task times are all realized, what will be the net fee earned by the corporation?

**c.** How much can the corporation save by completing the project in its most cost-effective time?

**10-26 PERT/Cost: Resource allocation.**

The following times and costs have been estimated to complete an airborne radar guidance system for the Defense Department. In addition to the costs listed, the firm will incur a $200 per week fine if the project takes more than 20 weeks to complete. The firm further estimates that it will be able to save $400 per week in administrative overhead for every week this project can be shortened.

| Task | Least-Cost Time to Complete (weeks) | Least Cost | Cost to Shorten by 1 Week |
|---|---|---|---|
| 1–2 | 4 | $1,600 | $200 |
| 1–3 | 5 | 2,200 | 200 |
| 2–4 | 6 | 2,500 | 100 |
| 2–5 | 7 | 3,000 | 300 |
| 3–5 | 3 | 1,100 | 500 |
| 3–6 | 2 | 800 | 100 |
| 4–8 | 5 | 1,900 | 200 |
| 5–7 | 6 | 3,700 | 420 |
| 5–8 | 4 | 1,800 | 700 |
| 7–8 | 5 | 1,100 | 200 |
| 6–7 | 5 | 1,800 | 300 |

Task 1–2 can be shortened by 3 weeks; all other tasks can be shortened only 1 week each. Note that each task requires four laborers.

**Required**

**a.** Determine the least-cost time to complete this project.

**b.** Schedule the activities to minimize labor fluctuations.

**c.** Prepare a weekly budget assuming that all costs are incurred uniformly over time.

**10-27 Drawing a network of activities for an ad agency.**[3]

The preparation of a television commercial begins with a storyboard, a detailed sketching of each of the scenes in the commercial. When the story has been approved by a client's marketing department, it must then be approved by three different legal departments: (1) the ad agency's, (2) the client's, and (3) one rep-

[3]Adapted from facts given in "Cutting the Cost of Commercials," *Business Week* (February 15, 1982), pp. 118–121.

resenting the TV networks. Upon approval by all three legal departments, the agency typically submits the story to three production companies for bids.

After the production contract has been awarded, the producer must search for an ideal cast and filming location. The actual filming is followed by a lengthy process of editing and sound mixing.

Normally the preparation of the storyboard and client approval takes 8 weeks. The client is consulted on major decisions as the storyboard is being prepared, so there is no separate final approval. The ad agency's legal department is usually familiar with the story and can approve the story in 1 week. Similarly, the client's legal department takes only 1 week for approval. However, the network's legal representative usually takes 2 weeks. The production companies typically desire 2 weeks to prepare a bid for producing the commercial. Once the contract is awarded to the low bidder, the producer needs 2 weeks to choose a cast and find an appropriate site. Actual filming takes 1 week, but editing and sound mixing take another 3 weeks.

**Required**
Sketch the network of activities and determine the length of time required to complete a commercial.

**10-28 Extension of 10-27: Determination of least cost.**
Assume that the ad agency in 10-27 has been approached by a client who has contracted for some commercial time during the next Super Bowl football game. The client wants a new commerical ready for these time slots. However, the Super Bowl game is just 12 weeks away. The normal cost to produce this commercial would be $60,000. But since the cost of air time will exceed $250,000, the client is not overconcerned with the production cost of the commercial. Nonetheless, the client does expect the agency to minimize cost.

The ad agency can cut the time in half to prepare the story board by working overtime and adding extra personnel. This would increase costs by $6,000. Adding a legal liaison at a cost of $1,000 would enable them to get the agency's and client's legal staffs to approve the story while the story board is being prepared. The agency has no control over the time required to gain the network's legal approval.

If the agency indicates to producers that it will accept the first reasonable bid received, it can expect to receive a bid and sign the contract in 1 week. But doing so will probably result in a bid about $5,000 higher than what would otherwise be paid. Similarly, the producer can be told to simply hire some big-name stars instead of searching for the best cast. This would reduce casting and site selection time by 1 week, but the agency would need to pay an extra $10,000 for the stars.

By putting on extra staff costing $7,000, the agency can cut 1 week off the time to edit the commercial. It would cost an additional $15,000 to cut another week off the time required for editing and sound mixing.

**Required**
Determine the optimal cost for producing the commercial in time for the Super Bowl game.

**10-29 Developing a network and estimating time and cost to complete the activity.**
Chi Pi Alpha is considering whether to enter a float in the campuswide Spring Parade, to be held on April 15. The Independent Registrar's Service will award a

$1,000 prize to the best entry. A committee has determined that the following activities must be undertaken to complete the entry. First, an acceptable idea for the design must be agreed upon. This will take 2 weeks if assigned to a committee. If a contest were run instead and a $100 prize were offered, an acceptable idea would be forthcoming in 7 days. Once the idea is settled upon, construction of the basic framework for the float can begin. This will take 8 days if the fraternity members do it themselves. Alternatively, some professional carpenters can be hired for $800 to finish the framework in 3 days. Also, as soon as the idea is accepted, Chi Pi Alpha can go about the task of acquiring props (manikins, costumes, lights, and so forth). It will take a week to acquire these items by scavenging and borrowing, but 1 day if everything is bought or rented, at a cost of $300. Once the framework is complete, a chicken-wire mesh can be installed over the float in 2 days. When the mesh is installed, the props can be wired. This will take 1 day. Also, as soon as the chicken wire is installed, the fraternity members can start stuffing it with colored tissue (to look like flowers). It will take 4 days to install the tissue unless it is decided to spend $150 for beverages and make a party out of it, in which case it will take just 1 day. When the tissue and props are installed, the Student Endorsement Committee must inspect the float for safety. The inspection takes 1 day, but could be reduced to zero for $800.

According to "Graft Almost Always Prevails," applied consistent with last year's lack of principles, it is Chi Pi Alpha's opinion that they will win the prize for the float if it can be completed by the April 15 deadline.

**Required**

**a.** Draw the network of activities.

**b.** If Chi Pi Alpha completes each activity in its cheapest time, how long is the critical path?

**c.** If the project is begun on March 27, what should be done?

**d.** If it is already March 31, should the project be undertaken?

**10-30 Critical path analysis with slack—difficult.**

Alpha Air Research anticipates receiving a contract to build a prototype lightweight jet fighter. You are now preparing the budget for this contract. Activities with regard to this project will begin once the contract is received. The obligation will end with the delivery of this prototype to the military. Management has identified nine critical activities for this project, and has estimated the time to complete each activity.

1. Preparation of detailed design specifications for the jet—3 months.
2. Upon completion of the design specifications, the designs will be tested extensively by computer simulation—2 months.
3. Prior to beginning construction of the prototype, the firm must build an assembly facility—6 months.
4. The firm does not have sufficient capital to finance the construction of the prototype. Thus, prior to beginning actual construction of the prototype, the firm must arrange to borrow $4 million. It will take 1 month to find a lender.
5. Construction of the prototype can begin after the design specifications have been tested by simulation. Actual construction will take 8 months.
6. The firm will engage in an extensive marketing campaign to sell this aircraft to various foreign governments. Management refuses to begin the marketing pro-

gram until actual construction of the prototype has begun. It has been stung by past criticisms from some foreign buyers who have said that they do not even hear about new equipment until after the U.S. military has actually received delivery of the equipment. Therefore management feels that it is important for the entire marketing campaign for foreign sales to be completed before any deliveries are made. The marketing program takes 1 year.

7. The firm must train two test pilots to fly the aircraft. Training can begin as soon as the testing of the design specifications is complete. Training will take 3 months.
8. When construction of the prototype is complete, it must be inspected by the FAA for approval. Inspection will take 1 month.
9. After the prototype has been inspected, and when the pilots are ready, the prototype can be flight-tested. This testing will take 2 months.

Upon completion of the flight tests, the prototype is ready for delivery to the military. Payment for the aircraft is made upon delivery.

**Required**

a. Prepare a PERT diagram for this project; identify the critical path.
b. Alpha Air Research is short of cash. What is the earliest date on which they can expect to receive payment for the prototype if they stick to the plans outlined above?
c. Management agrees to make delivery on the date indicated in (b), but would like to postpone the incurrence of expenses as long as possible. What is the latest date on which pilot training can begin and not affect the completion date for the project?
d. The situation described in this problem forces some slack time in the noncritical paths. This slack could be eliminated by shortening the critical path. What kinds of costs should you estimate to determine whether the critical path should be shortened?

**10-31 PERT/Cost: Normal time and least-cost time—difficult.**

The network shown describes a project a firm will undertake. There is a $300-per-day fine for each day in excess of 9 that it takes to complete the project.

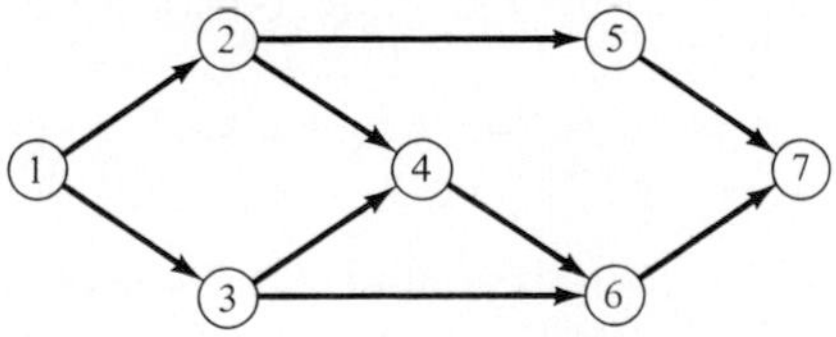


| Activity | Normal Time | Cost to Shorten by 1 Day | Fastest Time Possible |
|---|---|---|---|
| 1–2 | 3 days | $200 | 1 day |
| 1–3 | 2 | 300 | 1 |
| 2–5 | 6 | 75 | 5 |
| 2–4 | 4 | 125 | 2 |
| 3–4 | 3 | 400 | 2 |
| 3–6 | 3 | 200 | 1 |
| 4–6 | 2 | 100 | 1 |
| 5–7 | 5 | 50 | 3 |
| 6–7 | 6 | 200 | 3 |

**Required**

**a.** What is the critical path?

**b.** If each activity is finished in its normal time, how large a fine will the firm incur?

**c.** What is the least-cost time to finish the entire project? What activities will be shortened to accomplish this time?

10-32 **Network, Gantt chart and zero-stock inventory—requires study of Chapter 7.** Eastern Electronics has promised a customer delivery of 1,000 units of a product on day 80. The firm has adopted a zero-stock inventory policy, so it must carefully plan the timing of its orders for parts. The completed product consists of three subassemblies. The parts required for each subassembly and the lead times for each part are provided below.

| Subassembly | Part | Lead Time |
|---|---|---|
| DRW | K-12 | 4 days |
| DRW | K-14 | 6 days |
| LSM | Y-7 | 3 days |
| SLD | H-5 | 6 days |
| SLD | H-9 | 9 days |

It will take 7 days to assemble the DRW subassemblies and another 2 days to test them. The LSM subassembly requires 3 days. Testing the LSMs requires one day. When both the DRW and LSM subassemblies are complete, they are linked together. This operation will take 4 days. The SLD assembly requires 6 days. After assembly there is a 4-day testing period. The last step is to combine the SLD with the already linked DRW-LSM. This step requires 3 days. All parts for a subassembly must be available when the assembly of it is begun.

**Required**

Determine when purchase orders for each part should be released. (*Hint:* This amounts to preparing a Gantt chart with all slack time squeezed out.)

# PART THREE

## PRODUCT COSTING

# CHAPTER 11

# ALLOCATING COMMON COSTS

Part Three of the text, Chapters 11 to 17, is devoted to measuring the actual cost of producing a firm's products or services. While this cost information is required for external reporting, it is also derived for two major managerial purposes: (1) cost control and (2) marketing decisions.

## OBJECTIVES OF COST ACCUMULATION

Production managers need to monitor the cost of manufacturing the firm's products to ensure efficiency. A sudden change in costs may signal a production problem that requires attention.

Sales managers need cost information to evaluate the relative profitability of products. This will allow marketing personnel to channel their efforts toward promoting the firm's most profitable products. Further, if price competition intensifies, cost data will provide guidance on the amount of discounting that can be offered while still maintaining profitability.

In Chapter 2 we distinguished inventoriable (product) costs from period costs. Inventoriable costs were identified as all costs necessary to produce the firm's products and are therefore included in the computation of the products' unit costs. Period costs, in contrast, are those that expire in the period incurred; they are expensed independently of the movement of the firm's products. Our task in these next several chapters is to accumulate the product costs for each of the firm's products so that unit costs can be calculated. As we do so, we will also accumulate costs by responsibility center so that the efficiency of operations may be monitored.

### Overview of Cost Accumulation

The cost accumulation process is complicated by three factors: (1) Firms frequently incur common costs; (2) many production costs are incurred to provide intermediate services to manufacturing departments; and (3) many firms incur joint production costs.

**Common costs** are those that provide benefits to many (or all) of the firm's products but do not vary with small changes in the volume of the production of the products. For example, the building in which a firm manufactures products provides protection from the elements for all manufacturing operations. But tracing these costs to the individual products requires that we go through several steps. The first step is examined in the current chapter.

In the next chapter we examine the treatment of the cost to provide services to manufacturing departments. For example, a firm may produce its own electricity, which is used throughout the plant. Part of the costs to provide electricity will be the common costs assigned to the department producing the electricity. Getting this department's costs assigned to production departments is the subject of Chapter 12.

When we get to Chapter 13 we will have assigned all manufacturing costs to production departments. But a production department may well produce more than one end product. Chapter 13 addresses the problem of how to assign **joint costs** to product lines when two or more products are simultaneously derived from an operation.

Once we have all manufacturing costs charged to a product line, the final step is the calculation of the unit cost for each type of product. Chapters 14 to 17 examine these latter computations. Figure 11-1 summarizes the flow of the cost accumulation process and indicates the chapter numbers devoted to each step in the process. While we address the complications that occur in cost accumulation in the natural order in which firms must make the calculations, be aware that it is easy to get lost in the details and lose sight of the eventual objective: the determination of unit costs.

Let us illustrate the cost accumulation process with an example using a single common cost. Consider a firm that purchases a single insurance policy to cover property damage. A portion of the premium for the policy will be charged to each responsibility center benefiting from the coverage. Assuming that the firm's insurance premium is $50,000 and that the firm has only four responsibility centers, the initial charge to each center might be as follows:

| | |
|---|---|
| Selling and administration | $ 5,000 |
| Computer services | 10,000 |
| Engineering services | 5,000 |
| Production | 30,000 |

Now for the computer services center, the insurance premium becomes one of its costs for providing service. Other departments that use the computer facilities will be charged for the cost of services provided. In effect, then, the insurance premium charged to computer services will be passed on to the other departments. Assuming that 40% of the computer use was devoted to administration, 10% to engineering, and 50% to production, the amount of the insurance premium included in the computer center's charges to other departments would be

| | |
|---|---|
| Selling and administration | $4,000 |
| Engineering services | 1,000 |
| Production | 5,000 |

At this point the total insurance premium included in the cost to provide engineering services is $6,000 ($5,000 direct + $1,000 included in computing charges). These costs, in turn, are included as a cost to provide engineering services. Assuming that 20% of engineering's services went to administration and 80% to production, the total amount of insurance premiums included in the engineering department's charges to the other centers would be

| | |
|---|---|
| Selling and administration | $1,200 |
| Production | 4,800 |

Through this process of charging and recharging for services, the total amount of the insurance premium charged to the final user departments would be

| | |
|---|---|
| Selling and administration | |
| Direct charge | $ 5,000 |
| From computer services | 4,000 |
| From engineering | 1,200 |
| | $10,200 |
| Production | |
| Direct charge | $30,000 |
| From computer services | 5,000 |
| From engineering | 4,800 |
| | $39,800 |

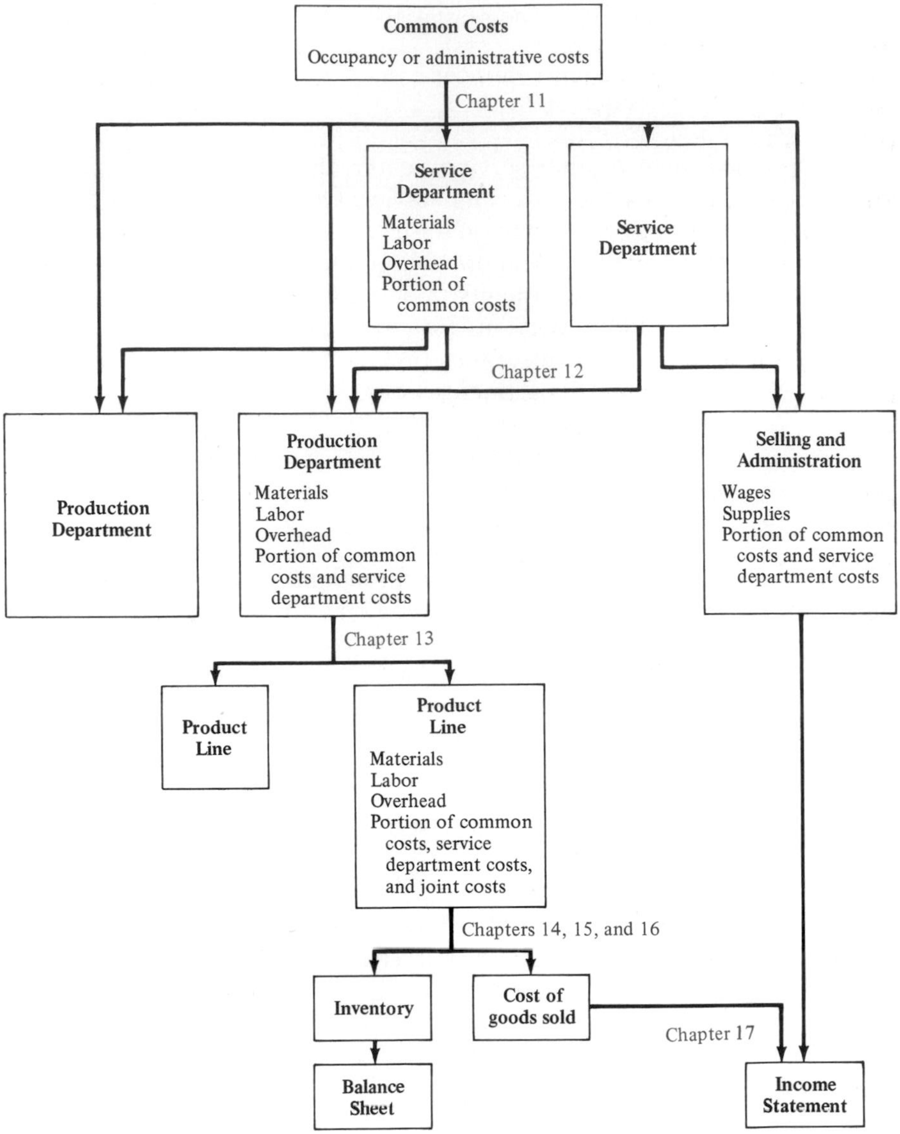


**FIGURE 11-1 An overview of the process for calculating manufacturing costs per unit.**

The entire $50,000 premium has eventually been charged in total to administration and production. The $10,200 charged to administration will be included in the income statement as a period expense. The $39,800 cost to production, however, will be included as a cost to produce the firm's products. If the department produced 79,600 units of product during the period, the cost of a unit would include a charge of $39,800/79,600 = $0.50 per unit for insurance. If 70,000 units were sold, then cost of goods sold would include 70,000 × $0.50 = $35,000 for insurance, while the remaining 9,600 × $0.50 = $4,800 would be included as part of the cost of inventory on the balance sheet.

Note that at every step, whenever a product or service is used by more than one department, the total cost to provide the product or service must be allocated to the user departments. Similarly, if a department provides more than one product or service, the department's total costs will have to be allocated to each product or service to determine the cost of providing those products and services. **Allocation,** the process of assigning a single cost to more than one object, is the very core of the process of cost accumulation. In the remainder of this chapter we will concentrate on the first two steps in Figure 11-1, assigning costs to the goods and services acquired and assigning the costs of the goods and services to the initial responsibility center using the goods or services.

## COST ALLOCATION

If goods and services were always purchased in individual units and all the goods and services of a particular type were always used by only one responsibility center, our job would simply be that of tracing the flow of costs. But firms rarely purchase individual units of goods and services, and these same items are often used by many departments. In these cases we generally allocate the common costs incurred. In every case there will be three questions that must be answered when making allocations:

1. What basis should be used for allocation?
2. Which costs should be allocated?
3. What procedures should be used for allocating common costs?

### What Basis to Use for an Allocation

By **allocation basis** we mean the unit of measure that is multiplied by a cost per unit to determine the total cost assigned to a cost object. For example, if we are trying to allocate the cost of running a computer to the users of the computer's services, the allocation base might be the number of requests for service made, the number of pages of output printed for each user, or the number of hours of central processor time devoted to each user. Our criteria for selecting among possible bases will be the existence of a cause-and-effect relationship. That is, we would like a measure that reflects a factor that causes the incurrence of most of the cost being allocated. Thus, if we find that almost all of the costs for running a computer vary with the number of hours that the central processing unit is run, CPU operating time would seem to be an excellent basis for allocating the computer costs. Some examples of allocation bases, drawn from a hospital, are listed in Exhibit 11-1.

Fortunately, cause-and-effect relationships tend to be identifiable for most costs. We tend to receive one bill for a single activity that caused the cost. However, cause and effect can be very difficult to determine when several services are obtained simultaneously and we are billed for a single amount. In these cases we need to analyze the situation to consider what the actual causes are. Consider, for example, the cost of electricity. Say our firm is currently paying $5,000 a month plus $0.20 per kilowatt-hour used. In this case, the variable service charge has a clear cause-and-effect relationship with the amount of electricity used by each department. But what of the "fixed" fee of $5,000? The $5,000 monthly charge is fixed relative to the use of electricity, but it is likely that the charge is variable with respect to the total capacity to provide electricity. That is, the monthly charge to provide a single 110-volt line to the firm will be quite different than that for supplying fifty 220-volt lines. Thought of in this way, we can see that we are really acquiring two different services: (1) actual electrical usage and (2) the capacity or capability to make use of the electricity. Very often, in these types of cases we need two allocation bases to reflect the two different causal factors: one based on departmental use and the second based on the capacity provided to each department.

Recall that one of our objectives for allocation is cost control. We want to choose allocation bases that reflect a cause-and-effect basis so that our charges to cost objects coincide with the actions that managers can take to actually reduce costs. If, in our electricity example, we allocate the total actual electricity bill solely on the basis of relative usage of electricity, managers can reduce the costs charged to them only by reducing usage. With this allocation basis, reducing the demand for capacity will not affect the costs allocated to the department. Thus managers will not be motivated to reduce demand for capacity even though such an action might reduce the firm's monthly fixed charge.

By identifying, to the extent practical, all cause-and-effect relationships and establishing separate allocation bases for each, we will better achieve our objective of cost control. Consider what will happen if we allocate our electricity bill on two bases: the fixed charge based on capacity and the variable charge based on usage. Now managers can reduce the

**EXHIBIT 11-1 Typical Cost Allocation Bases**[a]

| Cost Pool | Allocation Basis |
|---|---|
| Building depreciation | Square feet |
| Employee fringe benefits | Gross departmental salaries |
| Administration and general | Accumulated cost |
| Operation of plant | Square feet |
| Laundry service | Pounds of laundry[b] |
| Housekeeping | Hours of service[b] |
| Dietary | Meals served to patients |
| Cafeteria | Average number of employees |
| Nursing administration | Number of nursing hours per department |
| Central control supply service | Costed requisitions |
| Pharmacy | Costed requisitions |
| Medical records and library | Time spent |

[a]These are the actual bases used by a medium-sized hospital located in central Oklahoma.
[b]As derived from occasional studies of actual activity.

costs charged to them both by conserving the actual use of electricity and by minimizing the demand for capacity.[1]

Let us temper our previous statement by recognizing that just because we can identify a cause-and-effect relationship does not imply that we can always justify the expense of accurately allocating costs based on that relationship. Where electricity is cheap, we may well be better off to allow some waste rather than incur the cost of installing usage meters in every department. In this case electricity is included in plantwide overhead. But as electricity becomes expensive, we will get better cost control if every department is charged for actual usage. But even then we may not need an accurate measure of usage; instead we may settle for an estimate. For electricity we might allocate the cost on the basis of the number of outlets in each department, arguing that both capacity and use are related to the number of outlets. Another possibility is to add the rated wattage of all the equipment in a department. By using an estimate we are trading off the cost of gathering information with the value of having accurate infor-

[1]Note that, from a practical point of view, we may not be able to adjust capacity quickly. The cost of removing an excess line may be prohibitive. The firm may well want to wait until there are several changes to be made to its electrical system before deleting the extra line. Nonetheless, the cost of having the excess line is not producing an asset. As such, it theoretically should not be part of the product cost but rather should be written off as a loss. Including such a loss on management reports has the added benefit of periodically reminding management to get rid of the excess line as soon as it is practical to do so. Further, reporting the loss separates the continuing costs for which we will hold a manager responsible from those costs that should be deleted but are beyond the manager's authority to control.

mation. Only when the cost of electricity becomes significant will we be able to justify the cost of metering departmental usage and capacity.

For resources whose costs are predominantly fixed or variable, management may choose to treat all the costs as fixed or variable. In this situation the error introduced in the accounting information will be small and we will save the effort (and cost) of having to allocate fixed and variable costs separately. However, we must be careful not to overdo the savings of accounting effort to the detriment of the information. Two significant problems can (and frequently do) arise when we fail to treat fixed and variable costs separately.

If we treat all of a resource's costs as variable, even when they are not, fixed costs will be allocated in proportion to the user department's actual demands for service in the current period. In this case a manager of a user department does not have total control over the amount of cost that will be charged to the manager's department. The problem is that the amount of fixed cost charged to any department will be a function of the total use of services made by all departments. Thus it is possible for a department to maintain a constant demand for service but have its charges increase if another department decreases its demand for service. In Exhibit 11-2, Allocation 1, department A maintains demand at 200 units of service but its charge for service increases from $4,353 to $4,667 from year 1 to year 2 because department B's demand has fallen from 225 to 175 units of service. Holding a manger responsible for a cost that is substantially not under the manager's control can lead to frustration and distrust of the accounting system. If a manager ignores the accounting system, a significant portion of the financial control system is destroyed.

A similar problem happens if all costs are treated as fixed costs. When all costs were treated as variable, department A's total charge varied inversely with the total demand for service. When all costs are treated as fixed, department A's charge will vary directly with the total demand for service. When costs are considered fixed, each user department is typically charged a set proportion of costs. For example, in Allocation 2 of Exhibit 11-2 we see that each user department is charged one-half of the service department's costs. If department A maintains its demand at 200 units of service but department B increases demand from 175 units to 225 units (reverse the order of years 1 and 2 in the exhibit), we see that A's costs will go from $4,375 to $4,625. Department B has increased demand by 50 units, causing an increase of $500 in costs, but because of the fixed allocation proportion, $250 of this cost is charged to A. Once again, department A is charged for a cost that is not under the manager's control.

Another problem with erroneously treating all costs as fixed or variable arises when we look at the behavioral implications for a manager trying to optimize performance. When all costs are treated as variable, the

**EXHIBIT 11-2 Effect of Using a Single Allocation Base for a Resource with a Mixed Cost Function**

Cost function for the acquired resource = \$5,000 per period + \$10 per unit of service

| Year 1 | Year 2 |
|---|---|
| Department A uses 200 units of service | Department A uses 200 units of service |
| Department B uses 225 units of service | Department B uses 175 units of service |
| Total cost: \$5,000 + \$10(425) = \$9,250 | Total cost: \$5,000 + \$10(375) = \$8,750 |

**ALLOCATIONS**

1. All costs treated as variable per unit of service

| | Year 1 | | Year 2 | |
|---|---|---|---|---|
| To department A | (200/425)(\$9,250) = | \$4,353 | (200/375)(\$8,750) = | \$4,667 |
| To department B | (225/425)(\$9,250) = | 4,897 | (175/375)(\$8,750) = | 4,083 |
| | | \$9,250 | | \$8,750 |

2. All costs treated as fixed, equal long-run expected demand

| | Year 1 | | Year 2 | |
|---|---|---|---|---|
| To department A | (1/2)(\$9,250) = | \$4,625 | (1/2)(\$8,750) = | \$4,375 |
| To department B | (1/2)(\$9,250) = | 4,625 | (1/2)(\$8,750) = | 4,375 |
| | | \$9,250 | | \$8,750 |

3. Fixed and variable costs allocated separately

| | Year 1 | | Year 2 | |
|---|---|---|---|---|
| To department A | (1/2)(\$5,000) + \$10(200) = | \$4,500 | (1/2)(\$5,000) + \$10(200) = | \$4,500 |
| To department B | (1/2)(\$5,000) + \$10(225) = | 4,750 | (1/2)(\$5,000) + \$10(175) = | 4,250 |
| | | \$9,250 | | \$8,750 |

marginal cost charged to a user is higher than the true marginal cost of the service. By lowering demand for a service, a user's costs drop by more than the marginal cost because some fixed costs are transferred to other user departments. The result is that there will be a tendency to underutilize services.

Exactly the reverse happens when all costs are treated as fixed. Now when a department increases its demand for service, part of the marginal costs it causes are allocated to other departments. Since the department using the services is not fully charged for the additional costs, it will tend to overutilize the resource.

### Which Costs to Allocate

The next question arises when we record the actual results of operations. Should we charge cost objects for the *actual* costs incurred or for *budgeted* costs? Charging actual costs may penalize a responsibility center for inefficiencies not under its control. This occurs when a responsibility center uses a product or service provided by another responsibility center. For example, assume that the purchasing department, through an error, pays too high a price for a material and the actual cost is assigned to the production department assembling the product. Then when we evaluate the assembly department's performance by comparing budgeted costs to actual costs, the department's cost will be "above budget." On the other hand, by charging only the costs that should have been incurred for the quantity of goods or services provided to the department, we escape this problem. While charging a budgeted cost figure seems simple for this example, the decision to use budgeted costs can result in quite an increase in accounting effort since we will have to determine a budgeted cost for the services provided by every department that passes its costs to other departments.

## PROCEDURES FOR ALLOCATING COMMON COSTS

So far our discussion has centered on separable costs. **Separable costs** are costs that are capable of being traced, on a cause-and-effect basis, to a particular cost object (although it may be uneconomic to do so). When the incurrence of a single cost provides two or more products or services and we are unable to determine a clear cause-and-effect relationship between the individual items acquired and the cost incurred, the cost is referred to as a common cost or joint cost.[2] An example of a common cost is a Wide Area Telephone Service (WATS) line. With a WATS line, a firm pays a flat monthly fee for the right to make long-distance telephone calls within a specified area. Since the cost is not related to the specific calls made, it is difficult to determine a cause-and-effect relationship for assigning the cost of the WATS line to the various user departments.

### Reasons for Allocating Costs

Although it may be difficult to determine a proper allocation basis for a common cost, the broad objectives for allocating common costs are the

[2]Some writers make a distinction between common costs and joint costs. When this is so, *common costs* usually refer to the costs to acquire two or more products and services only indirectly related to the firm's final outputs. *Joint costs,* in contrast, usually refer to the costs of simultaneously producing two or more final products, or major components of final products. The reader should realize, however, that the practical and theoretical problems encountered in the treatment of common and joint costs are identical.

same as those for separable costs—cost control and income measurement. Although we may not be able to identify a cause-and-effect relationship between services used and the specific common cost incurred, we know that use and cost are at least indirectly related. If a firm acquires a WATS line and charges the entire cost to the administrative unit that chose to acquire the line, what can be expected to happen? Other user departments will have been provided a free good. Simple economics tell us there will be a great deal of demand for this good. Users in departments not charged for the service will use it anytime the perceived payoff is greater than zero (the payoff may be personal—the chance to talk to an old friend). Under these conditions the demand for the service is likely to exceed supply (the line is always busy), so one or more additional lines are added, thereby increasing the monthly WATS bill. One means for preventing nonproductive calls, and thus controlling costs, is to charge for them. By allocating a cost for each call, we are in effect establishing a price for each call. In theory this should give us some assurance that departments use the telephone service only when perceived benefits exceed the allocated charge.

The second objective for allocating common costs is to determine product costs. GAAP defines the cost of an asset as all costs necessary to acquire an asset and get it ready for its intended use. Common costs incurred in a firm's manufacturing process are part of the costs to acquire the firm's inventory and should therefore become part of the cost of the inventory.

Although allocations are required for external reporting, they are not required for internal use. Yet most large firms allocate common costs for internal purposes as well. One possible explanation for this behavior is that allocations may make it easier to monitor the profitability of products. In a large firm it may be uneconomic to attempt to make a periodic marginal analysis of the profitability of each of hundreds of thousands of products. Instead, the firm can use its accounting system for external reporting, which includes allocated costs, to generate product line income statements. Products that show a loss, or very small income, can then be more carefully analyzed to determine if they are profitable. In this case the accounting reports serve as an attention-directing device. The reports alert managers to potential problem areas. But, as we point out in Chapter 5, average costs, including allocated costs, should not be used for decisions such as dropping a product. The correct approach is to compare differential revenues to differential costs.

Although the objectives for allocating common costs are clear, the means are not. Because, by definition, clear cause-and-effect relationships cannot be found, a variety of arbitrary estimation procedures have been proposed and used. We briefly describe several of the more popular procedures.

### Physical Basis

Earlier when we were approximating cause-and-effect relationships we tended to use a measure of some physical attribute of the user of a service (see Exhibit 11-1). The major advantages of **physical measures** are that they are unambiguous and inexpensive to use. For the most part, physical measures need little additional information beyond what would be available for other purposes anyway. In addition, physical means often have an indirect relationship to total cost for common costs. As such, common costs are frequently allocated to users of a resource in proportion to physical measures.

For example, a firm might choose to allocate its heating costs to factory overhead and general and administrative expense based on the relative volume of space occupied by the factory and the office. If manufacturing operations utilized 80,000 cubic feet of space, whereas approximately 20,000 cubic feet were occupied by administrative offices, the monthly heating bill would be charged 80% to factory overhead control and 20% to administrative overhead. Note that the measurement of relative space would need to be made only once. We could use the same relative proportions every month as long as there were no changes in the size of the manufacturing or office facilities.

Physical measures are often used as a means for charging multiple users for services. Many state-owned toll roads and toll bridges impose user charges to recover the cost of construction plus repairs. These charges are frequently based on the number of axles per vehicle. The rationale is that both construction costs and wear and tear depend on the weight of vehicles using the facility. However, the cost to weigh each vehicle (both in terms of the cost to monitor a scale and in delay costs for the users) is prohibitive. However, the number of axles on a vehicle is generally related to the gross weight of the vehicle, and is much easier to observe. Thus the number of axles is used as the basis for the charge on the assumption that this is a cost-effective estimate of the relative weight of vehicles.

### Relative Sales Value

Oftentimes cause and effect are not clear at all. For example, in a multidivisional firm, what is the cause of central office administrative expenses? Intuition suggests that these costs are related to the size of activities, but measuring size is difficult. In these situations, many firms use divisional sales as the measure of divisional sizes. Central administrative expenses are then allocated to each division in the proportion of each division's sales to the firm's total sales.

The **relative sales value** method seems to be particularly common in the motion picture and television industries. Firms on the production side of these industries tend to have very large facilities costs (the costs of maintaining sound stages and very expensive audio and visual recording equipment). These facilities are used for the production of many scripts, and their costs are frequently allocated to the individual project based on the gross revenue produced by the project. Thus if a studio incurred general production costs of $2,100,000 in a period in which four scripts were completed, the common costs might be allocated as follows:

| Script | Gross Lease Revenue | Proportion of Total Revenue | Allocated General Production Costs |
|---|---|---|---|
| A | $ 500,000 | 5/30 | $ 350,000 |
| B | 1,000,000 | 10/30 | 700,000 |
| C | 1,400,000 | 14/30 | 980,000 |
| D | 100,000 | 1/30 | 70,000 |
| Total | $3,000,000 | | $2,100,000 |

To these allocated general production costs the specific separable costs traced to each project would be added. These latter costs might include the cost of actors, props, and specific promotional costs. After accumulating these costs, we could then determine the profits earned by each project.

There are two significant problems with using the relative sales value approach. First, we need to know the actual sales generated by each cost object. If we are producing products with known selling prices, this may not be a large problem. But when used as in our movie industry example, there may be a significant delay before we determine the gross receipts from a cost object. This delay means we cannot report the results of operations for quite some time.

A more important objection is the inherent arbitrariness of the allocation. Successful (in terms of gross receipts) scripts are allocated much larger costs than unsuccessful scripts. In effect, the large revenue generators subsidize the less profitable projects. When separable costs are then added, the "most successful" projects may actually show losses. This, of course, can be devastating to anyone who has a profit-sharing agreement for a specific script (for example, the leading stars of a successful film). On the other hand, the relative sales value method is very easy to implement and thus the cost of doing the accounting is minimal.

### Relative Cost

Another approach related to the user's size is to allocate on the basis of the other costs incurred by users—that is, on the basis of **relative costs.** Thus corporate administrative costs might be allocated to the firm's operating divisions in proportion to each division's total separable costs.

For example, assume that Division 1 has total cost of goods sold of \$800,000, and selling and administrative costs of \$200,000, while Division 2's cost of goods sold was \$1,900,000 and selling and administrative costs were \$100,000. If corporate administrative costs were \$120,000, they might be allocated to the divisions as follows:

$$\text{Division 1: } \frac{\$1{,}000{,}000}{\$1{,}000{,}000 + \$2{,}000{,}000} \times \$120{,}000 = \$40{,}000$$

$$\text{Division 2: } \frac{\$2{,}000{,}000}{\$1{,}000{,}000 + \$2{,}000{,}000} \times \$120{,}000 = \$80{,}000$$

But note that by using total costs, the allocation of corporate administrative costs is heavily influenced by each division's cost of goods sold. But cost of goods sold may not be an accurate reflection of a division's relative size in terms of investment or of personnel. To avoid this problem, specific costs like total divisional payroll are often picked as the basis for allocating home office expense. Note, by the way, how similar this is to the allocation of departmental overhead to products on the basis of direct labor hours or direct labor cost.

The relative sales value and relative cost approaches are sometimes called "ability to bear" allocations. This terminology recognizes that these allocations are based more on size and the ability of a division or responsibility center to absorb the allocation than on a cause-and-effect relationship. While acceptable for external reporting, these approaches can be very misleading to management for decision making.

### Incremental Cost

The fact that we are going to incur a specific cost anyway often leads us to adding another cost. For example, if a firm is sending an employee across the country to transact business, the employee might choose to stop en route to visit friends. That is, the employee would not have made the visit had it not been for the fact that it could be made for a very small additional cost over what the employer was going to pay anyway. In these circumstances it is typical for the joint transportation cost to be allocated such that the employer pays the full cost that would have been incurred for just the business trip, while the employee pays for any incremental costs caused by the side trip. Similarly, if an employee takes a spouse on a business trip, the employee usually needs to pay only **incremental costs.**

Although the incremental cost approach is generally considered fair when it is obvious which cost was tacked onto the other cost, the approach falls apart when there is no clear indication of the ordering in which the costs were incurred. For example, consider an engineer based in Los Angeles who must inspect two different construction projects. One of the projects is located in Minneapolis and the other is in Atlanta. Assume that a round-trip fare to Minneapolis would cost $400 while a roundtrip fare from Los Angeles to Atlanta would cost $600. To save money and time, the engineer actually travels in a triangle from Los Angeles to Minneapolis to Atlanta and back to Los Angeles. The total cost amounts to $750. If we use the incremental cost approach to allocate the joint cost to the projects, we might charge $400 to the Minneapolis project and the incremental cost of $350 to the Atlanta project. Unfortunately, it could just as easily be argued that we should charge $600 to the Atlanta project and the incremental cost of $150 to the Minneapolis project. When one trip has not been clearly added onto the other, there is no basis for choosing between the possible alternative incremental cost allocations. But when the ordering of costs is clear, such as taking a spouse on a business trip, the incremental cost approach appropriately captures the cause-and-effect relationship.

### Shapley Value

**Shapley value allocations** are an average of all possible incremental cost allocations. The incremental costs for each cost object are calculated for every possible expansion path. An **expansion path** is a presumed ordering of the sequence in which decisions were made by users to join in acquiring a common resource. If there are two users, A and B, there are two possible expansion paths: AB and BA. That is, either user A or user B is assumed to have made the first decision to acquire the resource and then the other joined in to acquire the resource jointly. If there are three users, A, B, and C, then there are six possible expansion paths: ABC, ACB, BAC, BCA, CAB, and CBA. In general, for $n$ users there are $n!$ expansion paths. After each user's incremental costs are calculated for every possible expansion path the incremental costs are averaged to yield the Shapley allocation.

Using the facts in the example in which an engineer travels to Minneapolis and Atlanta, there are two possible expansion paths:

| | Incremental Costs | | |
|---|---|---|---|
| **Expansion Path** | **Minneapolis** | **Atlanta** | **Total** |
| Minneapolis first | $400 | $350 | $ 750 |
| Atlanta first | 150 | 600 | 750 |
| Total | $550 | $950 | $1,500 |
| Average incremental cost | $275 | $475 | $ 750 |

To determine the Shapley allocation, we total the possible incremental allocations for each site and divide by the number of possible allocations.

For our example, $275 of the $750 cost would be charged to Minneapolis and $475 would be charged to Atlanta.

The Shapley allocation is an improvement over the incremental cost approach when there is no clear order in which decisions to add costs were made. Instead of one cost object being charged for the full cost to acquire services separately, and other objects being charged incremental costs, the Shapley method gives all users a portion of the benefits arising from the combined acquisitions through an averaging process.

### Alternative Cost

The **alternative cost allocation** procedure is very similar to the Shapley allocation. It also allocates the savings from making a combined purchase to the cost objects involved. However, instead of the averaging process, the savings are allocated in proportion to the cost of the best alternative means of acquiring each user's products or services. For our traveling engineer, the alternative would be to make each trip separately. The alternative costs were $400 for Minneapolis and $600 for Atlanta, or a total of $1,000. Because the actual cost for the combined trip was $750, the combination yielded a savings of $250. These savings are allocated to the two sites in proportion to the alternative costs. Thus 40% of the savings will be allocated to Minneapolis and 60% to Atlanta. The resulting allocation is as follows:

| | Minneapolis | Atlanta | Total |
|---|---|---|---|
| Costs if trips were not combined | $400 | $600 | $1,000 |
| Savings from combined trip | 100 | 150 | 250 |
| Allocation and net cost | $300 | $450 | $ 750 |

Although the approach just outlined stresses that we are allocating the savings arising from the combined purchase, the same resulting allocations can be obtained by simply allocating the actual cost in proportion to the alternative costs:

| | | |
|---|---|---|
| Minneapolis | ($400 ÷ $1,000)($750) = | $300 |
| Atlanta | ($600 ÷ $1,000)($750) = | 450 |
| Total | | $750 |

The alternative cost procedure gets quite cumbersome if more than two products or services are acquired simultaneously. When it is time to determine the best alternative cost for acquiring the product or service for each cost object, we must evaluate all of the available subcombinations. For example, if the engineer is traveling to four cities—Minneapolis, Atlanta,

Dallas, and Denver—it is necessary with the alternative cost method to compute all of the following alternative costs:

| Independent | Pairs | Triples |
|---|---|---|
| Minneapolis | Minneapolis-Atlanta | Minneapolis-Atlanta-Dallas |
| Atlanta | Minneapolis-Dallas | Minneapolis-Atlanta-Denver |
| Dallas | Minneapolis-Denver | Minneapolis-Dallas-Denver |
| Denver | Atlanta-Dallas | Atlanta-Dallas-Denver |
| | Atlanta-Denver | |
| | Dallas-Denver | |

Through a series of steps we eventually will get the best alternative cost for going to each city. How we do so is illustrated in the demonstration problem at the end of the chapter.

The alternative cost and Shapley methods usually result in very similar allocations. They differ in that the alternative cost method gives more of the benefits (cost savings) to cost objects with higher alternative costs. The rationale is that larger (more costly) cost objects cause more of the savings when a combined purchase is made.

## CHOOSING THE PROCEDURE TO USE

Which allocation procedure is to be preferred in a situation depends upon the nature of the common cost involved and the availability of data. When cause-and-effect relationships cannot be determined, the Shapley and alternative cost approaches use market prices to acquire products or services separately as a guide to the allocation. In this way the resources acquired are valued in relation to their value to society as a whole, as reflected by their market prices. If the savings from a combined purchase are thought to be a function of the amount of resources acquired, the alternative cost approach is preferred.

In some cases the data needed for the Shapley and alternative cost methods are not available. For example, it is unlikely that an accurate measure can be obtained for the corporate headquarters costs that would be incurred by the Chevrolet Division of General Motors if it were an independent company. In these cases we are generally forced to use an ability-to-bear basis. But whether we use sales, total costs, or a component of costs is a matter of judgment. The choice depends on what we believe the underlying cause-and-effect relationship to be.

Physical bases are best when we have a good, but not perfect, understanding of the cause-and-effect relationship. Here the choice of a basis is frequently tempered by the need for accurate information and the cost to acquire it. Thus the cost of a janitorial service may be allocated to departments based upon square footage instead of time spent in each department. Such a choice is justified if the amount of janitorial costs allocated to each department is too minor to affect decisions and the cost to do a time study is high.

## SUMMARY

The common costs to provide goods or services to many users are allocated to the users to encourage cost control and to determine the cost of a firm's final products or services. The ultimate goal in choosing an allocation basis is to capture the underlying cause-and-effect relationship that governs the level of cost incurred. In many cases identifying a cause-and-effect relationship may be elusive. In other cases, the cost of monitoring a basis known to be related to the incurrence of a common cost may be too high. In either of these cases, management may have to use one of the arbitrary allocation bases described in the chapter.

## DEMONSTRATION PROBLEM

Over lunch one day, the manager of federal government sales (FGS) for the Software Development Corporation was complaining to the manager of the sales to state and local governments (SLS): "Our hotel costs in the state capital are getting out of hand. Last year I spent 80 nights there. The hotel I prefer costs $55 per night, but sometimes I have to stay in a more expensive hotel, and on other occasions I've had to stay in some pretty run-down places. In total my lodging costs for last year were $4,400. That's really chewing up my travel budget."

The manager of state and local sales agreed. "I'm in the state capital even more than you. My major customer is the state government, so I'm there at least a couple of nights a week. I believe I spent 120 nights last year in the capital city. Your average night's cost is probably about what I paid."

After lunch the FGS manager thought about leasing a hotel room in the capital on a year-round basis and sharing the cost with the state and local sales division. A call placed to the manager of commercial sales (CS) revealed that the commercial sales manager spent an average of 75 nights a year in the city. However, the CS manager insisted on a suite. The explanation was that customers often called the hotel or met the manager at the hotel and the manager felt an impressive showing helped business. The commercial sales manager estimated that a suite averaged $100 per night.

The FGS manager then contacted a comfortable, well-located hotel in the city. The manager found that the hotel was willing to lease a room on an annual basis and would charge a greatly reduced per-day fee. A single room normally renting for $55 per night could be leased for an annual fee of $8,030 (or $22 per night). The hotel was also willing to lease a three-room suite (two bedrooms and a parlor) for $12,775 per year ($35 per night). From this information the manager laid out the following alternatives.

**1.** Continue as we are now:

| | |
|---|---|
| FGS | $ 4,400 |
| SLS | 6,600 |
| CS | 7,500 |
| Total | $18,500 |

**2.** Lease a room and share with SLS:

| | |
|---|---|
| FGS + SLS | $ 8,030 |
| CS | 7,500 |
| Total | $15,530 |

**3.** Lease a suite and share with SLS and CS:

| | |
|---|---|
| FGS + SLS + CS | $12,775 |

Then the FGS manager noticed that the other managers might also consider the following.

**4.** SLS and CS lease a suite:

| | |
|---|---|
| FGS | $ 4,400 |
| SLS + CS | 12,775 |
| Total | $17,175 |

The next day the FGS manager invited the other two managers to lunch. All three agreed that leasing a suite made sense. They then proceeded into a discussion of how to share the cost.

**Required**

Determine the costs to be allocated to each manager, assuming that last year's usage rates would continue for the next year, under each of the following proposals:

**a.** Costs would be shared based on an equal charge per use of the suite.

**b.** Costs would be shared in proportion to the total dollar sales each division made in the capital city. Last year's sales by division were as follows:

| | |
|---|---|
| FGS | $ 5,600,000 |
| SLS | 14,375,000 |
| CS | 4,285,000 |

**c.** Costs would be shared based on the Shapley allocation.

**d.** Costs would be allocated in proportion to the best alternative cost.

**Solution**

**a.** The managers are anticipating a total of 275 days' use of the suite. This implies an average cost per day of $12,775 ÷ 275 = $46.455. The charge to each division would be

| Division | Days | Charge | Total |
|---|---|---|---|
| FGS | 80 | $46.455 | $ 3,716 |
| SLS | 120 | 46.455 | 5,575 |
| CS | 75 | 46.455 | 3,484 |
| Total | 275 | | $12,775 |

While everyone benefits from this allocation, the big winner is commercial sales. CS insisted on the more expensive room, yet pays the same daily fee as the other users.

**b.** With the relative sales value allocation each division is charged a percent of the total cost determined by each division's sales as a percent of total sales. The resulting allocation is

| Division | Sales | Sales (%) | Cost | Total |
|---|---|---|---|---|
| FGS | $ 5,600,000 | 23 | $12,775 | $ 2,938.25 |
| SLS | 14,375,000 | 59 | 12,775 | 7,537.25 |
| CS | 4,285,000 | 18 | 12,775 | 2,299.50 |
| Total | $24,260,000 | 100 | | $12,775.00 |

Although this allocation will appeal to two of the managers, the manager of SLS will find it unacceptable. The allocation charges SLS more than the cost SLS is currently incurring by renting rooms as needed.

**c.** The Shapley allocation requires us to calculate the incremental cost which each division adds along all possible expansion paths.

| | Incremental Costs | | | |
|---|---|---|---|---|
| Expansion Paths | FGS | SLS | CS | Total |
| FGS,SLS, CS | $ 4,400 | $ 3,630 | $ 4,745 | $12,775 |
| FGS, CS, SLS | 4,400 | 875 | 7,500 | 12,775 |
| SLS, FGS, CS | 1,430 | 6,600 | 4,745 | 12,775 |
| SLS, CS, FGS | 0 | 6,600 | 6,175 | 12,775 |
| CS, FGS, SLS | 4,400 | 875 | 7,500 | 12,775 |
| CS, SLS, FGS | 0 | 5,275 | 7,500 | 12,775 |
| Total | $14,630 | $23,855 | $38,165 | $76,650 |
| Average (÷ 6) | $ 2,438 | $ 3,976 | $ 6,361 | $12,775 |

The entries in the first row were determined as follows: If FGS operates on its own, then it must pay $4,400 in lodging costs. If FGS and SLS combine to lease a room for $8,030, the incremental cost that SLS has caused is $8,030 − $4,400 = $3,630. When CS joins the group they rent the suite for $12,775. The incremental cost caused by CS is $12,775 − $8,030 = $4,745.

Note an interesting result in the fourth row. In this row SLS is considered to be the first division in the expansion path. Operating alone SLS incurs a cost of $6,600. When SLS and CS combine, their best alternative is to rent the suite. That is, the suite's cost of $12,775 is less than the cost for these two divisions operating independently. Thus CS adds $12,775 − $6,600 = $6,175 as the incremental cost. But now when FGS joins the group there is no additional cost. The cost stays at $12,775, so FGS's incremental cost is zero. The average incremental cost, the last row, is the Shapley allocation of costs to each division.

**d.** The best alternative cost allocation requires us to calculate each division's best alternative relative to all three sharing the cost of the suite. This means we must calculate the cost allocated to each division under the best possible sharing arrangement between any two pairs of divisions.

| | | Allocated Cost | | |
|---|---|---|---|---|
| **Combination** | **Best Alternative** | **FGS** | **SLS** | **CS** |
| FGS and SLS | $ 8,030 | $3,212 | $4,818 | — |
| FGS and CS | 11,900 | 4,400 | — | $7,500 |
| SLS and CS | 12,775 | — | 5,980 | 6,795 |
| All independent | 18,500 | 4,400 | 6,600 | 7,500 |
| Best alternative cost | | $3,212 | $4,818 | $6,795 |

In the first row, if FGS and SLS combine they will share a single room costing $8,030. Each division's best alternative cost to that arrangement is to acquire rooms independently. If they acquire rooms independently, they will incur costs of $4,400 and $6,600, respectively. The $8,030 is then allocated to each division in proportion to the independent costs:

$$\text{To FGS} \quad \frac{\$4,400}{\$11,000} \times \$8,030 = \$3,212$$

$$\text{To SLS} \quad \frac{\$6,600}{\$11,000} \times \$8,030 = \$4,818$$

In the second row, even if FGS and CS wanted to combine, their best strategy is to acquire rooms independently. There is no common cost to allocate.

In the third row, if SLS and CS combine they would rent the suite for $12,775. Each division's best alternative cost is to acquire rooms independently at a cost of $6,600 and $7,500. The $12,775 is allocated to each division in proportion to the independent costs. The last row indicates each division's best alternative cost if the division chooses not to cooperate with all other divisions.

Finally, the actual common cost of $12,775 is allocated to each division in proportion to the best of its alternative costs.

| Division | Best Alternative | Proportion | Cost | Allocation |
|---|---|---|---|---|
| FGS | $ 3,212 | 0.22 | $12,775 | $ 2,810.50 |
| SLS | 4,818 | 0.32 | 12,775 | 4,088.00 |
| CS | 6,795 | 0.46 | 12,775 | 5,876.50 |
| Total | $14,825 | 1.00 | | $12,775.00 |

## KEY TERMS AND CONCEPTS

- Common cost
- Joint cost
- Allocation
- Allocation basis
- Separable costs
- Physical measures
- Relative sales value
- Relative costs
- Incremental costs
- Shapley value allocations
- Expansion path
- Alternative cost allocation

Some authors consider these terms equivalent, whereas others distinguish between them.

## FURTHER READING


Ayres, Frances L. "Models of Coalition Formation, Reward Allocation and Accounting Cost Allocations: A Review and Synthesis," *Journal of Accounting Literature* (Spring 1985), p. 1.

Cohen, Susan I., and Martin Loeb. "Public Goods, Common Inputs, and the Efficiency of Full Cost Allocations," *The Accounting Review* (April 1982), p. 336.

Hughes, John S., and James H. Scheiner. "Efficiency Properties of Mutually Satisfactory Cost Allocations," *The Accounting Review* (January 1980), p. 85.

Jensen, Daniel L. "A Class of Mutually Satisfactory Allocations," *The Accounting Review* (October 1977), p. 842.

Mautz, Robert K., and K. Fred Skousen. "Common Cost Allocation in Diversified Companies," *Financial Executive* (June 1968), p. 15.

Moriarity, Shane. "Another Approach to Allocating Joint Costs," *The Accounting Review* (October 1975), p. 791.

Reinstein, Alan. "Improving Cost Allocations for Auto Dealers," *Management Accounting* (June 1982), p. 52.

Roth, Alvin E., and Robert Verrecchia. "The Shapley Value as Applied to Cost

Allocations: A Reinterpretation," *Journal of Accounting Research* (Spring 1979), p. 295.

Shapley, Lloyd. "A Value for n-Person Games," in H. W. Kuhn and H. W. Tucker (eds). *Contributions to the Theory of Games II* (Annals of Mathematics Study No. 28), Princeton, N.J.: Princeton University Press, 1953.

Zimmerman, Jerold L. "The Costs and Benefits of Cost Allocations," *The Accounting Review* (July 1979), p. 504.

## QUESTIONS AND EXERCISES

**11-1** What is a responsibility center and what are its implications for accounting?

**11-2** What is being assumed when an allocation is made for purposes of cost control?

**11-3** Simple allocation schemes achieve product costing purposes but are not very effective for control purposes. Explain.

**11-4** Briefly, what is the advantage and the disadvantage of using a single allocation base for a variety of costs?

**11-5** What are the limitations attending to the use of "fairness" as a basis for allocating common costs?

**11-6** What is wrong with "ability to bear" as a basis for allocating common costs?

**11-7** A college receives a telephone bill (which includes charges for basic service, local tolls, long distance, and WATS service) monthly. The total is divided by the number of telephones on campus, and each department is billed accordingly. The college also sends out a monthly memo exhorting faculty and staff to minimize use of the telephone. What is wrong with this?

**11-8** The budget for the firm's internal auditing department consists primarily of fixed costs that represent salaries. How would you recommend allocating this cost to using departments?

**11-9** When a fixed cost is allocated as a rate (per unit of service), the user views this as a variable cost. Furthermore, the amount charged to a particular department can depend on usage in other departments. How can this problem be avoided?

**11-10** The cost of providing routine maintenance is charged on a per-hour basis. How can this operate to the disadvantage of the firm?

**11-11** Your employer has asked you to go to Mexico City on business. Your meetings are scheduled on Monday and Thursday. Because you will have some free time available and would like to do some sightseeing, you invite a friend to accompany you. The round-trip airfare to Mexico City is $400 per person. A single hotel room for the week would cost $50 per night. The double you rented actually cost $300 for the week. How much should your employer reimburse you for transportation and lodging? Why is your approach preferable to some of the other approaches discussed in the text?

**11-12** A graduate student interviewing for a full-time teaching position has just returned from visiting three institutions on a single trip costing $864. Each school has offered to reimburse the student its "fair share." If the schools had been visited individually, travel costs and time would have been as follows:

| | |
|---|---|
| State university | $ 400 (3 days) |
| City college | 600 (1 day) |
| Private university | 800 (2 days) |
| Total | $1,800 (6 days) |

You are to determine (a) how the travel cost could be allocated among the three, and (b) which method appears to be most "equitable."

**11-13** A business school shares a WATS line that costs $1,000 per month. During March, the accounting department made calls that would have cost $500 at normal toll rates. The finance department and the management department made calls that would have cost $400 and $300, respectively. Allocate the cost of the WATS line using the alternative cost method.

**11-14** Baja, Inc., operates as an importer in a free-trade zone (no taxes). It has three wholly owned subsidiaries in other countries, which produce the goods that are imported to Baja and sold there. Corporate headquarters are in Baja and corporate expenses for the coming year are estimated at $600. The income statements for the subsidiaries (before corporate expenses) are as follows:

| | Japan | Canada | Australia |
|---|---|---|---|
| Sales | $800 | $700 | $600 |
| Expenses | 400 | 420 | 240 |
| Net income | $400 | $280 | $360 |

What will be the effect on each subsidiary's income if corporate expenses are allocated on the basis of (a) sales, (b) expenses, and (c) net income before corporate costs? (d) What do you recommend?

**11-15** International Cheese Enterprises (ICE) is a mail order company with headquarters in North America. It exports various cheeses to South America. ICE has producing operations in Wisconsin, Minnesota, Oklahoma, and Louisiana. Each of the states is responsible for its own profitability *subject to* the allocation of ICE headquarter's expenses of $2,000. The state operations report the following results for the second quarter (before the allocation of ICE expenses):

| | Wisconsin | Minnesota | Oklahoma | Louisiana |
|---|---|---|---|---|
| Tons shipped | 400 | 300 | 150 | 50 |
| Net income | $1,600 | $1,500 | $900 | $350 |

What will income be for each state operation if ICE's expenses of $2,000 are allocated on (a) a physical basis and (b) an income basis?

**11-16** For August the central office of a small local chain has expenses (all fixed) amounting to $300. The three stores in the chain report income, before allocation of central office expense, as follows:

| | Store 1 | Store 2 | Store 3 |
|---|---|---|---|
| Sales | $800 | $900 | $750 |
| Cost of goods sold | 480 | 675 | 375 |
| Gross profit | $320 | $225 | $375 |
| Other expenses | 200 | 100 | 200 |
| Net income | $120 | $125 | $175 |

What is each store's net income if home office expense is allocated on the basis of (a) sales, (b) cost of goods sold, and (c) gross profit?

**11-17** Departments 1 and 2 share a common facility. The total cost is $10,000. Department 1 could acquire the necessary services from this facility alone at a cost of $8,000. Department 2 operating alone could get the needed services for $7,000. Allocate the common cost using (a) the Shapley method and (b) the alternative cost method.

**11-18** Departments A, B, and C share a common resource at a total cost of $25,000. The costs that each department would need to incur for this resource by operating independently are

| | |
|---|---|
| Department A | $20,000 |
| Department B | $15,000 |
| Department C | $ 5,000 |

However, the departments could also choose to operate in pairs. The cost for each pair of departments to acquire the needed resources would be

| Pairs of Departments | Common Cost for Resource |
|---|---|
| A and B | $24,000 |
| A and C | 22,000 |
| B and C | 16,000 |

Allocate the actual common cost of $25,000 to the three departments using (a) the Shapley method and (b) the alternative cost method.

**11-19** The local telephone company charges $8 per month for each telephone plus $0.02 per "message unit" (a message unit is a measure of the amount of time the phone is used). A firm has 45 telephones in its offices, including 15 in the sales department and 30 in the general administrative offices. Last month the sales department used 1,200 messages units, while general administration used 300 message units. Allocate the telephone costs to sales and general administration using (a) the number of telephones as the basis, (b) the number of message units as the basis, and (c) a dual-rate basis.

## PROBLEMS AND CASES

**11-20 Separate allocation rates.**

A factory averages total employment of 700 people. The administrative force averages 150 people. The company operates a cafeteria for all employees. They must, of course, have sufficient capacity to serve all employees. The cafeteria's monthly costs are $12,000 plus $1.75 per meal served. In July the plant was closed for retooling. The cafeteria provided 3,200 meals to administrative personnel in July and 1,000 meals to production employees.

**Required**
Allocate the cafeteria costs to production and administration based on:
**a.** Actual meals served.
**b.** Separate rates for fixed and variable costs.

**11-21 Separate allocation rates and inefficiencies.**
Spencer Manufacturing operates its own steam plant, providing steam for heating and for the manufacturing process. The steam plant's budgeted operating costs per month are $8,000 plus $0.40 per thousand cubic feet (mcf) of steam. The annual average demand for steam is 50,000 mcf for heating and 450,000 mcf for manufacturing. In January, 6,000 mcf were needed for heating and 30,000 mcf for manufacturing. The new manager of the steam plant made several staff planning errors resulting in a total cost for operating the steam plant in January of $27,000.

**Required**
Determine the cost that should be charged to manufacturing and heating for steam in January.

**11-22 Rework demonstration problem.**
Refer to the demonstration problem at the end of the chapter. Assume that the manager of sales to state and local governments has been renting a hotel room for $50 per night. The manager of federal government sales has still been renting at $55 per night.

**Required**
Allocate the cost of the suite to the three managers using the Shapley and alternative cost methods.

**11-23 Alternative cost allocation.**
The president of Taylor Industries must fly from the firm's headquarters in Tennessee to Atlanta, Georgia. The president will use the corporate aircraft, at a cost of $1,000. The president sent a memo to other departments asking whether anyone needed a lift. An internal auditor, who also needed to go to Atlanta, canceled an airline ticket costing $250 and joined the flight. A salesman who planned to drive to Atlanta (and who would have been reimbursed for 400 miles at $0.20 per mile) also joined the flight.

**Required**
Allocate the cost of using the corporate airplane to the three travelers using:
**a.** A physical measure (number of people).
**b.** The alternative cost approach.

**11-24 Shapley allocation.**
The engineering department of Northeast Industries decided to buy eight personal computers for the staff. The cost was to be $1,000 per computer. The manager of the engineering department noted that if the firm bought 10 or more of the computers the per-unit price would drop to $900. The manager circulated a note to other departments to the effect that if anyone else wanted to acquire this type of computer, this would be the ideal time to do so. The marketing department responded that they would like to acquire three of these computers.

**Required**
Allocate the total purchase cost of the computers to engineering and marketing assuming that:
**a.** Marketing is charged incremental cost.
**b.** The Shapley allocation is used.

**11-25 Allocation of actual or budgeted costs.**
The actual and budgeted costs and hours of a personnel department are shown as follows:

| Costs or Hours | Budget | Actual |
|---|---|---|
| Fixed costs | $40,000 | $41,000 |
| Variable costs | $35,000 | $42,200 |
| Hours to A | 1,000 | 1,200 |
| Hours to B | 1,500 | 1,400 |

**Required**
**a.** What allocation basis would the managers of personnel, department A, and department B, individually, prefer?
**b.** How do you suggest that the conflicts in (a) be resolved?

**11-26 Standard allocation rates.**
You have been called in as a consultant to assist in setting forth some budgetary relationships between service and producing departments. You are to consider the service department and only one of the departments it serves.

The flexible budget for the service department is $4,000 plus $5 per hour worked in the service department. The flexible budget for the producing department requires 100 service department hours plus 1 service department hour for every 100 hours worked in the producing department. (For simplicity, assume that the service department costs allocated to this department are its only indirect manufacturing costs.)

It is normally expected that 4,000 hours will be worked in the service department and 20,000 hours in the producing department.

**Required**
**a.** Find a single standard rate whereby the service department can allocate its costs to the departments being served.
**b.** Prepare a flexible budget for the producing department that sets forth its budgeted service department costs, both fixed and variable.
**c.** Determine a single standard rate whereby the costs in (b) can be allocated to the producing department's product.

**11-27 Calculation of four different allocations.**
R. Tripp, CPA, must visit two clients this week. Tripp works in Cleveland, but the clients are located in Chicago and St. Louis. If Tripp flies to Chicago and returns, the cost will be $120. If Tripp flies to St. Louis and returns, the cost will be $180. If Tripp flies to Chicago, then to St. Louis, and then returns, the cost will be $250. The distance from Cleveland to Chicago is 340 miles; from Chicago to St. Louis, 290 miles; and from St. Louis to Cleveland, 550 miles. Tripp actually flew from Cleveland to Chicago to St. Louis to Cleveland.

**Required**

Allocate the travel costs to the Chicago and St. Louis clients using each of the following as a basis.

**a.** Mileage

**b.** Alternative costs

**c.** The Shapley method

**d.** Incremental costs

**11-28 Alternative cost allocation.**

Universal University has three academic budget units: the College of Arts, the College of Business, and the College of Engineering. The university maintains a large computer to serve the academic units. It costs $20,000 per month plus $50 per hour to maintain the computer. The amount of computer time used by each academic unit varies only slightly from month to month. In March the Engineering College used 500 hours of time; the Business College used 150 hours; and the Arts College used 50 hours of computer time.

The Engineering College has determined that it could satisfy its computation needs separately at a cost of $16,000 per month plus $60 per hour. The Business College could contract with a service bureau to meet its needs at a cost of $3,000 per month plus $70 per hour. The Arts College can meet its needs through a service bureau for $75 per hour with no fixed costs. However, the service bureau will also contract with both the Arts College and the Business College to provide service for $3,500 per month plus $65 per hour. The service bureau's computer is not compatible with the needs of the Engineering College.

**Required**

**a.** Determine the amount of computer costs that should be charged to each academic unit, assuming that the alternative cost method of allocation is used.

**b.** Assume that the Engineering College uses only 400 hours per month and can meet this need by incurring a cost of $9,000 per month plus $60 per hour, but central administration bought the large computer to provide "room for future growth." Assume that 700 hours is the maximum usage available per month. How would you now charge the computer costs?

**11-29 Allocations and decision making.**

In 19X0 Haley's Department Store devoted 6,000 square feet to the display and sale of clothes, 1,500 square feet to linen and bedding, and 2,000 square feet to jewelry and cosmetics. This left empty 500 square feet of its 10,000-square-foot store. The $47,500 annual cost to maintain the store building was allocated to the three departments based on the 9,500 square feet of occupied space. In 19X1 management put in a confectionery shop in the previously unoccupied space. The allocation of the building costs was left unchanged. In 19X1 the four departments' earnings before allocated building costs were

| | |
|---|---|
| Clothes | $36,000 |
| Bedding | 9,750 |
| Jewelry | 20,000 |
| Confections | 2,000 |

In 19X2 the four departmental managers each requested that they be allowed to expand their floor space. They argued that one of the other department's floor space should be reduced so that their own department could be expanded.

**Required**

**a.** Determine net income after the allocated building costs for 19X1 for each department (the firm allocated costs to only three departments). What would be the reported net income per unit of scarce resource (per square foot)? Which department does this suggest should be reduced in size?

**b.** Allocate building costs to all four departments. Calculate net income per square foot of space. Which department does this allocation suggest should be reduced?

**c.** How should the decision be made for determining which department should be reduced in size?

**11-30 Physical, Shapley, and alternative cost allocations.**

Dak and Blecker is a small engineering consulting firm specializing in bridge engineering, but they do some other work. The owners are interested in the relative profitability of the bridge work versus all other services. Hence, they try to allocate all costs either to "bridge contracts" or to "everything else." The firm has a company-owned automobile that cost $3,500 to operate this year. They now wish to allocate this cost to the firm's two categories of contracts.

The car was used by people working on bridge contracts for 80 days. These people put 20,000 miles on the car. People working on nonbridge contracts used the car 130 days and put 15,000 miles on the car. If the car is not available when someone needs it, the firm either rents a car for $35 per day (unlimited mileage) or pays the employee $0.20 per mile to use the employee's own car, whichever is less.

For simplicity, base your calculations for the following questions on averages (for example, assume that every use of the car for a bridge contract involved the same mileage per day that the car was used).

**Required**

**a.** What is the lowest alternative cost for the bridge contracts for having automobile services? What is the lowest alternative cost to acquire car services for "everything else"?

**b.** Allocate the $3,500 to the two types of contracts based on mileage.

**c.** Allocate the $3,500 to the two types of contracts using the Shapley method.

**d.** Allocate the $3,500 to the two types of contracts using the alternative cost method.

**11-31 Shapley and alternative cost allocations.**

Tristate Bonded Warehouses, Inc., provides secure warehouse space to firms. Customers contract for a specified amount of space for a 6-month period. Tristate's pricing depends on the total amount of space required by a customer. Their current pricing formula per half year is

| Cubic Feet Contracted for | Price |
|---|---|
| 1,000 or less | $100 |
| 1,000 to 5,000 | $100 + $0.10/cu ft in excess of 1,000 |
| 5,000 to 10,000 | $500 + $0.07/cu ft in excess of 5,000 |
| 10,000 to 25,000 | $850 + $0.06/cu ft in excess of 10,000 |
| 25,000 or more | $1,750 + $0.05/cu ft in excess of 25,000 |

Thrifty Supermarkets has three stores that use the Tristate Warehouse. The Main Street store contracts for 8,000 cu ft of space; the Broad Street Store contracts for 16,000 cu ft; and the Mission Street store contracts for 3,000 cu ft of space.

**Required**

**a.** Determine the cost to each store of warehouse space if each contracts separately with Tristate.

**b.** Determine the total cost to Thrifty Supermarkets if the three stores cooperate and sign one contract jointly for the total needed space.

**c.** Allocate the cost in (b) using the

**1.** Shapley allocation

**2.** alternative cost allocation.

11-32 **Allocation bases** (CMA adapted).

Bonn Company recently organized its computer and data processing activities. The small installations located within the accounting departments at its plants and subsidiaries have been replaced with a single data processing department at corporate headquarters responsible for the operations of a newly acquired large-scale computer system. The new department has been in operation for 2 years and has been regularly producing reliable and timely data for the past 12 months. Company management has required that the departmental manager recommend a cost accumulation system to facilitate cost control and the development of suitable rates to charge users for service.

For the past 2 years, the departmental costs have been recorded in one account. The costs have then been allocated to user departments on the basis of computer time used. The schedule below reports the costs and charging rate for the year.

**BONN COMPANY**
**Data Processing Department**
**Costs for the Year-Ended December 31**

| | |
|---|---|
| 1. Salaries and benefits | $ 622,600 |
| 2. Supplies | 40,000 |
| 3. Equipment maintenance contracts | 15,000 |
| 4. Insurance | 25,000 |
| 5. Heat and air conditioning | 36,000 |
| 6. Electricity | 50,000 |
| 7. Equipment and furniture depreciation | 285,400 |
| 8. Building improvements depreciation | 10,000 |
| 9. Building occupancy and security | 39,300 |
| 10. Corporate administrative charges | 52,700 |
| Total costs | $1,176,000 |
| | |
| Computer hours for user processing[a] | 2,750 |
| Hourly rate ($1,176,000 ÷ 2,750) | $ 428 |

[a]Use of available computer hours

| | |
|---|---|
| Testing and debugging programs | 250 |
| Set-up of jobs | 500 |
| Processing jobs | 2,750 |
| Downtime for maintenance | 750 |
| Idle time | 742 |
| Total hours | 4,992 |

The department manager recommends that the department costs be accumulated by five activity centers within the department: systems analysis, programming, data preparation, computer operations (processing), and administration. He then suggests that the costs of the administration activity should be allocated to the other four activity centers before a separate rate for charging users is developed for each of the first four activities.

The manager made the following observations regarding the charges to the several subsidiary accounts within the department after reviewing the details of the accounts:

1. *Salaries and benefits.* Records the salary and benefit costs of all employees in the department.
2. *Supplies.* Records paper costs for printers, and a small amount for miscellaneous other costs.
3. *Equipment maintenance contracts.* Records charges for maintenance contracts; all equipment is covered by maintenance contracts.
4. *Insurance.* Records cost of insurance covering the equipment and the furniture.
5. *Heat and air conditioning.* Records a charge from the corporate heating and air conditioning department estimated to be the incremental costs to meet the special needs of the computer department.
6. *Electricity.* Records the charge for electricity, based upon a separate meter within the department.
7. *Equipment and furniture depreciation.* Records the depreciation charges for all owned equipment and furniture within the department.
8. *Building improvements depreciation.* Records the amortization charges for the building changes which were required to provide proper environmental control and electrical service for the computer equipment.
9. *Building occupancy and security.* Records the computer department's share of the depreciation, maintenance, heat, and security costs of the building; these costs are allocated to the department on the basis of square feet occupied.
10. *Corporate administrative charges.* Records the computer department's share of the corporate administrative costs. They are allocated to the department on the basis of number of employees in the department.

**Required**

**a.** For each of the 10 cost items, state whether or not it should be distributed to the five activity centers, and for each cost item that should be distributed recommend the basis upon which it should be distributed. Justify your conclusion in each case.

**b.** Assume the costs of the computer operations (processing) activity will be charged to the user departments on the basis of computer hours. Using the analysis of computer utilization shown as a footnote to the department cost schedule presented in the problem, determine the total number of hours that should be employed to determine the charging rate for computer operations (processing). Justify your answer.

**11-33 Relevant costing and allocation.**

Timetech manufactures two lines of watches. The Exclusiva line sells for $295, while the Commoner sells for $19.95. The firm has prepared the following pro forma product line income statement for next year.

| | Exclusiva | Commoner | Total |
|---|---|---|---|
| Sales | $885,000 | $3,990,000 | $4,875,000 |
| Cost of goods sold | | | |
| Variable costs | 330,000 | 2,200,000 | 2,530,000 |
| Fixed costs | 246,900 | 1,113,100 | 1,360,000 |
| Gross margin | $308,100 | $ 676,900 | $ 985,000 |
| Advertising | 245,000 | 5,000 | 250,000 |
| Sales commissions | 44,250 | 199,500 | 243,750 |
| Administration | 99,000 | 99,000 | 198,000 |
| Net income | $ (80,150) | $ 373,400 | $ 293,250 |

These projected results are fairly typical of the firm's results for the past few years. Management has attempted to boost the sales of Exclusiva, but is now convinced that demand is rather steady at 3,000 units per year. Management wants to consider several alternatives.

Variable manufacturing costs are those directly traceable to each product. The fixed manufacturing costs are mostly capacity costs (depreciation, property taxes, heat, and so forth) and have been allocated to the products using the gross sales method. The advertising costs are mostly magazine ads. The ads prominently display the Timetech name, but each ad features only one of the two products. The ads are charged to the product line on the basis of which product is featured in the ad. Sales commissions are 5% of sales. The administrative costs (executive salaries, accounting costs, and so on) are arbitrarily charged 50% to each product line.

**Required**

**a.** In the short run, when production and administrative capacity cannot be altered, what will be the dollar effect on income if we drop the Exclusiva line?

**b.** A consultant has questioned our allocation bases for fixed manufacturing costs and administrative costs. A study reveals that fixed manufacturing costs over the years are a direct function of the number of units produced (without regard to the type of product). Clearly, an allocation based on physical units would better reflect cause-and-effect relationships. On the other hand, administrative costs ought to be allocated in proportion to the gross margin earned on each product (the consultant did not explain why, but the firm's president is convinced that this is the right approach). Prepare a new product line income statement incorporating these two changes.

**c.** Management proposes to slash advertising costs on the Exclusiva line to $100,000. Sales of Exclusiva are expected to fall only 1%, but sales of the Commoner line will likely fall 10% (people identify the Commoner with the Timetech name and quality image portrayed in the Exclusiva ads). What will be the dollar effect on net income of slashing advertising costs?

**11-34 Allocation of head office costs** (SMA adapted).
Quality Department Stores Limited has always followed the policy of fully allocating *all* costs to its various stores. Such costs have included head office central and administrative costs, consisting of executive and office salaries, travel expenses, accounting costs, audit fees, legal fees, office supplies, charitable donations, rentals, depreciation, and postage.

All of these costs have been difficult to trace directly to the individual stores benefited; therefore, the basis of allocation has been that of the total revenue of each store. For example, during fiscal and calendar 19X0, the following allocations were made.

| Store | Revenue (in millions) | Costs Allocated on the Basis of Revenue (in millions) |
|---|---|---|
| Alpha | $ 75 | $ 8.25 |
| Beta | 15 | 1.65 |
| Gamma | 45 | 4.95 |
| Delta | 45 | 4.95 |
| | $180 | $19.80 |

In 19X1, the Alpha store's revenue was expected to rise; however, the store encountered severe competitive conditions and its revenue remained at $75 million. In contrast, the Delta store enjoyed unprecedented growth in business because of large influxes of population to that city. Its revenue rose to $105 million. Beta and Gamma revenues remained unchanged. Staff cutbacks and careful supervision and control reduced the total costs allocated on the basis of revenue to $18.0 million.

**Required**

**a.** What costs were allocated to each store in 19X1?

**b.** Using the results in (a), fully explain the limitations of using revenue as a basis for cost allocation, and describe a more appropriate alternative approach that Quality Department Stores Limited might adopt.

**11-35 Physical and relative sales value allocation.**

This is the time of the year for Mammoth University to allocate its athletic recruiting cost to its various sports programs. For ease, assume that there are only three programs: (1) men's major sports, (2) men's minor sports, and (3) women's sports. The recruiting process goes through two stages: (1) an on-site visit wherein recruiters are sent to high schools and (2) on-campus visits in which prospective athletes are brought to campus. In January the university sent recruiters to 200 high schools at a total cost of $150,000. The recruiters extended invitations for campus visits to 200 men for major sports, 300 men for minor sports, and 100 women. In March the women recruits were brought to campus by bus at a total cost of $5,000. They were housed in some abandoned military barracks at a total cost of $1,000 for two nights' lodging. In April, the university chartered some jets to bring the male students to campus at a total cost of $500,000. These athletes were housed in a nearby hotel at a cost of $25,000 for one night's lodging. After the students returned home, the university gave each of the male recruits for major sports $500 (total $100,000) to cover their out-of-pocket costs for incidentals during the campus visit. Assume (for simplicity) that all recruits accepted the offer to attend the university.

The university department charged with compliance with government regulations calculates that it cost $781,000 ÷ 600 = $1,301.67 for each recruit, or $260,334 for major sports, $390,501 for men's minor sports, and $130,167 for women's sports.

**Required**

**a.** Determine the costs to be charged to each sports program if the university uses a physical basis (number of bodies) for allocation of common costs.

**b.** Determine the costs to be charged to each sports program if the university uses the relative sales value method to allocate common costs. Assume that each male in a major sport will generate net revenue of $5,000, each male in minor sports $1,000, and each female $500.

**11-36 Calculate three types of allocations.**

RLN Industries engages in the manufacture of sophisticated electronic systems. The firm is organized consistent with its major markets. The firm consists of three divisions: (1) military sales, (2) law enforcement agency sales, and (3) industrial sales. Each division is totally responsible for its own sales, production, and product development. Each division requires large amounts of computer time both for production and product development. The firm rents a large computer, which is used by all three divisions. The computer costs the firm $600,000 per year plus $15 per hour to operate. (The hourly charge covers the cost of electricity, wages for the machine operator, paper, and so on.) During the previous year the military division had sales of $3,500,000 and used 4,000 hours of computation time. The law enforcement division used 1,000 hours of computation time and generated sales of $500,000. Industrial sales totaled $4,000,000 and used 3,000 hours of computer time. The computation needs of the military division could be obtained separately for $500,000. The law enforcement division does not really need very sophisticated computation capabilities and its needs could be obtained separately for $50,000. The industrial sales division's needs could be obtained for $200,000. (Note that these costs for obtaining services separately are for everything; i.e., they include cost of paper, labor, and so on.)

**Required**

Allocate the computer costs based upon

**a.** Ability to bear (sales)

**b.** Physical basis (time)

**c.** Alternative costs

**11-37 Effect of the allocation of corporate costs on state taxes.**

Due to the potential for manipulating net income earned in a state, and thereby state income taxes, many states require those firms operating within their borders to allocate general corporate overhead costs to operating units based upon a legislated formula. General corporate overhead costs are often very substantial because they include not only the costs of corporate administrative personnel but also interest on corporate debt and federal income taxes. A popular formula for allocating these costs is to allocate the following proportion of corporate overhead to each operating unit.

$$\begin{aligned}\frac{\text{unit's share of}}{\text{corporate costs}} \; &= \frac{1}{3}\left(\frac{\text{unit's sales}}{\text{corporate sales}} + \frac{\text{unit's assets}}{\text{total corporate assets}}\right.\\ &\qquad \left. + \frac{\text{unit's payroll costs}}{\text{total corporate payroll}}\right)\end{aligned}$$

The Porter-Harris Company manufactures large scale computer storage devices in states A and B. In addition, the firm maintains sales offices in states A and

B as well as a third office in state C. State C also houses the firm's corporate headquarters. The offices are geographically dispersed and sell to customers in all states in their region.

The chart below summarizes the past year's operations (in thousands), which are fairly typical of normal operations. Additional information is also included.

| | State A | State B | State C | Corporate Total |
|---|---|---|---|---|
| Sales | $22,500 | $31,000 | $18,500 | $72,000 |
| Cost of good sold | 14,200 | 22,600 | 12,300 | 49,100 |
| Gross margin | $ 8,300 | $ 8,400 | $ 6,200 | $22,900 |
| Other direct costs | 2,100 | 1,800 | 1,500 | 5,400 |
| Net income before corporate costs | $ 6,200 | $ 6,600 | $ 4,700 | $17,500 |
| Corporate costs | | | | 11,200 |
| Net income | | | | $ 6,300 |
| Total assets | $20,000 | $22,000 | $16,000 | $58,000 |
| Total payroll | $ 7,000 | $12,000 | $ 5,000 | $24,000 |
| State tax rate | 8% | 0% | 10% | NA |

State A allows any reasonable allocation of corporate overhead costs. State B does not have an income tax, so it is unconcerned with the determination of income. State C requires that the firm use the allocation formula given in the introduction to this problem.

Recently management was approached by the Economic Development Office from state D (which is adjacent to state C). These officials want the firm to move the sales office and corporate headquarters to state D. State D has an income tax of 10% also, but it allows a different approach for allocating corporate costs. Federal income taxes (which amount to $9,000 of the $11,200 of corporate costs) must be allocated to units in proportion to net income before corporate costs. But all remaining corporate costs are deductible in the state in which they were incurred (which would be state D if corporate headquarters were moved). Management expects that there would be no effect on sales or operating costs if the sales office and corporate headquarters were moved to state D.

**Required**

Determine the annual savings in state taxes that the firm would achieve if it moved its offices from state C to state D.

**11-38 Effect of accounting system choice on performance.**

Tartan Industries has had a goal of increasing net income by 5% each year for the past several years. To encourage attainment of this goal the top managers of each of the firm's subsidiaries are given a bonus of 30% of their base salary if their subsidiary's net income increases by 5% or more. Most managers expect the goal and bonus system will continue, unchanged, into the indefinite future.

The firm's income statement for 19X8 is given below. Although each subsidiary is in a different business, their cost structures are quite similar. The fixed costs listed in the income statement are those directly traceable to each subsidiary.

All common costs, including corporate administrative costs and interest on long-term debt, are included in the item corporate costs. Corporate costs are arbitrarily allocated evenly to all three divisions. Assume that corporate costs and fixed costs will remain essentially unchanged for 19X9.

**TARTAN INDUSTRIES**
**Segment Income Statement**
**19X8 (in thousands)**

| | Green Company | Red Company | Yellow Company | Corporate Total |
|---|---|---|---|---|
| Sales | $45,000 | $38,000 | $52,000 | $135,000 |
| Variable costs | 27,000 | 22,800 | 31,200 | 81,000 |
| Fixed costs | 5,000 | 4,000 | 6,000 | 15,000 |
| Corporate costs | 7,000 | 7,000 | 7,000 | 21,000 |
| Net income | $ 6,000 | $ 4,200 | $ 7,800 | $ 18,000 |

**Required**

**a.** Under the present accounting system, what level of 19X9 sales will each division strive for? Is there any motivation for a division to exceed its goal for sales?

**b.** Assume that in 19X9 the Red and Yellow Companies exactly met their sales goals as calculated in part (a), but the Green Company's sales fell by 10% from the 19X8 level. Determine corporate net income. Will any of the managers earn bonuses?

**c.** Prepare an income statement by segments for 19X8 assuming that the firm allocates corporate costs to the companies in proportion to sales.

**d.** What level of sales will each company strive for in 19X9 given that the firm allocates corporate costs relative to sales?

**e.** Assume that the Red and Yellow Companies exactly met their sales goals as calculated in part (d), but the Green Company's sales fell by 10% from the 19X8 level. Determine net income with corporate costs allocated relative to sales. Will any of the managers earn bonuses?

**f.** Assume that at the end of the third quarter in 19X9, corporate management announces that it appears that the Green Company's sales will fall by 10% from the 19X8 level. The manager of the Red Company believes that the manager of the Yellow Company will strive for the level of sales calculated in part (d) for the Yellow Company. Similarly, the manager of the Yellow Company believes the manager of the Red Company will strive for Red's level of sales in part (d). Determine the level of sales that the managers of the Red and Yellow Companies will strive for to get their bonuses.

**g.** Assume that Red and Yellow's sales in 19X9 are as calculated in part (f), and Green's sales fall by 10% from the 19X8 level. Prepare an income statement. Will any bonuses be paid?

# CHAPTER 12

# ALLOCATING SERVICE CENTER COSTS

In the preceding chapter we assigned all the costs for goods and services to the responsibility center that initially incurred the cost. This first center is usually in the best position to exert control over the prices, quality, and quantity of items acquired. However, these acquisitions are not necessarily caused by a demand for the resources by the initial responsibility center. For example, we may establish a computer services department to control the costs and supply of those services, but the computer services are acquired for the benefit of (are caused by) other departments. How we charge these latter departments for the costs they cause is the subject of this chapter.

Because many of the costs charged to initial responsibility centers are common costs allocated to them (for example, building depreciation and insurance) and because we are now going to allocate these costs to users, the process is often called the reallocation problem. Further, since the problem is usually what to do with the costs for centers that provide services to other centers, the problem is often called the service center reallocation problem.

## ALLOCATING SERVICE DEPARTMENT COSTS

Three problems must be addressed in solving the service center reallocation problem. We must decide (1) what allocation base should be used, (2) which costs to allocate, and (3) what procedure to use for treating any interactions between service departments. We examine each question in turn.

### The Basis for Allocating Service Department Costs

The measure of how much of a service department's services were provided to other departments will usually be based on a measure of the services provided to each user. However, any of the bases described in Chapter 11 may be used if management feels they accurately capture cause-and-effect relationships or can be justified in a cost-benefit sense.

In Chapter 11 we stated that if we wished to allocate both fixed and variable costs, we should try to allocate them separately. If so, we must specify fixed or variable with respect to what? Normally we distinguish fixed and variable costs with respect to the number of units of final product produced. But it is unlikely that we will be able to determine which service department costs are variable with respect to the products made by the firm. On the other hand, it is likely that we can identify the service department costs that are variable with respect to the service it provides. Thus the cost of a personnel department may be variable with respect to the number of new hires, but a direct relationship between variable personnel costs and the number of units of product produced may not exist.

If we decide to allocate variable personnel costs to other departments on the basis of new hires, should these costs be considered a variable cost for the other departments? The answer is generally yes, based on two rationalizations. First, we know that the distinction between variable and fixed costs is rather vague. When a cost is incurred, a judgment has to be made whether it is classified as a fixed or variable item. Once the judgment is made, the cost will continue to be treated as fixed or variable no matter how many times it is reallocated. A second rationalization notes that variable costs are generally considered more controllable by management. By treating the personnel cost as variable for, say, the computer services center, we are highlighting this cost as controllable by the manager of computer services (that is, if there had been no new hires we would not have incurred some of these costs).

### Which Costs to Allocate

Another issue is whether we should allocate actual costs or budgeted costs. When we allocate part of the personnel department's cost to the equipment maintenance department, we are holding the manager of equipment maintenance responsible for the level of personnel costs incurred. The maintenance manager has some control over the quantity of services demanded and should be held responsible for the use made of services. But how much control does the manager have over the cost per unit of service? The major argument against allocating actual cost is that the user department cannot control the efficiency of the service department and should not be held responsible for the actual cost per unit of service. However, others argue that the manager of the user department should try to keep the total cost of services under control. If prices rise, the manager should adjust demand accordingly. In this way, the user controls total cost and puts pressure on the provider of the service to keep costs in line.

Unfortunately, since the actual price (cost) of services often is not known until long after the services have been rendered, the using manager cannot react to price changes. To counteract this effect, many firms allocate service department costs on the basis of the budgeted or standard cost per unit of service rendered. The user department then knows beforchand the cost per unit of service and can adjust the demand for services accordingly. The department providing the service will also be aware of the "selling price" or transfer price of each unit of service it provides. It then becomes the supplying department's objective to provide its service at the budgeted cost per unit of service. The difference between its total actual costs and the total standard costs charged to other departments becomes a measure of the department's efficiency. The use of budgeted or standard costs works well as long as the standards are updated frequently to ensure that the price per unit of service accurately reflects the most efficient cost per unit for providing services at a particular point in time. Of course, for new firms or new ventures we usually have to operate an actual cost accounting system for several periods in order to build a history from which we can derive standards.

## PROCEDURES FOR HANDLING SERVICE DEPARTMENT INTERACTIONS

If service departments only provided services to production departments, the allocation problem would be no different from that in Chapter 11. Unfortunately we find that service departments often serve other service departments. The people in the equipment maintenance department use the services of the personnel department but also provide service to the equipment in the personnel department. When we allocate the personnel department's costs, not all of the costs should be charged to production departments; some costs should be charged to the equipment maintenance department. Then when we allocate the equipment maintenance department's costs, some costs should be charged back to the personnel department. Exhibit 12-1 lists all the cost centers for a midwestern hospital.

**EXHIBIT 12-1 Cost Centers for a Medium-Sized Central Oklahoma Hospital**

| Service Centers | Revenue Centers[a] |
|---|---|
| 1. Administration and general | 12. Operating room |
| 2. Nursing administration | 13. Recovery room |
| 3. Operation of plant | 14. Delivery room |
| 4. Pharmacy | 15. Anesthesiology |
| 5. Employee benefits | 16. Radiology |
| 6. Medical records | 17. Laboratory |
| 7. Laundry | 18. Oxygen therapy |
| 8. Cafeteria | 19. Physical therapy |
| 9. Housekeeping | 20. Pulmonary |
| 10. Central supply | 21. Electrocardiology |
| 11. Dietary | 22. Electroencephalography |
| | 23. Medical supplies |
| | 24. Drugs |
| | 25. General routine care |
| | 26. Intensive care unit |
| | 27. Coronary care unit |
| | 28. Nursery |
| | 29. Emergency room |
| | 30. Coffee shop |

[a]A revenue center for a service organization is the rough equivalent of a production department for a manufacturer.

Reading down the list of service centers, we can see that many of the service centers would provide and use services to or from several of the other centers (e.g., employee benefits would serve all other departments and central supply would serve most of the other departments).

To handle these interactions between service departments, several allocation procedures have been developed. Using any of them will eventually charge all costs to production and administrative departments. As always, our choice of which procedure to use must be based on the cost of implementing the procedure, balanced against the level of accuracy we achieve. We will consider the procedures in order of increased difficulty and will illustrate each procedure using the data that follow.

Consider a firm that has three service departments: personnel (PL), security (S), and equipment maintenance (EM). The firm also has two production departments: manufacturing (M) and assembly (A). The costs charged to the service departments are summarized in Exhibit 12-2. Although the firm allocates both fixed and variable costs, it does so using separate allocation bases. Our illustration will be concerned solely with the allocation of variable costs; fixed costs would receive a parallel treatment.

Exhibit 12-3 provides data for several potential allocation bases. The first step is to identify the most likely base that would explain changes in

**EXHIBIT 12-2 Direct Costs to Operate Service Departments**

| | Personnel | Security | Equipment Maintenance |
|---|---|---|---|
| Variable costs | | | |
| Wages | $30,000 | $42,000 | $13,000 |
| Supplies | 7,000 | 1,000 | 10,500 |
| Miscellaneous | 3,000 | 2,000 | 1,500 |
| Subtotal | $40,000 | $45,000 | $25,000 |
| Fixed costs | | | |
| Rent | $ 3,000 | $ 8,000 | $ 1,000 |
| Depreciation | 5,000 | 14,000 | 3,500 |
| Other | 2,000 | 3,000 | 500 |
| Subtotal | $10,000 | $25,000 | $ 5,000 |
| Total direct costs | $50,000 | $70,000 | $30,000 |

variable costs for each department. In our judgment, the number of new hires, the number of requests for security assistance (abbreviated as security requests in Exhibit 12-3), and the maintenance hours logged would best explain changes in the variable costs for personnel, security, and equipment maintenance, respectively.

The next step is to convert the raw data in Exhibit 12-3 to proportions. That is, we want to know the percentage of each service department's costs that will be allocated to each user department. The proportions are given in Exhibit 12-4. Note that the proportions are derived from the data in Exhibit 12-3 after ignoring any service that a department provides to itself. For example, four people were hired for the assembly department out of a total of 11 hires (see Exhibit 12-3). But one of the new hires was made for the personnel department itself. We disregard the hire for the

**EXHIBIT 12-3 Allocation-Basis Measures**

| | Department | | | | | |
|---|---|---|---|---|---|---|
| | Personnel | Security | Equipment Maintenance | Manufacturing | Assembly | Total |
| Number of employees | 5 | 40 | 20 | 80 | 60 | 205 |
| Number of new hires | 1 | 1 | 3 | 2 | 4 | 11 |
| Square feet of space | 4,500 | 1,000 | 1,500 | 4,500 | 4,500 | 16,000 |
| Security requests | 4 | 0 | 2 | 8 | 6 | 20 |
| Cost of equipment | $ — | $50,000 | $75,000 | $150,000 | $50,000 | $325,000 |
| Maintenance hours logged | 260 | 260 | — | 1,300 | 780 | 2,600 |

**EXHIBIT 12-4 Cost Allocation Proportions**

| | | Proportion of Service Provided to | | | | |
|---|---|---|---|---|---|---|
| Variable Costs | Department | PL | S | EM | M | A |
| $40,000 | PL[a] | — | 0.1 | 0.3 | 0.2 | 0.4 |
| 45,000 | S | 0.2 | — | 0.1 | 0.4 | 0.3 |
| 25,000 | EM | 0.1 | 0.1 | — | 0.5 | 0.3 |

[a]The costs for the personnel department are allocated to users relative to the number of new hires (after excluding any new hires in the personnel department). Thus one of ten, or 0.1 of personnel's service is allocated to security.

personnel department and say that there were 10 new hires provided to all other departments. Of these, four (or 40%) were for assembly. Thus 40% of the personnel department's variable costs will be assigned to assembly.

Self-service costs are usually ignored when allocating service department costs to assure that all costs are allocated to final users. Occasionally, we may wish to account for self-service costs. How we do so is addressed in the demonstration problem at the end of the chapter.

We now turn to a discussion of four procedures for allocating service department costs to final users. They are the direct method, the step method, the two-step direct method, and the simultaneous-equations method.

### The Direct Method

The **direct allocation method** concentrates solely on the objective of assigning all service departments' costs to final users. Thus a service department's costs are allocated only to final users; none of its costs are assigned to other service departments. Therefore the first step we must take is to adjust the percentages in Exhibit 12-4 so that the percentage of costs assigned to the production departments totals 100% for each service department. To do so, we take the proportion of a service department's costs being assigned to a particular production department and divide by the sum of the proportions of the service department's cost being assigned to all production departments. In Exhibit 12-4 we see that 20% of the personnel department's costs were provided to manufacturing and 40% went to assembly. Therefore we act as if 20/60 of the service department's costs went to manufacturing and 40/60 went to assembly. Making similar adjustments for the other departments, the revised proportions of service for the direct method are as follows:

| Service Department | Proportion of Service Provided to Manufacturing | Assembly |
|---|---|---|
| PL | 1/3 | 2/3 |
| S | 4/7 | 3/7 |
| EM | 5/8 | 3/8 |

The next step is to assign service department costs to the production departments on the basis of these revised percentages. For example, 1/3 of the $40,000 personnel department costs goes to manufacturing and 2/3 to assembly. The allocation of the costs becomes

| | | Costs Allocated to Production Departments | |
|---|---|---|---|
| Costs Traced Directly to Service Departments | Services Provided from | Manufacturing | Assembly |
| $40,000 | PL | $13,333.33 | $26,666.67 |
| 45,000 | S | 25,714.29 | 19,285.71 |
| 25,000 | EM | 15,625.00 | 9,375.00 |
| Total | | $54,672.62 | $55,327.38 |

Thus we would add $54,672.62 to the manufacturing department's variable overhead costs to reflect usage of the services of the personnel, security, and equipment maintenance departments. We would also add $55,327.38 to the assembly department's variable overhead account to reflect these services.

The direct method is an easy and, consequently, inexpensive accounting procedure to use. It is the most widely used service department allocation procedure in manual accounting systems. However, the direct method fails to meet our objective for cost allocation. In Chapter 11 we gave the objectives for allocation as cost control and product costing.

Because the direct method fails to charge service departments for the use of services from other service departments, these services are a free good. Consequently, service department managers are motivated to overuse services. For product-costing purposes we attempt to trace cause-and-effect relationships. By ignoring transactions between service departments, the direct method breaks the cause-and-effect linkage between demand for services by final users and the cost of providing those services. Nonetheless, in a noncomputerized accounting environment, the cost of implementing the direct method may be sufficiently less than the cost of alternative approaches that its use can be justified.

### The Step Method

The **step method of allocation** (also called the **step-down method**) is a compromise approach. It recognizes about half of the interactions between service departments. Under this approach the costs of the service departments are allocated sequentially. The costs for the department that is allocated first are allocated to every other department. When we allocate the second department's costs, however, we do not allocate costs back to the first department. In fact, the general rule is that once a department's costs have been allocated, no costs are ever allocated back to it.

As we eliminate departments through the allocation procedure, we must adjust the proportions of service each remaining service department provides to other departments. At each step we want the total of the percentages of a service department's costs assigned to the remaining departments to be 100%. Let us demonstrate the procedure with our example. We start with the information in Exhibit 12-4.

| | | Services Provided to | | | | |
|---|---|---|---|---|---|---|
| **Variable Costs Traced Directly to Service Departments** | **Services Provided from** | **PL** | **S** | **EM** | **M** | **A** |
| $40,000 | PL | — | 0.1 | 0.3 | 0.2 | 0.4 |
| 45,000 | S | 0.2 | — | 0.1 | 0.4 | 0.3 |
| 25,000 | EM | 0.1 | 0.1 | — | 0.5 | 0.3 |

Our first task is to determine the order in which the departments' costs should be allocated. There are several rules of thumb for making this choice. One common rule selects first the department that serves the most other departments. If ties occur, the rule picks the department with the highest costs traced to it. Unfortunately, the rule is entirely arbitrary, lacking any justification. Another approach is to select first that department whose costs we want to control most. Every other department will be charged, and held responsible, for the costs of the first department to be allocated. Thus all users of the first department's services will pay more attention to the cost of its services. In sequence, there will be more users paying attention to the cost of services from those departments whose costs are being allocated early in the procedure.

For example, assume that management has determined that we should assign the equipment maintenance costs first, then security, and finally personnel. Begin the allocation by listing the service departments and their costs in the order in which they are to be allocated. The step procedure then assigns the first department's costs to all other departments.

| Costs Traced Directly to Service Departments | Costs Allocated | Production Departments | |
|---|---|---|---|
| | | Manufacturing | Assembly |
| $25,000 | EM ($25,000) | $12,500 | $7,500 |
| 45,000 | S 2,500 | | |
| 40,000 | PL 2,500 | | |

At this point the total costs assigned to security are $47,500: the $45,000 traced directly to it and the $2,500 allocated from equipment maintenance. We now allocate the security costs to the remaining departments, excluding equipment maintenance. But when we exclude equipment maintenance the remaining allocation percentages in Exhibit 12-4 will no longer total 100%. We adjust them by dividing the percent of cost assigned to each remaining department by the sum of the percentages for all the remaining departments. The new proportions for security become 2/9 to personnel, 4/9 to manufacturing, and 3/9 to assembly. After the allocation we have

| Costs Traced Directly to Service Departments | Costs Allocated | Production Departments | |
|---|---|---|---|
| | | Manufacturing | Assembly |
| $25,000 | EM ($25,000) | $12,500 | $ 7,500 |
| 45,000 | S 2,500 (47,500) | 21,111 | 15,833 |
| 40,000 | PL 2,500 10,556 | | |

Now the total cost for the personnel department is $53,056 (the original $40,000 plus $2,500 from equipment maintenance plus $10,556 from security). Revising personnel's remaining percentages, we allocate 2/6 of the personnel costs to manufacturing and 4/6 to assembly, giving as the final allocation:

| Costs Traced Directly to Service Departments | Costs Allocated | Production Departments | |
|---|---|---|---|
| | | Manufacturing | Assembly |
| $ 25,000 | EM ($25,000) | $12,500 | $ 7,500 |
| 45,000 | S 2,500 (47,500) | 21,111 | 15,833 |
| 40,000 | PL 2,500 10,556 (53,056) | 17,685 | 35,371 |
| $110,000 | Totals | $51,296 | $58,704 |

The solution format used above for the step method was devised to save space. In practice you are more likely to see the following format.

| | Service Departments | | | Production Departments | |
|---|---|---|---|---|---|
| | Maintenance | Security | Personnel | Manufacturing | Assembly |
| Direct costs | $ 25,000 | $ 45,000 | $ 40,000 | $ — | $ — |
| Allocations | (25,000) | 2,500 | 2,500 | 12,500 | 7,500 |
| | | (47,500) | 10,556 | 21,111 | 15,833 |
| | | | (53,056) | 17,685 | 35,371 |
| Total | | | | $51,296 | $58,704 |

One advantage of the latter format is that if the direct costs of the production departments are included in the first line (where we have placed dashes), then the final cost for each production department will be the department's total costs. As always, which format you choose to use is a matter of personal preference.

The step method still does not fully meet our objectives for cost control and product costing. The services provided by some departments are still free goods to the managers of a portion of the other departments. For product costing, not only is the cause-and-effect linkage broken, but in addition, the amount of cost charged to a final user can be manipulated by the choice of the order in which service department costs are allocated.[1] This latter problem is sufficiently severe that when hospitals were reimbursed for actual costs for medicare patients, agencies in some parts of the country required a specific departmental allocation sequence by hospitals that used the step method.

The step method is considerably more costly to use than the direct method. We are aware of an organization that uses the method that has approximately 20 service departments and 20 final user departments. It takes an accountant nearly two full days to do the allocation—and cost reports are prepared monthly! Nonetheless, the method is still widely used in manual accounting environments.

### The Two-Step Direct Method

As the name implies, the **two-step direct allocation method** proceeds in two steps. In the first step each service department's costs are allocated to every other department. After this first round, the costs that have been allocated to a service department are allocated directly to the production

[1]The OPSTPAL program on the disk that accompanies this text will determine the order in which to allocate service departments, when using the step method, to maximize or minimize the costs allocated to a particular department.

departments. Let us illustrate the procedure with our sample data. The first allocation is made using the proportions in Exhibit 12-4. No adjustments of the proportions are required yet.

| | | Costs Allocated to | | | | |
|---|---|---|---|---|---|---|
| | | Service Departments | | | Production Departments | |
| Costs Traced Directly to Service Departments | Services Provided from | PL | S | EM | M | A |
| $ 40,000 | PL | $ — | $4,000 | $12,000 | $ 8,000 | $16,000 |
| 45,000 | S | 9,000 | — | 4,500 | 18,000 | 13,500 |
| 25,000 | EM | 2,500 | 2,500 | — | 12,500 | 7,500 |
| $110,000 | Totals | $11,500 | $6,500 | $16,500 | $38,500 | $37,000 |

We have now charged each service department for the direct cost of using the services of other service departments. But we have not allocated all costs to final users. This can be accomplished if we take the total costs allocated to each service department and reallocate them to the production departments. Under the two-step direct method, we reallocate the costs charged to the service departments using the direct method. Once again we must adjust the percentages of services provided to the production departments so that the percentages total 100%. This adjustment provides us with the same percentages as we derived for the direct method. Then we allocate as follows:

| | | Costs Reallocated to Production Departments | |
|---|---|---|---|
| Costs Allocated to Service Departments | Services Provided from | Manufacturing | Assembly |
| $11,500 | PL | $ 3,833 | $ 7,667 |
| 6,500 | S | 3,714 | 2,786 |
| 16,500 | EM | 10,312 | 6,188 |
| $34,500 | Totals | $17,859 | $16,641 |

To get the total costs charged to each production department we combine this second allocation with the first, as follows:

| | Production Departments | |
|---|---|---|
| | Manufacturing | Assembly |
| First step | $38,500 | $37,000 |
| Second step | 17,859 | 16,641 |
| Total | $56,359 | $53,641 |

**EXHIBIT 12-5 Service Department Cost Report: Variable Costs, Two-Step Direct Allocation**

| | Personnel | Security | Equipment Maintenance | Total |
|---|---|---|---|---|
| Direct costs incurred | $40,000 | $45,000 | $25,000 | $110,000 |
| Allocated costs | | | | |
| From personnel | — | 4,000 | 12,000 | 16,000 |
| From security | 9,000 | — | 4,500 | 13,500 |
| From equipment maintenance | 2,500 | 2,500 | — | 5,000 |
| Total cost to provide services | $51,500 | $51,500 | $41,500 | $144,500 |
| Costs charged to | | | | |
| Production departments | | | | |
| Manufacturing | $11,833 | $21,714 | $22,812 | $ 56,359 |
| Assembly | 23,667 | 16,286 | 13,688 | 53,641 |
| Total | $35,500 | $38,000 | $36,500 | $110,000 |
| Other service departments | 16,000 | 13,500 | 5,000 | 34,500 |
| Grand total | $51,500 | $51,500 | $41,500 | $144,500 |

A summary report is given in Exhibit 12-5. The report presents the total costs required to provide the services of each department. Note that after the allocation of service department costs between service departments, the total costs to provide all services, $144,500, exceed the actual total costs of $110,000. This occurs because the allocated costs are counted twice: once as a direct cost to the originating department and once as an indirect cost to the using department.

The report illustrated in Exhibit 12-5 also summarizes the distribution of each service department's costs to other departments. We can see that the costs assigned to the production departments equal the total of the direct costs incurred by the service departments. Thus all costs eventually have been assigned to the production departments. For the example we have used, these costs would be assigned to the variable overhead costs of the production departments.

The advantage of the two-step direct method is that every department using the services of another department is charged for the use of those services. This should lead to much more awareness and control over the costs of providing services than can be expected under the direct method or the step method.

Although it is an improvement, this method does not charge users for the full cost of providing a service. Other service departments are allocated a charge based solely on direct costs. In addition, the major drawback of the method is that it requires too many computations for a manual system. If a firm chooses to computerize service department allocations, they should use the next, and best, method.

### The Simultaneous-Equations Method

The major problem in trying to charge each user department with the full cost of using a service is to find the full cost of providing the service. Fortunately, we can express this cost in equation form. First, let $S_1$ represent the total variable cost of the personnel department, let $S_2$ be the total cost of the security department, and $S_3$ be the total cost of operating the equipment maintenance department. Then the total variable cost to operate the personnel department includes not only the $40,000 of costs traced directly to it but also a portion of the costs of the security department and a portion of the maintenance department's costs. In our example, 20% of the security department's costs are chargeable to the personnel department. Then the total cost of the personnel department must include 20% of the security costs; but this will be 20% of the security department's total cost, which we have chosen to label $S_2$. Thus the amount of the costs chargeable to personnel will be 20% of $S_2$ or $0.2S_2$. Similarly, 10% of the total maintenance costs, or $0.1S_3$, will also be charged to the personnel department. After consideration of the allocations from the other service departments, the total cost of operating the personnel department can be represented in notation form as

$$S_1 = \$40,000 + 0.2S_2 + 0.1S_3$$

In the same manner, the cost of the security and maintenance departments can be represented by

$$S_2 = \$45,000 + 0.1S_1 + 0.1S_3$$
$$S_3 = \$25,000 + 0.3S_1 + 0.1S_2$$

which results in a system of three equations and three unknowns.

Setting up the equations is not particularly difficult. The data requirements are the same as for the two-step direct method. We need only know (1) the costs charged directly to each service department, which would be readily available in the accounting records, and (2) the proportions of each service department's costs chargeable to the other service departments. These latter figures can be derived using the methods described in Chapter 11.

The difficult problem is solving the set of simultaneous equations to find the total costs of service. The next few paragraphs describe the algebraic technique for solving the equations by hand. The appendix at the end of this chapter describes a far less onerous procedure for use with a computer. In either case, the technique is called the **simultaneous-equations allocation method**, also frequently referred to as the **dual allocation method** or the **reciprocal allocation method.**

To solve the equations by hand, we first substitute one equation into the other two and gather like terms. Substituting the equation for the personnel department's costs into the other two equations yields

$$S_2 = 45{,}000 + 0.1(40{,}000 + 0.2S_2 + 0.1S_3) + 0.1S_3$$
$$S_3 = 25{,}000 + 0.3(40{,}000 + 0.2S_2 + 0.1S_3) + 0.1S_2$$

or

$$S_2 = 45{,}000 + 4{,}000 + 0.02S_2 + 0.01S_3 + 0.1S_3$$
$$S_3 = 25{,}000 + 12{,}000 + 0.06S_2 + 0.03S_3 + 0.1S_2$$

Rearranging,

$$0.98S_2 = 49{,}000 + 0.11S_3$$
$$0.97S_3 = 37{,}000 + 0.16S_2$$

We now have two equations and two unknowns. Once again we can substitute one equation into the other, but first we divide both sides of the second equation by 0.97 to get[2]

$$S_3 = 38{,}144.33 + 0.1649S_2$$

then substitute this equation into the equation for $S_2$ to get

$$0.98S_2 = 49{,}000 + 0.11(38{,}144.33 + 0.1649S_2)$$
$$0.98S_2 = 49{,}000 + 4{,}195.88 + 0.0181S_2$$
$$0.9619S_2 = 53{,}195.88$$

Therefore,

$$S_2 = 55{,}305.47$$

Substituting $S_2$ into our equation for $S_3$ we get

$$S_3 = 38{,}144.33 + 0.1649(55{,}305.47)$$
$$S_3 = 47{,}266.88$$

and substituting $S_2$ and $S_3$ into our equation for $S_1$ provides

$$S_1 = 40{,}000 + 0.2(55{,}305.47) + 0.1(47{,}266.88)$$
$$S_1 = 55{,}787.78$$

[2]To save space we have rounded numbers to four decimals, but subsequent calculations were made using unrounded numbers.

Now that we have the total cost of providing each service, it is a relatively trivial matter to allocate these total costs to the departments using the services. We can simply use the unadjusted percentages given in Exhibit 12-4 to allocate the service department's full costs to user departments. For example, 20% of personnel's full cost ($0.2 \times \$55{,}787.78 = \$11{,}157.55$) will be assigned to manufacturing. With rounding, our allocation becomes

| | | Service Departments | | | Production Departments | |
|---|---|---|---|---|---|---|
| **Total Cost of Service Departments** | **Services Provided from** | **PL** | **S** | **EM** | **M** | **A** |
| $55,787.78 | PL | $ — | $5,579 | $16,736 | $11,158 | $22,315 |
| 55,305.47 | S | 11,061 | — | 5,531 | 22,122 | 16,592 |
| 47,266.88 | EM | 4,727 | 4,727 | — | 23,633 | 14,180 |
| | Total | | | | $56,913 | $53,087 |

From this allocation we can prepare a service department cost report as before. The report is illustrated in Exhibit 12-6. Once again the total cost to provide all services exceeds the total direct cost because of double counting. But we can also see that the total costs allocated to the production departments are the total of the direct costs incurred by the service departments.

**EXHIBIT 12-6 Service Department Cost Report: Variable Costs, Simultaneous Allocation**

| | Personnel | Security | Equipment Maintenance | Total |
|---|---|---|---|---|
| Direct costs incurred | $40,000 | $45,000 | $25,000 | $110,000 |
| Allocated costs | | | | |
| From personnel | — | 5,579 | 16,736 | 22,315 |
| From security | 11,061 | — | 5,531 | 16,592 |
| From equipment maintenance | 4,727 | 4,727 | — | 9,454 |
| Total cost to provide services | $55,788 | $55,306 | $47,267 | $158,361 |
| Costs charged to | | | | |
| Production departments | | | | |
| Manufacturing | $11,158 | $22,122 | $23,633 | $ 56,913 |
| Assembly | 22,315 | 16,592 | 14,180 | 53,087 |
| Total | $33,473 | $38,714 | $37,813 | $110,000 |
| Other service departments | 22,315 | 16,592 | 9,454 | 48,361 |
| Grand total | $55,788 | $55,306 | $47,267 | $158,361 |

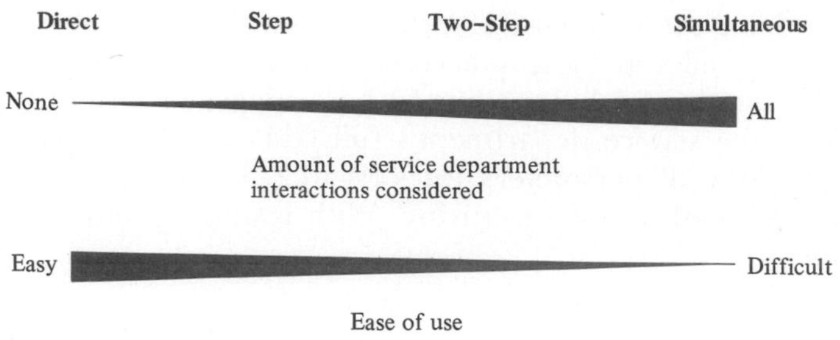


**FIGURE 12-1 Comparison of service department allocation methods.**

The simultaneous allocation is the theoretically correct procedure to use. It charges all users for the full cost of providing services. In addition, it accurately captures the cause-and-effect relationships between final users and the costs incurred by the service departments.[3] However, the simultaneous method cannot, as a practical matter, be used in a manual system. It must be computerized. The appendix to this chapter provides further discussion on the use of this method in a computerized environment. The four procedures we have discussed are compared in Figure 12-1.

## STANDARD COSTS AND ALLOCATIONS

We have implicitly presumed that we have been allocating actual service department costs. However, we would have to go through the same process if our firm used a standard cost system. The difference is that the allocation would be performed with budgeted figures, prior to the period of operation, to establish the standard costs. These budgeted figures would then provide the standard rate per unit of service for each service department. Knowing the rates ahead of time allows the user departments to know precisely what they will be charged when they use a service.

In a standard cost system, these predetermined standard costs for services will be included in the budget for each production department. These costs are then added to each production department's overhead budget. The departmental overhead budget along with our budgeted production will then yield each production department's standard overhead application rate.

[3]For a proof of this statement, see the article by Kaplan referenced in the Further Reading section at the end of the chapter.

**EXHIBIT 12-7 Budgeted Direct Costs per Department**

| | Engineering | Computer | Development | Drafting |
|---|---|---|---|---|
| Materials | $10,000 | $ 5,000 | $15,000 | $ 40,000 |
| Labor | 35,000 | 20,000 | 70,000 | 50,000 |
| Overhead | 8,000 | 15,000 | 12,000 | 18,000 |
| Total | $53,000 | $40,000 | $97,000 | $108,000 |

## SUMMARY

Knowledge of the full cost of providing a service can help management decide whether to continue providing a service internally or to contract for the service externally. But the full cost of providing a service includes not only the costs charged directly to the service department, but also the cost of services provided to the department from other service departments. Although the simultaneous-equations approach to allocating service department costs is the best way to capture the interrelationships between service departments, organizations without access to a computer may find that the less accurate allocation methods provide a cost-benefit advantage over the simultaneous-equations approach. Whichever approach is used, once service department costs have been allocated, all manufacturing costs will have been charged to production departments. The next chapter assigns these costs to specific product lines.

## DEMONSTRATION PROBLEM

Anderson's Blue Line, Inc., provides architectural blueprints. The firm has two service departments: a computer center and an engineering department. The firm's revenue generating centers (final users of services) are the development department and the drafting department.

The budgeted direct costs for each department for the next period are given in Exhibit 12-7. The costs for the service departments are allocated based upon the hours of service devoted by each to users. The budgeted hours of use are given in Exhibit 12-8.

**EXHIBIT 12-8 Hours of Service Provided to Users**

| | Engineering | Computer | Development | Drafting |
|---|---|---|---|---|
| Engineering | 100 | 200 | 500 | 300 |
| Computer | 150 | 300 | 300 | 100 |

During the coming period the computer department plans on developing a piece of software that the firm hopes to be able to sell to architects. Management estimates that 250 of the computer department's self-service hours in Exhibit 12-8 will be devoted to producing the software.

**Required**

Determine the cost to develop the software and the overhead rate per direct labor dollar for the drafting department if service department costs are allocated using:

**a.** The direct method.
**b.** The step method (allocate engineering costs first).
**c.** The two-step direct method.
**d.** The simultaneous-equations method.

**Solution**

As promised, this demonstration problem involves the rare situation in which we separately want to account for a portion of self-service. It also ties in the allocation of service costs to departmental overhead rates. The procedure for accounting for self-service is to set up another final user. In this case the new final user is the software project. It will be treated as if it were a separate department.

Exhibit 12-9 recasts the hours of service provided and presents the proportions of each service department's service provided to users. It incorporates the addition of the software as a separate user and ignores the remaining self-service. These proportions are used in the allocation procedures.

**a.** For the direct method 5/8 of engineering's costs go to development, 3/8 to drafting and none to the software. For the computer department the respective percentages are 0.375/0.8125; 0.125/0.8125; and 0.3125/0.8125. The allocation is:

| Direct Service Department Costs | | Development | Drafting | Software |
|---|---|---|---|---|
| $53,000 | Engineering | $33,125 | $19,875 | $ 0 |
| 40,000 | Computer | 18,461 | 6,154 | 15,385 |
| | Total | $51,586 | $26,029 | $15,385 |

**EXHIBIT 12-9 Restated Hours of Service Provided and Proportions of Service Devoted to Each User**

| | Hours of Service | | | | |
|---|---|---|---|---|---|
| | Engineering | Computer | Development | Drafting | Software |
| Engineering | — | 200 | 500 | 300 | — |
| Computer | 150 | — | 300 | 100 | 250 |

| | Proportions of Service | | | | |
|---|---|---|---|---|---|
| | Engineering | Computer | Development | Drafting | Software |
| Engineering | — | 0.2 | 0.5 | 0.3 | — |
| Computer | 0.1875 | — | 0.375 | 0.125 | 0.3125 |

The cost of the software is $15,385, using the direct method.

The total overhead for drafting is the $18,000 in direct costs (see Exhibit 12-7) plus the $26,029 in allocated service department costs, or $44,029. The budgeted labor cost for drafting is $50,000, so the overhead rate per labor dollar would be:

$$\$44{,}029/\$50{,}000 = \$0.88 \text{ per labor dollar.}$$

**b.** For the step method, we have:

| Direct Service Department Costs | Costs Allocated | Development | Drafting | Software |
|---|---|---|---|---|
| $53,000 | Engineering (53,000) | $26,500 | $15,900 | $ 0 |
| 40,000 | Computer 10,600 (50,600) | 23,354 | 7,785 | 19,461 |
| | Total | $49,854 | $23,685 | $19,461 |

This time the cost of the software is $19,461. The overhead rate for drafting is:

$$\frac{\$18{,}000 + \$23{,}685}{\$50{,}000} = \$0.83 \text{ per labor dollar}$$

**c.** The two-step direct method yields

**FIRST STEP**

| Direct Service Department Costs | | Engineering | Computer | Development | Drafting | Software |
|---|---|---|---|---|---|---|
| $53,000 | Engineering | $ 0 | $10,600 | $26,500 | $15,900 | $ 0 |
| 40,000 | Computer | 7,500 | 0 | 15,000 | 5,000 | 12,500 |
| | Total | $7,500 | $10,600 | $41,500 | $20,900 | $12,500 |

**SECOND STEP**

| Costs Allocated to Service Departments | | Development | Drafting | Software |
|---|---|---|---|---|
| $ 7,500 | Engineering | $4,688 | $2,812 | $ 0 |
| 10,600 | Computer | 4,892 | 1,631 | 4,077 |
| | Total | $9,580 | $4,443 | $4,077 |

**TOTAL ALLOCATION**

| | Development | Drafting | Software |
|---|---|---|---|
| First step | $41,500 | $20,900 | $12,500 |
| Second step | 9,580 | 4,443 | 4,077 |
| Total | $51,080 | $25,343 | $16,577 |

The two-step direct method yields a cost of $16,577 for the software and an overhead rate for drafting of

$$\frac{\$18{,}000 + \$25{,}343}{\$50{,}000} = \$0.87 \text{ per labor dollar}$$

**d.** Letting $E$ represent the full cost for engineering and $C$ represent the full cost to operate the computer center, the simultaneous equations are

$$E = 53{,}000 + 0.1875C$$
$$C = 40{,}000 + 0.2E$$

or

$$E = 53{,}000 + 0.1875(40{,}000 + 0.2E)$$
$$0.9625E = 60{,}500$$
$$E = 62{,}857.14$$

and

$$C = 40{,}000 + 0.2(62{,}857.14)$$
$$C = 52{,}571.43$$

The allocation to user departments is

| Total Service Department Cost | | Development | Drafting | Software |
|---|---|---|---|---|
| $62,857.14 | Engineering | $31,429 | $18,857 | $ 0 |
| 52,571.43 | Computer | 19,714 | 6,571 | 16,429 |
| | Total | $51,143 | $25,428 | $16,429 |

Thus the theoretically correct cost for the software is $16,429. The overhead rate for drafting is

$$\frac{\$18{,}000 + \$25{,}428}{\$50{,}000} = \$0.87 \text{ per labor dollar}$$

## KEY TERMS AND CONCEPTS

Direct allocation method
[ Step method
[ Step-down method
Two-step direct allocation method

[ Simultaneous-equations allocation method
[ Dual allocation method
[ Reciprocal allocation method

[ Bracketed terms are equivalent in meaning.

## FURTHER READING

Baker, Kenneth R., and Robert E. Taylor. "A Linear Programming Framework for Cost Allocation and External Acquisition when Reciprocal Services Exist," *The Accounting Review* (October 1979), p. 784.

Bentz, William F. "Computer Extended Reciprocal Allocation Methods," *The Accounting Review* (July 1979), p. 595.

Capettini, Robert, and Gerald L. Salamon. "Internal Versus External Acquisition of Services when Reciprocal Services Exist," *The Accounting Review* (July 1977), p. 690.

Churchill, Neil. "Linear Algebra and Cost Allocations: Some Examples," *The Accounting Review* (October 1964), p. 894.

Kaplan, Robert S. "Variable and Self Service Costs in Reciprocal Allocation Models," *The Accounting Review* (October 1973), p. 738.

Manes, Rene P., Soong H. Park, and Robert Jensen. "Relevant Costs of Intermediate Goods and Services," *The Accounting Review* (July 1982), p. 594.

## QUESTIONS AND EXERCISES

**12-1** How are service department costs similar to manufacturing overhead?

**12-2** If service department costs and manufacturing overhead are both indirect costs, what distinguishes the two?

**12-3** What should determine which method of cost allocation discussed in this chapter is chosen?

**12-4** What are the advantages and disadvantages of using separate bases for allocating departmental costs rather than a single basis (plantwide) for this purpose?

**12-5** A supervisor of a responsibility center declared at a budget meeting, "I don't care how much of maintenance's fixed costs are actually allocated to my department, as long as it is the same amount for which I am budgeted." What is the supervisor's point?

**12-6** At a budget meeting a department head said, "If you agree not to use allocated costs when evaluating performance, then I don't care if tide tables are used for the allocation." Do you agree?

**12-7** It has been decided that it is appropriate to allocate the costs incurred by one service department to all the other departments that benefit from its service. Why would it be better to use a charging rate based on budgeted costs, rather than a rate based on actual costs?

**12-8** A product is begun in department 1 and completed in department 2. Is department 1 a service department or a production department? Why?

**12-9** "The direct method of allocation is simpler than the step method but it is not as accurate since it ignores the fact that service departments do serve one another." How does the step method overcome this limitation?

**12-10** A firm is going to implement the step method for allocating service department costs. Each service manager wants to be first in the allocation process since subsequent departmental totals will be inflated by previously allocated service department costs, thereby making the department appear to have costs in excess of those that were directly incurred. Naturally, none of the managers wants to be last. As the accountant in charge, how would you respond?

**12-11** A service department budgets its costs at $40,000 per month plus $10 per hour. For November the following were the planned and actual hours provided by the service department to three producing departments.

| | Planned | Actual |
|---|---|---|
| Department A | 1,600 | 1,500 |
| Department B | 1,400 | 1,600 |
| Department C | 2,000 | 1,800 |
| Total | 5,000 | 4,900 |

You are to determine the rate(s) whereby the service department can allocate its costs according to (a) planned activity and (b) actual activity.

**12-12** Refer to 12-11. The service department had actual fixed costs of $42,000 and actual variable costs of $48,000. How much was not allocated under each of the rates developed in 12-11?

**12-13** A local hospital is required to account for the full cost of patient care. Patients are assigned *all direct costs*. Indirect costs are $240,000 per month plus $90 per patient day. This is a 120-bed hospital, which averages 80% occupancy. What is the average daily charge per patient for indirect costs? (Assume that there are 30 days in a month.)

**12-14** Shadee, Inc., allocates service department costs on the basis of what it would cost to purchase the services from an outside source.

| | Cost of Purchasing Service Outside | | |
|---|---|---|---|
| **Using Department** | **Department A** | **Department B** | **Department C** |
| Production department X | $50,000 | $40,000 | $20,000 |
| Production department Y | 60,000 | 30,000 | 30,000 |

Service department costs are budgeted at $88,000 for A, $63,000 for B, and $40,000 for C. Allocate service department costs using (a) alternative cost as the basis and (b) the direct method of allocation.

**12-15** Plethora, Inc., employs the direct method for allocating service department costs to production departments X and Y. The bases for allocation are as follows:

| | |
|---|---|
| Physical plant: | $60,000 fixed costs on the basis of square feet occupied; $20,000 variable costs on the basis of number of employees |
| Equipment maintenance: | $80,000 fixed costs on the basis of budgeted machine hours; $40,000 variable costs on the basis of expected maintenance hours |

| | Square Feet | Number of Employees | Budgeted Machine Hours | Budgeted Maintenance Hours |
|---|---|---|---|---|
| Physical plant | 1,600 | 10 | — | 10 |
| Equipment maintenance | 3,900 | 12 | 100 | 20 |
| Department X | 5,000 | 40 | 10,000 | 200 |
| Department Y | 8,000 | 50 | 15,000 | 400 |

Assign the service department costs to departments X and Y using (a) the direct method, (b) the step method with the physical plant's costs allocated first, and (c) the step method with equipment maintenance's costs allocated first.

**12-16** Phlora, Inc., has two service departments, personnel and financial, that provide services for one another as well as for two production departments, assembly and finishing. Data for the month are as follows:

| | Personnel | Financial | Assembly | Finishing |
|---|---|---|---|---|
| Employees | 6 | 8 | 20 | 15 |
| Payroll | $12,000 | $14,000 | $30,000 | $27,000 |

The personnel department had total costs of $30,000, and the financial department had total costs of $40,000. Personnel costs are related to the number of employees and financial costs are related to payroll. Allocate these costs using (a) the step method with personnel's costs allocated first and (b) the two-step direct method of allocation.

**12-17** The following data summarize recent operations.

| | Service Departments | | Production Departments | |
|---|---|---|---|---|
| | A | B | C | D |
| Costs incurred | $2,700 | $2,400 | $4,400 | $2,100 |
| Space occupied | — | 25% | 45% | 30% |
| Employees | 2 | 4 | 7 | 8 |
| Area temperature, °F | 70 | 74 | 69 | 72 |
| Units produced | — | — | 200 | 200 |

Department A's costs are allocated on the space-occupied basis, whereas department B's costs are allocated according to the number of employees. The number of units produced is used as the basis for applying overhead. You are to allocate all service department costs and determine overhead rates for the production departments using (a) the direct method of allocation and (b) the step method of allocation. (Allocate department A's cost first.)

**12-18** Redi, Inc., leases a manufacturing facility at a cost of $30,000 per month. There are two service departments at this plant, personnel and plant office, and two producing departments, assembly and finishing. The following data represent the budget for a normal month.

| | Personnel | Plant Office | Assembly | Finishing |
|---|---|---|---|---|
| Overhead incurred | $16,000 | $18,000 | $25,000 | $30,000 |
| Floor space area | 5% | 15% | 50% | 30% |
| Number of employees | 2 | 8 | 45 | 35 |
| Direct labor hours | — | — | 7,500 | 5,000 |
| Machine hours | — | — | 500 | 200 |

Facility costs are related to floor space, personnel costs are related to the number of employees, and plant office costs are related to direct labor hours. Determine the monthly overhead rate for each department (based on direct labor hours) using (a) the direct allocation method for service department costs and (b) the step method of allocation for service department costs (personnel first and plant office second). (c) What do you conclude?

## PROBLEMS AND CASES

**12-19 Cost allocation: Service departments** (CPA adapted).
The Parker Manufacturing Company has two production departments (fabrication and assembly) and three service departments (general factory administration, factory maintenance, and factory cafeteria). The following is a summary of costs and other data for each department prior to allocation of service department costs for the year ended June 30.

| | Fabrication | Assembly | General Factory Administration | Factory Maintenance | Factory Cafeteria |
|---|---|---|---|---|---|
| Direct labor costs | $1,950,000 | $2,050,000 | $90,000 | $82,100 | $87,000 |
| Direct materials costs | $3,130,000 | $ 950,000 | — | $65,000 | $91,000 |
| Manufacturing overhead costs | $1,650,000 | $1,850,000 | $70,000 | $56,100 | $62,000 |
| Direct labor hours | 562,500 | 437,500 | 31,000 | 27,000 | 42,000 |
| Number of employees | 280 | 200 | 12 | 8 | 20 |
| Square footage occupied | 88,000 | 72,000 | 1,750 | 2,000 | 4,800 |

The costs of the general factory administration department, factory maintenance department, and factory cafeteria are allocated on the basis of direct labor hours, square footage occupied, and number of employees, respectively. There are no manufacturing overhead variances. Round all final calculations to the nearest dollar.

**Required**

**a.** Assume that Parker elects to distribute service department costs directly to production departments without interservice department cost allocation. The amount of factory maintenance department costs that would be allocated to the fabrication department would be

1. $0
2. $111,760
3. $106,091
4. $91,440

**b.** Assume the same method of allocation as in the foregoing item. The amount of general factory administration department costs that would be allocated to the assembly department would be
**1.** $0
**2.** $63,636
**3.** $70,000
**4.** $90,000

**c.** Assuming that Parker elects to distribute service department costs to other service departments using the step method (starting with the service department with the greatest total costs) as well as the production departments, the amount of factory cafeteria department costs that would be allocated to the factory maintenance department would be
**1.** $0
**2.** $96,000
**3.** $3,840
**4.** $6,124

**d.** Assume the same method of allocation as in the foregoing item. The amount of factory maintenance department costs that would be allocated to the factory cafeteria would be
**1.** $0
**2.** $5,787
**3.** $5,856
**4.** $148,910

**12-20 Step method allocation.**
Baker Engineering uses the step method for allocating its service department costs to production departments. The firm operates three service departments: (1) computer services, (2) personnel, and (3) janitorial services. The computer costs are allocated based on a log of computer hours used for each department; the personnel costs are allocated based on the number of employees in each department; and the janitorial costs are allocated based on the number of square feet occupied by each department. Relevant cost and operating data for the service departments and the firm's two production departments are as follows:

| | Service Departments | | | Production Departments | |
|---|---|---|---|---|---|
| | Computer | Personnel | Janitor | Development | Assembly |
| Labor costs | $95,000 | $60,000 | $22,000 | $315,000 | $286,000 |
| Materials costs | $12,000 | $ 5,000 | $ 1,000 | $ 75,000 | $412,000 |
| Overhead costs | $40,000 | $10,000 | $ 3,000 | $110,000 | $112,000 |
| Computer hours used | 1,500 | 100 | — | 1,800 | 100 |
| Number of employees | 6 | 9 | 3 | 15 | 21 |
| Square feet occupied | 1,000 | 2,000 | 500 | 5,000 | 10,000 |

**Required**
Determine the amount of service department costs to be allocated to each of the production departments using the step method. Allocate the computer center costs first, then the personnel costs, and finally the janitorial costs.

**12-21 Allocation of service department costs.**
EFG, Inc., has three service departments and two production departments. The three service departments are a cafeteria, a janitorial department, and a nursing department. The cafeteria's costs are allocated on the basis of the number of employees in each department; the janitorial department on the basis of the number of square feet in each department; and the nursing department on the number of cases treated for each department. The following table summarizes the costs and pertinent information for each department.

| | Cafeteria | Janitor | Nurse | Assembly | Finishing |
|---|---|---|---|---|---|
| Costs traced directly | \$40,000 | \$30,000 | \$10,000 | \$80,000 | \$70,000 |
| Number of employees | 20 | 10 | 2 | 30 | 38 |
| Square feet | 10,000 | 2,000 | 5,000 | 10,000 | 25,000 |
| Visits to nurse | 6 | 2 | — | 24 | 8 |

**Required**
Determine the service department costs to be charged to the production departments (assembly and finishing), as well as the total production department costs under the following methods.

**a.** The direct method.

**b.** The step method of allocating service department costs. (The cafeteria costs are to be allocated first, the janitorial costs second, and the nursing costs third.)

**12-22 Step method of allocation.**
Klose Inc., has three service departments ($S_1$ through $S_3$) and two production departments ($P_1$ and $P_2$). The following chart describes the usage of each department's services and the costs incurred by each.

| | | Proportion of Services Provided to | | | | |
|---|---|---|---|---|---|---|
| Costs Traced Directly to Service Departments | | $S_1$ | $S_2$ | $S_3$ | $P_1$ | $P_2$ |
| \$90,000 | $S_1$ | — | 0.2 | 0.1 | 0.3 | 0.4 |
| 25,000 | $S_2$ | 0.5 | — | 0.1 | 0.2 | 0.2 |
| 35,000 | $S_3$ | 0.2 | 0.4 | — | 0.1 | 0.3 |

**Required**

**a.** Allocate the service department costs to the production departments using the step method. Allocate Department $S_1$ first, $S_2$ second, and $S_3$ last.

**b.** Allocate the service department costs to the production departments using the two-step direct method.

**12-23 Step and direct allocation method.**
Holiday's has five service departments and two production departments. The following chart gives the costs directly traceable to each service department and the proportion of each service department's services used by each of the other departments in the firm.

| Traceable Costs | | Service Departments A | B | C | D | E | Production Departments 1 | 2 |
|---|---|---|---|---|---|---|---|---|
| $10,000 | A | — | — | — | — | 0.4 | 0.6 | — |
| 60,000 | B | — | — | 0.2 | 0.3 | — | 0.3 | 0.2 |
| 30,000 | C | 0.1 | 0.2 | — | 0.3 | 0.1 | 0.2 | 0.1 |
| 20,000 | D | 0.2 | 0.1 | 0.3 | — | — | — | 0.4 |
| 30,000 | E | 0.2 | — | — | 0.3 | — | 0.2 | 0.3 |

**Required**

**a.** Determine the costs to be assigned to departments 1 and 2 assuming direct allocation.

**b.** Determine the costs to be assigned to departments 1 and 2 assuming the step method of allocation. Allocate the departmental costs in the order in which they are listed.

**12-24 Step and two-step methods of allocation.**

Anaid Industries' accounting records reveal the following distribution of costs where $S_1$, $S_2$, and $S_3$ are service departments and $P_1$ and $P_2$ are production departments.

| | Department $S_1$ | $S_2$ | $S_3$ | $P_1$ | $P_2$ |
|---|---|---|---|---|---|
| Direct materials | $ — | $ — | $ — | $30,000 | $25,000 |
| Other materials | 8,000 | 16,000 | 5,000 | 9,000 | 12,000 |
| Direct labor | — | — | — | 50,000 | 80,000 |
| Other labor | 15,000 | 8,000 | 21,000 | 11,000 | 7,000 |
| Overhead | 14,000 | 17,000 | 11,000 | 38,000 | 55,000 |

Department $S_1$ is the janitorial department; its costs are allocated equally to all departments. $S_2$ is the payroll office; its costs are based on the number of employees in each department. There are 6 employees in department $S_1$, 5 in department $S_2$, 10 in department $S_3$, 14 in $P_1$, and 20 in $P_2$. Department $S_3$ is the lunchroom; it provides 10% of its service to department $S_2$, 30% to $P_1$, and 60% to $P_2$.

**Required**

**a.** Allocate the service department costs to the production departments using the step method. Allocate in the order in which the departments are listed.

**b.** Allocate the service department costs to the production departments using the two-step direct method.

**12-25 Cross-allocations, rates given.**

Pyrrhic, Inc., has two service departments (A and B). It also has two production departments (X and Y), each of which produces a different product. The flexible budget for A totals $1,000 and for B totals $2,500. The hours of service provided by the service departments are tabled as follows:

| | Provided to A | B | X | Y |
|---|---|---|---|---|
| By A | — | 100 | 100 | 300 |
| By B | 100 | — | 1,500 | 400 |

Interservice departmental charges are determined by simultaneously solving:

$$SR_A = \frac{\$1{,}000 + 100SR_B}{500}$$

$$SR_B = \frac{\$2{,}500 + 100SR_A}{2{,}000}$$

A company engineer has solved these and found $SR_A = \$2.2727$ and $SR_B = \$1.3636$. ($SR_A$ indicates the standard rate charged by department A.)

**Required**

**a.** Assuming that the expectations of the first paragraph and the table are achieved, enter all transactions into the following accounts (index your entries).

| | Departmental Accounts | | | |
|---|---|---|---|---|
| **All Other Accounts** | **A** | **B** | **X** | **Y** |
| | | | | |

**b.** What purpose is served by using an interservice charge?

**12-26 Direct and simultaneous-equations allocation methods with self-service.**
Accpubs, Inc., is a small publishing company dealing in specialized monographs. It provides two services: general editing and technical writing. The priority for each department is to service outsiders. However, during slack periods, the firm's technical department writes material to be published under the firm's own imprint; such material is edited in-house. The editing department also services both outside and inside manuscripts. In other words, the departments service one another as well as outsiders. During the past month, editing costs were $23,040 and writing costs were $18,000. The hours provided by each department are as follows:

| By \ To | Editing | Writing | Outside | Totals |
|---|---|---|---|---|
| **Editing** | — | 120 | 360 | 480 |
| **Writing** | 20 | 100 | 200 | 320 |
| **Totals** | 20 | 220 | 560 | 800 |

Total costs are allocated between inside work (to be sold by the firm) and outside work (done for others).

**Required**

Distribute total costs between work done on the firm's own publications (in-house) and work done for outsiders using:

**a.** the direct method of allocation.

**b.** the dual method of allocation.

**12-27 Simultaneous-equations allocation method.**
Vern's Protection Service has three service departments ($S_1$, $S_2$, $S_3$) and three production departments ($P_1$, $P_2$, $P_3$). The direct costs of each department and the

proportions of service provided by each department to the others are given by the following table.

| Direct Costs | | $S_1$ | $S_2$ | $S_3$ | $P_1$ | $P_2$ | $P_3$ |
|---|---|---|---|---|---|---|---|
| $20,000 | $S_1$ | — | 0.4 | 0.1 | 0.2 | 0.2 | 0.1 |
| 10,000 | $S_2$ | 0.1 | — | 0.2 | 0.2 | — | 0.5 |
| 40,000 | $S_3$ | 0.2 | 0.2 | — | 0.1 | 0.4 | 0.1 |

**Required**

**a.** Determine the costs to be allocated to each production department using simultaneous equations.

**b.** Prepare a service department cost report such as that given in Exhibit 12-6.

**12-28 Simultaneous-equations allocation method.**

The following chart summarizes the portion of service department services used by other departments, where $S_1$, $S_2$, and $S_3$ are service departments and $P_1$ and $P_2$ are production departments.

| Department | Proportion of Services Used by | | | | |
|---|---|---|---|---|---|
| | $S_1$ | $S_2$ | $S_3$ | $P_1$ | $P_2$ |
| $S_1$ | — | 0.3 | 0.1 | 0.4 | 0.2 |
| $S_2$ | 0.1 | — | 0.4 | 0.2 | 0.3 |
| $S_3$ | 0.2 | 0.4 | — | 0.3 | 0.1 |

The costs accumulated during the period for the service departments were $12,000 for $S_1$, $20,000 for $S_2$, and $9,000 for $S_3$.

**Required**

**a.** Allocate the service department costs to the producing departments using the simultaneous-equations method.

**b.** Allocate the service department costs using the two-step direct method.

**12-29 Simultaneous-equations method** (CIA).

The Barnes Company has two service departments and three production departments, each producing a separate product. For a number of years, Barnes has allocated the costs of the service departments to the production departments on the basis of the annual sales revenue dollars. In a recent audit report, the internal auditor stated that the distribution of service department costs on the basis of annual sales dollars would lead to serious inequities. It was recommended that maintenance and engineering service hours be used as a better service cost allocation basis. For illustrative purposes, the following information was appended to the audit report.

| | Service Departments | | Production Departments | | |
|---|---|---|---|---|---|
| | Maintenance | Engineering | Product A | Product B | Product C |
| Maintenance hours used | — | 400 | 800 | 200 | 200 |
| Engineering hours used | 400 | — | 800 | 400 | 400 |
| Department direct costs | $12,000 | $54,000 | $80,000 | $90,000 | $50,000 |

**Required**

**a.** Give two reasons to justify the internal auditor's criticism of using sales revenue as the basis for allocating costs of the service departments to the production departments.

**b.** Because the service departments perform work for each other, it is necessary to use simultaneous equations when hours are used as a basis for determining allocatable service department costs. Calculate the total engineering department's cost after the allocation of interservice department costs but before allocation to the maintenance and production departments. Show the components of your calculations.

**c.** Cite a condition under which sales dollars might represent a satisfactory basis for allocating service department costs to the production departments.

**12-30 Simultaneous allocation for a hospital.**

Small Town Hospital splits its service into two categories: general care and obstetrics. Medicare will pay the hospital 120% of the total costs incurred to treat Medicare patients. The hospital has two service departments: general records and dietary. The general records' costs are allocated to departments based upon a log of hours spent for each department. Dietary costs are allocated on the basis of the number of meals served. Results for the past period are summarized below.

| | Records | Dietary | General Care | Obstetrics |
|---|---|---|---|---|
| Labor cost | $3,000 | $ 8,000 | $40,000 | $60,000 |
| Supplies, etc. | $4,000 | $35,000 | $25,000 | $15,000 |
| Meals served | 100 | 100 | 700 | 200 |
| Record hours | 40 | 50 | 100 | 50 |

During the period 60% of the general care patients were Medicare patients. None of the obstetrics patients were Medicare patients.

**Required**

Determine the amount of the Medicare reimbursement if the hospital uses the simultaneous-equations method for allocating service department costs.

**12-31 Simultaneous allocation for a CPA firm.**

Jones and Lakso, CPAs, offer two types of services: auditing and tax work. Clients are billed at a rate equal to 200% of the costs incurred for auditing and 150% of the costs incurred for tax work. All costs incurred by the firm are classified into direct costs (charged directly to the clients) or overhead. Overhead is accumulated into two accounts: one for auditing and another for tax. These overhead costs are then treated as service department costs and are allocated to clients using the simultaneous-equations allocation method. The allocation basis is the number of hours worked by the departments. Appropriate data for the most recent accounting period is summarized below:

| | Audit Overhead | Tax Overhead | Client 1 | Client 2 | Client 3 | Client 4 |
|---|---|---|---|---|---|---|
| Audit costs | $12,000 | — | $3,000 | $5,000 | $2,000 | $6,000 |
| Tax costs | — | $8,000 | $1,000 | — | $3,000 | $2,000 |
| Audit hours | — | 50 hr | 90 hr | 125 hr | 60 hr | 175 hr |
| Tax hours | 80 hr | 45 hr | 30 hr | — | 180 hr | 110 hr |

**Required**

Determine this period's total billing to each client.

**12-32 Allocation with self-service as a separate cost.**

R. D. Smith, Inc., is a management consulting firm providing a wide range of services to its clients. Most of the costs incurred by the firm are for personnel, and these costs are easily traceable to the clients for whom services have been rendered. However, the firm also operates two departments that are considered service departments. These are an engineering department and a computer department. The costs of operating the engineering department are charged to users based upon a log of hours devoted to each user. The costs for the computer department are allocated on the basis of a record of CPU hours devoted to each user.

During the current month, the computer department worked on developing an automated inventory control system. This was in addition to its normal operations and normal services to other users in the firm. The company expects to be able to lease the inventory control system to many of its clients. Consequently, management wishes to capitalize the costs of preparing the program.

Relevant data for the service departments are given in the schedules below.

**Engineering Department**

| | |
|---|---|
| Costs incurred | |
| Materials and supplies | $ 3,000 |
| Wages and salaries | 26,000 |
| Overhead and miscellaneous | 5,000 |
| Total costs | $34,000 |
| Services provided (in hours) | |
| To client A | 45 |
| To client B | 50 |
| To the computer department | 25 |
| Not charged to a specific user | 40 |
| Total hours | 160 |

**Computer Department**

| | |
|---|---|
| Costs incurred | |
| Materials and supplies | $ 4,000 |
| Wages and salaries | 55,000 |
| Overhead and miscellaneous | 26,000 |
| Total costs | $85,000 |
| Services provided (CPU hours) | |
| To client A | 80 |
| To client B | 70 |
| To engineering | 50 |
| For inventory control system | 100 |
| For normal reliability checks and maintenance | 20 |
| Total hours | 320 |

**Required**

Determine the cost of developing the inventory control system if the firm uses the following methods for allocating service department costs. (*Hint:* Set up an additional final user in addition to clients A and B.)

**a.** Step method, engineering first.

**b.** Simultaneous method.

**12-33 Manipulating step-method allocations—computer required.**

In the chapter we mentioned that when using the step method, the selection of the order for allocating service departments is arbitrary. Yet the order of allocation can have a substantial effect on the amount of costs assigned to an end user. This, unfortunately, opens an opportunity to manipulate the amount of costs assigned to end users.

Refer to Problem 12-23. Assume that the products produced by Holiday are all sold to the government on a cost-plus basis. The products produced by production department 1 are sold for 150% of cost, while the products produced by production department 2 are sold for 225% of cost.

**Required**

Ignoring any direct production costs, determine the company's revenue if the service department costs are allocated in the order that:

**a.** maximizes the costs charged to production department 1.

**b.** maximizes the costs charged to production department 2.

Use the program OPSTPAL to determine the appropriate service department allocation sequences.

**12-34 Step method; product and period costs—computer required.**

A firm has three service departments (A, B, C), two production departments (D, E) and a marketing department (F). Service department costs and proportions of service to each department are shown below.

| Costs | | A | B | C | D | E | F |
|---|---|---|---|---|---|---|---|
| $30,000 | A | — | 0.1 | 0.2 | 0.2 | 0.15 | 0.35 |
| 20,000 | B | 0.15 | — | 0.1 | 0.2 | 0.25 | 0.3 |
| 10,000 | C | 0.2 | 0.05 | — | 0.3 | 0.2 | 0.25 |

**Required**

**a.** Using the computer program OPSTPAL determine the order in which service department costs should be distributed if the objective is to maximize the amount of service department costs to be assigned as product costs. Allocate the costs using these results according to the step method.

**b.** Using the program OPSTPAL, determine the order in which the costs should be allocated if the objective is to maximize the amount of service department costs to be assigned as period costs. Allocate the costs using these results according to the step method.

# APPENDIX 12

# SIMULTANEOUS ALLOCATION USING MATRIX ALGEBRA

The simultaneous-equations procedure for allocating service department costs best meets our objectives for allocation. Every department is charged for the full cost of the services it uses, and all costs are allocated to the production departments based on a cause-and-effect relationship between cost and the demands for services. Until recently, however, few firms used this approach. The cost, in terms of labor, to solve the system of equations was simply too high. Solving a system of three equations is not overly difficult, but in a realistic setting with, say, 10 service departments, the algebra gets very complex, and the likelihood of solving a system of 10 equations, by hand, without making an arithmetic error is very low. However, the ready availability of computers now makes the simultaneous allocation of service department costs very easy. A set of simultaneous equations can be solved by means of matrix algebra, and computers are particularly adept at the required manipulations.

While the computer will do all of the work, it is necessary to have a basic knowledge of what it is doing. This knowledge will allow you to enter the data properly and to interpret the output. Let us solve a problem manually, using the data from the example in Exhibit 12-4 in the chapter. There are two solution approaches available, which we label the gross method and the net method.

## THE GROSS METHOD

We start by first rearranging our equations describing full service department costs, so that all the terms involving an $S$ are on one side of the equals sign and all the direct costs are on the other side. Using the data from Exhibit 12-4, the allocation equations become:

$$\begin{aligned} S_1 - 0.2S_2 - 0.1S_3 &= 40{,}000 \\ -0.1S_1 + S_2 - 0.1S_3 &= 45{,}000 \\ -0.3S_1 - 0.1S_2 + S_3 &= 25{,}000 \end{aligned}$$

we then notice that this can be expressed in matrix terms as

$$\begin{pmatrix} 1.0 & -0.2 & -0.1 \\ -0.1 & 1.0 & -0.1 \\ -0.3 & -0.1 & 1.0 \end{pmatrix} \begin{pmatrix} S_1 \\ S_2 \\ S_3 \end{pmatrix} = \begin{pmatrix} 40{,}000 \\ 45{,}000 \\ 25{,}000 \end{pmatrix}$$

or, equivalently,

$$\left[ \begin{pmatrix} 1 & 0 & 0 \\ 0 & 1 & 0 \\ 0 & 0 & 1 \end{pmatrix} - \begin{pmatrix} 0.0 & 0.2 & 0.1 \\ 0.1 & 0.0 & 0.1 \\ 0.3 & 0.1 & 0.0 \end{pmatrix} \right] \begin{pmatrix} S_1 \\ S_2 \\ S_3 \end{pmatrix} = \begin{pmatrix} 40{,}000 \\ 45{,}000 \\ 25{,}000 \end{pmatrix}$$

The first matrix inside the brackets is an identity matrix, conventionally labeled **I.** Note that the second matrix consists of the proportions of service department costs going to other service departments, as given in Exhibit 12-4, but flipped on its diagonal. Flipping a matrix on its diagonal is called taking its transpose, labeled with a superscript $t$. If we label the original matrix of service department percentages allocated to the other service departments as $\mathbf{B}^t$, then because $(\mathbf{A}^t)^t = \mathbf{A}$, we can refer to the transposed matrix above as **B**. This means that the expression in the brackets can be expressed in notation as $[\mathbf{I} - \mathbf{B}]$. If we also let **S** represent the vector (a matrix with only one row or column) of $S_i$'s and **b** represent the vector of direct costs, then the entire expression can be put into the notation form: $(\mathbf{I} - \mathbf{B})\mathbf{S} = \mathbf{b}$. Exhibit 12-10 summarizes our notation.

To get the solution, we premultiply both sides of the equation by the inverse of $(\mathbf{I} - \mathbf{B})$:

$$(\mathbf{I} - \mathbf{B})^{-1} (\mathbf{I} - \mathbf{B})\mathbf{S} = (\mathbf{I} - \mathbf{B})^{-1}\mathbf{b}$$

The inverse of a matrix, represented by a superscript $-1$, is the matrix that, when multiplied by the original matrix, results in an identity matrix; that is, $\mathbf{A}^{-1}\mathbf{A} = \mathbf{I}$. Therefore, the equation reduces to

$$\mathbf{IS} = (\mathbf{I} - \mathbf{B})^{-1}\mathbf{b}$$

**EXHIBIT 12-10 Matrix Notation for the Variable Cost Allocation**

| Direct Costs | Service Departments | PL | S | EM | M | A |
|---|---|---|---|---|---|---|
| $40,000 | PL | — | 0.1 | 0.3 | 0.2 | 0.4 |
| 45,000 | S | 0.2 | — | 0.1 | 0.4 | 0.3 |
| 25,000 | EM | 0.1 | 0.1 | — | 0.5 | 0.3 |
| **b** | | | $\mathbf{B}^t$ | | $\mathbf{C}^t$ | |

where $\mathbf{b}$ = vector of direct costs
$\mathbf{B}^t$ = interservice department proportions
$\mathbf{C}^t$ = all service department proportions

and because multiplying any matrix by an identity matrix results in the same matrix, $\mathbf{IA} = \mathbf{A}$, we get

$$\mathbf{S} = (\mathbf{I} - \mathbf{B})^{-1}\mathbf{b}$$

The solution to this equation provides the full cost for operating each service department. To get the costs allocated to each production department, we multiply each value of **S** by the proportions of service going to each production department. If we refer to the array of percentages of service department costs allocated to production departments as $\mathbf{C}^t$, and if we let **y** represent the costs allocated to the production departments, then our final allocation can be represented as

$$\mathbf{y} = \mathbf{C} \times \mathbf{S}$$

To solve our cost allocation example we substitute the following data into the equation

$$\mathbf{C} = \begin{pmatrix} 0.2 & 0.4 & 0.5 \\ 0.4 & 0.3 & 0.3 \end{pmatrix}$$

$$(\mathbf{I} - \mathbf{B}) = \begin{pmatrix} 1.0 & -0.2 & -0.1 \\ -0.1 & 1.0 & -0.1 \\ -0.3 & -0.1 & 1.0 \end{pmatrix}$$

$$\mathbf{b} = \begin{pmatrix} 40{,}000 \\ 45{,}000 \\ 25{,}000 \end{pmatrix}$$

Solving in two steps, we get

$$\mathbf{S} = \begin{pmatrix} 1.0 & -0.2 & -0.1 \\ -0.1 & 1.0 & -0.1 \\ -0.3 & -0.1 & 1.0 \end{pmatrix}^{-1} \begin{pmatrix} 40{,}000 \\ 45{,}000 \\ 25{,}000 \end{pmatrix}$$

$$\mathbf{S} = \begin{pmatrix} 55{,}787.78 \\ 55{,}305.46 \\ 47{,}266.88 \end{pmatrix}$$

and solving we get

$$\mathbf{y} = \begin{pmatrix} 0.2 & 0.4 & 0.5 \\ 0.4 & 0.3 & 0.3 \end{pmatrix} \begin{pmatrix} 55{,}787.78 \\ 55{,}305.46 \\ 47{,}266.88 \end{pmatrix}$$

$$\mathbf{y} = \begin{pmatrix} 56{,}913 \\ 53{,}087 \end{pmatrix}$$

The **S** vector provides the full cost of each service department and the **y** vector gives the total service department costs allocated to each production department. Instead of solving the problem in two steps, the final allocation could have been obtained in one step as

$$\mathbf{y} = \mathbf{C}(\mathbf{I} - \mathbf{B})^{-1}\mathbf{b}$$

However, the two-step procedure gives us the information needed to prepare a report such as that in Exhibit 12-6.

## THE NET METHOD

The gross method is by far the more popular solution procedure. It directly parallels the manual solution of a set of simultaneous equations, so the logic is easy to understand. The net method provides more useful information, but the underlying logic is mathematical rather than intuitive.

It turns out that

$$\mathbf{ABC} = \mathbf{C}^t\mathbf{B}^t\mathbf{A}^t$$

Thus making the appropriate substitutions, the allocation problem can also be represented as

$$\mathbf{y} = \mathbf{b}^t(\mathbf{I} - \mathbf{B}^t)^{-1}\mathbf{C}^t$$

This equation can also be solved in two steps, with

$$\mathbf{N} = (\mathbf{I} - \mathbf{B}^t)^{-1}\mathbf{C}^t$$

and

$$\mathbf{y} = \mathbf{b}^t\mathbf{N}$$

where **N** is a matrix that provides the proportion of each service department's direct costs that will be allocated to the final users. For the example, we have

$$\mathbf{N} = \begin{pmatrix} 1.0 & -0.1 & -0.3 \\ -0.2 & 1.0 & -0.1 \\ -0.1 & -0.1 & 1.0 \end{pmatrix}^{-1} \begin{pmatrix} 0.2 & 0.4 \\ 0.4 & 0.3 \\ 0.5 & 0.3 \end{pmatrix}$$

$$\mathbf{N} = \begin{pmatrix} 0.4341 & 0.5659 \\ 0.5466 & 0.4534 \\ 0.5981 & 0.4019 \end{pmatrix}$$

In the second step,

$$\mathbf{y} = (40{,}000 \quad 45{,}000 \quad 25{,}000) \begin{pmatrix} 0.4341 & 0.5659 \\ 0.5466 & 0.4534 \\ 0.5981 & 0.4019 \end{pmatrix}$$

$$\mathbf{y} = (56{,}913 \quad 53{,}087)$$

The final allocation to user departments is the same, but the intermediate results, **N**, allows us to prepare a report showing exactly how much of each service department's direct costs are charged to final users. That is, for the example, the matrix **N** tells us that 43.41% of personnel's $40,000 direct costs will be charged to machining, and 56.59% to assembly. This information allows us to prepare the report in Exhibit 12-11.

This exhibit allows us to provide managers a report that ties directly to the cost incurred by the service departments. It is far less confusing to

**EXHIBIT 12-11 Service Department Cost Report: Net Method**

| Direct Cost | Service Department | Manufacturing | Assembly | Total |
|---|---|---|---|---|
| $ 40,000 | Personnel | $17,364 | $22,636 | $ 40,000 |
| 45,000 | Security | 24,597 | 20,403 | 45,000 |
| 25,000 | Equipment maintenance | 14,952 | 10,048 | 25,000 |
| $110,000 | Totals | $56,913 | $53,087 | $110,000 |

managers than the previous report given in Exhibit 12-6. That report explained total costs but could not reconcile the costs incurred by a single department with the costs charged to other departments.

Because the **N** matrix gives us the percentages of each service department's costs charged to users, we can easily determine the effect of a change in a service department's costs. For every additional dollar incurred by personnel, the manufacturing department will be charged with an additional \$0.43. Similarly, if the costs of the security department increase by \$10, an additional \$4.53 will be charged to assembly.

The most convenient aspect of the net version of the allocation is realized when we make journal entries. If the gross method is used, the following single entry must be made to close the service department accounts (note, we are assuming that the detailed accounts within a department for materials, wages and so forth have been first closed to a summary account).

| | | |
|---|---|---|
| Overhead control—manufacturing | 56,913 | |
| Overhead control—assembly | 53,087 | |
| Cost summary—personnel | | 40,000 |
| Cost summary—security | | 45,000 |
| Cost summary—equip. maint. | | 25,000 |

In contrast, the use of the net method allows us to break the entry into its parts:

| | | |
|---|---|---|
| Overhead control—manufacturing | 17,364 | |
| Overhead control—assembly | 22,636 | |
| Cost summary—personnel | | 40,000 |
| Overhead control—manufacturing | 24,597 | |
| Overhead control—assembly | 20,403 | |
| Cost summary—security | | 45,000 |
| Overhead control—manufacturing | 14,952 | |
| Overhead control—assembly | 10,048 | |
| Cost summary—equip. maint. | | 25,000 |

For this simple example the gross approach yields a more compact entry. But in realistic situations with 10 to 15 service departments and 20 to 30 production departments, the second approach is more easily followed both by preparers and auditors.

We prefer the net method and hope it becomes more widely adopted. But you should be aware that the gross method is more commonly used. It has been the only method to appear on professional certification exams in recent years. We hope that this situation too will change in the near future.

## PROBLEMS AND CASES: APPENDIX 12

**12-35 Simultaneous-equations allocation method.**

Berkshire Equipment has three service departments—engineering, maintenance, and personnel—and two production departments—casting and assembly. Engineering's costs are allocated in proportion to each department's materials cost; maintenance is allocated on the basis of square footage of space occupied; personnel costs are allocated on the number of employees in each department. The firm has a computer to solve the allocation problem using the simultaneous-equations (matrix) approach, but we must determine the appropriate input. Appropriate data for Berkshire's most recent accounting period are as follows:

| | Engineering | Maintenance | Personnel | Casting | Assembly |
|---|---|---|---|---|---|
| Labor cost | $150,000 | $25,000 | $60,000 | $208,000 | $320,000 |
| Materials cost | $ 20,000 | $15,000 | $10,000 | $103,000 | $ 72,000 |
| Overhead cost | $ 65,000 | $22,000 | $35,000 | $110,000 | $176,000 |
| Square feet | 1,000 | 600 | 800 | 6,300 | 1,900 |
| Number of employees | 5 | 2 | 4 | 13 | 20 |

**Required**

Representing the problem with the equation, $\mathbf{y} = \mathbf{C}(\mathbf{I} - \mathbf{B})^{-1}\mathbf{b}$, write out the elements of the matrices or vectors for $(\mathbf{I} - \mathbf{B})$, $\mathbf{b}$, and $\mathbf{C}$.

**12-36 Simultaneous allocation: Net method—computer recommended.**

Refer to the data in Problem 12-35.

**Required**

Determine the amount of each service department's costs that will be allocated to casting and assembly using the computer program MATALLOC for the simultaneous method of allocation.

**12-37 Simultaneous-equations allocation method and sensitivity.**

Wooley's, Inc., has four service departments and two production departments. The following table gives the proportion of each service department's costs that is assigned to the other service and production departments.

| Service Department Direct Costs | | $S_1$ | $S_2$ | $S_3$ | $S_4$ | $P_1$ | $P_2$ |
|---|---|---|---|---|---|---|---|
| $85,000 | $S_1$ | — | 0.1 | 0.2 | 0.2 | 0.3 | 0.2 |
| 30,000 | $S_2$ | 0.3 | — | 0.2 | 0.2 | 0.1 | 0.2 |
| 65,000 | $S_3$ | 0.1 | 0.3 | — | — | 0.2 | 0.4 |
| 12,000 | $S_4$ | 0.2 | 0.1 | 0.6 | — | 0.1 | — |

The costs to be allocated to each production department can be expressed by the formula $\mathbf{y} = \mathbf{C}(\mathbf{I} - \mathbf{B})^{-1}\mathbf{b}$.

**Required**

**a.** Define the vectors or matrices for **C** and **b** by writing out their elements.

**b.** If

$$(\mathbf{I} - \mathbf{B})^{-1} = \begin{pmatrix} 1.19 & 0.50 & 0.27 & 0.45 \\ 0.29 & 1.25 & 0.40 & 0.42 \\ 0.47 & 0.56 & 1.21 & 0.88 \\ 0.29 & 0.35 & 0.13 & 1.17 \end{pmatrix}$$

what effect would a \$1 increase in costs for $S_1$ have on the final cost allocated to $P_1$ and $P_2$?

**12-38 Simultaneous-equations method of allocation.**

The following table represents the uses of service departments for a recent period.

| Costs | | $S_1$ | $S_2$ | $S_3$ | $P_1$ | $P_2$ |
|---|---|---|---|---|---|---|
| \$30,000 | $S_1$ | — | [a] | [a] | 0.2 | 0.3 |
| 50,000 | $S_2$ | [a] | — | [a] | 0.3 | 0.2 |
| 10,000 | $S_3$ | [a] | [a] | — | 0.5 | 0.1 |

[a]These numbers are not necessary for the solution.

Assume

$$(\mathbf{I} - \mathbf{B})^{-1} = \begin{pmatrix} 1.1 & 0.4 & 0.3 \\ 0.5 & 1.2 & 0.2 \\ 0.2 & 0.4 & 1.3 \end{pmatrix}$$

**Required**

Determine the service department costs to be allocated to departments $P_1$ and $P_2$.

**12-39 Simultaneous-equations allocation method.**

APC has two service departments that provide service to each of its three product lines. For the upcoming season, the firm anticipates the costs incurred by each department and the proportion of services provided to other departments will be as follows:

| | | Service Departments | | Production Departments | | |
|---|---|---|---|---|---|---|
| Service Department Costs | | A | B | Gas | Residual | Heating Oil |
| \$60,000 | A | — | 0.2 | 0.3 | 0.3 | 0.2 |
| 40,000 | B | 0.3 | — | 0.1 | 0.1 | 0.5 |

Using the matrix notation, the simultaneous allocation of costs can be represented as $\mathbf{y} = \mathbf{C}(\mathbf{I} - \mathbf{B})^{-1}\mathbf{b}$.

**Required**

**a.** Identify **C**, (**I** − **B**), and **b** by writing out their elements.

PROBLEMS AND CASES: APPENDIX 12

**b.** If

$$(\mathbf{I} - \mathbf{B})^{-1} = \begin{pmatrix} 1.0638 & 0.3191 \\ 0.2128 & 1.0638 \end{pmatrix}$$

determine the service department costs to be allocated to each of the other departments.

**c.** Determine the service department costs allocated to home heating oil if the firm uses the two-step direct method.

**12-40 Simultaneous-equations allocation method.**

Gauss Gears operates a small manufacturing firm. It has two manufacturing divisions: molding and machining. The firm also operates two service departments: engineering and maintenance. Engineering costs are allocated based on a log of hours worked for each department, and maintenance costs are based on square footage. Next period the firm expects to incur the following costs per department and utilize services as indicated.

| | Molding | Machining | Engineering | Maintenance | Total |
|---|---|---|---|---|---|
| Direct labor | $ 80,000 | $150,000 | $40,000 | $10,000 | $280,000 |
| Direct materials | $240,000 | $ 20,000 | $ 5,000 | $ 2,000 | $267,000 |
| Overhead | $175,000 | $ 90,000 | $25,000 | $18,000 | $308,000 |
| Square footage | 1,000 | 3,000 | 1,000 | 500 | 5,500 |
| Engineering hours | 2,600 | 1,000 | 100 | 400 | 4,100 |

**Required**

Using matrix algebra for simultaneous allocation, determine the standard cost per unit of service for next period and the standard overhead application rate for the production departments assuming that overhead is applied on a per-direct-labor-dollar basis.

**12-41 Simultaneous equations method** (CMA adapted).

Balou Company is developing departmental overhead rates based upon direct labor hours for its two production departments. The molding department employs 20 people and the assembly department employs 80 people. Each person in these two departments works 2,000 hours per year. The production-related overhead costs for the molding department are budgeted at $200,000, and the assembly department costs are budgeted at $320,000. Two service departments—repair and power—directly support the two production departments and have budgeted costs of $48,000 and $250,000, respectively. The production departments' hourly overhead rates cannot be determined until the service departments' costs are properly allocated. The following schedule reflects the use of the repair department's and power department's output by the various departments.

| | Repair | Power | Molding | Assembly |
|---|---|---|---|---|
| Repair hours | 0 | 1,000 | 1,000 | 8,000 |
| Kilowatt-hours | 240,000 | 0 | 840,000 | 120,000 |

**Required**

**a.** Calculate the charges to molding and assembly using the direct allocation method to charge the production departments for service department costs.

**b.** Calculate the overhead rates per direct labor hour for the molding and assembly departments using simultaneous equations (sometimes called the reciprocal or algebraic method) to charge service department costs to each other and to the production departments.

**c.** Explain the difference between the methods and indicate the arguments that are generally presented to support the reciprocal method over the direct allocation method.

**12-42 Matrix allocation for a university—computer recommended.**

The University's Center for Continuing Education offers both credit and noncredit programs. The fees for the credit programs consist solely of tuition, the level of which are set by the regents. The center bills the noncredit programs for 225% of the total cost for putting on the programs. The following chart provides some data for the most recent term.

| | Administration | Reproduction | Supplies | Credit Programs | Noncredit Programs |
|---|---|---|---|---|---|
| Salaries | $225,000 | $ 26,000 | $ 14,000 | $160,000 | $250,000 |
| Other costs | $ 80,000 | $120,000 | $160,000 | $ 90,000 | $110,000 |
| Copy pages | 5,000 | 6,000 | 9,000 | 42,000 | 44,000 |

The Continuing Education Center uses the simultaneous-equations method for allocating service department costs. The administration costs are allocated based on salaries, reproduction costs are allocated on the number of pages copied for each user, and the supplies department's costs are allocated on the basis of "other costs."

**Required**

Determine the total fees to be billed this term for noncredit programs.

**12-43 Simultaneous allocation—computer recommended.**

Use the information given in Problem 12-23.

**Required**

Allocate Holiday's service department costs to the production departments using matrix allocation. Use the net method and develop a report that shows the amount of each service department's costs that are assigned to final users.

**12-44 Step and simultaneous-equations allocation—computer recommended.**

Eudora International Airlines wishes to allocate the cost of its four major service departments—personnel, janitorial, equipment maintenance, and payroll—to its major revenue-producing activities: freight service, domestic passenger service, and international passenger service. Personnel costs are allocated on the basis of the number of employees hired by each department. The following number of persons were hired by each department this period: janitorial, 2; maintenance, 5; payroll, 3; freight, 6; domestic passenger, 12; international passenger, 7. Janitorial costs are based on square footage of office and terminal space. The square-footage figures are as follows: personnel, 5,000; maintenance, 20,000; payroll, 4,000; freight,

30,000; domestic, 5,000; and international, 2,000. Equipment maintenance is based upon a log of labor hours to each department. These were: personnel, 100; janitorial, zero; payroll, 200; freight, 3,000; domestic, 2,000; and international, 1,700. Payroll is based upon number of employees. Employment by department was: personnel, 15; janitorial, 12; maintenance, 30; freight, 25; domestic, 150; and international, 20. Costs traced to each service department were: personnel, $110,000; janitorial, $100,000; maintenance, $435,000; and payroll, $90,000.

**Required**

**a.** Allocate these costs using the step method. Use the order in which the service departments are listed.

**b.** Allocate these costs using matrix allocation (reciprocal service).

**12-45 Simultaneous equations and step methods of allocation—computer required.** Pixy Company has five lettered service departments and three numbered production departments. The costs incurred by each service department and the proportions of service rendered are as follows:

| | | A | B | C | D | E | 1 | 2 | 3 |
|---|---|---|---|---|---|---|---|---|---|
| $500,000 | A | — | 0.05 | 0.1 | 0.15 | 0.02 | 0.15 | 0.23 | 0.3 |
| 400,000 | B | 0.1 | — | 0.07 | 0.03 | 0.15 | 0.15 | 0.3 | 0.2 |
| 300,000 | C | 0.05 | 0.1 | — | 0.2 | 0.15 | 0.2 | 0.1 | 0.2 |
| 200,000 | D | 0.15 | 0.1 | 0.05 | — | 0.2 | 0.1 | 0.3 | 0.1 |
| 100,000 | E | 0.01 | 0.04 | 0.15 | 0.1 | — | 0.2 | 0.2 | 0.3 |

**Required**

**a.** Use the MATALLOC program to allocate the above costs.

**b.** Use the OPSTPAL program to determine the order in which to allocate costs using the step method if the objective is to maximize the costs allocated to 2.

**c.** Use the MATALLOC program to perform the allocation for (b) above.

# CHAPTER 13

# ALLOCATING JOINT PRODUCTION COSTS

In the preceding chapter we got to the point where all production costs were assigned to production departments. In this chapter we assign the production costs to product lines within departments. The following three chapters will assign the product line costs to the individual units produced.

Once again most costs are easily traceable to product lines. An exception is joint costs. A **joint cost** is a variable cost that simultaneously results in two or more unique products or services. The issues involved in assigning these costs to product lines are essentially equivalent to those discussed in Chapter 11 for common costs. However, with joint production costs more emphasis is usually placed on the product costing objective (determining the cost of products in inventory) than on the cost control or performance measurement objective.

Although joint production costs are clearly necessary to acquire a firm's inventory, it frequently is not clear which portion of the costs was incurred to get which products. The cost of a steer for a meat processor is a prime (or choice) example of a joint production cost. The purchase price of the steer is certainly a necessary cost to produce the firm's end products. But finding a clear cause-and-effect relationship that would provide the basis for allocating the cost of the steer to the eventual products—hides, hamburger, steaks, and so forth—has proved elusive.

## JOINT COST ALLOCATION PROCEDURES

Although clear cause-and-effect relationships are usually difficult or impossible to identify for joint costs, a number of allocation procedures have been developed and are commonly used in practice. Each method intuitively makes sense in certain situations, but none of the approaches provides meaningful results in all situations. Let us now turn to an examination of the more popular methods.

### Physical Basis

As with common costs, joint costs are frequently allocated in proportion to a measure of some physical characteristic of the resulting products. **Physical measures** are generally appealing when the products emerging from a joint process are very similar and differ only by size. For example, consider a machining operation that cuts steel rods into drive shafts for electric motors. The firm cuts a 24-inch rod into a 7-inch drive shaft and a 17-inch drive shaft. In this case the joint costs consist of the cost of the rod and the cutting operation. One physical allocation might be to allocate the costs in proportion to the size of the drive shafts produced. An alternative is to allocate the cost of the rod in proportion to the size of the outputs but allocate the cutting cost equally between the two products. As before, physical measures are appealing because they are generally inexpensive to use.

### Relative Sales Value

If products emerging from a joint process are immediately salable, joint costs are frequently allocated to the products in proportion to their **relative sales value.** For example, a dairy processor might allocate the joint cost of raw milk and the cost of processing it through a separator to the resulting cream and milk in proportion to the sales value of the two products. In this way the carrying value of inventories will reflect the fact that some products are more valuable than others.

However, many joint processes result in products that are not immediately salable at the split-off point. The **split-off point** is that point in the process at which the individual products or services become separately identifiable. Instead, firms frequently must incur separate processing costs to make the products or services salable. **Separate processing costs** are costs incurred after the split-off point that are traceable to the individual products.

Of course, products may pass through several joint processes before they become salable. In that case, costs considered separable relative to one split-off point may be joint costs relative to a later split-off point. For

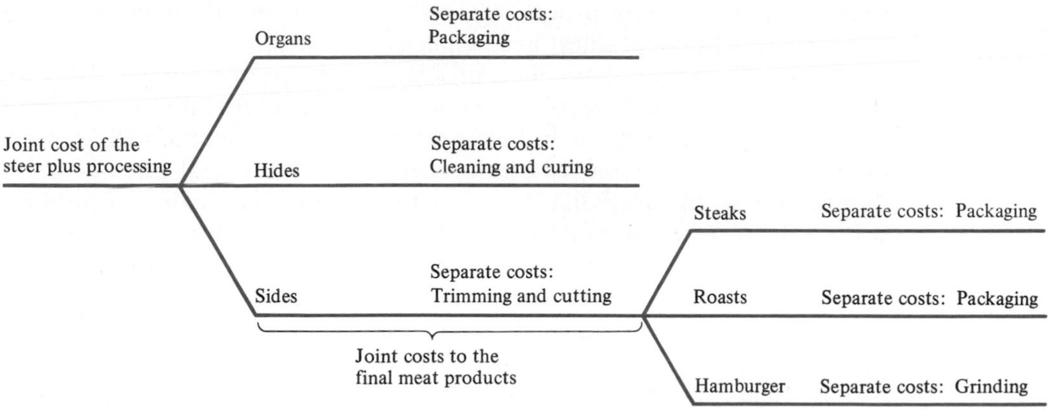


**FIGURE 13-1 Joint and separate processing costs for a beef packer.**

example, in a beef-packing plant the first stage of the process may be to separate the hides, organs, and beef sides. At this point, the joint costs are the cost of the steer and the costs to process it to the split-off point. These costs will be allocated to the resulting products. The separate processing costs for the organs may amount to nothing more than the cost to package and ship the products to a dog food company; the separate processing costs for the hides may include cleaning and curing costs; and there may be substantial separate processing costs for the beef sides if they are trimmed and cut into eventual end products (steaks, roasts, hamburger, and so on).

If the sides are cut into individual products, we have another joint process. The joint costs will be the costs allocated to the sides plus the separate processing costs for the sides. These costs will then be allocated to the final products that result at the second split-off point. We may then have additional further processing costs for the individual products. These might include packaging costs for steaks and roasts and grinding costs to obtain hamburger. The relationships of these costs are illustrated in Figure 13-1. When separate processing costs must be incurred to make joint products marketable, the relative sales value approach is usually modified into a net realizable value approach.

### Net Realizable Value

The relative sales value method allocated joint costs based on the final eventual selling price of the cost objects. Unfortunately, the relative sales value method ignores the possibility that much of the sales value of an object may have arisen from the value added by separate processing costs incurred for the cost object. Thus cost objects that benefit from the incurrence of large separate processing costs (to the extent these costs can be reflected in additional sales) are penalized by having a larger portion of joint costs allocated to them. This problem can be partially alleviated if we adjust the eventual selling price for cost objects by subtracting out separate processing costs. By subtracting these separable costs from the selling price, we are estimating the **net realizable value** of the individual cost objects at the split-off point. Note that the estimate need only be made if a product is not salable at the split-off point. If a product is salable at split-off, its actual selling price is a better indication of relative value than the estimated net realizable value after separate processing.

To illustrate the calculations consider a canner who is processing green beans. First, the beans are cleaned and sliced. The sliced beans are then mechanically sorted into "full cuts" and "short cuts" (ends and pieces). The separate products are then canned, cooked, labeled, and distributed. The full-cut beans use fancier packaging and are subject to higher promotion costs. Given the data in Exhibit 13-1, let us determine the cost per case for each product using the net realizable value allocation.

We begin by allocating the joint cost of the beans to the two products. These costs are allocated in proportion to the net realizable value of the products at the point they are sorted (the split-off point). Our estimate of the net realizable value is obtained by determining the *total* (not per unit) sales value of all the products obtained from the joint process (45 cases of full cuts and 50 cases of short cuts). From the total sales value of each product line we subtract the separate processing costs incurred for each to make them salable. The $200 joint cost is then allocated to the products in proportion to their net realizable values (see Figure 13-2 for a schematic diagram) as follows:

| Product | Eventual Sales Value | Further Processing Costs | Net Realizable Value | Proportion | Joint Cost | Allocation |
|---|---|---|---|---|---|---|
| Full cut | $324 | $171 | $153 | 153/260 | $200 | $117.69 |
| Short cut | 252 | 145 | 107 | 107/260 | 200 | 82.31 |
| | | | $260 | | | $200.00 |

This provides us with the total joint cost to be allocated to each of the products. To get the full cost of each product on a per-case basis, we add the separate processing costs to the allocated costs and divide by the number of cases of each product that we produced.

| Product | Allocated Joint Cost | Separate Processing Cost | Total Cost | Number of Cases Produced | Cost per Case |
|---|---|---|---|---|---|
| Full cut | $117.69 | $171 | $288.69 | 45 | $6.42 |
| Short cut | 82.31 | 145 | 227.31 | 50 | 4.55 |

**EXHIBIT 13-1 Data for a Bean Processor**

Cost per ton of fresh beans: $200

| | Products | |
|---|---|---|
| | **Full Cuts** | **Short Cuts** |
| Output | 45 cases (24 cans @ 16 oz) | 50 cases (24 cans @ 12 oz) |
| Cost to cook, label and distribute | $3.80 per case | $2.90 per case |
| Selling price | $7.20 per case | $5.04 per case |

The per-unit case costs are then used for valuing ending finished goods inventory and determining the cost of goods sold.

### Shapley and Alternative Cost Allocations

Both the **Shapley value allocation** and the **alternative cost allocation** can be used to allocate joint production costs if we know what the alternative costs to acquiring the products jointly would be. Returning to the dairy processor example, if the firm can determine the cost of acquiring milk and cream separately, then the joint cost of purchasing and processing raw milk can be allocated to the two products by using either the Shapley or alternative cost allocations. The computational procedures are unchanged from those described in Chapter 11, so we will not repeat that discussion here, but we do provide an illustration in the demonstration problem.

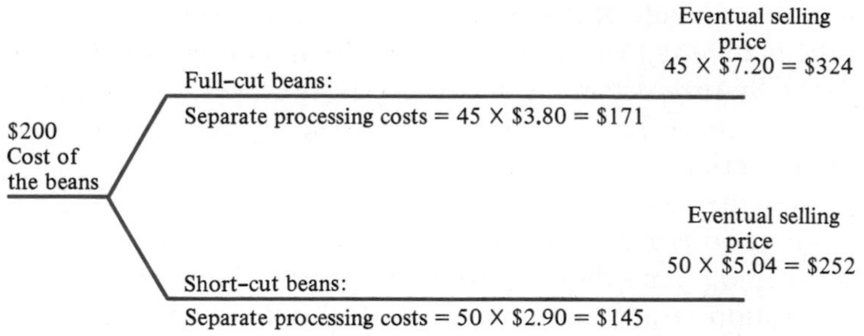

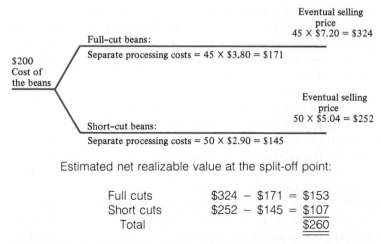

Estimated net realizable value at the split-off point:

| | | |
|---|---|---|
| Full cuts | $324 − $171 = | $153 |
| Short cuts | $252 − $145 = | $107 |
| Total | | $260 |

**FIGURE 13-2 Schematic diagram for the bean-canning example.**

## ACCOUNTING FOR BY-PRODUCTS

When one or more of the products that are acquired by a joint process are considered immaterial relative to the main products, the immaterial products are called by-products. **By-products** are products for which we choose not to measure profitability. The rationale for this choice is that we are not intentionally in the business to produce by-products. Thus knowing the profitability or lack thereof will have no effect on the amount of by-products we produce. Given the immaterial status of by-products (by definition), our accounting for them is a mixture of expediency tempered by the need for internal control.

In many cases the value of by-products is immaterial both relative to our main product and in absolute dollar terms. In these cases we often cannot justify the cost to account for inventories of by-products formally. When such is the case, no accounting recognition is given to the by-products until they are sold. When sold, the net proceeds of the sale are frequently treated as miscellaneous income. Since no joint costs are assigned to the by-products, all costs attributable to the joint process are allocated solely to the main products.

A slight variation is to treat the proceeds from sale of the by-product as a reduction in the cost of the joint process. If it costs $500 to operate the joint process and we sell by-products for $10, the $10 proceeds are credited to production costs to yield a net joint cost of $490. The $490 net joint cost will then be allocated to our main products. The entry to record the sale of our by-products would be

| | | |
|---|---|---|
| Cash | 10 | |
| Work-in-Process | | 10 |

Note that if this entry is made at the time the by-products are sold, we are likely violating the matching principle. For sales may not occur in the same period in which the by-products were produced. If, however, the amounts are immaterial, then the effect of our violating the matching principle should also be immaterial.

In some cases the value of by-products may be immaterial relative to the firm's main products and yet be sufficiently material in absolute terms to justify keeping records for control purposes. For example, in many mining operations trace amounts of gold may be produced even though another ore is considered to be the main product. We may wish to treat the gold as a by-product for income measurement purposes, and yet we may also want to keep close inventory control over the gold to prevent its loss or theft. In these cases, we establish a formal inventory record of the by-product, carrying it at an estimate of its net realizable value. As before, the offsetting credit could be to miscellaneous income or used to reduce the cost of the joint process. For example, in the latter case, if our firm spends $1,000 to produce a main product and a by-product estimated to be worth $20, our accounting treatment to record the joint manufacturing costs would be

| | | |
|---|---|---|
| (1) Work-in-Process | 1,000 | |
| Various accounts | | 1,000 |

to record the acquisition of the by-product

| | | |
|---|---|---|
| (2) By-product Inventory | 20 | |
| Work-in-Process | | 20 |

and the entry for the sale of the by-product

| | | |
|---|---|---|
| (3) Cash | 22 | |
| Miscellaneous Income | | 2 |
| By-product Inventory | | 20 |

In this last entry we presume that our actual sales price was not exactly equal to our estimated net realizable value (the typical case). Any differences would generally be recorded as miscellaneous income or expense. Notice also that when we record an inventory value for by-products we avoid the matching principle violation we had seen previously. For now we reduce our processing costs at the same time as by-products are produced, even if they are sold much later.

There are many variations on accounting for by-products. The timing of recognition and the treatment for the proceeds from sales that we described lead to four variations. They are summarized in Exhibit 13-2. To complicate matters further, some accountants try to distinguish between by-products and scrap. In such cases scrap are items with virtually no value or negative value. The cost to dispose of scrap is usually charged to overhead.

## RELATIONSHIP BETWEEN SCRAP, BY-PRODUCTS, AND MAIN PRODUCTS

The distinction between scrap, by-products, and main products frequently change as conditions change. Consider the following case, modeled after a real situation.

The Chocolate Cookie Company (CCC) has produced a popular line of chocolate cookies for decades. Currently, it costs the firm $300 to process a batch of 10,000 cookies. The company sells the cookies for $1 for a

**EXHIBIT 13-2 Four Common Approaches to Accounting for By-products**

| Treatment of Proceeds from Sales | Timing of Recognition: At Production | Timing of Recognition: At Sale |
|---|---|---|
| Miscellaneous income | A | B |
| Reduction in joint cost | C | D |

Valuation of ending inventory of by-products
A and C: Estimated market value
B and D: Separable cost per unit (zero if there are no separable costs)

**JOURNAL ENTRIES**[a]

| Approach | When By-product Is Produced | When By-product Is Sold |
|---|---|---|
| A | By-product Inventory<br>  Miscellaneous income | Cash<br>  By-product Inventory |
| B | No entry | Cash<br>  Miscellaneous Income |
| C | By-product Inventory<br>  Work in Process | Cash<br>  By-product Inventory |
| D | No entry | Cash<br>  Work in Process |

[a]These entries presume that there are no separable costs required to make the by-product salable.

package of 20 (or $0.05 each). For years the company threw away its broken or imperfect cookies. In a batch of 10,000 cookies, 500 units would be thrown away. Management attempted to find uses for the broken cookies (such as for livestock feed), but was unsuccessful. In this situation, the appropriate accounting treatment is to consider the broken cookies as scrap. No costs are allocated to the units thrown away. The $300 of costs are attributed solely to the 9,500 good cookies to yield a unit cost of $0.0316.

One day the sales manager observed her children breaking up the company's cookies and mixing them with ice cream. Tasting the mixture, she was impressed. Soon after, the firm approached an ice cream manufacturer and entered an agreement to produce "Cookies and Cream." As part of the agreement, CCC sells the broken and imperfect cookies to the ice cream company for $0.035 each. Now, the firm's revenues per batch are $475 from the sale of good cookies and $17.50 from the sale of imperfect cookies. Due to the relatively immaterial size of the revenues from the imperfect cookies, they would now be considered a by-product. The sales value of the imperfect cookies is subtracted from the total production cost and the net production cost is allocated to the good cookies. Now the cost per good cookie becomes ($300 − $17.50)/9,500 = $0.0297.

Soon the Cookies and Cream became very popular. The amount of imperfect cookies occurring naturally was insufficient to produce the amount of Cookies and Cream demanded. Consequently, CCC began breaking good cookies and selling them to the ice cream company. From a batch, CCC now sells 4,000 good cookies to traditional customers, and 5,500 good cookies (after being intentionally broken) plus 500 imperfect cookies to the ice cream company. It costs CCC $25 to break the 5,500 good cookies. Total revenues per batch from traditional customers are now $200 and from the ice cream company $210. Because both products are now significant, they would be considered joint products. The joint production costs can be allocated to each product line using any of several methods.

Income statements per batch for CCC under each situation are presented in Exhibit 13-3. For the joint product case, the joint costs were allocated using the net realizable value method. That is,

| Product | Eventual Sales Value | Separate Processing | Net Realizable Value | Proportion | Allocation |
|---|---|---|---|---|---|
| Good | $200 | $ 0 | $200 | 200/385 | $155.84 |
| Imperfect | 210 | 25 | 185 | 185/385 | 144.16 |
| | | | $385 | | $300.00 |

Part C of Exhibit 13-3 indicates that when the products are treated as main products, each product line is profitable. This may or may not be the case. Comparing the total net income in parts (b) and (c) of Exhibit 13-3, we see that net income *per batch* declined as more cookies were sold as imperfect. If capacity is not a constraint, so that the firm is producing enough batches to satisfy its demand for good cookies, then both product lines are profitable. But if capacity is a constraint and there is unfilled demand for good cookies, the sale of the cookies as imperfect is not the most profitable alternative. That is, CCC would be better off selling the good cookies as good cookies for $0.05 each rather than as imperfects for $0.035 each.

If capacity is a constraint, the unprofitable status of the sales to the ice cream company can be revealed to management by using an altered allocation procedure. Exhibit 13-4 presents a new product line income statement. This time the allocated joint cost has been adjusted for the opportunity cost from selling the cookies to the ice cream company instead of traditional customers. The opportunity cost is

$$(\$0.05 - \$0.035)5{,}500 = \$82.50$$

**EXHIBIT 13-3 Income Statements as the Treatment of Joint Products Changes**

**a.** Imperfect cookies are scrap:

| | | |
|---|---|---|
| Sales (9,500 × $0.05) | | $475.00 |
| Cost of goods sold | | 300.00 |
| Net income | | $175.00 |

**b.** Imperfect cookies are sold as a by-product:

| | | |
|---|---|---|
| Sales (9,500 × $0.05) | | $475.00 |
| Production costs | $300.00 | |
| By-product sales | 17.50 | |
| Cost of goods sold | | 282.50 |
| Net income | | $192.50 |

**c.** Imperfect cookies are treated as a main product:

| | Good | Imperfect | Total |
|---|---|---|---|
| Sales | $200.00 | $210.00 | $410.00 |
| Joint cost | 155.84 | 144.16 | 300.00 |
| Separable cost | — | 25.00 | 25.00 |
| Cost of goods sold | $155.84 | $169.16 | $325.00 |
| Net income | $ 44.16 | $ 40.84 | $ 85.00 |

The new joint costs are as follows:

| Product | NRV Joint Cost | Opportunity Cost | Joint Cost |
|---|---|---|---|
| Good | $155.84 | ($82.50) | $ 73.34 |
| Imperfect | 144.16 | 82.50 | 226.66 |
| | $300.00 | | $300.00 |

The income statement in Exhibit 13-4 is a useful attention-directing device. It points out that in the short run the firm should concentrate on selling the cookies to traditional customers if they wish to maximize profits. Even if management chooses to continue to sell to the ice cream company for long-run considerations,[1] the report shows that there is a short-run cost from choosing to do so. Unfortunately, the approach used is arbitrary. We tried several allocations before getting the results presented in Exhibit 13-4.

[1]Presumably, when capacity becomes a constraint, capacity will be increased. During the expansion period management must weigh the damage on future lost sales from not meeting the demand for each product. For a new product, such as the Cookies and Cream, maintaining market share for the new product may be far more important than meeting demand for the old product.

**EXHIBIT 13-4 Allocation with Opportunity Cost**

| | Good | Imperfect | Total |
|---|---|---|---|
| Sales | $200.00 | $210.00 | $410.00 |
| Joint cost | 73.34 | 226.66 | 300.00 |
| Separable cost | — | 25.00 | 25.00 |
| Cost of goods sold | $ 73.34 | $251.66 | $325.00 |
| Net income | $126.66 | $ (41.66) | $ 85.00 |

By choosing arbitrary allocations we should always be able to prepare reports that reflect the relative profitability of products. But, in order to know whether we are sending the proper signals on profitability, we must do an appropriate *relevant cost analysis* for each product.

But, if we have done the appropriate analysis, why bother with allocations? It would be simpler to just tell management what the actual situation is. Further, once an allocation procedure is chosen, it is likely to be used continuously, even after conditions change. For CCC, once the capacity constraint is relieved, both products are profitable. The report in Exhibit 13-4 would then be misleading.

## THE OBJECTIVE FOR JOINT COST ALLOCATIONS

When we have situations like the Chocolate Cookie Company, where the proportion of the joint products produced can be altered, a perfect allocation procedure would consistently provide accurate information on the relative profitability of the products. Such information would allow managers to take actions such as adjusting production proportions.[2] However, to date, no allocation procedure has been found that meets this objective. All existing procedures are arbitrary and therefore cannot be relied upon to be useful for decision making.

When the relative proportions of joint products can be varied, management is faced with the problem of evaluating the relative profitability of products. In this case, joint cost allocations have the potential of being useful attention-directing devices if an appropriate allocation procedure is ever found. But if management faces a situation in which the joint products are produced in fixed proportions, allocations do not even have the po-

[2] If you studied Appendix 5A, you should see that linear programming is very useful in determining joint production proportions. There have been allocations proposed based on the shadow prices from linear-programming solutions, but they are not always perfect either. The discussion of these latter procedures is beyond the scope of our text.

tential for being useful to management. For in that case, the only decision faced by management is either to produce the joint products or not to produce them. Here the only information needed to reach the correct decision is to compare total revenues from the joint products to the total cost of producing them.

## WHY ARE JOINT COSTS ALLOCATED?

There are two rationales for allocating joint costs. The first is a cost-benefit argument. It says that the cost of making appropriate analyses of the relative profitability of products is too expensive (actual situations may involve hundreds of products and dozens of joint processes). In such a case, this argument claims that we are better off using arbitrary allocations because the cost arising from incorrect decisions will be less than the cost of undertaking hundreds of individual analyses of product costs. Although this argument sounds good, we can never be certain that its conclusion is true for a particular firm.

The second rationale is more convincing. It argues that joint cost allocations are necessary for external reporting. When we prepare a balance sheet, we must value inventories. In a pure joint process with no separable costs, if we do not allocate joint costs, the cost of ending inventory will be zero. All costs will be written off as a period cost and income will be understated. Another extreme approach that avoids allocations is to value inventory at market value. But this approach recognizes a profit for the products in inventory. Thus net income is overstated. The compromise is to allocate costs arbitrarily to the products. Although we may not be able to defend the precise unit costs generated, they are preferable to the extreme alternatives of valuing inventory at zero or at market value.

It is this latter argument that leads to the net realizable value allocation. In effect, inventories of joint products are first valued at estimated market value less the cost to sell them. This yields the net realizable value for inventory. Next, the lower of cost or market rule is applied to lower inventory values to cost. These costs are approximated by allocating costs to the units sold and the ending inventory in proportion to the net realizable values of the units sold and the units still on hand. Even though these allocations may not be useful for managerial decision making, they do result in a better financial statement presentation than the alternatives.

## JOINT COSTS AND FURTHER PROCESSING DECISIONS

The financial statements prepared for external use are frequently used internally as well. They are often used as the basis for identifying actions that can be taken to improve the results reported in external financial statements. However, extreme care must be used when evaluating product lines that include significant allocated joint costs.

If the products produced by a joint process are profitable as a total, the managerial question is not whether to produce the joint products, but rather what to do with them once they are produced. That is, should some of the products be sold "as is" at the split-off point, discarded at the split-off point, or further processed into another product? For these questions, allocated joint costs are *irrelevant* and should be *ignored.*

Consider the per-unit data given in Exhibit 13-5. The top set is typical of data developed from product line income statements prepared for external use. The last line of data was made available for managerial use. From the net income line, it would appear to a naive manager that products A, B, and C are profitable and products D and E are not. One reaction would be to stop completing products D and E and sell them at split-off. But when joint costs are involved, net income figures cannot be relied upon as a guide to action.

Rather than referring to net income to determine which products to complete, the appropriate analysis is to compare the value added by incurring further processing costs to the amount of those costs. If the increase in the selling price of the products exceeds the additional processing costs, the units should be processed further.

Exhibit 13-6 compares the increase in selling price from further processing to the cost of further processing for each product. Note that the increase in the selling price is simply the difference between the selling price of the finished product and the selling price of the product at the split-off point (the first and last lines in Exhibit 13-5, respectively). The further processing cost is the same as that given in Exhibit 13-5.

The final line in Exhibit 13-6 now gives us the appropriate information for deciding which products to complete and which to sell at split-

**EXHIBIT 13-5 Income per Unit for Joint Products**

| | Product | | | | | |
|---|---|---|---|---|---|---|
| | A | B | C | D | E | Total |
| Selling price | $40 | $35 | $45 | $ 60 | $44 | $224 |
| Joint cost[a] | 15 | 10 | 20 | 40 | 30 | 115 |
| Further processing cost | 10 | 20 | 15 | 30 | 20 | 95 |
| Net income | $15 | $ 5 | $10 | $(10) | $ (6) | $ 14 |
| Selling price at split-off point | $25 | $24 | $28 | $ 26 | $27 | |

[a]Allocated based on the weight of the resulting joint products.

**EXHIBIT 13-6 Increased Cost and Revenue from Further Processing**

| | Product | | | | |
|---|---|---|---|---|---|
| | A | B | C | D | E |
| Increased selling price | $15 | $11 | $17 | $34 | $17 |
| Further processing cost | 10 | 20 | 15 | 30 | 20 |
| Gain (loss) from further processing | $ 5 | $ (9) | $ 2 | $ 4 | $ (3) |

off. The further processing costs are justified for products A, C, and D as the additional revenues exceed additional costs. But products B and E should not be completed. The costs for these products exceeds the incremental revenue from further processing.

Exhibit 13-7 presents revised per-unit income figures for the example. This exhibit reflects the income that would be earned if the correct further processing decisions were made for each product. Note that whereas total revenue has fallen, overall net income has risen. Note also that although product E still shows a book loss, the loss is smaller than what it was before.

The income statement that reflects the optimal further processing decisions still shows a net loss for products D and E. This might tempt management to discontinue these products entirely. But because these products are produced as part of a joint process, our only choice is whether to throw them away or sell them. If we discard them, we give up the revenue they generate, but the total joint cost will be unaffected. Giving up revenue for no cost saving is silly, so the products should be produced.

## SUMMARY

As with common costs, the ultimate goal in choosing an allocation basis for joint costs is to find a basis that captures the cause-and-effect relationship between the joint cost and the resulting products. But, typically, manage-

**EXHIBIT 13-7 Per-Unit Income for Joint Products with Optimal Further Processing Decisions**

| | A | B[a] | C | D | E[a] | Total |
|---|---|---|---|---|---|---|
| Selling price | $40 | $24 | $45 | $ 60 | $27 | $196 |
| Joint cost | 15 | 10 | 20 | 40 | 30 | 115 |
| Further processing cost | 10 | 0 | 15 | 30 | 0 | 55 |
| Net income | $15 | $14 | $10 | $(10) | $ (3) | $ 26 |

[a]Sold at split-off, not processed further.

ment is unable to determine such a relationship. For inventory valuation for external financial statements, managers are generally forced to use one of the arbitrary allocations described in this chapter. To date, cost accounting theory has been unable to provide much guidance in choosing among the procedures. However, it is known that whichever method is used, the resulting unit product costs should be viewed with caution when making operating decisions.

## DEMONSTRATION PROBLEM

The Louisiana Chemical Company processes a residual oil into three chemicals, A, B, and C. Each day the firm processes 1,000 gallons of residual oil. The process yields 500 gallons of A, 200 gallons of B, and 100 gallons of C. The cost of the oil and the cost to process it into the three separate products totals $2,000. It costs $1 per gallon in additional processing costs to make product A salable, while product B requires $3 per gallon of additional processing costs. In contrast, product C emerges from the process ready for sale. Product A sells for $3 per gallon, B sells for $10 per gallon, and C sells for $18 per gallon to retail customers. In the wholesale market, unfinished product A can be bought for $1.50 per gallon, unfinished B for $5 per gallon, and C for $10 per gallon. It is not considered economically feasible to process the residual oil to produce only one of the products. However, if the firm adjusted the process to obtain only chemicals A and B, it could process 1,000 gallons of input for $1,500. Similarly, processing to obtain only B and C could be done for $1,600 and to obtain only A and C would cost $1,700 per day. These alternative arrangements still only produce 500 gallons of A, 200 gallons of B, or 100 gallons of C. Assume there is no cost to dispose of waste. These facts are summarized in Figure 13-3.

**Required**

Determine net income for each product from the sale of 1 day's output using each of the methods described in the chapter for allocating the joint costs.

**Solution**

***Physical measure.*** For our example, the physical measure for the product would likely be gallons of product resulting from the joint process. In this case the joint cost allocated to each product is a simple proportion:

| Product | Gallons | Proportion | Joint Cost | Allocated Cost | Cost per Gallon | Further Processing per Gallon | Final Cost per Gallon |
|---|---|---|---|---|---|---|---|
| A | 500 | 5/8 | $2,000 | $1,250 | $2.50 | $1.00 | $3.50 |
| B | 200 | 2/8 | 2,000 | 500 | 2.50 | 3.00 | 5.50 |
| C | 100 | 1/8 | 2,000 | 250 | 2.50 | — | 2.50 |
| Totals | 800 | | | $2,000 | | | |

The physical basis results in each physical unit being allocated the same cost per unit ($2.50 in the example). The only difference in the final per-unit cost among

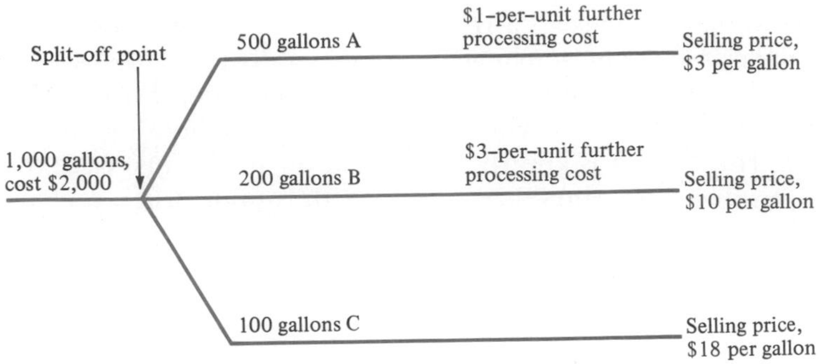


**ALTERNATIVE ACQUISITION COSTS**

| Purchase of Products in Wholesale Market | | | |
|---|---|---|---|
| **Product** | **Cost per Gallon** | **Produce Pairs of Products** | **Total Joint Cost** |
| A | $ 1.50 | AB | $1,500 |
| B | 5.00 | AC | 1,700 |
| C | 10.00 | BC | 1,600 |

**FIGURE 13-3 Summary of facts for the demonstration problem.**

the products is a result of the further processing costs charged directly to a product. A product line income statement for 1 day's sale of production for this firm would be as follows:

| Product | Units Sold | Selling Price | Total Sales | Allocated Cost | Further Processing Costs | Net Income |
|---|---|---|---|---|---|---|
| A | 500 | $ 3 | $1,500 | $1,250 | $ 500 | $ (250) |
| B | 200 | 10 | 2,000 | 500 | 600 | 900 |
| C | 100 | 18 | 1,800 | 250 | — | 1,550 |
| Totals | | | $5,300 | $2,000 | $1,100 | $2,200 |

*Relative sales value.* To avoid the problem of assigning equal value to disparate units the joint cost might be allocated in proportion to each product's ultimate sales value. Again, the actual allocation is a simple proportion based on the sales value of the products resulting from the process.

| Product | Units | Selling Price | Total Sales | Allocated Costs | Further Processing Costs | Net Income |
|---|---|---|---|---|---|---|
| A | 500 | $ 3 | $1,500 | $ 566.04 | $ 500 | $ 433.96 |
| B | 200 | 10 | 2,000 | 754.72 | 600 | 645.28 |
| C | 100 | 18 | 1,800 | 679.24 | — | 1,120.76 |
| Totals | | | $5,300 | $2,000.00 | $1,100 | $2,200.00 |

*Net realizable value.* Although the relative sales value allocation recognizes a difference in the value of the products, it does so based on their final selling price. However, some of the final value of each product will be due to the further processing costs incurred for each. The relative value of the products as they are received from the joint process might be more accurately reflected by using the estimated relative sales value at the split-off point.

As we have seen, the net realizable value is simply the eventual selling price of each product less any costs incurred between the split-off and final sale. For our example we would get the following allocation.

| Product | Eventual Sales Value | Further Processing Costs | Net Realizable Value at Split-off | Proportion | Allocated Cost | Cost per Gallon | Further Processing | Final Cost per Gallon |
|---|---|---|---|---|---|---|---|---|
| A | $1,500 | $500 | $1,000 | 10/42 | $ 476.19 | $0.95 | $1.00 | $1.95 |
| B | 2,000 | 600 | 1,400 | 14/42 | 666.67 | 3.33 | 3.00 | 6.33 |
| C | 1,800 | — | 1,800 | 18/42 | 857.14 | 8.57 | — | 8.57 |
| Totals | | | $4,200 | | $2,000.00 | | | |

This time the product line income statement shows net income strictly in proportion to the product's net realizable value. That is, product A's share of the total $2,200 in income is 10/42.

| Product | Total Sales | Allocated Cost | Further Processing Costs | Net Income |
|---|---|---|---|---|
| A | $1,500 | $ 476.19 | $ 500 | $ 523.81 |
| B | 2,000 | 666.67 | 600 | 733.33 |
| C | 1,800 | 857.14 | — | 942.86 |
| Totals | $5,300 | $2,000.00 | $1,100 | $2,200.00 |

*Shapley value.* For the Shapley value we need to calculate the incremental cost of producing each product along all possible expansion paths. The six possible expansion paths and the implied incremental costs for each product are as follows:

| | Incremental Cost | | | |
|---|---|---|---|---|
| Expansion Path | A | B | C | Total |
| ABC | $ 750 | $ 750 | $ 500 | $ 2,000 |
| ACB | 750 | 300 | 950 | 2,000 |
| BAC | 500 | 1,000 | 500 | 2,000 |
| BCA | 400 | 1,000 | 600 | 2,000 |
| CAB | 700 | 300 | 1,000 | 2,000 |
| CBA | 400 | 600 | 1,000 | 2,000 |
| Totals | $3,500 | $3,950 | $4,550 | $12,000 |
| Average | $ 583.33 | $ 658.33 | $ 758.34 | $ 2,000 |

The incremental costs for the first expansion path are determined as follows: If A is acquired separately it would be purchased for $1.50 per gallon for the 500 gallons acquired, or $750. If A and B are both to be acquired, the best alternative is to use the adjusted process that produces A and B for $1,500. B's incremental cost then is $750. When all three products are acquired, the cost rises to $2,000, so C's incremental cost for the first expansion path is $500. The average incremental costs for all possible paths yield an allocated cost of $583.33 for A, $658.33 for B, and $758.34 for C.

A product line income statement for the Shapley allocation would be

| Product | Total Sales | Allocated Cost | Further Processing Costs | Net Income |
|---|---|---|---|---|
| A | $1,500 | $ 583.33 | $ 500 | $ 416.67 |
| B | 2,000 | 658.33 | 600 | 741.67 |
| C | 1,800 | 758.34 | — | 1,041.66 |
| Totals | $5,300 | $2,000.00 | $1,100 | $2,200.00 |

***Alternative cost.*** For our example we calculate the alternative cost allocation as follows. If product A were not part of the joint process, there are three possible alternatives for getting it: Product A can be purchased singly, acquired jointly with B, or acquired jointly with C. If purchased singly it would cost $750 to acquire the units of A. But if A is acquired jointly with B, the package will cost $1,500. To determine the alternative cost for A when acquired with B, we must allocate the $1,500 between A and B. To do so, we look at the alternative costs to the acquisition of A and B jointly. There is only one alternative to this coalition, acquiring the units singly. Product A would cost $750, whereas B would cost $1,000 if purchased separately. Therefore the $1,500 joint cost is allocated in proportion to these alternative costs as

$$\text{To A:} \quad \frac{\$750}{\$1,750} \times \$1,500 = \$642.86$$

$$\text{To B:} \quad \frac{\$1,000}{\$1,750} \times \$1,500 = \$857.14$$

A similar calculation must be done for the A and C joint acquisition. These products can be acquired jointly for $1,700, whereas C can be purchased singly for $1,000. The allocated cost then is

$$\text{To A:} \quad \frac{\$750}{\$1,750} \times \$1,700 = \$728.57$$

$$\text{To C:} \quad \frac{\$1,000}{\$1,750} \times \$1,700 = \$971.43$$

We have now determined the cost of every alternative means of obtaining A ($750 if alone, $642.86 with B, or $728.57 with C). The cheapest alternative means of acquiring product A is $642.86.

Next we perform similar calculations for B. If B is acquired singly it will cost $1,000, while if acquired with A, its cost was determined earlier to be $857.14. The only alternative left is to acquire B and C together. The joint acquisition of B and C was said to cost $1,600. The cost to acquire C separately is also $1,000. Therefore we allocate the $1,600 joint cost in proportion to the cost of getting B and C separately, which yields

$$\text{To B:} \quad \frac{\$1{,}000}{\$2{,}000} \times \$1{,}600 = \$800$$

$$\text{To C:} \quad \frac{\$1{,}000}{\$2{,}000} \times \$1{,}600 = \$800$$

The three alternative costs for getting B are $800 if acquired with C, $857.14 with A, and $1,000 singly. The cheapest alternative cost is $800.

We now determine the cheapest alternative means to acquire C. Fortunately, at this point there are no new calculations. The cost to get C with B was determined to be $800, with A to be $971.43, and alone $1,000. The cheapest alternative is $800.

The last step is to allocate the actual joint cost being incurred, $2,000 to the three products in proportion to their best alternative cost.

| Product | Best Alternative Cost | Proportion | Joint Cost | Allocated Cost | Cost per Gallon | Further Processing Cost per Gallon | Final Cost per Gallon |
|---|---|---|---|---|---|---|---|
| A | $ 642.86 | 642.86/2,242.86 | $2,000 | $ 573.26 | $1.15 | $1.00 | $2.15 |
| B | 800 | 800.00/2,242.86 | 2,000 | 713.37 | 3.57 | 3.00 | 6.57 |
| C | 800 | 800.00/2,242.86 | 2,000 | 713.37 | 7.13 | — | 7.13 |
| | $2,242.86 | | | $2,000.00 | | | |

The product line income statement for 1 day's sales would be

| Product | Sales | Allocated Cost | Further Processing Costs | Net Income |
|---|---|---|---|---|
| A | $1,500 | $ 573.26 | $ 500 | $ 426.74 |
| B | 2,000 | 713.37 | 600 | 686.63 |
| C | 1,800 | 713.37 | — | 1,086.63 |
| Totals | $5,300 | $2,000.00 | $1,100 | $2,200.00 |

Exhibit 13-8 summarizes the results of each approach. As can be seen, the methods can yield substantially different results. Unfortunately, theory has not progressed to the point where we can say that one approach is definitely superior to the others.

**EXHIBIT 13-8 Comparison of Allocation Methods**

| Method | Allocated Joint Cost per Product[a] A | B | C |
|---|---|---|---|
| Physical (gallons) | $1,250 | $500 | $250 |
| Relative sales value | 566 | 755 | 679 |
| Net realizable value | 476 | 667 | 857 |
| Shapley | 583 | 658 | 758 |
| Alternative costs | 573 | 713 | 713 |

[a]Not including the separate processing cost.

In many industries a particular method has become established as "accepted practice," such as the net realizable value method in the meat packing industry. Firms in the industry use the established method so that their external financial statements will be comparable with those of other firms in the industry. In other cases it appears that firms use the method that management feels is the easiest to apply (usually a physical measure).

## KEY TERMS AND CONCEPTS

Joint cost
Physical measures
Relative sales value
Split-off point
Separate processing costs
Net realizable value
Shapley value allocation
Alternative cost allocation
By-products

## FURTHER READING

Balachandran, Bala V., and Ram T. S. Ramakrishnan. "Joint Cost Allocation: A Unified Approach," *The Accounting Review* (January 1981), p. 85.

Biddle, Gary C., and Richard Steinberg. "Allocations of Joint and Common Costs," *Journal of Accounting Literature* (Spring 1984), p. 1.

Billera, Louis J., David C. Heath, and Robert E. Verrecchia. "A Unique Procedure for Allocating Common Costs from a Production Process," *Journal of Accounting Research* (Spring 1981), p. 185.

Cats-Baril, William L., James F. Gatti, and D. Jacque Grinnell. "Joint Product Costing in the Semiconductor Industry," *Management Accounting* (February 1986), p. 28.

Feller, Robert E. "Accounting for Joint Products in the Petroleum Industry," *Management Accounting* (September 1977), p. 41.

Hamlen, Susan S., William A. Hamlen, Jr., and John Tschirhart. "The Use of the Generalized Shapley Allocation in Joint Cost Allocation," *The Accounting Review* (April 1980), p. 269.
Hartley, Ronald V. "Decision Making when Joint Products Are Involved," *The Accounting Review* (October 1971), p. 746.
Jensen, Daniel L. "The Role of Cost in Pricing Joint Products: A Case of Production in Fixed Proportions," *The Accounting Review* (July 1974), p. 465.

## QUESTIONS AND EXERCISES

**13-1** How do joint and separable costs relate to direct and indirect costs?

**13-2** What is meant by the separation or split-off point, and what is its significance for product costing?

**13-3** Can the notion of joint products be extended to include joint services? Give an example.

**13-4** A decision as to whether to process a product further should not be influenced by joint cost allocation, but instead should be based on differential or incremental factors. Explain.

**13-5** The allocation of a joint cost among joint products is essentially an arbitrary process. If this is so, then why allocate?

**13-6** The owner of a business says, "I cannot uniquely determine the profitability of one of my joint products, but I can uniquely determine how much it contributes toward joint costs and profit." Explain.

**13-7** What determines whether a joint product is classified as a main product or a by-product?

**13-8** A specialty chemical company obtains 73 different products of relatively equal value from processing a single input. Should these products be treated as main products or by-products?

**13-9** A by-product is not further processed and can be sold at separation for $10. This is considered a significant amount, so a value is placed on the by-product at the time of production and formal inventory records of the by-product are kept. Give the journal entries at production and at sale if the by-product is handled using (a) the other-income approach and (b) the cost reduction approach. (c) Repeat parts (a) and (b) assuming that the sales value of the by-product is considered an immaterial amount and no inventory records are kept for it.

**13-10** A packing company in the upper Midwest sells, as its main product, "boxed beef." The boxed beef is shipped to retail outlets, which prepare the final retail cuts for sale without waste. Management has emphasized the importance of by-products (the things that do not go into boxed beef) by pointing out that "our profit is equal to the revenues produced by the by-products." What cost allocation method is being assumed and are by-products more important to this firm than main products?

**13-11** Department N receives material from department M, which it processes into two main products: goh and nogoh. During March, $24,000 was transferred in from department M, and department N incurred costs of its own amounting to $28,000. Additional information is as follows:

| | Goh | Nogoh |
|---|---|---|
| Units produced | 1,000 | 2,000 |
| Further processing costs | $8,000 | $4,000 |
| Unit selling price | $ 40 | $ 20 |
| Units sold | 800 | 1,200 |

Determine the cost per unit of each product using net realizable value.

**13-12** Prentis Processors produces two products using three ingredients:

A: 2 gallons @ $3.00
B: 3 gallons @ $7.00
C: 1 gallon @ $5.00

During processing, one-third of the inputs is lost to evaporation. The balance yields 60% torp, which sells for $14 per gallon, and 40% trin, which sells for $12 per gallon. Determine the cost per gallon of torp and trin using (a) physical allocation and (b) sales value allocation.

**13-13** A firm processes a particular animal, obtaining from it two main products and a by-product. The by-product is sold as is, and the revenues are treated as a reduction in the cost of the main products at the time of sale. Joint costs are allocated to the main products according to final sales value. For the week, manufacturing costs totaled $30,000 and by-product sales were $3,200. Other data concerning the main products were as follows:

| | Product 17 | Product 18 |
|---|---|---|
| Units produced | 5,000 | 4,000 |
| Units sold | 4,000 | 2,500 |
| Sales revenues | $28,000 | $20,000 |
| Separable processing costs | $2 per unit | $3 per unit |
| Color | red | green |

(a) Determine the unit cost of each product to be inventoried as finished goods.
(b) What was gross margin for the period?

**13-14** A firm produces two products jointly in department A, which are then transferred for further processing to separate departments. For the month, total costs in department A were $14,000, and 8,000 liters were produced. The subsequent departments had results as follows:

| | Department B | Department C |
|---|---|---|
| Liters produced | 4,000 | 4,000 |
| Liters sold | 3,000 | 2,000 |
| Sales value of production | $25,000 | $13,600 |
| Additional processing costs | $ 7,000 | $ 3,600 |
| Revenue from liters sold | $18,750 | $ 6,800 |

Determine the cost per liter (at separation and after further processing) for each product produced by B and C. The firm uses the net realizable value method for cost allocation purposes.

**13-15** Zipfect, Inc., processes a material in batches. For every 1,000 liters of the material processed, the following main products emerge.

| | $MP_1$ | $MP_2$ |
|---|---|---|
| Production by volume | 300 liters | 700 liters |
| Sales value at separation | \$5 per liter | \$4 per liter |
| Further processing costs | \$1 per liter | \$2 per liter |
| Sales value after processing | \$8 per liter | \$7 per liter |

The material costs \$300 per 1,000-liter batch and the joint cost of processing a batch is \$560. For each of the two products, determine the cost per unit using (a) volume, (b) sales value at separation, (c) sales value after processing, and (d) net realizable value.

**13-16** A broker purchased 10,000 bushels of apples for \$20,000 plus transportation costs of \$2,000. The fruit was graded as extra fancy, 1,000 bushels; fancy, 7,000 bushels; and rejects, 2,000 bushels. He feeds the rejects to his hogs, figuring that each bushel saves \$1 on hog feed. The cost of grading was \$4,000 plus \$1 per bushel. The rejects are treated as a reduction of the cost of the main products. Extra fancy apples sell for \$9.00 per bushel, and fancy apples sell for \$5.00 per bushel. (a) What are the unit costs of the main products if sales value is used to allocate joint costs? (b) What are the unit costs of the main products if the joint costs are allocated using net realizable value? (c) Should the broker be selling the fancy grade or feeding them to his hogs? (d) Which is his most profitable product?

**13-17** Bio-Local processes a chemical into two main products (X and Y) and one by-product (Z). The revenue from the by-product is treated as miscellaneous income at the time of sale, and all joint costs are allocated to the main products according to their net realizable value. During the period, 20,000 gallons were processed at a cost (materials and processing) of \$99,000, yielding 20% X, 15% Y, and 50% Z, with the balance as waste that can be safely disposed down the drain. Product X sells for \$30 per gallon and requires further processing costs of \$8 per gallon; product Y sells for \$15 per gallon and requires no further processing costs; and product Z sells for \$3 per gallon and requires further processing costs of \$1 per gallon.

At what unit cost will X, Y, and Z be carried in inventory (a) if they have not been further processed, and (b) if they have been further processed?

## PROBLEMS AND CASES

**13-18 Joint costs and performance.**
The newly appointed vice-president of the firm is greatly troubled over the firm's future. (a) He feels strongly that an equitable allocation of joint costs among products is necessary if the firm is to know how profitable each of its products is. (b)

He is also dissatisfied with the treatment accorded by-products. Specifically, he asks, "How is it possible to evaluate the producing branch of the firm, on the one hand, and the marketing branch, on the other, if the net realizable value of the by-product is used to reduce the cost of the main product? How can I evaluate the performance of each of the individuals responsible for these functions, if all I get is the net result?"

**Required**
Comment on each of the two problems. Consider the type of information that the vice-president is searching for and how you, as the accountant, would provide it.

**13-19 Joint costs and pricing.**
Assume a production process with joint costs of $100 and separable costs of $30 to product A and $50 to product B. The process yields 5 units of A and 10 units of B. Management has learned that its closest competitor prices A and B as follows: It establishes selling prices for each product equal to 1.5 times its cost, where the cost of the product consists of its separable cost *plus* joint costs allocated to it on the basis of total revenues.

**Required**
Using this formula, what would be the prices of A and B?

**13-20 Profitability of joint products.**
Larry Dean raises registered Labrador retrievers. Dean's prize dog has just given birth to six pups. There were two chocolate males, two yellow males, and two yellow females in the litter. The stud fee, veterinary bills, and other costs associated with the dog's pregnancy amounted to $350. The pups had to be kept with their mother for 6 weeks before they could be sold. During this time, feeding and medical bills for each of the pups amounted to $80. In addition, the female pups required additional veterinary costs of $20 each (these costs are always incurred for female pups). At the end of the 6-week waiting period, the chocolate males were sold for $150 each, the yellow males for $200 each, and the females for $225 each.

**Required**
Using the net realizable value method for allocating joint costs, determine the profit to be recognized on the sale of each type of dog.

**13-21 Net realizable value, alternative cost allocation.**
Bennett Industries retails three products: A, B, and C. Bennett can purchase product A for $12 per unit, B for $18, and C for $26, through normal distribution channels. However, Bennett has just purchased the entire stock of a competitor who has gone bankrupt. The inventory purchased was 5,000 units of A, 4,000 units of B, and 8,000 units of C. The purchase price of the inventory was $280,000. Bennett incurs marketing costs of $1 per unit for A, $2 per unit for B, and $3 per unit for C. Bennett's selling prices for the products are $20 for A, $30 for B, and $50 for C.

**Required**
If Bennett sells 2,000 A's, 2,000 B's, and 3,000 C's, determine the cost of goods sold per product, in total and per unit, using:

**a.** The net realizable value method of allocation.
**b.** The alternative cost allocation method.

**13-22 Net realizable value, alternative cost, and Shapley allocations.**
Colonel Mills is a large food processing company. One of its major products is "instant rice." The firm buys unprocessed rice for $300 per ton. The rice is then sent through a separator, which scrapes the hulls off the rice. It costs $50 per ton to process the rice through the separator. From a ton of rice, the separator produces 1,900 pounds of white rice and 100 pounds of hulls. The hulls are then pulverized into a powder and sold to health food stores as a vitamin supplement for $2 per pound. It costs $40 per 100 pounds to pulverize the hulls. The white rice is cooked, freeze dried, and packed into 5-pound bags. It costs the firm $325 to cook, dry, and package 1,900 pounds of rice. The processed rice is sold to grocery wholesalers for $3 per 5-pound bag.

As an alternative to buying unprocessed rice, the firm could buy hulls for $75 per 100 pounds and could buy uncooked white rice for $18 per 100 pounds.

**Required**

Determine the income this firm would earn on pulverized hulls and instant rice if it processes 15 tons of unprocessed rice, assuming:

**a.** The firm uses the net realizable value method to allocate joint costs.
**b.** The firm uses the alternative cost approach to allocate joint costs.
**c.** The firm uses the Shapley method to allocate joint costs.

**13-23 Net realizable value and alternative cost allocation.**
Diamond Petroleum purchases crude oil from which it refines three products: gasoline, jet fuel, and naphtha. The firm purchases 100,000 barrels of crude oil at a time for a cost of $1,600,000. From this input, the firm gets 4,500,000 liters of gasoline, 400,000 liters of jet fuel, and 100,000 liters of naphtha. The gasoline is sold for $0.36 per liter after incurring separate costs of $0.01 per liter; the jet fuel is sold for $0.60 per liter after incurring separate costs of $0.05 per liter; and the naphtha is sold as is for $0.40 per liter. The firm can buy gasoline for $0.324 per liter, jet fuel for $0.51 per liter, and naphtha for $0.37 per liter.

**Required**

Allocate the cost of crude oil to each of the products using:

**a.** The alternative cost method.
**b.** The net realizable value method.

**13-24 Unit costing: Multiple products with multiple separation points.**
Products J and M are jointly produced in department 1. Product J is sent to department 2, where it yields two main products, K and L. Product M is sent to department 3, where it yields main product N and by-product Q. By-product revenues are treated as a reduction or recovery of the initial joint costs; net realizable value is used to cost main products. None of the products is marketable at the point of separation. There are no physical gains or losses in processing. Operations for the month are expected to be as follows:

| Product | Pounds | Selling Price per Pound |
|---|---|---|
| K | 20,000 | $6 |
| L | 10,000 | 4 |
| N | 12,000 | 6 |
| Q | 12,000 | 1 |

Processing costs in each department are expected to be as follows: department 1, $74,400; department 2, $60,000; and department 3, $48,000.

**Required**
At what unit cost will each of products J, K, L, M, N, and Q be carried in inventory if results are as planned?

**13-25 Cost allocation: Multiple split-off points with by-products.**
Phauna, Inc., processes an animal product into consumer and commercial products. Relevant data are as follows:

*Physical Flow:* Department 1 begins with 1,000 pounds of raw material, which results in main products A (50%) and B (30%), by-product C (10%), and waste (10%). Department 2 receives product A and processes it further, resulting in main products D (60%) and E (40%). Department 3 receives product B and processes it further (adding sufficient material to double the weight), resulting in main product F (70%), by-product G (20%), and waste (10%). All waste is normal and there are no in-process inventories at the end of the period.

*Cost Data:*

| | Department 1 | Department 2 | Department 3 |
|---|---|---|---|
| Prior department cost | $ — | $ ? | $ ? |
| Material | 1,000 | — | 200 |
| Processing | 2,600 | 800 | 400 |

All selling and administration costs are fixed.

*Sales Data:* Owing to the nature of the process, there is no market for the intermediate (in-process) goods, nor can they be purchased from others. The sales value of Phauna's end products follows:

| Product | Per Pound |
|---|---|
| C | $ 1.00 |
| D | 5.00 |
| E | 4.00 |
| F | 10.00 |
| G | 2.00 |

*Cost Allocation:* Products D, E, and F are main products, for which the net realizable value method is used to allocate joint costs. The sales of by-product C are treated as other income, whereas the sales of by-product G are treated as a reduction of department 3's joint costs.

**Required**

**a.** Draw a physical flow chart that traces an initial 1,000 pounds of input through the departments. Be sure to indicate how many pounds emerge at every stage.

**b.** From an initial input of 1,000 pounds, determine the total *and* unit costs of each end product.

**c.** Prepare an income statement based on the production and sale of the products resulting from an initial input of 1,000 pounds.

**13-26 Joint cost allocation using net realizable value.**
Detox Industries has recently undertaken to convert leftover Agent Orange into several chemical products. The defoliant is acquired free from the government. It is then passed through several refining processes. The first process costs $500 per canister. This results in 100 pounds of Yellow Food Coloring and 40 gallons of Agent Red. Agent Red is then refined further into 10 pounds of Pink Pigment and 15 pounds of Magenta Mass at a cost of $25 per gallon of Agent Red. Finally, the Magenta Mass is separated into two quarts of a herbicide designed to kill violets and 10 pounds of Black Goop used to seal asphalt driveways. This separation process costs $10 per pound of Magenta Mass. Selling prices for each of the products are

| | |
|---|---|
| Yellow Food Coloring | $ 5 per pound |
| Pink Pigment | 45 per pound |
| Violet Killer | 400 per quart |
| Black Goop | 10 per pound |

In January the firm ended the month with 4 pounds of Yellow Food Coloring and 20 pounds of Black Goop in inventory.

**Required**
Assuming that joint costs are allocated using the net realizable value method, determine the cost of ending inventory.

**13-27 Joint product cost allocation with by-products and waste.**
Recyclers, Inc., reprocesses newspapers, obtaining two main products, a by-product, and waste. By-product revenues are treated as other income. During the period, 1,000 tons were processed at a cost of $12,000 for materials and processing, resulting in the following:

| Product | Tons | Sales Value at Separation | Costs after Separation | Final Value |
|---|---|---|---|---|
| Main 1 | 200 | $4,000 | $2,000 | $10,000 |
| Main 2 | 400 | 5,000 | 6,000 | 12,000 |
| By-product | 300 | 1,000 | 1,000 | 3,000 |
| Waste | 100 | — | — | — |

**Required**
**a.** Account for all costs using a physical basis for allocation.
**b.** Account for all costs using net realizable value as the basis for allocation.
**c.** Account for all costs using final sales value as the basis for allocation.

**13-28 Joint product costs: Multiple choice** (CPA adapted).
Miller Manufacturing Company buys zeon for $0.80 a gallon. At the end of processing in Department 1, zeon splits off into products A, B, and C. Product A is sold at the split-off point, with no further processing. Products B and C require further processing before they can be sold; product B is processed in Department 2 and product C is processed in Department 3. Following is a summary of costs and other related data for the year ended June 30, 19X3.

| | Department | | |
|---|---|---|---|
| | 1 | 2 | 3 |
| Cost of zeon | $96,000 | $ — | $ — |
| Direct labor | 14,000 | 45,000 | 65,000 |
| Manufacturing overhead | 10,000 | 21,000 | 49,000 |

| | Products | | |
|---|---|---|---|
| | A | B | C |
| Gallons sold | 20,000 | 30,000 | 45,000 |
| Gallons on hand at June 30, 19X3 | 10,000 | — | 15,000 |
| Sales in dollars | $30,000 | $96,000 | $141,750 |

There were no inventories on hand at July 1, 19X2, and there was no zeon on hand at June 30, 19X3. All gallons on hand at June 30, 19X3, were complete as to processing. Miller uses the net realizable value method of allocating joint costs.

**Required**

**a.** For allocating joint costs, the net realizable value of product A for the year ended June 30, 19X3, would be
   **1.** $30,000
   **2.** $45,000
   **3.** $21,000
   **4.** $6,000

**b.** The joint costs for the year ended June 30, 19X3, to be allocated are
   **1.** $300,000
   **2.** $95,000
   **3.** $120,000
   **4.** $96,000

**c.** The cost of product B sold for the year ended June 30, 19X3, is
   **1.** $90,000
   **2.** $66,000
   **3.** $88,857
   **4.** $96,000

**d.** The value of the ending inventory for product A is
   **1.** $24,000
   **2.** $12,000
   **3.** $8,000
   **4.** $13,333

**13-29 Net realizable value and cost allocation** (SMA adapted).
Lafferty Ltd. has three products derived from the same manufacturing operation. However, each product requires additional processing beyond the split-off point. The main products are X and Y. The by-product is ZZ. The costs incurred before the split-off point were $320,000. Costs incurred beyond the split-off point were recorded as follows:

| | |
|---|---|
| Product X | $300,000 |
| Product Y | 250,000 |
| By-product ZZ | 11,200 |

During a review of costs, it is ascertained that product Y was overcharged with an amount of $50,000 representing direct labor. The following additional information was obtained.

| | Weight (pounds) | Selling Price per Pound | Anticipated Net Profit (percent of sales) |
|---|---|---|---|
| Product X | 200,000 | $4.00 | 15 |
| Product Y | 200,000 | $2.20 | 15 |
| By-product ZZ | 30,000 | $1.20 | 15 |

Selling and administrative expenses, all variable, amount to 20% of sales.

**Required**

**a.** Prepare a schedule of production costs showing the allocation of costs incurred prior to the split-off point. Use net realizable value less a normal profit margin for the allocation basis. By-product sales are treated as miscellaneous income.

**b.** Assuming that all three products are main products, present a schedule of profits for each product using the net realizable value method (sales less separable costs) as the cost allocation basis.

**c.** List and briefly describe two different methods of accounting for by-products.

**13-30 By-product costing: Timing the credit for NRV.**

Fine Foods Industries works on a batch processing basis. Each batch begins with 10 tons of a vegetable product. The firm purchases the product for $65,000. The input is separated into three products at a cost of $15,000. The typical batch yields 5,000 pounds of product A. Product A is treated at a cost of $1 per pound, after which it is ready for sale for $12 per pound. A batch of input also yields 2,000 pounds of product B. Product B must be sterilized at a cost of $2 per pound and then it is sold for $5 per pound. The remaining 13,000 pounds of output from a batch are sent through a second separator at a cost of $15,000. From this process the firm obtains 6,000 pounds of product C, which sells for $10 per pound, and 7,000 pounds of product D, which sells for $8 per pound.

The firm started the current period with no inventories. They processed one batch of input (all units were completed). Their sales, in pounds, were as follows:

| | |
|---|---|
| A | 4,500 |
| B | 1,800 |
| C | 4,000 |
| D | 6,200 |

Product B is considered a by-product.

**Required**

Determine the net income for the period and the cost of ending inventory if:

**a.** The firm credits the net realizable value of the by-product against the joint processing cost at the time the by-product is produced. Also give the journal entry for the sale of one unit of the by-product.

**b.** The firm credits the net realizable value of the by-product against the joint processing costs at the time the by-product is sold. Also give the journal entry for the sale of one unit of the by-product.

**13-31 By-product costing: Cost reduction versus miscellaneous income.**
Jor-Dan Industries began the current period with no inventories. During the period they processed 25,000 pounds of materials costing $75,000. Conversion costs incurred during the period amounted to $110,000. The firm ended the period with no work-in-process. During the period 8,000 units of Trylene, 12,000 units of Coldron and 5,000 units of Strold were produced. All costs are considered joint costs. The firm sold 6,000 units of Trylene, 8,000 units of Coldron, and 4,500 units of Strold. Trylene sells for $15 per unit, Coldron for $22 per unit, and Strold for $2 per unit. The firm uses the net realizable value method for cost allocation. Strold is considered a by-product.

**Required**

**a.** If the firm credits the proceeds of the sales of the by-product as an offset against conversion costs at the time the by-products are sold, determine the firm's net income and cost of ending inventory.

**b.** If the firm recognized the sale of the by-product as miscellaneous income at the time of sale, would net income be higher, lower, or the same as in part (a)?

**c.** If the firm credits the net realizable value of the by-product as an offset against conversion costs at the time the by-products are produced, determine the firm's net income and cost of ending inventory.

**13-32 Net realizable value, alternative cost, and Shapley allocations.**
Tammyland, Inc., manufactures two products from a single input. The firm pays $100 to acquire a unit of resource. The firm incurs a processing cost of $50, which converts the input into 3 units of product A and 2 units of product B. Instead of processing the material itself, the firm can acquire units of product A for $20 each and B for $70 each. Whichever way acquired, the firm must also incur separate processing costs to get the products ready for sale. The separate processing costs are $5 per unit for A and $10 per unit for B. The units are eventually sold for $40 per unit for A and $75 per unit for B.

**Required**

**a.** What is the contribution margin per unit for each product? Does it depend on how joint costs are allocated?

**b.** What is the unit cost per product using the alternative cost approach to allocation?

**c.** What is the unit cost per product using the net realizable value approach to allocation?

**d.** What is the unit cost per product using the Shapley approach to allocation?

**13-33 Joint cost and decision making.**
Luris Industries has two separate profit centers: division A and division B. The firm acquires its major input for both divisions jointly. Currently, the firm purchases this material in 1,000-pound lots for $2,000. The material is passed through an exclusive separator process. After separation, division A gets 300 pounds of chemical J-52A and division B gets 200 gallons of Quitoban. Division A incurs separate processing costs of $150 to get the chemical ready for sale. Division B incurs a cost of $250 to bottle and package the Quitoban as an antiperspirant. After the additional processing, division A sells the 300 pounds of chemicals for $5 per pound and division B sells the antiperspirant for $7 per gallon.

**Required**

**a.** Determine the income per lot to be reported by each division if joint costs are allocated on a net realizable value basis.

**b.** The firm has the opportunity to buy a higher-quality lot of raw material for $3,000. If it does so, division A's separate processing costs will increase to $400 but the selling price of its product will remain the same. Division B's selling price will increase to $15 per gallon and its separate processing costs will stay the same. If you were the manager of division A, would you want the firm to buy the higher-quality material? What if you were the manager of division B? (Show new net income figures to justify your answer.)

**c.** As president of the company, do you think the higher-quality materials should be purchased? How do you resolve the conflict in (b)?

**13-34 Physical, net realizable value, and alternative cost allocations.**

With winter approaching, it is time for the Ayagru Petroleum Consortium (APC) to set prices for its products. The firm refines three products from crude oil: gasoline, home heating oil, and a residual that it sells to other companies for further processing. The market for the residual is extremely competitive, so the firm cannot affect the current market price of $30 per barrel (this is the price at which APC can either buy or sell the product). In addition, the firm has chosen not to raise its gasoline price of $33.60 per barrel. APC can purchase gasoline in bulk for $31 per barrel. The firm, through predatory pricing practices, has been able to achieve a near monopoly in the home heating oil market in its region. The firm's consumer relations department has determined that a price of $38 per barrel for heating oil will allow the firm to sell all the oil it anticipates having available during the season, and yet still be able to capture 80% of the disposable income of the families in the marketing region. APC can acquire heating oil in the wholesale market for $27 per barrel.

For the upcoming season, the firm expects to refine 200,000 barrels of crude oil. APC's cracking process will produce one-half barrel of gasoline, three-eighths barrel of residual, and one-eighth barrel of heating oil per barrel of crude. After the products are refined, it costs $1 per barrel for gasoline, zero per barrel for residual, and $0.25 per barrel of heating oil to make the products available for sale. (These costs must also be incurred if we purchase the products individually.) It costs the firm $25 per barrel to buy crude oil and $400,000 to operate the refinery for the season.

**Required**

Determine the season's profit on the sale of heating oil under each of the following bases for allocating the cost of crude oil.

**a.** Physical basis, using barrels

**b.** Net realizable value

**c.** Alternative cost

**13-35 Alternative costs and Shapley allocations.**

The manager of Coleen's Coin Coop can purchase bulk coins (dimes) in three forms. A hundred dollars face value of "mixed coins" can be purchased for $104. This bag contains an average of 80% silver-clad coins (worth only face value). Silver-clad coins are simply deposited in the bank. The remaining 20% of the mixed coins are silver coins less than 30 years old. Since the manager wants only the silver coins, this option, in effect, means paying $120 to receive $100 face value of silver coins less than 30 years old.

The manager could instead, buy a bag of "old" silver coins. The bag of "old" silver coins contains $100 face value of silver coins more than 30 years old. This bag can be purchased for $170.

The manager in fact purchases the coins in a third form: "mixed silver" coins. This bag can be purchased for $130 and contains $100 face value of silver coins, 60% of which are less than 30 years old and 40% of which are more than 30 years old.

Coleen's Coin Coop can sell $100 face value of silver coins under 30 years old for $145, by incurring an additional marketing cost of $10. Silver coins more than 30 years old sell for $200 per $100 of face value after incurring a $20 marketing cost.

**Required**

**a.** Is the manager now buying the coins in the most optimal manner?

**b.** Given the manner in which the firm is now, in fact, buying the coins, what is the cost to be assigned to Coleen's ending inventory of 3,000 silver dimes under 30 years old, and 1,000 silver dimes over 30 years old? The net realizable value method is used.

**c.** What is the cost assigned to ending inventory in (b) if the Shapley allocation is used?

**13-36 Main products and by-products.**

Nyles, Inc., manufactures a number of joint products. The process begins in department 1 with 100,000 pounds, of which 30% goes to department 2, 60% goes to department 3, and the remainder is lost. From department 2, five-sixths goes to department 4 and one-sixth goes to department 5.

There is no market for intermediate products; only the end products of department 3 (a by-product), department 4 (a main product), and department 5 (a main product) are sold. Joint costs are *not* assigned to the by-product; by-product sales are treated as miscellaneous income. Cost and sales data are as follows:

| Department | Costs | Sales | Product |
|---|---|---|---|
| 1 | $10,000 | | |
| 2 | 10,000 | | |
| 3 | 2,000 | $10,000 | C |
| 4 | 25,000 | 40,000 | A |
| 5 | 5,000 | 6,000 | B |

**Required**

**a.** Account for all costs (total and per pound) of products A, B, and C, assuming that joint costs are allocated by (1) the physical method, (2) the sales value method, and (3) the net realizable value method.

**b.** What (opportunity) cost should be assigned to product B for purposes of determining whether or not it should be processed further?

**13-37 Joint cost allocation: Main products.**

Terrco is a bulk buyer of soap by-products. These by-products are combined with Terrco's secret mystery ingredient; the result is three separately identifiable products. Data concerning the operation follow:

| | | | Further Processing Data | |
|---|---|---|---|---|
| Product | Units Produced | Selling Price per Unit at Split-off | Additional Costs | Total Revenues after Processing |
| K | 3,000 | $2 | $ 8,000 | $15,000 |
| L | 12,000 | 4 | 20,000 | 72,000 |
| M | 33,000 | 2 | 10,000 | 73,000 |

Joint input costs total $90,000. The firm treats all its products as main products.

**Required**

**a.** Which of the products should be further processed? Why?

**b.** If Terrco pursues the best product mix, what is the maximum profit that can be achieved from a joint input costing $90,000?

**c.** If Terrco allocates joint costs on the basis of the final sales value of its end products, how much will be allocated to each product?

**d.** If Terrco allocates joint costs on the basis of the net realizable value of its products, how much will be allocated to each product?

**e.** If Terrco allocates joint costs on the basis of units produced, how much will be allocated to each product?

**f.** How do the allocations required in (c), (d), and (e) affect your answer to (b)? Why?

**13-38 Joint costs and decision making** (SMA).

A pharmaceutical company manufactures two products, A and B, in a joint process. The joint costs amount to $12,000 per batch of finished goods. Each batch amounts to 10,000 litres, of which 25% are product A and 75% are product B. The two products are processed further, but without any gain or loss in volume. The costs of additional processing are $0.30 per litre for product A and $0.40 per litre for product B. After the additional processing, the selling price of product A is $2.10 per litre, and the selling price of product B is $1.60 per litre.

**Required**

**a.** If the joint costs are to be allocated on the basis of the net realizable value of each product at the split-off point, what amount of joint costs will be allocated to each product?

**b.** Prepare a schedule of gross profit by product and by batch using the preceding allocation and assuming that 80% of product A and 60% of product B were sold, with no opening inventories of either product.

**c.** The company has discovered an additional process by which product A can be transformed into product AA, which could be sold for $6 per litre. On the other hand, this additional processing would increase costs by $2.10 per litre. Assuming that there is no other change in costs, should the company use the new process? Show supporting calculations.

**13-39 Joint products and decision making: Comprehensive.**

Knits, Inc., processes a common input costing $100 that results in three distinct products at separation. Data regarding the products at separation and their sales values, further processing costs, and the resulting products after further processing with their sales values are as follows:

| At Separation | Sales Value | Further Processing Costs | After Processing | Sales Value |
|---|---|---|---|---|
| A | $50 | $100 | X | $190 |
| B | 10 | 30 | Y | 35 |
| C | 60 | 150 | Z | 220 |

**Required**

**a.** What is net income if all products are sold at the point of separation?
**b.** What is net income if all products are sold after further processing?
**c.** Which product(s) should be sold at split-off, rather than being further processed? Why or why not?
**d.** What is net income with the best product mix?
**e.** If there is no market for B at split-off, should it be processed further?
**f.** If an A can be processed directly (at no cost) into a C, at what opportunity cost should A be valued for purposes of making this decision?
**g.** Refer to (f) above. Should A be processed into a C?
**h.** Assume that C can be processed directly into an X. If the firm is not to be any worse off as a result, the cost of processing should not exceed how much?
**i.** Assume that A can be processed into Z at a cost of $155. If the sales value of Z is stable, to what level would the price of X have to fall before the firm is justified in taking this course of action?
**j.** In addition to the costs shown, fixed costs per period are $35,000. How many units of input must be processed per period to break even?
**k.** Identify, by letter, the questions for which the joint cost of $100 per unit is not relevant.

**13-40 Joint costs: Further processing.**
Tandem Technology manufactures two products using a joint process. The cost of materials going into the joint process for a typical period is $55,000, while labor and overhead to operate the process amount to $65,000. For this level of operations the firm obtains 10,000 pounds of product 1 and 30,000 pounds of product 2. Product 1 can be sold "as is" for $4 per pound. Product 2 requires further processing costs of $2 per pound and is eventually sold for $7 per pound.

**Required**

**a.** Determine net income by product line, if Tandem sells 7,000 pounds of product 1 and 26,000 pounds of product 2 in a particular period (assume Tandem has sufficient inventory and always produces the quantities stated above). Use the net realizable value method for allocating joint costs.
**b.** Assume the firm does not sell product 1 "as is," but instead incurs separate processing costs of $20,000 per batch to "finish" the product. The finished products sell for $5 per pound. Assume Tandem started a period with no beginning inventory and sold all 10,000 pounds of product 1 and all 30,000 pounds of product 2. What is the net income by product line for the period, again using the net realizable value method for allocating joint costs?
**c.** Assuming Tandem would sell the same number of "unfinished" units of product 1 as "finished" units, should it sell the product in its finished or unfinished form? Why?

**13-41 Joint products and relevant costing** (CPA adapted).
The McLean Processing Company produces a chemical compound, Supergro, that is sold for $4.60 per gallon. The manufacturing process is divided into the following departments.

1. *Mixing department.* The raw materials are measured and mixed in this department.
2. *Cooking department.* The mixed materials are cooked for a specified period in this department. In the cooking process there is a 10% evaporation loss in materials.
3. *Cooling department.* After the cooked materials are cooled in this department under controlled conditions, the top 80% in the cooling tank is siphoned off and pumped to the packing department. The 20% residue, which contains impurities, is sold in bulk as a by-product, Groex, for $2.00 per gallon.
4. *Packing department.* In this department, special one-gallon tin cans costing $0.60 each are filled with Supergro and shipped to customers.

The company's research and development department recently discovered a new use for the by-product if it is further processed in a new boiling department. The new by-product, Fasgro, would sell in bulk for $5.00 per gallon.

In processing Fasgro the top 70% in the cooling tank would be siphoned off as Supergro. The residue would be pumped to the boiling department, where one-half gallon of raw material, SK, would be added for each gallon of residue. In the boiling department process there would be a 40% evaporation loss. In processing Fasgro the following additional costs would be incurred:

| | |
|---|---|
| Material SK | $1.10 per gallon |
| Boiling department variable processing costs | $1.00 per gallon of input |
| Boiling department fixed processing costs | $2,000 per month |

In recent months, because of heavy demand, the company has shipped Supergro and Groex on the same day that their processing was completed. Fasgro would probably be subject to the same heavy demand.

During the month of July 19X3, which was considered a typical month, the following raw materials were put into process in the mixing department:

| | |
|---|---|
| Material FE | 10,000 gallons @ $0.90 per gallon |
| Material QT | 4,000 gallons @ $1.50 per gallon |

July processing costs per gallon of departmental input were as follows:

| | |
|---|---|
| Mixing department | $0.40 |
| Cooking department | 0.50 |
| Cooling department | 0.30 |
| Packing department | 0.10 |

For accounting purposes the company assigns joint or common costs to its by-products equal to their net realizable value.

**Required**

**a.** Prepare a statement computing total manufacturing costs and gross profit for the month of July.

  **1.** Assume that Groex is the by-product.

  **2.** Assume that Fasgro is the by-product.

**b.** Which by-product should be produced?

**13-42 Joint product costing** (CMA adapted).

Doe Corporation grows, processes, cans, and sells three main products—sliced pineapple, crushed pineapple, and pineapple juice. The cutting department washes, peels, cores and trims the pineapples. The trimmed pineapples are forwarded to the slicing department to be sliced and canned. The pieces of pineapple trimmed from the fruit are diced and canned in the crushing department. The core and surplus pineapple generated from the cutting department are pulverized into a liquid in the juicing department; there is an evaporation loss equal to 8% of the weight of the good output produced in the juicing department, which occurs as the juices are heated. The outside skin is chopped into animal feed in the feed department.

Doe uses the net realizable value method to assign costs of the joint process to its main products. The by-product (animal feed) is inventoried at its market value with a credit to other income.

A total of 270,000 pounds were entered into the cutting department during May. The following schedule shows the costs incurred in each department, the proportion (by weight) transferred to the four final processing departments and the selling price of each end product.

| Department | Costs Incurred | Proportion (by weight) | Selling Price per Pound |
|---|---|---|---|
| Cutting | $60,000 | — | none |
| Slicing | 4,700 | 35% | $0.60 |
| Crushing | 10,580 | 28 | 0.55 |
| Juicing | 3,250 | 27 | 0.30 |
| Animal feed | 700 | 10 | 0.10 |
| | $79,230 | 100% | |

**Required**

**a.** How many pounds of pineapple result as output for pineapple slices, crushed pineapple, pineapple juice, and animal feed?

**b.** What is the net realizable value at the split-off point of each of the main products?

**c.** What is the amount of the cost of the cutting department assigned to each of the main products and the by-product?

**d.** What is the gross margin for each of the three main products?

**e.** Comment on the significance to management of the gross margin information by main product.

**f.** If there is no market for the outside skin as animal feed and, instead, it must be disposed of at a cost of $800, what effect will this have on the costs allocated to the main products?

# CHAPTER 14

# JOB COSTING

In the preceding chapter we finally got all product costs assigned to individual product lines within production departments. In this chapter and the next two we complete the last step, assigning costs to the individual units produced.

## JOB VERSUS PROCESS COSTING

The firm's operating environment dictates the approach we must take to assigning production costs to products. If we work on many dissimilar products or activities, we will need to accumulate the cost of each separately, at the time we do the work. In contrast, if we provide a uniform service or produce a uniform product, we will only need to determine product costs on a periodic basis. It is the environment that dictates the form of the accounting system that is appropriate.

**Job costing** refers to accounting systems that determine the cost of individual orders (jobs). Typical job costing situations include the following:

1. Auto repair shops, where each job is usually different, requiring different amounts of material and labor.

2. Automobile assembly, where each car includes a variety of different options.
3. Printing shops, where each order will be for a different type of product and will use different quality paper, inks, and so forth.
4. Public accounting firms, where each audit, tax return, or management services engagement will require different amounts of professional time.

Note that the common characteristic is the relative uniqueness of the work performed for each customer. In each case we need to know the cost of each particular job for pricing and performance evaluation. Almost all service industries operate in a job cost environment.

If job costing is at one extreme, process costing is at the other. **Process costing** refers to those accounting systems that determine an average cost for all units of product or service performed in a particular time period. Process costing is appropriate when we provide a similar product or service to all customers. Typical process costing situations include the following:

1. An aspirin manufacturer; here each unit of product is essentially identical.
2. Breweries; although there may be more than one product line, each line is a separate, continuous process.
3. Telephone directory assistance; here each request for service is considered the same.
4. Commercial laundries, which wash *pounds* of fabric; they do not distinguish among the objects being washed.

The distinguishing characteristic of a process costing situation is the similarity of the products or services produced for all customers. In these cases we can calculate our units on a periodic basis. We do not need to know the particular cost of a unit processed in a particular production run or sold to a particular customer.

Exhibit 14-1 contrasts some general tendencies in the operating environment that lead to the choice of job costing versus process costing. Although it is easy to distinguish job and process costing environments at the extremes, many firms will fall in between. Many accounting systems will employ both systems. In an auto assembly plant, for example, the construction cost of the basic auto frame will be done on a process costing basis. Similarly, the unit cost of most subassemblies and options will also be determined on a process costing basis. However, when all these parts are assembled into a finished product, the accounting for the completed car will be done on a job cost basis. In spite of the lack of total independence between the two systems, we will discuss them separately. We turn

**EXHIBIT 14-1 Characteristics of Job versus Process Costing Environments**

| | Job Costing Environment | Process Costing Environment |
|---|---|---|
| Sales/production | Sales precede production; production is for a specific order | Production precedes sales; production is for inventory |
| Materials inventory | Required materials for jobs often unknown; minimal materials inventory kept on hand | Materials needed are known; inventory size is a function of ordering costs and carrying costs |
| Direct labor | Generally skilled; employees need to be able to perform a wide range of tasks | Generally less skilled; tasks are routine and well defined |
| Overhead | Relatively low; most costs are direct costs | Automation is more feasible; leading to higher overhead costs |
| Production runs | Short; number of units produced each time depends on specific orders received | Long; often continuous |
| Costing | Unit costs are determined perpetually (as each job is completed) | Unit costs are determined periodically (monthly, quarterly) |

now to a discussion of job costing. Process costing will be covered in Chapters 15 and 16.

## THE JOB COST SHEET

When an order is received by a firm employing job costing, a **job cost sheet** is prepared. The job cost sheet (or job sheet) lists the appropriate quantities of final product to be produced, the materials needed, and the specific labor and machine operations to be performed.

In some job cost situations the job sheet follows the job physically through the production process, serving not only to accumulate costs, but also to provide the appropriate routing for the job. As each production department works on the job, the labor and materials used by that department are recorded on the job sheet. If overhead is to be applied to jobs on a basis other than materials or labor, a record of the overhead basis (such as machine hours used) is also recorded on the job card. Finally, when a department completes its work on the order, the costs are extended (prices and quantities multiplied together). The goods are then transferred to the next department with the job sheet. Eventually all departments finish working on the order, and the job sheet has accumulated all the costs incurred. An example of a completed job sheet is given in Figure 14-1.

**BRADY'S PRINT SHOP**

Customer Bill Williamson Job Number 246b

Description of order 500 wedding announcements, text attached double envelopes; film insert

Order date 6/22 Promise date 6/30 Quoted Price $275

| Engraving Department | Labor | Overhead |
|---|---|---|
| Materials<br>1 plate $78 | 2 hours @ $8 = $16 | 2 hours @ $6 = $12 |

| Printing Department | Labor | Overhead |
|---|---|---|
| Materials<br>High gloss ink 1 lb @ $20 $20<br>½ Ream Prestige paper @ $14 $ 7 | ½ hour @ $10 = $5 | ½ hour @ $25 = $12.50 |

| Binding Department | Labor | Overhead |
|---|---|---|
| Materials | | |

Stock Supplies
500 J-16 envelopes @ $3/100 $15
500 J-17 envelopes @ $3/100 $15
500 film inserts @ $.50/100 = $2.50

**Cost Summary**

| | Materials | Labor | Overhead | Total |
|---|---|---|---|---|
| Engraving | $78.00 | $16.00 | $12.00 | $106.00 |
| Printing | 27.00 | 5.00 | 12.50 | 44.50 |
| Binding | | | | |
| Supplies | 32.50 | | | 32.50 |

Total $183.00

**FIGURE 14-1 An example of a completed job cost sheet.**

In other situations the job cost sheets are maintained by the cost accounting department, and a work order form becomes the routing document for the job. Employees maintain a record of their time spent on jobs via work tickets. These tickets are then forwarded to the cost accounting

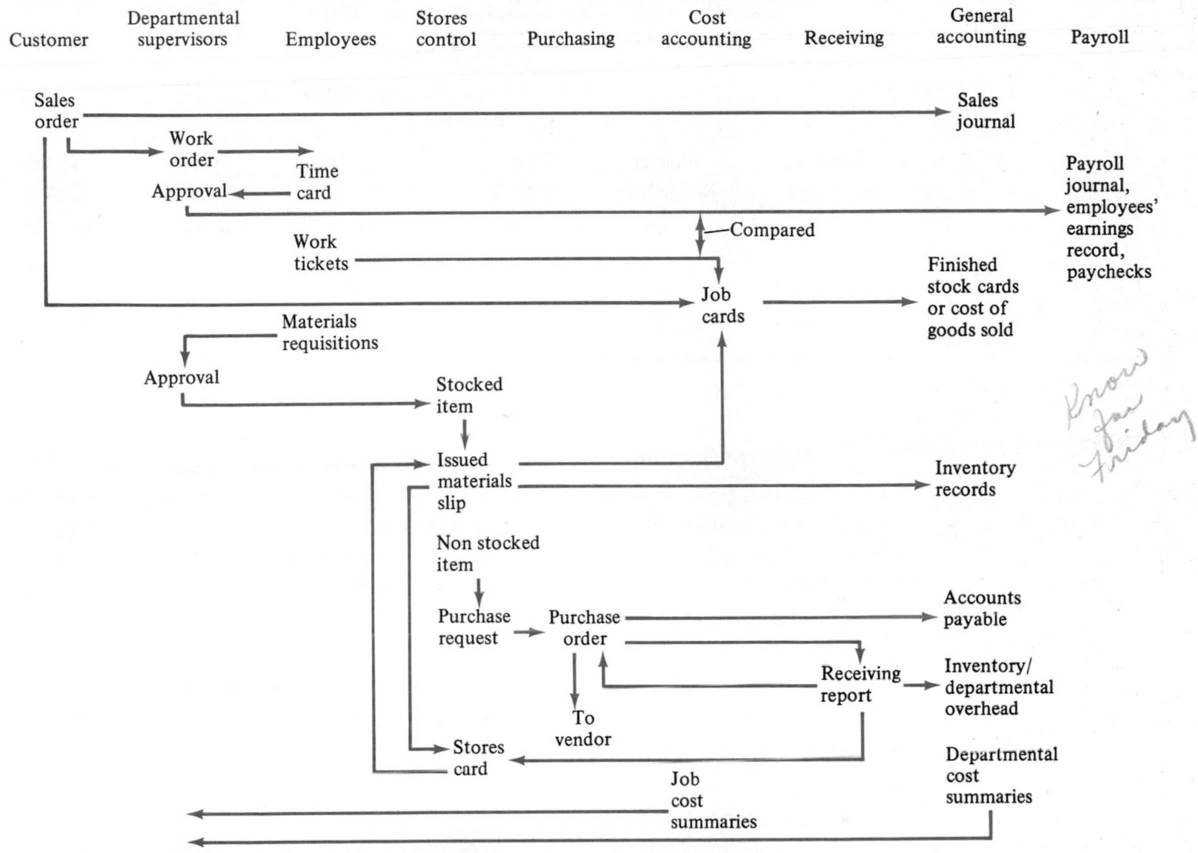


**FIGURE 14-2 Paperwork flow for job costing.**

department for posting labor costs to jobs. Similarly, as materials are issued for each job, copies of the materials-issue slips are forwarded to cost accounting. As you can imagine, in a firm with many departments working on hundreds of jobs, a job cost system generates a flurry of paperwork. Figure 14-2 illustrates just a portion of the paperwork flow in a typical job shop firm.

## ILLUSTRATION OF JOB COSTING

Job costing systems are not conceptually difficult to understand, but they require considerable accounting effort. To illustrate the required accounting treatment, we will use the following data for Wright, Inc., a firm that specializes in assembling electronic components.

**EXHIBIT 14-2 Description of Beginning Work-in-Process**

**WRIGHT, INC.**
**Work-in-Process Inventory**
**August 1**

| Job Number | Direct Materials | Direct Labor | Variable Overhead | Fixed Overhead | Total Costs |
|---|---|---|---|---|---|
| 712 | $ 400 | $ 600 | $450 | $ 675 | $2,125 |
| 715 | 550 | 400 | 300 | 450 | 1,700 |
| 716 | 650 | 240 | 180 | 270 | 1,340 |
| Total costs | $1,600 | $1,240 | $930 | $1,395 | $5,165 |

Wright's beginning balance for work-in-process on August 1 is $5,165. The specific jobs and costs in process on August 1 are given in Exhibit 14-2, and additional operating data are given in Exhibit 14-3. During the first week in August, work was begun on two new jobs, 717 and 718, while jobs 712, 716, and 717 were completed. Let us now turn to the accounting transactions needed to record Wright's activities for the first week in August.

Exhibit 14-3 indicates that total purchases of materials during the week amounted to $5,260. This amount is assigned to Raw Materials Inventory as the acquisition cost of the goods.

| | | |
|---|---|---|
| (1) Raw Materials Inventory | 5,260 | |
| Accounts or Vouchers Payable | | 5,260 |

Note that only the total is entered in the general ledger. The details concerning type of item, quantity, and unit cost will be entered on the appropriate stores card included in the subsidiary ledger.

Raw materials are requisitioned by the department responsible for employing them in production. During the period, total requisitions for materials were $4,280, so the journal entry is

| | | |
|---|---|---|
| (2) Work-in-Process Inventory | 4,280 | |
| Raw Materials Inventory | | 4,280 |

Again, only the total is entered in the general ledger. The cost of the specific materials used will be charged to the appropriate job cost sheets for the jobs in process.

Each employee fills out a daily time card indicating the hours worked and the jobs worked on. Assuming that employees earn $8 per hour, the

**EXHIBIT 14-3 Data for Wright, Inc.**

**BUDGET INFORMATION AS OF AUGUST 1**

| | |
|---|---|
| Variable overhead cost per direct labor hour | $6 |
| Fixed overhead cost per direct labor hour | $9 |

**SUMMARY OF OPERATIONS—AUGUST 1 TO AUGUST 7**

| | |
|---|---|
| Total purchases of materials | $5,260 |
| Total cost of variable overhead items | 2,620 |
| Total cost of fixed overhead items | 3,850 |

| Job | Material Requisitions Summary | Time Card Summary |
|---|---|---|
| 712 | $ 400 | 60 hr |
| 715 | 100 | 20 |
| 716 | 2,650 | 250 |
| 717 | 900 | 55 |
| 718 | 230 | 15 |
| Total | $4,280 | 400 hr |

information given in Exhibit 14-3 implies that labor earned 400 × $8 = $3,200 during the week; giving rise to the following entry:

| | | |
|---|---|---|
| (3) Payroll Clearing | 3,200 | |
| Vouchers or Payroll Payable | | 3,200 |

A word is in order with respect to the account titled Payroll Clearing. The function of any "clearing" account is to facilitate the recording of information; such accounts or their balances are not balance sheet or income statement items. In the case of payroll accounting, it is usual for one individual to be responsible for accumulating the actual payroll information (the foregoing entry) for pay purposes, and another to be responsible for distributing the payroll costs to the jobs or departments affected (the following entry). In such a case, one person is debiting the Payroll Clearing account, while another is crediting the same account. The clearing account facilitates the process. If all information is current and correct, the balance of this account will be zero; otherwise there is an indication that an adjusting journal entry is required, or, if not, that an error has been made.

We have assumed that the entire direct labor cost for the week can be charged to the specific jobs worked on. As different workers perform their tasks, this is noted on the job order cost sheet as well as being entered in the general ledger.

| | | |
|---|---|---|
| (4) Work-in-Process Inventory | 3,200 | |
| Payroll Clearing | | 3,200 |

Variable overhead consists of such items as indirect materials, indirect labor, utilities, payroll taxes, and so forth. The actual cost of each is credited to the individual asset or liability account affected and debited to Variable Overhead Control. Since this is a control account, a more detailed entry will be made in the corresponding subsidiary ledger for each department's variable overhead. These costs are recorded during the period as incurred and at the end of the period as accrued. The total variable overhead[1] costs for the week amounted to $2,620.

| | | |
|---|---|---|
| (5) Variable Overhead Control | 2,620 | |
| Various asset and liability accounts | | 2,620 |

Assume that Wright applies variable overhead to each job at the rate of $6 per direct labor hour. This rate reflects management's best estimate of how overhead varies with labor usage. Because 400 direct labor hours were worked during the week, variable overhead in the amount of $2,400 will be assigned to work-in-process.

| | | |
|---|---|---|
| (6) Work-in-Process Inventory | 2,400 | |
| Variable Overhead Applied | | 2,400 |

Note that we have used two separate accounts for variable overhead. One account is used to accumulate the actual costs and the other is used to record the costs assigned to production. Some firms use only one account, simply titled Overhead, but the use of two separate accounts emphasizes that there is no direct relationship between the costs incurred during a period and the costs assigned to jobs during the same period.

The actual fixed overhead costs are also recorded in a general ledger control account as they are incurred or accrued. As with variable overhead, the appropriate asset or liability account is credited and Fixed Overhead Control is debited. Appropriate detailed entries are made in the corresponding subsidiary ledger. The total cost of fixed overhead items for the week was $3,850, recorded with the following entry.

| | | |
|---|---|---|
| (7) Fixed Overhead Control | 3,850 | |
| Various asset and liability accounts | | 3,850 |

[1]At this point in the text, maintaining a distinction between variable and fixed overhead is not necessary. However, the distinction will prove valuable later on.

Wright also applies fixed overhead to jobs based on the direct labor hours worked. For the current period, fixed overhead is charged at $9 per labor hour. For the 400 hours worked, the entry to apply fixed overhead is:

| | | |
|---|---|---|
| (8) Work-in-Process Inventory | 3,600 | |
| Fixed Overhead Applied | | 3,600 |

For the remaining entries we need a summary of Wright's job cost sheets, as given in Exhibit 14-4, where the current costs (determined from the data in Exhibit 14-3) have been added to the beginning inventory costs listed in Exhibit 14-2.

During the period, jobs 712, 716, and 717 were said to have been completed. Summing the costs for these jobs as given in Exhibit 14-4 yields a total cost of goods completed of $3,905 + $9,740 + $2,165 = $15,810. With this information we can now prepare the following journal entry.

| | | |
|---|---|---|
| (9) Finished Goods Inventory | 15,810 | |
| Work-in-Process Inventory | | 15,810 |

The ending inventory for work-in-process according to the general ledger is $2,835 ($5,165 for beginning inventory plus $4,280 for materials, $3,200 for labor, $2,400 for variable overhead, and $3,600 for fixed overhead less the $15,810 cost of goods manufactured). This balance is proved against (reconciled with) the subsidiary ledger by summing the amounts assigned to jobs still in process at the end of the week. The jobs still in process are jobs 715 and 718. From Exhibit 14-4 we can see that the total on these job sheets, $2,260 + $575 = $2,835, agrees with the general ledger balance.

Assume that jobs 712 and 717 were delivered (sold) to the customers ordering the work. Job 716 was produced for inventory and half of those

**EXHIBIT 14-4 Summary of Job Cost Sheets for Wright, Inc.**

| | | Current Cost | | | | |
|---|---|---|---|---|---|---|
| Job Number | Beginning Cost | Materials | Labor | Variable Overhead | Fixed Overhead | Ending Total Cost |
| 712 | $2,125 | $ 400 | $ 480 | $ 360 | $ 540 | $ 3,905 |
| 715 | 1,700 | 100 | 160 | 120 | 180 | 2,260 |
| 716 | 1,340 | 2,650 | 2,000 | 1,500 | 2,250 | 9,740 |
| 717 | — | 900 | 440 | 330 | 495 | 2,165 |
| 718 | — | 230 | 120 | 90 | 135 | 575 |
| Total | $5,165 | $4,280 | $3,200 | $2,400 | $3,600 | $18,645 |

**EXHIBIT 14-5 Posting of Journal Entries to the General Ledger**

| Raw Materials Inventory | | Work-in-Process Inventory | | Finished Goods Inventory | | Cost of Goods Sold | |
|---|---|---|---|---|---|---|---|
| Bal. 0 | | Bal. 5,165 | | Bal. 0 | | | |
| (1) 5,260 | (2) 4,280 | (2) 4,280 | (9) 15,810 | (9) 15,810 | (10) 10,940 | (10) 10,940 | |
| | | (4) 3,200 | | | | | |
| | | (6) 2,400 | | | | | |
| | | (8) 3,600 | | | | | |
| 980 | | 2,835 | | 4,870 | | 10,940 | |

| Variable Overhead Control | | Variable Overhead Applied | | Fixed Overhead Control | | Fixed Overhead Applied | |
|---|---|---|---|---|---|---|---|
| (5) 2,620 | | | (6) 2,400 | (7) 3,850 | | | (8) 3,600 |

items were also sold. Using the information in Exhibit 14-4 the general journal entry to record the cost of sales is

| | | |
|---|---|---|
| (10) Cost of Goods Sold | 10,940 | |
| Finished Goods Inventory | | 10,940 |

where $\$10{,}940 = \$3{,}905 + \$2{,}165 + \frac{1}{2}(\$9{,}740)$.

This entry completes the entries that would be made during the period. Those related to cost flows have been posted to the general ledger accounts in Exhibit 14-5, and the account balances have been determined. The flow of manufacturing costs is further summarized in the Statement of Cost of Goods Manufactured and Sold provided in Exhibit 14-6.

The next set of entries are adjusting entries to close out the overhead control and applied accounts. As can be seen in Exhibit 14-5, the balances in the overhead control and applied accounts are not equal. This should come as no surprise because overhead was applied to jobs independently from the actual accumulation of overhead costs. This difference gives rise to over- or underapplied overhead. If more overhead was applied to work-in-process than was actually incurred, we have **overapplied overhead.** In this case our cost of goods sold and the values of work-in-process and finished goods inventory will have been overstated. Alternatively, if we applied less overhead than actually incurred, we have **underapplied overhead.** In the latter case, cost of goods sold and inventories are understated.

**EXHIBIT 14-6 Statement of Cost of Goods Manufactured and Sold**

| | | | |
|---|---|---|---|
| Raw materials, August 1 | $ 0 | | |
| Materials purchased | 5,260 | | |
| Materials available for use | $5,260 | | |
| Raw materials, August 7 | 980 | | |
| Raw materials used | | $ 4,280 | |
| Direct labor | | 3,200 | |
| Variable overhead applied | | 2,400 | |
| Fixed overhead applied | | 3,600 | |
| Total manufacturing costs | | $13,480 | |
| Work-in-process, August 1 | | 5,165 | |
| Total work-in-process | | $18,645 | |
| Work-in-process, August 7 | | 2,835 | |
| Cost of goods manufactured | | | $15,810 |
| Finished goods, August 1 | | | 0 |
| Cost of goods available for sale | | | $15,810 |
| Finished goods, August 7 | | | 4,870 |
| Cost of goods sold | | | $10,940 |

Wright's overhead accounts can be closed with the following entries.

| | | | |
|---|---|---|---|
| (11) | Underapplied Variable Overhead | 220 | |
| | Variable Overhead Applied | 2,400 | |
| | Variable Overhead Control | | 2,620 |
| (12) | Underapplied Fixed Overhead | 250 | |
| | Fixed Overhead Applied | 3,600 | |
| | Fixed Overhead Control | | 3,850 |

The last step in the process is to dispose of the over- or underapplied overhead. Wright takes the easiest approach and closes these accounts to cost of goods sold. Thus the last entry is

| | | | |
|---|---|---|---|
| (13) | Cost of Goods Sold | 470 | |
| | Underapplied Variable Overhead | | 220 |
| | Underapplied Fixed Overhead | | 250 |

These final results have been posted to the general ledger accounts in Exhibit 14-7.

This completes the overview of the job-cost accounting system. However, we have glossed over several troublesome points. Let us now turn to an examination of some of these points in detail.

**EXHIBIT 14-7 Closing the Overhead Accounts**

| Raw Materials Inventory | | Work-in-Process Inventory | | Finished Goods Inventory | | Cost of Goods Sold | |
|---|---|---|---|---|---|---|---|
| Bal. 0 | | Bal. 5,165 | | Bal. 0 | | | |
| (1) 5,260 | (2) 4,280 | (2) 4,280 | (9) 15,810 | (9) 15,810 | (10) 10,940 | (10) 10,940 | |
| | | (4) 3,200 | | | | (13) 470 | |
| | | (6) 2,400 | | | | | |
| | | (8) 3,600 | | | | | |
| 980 | | 2,835 | | 4,870 | | 11,410 | |

| Variable Overhead Control | | Variable Overhead Applied | | Fixed Overhead Control | | Fixed Overhead Applied | |
|---|---|---|---|---|---|---|---|
| (5) 2,620 | | | (6) 2,400 | (7) 3,850 | | | (8) 3,600 |
| | (11) 2,620 | (11) 2,400 | | | (12) 3,850 | (12) 3,600 | |

## ACTUAL, NORMAL, AND STANDARD COST SYSTEMS

In an **actual cost system** we record the actual costs required to complete each job. For materials and labor this creates no particular difficulty because we can determine at the time the jobs are completed what the actual materials and labor costs were. We simply need to be able to determine actual materials used and their prices, as well as actual hours worked and actual wage rates. Materials costs can be obtained by using materials requisitions slips. When materials are taken from stores, a slip is issued by the stores clerk indicating the quantity of materials issued, their cost, and the job to be charged. If any materials are returned, an additional slip noting the returns is issued. These slips are then used to cost jobs. Similarly, production workers can keep a time card indicating the jobs worked on and the number of hours devoted to each. The time card will have the employee's wage rate, so actual labor costs can easily be charged to jobs.

The primary difficulty with an actual cost system is what to do about overhead. At the time jobs are being worked on, we will not know actual overhead costs. We can determine the actual total overhead only at the end of the accounting period. At the end of the period we can calculate an actual overhead rate per machine hour or labor hour and then determine the actual cost of each job. But, for most firms, the information would arrive too late to be useful. In fact, the only job-oriented firms that we are aware of that use actual cost systems are defense contractors. Even they use a normal cost system for progress billing and then make a final billing or refund based upon a restatement to an actual cost system (months or even years after the accounting period is over).

In a normal cost system, actual materials and labor costs are recorded in the same manner as an actual cost system. The difference is in the treatment of overhead. A **normal cost system** uses predetermined overhead rates. A predetermined rate is determined at the beginning of the accounting period by estimating the overhead costs that will be incurred and dividing by the estimated level of activity as represented by the overhead application basis (usually machine hours or labor hours). Because these estimates are typically taken from the firm's master budget, the overhead rate might be represented as

$$\text{variable overhead application rate} = \frac{\text{master budget variable overhead}}{\text{master budget labor hours}}$$

$$\text{fixed overhead application rate} = \frac{\text{master budget fixed overhead}}{\text{master budget machine hours}}$$

In a normal cost system, as we work on jobs, overhead is applied to them by multiplying the predetermined overhead rates by the actual amount of machine or labor hours used on each job. The example using the Wright company employed a normal cost system.

In a **standard cost system,** predetermined rates and quantities are used for all three types of manufacturing costs. For each potential job there will be standards specifying the amount of materials that should be used and their cost. Similarly, there are standards for the number of labor hours to be used, and the standard wage rate for the class of labor that should be used, for each type of job. In a standard cost system, the total standard cost for a job is determined as soon as the number of units produced is known. Once production is known, the standard cost for materials for a job is determined by multiplying the standard quantity of materials allowed per unit by the units produced and by the standard price for materials. A similar calculation is made for labor. The charge for overhead differs from normal costing in that the standard overhead rates are multiplied by the standard labor or machine hours allowed for good production (normal costing multiplies the predetermined overhead rate by the actual hours).

Actual cost systems are rarely used in a job cost environment. When they are used, it is usually because an actual cost system is required by contract, such as a defense contract that is priced at actual cost plus a percentage of cost for profit. Normal cost systems are the most commonly used systems. A normal cost system provides a timely estimate of the cost of producing each job. Standard cost systems are most often used by mature firms whose technology and product lines are quite stable. Standard cost systems provide excellent cost control (the subject of Chapters 18 and 19), but are more expensive to implement because of the need to have detailed standards for every product the firm manufactures.

go over w/chap 18

## THE VOLUME VARIANCE

In an actual cost system there can be no over- or underapplied overhead because actual overhead is charged to jobs after the fact. In normal and standard cost systems, over- or underapplied *variable* overhead arises when actual spending for overhead items differs from the budget (because of either poor spending control or an error in the estimate of the level of spending required). In addition to differences in spending, over- or underapplied *fixed* overhead will arise whenever the actual volume of production differs from that planned in the master budget.

Consider the following example. A firm's fixed overhead consists solely of depreciation amounting to $50,000 per period (a number that we can predict exactly). The firm allocates fixed overhead based on machine hours and predicts that customers will bring in orders requiring 25,000 hours of machine time next period. With these facts, the firm's fixed overhead application rate will be

$$\text{fixed overhead application rate} = \frac{\$50{,}000}{25{,}000 \text{ hr}}$$
$$= \$2 \text{ per machine hour}$$

Now assume that customer orders during the period required only 23,500 hours of machine time for production. During the period, as we produced the products, we applied overhead to each job at $2 for each machine hour used. In total we would have applied $2 × 23,500 hr = $47,000. But the actual fixed overhead incurred was $50,000, so we underapplied overhead by $3,000. Note that the cost was exactly as budgeted. The sole cause of the underapplied overhead was that we used 23,500 machine hours instead of 25,000. Had customers brought in orders requiring the use of 26,000 machine hours, we would have applied $52,000 of overhead to jobs and would have overapplied overhead by $2,000. In fact, with costs being exactly at budget, the only way not to have over- or underapplied fixed overhead is to operate exactly at the 25,000 hours planned (see Figure 14-3). But because predicting actual customer demand is extremely difficult, it would be highly unusual to operate exactly at the volume of operations planned in the master budget.

The **volume variance** (also called the **capacity variance** or the **denominator variance**) is calculated to capture the over- or underapplied fixed overhead arising because actual production volume differs from the master budget predicted volume. The formula for the calculation is

$$\text{volume variance} = \text{fixed overhead rate (actual volume} - \text{budgeted volume)}$$

where the fixed overhead application rate is determined from the estimates of cost and volume in the master budget and volumes are measured in

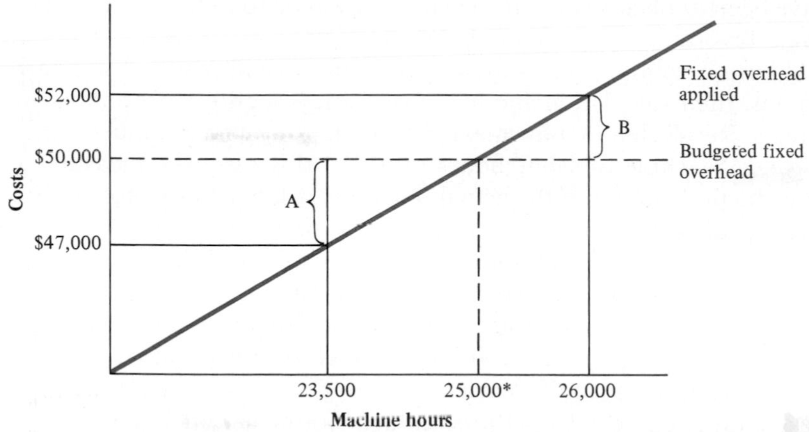


*Planned activity level in the master budget

Line segment A represents the unfavorable volume variance of $3,000 if actual activity during the period was 23,500 machine hours.

Line segment B represents the favorable volume variance of $2,000 if actual activity during the period was 26,000 machine hours.

**FIGURE 14-3 The volume variance.**

terms of the base on which overhead is applied (usually machine hours or labor hours). For the example, when the firm actually used 23,500 machine hours, the calculation would be

$$\text{volume variance} = \$2(23{,}500 - 25{,}000)$$
$$= \$3{,}000 \text{ U}$$

If 26,000 machine hours were used, the variance would be

$$\text{volume variance} = \$2(26{,}000 - 25{,}000)$$
$$= \$2{,}000 \text{ F}$$

Note that we have added a letter to each variance. The U stands for unfavorable and the F stands for favorable. Underapplied variances are traditionally called unfavorable because they indicate that we have failed to reach our planned volume. Further, because we have not applied enough costs to jobs, the correction for our error will be to increase costs (which has an unfavorable effect on earnings). In contrast, a favorable volume variance arises because we overapplied fixed overhead. This indicates that we surpassed our planned volume level. Because too many costs have been applied to jobs, the correction will be to reduce costs, which will have a favorable effect on net income.

Although volume variances arise in both normal cost and standard cost systems, their calculation and interpretation is slightly different in the two systems. Recall that in a normal cost system overhead is applied based on the *actual* machine or labor hours used. In this case, the measure of actual production volume is the actual machine or labor hours used. Thus when we calculate the volume variance as the fixed overhead rate times the difference between actual hours and master budget hours, the resulting volume variance may not be due solely to changes in the volume of products produced. For example, if more labor or machine hours were used due to inefficiencies, the volume variance in a normal cost system would be affected by the inefficiencies. However, in a standard cost system, overhead is applied based on the standard hours *allowed* for the good output achieved. Thus the measure of the actual volume achieved in a standard cost system is the standard number of machine hours allowed for production. Therefore in a standard cost system the volume variance arises solely from changes in the level of output.

The volume variance arises because we apply fixed overhead to jobs as if they were variable costs. The difference in the calculation of the volume variance between normal and standard cost systems is attributable to the fact that the two systems apply overhead slightly differently.

### Disposition of the Volume Variance

The accounting treatment given to the volume variance depends on its cause and its size. Regardless of cause, if the size of the volume variance is immaterial, it is usually written off to the income statement as an adjustment to cost of goods sold.

If the volume variance is large, three different approaches are taken dependent on the cause. If a firm faces cyclical demand, the volume variance is usually carried forward in the balance sheet as a deferred charge. Over the demand cycle we expect the favorable and unfavorable volume variances to cancel out. This allows us to use a single fixed overhead application rate over the cycle, resulting in stable average costs for our products.

If the volume variance arose from an unusual, nonrecurring event such as a natural disaster that curtailed production, it is usually written off as a period cost. That is, the volume variance is reported as a loss on the income statement. In the more common case, where the volume variance is due to an error in predicting the actual level of activity achieved, we prorate the volume variance to cost of goods sold, work-in-process, and finished goods inventory. This approach recognizes the volume variance as an estimation error. In effect, we are saying the fixed overhead rate was wrong and we will now use an approximation to correct the error. On the

**EXHIBIT 14-8 Four Approaches to Disposing of the Volume Variance**

| | |
|---|---|
| Assumed data: | |
| Budgeted (and actual) fixed overhead | $50,000 |
| Fixed overhead applied to production | $47,000 |
| Current balances in selected accounts | |
| Work-in-Process | $10,000 |
| Finished Goods | 20,000 |
| Cost of Goods Sold | 70,000 |

The initial entry to recognize the volume variance would be the same under all four approaches. It is

| | | |
|---|---|---|
| Fixed Overhead Applied | 47,000 | |
| Volume Variance | 3,000 | |
| Fixed Overhead Control | | 50,000 |

1. If the unfavorable volume variance were considered immaterial, the closing entry would be

| | | |
|---|---|---|
| Cost of Goods Sold | 3,000 | |
| Volume Variance | | 3,000 |

2. If the unfavorable volume variance were due to cyclical demand which will reverse in the future, the entry would be

| | | |
|---|---|---|
| Deferred Charges | 3,000 | |
| Volume Variance | | 3,000 |

3. If the volume variance were due to a flood that closed the plant, the entry would be

| | | |
|---|---|---|
| Flood Loss | 3,000 | |
| Volume Variance | | 3,000 |

4. If the variance is due to an error in predicting demand levels, the entry would be

| | | |
|---|---|---|
| Cost of Goods Sold | 2,100 | |
| Finished Goods Inventory | 600 | |
| Work-in-Process Inventory | 300 | |
| Volume Variance | | 3,000 |

assumption that fixed overhead is included in jobs in work-in-process, finished goods and cost of goods sold in the same proportion as other costs, the volume variance is usually prorated to these accounts in proportion to their ending balances.[2] Exhibit 14-8 presents the journal entries for the

[2]It would be possible to determine the actual amount of fixed overhead in each of these accounts by going to the job sheets. Then the volume variance could be allocated to each account based on the fixed overhead in each. But it would be extremely rare for the value of this more accurate information to justify the cost of obtaining it.

four approaches to disposing of the volume variance based on the assumed data given.

### Disposition of Over- or Underapplied Overhead

The over- or underapplied variable overhead and the remaining over- or underapplied fixed overhead after the volume variance has been extracted is due to actual spending for overhead not being equal to the budgeted amount. If these amounts are small, they are usually closed to cost of goods sold. If large, they are prorated to work-in-process, finished goods and cost of goods sold.[3] Except where the volume variance is set up as a deferred charge or written off as a loss, the volume variance and the other over- or underapplied overhead are typically given the same treatment. In these cases the volume variance may not be identified. Instead, total over- or underapplied overhead is treated as a single figure.

## SUMMARY

In a job cost environment either actual or standard direct materials and direct labor costs are traced directly to the job sheet for an order. Overhead, typically, is applied to jobs, as they are being produced, by means of a predetermined overhead application rate. This, in turn, means that at the end of the accounting period there will be an over- or underapplied overhead balance. If this difference is immaterial in amount, it is usually closed to cost of goods sold, but material amounts may need to be prorated to appropriate accounts. Although job costing is not a conceptually difficult accounting system, the required paperwork and bookkeeping loads are massive.

## DEMONSTRATION PROBLEM

D. Ratcliffe, Inc., CPA, is a small firm employing seven professionals. Most of the firm's revenues come from tax work, but they do have a dozen audit clients. The firm uses job costing to determine the income or loss from each of its professional engagements.

Professional salaries are the firm's biggest cost. The primary document for recording the use of professional time is a daily time log. Each employee is required

[3]Earlier we mentioned that most firms that are required by contract to use an actual cost system will use a normal cost system and adjust it. They do so by determining the overhead basis for each job (machine or labor hours) and then prorating the total of the volume variance and the other over- or underapplied overhead to each job in proportion to the overhead basis. This converts the normal cost of each job to an actual cost.

Name: D. Ratcliffe Position: Partner

| Times | Activity | Client | Hours | Fee | Charge To |
|---|---|---|---|---|---|
| 8:15–9:00 | Open mail | – | 0.75 | $ 56.25 | Miscellaneous |
| 9:00–10:00 | Meet prospective client | B. Jones | 1 | 75.00 | Practice development |
| 10:00–10:30 | Telephone call | D. Nevins | 0.5 | 37.50 | Client |
| 11:30–3:00 | Review tax return, lunch | H. Rolfe | 3.5 | 262.50 | Client |
| 3:00–4:00 | Review audit plan | FNB | 1 | 75.00 | Client |
| 4:00–5:30 | Discuss tax strategy | D. Nevins | 1.5 | 112.50 | Client |
| 7:00–8:30 | Attend University Accounting Club meeting | – | 1.5 | 112.50 | Staff recruiting |

**Summary**

| | |
|---|---|
| Total hours | 9.75 |
| Client hours | 6.5 |
| Overtime | N/A |

$$\frac{\text{Client hours}}{\text{Total hours}} = 67\%$$

**FIGURE 14-4 Daily time log.**

to submit a daily record of activities (see Figure 14-4). The daily record serves both as the source document for charging costs to jobs and as a performance measurement report. In the report all activities are recorded at the employee's billing rate. This is done to call to the employee's attention the opportunity cost of devoting time to nonrevenue-generating activities.

Once a week the daily time logs are summarized. At this point the *cost* of professional time is computed and charged to each client's job sheet or to an appropriate nonrevenue account. Currently, partners earn $38 per hour, managers $16.50 per hour, and staff members $11 per hour.

The only other direct cost is travel and entertainment. All employees submit weekly expense reports for reimbursement. The employee must indicate for each expense item the appropriate client or nonrevenue-generating account to be charged.

During the past month the firm worked on several tax engagements plus two audits: Nevins Pharmaceuticals and the First National Bank. A summary of the time reports and the expense reports for the month is as follows:

| | Clients | | | Nonrevenue Activities | | | |
|---|---|---|---|---|---|---|---|
| | Nevins | FNB | All Others | Practice Development | Staff Recruiting | Training and Seminars | Miscellaneous |
| Professional time | | | | | | | |
| Partner | 36 | 22 | 68 | 16 | 5 | 8 | 21 |
| Manager | 78 | 86 | 100 | 12 | 20 | 24 | 32 |
| Staff | 175 | 125 | 292 | — | — | 96 | 16 |
| Travel and entertainment | $750 | $675 | $900 | $450 | $300 | $1,200 | — |

Tax clients are billed for the actual hours devoted to a task, but audit clients are billed based on a budget of the number of hours of professional time expected to be required for each engagement. The budget for Nevins Pharmaceuticals called for the use of 20 hours of partner time, 80 hours of manager time, and 160 hours of staff time. The billing rates are $75 per hour for partners, $32 per hour for managers, and $20 per hour for staff time billed.

Costs of nonrevenue activities are accumulated to facilitate control and future budgeting. Once accumulated they are all treated as overhead. Overhead is charged to jobs at the rate of $0.65 per dollar of cost for professional time billed.

During the month the Nevins engagement and all the work for tax clients were completed and billed to clients. At month-end the audit of the bank is still in progress. The overhead related to maintaining the firm's office (rent, secretarial support, and so forth) was $3,480 for the month.

**Required**

**a.** Determine the profit or loss on the Nevins engagement using a normal cost basis.

**b.** Determine the cost of audits in progress using a normal cost basis.

**c.** Determine the firm's overall profit or loss for the period using normal costs adjusted for over- or underapplied overhead.

**d.** If the firm used an actual cost basis, what would be the profit or loss on the Nevins engagement?

**Solution**

**a.** From the time summary and the billing and cost rates the following job summary for the Nevins engagement can be prepared.

| | Budget Hours | Billing Rate | Fee | Actual Hours | Labor Rate | Cost |
|---|---|---|---|---|---|---|
| Professional time | | | | | | |
| Partners | 20 | $75 | $1,500 | 36 | $38.00 | $ 1,368 |
| Managers | 80 | 32 | 2,560 | 78 | 16.50 | 1,287 |
| Staff | 160 | 20 | 3,200 | 175 | 11.00 | 1,925 |
| Totals | | | $7,260 | | | $ 4,580 |
| Overhead @ $0.65 per dollar | | | | | | 2,977 |
| Travel and entertainment | | | | | | 750 |
| Total cost | | | | | | $ 8,307 |
| Total fee | | | | | | 7,260 |
| Profit (loss) | | | | | | $ (1,047) |

**b.** The cost of the First National Bank audit in process can also be determined from the summary of time reports and expenses. Because the firm uses a normal cost system, the overhead is assigned using the $0.65 per dollar of professional cost rate.

| | Hours | Labor Rate | Cost |
|---|---|---|---|
| Professional time | | | |
| Partners | 22 | $38.00 | $ 836.00 |
| Managers | 86 | 16.50 | 1,419.00 |
| Staff | 125 | 11.00 | 1,375.00 |
| Total | | | $3,630.00 |
| Overhead @ $0.65 per dollar | | | 2,359.50 |
| Travel and entertainment | | | 675.00 |
| Total cost of audit in process | | | $6,664.50 |

**c.** The revenues and normal costs for the tax engagements can be calculated from the time and expense summary.

| | Hours | Billing Rate | Fee | Labor Rate | Cost |
|---|---|---|---|---|---|
| Professional time | | | | | |
| Partners | 68 | $75 | $ 5,100 | $38.00 | $ 2,584.00 |
| Managers | 100 | 32 | 3,200 | 16.50 | 1,650.00 |
| Staff | 292 | 20 | 5,840 | 11.00 | 3,212.00 |
| Total | | | $14,140 | | $ 7,446.00 |
| Overhead @ $0.65 per dollar | | | | | 4,839.90 |
| Travel and entertainment | | | | | 900.00 |
| Total cost | | | | | $13,185.90 |
| Total fee | | | | | 14,140.00 |
| Income (loss) from tax clients | | | | | $ 954.10 |

Adding the $954.10 income from the tax clients to the $1,047 loss on the Nevins audit yields a total net loss of $92.90 for the month. However, this figure is before calculating over- or underapplied overhead.

The actual overhead costs incurred include the $3,480 for maintaining the office plus all the costs of nonrevenue-generating activities. The nonrevenue-generating activity costs and total overhead incurred were as follows:

| | | Practice Development | | Staff Recruiting | | Training and Seminars | | Miscellaneous | | |
|---|---|---|---|---|---|---|---|---|---|---|
| | Rate | Hours | Cost | Hours | Cost | Hours | Cost | Hours | Cost | Total |
| Professional time | | | | | | | | | | |
| Partners | $38.00 | 16 | $ 608 | 5 | $190 | 8 | $ 304 | 21 | $ 798 | $ 1,900 |
| Managers | 16.50 | 12 | 198 | 20 | 330 | 24 | 396 | 32 | 528 | 1,452 |
| Staff | 11.00 | — | — | — | — | 96 | 1,056 | 16 | 176 | 1,232 |
| Total | | | $ 806 | | $520 | | $1,756 | | $1,502 | $ 4,584 |
| Travel and entertainment | | | 450 | | 300 | | 1,200 | | — | 1,950 |
| Office maintenance | | | — | | — | | — | | 3,480 | 3,480 |
| Total | | | $1,256 | | $820 | | $2,956 | | $4,982 | $10,014 |

The total overhead applied to jobs during the month can be obtained from our previous calculations as follows:

| | |
|---|---|
| **a.** To Nevins | $ 2,977.00 |
| **b.** To First National Bank | 2,359.50 |
| **c.** To all tax clients | 4,839.90 |
| Total applied | $10,176.40 |

Comparing the $10,176.40 of overhead costs applied to jobs to the $10,014 of actual overhead costs incurred, we see that overhead was overapplied by $162.40. If this amount is closed to cost of services rendered, the firm will show a net income for the month of $69.50.

| | | |
|---|---|---|
| Professional fees | | |
| Nevins audit | $ 7,260.00 | |
| Tax clients | 14,140.00 | $21,400.00 |
| Cost of services rendered | | |
| Nevins audit | $ 8,307.00 | |
| Tax clients | 13,185.90 | |
| Overapplied overhead | (162.40) | 21,330.50 |
| Net income | | $ 69.50 |

**d.** The actual overhead rate is found by dividing the actual overhead incurred, $10,014, by the actual costs of professional time devoted to revenue-generating activities. The actual professional costs were

| | |
|---|---|
| Nevins Pharmaceuticals | $ 4,580 |
| First National Bank | 3,630 |
| Tax clients | 7,446 |
| Total | $15,656 |

Thus the actual overhead rate is $10,014 ÷ $15,656 = $0.6396 per dollar billed. The revised total costs for the Nevins audit would be

| | |
|---|---|
| Professional time | $4,580 |
| Overhead (actual rate) | 2,929 |
| Travel and entertainment | 750 |
| Total | $8,259 |

Comparing the new cost of $8,259 to the revenue generated from the Nevins audit, $7,260, shows that the loss on the engagement drops to $999.

## KEY TERMS AND CONCEPTS

Job costing
Process costing
Job cost sheet
Overapplied overhead
Underapplied overhead
Actual cost system
Normal cost system
Standard cost system
[ Volume variance
[ Capacity variance
[ Denominator variance

[ Bracketed terms are equivalent in meaning.

## FURTHER READING


Brown, Robert G. "Small Business Controls: The Case of a Job Shop," *Management Accounting* (March 1976), p. 51.

Carbone, Frank J. "Automated Job Costing Helps Mulach Steel Stay Competitive," *Management Accounting* (June 1980), p. 29.

NAA. *Accounting for Labor Costs and Labor-Related Costs,* Research Series No. 32 (New York: National Association of Accountants, 1957).

Reiter, Stanley. "System for Managing Job Shop Production," *Journal of Business* (July 1966), p. 371.

Riley, Kevin. "Productive Hours Analysis for a Small Shop," *Management Accounting* (January 1973), p. 7.

Smith, Alan F. "Target Pricing: The Job Coster's Dilemma," *Management Accounting (Eng.)* (May 1979), p. 18.

Wise, Ronald L. "Cost Reporting for the Small and Medium Size Job Shop Operation," *Management Accounting* (February 1970), p. 20.

Wolk, Harry I., and Michael G. Tearney. "Job Order Costing and Normal Spoilage: An Equational Approach," *Government Accounting Journal* (Fall 1977), p. 53.


## QUESTIONS AND EXERCISES

**14-1** In a job order situation, Work-in-Process is a control account. What form does the subsidiary ledger take?

**14-2** What is the similarity and what is the difference between actual and normal cost systems?

**14-3** Given your local area, name five businesses that operate under job order conditions and five that operate under process conditions.

**14-4** Give five examples of job order cost sheets that you have personally received recently. (*Hint:* An itemized dental bill made out to you is a job order cost sheet.)

**14-5** Of what significance is a volume variance to an actual cost system and to a normal cost system?

**14-6** What determines how over- or underapplied overhead should be handled in a normal cost system?

**14-7** A local auto repair shop charges customers $35 per hour for labor. A sign posted in the service area indicates that each customer will be charged $1.50 or 10% of the repair bill, whichever is lower, for "miscellaneous." Should a customer insist that "miscellaneous" be itemized in detail?

**14-8** Overtime premiums may be a product cost, chargeable to a particular job or to overhead, or a period cost. Under what conditions would each approach be used? Give examples.

**14-9** As part of the contract between a union and a firm, all production employees are guaranteed 5 hours of overtime per week. Should overtime be treated as a direct or an indirect cost?

**14-10** The accounting records of Pixie, Inc., show overhead as $15,275 in a month when production was 825 units and $15,950 when production was 1,050 units. Determine (a) the variable overhead per unit, (b) the fixed overhead per month, (c) budgeted overhead for 1,000 units, and (d) the overhead rate based on 1,000 units.

**14-11** Refer to the demonstration problem at the end of the chapter. If the firm recognizes revenue and matches expenses on a progress basis, rather than when an engagement is completed, what would be the profit or loss for the month on the audit in progress? (Assume that the hours spent so far are consistent with the budget for the audit.)

**14-12** NML Enterprises uses a predetermined rate to apply overhead to production. This rate is based on direct labor hours and has been calculated as follows:

$$\text{overhead application rate} = \frac{\text{budgeted overhead costs}}{\text{budgeted direct labor hours}} = \frac{\$900{,}000}{100{,}000} = \$9.00$$

The indirect manufacturing costs are incurred more or less uniformly over the year. On the other hand, actual production fluctuates as evidenced by direct labor costs (the plant is not unionized and management can acquire direct labor talent as required for production). Direct labor hours are budgeted, quarter by quarter, as follows:

| | |
|---|---|
| First quarter | 28,000 |
| Second quarter | 20,000 |
| Third quarter | 25,000 |
| Fourth quarter | 27,000 |

For each quarter and for the year, determine whether overhead is over- or underapplied and by what amount.

**14-13** People's Corporation allocates overhead by using a burden rate of $1 per direct labor hour. In April, when actual overhead was $1,250, overhead costs were overabsorbed by $250. The master budget operating volume is 1,000 direct labor hours and variable overhead cost is $0.20 per direct labor hour. Determine (a) budgeted fixed overhead per month and (b) the volume or denominator variance for the month.

**14-14** Machine Shop, Inc., does custom work employing a cost system in which overhead is allocated at a predetermined rate of 200% of direct costs. When direct costs are $4,000, indirect costs are budgeted at $9,200; when direct costs are budgeted at $6,200, indirect costs are budgeted at $11,950. (a) What are the budgeted variable and fixed costs? (b) If actual direct costs are $5,700 and actual indirect costs are $11,600, by how much is overhead over- or underapplied?

**14-15** A firm applies indirect product costs on the basis of direct labor payroll. It has been estimated that at the firm's normal volume, when the payroll is $420,000, nonvariable overhead is $294,000 and variable overhead is $168,000. Actual results for the period resulted in a payroll of $580,000 (of which 25% is indirect labor and supervision) and total overhead was $450,800. Determine (a) the overhead rate, (b) the volume variance, (c) the total over- or underapplied overhead.

**14-16** For purposes of obtaining an overhead rate, a firm has budgeted the following:

| | |
|---|---|
| Direct labor hours | 20,000 |
| Nonvariable overhead | $200,000 |

At the end of the period, a favorable volume variance of $15,000 was reported. How many direct labor hours were recorded?

**14-17** Job 87M had direct material costs of $400 and a total cost of $2,100. Overhead is applied at the rate of 75% of prime cost (direct material plus direct labor). (a) How much direct labor was incurred on this job, and (b) how much overhead was applied?

**14-18** JTW manufactures cogs for tracked vehicles. Budgeted nonvariable overhead for the year is $200,000 and is applied at the rate of 80% of direct labor cost. The volume (capacity) variance for the year is unfavorable to the extent of $12,000. Determine (a) the originally budgeted direct labor cost, (b) the applied fixed overhead, and (c) the actual direct labor cost.

**14-19** The flexible budget for indirect manufacturing costs (factory overhead) is $50,000 plus $1 per unit produced; indirect manufacturing costs are applied at a rate of $3 per unit of finished product. If the volume variance for the period indicated $1,000 underabsorbed, how many units were produced?

**14-20** Froogle, Inc., incurs indirect costs uniformly throughout the year, although production peaks during the second and third quarters. Fixed overhead is budgeted at $42 million and machine hours (used as the basis for applying overhead) are budgeted at 100,000. Production for the year (in percentage terms) is 15-35-40-10 by quarter. What is the planned volume variance for each quarter, individually and cumulatively?

**14-21** In its first year of operations, Blythe Manufacturing Company estimated overhead costs and activity in order to obtain a predetermined overhead rate. At year-end, overhead was overapplied by $12 million. It has been decided that this is the result of faulty estimates. Of the year's production, 10% is in work-in-progress, 25% is in finished goods, and the rest has been sold. Give the journal entry to close out the overapplied overhead.

**14-22** Hubris, Inc., operates under job order conditions. The firm began the month with $23 of work-in-process, and cost of goods manufactured was $262. A summary of the transactions for the month is as follows:

| | |
|---|---|
| Direct materials requisitions | $ 67 |
| Direct labor | 112 |
| Actual overhead | 89 |
| Applied overhead | 91 |

Using the data, (a) prepare simple journal entries to record the above transactions, (b) determine and close to Cost of Goods Sold any over- or underapplied overhead, and (c) determine the ending Work-in-Process inventory.

**14-23** Job 280Z has costs accumulated to date as follows:

| | |
|---|---|
| Direct materials | $13,200 |
| Direct labor ($7 per hour) | 2,800 |
| Overhead (80% of direct labor) | 2,240 |
| | $18,240 |

Completing the job required additional materials of $2,000 and 150 direct labor hours (of which 10 were the result of an abnormal inefficiency). (a) What was the total (normal) cost of this job, and (b) assuming all costs were entered in the Work-in-Process account, what is the proper entry to transfer costs from Work-in-Process on completion of the job?

**14-24** Opinion Research, Inc., has developed a flexible budget for indirect costs of $30,000 per month plus $20 per client hour. In July the firm based its overhead rate on the assumption that it would work 3,000 hours. For July the actual overhead costs were $90,000 and client hours amounted to 2,800. Determine the total cost charged to Job 717 if direct costs were $26,000 and 850 hours were worked for the client.

**14-25** Health Care, Inc., is a consulting firm. It applies indirect costs to contracts on the basis of billable hours, which represents its best measure of output. For the year the firm projected 18,000 billable hours and indirect costs as $243,000 fixed and $162,000 variable. Direct costs are estimated as $25 per billable hour. Determine (a) the rate for applying variable and fixed overhead and (b) the cost assigned to contract 117, which is estimated to require 360 total billable hours and is 70% complete.

**14-26** Home Contracting, Inc., does additions and remodeling work. Each contract is treated as a separate job. The firm's pricing policy is to estimate the direct costs of the job, apply overhead as a percentage of the direct costs, and then add 40% to this for profit. For the next year, direct costs are estimated at $800,000 and indirect costs are estimated at $1,300,000. Determine (a) the overhead rate to be used: (b) the price to be quoted to a customer for a gazebo that is expected to have direct materials costs of $2,500 and direct labor costs of $1,500; and (c) the under- or overapplied overhead for the year if actual direct costs are $720,000 and overhead is $1,200,000.

## PROBLEMS AND CASES

**14-27 Cost flow.**

Pedco uses a job order cost accounting system. Overhead is applied at the rate of $2.50 per direct labor hour. Inventory data are as follows:

| | December 1 | December 31 |
|---|---|---|
| Raw materials | $12,000 | $ ? |
| Work-in-process | 14,000 | ? |
| Finished goods | 21,000 | 24,000 |

During December, the following data were recorded:

| | |
|---|---|
| Materials purchased | $ 40,000 |
| Raw materials used | 42,000 |
| Direct labor (12,000 hours) | 36,000 |
| Manufacturing overhead (actual) | 31,000 |
| Cost of goods completed | 105,000 |
| Selling and administration expense | 2,000 |
| Sales | 98,000 |

**Required**

Prepare a statement of cost of goods manufactured and an income statement. Overapplied or underapplied overhead is closed monthly to the income statement.

**14-28 Job order: Cost flow** (CPA adapted).

The Rebecca Corporation is a manufacturer of machines made to customer specifications. All production costs are accumulated by means of a job order costing system. The following information is available at the beginning of the month of October 19X0.

| | |
|---|---|
| Direct materials inventory, October 1 | $16,200 |
| Work-in-process, October 1 | $ 3,600 |

A review of the job order cost sheets revealed the composition of the work-in-process inventory on October 1, as follows:

| | |
|---|---|
| Direct materials | $1,320 |
| Direct labor (300 hours) | 1,500 |
| Factory overhead applied | 780 |
| | $3,600 |

Activity during the month of October was as follows:

Direct materials costing $20,000 were purchased.
Direct labor for job orders totaled 3,300 hours at $5 per hour.
Factory overhead was applied to production at the rate of $2.60 per direct labor hour.

On October 31, inventories consisted of the following components.

| | |
|---|---|
| Direct materials inventory | $17,000 |
| Work-in-process inventory | |
| Direct materials | $4,320 |
| Direct labor (500 hours) | 2,500 |
| Factory overhead applied | 1,300 |
| | $8,120 |

**Required**
Prepare in good form a detailed statement of the cost of goods manufactured for the month of October.

**14-29 Job order cost entries.**
S-F Manufacturing Company performs a variety of activities under job order conditions. During the week, the following activities took place.

1. Received 600 units of material at a cost of $12 each.
2. Issued 120 units of material for Job 26M and 80 units for Job 27N.
3. Received miscellaneous supplies amounting to $420. These are not inventoried but are sent directly to the departments. The cost is treated as overhead.
4. Job 26M required 110 hours of direct labor and Job 27N required 80 hours. Direct labor receives $11 per hour.
5. Overhead is applied at the rate of 120% of direct labor.
6. Other indirect costs were

| | |
|---|---|
| Utilities | $500 |
| Depreciation | 900 |
| Supervision | 600 |

7. Beginning work-in-process (Job 26M) was $1,700.
8. Job 26M was completed during the week.
9. Half the units produced on Job 26M were delivered to customers.

**Required**
Set up T-accounts and record the data for the week. Use the following titles.

| | |
|---|---|
| Direct Materials | Finished Goods |
| Payroll Clearing | Cost of Goods Sold |
| Overhead Control | Job 26M |
| Overhead Applied | Job 27N |
| Work-in-Process | |

**14-30 Job costing: Disposition of overhead.**
At the beginning of the year, Floyd's Body Shop estimated that its total overhead would be $175,000 for the current year. It was also estimated that the firm would use 25,000 hours of direct labor. In fact, total overhead turned out to be $190,000, and the firm used 26,000 hours of direct labor.

**Required**

**a.** Determine the total cost that would be charged to Work-in-Process during the period for job 86-244, which required materials of $450 and 5 hours of labor. Labor is paid $6 per hour.

**b.** For the year in total, determine the amount of over- or underapplied overhead.

**c.** During the year the firm's cost of goods sold totaled $650,000. At the end of the year there were jobs amounting to $10,000 in ending work-in-process and $40,000 in finished goods. Sales for the period were $1,000,000. Prepare the journal entry to dispose of over- or underapplied overhead if it is allocated among ending inventories and cost of goods sold.

**14-31 Journal entries for under- or overapplied overhead.**
A firm began the month of March with the following inventory balances.

| | |
|---|---|
| Raw materials | $22,000 |
| Work-in-process | 5,000 |
| Finished goods | 45,000 |

During March, $50,000 of materials were put into production. Direct labor costs amounted to $40,000. The cost of goods completed during March was $135,000, and the cost of goods sold was $150,000. Overhead was applied to production at the rate of $1.50 for each dollar of direct labor. The actual overhead costs for March amounted to $66,000. Materials purchases were $40,000.

**Required**
Prepare the journal entry that allocates over- or underapplied overhead to inventories and cost of goods sold in proportion to the ending balance in the appropriate accounts.

**14-32 Indirect costs.**
Garages, Inc., constructs garages employing job order cost techniques. It applies indirect costs based on a percentage of direct costs. Costs for the third quarter have been budgeted as follows:

| | |
|---|---|
| Direct materials costs | $60,000 |
| Direct labor costs | 30,000 |
| Indirect costs | 45,000 |

During the third quarter, actual costs were recorded as follows:

| | |
|---|---|
| Direct materials costs | $50,000 |
| Direct labor costs | 35,000 |
| Indirect costs | 45,000 |

**Required**

**a.** At what rate are indirect costs applied?

**b.** For the third quarter, how much overhead was applied?

**c.** Was overhead over- or underapplied, and by how much?
**d.** Give the summary entries for actual and applied overhead.

**14-33 Overhead variances.**
Pesces, Inc., manufactures nets for shrimp trawls. These are produced on a job lot basis. The overhead rate in the assembly department is $0.80 for fixed overhead and $1.20 for variable overhead per direct labor hour. During the month of February the assembly department was charged with 10,000 direct labor hours. Actual overhead costs for the month were $13,100 variable and $9,400 fixed. Variable overhead was budgeted at $1.20 per hour, and fixed overhead was budgeted at $9,600 per month.

**Required**
**a.** What was the monthly budgeted level of activity?
**b.** How much overhead was applied to work-in-process?
**c.** What is the amount of over- or underapplied overhead?
**d.** What is the volume (or denominator) variance for fixed overhead?

**14-34 Overhead application and disposition.**
Custom, Inc., manufactures and assembles various types of small subassemblies for other manufacturers. Owing to the diversity of the work, units produced is not a good measure of activity or output.

The firm operates a job order system employing normal costing. In machining, overhead is applied at a predetermined rate based on machine hours. In assembly, overhead is applied at a predetermined rate based on direct labor cost in that department.

The originally *projected* data for the second quarter are as follows:

| | Machining | Assembly | Totals |
|---|---|---|---|
| Materials cost | $200,000 | — | $200,000 |
| Direct labor cost | $ 50,000 | $100,000 | $150,000 |
| Overhead cost | $ 50,000 | $ 40,000 | $ 90,000 |
| Machine hours | 2,000 | — | 2,000 |
| Direct labor hours | 2,500 | 5,000 | 7,500 |
| Number of employees | 5 | 10 | 15 |
| Average temperature, °F | 65 | 70 | 135 |

The *actual* costs and hours for the quarter were as follows:

| | Machining | Assembly | Totals |
|---|---|---|---|
| Materials cost | $210,000 | $ 10,000 | $220,000 |
| Direct labor cost | $ 55,000 | $110,000 | $165,000 |
| Overhead cost | $ 56,000 | $ 42,000 | $ 98,000 |
| Machine hours | 2,000 | — | 2,000 |
| Direct labor hours | 2,600 | 5,100 | 7,700 |
| Number of employees | 5.5 | 11.0 | 16.5 |
| Average temperature, °F | 68 | 72 | 140 |

**Required**
**a.** Calculate predetermined overhead rates for each department.
**b.** Record entries to apply overhead in each department.

**c.** Record entries to close over- or underapplied overhead in each department to Cost of Goods Sold.

**14-35 Income statement with allocation of over- or underapplied overhead** (SMA adapted). Nicole Limited is a company that produces machinery to customer orders, using a job order cost system. Manufacturing overhead is applied to production using a predetermined rate. This overhead rate is set at the beginning of each fiscal year by forecasting the year's overhead and relating it to direct labour dollars. The budget for the company's last fiscal year was as follows:

| | |
|---|---|
| Direct labour | $1,200,000 |
| Manufacturing overhead | $ 720,000 |

As at the end of the year, two jobs were complete. These were 1768B, with total direct labour charges of $11,000, and 1819C, with total direct labour charges of $39,000. On these jobs, machine hours were 287 hours for 1768B and 647 hours for 1819C. Direct materials issued to 1768B amounted to $22,000 and to 1819C amounted to $42,000.

Total charges to the Manufacturing Overhead Control account for the year were $897,000, and direct labour charges made to all jobs amounted to $1,583,600, representing 247,216 direct labour hours.

There were no beginning inventories. In addition to the ending Work-in-Process just described, the ending Finished Goods showed a balance of $72,000.

Sales for the year amounted to $2,700,680, cost of goods sold totaled $648,000, and selling, general, and administrative expenses were $1,857,870.

The amounts for inventories and cost of goods sold were not adjusted for any over- or underapplication of manufacturing overhead to production. It is the company's practice to allocate any over- or underapplied overhead to inventories and cost of goods sold.

**Required**

Prepare an income statement for the company for the year. Your answer should include supporting schedules for the amount of over- or underapplied overhead, the allocation of such an amount, and the amount of work-in-process before this allocation. Income tax is to be provided for at the rate of 40%.

**14-36 Normal and actual costing.**

The following data are for the third-quarter operations of the Guinn Brewery.

| | Planned Costs and Hours | Actual Costs and Hours |
|---|---|---|
| Direct materials costs | Not given | $ 80,000 |
| Direct labor cost | Not given | $120,000 |
| Factory overhead[a] | $50,000 | $ 60,000 |
| Direct labor hours | 10,000 | 11,000 |

[a]Factory overhead is applied on the basis of direct labor hours.

The firm produces only one product, although it employs job order cost techniques. The product is produced in batches, and each batch is accounted for as a separate job. During the third quarter, 1,000 batches were produced and 900 batches were sold. There were no beginning inventories.

**Required**

**a.** Assume Guinn employs *normal costing*.

1. What is the overhead rate?
2. Give the entries for overhead and direct costs.
3. Using normal costing, what was the manufacturing cost per job?
4. Under- or overapplied overhead is to be prorated between ending inventory and cost of goods sold. Provide the entry.

**b.** Assume Guinn employs *actual costing*.

1. What is the actual overhead rate?
2. Give the entries for overhead and direct costs.
3. Using actual costing, what was the manufacturing cost per job?

**14-37 Actual, normal, and standard costing compared.**

For the current period Mason Metals had budgeted variable overhead costs to be $150,000 and fixed overhead to be $90,000. The firm anticipated using 75,000 machine hours during the period to produce 10,000 units of product.

During the period the firm actually produced 11,200 units of product. Actual variable overhead costs amounted to $165,000, and actual fixed overhead was $92,000. The firm used 85,120 machine hours to produce the products.

**Required**

Determine the amount of variable and fixed overhead that would be charged to the units produced, the amount of over- or underapplied variable and fixed overhead, and the volume variance if the firm uses

**a.** An actual cost system.

**b.** A normal cost system with overhead applied on the basis of machine hours.

**c.** A standard cost system with overhead applied on the basis of machine hours (the standards are derivable from the initial budget data).

**14-38 Straightforward job order costing.**

Beckke Machine Tools, Inc., uses a job cost system. During March, the firm worked on three orders: A, B, and C. The budget for March anticipated that the firm would use 400 direct labor hours and that total overhead would be $2,000. During March the firm used $4,000 of materials for job A; $6,000 for job B; and $9,000 for job C. Labor is paid $8 per hour. The firm used 125 direct labor hours for job A, 210 for job B, and 80 for job C. Job A was completed and sold, job B was completed and is in finished goods inventory, and job C is not yet complete. Overhead is applied to jobs on the basis of direct labor hours. Actual overhead for March was $2,050.

**Required**

**a.** Determine the cost of ending work-in-process inventory.

**b.** Determine the amount of over- or underapplied overhead for March.

**14-39 Job costing and pricing.**

State Printing Ink provides all of the routine printing for state agencies. It is operated as a profit center; full normal cost is 80% of the amount charged to agencies using its services. Overhead is charged at a rate equal to 40% of prime costs.

**Required**

**a.** A recent job for the agency required direct materials costing $2,000 and direct labor costing $5,200. What was the total cost of this job?

**b.** What amount would have been billed on the job in (a)?

**c.** For the month, the printing operation accumulated actual costs as follows: direct material of $310,000, direct labor of $520,000, and overhead of $348,000. What was over- or underapplied overhead?

**d.** Assuming that over- or underapplied overhead is closed to the income statement monthly, what was income for the month?

**14-40 Cost accumulation.**

The MN Company is a machine shop specializing in custom lathe work. All materials are provided by MN's customers. MN incurs only direct labor and indirect manufacturing costs. These costs for the month, both budgeted and actual, are as follows:

| | Actual | Budget |
|---|---|---|
| Direct labor | $45,000 | $50,000 |
| Indirect manufacturing | 30,000 | 40,000 |

Overhead is applied using a predetermined rate based on labor cost. The only job still in process at the end of the month, job 7-11, has involved direct labor to the extent of $4,000 to date.

**Required**

**a.** What is MN's overhead rate?

**b.** Give the entries to record actual and applied overhead for the month. Also, determine whether overhead is overapplied or underapplied, and by how much.

**c.** What is the total cost to date of job 7-11?

**d.** If MN had used an actual rate to apply overhead, what would be the effect on the total cost of the one job still in process?

**14-41 Job order entries** (SMA adapted).

Laramie Ltd. uses a job cost system. At the beginning of the month of June, two orders were in process, as follows:

| | Order 88 | Order 105 |
|---|---|---|
| Raw materials | $1,000 | $900 |
| Direct labour | 1,200 | 200 |
| Manufacturing overhead absorbed | 1,800 | 300 |

There was no inventory of finished goods on June 1. During the month of June, orders 106 to 120, inclusive, were put into process.

Raw materials requirements amounted to $13,000, direct labour expenses for the month were $20,000, and actual manufacturing overhead recorded during the month amounted to $28,000.

The only order in process at the end of June was order 120, and the costs incurred for this order were $1,150 of raw materials and $1,000 of direct labour. In addition, order 118, which was 100% complete, was still on hand as of June 30. Total costs allocated to this order were $3,300. The firm's overhead allocation rate in June was the same as that used in May and is based on labour cost.

**Required**

**a.** Prepare journal entries, with supporting calculations, to record the cost of goods manufactured, the cost of goods sold, and the closing of the over- or underabsorbed manufacturing overhead to Cost of Goods Sold.

**b.** Explain another method of dealing with the over- or underabsorbed manufacturing overhead.

**14-42 Cost of goods manufactured.**

Archie's Auto Customizing Service had the following activity for the week.

| Date | Job Number | Materials Requisitions | Labor Hours |
|---|---|---|---|
| 8/1[a] | 116 | $3,400 | 110 |
| 8/1[a] | 117 | 2,600 | 80 |
| 8/4 | 116 | 700 | 15 |
| 8/4 | 117 | 900 | 30 |
| 8/4 | 118 | 2,100 | 50 |
| 8/5 | 117 | 400 | 35 |
| 8/5 | 118 | 2,600 | 40 |
| 8/6 | 119 | 1,500 | 80 |
| 8/7 | 118 | — | 30 |
| 8/7 | 119 | 700 | 45 |
| 8/8 | 120 | 2,300 | 40 |
| 8/8 | 121 | 1,700 | 30 |

[a]Beginning inventory of jobs in process.

Direct labor is paid $20 per hour and overhead is charged at the rate of $15 per hour. Jobs 116, 117, 118, and 120 were completed during the week.

**Required**

Prepare, in summary form, a statement of cost of goods manufactured with supporting calculations.

**14-43 Journal entries.**

At the beginning of the accounting period, ABC estimated that its total overhead would be $80,000. Overhead is applied to jobs on the basis of direct labor cost. Direct labor was budgeted to cost $200,000 this period. During the period only three jobs were worked on. The following summarizes the direct materials and labor costs of each.

| | Job 1231 | Job 1232 | Job 1233 |
|---|---|---|---|
| Direct materials | $45,000 | $70,000 | $30,000 |
| Direct labor | 70,000 | 90,000 | 50,000 |

Job 1231 was finished and sold: job 1232 was finished but is awaiting sale; and job 1233 is still being worked on. Actual overhead for the period was $82,000.

**Required**

Prepare journal entries as follows:

**a.** Costs incurred in production

**b.** Cost of goods manufactured

**c.** Cost of goods sold

**d.** Allocation of over- or underapplied overhead in proportion to the *ending balance* in Work-in-Process, Finished Goods, and Cost of Goods Sold

**14-44 Job order costs.**

Vern's Van Service customizes light trucks to customers' orders. This month they worked on five jobs, numbered 207 through 211. Materials requisitions for the month were as follows:

| Ticket | Carpet | Paint | Electronics | Other | Total |
|---|---|---|---|---|---|
| 207 | $ 40 | $350 | $580 | — | $ 970 |
| 208 | 75 | 200 | 375 | — | 650 |
| 209 | 200 | 400 | 200 | — | 800 |
| 210 | 30 | 150 | 770 | — | 950 |
| 211 | 60 | — | 50 | — | 110 |
| Indirect | — | — | — | 750 | 750 |
| Total | | | | | $4,230 |

An analysis of the payroll records revealed the following distribution for labor costs.

| | Job | | | | | | |
|---|---|---|---|---|---|---|---|
| | 207 | 208 | 209 | 210 | 211 | Other | Total |
| Direct labor | $1,400 | $1,200 | $800 | $1,700 | $400 | — | $5,500 |
| Indirect labor | — | — | — | — | — | $2,200 | 2,200 |
| Total | | | | | | | $7,700 |

Other overhead costs (consisting of rent, depreciation, taxes, insurance, utilities, and so forth) amounted to $3,600. At the beginning of the period, management anticipated that total overhead would amount to $6,400 and total direct labor would amount to $5,000. Overhead is applied on the basis of direct labor dollars.

Jobs 207 through 210 were finished during the month; job 211 is still being worked on. Jobs 207 through 209 were picked up and paid for by customers. Job 210 is still on the lot waiting to be picked up.

**Required**

**a.** Prepare all the journal entries to reflect the incurrence of materials, labor, and overhead cost, the application of overhead, and the transfer of units to finished goods and cost of goods sold.

**b.** Close over- or underapplied overhead to Cost of Goods Sold.

**14-45 Accounting for job costs: Predetermined overhead rates.**

Hour House Clockworks manufactures its different products in batches of 100, using job order costing for each batch. Three departments are involved. The budget data for each department for November are as follows:

| | Department M | Department N | Department O |
|---|---|---|---|
| Direct materials cost | $44,000 | $52,000 | $18,000 |
| Direct labor cost | $60,000 | $48,000 | $50,000[a] |
| Overhead cost | $63,000 | $36,000 | $40,000 |
| Direct labor hours | 5,000 | 4,000[a] | 4,000 |
| Machine hours | 3,000[a] | 1,000 | — |

[a]Overhead is applied in this department on the basis of this item.

**Required**

**a.** What is the predetermined overhead rate for each department?

**b.** Job K-63 was started and completed during the month. The summary job cost sheet showed the following:

| | Department M | Department N | Department O |
|---|---|---|---|
| Materials | $4,500 | $5,100 | $1,900 |
| Labor | $5,800 | $4,900 | $5,200 |
| Labor hours | 480 | 410 | 420 |
| Machine hours | 310 | 90 | — |

What was the total cost of Job K-63?

**c.** Department N had actual overhead costs for the month of $38,700. Actual labor hours were 3,900 and actual machine hours were 950. What was the over- or underapplied overhead for the month?

**14-46 Job order: Services.**

Promo, Inc., provides incentive programs for a variety of clients. Clients are billed at 150% of cost, where cost is defined as direct costs plus indirect costs applied at a rate equal to 90% of direct costs. There were no contracts in progress at the beginning of the period. The following events took place during the period.

1. Received 4,000 volumes of the Founder's "Inspirational Handbook" at a cost of $15 each.
2. Issued 80 volumes to client A, 60 to client B, and 110 to client C.
3. Salary distribution was $6,000 to client A, $4,200 to client B, and $4,800 to client C.
4. Other direct costs were $1,800 to client A, $1,200 to client B, and $1,400 to client C.
5. Indirect costs totaled $23,000. Over- or underapplied overhead is closed to cost of completed contracts.
6. The work for client B was completed.

**Required**

**a.** Journalize the foregoing transactions.

**b.** Promo uses the completed-contract method for reporting income; that is, revenues and matching expenses are not reported until an engagement is finished. Prepare an income statement for the period.

**14-47 Job order: Comprehensive** (CMA adapted).

The following data apply to department 203 of the Acee Electric Company.

**DEPARTMENT 203: WORK-IN-PROCESS, BEGINNING OF THE YEAR**

| Job Number | Material | Labor | Overhead | Total |
|---|---|---|---|---|
| 1376 | $17,500 | $22,000 | $33,000 | $72,500 |

**DEPARTMENT 203: COSTS FOR THE YEAR**

| | Material | Labor | Other | Total |
|---|---|---|---|---|
| Incurred by jobs | | | | |
| 1376 | $ 1,000 | $ 7,000 | $ — | $ 8,000 |
| 1377 | 26,000 | 53,000 | — | 79,000 |
| 1378 | 12,000 | 9,000 | — | 21,000 |
| 1379 | 4,000 | 1,000 | — | 5,000 |
| Not incurred by jobs | | | | |
| Indirect materials and supplies | 15,000 | — | — | 15,000 |
| Indirect labor | — | 53,000 | — | 53,000 |
| Employee benefits | — | — | 23,000 | 23,000 |
| Depreciation | — | — | 12,000 | 12,000 |
| Supervision | — | 20,000 | — | 20,000 |
| Total | $58,000 | $143,000 | $35,000 | $236,000 |

**DEPARTMENT 203: OVERHEAD RATE FOR THE YEAR**

| | |
|---|---|
| Budgeted overhead | |
| Variable | |
| Indirect materials | $ 16,000 |
| Indirect labor | 56,000 |
| Employee benefits | 24,000 |
| Fixed | |
| Supervision | 20,000 |
| Depreciation | 12,000 |
| Total | $128,000 |
| Budgeted direct labor dollars | $ 80,000 |
| Rate per direct labor dollar ($128,000 ÷ $80,000) | 160% |

**Required**

**a.** What is the algebraic form of the flexible budget for overhead?

**b.** What are the fixed *and* variable components of the overhead rate?

**c.** What are the actual, budgeted, and absorbed overhead costs?

**d.** For the year, determine whether overhead was over- or underapplied. Also, determine the overhead volume variance.

**e.** Job 1376 was the only job completed during the year; it was also the only job sold. What was the "normal" cost of goods manufactured and sold for this job?

**f.** What is the work-in-process inventory in department 203 at the end of the year, by job and by cost?

**14-48 Multiple jobs: Comprehensive** (CMA adapted).
Baehr Company is a manufacturing company with a fiscal year that runs from July 1 to June 30. The company uses a job order accounting system for its production costs.

A predetermined overhead rate based upon direct labor hours is used to apply overhead to individual jobs. A flexible budget of overhead costs was prepared for the 19X7–X8 fiscal year as follows:

| Direct labor hours | 100,000 | 120,000 | 140,000 |
|---|---|---|---|
| Variable overhead costs | $325,000 | $390,000 | $455,000 |
| Fixed overhead costs | 216,000 | 216,000 | 216,000 |
| Total overhead | $541,000 | $606,000 | $671,000 |

Although the annual ideal capacity is 150,000 direct labor hours, company officials have determined 120,000 direct labor hours as normal capacity for the year.

The following information is for November 19X7. Jobs X7-50 and X7-51 were completed during November.

| | |
|---|---|
| Inventories, November 1 | |
| Raw materials and supplies | $ 10,500 |
| Work-in-process (job X7-50) | 54,000 |
| Finished goods | 112,500 |
| Purchases of Raw Materials and Supplies | |
| Raw materials | $135,000 |
| Supplies | 15,000 |
| Materials and Supplies Requisitioned for Production | |
| Job X7-50 | $ 45,000 |
| Job X7-51 | 37,500 |
| Job X7-52 | 25,500 |
| Supplies | 12,000 |
| | $120,000 |
| Factory Direct Labor Hours | |
| Job X7-50 | 3,500 DLH |
| Job X7-51 | 3,000 DLH |
| Job X7-52 | 2,000 DLH |
| Labor Costs | |
| Direct labor wages | $ 51,000 |
| Indirect labor wages (4,000 hours) | 15,000 |
| Supervisory salaries | 6,000 |
| | $ 72,000 |
| Building Occupancy Costs (heat, light, depreciation) | |
| Factory facilities | $ 6,500 |
| Sales offices | 1,500 |
| Administration offices | 1,000 |
| | $ 9,000 |

| | |
|---|---|
| Factory Equipment Costs | |
| Power | $ 4,000 |
| Repairs and maintenance | 1,500 |
| Depreciation | 1,500 |
| Other | 1,000 |
| | $ 8,000 |

**Required**

**a.** What is the predetermined rate to be used to apply overhead to individual jobs during the fiscal year?

**b.** Prepare a schedule showing the costs assigned to each of jobs X7-50, X7-51, and X7-52.

**c.** What is cost of goods manufactured for November?

**d.** What is the cost assigned to work-in-process on November 30?

**e.** Determine whether overhead for November is overapplied or underapplied, and by what amount.

**14-49 Effects of automation on overhead rates.**

"Our costs are out of control, our accounting system is screwed up, or both!" screamed the sales manager. "We are simply noncompetitive on a great many of the jobs we bid on. Why just last week we lost a customer when a competitor underbid us by 35%! And I bid the job at *cost* because the customer has been with us for years but has been complaining about our prices."

This problem, raised at the weekly management meeting, has been getting worse over the years. The Johnson Tool Company produces parts to customer orders. When the firm first became successful, it employed nearly 500 skilled machinists. Over the years the firm has become increasingly automated. The firm now employs only 75 production workers, but output has quadrupled.

The problems raised by the sales manager are typified by the portions of two bid sheets reproduced on page 668. These figures are from the cutting department, but the relative size of the three types of manufacturing costs are similar for other departments.

The cutting department charges overhead to products based upon direct labor hours. For the current period, the department expects to use 4,000 direct labor hours. Departmental overhead, consisting mostly of depreciation on the highly automated equipment, is expected to be $1,480,000.

An employee can typically set up any job on the appropriate equipment in about 15 minutes. Once machines are operating, an employee can tend five to eight machines simultaneously. All that is required is to load or unload materials and monitor calibrations. The department's equipment will log a total of 25,000 hours of run time in the current period.

Bid 74683 was one on which the firm was substantially underbid by a competitor. The firm did get the job for bid 74687, but the larger jobs are harder to find. Small jobs arise frequently, but the firm is rarely successful in obtaining them.

**Required**

Critique the current cost accounting system. Suggest a better approach. What would be the costs of the jobs, using your improved approach?

**CUTTING DEPARTMENT**

Bid # 74683 Machine Run Time 3 Hours

| | | |
|---|---|---|
| Materials | | |
| Steel sheeting | | $280.25 |
| Direct labor | | |
| Equipment setup | ¼ hour @ $12.50 | 3.13 |
| Equipment tending | 1 hour @ $12.50 | 12.50 |
| Overhead | 1¼ hours @ $370 | 462.50 |
| Total cost | | $758.38 |

**CUTTING DEPARTMENT**

Bid # 74687 Machine Run Time 11 Hours

| | | |
|---|---|---|
| Materials | | |
| Steel sheeting | | $2,440.50 |
| Direct labor | | |
| Equipment setup | ¼ hour @ $12.50 | 3.13 |
| Equipment tending | 1¼ hours @ $12.50 | 15.63 |
| Overhead | 1½ hours @ $370 | 555.00 |
| Total cost | | $3,014.26 |

**14-50 Job costing: International financial institution—difficult.**
The International Money Fund invests customers' funds in high-yield, short-term loans to the central banks of numerous countries. The loans are denominated in the currency of the borrowing country. Although the yields are high, there is considerable risk due to fluctuating exchange rates.

Income and expenses for each customer's account are accrued daily. Foreign exchange gains or losses are apportioned to customer accounts based on the end-of-the-day balance in each account (after the account has been adjusted for expenses, investments, withdrawals, and earned interest).

There is a $100 transaction fee for deposits and withdrawals. In addition, the fund charges a management fee of 0.003% of each customer's daily beginning account balance. Deposited funds begin to earn interest on the day following deposit (funds deposited on Monday do not receive interest for Monday; the first interest is accrued on Tuesday). However, withdrawn funds do earn interest for the day of withdrawal. Thus interest is accrued on the beginning daily balance in each customer's account. All customer account records are maintained by the fund in U.S. dollars (rounded to the nearest dollar).

Interest income is calculated by multiplying the beginning loan balance by the daily interest rate. The accrued interest is converted to dollars using the end-of-the-day foreign exchange rate. Foreign exchange gains and losses are calculated by converting the beginning loan balance at both the beginning- and end-of-the-day exchange rates and finding the difference. The beginning balance for a loan for the next day is today's balance plus accrued interest denominated in the foreign currency (that is, loans are compounded daily). Data for Thursday, July 20, are as follows:

**Loans Outstanding to Central Banks**

| Country | Amount (currency) | Daily Interest Rate |
|---|---|---|
| Argentina | 1,640,000,000,000 (peso) | 0.0025 (0.25%) |
| Brazil | 27,869,000,000 (cruzeiro) | 0.00139 |
| Ecuador | 6,600,000,000 (sucre) | 0.0005 |
| Peru | 50,722,000,000 (sol) | 0.00111 |
| Venezuela | 214,690,000 (bolivar) | 0.00194 |

Total customer deposits at the beginning of the day were $575,000,000. No new loans were made on July 20, nor did any loan mature.

Only two customers made transactions during the day. Mahatma Prospet n.v. deposited 115,540,000 Pakistan rupees, and Krykstalis Shipping withdrew 296,920,000 Greek drachmas. The Mahatma account balance at the beginning of the day as reflected in the fund's records was $10,750,000; the Krykstalis beginning balance was $22,380,000. Transactions are recorded using the end-of-the-day foreign exchange rate. Applicable exchange rates for the day were as follows:

| | Currency per U.S. Dollar | |
|---|---|---|
| Country (currency) | Beginning of the Day | End of the Day |
| Argentina (peso) | 20,500.00 | 21,000.00 |
| Brazil (cruzeiro) | 185.79 | 184.50 |
| China (yuan) | 1.9563 | 1.970 |
| Ecuador (sucre) | 33.00 | 33.00 |
| Greece (drachma) | 70.75 | 74.23 |
| Pakistan (rupee) | 12.3178 | 11.554 |
| Peru (sol) | 742.60 | 725.30 |
| South Korea (won) | 741.20 | 739.60 |
| Thailand (baht) | 23.00 | 23.00 |
| Venezuela (bolivar) | 4.2937 | 4.2265 |

**Required**

**a.** Determine the total interest accrued for the fund on July 20.

**b.** Determine the total foreign exchange gain or loss for the fund on July 20.

**c.** Determine the ending balance in the Mahatma and Krykstalis accounts as well as the total ending balance of all customers' accounts for July 20.

**d.** Determine the net income earned by Mahatma Prospet n.v. and Krykstalis Shipping for July 20 from the fund.

# APPENDIX 14

# PAYROLL ACCOUNTING

The required record keeping and number of calculations required for payroll accounting, even in small firms, is burdensome. As such, it is not surprising that payroll accounting is generally one of the first areas to be computerized or subcontracted to a computer service bureau. However, to illustrate the complexity and data requirements of payroll accounting, this appendix examines a manual payroll system.

A payroll accounting system must be tailored to provide the specific information desired by management, while keeping in mind government-mandated record-keeping requirements. Although we cannot possibly cover every variation that is possible in payroll systems, the description that follows is a fairly common system for a manufacturing firm. A few alternatives to the system are mentioned at appropriate points.

The system presented in this appendix is for a manufacturing firm that uses standard costing. For this system, only one time-keeping record is used per employee: This record shows total hours worked, nonproductive time, and overtime hours. A simple clock card such as that shown in Figure 14-5 can be used to gather this information. Each day the employee punches in for regular hours worked and separately for any overtime. Daily the foreman notes any nonproductive time and the reason for it.

Once a week the time cards are forwarded to a cost clerk for summarizing the hours worked in each department. Initially, only the hours worked and a breakdown into productive and nonproductive time needs to be recorded. The top portion of Figure 14-6 presents data for an example that follows shortly.

***Variation***

*Note that if management wished to charge specific jobs with the actual cost of labor used on each job, an additional form would be required. A record would be needed for each employee of the time spent on specific jobs. These daily time reports would then need to be collated, and*

Employee ______________________ Rate Scale ______________________

Department ______________ From ______________ To ______________

| | Regular | | Overtime | | Total Hours | |
|---|---|---|---|---|---|---|
| | In | Out | In | Out | Regular | Overtime |
| Monday | | | | | | |
| Tuesday | | | | | | |
| Wednesday | | | | | | |
| Thursday | | | | | | |
| Friday | | | | | | |
| Saturday | | | | | | |
| | | | | Weekly total | | |

Nonproductive time (list) ______________________________

Employee's signature ______________________ Supervisor's signature ______________________

**FIGURE 14-5 Employee's time card.**

*appropriate times and costs charged to each job. In addition, it would be necessary to verify that each employee's individual time reports accounted for all the time recorded on the clock card. The report in Figure 14-6 would then be prepared from the individual time reports, and the clock cards could be sent straight to payroll.*

***Variation***

*If an employee works for more than one department, or is temporarily transferred to a department other than the one in which he or she normally works, a notation should be made on the time card. This notation then allows the cost clerk to assign the employee properly to the appropriate department when preparing the departmental summary forms.*

Once the labor hours have been summarized as in Figure 14-6, the time cards can be forwarded to the payroll department. The cost clerk can then prepare the cost distribution for departmental labor.

In the system illustrated here, only the base wage rate is included as the cost of direct labor. For each employee, the cost clerk can then note the employee's wage scale and multiply by the hours worked to get direct labor costs. Note that a distinction is made between the amount paid for labor at the base rate and the amount of overtime premium paid. This

**Departmental Labor Summary**

Department 215 Date Jan. 15

| Employee | Rate | Hours Reg. | Hours Over. | Base Pay | Overtime Premium | Nonproductive Hours | Cost | Expln* | Total |
|---|---|---|---|---|---|---|---|---|---|
| Jim Jones | $7.50 | 40 | | $300.00 | | | | | $300.00 |
| Sally Smith | 7.50 | 40 | 5 | 337.50 | $18.75 | | | | 356.25 |
| Bill Wilson | 8.00 | | | | | 40 | $320 | V | 320.00 |
| Total | | | | $637.50 | $18.75 | | $320 | | $976.25 |

*S = sick leave  MB = machine breakdown  O = other (explain) ______
V = vacation  MU = materials unavailable

**Labor Cost Distribution**

| | | |
|---|---|---|
| Direct labor cost – Dept. 215 | 637.50 | |
| Overhead control – Dept. 215 | 18.75 | |
| Accrued holiday pay | 320.00 | |
| Payroll clearing | | 976.25 |

**FIGURE 14-6 Cost accounting time summary and distribution.**

allows the clerk to charge the overtime premium to departmental overhead.

The cost distribution at the bottom of the form in Figure 14-6 shows that all productive time is charged at straight rates to a departmental direct labor cost account. Recall that we are presuming that the firm is using a standard cost system, in which case the charges to Work-in-Process inventory are made at standard cost. Any difference between the total departmental labor costs charged to Work-in-Process and the total departmental labor cost will be reconciled as variances. These variances are the subject of Chapters 18 and 19.

The cost distribution also indicates that overtime premiums are charged to the department's overhead control account. The pay for the employee on vacation is charged against an accrual account. That is, the firm accrues holiday pay as earned, so when an employee actually takes holiday pay there is no labor charge to the department. Finally, as indicated in the main body of this chapter, the total labor cost is charged to the payroll clearing account.

While the cost clerk prepares the labor cost distribution, the time cards go to the payroll department for the actual preparation of checks. The payroll department prepares a payroll journal such as the one in

**EXHIBIT 14-9 Payroll Journal: Employee Deductions**

| | | Deductions | | | | | |
|---|---|---|---|---|---|---|---|
| **Employee** | **Gross Wages** | **FICA** | **Federal Withholding** | **State Withholding** | **Union Dues** | **Stock Purchase** | **Net Pay** |
| Jim Jones | $300.00 | $18.00 | $ 66.00 | $ 5.28 | $10.00 | $ — | $200.72 |
| Sally Smith | 356.25 | 21.37 | 78.33 | 6.27 | 10.00 | 25.00 | 215.28 |
| William Wilson | 320.00 | 19.20 | 70.40 | 5.63 | 10.00 | — | 214.77 |
| Total | $976.25 | $58.57 | $214.73 | $17.18 | $30.00 | $25.00 | $630.77 |

Exhibit 14-9. In addition, the same information that appears in the payroll journal will also have to be accumulated on an earnings statement for each employee. These latter records are needed to show compliance with government wage-and-hour rules as well as to form the basis for preparation of W-2 reports at year-end.

The payroll journal also records all the deductions that the employer withholds from an employee's paycheck. In the illustration we have assumed deductions for the employee's contribution to FICA, state and federal income tax withholding, a deduction for union dues, and a deduction for a stock purchase plan. Other possible deductions include payments to a credit union, purchase of savings bonds, and purchase of insurance. The amounts of the deductions for taxes are determined by law, while many of the others are voluntary choices made by the employee. Payroll must, of course, keep a record of each employee's desired deductions.

As the payroll journal indicates, the employee's base wage rate is only one part of the total cost to employ a worker. The columns in Exhibit 14-10 indicate that the employer must also pay a FICA tax, federal and state unemployment tax, and workmen's compensation insurance. As mentioned previously, this firm also accrues holiday pay as it is earned.

The specific dollar amounts for additional employer costs in Exhibit 14-10 were calculated as follows:

*Employer FICA:* 6% of gross wages. The actual rate is higher, but it has been changing annually. In addition, there is a maximum annual tax per employee, but we are assuming that all employees are currently below the maximum for the illustration.

*Federal and State Unemployment Insurance:* Typically firms pay 0.5% of gross wages, subject again to a maximum, for federal unemployment insurance. State rates vary. For this example, we have assumed a state rate of 2.1%.

**EXHIBIT 14-10 Payroll Journal: Additional Employer Costs**

| | Employer Costs | | | | | |
|---|---|---|---|---|---|---|
| Employee | FICA | Federal Unemployment | State Unemployment | Accrued Holiday Pay | Workmen's Compensation | Total |
| Jim Jones | $18.00 | $1.50 | $ 6.30 | $19.67 | $1.20 | $ 46.67 |
| Sally Smith | 21.37 | 1.78 | 7.48 | 19.67 | 1.42 | 51.72 |
| William Wilson | 19.20 | 1.60 | 6.72 | — | 1.28 | 28.80 |
| Total | $58.57 | $4.88 | $20.50 | $39.34 | $3.90 | $127.19 |

*Accrued Holiday Pay:* The illustration presumes that the firm's employees receive 16 paid holiday and vacation days per year. This, in turn, implies that employees actually work 244 days (52 × 5 − 16). Holiday and vacation costs are accrued as 6.557% of base pay (16 ÷ 244). However, holiday pay accrues only on straight time (40 hours per week). It is assumed that employees do not earn additional days off for overtime or while on vacation.

*Workmen's Compensation:* Workmen's compensation insurance rates depend on the risk of the particular jobs being performed. The illustration assumes a rate of 0.4% of gross pay.

Once the payroll journal has been completed, the payroll department can make the following entry.

| | | |
|---|---|---|
| Payroll Clearing | 976.25 | |
| Overhead Control: Department 215 | 127.19 | |
| FICA Taxes Payable | | 117.14 |
| Federal Withholding Payable | | 214.73 |
| State Withholding Payable | | 17.18 |
| Union Dues Payable | | 30.00 |
| Stock Purchase | | 25.00 |
| Federal Unemployment Payable | | 4.88 |
| State Unemployment Payable | | 20.50 |
| Accrued Holiday Pay | | 39.34 |
| Workmen's Compensation Payable | | 3.90 |
| Cash | | 630.77 |

The debit to Payroll Clearing should exactly offset the credit made by the cost clerk. These two figures should be reconciled prior to the actual preparation of paychecks. In the system described, two people have independently calculated gross wages. This comparison should reveal any errors made in gross pay. Throughout this text we have commented on the motivational and morale effects of the accounting system on employees. No error is likely to be as costly in terms of employee morale as an error in a paycheck. Thus the duplicate calculation of gross pay is intentional in order to try to minimize errors in paychecks.

The debit to Overhead Control charges all the additional employer's costs to the appropriate department's overhead account. The credit to FICA taxes payable reflects that both the employee and employer contributions must be forwarded to the government. The remaining entries follow directly from Exhibits 14-9 and 14-10.

***Variation***

*In the preceding illustration holiday pay was treated as an overhead item. It could easily have been included as a direct labor cost. To do so, a new labor rate must be supplied to the cost clerk for the labor cost distribution. Instead of using a labor rate of $7.50 per hour for Jim Jones, a rate of $7.99 ($7.50 × 1.06557) would be used. This rate, which reflects the accrual for holiday pay, would be used to accumulate direct labor cost. At the same time the holiday accrual would be reflected in the credit to the Payroll Clearing account. With this system, the payroll department's payroll journal would be unchanged, but accrued holiday pay would be charged to the Payroll Clearing account instead of Departmental Overhead. Any of the other employer tax or fringe benefits could also be treated as a direct cost in a similar manner.*

Payroll accounting requires a tremendous amount of routine calculations. Further, employees insist on absolute accuracy. Not surprisingly, payroll systems were among the very first applications of computers in business. An integrated payroll system program, PAY, is included on the disk that accompanies the text.

## QUESTIONS AND EXERCISES: APPENDIX 14

**14-51** At the end of the month the Payroll Clearing account is observed to have a credit balance. Assuming that no clerical mistakes have been made, how would you account for this?

**14-52** A new payroll clerk prepared the following (summary) entry for payroll.

| | | |
|---|---|---|
| Work-in-Process | 6,400 | |
| Overhead Control | 1,200 | |
| Payroll Clearing | | 7,600 |
| To record 800 regular hours at $8 and 100 overtime hours at $12. | | |

What would be a more appropriate way of recording payroll?

**14-53** Wink Mattress, Inc., reports payroll data for the week as follows:

| | | |
|---|---|---|
| Direct labor | | |
| Regular time | 600 hours @ $10 | $6,000 |
| Overtime | 50 hours @ $15 | 750 |
| Indirect labor | | 1,500 |
| Total | | $8,250 |

Overtime is considered to be a normal cost of production. During the week, 40 hours of direct labor (included in the above summary) were lost due to idle time caused by an abnormal power failure.

Payroll taxes to the employer averaged 10% of the total payroll. In addition, holiday and vacation pay are accrued at 5% of gross wages earned. Taxes and fringe benefits are considered to be overhead. You are to prepare entries to distribute payroll costs to general ledger accounts.

## PROBLEMS AND CASES: APPENDIX 14

**14-54 Payroll.**
Labor Intensive Products, Inc., has accumulated the following hours for direct labor.

| | Total | Job 6 |
|---|---|---|
| Regular | 2,000 | 350 |
| Overtime | 300 | 50 |

The following information is available regarding direct labor.

| | |
|---|---|
| Hourly rate | $12 |
| Payroll tax rate, employer | 10% |
| Payroll tax rate, employee | 6% |
| Federal income tax withholding | 20% |
| State income tax withholding | 4% |
| Overtime rate | 150% of straight time |

Only the straight hourly rate is treated as direct labor cost. The overtime premium and employer taxes are treated as overhead. The overhead rate is 50% of direct labor cost. Job 6 was started and completed during the week, requiring materials costing $7,200.

**Required**

**a.** Record the general journal entry summarizing direct labor for the period.

**b.** What is the total cost assigned to job 6?

**14-55 Direct labor costs and entries.**
Bob has one clerical employee, who is paid $3.85 per hour for 8 hours per day. Bob treats the $3.85 as the direct wage rate (implying that all fringe benefits are considered overhead). FICA taxes are 6% of gross earnings (paid by both the

employer and employee). The employee receives 2 weeks of paid vacation and 6 paid holidays. There are no fringes or taxes. Holiday and vacation pay is accrued monthly as one-twelfth of anticipated annual cost. In January the employee worked 21 days and got one day's vacation pay.

**Required**
Prepare the summary journal entry to recognize labor expense, holiday pay, and the payment of wages during January.

**14-56 Determining payroll cash requirements—computer required.**
It is Monday, September 22, and sales have not been good for Huskie Motors. The accountant is concerned whether the firm will have sufficient cash to meet its payroll obligations. The following list provides payroll data for the employees who are to be paid this week.

| Name | Jay Smith | Pat Jones | Gerry Kwon |
|---|---|---|---|
| Social security number | 123-45-6543 | 098-76-4678 | 777-66-4444 |
| Department | 2A | 2A | 3B |
| Hourly pay rate | $15.00 | $9.00 | $8.75 |
| Credit union deduction | $40 | $0 | $15 |
| Year-to-date gross | $22,500 | $17,500 | $13,300 |
| Year-to-date deductions | $ 8,200 | $ 7,800 | $ 6,000 |
| Current hours worked | 47 | 50 | 40 |

Jay Smith is a supervisor and does not receive an overtime bonus and does not belong to the union. The other employees are union members and are paid overtime at 150% of their base pay. The company pays $25 for health insurance. Union dues paid by employees are $75. The federal tax rate for all employees is 18%, state tax is 5%, FICA 7.15%, federal unemployment 0.8%, and the state unemployment rate is 2.7%. FICA taxes are paid on wages up to $37,800, and federal and state unemployment taxes are paid on wages up to $7,000.

State and federal taxes and withholding do not have to be paid until next month. Net wages, health insurance, credit union payments, and union dues must be paid in the current week.

**Required**
Determine the amount of cash needed during the current week to meet payroll-related costs. The use of the program PAY on the disk that accompanies the text is recommended.

**14-57 Payroll distribution adjusting entry—computer recommended.**
Refer to the data given in Problem 14-56. The firm was able to meet its payroll. However, on October 1, after the payroll was completed and the appropriate journal entries were made, it was discovered that Pat Jones really works in department 3B. All other information was correct.

**Required**
Prepare the journal entry required to adjust the firm's books for the error. (*Hint:* Run the program PAY with the incorrect information and then with the correct information and compare the resulting entries.)

## PROBLEMS AND CASES: APPENDIX 14

**14-58 Journal entries to correct wages—computer recommended.**
Highland Market just began business and the accountant has prepared the first payroll. The following rates and data, all correct, were used.

| | |
|---|---|
| overtime pay rate | = 1.5 |
| federal tax rate | = 0.18 |
| state tax rate | = 0.05 |
| FICA rate | = 0.0715 |
| federal unemployment tax rate | = 0.008 |
| state unemployment tax rate | = 0.027 |
| health insurance premium | = $25.00 |
| union dues | = $75.00 |
| FICA cutoff | = $37,800.00 |
| federal unemployment tax cutoff | = $7,000.00 |
| state unemployment tax cutoff | = $7,000.00 |

The firm has three employees. Personal data and hours worked during the period were entered in the computer program as follows:

| Name | Bill Dyl | Jane Ochs | Fred Sill |
|---|---|---|---|
| Social security number | 222-44-1111 | 321-01-2345 | 654-00-2211 |
| Department | 170 | 170 | 175 |
| Hourly pay rate | $6.50 | $.70 | $4.00 |
| Credit union | $10 | $0 | $8 |
| Hours worked | 42 | 40 | 35 |

None of the employees is a union member, but they all qualify for overtime pay.

After the payroll program was run, the journal entries made, and the paychecks distributed, Jane Ochs pointed out (rather heatedly) that her pay rate was really $7.00 per hour not $0.70 per hour.

**Required**

Prepare the necessary adjusting entries to reflect the correction of this error and the issuance of additional pay. (*Hint:* Run the program PAY with the incorrect data and then again with the correct data and compare the results.)

# CHAPTER 15

# PROCESS COSTING

Job costing is used primarily when firms produce dissimilar products in relatively small production runs. In these situations, each product or service may require differing amounts of material, labor, and overhead items. Quick feedback on the costs of specific jobs is necessary for management to keep prices competitive and adequate. In contrast, firms that continuously manufacture only a few products do not require feedback on the cost of specific batches of product but instead can rely on average costs determined on a periodic basis. The accounting procedure for periodically determining average unit costs is called process costing.

Chapter 14 contrasted the characteristics of operating environments that would lead to the need to use process versus job costing. If you have not read it recently, or at all, you may wish to look at the first part of that chapter.

## MEASURING OUTPUT

With process costing our first task is to determine the amount of production accomplished during the period. Although this seems like it ought to be rather easy, there is a problem with determining the amount of effort represented by the incomplete products that are in work-in-process.

### Equivalent Units

To accommodate partially completed units, we introduce the concept of an equivalent unit of production. An **equivalent unit of production,** also called an **effective unit of production,** is the amount of production effort that, if concentrated on a single unit of product, would result in a completed unit. Thus if there are two units of product in work-in-process, each 50% complete, we say that the total effort represented by these two units equals the equivalent of one complete unit, or represents one equivalent unit of production.

At the end of each period, then, we need to determine the total number of equivalent units represented by the products in ending work-in-process. If a firm processes its products in batches, the number of equivalent units represented by each batch in ending work-in-process can be determined and summed. If a firm has a group of 200 units of product that are 10% complete and another batch of 300 units that are 70% complete, then the first batch represents 20 equivalent units of effort and the second batch 210 equivalent units of effort, for a total of 230 equivalent units in ending work-in-process.

However, if a firm works on discrete units that at the end of a period are in a large number of different states of completion, it would generally be too great a task to determine the stage of completion for each unit and then sum to get the total equivalent units. In these cases, we typically estimate the average stage of completion for all units and treat them all as if they were at the average state of completion. For example, if our firm has 400 units in process, ranging from 25% to 80% complete, and most of the units are in the more advanced stages of completion, we may estimate that the units on average are 60% complete, thus representing 240 equivalent units of effort. At the extreme, if a firm produces its product on an assembly line, so that at the end of each period goods will be in every conceivable state of completion, all units are typically treated as if they were 50% complete.

Let us now do an example, showing the calculation of the equivalent units of effort accomplished in a period. Assume our firm began a period with 4,000 units of product in work-in-process. Each of these units in beginning work-in-process inventory was 25% complete. During the period, the firm began work on an additional 20,000 units. At the end of the period there were 5,000 units in the ending work-in-process inventory, each unit 70% complete.

We start by analyzing the physical flow of units through work-in-process. We will need to know how many units were ever in work-in-process during the period and their location at the end of the period. In this way we assure ourselves that we have not overlooked any units (for more complicated problems, this is a very real danger).

**EXHIBIT 15-1 Three Approaches to Accounting for Physical Flow**

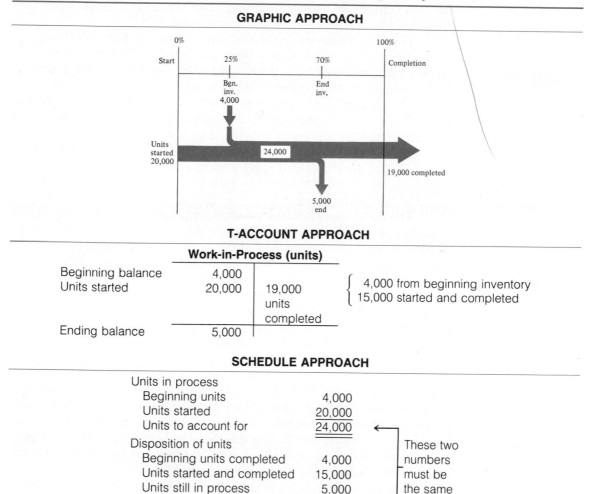

**GRAPHIC APPROACH**

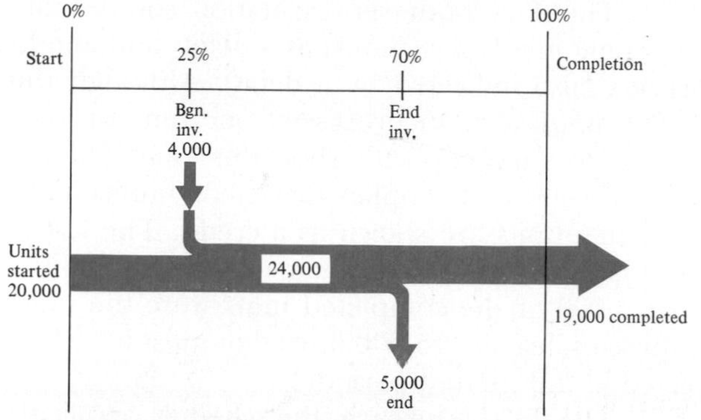


**T-ACCOUNT APPROACH**

**Work-in-Process (units)**

| | | | |
|---|---|---|---|
| Beginning balance | 4,000 | | |
| Units started | 20,000 | 19,000 units completed | { 4,000 from beginning inventory; 15,000 started and completed } |
| Ending balance | 5,000 | | |

**SCHEDULE APPROACH**

| | | |
|---|---|---|
| Units in process | | |
| Beginning units | 4,000 | |
| Units started | 20,000 | |
| Units to account for | 24,000 | ← These two numbers must be the same |
| Disposition of units | | |
| Beginning units completed | 4,000 | |
| Units started and completed | 15,000 | |
| Units still in process | 5,000 | |
| Units accounted for | 24,000 | ← |

Exhibit 15-1 presents three alternative approaches to tracing the physical flow of units. In the graphic approach, we represent the process by a line showing stages of completion from 0% (units started) to 100% (the completion point). The status of beginning and ending inventories are noted by placing a slash at the appropriate percentage completion point. The 20,000 units started are shown by a horizontal line. These units join the 4,000 units that were already 25% complete at the beginning of the period to yield 24,000 units in process. The units progress through the process (moving to the right). At the 70% complete point, 5,000 units are "left behind" in ending inventory. The remaining 19,000 units progressed out of the process (they were completed).

The T-account representation shows that we had 4,000 units in beginning inventory (shown as a debit) and another 20,000 were put into process (also indicated by a debit). Although this means that a total of 24,000 units were in process at one time or another, the T-account approach does not explicitly show this total. The ending balance, below the line, of 5,000 units implies that 19,000 units left the process. The 19,000 departing units are shown as a credit. The last step is to indicate where the 19,000 completed units came from. Assuming a first-in, first-out (FIFO) flow, 4,000 of the completed units were the units from beginning work-in-process, leaving 15,000 units that must have been both started and completed in the current period.

The third approach, the schedule, explicitly shows the total 24,000 units that were in process. The second part of the schedule shows the location of these units at the end of the period. It indicates that the 4,000 units in beginning inventory were completed, an additional 15,000 units were started and completed, and 5,000 units are in ending work-in-process. The schedule approach also explicitly shows that we must account for all units that were ever in the process.

You should use the approach to tracing physical flows that you find easiest to understand. We find that with complicated problems (such as those in the next chapter), the graphic approach greatly clarifies the problem. However, it is easy to overlook units when using the graphic approach. Consequently, we use both the graphic approach and the T-account approach to assure that all units are accounted for. Most other accountants prefer the schedule approach because it explicitly shows whether all units have been accounted for. If you use the schedule approach, we suggest that you also use the graphic approach. We believe you will find it a significant aid in solving the more difficult problems.

Whichever approach was used, we find for our example that 19,000 units were completed during the period. But our actual effort, in terms of equivalent units of work accomplished during the period, may be higher or lower than 19,000 units, depending on the status of beginning and ending work-in-process inventory. That is, some of the work done on the units in beginning work-in-process was really done in the previous accounting period. Thus this effort must be subtracted from the total units completed to get just the current period's work. Since the 4,000 units in beginning work-in-process were 25% complete, the equivalent of 1,000 full units of effort must have been completed last period. The effort represented by the completed units for the current period, then, is 18,000 equivalent units.

| | |
|---|---|
| Total units completed | 19,000 |
| Less the work done on beginning inventory units last period | (1,000) |
| Current period equivalent units of effort for the units completed | 18,000 |

But we have not finished. We have only found the current period's effort associated with those units that were completed and transferred. There are also some partially completed units in ending work-in-process. Presumably, the effort in these units was also performed in the current period. Since the 5,000 ending units were estimated to be 70% complete, we add 3,500 equivalent units of effort to our previous balance to get a total of 21,500 equivalent units of effort accomplished in the current period.

| | |
|---|---|
| Total units completed | 19,000 |
| Less work done on beginning inventory units last period | (1,000) |
| Plus the current period's effort in ending inventory units | 3,500 |
| Total current period equivalent units of effort | 21,500 |

We can also determine the equivalent units of effort using a slightly different analysis. Our second approach determines directly the units of effort accomplished in the current period. We again start by examining the physical flow of units in Exhibit 15-1. This time we note that of the 19,000 units completed, 4,000 units would be the units from beginning work-in-process, leaving the 15,000 units that we both started and completed in the current period. Noting that the 4,000 beginning units were 25% complete at the start of the period, we must have performed the remaining 75% of the effort for these units in the current period. Thus 3,000 equivalent units of effort were needed to *complete* beginning work-in-process. Of course, all of the effort for the 15,000 units both started and completed in the current period must have been performed in the current period. These 15,000 units then represent 15,000 current-period equivalent units of effort. Adding this effort to the effort to complete beginning work-in-process gives us the total current effort, associated with completed units, of 18,000.

| | |
|---|---|
| Effort in current period to complete units in beginning inventory | 3,000 |
| Plus effort for units started and completed in the current period | 15,000 |
| Current period equivalent units of effort for the units completed | 18,000 |

This is the same result that we had from the first analysis. Once again, we add to the current effort for completed units the equivalent units of effort represented by the units in ending inventory. The effort in ending inventory still represents 70% of 5,000, or 3,500 equivalent units. Adding this to the 18,000 units of effort for completed units gives us a total of 21,500 units of effort for the period.

| | |
|---|---|
| To complete beginning inventory | 3,000 |
| Plus units started and completed | 15,000 |
| Plus effort in ending inventory | 3,500 |
| Total current period effort | 21,500 |

Although both analyses provide the same total effort for the period, the second analysis will turn out to be more useful to us when it is time to determine the cost of the units completed. Therefore, we will use the second approach hereafter.

### Uneven Cost Incurrence

If units that were considered 50% complete were actually half done with regard to all types of cost, the determination of the equivalent units of production for a period would be reasonably simple. Unfortunately, a unit described as 50% complete may include 100% of one type of raw material, 0% of a second type, and 33% of the direct labor required for its completion. In this case when we say a unit is half done we probably mean it is halfway through the process, but more or less than half of a specific type of cost may have been incurred. To accurately determine the cost of a unit of product we will need to calculate the equivalent units of production achieved during a period for each major type of cost.

Let us demonstrate with an example. Assume that a firm starts a period with 300 units in work-in-process. These units are totally complete with regard to materials, two-thirds complete with regard to labor, and half complete with regard to overhead. The firm completes 1,000 units during the period and ends the period with 400 units that are 50% complete with regard to materials, 30% complete with regard to labor, and 25% complete with regard to overhead.

To determine the equivalent units of effort for the current period we again analyze three components: the effort to complete beginning work-in-process, the effort for units that were produced completely in the current period, and the effort for the units in ending work-in-process. But now we must also perform the analysis for each type of cost.

| | Equivalent Units of Effort | | |
|---|---|---|---|
| **Current Period Effort** | **Materials** | **Labor** | **Overhead** |
| To complete beginning units | — | 100 | 150 |
| Started and completed | 700 | 700 | 700 |
| In ending inventory | 200 | 120 | 100 |
| Current equivalent units | 900 | 920 | 950 |

**EXHIBIT 15-2 Computation of Current Effort**

**Physical Flow**

| | | |
|---|---|---|
| 300 | 1,000 | 300 from beginning inventory; 700 units started and completed |
| 1,100 | | |
| 400 | | |

| | Type of Cost | | |
|---|---|---|---|
| | **Materials** | **Labor** | **Overhead** |
| Completed units from beginning inventory | 300 | 300 | 300 |
| Effort done last period (100%, 66.7%, and 50%, respectively) | (300) | (200) | (150) |
| Current effort to complete the units in beginning inventory | — | 100 | 150 |

Note that although the firm completed 1,000 physical units during the period, there are not 1,000 equivalent units of effort for any of the costs in the current period. This is because much of the work for the units completed this period was actually performed in the previous period. This is particularly noticeable with materials. From Exhibit 15-2 we can see that 700 units of product were started and completed during the period. The additional 300 units completed came from beginning work-in-process, and the problem stated that the beginning units were complete last period with regard to materials. Therefore, no additional effort with respect to materials was performed in the current period to complete the beginning inventory. The problem also states that the units in ending inventory were only half complete with respect to materials, so 200 equivalent whole units of material are reflected in ending work-in-process. In contrast, for labor there were 100 units worth of effort needed to complete beginning work-in-process (one-third of the effort for 300 units) and the ending inventory represents 120 equivalent units of effort for labor costs (30% × 400). Adding these amounts to the 700 units of effort for the products started and completed during the period yields a total effort for labor of 920 equivalent units. We leave it to you to work through the calculation of equivalent units for overhead.

## COST PER UNIT OF EFFORT

Once we have determined the amount of effort accomplished during the period, we then turn to determining the cost of each equivalent unit of effort for each type of cost. The accounting records will have accumulated all production costs by department. Further, the direct materials and labor costs (by definition) will be segregated by product. Similarly we presume departmental overhead costs have been allocated to product lines (see Chapters 12 and 13).

In calculating unit costs we must decide whether to use actual costs, normal costs, or standard costs. If we use standard costing, all unit costs will have been predetermined. Valuing cost of goods completed and cost of ending work-in-process amounts to nothing more than multiplying the equivalent units by the predetermined unit standard costs.

With normal costing we would need to calculate actual unit costs for materials and labor but would use a predetermined overhead cost. Although there are times when normal costing is used in a process costing environment, actual cost systems are more common. Unlike job costing, actual costing is practical in a process situation because the accounting is done at the end of the period when actual overhead costs are known. Because actual cost systems are so common, the remainder of our discussion of process costing will assume that we are accounting for actual costs.

Even after deciding to use an actual cost system, we still have a choice concerning the presumed cost flows. Should manufacturing costs be assumed to follow a LIFO, FIFO, or average pattern? Although many firms use LIFO for valuing raw materials and finished goods inventories, the use of LIFO for work-in-process inventories is rare. Similarly, the use of a FIFO assumption is also rare. However, it has been our experience that students grasp the process costing concepts more easily in a FIFO situation than when average costs are used. Consequently we look at FIFO costing first and then move to average process costing.

### FIFO Process Costing

Assume that for the previous example, the firm's accounting records show total materials costs of \$2,700 for the period, total labor cost of \$3,680, and total overhead for the period of \$4,750. Then the cost per equivalent unit of product for each type of cost for the current period would be as follows:

| | Materials | Labor | Overhead |
|---|---|---|---|
| Current period equivalent units | 900 | 920 | 950 |
| Current period costs | \$2,700 | \$3,680 | \$4,750 |
| Current cost per equivalent unit | \$3 | \$4 | \$5 |

That is, in the *current* period each complete unit of product required materials costing \$3, labor costing \$4, and \$5 of overhead. On the presumption that the effort in ending work-in-process was accomplished in the current period, we determine the total cost of ending work-in-process by multiplying the equivalent units of effort represented in ending inventory by the current cost per equivalent unit.

**Cost of Ending Work-in-Process**

| | Materials | Labor | Overhead | Total |
|---|---|---|---|---|
| Equivalent units of effort | 200 | 120 | 100 | |
| Cost per equivalent unit | × $3 | × $4 | × $5 | |
| Inventory cost | $600 | $480 | $500 | $1,580 |

Summing the resulting figures for each type of cost gives us the total cost of ending work-in-process of $1,580.

The current costs per equivalent unit of effort are also used to determine the current costs attached to units completed. When these costs are added to the cost of beginning work-in-process, we get the total cost of goods completed and transferred to finished goods inventory. Returning to the example, assume that the cost of the beginning work-in-process inventory was $2,622 ($750 for materials, $968 for labor, and $904 for overhead). Then the cost of goods completed in the current period is determined as follows:

| | Materials | Labor | Overhead | Total |
|---|---|---|---|---|
| Current Period Effort | | | | |
| To complete beginning units | — | 100 | 150 | |
| Started and completed | 700 | 700 | 700 | |
| Current effort for units finished | 700 | 800 | 850 | |
| Current cost per equivalent unit | × $3 | × $4 | × $5 | |
| Current cost of units completed | $2,100 | $3,200 | $4,250 | $ 9,550 |
| Plus beginning costs | 750 | 968 | 904 | 2,622 |
| Total cost of goods completed | $2,850 | $4,168 | $5,154 | $12,172 |

Again, summing across the three types of manufacturing costs gives us the cost of goods completed and transferred to finished goods as $12,172.

## A FIFO Format

In presenting and solving our example of a process costing problem, we broke the solution into small steps to be able to discuss each step. In actually solving these problems, the approach we took involves too much duplication of effort; therefore, a number of shortcut solution formats have been proposed. The objective of all the formats is to minimize the number of times information must be copied, and yet present the information in an orderly manner to facilitate solution of the problem. We present our ex-

**EXHIBIT 15-3 FIFO Process Costing Solution Format**

**EQUIVALENT UNITS**

| Current Effort | Materials | Labor | Overhead |
|---|---|---|---|
| To finish beginning work-in-process | — | 100 | 150 |
| Units started and completed | 700 | 700 | 700 |
| Effort in ending work-in-process | 200 | 120 | 100 |
| Total effort | 900 | 920 | 950 |
| Current costs | $2,700 | $3,680 | $4,750 |
| Cost per equivalent unit | $3 | $4 | $5 |

**COST DISTRIBUTION**

| | | |
|---|---|---|
| Cost of goods completed | | |
| Cost of beginning work-in-process | | $ 2,622 |
| Costs to complete beginning inventory | | |
| Materials (0 × $3) | $ 0 | |
| Labor (100 EU × $4) | 400 | |
| Overhead (150 EU × $5) | 750 | 1,150 |
| Costs of units started and completed [700 EU × ($3 + $4 + $5)] | | 8,400 |
| Total cost of goods completed | | $12,172 |

| | |
|---|---|
| Cost of ending work-in-process | |
| Materials (200 EU × $3) | $ 600 |
| Labor (120 EU × $4) | 480 |
| Overhead (100 EU × $5) | 500 |
| Total | $1,580 |

**CHECK**

| | |
|---|---|
| Costs incurred | |
| Beginning inventory cost | $ 2,622 |
| Current period costs | |
| Materials | 2,700 |
| Labor | 3,680 |
| Overhead | 4,750 |
| Total costs to account for | $13,752 |
| Costs distributed | |
| Cost of goods completed | $12,172 |
| Cost of ending work-in-process | 1,580 |
| Total costs distributed | $13,752 |

ample in one such format in Exhibit 15-3. It is no better or worse than most formats that have been proposed, but it is the one with which we feel comfortable. Exhibit 15-4 illustrates an alternative approach that is frequently used with computer spreadsheet programs.

The top portion of Exhibit 15-3 determines the equivalent units of effort accomplished, followed by the determination of the cost per equiv-

**EXHIBIT 15-4 Alternate FIFO Process Costing Solution Format**

| | EQUIVALENT UNITS | | | |
|---|---|---|---|---|
| **Current Effort** | **Materials** | **Labor** | **Overhead** | **Physical Units** |
| To finish beginning work-in-process | — | 100 | 150 | 300 |
| Units started and completed | 700 | 700 | 700 | 700 |
| Effort in ending work-in-process | 200 | 120 | 100 | 400 |
| Total effort | 900 | 920 | 950 | 1,400 |
| Current costs | $2,700 | $3,680 | $4,750 | $11,130 |
| Costs per equivalent unit | $3 | $4 | $5 | NA |

**COST DISTRIBUTION**

| | **Materials** | **Labor** | **Overhead** | **Total Costs** |
|---|---|---|---|---|
| Cost of goods completed | | | | |
| Cost of beginning work-in-process | $ 750 | $ 968 | $ 904 | $ 2,622 |
| Cost to complete | 0 | 400 | 750 | 1,150 |
| Cost of units started and completed | 2,100 | 2,800 | 3,500 | 8,400 |
| Total cost of goods completed | $2,850 | $4,168 | $5,154 | $12,172 |
| Cost of ending work-in-process | | | | |
| Total cost | $ 600 | $ 480 | $ 500 | $ 1,580 |

alent unit. The costs are distributed to cost of goods completed and ending work-in-process in the center section. The cost distribution uses the information from the equivalent units section of the solution as well as the costs per equivalent unit. The last item in the solution is a check to ensure that all costs have been accounted for—that all costs that went into Work-in-Process have been distributed to either ending inventory or Cost of Goods Completed.

Note that in **FIFO process costing** the costs attached to beginning work-in-process are assumed to flow directly to Cost of Goods Completed, while ending work-in-process is valued at the current period costs per equivalent unit of production. Another approach, average process costing, will be examined next.

### Weighted-Average Process Costing

With FIFO process costing we went to a great deal of trouble to identify only the effort and costs associated with the current period. This approach provides accurate information on the current cost of materials, labor, and overhead per unit of product. However, if we average the costs incurred in the current period with the costs in beginning inventory, the per-unit costs generally will not change much (because beginning inventory is usually quite small relative to current production), but the calculations will be greatly simplified. Most firms in fact feel the slight loss of accuracy in per-unit cost is easily justified by the reduced effort required by weighted-average process costing. The only place FIFO process costing routinely appears is in accounting exams (including professional certification exams).

With **weighted-average process costing,** the current period's costs will be added to the beginning work-in-process costs. The total of beginning and current costs will then be divided by the total of the effort in beginning inventory plus the current effort. The result will be an average cost per equivalent unit of effort. Using the data from the previous example, let us solve the problem again using average process costing.

| | Equivalent Units | | |
|---|---|---|---|
| **Total Effort** | **Materials** | **Labor** | **Overhead** |
| Effort in beginning inventory from last period | 300 | 200 | 150 |
| Effort to complete beginning units | — | 100 | 150 |
| Started and completed | 700 | 700 | 700 |
| Effort in ending inventory | 200 | 120 | 100 |
| Total equivalent units | 1,200 | 1,120 | 1,100 |

Here the first line is the effort in beginning work-in-process. Although this effort was done last period, it will be averaged in with the current period's effort. Note that if we add the first three lines (beginning effort, effort to complete beginning units, and effort for units started and completed) the result is simply the total number of units completed during the period. That is, the averaging process results in our including in the total effort calculation all the effort for all the units completed during the period. Thus a shortcut to determining total equivalent units of effort for average process costing is as follows:

| | Equivalent Units | | |
|---|---|---|---|
| **Total Effort** | **Materials** | **Labor** | **Overhead** |
| Units completed | 1,000 | 1,000 | 1,000 |
| Ending inventory | 200 | 120 | 100 |
| Total equivalent units | 1,200 | 1,120 | 1,100 |

Similar to the effort calculation, we include both the costs for beginning inventory and the current costs to get total costs. The total costs in turn are divided by the total effort to get an average cost per equivalent unit of effort. That is,

| | Materials | Labor | Overhead |
|---|---|---|---|
| Beginning inventory costs | $ 750 | $ 968 | $ 904 |
| Current costs | 2,700 | 3,680 | 4,750 |
| Total costs | $3,450 | $4,648 | $5,654 |
| Total equivalent units | 1,200 | 1,120 | 1,100 |
| Average cost per equivalent unit | $2.875 | $ 4.15 | $ 5.14 |

The cost of ending work-in-process is determined just as we did with FIFO process costing, but now using average-cost-per-equivalent-unit figures.

| Ending Work-in-Process | Materials | Labor | Overhead | Total |
|---|---|---|---|---|
| Equivalent units | 200 | 120 | 100 | |
| Cost per equivalent unit | $2.875 | $4.15 | $5.14 | |
| Inventory cost | $575 | $498 | $514 | $1,587 |

Hence, with average process costing, the cost of ending work-in-process inventory becomes $1,587.

The major computational savings in using average process costing comes when it is time to determine the cost of goods completed. Since we are no longer maintaining a distinction between current and previous period effort, all units completed are simply valued at average cost.

| Cost of Goods Completed | Materials | Labor | Overhead | Total |
|---|---|---|---|---|
| Units completed | 1,000 | 1,000 | 1,000 | |
| Cost per equivalent unit | $2.875 | $4.15 | $5.14 | |
| Total cost of goods completed | $2,875 | $4,150 | $5,140 | $12,165 |

This time cost of goods completed is valued at $12,165. Referring back to our FIFO calculations we can see that the costs distributed to ending work-in-process and cost of goods completed with average costing differ only slightly from the figures derived using FIFO process costing. But the average costing approach requires far less work.

Exhibit 15-5 presents a solution format for average process costing, again incorporating some shortcuts. The equivalent units of effort in the cost distribution comes from the top portion of the solution, and once again we end with a check to ensure that all costs going into Work-in-Process are either in ending inventory or Cost of Goods Completed.

## USING PROCESS COSTING

Before proceeding to some additional variations on process costing, let us pause for a moment to consider what we are doing. We have presumed

**EXHIBIT 15-5 Average Process Costing Solution Format**

**EQUIVALENT UNITS**

| | Materials | Labor | Overhead |
|---|---|---|---|
| Total effort | | | |
| For units completed | 1,000 | 1,000 | 1,000 |
| For ending inventory | 200 | 120 | 100 |
| Total effort | 1,200 | 1,120 | 1,100 |
| Total costs | | | |
| From beginning inventory | $ 750 | $ 968 | $ 904 |
| Current costs | 2,700 | 3,680 | 4,750 |
| Total costs | $3,450 | $4,648 | $5,654 |
| Average cost per equivalent unit | $2.875 | $4.15 | $5.14 |

**COST DISTRIBUTION**

| | | | |
|---|---|---|---|
| Cost of goods completed[a] | | Cost of ending work-in-process | |
| Materials (1,000 EU × $2.875) | $ 2,875 | Materials (200 EU × $2.875) | $ 575 |
| Labor (1,000 EU × $4.15) | 4,150 | Labor (120 EU × $4.15) | 498 |
| Overhead (1,000 EU × $5.14) | 5,140 | Overhead (100 EU × $5.14) | 514 |
| Total | $12,165 | Total | $1,587 |

**CHECK**

| | |
|---|---|
| Costs incurred | |
| Beginning inventory cost | $ 2,622 |
| Current period costs | |
| Materials | 2,700 |
| Labor | 3,680 |
| Overhead | 4,750 |
| Total costs to account for | $13,752 ← |
| Costs distributed | |
| Cost of goods completed | $12,165 |
| Cost of ending work-in-process | 1,587 |
| Total costs distributed | $13,752 ← |

[a]In solving these, it is not necessary to write out all of this information. We know 1,000 units were completed and they will be charged for materials, labor, and overhead. An easier approach is simply:

cost of goods completed = 1,000 EU × ($2.875 + $4.15 + $5.14) = $12,165 that all of a department's costs have been accumulated in that department's Work-in-Process account. However, at the end of the period we want to allocate the department's production costs to the units that have been completed and to the units that are still in process. For the preceding example, the department's Work-in-Process account at the end of the period would have accumulated a total of $13,752 in costs (the beginning balance of $2,622 plus $11,130 in current costs). We use our process costing technique to split this total between Cost of Goods Completed and ending Work-in-Process.

### Journal Entries for Process Costing

Once we know the cost of goods completed, we can then prepare the journal entry to transfer these costs from the department's Work-in-Process account to the Finished Goods account. Using the result from the average process costing example, our journal entry would be

| | | |
|---|---|---|
| Finished Goods | 12,165 | |
| Work-in-Process | | 12,165 |

The balance in ending Work-in-Process is simply the residual amount left in the account after we subtract out the cost of goods completed, so no specific entry is needed to set up the ending Work-in-Process balance. Thus, we can see that the bookkeeping (the journal entry) for process costing is trivial, but the accountant will need to go to considerable effort to determine the proper dollar amount for the entry. Note also, by the way, that the average cost per unit of goods completed using FIFO process costing may not be the same as the cost per equivalent unit of ending work in process. These unit costs will differ if the cost per unit in beginning inventory differs from the current period's unit costs. Ending inventory is costed at current period costs, whereas the cost of goods completed includes the costs carried forward from beginning inventory.

### Costs Incurred at Specific Points

Rather than try to figure out precisely how complete the units in inventory are with regard to each major cost item, firms sometimes will specify a specific point in the production process for each department at which a cost is *deemed* to be incurred in its entirety. If, for example, in an assembly department, most direct materials are added early in the process, we might arbitrarily decide that all materials are added in this department when units are 10% complete. At the end of the period, if the department's ending inventory averages more than 10% complete, ending inventory is treated as if all direct materials have been added to these units. Similarly, we can determine points at which labor and overhead will be assumed to be incurred. Alternatively, labor and overhead are sometimes deemed to be added to production in strict proportion to how far through the process the units have progressed. If ending inventory is on the average 40% through the process, then 40% of labor and overhead costs will be presumed to have been incurred for these units. As always, the willingness to make these assumptions depends on the importance of having precise unit cost figures and the computational savings achieved by making the assumptions.

### Process Costing with Multiple Departments

When units pass through several departments, the costs attached to units in previous departments must be carried forward to subsequent departments. This is accomplished by introducing another cost item (in addition to materials, labor, and overhead) called transferred-in costs. For subsequent departments this cost item behaves exactly as a raw material added at the beginning of the manufacturing process.

Consider, for example, a firm that manufactures electronic components. Department A attaches connectors to printed circuit boards. The units are then transferred to department B, which adds memory units and a processor. From here the units are transferred to department C, and so on. A unit is considered begun in department A when the first connection is attached to a circuit board. Since the circuit board is by far the most expensive material dealt with by A, all materials costs are deemed added at the beginning of the process. Conversion costs (direct labor plus overhead) are considered to be added uniformly in proportion to how complete the units are in A. Department A started the period with 200 units 25% complete, ended the period with 800 units 75% complete, and began work on 3,000 units during the period. Costs attached to beginning work-in-process were $600. Current period costs were $3,000 for materials and $8,850 for conversion costs. Department A uses FIFO process costing.

Assume further that department B began the period with 400 units in inventory 30% complete and ended with 100 units 10% completed. The materials added by department B are deemed added when units are 50% complete, whereas conversion costs are assumed to be incurred uniformly. Costs attached to beginning inventory were $1,630 for transferred-in costs, zero for materials, and $884 for conversion costs. Current costs for the period were $8,100 for materials and $13,750 for conversion costs. Department B uses weighted-average process costing (of course, it is highly unlikely that a firm would use different costing techniques in different departments, but this example gives us the opportunity to demonstrate each approach once more).

The computation of cost of goods completed and ending work-in-process for department A is not affected by the multidepartmental nature of the firm. The solution given in Exhibit 15-6 parallels that in Exhibit 15-3. We have used both the graphic and T-account approaches to tracing the physical flow of units through department A. Note that we have added to the graph an indication of the point at which materials are added to the process. In more difficult problems with several materials and labor added at discrete points, the indication on the graph of when they are incurred will help us tell at a glance whether the effort for these items is included in beginning and ending inventories.

The cost computations for department B are presented in Exhibit 15-7. Notice that we have added a column for the new cost item: transferred-in costs. **Transferred-in costs** are the accumulated costs associated with the materials (partially completed units) received from the previous production department. The transferred-in units are treated just like any material added at the beginning of the process. Being added at the beginning of the new department's process, all units in work-in-process must include the effort for transferred-in materials. Department B's current cost for transferred-in units is the cost of the units completed and transferred from department A. Because of this relationship, the process cost reports must be prepared in the same sequence that products flow through the departments.

The journal entries for the completion and transfer of these products would be

| | | |
|---|---|---|
| Work-in-Process: Department B | 9,850 | |
| Work-in-Process: Department A | | 9,850 |
| To record the completion and transfer of units from department A. | | |
| Work-in-Process: Department C | 33,750 | |
| Work-in-Process: Department B | | 33,750 |
| To record the completion and transfer of units from department B. | | |

As you can see, the transfer of costs to subsequent departments accumulates total production costs. When units are completed in the last department, the cost of goods completed in that department will be the total cost for the units.

### Simplifications Available with a Just-in-Time Philosophy

Many firms are following the lead of Japanese manufacturers and adopting a just-in-time operating philosophy. As mentioned in Chapter 7, when this approach is properly implemented there are virtually no inventories. Goods

**EXHIBIT 15-6 Department A: FIFO Process Costing**

**Timing of Costs and Status of Inventories**

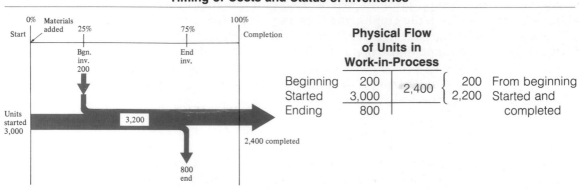

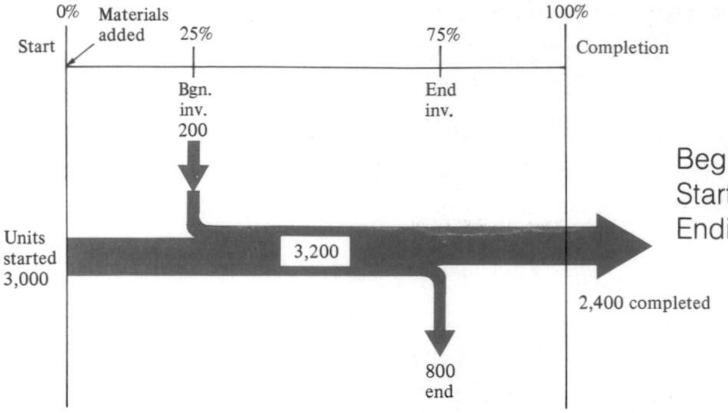


**Physical Flow of Units in Work-in-Process**

| | | | | |
|---|---|---|---|---|
| Beginning | 200 | 2,400 | 200 | From beginning |
| Started | 3,000 | | 2,200 | Started and completed |
| Ending | 800 | | | |

**EQUIVALENT UNITS**

| Current Effort | Materials | Conversion Costs |
|---|---|---|
| To finish beginning | — | 150 |
| Started and completed | 2,200 | 2,200 |
| In ending inventory | 800 | 600 |
| Total effort | 3,000 | 2,950 |
| Current costs | \$3,000 | \$8,850 |
| Cost per equivalent unit | \$1 | \$3 |

**COST DISTRIBUTION**

| | |
|---|---|
| Cost of goods completed | |
| From beginning inventory | \$ 600 |
| To finish beginning (150 EU × \$3) | 450 |
| Started and completed [2,200 EU × (\$1 + \$3)] | 8,800 |
| Total cost of goods completed | \$9,850 |

Cost of ending work-in-process
800 EU × \$1 + 600 EU × \$3 = \$2,600

**CHECK**

| | |
|---|---|
| Costs incurred | |
| Beginning inventory cost | \$ 600 |
| Current period costs | |
| Materials | 3,000 |
| Conversion | 8,850 |
| Total costs to account for | \$12,450 |
| Costs distributed | |
| Cost of goods completed | \$ 9,850 |
| Cost of ending work-in-process | 2,600 |
| Total costs distributed | \$12,450 |

**EXHIBIT 15-7 Department B: Average Process Costing with Transferred-In Costs**

**Timing of Costs and Status of Inventories**

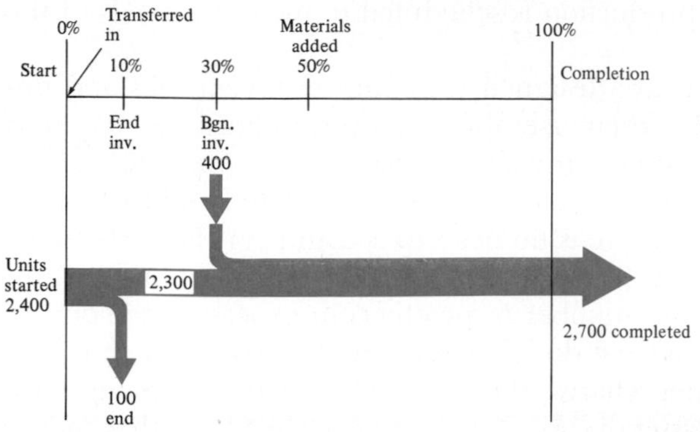


| | Physical Flow | |
|---|---|---|
| Beginning | 400 | |
| From A | 2,400 | 2,700 units completed |
| Ending | 100 | |

**EQUIVALENT UNITS**

| | Transferred In | Materials | Conversion Costs |
|---|---|---|---|
| Total effort | | | |
| Units completed | 2,700 | 2,700 | 2,700 |
| Ending inventory | 100 | — | 10 |
| Total effort | 2,800 | 2,700 | 2,710 |
| Total costs | | | |
| Beginning costs | $ 1,630 | $ — | $ 884 |
| Current costs | 9,850[a] | 8,100 | 13,750 |
| Total costs | $11,480 | $8,100 | $14,634 |
| Cost per equivalent unit | $4.10 | $3.00 | $5.40 |

**COST DISTRIBUTION**

Costs of goods completed
2,700 EU × ($4.10 + $3.00 + $5.40) = $33,750

Cost of ending work-in-process
100 EU × $4.10 + 10 EU × $5.40 = $464

**CHECK**

| | |
|---|---|
| Costs incurred | |
| Beginning inventory cost | $ 2,514 |
| Current period costs | |
| Transferred-in | 9,850 |
| Materials | 8,100 |
| Conversion | 13,750 |
| Total costs to account for | $34,214 |
| Costs distributed | |
| Cost of goods completed | $33,750 |
| Cost of ending work-in-process | 464 |
| Total costs distributed | $34,214 |

[a]Note that this is the figure for cost of goods completed in department A; see Exhibit 15-6.

are produced to specific orders and shipped immediately upon completion. In multiple department settings, departments assemble goods just in time to be sold, and subassemblies are produced just in time for final assembly. Thus each department's production is scheduled to meet the needs of the subsequent department.

Just-in-time systems are designed to minimize inventories and improve quality control.[1] But their use also greatly simplifies the required accounting. If work-in-process at the end of the period is immaterial, it is unnecessary to split costs between cost of goods completed and the cost of ending inventory. Further, there is no need to account for the costs transferred from one department to the next (again, this information is useful only if there are a significant number of products in process at the end of the period). Instead, all we need do is accumulate departmental costs (for control purposes) and then charge them directly to cost of goods sold. Indeed, even when the system is not functioning perfectly (so that inventories are sufficiently material to require valuation for external reporting), the amount of inventories on hand is still frequently so insignificant that a formal system for costing specific units cannot be justified. In these instances, firms simply make an adjusting entry to cost of goods sold to set up the cost of inventories based on very rough estimates.

## SUMMARY

Although process costing seems quite different from job costing, the two systems are really very similar. In job costing, the cost object is the group of products produced for a particular order. In process costing, the cost object consists of all the units manufactured during a period of time. In both cases direct costs must be traced to a particular department and then to the cost object. In both cases overhead is traced to a department and then allocated to production. The major difference is that under job costing a department may work on hundreds of cost objects (jobs) during a period, whereas with process costing a department typically works on only one cost object during the period. As such, job costing tends to require considerably more clerical effort to trace costs to final cost objects. With process costing our task is limited to determining the amount of production a department has accomplished during a period and then charging the department's costs to those units produced. Although the processing of units may be done on a continuous basis, our costing is done only periodically.

[1]The quality control aspects are beyond the scope of this text, but involve using small production lot sizes so that errors are found quickly and affect relatively few units.

## DEMONSTRATION PROBLEM

In this demonstration problem we add a new wrinkle: process costing when two products are produced simultaneously. Drelco manufactures two models of an electric air cleaner: plain and deluxe. The assembly operations and mechanical parts for the two units are identical. The only significant difference is in the quality of the cabinet in which the units are placed. The plain model has a cabinet made of white plastic, whereas the deluxe model's cabinet is made from a brown plastic with a simulated wood grain.

The assembly process begins with a worker taking a brown or white chassis, inserting a filter, attaching and wiring an electric motor, and finally attaching a brown or white cabinet. The mix between brown and white models is changed daily depending on market demand. The current period began with 300 white models in work-in-process. These units were considered to be 20% complete with regard to materials and 30% complete with regard to conversion costs. During the period, work was begun on 4,000 white models and 3,000 brown models. The period ended with 200 brown models in ending work-in-process, approximately 50% complete with regard to materials and 70% complete with regard to conversion costs.

The costs attached to beginning work-in-process were $90 for parts unique to the white unit, $300 for common parts (filters and motors), and $350 for conversion costs. During the period the firm incurred costs of $4,210 for materials unique to the plain model, $5,800 of costs for parts for the deluxe model, $35,700 for other materials costs, and $21,370 for conversion costs. The firm uses weighted-average process costing.

**Required**
Determine the cost of goods completed for each model and the cost of ending work-in-process.

**Solution**
The solution to the problem is given in Exhibit 15-8. The major task in solving this problem is to segregate the materials unique to one of the products from the materials common to both products. In addition, we must trace the physical flow of the two products separately.

Because there are no plain units in ending work-in-process, all the units in beginning inventory (300) and the plain units put into production (4,000) must have been completed. Thus a total of 4,300 equivalent units of effort for plain materials must have been completed. These units also required 4,300 units of effort for the common materials and conversion costs.

For the deluxe units, 3,000 units were started, but 200 are still in process. Hence 2,800 units must have been completed. These units require 2,800 equivalent units of deluxe materials. They also represent 2,800 units of common materials and conversion costs. Thus the total effort for the common costs for all units completed can be found by adding together the 4,300 plain units to the 2,800 deluxe units to get 7,100 equivalent units for the common cost elements.

Ending work-in-process represents only deluxe units, so no additional effort for the plain materials is incorporated into the ending inventory. The deluxe units were said to be 50% complete with regard to materials. Assuming that this means with regard to all materials, we add 100 equivalent units of effort to both the

**EXHIBIT 15-8 Solution to the Demonstration Problem**

**EQUIVALENT UNITS**

| | Common Costs | | Separate Materials | |
|---|---|---|---|---|
| | **Materials** | **Conversion Costs** | **Plain Model** | **Deluxe Model** |
| Units completed | 7,100 | 7,100 | 4,300 | 2,800 |
| Ending work-in-process | 100 | 140 | 0 | 100 |
| Total effort | 7,200 | 7,240 | 4,300 | 2,900 |
| Beginning costs | $ 300 | $ 350 | $ 90 | $ — |
| Current costs | 35,700 | 21,370 | 4,210 | 5,800 |
| Total costs | $36,000 | $21,720 | $4,300 | $5,800 |
| Cost per equivalent unit | $5 | $3 | $1 | $2 |

**COST DISTRIBUTION**

Cost of goods completed

**Plain Model**

| | | |
|---|---|---|
| Plain materials | (4,300 EU × $1) | $ 4,300 |
| Common materials | (4,300 EU × $5) | 21,500 |
| Conversion costs | (4,300 EU × $3) | 12,900 |
| Total | | $38,700 |

**Deluxe Model**

| | | |
|---|---|---|
| Deluxe materials | (2,800 EU × $2) | $ 5,600 |
| Common materials | (2,800 EU × $5) | 14,000 |
| Conversion costs | (2,800 EU × $3) | 8,400 |
| Total | | $28,000 |

Cost of ending work-in-process

**Deluxe Model**

| | | |
|---|---|---|
| Deluxe materials | (100 EU × $2) | $ 200 |
| Common materials | (100 EU × $5) | 500 |
| Conversion costs | (140 EU × $3) | 420 |
| Total | | $1,120 |

**CHECK**

| | |
|---|---|
| Costs incurred | |
| Beginning inventory cost | $ 740 |
| Current period costs | |
| Common materials | 35,700 |
| Conversion | 21,370 |
| Plain cabinets | 4,210 |
| Deluxe cabinets | 5,800 |
| Total costs to account for | $67,820 |
| Costs distributed | |
| Cost of goods completed | |
| Plain models | $38,700 |
| Deluxe models | 28,000 |
| Cost of ending work-in-process | 1,120 |
| Total costs distributed | $67,820 |

common materials and the materials unique to the deluxe model. Ending work-in-process was also said to be 70% complete with regard to conversion costs, so 140 equivalent units of conversion effort is represented by ending inventory.

The computation of the cost of an equivalent unit of effort is just as before. But now the cost distribution must take into account the different units being produced. Thus in the calculation of cost of goods completed we determine separately the cost of the plain units completed from the cost of the deluxe units.

## KEY TERMS AND CONCEPTS

[Equivalent unit of production
[Effective unit of production
FIFO process costing
Weighted-average process costing
Transferred-in costs

[Bracketed terms are equivalent in meaning.

## FURTHER READING

Corcoran, Wayne A., and Wayne E. Leininger. "Stochastic Process Costing Models," *The Accounting Review* (January 1973), p. 105.

Frank, Werner. "A Computer Application in Process Cost Accounting," *The Accounting Review* (October 1965), p. 854.

Franke, Reimund. "Process Model for Costing," *Management Accounting* (January 1975), p. 45.

Horngren, Charles T. "Process Costing in Perspective: Forget FIFO," *The Accounting Review* (July 1967), p. 593.

Schwan, Edward S. "Process Costing via Reaction Accounting," *Management Accounting* (September 1974), p. 45.

Stallman, James C. "Framework for Evaluating Cost Control Procedures for a Process," *The Accounting Review* (October 1972), p. 774.

## QUESTIONS AND EXERCISES

**15-1** What is meant by an equivalent finished unit?

**15-2** Under what conditions will FIFO and weighted-average process costing consistently produce similar unit cost figures?

**15-3** A department in a processing operation has some finished units physically on hand. Should they be counted as completed units or as ending inventory?

**15-4** In a process cost situation, Work-in-Process is a control account. What form docs the subsidiary ledger take?

**15-5** What is the effect, this period and next, of overestimating the degree of completion of ending inventory in a process cost situation?

**15-6** Under what conditions could a process complete more units during the period than it started?

**15-7** International University has 30,000 students enrolled around the world. On average, they carry six units each. Fifteen units is considered a full load. Using the notion of equivalent units as developed in the chapter, how many full-time equivalent students does IU have?

**15-8** In process situations involving pipeline operations or assembly line operations, if the pipeline or assembly line is always full, then beginning and ending inventories are always 50% complete with regard to processing. Explain.

**15-9** What are the similarities and differences between process costing and percentage-of-completion accounting as studied in financial accounting?

**15-10** A firm has one machine through which is drawn a standard type of wire to make nails. With very minor adjustments, different size nails are produced. Would you recommend that the firm employ job order or process cost techniques?

**15-11** At the beginning of the period there were 2,000 units in process, which averaged 50% complete. At the end of the period there were 3,000 units in process, which averaged 40% complete. During the period, 20,000 units were completed and transferred to the next department. This department produced "the equivalent" of how many finished units?

**15-12** The beginning inventory has 4,000 units, averaging 50% complete. The ending inventory has 3,000 units, averaging 60% complete. During the period, work was begun on 40,000 units. In terms of output for the period, how many effective units did this department produce?

**15-13** At the start of the period there were 5,000 units in process, which were 60% complete as to materials and 40% complete as to conversion. An additional 45,000 units were started during the period. At the end of the period, there were 8,000 units in process, which were 50% complete as to materials and 30% complete as to conversion. Assuming no units were lost or gained in production, how many units were transferred out during the period? What was equivalent production for the period with regard to materials and conversion?

**15-14** A department began the month with no beginning inventory. During the month it started work on 15,000 units and completed 10,000; the 5,000 units in ending inventory were 80% complete for material and 60% complete for conversion. Total costs for the month were $29,400 for material and $25,350 for conversion. What is the cost of ending inventory and completions?

**15-15** Department J had the following units in process during the month.

| | |
|---|---|
| Beginning | 4,000 units, 75% processed |
| Units started | 24,000 |
| Units completed | 20,000 |
| Ending | 8,000 units, 50% processed |

The processing costs associated with the beginning inventory amounted to $7,000, and during the month processing costs of $65,000 were incurred. Using weighted-average costing, what are the total processing costs assigned to the ending inventory and completions?

**15-16** Department O receives material from department N for further processing; it does not add further material to the product. There was no beginning inventory; 6,000 units were started, of which 5,000 were completed and transferred to department P. The ending inventory averaged 50% complete. Processing costs in department O for the period amounted to $17,050. Determine the current unit cost of processing and the division of processing costs between ending inventory and cost of goods manufactured for department O.

**15-17** Department G receives material from a previous department but adds none of its own. The beginning inventory of 5,000 units was 80% processed and the ending inventory of 10,000 units was 60% processed. During the period, 30,000 units were transferred in and 25,000 were transferred out. The processing costs attached to the beginning inventory were $28,000 and costs incurred during the period amounted to $175,500. Determine the cost per unit for processing in the current period.

**15-18** Refer to 15-17. The costs attached to beginning inventory for materials from the previous department were $15,000. The cost of materials transferred to department G during the current period was $93,000. Using the FIFO method, determine the unit cost and total cost of ending inventory and transfers out. Prepare the journal entry for costs transferred out of the department.

**15-19** Refer to 15-17. The costs attached to beginning inventory for materials from the previous department were $15,000. The cost of material transferred to department G during the current period was $93,000. Using the weighted-average method, determine the unit cost of ending inventory and transfers out. Also, prepare the journal entry for costs transferred out of the department.

**15-20** Refer to the demonstration problem at the end of the chapter. Assume that the deluxe units in ending inventory are 60% complete with regard to materials costs and 75% complete with regard to conversion costs. Determine the cost of goods completed and the cost of ending work in process (the numbers will not come out even).

## PROBLEMS AND CASES

**15-21 Physical units.**

Below are several short problems dealing with processing situations.

**Required**

For each problem, prepare a physical production report that accounts for all whole units as well as a FIFO calculation of equivalent units wherever appropriate.

**a.** Department K receives material from department J. At the start of the period there were 10,000 units being worked on that were 40% complete with respect to processing. During the period an additional 60,000 units entered department K. At the end of the period there were 9,000 units being worked on that averaged 60% complete with respect to processing. Department K does not add any material to the product.

**b.** Department N began the period with 5,000 units, which were 60% processed. An additional 30,000 units were started during the period. During the period 32,000 units were completed and transferred out of the department. The ending inventory was 40% processed. Department N adds material to the initial product when it is 50% complete.

**c.** Department X began the period with 6,000 units in inventory, which averaged 50% complete with respect to materials and 40% complete with respect to processing. At the end of the period, there were 8,000 units in inventory, which averaged 60% complete with respect to materials and 50% with respect to processing. The department shipped 60,000 units to finished goods during the period.

**d.** Department P started the period with 10,000 units that were 60% converted. During the period, it began work on another 50,000 units. The ending inventory has 6,000 units that are 40% converted. Material A is introduced at the start of the process and material B is introduced when the units are 45% processed.

15-22 **Equivalent units** (CPA adapted).

The Jorcano Manufacturing Company uses a process cost system to account for the costs of its only product, product D. Production begins in the fabrication department, where units of raw material are molded into various connecting parts. After fabrication is complete, the units are transferred to the assembly department. There is no material added in the assembly department. After assembly is complete, the units are transferred to a packaging department, where packing material is placed around the units. After the units are ready for shipping, they are sent to a shipping area.

At year-end, June 30, 19X3, the following inventory of product D is on hand.

No unused raw material or packing material.

Fabrication department: 300 units, one-third complete as to raw material and 50% complete as to direct labor.

Assembly department: 1,000 units, 40% complete as to direct labor.

Packaging department: 100 units, 75% complete as to packing material and 25% complete as to direct labor.

Shipping area: 400 units.

**Required**

Select the correct response to each of the following:

**a.** The number of equivalent units of raw material in all inventories at June 30, 19X3, is

**1.** 300
**2.** 100
**3.** 1,600
**4.** 925

**b.** The number of equivalent units of fabrication department direct labor in all inventories at June 30, 19X3, is

1. 1,650
2. 150
3. 300
4. 975

c. The number of equivalent units of packing material in all inventories at June 30, 19X3, is
1. 75
2. 475
3. 100
4. 425

**15-23 Costing multiple services.**
Determining the cost to perform services in a service-oriented firm is often difficult because employees frequently engage in a variety of tasks on any given day. Nonetheless, process costing concepts can still be used.

The Social Security Administration just opened a new claims office in the city of Moore. This gives the administration an opportunity to estimate the costs of providing services, as there were no claims in process at the beginning of the period.

All costs of the office are considered direct labor or overhead. Overhead will be charged to services based on labor. During the current period the office used 8,100 hours of labor at a cost of $101,250. Overhead for the period was $76,500. The use of work sampling methods (see Chapter 3) revealed that employees spent the following percentages of their time devoted to the tasks indicated.

| | |
|---|---|
| Process application for ID number | 10% |
| Process claim for retirement benefits | 35% |
| Process claim for disability benefits | 40% |
| Process claim for survivor's benefits | 15% |

The following chart summarizes the case activity during the period and the number of cases still in process at the end of the period. The number in parentheses below the in-process cases is an estimate of the average degree of completion for the cases.

| Task | Cases Completed | Cases in Process | Total Cases |
|---|---|---|---|
| Process application for ID number | 4,800 | 300 (70%) | 5,100 |
| Process claim for retirement benefits | 6,000 | 250 (20%) | 6,250 |
| Process claim for disability benefits | 1,200 | 700 (40%) | 1,900 |
| Process claim for survivor's benefits | 2,700 | 300 (90%) | 3,000 |

**Required**
Estimate the cost to process each type of case. What is the approximate cost invested in the cases still in process?

**15-24 Accounting for physical units.**

Wege, Inc., manufactures circuit boards under process conditions. During February, department M operated as follows:

In process, February 1: 2,000 boards, 50% complete as to materials and 40% complete as to processing.

In process, February 28: 4,000 boards, 70% complete as to materials and 40% complete as to processing.

During February, 12,000 boards were started in process and no units were lost.

**Required**

**a.** Prepare a production report for February showing the equivalent units of effort if the firm uses FIFO process costing.

**b.** Prepare a weighted-average production report for February.

**15-25 FIFO Costing.**

Yellow Crate Company uses first-in, first-out process costing for its inventory. The firm makes soft drink containers. Materials are added at the beginning of the process, whereas labor and overhead costs are incurred uniformly. The firm had 6,000 units in beginning work-in-process. These units were 75% complete. During the period the firm began work on an additional 98,000 units, and completed the period with 10,000 units 30% complete in ending work-in-process inventory.

Costs attached to beginning inventory were $2,000 for materials and $600 for labor and overhead. Costs added during the period were $29,400 for materials and $13,875 for labor and overhead.

**Required**

Determine the cost of goods completed and the total and unit costs of ending work-in-process.

**15-26 FIFO costing.**

Bengal Chemicals uses FIFO process costing for determining the cost of its products. A unit of product is considered to be 1 gallon of lawn killer W. At the beginning of the quarter, the firm had 7,000 gallons of product in process. This batch was 30% complete. During the quarter, an additional 90,000 gallons of product were put into process and 86,000 gallons were completed. At the end of the quarter there was a batch of 11,000 gallons of product, 60% complete in process.

Raw material (crude oil) is added at the beginning of the process. Direct labor is required when the units are 50% complete. Overhead costs are presumed to be incurred uniformly with production. The cost of beginning work-in-process was $14,000 for materials and $5,000 for overhead. Costs incurred for the current period were $193,500 for materials, $131,920 for labor, and $220,820 for overhead.

**Required**

Determine the cost of goods completed and the cost of ending work-in-process for the first quarter of 19X1 for the product lawn killer W.

**15-27 Prior department: FIFO costing.**

Benton Industries began 19X7 with 15,000 units in work-in-process in department 3. These units were one-third complete and were costed at $40,470 for prior department costs and $14,322 for conversion costs. During 19X7, 93,000 additional units were transferred into department 3 from department 2. These units were transferred from department 2 at a cost of $224,130. Department 3 incurred additional materials costs of $166,840 and conversion costs of $315,228 during the year. Department 3 ended the year with 11,000 units in ending work-in-process. These units were 40% complete.

**Required**

Determine the cost of goods completed and the cost of ending work-in-process in department 3 using FIFO process costing. Assume that conversion costs are incurred uniformly and materials are added in department 3 when the units are 60% complete.

**15-28 Weighted-average costing.**

Spurrier, Inc., manufactures a single product under carefully controlled conditions. Data for the period are as follows:

Beginning inventory: 20,000 units are being worked on. They are 60% complete as to materials at a cost of $24,000. They are 50% complete as to processing at a cost of $50,000.

During the period, work was begun on an additional 60,000 units and 70,000 units were completed and transferred out.

Ending inventory: 10,000 units are being worked on. They are 40% complete as to materials and 30% complete as to processing.

During the period the cost of materials added was $130,200 and the cost of processing was $327,600.

**Required**

Using weighted-average methods, account for all units, total costs, and unit costs.

**15-29 Prior department costs: Weighted-average costing.**

A department processes material received from a prior department. Data for the period are as follows:

The beginning inventory consists of 5,000 units transferred in at a cost of $15,000. They have been 50% processed at a cost of $5,000.

During the period an additional 20,000 units were transferred in at a cost of $62,000.

During the period 22,000 units were completed and transferred out.

The ending inventory consists of 3,000 units, two-thirds processed.

Processing costs incurred during the period amounted to $45,400.

**Required**

Using the weighted-average method of costing, account for all units and costs.

**15-30 Weighted-average costing.**

Amdarco Industries began 19X7 with 12,000 units in work-in-process in department 38. These units were one-third complete and were costed at $44,560 for prior department costs and $12,276 for conversion costs. During 19X7, 80,000 additional units were transferred into department 38. These units were transferred from department 37, and had a cost of $340,000. Department 38 incurred materials costs of $136,850 and conversion costs of $220,394 during the year. Department 38 ended the year with 7,000 units in ending work-in-process. These units were 40% complete.

**Required**
Determine the cost of goods completed and the cost of ending work-in-process in department 38 using weighted-average process costing. Assume that conversion costs are incurred uniformly and materials are added in department 38 when the units are 60% complete.

**15-31 FIFO and weighted average.**
Andouille Packing has several departments, one of which is of immediate interest. In this department all material is added at the start of the process.

Operations for February are as follows:

| | |
|---|---|
| Work-in-process, February 1 | 8,000, three-fourths processed |
| Transfers in | 34,000 |
| Transfers out | 30,000 |
| Work-in-process, February 28 | 12,000, two-thirds processed |

Costs to be accounted for are as follows:

| | Materials | Processing |
|---|---|---|
| Work-in-process, February 1 | $32,000 | $18,000 |
| Costs added, February | 13,940 | 95,680 |

**Required**
Account for physical units, unit costs, and total costs assuming that the firm uses
**a.** weighted-average costing.
**b.** FIFO costing.

**15-32 Determining the status of work-in-process, and system choice.**
Several years ago the city's police commissioner requested that the department estimate the cost of a typical murder investigation. The commissioner uses this, and similar, information when submitting the department's budget request to the city council.

At the beginning of the year there were 10 murder cases still open. Details are provided in the following schedule.

| | | Investigation Hours (estimated) | | |
|---|---|---|---|---|
| Case Number | Principal Investigator | To Date | To Complete | Status |
| 83-12 | Doolin | 2,000 | 0 | Inactive |
| 85-9 | Barber | 3,000 | 0 | Inactive |
| 86-7 | Stutts | 1,800 | 300 | Active |
| 86-11 | Barber | 1,500 | 500 | Active |
| 86-14 | Ross | 2,500 | 0 | Inactive |
| 87-2 | Pippin | 1,000 | 1,000 | Active |
| 87-4 | Pippin | 800 | 50 | Imminent |
| 87-5 | Ross | 200 | 100 | Imminent |
| 87-6 | Stutts | 500 | 1,000 | Active |
| 87-10 | Ross | 100 | 1,000 | Active |

During the year the city experienced 35 additional murders. As of the end of the year there were 8 cases still being held open. Summary data are presented in the schedule below.

| | | Investigation Hours (estimated) | | |
|---|---|---|---|---|
| Case Number | Principal Investigator | To Date | To Complete | Status |
| 83-12 | Doolin | 2,000 | 0 | Inactive |
| 86-11 | Barber | 2,200 | 300 | Active |
| 87-2 | Pippin | 1,800 | 0 | Inactive |
| 87-10 | Ross | 2,000 | 100 | Imminent |
| 88-5 | Ross | 1,000 | 2,000 | Active |
| 88-10 | Pippin | 100 | 100 | Imminent |
| 88-11 | Stutts | 700 | 1,300 | Active |
| 88-15 | Pippin | 300 | 2,500 | Active |

The costs incurred by the police department are segregated into just two categories: wages and overhead. Officers keep a daily log of the number of hours devoted to various activities. There are no actual logs of hours spent on specific cases. The year-end reports on open cases represent estimates by each case's principal investigator.

During the year 30,000 hours of investigative time were spent on murder cases. This represents wages for the year of $410,000. Overhead of $82,000 was allocated on the basis of wages. The case load in process at the beginning of the year was costed at $37,500.

**Required**

**a.** Determine the average cost to complete a murder investigation (1) using FIFO process costing (use the FIFO *assumption* even though the actual flow of cases is not FIFO) and (2) using weighted-average process costing.

**b.** An officer has observed that the cost to complete a murder investigation varies widely. "Some cases are solved nearly instantaneously, while others may drag on for years. Why don't we use job costing?" (Apparently, the officer is a part-time accounting student.) What is your reply?

**15-33 Two departments, two periods: FIFO and weighted average.**

Rausher Industries began a new product line this year. Management wants a cost report for the current year and a budget for next year.

The product requires processing in two departments. Materials are added at the beginning of the process in department 1. Department 2 finishes the product but adds no direct materials. During the year work was begun on 12,000 units in department 1, and 9,000 of these units were transferred to department 2. The remaining 3,000 units were 60% complete with regard to conversion costs in department 1, which incurred $36,000 of materials costs and $14,040 of conversion costs.

Department 2 completed and sent 7,000 units to the finished goods warehouse. It ended the period with 2,000 units 40% complete with regard to department 2's conversion costs, which were $32,760 for the period.

The plan for next year is to begin an additional 15,000 units in department 1. Management expects to finish the year with 5,000 units one-half converted in department 1. Department 2 is expected to complete 14,000 units, and its ending inventory is expected to be 70% complete. Materials are expected to be $48,600 and conversion costs for departments 1 and 2 are expected to be $14,545 and $59,075, respectively.

**Required**

Prepare a cost report for the current year and a budgeted cost report for next year assuming the firm uses

**a.** FIFO processing costing.
**b.** weighted-average process costing.

**15-34 Process costing, actual cost distribution.**

Grievance, Inc., specializes in pest control products. The following schedule for one of the firm's products shows the equivalent or effective production for a period of time and the costs accumulated. The questions that follow have to do with how these costs would be *distributed* under various cost flow assumptions.

| | Equivalent Units | Total Costs | Unit Cost |
|---|---|---|---|
| Beginning | 3,000 | $120,000 | $40.00 |
| Increases | 10,000 | 387,000 | 38.70 |
| Total | 13,000 | $507,000 | $39.00 |
| Ending | 2,000 | ? | ? |
| Decreases | 11,000 | $ ? | $ ? |

**Required**

Determine the total cost and the unit cost to be assigned to ending work-in-process inventory and to cost of goods manufactured assuming

**a.** weighted-average costing.
**b.** FIFO costing.

**15-35 Unit costing: Objective.**

Massprod, Inc., produces a single product under process costing conditions. You are to use the data below to distribute department W's conversion costs at the end of the period.

| | Whole Units | Conversion: Department W — Equivalent Units | Total Costs | Unit Cost |
|---|---|---|---|---|
| Inventory, February 1 | 200 | 100 | $ 210 | $2.100 |
| Additions | 900 | 800 | 1,800 | 2.250 |
| Total | 1,100 | 900 | $2,010 | $2.233 |
| Inventory, February 28 | 400 | 200 | ? | ? |
| Completions | 700 | 700 | ? | ? |

**Required**

**a.** Was department W efficient during the period insofar as conversion costs are concerned? Explain.
**b.** Use one of the following responses for each of the next four questions: (a) $2.175 (b) $2.229 (c) $2.233 (d) $2.250 (e) something else.

1. Using FIFO costing, what is the cost per physical unit to be assigned to the ending inventory?
2. Using FIFO costing, what is the cost per physical unit to be assigned to the completed units?
3. Using weighted-average costing, what is the cost per physical unit to be assigned to the ending inventory?
4. Using weighted-average costing, what is the cost per physical unit to be assigned to the completed units?

15-36 **Physical units: Weighted-average and FIFO costing** (CPA adapted).
Lakeview Corporation is a manufacturer using process costing techniques. It manufactures a product that is produced in three separate departments: molding, assembly, and finishing. The following information was obtained for the assembly department for the month of June.

| | |
|---|---|
| Beginning inventory | |
| 2,000 units transferred in from molding | $ 32,000 |
| 100% complete as to direct materials | 20,000 |
| 60% complete as to direct labor | 7,200 |
| 50% complete as to factory overhead | 5,500 |
| | $ 64,700 |
| Costs incurred during June | |
| 10,000 units transferred in from molding | $160,000 |
| Direct materials | 96,000 |
| Direct labor | 36,000 |
| Factory overhead | 18,000 |
| | $310,000 |
| Ending inventory | |
| 4,000 units still in work-in-process | |
| 90% complete as to direct materials | |
| 70% complete as to direct labor | |
| 35% complete as to factory overhead | |

Eight thousand units were completed and transferred to the finishing department.

**Required**

Account for all costs according to

**a.** weighted-average costing.

**b.** FIFO costing.

15-37 **Process costing: Two departments with by-product—requires prior study of Chapter 13** (CPA adapted).
The Adept Company is a manufacturer of two products known as "prep" and "pride." Incidental to the production of these two products, it produces a by-product known as "wilton." The manufacturing process covers two departments, grading and saturating.

The manufacturing process begins in the grading department when raw materials are started in process. Upon completion of processing in the grading department, the by-product wilton is produced, which accounts for 20% of the material output. This by-product needs no further processing and is transferred to finished goods.

The net realizable value of the by-product wilton is accounted for as a reduction of the cost of materials in the grading department. The current selling price of wilton is $1.00 per pound, and the estimated selling and delivery costs total $0.10 per pound.

The remaining output is transferred to the saturating department for the final phase of production. In the saturating department, water is added at the beginning of the production process, which results in a 50% gain in weight of the materials in production.

The following information is available for the month of November 19X9.

| | November 1 | | November 30 |
|---|---|---|---|
| **Inventories** | **Quantity (pounds)** | **Amount** | **Quantity (pounds)** |
| Work-in-process | | | |
| Grading department | None | $ — | None |
| Saturating department | 1,600 | 17,600 | 2,000 |
| Finished goods | | | |
| Prep | 600 | 14,520 | 1,600 |
| Pride | 2,400 | 37,110 | 800 |
| Wilton | None | — | None |

The work-in-process inventory (labor and overhead) in the saturating department is estimated to be 50% complete both at the beginning and end of November. Costs of production for November are as follows:

| Costs of Production | Materials Used | Labor and Overhead |
|---|---|---|
| Grading department | $265,680 | $86,400 |
| Saturating department | — | 86,000 |

The material used in the grading department weighed 36,000 pounds. Adept uses the first-in, first-out method of process costing.

**Required**

Prepare a cost-of-production report for both the grading and saturating departments for the month of November. Show supporting computations in good form. The answer should include the following:

Equivalent units of production (in pounds)
Total manufacturing costs
Cost per equivalent unit (pounds)
Dollar amount of ending Work-in-Process
Dollar amount of inventory cost transferred out

15-38 **Comprehensive: Joint products, process costing, weighted-average costing—requires prior study of Chapter 13.**

S-T, Inc., processes material in 1,000-gallon batches. Each batch results in 400 gallons of main product X, 500 gallons of main product Y, and 100 gallons of by-product Z. Material is added at the start of the process. The joint products emerge at the end of the process. By-product revenues are treated as a recovery of joint cost (cost reduction) at the time of production and main products are costed according to net realizable value. Product X sells for $8 per gallon and has separable costs of $2 per gallon. Product Y sells for $11 per gallon and has separable costs of $3 per gallon. By-product Z sells for $1 per gallon.

The beginning inventory consists of two batches averaging 30% and 80% converted, material costs are $8,550, and conversion costs are $3,007. The ending inventory consists of one batch, which is 50% converted. During the week 20 batches were completed and transferred out; there was no gain or loss during the week.

During the week materials placed into production had a cost of $71,250, and conversion costs totaled $40,740.

**Required**
Using weighted-average costing, what is the unit cost to be assigned to the completed products X, Y, and Z?

**15-39 Comprehensive: Service department allocation, step method, overhead rates, and process costing—requires prior study of Chapter 12.**
Byron Brothers operates two production departments and three service departments (labeled $P_1$, $P_2$, $S_1$, $S_2$, and $S_3$ for simplicity). Costs incurred by each department are summarized here.

| | Department | | | | |
|---|---|---|---|---|---|
| | $S_1$ | $S_2$ | $S_3$ | $P_1$ | $P_2$ |
| Materials | $20,000 | $50,000 | $100,000 | $62,500 | $ 37,500 |
| Labor | 56,250 | 14,250 | 93,750 | 18,750 | 187,500 |
| Overhead | 32,000 | 41,000 | 63,200 | 48,250 | 112,200 |

Department $S_1$'s costs are allocated in proportion to the materials costs incurred by each department, $S_2$'s costs are allocated relative to each department's labor costs, and $S_3$'s costs are allocated evenly to all user departments.

**Required**
**a.** Allocate the service department costs to the two production departments using the step method (allocate $S_1$ first, then $S_2$, and $S_3$ last).
**b.** Department $P_1$'s overhead costs are allocated to products based on labor costs. What is $P_1$'s overhead application rate per dollar of labor costs?
**c.** Production department $P_1$ started the period with 600 units of product, 20% complete with regard to materials and 40% complete with regard to conversion costs. These units were valued at $4,860. During the period the department began work on 12,000 units of product. The period ended with 200 units still in process in department $P_1$. These ending units were 100% complete with regard to materials and 90% complete with regard to conversion costs. If the firm uses FIFO process costing, determine the cost of ending work-in-process and cost of goods completed.

**15-40 Comprehensive: service department allocation, multidepartment weighted-average process costing—requires prior study of Chapter 12.**
The JCI Company has two service departments and two production departments. The service departments are materials handling and engineering, and the production departments are regular processing and deluxe processing. The percent-

age of each service department's services provided to other departments during the current period were

| | Materials Handling | Engineering | Regular Processing | Deluxe Processing |
|---|---|---|---|---|
| Materials handling | — | 0.2 | 0.3 | 0.5 |
| Engineering | 0.3 | — | 0.4 | 0.3 |

The costs charged directly to each department during the period were

| | Direct Materials | Direct Labor | Overhead | Total |
|---|---|---|---|---|
| Materials handling | $ 2,000 | $ 27,000 | $11,000 | $ 40,000 |
| Engineering | 4,000 | 55,000 | 16,000 | 75,000 |
| Regular processing | 85,000 | 30,000 | 25,000 | 140,000 |
| Deluxe processing | 24,000 | 28,000 | 16,000 | 68,000 |
| Total | $115,000 | $140,000 | $68,000 | $323,000 |

The period began with 1,500 units of product in work-in-process in the regular processing department. These units were 70% complete with regard to materials and 40% complete with regard to conversion costs. They were valued at $2,290 for materials and $2,234.04 for conversion costs. During the period 30,000 additional units were put into regular processing. The period ended with 2,000 units in regular processing. These units were 30% complete with regard to materials and 25% complete with regard to conversion costs.

The firm sells some of the units "as is" when they are finished with regular processing; the additional units are sent to the deluxe processing department where additional components are added. The deluxe processing department started the period with 500 units in process. They were 20% complete with regard to deluxe materials and 30% complete with regard to deluxe conversion costs. These units were valued at $3,202 for transferred-in units, $440 for materials, and $1,155.56 for conversion costs. During the period 40% of the units completed by the regular processing department were transferred to the deluxe processing department. The remaining 60% of the units were transferred to the finished goods warehouse. The period ended with 800 units in process in the deluxe processing department. These units were 90% complete with regard to materials and 80% complete with regard to conversion costs.

**Required**

**a.** Allocate the service department costs to the production departments using the simultaneous-equations method.

**b.** Determine the cost of goods completed for each of the products and the costs of the ending work-in-process inventories. The firm uses weighted-average process costing.

# CHAPTER 16

# PROCESS COSTING WITH SPOILAGE AND REWORK

In the previous chapter it was assumed that all units put into a production process were finished without incident as good units. This chapter examines the complications that arise when some units are spoiled and some units must be reworked. Given the predominance of the use of average process costing, we will restrict our discussion to average costing.

## SPOILAGE

Whether as the result of accidents, machine malfunctions, poor workmanship, or substandard materials, from time to time some portion of the production in any process will have to be scrapped. To the extent that this spoilage is unavoidable it is properly included as one of the costs of obtaining good units of inventory. On the other hand, avoidable spoilage is properly treated as a loss. Thus one of our tasks in dealing with spoilage is to segregate normal from abnormal spoilage. **Normal spoilage** is defined as the average spoilage unavoidable in the production process and its cost will be included as an inventoriable cost. **Abnormal spoilage** is defined as the actual spoilage in excess of (or below) the normal rate and it will be treated as a period loss (gain).

A second problem is to determine whether normal spoilage costs should be partially charged to ending work-in-process inventory or whether the total normal spoilage cost is charged only to the cost of the goods completed. The general rule will be that an allowance for spoilage will be attached to ending work-in-process only if the ending inventory is, on the average, beyond the point at which inspection for spoilage occurs. Let us demonstrate with an example.

A firm began a period with 500 units in work-in-process considered, on the average, to be 25% complete. An additional 4,000 units were begun. The period ended with 600 units considered to be 80% complete. Materials are added at the beginning of the process while conversion costs are assumed to be incurred in proportion to the stage of completion of the products. The units are inspected when they are 75% complete. Normal spoilage is considered to be 5% of the units inspected. This period 250 units were rejected and thrown away. Costs attached to beginning inventory were $3,000 for materials and $1,000 for conversion costs. Current period costs were $20,625 for materials and $33,971.75 for conversion costs. Let us now use average process costing to determine the cost of goods completed, cost of ending work-in-process, and the loss from abnormal spoilage.

The complete solution is given in Exhibit 16-1. As usual, we begin by determining the effort exerted during the period. This time we account for the good units completed, the units spoiled, and the effort in ending work-in-process. The spoiled units are further divided into those that constitute normal spoilage and the remainder, which are considered abnormal spoilage.

Normal spoilage was said to be 5% of the units inspected. Therefore, we must determine how many units were inspected. The maximum possible would be the beginning units plus all units on which work was started. From the total units that might have been inspected we subtract any units that, in fact, were not inspected. There are only two possible groups of units that may not have been inspected: (1) Units in beginning inventory may have been inspected in the preceding period, and (2) units in ending inventory may not have reached the inspection point.

For this particular example both the units in the beginning and ending inventory were inspected in the current period resulting in 4,500 units being inspected. That is, the beginning units were said to be 25% complete, but inspection occurs at the 75% complete point. Therefore, they cannot have been inspected in the previous period. Our ending work-in-process is 80% complete so these units made it beyond the inspection point and must have been inspected. Finally, the units started and completed in the period must also have been inspected.

Normal spoilage, then, is 5% of the 4,500 units inspected, or 225. Because actual spoilage was 250 units, there must be 25 units of abnormal spoilage. When entering the equivalent units of effort represented by the spoiled units on the worksheet, we must be careful to portray the actual

## EXHIBIT 16-1 Process Costing with Spoilage

### Timing of Costs and Inventory Status

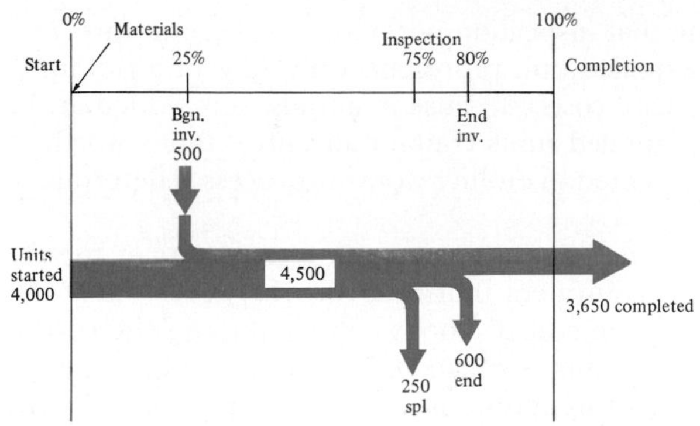

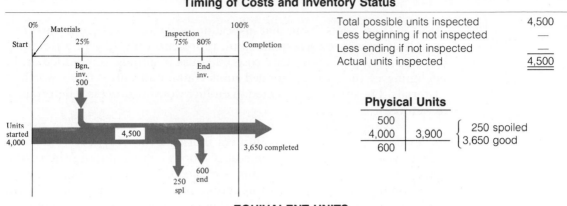

| | |
|---|---|
| Total possible units inspected | 4,500 |
| Less beginning if not inspected | — |
| Less ending if not inspected | — |
| Actual units inspected | 4,500 |

**Physical Units**

| | | |
|---|---|---|
| 500 | | |
| 4,000 | 3,900 | { 250 spoiled; 3,650 good } |
| 600 | | |

### EQUIVALENT UNITS

| | Materials | | Conversion Costs | |
|---|---|---|---|---|
| Effort | | | | |
| Good units completed | 3,650 | | 3,650.00 | |
| Normal spoilage | 225 | 5% of 4,500 = 225 | 168.75 | 225 × .75 |
| Abnormal spoilage | 25 | 250 − 225 = 25 | 18.75 | 25 × .75 |
| Ending work-in process | 600 | | 480.00 | |
| Total effort | 4,500 | | 4,317.50 | |
| Costs | | | | |
| Beginning costs | $ 3,000 | | $ 1,000.00 | |
| Current costs | 20,625 | | 33,971.75 | |
| Total costs | $23,625 | | $34,971.75 | |
| Cost per equivalent unit | $5.25 | | $8.10 | |

### COST DISTRIBUTION

| | |
|---|---|
| Cost of goods completed | |
| 3,650 ($5.25 + $8.10) | $48,727.50 |
| Plus normal spoilage | 2,188.39 |
| Total cost of goods completed | $50,915.89 |
| Cost of ending work-in-process | |
| 600($5.25) + 480($8.10) | $ 7,038.00 |
| Plus normal spoilage | 359.74 |
| Total ending work-in-process | $ 7,397.74 |
| Loss from abnormal spoilage | |
| 25($5.25) + 18.75($8.10) | $ 283.12 |

| | |
|---|---|
| Normal spoilage | |
| 225($5.25) + 168.75($8.10) | $2,548.13 |
| Allocation[a] | |
| To cost of goods completed: | |
| $\frac{3,650}{4,250}$ ($2,548.13) | $2,188.39 |
| To ending work-in process: | |
| $\frac{600}{4,250}$ ($2,548.13) | 359.74 |
| Total | $2,548.13 |

### CHECK

| | |
|---|---|
| Costs incurred | |
| Beginning inventory cost | $ 4,000.00 |
| Current period costs | |
| Materials | 20,625.00 |
| Conversion | 33,971.75 |
| Total costs to account for | $58,596.75 |
| Costs distributed | |
| Cost of goods completed | $50,915.89 |
| Cost of ending work-in-process | 7,397.74 |
| Loss from abnormal spoilage | 283.12 |
| Total costs distributed | $58,596.75 |

[a]Note that the cost of normal spoilage is allocated to physical units, not equivalent units.

effort in those units. Note that inspection occurs when the units are 75% complete; therefore each spoiled unit represents only 75% of a full unit's worth of effort for conversion costs. Because materials were added at the beginning of the process, spoiled units contain an entire unit's worth of materials. The effort represented in ending work-in-process is determined as before.

Having spoilage does not change our treatment of costs or the determination of the cost per equivalent unit of effort. However, there is a change when we determine the cost of goods completed and the cost of inventory. The cost of good units is calculated as before: The effort in units completed and the effort in ending inventory are multiplied by the cost per unit of effort. But now, in addition, we add a cost component for normal spoilage. The cost of normal spoilage is found by multiplying the effort represented by the spoiled units times the cost per unit of effort. Having determined the cost of normal spoilage we then determine to which units normal spoilage should be applied.

Normal spoilage costs are assigned to all units that have *survived* inspection. In our example, 3,650 completed good units have survived. In addition, since ending inventory is beyond the inspection point, the 600 units of ending inventory have also survived inspection for a total of 3,650 + 600 = 4,250. Therefore in Exhibit 16-1 the normal spoilage cost of $2,548.13 is spread equally over all 4,250 *physical* units that have survived inspection.

Next we determine the loss from abnormal spoilage by multiplying the effort in those units by the cost of each equivalent unit of effort. Finally, the check at the bottom of Exhibit 16-1 assures us that all costs are accounted for either in ending work-in-process, cost of goods completed, or loss from abnormal spoilage.

### Ending Work-in-Process before the Inspection Point

If in the previous example we change the inspection point to occur when units are 85% complete (beyond the stage of completion of ending work-in-process), two items would change. First, in determining the number of units inspected, ending work-in-process would not have been inspected. This, in turn, would mean that normal spoilage would be 5% of 3,900, or 195 units. Later, when it is time to determine which units get charged for normal spoilage, only the 3,650 good units completed will have survived inspection (ending work-in-process has not been inspected so those units have not survived inspection). Therefore, all normal spoilage costs would be charged to cost of goods completed. Exhibit 16-2 presents the solution to our example if inspection occurs at the 85% completion point.

## EXHIBIT 16-2 Ending Inventory before the Inspection for Spoilage

### Timing of Costs and Inventory Status

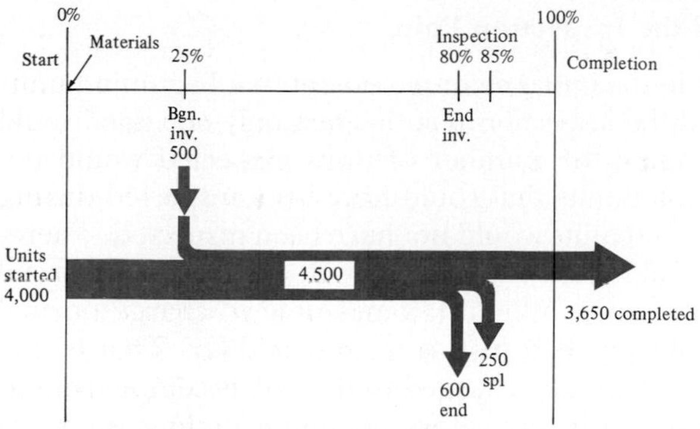


| | |
|---|---|
| Total possible units inspected | 4,500 |
| Less beginning if not inspected | — |
| Less ending if not inspected | 600 |
| Actual units inspected | 3,900 |

**Physical Units**

| | | |
|---|---|---|
| 500 | 3,900 | 250 spoiled |
| 4,000 | | 3,650 good |
| 600 | | |

### EQUIVALENT UNITS

| | Materials | | Conversion Costs | |
|---|---|---|---|---|
| Effort | | | | |
| Good units completed | 3,650 | | 3,650.00 | |
| Normal spoilage | 195 | 5% of 3,900 = 195 | 165.75 | 195 × .85 |
| Abnormal spoilage | 55 | 250 − 195 = 55 | 46.75 | 55 × .85 |
| Ending work-in-process | 600 | | 480.00 | |
| Total effort | 4,500 | | 4,342.50 | |
| Costs | | | | |
| Beginning costs | $ 3,000 | | $ 1,000.00 | |
| Current costs | 20,625 | | 33,971.75 | |
| Total costs | $23,625 | | $34,971.75 | |
| Cost per equivalent unit | $5.25 | | $8.0533679 | |

### COST DISTRIBUTION

| | |
|---|---|
| Cost of goods completed | |
| 3,650 ($5.25 + $8.053) | $48,557.29 |
| Plus normal spoilage | 2,358.60 |
| Total cost of goods completed | $50,915.89 |
| Cost of ending work-in-process | |
| 600($5.25) + 480($8.053) | $ 7,015.62 |
| Loss from abnormal spoilage | |
| 55($5.25) + 46.75($8.053) | $ 665.24 |

| | |
|---|---|
| Normal spoilage | |
| 195($5.25) + 165.75($8.053) | $2,358.60 |
| All to cost of goods completed | |

### CHECK

| | |
|---|---|
| Costs incurred | |
| Beginning inventory cost | $ 4,000.00 |
| Current period costs | |
| Materials | 20,625.00 |
| Conversion | 33,971.75 |
| Total costs to account for | $58,596.75 |
| Costs distributed | |
| Cost of goods completed | $50,915.89 |
| Cost of ending work-in-process | 7,015.62 |
| Loss from abnormal spoilage | 665.24 |
| Total costs distributed | $58,596.75 |

### Beginning Units beyond the Inspection Point

Assume the same facts as in the initial example except that beginning units are 90% complete (beyond the inspection point). Then only one item would change in the solution. Again the number of units inspected would decrease. Out of the 4,500 total units that could have been inspected during this period, the beginning 500 units would not have been inspected. Therefore, only 4,000 units would have been inspected, resulting in normal spoilage this period of 200 units. When it comes time to charge normal spoilage to units, we would proceed just as we did initially. That is, the cost of the normal spoilage would be charged to the goods completed and the units in ending work-in-process (we are assuming ending units are 80% complete, as specified in the original example).

This may seem strange. In the original example we spread the cost of the 225 units of normal spoilage over cost of goods completed and ending work-in-process. Why is it the same now that there are only 200 units of normal spoilage? The answer is that we are still spreading the cost of approximately 225 units as normal spoilage. Our revised example stated that the units in beginning inventory were beyond the inspection point. That means that an allowance for normal spoilage would have been assigned to these units last period. This allowance would be approximately 5% of the units in inventory (500) or 25 units. The cost of normal spoilage on these units would have been included last period in the cost of Work-in-Process inventory. When we add the beginning inventory costs to the current period costs, we are in effect averaging last period's and this period's normal spoilage costs together. Thus the costs for normal spoilage in beginning inventory are spread over all production in the current period along with the costs of the current 200 units of normal spoilage, which we also spread over all units.

### Actual Spoilage Less than Normal Spoilage

Returning to the original example we can note that actual spoilage, 250 units, was greater than normal spoilage, 225 units. What would change if actual spoilage was less than normal, say 190 units? Not much. Normal spoilage is based on what we expect to happen in the long run. Therefore the amount of normal spoilage included in the determination of the current period's effort would be the same as before (225 units). Abnormal spoilage is just the difference between actual and normal spoilage, so the effort for abnormal spoilage shows up as a negative 35 units in the effort computation (see Exhibit 16-3). When it is time to distribute costs to goods completed and ending inventory, the normal spoilage is treated exactly as before. However, when it is time to calculate the loss from abnormal spoil-

**EXHIBIT 16-3 Determination of Equivalent Units of Effort When Actual Spoilage Is Less than Normal Spoilage**

| | Materials | Conversion Cost |
|---|---|---|
| Good units completed | 3,650 | 3,650.00 |
| Normal spoilage | 225 | 168.75 |
| Abnormal spoilage | (35) | (26.25) |
| Ending work-in-process | 600 | 480.00 |
| Total equivalent units | 4,440 | 4,272.50 |

age, the negative effort numbers convert the loss to a "gain from less than normal spoilage." As with over- or underapplied overhead, firms will typically accumulate monthly gains and losses from abnormal spoilage in a deferred charge account under the assumption that they will tend to cancel each other out over time. The balance in the account is then closed to the income statement on an annual basis.

### Spoilage with Salvage Value

If, instead of throwing spoiled goods away, we are able to sell them, the cost of spoilage should be reduced by the proceeds of such sales. We calculate the cost of normal spoilage and abnormal spoilage as before, but then subtract a pro rata share of salvage proceeds from each. For example, in Exhibit 16-1, the cost of normal spoilage had been determined to be $2,548.13 for the 225 units of normal spoilage and $283.12 for the 25 units of abnormal spoilage. If these units could be sold for $2 each, the net spoilage costs would be

| | |
|---|---|
| Normal spoilage | $2,548.13 |
| Less salvage value ($2 × 225) | 450.00 |
| Net normal spoilage | $2,098.13 |

and

| | |
|---|---|
| Loss from abnormal spoilage | $283.12 |
| Less salvage value ($2 × 25) | 50.00 |
| Net loss from abnormal spoilage | $233.12 |

The net normal spoilage figure would then be allocated to the cost of goods completed and ending work-in-process inventories using the same ratios as in Exhibit 16-1.

## REWORK

In some processes goods rejected at inspection are not thrown away or sold as is, but rather are returned to the process to be repaired or reassembled into a good unit. In this situation the additional effort to put the unit into acceptable condition is called rework. As with spoilage, there are two major factors to consider in accounting for rework: (1) How much is **normal rework,** which is properly charged to inventory, and how much is **abnormal rework,** which is a loss? (2) Should ending work-in-process inventory be charged an allowance for normal rework?

Both questions are answered as before. Normal rework is determined from a firm's experience and its estimate of the unavoidable rework rate. Ending work-in-process is allocated a charge for normal rework only if it has survived the rework inspection. On the other hand, what constitutes rework effort is different from spoilage. **Rework** is the effort incurred above and beyond the effort that would have been incurred had the unit passed the inspection. That is, rework is only the duplicate effort required to fix the rejected unit. An example may clarify the point.

Suppose a firm began the current period with 500 units in work-in-process considered on average to be 25% complete. An additional 4,000 units were begun. The period ended with 600 units considered to be 80% complete. Materials are added at the beginning of the process, whereas conversion costs are assumed to be incurred in proportion to the stage of completion of the products. The units are inspected when they are 60% complete. Rejected units are returned to the 20% complete point to go through the process again for rework. Normal rework is considered to be 2% of the units that ultimately pass the inspection.[1] This period 4,650 units were inspected. Costs attached to beginning inventory were $3,000 for materials and $1,000 for conversion costs. Current period costs were $20,625 for materials and $33,987.20 for conversion costs. We wish to determine the cost of goods completed, cost of ending work-in-process, and the loss from abnormal rework using average process costing.

The physical flow in Exhibit 16-4 indicates that 3,900 good units were apparently completed during the period. To determine the number of actual units reworked we first calculate the number of units that would have been inspected had there been no rework. This can be found by taking the total number of units that were ever in work-in-process and subtracting from this the total units that would not have passed the in-

[1]Be careful with definitions of normal rework and normal spoilage. Firms (and people who write professional exams) use different definitions. Sometimes normal rework is given as a percentage of units started, total units inspected, or total units completed. We feel that basing normal spoilage on the units surviving inspection is the most theoretically defensible method, but if you encounter other definitions be sure to make the calculation correctly. Problems 16-33, 16-34, and 16-38 include alternative definitions of normal rework.

spection point in the current period. Beginning work-in-process units would not be inspected this period if they had been inspected last period. But the chart in Exhibit 16-4 shows that the beginning work-in-process had not reached the inspection point. Therefore, the beginning units in the example must have been inspected in the current period. In contrast, units in ending work-in-process would not have been inspected if they had not yet reached the inspection point. However, for the example, ending work-in-process is beyond the inspection point, so these units also must have been inspected. Had there been no rework, the total units inspected should have been 4,500. However, we are told that 4,650 were inspected. Hence, some units must have gone through the inspection more than once. This would occur if units were reworked, so we conclude that there were 4,650 − 4,500 = 150 units worth of rework in the current period. Note that this says nothing about whether 1 unit was reworked 150 times, 2 units were reworked 75 times each, or 150 units were reworked once. We do not care what the actual physical flow of units was; we are interested only in the number of units' worth of rework effort that was expended in the current period.

Given that 4,500 units passed inspection, 2% or 90 units are considered normal rework. Subtracting this from the actual total of 150 units reworked leaves 60 units of abnormal rework. Knowing the units, we now determine the equivalent units' worth of effort, by each cost category, required to rework the units. In this problem, materials are added at the beginning of the process, but reworked items are returned to the 20% complete point in the process. Therefore, no new direct materials were added during rework. However, units returned for rework do pass through the process from the 20% complete point to the 60% complete point for a second time. That is, if these units were not reworked, they would have continued in the process until complete, having passed through all phases of the process only once. Rework causes the units to pass through a portion of the process twice. It is this duplicate effort that gives rise to a cost for rework. Each unit reworked required 40% of an equivalent unit of effort for conversion costs (that is, 60% − 20% for costs considered to be incurred in proportion to the stage of completion). Therefore, the 90 units of normal rework constitute 90 × 0.4 = 36 equivalent units of conversion cost effort and the 60 units of abnormal rework represent 24 equivalent units of conversion effort.

From this point on, the treatment of rework costs is similar to spoilage. The cost of normal rework is allocated to all units surviving inspection (in this case, both goods completed and ending inventory). The cost of abnormal rework is considered a loss.

As with spoilage it is also possible for there to be a gain from less than normal rework. We would again include as effort for normal rework the total effort we expect to incur on the average for rework. The effort

## EXHIBIT 16-4 Average Process Costing with Rework

### Timing of Costs and Inventory Status

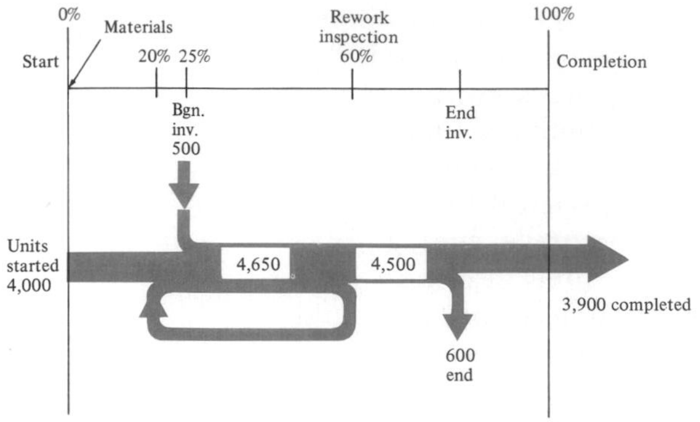


| | |
|---|---|
| Total possible inspection (no rework) | 4,500 |
| Less beginning if not inspected | — |
| Less ending if not inspected | — |
| Total inspected if no rework | 4,500 |
| Actual inspection | 4,650 |
| Number of units reworked | 150 |

**Physical Units**

| | | |
|---|---|---|
| 500 | | |
| 4,000 | 3,900 | good |
| 600 | | |

### EQUIVALENT UNITS

| | Materials | Conversion Costs | |
|---|---|---|---|
| Effort | | | |
| Good units completed | 3,900 | 3,900 | |
| Normal rework | — | 36 | 4,500 × 0.02 × 0.4 = 36 |
| Abnormal rework | — | 24 | (150 − 90) × 0.4 = 24 |
| Ending work-in-process | 600 | 480 | |
| Total effort | 4,500 | 4,440 | |
| Costs | | | |
| Beginning costs | $ 3,000 | $ 1,000.00 | |
| Current costs | 20,625 | 33,987.20 | |
| Total costs | $23,625 | $34,987.20 | |
| Cost per equivalent unit | $5.25 | $7.88 | |

### COST DISTRIBUTION

| | |
|---|---|
| Cost of goods completed | |
| 3,900($5.25 + $7.88) | $51,207.00 |
| Plus normal rework | 245.86 |
| Total cost of goods completed | $51,452.86 |
| Cost of ending work-in-process | |
| 600($5.25) + 480($7.88) | $ 6,932.40 |
| Plus normal rework | 37.82 |
| Total ending work-in process | $ 6,970.22 |
| Loss from abnormal rework | |
| 24 × $7.88 | $ 189.12 |

| | |
|---|---|
| Normal rework 36 × $7.88 | $283.68 |
| Allocation | |
| To cost of goods completed: $\frac{3{,}900}{4{,}500}$ ($283.68) | $245.86 |
| To ending work-in-process: $\frac{600}{4{,}500}$ ($283.68) | 37.82 |
| Total normal rework | $283.68 |

### CHECK

| | |
|---|---|
| Costs incurred | |
| Beginning inventory cost | $ 4,000.00 |
| Current period costs | |
| Materials | 20,625.00 |
| Conversion | 33,987.20 |
| Total costs to account for | $58,612.20 |
| Costs distributed | |
| Cost of goods completed | $51,452.86 |
| Cost of ending work-in-process | 6,970.22 |
| Loss from abnormal rework | 189.12 |
| Total costs distributed | $58,612.20 |

for abnormal rework then shows up as negative numbers for the effort not required because rework was less than normal.

## REWORK AND SPOILAGE

It is, of course, possible that a department reworks some units and also scraps units. These situations get complicated.[2] It is necessary to determine the relationship between spoiled and reworked units to see, for example, whether normal rework should be charged to spoiled units. If we add to this the necessity to separate normal from abnormal spoilage, normal from abnormal rework, and also whether ending work-in-process should be charged for normal rework, normal spoilage, or both, we can see that there are a number of decisions to be made. In these problems, a chart showing the timing of costs and status of inventories is a virtual necessity. We demonstrate one set of decisions by combining the facts given in the previous two examples.

The firm still began the period with 500 units in work-in-process, 25% complete. An additional 4,000 units were begun during the period. The period ended with 600 units approximately 80% complete. Materials are added at the beginning of the process, whereas conversion costs are assumed to be incurred in proportion to the stage of completion of the products. Units are inspected for rework when they are 60% complete. Rejected units are returned to the 20% complete point for rework. Normal rework is considered to be 2% of the units that pass inspection. This period 4,650 units were inspected for rework. Units are inspected again when they are 75% complete. Units failing this inspection are thrown away as scrap. Normal spoilage is considered to be 5% of the units inspected. This period 250 units were rejected as spoiled. Costs attached to beginning inventory were $3,000 for materials and $1,000 for conversion costs. Current period costs were $20,625 for materials and $34,020 for conversion costs. Our task is to determine the cost of goods completed, the cost of ending work-in-process, the loss from abnormal rework and the loss from abnormal spoilage.

The determination of the units of effort accomplished during the period is unchanged from the previous examples. This information is reproduced in Exhibit 16-5. The change that does occur is in the distribution of costs to the various cost objects. Normal rework is assigned to *all units* that survive the rework inspection, but some of these units eventually are discarded as spoiled. Therefore, normal rework must be allocated to units completed, ending work-in-process, and the spoiled units. Once the nor-

[2]There is a computer program, PROCESS, on the disk that accompanies the text that will solve these problems. Before relying on the computer program, however, you should understand the computations.

## EXHIBIT 16-5 Process Costing with Rework and Spoilage

### Timing of Costs and Inventory Status

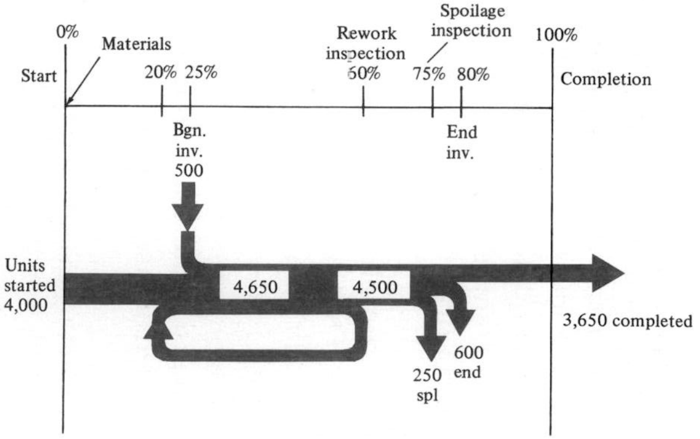


| | |
|---|---|
| Actual units inspected for rework | 4,650 |
| Units inspected if no rework | 4,500 |
| Actual rework | 150 |
| Units inspected for spoilage | 4,500 |

**Physical Units**

| | |
|---|---|
| 500 | |
| 4,000 | 3,900 {3,650 good, 250 spoiled} |
| 600 | |

### EQUIVALENT UNITS

| | Materials | Conversion Costs | |
|---|---|---|---|
| Effort | | | |
| Good units completed | 3,650 | 3,650.00 | |
| Normal rework | — | 36.00 | $4{,}500 \times 0.02 \times 0.4 = 36$ |
| Abnormal rework | — | 24.00 | $(150 - 90) \times 0.4 = 24$ |
| Normal spoilage | 225 | 168.75 | $225 \times 0.75 = 168.75$ |
| Abnormal spoilage | 25 | 18.75 | $25 \times 0.75 = 18.75$ |
| Ending work-in-process | 600 | 480.00 | |
| Total effort | 4,500 | 4,377.50 | |
| Costs | | | |
| Beginning costs | $ 3,000 | $ 1,000 | |
| Current costs | 20,625 | 34,020 | |
| Total costs | $23,625 | $35,020 | |
| Cost per equivalent unit | $5.25 | $8.00 | |

## COST DISTRIBUTION

| | |
|---|---|
| Cost of goods completed | |
| 3,650($5.25 + $8.00) | $48,362.50 |
| Plus normal rework | 233.60 |
| Plus normal spoilage | 2,186.26 |
| Total cost of goods completed | $50,782.36 |
| | |
| Cost of ending work-in-process | |
| (600 × $5.25) + (480 × $8) | $ 6,990.00 |
| Plus normal rework | 38.40 |
| Plus normal spoilage | 359.39 |
| Total ending work-in-process | $ 7,387.79 |
| | |
| Loss from abnormal rework | |
| 24 × $8 | $ 192.00 |
| | |
| Loss from abnormal spoilage | |
| (25 × $5.25) + (18.75 × $8) | $ 281.25 |
| Plus normal rework | 1.60 |
| Total | $ 282.85 |

| | |
|---|---|
| Normal rework 36 × $8 | $ 288.00 |
| Allocation of normal rework | |
| To cost of goods completed: $\frac{3,650}{4,500}$ ($288.00) | $ 233.60 |
| To ending work-in-process: $\frac{600}{4,500}$ ($288.00) | 38.40 |
| To abnormal spoilage: $\frac{25}{4,500}$ ($288.00) | 1.60 |
| To normal spoilage: $\frac{225}{4,500}$ ($288.00) | 14.40 |
| Total | $ 288.00 |
| Normal spoilage | |
| (225 × $5.25) + (168.75 × $8) | $2,531.25 |
| Plus normal rework | 14.40 |
| Total | $2,545.65 |
| Allocation of normal spoilage | |
| To cost of goods completed: $\frac{3,650}{4,250}$ ($2,545.65) | $2,186.26 |
| To ending work-in-process: $\frac{600}{4,250}$ ($2,545.65) | 359.39 |
| Total | $2,545.65 |

## CHECK

| | |
|---|---|
| Costs incurred | |
| Beginning inventory cost | $ 4,000.00 |
| Current period costs | |
| Materials | 20,625.00 |
| Conversion | 34,020.00 |
| Total costs to account for | $58,645.00 ← |
| | |
| Costs Distributed | |
| Cost of goods completed | $50,782.36 |
| Cost of ending work-in-process | 7,387.79 |
| Loss from abnormal rework | 192.00 |
| Loss from abnormal spoilage | 282.85 |
| Total costs distributed | $58,645.00 ← |

mal rework costs are allocated, we can then determine the total cost of normal spoilage and allocate it to the units completed and ending work-in-process. These calculations are all illustrated in Exhibit 16-5.

When a process involves multiple inspections for spoilage and/or rework, the question arises as to whether normal spoilage/rework should be assigned to the units identified as normal/abnormal spoilage or rework in subsequent inspections. The rule is that at each inspection normal spoilage and rework is charged to the *physical* units that survive the inspection. If some of these physical units are found to be spoiled in a later inspection, then the normal spoilage or rework from the first inspection is allocated to both the normal and abnormal spoiled units in the second inspection. Note, however, that subsequent rework does not alter the number of physical units in the process, so normal spoilage or rework in one inspection would not be allocated to normal and abnormal rework in a later inspection. That is, spoilage involves a physical unit leaving the process; rework does not.

### Journal Entries for Rework and Spoilage

As we saw in Chapter 15, the journal entries required for process costing are very straightforward. The same continues to be true even when we have rework and spoilage. The journal entry to record the results of the calculations in Exhibit 16-5 would be

| | | |
|---|---|---|
| Finished Goods Inventory | 50,782.36 | |
| Loss from Abnormal Rework | 192.00 | |
| Loss from Abnormal Spoilage | 282.85 | |
| Work-in-Process Inventory | | 51,257.21 |

Once again, no specific entry is required to record the ending balance for work-in-process. It will simply be the residual left in the account after the above entry has been made.

### Rework as a Separate Process

In the preceding discussion of rework, we presumed that items that had to be reworked were sent back through the original process a second time. In many processes this will not be the case. Instead, items to be reworked will be pulled from the production line and sent to a separate rework center. In these situations, the accounting for rework is far easier than with the approach described earlier because in the latter case we will know precisely what the rework costs have been (they will have been accumulated in the separate department). Similarly, we will have a precise count of the units actually transferred to the rework department, so there is no need to estimate the amount of rework. In this case the task is limited to distinguishing normal from abnormal rework and calculating an average cost for rework. The abnormal rework is still written off as a loss, and the normal rework is added to cost of goods completed and ending work-in-process (if beyond the inspection point) as a product cost. Accounting for rework performed in a separate department is illustrated in the demonstration problem at the end of the chapter.

## ZERO-DEFECT POLICY

Normal rework and normal spoilage were defined as the defects that are thought to be unavoidable in the production process. Being necessary costs to produce the good units resulting from the process, these costs were included as a product cost. But in recent years the assumption that defects are unavoidable has been seriously questioned. It is common, for example, for Japanese firms to have a **zero-defect policy,** wherein every unit produced is expected to be a good unit. Consequently, any spoilage or rework is written off as a loss.

Advocates of zero-defect policies claim that such policies lead to higher-quality products and lower unit costs in the long run. That is, when management acquiesces to the acceptance of defects, production personnel become sloppy. Two results then occur. Defect rates tend to become higher, leading to higher unit costs, and even the good units produced tend toward shoddiness. Inferior products, in turn, lead to customer dissatisfaction.

The actual determination of whether some defects are, indeed, unavoidable depends upon the actual product being produced. Nonetheless, there is some behavioral support for reporting all defects as losses even if they are unavoidable. The segregation of the loss will constantly remind management of the cost of defects (as opposed to being buried in the product cost). This should lead management to monitor defects more closely and prevent production personnel from becoming careless.

If a zero-defect policy is implemented, our accounting for rework and spoilage is greatly simplified. None of the rework or spoilage costs are charged to completed units or work in process. Instead, all such costs are written off directly as losses.

## SUMMARY

If some rework or spoilage is unavoidable in a production process, then the cost of normal rework and spoilage should be included as a cost of production. The amount of normal rework and spoilage represents management's estimate of the average amount of rework and spoilage that will be incurred when the process is operating efficiently. In any particular period actual rework or spoilage will likely deviate from average. This deviation is known as abnormal rework or spoilage. In the short run, abnormal rework and spoilage costs can be accumulated in a deferred charge account under the assumption that favorable and unfavorable deviations will tend to balance out. But at year-end the balance of the deferred charge account is typically written off as a period cost in the income statement.

## DEMONSTRATION PROBLEM

The W. L. Smith Machine Shop specializes in manufacturing precision parts for jet aircraft. One of the firm's major products is a bevel-shaped roller. The firm cuts high-quality stainless steel rods into 1-inch lengths and then lathes a bevel into the middle of the roller.

The cutting and machining of the rollers is done on semiautomatic equipment. Although the equipment is capable of producing rollers to the close tolerances demanded by the firm's customers, it requires constant attention and frequent resettings as the cutting tools wear. All units produced by the equipment are inspected for conformity to specified dimensions. Units cut to smaller than desired dimensions must be thrown away. Units cut larger than the specifications can be machined by hand to the correct dimensions and then returned to the process. The last step in the process is to cut a slit into one end of those rollers meeting specifications.

For the current period, the machining department began with 1,500 rollers in process. The units were complete with regard to materials, but only 40% complete with regard to conversion costs. Work was begun on another 40,000 rollers during the period. The department ended the period with 2,000 rollers in process, 70% complete with regard to conversion costs and totally complete with regard to materials.

The inspection of units is considered the point at which units are 85% complete with regard to conversion costs. Management normally expects 20% of the units inspected to fail to meet specifications. Half of these units can usually be reworked; the other half must be discarded. During the period, 3,500 units were discarded and 4,200 units were reworked.

The beginning work-in-process for this department was $4,600 for materials and $2,200 for conversion costs. During the period materials totaling $130,275 were put into process and conversion costs were $167,375. It cost another $14,910 to operate the rework station.

**Required**
Determine cost of goods completed, the cost of ending work-in-process, and the gain or loss from abnormal rework and spoilage.

**Solution**
The complete solution is given in Exhibit 16-6. The chart of the process indicates that ending inventory has not passed the inspection point. Therefore, only 39,500

**EXHIBIT 16-6 Solution to the Demonstration Problem**

## Timing of Costs and Inventory Status

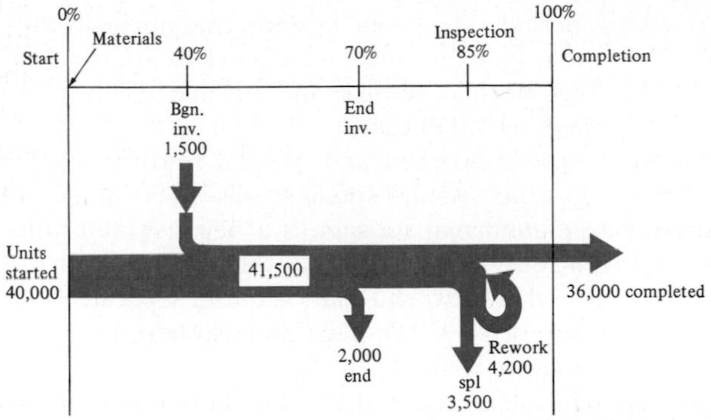


| | |
|---|---|
| Units inspected | 39,500 |
| Normal rework (10%) | 3,950 |
| Normal spoilage (10%) | 3,950 |

**Physical Flow**

| | | |
|---|---|---|
| 1,500 | | |
| 40,000 | 39,500 | 36,000 good; 3,500 spoiled |
| 2,000 | | |

## EQUIVALENT UNITS

| | Materials | Conversion | Rework |
|---|---|---|---|
| Effort | | | |
| Good units completed | 36,000 | 36,000 | — |
| Normal rework | — | — | 3,950 |
| Abnormal rework | — | — | 250 |
| Normal spoilage | 3,950 | 3,357.5 | — |
| Abnormal spoilage | (450) | (382.5) | — |
| Ending work-in-process | 2,000 | 1,400 | — |
| Total effort | 41,500 | 40,375 | 4,200 |
| Costs | | | |
| Beginning | $ 4,600 | $ 2,200 | $ — |
| Current | 130,275 | 167,375 | 14,910 |
| Total | $134,875 | $169,575 | $14,910 |
| Cost per equivalent unit | $3.25 | $4.20 | $3.55 |

## COST DISTRIBUTION

| | |
|---|---|
| Cost of goods completed | |
| 36,000 × ($3.25 + $4.20) | $268,200.00 |
| Plus normal rework (3,950 × $3.55) | 14,022.50 |
| Plus normal spoilage | |
| Materials (3,950 × $3.25) | 12,837.50 |
| Conversion (3,357.5 × $4.20) | 14,101.50 |
| Total | $309,161.50 |

| | |
|---|---|
| Cost of ending inventory | |
| Materials (2,000 × $3.25) | $ 6,500.00 |
| Conversion (1,400 × $4.20) | 5,880.00 |
| Total | $12,380.00 |
| Loss from abnormal rework (250 × $3.55) | $ 887.50 |
| Gain from less than normal spoilage | |
| Materials (450 × $3.25) | $ 1,462.50 |
| Conversion (382.5 × $4.20) | 1,606.50 |
| Total | $ 3,069.00 |

## CHECK

| | |
|---|---|
| Costs incurred | |
| Beginning inventory cost | $ 6,800.00 |
| Current period costs | |
| Materials | 130,275.00 |
| Conversion | 167,375.00 |
| Rework | 14,910.00 |
| Total costs to account for | $319,360.00 |
| Costs distributed | |
| Cost of goods completed | $309,161.50 |
| Cost of ending work-in-process | 12,380.00 |
| Loss from abnormal rework | 887.50 |
| Gain for less than normal spoilage | (3,069.00) |
| Total costs distributed | $319,360.00 |

units could have been inspected this period. The problem states that normally 20% of the units fail the inspection and that half the units are reworked and half are scrapped. This of course implies that normal rework and normal spoilage are individually 10% of the units inspected, or 3,950 each.

Because 4,200 units were actually reworked and normal rework is 3,950 units, abnormal rework must be 250 units. Actual spoilage was 3,500 units, but normal spoilage is 3,950 units; hence abnormal spoilage is a negative 450 units. Note that the spoiled units represent only 85% of an equivalent whole unit for conversion costs. We can also see that when rework is handled as a separate operation we can treat rework as a separate process. We have done so here by cumulating rework effort and costs in a separate column.

The calculation of costs per equivalent unit and the distribution of costs are the same as we have seen several times before. Hence we will refrain from discussing the solution further.

## KEY TERMS AND CONCEPTS

Normal spoilage
Abnormal spoilage
Normal rework
Abnormal rework
Rework
Zero-defect policy

## FURTHER READING

Dugdale, Harry. "Process Cost Accounting: Procedural Outline," *Accountants Review* (December 1974), p. 308.

Gossett, Thomas E., and Milton F. Usry. "Process Cost Accounting and Diagrammatical Outlines," *The Accounting Review* (January 1968), p. 133.

Luh, Frank S. "Graphical Approach to Process Costing," *The Accounting Review* (July 1967), p. 600.

NAA. *Cost Control of Spoiled Work,* Accounting Practice Report No. 12 (New York: National Association of Accountants, 1961).

## QUESTIONS AND EXERCISES

**16-1** How may the point at which spoilage occurs affect unit costing?

**16-2** In continuous processing situations (such as a refinery), the beginning and ending work-in-process inventories are frequently the same. How does this simplify determination of equivalent product, completed product, and gains or losses?

**16-3** "We treat spoiled units as fully completed regardless of when the spoiled units are discovered. This makes unit costing much simpler." What is wrong with this approach?

**16-4** "Approximately 20% of what we produce is graded as 'seconds' after inspection. We treat these as by-products." Is this a misapplication of joint costing to process costing?

**16-5** A finished unit that requires rework is one for which additional costs must be incurred. At what cost should a unit that has been reworked be inventoried?

**16-6** A process has resulted in 200 defective units at a cost of $90 each. These units, which ordinarily sell for $150, can be sold "as is" for $50 each. Alternatively, they can be reworked at a cost of $60 each and sold as "firsts," or they can be reworked at a cost of $20 each and sold as "seconds" for $120 each. What should be done?

**16-7** Spoilage in a department is discovered after inspection when the units are complete. This month's production was done at a cost per unit of $10. Of the 10,000 units completed, 8% were rejected as spoiled; additionally, the ending inventory had the equivalent of 400 units in process. Spoilage is normal. Determine the cost of (a) ending inventory and (b) goods completed.

**16-8** Rejected castings in a foundry are treated as scrap. During the current period, 80 castings (which cost $200 each to produce) were scrapped for $25 each. Prepare the journal entry assuming that the scrapped castings are an abnormal loss.

**16-9** For each of the following four independent cases provide the journal entry to record the total cost (and unit cost) of goods manufactured. Assume that there are no beginning or ending work-in process inventories.

| | Case 1 | Case 2 | Case 3 | Case 4 |
|---|---|---|---|---|
| Total costs assigned to work-in-process | $1,000 | $1,000 | $1,000 | $1,000 |
| Total units produced | | | | |
| Good units | 1,000 | 800 | 800 | 800 |
| Normal loss | — | 200 | — | 100 |
| Abnormal loss | — | — | 200 | 100 |

**16-10** During February a firm began a new process. Of the 12,000 units started during the month, 9,000 were completed, 1,000 were spoiled (considered normal during this start-up period), and 2,000 were in ending inventory (100% complete as to materials and 50% complete as to processing). Spoiled units are discovered upon inspection at the end of the process. Material costs of $88,000 were incurred, as were processing costs of $70,000. Prepare journal entries for all costs for the month.

**16-11** A department placed 10,000 units of materials in process at a cost per unit of $5.00. One unit of material is required per finished unit. The department completed the equivalent of 8,000 units. There are no beginning or ending inventories. Prepare the journal entry to transfer these costs out of the department to finished goods assuming that (a) the loss is normal and (b) the loss is abnormal.

**16-12** In the cooking department it is normal that 20% of the material placed into process is lost through evaporation. Any departures from this are treated as gains or losses. The final product contains 5 liters of material. During the period, the equivalent product actually produced was 1,000 units, and 6,500 liters were actually used. Determine (a) actual shrinkage, (b) normal shrinkage, and (c) the gain or loss, if any.

**16-13** A department calculates a "processing yield" for the material it places into process as the weight of finished equivalent product divided by the weight of material placed into process. It expects a normal yield of 75% and deviations from this are treated as gains or losses in processing. During November it placed 50,000 pounds into process, which yielded 38,500 pounds of finished equivalent product. Determine (a) acceptable shrinkage and (b) the gain or loss.

**16-14** Refer to 16-13. If the material costs $2 per pound of input, determine (a) the material cost assigned to the good product and (b) the cost assigned to the gain or loss.

**16-15** Complex, Inc. produces a product that passes through 317 departments; all departments employ weighted-average costing. Department 112 does not add any material; it works on what it receives from Department 111 and passes its (good) product to Department 113. During February, Department 112 had the following:

| | |
|---|---|
| Inventory, February 1 | 3,000 units; 40% processed |
| Received from Department 111 | 22,000 units |
| Inventory, February 29 | 4,000 units; 50% processed |
| Spoiled units | 2,000 |
| Transferred to Department 113 | 19,000 |

What is the weighted-average cost divisor for transferred-in units and for processing if the spoilage is (a) normal and discovered at the start of the process, (b) normal and discovered at the end of the process, (c) abnormal and discovered at the start of the process, and (d) abnormal and discovered at the end of the process?

**16-16** Refer to the demonstration problem at the end of the chapter. Assume that the firm discarded 4,100 units and reworked 3,800 units. Calculate new figures for cost of goods completed, cost of ending work-in-process, and gains or losses from abnormal rework and spoilage.

## PROBLEMS AND CASES

**16-17 Physical units: Normal and abnormal losses.**
Procest, Inc., employs a process cost system, using weighted-average costing. One of the departments adds material at the start of the process and has the following physical production record for the period.

| | |
|---|---|
| Beginning inventory | 1,000, 50% converted |
| Units started | 12,000 |
| Normal loss or spoilage | 1,500 |
| Abnormal loss or spoilage | 1,000 |
| Units completed | 10,000 |
| Ending inventory | 500, 50% converted |

Procest discovers its losses at the end of the process during final inspection.

**Required**

**a.** Over how many units will the total cost of materials be spread this period?
**b.** Over how many units will the total cost of converting or processing be spread this period?

**16-18 Effect of timing of normal and abnormal losses on weighted-average unit costs.** Tharp, Inc., employs several departments in a process cost situation. One of its departments operated during the previous period as follows:

1. Materials were added at the start of the process; processing was uniform.
2. The beginning inventory consisted of 1,000 units in process, 50% complete; 12,000 units were started; 9,000 good units were completed; 3,000 units, 50% complete, were in ending inventory; and 1,000 units were lost.
3. The costs were as follows:

| | Materials | Conversion |
|---|---|---|
| Beginning inventory | $ 1,000 | $ 1,000 |
| Costs added | 12,000 | 22,000 |

4. The department employs weighted-average cost techniques.

**Required**

Account for all units, total costs, and unit costs assuming that:

**a.** The losses are normal and are discovered at the start of the process.
**b.** The losses are normal and are discovered at the end of the process.
**c.** The losses are abnormal and are discovered at the start of the process.
**d.** The losses are abnormal and are discovered at the end of the process.

**16-19 Evaluation and costing.**

The Tire Division of Recycling, Inc., collects used razor blades for purposes of manufacturing the steel edging found on curbs at corners. The blades are smelted and poured into rough castings at the Bladex Division. These castings are received at the plant, which grinds the rough castings (grinding department) and then hones them to a fine edge (milling department).

Our immediate concern is with the grinding department. Losses there are normal unless otherwise stated. In this department all materials are put into process at the beginning, and any defective units are discovered at the end of the process; that is, all defects are 100% complete with respect to processing.

Grinding had an opening inventory of 150 castings, two-thirds converted, for which material costs were $750 and conversion costs were $390. During October an additional 1,000 castings costing $5,000 were received from Bladex and placed into process. Conversion costs for October were $3,000. The ending inventory consisted of 250 castings complete with respect to materials and four-fifths converted; 860 units were transferred to milling.

**Required**

**a.** For purposes of planning and control, management is interested *only* in the current cost of producing the period's equivalent or effective product. Accordingly, for managerial purposes what is the current unit cost of conversion?
**b.** For purposes of financial accounting (balance sheet and income statement), management has decided on a flow of costs that can be described as weighted average. For this purpose, again, using conversion costs only, what unit cost and total cost will be assigned to the ending inventory and transfers out, respectively?

**16-20 Weighted average: Normal and abnormal spoilage** (SMA adapted).

Wright Ltd., following process costing procedures, manufactures a single product in one department. On April 1, 19X1, the balances in the company's Work-in-Process account, representing the costs of 5,000 units, were as follows:

| | |
|---|---|
| Materials | $ 58,400 |
| Conversion | 88,000 |
| | $146,400 |

During April, 20,000 units were placed in process; 19,000 units were completed and transferred to finished goods; 2,000 units were scrapped (of which "normal spoilage" was 1,200 units) at a point when all materials had been applied and 10% of the conversion work was done; and 4,000 units remained in process at month-end. The closing work-in-process units were 100% complete as to materials and 50% complete as to conversion work. There was no inventory of finished goods on April 1, and 50% of April's completed production was sold during the month.

Costs applied to production during the month were as follows:

| | |
|---|---|
| Materials | $ 491,600 |
| Conversion | 760,000 |
| | $1,251,600 |

**Required**

Prepare an appropriate schedule showing equivalent production, unit costs, and cost disposition. Wright Ltd. uses weighted-average costing. The last item should show clearly a *detailed* breakdown of the total costs of $1,398,000 ($146,400 + $1,251,600) charged to the department between closing work-in-process, finished goods, cost of goods sold, and so forth.

**16-21 Weighted average: Abnormal spoilage** (SMA adapted).

Genie Company manufactures a product that requires processing in two different departments: A and B. In department B, raw materials are added to production received from department A in the proportion of 1 kilogram (kg) of raw material to 5 kg of material received from department A; the resulting mixture is then refined. During this process, a quantity equal to 10% of the total input weight is lost. Under normal conditions there is no additional loss. The loss of weight occurs at the beginning of processing.

In January, department B received 50,000 kg of material from department A at a cost of $162,000. Refining costs in department B were as follows:

| | |
|---|---|
| Raw materials | $10,800 |
| Conversion costs | 15,600 |

The following data describe the activities of department B of Genie Company for the month of January.

| | |
|---|---|
| Units in process on January 1 | None |
| Units completed during the month | 50,000 kg |
| Units in process in department B at January 31, composed of 1,000 kg, 30% complete as to conversion costs and 100% complete as to raw materials; 2,000 kg, 35% complete as to conversion costs and 100% complete as to raw materials | 3,000 kg |
| Spoiled units | 1,000 kg |

The spoiled units were discovered during the final inspection when their processing was complete in department B; these units are not recoverable. It was demonstrated that these units were spoiled as a result of negligence, and their cost should be posted directly to the income statement.

**Required**

Prepare a cost-of-production report using weighted-average costing for department B for the month of January. Your answer should indicate the value of work-in-process inventory at the end of January, as well as a schedule of quantities and equivalent production.

**16-22 Determining total costs charged** (SMA adapted).

Benedict Company Ltd. uses a process costing system. The company has two manufacuring departments: A and B. Raw materials are added in department B at 50% of completion. Direct labour and manufacturing overhead are applied uniformly throughout the manufacturing process. Inspection takes place at the end of the process and all waste is considered abnormal. Unit costs are as follows:

| | Department A | Department B |
|---|---|---|
| Raw materials | $ 8 | $ 4 |
| Direct labour | 6 | 6 |
| Manufacturing overhead | 6 | 5 |
| | $20 | $15 |

Production statistics for department B for the period were as follows:

| | |
|---|---|
| Beginning inventory ($33\frac{1}{3}$% complete) | 3,000 units |
| Received from department A | 17,000 units |
| Transferred to finished goods inventory | 15,000 units |
| Ending inventory (75% complete) | 4,000 units |

**Required**

Calculate the following for department B:

**a.** The total cost of the units received from department A during the period.
**b.** The total cost of the raw materials charged to department B during the period.
**c.** The total cost of direct labour charged to department B during the period.
**d.** The total cost of manufacturing overhead charged to department B during the period.
**e.** The total cost of abnormal waste.
**f.** The total cost of ending inventory in department B.

**16-23 Normal and abnormal spoilage.**

Bertson, Inc., uses average process costing to determine the cost of producing its products. The firm began March with 300 units in work-in-process inventory, approximately one-third complete. During March, the firm began work on another 1,500 units. Ending work-in-process consists of 400 units, 40% complete. The firm transferred 1,200 good units to finished goods during March. The firm considers 10% of the number of good units completed to be the normal number of units that will be spoiled. Spoiled units are discovered when they are 70% complete. Direct materials are added when the units are 50% complete. Labor and overhead costs are incurred uniformly through the process. The costs attached to beginning work-in-process were zero for materials and $23,930 for conversion costs. Material costs incurred during the period were $224,000, and conversion costs were $336,070.

**Required**
Determine the cost of goods completed in March, the loss from abnormal spoilage, and the cost of ending work-in-process.

16-24 **Weighted-average costing, prior department: Normal and abnormal spoilage.** Skipton Novelties uses average process costing for its line of children's phonograph records. During its most recent accounting period the firm began with 12,000 units in the packaging department. An additional 176,000 units were transferred into the packaging department from the pressing department during the period. At the end of the period there were 15,000 units in process. The packaging department first trims excess plastic off the records, then inspects them, and finally puts them into an album cover and wraps them in plastic. Thus transferred-in units signify the start of the process. Labor is used when the units are considered 20% complete, inspection is considered to be the 50% complete point, packaging materials are added at the end of the process, and overhead costs are incurred uniformly.

This period 6,000 units were rejected as spoiled. The spoiled units are sold as is to TV Record Sales, Inc., for $0.50 each. Normal spoilage is considered to be 5% of the units inspected. Beginning inventory was estimated to average 60% complete, and ending inventory averages 80% complete. Costs attached to beginning work-in-process were: transferred-in costs, $8,400; labor, $2,400; and overhead, $3,600. Costs for the current period were $123,200 for transferred-in units, $44,600 for labor, $58,450 for packaging materials, and $105,600 for overhead.

**Required**
Determine the cost of goods completed, cost of ending work-in-process, and the gain or loss from abnormal spoilage.

16-25 **Weighted-average, prior department, normal and abnormal defects** (CMA adapted). APCO manufactures various lines of bicycles employing a process cost system using the weighted-average method to determine unit costs. Parts are consolidated into a single bike unit in the molding department and transferred to the assembly department where they are partially assembled. After assembly the bicycle is sent to the packing department.

Defective bicycles are identified at an inspection point when the assembly labor process is 70% complete; all assembly material has been added at this point of the process. The normal rejection percentage for defective bicycles is 5% of those reaching the inspection point. The presence of any defective bicycles over and above the 5% quota is considered abnormal. All defective bikes are removed from the production process and destroyed.

Annual cost and production figures for a particular style of bike in the assembly department follow.

**ASSEMBLY DEPARTMENT COST DATA**

| | Transferred In from Molding Department | Assembly Material | Assembly Conversion Cost | Total Cost of Dirt Bike through Assembly |
|---|---|---|---|---|
| Prior period costs | $ 82,200 | $ 6,660 | $ 11,930 | $ 100,790 |
| Current period costs | 1,237,800 | 96,840 | 236,590 | 1,571,230 |
| Total costs | $1,320,000 | $103,500 | $248,520 | $1,672,020 |

**ASSEMBLY DEPARTMENT PRODUCTION DATA**

| | | Percent Complete | | |
|---|---|---|---|---|
| | Bicycles | Transferred In | Assembly Material | Assembly Conversion |
| Beginning inventory | 3,000 | 100 | 100 | 80 |
| Transferred in from molding during year | 45,000 | 100 | — | — |
| Transferred out to packing during year | 40,000 | 100 | 100 | 100 |
| Ending inventory | 4,000 | 100 | 50 | 20 |

**Required**

How much of the total production cost of $1,672,020 will be associated with each of normal defects, abnormal defects, good units completed, and ending work-in-process?

**16-26 Weighted-average costing, spoilage: Two inspections.**

RST uses weighted-average process costing for inventory. At the beginning of the year the firm had 2,000 units, 20% complete, in work-in-process. During the year work was begun on an additional 12,000 units. Ending work-in-process consisted of 3,000 units, 80% complete. Units go through two inspections. The first inspection occurs when the units are 50% complete. Units rejected are thrown away. Normally, 5% of units inspected are considered normal spoilage. This period 1,000 units were rejected at the first inspection. The second inspection occurs when units are complete. Normally, 1% of these units are rejected. This year 150 units were rejected. Rejected units are sold for $5 each. The cost attached to beginning work-in-process was $1,600. Current costs were as follows: materials, $70,000; labor, $104,000; and overhead, $50,000. Materials are added when the units are 25% complete, labor when the units are 75% complete, and overhead is incurred uniformly.

**Required**

Determine ending work-in-process, cost of goods manufactured, and loss from abnormal spoilage.

**16-27 Normal and abnormal spoilage with salvage value.**

Paget, Inc., produces under process conditions. Beginning work-in-process consists of 4,000 units, 40% complete. Costs for the beginning inventory are: materials, $12,250; labor, $15,000; and overhead, $18,150. During the current period the firm began work on an additional 25,000 units. Current period costs were: materials, $73,800; labor, $81,500; and overhead, $106,250. Ending work-in-process consists of 3,000 units, 90% complete. During the period, 24,000 units were transferred to finished goods inventory. Materials are added at the beginning of the process, labor is added when the units are 25% complete, and overhead is incurred uniformly. Units are inspected when they are 80% complete. Normally, 6% of the units inspected are rejected as spoiled. Spoiled units have a salvage value of $2.

**Required**

Using average process costing, determine the cost of goods completed, the cost of ending work-in-process, and the loss from abnormal spoilage.

**16-28 Normal and abnormal spoilage with salvage value.**
Vernies Inc. started the year with 3,000 units in work-in-process. These units were 10% complete and valued at $250 for the overhead costs incurred last period. During the current period the firm put 37,000 additional units into the process. The firm ended the period with 32,500 good units completed and 6,000 units in ending work-in-process, 70% complete. The missing units were spoiled. Spoilage is discovered when the units are inspected. Inspection occurs when the units are 50% complete. Spoiled units are sold for $2 each to a scrap dealer. During the period, the firm incurred materials costs of $98,000, labor costs of $63,700, and overhead costs of $29,710. Materials are added when the units are 20% complete, labor is added when the units are 80% complete, and overhead costs are incurred uniformly. Normal spoilage is considered to be 3% of the units inspected.

**Required**
Using weighted-average process costing, determine the cost of ending work-in-process, the cost of goods completed, and the loss from abnormal spoilage.

**16-29 Weighted-average costing: Normal and abnormal spoilage** (CMA adapted).
Ranka Company manufactures high-quality leather products. The company's profits have declined during the past 9 months. Ranka has used unit cost data that were developed 18 months ago in planning and controlling its operations. In an attempt to isolate the causes of poor profit performance, management is investigating the manufacturing operations of each of its products.

One of Ranka's main products is fine leather belts. The belts are produced in a single, continuous process. During the process, leather strips are sewn, punched, and dyed. Buckles are attached by rivets when the belts are 70% complete as to direct labor and overhead (conversion costs). The belts then enter a final finishing stage to conclude the process. Labor and overhead are applied continuously during the process.

The leather belts are inspected twice during the process: (1) right before the buckles are attached (the 70% point in the process) and (2) at the conclusion of the finishing stage (the 100% point in the process). Ranka uses the weighted-average method to calculate its unit costs. The cost per equivalent unit being used for planning and controlling purposes is $5.35 per unit.

The work-in-process inventory consisted of 400 partially completed units on October 1. The belts were 25% complete as to conversion costs. The costs included in the inventory on October 1 were as follows:

| | |
|---|---|
| Leather strips | $1,000 |
| Conversion costs | 300 |
| Total | $1,300 |

During October, 7,600 leather strips were placed in production. A total of 6,800 good leather belts were completed. A total of 300 belts were identified as defective at the two inspection points: 100 at the first inspection point (before buckle is attached) and 200 at the final inspection point (after finishing). This quantity of defective belts was considered normal. In addition, 200 belts were removed from the production line when the process was 40% complete as to conversion costs because they had been damaged as a result of a malfunction during the sewing operation. Since this malfunction was considered an unusual occurrence, the spoilage was classified as abnormal. Defective (spoiled) units are not reprocessed and have zero salvage value. The work-in-process inventory on October 31 consisted of 700 belts, which were 50% complete as to conversion costs.

The costs charged to production during October were as follows:

| | |
|---|---|
| Leather strips | $20,600 |
| Buckles | 4,550 |
| Conversion costs | 20,700 |
| Total | $45,850 |

**Required**

**a.** Determine the equivalent units for each factor of production.
**b.** Calculate the cost per equivalent whole unit for each factor of production.
**c.** Determine the assignment of total production costs to the work-in-process inventory and to goods transferred out.
**d.** Calculate the average unit cost of the 6,800 good leather belts completed and transferred to finished goods.

**16-30 Weighted-average costing: Losses** (CMA adapted).
West Corporation is a divisionalized manufacturing company. A product called aggregate is manufactured in one department of the California Division. Aggregate is transferred upon completion to the Utah Division, where it is used in the manufacture of other products.

The raw material is added at the beginning of the process. Labor and overhead are added continuously throughout the process. Shrinkage of 10% to 14%, all occurring at the beginning of the process, is considered normal. In the California Division all departmental overhead is charged to the departments, and divisional overhead is allocated to the departments on the basis of direct labor hours. The divisional overhead rate for the year is $2 per direct labor hour.

The following information relates to production during November:

| | |
|---|---|
| Work-in-process, November 1: 4,000 pounds, 75% complete | |
| Raw materials | $22,800 |
| Direct labor at $5.00 per hour | 24,650 |
| Departmental overhead | 12,000 |
| Divisional overhead | 9,860 |
| Raw material | |
| Inventory, November 1: 2,000 pounds | $10,000 |
| Purchases, November 3: 10,000 pounds | 51,000 |
| Purchases, November 18: 10,000 pounds | 51,500 |
| Released to production during November: 16,000 pounds | ? |

Direct labor costs at $5.00 per hour: $103,350
Direct departmental overhead costs: $52,000
Transferred to Utah Division: 15,000 pounds
Work-in-process, November 30: 3,000 pounds, $33\frac{1}{3}$% complete

The FIFO method is used for materials inventory valuation and the weighted-average method is used for work-in-process inventories.

**Required**

**a.** Prepare for November a cost of production report for the department of the California Division producing aggregate, presenting the following:

1. The equivalent units of production by cost factor of aggregate.
2. The equivalent unit costs for each cost factor of aggregate.
3. The cost of aggregate transferred to the Utah Division.
4. The cost of abnormal shrinkage, if any.
5. The cost of the work-in-process inventory at November 30.

**b.** The California Division intends to implement a flexible budgeting system to improve cost control over direct labor and departmental overhead. The basis of the flexible budget will be the production that occurs in the budget period. For the department producing aggregate, what amount reflects the best measure of production activity for the November flexible budget? Explain your answer.

**16-31 Normal and abnormal rework.**

Prall Inc. began the year with 9,000 units in beginning work-in-process. These units were 20% complete. During the period the firm began work on an additional 56,000 units. Beginning work-in-process was valued at $5,400 for the overhead costs incurred last period. During the year the firm incurred costs of $142,975 for materials, $107,900 for labor, and $203,320 for overhead. The firm ended the period with 3,000 units in process 90% complete. The units are inspected when they are 60% complete. Rejected units are returned to the 25% complete point in the process for rework. The firm considers 2% of the units surviving inspection to be normal for rework. Direct materials are added to the process when the units are 40% complete and labor when the units are 75% complete; overhead is incurred uniformly. This period 66,500 units were inspected.

**Required**

Using weighted-average process costing, determine the cost of goods completed, the cost of ending work-in-process, and the loss from abnormal rework.

**16-32 Normal and abnormal rework.**

Sigh-Lon, Inc., uses weighted-average process costing. Materials are added at the beginning of the process, labor is added when the units are 50% complete, and overhead is incurred uniformly. The firm started the period with 3,000 units, 25% complete. Work was begun on an additional 35,000 units. The firm ended the period with 7,000 units, 80% complete. When the units are 60% complete, they are inspected. Any rejected units are returned for rework to the point at which they are 40% complete. Normal rework is considered to be 1% of the units surviving inspection. This period 39,000 units were inspected. The costs attached to beginning work-in-process were $15,000 for materials and $3,500 for overhead. Current costs were $178,800 for materials, $228,150 for labor, and $116,100 for overhead.

**Required**

Determine the cost of goods completed, the cost of ending work-in-process, and the loss from abnormal rework.

**16-33 Normal and abnormal rework: Alternate definition of normal rework.**

Gil Glass Designers uses average process costing to cost its products. The firm began the current period with 6,000 units in work-in-process, 30% complete. During the period, work was begun on an additional 40,000 units. The firm ended the period with 7,000 units in ending work-in-process, 80% complete. Materials are added at the beginning of the process, labor is added when the units are 40% complete, and overhead is incurred uniformly. Units are inspected for rework when they are 60% complete. Rejected units are returned to the 20% complete point for rework. Normal rework is 1% of the units inspected. This period 46,400 units were inspected. Costs attached to beginning work-in-process were $15,000 for materials, zero for labor, and $14,000 for overhead. Current period costs were $141,400 for materials, $278,400 for labor, and $377,650 for overhead.

**Required**

Determine the cost of goods completed, cost of ending work-in-process, and the gain or loss from abnormal rework.

**16-34 Normal and abnormal rework: Alternate definition of normal rework.**

Gherta Industries began 19X6 with 300 units in work-in-process. These units were 60% complete. Costs attached to these units were $2,700 for materials, $3,600 for labor, and $1,440 for overhead. During 19X6, work was begun on an additional 1,800 units. The firm ended the year with 500 units, 20% complete. The costs incurred during the period were $17,250 for materials, $18,450 for labor, and $13,059 for overhead. Units are inspected when they are 80% complete. Rejected units are returned to the point where units are 35% complete for rework. Management considers 10% of the number of good units completed in a year to be the normal number of units reworked. During the year, 200 units were reworked. Materials are added at the beginning of the process, direct labor is added when the units are 50% complete, and overhead costs are incurred uniformly. The firm uses weighted-average process costing.

**Required**

Determine the cost of goods completed, the cost of ending work-in-process, and the loss from abnormal rework.

**16-35 Spoilage with salvage followed by rework.**

Taxco, Inc., began the current period with 8,000 units in beginning work-in-process. These units were 60% complete and had costs attached of $4,000 for materials, $10,000 for labor, and $45,000 for overhead. During the period, work was begun on an additional 45,000 units. Direct materials are added when the goods are 50% complete, labor is added when the units are 30% complete, and overhead is incurred uniformly. Units are inspected for rework when they are 75% complete. Rejected units are returned to the 40% complete point for rework. Normal rework is 2% of the units surviving inspection. During the period, 49,000 units were inspected for rework. An inspection for spoilage occurs when the units are 20% complete. Spoiled units are sold to a scrap dealer for $1 each. Normal spoilage is 1% of the units inspected. This period 500 units were scrapped. Ending work-in-process consists of 5,000 units, 25% complete. Current costs were $22,950 for materials, $47,000 for labor, and $300,625 for overhead.

**Required**

Using average process costing determine the cost of goods completed, the cost of ending work-in-process, the loss from abnormal spoilage, and the loss from abnormal rework.

**16-36 Rework followed by spoilage.**

Diversy, Inc., began the current period with 5,000 units in beginning work-in-process. These units were 60% complete. Costs attached to beginning work-in-process were $15,000 for materials, $10,500 for labor, and $25,000 for overhead. During the period, work was begun on an additional 25,000 units. Materials are added at the beginning of the process, labor is added when the units are 40% complete, and overhead is incurred uniformly. Units are inspected for rework when they are 50% complete. Rejected units are returned to the 30% complete point for rework. Normal rework is 3% of the units surviving inspection. Units are inspected again when they are 70% complete. Rejected units are thrown away. Normal spoilage is 1% of the units inspected. There were 26,000 units inspected for rework and 400 units were rejected at the spoilage inspection. Ending work-in-process consists of 3,000 units, 80% complete. Current costs were $75,000 for materials, $53,050 for labor, and $210,840 for overhead.

**Required**

Using average process costing determine the cost of goods completed, the cost of ending work-in-process, the loss from abnormal rework, and the loss from abnormal spoilage.

**16-37 Rework followed by spoilage: Zero-defect policy.**

The Mashiti Company produces a remote control device for home entertainment systems. Direct materials are deemed to be added when the units are 25% complete. Labor and overhead costs are incurred uniformly. The units are inspected when they are 60% complete, and any rejected units are returned to the 35% complete point for rework. A tricky soldering operation occurs when the units are 80% complete. They are inspected again at this point. Units soldered incorrectly are ruined and must be thrown away.

The firm began the current period with 7,000 units in process one-half complete. These units were costed at $21,000 for materials and $35,000 for conversion costs. During the period the firm completed 58,000 good units. There were 200 units reworked and 375 units were discarded as spoiled. The period ended with 6,000 units in process approximately 70% complete. The firm uses weighted-average process costing. Management is attempting to instill a zero-defect attitude among employees and hence considers all rework and spoilage to be abnormal. Costs incurred during the period were $185,000 for materials and $579,241 for conversion costs.

**Required**

Determine the cost of goods completed, the cost of ending work-in-process, and the loss from rework and spoilage.

**16-38 Rework followed by spoilage: Alternate definition of normal rework.**

APC uses average process costing to determine the cost per unit of heating oil as it leaves the mixing department (a unit is defined as a barrel of product). The refined heating oil enters the mixing department and is strained, an additive is added, and the resulting mixture is pumped into tanks awaiting sale.

Only the refined oil is considered a direct material; it, of course, is added at the beginning of the process. Direct labor for mixing in the additive occurs at the midpoint of the process. Overhead is considered to be incurred uniformly. For the current period, the firm began with 10,000 units in beginning work-in-process, 70% complete. Work was begun on an additional 30,000 units. The firm ended the period with 5,000 units in work-in-process, 80% complete. Units are inspected when they are 60% complete. Units rejected at this inspection are returned to the 40% complete point for rework (increasing the additive). Normal rework is considered to be 2% of units inspected. During the period, 31,000 units were inspected for rework. A second inspection occurs when the units are 90% complete. Units rejected at this inspection (spoilage) are discarded. Normal spoilage is considered to be 1% of units inspected for spoilage. This period 500 units were discarded. Costs attached to beginning work-in-process were $300,000 for materials, $2,000 for labor, and $600 for overhead. Current costs were $900,000 for materials, $6,200 for labor, and $1,357.50 for overhead.

**Required**

Determine the cost of goods completed, cost of ending work-in-process, and the loss from abnormal spoilage and abnormal rework.

**16-39 Rework followed by spoilage.**

Champion, Inc., began the current period with 3,000 units in work-in-process. These units were 40% complete. Costs attached to beginning work-in-process were $6,000 for materials, $9,000 for labor, and $10,000 for overhead. During the period, work was begun on an additional 8,000 units. Materials are added at the beginning of the process, labor is added when the units are 30% complete, and overhead is incurred uniformly. Units are inspected when they are 60% complete. Rejected units are returned to the 20% complete point for rework. Normal rework is 1% of the units surviving inspection. Units are inspected again when they are 75% complete. Rejected units are thrown away. Normal spoilage is considered to be 2% of the units inspected. There were 11,150 units inspected for rework and 250 units were rejected for spoilage. Ending work-in-process consists of 1,750 units, 90% complete. Current costs incurred were $16,000 for materials, $24,450 for labor, and $44,112.50 for overhead.

**Required**

Using average process costing determine cost of goods completed, cost of ending work-in-process, loss from abnormal spoilage, loss from abnormal rework.

**16-40 Two inspections for spoilage, one for rework.**

Dynamic General makes a critical part for some military equipment. The material for this part is introduced at the start of the process. Conversion costs are incurred uniformly. When the units are 20% complete, they are inspected. Rejected units are thrown away. When the units are 50% complete, they are inspected again, and once again the spoiled units are thrown away. When the units are 90% complete, they are inspected a third time. Units that fail this last inspection are returned to the 70% complete point for rework.

The firm began the current period with 12,000 units in process, 40% complete. Work was begun on another 125,000 units and 9,000 units were in ending work in process, 60% complete. During the period, 14,000 units were rejected at the first inspection, 15,000 were rejected at the second inspection, and a total of 110,000 units were inspected for rework. A rejection rate of 10% of the units inspected is considered normal for each of the three inspections.

Costs attached to beginning work-in-process were $35,000 for materials and $10,800 for conversion costs. Current period costs were $376,000 for materials and $281,450 for conversion costs.

**Required**

Distribute the costs as appropriate using weighted-average process costing.

**16-41 Comprehensive problem—requires prior study of Chapters 11 and 12.** The General Eastmoreland Air Force Base trains new pilots and aircraft maintenance personnel. The base commander requires a quarterly report on the actual cost incurred to train a pilot and a maintenance person.

Fortunately, for those of us who have to determine these costs, the air base maintains only four cost centers: staff administration, personnel services, pilot training, and maintenance training. The direct costs incurred by each of these cost centers for the quarter just ended were as follows:

| | Staff Administration | Personnel Services | Pilot Training | Maintenance Training |
|---|---|---|---|---|
| Salaries and wages | $800,000 | $560,000 | $ 640,000 | $400,000 |
| Materials costs | 150,000 | 100,000 | 1,300,000 | 200,000 |
| Other costs | 500,000 | 300,000 | 255,880 | 300,000 |

In addition to these direct costs, staff administration and personnel services share a computer facility. The costs for operating the computer this period were $120,000. It is estimated that, if staff administration had acquired computational services independently, its cost would have been $80,000, whereas if personnel services had acquired computer services independently, its cost would have been $60,000.

Staff administration costs are allocated to other cost centers in proportion to each cost center's salaries and wages. Personnel costs are allocated to cost centers in proportion to the number of people employed in each cost center. For the quarter, 24% of the base employees were assigned to staff administration, 20% were in personnel services, 24% in pilot training, and 32% in maintenance training.

A pilot trainee goes through two steps. The first is ground school in which a trainee learns about the mechanics of an airplane, navigation, flight rules, and so forth. At the completion of this step, trainees are given a written exam. Persons failing the exam must go through the entire ground school course a second time. Normally 20% of the trainees taking the exam fail the exam (although eventually everyone does pass after enough tries).

Upon completion of ground school, the trainees enter flight training. They must accumulate a total of 200 hours of flying time to be awarded a pilot's license. After 100 hours of flying experience, the trainees are given a flight test. Persons passing the exam are allowed to complete training, while failures are transferred out of the pilot program to the aircraft maintenance program. Normally 25% of the trainees fail the flight test.

Both the salaries and wages and the overhead costs for pilot training are assigned uniformly over the training process. Training is assumed to be 20% complete when ground training is completed and 60% complete when the flight test is given. The total materials costs of $1,300,000 consists of two different types of costs. That is, $200,000 of the costs are for flight manuals, maps, and student manuals used in ground training. These materials are given to students as they begin ground school. Persons repeating the ground school course are given an entire new set of materials. The remaining $1,100,000 in materials costs is for jet fuel, repairs, destroyed aircraft, and so forth incurred for flight training. These materials are assumed to be uniformly incurred over the 200 hours of flight training.

Although there are usually trainees in virtually all stages of training at any one time, for costing purposes, the air base estimates the average stage of completion of all persons in the program at the end of each quarter. It then treats all of these people as if they were in the same stage of completion. The quarter began with 100 trainees considered to be 40% through the entire program; that is, on the average, all trainees have finished ground school and have 50 hours of flight training time completed (50 hours is 25% of the flight training, but flight training only represents 80% of the entire process; therefore the 50 hours represents 25% × 80% = 20% of the entire process).

During the quarter, 800 trainees began the pilot training program. The quarter ended with 50 people about 30% of the way through the entire program (finished with ground school and with 25 hours of flying time). Ground school exams were given to 1,100 persons and 250 trainees failed the flight test. The training costs attached to the persons in the midst of training at the beginning of the quarter were as follows: ground school materials costs, $40,000; flight training materials costs, $216,250; and labor and overhead costs, $247,500.

**Required**

**a.** Determine the total staff administration and personnel services costs assuming that the computer costs are allocated using the Shapley method.

**b.** Allocate the staff administration and personnel services costs to pilots and maintenance training using the simultaneous-equations approach.

**c.** Using weighted-average process costing, determine the cost to train a pilot this period, the training costs attached to persons still in training at the end of the period, the loss from above normal repeats of ground school training, and the loss from the abnormal flight training failure rate.

**16-42 Two departments: Process and job costing with spoilage and rework—difficult, but interesting.**

The Christler Motor Company uses process costing to determine the cost of subassemblies, but job costing to determine the cost of a particular car. This problem examines the determination of the cost to manufacture left front doors for intermediate sized cars (the firm has three models that use the same doors: the Gibraltar, the Wichita, and the Bluebird).

Department 1 assembles the door. Workers construct a metal frame, which is spot-welded together. Then internal parts are added, and finally an outer shell is welded to the unit. A unit is defined as existing when the first pieces are welded together as a frame. When internal parts are added, units are considered 50% complete. When the outer shell is added, the units are 90% complete. As soon as the units have the outer shell, they are inspected. Units that pass inspection go to a finishing area. Some of the units that fail inspection are discarded as spoiled, and others are sent to a rework station to have new internal parts installed. Management estimates that it takes 20% as much time to replace these parts as to construct an

## DEPARTMENT 2: SUMMARY OF PERIOD'S PRODUCTION

| Order Number | Door | Model Trim G | Model Trim W | Model Trim B | Lining Plastic | Lining Cloth | Lining Leather | Courtesy Lights | Chrome Edging | Total Unit Cost |
|---|---|---|---|---|---|---|---|---|---|---|
| | Cost (in dollars): | 12 | 18 | 21 | 17 | 30 | 80 | 5 | 8 | |
| 3582130 | | X | | | | X | | | | |
| 3582131 | | | | X | X | | | X | | |
| 3582132 | | X | | | X | | | | | |
| 3582134 | | | X | | | | X | X | X | |
| 3582135 | | | | X | | X | | | X | |
| 3582137 | | X | | | X | | | | | |
| 3582138 | | X | | | | X | | X | | |
| 3582140 | | | X | | X | | | | | |
| 3582141 | | X | | | | | X | X | | |
| 3582142 | | | | X | | X | | | X | |
| 3582145 | | X | | | X | | | | | |
| 3582146 | | | X | | | | X | X | | |
| 3582149 | | | X | | X | | | | | |
| 3582150 | | X | | | X | | | | X | |
| 3582155 | | | | X | | X | | | | |
| 3582157 | | | | X | | | X | X | X | |
| 3582159 | | | X | | X | | | | | |
| 3582160 | | X | | | | X | | | X | |
| 3582161 | | X | | | X | | | | | |
| 3582162 | | | X | | X | | | | | |
| 3582165 | | X | | | | X | | | | |
| 3582166 | | X | | | X | | | X | | |
| 3582167 | | | | X | | X | | | X | |
| 3582168 | | X | | | X | | | | | |
| 3582170 | | | X | | X | | | X | | |
| 3582171 | | | X | | | | X | | X | |
| 3582174 | | X | | | | X | | | | |
| 3582176 | | | X | | X | | | | | |
| 3582177 | | X | | | | | X | | | |
| 3582179 | | | | X | X | | | | | |
| 3582181 | | X | | | | | | | | |
| 3582182 | | | X | | | | | | | |
| 3582184 | | | X | | | | | | | |
| 3582185 | | | | X | | | X | | | |
| 3582187 | | X | | | X | | | | | |
| 3582188 | | | | | | | | | | |

Uni stil in proc

entire door. Note that reworked units go directly to the finishing area; they are not inspected a second time.

Department 1 began the period with 10 doors in process, estimated to be 60% complete. Work was begun on 40 more units, and the department ended the period with 12 units, 95% complete in process. Normal spoilage is considered to be 1.5% of the units inspected, and normal rework is 10% of the units inspected. This period 1 unit was scrapped and 3 units were reworked. Labor and overhead costs are incurred uniformly through the process.

Costs attached to beginning work-in-process were: frames, $200; internal parts, $150; outer shells, $0; and conversion costs, $210. Current period costs were: frames, $800; internal parts, $671.50; outer shells, $1,550; and conversion costs, $1,536.50.

Department 2 makes the doors ready for assembly on a particular car. Appropriate trim is added for each model, and any options ordered by the customer are installed. Department 2, which uses job costing, started the period with no inventory. The chart on page 750 summarizes the period's production.

Department 2 draws parts as needed from central stores, with the exception of the unfinished doors, which it inventories (as work-in-process). A unit of labor is defined as the total labor required to attach model trim and lining; specifically, trim and lining each require $\frac{1}{2}$ unit of labor time. The amount of time is unaffected by the type of lining used or the model. Installing courtesy lights or chrome edging requires $\frac{1}{4}$ unit of labor time. Overhead is assigned to products on the basis of labor units. Total labor costs for the period were $1,100, and overhead amounted to $875.

**Required**
Determine the period's cost of production for each department, the costs of ending work-in-process, and the gain or loss from abnormal rework and spoilage.

CHAPTER

# 17

# ABSORPTION AND DIRECT COSTING

In accumulating costs in Chapters 11 through 13 we were careful to maintain a distinction between fixed and variable manufacturing costs. By doing so we are now able to prepare two different types of income statements. The first, called an absorption costing income statement, includes the firm's fixed manufacturing costs as a product cost (part of the cost of producing inventory). The second, direct costing, treats fixed manufacturing costs as a period cost (expensed in the period incurred).

## ABSORPTION COSTING

**Absorption costing,** also known as **full costing,** is the approach we used in Chapters 14 through 16. Whether using process costing or job costing we included fixed manufacturing costs as part of the cost to acquire inventory. Since the fixed costs are considered part of the inventory cost, they become expenses in the income statement as part of cost of goods sold only when the units are sold. For example, if fixed costs are \$40,000 for a particular year and we produce 10,000 units of product, then each unit of product will be assigned a fixed cost charge of \$4. If we sell 8,000 units during the year, then cost of goods sold will include 8,000 units × \$4 = \$32,000 of fixed costs. The remaining 2,000 units × \$4 = \$8,000 of fixed costs will be included as part of the cost of inventory still on hand.

Because of this, we say that absorption costing defers a portion of the fixed manufacturing costs into inventory whenever production in a period exceeds sales.

This "inventorying" of fixed costs creates a problem that many people find objectionable. Net income becomes a function of the firm's level of production as well as sales. For example, assume that variable manufacturing costs are $6 per unit, the product sells for $15 per unit, and fixed manufacturing costs are $40,000. Further, variable selling costs are $1 per unit sold and fixed administrative costs are $15,000. Then if 10,000 units are produced and 8,500 units are sold, the absorption costing net income (assuming no beginning inventories) will be as shown in Exhibit 17-1. Notice that the cost per unit of product in ending inventory is $10. This is the sum of the $6 per unit of variable costs plus the $4 per unit of fixed costs.

Now let us see what happens if the firm produces 20,000 units of product but still sells only 8,500 units. Assuming that variable costs are still $6 per unit and fixed costs remain unchanged at $40,000, the absorption cost income statement is provided in Exhibit 17-2. Note that net income has increased from $19,000 to $36,000. This increase is not due to more efficient operations or increased sales, however. It is due solely to the fact that the amount of production doubled. Notice that this time the cost per unit of ending inventory is $8. This consists of the same $6 per unit variable cost as before, but now the fixed cost is just $40,000 ÷ 20,000 units = $2 per unit. Whereas, previously, fixed costs of $4 per unit for 1,500 units were deferred in ending inventory (a total of $6,000), the new plan would defer $2 per unit for 11,500 units—a total of $23,000. Thus the higher production takes $23,000 − $6,000 = $17,000 of fixed costs out

**EXHIBIT 17-1 Absorption Costing Income Statement for the Production of 10,000 Units and the Sale of 8,500 Units**

| | | |
|---|---|---|
| Sales (8,500 units @ $15) | | $127,500 |
| Cost of goods sold | | |
| Beginning inventory | $ — | |
| Variable manufacturing costs (10,000 @ $6) | 60,000 | |
| Fixed manufacturing costs[a] | 40,000 | |
| Ending inventory (1,500 @ $10) | (15,000) | 85,000 |
| Gross margin | | $ 42,500 |
| Selling and administrative costs | | |
| Variable selling (8,500 @ $1) | | 8,500 |
| Fixed administrative | | 15,000 |
| Net income | | $ 19,000 |

[a]Fixed overhead is $40,000/10,000 = $4 per unit.

**EXHIBIT 17-2 Absorption Costing Income Statement for the Production of 20,000 Units and the Sale of 8,500 Units**

| | | |
|---|---|---|
| Sales (8,500 units @ $15) | | $127,500 |
| Cost of goods sold | | |
| Beginning inventory | $ — | |
| Variable manufacturing costs (20,000 @ $6) | 120,000 | |
| Fixed manufacturing costs[a] | 40,000 | |
| Ending inventory (11,500 @ $8) | (92,000) | 68,000 |
| Gross margin | | $ 59,500 |
| Selling and administrative costs | | |
| Variable selling costs (8,500 @ $1) | | 8,500 |
| Fixed administrative costs | | 15,000 |
| Net income | | $ 36,000 |

[a]Fixed overhead is $40,000 ÷ 20,000 = $2 per unit.

of the income statement (as compared to the lower production level) and places them on the balance sheet as the cost of inventory (see Exhibit 17-3). This deferral of course raises net income when more units are produced and exactly explains the difference between the two income figures ($36,000 − $19,000 = $17,000). Many accountants object to absorption costing because it allows management to manipulate reported net income by varying production levels even if sales are unchanged.

## DIRECT COSTING

To avoid the problem of unit costs being a function of production, some accountants have argued that we should use **direct costing** (also called **variable costing**). In direct costing, only variable manufacturing costs (di-

**EXHIBIT 17-3 Ending Inventory as a Function of Production**

| Production of 10,000 Units | | | Production of 20,000 Units | |
|---|---|---|---|---|
| Ending Inventory | | | Ending inventory | |
| Variable costs (1,500 @ $6) | $ 9,000 | | Variable costs (11,500 @ $6) | $69,000 |
| Fixed costs (1,500 @ $4) | 6,000 | | Fixed costs (11,500 @ $2) | 23,000 |
| | | $17,000 Additional deferred fixed costs | | |
| Total ending inventory | $15,000 | | Total ending inventory | $92,000 |

**EXHIBIT 17-4 Direct Costing Income Statement for the Production of 10,000 Units and the Sale of 8,500 Units**

| | | |
|---|---|---|
| Sales (8,500 @ $15) | | $127,500 |
| Variable cost of goods sold | | |
| Beginning inventory | $ — | |
| Variable manufacturing costs (10,000 @ $6) | 60,000 | |
| Ending inventory (1,500 @ $6) | (9,000) | 51,000 |
| Variable selling costs (8,500 @ $1) | | 8,500 |
| Contribution margin | | $ 68,000 |
| Fixed expenses | | |
| Manufacturing | | 40,000 |
| Administrative | | 15,000 |
| Net income | | $ 13,000 |

rect materials, direct labor, and variable overhead)[1] are included as costs to produce inventory. Fixed costs do not become a product cost, but instead are written off as an expense in the period in which they are incurred. Under direct costing the treatment of fixed manufacturing costs parallels the treatment of fixed selling and administrative costs. Let us illustrate a direct cost income statement using our previous example. When we produce 10,000 units of product and sell 8,500, our direct costing net income statement would be as shown in Exhibit 17-4.

With absorption costing, income increased when production was doubled. But with direct costing, income will not change if production alone is changed. Using the earlier example in which 20,000 units are produced and 8,500 are sold, the direct cost income statement yields the same income as when 10,000 units were produced. The reason that net income is the same is that the total fixed costs of $40,000 are expensed regardless of production level. None of these costs is deferred to ending inventory.

### Format of the Direct Costing Income Statement

The format of the absorption costing statement should be quite familiar now. It starts by subtracting cost of goods sold from sales to yield gross margin. From the gross margin we subtract our other selling and administrative expenses to yield net income. In effect, the absorption costing

[1]Note that the inclusion of variable overhead as a product cost means that the name *direct costing* is really inappropriate. But so is the term *variable costing* since we only include variable manufacturing costs. We presumably could develop our own more appropriate name, but the term *direct costing* is very well entrenched; hence, we will stick with this commonly used term.

**EXHIBIT 17-5 Direct Costing Income Statement for the Production of 20,000 Units and the Sale of 8,500 Units**

| | | |
|---|---|---|
| Sales (8,500 @ $15) | | $127,500 |
| Variable cost of goods sold | | |
| Beginning inventory | $ — | |
| Variable manufacturing costs (20,000 @ $6) | 120,000 | |
| Ending inventory (11,500 @ $6) | (69,000) | 51,000 |
| Variable selling costs (8,500 @ $1) | | 8,500 |
| Contribution margin | | $ 68,000 |
| Fixed expenses | | |
| Manufacturing | | 40,000 |
| Administrative | | 15,000 |
| Net income | | $ 13,000 |

income statement groups all manufacturing costs (in cost of goods sold) separately from nonmanufacturing costs. However, the previous examples reveal that the format of the direct costing income statement is quite different. In the direct costing statement manufacturing and nonmanufacturing expenses are mixed. Rather than grouping costs by function, we group them by variability. All variable costs (both manufacturing and nonmanufacturing) are segregated first and subtracted from sales to yield total contribution margin. Once the contribution margin has been determined, we then subtract out all fixed costs to yield net income. A major advantage cited for the direct costing approach is that, by concentrating on the behavior of costs, the format of the statement permits an easy comparison of the actual operating results with the preliminary plans that were based on cost-volume-profit analysis (see Chapter 4).

## CONVERTING FROM ONE COSTING METHOD TO THE OTHER

Once we understand how income statements are prepared under each of the two costing methods, we should be able to convert an income statement prepared under one approach to the other. Since the only difference between absorption and direct costing is in the treatment of fixed manufacturing costs, we need only reconcile the treatment of these costs. Figure 17-1 indicates the difference in the timing of the expensing of fixed costs under the two approaches. As illustrated, absorption costing net income will be *less than* direct costing net income by the amount of fixed costs deferred under absorption costing from a prior period to the current period. In contrast, the absorption costing net income figure will be *higher than* the direct costing income figure by the amount of current period fixed costs deferred to the next period under absorption costing. Thus the steps

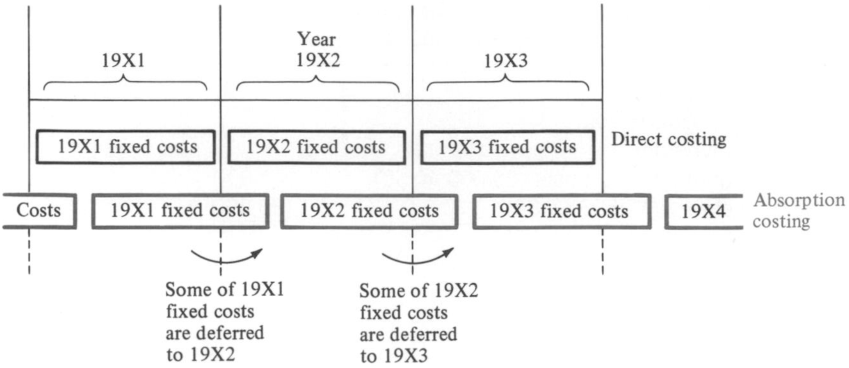


**FIGURE 17-1 Timing of the expensing of fixed manufacturing costs with direct versus absorption costing.**

necessary to reconcile direct costing net income with absorption costing net income are

Direct costing net income
− Fixed costs in beginning inventory: Absorption costing
+ Fixed costs in ending inventory: Absorption costing
= Absorption costing net income

Of course to reconcile absorption costing income with a direct costing net income, we reverse the sign of our adjustments to get

Absorption costing net income
+ Fixed costs in beginning inventory: Absorption costing
− Fixed costs in ending inventory: Absorption costing
= Direct costing net income

Let us illustrate these calculations with the data from the previous examples. When we produced 10,000 units and sold 8,500, we had an absorption costing net income of $19,000 but a direct costing net income of $13,000. In that example we did not have any beginning inventory, and our ending inventory consisted of 1,500 units. The fixed costs per unit of product in ending inventory under absorption costing were $4, so ending absorption costing inventory contained a total of $6,000 in fixed costs. The reconciliation of direct costing to absorption costing net income is

| | |
|---|---|
| Direct costing net income | $13,000 |
| − Beginning inventory fixed costs | — |
| + Ending inventory fixed costs | 6,000 |
| = Absorption costing net income | $19,000 |

For the second example, 20,000 units were produced and 8,500 were sold. In that example there was an absorption costing net income of \$36,000 and a direct costing net income of \$13,000. Let us now reverse the order and reconcile direct costing with absorption costing net income. There is still no beginning inventory, but now the ending inventory contains 11,500 units. Under absorption costing there were fixed costs of \$2 per unit, or a total of \$23,000 in ending inventory, yielding

| | |
|---|---|
| Absorption costing net income | \$36,000 |
| + Beginning inventory fixed costs | — |
| − Ending inventory fixed costs | 23,000 |
| = Direct costing net income | \$13,000 |

### Inventory Flow and Reconciliation

You may have noticed that we did not mention whether the firm used FIFO, LIFO, or some other inventory flow assumption for costing inventory. We did not have to because the nature of the adjustments is the same under each flow assumption. However, the actual calculation of the amount of fixed cost in beginning and ending inventory does differ depending on the flow assumption. Let us illustrate the calculations using the following data.

| Year | Units Produced | Units Sold | Fixed Cost (total) | Variable Cost (per unit) | Selling Price |
|---|---|---|---|---|---|
| 19X1 | 10,000 | 8,000 | \$21,000 | \$3.00 | \$7 |
| 19X2 | 12,000 | 11,000 | \$21,000 | \$3.50 | \$7 |
| 19X3 | 14,000 | 15,000 | \$21,000 | \$4.00 | \$7 |

We will now prepare income statements for 19X3. Note that beginning inventory will consist of 3,000 units (2,000 more units were produced than sold in 19X1 and another 1,000 units were added in 19X2 when production again exceeded sales). The 19X3 ending inventory will consist of 2,000 units since sales in 19X3 exceeded production by 1,000 units.

Under a FIFO flow assumption, the *beginning* direct cost inventory will be valued at the then most recently incurred variable costs, or the \$3.50 from year 19X2. Under absorption costing, however, the units will also be valued at 19X2 costs, but will include an additional fixed cost of \$21,000 ÷ 12,000 = \$1.75 per unit for a total absorption cost of \$5.25 per unit.

FIFO direct costing *ending* inventory will be at 19X3 variable costs of \$4.00 per unit, whereas the absorption cost for 19X3 will add 19X3's fixed cost of \$21,000 ÷ 14,000 = \$1.50 per unit for a total absorption cost of $5.50. The direct and absorption costing income statements then are as follows:

| **Direct Costing** | | | **Absorption Costing** | | |
|---|---|---|---|---|---|
| Sales (15,000 @ $7) | | $105,000 | Sales (15,000 @ $7) | | $105,000 |
| Variable cost of goods sold | | | Cost of goods sold | | |
| Beginning inventory | | | Beginning inventory | | |
| (3,000 × $3.50) | $10,500 | | (3,000 × $5.25) | $15,750 | |
| Cost of goods manufactured | | | Cost of goods manufactured | | |
| (14,000 × $4.00) | 56,000 | | (14,000 × $4.00 + | | |
| Available for sale | $66,500 | | $21,000) | 77,000 | |
| Ending inventory | | | Available for sale | $92,750 | |
| (2,000 × $4.00) | (8,000) | 58,500 | Ending inventory | | |
| Contribution margin | | $ 46,500 | (2,000 × $5.50) | (11,000) | 81,750 |
| Fixed costs | | 21,000 | Net income | | $ 23,250 |
| Net income | | $ 25,500 | | | |

The reconciliation of absorption costing with direct costing net income proceeds as before.

| | |
|---|---|
| Direct costing net income | $25,500 |
| + Ending inventory fixed costs (2,000 × $1.50) | 3,000 |
| − Beginning inventory fixed costs (3,000 × $1.75) | 5,250 |
| = Absorption costing net income | $23,250 |

If our firm uses LIFO, the calculation of beginning and ending inventory costs is more complex. The 19X3 beginning LIFO inventory consists of two layers: 2,000 units from 19X1 and 1,000 units from 19X2. For direct costing the 19X1 units are valued at $3.00 per unit and the 19X2 units at $3.50, for a beginning direct cost LIFO inventory of

$$2{,}000 \times \$3 + 1{,}000 \times \$3.50 = \$9{,}500$$

Absorption costing adds a fixed cost per unit of $21,000 ÷ 10,000 = $2.10 for the 19X1 units and $1.75 for the 19X2 units. The LIFO absorption cost beginning inventory then is

$$2{,}000 \times (\$3.00 + \$2.10) + 1{,}000 \times (\$3.50 + \$1.75) = \$15{,}450$$

The 19X3 ending LIFO inventory consists of 2,000 units, which would be from 19X1. Thus the direct cost ending inventory would be $6,000 and the absorption cost ending inventory would be $10,200.

The LIFO income statements then are as follows:

**Direct Costing**

| | | |
|---|---|---|
| Sales (15,000 @ $7) | | $105,000 |
| Variable cost of goods sold | | |
| Beginning inventory | $ 9,500 | |
| Cost of goods manufactured | 56,000 | |
| Available for sale | $65,500 | |
| Ending inventory | (6,000) | 59,500 |
| Contribution margin | | $ 45,500 |
| Fixed costs | | 21,000 |
| Net income | | $ 24,500 |

**Absorption Costing**

| | | |
|---|---|---|
| Sales | | $105,000 |
| Cost of goods sold | | |
| Beginning inventory | $15,450 | |
| Cost of goods manufactured | 77,000 | |
| Available for sale | $92,450 | |
| Ending inventory | (10,200) | 82,250 |
| Net income | | $ 22,750 |

And once again the reconciliation of direct and absorption net income is

| | |
|---|---|
| Direct costing net income | $24,500 |
| + Fixed costs in ending inventory (2,000 × $2.10) | 4,200 |
| − Fixed costs in beginning inventory (2,000 × $2.10 + 1,000 × $1.75) | 5,950 |
| = Absorption costing net income | $22,750 |

### Journal Entries for the Conversion

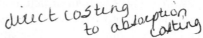

direct costing to absorption costing

The most common need for converting from one costing approach to the other arises when a firm uses direct costing for internal reports. Then, at year-end, the internal reports are adjusted to provide absorption costing statements for external financial statements and the firm's income tax return. The journal entries required to make the conversion are fairly straightforward. Using the data from the previous LIFO example, the direct-cost accounting records would be converted to absorption costs with the following entry.

| | | |
|---|---|---|
| Finished Goods Inventory | 4,200 | |
| Cost of Goods Sold | 22,750 | |
| Fixed Cost Expense | | 21,000 |
| Retained Earnings | | 5,950 |

The debit to Finished Goods increases the carrying value of inventory to absorption cost. Similarly, the debit to Cost of Goods Sold reflects the addition of a portion of the fixed costs. The credit to the Fixed Cost account closes out that account as it is not considered an expense account under absorption costing. Finally, the credit to Retained Earnings reflects the effect on the prior year's earnings for the difference in the carrying value of beginning inventory.

At the beginning of the next period, the following entry would be made to restore the books to a direct cost basis.

| | | |
|---|---|---|
| Retained Earnings | 4,200 | |
| Finished Goods Inventory | | 4,200 |

This entry restates the carrying value of inventory to direct costing and restores Retained Earnings to a direct cost basis. In the example, there was no work-in-process inventory. If there had been, work-in-process would have to be adjusted in the same manner as finished goods inventory.

## ABSORPTION COSTING AND THE VOLUME VARIANCE

In the earlier illustrations of absorption costing we have implicitly assumed the use of actual costing (actual fixed overhead was assigned to the actual products manufactured). But in Chapter 14 we mentioned that in job cost environments the use of predetermined overhead rates is more common for assigning fixed costs to production. Let us briefly examine the effect of predetermined overhead rates on our previous analysis.

Exhibits 17-6 and 17-7 present absorption cost income statements using the data from Exhibits 17-1 and 17-2. However, this time we have presumed that the firm anticipated producing 16,000 units. Thus its predetermined fixed overhead rate is $40,000 ÷ 16,000 = $2.50 per unit. We can see from Exhibits 17-6 and 17-7 that net income is still affected by production (income changes from $16,750 to $41,750). It is also still true that we can reconcile absorption cost net income to direct cost net income by concentrating solely on the fixed costs in ending inventory:

| | |
|---|---|
| Absorption costing net income (Exhibit 17-6) | $16,750 |
| + Beginning inventory fixed costs | — |
| − Ending inventory fixed costs (1,500 @ $2.50) | 3,750 |
| = Direct costing net income (Exhibit 17-4) | $13,000 |

However, there is an interesting change when we use predetermined overhead rates. Note that the gross margins in Exhibits 17-6 and 17-7 are equal. As long as the denominator volume on which the predetermined overhead rate is based remains constant and total fixed overhead stays constant, the fixed cost applied per unit will remain constant. Thus in this case, the gross margin will be unaffected by the level of production. In fact, now the total effect of volume on net income is captured by the volume variance (the difference between the fixed overhead applied to production and budgeted fixed overhead):

| | |
|---|---|
| Net income from Exhibit 17-6 | $16,750 |
| Volume variance, Exhibit 17-6 | 15,000 |
| Volume variance, Exhibit 17-7 | 10,000 |
| Net income in Exhibit 17-7 | $41,750 |

**EXHIBIT 17-6 Absorption Costing Income Statement with Predetermined Fixed Overhead Rate[a]**

| | | |
|---|---|---|
| Sales (8,500 @ $15) | | $127,500 |
| Cost of goods sold | | |
| Beginning inventory | $ — | |
| Variable manufacturing costs | 60,000 | |
| Fixed costs applied (10,000 @ $2.50) | 25,000 | |
| Ending inventory (1,500 @ $8.50) | (12,750) | 72,250 |
| Gross margin | | $ 55,250 |
| Less: | | |
| Selling and administrative costs | | |
| Variable selling | | 8,500 |
| Fixed administrative | | 15,000 |
| Unfavorable volume variance ($25,000 − $40,000) | | 15,000 |
| Net income | | $ 16,750 |

[a]Assumptions: Produce 10,000 units; sell 8,500 units; denominator volume 16,000 units; predetermined overhead rate $40,000 ÷ 16,000 = $2.50 per unit.

**EXHIBIT 17-7 Absorption Costing Income Statement with Predetermined Fixed Overhead Rate[a]**

| | | |
|---|---|---|
| Sales (8,500 @ $15) | | $127,500 |
| Cost of goods sold | | |
| Beginning inventory | $ — | |
| Variable manufacturing costs | 120,000 | |
| Fixed costs applied (20,000 @ $2.50) | 50,000 | |
| Ending inventory (11,500 @ $8.50) | (97,750) | 72,250 |
| Gross margin | | $ 55,250 |
| Less: | | |
| Selling and administrative costs | | |
| Variable selling | | 8,500 |
| Fixed administrative | | 15,000 |
| Plus: | | |
| Favorable volume variance ($50,000 − $40,000) | | 10,000 |
| Net income | | $ 41,750 |

[a]Assumptions: Produce 20,000 units; sell 8,500 units; denominator volume 16,000 units; predetermined overhead rate $40,000 ÷ 16,000 = $2.50 per unit.

This observation has led many firms to adopt a procedure that eliminates production volume as a determinant in quarterly (or monthly) earnings. Instead of using a different denominator volume based on each period's anticipated level of operations, they make a single prediction of volume for the year. Then a constant fixed overhead application rate is used for the entire year. The volume variance for each quarter (or month) is not closed to the income statement. Instead, it is carried as a deferred charge in the balance sheet. In this way the periodic income reported during the year will be unaffected by changes in activity level. Some firms go a step further and extend this approach to a 3- to 5-year cycle. They adopt an average denominator activity level for several years and defer volume variances over the period. Such an approach largely eliminates the swings in net income arising from changes in activity. Of course, there will come a time when the accumulated volume variance will have to be closed to net income. If the denominator activity is consistently above or below actual activity, the accumulated volume variance can have a very significant effect on net income when it is closed out.

## ABSORPTION VERSUS DIRECT COSTING

As we have just seen, in a single-product firm we can easily convert from one costing method to the other. But for firms with hundreds of products, the task would be quite time-consuming. Thus most firms choose to use only one approach or the other.

The debate over which accounting system should be adopted has gone on for decades. While many issues have been raised in these debates, the two central issues involve the effect on manager's decisions and the effect on inventory valuations.

For decision making, the debate concerns whether variable costs or full costs more frequently approximate the relevant costs for decisions. This is of particular concern to highly automated firms in which fixed costs are significant and variable costs are minimal. In such a firm a product's variable cost might be \$1 while its fully absorbed cost might be \$10. Many accountants worry that only reporting variable costs might lead managers to serious pricing errors or the acceptance of unprofitable orders. Unfortunately, as we noted in Chapter 5, such determinations are very situation-specific and must include an estimate of the opportunity cost for using capacity (a portion of the demonstration problem at the end of the chapter reinforces this point).

For inventory valuation, the debate centers on whether it is appropriate, in effect, to capitalize a portion of fixed overhead. Absorption costers are in favor of this approach, saying that the fixed costs are a necessary cost to acquire the inventory. Direct costers argue negatively, saying that the fixed costs do not represent future service value and thus are not an asset. Although we cannot resolve the debate, in the United States, GAAP currently favors absorption costing for external reports,[2] and the Internal Revenue Service requires absorption costing for tax returns.[3] Thus most firms use an absorption costing system to prepare external reports and use them internally as well in order to minimize accounting costs.

For many firms the distinction between absorption and direct costing is becoming moot. Firms that have successfully adopted just-in-time production systems (see Chapter 7) will not have significant inventories. Without inventories, both accounting systems provide similar results.

## SUMMARY

External financial statements are almost always prepared using an absorption costing basis. However, absorption costing financial statements must be used with great care for performance measurement or short-run decision making. As a performance measure, absorption costing statements are too easily subject to manipulation through the choice of the level of production and the definition of capacity. For short-run decisions, absorption costing overstates marginal costs. Direct costing, on the other hand, avoids the income manipulation problem and facilitates the use of the contribution margin approach to analyzing short-run decisions. But care must be used with the direct cost approach, too, because it understates marginal costs when opportunity costs exist for using capacity.

## DEMONSTRATION PROBLEM

In establishing the current year's budget, Kirchoff Industries had segregated all its costs into fixed and variable costs. Management determined that direct materials costs would be $4 per unit of product manufactured; direct labor, $2.50 per unit; variable overhead, $1.00 per unit; and fixed overhead, $300,000. Administration and selling costs were expected to have a fixed component of $100,000 and a variable component of $1.50 per unit sold.

After detailed market studies, management determined that a selling price of $25 per unit would likely result in a sales volume of 30,000 units. Based on this analysis the budget in Exhibit 17-8 was prepared.

During the year the firm produced 30,000 units, as budgeted. However, the market for the product turned out to be softer than anticipated. Only 20,000 units were sold at $25. Just before the end of the year an additional 3,000 units were sold for $15 to a foreign distributor. The year's actual income statement is given in Exhibit 17-9.

[2]*FASB Accounting Standards Current Text*, Section I78, paragraphs 104–106.

[3]Internal Revenue Code Section 1.471-11(b)(3)(ii).

**EXHIBIT 17-8 Budgeted Income Statement (Absorption Costing)**

| | | |
|---|---|---|
| Sales (30,000 units @ $25) | | $750,000 |
| Costs of goods sold | | |
| Beginning inventory | $ — | |
| Direct materials | 120,000 | |
| Direct labor | 75,000 | |
| Variable overhead | 30,000 | |
| Fixed overhead | 300,000 | |
| Ending inventory | ( — ) | 525,000 |
| Gross margin | | $225,000 |
| Fixed selling and administration | | 100,000 |
| Variable selling and administration | | 45,000 |
| Net income | | $ 80,000 |

Upon reviewing the income statement for the period, the president had mixed emotions: "I'm pleased that we were able to show a profit in spite of the depressed market, but I see that we sold 3,000 units at less than cost. Our manufacturing cost is $17.50 per unit. If we add our variable selling cost of $1.50 per unit, we can see it costs us $19 to get a unit into our customers' hands. We lost $4 a unit on that foreign sale of 3,000 units. If we hadn't made that sale, our profits would have been $20,000; a 250% better performance. That special sale was a big mistake!"

**Required**

**a.** Prepare the absorption cost income statement that would have resulted if the firm had rejected the foreign sale and only sold 20,000 units at $25.

**EXHIBIT 17-9 Actual Income Statement (Absorption Costing)**

| | | |
|---|---|---|
| Sales (20,000 @ $25 + 3,000 @ $15) | | $545,000 |
| Cost of goods sold | | |
| Beginning inventory | $ — | |
| Direct materials | 120,000 | |
| Direct labor | 75,000 | |
| Variable overhead | 30,000 | |
| Fixed overhead | 300,000 | |
| Cost of goods available | $525,000 | |
| Ending inventory | (122,500)[a] | 402,500 |
| Gross margin | | $142,500 |
| Fixed selling and administration | | 100,000 |
| Variable selling and administration | | 34,500 |
| Net income | | $ 8,000 |

[a]Ending inventory consists of 7,000 units @ $17.50 each:

$$\frac{\text{cost of goods manufactured}}{\text{units manufactured}} = \frac{\$525{,}000}{30{,}000} = \$17.50$$

**EXHIBIT 17-10 Income Statement for Reduced Sales (Absorption Costing)**

| | | |
|---|---|---|
| Sales (20,000 @ $25) | | $500,000 |
| Cost of goods sold | | |
| Beginning inventory | $ — | |
| Direct materials | 120,000 | |
| Direct labor | 75,000 | |
| Variable overhead | 30,000 | |
| Fixed overhead | 300,000 | |
| Cost of goods available | $525,000 | |
| Ending inventory | (175,000) | 350,000 |
| Gross margin | | $150,000 |
| Fixed selling and administration | | 100,000 |
| Variable selling and administration | | 30,000 |
| Net income | | $ 20,000 |

**b.** Prepare a direct cost income statement based on actual sales and reconcile it to the actual absorption cost income statement.
**c.** Prepare a direct cost income statement if the firm only sold the 20,000 units at $25. Reconcile this statement to the comparable absorption cost statement.
**d.** Is the firm better or worse off for having made the foreign sale?

**Solution**

**a.** The absorption costing income statement assuming the sale of 20,000 units is presented in Exhibit 17-10. Although sales are lower than what the firm actually experienced, these lower sales are more than offset by a lower cost of goods sold and lower variable selling and administrative expenses. As the president indicated, reported profits on an absorption cost basis would have been increased to $20,000 had the foreign sale not been made.
**b.** The direct costing income statement for actual sales is given in Exhibit 17-11. The very large difference between the direct and absorption costing income

**EXHIBIT 17-11 Income Statement for Actual Sales (Direct Costing)**

| | | |
|---|---|---|
| Sales (20,000 × $25 + 3,000 × $15) | | $545,000 |
| Variable cost of goods sold | | |
| Beginning inventory | $ — | |
| Direct materials | 120,000 | |
| Direct labor | 75,000 | |
| Variable overhead | 30,000 | |
| Cost of goods available | $225,000 | |
| Ending inventory | (52,500) | 172,500 |
| Variable selling and administration | | 34,500 |
| Contribution margin | | $338,000 |
| Fixed overhead | | 300,000 |
| Fixed selling and administration | | 100,000 |
| Net income | | $ (62,000) |

**EXHIBIT 17-12 Income Statement for Reduced Sales (Direct Costing)**

| | | |
|---|---|---|
| Sales (20,000 × $25) | | $500,000 |
| Variable cost of goods sold | | |
| Beginning inventory | $ — | |
| Direct materials | 120,000 | |
| Direct labor | 75,000 | |
| Variable overhead | 30,000 | |
| Cost of goods available | $225,000 | |
| Ending inventory | (75,000) | 150,000 |
| Variable selling and administration | | 30,000 |
| Contribution margin | | $320,000 |
| Fixed overhead | | 300,000 |
| Fixed selling and administration | | 100,000 |
| Net income | | $ (80,000) |

statements is due to the large amount of fixed production costs deferred in ending inventory under absorption costing. That is, under absorption costing the $300,000 of fixed overhead costs is spread over the 30,000 units manufactured. This results in a fixed charge of $10 per unit attached to ending inventory under absorption costing. Since there is an ending inventory of 7,000 units, absorption costing income is $70,000 higher than direct costing income; that is,

| | |
|---|---|
| Absorption costing net income | $ 8,000 |
| − Fixed costs deferred in ending inventory | 70,000 |
| = Direct costing net income | $ (62,000) |

**c.** The difference between absorption and direct costing net income is even larger when we look at the reduced sales case. Exhibit 17-12 shows a direct costing loss of $80,000 as compared to the $20,000 net income shown in Exhibit 17-10. Once again, the difference is due solely to the fixed costs in inventory. With reduced sales, there would be 10,000 units in ending inventory, each with a $10 charge for fixed overhead when absorption costing is used.

| | |
|---|---|
| Absorption costing net income | $ 20,000 |
| − Fixed costs deferred in ending inventory | 100,000 |
| = Direct costing net income | $ (80,000) |

**d.** The absorption costing income statements suggest that the sale to foreigners was not a good deal, but the direct cost income statements suggest it was (our loss was reduced from $80,000 to $62,000). Which approach better measures the actual effect of the sale? In this case the direct costing statements are probably a better reflection of the effect on the firm's financial position. Although the units were sold for less than the firm's full cost of $19, the $15 selling price is higher than the firm's variable costs. The variable costs are just $9 per unit (direct materials $4, plus direct labor $2.50, plus variable overhead $1, plus variable selling and administrative expense of $1.50). Thus each unit sold did contribute $6 toward coverage of the firm's fixed costs.

But even the foregoing analysis is not really correct. For in this case we are examining a decision to sell products *after they have been produced.* Once we have the products, *all* production costs are irrelevant. The only costs relevant to the sale at this point are the $1.50 per unit in selling and administrative expenses that must be incurred if we make a sale. If there are no other outlets for the products, any sale for more than $1.50 per unit will make the firm better off. Of course, before deciding to dump the products at distress prices now, management should give consideration to holding the products if it is felt that a better market will exist for them in the future.

## KEY TERMS AND CONCEPTS

[ Absorption costing
Full costing ]

[ Direct costing
Variable costing ]

[Bracketed terms are equivalent in meaning.

## FURTHER READING

Abel, Rein. "The Role of Costs and Cost Accounting in Price Determination," *Management Accounting* (April 1978), p. 29.

Eichhorn, Frederic G. "A Direct Allocation Financial Data Base for Manufacturing," *Management Accounting* (May 1978), p. 39.

Fremgen, James M. "The Direct Costing Controversy—An Identification of the Issues," *The Accounting Review* (January 1964), p. 43.

Grinnell, D. Jacque. "Using Linear Programming to Compare Direct and Absorption Costing," *The Accounting Review* (July 1977), p. 485.

Hanks, George F. "The Income Statement: A Dark Cloud Over Management Accounting," *Cost and Management* (January–February 1985), p. 25.

Parker, John R. E. "Perspectives on Direct Costing," *The Canadian Chartered Accountant* (March 1961), p. 225.

Stallman, James C. "A Simplified Graphical Display of Production Sales Volume Effects on Absorption Costing Income," *The Accounting Review* (April 1979), p. 390.

## QUESTIONS AND EXERCISES

**17-1** What danger is inherent in the use of direct costing techniques exclusively?

**17-2** A firm employs direct costing on a day-to-day basis. It must convert direct costing results to full costing results for external purposes. How can this be accomplished?

**17-3** The level of production attained will have an effect on income as determined using absorption costing but will have no effect on income as determined using variable costing. Explain.

**17-4** What happens to the volume variance if direct costing is employed?

**17-5** The basic issue in variable and absorption costing can be said to be one of timing rather than amount. Explain.

**17-6** What is the difference between direct costs and direct costing?

**17-7** Will the use of direct costing avoid the problem of joint cost allocation?

**17-8** Breakeven is unique when variable costing is employed, but multiple breakeven points are possible when absorption costing is employed. Explain.

**17-9** What is the relationship between the quantity required to break even and the quantity used for denominator volume to determine the overhead rate?

**17-10** If inventory physically increases during the period, income under absorption costing will be higher than income using variable costing. Explain.

**17-11** A firm has prepared the following budget for a new product.

| | Variable Costs per Unit | Fixed Costs per Period |
|---|---|---|
| Direct material | $ 6 | $ — |
| Direct labor | 13 | — |
| Overhead | 7 | 20,000 |
| Selling | 2 | 10,000 |
| Administration | 1 | 15,000 |
| Total | $29 | $45,000 |

During the first period, the firm plans on producing and selling 1,000 units. What is the expected inventoriable cost per unit under (a) direct costing and (b) full costing?

**17-12** A firm has prepared financial statements on both a direct costing and a full costing basis. The differences are as follows:

| | Basis 1 | Basis 2 |
|---|---|---|
| Income | $500,000 | $440,000 |
| Inventory change | 140,000 (decrease) | 200,000 (decrease) |

Which basis is being used for direct and for full costing? Why?

**17-13** Using method A, a firm would report income of $20,000 and an increase in inventory of $5,000. Using method B, it would report income of $22,000 and an increase in inventory of $7,000. Which method corresponds to variable costing and which to absorption costing? Why?

**17-14** A firm is planning to introduce a new product and provides you with the following data.

| | Variable Costs per Unit | Fixed Costs per Period |
|---|---|---|
| Production costs | $40 | $10,000 |
| Selling and administration | 10[a] | 25,000 |

[a]Per unit sold.

| | |
|---|---|
| Selling price | $90 |
| Production | 1,000 units |
| Sales | 900 units |

What is projected income using (a) direct costing and (b) full costing?

**17-15** A firm establishes a predetermined rate for overhead at the start of the year and closes any over- or underapplied overhead at the end of the year. The firm produces and sells one product. The physical inventories for the first half of the year are as follows:

| Month | Units |
|---|---|
| January 1 | 800 |
| February 1 | 900 |
| March 1 | 850 |
| April 1 | 875 |
| May 1 | 875 |
| June 1 | 825 |
| July 1 | 900 |

During which months will absorption costing income be (a) higher than, (b) equal to, and (c) less than variable costing income?

**17-16** Normal monthly volume is 500 units and fixed overhead is $100 per unit. When 500 units are produced and sold, expected income is $10,000. Volume variances are carried forward monthly and closed to the income statement at the end of the year. Data for the first 9 months of the year are as follows:

| Month | Units Produced | Units Sold |
|---|---|---|
| January | 500 | 400 |
| February | 500 | 600 |
| March | 500 | 500 |
| April | 600 | 500 |
| May | 400 | 500 |
| June | 500 | 500 |
| July | 600 | 400 |
| August | 300 | 400 |
| September | 400 | 500 |

Determine income for each month using (a) variable costing and (b) absorption costing.

**17-17** At a level of activity of 5,000 units produced and sold, fixed costs are budgeted at $60,000 for manufacturing and $50,000 for selling and administration, and variable costs are budgeted at $40,000 for manufacturing and $30,000 for selling and administration (these latter costs vary with units sold).

In a period in which 5,000 units are produced and 4,000 are sold, how much will appear as expense for each type of cost on an income statement prepared using (a) direct or variable costing and (b) full or absorption costing? At what cost will the 1,000 units added to inventory be carried under (c) variable costing and (d) absorption costing?

**17-18** Lopro uses absorption costing. The overhead absorption rate and variable manufacturing costs have not changed in the past 2 years. Work-in-progress inventories and beginning finished goods inventory are zero. Some of the data for the current year are as follows:

| | |
|---|---|
| Finished goods, ending | $ ? |
| Cost of goods sold | 162,000 |
| Volume variance (favorable) | 4,000 |
| Net income after adjusting for volume variance | 30,000 |
| Budgeted fixed manufacturing overhead | 80,000 |
| Units employed for overhead rate | 20,000 |
| Units sold | 18,000 |

Prepare a statement of cost of goods manufactured and sold using (a) absorption costing and (b) variable costing. Also (c) determine net income using variable costing and (d) reconcile the two income figures.

**17-19** B.A.V., Inc., has budgeted for its first year of operations as follows:

| | |
|---|---|
| Unit selling price | $ 25 |
| Variable manufacturing cost per unit | 10 |
| Variable selling and administrative cost per unit | 5 |
| Fixed manufacturing cost | 200,000 |
| Fixed selling and administrative cost | 150,000 |

The firm will use an annual volume of 50,000 units to apply overhead. In the first year it expects to produce 40,000 units and to sell 35,000. Volume variances will be closed to the income statement. Variable selling and administrative costs vary with the number of units sold.

Project (a) breakeven using conventional CVP techniques, (b) income using absorption costing, and (c) income using direct costing.

## PROBLEMS AND CASES

**17-20 Absorption and direct cost income statements and special sale.** Refer to the demonstration problem at the end of the chapter. Assume that Kirchoff expects to sell 27,000 units next year for $25 per unit. Its cost will remain unchanged from last year.

**Required**

**a.** Prepare absorption and direct cost income statements for the next year assuming that the firm sells 27,000 units but produces 20,000 units (that is, it will sell its beginning inventory of 7,000 units and end the period with no inventory).

**b.** Assume Kirchoff had not made the foreign sale described in the demonstration problem. For the current year prepare absorption and direct cost income statements assuming that the firm sells 27,000 units and produces 17,000 units.

**c.** Given your results from (a) and (b), should Kirchoff have made the foreign sale last year?

**17-21 Physical data.**

Yoda Enterprises specializes in genetic engineering. It employs a variable cost system in the production of its only product. Physical inventories for the past few months were as follows:

| | Work-in-Process (equivalent units) | Finished Goods | Total Units |
|---|---|---|---|
| January 1 | 3,000 | 3,000 | 6,000 |
| February 1 | 4,000 | 3,000 | 7,000 |
| March 1 | 5,000 | 2,000 | 7,000 |
| April 1 | 2,000 | 4,000 | 6,000 |
| May 1 | 3,000 | 5,000 | 8,000 |
| June 1 | 4,000 | 4,000 | 8,000 |

Yoda's cost and revenue functions were unchanged over this period. It has fixed and variable costs, both in production and in selling.

**Required**

**a.** In which of the 5 months will variable costing income exceed absorption costing income?

**b.** In which of the 5 months will absorption costing income exceed variable costing income?

**c.** In which of the 5 months will income be the same under either method?

**d.** For the 5-month period taken as a whole, which costing method will produce the higher income? Explain.

**17-22 Variable and absorption costing using actual rates.**

Chorleywood Metalworks is a British manufacturing subsidiary of a Dutch merchandising house. The firm uses an actual (FIFO) cost system, allocating actual fixed overhead for the year to actual production. Data for the first 2 years of operation are as follows:

| | 19X1 | 19X2 |
|---|---|---|
| Units produced | 1,000 | 900 |
| Units sold | 700 | 800 |
| Total sales | £7,000 | £8,000 |
| Total costs | | |
| Production | | |
| Variable | 2,000 | 1,800 |
| Fixed | 1,800 | 1,800 |
| Selling and administration | | |
| Variable | 700 | 800 |
| Fixed | 2,800 | 2,800 |

**Required**
**a.** Prepare income statements for both years using variable costing.
**b.** Prepare income statements for both years using absorption costing.
**c.** Reconcile (through inventory) the differences in income.

**17-23 Income statement data.**
You are on your way to a meeting with the board of directors. Your assistant provides you with last month's income statements—one based on variable costing procedures and one based on absorption costing procedures. Unfortunately, your assistant is new and has used absorption costing terminology for both income statements. What you got is as follows:

| | Income Statement 1 | | Income Statement 2 | |
|---|---|---|---|---|
| Sales | | $8,672 | | $8,672 |
| Cost of goods sold | $3,000 | | $4,032 | |
| Other expenses | 4,180 | 7,180 | 3,100 | 7,132 |
| Net income | | $1,492 | | $1,540 |

**Required**
**a.** Which income statement is based on variable costing procedures?
**b.** Was production equal to, greater than, or less than sales for the month? Explain.
**c.** What was the amount of fixed overhead for the month?

**17-24 Balance sheet data.**
You are given the following inventory data for a firm. The data are both for the month of January. One set of figures is based on variable costing, and the other set is based on absorption costing.

| | Balance Sheet 1 | Balance Sheet 2 |
|---|---|---|
| Inventory, January 1 | $17,000 | $38,000 |
| Inventory, January 31 | 8,000 | 19,000 |

**Required**
**a.** Which of the two balance sheets is based on absorption costing procedures?
**b.** During January, what was the number of units produced in relation to the number of units sold?
**c.** What was the dollar difference between net income on income statement 1 and income statement 2 for January?

**17-25 Conversion from direct to full costing.**
Converto, Inc., has employed variable (direct) costing throughout the year. The finished goods inventory, *at standard variable cost*, is as follows:

| | Finished Goods |
|---|---|
| Beginning inventory | $10,000 |
| Cost of goods manufactured | 80,000 |
| Finished goods available for sale | $90,000 |
| Ending inventory | 20,000 |
| Cost of goods sold | $70,000 |

There are no work-in-process inventories.

The firm desires to allocate fixed manufacturing overhead costs of $60,480 in order to conform with full or absorption costing for external financial statement purposes. A similar procedure last year allocated $18,000 to ending inventory.

**Required**

Determine the cost of ending inventory and cost of goods sold:

**a.** According to FIFO methods.

**b.** According to LIFO methods.

**c.** According to weighted-average costing (assume that the standard variable cost per unit has not changed since last year).

**17-26 Proration: Variable to absorption costing.**

Tom Halliday has been in business for a year. At the start, it was not known precisely what costs for the year would be. However, the product is sufficiently unique and patent-protected that any cost increases could easily be passed on to the customer; hence, profitability is assured. Accordingly, it was decided to use actual direct costing throughout the year and to adjust the relevant accounts at the end of the year to conform with IRS requirements for absorption costing. Tom's company also uses process cost accounting even though it has only one department. Inventory data for the year are as follows:

| | Work-in-Process (equivalent units) | Finished Goods (units) |
|---|---|---|
| Beginning | — | — |
| Increases | 54,000 | 48,000 |
| Total | 54,000 | 48,000 |
| Ending | 6,000 | 8,000 |
| Decreases | 48,000 | 40,000 |

Fixed manufacturing costs for the year totaled $124,416. Variable manufacturing costs were $120 per unit.

**Required**

**a.** Using units as the basis for allocation, prorate the fixed manufacturing costs so as to approximate full or absorption costing.

**b.** As a result of the allocation, will Tom's absorption-costing income be higher or lower than direct-cost income, and by how much?

**17-27 Comparative effects of costing methods.**

Conic, Inc., uses absorption costing and bases its fixed overhead rate of $5 per unit on normal volume of 10,000 units per quarter. In a quarter in which 10,000 units are produced and sold, income is expected to be $30,000. Volume variances, if any, are carried forward quarterly and closed to the income statement at year-end. Projected data for the year by quarter are as follows:

| Quarter | Production | Sales |
|---|---|---|
| First | 12,000 | 9,000 |
| Second | 10,000 | 11,000 |
| Third | 9,000 | 9,000 |
| Fourth | 11,000 | 10,000 |

**Required**

**a.** What will reported income be in each quarter under absorption costing and variable costing methods?

**b.** For the year, which method will produce the higher income and by how much?

**17-28 Absorption and variable cost income.**

Fein, Inc., budgets costs quarterly as follows:

| | Nonvariable | Variable |
|---|---|---|
| Manufacturing | $200,000 | $10 per unit |
| Selling | 80,000 | 3 per unit sold |
| Administration | 50,000 | 1 per unit sold |

Overhead rates are based on a normal quarterly volume of 10,000 units; volume variances, if any, are closed to the income statement quarterly. The product sells for $50 per unit. There are 1,000 units in inventory at the beginning of the year, valued at the same cost per unit as is being budgeted for the current year.

Activity for the year is planned as follows:

| Quarter | Units Produced | Units Sold |
|---|---|---|
| First | 10,000 | 8,000 |
| Second | 12,000 | 9,000 |
| Third | 8,000 | 12,000 |
| Fourth | 10,000 | 10,000 |

**Required**

**a.** Determine budgeted income by quarter under (1) variable costing and (2) absorption costing.

**b.** What is the cost of the end of the year inventory using (1) variable costing and (2) absorption costing?

**17-29 Converting from absorption to variable costing.**

Conglomerate, Inc., has income statements for 19X2 and 19X3 that have been prepared on the basis of absorption costing with the volume variance taken to the income statement in full.

| | 19X2 | | 19X3 | |
|---|---|---|---|---|
| Sales | | $950,000 | | $1,000,000 |
| Less cost of goods sold | | | | |
| Direct | $380,000 | | $400,000 | |
| Indirect | 380,000 | | 400,000 | |
| Volume variance | (20,000) | 740,000 | 40,000 | 840,000 |
| Gross margin | | $210,000 | | $ 160,000 |
| Less other expenses | | | | |
| Selling | $ 49,000 | | $ 50,000 | |
| Administration | 52,100 | 101,100 | 51,800 | 101,800 |
| Net operating income | | $108,900 | | $ 58,200 |

All cost functions are linear and unchanged for both years. Fixed indirect overhead is $2 per unit. Selling expenses are linearly related to sales; selling expenses are a mixed cost. Administration expenses are linearly related to production.

| | 19X2 | 19X3 |
|---|---|---|
| Units sold | 190,000 | 200,000 |
| Units produced | 210,000 | 180,000 |

**Required**

**a.** Fill in the correct amounts on the following variable-costing-based income statement for *19X3* (note: *not* 19X2).

| | | |
|---|---|---|
| Sales | | $ ______ |
| Less: | | |
| Variable direct expenses | $ ______ | |
| Variable selling expenses | $ ______ | |
| Variable administration expenses | $ ______ | $ ______ |
| Contribution margin | | $ ______ |
| Less: | | |
| Fixed indirect expenses | $ ______ | |
| Fixed selling expenses | $ ______ | |
| Fixed administration expenses | $ ______ | $ ______ |
| Net operating income | | $ ______ |

**b.** Consider 19X2. Assume the volume variance is to be distributed between inventories (balance sheet) and cost of goods sold (income statement) in a manner to adjust inventories and cost of goods sold to approximate actual FIFO cost. Assume that there were 10,000 units in beginning inventory for 19X2. What *proportion* of the 19X2 volume variance would be assigned to cost of goods sold?

**17-30 Absorption to direct costing.**

As controller of Conglomerate's Fern Division, you are on your way to present the division's first-quarter statements. These statements are based on full (absorption) costing, but are detailed insofar as fixed and variable cost classifications are concerned. You anticipate the possibility that one of the new board members, an accounting professor, will ask for income as determined through the use of variable costing.

The following information is available.

A predetermined overhead rate established 2 years ago is in use.
The beginning inventory includes fixed costs of $230,000.
The ending inventory includes fixed costs of $270,000.
LIFO (periodic) costing is employed.
Ferns sell for $100 per carload.
Absorption costing income is $115,000.

**Required**

**a.** What is variable costing income?

**b.** On your way back from the (successful) presentation, you discover that the balance sheet shows a credit balance of $20,000 with the caption "Overabsorbed Overhead." This is shown on the right-hand side of the balance sheet. It is your division's practice to carry any over- or underapplied overhead forward from quarter to quarter and to close it out at the end of the fiscal year to cost of goods sold. If this is relevant to the calculation of variable costing income, give the new income figure. If this is not relevant to the calculation of variable costing income, briefly explain why. If the effect of this on variable costing income cannot be determined, briefly explain why.

**17-31 Direct and absorption costing.**
Brobst Electric Company manufactures a single specialty item, which sells for $200. Production costs are $40,000 quarterly plus $50 per unit; normal volume (used for product costing) is 1,000 units per quarter. Selling and administrative costs are fixed and amount to $80,000 per quarter. Over- or underapplied overhead is closed to the income statement quarterly. Brobst begins with 300 units in inventory on January 1, valued at the same unit cost that is being budgeted for the next year.

**Required**

**a.** What is Brobst's breakeven point?

**b.** Determine Brobst's projected income for the next four quarters, using both variable (direct) and full (absorption) costing techniques. Unit production and sales are as follows:

| Quarter | Sales | Production |
|---|---|---|
| First | 900 | 1,000 |
| Second | 1,200 | 1,000 |
| Third | 800 | 900 |
| Fourth | 1,000 | 1,200 |

**c.** Reconcile the differences in quarterly income figures through inventory balances as they would appear under each method.

**17-32 Product costing and income.**
Wilson, Inc., budgets the following costs for a normal monthly volume of 200 units of a product that sells for $1,000 each.

| | Manufacturing | Nonmanufacturing |
|---|---|---|
| Fixed costs per month | $40,000 | $20,000 |
| Variable costs per unit | 400 | 150[a] |

[a]Per unit sold.

**Required**

**a.** What is the unit product cost using variable costing?

**b.** What is the unit product cost using absorption costing?

**c.** What will absorption and direct costing income be in a month in which 200 units are produced and 210 are sold?

**d.** What will absorption and direct costing income be in a month in which 200 units are produced and 180 are sold?

**e.** Using conventional cost-volume-profit analysis, how many units must be sold monthly to break even?

**17-33 Evaluating direct and absorption costing.**
The following discussion took place at an executive meeting of Conglomerate, Inc., a widely diversified firm.

14th VP: *Absorption costing* was good enough in the past and it is good enough now.

37th VP: But virtually all the incoming talent of late argue in favor of *variable costing*.

| | |
|---|---|
| 25th VP: | We are not going to resolve our differences unless we *compromise*. I suggest we stop our practice of closing out the volume variance to the income statement and, instead, carry it forward on the balance sheet. |
| 14th VP: | That is OK with me, but it is still absorption costing. |
| 37th VP: | I have no objection to the proposal either, but only because it looks like variable costing to me. |
| 25th VP: | 37th VP, would you please elaborate? |
| 37th VP: | Well, the volume variance results from the level of production attained, and hence the proposal removes this as a determinant of income. |
| 25th VP: | Thank you. |
| President: | We shall adopt the proposal of the 25th VP. He thinks it is a compromise and neither of you thinks your position has been compromised at all. Since it is apparently a perfect solution, we shall adopt it. All in favor say Aye. |
| 52 VPs: | Aye! |
| President: | The meeting is adjourned. |

**Required**
Which, if any, of the three vice-presidents is correct? Why? In your explanation, indicate why the others are not correct.

**17-34 Converting from variable to absorption costing** (CMA adapted).
The vice-president for sales of Huber Corporation has received the following income statement for November, which was prepared on a direct costing basis. The firm has just adopted a direct costing system for internal reporting purposes.

**HUBER CORPORATION**
**Income Statement**
**For the Month of November**
**(000s omitted)**

| | |
|---|---|
| Sales | $2,400 |
| Less variable cost of goods sold | 1,200 |
| Contribution margin | $1,200 |
| Less fixed manufacturing costs at budget | 600 |
| Gross margin | $ 600 |
| Less fixed selling and administrative costs | 400 |
| Net income before taxes | $ 200 |

The controller attached the following notes to the statements.

The unit sales price for November averaged $24.
The unit manufacturing costs for the month were

| | |
|---|---|
| Variable cost | $12 |
| Fixed cost applied | 4 |
| Total cost | $16 |

The unit rate for fixed manufacturing costs is a predetermined rate based upon a normal monthly production of 150,000 units.
Variable costs per unit have been stable all year.

Production for November was 45,000 units in excess of sales.
The inventory at November 30 consisted of 80,000 units.

**Required**

**a.** The vice-president for sales is not comfortable with the direct costing basis and wonders what the net income would have been under the prior absorption costing basis.
   **1.** Present the November income statement on an absorption costing basis.
   **2.** Reconcile and explain the difference between the direct costing and the absorption costing net income figures.

**b.** Explain the features associated with direct cost income measurement that should be attractive to the vice-president for sales.

**17-35 Conversion to variable costing.**

Shotgun Enterprises is a widely diversified conglomerate dealing in shipping, medical supplies, and food processing. The following data apply to one of the firm's divisions.

| | |
|---|---|
| Actual factory overhead, April | $29,000 |
| Overhead applied, April | $27,000 |
| Overhead in work-in-process | |
| Beginning of April | $ 5,000 |
| End of April | $ 8,000 |

Volume variances are carried forward on the balance sheet from month to month and closed to the income statement at the end of the calendar year. The volume variance has the following balances.

| | |
|---|---|
| Beginning of April | $400 debit |
| End of April | $700 debit |

The flexible budget is defined in terms of actual labor hours and overhead is applied accordingly.

| | |
|---|---|
| Absorption rate | $3.00 per hour |
| Variable portion of absorption rate | $1.50 per hour |

In addition to monthly absorption costing income statements, management is given monthly variable costing income statements. Since the division produces only for large chains on long-term contracts, it has no finished goods inventories; goods are shipped (and, hence, sold) as produced.

**Required**

What adjustment or adjustments will have to be made to the absorption costing income figure to obtain variable costing income for April?

**17-36 Absorption and variable costing income statements.**

The management of Stanley Coso, Inc., provides you with the following information.

Manufacturing costs: $100,000 per quarter plus $5 per unit
Selling and administrative costs: $50,000 per quarter plus $2 per unit
Selling price: $30 per unit
Normal capacity: 10,000 units per quarter for absorption costing purposes
Physical units:

| Quarter | Produced | Sold |
|---|---|---|
| First | 10,000 | 8,000 |
| Second | 9,000 | 9,000 |
| Third | 9,000 | 10,000 |
| Fourth | 8,000 | 6,000 |

Volume variances: These are closed to the income statement quarterly.

**Required**

**a.** What is breakeven volume in units?

**b.** Without doing any calculating, determine in which quarters absorption costing income will be higher than, the same as, and lower than variable costing income.

**c.** Prepare quarterly income statements under both variable costing and absorption costing.

**d.** Reconcile the quarterly differences in income with the quarterly difference in inventory (on the balance sheet).

**e.** How do you reconcile results of the fourth quarter with your answer to (a)?

**17-37 Variable and absorption cost income** (SMA adapted).
The following data relate to a year's budgeted activity for Rickuse Limited, a company manufacturing a single product.

| | |
|---|---|
| Units | |
| Beginning inventory | 30,000 |
| Production | 120,000 |
| Available for sale | 150,000 |
| Sales | 110,000 |
| Ending inventory | 40,000 |
| Per unit | |
| Selling price | $5.00 |
| Variable manufacturing costs | 1.00 |
| Variable selling, general, and administrative expenses | 2.00 |
| Fixed manufacturing costs (based on 100,000 units) | 0.25 |
| Fixed selling, general, and administrative expenses (based on 100,000 units) | 0.65 |

Total fixed costs and expenses remain unchanged within the relevant range of 25,000 units to a total capacity of 160,000 units.

**Required**

**a.** Calculate the projected annual breakeven sales in units.

**b.** Calculate the projected net income for the year under direct (variable) costing.

**c.** Determine the company's net income for the year under absorption (full) costing assuming the volume variance is closed to cost of goods sold.

**d.** Determine the price per unit that should be charged for a special order for 10,000 units (to be sold in an unrelated market) in order to increase the company's net income by $5,000.

**17-38 Adjusting journal entry to convert from variable to absorption costing.**
D.C. Lighting, Inc., employs variable costing internally with an annual adjusting journal entry (to inventory valuation adjustment accounts) in order to report results on an absorption cost basis. These contra accounts have the fixed manufacturing

costs necessary to restate inventories on a full costing basis. D.C. Lighting allocates the fixed manufacturing costs for the year in proportion to variable manufacturing costs.

Work-in-process and finished goods inventories on a variable cost basis at the beginning and end of the year were as follows:

| | Work-in-Process | Finished Goods |
|---|---|---|
| January 1 | $1,000 | $2,000 |
| December 31 | 3,000 | 4,000 |

The January 1 balances of the inventory adjustment accounts for fixed manufacturing overhead were $300 for work-in-process and $600 for finished goods.

Variable manufacturing costs incurred during the year were $20,000 and fixed manufacturing costs were $4,950.

**Required**

**a.** Determine the variable cost of goods manufactured and the variable cost of goods sold.

**b.** Prepare the adjustment necessary for D.C. Lighting to approximate actual full cost on a (1) FIFO basis, (2) LIFO basis, and (3) weighted-average basis.

**c.** Prepare the adjusting journal entry for the FIFO basis.

**17-39 Absorption versus direct costing and the effect of adopting a zero-stock policy.** The Auto Supply Company was started in 19X6 by two former employees of a major automobile manufacturer. They decided they could produce a pollution control valve for much less than it cost their former employer.

The Auto Supply Company's fixed overhead costs are $500,000 per year and variable costs are $3 per unit. For 19X6 the firm expected to sell 90,000 valves, but decided to produce 100,000 to have extra inventory. They set their overhead application rates accordingly. They established the selling price of the valve at $9. During 19X6 administrative costs were $75,000 including $10,000 of interest needed to finance inventory carrying costs. During the year the firm produced 95,000 valves, but sold only 80,000.

In 19X7 the firm expected to sell 190,000 units and decided to produce 200,000. This time administrative costs were $140,000 including interest costs for inventory of $30,000. The firm produced 210,000 units, but sold 185,000 units.

On January 2, 19X8, the firm had to dispose of 70% of its finished goods inventory as those units had become obsolete due to a design change. Shocked by this loss, the partners negotiated a contract to deliver prespecified quantities of the valves to their former employer at prespecified times. In exchange, they lowered their price to $8.00 per unit. During 19X8 they sold 250,000 units and produced 238,000 units (exactly in line with the plans developed from the contract at the beginning of the year). Administrative costs were $120,000 including $5,000 for interest on inventory.

In 19X9 the firm continued its policy of producing only to order. In 19X9 they contracted for, produced, and sold 300,000 units. Administrative costs were $115,000 with no interest costs for inventory.

The firm uses FIFO for inventories. Volume variances, if any, are expensed in the year they arise.

**Required**

**a.** Prepare absorption cost income statements for each of the 4 years.

**b.** Prepare direct cost income statements for each of the 4 years.
**c.** Reconcile the annual statements prepared in (a) and (b).

**17-40 Variable and absorption cost income** (CMA adapted).
BBG Corporation manufactures a synthetic element, pixie dust. Management expressed surprise to learn that income before taxes had dropped even though sales volume had increased. Steps had been taken during the year to improve profitability. The steps included raising the selling price by 12% because of a 10% increase in production costs and instructing the selling and administrative departments to spend no more this year than last year. Both changes were implemented at the beginning of this year.

BBG's accounting department prepared and distributed to top management the comparative income statements and related financial information shown below. BBG uses the FIFO inventory method for finished goods.

**BBG CORPORATION**
**Statements of Operating Income**
**(in thousands)**

| | 19X1 | 19X2 |
|---|---|---|
| Sales revenue | $9,000 | $11,200 |
| Cost of goods sold | $7,200 | $ 8,320 |
| Manufacturing volume variance | (600) | 495 |
| Adjusted cost of goods sold | $6,600 | $ 8,815 |
| Gross margin | $2,400 | $ 2,385 |
| Selling and administrative expenses | 1,500 | 1,500 |
| Income before taxes | $ 900 | $ 885 |

**BBG CORPORATION**
**Selected Operating and Financial Data**

| | 19X1 | 19X2 |
|---|---|---|
| Sales price | $ 10.00/kg | $ 11.20/kg |
| Material cost | $ 1.50/kg | $ 1.65/kg |
| Direct labor cost | $ 2.50/kg | $ 2.75/kg |
| Variable overhead cost | $ 1.00/kg | $ 1.10/kg |
| Fixed overhead cost | $ 3.00/kg | $ 3.30/kg |
| Total fixed overhead costs | $3,000,000 | $3,300,000 |
| Selling and administrative (all fixed) | $1,500,000 | $1,500,000 |
| Sales volume | 900,000 kg | 1,000,000 kg |
| Beginning inventory | 300,000 kg | 600,000 kg |

**Required**

**a.** Explain verbally for management why net income decreased despite the sales price and sales volume increases.
**b.** It has been proposed that the firm adopt variable (direct) costing for internal reporting purposes. Prepare the income statement for 19X2.

**c.** Present a numerical reconciliation of the difference in income before taxes using the absorption costing method as currently employed by BBG and the variable costing method as proposed for 19X2.

**17-41 Interpreting full costing results** (CMA adapted).
Sun Company, a wholly owned subsidiary of Guardian, Inc., produces and sells three main product lines.

At the beginning of 19X4, the president of Sun Company presented the budget to the parent company and accepted a commitment to contribute $15,800 to Guardian's consolidated profit in 19X4. The president has been confident that the year's profit would exceed budget target, since the monthly sales reports have shown that sales for the year will exceed budget by 10 percent. The president is both disturbed and confused when the controller presents an adjusted forecast as of November 30, 19X4, indicating that profit will be 11 percent under budget. The two forecasts are presented below.

**SUN COMPANY**
**Forecasts of Operating Results**

| | Forecasts as of | |
|---|---|---|
| | **1/1/X4** | **11/30/X4** |
| Sales | $268,000 | $294,800 |
| Cost of sales | 212,000[a] | 233,200 |
| Gross margin | $ 56,000 | $ 61,600 |
| Overabsorbed (underabsorbed) fixed manufacturing overhead | — | (6,000) |
| Actual gross margin | $ 56,000 | $ 55,600 |
| Selling expenses | $ 13,400 | $ 14,740 |
| Administrative expenses | 26,800 | 26,800 |
| Total operating expenses | $ 40,200 | $ 41,540 |
| Earnings before tax | $ 15,800 | $ 14,060 |

[a]Includes fixed manufacturing overhead of $30,000.

There have been no sales price changes or product mix shifts since the 1/1/X4 forecast. Variable costs have remained constant throughout the year. The only cost variance on the income statement is the underabsorbed manufacturing overhead. This arose because the company produced only 16,000 machine hours (budgeted machine hours were 20,000) during 19X4 as a result of a shortage of raw materials while its principal supplier was closed by a strike. Fortunately, Sun Company's finished goods inventory was large enough to fill all sales orders received.

**Required**

**a.** Analyze and explain why the profit has declined in spite of increased sales and good control over costs.

**b.** What plan, if any, could Sun Company adopt during December to improve the reported profit at year-end? Explain your answer.

**c.** Illustrate and explain how Sun Company could adopt an alternative internal cost reporting procedure that would avoid the confusing effect of the present procedure.

**d.** Would the alternative procedure described in (c) be acceptable to Guardian, Inc., for financial reporting purposes? Explain.

# COMPREHENSIVE CASE 2

# COST ACCUMULATION

Norman Metals was established at the beginning of last year to manufacture two types of valve housings, known as alpha and beta. The manufacturing process involves two departments. The first casts the housing and the second machines smooth the coupling joints. There are also two service departments—personnel and maintenance ($SD_1$ and $SD_2$). Selling and administrative activities are treated as a single department.

The firm has now completed its first year of operations. Production amounted to 5,000 units of alpha and 8,000 units of beta. The firm sold 4,600 units of alpha for $20 each and 7,300 units of beta at $30. We have been asked to prepare the firm's income statement on both an absorption and direct costing basis. Since this is a new firm, we do not have a great deal of confidence in the budgeted costs. Therefore we will prepare the income statements on an actual cost basis; however, we will use the master budget predetermined overhead rates. The complete master budget for Norman Metal's first year of operations is given in Comprehensive Case 1: Budgeting. But the information from that budget of interest to us now is that the variable overhead application rate for the casting department was budgeted to be $4.30 per direct labor hour, while the fixed overhead application rate for casting was $4.00 per unit of alpha and $2.40 per unit of beta. The application rates for the machining department were budgeted to be $5.00 per direct labor hour for the variable overhead while the fixed overhead rates were $1.25 per unit of alpha and $0.50 per unit for beta.

**EXHIBIT CC2-1 Summary of Actual Costs Incurred by Department**

| | Service Department 1 | Service Department 2 | Casting Department | Machining Department | Selling and Administration |
|---|---|---|---|---|---|
| Direct materials | | | | | |
| For alpha | $ — | $ — | $10,710.00 | $ — | $ — |
| For beta | — | — | 20,475.00 | — | — |
| Direct labor | | | | | |
| For alpha[a] | — | — | 9,296.40 | 6,197.60 | — |
| For beta[a] | — | — | 29,554.50 | 19,703.00 | — |
| Variable overhead items | 7,400 | 9,300 | 18,780.00 | 12,800.00 | — |
| Fixed overhead items | 8,700 | 6,100 | 31,000.00 | 4,500.00 | — |
| Sales commissions | — | — | — | — | 31,100 |
| Other selling and administrative costs | — | — | — | — | 35,000 |

[a]The costs for direct labor are for the following number of hours.

| | Casting | Machining |
|---|---|---|
| For alpha | 1,524 | 1,016 |
| For beta | 4,845 | 3,230 |

## The Absorption Costing Income Statement

With the predetermined overhead rates and the summary of actual costs incurred by each department, summarized in Exhibit CC2-1, we can begin the process of accumulating data for the income statement. As we do so, we will prepare the journal entries that record the result of operations in the formal accounting records.

The actual cost information reflected in Exhibit CC2-1 enters the accounting records through a large number of transactions occurring throughout the accounting period. We summarize these with entries (a) through (f).

| | | Debit | Credit |
|---|---|---|---|
| (a) | Raw Materials Inventory | 31,185 | |
| | Cash | | 31,185 |
| | To record purchase of inventory. (We assume that we purchased only the materials actually used.) | | |
| (b) | Work-in-Process: Casting | 31,185 | |
| | Raw Materials Inventory | | 31,185 |
| | To record the transfer of materials into production. | | |

| | | | |
|---|---|---|---|
| (c) | Work-in-Process: Casting | 38,850.90 | |
| | Work-in-Process: Machining | 25,900.60 | |
| | Accrued Payroll | | 64,751.50 |
| | To recognize direct labor costs. | | |
| (d) | Variable Overhead Control: $SD_1$ | 7,400 | |
| | Variable Overhead Control: $SD_2$ | 9,300 | |
| | Variable Overhead Control: Casting | 18,780 | |
| | Variable Overhead Control: Machining | 12,800 | |
| | Fixed Overhead Control: $SD_1$ | 8,700 | |
| | Fixed Overhead Control: $SD_2$ | 6,100 | |
| | Fixed Overhead Control: Casting | 31,000 | |
| | Fixed Overhead Control: Machining | 4,500 | |
| | Various accounts (Accumulated Depreciation, Cash, Accounts Payable, and others) | | 98,580 |
| | To summarize the various actual overhead costs incurred. | | |
| (e) | Sales Commissions | 31,100 | |
| | Cash | | 31,100 |
| | To recognize sales commissions paid. | | |
| (f) | Selling and Administrative Expenses | 35,000 | |
| | Various accounts | | 35,000 |
| | To record summary of other costs incurred. | | |

We now have recorded the costs to operate each of the departments. The next step is to allocate the cost of the service departments to the production departments. To do so we will use the step method (see Chapter 12), with predetermined rates for variable charges and lump sum charges for the service department's fixed costs.

The firm's master budget (see Comprehensive Case 1 for details) established $SD_1$'s predetermined variable cost charge to the other departments at a rate of \$750 per employee. Fixed costs were to be charged \$1,800 to $SD_2$, \$2,700 to casting, and \$4,500 to machining. During the period there were two employees working in $SD_2$, three in casting, and five in machining. Similarly, $SD_2$'s variable costs were budgeted to be charged to the other departments at the rate of \$100 per service call and fixed costs were to be charged \$4,200 to casting and \$4,200 to machining. During the period, casting made 60 requests for service and machining made 40 requests for service. Using the predetermined service department rates,[1] the following entries summarize the service department charges to the other departments.

[1]An alternative approach is to allocate actual service department costs to the production departments. This is analogous to using actual overhead rates.

| | | | |
|---|---|---|---|
| (g) | Variable Overhead Control: $SD_2$ | 1,500 | |
| | Variable Overhead Control: Casting | 2,250 | |
| | Variable Overhead Control: Machining | 3,750 | |
| | Fixed Overhead Control: $SD_2$ | 1,800 | |
| | Fixed Overhead Control: Casting | 2,700 | |
| | Fixed Overhead Control: Machining | 4,500 | |
| | Variable Overhead Applied: $SD_1$ | | 7,500 |
| | Fixed Overhead Applied: $SD_1$ | | 9,000 |
| | To record the application of $SD_1$'s costs to other departments. | | |
| (h) | Variable Overhead Control: Casting | 6,000 | |
| | Variable Overhead Control: Machining | 4,000 | |
| | Fixed Overhead Control: Casting | 4,200 | |
| | Fixed Overhead Control: Machining | 4,200 | |
| | Variable Overhead Applied: $SD_2$ | | 10,000 |
| | Fixed Overhead Applied: $SD_2$ | | 8,400 |
| | To record the application of $SD_2$'s costs to the other departments. | | |

Let us pause to notice that although the credits to the service department accounts go to the respective overhead applied accounts, the debits are charged to control accounts. Since we are applying overhead using a predetermined rate, the service department costs applied will not necessarily equal the actual costs incurred by each service department. The

**EXHIBIT CC2-2 Application of Departmental Overhead to Products**

| | Alpha | Beta | Total |
|---|---|---|---|
| A. Casting department | | | |
| 1. Labor hours used | 1,524 | 4,845 | |
| 2. Variable overhead rate per hour | $4.30 | $4.30 | |
| 3. Variable overhead applied | $ 6,553.20 | $20,833.50 | $27,386.70 |
| 4. Units produced | 5,000 | 8,000 | |
| 5. Fixed overhead per unit | $4.00 | $2.40 | |
| 6. Fixed overhead applied | $20,000.00 | $19,200.00 | $39,200.00 |
| 7. Total overhead applied | $26,553.20 | $40,033.50 | $66,586.70 |
| B. Machining department | | | |
| 1. Labor hours used | 1,016 | 3,230 | |
| 2. Variable overhead rate per hour | $5.00 | $5.00 | |
| 3. Variable overhead applied | $ 5,080.00 | $16,150.00 | $21,230.00 |
| 4. Units produced | 5,000 | 8,000 | |
| 5. Fixed overhead per unit | $1.25 | $0.50 | |
| 6. Fixed overhead applied | $ 6,250.00 | $ 4,000.00 | $10,250.00 |
| 7. Total overhead applied | $11,330.00 | $20,150.00 | $31,480.00 |
| C. Total overhead, both departments | $37,883.20 | $60,183.50 | $98,066.70 |

actual costs incurred by a service department will be accumulated in a control account for that department; see entry (d). In a few moments we will close out the applied and control accounts as over- or underapplied overhead. The difference will be an indication of how well the service department was able to control its costs.

When a service department's costs are applied to the production departments or to other service departments, these applied costs become part of the actual costs of the receiving departments. That is, the receiving department is held responsible for its use of actual services, but at a predetermined price (rate); hence the charge to the appropriate control account.

The next step is to use the predetermined production department overhead rates to assign the production department overhead costs to the products. We do so by multiplying the appropriate variable overhead rates by the direct labor hours for each product used, and the fixed overhead rates by the number of units of each product produced. These calculations, which are presented in Exhibit CC2-2, provide the support for the following journal entry:

| | | | |
|---|---|---|---|
| (i) | Work-in Process: Casting | 66,586.70 | |
| | Work-in-Process: Machining | 31,480.00 | |
| | Variable Overhead Applied: Casting | | 27,386.70 |
| | Fixed Overhead Applied: Casting | | 39,200.00 |
| | Variable Overhead Applied: Machining | | 21,230.00 |
| | Fixed Overhead Applied: Machining | | 10,250.00 |
| | To record the application of departmental overhead to production. | | |

Entries (a) through (i) summarize the transactions that would have occurred during the year. At the end of the year, before we make any adjusting or closing entries, the balances in the Work-in-Process accounts would be as given in Exhibit CC2-3. Because the firm manufactures only two products, and does so continuously, the firm uses process costing. Thus the value of ending work-in-process and cost of goods completed is deter-

**EXHIBIT CC2-3 Preclosing Departmental Work-in-Process Accounts[a]**

| | Work-in-Process: Casting | | | Work-in-Process: Machining | |
|---|---|---|---|---|---|
| (b) | 31,185.00 | | (c) | 25,900.60 | |
| (c) | 38,850.90 | | (j) | 31,480.00 | |
| (i) | 66,586.70 | | | 57,380.60 | |
| | 136,622.60 | | | | |

[a]The letters in parentheses correspond with the journal entries given in the text.

**EXHIBIT CC2-4 Cost of Goods Completed for Each Department Using Absorption Costing**

| | Alpha | Beta | Total |
|---|---|---|---|
| Casting department | | | |
| Direct materials (Exhibit CC2-1) | $10,710.00 | $ 20,475.00 | $ 31,185.00 |
| Direct labor (Exhibit CC2-1) | 9,296.40 | 29,554.50 | 38,850.90 |
| Overhead (Exhibit CC2-2, line A-7) | 26,553.20 | 40,033.50 | 66,586.70 |
| Cost of goods completed and transferred to the machining department | $46,559.60 | $ 90,063.00 | $136,622.60 |
| Machining department | | | |
| Transferred in from casting (above) | $46,559.60 | $ 90,063.00 | $136,622.60 |
| Direct labor (Exhibit CC2-1) | 6,197.60 | 19,703.00 | 25,900.60 |
| Overhead (Exhibit CC2-2, line B-7) | 11,330.00 | 20,150.00 | 31,480.00 |
| Cost of goods completed | $64,087.20 | $129,916.00 | $194,003.20 |

mined at the end of the period. However, since Norman Metals had no beginning or ending work-in-process, all manufacturing costs incurred during the period are attributable to cost of goods completed. The cost of the completed production is summarized in Exhibit CC2-4, which provides the support for entries (j) and (k)

| | | Debit | Credit |
|---|---|---|---|
| (j) | Work-in-Process: Machining | 136,622.60 | |
| | Work-in-Process: Casting | | 136,622.60 |
| | To record the transfer of products from the casting to machining department. | | |
| (k) | Finished Goods Inventory | 194,003.20 | |
| | Work-in-Process: Machining | | 194,003.20 |
| | To record the cost of goods completed and transferred to finished goods inventory. | | |

The costs transferred to finished goods are for the 5,000 units of alpha and 8,000 units of beta completed during the period. Calculating a unit cost and recalling that the firm sold 4,600 units of alpha and 7,300 units of beta, Exhibit CC2-5 provides the basis for the entry:

| | | Debit | Credit |
|---|---|---|---|
| (l) | Cost of Goods Sold | 177,508.57 | |
| | Finished Goods Inventory | | 177,508.57 |
| | To record the cost of goods sold. | | |

The next set of entries will close the various departmental overhead control and applied accounts. Exhibit CC2-6 summarizes the information in the previous journal entries to give us the current balance in each of these accounts. Once we know the balances, the following entries will close the accounts:

| | | | |
|---|---|---|---|
| (m) | Variable Overhead Applied: $SD_1$ | 7,500 | |
| | Overapplied Overhead: $SD_1$ | | 100 |
| | Variable Overhead Control: $SD_1$ | | 7,400 |
| | Fixed Overhead Applied: $SD_1$ | 9,000 | |
| | Overapplied Overhead: $SD_1$ | | 300 |
| | Fixed Overhead Control: $SD_1$ | | 8,700 |
| | Variable Overhead Applied: $SD_2$ | 10,000 | |
| | Underapplied Overhead: $SD_2$ | 800 | |
| | Variable Overhead Control: $SD_2$ | | 10,800 |
| | Fixed Overhead Applied: $SD_2$ | 8,400 | |
| | Overapplied Overhead: $SD_2$ | | 500 |
| | Variable Overhead Control: $SD_2$ | | 7,900 |
| | Variable Overhead Applied: Casting | 27,386.70 | |
| | Overapplied Overhead: Casting | | 356.70 |
| | Variable Overhead Control: Casting | | 27,030.00 |
| | Fixed Overhead Applied: Casting | 39,200 | |
| | Overapplied Overhead: Casting | | 1,300 |
| | Fixed Overhead Control: Casting | | 37,900 |
| | Variable Overhead Applied: Machining | 21,230 | |
| | Overapplied Overhead: Machining | | 680 |
| | Variable Overhead Control: Machining | | 20,550 |
| | Fixed Overhead Applied: Machining | 10,250 | |
| | Underapplied Overhead: Machining | 2,950 | |
| | Fixed Overhead Control: Machining | | 13,200 |
| | To close the overhead applied and control accounts. | | |

Although the foregoing entries provide us with an indication of how well departmental overhead costs were controlled, the over- and underapplied overhead amounts must also be closed. Generally the choice is to allocate these amounts to inventory and cost of goods sold or simply to write them all off to cost of goods sold. Norman Metals has chosen to do the latter. The last entry then is as follows:

| | | | |
|---|---|---|---|
| (n) | Cost of Goods Sold | 513.30 | |
| | Overapplied Overhead: $SD_1$ | 400.00 | |
| | Overapplied Overhead: Casting | 1,656.70 | |
| | Underapplied Overhead: $SD_2$ | | 300.00 |
| | Underapplied Overhead: Machining | | 2,270.00 |
| | To close the over- and underapplied overhead accounts to cost of goods sold. | | |

**EXHIBIT CC2-5 Cost of Goods Sold and Ending Inventory Using Absorption Costing**

| | Alpha | Beta | Total |
|---|---|---|---|
| Cost of goods completed (Exhibit CC2-4) | $64,087.20 | $129,916.00 | $194,003.20 |
| Number of units completed | 5,000 | 8,000 | |
| Current cost per unit[a] | $12.81744 | $16.2395 | |
| Beginning inventory (units) | — | — | |
| Units completed | 5,000 | 8,000 | |
| Units sold | 4,600 | 7,300 | |
| Ending inventory (units) | 400 | 700 | |
| Units sold | 4,600 | 7,300 | |
| Current cost per unit | $12.81744 | $16.2395 | |
| Cost of goods sold | $58,960.22 | $118,548.35 | $177,508.57 |
| Ending inventory | 400 | 700 | |
| Current cost per unit | $12.81744 | $16.2395 | |
| Cost of ending inventory | $ 5,126.98 | $ 11,367.65 | 16,494.63 |
| Total costs accounted for (cost of goods sold plus ending inventory) | $64,087.20 | $129,916.00 | $194,003.20 |

[a]Typically, unit costs would not be calculated to such precision. We do so to avoid having to round calculations, in the hope that the reader can more easily follow our derivations.

We see in this example a situation that is often encountered: Even though over- or underapplied overhead is fairly large for some of the departments, the net balance for all departments—in this case, $513.30—is quite small.

With the overhead accounts closed, we can now prepare the absorption costing income statement. Adding the underapplied overhead from entry (n) to the cost of goods sold in entry (1) yields the adjusted cost of goods sold of $178,021.87. Finally, by subtracting the sales commission and other administration costs, listed in Exhibit CC2-1, from the gross margin we get the absorption costing net income of $66,878.13. The statement is presented in Exhibit CC2-7.

## The Direct Costing Income Statement

Let us now derive a direct costing income statement for Norman Metals. The only difference between an absorption costing income statement and a direct costing income statement is the treatment of fixed overhead. Therefore we can use most of the figures already computed for the absorption costing income statement.

**EXHIBIT CC2-6 Summary of the Overhead Account Balances at Year-End before Adjustment[a]**

**Variable Overhead Control: $SD_1$**

| | Debit | Credit |
|---|---|---|
| (d) | 7,400 | |

**Variable Overhead Applied: $SD_1$**

| Debit | Credit | |
|---|---|---|
| | 7,500 | (g) |

**Fixed Overhead Control: $SD_1$**

| | Debit | Credit |
|---|---|---|
| (d) | 8,700 | |

**Fixed Overhead Applied: $SD_1$**

| Debit | Credit | |
|---|---|---|
| | 9,000 | (g) |

**Variable Overhead Control: $SD_2$**

| | Debit | Credit |
|---|---|---|
| (d) | 9,300 | |
| (g) | 1,500 | |
| | 10,800 | |

**Variable Overhead Applied: $SD_2$**

| Debit | Credit | |
|---|---|---|
| | 10,000 | (h) |

**Fixed Overhead Control: $SD_2$**

| | Debit | Credit |
|---|---|---|
| (d) | 6,100 | |
| (g) | 1,800 | |
| | 7,900 | |

**Fixed Overhead Applied: $SD_2$**

| Debit | Credit | |
|---|---|---|
| | 8,400 | (h) |

**Variable Overhead Control: Casting**

| | Debit | Credit |
|---|---|---|
| (d) | 18,780 | |
| (g) | 2,250 | |
| (h) | 6,000 | |
| | 27,030 | |

**Variable Overhead Applied: Casting**

| Debit | Credit | |
|---|---|---|
| | 27,386.70 | (i) |

**Fixed Overhead Control: Casting**

| | Debit | Credit |
|---|---|---|
| (d) | 31,000 | |
| (g) | 2,700 | |
| (h) | 4,200 | |
| | 37,900 | |

**Fixed Overhead Applied: Casting**

| Debit | Credit | |
|---|---|---|
| | 39,200 | (i) |

**Variable Overhead Control: Machining**

| | Debit | Credit |
|---|---|---|
| (d) | 12,800 | |
| (g) | 3,750 | |
| (h) | 4,000 | |
| | 20,550 | |

**Variable Overhead Applied: Machining**

| Debit | Credit | |
|---|---|---|
| | 21,230 | (i) |

**Fixed Overhead Control: Machining**

| | Debit | Credit |
|---|---|---|
| (d) | 4,500 | |
| (g) | 4,500 | |
| (h) | 4,200 | |
| | 13,200 | |

**Fixed Overhead Applied: Machining**

| Debit | Credit | |
|---|---|---|
| | 10,250 | (i) |

[a]The letters in parentheses correspond with the journal entries in the text.

**EXHIBIT CC2-7 Absorption Cost Income Statement**

| | |
|---|---|
| Sales (4,600 × \$20 + 7,300 × \$30) | \$311,000.00 |
| Cost of goods sold | 178,021.87 |
| Gross margin | \$132,978.13 |
| Sales commissions | 31,100.00 |
| Other selling and administration costs | 35,000.00 |
| Net income | \$ 66,878.13 |

We would still accumulate all costs by department for control purposes (i.e., we want departmental managers to monitor and control the level of all costs incurred). Therefore, even with direct costing, entries (a) through (f) would be made as previously. The first difference from absorption costing occurs when it is time to charge service department costs to production departments. Under direct costing, only variable costs will be charged to departments using the service department's services. Since the variable costs are the same as in entries (g) and (h), we give the new entries, without documentation, as follows:

| | | | |
|---|---|---|---|
| (g′) | Variable Overhead Control: $SD_2$ | 1,500 | |
| | Variable Overhead Control: Casting | 2,250 | |
| | Variable Overhead Control: Machining | 3,750 | |
| | Variable Overhead Applied: $SD_1$ | | 7,500 |
| | To record the application of $SD_1$'s costs to the other departments. | | |
| (h′) | Variable Overhead Control: Casting | 6,000 | |
| | Variable Overhead Control: Machining | 4,000 | |
| | Variable Overhead Applied: $SD_2$ | | 10,000 |
| | To record the application of $SD_2$'s costs to the other departments. | | |

Similarly, when we apply the production departments' overhead to the units produced, we apply only the variable overhead. Thus the charge to Work-in-Process uses the same information as entry (i) to yield

| | | | |
|---|---|---|---|
| (i′) | Work-in-Process: Casting | 27,386.70 | |
| | Work-in-Process: Machining | 21,230.00 | |
| | Variable Overhead Applied: Casting | | 27,386.70 |
| | Variable Overhead Applied: Machining | | 21,230.00 |
| | To record application of overhead to production. | | |

The calculation of cost of goods completed is given in Exhibit CC2-8. The only difference between Exhibits CC2-4 and CC2-8 is the exclusion of fixed overhead costs in the latter.

**EXHIBIT CC2-8 Calculation of Cost of Goods Completed Using Direct Costing**

| | Alpha | Beta | Total |
|---|---|---|---|
| Casting department | | | |
| Direct materials (Exhibit CC2-1) | $10,710.00 | $ 20,475.00 | $ 31,185.00 |
| Direct labor (Exhibit CC2-1) | 9,296.40 | 29,554.50 | 38,850.90 |
| Variable overhead (Exhibit CC2-2) | 6,553.20 | 20,833.50 | 27,386.70 |
| Cost of goods completed and transferred to machining | $26,559.60 | $ 70,863.00 | $ 97,422.60 |
| Machining department | | | |
| Transferred in from casting (above) | $26,559.60 | $ 70,863.00 | $ 97,422.60 |
| Direct labor (Exhibit CC2-1) | 6,197.60 | 19,703.00 | 25,900.60 |
| Variable overhead (Exhibit CC2-2) | 5,080.00 | 16,150.00 | 21,230.00 |
| Cost of goods completed | $37,837.20 | $106,716.00 | $144,553.20 |

Exhibits CC2-8 and CC2-9 provide the documentation for entries (j′) through (l′).

| | | | |
|---|---|---|---|
| (j′) | Work-in-Process: Machining | 97,422.60 | |
| | Work-in-Process: Casting | | 97,422.60 |
| | To record transfer of products from casting to machining. | | |
| (k′) | Finished Goods Inventory | 144,553.20 | |
| | Work-in-Process: Machining | | 144,553.20 |
| | To record cost of goods completed. | | |
| (l′) | Cost of Goods Sold | 132,188.57 | |
| | Finished Goods Inventory | | 132,188.57 |
| | To record cost of goods sold. | | |

**EXHIBIT CC2-9 Cost of Goods Sold and Ending Inventory Using Direct Costing**

| | Alpha | Beta | Total |
|---|---|---|---|
| Cost of goods completed (Exhibit CC2-8) | $37,837.20 | $106,716.00 | $144,553.20 |
| Number of units completed | 5,000 | 8,000 | |
| Cost per unit | $7.56744 | $13.3395 | |
| Units sold | 4,600 | 7,300 | |
| Cost per unit | $7.56744 | $13.3395 | |
| Cost of goods sold | $34,810.22 | $ 97,378.35 | $132,188.57 |
| Ending inventory | 400 | 700 | |
| Cost per unit | $7.56744 | $13.3395 | |
| Cost of ending inventory | $ 3,026.98 | $ 9,337.65 | 12,364.63 |
| Total costs accounted for (cost of goods sold plus ending inventory) | $37,837.20 | $106,716.00 | $144,553.20 |

The closing of the overhead accounts will be different from in absorption costing. The fixed overhead costs have not been applied to production, but we do have the fixed overhead control accounts. To close these accounts we will charge them to a new income statement account—Fixed Manufacturing Expenses. Thus the comparable entry to entry (m) becomes

| | | |
|---|---|---|
| (m′) Fixed Manufacturing Expenses | 50,300 | |
| Fixed Overhead Control: $SD_1$ | | 8,700 |
| Fixed Overhead Control: $SD_2$ | | 6,100 |
| Fixed Overhead Control: Casting | | 31,000 |
| Fixed Overhead Control: Machining | | 4,500 |
| Variable Overhead Applied: $SD_1$ | 7,500 | |
| Overapplied Overhead: $SD_1$ | | 100 |
| Variable Overhead Control: $SD_1$ | | 7,400 |
| Variable Overhead Applied: $SD_2$ | 10,000 | |
| Underapplied Overhead: $SD_2$ | 800 | |
| Variable Overhead Control: $SD_2$ | | 10,800 |
| Variable Overhead Applied: Casting | 27,386.70 | |
| Overapplied Overhead: Casting | | 356.70 |
| Variable Overhead Control: Casting | | 27,030.00 |
| Variable Overhead Applied: Machining | 21,230 | |
| Overapplied Overhead: Machining | | 680 |
| Variable Overhead Control: Machining | | 20,550 |
| To close overhead accounts. | | |

As before, we will close the over- and underapplied overhead accounts to Cost of Goods Sold. Since we only have over- or underapplied overhead with respect to the variable overhead accounts, the net effect on cost of goods sold changes. The net balance charged to Cost of Goods Sold under direct costing is a credit of $336.70, reflected in the following entry.

| | | |
|---|---|---|
| (n′) Overapplied Overhead: $SD_1$ | 100.00 | |
| Overapplied Overhead: Casting | 356.70 | |
| Overapplied Overhead: Machining | 680.00 | |
| Underapplied Overhead: $SD_2$ | | 800.00 |
| Cost of Goods Sold | | 336.70 |

Combining the adjustment to cost of goods sold in entry (n′) with the original cost of goods sold determined in entry (l′), we get an adjusted cost of goods sold of $131,851.87; that is,

| | |
|---|---|
| Original amount | $132,188.57 |
| Less adjustment | 336.70 |
| Adjusted amount | $131,851.87 |

**EXHIBIT CC2-10 Direct Costing Income Statement**

| | |
|---|---|
| Sales (4,600 × $20 + 7,200 × $30) | $311,000.00 |
| Variable expenses | |
| Cost of goods sold | 131,851.87 |
| Sales commissions | 31,100.00 |
| Contribution margin | $148,048.13 |
| Fixed expenses | |
| Fixed manufacturing expenses | 50,300.00 |
| Other selling and administrative costs | 35,000.00 |
| Net income | $ 62,748.13 |

This figure appears in Exhibit CC2-10 as the variable cost of goods sold in the direct costing income statement. Note also that in Exhibit CC2-10 we combine all variable costs, including variable selling and administrative costs, to calculate a contribution margin. From the contribution margin we then subtract the fixed manufacturing expenses and fixed selling and administrative expenses to get the direct costing net income of $62,748.13.

## Reconciling Direct and Absorption Costing Income

We now have both the direct costing and absorption costing net income figures for Norman Metal's first year of operation. Let us end the cost accumulation illustration by reconciling the two income numbers.

**EXHIBIT CC2-11 Reconciliation of Absorption and Direct Costing Net Income**

| | Alpha | Beta | Total |
|---|---|---|---|
| Cost per unit of product, absorption basis (Exhibit CC2-5) | $12.81744 | $16.2395 | |
| Cost per unit of product, direct cost basis (Exhibit CC2-9) | 7.56744 | 13.3395 | |
| Fixed cost per unit, absorption basis | $ 5.25 | $ 2.90 | |
| Ending inventory (units) | 400 | 700 | |
| Fixed cost per unit | $ 5.25 | $ 2.90 | |
| Total fixed costs in ending inventory | $2,100 | $2,030 | $ 4,130.00 |
| Absorption costing net income (Exhibit CC2-7) | | | $66,878.13 |
| Fixed costs deferred in ending inventory | | | (4,130.00) |
| Direct costing net income (Exhibit CC2-10) | | | $62,748.13 |

The only difference between absorption and direct costing net income is in the treatment of fixed manufacturing overhead. These costs are expensed under direct costing when incurred, but deferred to inventory and expensed only when sold under absorption costing. Thus, to reconcile the two we need only adjust for the amount of fixed cost deferred under absorption costing. Since there were no beginning inventories, no fixed costs from previous periods have been expensed in the current period's absorption costing income statement. However, under absorption costing some of the current period's fixed costs will be deferred to the next period via ending inventory. To determine the amount, we need to determine the fixed costs assigned to each unit of product under absorption costing.

From Exhibit CC2-5 we can get the full cost (variable plus fixed) of each product produced. If we subtract the variable cost per unit (determined in Exhibit CC2-9), the difference will be the fixed cost per unit assigned under absorption costing. Finally, multiplying these fixed costs per unit by the number of units in ending inventory will provide the total fixed costs deferred under absorption costing. This difference will exactly explain the difference in absorption and direct costing net income, as shown in Exhibit CC2-11.

# PART FOUR

# MEASURING AND EVALUATING PERFORMANCE

# CHAPTER 18

# STANDARD COSTS AND VARIANCE ANALYSIS

In Part Two we were concerned primarily with the planning process: budgeting what the firm hopes to achieve. In Part Three we shifted our emphasis to the accumulation of the actual costs incurred by the firm. In this part we will tie the two processes together. We compare actual performance with the budget and assign responsibility for differences to the appropriate managers.

## STANDARD COSTS

In Chapter 3 we developed standard costs. In case it has been a while since you have read that chapter, let us briefly review the setting of standards. For each direct material used, and for each class of direct labor, we estimate the amount of the resource required to produce a unit of product. These **standard quantities** are the amount of each *input* required to produce a single unit of *output.* They may be **ideal standards** that allow for no spoilage or waste or, more commonly, **attainable standards** that include an allowance for the amount of spoilage and waste expected when the firm operates at normal efficiency.

**Standard prices** are the expected costs per unit of *input* (pound of material, hour of labor). They may reflect the costs being incurred at the time the standard is established, but more often represent the average cost per unit of input expected to be incurred during the budget period. Standard cost must be carefully distinguished from standard price. The **standard cost** for an input is the product of the standard quantity for the input multiplied by the standard price for the input. The resulting standard cost is the total amount that should be spent on an input to produce a unit of output.

Standards are also established for overhead. However, overhead is usually allocated to products on some measure of activity common to all products (usually machine hours or labor hours). Thus for overhead the standard quantity is not a physical measure of the actual overhead resources used, but instead is a measure of the amount of the application base (machine or labor hours) required per unit of output. Similarly, the standard price for overhead is our best estimate of the amount of overhead costs that will be required per hour of the application base.

So far we have talked solely about the standard manufacturing costs for the firm's end products. In the budgeting process we also establish budgets for major cost centers. If the costs incurred in these centers are sufficiently large to justify establishing an elaborate cost control system, we can set standards for centers too. For example, for an equipment maintenance department we might establish standards for material, labor, and overhead items relative to the services provided. This, in turn, permits the pricing of equipment maintenance services at a standard cost. These standards are then used to charge other departments for the use of maintenance services. In any case, all of the standards we have identified are used to help measure operating efficiency.

The differences between the standard costs we expected to incur and the actual costs incurred are called **variances.** The timing for variance calculations and how they are recorded in the accounting records depends on whether a job or process cost system is being used. These issues are addressed in the appendix to this chapter. For now, let us just concentrate on the calculations using the following example.

The Windsor division of Supertech, Inc., manufactures computer diskettes for a large number of distributors. The vinyl disks are all the same and are produced by the manufacturing department. The sleeves are produced to customers' specifications. The fabricating department constructs the sleeve, inserts a vinyl disk, and tests the completed disks. From the fabricating department the completed disks are sent to customers. Let us use the data given in Exhibit 18-1 to illustrate the computation of variances for the fabricating department.

### Master Budget

The standard cost data in Exhibit 18-1 is given on a per-unit basis. The allowance of 1.02 vinyl disks per completed disk implies that these are

**EXHIBIT 18-1 Standards and Actual Costs for the Fabricating Department**

**STANDARD COST PER COMPLETED DISK**
**ANTICIPATED PRODUCTION: 60,000 COMPLETED DISKS**

| | | |
|---|---|---|
| Vinyl disk | 1.02 disks @ $0.35 | $0.357 |
| Sleeve materials | 31 sq in @ $0.003 | 0.093 |
| Direct labor | 0.024 hr @ $6.00 | 0.144 |
| Variable overhead | 0.024 hr @ $3.50 | 0.084 |
| Fixed overhead | 0.024 hr @ $2.00 | 0.048 |
| Standard cost per unit | | $0.726 |

**ACTUAL COSTS INCURRED FOR THE WEEK ENDING 3/30**
**TOTAL PRODUCTION: 58,500 COMPLETED DISKS**

| | | |
|---|---|---|
| Vinyl disks | 59,600 disks | $21,754 |
| Sleeve materials | 1,310,000 sq in | 5,068 |
| Direct labor | 1,450 hr | 8,642 |
| Variable overhead | 1,450 hr | 5,249 |
| Fixed overhead | | 2,810 |
| Total costs | | $43,523 |

normally attainable standards. It is instructive to begin our analysis by constructing the department's apparent master budget for the week. The **master budget** is the budget prepared prior to the beginning of the period. It incorporates forecasts of the costs to be incurred by the department for the anticipated level of operations. Its main function is a guide to the amount of resources to be obtained and the determination of the fixed overhead application rate. That is, the department's budgeted fixed overhead will be applied to products on the basis of the anticipated activity level (frequently referred to as the denominator level of activity, or denominator volume, because it is the denominator in the fraction that determines the final overhead rate).

The master budget activity rate is given in the top of Exhibit 18-1 as 60,000 disks. Thus we can multiply the standard quantity for each input by 60,000 and then multiply by the standard price of the input to derive the master budget amounts for the department as presented in Exhibit 18-2.

Comparing the total cost called for in the master budget, $43,560, to the actual costs incurred, $43,523, seems to imply that the fabricating department has performed well, since it came in at almost exactly budget (actually $37 less). However, such an analysis ignores the actual level of activity achieved. The master budget called for the production of 60,000 disks, whereas actual output was only 58,500 disks.

**EXHIBIT 18-2 Fabricating Department's Master Budget**

| TOTAL BUDGETED PRODUCTION: 60,000 DISKS | | |
|---|---|---|
| Vinyl disks | 61,200 @ $0.35 | $21,420 |
| Sleeve materials | 1,860,000 sq in @ $0.003 | 5,580 |
| Direct labor | 1,440 hr @ $6.00 | 8,640 |
| Variable overhead | 1,440 hr @ $3.50 | 5,040 |
| Fixed overhead | | 2,880 |
| Total budgeted cost | | $43,560 |

### Flexible Budget

To accurately evaluate performance we must prepare a flexible budget for the actual output attained. The **flexible budget** provides the total costs that should have been incurred given actual output (referred to as the **standard cost allowed** or the **standard cost earned**). It uses the same per-unit standards for variable costs as the master budget but now the standards are multiplied by the actual number of units produced. However, because fixed costs are not supposed to vary with changes in activity, the flexible budget figure for fixed overhead is the same as that called for in the master budget.

## VARIANCES

Exhibit 18-3 presents the flexible budget for the fabricating department based on the actual output of 58,500 disks. The flexible budget amounts

**EXHIBIT 18-3 Actual Costs Compared to Flexible Budget for the Fabricating Department**

| | Actual Costs (58,500 units) | Flexible Budget (58,500 units)[a] | Budget Variance |
|---|---|---|---|
| Vinyl disks | $21,754 | $20,884.50 | $869.50 U |
| Sleeve materials | 5,068 | 5,440.50 | 372.50 F |
| Direct labor | 8,642 | 8,424.00 | 218.00 U |
| Variable overhead | 5,249 | 4,914.00 | 335.00 U |
| Fixed overhead | 2,810 | 2,880.00 | 70.00 F |
| Total costs | $43,523 | $42,543.00 | $980.00 U |

[a]Flexible budget calculations:

| | |
|---|---|
| Vinyl disks | 58,500 × $0.357 = $20,884.50 |
| Sleeve materials | 58,500 × $0.093 = $ 5,440.50 |
| Direct labor | 58,500 × $0.144 = $ 8,424.00 |
| Variable overhead | 58,500 × $0.084 = $ 4,914.00 |
| Fixed overhead | 60,000 × $0.048 = $ 2,880.00 |

are also compared to the actual costs incurred and the differences are labeled **budget variances.**[1]

In addition to calculating these differences and naming them, we also refer to the variances as favorable (F) or unfavorable (U). If a cost is less than anticipated, the variance is labeled as a **favorable variance.** If the cost is higher than anticipated, it is an **unfavorable variance.** In Exhibit 18-3 we see that when actual costs are higher than the costs allowed in the flexible budget, we called the variance unfavorable. The name is appealing in that our costs were higher than what the budget allowed and the effect is to decrease what profits would otherwise have been (an unfavorable effect).[2]

The budget variances resulting from the comparison of actual costs to the flexible budget now give us a different perspective on the fabricating department's performance. Overall, the department spent $980 more than called for, but the department did spend less for the sleeve materials and fixed overhead items than anticipated. While the budget variances are helpful for identifying areas of spending in which the department performed well or poorly, they do not provide information as to the precise source of the variances or who is responsible for them. To obtain this latter information we need to examine the flexible budget and actual cost figures in more detail.

For the fabricating department the standard price (*SP*) for vinyl disks is $0.35 per disk. The standard quantity (*SQ*) per completed unit is 1.02 disks. Thus when 58,500 units of output (*UO*) were produced, the flexible budget allowance for vinyl disks was calculated as follows:

$$\begin{aligned}\text{flexible budget} &= SP \times SQ \times UO \\ &= \$0.35 \times 1.02 \times 58{,}500 \\ &= \$20{,}884.50\end{aligned}$$

Similarly, we can represent the actual costs incurred as

$$\text{actual cost amount} = AP \times AQ \times UO$$

where *AP* is the actual price paid for each vinyl disk and *AQ* is the actual average number of disks required per unit of output.

[1]The term *budget variance* is fairly well entrenched in the accounting literature. It might more appropriately be called an efficiency variance, but the term efficiency variance is generally accepted as referring to just part of the budget variance.

[2]A word of caution: The words *favorable* and *unfavorable* are being used in a technical way having to do with financial accounting rather than managerial accounting. They should *not* be interpreted indiscriminately as "good" and "bad." Whether a variance is good or bad depends on *what caused it;* whereas, whether a variance is favorable or unfavorable depends on the effect on income. For example, changed economic conditions may have led us to expect an unfavorable variance of $1,500, whereas we actually incurred an unfavorable variance of $1,200. Although the variance is unfavorable, it is "better" than we expected.

For the fabricating department, 59,600 vinyl disks costing \$21,754 were actually used; division yields the actual price per disk as \$21,754 ÷ 59,600 = \$0.365 per disk. Similarly, the actual number of vinyl disks per unit of completed product turned out to be 59,600 ÷ 58,500 = 1.0188 per completed disk. Thus the total actual cost can also be represented as[3]

$$\begin{aligned}\text{actual cost} &= AP \times AQ \times UO \\ &= \$0.365 \times 1.0188 \times 58{,}500 \\ &= \$21{,}754\end{aligned}$$

Next, let us consider the cost that would have been incurred by the department had it been able to acquire the resources actually used at their standard prices. This figures is represented as

$$\text{actual inputs at standard prices} = SP \times AQ \times UO$$

For the fabrication department the standard cost of the vinyl disks actually used is[3]

$$\begin{aligned}\text{actual inputs at standard prices} &= SP \times AQ \times UO \\ &= \$0.35 \times 1.0188 \times 58{,}500 \\ &= \$20{,}860\end{aligned}$$

With these three definitions of costs, we can now gain further information about the efficiency of operations by examining two possible sources of variances: (1) The price actually paid per unit of resource may be different than our standard price, and (2) the amount of resources used per unit of product may differ from the standard quantities allowed. In most firms different people are responsible for each variance. A purchasing agent is generally responsible for obtaining resources at budgeted costs, whereas production supervisors are responsible for the efficient use of the resources. Fortunately, it is very easy to separate the budget variances into these two sources.

### Quantity Variance

Compare the expression for actual resources used at standard prices ($SP \times AQ \times UO$, sometimes called the flexible budget for inputs) to the flexible budget ($SP \times SQ \times UO$, which is also the standard cost allowed for production achieved). Notice that the only term that is different in the two

[3]Calculating actual quantities per unit of output and actual costs per unit of input frequently introduces a rounding error. Shortly we will illustrate an alternative approach that avoids the problem.

formulations is the quantity of resources used per unit of output. Thus by comparing these two figures, we have isolated the effect of using an inappropriate quantity of resources. We call the difference between the flexible budget and actual inputs at standard price the **quantity variance.** Algebraically, the variance can be represented as

$$\begin{aligned} \text{quantity variance} &= \text{flexible budget} - \text{actual inputs at standard price} \\ &= SP \times (SQ \times UO) - SP \times (AQ \times UO) \\ &= SP \times (SQ \times UO - AQ \times UO) \end{aligned}$$

This gives us the effect on total cost from using more or fewer units of resources than standard for all the units of output produced. If, instead, we wanted to know the effect on the cost of an individual unit of product, we could simply divide by the units of output (*UO*) to get a per-unit variance.

## Price Variance

Now let us compare the algebraic expression for actual inputs at standard price ($SP \times AQ \times UO$) with the expression for the actual cost incurred ($AP \times AQ \times UO$). We can see that the only term that differs is the price per unit of input. This comparison yields the effect from having paid prices different from standard. We call this variance the **price variance.**[4]

$$\begin{aligned} \text{price variance} &= \text{actual inputs at standard price} - \text{actual costs} \\ &= SP \times (AQ \times UO) - AP \times (AQ \times UO) \\ &= (SP - AP) \times AQ \times UO \end{aligned}$$

Again, the variance has been calculated in terms of the total effect for all output. Should we want the effect on a single unit of output we can divide by the units of output (*UO*).

The price and quantity variances sum to the budget variance. This relationship can be seen when we depict the variances in schematic form as follows:

| **Actual Cost** | **Actual Inputs at Standard Price** | **Flexible Budget** |
|---|---|---|
| ***(AP × AQ × UO)*** | ***(SP × AQ × UO)*** | ***(SP × SQ × UO)*** |
| Price variance (Actual Cost to Actual Inputs at Standard Price) | Quantity variance (Actual Inputs at Standard Price to Flexible Budget) | |
| Budget variance (Actual Cost to Flexible Budget) | | |

[4]We will usually call these variances price and quantity variances. Common alternatives are to call price variances **rate variances** or **spending variances.** Similarly you are likely to see quantity variances referred to as **usage variances** or **efficiency variances.** We will use these alternative terms from time to time so that you will become familiar with them.

### Graphic Depiction of Price and Quantity Variances

Figure 18-1 illustrates the price and quantity variances graphically. The flexible budget cost equation is shown as a straight line because we are assuming that variable costs are constant on a per-unit basis in the firm's relevant range. However, the graphic analysis is completely general for any flexible budget cost equation (curvilinear, step costs, or whatever). The price variance is still the difference between the actual costs incurred and the amount of standard costs allowed for the resources used. The quantity variance is the difference between the amount of standard costs allowed for the resources used and the amount of costs allowed in the flexible budget for the output achieved (the resources which should have been used). Figure 18-2 illustrates the variances for a resource whose costs are acquired in steps.

To make the equations for the variances completely general we must redefine the term *SP*. If the standard price per unit changes depending on the amount of resources acquired, then, in general terms, *SP* must represent the standard price allowed for resources in the flexible budget equation, adjusted for the appropriate level of resources that were used or should have been used. Although we will use this approach in the ap-

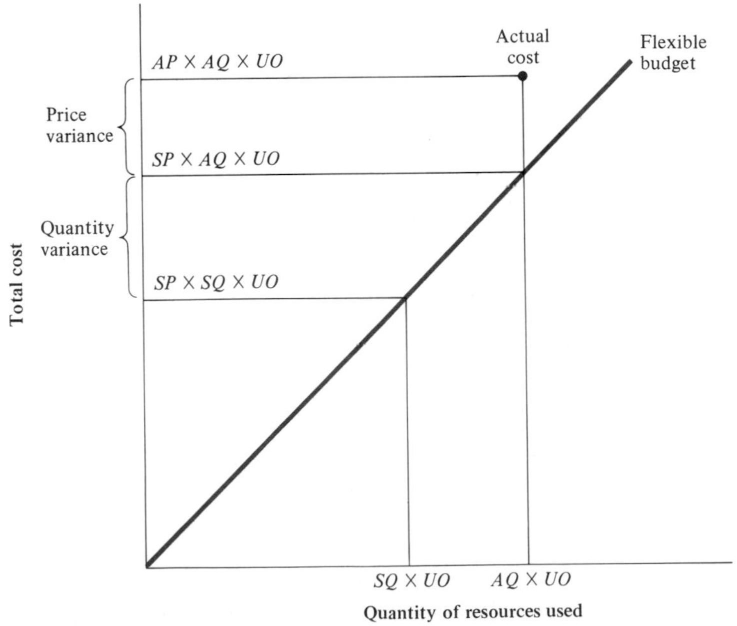


**FIGURE 18-1 Price and quantity variances for a variable cost.**

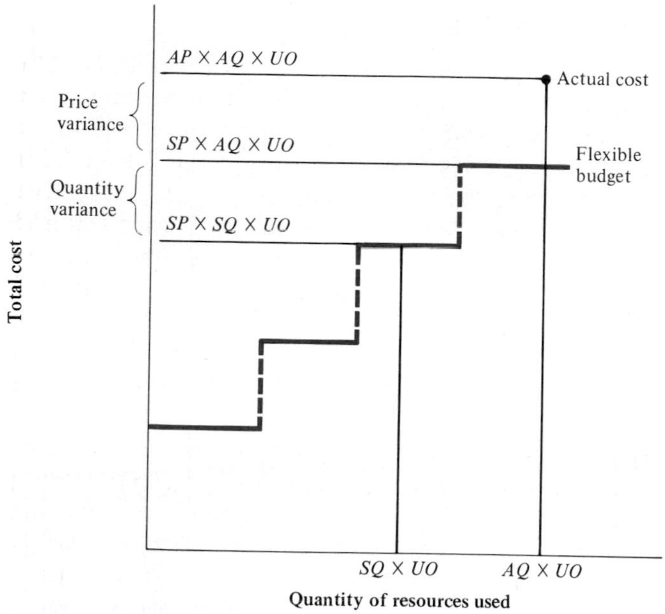


**FIGURE 18-2 Price and quantity variances for a step cost.**

pendixes in Chapter 19, in this chapter we assume that variable costs per unit are constant in the relevant range.

### Variance Calculations

Let us now return to the example for the fabricating department. The price and quantity variances for each cost are presented in schematic form in Exhibit 18-4. In each case we calculated the cost per unit of an input by dividing the actual cost incurred as given in Exhibit 18-1 by the number of units of the resource acquired. Similarly, the actual quantity of a resource used per unit of output was determined by dividing the quantities used as given in Exhibit 18-1 by the 58,500 finished units produced.

We can note that the budget variances for each cost are just as before. But now we also subdivided the budget variance into a price and quantity variance for each type of cost. Another feature that stands out is that we have not calculated a price and a quantity variance for fixed overhead. Why not? Recall that fixed overhead costs are not expected to vary with changes in level of output. That is, there is no standard quantity of fixed overhead per unit of output. Instead the entire fixed overhead budget variance can be thought of as a price or spending variance.

**EXHIBIT 18-4 Price and Quantity Variances for the Fabricating Department**[a]

| | Actual Costs $AP \times AQ \times UO$ | Price Variances | Actual Inputs at Standard Price $SP \times AQ \times UO$ | Quantity Variances | Flexible Budget $SP \times SQ \times UO$ |
|---|---|---|---|---|---|
| Vinyl disks | \$0.365 × 1.0188 × 58,500<br>\$21,754 | | \$0.35 × 1.0188 × 58,500<br>\$20,860 | | \$0.35 × 1.02 × 58,500<br>\$20,884.50 |
| | | \$894 U | | \$24.50 F | |
| | | | \$869.50 U | | |
| Sleeve materials | \$0.0028 × 30.9402 × 58,500<br>\$ 5,068 | | \$0.003 × 30.9402 × 58,500<br>\$ 5,430 | | \$0.003 × 31 × 58,500<br>\$ 5,440.50 |
| | | \$362 F | | \$10.50 F | |
| | | | \$372.50 F | | |
| Direct labor | \$5.96 × 0.024786 × 58,500<br>\$ 8,642 | | \$6.00 × 0.024786 × 58,500<br>\$ 8,700 | | \$6.00 × 0.024 × 58,500<br>\$ 8,424 |
| | | \$ 58 F | | \$276 U | |
| | | | \$218 U | | |
| Variable overhead | \$3.62 × 0.024786 × 58,500<br>\$ 5,249 | | \$3.50 × 0.024786 × 58,500<br>\$ 5,075 | | \$3.50 × 0.024 × 58,500<br>\$ 4,914 |
| | | \$174 U | | \$161 U | |
| | | | \$335 U | | |
| Fixed overhead | \$ 2,810 | | | | \$ 2,880 |
| | | | \$ 70 F | | |

[a]Unit cost figures are shown rounded; the actual calculations used unrounded figures.

As an alternative to the schematic approach, the price and quantity variances for the variable costs can also be calculated from the formulas we derived earlier. In formula form, the variances are as follows:[5]

| | **Price Variance**<br>**(*SP* − *AP*) × *AQ* × *UO*** | **Quantity Variance**<br>***SP* × (*SQ* × *UO* − *AQ* × *UO*)** |
|---|---|---|
| Vinyl disks | (\$0.35 − \$0.365) × 1.0188 × 58,500<br>= −\$0.015 × 59,600<br>= \$894 U | \$0.35(1.02 × 58,500 − 1.0188 × 58,500)<br>= \$0.35(59,670 − 59,600)<br>= \$24.50 F |
| Sleeve materials | (\$0.003 − \$0.0028) × 30.9402 × 58,500<br>= \$0.0002 × 1,810,000<br>= \$362 F | \$0.003(31 × 58,500 − 30.9402 × 58,500)<br>= \$0.003(1,813,500 − 1,810,000)<br>= \$10.50 F |
| Direct labor | (\$6.00 − \$5.96) × 0.024786 × 58,500<br>= \$0.04 × 1,450<br>= \$58 F | \$6.00(0.024 × 58,500 − 0.024786 × 58,500)<br>= \$6.00(1,404 − 1,450)<br>= \$276 U |
| Variable overhead | (\$3.50 − \$3.62) × 0.024786 × 58,500<br>= −\$0.12 × 1,450<br>= \$174 U | \$3.50(0.024 × 58,500 − 0.024786 × 58,500)<br>= \$3.50(1,404 − 1,450)<br>= \$161 U |

### A Shortcut

If you have followed our calculations closely, you will have noticed that we ran into rounding difficulties when calculating *AP* and *AQ*. We can avoid this problem and save some computations by making another observation. Whenever the term *AQ* is used in a variance calculation, whether using the schematic or formula approach, it is multiplied by *UO*. The product of these terms is the total amount of a resource used, and typically we will know this number. Similarly, whenever the term *AP* is used it is multiplied by both *AQ* and *UO*. The total product of these terms is the actual amount paid for resources. Again, this amount would normally be known.

When the amount of actual resources used and the actual amount paid for resources is known, we do not have to calculate *AP* and *AQ*. Instead, we can substitute the total products into the variance calculations. For example, using the data for the amount of labor used by the fabricating

[5] Unit cost figures are shown rounded. The actual calculations were made with unrounded figures.

department, we could calculate the price and quantity variances in schematic form as (see Exhibit 18-1 for the data):

| **Actual Costs** *AP* × *AQ* × *UO* | **Price Variance** | **Actual Inputs at Standard Price** *SP* × (*AQ* × *UO*) | **Quantity Variance** | **Flexible Budget** *SP* × *SQ* × *UO* |
|---|---|---|---|---|
| | | \$6.00 × (1,450) | | \$6.00 × 0.024 × 58,500 |
| \$8,642 | | \$8,700 | | \$8,424 |
| | \$58 F | | \$276 U | |
| | | \$218 U | | |

Similarly, the labor variances can be determined without calculating *AP* or *AQ* in formula form as:

| **Price Variance** | **Quantity Variance** |
|---|---|
| *SP*(*AQ* × *UO*) − (*AP* × *AQ* × *UO*) | *SP* × *SQ* × *UO* − *SP*(*AQ* × *UO*) |
| = \$6.00(1,450) − \$8,642 | = \$6.00 × 0.024 × 58,500 − \$6.00(1,450) |
| = \$8,700 − \$8,642 | = \$8,424 − \$8,700 |
| = \$58 F | = \$276 U |

The detailed approach in which *AP* and *AQ* are calculated is useful for understanding the calculation of variances. Further, there are times when it *must* be used (for example, when solving problems such as the demonstration problem at the end of the chapter). But for the most part, the shortcut approach is preferable. It saves a few calculations and avoids rounding problems.

### Interpretation of Variances

Let us now pause for a moment to interpret the variances for the fabricating department. Recall that the reason for calculating the price and quantity variances is to identify responsibility for variances. Normally, different people are responsible for the two variances. For example, look at the variance for the vinyl disks in Exhibit 18-4. Although the overall budget variance is unfavorable, most of it is not attributable to the fabricating department. Recall that the vinyl disks are produced by the manufacturing department. Presumably it is their responsibility to produce the vinyl disks at standard cost. Thus the price variance is really the responsibility of the manufacturing department.[6] The part of the budget variance that is controllable by the manager of the fabricating department is the quantity

[6]As explained in the appendix to this chapter, the price variance for the vinyl disks would normally be isolated in the manufacturing department and the disks would be transferred to the fabricating department at standard cost. In this case there would be no price variance for the vinyl disks in the fabricating department. We presumed them to be transferred at actual cost so that we could raise the responsibility issue.

variance. We can see from the variance that the department used fewer disks than were called for by the standard. Thus it appears that the fabricating department was efficient in its use of the disks. Note, however, that this interpretation is dependent on the standard being an attainable standard (it allows 1.02 disks per unit of output). If the quantity standard were an ideal standard (i.e., allowing only one disk per unit of output), a favorable variance would indicate a serious problem (because in this case a favorable quantity variance can arise only if some of the final products are missing the recording medium).

For materials, the price variance is usually the responsibility of a purchasing agent. The quantity variance is usually the responsibility of the departmental manager. However, if the purchasing agent acquired poor quality materials, some or all of the materials quantity variance and labor quantity variance may also be assigned to the purchasing agent.

If the departmental manager has the discretion to use different classes of labor (earning different wage rates), both the price and quantity variances may be attributable to the manager. That is, the manager is held responsible for both the total hours used and for matching the appropriate skill levels (and wage rates) to the required tasks. Frequently, however, price variances arise because of unanticipated wage increases. Because overall wage rates are usually not under the control of a departmental manager, the manager in this case is normally held responsible for only the quantity variance.

The interpretation of the variances for variable overhead is more difficult. The quantity variance is the amount of variance expected due to deviations in the amount of the application base used. In the fabricating department, overhead is applied on labor hours. Thus, in this example, the unfavorable quantity variance is the amount of excess overhead expected to be incurred due to the excessive use of labor. All other excess use of overhead items, as well as deviations in costs, are captured in the overhead price variance. Typically, departmental managers are held responsible for both the price and quantity variances for variable overhead.

Finally, the fixed overhead budget variance is the total difference between budgeted and actual fixed costs. It is usually small and due to errors in predicting the actual amount of fixed costs to be incurred. They are typically charged to the departmental manager, but being small they usually do not affect the manager's performance appraisal.

Overall, how did the fabricating department perform? It appears to have done quite well. Of the total unfavorable budget variance of $980, $894 is due to the excess costs of the disks transferred from the manufacturing department. Thus, on balance, the fabricating department has virtually met the standard (small deviations are to be expected). Nonetheless, the manager may wish to pay a bit closer attention to the use of labor and the amount of overhead items consumed.

### Another Approach to the Materials Price Variance

So far we have ignored a problem that can arise in calculating the direct materials variances. All of the variances we are calculating are derived for control purposes. That is, we want the firm's personnel to be aware of deviations from the company's standards so that they can strive to adjust their actions to bring performance in line with the standards. For the feedback information on performance to be effective, personnel must be made aware of any deviations as soon as practical. The sooner variances can be identified, the sooner corrective actions can be implemented. With labor and the majority of overhead items, the acquisition and the use of resources occur simultaneously. But materials are often purchased in advance of use and held in inventory until needed. To meet our control objective, we may want to identify any materials price variance in the period in which the materials are acquired rather than when used. In this case when we calculate the materials price variance it will be based on the quantity of materials *purchased*. In equation form,

$$\text{materials price variance} = (SP - AP) \times \text{units of materials purchased}$$

Without regard to how the price variance is calculated, our quantity variance should still be based on the amount of materials *used* in production for the output attained. Thus there will be no change in the quantity variance.

When we use the schematic approach for determining variances and the materials price variance is based on purchases, we must insert a second line for materials in the chart. For example, assume that our standards call for the use of 20 pounds of materials per unit of output at a cost of $2 per pound. This period we produced 12,000 units and used 250,000 pounds. Also, during the period we purchased 265,000 pounds at $1.90 per pound. The price and quantity variances, with the price variance related to purchases, can be represented schematically as follows:

| **Actual Costs Incurred for Units *Purchased*** | **Price Variance** | **Actual Inputs *Used* at Standard Price** | **Quantity Variance** | **Flexible Budget** |
|---|---|---|---|---|
| | | $2 × 250,000 | | $2 × 20 × 12,000 |
| | | $500,000 | | $480,000 |
| | | | $20,000 U | |
| | | **Actual Inputs *Purchased* at Standard Price** | | |
| $1.90 × 265,000 | | $2 × 265,000 | | |
| $503,500 | | $530,000 | | |
| | $26,500 F | | | |

and, in equation form,

$$\begin{aligned}\text{price variance} &= (SP - AP) \times \text{units of material purchased}\\ &= (\$2.00 - \$1.90) \times 265{,}000\\ &= \$26{,}500\ \text{F}\\ \text{quantity variance} &= SP(SQ \times UO - AQ \times UO)\\ &= \$2(20 \times 12{,}000 - 250{,}000)\\ &= \$20{,}000\ \text{U}\end{aligned}$$

Had the price variance been calculated only on the units of materials *used* during the period, it would have been as follows:

$$\begin{aligned}\text{price variance} &= (SP - AP) \times \text{units of materials used}\\ &= (\$2.00 - \$1.90) \times 250{,}000\\ &= \$25{,}000\ \text{F}\end{aligned}$$

An interesting question related to the theory of income measurement is whether the entire price variance on purchases ($26,500) should be charged to current period's income or whether only $25,000 should be charged to current income with the remaining $1,500 deferred to the period in which the materials are used. We will let you ponder that question.

### The Volume Variance

So far we have identified the variances related to manufacturing costs that explain the difference between the flexible budget and the actual level of costs incurred. There is another variance that arises from our bookkeeping practice. This variance, called the volume variance or denominator variance, should be distinguished from those discussed earlier. The volume variance does not explain a difference between actual costs incurred and budgeted costs. Rather, it is simply a bookkeeping adjustment to correct an error in the way in which we record overhead costs. Before explaining its calculation, let us reexamine the manner in which we charge overhead to production in our accounting records.

At the time the master budget is prepared, we have available our best estimate of the level of operations we expect to achieve for the upcoming period. In addition, we also will have estimated the fixed overhead costs that will be incurred. At this point we compute a fixed overhead application rate. Like variable overhead, fixed overhead will be charged to products on the basis of some common measure such as machine hours or labor hours. If the budget calls for $30,000 of fixed overhead, if we apply fixed overhead on the basis of labor hours, and if we anticipate producing

10,000 units of product each requiring 1 hour of labor time, then we will establish a **fixed overhead application rate** of $30,000 ÷ 10,000 hours = $3 per standard direct labor hour. Then during the period, as units of product are completed, we transfer the cost of completed units at standard cost to finished goods inventory. Included in this standard cost will be the standard cost for materials, labor, variable overhead, *and* a charge for fixed overhead.

Note that for the variable cost items the costs charged to inventory will coincide with the figures in the flexible budget. That is, both the flexible budget and our bookkeeping transfers of costs to inventory are based on the standard cost of units produced. But it is not generally true that we will have applied fixed overhead to inventory at the level called for in the flexible budget.

The figure for fixed overhead does not vary as we change the flexible budget for level of output. Whatever figure is called for in the master budget for fixed overhead will also be called for in the flexible budget. But in our bookkeeping, when we charge fixed overhead to inventory based on a fixed overhead application rate, we are treating fixed overhead as if it were a variable cost. That is, if 12,000 units of product are produced, we will charge into inventory $36,000 for fixed overhead (12,000 units at 1 direct labor hour per unit at $3 of fixed overhead per direct labor hour). If 11,000 units had been produced, we would have applied $33,000 of fixed overhead costs. Similarly, 9,000 units would lead to the application of $27,000 of fixed costs and 10,000 units would result in the application of $30,000 of fixed overhead to inventory. Note that only at the level of

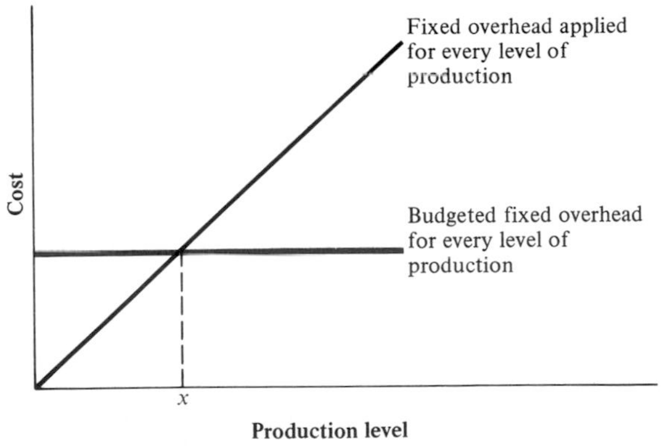


**FIGURE 18-3 The relationship between applied fixed overhead and budgeted fixed overhead, where x represents the level of production anticipated in the master budget.** The fixed overhead applied will be equal to budgeted fixed overhead only if the actual production level achieved coincides with the master budget planned level of production.

10,000 units (the level of output anticipated in the master budget) will the amount of the fixed costs applied to inventory be equal to the amount of fixed costs in the flexible budget. At production levels in excess of that budgeted in the master budget, the fixed costs applied will exceed the budgeted costs.[7] At levels of production below master budget, the fixed costs applied to production will be less than that called for in the budget. This relationship is depicted graphically in Figure 18-3. The **volume variance** or **denominator variance** is simply the difference between the amount of fixed costs applied to inventory and the amount of budgeted fixed costs.

Knowing how fixed costs are applied to production, we can now express the volume variance in equation form. The fixed costs are applied to production as simply the fixed overhead application rate times the measure of activity (labor hours, machine hours, or whatever) allowed for the output achieved. Budgeted fixed overhead can also be expressed as the fixed overhead application rate times the measure of activity called for in the master budget. That is, we know that

$$\text{fixed overhead application rate} = \frac{\text{budgeted fixed overhead}}{\begin{array}{c}\text{measure of activity anticipated}\\ \text{in the master budget}\end{array}}$$

Therefore,

$$\text{budgeted fixed overhead} = \begin{pmatrix}\text{fixed overhead}\\ \text{application rate}\end{pmatrix} \times \begin{pmatrix}\text{master budget}\\ \text{activity level}\end{pmatrix}$$

Similarly, since fixed overhead is applied to production using the fixed overhead application rate times the measure of output allowed for the production achieved (i.e., the flexible budget activity level), the fixed overhead applied to production is as follows:

$$\text{fixed overhead applied} = \begin{pmatrix}\text{fixed overhead}\\ \text{application rate}\end{pmatrix} \times \begin{pmatrix}\text{flexible budget}\\ \text{activity level}\end{pmatrix}$$

The volume variance, which is simply the difference between the fixed overhead applied and budgeted, becomes

$$\text{volume variance} = \begin{pmatrix}\text{fixed overhead}\\ \text{application rate}\end{pmatrix} \times \begin{pmatrix}\begin{array}{c}\text{flexible budget}\\ \text{activity level}\end{array} - \begin{array}{c}\text{master budget}\\ \text{activity level}\end{array}\end{pmatrix}$$

or, in words, the volume variance is calculated by simply multiplying the fixed overhead application rate by the difference between the activity level

[7]Since the amount of fixed costs will be the same in both the master budget and the flexible budget, we need not make a distinction as to which budget we are referring.

anticipated in the master budget and the level achieved, as reflected in the flexible budget.

Let us return to the example involving the fabricating department. The data in Exhibit 18-1 indicate that the fixed overhead application rate was $2.00 per labor hour. The master budget called for producing 60,000 disks, which translates into an activity level of

$$60{,}000 \times 0.024 \text{ hr} = 1{,}440 \text{ hr}$$

During the period, 58,500 disks were actually produced, so the flexible budget allowance for labor hours is

$$58{,}500 \times 0.024 = 1{,}404 \text{ hr}$$

Thus the volume variance is as follows:

$$\begin{aligned}\text{volume variance} &= \$2.00 \text{ per DLH} \times (1{,}404 \text{ DLH} - 1{,}440 \text{ DLH}) \\ &= \$72 \text{ U}\end{aligned}$$

That is, we have underapplied budgeted overhead by $72 because we failed to reach our planned level of output. To correct this bookkeeping error, we will have to expense more fixed overhead. This will have the effect of reducing earnings, so in this case the variance is called unfavorable.

## COMBINED OVERHEAD VARIANCES

To calculate a fixed overhead price variance (budget variance) separately from the variable overhead variances, it is necessary to maintain separate records of the fixed versus variable overhead costs incurred. Maintaining such a distinction can be difficult and expensive. It may be necessary to study carefully the behavior of cost items to determine whether they are fixed or variable. In addition, some costs are truly mixed, having a fixed and variable portion. Whenever an invoice is to be paid, the portion to be charged to fixed versus variable overhead would have to be determined.

Some firms feel the value of having separate variances for fixed and variable overhead cannot justify an elaborate record-keeping system. These firms are satisfied with determining combined overhead variances. It is still necessary to determine a budgeted overhead cost equation using tech-

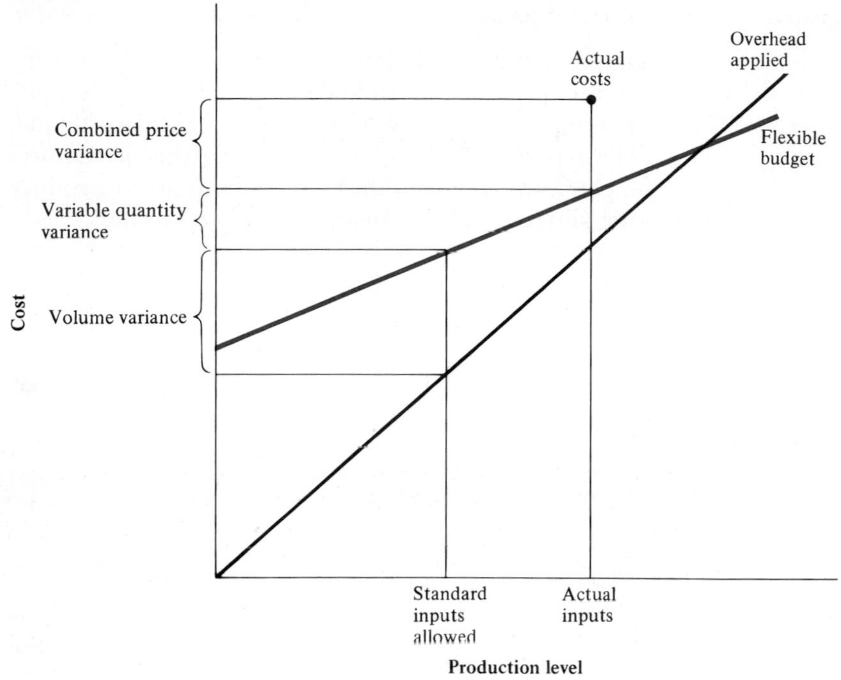


**FIGURE 18-4 Combined overhead variances.**

niques such as those described in Chapter 3. In addition, we will still need to determine a standard application rate for fixed and variable overhead. But when overhead costs are incurred, they are simply all accumulated in one overhead account. No attempt is made to separate fixed and variable costs. Nonetheless, when it is time to analyze overhead expenditures, we will still be able to determine the volume variance and the variable overhead quantity variance. However, the variable spending and fixed overhead budget variances will be combined.

The combined overhead spending variances will be the difference between the actual total overhead costs incurred and the flexible budget allowance for the actual inputs used (such as machine hours or direct labor hours). The variable overhead quantity variance is still the difference between the flexible budget allowance for inputs actually used and the allowance for the inputs that should have been used for the output obtained. Finally, the fixed overhead volume variance continues to be the difference between the overhead applied to outputs and the flexible budget allowance for overhead given the outputs. Each of these variances is illustrated in Figure 18-4.

### Computation of Combined Variances

Let us look at an example of the calculation of combined overhead variances. At the beginning of a period, an estimate of total overhead is made just as before for the master budget. Assume that the overhead cost equation is \$5 per direct labor hour plus \$30,000. Assuming that it requires 1 hour of direct labor per unit of output and that we intend to produce 10,000 units, the master budget total overhead is estimated to be

$$\begin{aligned}\text{total overhead} &= \$5 \times 10{,}000 + \$30{,}000 \\ &= \$80{,}000\end{aligned}$$

Similarly, the total standard overhead application rate is simply total overhead divided by master budget activity, or

$$\begin{aligned}\text{standard overhead application rate} &= \frac{\$80{,}000}{10{,}000 \text{ DLH}} \\ &= \$8 \text{ per DLH}\end{aligned}$$

It is important to note that the standard rate is the sum of the variable overhead application rate and the fixed overhead application rate. That is,

$$\begin{aligned}\text{total rate} &= \text{variable rate} + \text{fixed rate} \\ &= \frac{\$50{,}000}{10{,}000 \text{ DLH}} + \frac{\$30{,}000}{10{,}000 \text{ DLH}} \\ &= \$8 \text{ per DLH}\end{aligned}$$

Thus, although we do not apply fixed and variable overhead separately or accumulate fixed and variable costs separately, we can still calculate most of the overhead variances.

Assume that we actually produced 12,000 units of product using 12,100 direct labor hours and that total overhead was \$92,000. Since we know the actual output, we can calculate the flexible budget amount of overhead allowed for the output attained as

$$\begin{aligned}\text{flexible budget overhead allowance} &= \$5 \times 12{,}000 + \$30{,}000 \\ &= \$90{,}000\end{aligned}$$

Similarly we can calculate the inputs-at-standard figure for total overhead by noting that at 12,000 labor hours, fixed overhead would still be expected to be \$30,000, whereas variable overhead would be expected to be \$5 × 12,100 = \$60,500, for a total of \$90,500. Then in schematic form the analysis of the variances for total overhead becomes

| Actual Costs | Combined Price Variance | Actual Inputs at Standard Prices | Variable Quantity Variance | Flexible Budget |
|---|---|---|---|---|
| | | $30,000 + $60,500 | | $30,000 + $60,000 |
| $92,000 | | $90,500 | | $90,000 |
| | $1,500 U | | $500 U | |

To see how this differs from the previous, more detailed analysis, assume for the moment that we know that the actual amount of variable overhead costs incurred were $61,800 and the actual fixed overhead costs were $30,200. Our previous separate analysis would be

| | Actual Costs | Price Variance | Actual Inputs at Standard Prices | Quantity Variance | Flexible Budget |
|---|---|---|---|---|---|
| Variable overhead | $61,800 | | $60,500 | | $60,000 |
| | | $1,300 U | | $500 U | |
| Fixed overhead | $30,200 | | $30,000[a] | | $30,000 |
| | | $ 200 U | | — | |
| Totals | $92,000 | | $90,500 | | $90,000 |
| | | $1,500 U | | $500 U | |

[a]Previously we had left this spot blank for fixed overhead. We now add the fixed overhead that would have been budgeted for 12,100 hours, which is, of course, unchanged at $30,000.

As this latter analysis shows, the combined variances yield the appropriate variable overhead quantity variance and provides the sum of the fixed and variable overhead price variances.

The level of analysis for the spending variance has no effect on the volume variance. Total overhead was applied to production at $8 per direct labor hour. This rate includes a fixed overhead application rate of $3. Hence, the volume variance is

$$\begin{aligned}\text{volume variance} &= \begin{pmatrix}\text{fixed overhead}\\ \text{application rate}\end{pmatrix} \times \begin{pmatrix}\text{flexible budget} & - & \text{master budget}\\ \text{activity level} & & \text{activity level}\end{pmatrix}\\ &= \$3 \times (12{,}000 \text{ DLH} - 10{,}000 \text{ DLH})\\ &= \$6{,}000 \text{ F}\end{aligned}$$

With the combined analysis, a shortcut version for calculating the volume variance is sometimes employed. Note that the figure for total overhead under the flexible budget column is the sum of the budgeted fixed costs plus variable cost allowed. If we compare this to the overhead applied to production, which is the sum of the fixed cost applied and the variable cost allowed, the difference between the two figures is the volume variance. Thus a shortcut is to simply compare total flexible budget overhead, \$90,000, with total overhead applied, \$8 × 12,000 = \$96,000, to find the \$6,000 favorable volume variance.

## SUMMARY

The master budget, prepared at the beginning of a period, is used for planning purposes. To measure efficiency at the end of the period a flexible budget is constructed to reflect the costs that should have been incurred given the actual outputs produced. The difference between the actual costs incurred and the flexible budget allowance is then further divided into a price and quantity effect for variable costs. This subdivision of variances allows management to assign responsibility for the actual variances more effectively. For fixed overhead, only a budget variance is calculated to explain the difference between budgeted and actual fixed costs incurred. But in addition, a fixed overhead volume variance must be calculated to explain the difference between the fixed overhead assigned to production and the budgeted fixed overhead.

## DEMONSTRATION PROBLEM

The examples in the chapter demonstrate the calculation of variances when all costs and standards are known. But if we fully understand the underlying concepts of variance calculations, we should also be able to work backward from the variances to the underlying costs and standards. This demonstration problem takes that approach.

A firm's cost accountant called in ill this morning. However, the monthly performance reports are due out this afternoon. Fortunately the cost accountant had nearly completed the computation of variances for the assembly department. You have been asked to complete the report based on the information that the accountant has already compiled. The accountant's notes reveal the following facts for the assembly department for the current month:

| | |
|---|---|
| Standard cost of direct materials allowed | \$50,400 |
| Direct material usage variance | \$1,680 U |
| Actual price paid per pound of materials | \$4.05 |
| Standard direct labor wage rate | \$7/hr |
| Standard labor hours allowed per unit of output | 1.5 hr |
| Actual labor hours used at standard cost per hour | \$41,160 |
| Direct labor rate variance | \$294 F |

| | |
|---|---|
| Actual direct labor hours per unit of output | 1.4 hr |
| Standard variable overhead cost per direct labor hour | $3.50/hr |
| Actual variable overhead cost per direct labor hour | $3.65/hr |
| Actual fixed overhead costs incurred | $36,275 |
| Fixed overhead spending variance | $275 U |
| Fixed overhead volume variance | $1,800 F |
| Actual materials used per unit | 3.1 lb |

Note that both fixed and variable overhead are applied to products based on standard direct labor hours.

**Required**

Determine the following:

**a.** The standard price per pound of materials
**b.** The materials price variance
**c.** The actual cost of materials used
**d.** The labor usage variance
**e.** The actual wage rate per hour
**f.** The actual total labor cost
**g.** The flexible budget allowance for labor
**h.** The flexible budget allowance for variable overhead
**i.** The actual variable overhead costs
**j.** The variable overhead spending and efficiency variances
**k.** The budgeted amount of fixed overhead
**l.** The fixed overhead applied to production
**m.** The fixed overhead application rate per direct labor hour
**n.** The number of units of output anticipated in the master budget for the month

**Solution**

This is about as difficult a version of this type of problem as you are likely to see. With the amount of information given and the large number of answers required, it is generally best to take an organized approach to the solution of the problem. In our opinion, the most efficient approach is to place all of the known information into a schematic format. In Exhibit 18-5 we have used the same format as that used in the chapter. We have written all the known information into its proper place and indicated unknowns with question marks. Before proceeding, you should trace each piece of given information to the chart so that you understand where each number has come from. Note particularly that the figure for the actual direct labor hours per unit of product appears in four separate places on the chart. The 1.4 actual hours appears in the Actual Inputs at Standard Price and Actual Costs columns for both the direct labor row and the variable overhead row. The figure shows up in the variable overhead row because the problem stated that overhead is allocated to products on the basis of direct labor hours. Also note that the $7 standard wage rate for direct labor appears twice: once in the Flexible Budget column and once under Actual Inputs at Standard Price for the direct labor row. Similarly, several other figures show up in several places on the chart. Finally, note that we have not included the volume variance in Exhibit 18-5; we will consider it separately at the end of the solution.

**EXHIBIT 18-5 The Known Information for the Demonstration Problem**

| | Actual Costs<br>(*AP* × *AQ* × *UO*) | Price<br>Variances | Actual Inputs at<br>Standard Price<br>(*SP* × *AQ* × *UO*) | Quantity<br>Variances | Flexible<br>Budget<br>(*SP* × *SQ* × *UO*) |
|---|---|---|---|---|---|
| Direct materials | $4.05 × 3.1 × ?<br>? | | ? × 3.1 × ?<br>? | | ? × ? × ?<br>$50,400 |
| | | ? | | $1,680 U | |
| Direct labor | ? × 1.4 × ?<br>? | | $7 × 1.4 × ?<br>$41,160 | | $7 × 1.5 × ?<br>? |
| | | $294 F | | ? | |
| Variable overhead | $3.65 × 1.4 × ?<br>? | | $3.5 × 1.4 × ?<br>? | | $3.5 × 1.5 × ?<br>? |
| | | ? | | ? | |
| Fixed overhead | $36,275 | | | | ? |
| | | | $275 U | | |

Once we have recorded our known information, we now search for relationships where we know all the information except for one piece of data. For example, in the row for direct materials we know that the $1,680 unfavorable materials quantity variance is the difference between the flexible budget allowance of $50,400 and the value of inputs at standard. Therefore the total for inputs at standard must be $50,400 + $1,680 = $52,080. Unfortunately, even with this number now filled in, there are no other relationships in the direct materials row for which we know all but one figure.

Turning to direct labor we know that the difference between inputs at standard and actual costs is the $294 favorable price variance. Therefore actual labor costs must be $41,160 − $294 = $40,866. There is also a slightly less obvious relationship that will provide additional information. Note that by using the information in the column Inputs at Standard, we can solve for the units of output. That is, division of the $41,160 value of inputs at standard by the standard wage rate of $7 per hour and the actual hours used per unit of 1.4 will give us the number of units produced, which is 4,200. We can now substitute this value for units produced in every column for materials, labor, and variable overhead (in nine places). This gives us as known information the data represented in Exhibit 18-6.

Referring to Exhibit 18-6 we can see that we have made a great deal of progress. We can now find the actual cost for materials by multiplying together the actual cost of materials with the actual materials per unit and the 4,200 units produced. Actual materials costs must be $4.05 × 3.1 × 4,200 = $52,731. Comparing actual materials costs to inputs at standard now gives the materials price variance of $52,080 − $52,731 = $651 U. Next, dividing the inputs at standard for materials by the actual materials used per unit and the actual units produced gives us the standard price per pound of materials of $52,080 ÷ (3.1 × 4,200) = $4 per pound. Finally, we know that the flexible budget allowance is the product

**EXHIBIT 18-6 Partially Solved Demonstration Problem**

| | Actual Costs (*AP* × *AQ* × *UO*) | Price Variances | Actual Inputs at Standard Price (*SP* × *AQ* × *UO*) | Quantity Variances | Flexible Budget (*SP* × *SQ* × *UO*) |
|---|---|---|---|---|---|
| Direct materials | $4.05 × 3.1 × 4,200<br>? | ? | ? × 3.1 × 4,200<br>$52,080 | $1,680 U | ? × ? × 4,200<br>$50,400 |
| Direct labor | ? × 1.4 × 4,200<br>$40,866 | $294 F | $7 × 1.4 × 4,200<br>$41,160 | ? | $7 × 1.5 × 4,200<br>? |
| Variable overhead | $3.65 × 1.4 × 4,200<br>? | ? | $3.5 × 1.4 × 4,200<br>? | ? | $3.5 × 1.5 × 4,200<br>? |
| Fixed overhead | $36,275 | | $275 U | | ? |

of the $4 standard price for materials times the unknown standard quantity of materials per unit times the 4,200 units produced. Since we know this total is $50,400, we can divide to get the standard quantity of materials per unit as $50,400 ÷ ($4 × 4,200) = 3 pounds.

For labor we can multiply our known figures to get the flexible budget allowance for labor as $7 × 1.5 × 4,200 = $44,100. Comparing this figure to inputs at standard of $41,160 provides the labor usage variance of $44,100 − $41,160 = $2,940 F. In the Actual Costs column we can derive the actual wage rate by dividing actual costs by the actual labor hours and units produced to get $40,866 ÷ (1.4 × 4,200) = $6.95.

The values for the flexible budget allowance for variable overhead, inputs at standard, and actual variable overhead can now be found by multiplication. These figures are $22,050, $20,580, and $21,462, respectively. Once we have these totals, subtraction provides us with the variable overhead quantity variance $22,050 − $20,580 = $1,470 F and spending variance of $20,580 − $21,462 = $882 U.

Turning finally to fixed overhead, we know that the fixed overhead budget variance is the difference between the budget allowance for fixed overhead and the actual fixed overhead costs incurred. Therefore, we can find the budget allowance by subtraction to be $36,275 − $275 = $36,000.

Exhibit 18-7 presents the variance chart with all the data we have been able to derive so far. However, we have not yet determined the fixed overhead application rate, the fixed overhead applied to production, or the units of output anticipated in the master budget. To get this information we will need to look at the volume variance.

We know that the volume variance is the difference between the budgeted fixed overhead and the fixed overhead applied to production. Since our budget calls for fixed overhead of $36,000 and the volume variance is given as $1,800 F,

**EXHIBIT 18-7 Solution to the Demonstration Problem**

| | Actual Costs (*AP* × *AQ* × *UO*) | Price Variances | Actual Inputs at Standard Price (*SP* × *AQ* × *UO*) | Quantity Variances | Flexible Budget (*SP* × *SQ* × *UO*) |
|---|---|---|---|---|---|
| Direct materials | $4.05 × 3.1 × 4,200<br>$52,731 | | $4 × 3.1 × 4,200<br>$52,080 | | $4 × 3 × 4,200<br>$50,400 |
| | | $651 U | | $1,680 U | |
| Direct labor | $6.95 × 1.4 × 4,200<br>$40,866 | | $7 × 1.4 × 4,200<br>$41,160 | | $7 × 1.5 × 4,200<br>$44,100 |
| | | $294 F | | $2,940 F | |
| Variable overhead | $3.65 × 1.4 × 4,200<br>$21,462 | | $3.5 × 1.4 × 4,200<br>$20,580 | | $3.5 × 1.5 × 4,200<br>$22,050 |
| | | $882 U | | $1,470 F | |
| Fixed overhead | $36,275 | | | | $36,000 |
| | | | $275 U | | |

we must have applied $37,800 of fixed costs to production. In turn, the amount of fixed costs applied to production is the fixed overhead application rate multiplied by the standard direct labor hours allowed for the production actually achieved (because overhead was said to be applied on the basis of standard direct labor hours). The standard labor hours allowed for production is 1.5 hours per unit × 4,200 units = 6,300 hours, and the total fixed overhead applied was determined to be $37,800. Therefore, the fixed overhead application rate must be $37,800 ÷ 6,300 hours = $6 per labor hour.

Once we have the fixed overhead application rate, we can finally determine the number of units that were anticipated to be produced in the master budget. The fixed overhead application rate is determined by the master budget estimates. That is, the rate is determined by dividing budgeted fixed overhead by the number of standard labor hours called for in the master budget. We have determined that fixed overhead was budgeted to be $36,000 (recall that the budgeted amount of fixed overhead will be the same in both the flexible and master budgets). We have also determined that the fixed overhead application rate is $6 per direct labor hour. Therefore the master budget must have anticipated the use of 6,000 direct labor hours ($36,000/$6 per hour). Since we know that our standards call for 1.5 labor hours per unit, the master budget must have called for the production of 6,000 hours ÷ 1.5 hours per unit = 4,000 units.

The correct responses to each of the questions asked are as follows:

**a.** $4 per pound
**b.** $651 U
**c.** $52,731
**d.** $2,940 F
**e.** $6.95 per hour
**f.** $40,866
**g.** $44,100
**h.** $22,050
**i.** $21,462
**j.** $1,470 F efficiency, $882 U spending
**k.** $36,000
**l.** $37,800
**m.** $6 per labor hour
**n.** 4,000 units

## KEY TERMS AND CONCEPTS

Standard quantity
Ideal standard
Attainable standard
Standard price
Standard cost
Variances
Master budget
Flexible budget
[ Standard cost allowed
[ Standard cost earned
Budget variance
Favorable variance
Unfavorable variance
[ Quantity variance
[ Usage variance
[ Efficiency variance
[ Price variance
[ Rate variance
[ Spending variance
Fixed overhead application rate
[ Volume variance
[ Denominator variance

[Bracketed terms are equivalent in meaning.

## FURTHER READING

Demski, Joel S. "Analyzing the Effectiveness of the Traditional Standard Cost Variance," *Management Accounting* (October 1967), p. 9.

Guilfoyle, Harold B. "Measuring Production Efficiency," *The Canadian Chartered Accountant* (July 1964), p. 25.

Marcinko, David, and Enrico Petri. "Use of the Production Function in Calculation of Standard Cost Variances—An Extension," *The Accounting Review* (July 1984), p. 488.

Piper, Roswell M. "The Joint Cost Variance: A Comment," *The Accounting Review* (April 1977), p. 527.

Schaeberle, F. W., and Max Laudeman. "The Cost Accounting Practices of Firms Using Standard Costs," *Cost and Management* (July–August 1983), p. 21.

Solomons, David. "A Diagrammatic Representation of Standard Cost Variances," *Accounting Research* (January 1951), p. 46.

Truitt, Jack. "Does the Joint Variance Make Economic Sense?" *Cost and Management* (May–June 1985), p. 30.

Zannetos, Zenon S. "On the Mathematics of Variance Analysis," *The Accounting Review* (July 1963), p. 528.

## QUESTIONS AND EXERCISES

**18-1** What is meant by the term *standard cost earned* or *standard cost allowed?*

**18-2** What does the term *denominator volume* mean?

**18-3** Why would a firm use a combined approach for overhead variance analysis?

**18-4** When will the flexible budget variance for materials not be equal to standard materials cost earned less actual cost of purchases?

**18-5** What information is retained and what is lost if a combined approach is taken for the analysis of overhead variances?

**18-6** What purpose is achieved by separating the budget variance into price and quantity components?

**18-7** If fixed costs are fixed, how can a budget variance occur? Illustrate.

**18-8** How do price and quantity variances for materials differ if materials are carried at standard cost rather than actual cost?

**18-9** When a firm uses ideal material quantity standards, favorable quantity variances are usually bad. Why?

**18-10** If our firm purchased 90,000 pounds of materials at $2.10 per pound and the standard price for materials was $1.95 per pound, what is the price variance?

**18-11** Sisyphus, Inc., has had its ups and downs. To effect controls, it installed a standard cost system in its job shop. Data for a recent job are as follows:

| | Standard | Actual |
|---|---|---|
| Direct labor hours | 950 | 900 |
| Direct labor dollars | $1,900 | $1,850 |
| Units produced | 380 | 380 |

Compute the labor variances, label them, and indicate whether or not they are favorable.

**18-12** From the following information, determine the labor rate variance and the labor usage variance.

| | |
|---|---|
| Labor hours used at the standard wage rate | $1,680 |
| Labor hours used at the actual wage rate | $1,752 |
| Labor hours allowed at the standard wage rate | $1,750 |
| Labor hours allowed at the actual wage rate | $1,825 |

**18-13** Data concerning direct labor follow:

| | |
|---|---|
| Rate variance | $3,000 favorable |
| Budget variance | $8,000 unfavorable |
| Standard rate | $11 per hour |
| Actual hours | 6,000 |

Determine (a) the usage variance, (b) standard hours earned, and (c) the actual wage rate.

**18-14** In a normal day employees at Westside Packaging can produce 300 units per productive hour. The employees are paid for 8 hours a day, but only 7 hours of productive time is actually achieved. The remaining time is devoted to coffee breaks and set-up time. Employees are paid $7 per hour, which includes most fringe benefits. (a) What is the normally attainable standard labor hours allowed per unit?

(b) What is the normally attainable standard labor cost per unit? (c) During May the firm produced 46,200 units of product. Total wages of $1,352.40 were paid for 184 hours of work. Determine the labor efficiency and spending variances.

**18-15** From the following information determine the fixed overhead budget variance and the volume variance.

| | |
|---|---|
| Labor hours allowed for good output | 2,750 |
| Labor hours anticipated in the master budget | 3,000 |
| Fixed overhead anticipated in the flexible budget | $6,750 |
| Fixed overhead costs actually incurred | $7,000 |
| Actual labor hours used during the period | 2,800 |

**18-16** Robertson, Inc., applies overhead on the basis of output as measured by standard hours earned or allowed. At a standard capacity of 8,500 hours, overhead is $19,125 fixed and $14,875 variable. During the period, the following resulted.

| | |
|---|---|
| Actual hours | 8,200 |
| Standard hours | 8,300 |
| Fixed overhead | $19,000 |
| Variable overhead | $14,000 |

Determine (a) the overhead rates, (b) the budget and volume variances for combined overhead, and (c) the separate variances for fixed and variable overhead.

**18-17** (CPA). The following information pertains to Nell Company's production of one unit of its manufactured product during the month of June.

| | |
|---|---|
| Standard quantity of materials | 5 lb |
| Standard cost per pound | $0.20 |
| Standard direct labor hours | 0.4 |
| Standard wage rate per hour | $7.00 |
| Materials purchased | 100,000 lb |
| Cost of materials purchased | $0.17/lb |
| Materials consumed for manufacture of 10,000 units | 60,000 lb |
| Actual direct labor hours required for 10,000 units | 3,900 |
| Actual direct labor cost per hour | $7.20 |

The materials price variance is recognized when materials are purchased. Determine the price and quantity variances for materials and labor.

**18-18** Medal Metal Works operates on a job order basis. The firm does *not* inventory raw materials, they are purchased to order as a job requires with the provision that the supplier will take back any unused materials at the invoice price. Job TR-3 has the following unit standards.

| | |
|---|---|
| Direct materials (3 units @ $8) | $24 |
| Direct labor (2 hours @ $15) | 30 |
| Indirect costs (2 hours @ $10) | 20 |
| Total cost per finished unit | $74 |

The actual data on job TR-3 were as follows:

| | |
|---|---|
| Units produced | 1,000 |
| Direct materials purchased | 3,000 @ $9 each |
| Supplemental purchases of direct materials | 100 @ $9 each |
| Direct materials used | 3,050 |
| Direct labor (2,100 hours) | $31,000 |

Determine the price and quantity variances for direct materials and labor.

**18-19** Dirmat, Inc., produced at a level that resulted in $12,096 being the standard cost allowed for materials for the output level attained. One pound of material is allowed for each unit of output, but there was an unfavorable usage variance of $630 arising from the use of 100 excess pounds of material. The price variance (reported at the point of purchase) was $1,300 unfavorable, and the inventory of this material increased by 800 pounds during the period.

Determine (a) the standard price per pound, (b) the actual number of pounds placed into production, (c) the actual number of pounds purchased, and (d) the actual price paid per pound.

**18-20** A clinic charges its patients on the basis of direct costs incurred plus fixed costs at the rate of $20 per hour. The fixed cost rate of $20 is based on the assumption of 6,000 patient hours monthly. (It is assumed that the average patient requires $\frac{1}{2}$ hour.) For September, 11,000 patients were seen and the following costs were recorded.

| | |
|---|---|
| Assigned (applied) fixed costs | $126,000 |
| Budget variance (unfavorable) | 12,000 |

Determine (a) how many patient hours were recorded, (b) the budgeted fixed overhead, (c) the volume variance, and (d) the actual fixed overhead.

## PROBLEMS AND CASES

**18-21 Variances for step costs.**

KSM Electronics prides itself on the high quality of its products. To assure high quality, the firm's finished products are subject to rigid inspection. Inspectors are budgeted to inspect 500 units per month and are paid $1,500 per month. For the month of January, there were 10 inspectors who earned a total of $16,200.

**Required**

**a.** Calculate the appropriate variances under each of the following assumptions.

**1.** Units inspected during January were 4,900.

**2.** Units inspected during January were 5,720.

**b.** If 5,150 units were inspected in January and management chose to pay overtime to the existing inspectors (the spending variance is due solely to overtime) rather than hire another inspector, did management make a wise decision?

**18-22 Direct cost variances.**

To control costs, West Side Products employs a standard cost system for direct costs, and variances are recorded and reported as they occur. The standards for one of its products are

| | |
|---|---|
| Direct labor (2 hours @ $10) | $20 |
| Material A (4 liters @ $5) | 20 |
| Material B (5 kilograms @ $2) | 10 |
| Standard direct cost per unit | $50 |

During the period the firm produced 1,050 units, incurring the following costs.

| | |
|---|---|
| Direct labor | 2,050 hours at a cost of $21,000 |
| Material A | Purchased 5,000 liters at a cost of $26,000; used 4,500 liters |
| Material B | Purchased 4,800 kilograms at a cost of $9,500; used 5,000 kilograms |

**Required**

Determine, in good form, all variances from standard.

**18-23 Finding unknowns.**

The Chase Company's master budget for April called for the production of 7,000 units of product. At that level of activity direct labor was budgeted at $84,000. During April, 7,200 good units of product were actually produced. Labor was in fact paid $6.10 per hour, resulting in a $1,430 unfavorable rate variance. The direct labor budget variance for April turned out to be $830 unfavorable.

**Required**

Determine the standard wage rate, the standard number of labor hours allowed for each unit of product, the actual total number of direct labor hours used during April, and the direct labor usage variance for April (in dollars).

**18-24 Materials variances with normally attainable standards.**

Billion Burgers sells a large number of hamburgers. One of their keys to success is that they insist on freshness. Any hamburger not sold within 15 minutes of preparation is thrown away. The standard cost of a unit consists of the cost of 3 pickle slices, one-tenth of an ounce of condiments, 1 hamburger patty, and 1 bun. The total standard cost for these ingredients is $0.35. With good planning the firm estimates throwing away only 5% of the hamburgers produced.

**Required**

**a.** How many units' worth of materials per hamburger sold would be allowed in a normally attainable standard?

**b.** What would the standard cost per hamburger be with the standard in (a)?

**c.** In April, Billion Burgers sold 55,000 hamburgers. They had prepared 61,000 hamburgers and thrown away 6,000. If the total cost of pickles, condiments, patties, and buns was $22,000, determine the materials quantity and price variances for April.

**18-25 Direct cost standards and usage variances.**

State Institution Corporation is state-owned and manufactures license plates. Management of SIC has been confronted frequently with work stoppages and high materials losses. In order to assess the effects of these problems, a standard cost system has been installed. SIC sells the finished plates to several states at $3 per pair. The following standards have been set.

| | |
|---|---|
| Labor | $1.00 per hour |
| Materials | $1.00 per blank[a] |
| Other direct costs | $0.50 per plate |
| Output | 100 plates per hour per employee |

[a]Each blank makes four plates.

SIC has 200 employees assigned to this project who work 9 hours a day, 6 days per week (overtime is paid at the straight rate).

During a recent week the results were as follows:

| | |
|---|---|
| Output | 400,000 plates |
| Blanks | 110,000 |
| Hours | 9,400 |
| Other direct costs | $232,000 |

**Required**

**a.** Assuming that there are no problems, what is management's weekly production goal?

**b.** What is the standard cost of a pair of license plates?

**c.** Assuming there are no price variances, what are the usage variances for the week?

**18-26 Materials variances and exchange rates.**

The most important raw material used by the Alabama Fabricating Company is slab steel, which is imported from Argentina. The firm has four major product lines. The standard quantity of steel required per unit of each is provided in the following schedule.

| Product Line | Steel per Unit |
|---|---|
| KD casting | 400 pounds |
| XT casting | 600 pounds |
| RM casting | 200 pounds |
| LL casting | 300 pounds |

The standard cost per ton of steel is $270. This standard was set when the currency exchange rate with Argentina was expected to average 318 pesos = $1.

During the year the firm produced the following quantities of its products.

| Product Line | Production |
|---|---|
| KD casting | 2,000 units |
| XT casting | 2,500 units |
| RM casting | 5,000 units |
| LL casting | 8,000 units |

The firm purchased and used 2,920 tons of steel at a total cost of $735,000.

**Required**

**a.** Determine the traditional materials price and quantity variances.

**b.** Further analysis revealed that the actual average exchange rate during the year was 350 pesos = $1. Separate the materials price variance into two components—one due to the exchange rate change and the other due to all other causes.

**c.** Relying on your analysis in part (b), evaluate the performance of the firm's purchasing department.

**18-27 Standard direct cost variances: Working backward to actual input** (CMA adapted).
The Lonn Manufacturing Company produces two primary chemical products to be used as base ingredients for a variety of products. The 19X8 budget for the two products (000s omitted) was as follows:

| | X-4 | Z-8 | Total |
|---|---|---|---|
| Production output in gallons | 600 | 600 | 1,200 |
| Direct materials | $1,500 | $1,875 | $3,375 |
| Direct labor | 900 | 900 | 1,800 |
| Total prime manufacturing cost | $2,400 | $2,775 | $5,175 |

The following planning assumptions were used for the budget:

Direct materials yield of 96%.
Direct labor rate of $6 per hour.

The actual results for 19X8 were (000s omitted)

| | X-4 | Z-8 | Total |
|---|---|---|---|
| Production output in gallons | 570.0 | 658.0 | 1,228.0 |
| Direct materials | $1,368.0 | $2,138.5 | $3,506.5 |
| Direct labor | 936.0 | 1,092.0 | 2,028.0 |
| Total prime manufacturing cost | $2,304.0 | $3,230.5 | $5,534.5 |

The actual production yield was 95% for X-4 and 94% for Z-8. The direct labor cost per hour for both products was $6.50.

**Required**

**a.** Calculate for product X-4:
  **1.** The direct materials price variance.
  **2.** The direct materials efficiency (yield) variance.

**b.** Calculate for product Z-8:
  **1.** The direct labor rate variance.
  **2.** The direct labor efficiency variance.

**18-28 Direct labor: Comprehensive.**
A firm's master budget called for the production of 20,000 units, resulting in a total labor cost of $180,000. During the year labor was actually paid $6.20 per hour, yielding an unfavorable labor rate variance of $5,500. For the actual output achieved, 27,000 labor hours were allowed. The flexible budget allowance for labor was $18,000 less than the master budget allowance.

**Required**

Determine the following.

**a.** The total cost for direct labor per the flexible budget
**b.** The actual number of units of output achieved
**c.** The actual number of labor hours required per unit produced
**d.** The labor usage variance
**e.** The budgeted number of hours allowed per unit of output
**f.** Total actual labor costs
**g.** The budgeted cost per direct labor hour
**h.** The labor budget variance
**i.** The standard cost for the actual number of labor hours used

**18-29 Direct cost variances.**

The Tsingtao Company is a joint venture with the People's Republic of China. The assembly plant is located in Ningpo, on the eastern coast of China. The company expected to produce 20,000 units of product in April. At that level of output, the firm budgeted the following costs for April.

| | | |
|---|---|---|
| Materials | (@ 2.80 yuan per pound) | 173,600 Y |
| Labor | (@ 7 yuan per hour) | 350,000 |
| | | 523,600 Y |

During April the firm produced 19,100 units of product. The firm purchased and used 57,300 pounds of materials costing 163,305 yuan. Labor was paid 318,206 yuan for the 46,795 hours worked.

**Required**

**a.** Determine the price and quantity variances for materials and labor.

**b.** The government refuses to allow the company to profit from the exploitation of workers. Exploitation is defined as paying workers less than budgeted amounts or getting more production from employees than anticipated. Profits from the exploitation of labor are subject to a 150% tax. What is the amount of tax, if any, in April?

**18-30 Standard direct cost variances.**

Phizz is a specialty chemical produced in batches. Normal production as given by the master budget is 100 batches per week. The standard direct cost and usage per batch are as follows:

| | |
|---|---|
| Direct labor A (3 hours @ $8) | $ 24 |
| Direct labor B (2 hours @ $10) | 20 |
| Direct material X (6 pounds @ $6) | 36 |
| Direct material Y (5 gallons @ $4) | 20 |
| Total direct cost per batch | $100 |

All direct cost variances are isolated as they occur.

Data for the week just ended are as follows:

1. Production amounted to 103 batches.
2. For direct labor A, 315 hours costing $2,472 were used.
3. For direct labor B, 210 hours costing $2,050 were used.
4. For direct material X, 700 pounds were purchased at a cost of $4,130, and 650 pounds were used.

5. For direct material Y, 500 gallons were purchased at a cost of $2,060 and 510 gallons were used.

**Required**
Prepare, in good form, a schedule showing all variances for each type of labor and material.

**18-31 Standard indirect cost variances.**
Phizz is a specialty chemical produced in batches. Normal (denominator) volume is 100 batches per week. The weekly flexible budget for indirect costs is $3,600 plus $5 per standard hour of direct labor. Indirect costs are absorbed on the basis of standard hours of direct labor.

Data for the week just ended are as follows:

1. Production amounted to 103 batches.
2. There were 315 hours of direct labor used, at a cost of $2,472.
3. The standards allow for 3 hours of direct labor per batch.
4. Actual variable overhead for the week was $1,550.
5. Actual fixed overhead for the week was $3,700.

Management employs the three-way, or combined, approach to analyze indirect costs.

**Required**
a. Determine, in good form, the indirect cost variances for the week.
b. Calculate the fixed and variable components of the combined spending variance for indirect costs.

**18-32 Standard indirect cost variances.**
El Toro, Inc., manufactures bulk fertilizers. The following data for direct materials, direct labor, and overhead is for the third-quarter of operations.

| | Planned Costs and Hours at Denominator Volume | Actual Costs and Hours at Actual Activity | Standard Costs Charged to Work-in-Process for Actual Output |
|---|---|---|---|
| Direct materials cost | Not given | $ 55,000 | $ 57,000 |
| Direct labor cost | Not given | 46,000 | 47,500 |
| Overhead[a] | $50,000 | 40,000 | 47,500 |
| Total | ? | $141,000 | $152,000 |
| Direct labor hours | 10,000 | 9,000 | 9,500 |

[a]The flexible budget allows variable overhead costs in the amount of $2 per actual hour worked. Overhead is applied to work-in-process on the basis of standard hours.

The firm produces only one product, although it employs job order cost techniques. The product is produced in batches, and each batch is accounted for as a separate job. During the third quarter, 1,000 batches were produced and 900 batches were sold. There were no beginning inventories.

**Required**
Using the combined approach, determine (in as much detail as possible) all indirect cost variances.

18-33 **Graph for fixed overhead variances.**
The graph shown is for actual, budgeted, and absorbed fixed overhead.

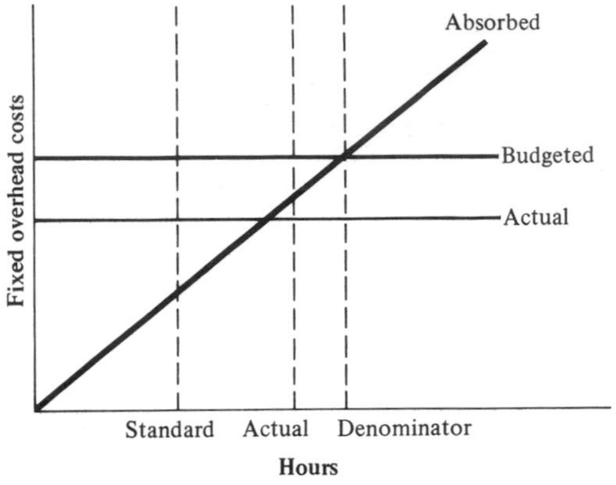


**Required**
Determine each of the following variances and indicate whether it is favorable, unfavorable, zero, or indeterminate.

**a.** The spending variance
**b.** The volume (or denominator) variance
**c.** The total or net variance (i.e., applied versus actual costs)

18-34 **Graph for combined overhead variances.**
The graph shown is for actual, budgeted, and absorbed overhead on a combined basis.

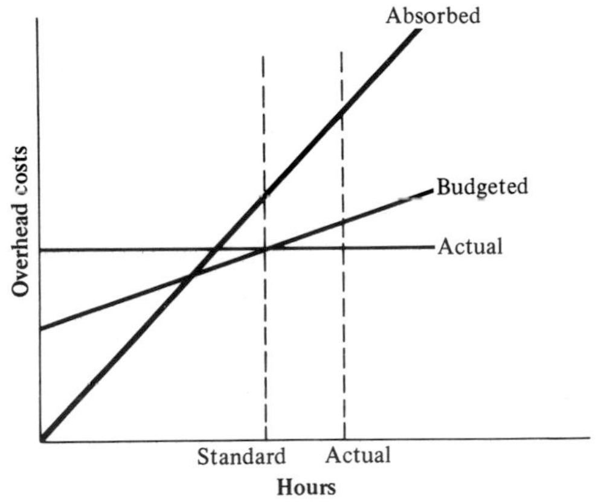


**Required**
Determine each of the following variances and indicate whether it is favorable, unfavorable, zero, or indeterminate.

**a.** The spending variance
**b.** The efficiency (usage) variance
**c.** The volume (denominator) variance
**d.** The budget variance
**e.** The total or net variance (i.e., applied versus actual costs)

**18-35 Finding unknown balances.**
Overhead is applied to production on the basis of standard labor hours. Find the values of the missing information, indicated by lowercase letters (a-r). Each case is independent of the other.

| | Phi Company | Pho Company |
|---|---|---|
| Number of labor hours expected in the master budget | a | 5,000 |
| Standard variable overhead rate per labor hour | $2 | j |
| Standard labor hours allowed per unit | 5 | 2 |
| Actual labor hours used per unit | b | 2.1 |
| Actual variable overhead rate per hour | c | k |
| Fixed overhead application rate per hour | $4 | l |
| Actual total variable overhead costs | d | $15,372 |
| Actual total fixed overhead costs | e | $23,750 |
| Variable overhead allowed in the flexible budget | $21,000 | m |
| Fixed overhead allowed in the flexible budget | $40,000 | n |
| Fixed overhead applied to production | f | $25,000 |
| Variable overhead spending variance | $504 F | o |
| Variable overhead efficiency variance | $840 F | $720 U |
| Fixed overhead volume variance | g | $1,000 F |
| Fixed overhead budget variance | $600 U | p |
| Number of units expected to be produced in master budget | h | q |
| Number of units actually produced during the period | i | r |

**18-36 Choice of capacity and variances for overhead** (SMA adapted).
The Multi-Rate Company uses a standard cost system and applies overhead to product using an average activity overhead rate. Proposals have been made to change to a practical capacity rate or to an expected activity rate for 19X1.

Average activity is 75% of practical capacity. The expected activity for 19X1 is only 60% of practical capacity. An overhead rate of $10.50 per direct labour hour has been calculated for 19X1 using an overhead budget at average activity. The overhead budget at an average activity of 13,500 direct labour hours (per year) is as follows:

| | |
|---|---|
| Variable overhead | $ 60,750 |
| Fixed overhead | 81,000 |
| Total budgeted overhead | $141,750 |

$$\text{Overhead rate} = \frac{\$141{,}750}{13{,}500} = \$10.50 \text{ per direct labour hour}$$

The actual activity in the month of January was 1,050 direct labour hours. Standard direct labour hours for output produced were 1,075 hours. The actual overhead for January was $11,635. Assume that January is 1/12 of the year.

**Required**

**a.** Determine the overhead rate if practical capacity is used as the base (denominator) activity.

**b.** Determine the overhead rate if activity expected for 19X1 is used as the base (denominator) activity.

**c.** Determine the combined overhead spending variance for January.

**d.** Determine the denominator (volume) variance, assuming the use of (1) an expected activity overhead rate and (2) a practical capacity overhead rate.

**e.** Briefly discuss the meaning of the variances determined in (d).

**18-37 Direct and indirect cost variances** (SMA adapted).
Arrow Ltd. uses a standard cost system in accounting for the cost of one of its products. The budgeted monthly production is 75 units per day for 22 working days per month. Standard cost for direct labour is 15 hours per unit at $5.00 per hour. Budgeted cost for manufacturing overhead is set as follows:

| | |
|---|---|
| Fixed overhead per month | $173,250 |
| Variable overhead per month | 74,250 |
| Total budgeted overhead | $247,500 |
| Manufacturing overhead rate per dollar of direct labour cost | 200% |

During the month of April the plant operated for only 21 days. Cost of production of 1,604 units was

| | |
|---|---|
| Direct materials (87,000 litres) | $ 870,000 |
| Direct labour (24,610 hours) | 125,511 |
| Fixed manufacturing overhead | 186,000 |
| Variable manufacturing overhead | 61,300 |
| | $1,242,811 |

**Required**
Determine all direct and indirect cost variances in as much detail as the data permit.

**18-38 Variances for direct materials and overhead.**
B. Backgammon, Inc., produces a well-known game by the same name. The firm prints a playing board, adds 30 checkerlike playing pieces and some dice, and puts it all into a fancy box. Only the playing pieces and boards are considered direct materials. The boxes and dice are considered part of overhead. All labor is also considered overhead. The master budget for March called for

| | |
|---|---|
| Sales (3,000 sets @ $10) | $30,000 |
| Playing pieces (90,000 @ $0.07) | 6,300 |
| Boards (3,000 @ $1.50) | 4,500 |
| Variable overhead (@ $0.80 per board) | 2,400 |
| Fixed overhead | 5,000 |
| Net income | $11,800 |

Overhead is applied on the basis of the number of playing boards produced. Actual production for the period turned out to be 2,800 sets. Actual costs incurred were as follows:

| | |
|---|---|
| Playing pieces (82,000) | $6,150 |
| Boards (2,875) | 4,025 |
| Variable overhead | 2,300 |
| Fixed overhead | 4,960 |

**Required**

**a.** Determine all standard cost variances, including the volume variance.

**b.** Evaluate the material usage variance for playing pieces. Is it good or bad?

**18-39 Variances from standard** (SMA adapted).
Angie's Manufacturing Company has recently adopted a standard costing system for product costing purposes. The following standards have been established.

| | |
|---|---|
| Direct materials | $5.00 per unit |
| Direct labour (2 hr @ $3.00) | $6.00 per unit |

Budgeted overhead for the month of April (based on expected activity of 4,000 direct labour hours) is as follows:

| | |
|---|---|
| Variable overhead | |
| Indirect labour (6,000 hr) | $15,000 |
| Indirect materials | 4,000 |
| | $19,000 |
| Fixed overhead | 8,000 |
| Total overhead | $27,000 |

Overhead is applied on the basis of labour hours. The average activity per month is 5,000 direct labour hours. The company calculates overhead rates based on average activity.

Results for the month of April are as follows:

| | |
|---|---|
| Units produced | 2,100 |
| Direct materials used | $11,000 |
| Direct labour (4,320 hr) | 13,250 |
| Indirect labour (6,400 hr) | 16,960 |
| Indirect materials | 4,450 |
| Fixed overhead | 8,125 |
| Total costs | $53,785 |

There was no beginning or ending work-in-process inventory.

**Required**

Calculate all variances in as much detail as the data permit.

**18-40 Variances from standards and plan** (CICA adapted).
Wilson Industries manufactures an industrial detergent. The firm has experienced severe cost pressures resulting from recent labour contract settlements, coupled with a deterioration in manufacturing efficiency. Equivalent unit inventories of work-in-process and finished goods have remained virtually unchanged during the past 4 years. Inventories are costed at "standard" and all manufacturing cost variances are charged to the Cost of Sales account at the end of each year.

An analysis of Cost of Sales revealed the following for the years ended September 30:

| | 19X7 Actual | 19X8 Actual | 19X8 Plan |
|---|---|---|---|
| Direct materials | $445,900 | $408,000 | $460,000 |
| Direct labour | 191,100 | 201,600 | 200,000 |
| Variable overhead | 100,100 | 88,200 | 100,000 |
| Fixed overhead | 100,100 | 112,000 | 100,000 |
| Total cost of sales | $837,200 | $809,800 | $860,000 |

Included in the foregoing analysis is a write-off of $10,100 during 19X8 as a result of spring flood damage. This charge was allocated to materials ($2,100) and fixed overhead ($8,000).

During 19X8, 82,000 pounds of materials and 42,000 direct labour hours were consumed in the manufacturing process. During the year, 80,000 units of good product were produced and sold.

The standard cost of the detergent is determined to be as follows:

| | |
|---|---|
| Direct materials (1 pound) | $4.60 |
| Direct labour ($\frac{1}{2}$ hour) | 2.00 |
| Variable overhead (@ $2.00 per direct labour hour) | 1.00 |
| Fixed overhead | 1.00 |
| Total standard cost per unit | $8.60 |

Combined variable and fixed overhead are applied to product on the basis of $2.00 per unit, based on a normal activity of 100,000 units, which represents 80% of the company's manufacturing capacity.

For the previous year, 19X7, manufacturing records revealed a net unfavorable cost variance from standard of approximately 7%. Direct materials variances are not recognized until after the manufacturing process commences.

**Required**

Prepare an analysis of all variances from standards for 19X8.

**18-41 Direct and indirect cost variances.**

Warren, Inc., has established unit standards and a weekly budget for its product as follows:

| | Unit Standard | Master Budget |
|---|---|---|
| Direct materials (3 units @ $10) | $30 | $30,000 |
| Direct labor (3 hours @ $5) | 15 | 15,000 |
| Variable overhead (3 hours @ $2)[a] | 6 | 6,000 |
| Fixed overhead (3 hours @ $8)[a] | 24 | 24,000 |
| Totals | $75 | $75,000 |

[a]The overhead is based on a weekly denominator volume of 3,000 standard hours, or 1,000 finished units. Denominator volume represents management's weekly production objective.

For the week in question, Warren actually produced 1,050 units. In doing so, they purchased 3,000 units of material at a cost of $31,000 and used 3,100 units. Direct laborers worked 3,000 hours and were paid $14,900. Variable overhead amounted to $6,300 and fixed overhead was $25,000.

**Required**
Determine all direct and indirect cost variances in as much detail as possible.

**18-42 Standard direct costs** (CPA adapted).
Vogue Fashions, Inc., manufactures ladies' blouses of one quality, produced in lots to fill each special order from its customers, comprised of department stores located in various cities. Vogue sews the particular stores' labels on the blouses. The standard direct costs for a dozen blouses are

| | |
|---|---|
| Direct materials (24 yards @ $1.10) | $26.40 |
| Direct labor (3 hours @ $4.90) | 14.70 |
| Standard direct cost per dozen | $41.10 |

During June, Vogue worked on three orders, for which the month's job cost records disclose the following:

| Lot Number | Units in Lot (dozens) | Material Used (yards) | Hours Worked |
|---|---|---|---|
| 22 | 1,000 | 24,100 | 2,980 |
| 23 | 1,700 | 40,440 | 5,130 |
| 24 | 1,200 | 28,825 | 2,890 |

The following information is also available.

1. Vogue purchased 95,000 yards of material during June at a cost of $106,400. The materials price variance is recorded when goods are purchased. All inventories are carried at standard cost.
2. Direct labor during June amounted to $55,000. According to payroll records, production employees were paid $5.00 per hour.
3. There was no work in process at June 1. During June, lots 22 and 23 were completed. All material was issued for lot 24, which was 80% completed as to direct labor.

**Required**
a. Prepare a schedule showing the computation of standard cost of lots 22, 23, and 24 for June.
b. Determine the materials price variance for June. Indicate whether the variance is favorable or unfavorable.
c. Prepare a schedule showing, for each lot produced during June, computations of the (1) materials quantity variance in yards, (2) labor efficiency variance in hours, and (3) labor rate variance in dollars. Indicate whether each variance is favorable or unfavorable.

**18-43 Standard indirect costs.**
Refer to 18-42. The standard indirect costs for a dozen blouses are 3 hours at $4.00, or $12.00 total.

Manufacturing overhead during June amounted to $45,600. A total of $576,000 was budgeted for manufacturing overhead for the year, based on estimated production at the plant's normal capacity of 48,000 dozen blouses annually. Manufacturing overhead at this level of production is 40% fixed and 60% variable. Production is budgeted to occur uniformly throughout the year. Manufacturing overhead is applied on the basis of direct labor hours.

**Required**

**a.** What is the algebraic flexible budget per month for manufacturing overhead?

**b.** Prepare a schedule showing computations of the manufacturing overhead variances for June. The firm calculates three variances for overhead: spending, usage (efficiency), and volume. Indicate whether the variances are favorable or unfavorable. Fixed overhead is incurred relatively uniformly over the year.

**18-44 Comprehensive variance problem.**

Encounters Three prepared the following master budget for the year.

| | |
|---|---|
| Sales (18,000 units @ $30) | $540,000 |
| Materials (9,000 lb @ $10) | 90,000 |
| Labor (36,000 hr @ $6) | 216,000 |
| Variable overhead (36,000 hr @ $2) | 72,000 |
| Fixed overhead | 90,000 |
| Gross margin | $ 72,000 |

At the end of the year the following actual results were achieved.

| | |
|---|---|
| Sales (20,000 units @ $30) | $600,000 |
| Materials (10,500 lb) | 99,750 |
| Labor ($6.25 per hr) | 243,750 |
| Variable overhead | 76,050 |
| Fixed overhead | 87,000 |
| Gross margin | $ 93,450 |

The flexible budget for overhead is related to the actual hours worked. There were no beginning or ending inventories, nor were any anticipated in the budget.

**Required**

Calculate the following variances:

**a.** Materials price variance
**b.** Materials usage variance
**c.** Labor rate variance
**d.** Labor efficiency variance
**e.** Variable overhead spending variance
**f.** Variable overhead efficiency variance
**g.** Fixed overhead budget variance
**h.** Fixed overhead volume variance

**18-45 Comprehensive standard costs** (CPA adapted).

The Groomer Company manufactures two products, florimene and glyoxide, used in the plastics industry. The company uses a flexible budget in its standard cost system to develop variances. Selected data are as follows:

| | Florimene | Glyoxide |
|---|---|---|
| Data on standard costs | | |
| Raw materials per unit | 3 lb @ $1.00 per lb | 4 lb @ $1.10 per lb |
| Direct labor per unit | 5 hr @ $2.00 per hr | 6 hr @ $2.50 per hr |
| Variable factory overhead per unit | $3.20 per direct labor hour | $3.50 per direct labor hour |
| Fixed factory overhead per month | $20,700 | $26,520 |
| Normal activity per month | 5,750 direct labor hours | 7,800 direct labor hours |
| Units produced in September | 1,000 | 1,200 |
| Costs incurred for September | | |
| Raw materials | 3,100 lb @ $0.90 per lb | 4,700 lb @ $1.15 per lb |
| Direct labor | 4,900 hr @ $1.95 per hr | 7,400 hr @ $2.55 per hr |
| Variable factory overhead | $16,170 | $25,234 |
| Fixed factory overhead | $20,930 | $26,400 |

**Required**

Prepare an analysis of the variances from standard costs for each product.

18-46 **Process and standard costing: Comprehensive and challenging—requires prior study of Chapter 15** (CPA adapted).

Hi-Vault, Inc., produces a special vaulting pole used in track and field events. Hi-Vault produces only one product and accounts for the production of this product using a standard cost system.

Following are the standards for the production of one pole.

| | |
|---|---|
| 3 units of item A at $1.00 per unit | $3.00 |
| 1 unit of item B at $0.50 per unit | 0.50 |
| 4 units of item C at $0.30 per unit | 1.20 |
| 20 minutes of direct labor at $4.50 per hour | 1.50 |
| Overhead applied at the rate of $9.00 per hour | 3.00 |
| Standard cost of one pole | $9.20 |

The flexible budget is $120,000 per year plus $5.00 per hour actually worked. At the time of purchase, raw materials are recorded at standard. The various inventories at December 31, 19X5, are as follows:

| | |
|---|---|
| Raw materials: | 15,000 units of item A, 4,000 units of item B, and 20,000 units of item C. |
| Work-in-process: | 9,000 poles, which were 100% complete as to items A and B, 50% complete as to item C, and 30% complete as to processing. |
| Finished goods: | 4,800 poles. |

Following is a schedule of raw materials purchased and direct labor and overhead incurred for the year ended December 31, 19X6:

| Item | Number of Units or Hours | Unit Cost | Total Amount |
|---|---|---|---|
| A | 290,000 | $1.15 | $333,500 |
| B | 101,000 | 0.49 | 49,490 |
| C | 367,000 | 0.35 | 128,450 |
| Labor | 34,100 | 4.60 | 156,860 |
| Overhead | — | — | 290,000 |

During the year Hi-Vault sold 90,000 units (finished poles sold). The various inventories at December 31, 19X6 are as follows:

| | |
|---|---|
| Raw materials: | 28,300 units of item A, 2,100 units of item B, and 28,900 units of item C. |
| Work-in-process: | 7,500 units, which were 100% complete as to items A and B, 60% complete as to item C, and 20% complete as to processing. |
| Finished goods: | 5,100 poles. |

**Required**

Determine the following:

**a.** The current period's equivalent units of product for each input

**b.** The current period's variances for all direct and indirect costs

**c.** The denominator volume

**18-47 Standard cost, job order, and flexible budgets** (CPA adapted).

The Smith Company uses a standard cost system. The standards are based on a budget for operations at the anticipated rate of production for the current period. The company records variances from standard as soon as they can be isolated. The flexible budget is based on actual direct labor hours; hence, three overhead variances are calculated at the end of the period. Current standards are as follows:

| | |
|---|---|
| Materials | |
| Material A | $1.20 per unit |
| Material B | 2.60 per unit |
| Direct labor | 2.05 per hour |

The contents of finished products are as follows:

| | Special Widgets | Deluxe Widgets |
|---|---|---|
| Material A | 12 units | 12 units |
| Material B | 6 units | 8 units |
| Direct labor | 14 hours | 20 hours |

The general ledger does not include a finished goods inventory account; costs are transferred directly from work-in-process to cost of sales at the time finished products are sold.

The budget and operating data for the month of August are summarized as follows:

| | |
|---|---|
| Budget | |
| Projected direct labor hours | 9,000 hr |
| Fixed manufacturing overhead | $ 4,500 |
| Variable manufacturing overhead | $13,500 |
| Operating data | |
| Sales | |
| 500 special widgets | $52,700 |
| 100 deluxe widgets | $16,400 |
| Purchases | |
| Material A (8,500 units) | $ 9,725 |
| Material B (1,800 units) | $ 5,635 |
| Direct labor hours | |
| Standard | 9,600 hr |
| Actual | 10,000 hr |
| Wages paid | |
| 500 hours @ $2.10 | |
| 8,000 hours @ $2.00 | |
| 1,500 hours @ $1.90 | |
| Manufacturing overhead | $20,125 |

Materials requisitions were as follows:

| | Material A (units) | Material B (units) |
|---|---|---|
| Issued from stores | | |
| Standard quantity | 8,400 | 3,200 |
| Over standard | 400 | 150 |
| Returned to stores | 75 | — |

**Required**

**a.** What is the predetermined overhead rate for variable overhead, fixed overhead, and combined overhead?

**b.** What is the standard cost of a special widget and a deluxe widget?

**c.** Prepare the following analyses of variances: (1) price and quantity variances for material A, material B, and direct labor; and (2) spending, usage, and volume variances for overhead.

**18-48 Cost-volume-profit pricing and standard cost variances** (CICA adapted). Zee Ltd. has several divisions and has just built a new plant which is capable of making up to 20,000 units of a product called zlip. Management has introduced a standard cost system to aid it in performance evaluation of its various managers and for establishing a selling price for zlip. At the present time, product zlip does not have any competition and management has priced it at standard variable and fixed manufacturing cost, plus 60%. Management hopes that this price can be maintained for several years.

For the first year of operations, ending July 31, 19X8, management plans to make 1,000 units of zlip each month. In 19X9 and subsequent fiscal years, production is expected to be 1,500 units per month. In the first month of operations, August 19X7, management expected that employees would not be familiar with the production methods. Thus, management budgeted for direct labor hours to be 20% in excess of standard hours per unit. In September 19X7 and in subsequent months, management is expecting standard direct labor to be attained.

The company's experience in its other plants and with similar products indicates that variable manufacturing overhead will vary in proportion to actual direct labor dollars. For the first several years only product zlip will be manufactured in the new plant. Fixed manufacturing costs of the new plant per year are expected to be $990,000 and incurred evenly throughout the year.

The standard variable manufacturing cost (after the break-in period) per unit of product zlip has been set as follows:

| | |
|---|---|
| Direct materials (4 pieces @ $10 per piece) | $ 40.00 |
| Direct labor (10 hours @ $15 per hour) | 150.00 |
| Variable manufacturing overhead (50% of direct labor cost) | 75.00 |
| Total | $265.00 |

At the end of August 19X7, the actual costs incurred in making 950 units of zlip were as follows:

| | |
|---|---|
| Direct materials (3,850 pieces @ $9.80) | $ 37,730 |
| Direct labor (12,000 hours @ $16.00) | 192,000 |
| Variable manufacturing overhead | 97,350 |
| Fixed manufacturing overhead | 86,110 |

Management now wishes to compare actual costs to budget and standards so as to ascertain what corrective action should be taken.

**Required**

**a.** What selling price should Zee Ltd. set for product zlip, in accordance with the stated pricing formula? Explain.

**b.** Compute all variances between actual and standard cost of direct labor using a flexible budget.

**c.** Compute all variances between actual and applied manufacturing overhead.

# APPENDIX 18

# RECORD KEEPING IN A STANDARD COST SYSTEM

Although standard cost systems are expensive to set up initially, they do provide valuable managerial information. In addition, the existence of a standard cost system simplifies record keeping. The accounting procedures differ slightly depending on whether we use job costing or process costing. Therefore we will examine both systems.

## STANDARD JOB COSTING

In a job shop environment the standards for each job are estimated at the time an order is accepted. You may have noticed, for example, that when you bring your car into a dealer's repair shop, the service manager will consult a manual that provides a list of all the parts necessary for a repair and also provides an average labor time to make the repair. Next, the service manager will price out the cost of the materials (parts) needed by consulting a supplier's current catalog. Finally, the labor cost is priced using the firm's labor rate. In this situation the labor rate usually consists of the firm's labor cost, an overhead application rate, and the firm's desired markup for profit. By including all these factors in the labor rate, the standard cost sheet can then be used as the customer invoice. Although they use a predetermined markup for profit, bookkeeping can easily convert the billed labor rate to a more traditional cost rate.

Many industries are similar to the auto repair business in that trade associations or profit-oriented service firms have developed estimates of standard costs for the products or services rendered by the industry. However, firms in many other industries will have to use the methods we described in Chapter 3 of this text to develop their own standards.

However determined, once the standards have been recorded on the job sheet, the job sheet or work order will follow the order through the production process. If the firm works on relatively few jobs, each of which has a major impact on profitability, we may wish to calculate variances on each job. On the other hand, if we work on a large number of relatively small jobs, we may wish to defer the calculation of variances and do them periodically. The calculation of variances on a periodic basis parallels the calculation under a process costing system, which we will discuss subsequently. So in this section we will restrict our attention to systems that report variances on a per-job basis.

### Materials Variances

When an order is accepted, a copy of the job sheet is forwarded to the materials storeroom so that the proper materials can be issued. We are likely to keep a stock of commonly used materials on hand. Unusual items, however, will have to be purchased. Typically, materials price variances will be identified at the time of purchase. Thus, regardless of whether the materials are special orders or common stock items, the bookkeeping will be the same. Let us assume that the storeroom purchased 1,000 units of product whose standard price was \$2, but due to an unexpected price change, we actually paid \$2.05. The purchase would then be recorded as follows:

| | | |
|---|---|---|
| Raw Materials Inventory | 2,000 | |
| Materials Price Variance | 50 | |
| Cash (or Accounts Payable) | | 2,050 |

We can note two things. First, unfavorable variances will show up as debits. An easy way to remember this is that an unfavorable variance increases our expenses, and increased expenses are represented by debits. Favorable variances will of course show up as credits. Second, note that separating the variance at the time of purchase means that we will carry our raw materials inventory at standard prices.

It is particularly important to separate materials price variances at the point of purchase for a job shop operation. Typically our standard costs will be used for the purpose of setting the selling price of jobs. If there are substantial materials price increases, we want to know about them as soon as possible so that we can adjust our standards for future pricing.

If the storeroom issues all anticipated materials for the job at its inception, the determination of materials usage variances can be quickly and easily noted. If more materials are required for the job, an excess materials requisition slip is issued. This notes at the time of incurrence that we are using more materials than the standard allows. The supervisor is thus put on notice that we are running over budget at the very earliest point. Similarly, if leftover materials are returned to the storeroom, the returned-goods receipt issued by the stores clerk serves as an indication of a favorable materials usage variance.

If materials are issued only as needed, we typically need to wait until the completion of the job before determining whether there has been a favorable or unfavorable usage variance. In any case, the recording of materials usage is the same. Let us assume that the standard for a job called for the use of 400 units of materials but we used only 390 units. Assuming that these are the same materials as in our previous example, we would record the usage as

| | | |
|---|---|---|
| Work-in-Process: Materials | 800 | |
| Materials Usage Variance | | 20 |
| Raw Materials Inventory | | 780 |

Note that since we recorded the price variance on materials at the point of purchase, we need only separate out the quantity variance at the point of usage.

### Labor Variances

Labor variances are likely to be calculated only at the completion of the job (rather than attempting to monitor usage on a continuous basis). At the completion of the job we will know the total number of hours worked for the job. Assume that a job was supposed to require 40 hours of direct labor. The firm's standard wage rate, the average earned by employees, is $6 per hour. In fact, the job required 45 hours of labor, costing $265.50. (That is, we recorded the actual wage rates for the workers who actually worked on the job. These actual rates will likely differ from the average standard rate.) Then the direct labor cost for this job would be recorded as follows:

| | | |
|---|---|---|
| Work-in-Process: Direct Labor | 240.00 | |
| Labor Usage Variance | 30.00 | |
| Labor Rate Variance | | 4.50 |
| Accrued Payroll | | 265.50 |

Once again we see that we are recording the work-in-process inventory at standard cost.

### Overhead Variances per Job

When jobs are finished, we will also be able to record the amount of overhead assigned to each. Assume that we apply overhead on the basis of direct labor hours. The variable overhead rate is \$3 per direct labor hour and the fixed overhead application rate is \$4 per hour. Since we are using direct labor hours as the basis for application, the following entry can be made at the same time as the labor entry.

| | | |
|---|---|---|
| Work-in-Process: Overhead | 280 | |
| Variable Overhead Usage Variance | 15 | |
| Variable Overhead Applied | | 135 |
| Fixed Overhead Applied | | 160 |

This entry presumes that we wish to identify the variable overhead usage variance on a per-job basis. To separate it out we apply variable overhead to work-in-process at the standard rate of \$3 per hour for the 40 standard hours allowed, for a total of \$120. But we charge the Overhead Applied account for the actual hours worked, 45, times the standard rate of \$3 for a total of \$135. This reflects the amount of variable overhead costs we expect were actually generated by working 45 hours. In contrast, the fixed overhead is applied to the Work-in-Process account and accumulated in the Fixed Overhead Applied account at the standard rate of \$4 per hour for the 40 standard hours allowed for the job.

During the period as we incur charges for overhead cost items we would make a series of entries to record actual overhead costs. For example, when we receive our property tax bill (\$200) and utility bills (\$100) we might make the following entry.

| | | |
|---|---|---|
| Fixed Overhead Control | 200 | |
| Variable Overhead Control | 100 | |
| Accounts Payable | | 300 |

Also, during the period when we finish particular jobs we will transfer the standard cost of the jobs from Work-in-Process to Finished Goods Inventory. If we finished a job whose total standard cost was \$1,320, we would make the entry:

| | | |
|---|---|---|
| Finished Goods Inventory | 1,320 | |
| Work-in-Process | | 1,320 |

Since all variances were segregated at the time we put costs into Work-in-Process, no new variances would be recognized when we transfer the products to Finished Goods.

Although we can calculate variances for prime costs on a per-job basis, we cannot calculate fixed overhead spending, fixed overhead volume, or variable overhead spending variances per job. These variances are incapable of being calculated on a per-job basis because we will not have timely information on the actual overhead costs that were incurred. Nor could we assign overhead costs to a particular job (if we could, they would, by definition, be direct costs). Instead we must wait until the end of the accounting period to calculate most of the overhead variances. At the end of the period the first step is to cost out any work-in-process. Recall that we have been recording costs only when jobs have been completed. Therefore, anything in process at the end of the period will not have any costs attached. We charge the goods with the standard materials and labor costs incurred to date and apply the appropriate overhead. At this point we will have the total Overhead Applied and the total Overhead Control balances.

Let us assume that we only worked on the one job that we have been using as our example. Let us further make the unreasonable assumption that property taxes and utilities were our only overhead costs for the period. Then if we had recognized the variable overhead usage variance when we applied overhead to work-in-process, our overhead accounts would have the following balances.

| | |
|---|---|
| Variable Overhead Applied | $135 cr |
| Fixed Overhead Applied | 160 cr |
| Variable Overhead Control | 100 dr |
| Fixed Overhead Control | 200 dr |

Since the variable overhead usage variance has already been recognized, the only remaining difference between the Variable Overhead Applied and Variable Overhead Control accounts must be the Variable Overhead Spending Variance. Therefore we close the variable overhead accounts with the entry

| | | |
|---|---|---|
| Variable Overhead Applied | 135 | |
| Variable Overhead Spending Variance | | 35 |
| Variable Overhead Control | | 100 |

The difference in the fixed overhead accounts can be due to two sources. We may have spent more or less than the budgeted amount for fixed overhead and we may have applied more or less fixed overhead than expected in the budget. Let us assume that our master budget had anticipated that we would spend $172 on fixed overhead and that we would use 43 standard direct labor hours. Our fixed overhead application rate of $4 per hour had been derived by dividing the $172 by the 43 budgeted hours. The fixed overhead volume variance then is the $4 per hour rate times the difference between the 43 master budget hours and the 40 standard hours allowed for the job we worked on (the flexible budget). The spending variance in turn is the difference between the actual fixed overhead of $200 and the budgeted amount of $172. The entry then to close the fixed overhead accounts is

| | | |
|---|---|---|
| Fixed Overhead Applied | 160 | |
| Fixed Overhead Volume Variance | 12 | |
| Fixed Overhead Spending Variance | 28 | |
| Fixed Overhead Control | | 200 |

We have now completed the recognition of all the production variances in our accounting records.

### Overhead Variances per Period

In the previous section we identified the variable overhead efficiency variance on a per-job basis. Although such an approach identifies the variance quickly, few firms go to the trouble of calculating the variance for each job. Instead, firms more commonly apply and accumulate the overhead applications strictly on the basis of the standard hours allowed for a job. In this latter case the entry to recognize the application of overhead would be as follows:

| | | |
|---|---|---|
| Work-in-Process: Overhead | 280 | |
| Variable Overhead Applied | | 120 |
| Fixed Overhead Applied | | 160 |

Then at the end of the period the balances in the overhead accounts would be as follows:

| | |
|---|---|
| Variable Overhead Applied | $120 cr |
| Fixed Overhead Applied | 160 cr |
| Variable Overhead Control | 100 dr |
| Fixed Overhead Control | 200 dr |

Nothing has changed that will affect the fixed overhead variances, so we will ignore them. But now there are two variances needed to explain the difference between the variable overhead control and applied balances. To calculate the variable overhead usage and spending variances, we would need to have available the total number of labor hours worked during the period. But this would not be a difficult number to derive even if we did not keep a running record of actual hours worked. All we need do is work backward through the labor usage variance to get the number. The records for the example will show an unfavorable labor usage variance of $30. We know that the standard labor rate is $6 per hour, and therefore we must have worked 5 hours more than the flexible budget allows. The variable overhead usage variance is then determined by multiplying this excess 5 hours by the standard variable overhead rate of $3 per hour to get the variable overhead usage variance of $15. The remaining variance between the applied and control accounts must be due to the spending variance so we can prepare the following entry.

| | | |
|---|---|---|
| Variable Overhead Applied | 120 | |
| Variable Overhead Usage Variance | 15 | |
| Variable Overhead Spending Variance | | 35 |
| Variable Overhead Control | | 100 |

As should be expected, this computation gives the same variances as when we calculated the usage variance on a per-order basis.

## STANDARD PROCESS COSTING

In a process costing situation we do not know total production until the period is over. Therefore we cannot transfer material, labor, and overhead into work-in-process at standard quantities during the period. However, we can identify price variances at the time resources are put into process. In this case the additions to the Work-in-Process account would reflect actual inputs used at standard prices. At the end of the period, when actual output is known, we can calculate the quantity variances and transfer units to Finished Goods at standard costs.

Alternatively, we could record additions to Work-in-Process at both actual quantities and actual prices. In this case all variances would be calculated at the end of the period.

Let us examine each recording system using the following facts. The firm purchased 1,000 units of raw materials for a total of $2,050. During the period, 390 units were put into process. In addition, 45 labor hours, costing $5.90 per hour, were used in production. Actual fixed overhead costs of $200 and actual variable overhead costs of $100 were incurred during the period. The standard costs per unit of output for the period based on the production of 215 units of output, were as follows:

| | |
|---|---|
| Material (2 lb @ $2 per pound) | $4.00 |
| Labor (0.2 hr @ $6 per hour) | 1.20 |
| Variable overhead (0.2 hr @ $3 per DLH) | 0.60 |
| Fixed overhead (0.2 hr @ $4 per DLH) | 0.80 |
| Standard cost per unit | $6.60 |

Using techniques described in Chapter 15, management determines at the end of the period that 200 equivalent units of production were completed during the period. All of these units were transferred to finished goods inventory.

### Recording Actual Quantities at Standard Prices

If management wishes to segregate variances early to facilitate control, price variances will be identified as resources are acquired. The entry to record the purchase of materials would be

| | | |
|---|---|---|
| Raw Materials Inventory | 2,000 | |
| Materials Price Variance | 50 | |
| Cash (or Accounts Payable) | | 2,050 |
| To record the purchase of 1,000 units of inventory at $2.05; standard price $2. | | |

Since materials are now at standard prices, the entry to record putting 390 units into process is

| | | |
|---|---|---|
| Work-in-Process: Materials | 780 | |
| Raw Materials Inventory | | 780 |

When 45 hours of labor costing $5.90 an hour is employed, the variance from the $6 per hour standard rate would be recognized as

| | | |
|---|---|---|
| Work-in-Process: Labor | 270 | |
| Labor Price Variance | | 4.50 |
| Wages Payable | | 265.50 |

During the period, the actual overhead cost would be accumulated in control accounts in the same manner as with job costing; that is,

| | | |
|---|---|---|
| Fixed Overhead Control | 200 | |
| Variable Overhead Control | 100 | |
| Miscellaneous accounts | | 300 |

Each of the previous entries summarizes a number of individual entries made during the period. These entries result in a balance of $1,050 in Work-in-Process. But since we do not know the standard quantities allowed until the end of the period, the following entries would have to await the calculation of the equivalent units of product manufactured.

Given the assumption that 200 equivalent units were produced during the period and given the unit standard costs, we can calculate the standard quantities of resources allowed. For materials, 2 pounds per unit, or a total of 400 pounds, were allowed. Similarly, the allowance for labor was 0.2 hour, or a total of 40 hours. We can now apply overhead to Work-in-Process.

| | | |
|---|---|---|
| Work-in-Process: Variable Overhead (40 hr @ \$3) | 120 | |
| Work-in-Process: Fixed Overhead (40 hr @ \$4) | 160 | |
| Variable Overhead Applied | | 120 |
| Fixed Overhead Applied | | 160 |

Next we segregate material and labor variances while transferring the cost of completed units to Finished Goods.

| | | |
|---|---|---|
| Finished Goods Inventory (200 units @ \$6.60) | 1,320 | |
| Direct Labor Usage Variance (5 hr @ \$6) | 30 | |
| Direct Materials Usage Variance (10 lb @ \$2) | | 20 |
| Work-in-Process (\$1,050 + \$120 + \$160) | | 1,330 |

The final entry is to close the overhead control and applied accounts, as follows:

| | | |
|---|---|---|
| Variable Overhead Applied | 120 | |
| Fixed Overhead Applied | 160 | |
| Variable Overhead Usage Variance | 15 | |
| Fixed Overhead Spending Variance | 28 | |
| Fixed Overhead Volume Variance | 12 | |
| Variable Overhead Price Variance | | 35 |
| Variable Overhead Control | | 100 |
| Fixed Overhead Control | | 200 |

Since the unit standard costs were based on the production of 215 units, budgeted fixed overhead must have been 215 units × \$0.80 = \$172. Hence the fixed overhead spending variance is (\$172 − \$200) = \$28 U. The volume variance, in turn, is (200 units − 215 units) × \$0.80 = \$12 U. The variable overhead price variance is (\$3 per hr − \$100/45 hr) × 45 hr = \$35 F, and the variable overhead usage variance is (40 hr − 45 hr) × \$3 per hr = \$15 U. Note that the entries to apply overhead, transfer costs to finished goods, and close the overhead applied and control accounts could all have been combined into one large entry since all these entries are being made at the same time.

### Recording Actual Quantities at Actual Prices

If management chooses to record actual costs in Work-in-Process, there is a slight saving in bookkeeping costs, but at the expense of not having price variances quickly available. The journal entries to reflect actual costs would be

| | | |
|---|---|---|
| Raw Materials Inventory | 2,050 | |
| Cash (or Accounts Payable) | | 2,050 |
| To record materials purchases. | | |

The entries to record the actual cost of materials, labor, and overhead would be as follows:

| | | |
|---|---|---|
| Work-in-Process: Materials | 799.50 | |
| (390 lb @ $2.05) | | |
| Raw Materials Inventory | | 799.50 |
| Work-in-Process: Labor | 265.50 | |
| (45 hr @ $5.90) | | |
| Wages Payable | | 265.50 |
| Work-in-Process: Fixed Overhead | 200 | |
| Work-in-Process: Variable Overhead | 100 | |
| Miscellaneous accounts | | 300 |

Finally at the end of the period, all variances would be calculated and the following single entry made (the variance calculations are the same as before):

| | | |
|---|---|---|
| Finished Goods Inventory | 1,320.00 | |
| Direct Materials Price Variance | 19.50 | |
| Direct Labor Usage Variance | 30.00 | |
| Variable Overhead Usage Variance | 15.00 | |
| Fixed Overhead Spending Variance | 28.00 | |
| Fixed Overhead Volume Variance | 12.00 | |
| Direct Materials Usage Variance | | 20.00 |
| Direct Labor Price Variance | | 4.50 |
| Variable Overhead Price Variance | | 35.00 |
| Work-in-Process | | 1,365.00 |

And we can see, all the variances are taken care of simultaneously.

## QUESTIONS AND EXERCISES: APPENDIX 18

**18-49** In process costing, what is the significance of equivalent units if standard costs are employed?

**18-50** Using the following information, prepare the journal entry that closes the overhead control and applied accounts.

| | |
|---|---|
| Variable Overhead Efficiency Variance | $ 1,700 F |
| Variable Overhead Spending Variance | 2,100 U |
| Fixed Overhead Budget Variance | 500 U |
| Fixed Overhead Volume Variance | 3,000 F |
| Overhead Applied | 28,000 |

**18-51** The following are the balances in a firm's inventory accounts at the end of an accounting period. In addition to the balances, you should know that the firm applies fixed overhead at the rate of $2 per standard direct labor hour, and variable overhead is applied at the rate of $3 per standard hour allowed. The master budget for this period had assumed that 5,000 standard labor hours would be used. The firm actually used 5,800 labor hours.

**Variable Overhead Applied**

| | |
|---|---|
| | 16,500 |

**Fixed Overhead Applied**

| | |
|---|---|
| | 11,000 |

**Variable Overhead Control**

| | |
|---|---|
| 17,000 | |

**Fixed Overhead Control**

| | |
|---|---|
| 9,850 | |

Prepare a journal entry that closes out the overhead accounts and separates out all appropriate variances.

## PROBLEMS AND CASES: APPENDIX 18

**18-52** **Journal entries and variances.**
Elvee's master budget called for the production of 5,000 units during the year. At that level of output costs were expected to be as follows:

| | |
|---|---|
| Materials (3 oz @ $8) | $120,000 |
| Labor (1.5 hr @ $3.50) | 26,250 |
| Variable overhead ($3 per hr) | 22,500 |
| Fixed overhead | 30,000 |
| Total costs | $198,750 |

Overhead is applied to production on the basis of direct labor hours. During the year the firm actually produced 4,800 units. The firm purchased and used 14,500 ounces of materials at a cost of $113,825. The firm used 7,008 direct labor hours costing $24,878.40. Variable overhead amounted to $21,900, and fixed overhead was $28,800.

**Required**
Prepare all the summary journal entries to record acquisition of materials and services, separating price and quantity variances at the earliest possible point. Include the year-end entries to close the overhead accounts and separate appropriate variances. Close all variances to cost of goods sold.

**18-53 Process and standard direct cost—requires prior study of Chapter 15.**
Phad, Inc., rides the waves of fashion. One of its current products passes through several departments, and FIFO process costing is employed. In department 47, three units of material (at a standard cost of $1.00 per unit of material) are added to the units received from department 46; it takes $1\frac{1}{2}$ hours of direct labor to process a unit in department 47 at a standard cost of $10 per hour.

Physical data for this week are as follows:

| | Units in Process | Percent Complete: Materials | Percent Complete: Direct Labor |
|---|---|---|---|
| Beginning of week | 400 | 70% | 50% |
| End of week | 600 | 70% | 60% |

During the week, work was started on 5,200 units and there was no spoilage. Department 47 used 15,000 units of material and worked 7,800 hours. There were no price variances.

**Required**
**a.** Determine the usage variances for the week for materials and labor.
**b.** Prepare the journal entries for the variances.

**18-54 Standard direct materials and process costing—requires prior study of Chapter 15.**
Redenbach, Inc., manufactures a single product under FIFO process costing conditions. The department in question is the last in the sequence and sends the completed product to finished goods.

The firm employs a standard cost system; all inventories are carried at full (absorption) standard costs. Variances, if any, are closed to the income statement at the end of the period. Denominator volume for the firm is 3,500 units per period.

The following inventory data—concerned with direct materials C and F and work-in-process—are for the last department in the sequence. The questions have to do with this department.

1. *Direct Material C.* 4,000 units in beginning inventory; 10,000 units purchased; 3,000 units in ending inventory; and 11,000 units used. The standards call for 2 units of material C per unit of finished product. The standard cost per unit of C is $10. Direct material C is added at the end of the process.

2. *Direct Material F.* 1,000 units in beginning inventory; 3,000 units purchased; 1,800 units in ending inventory; and 2,200 units used. The standards call for 1 unit of material F per unit of finished product. The standard cost per unit of F is $5. Direct material F is added when the product is 60% processed.
3. *Work-in-Process.* Beginning inventory 4,000 units, 75% processed; ending inventory 2,000 units, 50% processed. Units completed and transferred; 6,000. The standard processing cost per unit in this department is $30.

**Required**

**a.** Analyze direct materials usage variances for the period.
**b.** Prepare the journal entries to recognize the materials usage variances.

**18-55 General journal entry for normal and abnormal spoilage—requires prior study of Chapter 16** (CIA adapted).

The Pretty Pottery Company manufactures pitchers in two finishes, A and B. Pitcher B is made of higher-quality material and must pass through the hardening process twice (two cycles). Some specifics on each product's processing in the hardening department are as follows:

| | Product A | Product B |
|---|---|---|
| Number of hardening cycles per pitcher | 1 | 2 |
| Pitchers lost during hardening as a percentage of good output per cycle | 10% | 10% |
| Cost accumulated per pitcher prior to hardening | $3 | $4 |
| Cost per pitcher for each hardening cycle | $1 | $1 |

Assume that 121 units of each product go into hardening each day and none ever remains in hardening at the end of the day.

**Required**

**a.** Prepare the journal entry removing all direct costs from the hardening process and transferring completed product A and completed product B to their respective finished goods inventories at the end of a normal day.
**b.** On a particular day, the hardening process goes out of adjustment. Only 90 of product A pitchers and 90 of product B pitchers pass inspection at the end of the first hardening cycle, and only 70 of product B pitchers are accepted after the second cycle. Prepare the journal entry removing all direct costs from the hardening process and transferring completed product A and completed product B to their respective finished goods inventories at the end of this day.

# CHAPTER 19

# MORE ON VARIANCE ANALYSIS

Chapter 18 examined the computation of standard cost variances for manufacturing costs. In the present chapter we describe some additional variances related to sales and production. The appendixes discuss variances when costs are subject to a learning effect and variances from a PERT/Cost budget.

The production cost variances covered in Chapter 18 explain the difference between flexible budget manufacturing costs and the actual manufacturing costs incurred. If we can now calculate variances that explain the difference between the master budget and the flexible budget, we will be able to reconcile actual income to master budget income (except for a few items, which we will discuss shortly). We start by looking at the analysis for a single-product firm.

## RECONCILING ACTUAL RESULTS WITH THE MASTER BUDGET

Recall that both the master budget and the flexible budget are based on the same cost and revenue functions. The only difference between them is that the master budget is based on management's planned level of activity for a period, whereas the flexible budget is based on the actual level of activity obtained for the period. If cost and revenue functions are linear in the firm's relevant range, and we generally assume they are, the contribution margin per unit will be the same in both the master and the flexible budgets. That is, with linear functions the sales price per unit and the variable cost per unit will be constants; therefore their difference, the contribution margin per unit, will also be a constant. Finally, fixed costs are also assumed to be the same in both budgets. With these observations, we can represent net income in each budget as

$$\begin{matrix}\text{master budget}\\ \text{net income}\end{matrix} = \begin{pmatrix}\text{budgeted contribution}\\ \text{margin per unit}\end{pmatrix} \times \begin{pmatrix}\text{master budget}\\ \text{activity level}\end{pmatrix} - \begin{pmatrix}\text{fixed}\\ \text{costs}\end{pmatrix}$$

and

$$\begin{matrix}\text{flexible budget}\\ \text{net inome}\end{matrix} = \begin{pmatrix}\text{budgeted contribution}\\ \text{margin per unit}\end{pmatrix} \times \begin{pmatrix}\text{flexible budget}\\ \text{activity level}\end{pmatrix} - \begin{pmatrix}\text{fixed}\\ \text{costs}\end{pmatrix}$$

Subtracting the two expressions and factoring gives us the difference as

$$\begin{matrix}\text{difference in}\\ \text{net incomes}\end{matrix} = \begin{pmatrix}\text{budgeted contribution}\\ \text{margin per unit}\end{pmatrix} \times \begin{pmatrix}\text{master budget} & - & \text{flexible budget}\\ \text{activity level} & & \text{activity level}\end{pmatrix}$$

We will call this difference in incomes the sales quantity variance. Thus the **sales quantity variance** is the budgeted contribution margin per unit multiplied by the difference between the activity level anticipated in the master budget and the actual activity level achieved as reflected in the flexible budget. Before proceeding, a warning is called for. Much of the terminology in this chapter is not yet settled. For example, the sales quantity variance has also been called the **contribution margin variance**, the **activity variance**, the **sales volume variance**, and the **output adjustment variance**. You may encounter other terms too (such as on certification exams). If so, we hope the context of the question will lead you to understand the nature of the variance being called for.

### Marketing and Production Quantity Variances

As before, when we calculate variances we would like to do so in sufficient detail to be able to pinpoint responsibility. Although we have calculated the total effect on income from failure to operate at the master budget level of activity, we also want to determine who is responsible for the deviation from master budget activity. In a job cost environment there are two possibilities: (1) The marketing department may not have been able to generate the sales called for in the master budget or (2) the production department may not have been able to produce the products for which orders were received.[1] This suggests that we calculate two variances that

[1]In a process cost environment in which we produce to inventory, the inventory should act as a buffer, thus reducing the likelihood that sales were lost due to the production department's inability to meet demand.

explain the responsibility for the sales quantity variance. The first, the **marketing quantity variance**, is the difference between the number of units anticipated to be sold in the master budget and the quantity for which sales orders were received, multiplied by the budgeted contribution margin per unit. Second, the **production quantity variance** is the difference between the quantity of products for which sales orders were received and the quantity of products actually produced. Again, the difference is multiplied by the budgeted contribution margin to yield the dollar effect on budgeted income. A simple example should clarify the computations.

Assume that a firm's master budget called for the production of 3,000 units of product. The budgeted sales price was $10 per unit, budgeted variable costs were $6 per unit, and fixed costs were budgeted at $5,000. During the period the marketing department was able to generate sales orders for only 2,900 units. In addition, production scheduling problems restricted actual output to 2,700 units.

The net income anticipated in the master budget must have been as follows:

| | |
|---|---|
| Sales ($10 × 3,000 units) | $30,000 |
| Variable costs ($6 × 3,000 units) | 18,000 |
| Contribution margin | $12,000 |
| Fixed costs | 5,000 |
| Net income | $ 7,000 |

Net income in the flexible budget, based on the actual level of activity achieved, 2,700 units, would be

| | |
|---|---|
| Sales ($10 × 2,700 units) | $27,000 |
| Variable costs ($6 × 2,700 units) | 16,200 |
| Contribution margin | $10,800 |
| Fixed costs | 5,000 |
| Net income | $ 5,800 |

Given our budgeted contribution margin per unit of $10 − $6 = $4, we can explain the responsibility for the change in income in schematic form as follows:

| **Flexible Budget Contribution Margin (2,700 units)** | **Contribution Margin for Sales Orders Received (2,900 units)** | **Master Budget Contribution Margin (3,000 units)** |
|---|---|---|
| $10,800 | $11,600 | $12,000 |

$800 U — Production quantity variance

$400 U — Marketing quantity variance

$1,200 U — Sales quantity variance

In equation form the detailed variances are

$$\text{marketing quantity variance} = \$4 \text{ per unit} \times (3{,}000 \text{ units} - 2{,}900 \text{ units}) = \$400\text{ U}$$

$$\text{production quantity variance} = \$4 \text{ per unit} \times (2{,}900 \text{ units} - 2{,}700 \text{ units}) = \$800\text{ U}$$

In both cases the variances are labeled unfavorable because they have an unfavorable impact on net income. Since fixed costs are budgeted to be the same in both budgets, the marketing and production quantity variances explain the total change in budgeted net income; that is,

| | |
|---|---|
| Master budget income | \$7,000 |
| Marketing quantity variance | (400) |
| Production quantity variance | (800) |
| Flexible budget income | \$5,800 |

### The Marketing Price Variance

For production we have now seen two major types of variances: (1) the production quantity variance, just described, which isolates the effect on income from not being effective in the production of the desired quantity of products; and (2) all of the price and quantity variances, described in the previous chapter, which isolate the effects on *costs* from not efficiently using resources to produce the actual quantity of outputs achieved. Similarly, there are two major types of marketing variances: the marketing quantity variance identified in the preceding section and a marketing price variance. The **marketing price variance** accounts for any difference between the budgeted sales price per unit of product and the actual sales prices achieved.

To calculate the marketing price variance, we multiply the number of units actually sold, which is the flexible budget activity level, by the difference between the budgeted (standard) sales price per unit and the actual sales price per unit. In equation form the variance is as follows:

$$\text{marketing price variance} = \begin{pmatrix}\text{flexible}\\\text{budget sales}\end{pmatrix}\begin{pmatrix}\text{budgeted}\\\text{selling price}\end{pmatrix} - \begin{pmatrix}\text{actual}\\\text{selling price}\end{pmatrix}$$

Continuing our previous example, if the firm budgeted sales of 3,000 units at \$10 but actually sold 2,700 units at \$9.50, then the unfavorable effect from the reduced price is

$$\text{marketing price variance} = 2{,}700(\$10 - \$9.50)$$
$$= \$1{,}350\ \text{U}$$

### Variances for Selling and Administrative Costs

We have now explained the total difference between master budget and actual results, with the exception of deviations from budget in nonmanufacturing costs. The fixed selling and administrative (S&A) cost variances are straightforward. As with fixed overhead, there is no difference between the master budget and the flexible budget amounts for fixed S&A costs. Therefore, the only variance we need calculate is the fixed S&A budget variance: the difference between the budgeted and actual costs incurred. Unlike fixed overhead, the fixed S&A costs are not charged to inventory (they are simply period costs) so we do not have to calculate a volume variance to correct our bookkeeping practices.

If we have used the traditional definition for the contribution margin when calculating the sales quantity variance, the difference between the master budget and flexible budget allowance for variable selling and administrative costs will have been explained.[2] That is, the variable selling and administrative costs would have been subtracted from the sales price when calculating the contribution margin. In this case we need concern ourselves only with the difference between the actual variable selling and administrative costs incurred and the flexible budget allowance.

For example, assume that the master budget called for sales of \$200,000 and we budgeted variable selling and administrative expenses at 5% of sales or \$10,000. During the period sales of \$215,000 were actually achieved, and variable S&A expenses turned out to be \$10,500. The variable S&A variance would be as follows:

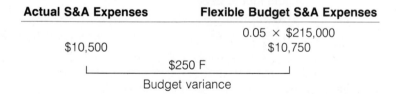

| **Actual S&A Expenses** | **Flexible Budget S&A Expenses** |
|---|---|
| | 0.05 × \$215,000 |
| \$10,500 | \$10,750 |
| \$250 F — Budget variance | |

That is, for a sales level of \$215,000, selling and administrative costs were budgeted to be \$10,750. The \$750 difference between this figure and

[2]Some firms choose to subtract only variable manufacturing costs from the selling price when calculating the contribution margin. In this case, an additional variance must be calculated to explain the change in the budget allowance from the master to flexible budget. If this approach is used, we call the variance an **output adjustment cost variance,** but any descriptive term will do.

the $10,000 allowance in the master budget is included in the sales quantity variance. Thus the only variance remaining is the difference between the actual costs incurred and the flexible budget.

Whereas most firms treat variable S&A costs as indicated in the previous paragraphs, some firms find that S&A costs are sufficiently important to attempt to institute tighter control over S&A spending. In these firms an attempt is made to relate groups of S&A costs to some measure of output. For example, a firm may budget the cost of its billing department as a function of the number of line items typed on invoices during a period, the costs of operating a payroll department may be budgeted as a function of the number of paychecks issued, and the costs of the bookkeeping department may be based on the number of account postings in a period.

In order to be able to calculate both a price and a quantity variance for these nonmanufacturing costs, we need to establish a relationship between the amount of inputs to be used for a task and the outputs obtained. The most likely means of doing so is to estimate the number of labor hours per unit of activity (lines typed, checks issued, or accounts posted). Then we can estimate the relationship between each department's costs and the number of labor hours incurred just as we did with overhead in Chapter 18.

For example, assume that a firm has determined that the standard time to type 100 invoice lines is 1 hour. Further, the firm has established a standard cost of $9 per labor hour to cover all the costs in the billing department. Then, if in a particular period the billing department actually typed 110,000 invoice lines using 1,050 labor hours, and if the total cost incurred by the billing department was $9,800, the billing department costs could be analyzed as follows:

| **Actual Cost** | **Actual Inputs Used at Standard Price** | **Flexible Budget** |
|---|---|---|
| | 1,050 hr × $9 | 110,000 lines × 0.01 hr × $9 |
| $9,800 | $9,450 | $9,900 |

$350 U — Price variance

$450 F — Quantity variance

It appears from the analysis that the department used less time per invoice line than standard, but the labor cost per hour was higher than standard.

Now that we have variances for nonmanufacturing costs, we are in a position where we can completely explain the difference between master budget and actual net income. Exhibit 19-1 is a schematic diagram illustrating all of the variances for a single-product firm.

The next section provides a comprehensive numerical illustration of all of the computations.

**EXHIBIT 19-1 Schematic Diagram Showing All Variances That Explain the Differences between Master Budget Net Income and Actual Net Income[a]**

| Actual Results | Inputs Used at Standard Price | Flexible Budget | Sales Orders Received | Master Budget |
|---|---|---|---|---|
| Actual sales | | Actual sales at budgeted selling prices | | |
| Marketing price variance | | No variance[c] | | |
| Manufacturing costs | | | | |
| Variable costs[b] | | | | |
| DM: Material price | Material quantity | No variance[c] | | |
| DL: Labor price | Labor quantity | No variance[c] | | |
| VO: VO price | VO quantity | No variance[c] | | |
| Fixed costs | | Budgeted fixed costs | | |
| Fixed overhead budget variance | | No variance[d] | | |
| Nonmanufacturing costs[b] | | | | |
| Variable S&A costs | | | | |
| Variable S&A budget variance | | No variance[c] | | |
| Fixed S&A costs | | Budgeted fixed costs | | |
| Fixed S&A budget variance | | No variance | | |
| Net income | | Net income | | Net income |
| Net price and cost variances | | Production quantity variance | Marketing quantity variance | |

[a]Drawn assuming no change in inventories.

[b]DM = direct materials; DL = direct labor; VO = variable overhead; S&A = selling and administration.

[c]Any differences are accounted for in the production and marketing quantity variances through the contribution margin.

[d]As indicated in Chapter 18, the volume variance does not help explain the difference between budgeted and actual costs.

## A COMPREHENSIVE EXAMPLE CALCULATING ALL VARIANCES FOR A SINGLE-PRODUCT FIRM

A job-oriented firm's master budget called for the production and sale of 10,000 units of product at $20 per unit. The detailed master budget was as follows:

| | | |
|---|---|---|
| Sales (10,000 @ $20) | | $200,000 |
| Cost of goods sold | | |
| Materials ($\frac{1}{2}$ lb @ $4 × 10,000) | $20,000 | |
| Labor ($\frac{1}{4}$ hr @ $6 × 10,000) | 15,000 | |
| Variable overhead ($\frac{1}{4}$ hr @ $4 × 10,000) | 10,000 | |
| Fixed overhead | 50,000 | 95,000 |
| Gross margin | | $105,000 |
| Variable S&A expenses ($2 per unit) | | 20,000 |
| Fixed S&A expenses | | 30,000 |
| Net income | | $ 55,000 |

During the period the marketing department generated sales orders for 9,800 units, but the firm was able to produce and sell only 9,500 units at an actual average selling price per unit of $19.50. The costs incurred are provided in the following actual cost income statement.

| | | |
|---|---|---|
| Sales (9,500 @ $19.50) | | $185,250 |
| Costs of goods sold | | |
| Materials (4,800 lb @ $3.90) | $18,720 | |
| Labor (2,600 hr @ $6.10) | 15,860 | |
| Variable overhead | 9,400 | |
| Fixed overhead | 49,200 | 93,180 |
| Gross margin | | $ 92,070 |
| Variable S&A expenses | | 19,100 |
| Fixed S&A expenses | | 30,600 |
| Net income | | $ 42,370 |

For this example, let us now calculate all variances that explain the difference between the anticipated master budget income and the actual net income achieved. We begin by calculating the variances that adjust the master budget to the flexible budget.

The marketing quantity variance is the difference between the units anticipated to be sold in the master budget and the number of sales orders received, multiplied by the standard contribution margin per unit. The standard contribution margin per unit is as follows:

| | |
|---|---|
| Selling price | $20.00 |
| Less: | |
| Direct materials | 2.00 |
| Direct labor | 1.50 |
| Variable overhead | 1.00 |
| Variable S&A costs | 2.00 |
| Standard contribution margin | $13.50 |

With this figure available we can calculate the marketing quantity variance as

marketing quantity variance = (10,000 − 9,800) × $13.50
= $2,700 U

Similarly, the production quantity variance is the difference between the sales orders received and the units actually produced multiplied by the standard contribution margin.

production quantity variance = (9,800 − 9,500) × $13.50
= $4,050 U

The difference between flexible budget net income and actual net income is explained by the marketing price variance and the cost variances. The marketing price variance is the difference between the budgeted selling price and the actual selling price multiplied by the number of units sold. It therefore is

marketing price variance = ($20.00 − $19.50) × 9,500
= $4,750 U

Because variable selling and administration costs were budgeted on a per-unit basis (as opposed to labor hours per task or some other basis), we can calculate only a variable S&A budget variance. It is the difference between the flexible budget and actual variable S&A costs; that is,

variable S&A budget variance = $19,000 − $19,100
= $100 U

Similarly, the fixed S&A budget variance is the difference between budgeted and actual fixed S&A costs:

fixed S&A budget variance = $30,000 − $30,600
= $600 U

Finally, we calculate the price and quantity variances for the manufacturing costs. Because we have done these calculations so many times before, they are simply presented in the following list without explanation:

| | |
|---|---|
| Direct materials price variance: ($4.00 − $3.90) × 4,800 | $ 480 F |
| Direct materials quantity variance: (4,750 − 4,800) × $4 | 200 U |
| Direct labor price variance: ($6.00 − $6.10) × 2,600 | 260 U |
| Direct labor quantity variance: (2,375 − 2,600) × $6 | 1,350 U |
| Variable overhead price variance: ($4.00 − $3.6154) × 2,600 | 1,000 F |
| Variable overhead quantity variance: (2,375 − 2,600) × $4 | 900 U |
| Fixed overhead spending variance: $50,000 − $49,200 | 800 F |

**EXHIBIT 19-2 Variances for the Comprehensive Example**

| | Actual Results | | Inputs Used at Standard Price | | Flexible Budget | | Sales Orders Received | | Master Budget |
|---|---|---|---|---|---|---|---|---|---|
| Sales | $185,250 | | | | $190,000 | | | | $200,000 |
| | | | $ 4,750 U | | | | No variance reported[a] | | |
| Variable manufacturing costs | | | | | | | | | |
| Direct materials | $ 18,720 | | $19,200 | | $ 19,000 | | | | $ 20,000 |
| | | $ 480 F | | $ 200 U | | | No variance reported[a] | | |
| Direct labor | $ 15,860 | | $15,600 | | $ 14,250 | | | | $ 15,000 |
| | | $ 260 U | | $1,350 U | | | No variance reported[a] | | |
| Variable overhead | $ 9,400 | | $10,400 | | $ 9,500 | | | | $ 10,000 |
| | | $1,000 F | | $ 900 U | | | No variance reported[a] | | |
| Fixed manufacturing costs | $ 49,200 | | | | $ 50,000 | | | | $ 50,000 |
| | | | $ 800 F | | | | No variance | | |
| Variable S&A costs | $ 19,100 | | | | $ 19,000 | | | | $ 20,000 |
| | | | $ 100 U | | | | No variance reported[a] | | |
| Fixed S&A costs | $ 30,600 | | | | $ 30,000 | | | | $ 30,000 |
| | | | $ 600 U | | | | No variance | | |
| Net income | $ 42,370 | | | | $ 48,250 | | $52,300 | | $ 55,000 |
| | | | $ 5,880 U[b] | | | $4,050 U | | $2,700 U | |

[a]Any differences are accounted for in the marketing and production quantity variances through the contribution margin.

[b]$5,880 = $4,750 − $480 + $200 + $260 + $1,350 − $1,000 + $900 − $800 + $100 + $600.

This completes our calculation of the variances needed to reconcile master budget income to actual income. The variances are summarized in Exhibit 19-2 in a schematic form.

## THE EFFECT ON VARIANCE ANALYSIS OF A CHANGE IN INVENTORY LEVELS

So far we have assumed that the firm has either sold everything it produced or that planned and actual inventory changes turned out to be the same. Of course, the more common situation will be that the actual change in inventory levels differs from that planned in the master budget. When this is true, we have to make an allowance for the difference between the amount of fixed costs expected to be residing in ending inventories versus the actual fixed costs assigned to ending inventories. Let us illustrate with a simple example in which we ignore materials costs and variable overhead.

Assume that the master budget for a firm called for the sale of 950 units of product. We started the period with no inventory but management wanted to end the period with a finished goods inventory of 50 units, resulting in total planned production of 1,000 units. Assume further that the standard quantity of labor for each unit is 2 hours at a standard cost of $3 per hour. The only other manufacturing cost is fixed overhead, budgeted at $5,000 for the operating period. The budgeted selling price is $20 per unit. Also assume that we actually produced 970 units of product and sold 930 units. Our inventory thus increased by 40 units instead of the planned increase of 50 units. In order to highlight the inventory change effect, we assume that our actual selling price per unit, actual standard labor costs per unit, and actual fixed overhead costs were as budgeted.

The master budget income statement for the period was as follows:

| | | |
|---|---|---|
| Sales (950 units @ $20) | | $19,000 |
| Cost of goods sold | | |
| Beginning inventory | $ — | |
| Direct labor ($3 × 2 hr × 1,000) | 6,000 | |
| Fixed overhead ($2.50 × 2 hr × 1,000) | 5,000 | |
| Cost of goods available | $11,000 | |
| Ending inventory (50 × $11) | (550) | 10,450 |
| Volume variance | | — |
| Master budget income | | $ 8,550 |

Note that we are presuming that fixed overhead is applied to production on the basis of the standard labor hours allowed for production. The fixed overhead application rate per hour is the budgeted fixed overhead of $5,000 divided by the 2,000 labor hours anticipated to be used during the period, or $2.50 per hour.

Let us now prepare the flexible budget income statement on the basis that we produced 970 units and sold 930 units. That income statement is as follows:

| | | |
|---|---|---|
| Sales (930 @ $20) | | $18,600 |
| Cost of goods sold | | |
| Beginning inventory | $ — | |
| Direct labor (2 hr × $3 × 970) | 5,820 | |
| Fixed overhead ($2.50 × 2 hr × 970) | 4,850 | |
| Cost of goods available | $10,670 | |
| Ending inventory (40 × $11) | (440) | 10,230 |
| Volume variance ($5,000 − $4,850) | | 150 |
| Flexible budget income | | $ 8,220 |

Note that once again we have applied fixed overhead to production using the fixed overhead application rate of $2.50 per standard direct labor hour. This time, however, because production was less than that anticipated in the master budget, we applied only $4,850 of overhead to production, not the $5,000 fixed overhead budgeted. The difference of $150 shows up as the unfavorable volume variance.

Without an inventory change, we could explain the difference between the master budget income and the flexible budget income by multiplying the difference in units sold (950 versus 930) by the budgeted contribution margin (the $20 selling price less the $6 variable labor cost or $14). However, that computation does not work here.

| | |
|---|---|
| Master budget income | $8,550 |
| Total sales quantity variance [$14 × (930 − 950)] | (280) |
| Adjusted income | $8,270 |
| Flexible budget income | 8,220 |
| Difference | $ 50 |

Our reconciliation is off by $50. This $50 represents the difference between the amount of fixed costs expected to be deferred into ending inventory in the master budget and the actual fixed costs attached to units in ending inventory. That is, the master budget anticipated that we would add 50 units of product to inventory. Each unit was assigned a fixed cost charge of $2.50 per hour for 2 standard hours of labor, or $5 per unit. In total, $250 of the period's fixed costs were to be charged to ending inventory. But instead of increasing inventory by 50 units, we only increased inventory by 40 units. The amount of the period's fixed costs actually deferred to ending inventory was thus only 40 units × $5 = $200. To fully reconcile master budget income to the flexible budget income we

**EXHIBIT 19-3 Reconciliation of Master Budget and Actual Income When Planned and Actual Inventory Changes Are Equal**

| Master Budget | | | Flexible Budget | | |
|---|---|---|---|---|---|
| Sales (950 @ $20) | | $19,000 | (920 @ $20) | | $18,400 |
| Cost of goods sold | | | | | |
| Beginning inventory | $ — | | | $ — | |
| Direct labor ($3 × 2 × 1,000) | 6,000 | | ($3 × 2 × 970) | 5,820 | |
| Fixed overhead ($2.50 × 2 × 1,000) | 5,000 | | ($2.50 × 2 × 970) | 4,850 | |
| Cost of goods available | $11,000 | | | $10,670 | |
| Ending inventory (50 × $11) | (550) | 10,450 | (50 × $11) | (550) | 10,120 |
| Volume variance | | — | | | 150 |
| Master budget income | | $ 8,550 | Flexible budget income | | $ 8,130 |

**Reconciliation**

| | |
|---|---|
| Master budget income | $8,550 |
| Total sales quantity variance [$14 × (920 − 950)] | (420) |
| Difference in fixed costs deferred in inventory | — |
| Flexible budget income | $8,130 |

must adjust for the difference in the amount of fixed costs being deferred in ending inventory, as follows:

| | |
|---|---|
| Master budget income | $8,550 |
| Total sales quantity variance [$14 × (930 − 950)] | (280) |
| Difference in fixed costs deferred in inventory [2 hr × $2.50 × (50 units − 40 units)] | (50) |
| Flexible budget income | $8,220 |

Exhibit 19-3 shows that if inventories change over the period, but the anticipated and actual changes are the same, the adjustment for fixed costs deferred in inventory is not needed. In Exhibit 19-3 we assume the same facts for the master budget, but that actual sales were only 920 units. Since we have also assumed that production remained at 970 units, the actual increase in inventory is 50 units—the same increase as expected in the master budget.

## VARIANCES FOR MULTIPRODUCT FIRMS

In Chapter 5 we briefly discussed profit planning for firms producing several products. One planning approach was to assume that sales of the firm's products would be made in constant proportions. For example, a fast-food restaurant might anticipate selling one soft drink for every two hamburgers sold. In setting unit prices, management may intentionally use a low markup on one product (hamburgers) to increase the total volume of customers and, hopefully, the total sales of the other product (soft drinks) with a higher contribution margin. In these cases, the evaluation of actual performance will be concerned not only with the total quantity of products sold but also with the relative mix of products.

### Sales Quantity and Mix Variances

In the multiproduct firm there are two variances that can be used to explain the difference between master budget and flexible budget net income. The first is the **sales quantity variance**, or **sales volume variance**, which adjusts budgeted income for the change in overall activity between the two budgets. The second variance, the **sales mix variance**, adjusts for the change in net income reflected in the flexible budget because products were not actually sold in the proportions anticipated in the master budget.

In the previous single-product case our calculation of the sales quantity variance involved multiplying the change in units between the master budget and the flexible budget by the budgeted contribution margin per unit. For that case the budgeted contribution margin per unit was the same in both budgets. In a multiproduct firm the computation is a bit more complex. We will now concentrate on the *weighted-average* budgeted contribution margin per unit. But this number will be different in the master and flexible budgets because the weighted-average budgeted contribution margin per unit is a function of the mix of products sold. The mix expected to be sold in the master budget is likely to be different from the mix in the flexible budget, which reflects actual sales. Thus the weighted-average budgeted contribution margin per unit will differ in the two budgets.

We calculate the sales quantity variance while holding sales mix constant. The *sales quantity variance* is calculated by multiplying the difference between total master budget unit sales and flexible budget unit sales by the weighted-average contribution margin per unit anticipated in the master budget.

Having isolated the sales quantity effect, we then turn to calculating the effect on income arising from a change in the mix of products sold. The change in mix is captured by the difference between the weighted-average budgeted contribution margin in the master budget versus the weighted-average budgeted contribution margin in the flexible budget. That is, the *sales mix variance* is found by multiplying the flexible budget unit sales by the difference between the master budget average contribution margin per unit and the flexible budget contribution margin per unit. Exhibit 19-4 illustrates these calculations in schematic form. A numerical example will show the rationale for these calculations.

Assume that a firm markets two products. Product A's contribution margin is $4 per unit while product B's contribution margin is $10 per

**EXHIBIT 19-4 Sales Mix and Quantity Variances**

| Flexible Budget: Actual Units Sold at Actual Mix times Standard Unit Contribution Margins | Flexible Budget: Actual Units Sold at Desired Mix times Standard Unit Contribution Margins | Master Budget: Budgeted Units to be Sold at Desired Mix times Standard Unit Contribution Margins |
|---|---|---|
| Sales mix variance | | Sales quantity variance |

unit. Management is attempting to maintain a sales ratio of 1 unit of B for every two units of A sold. The master budget called for total sales of 3,000 units, which implies sales of 2,000 units of A and 1,000 units of B. Actual sales for the period turned out to be 2,100 units consisting of 1,600 units of A and 500 units of B.

Because we are assuming linear cost and revenue functions, the selling prices and variable costs per unit are the same in both the master and flexible budgets. In addition, fixed costs are the same in both budgets; therefore we can explain changes in budgeted net income by looking solely at changes in contribution margins.

The contribution margin anticipated in the master budget is $18,000; that is,

| | | |
|---|---|---|
| A: | 2,000 units @ $4 | $ 8,000 |
| B: | 1,000 units @ $10 | 10,000 |
| | 3,000 units | $18,000 |

or $18,000 ÷ 3,000 = $6 per unit. The budgeted contribution margin in the flexible budget is $11,400; that is,

| | | |
|---|---|---|
| A: | 1,600 units @ $4 | $ 6,400 |
| B: | 500 units @ $10 | 5,000 |
| | 2,100 units | $11,400 |

or $11,400 ÷ 2,100 = $5.42857 per unit. The $6,600 difference in budgeted contribution margin arises because we sold 900 fewer units than anticipated and because, given the unit volume, we sold relatively more units of A. That is, had we maintained the ratio of 2 units of A for each unit of B *and* sold 2,100 units, the flexible budget contribution margin would have been $12,600:

| | | |
|---|---|---|
| A: | 1,400 units @ $4 | $ 5,600 |
| B: | 700 units @ $10 | 7,000 |
| | 2,100 units | $12,600 |

or $12,600 ÷ 2,100 = $6 per unit.

The difference between the \$12,600 contribution margin that would have been earned had 2,100 units been sold in the desired proportions and the \$18,000 master budget contribution margin for sales of 3,000 units reflects the change in income due to reduced unit sales with no change in mix. The difference between the actual flexible budget contribution margin of \$11,400 and the \$12,600 contribution margin for sales of 2,100 units in the desired proportions is the reduced income resulting from a change in product mix.

| Flexible Budget: Actual Mix | Flexible Budget: Desired Mix | Master Budget: Desired Mix |
|---|---|---|
| \$11,400 | \$12,600 | \$18,000 |

\$1,200 U — Sales mix variance

\$5,400 U — Sales quantity variance

These variances can also be calculated in equation form as:

$$\text{sales quantity variance} = \left(\begin{matrix}\text{master budget}\\ \text{units}\end{matrix} - \begin{matrix}\text{flexible budget}\\ \text{units}\end{matrix}\right) \times \begin{matrix}\text{master budget}\\ \text{average CM}\end{matrix}$$
$$= (3{,}000 - 2{,}100) \times \$6$$
$$= \$5{,}400 \text{ U}$$
$$\text{sales mix variance} = \left(\begin{matrix}\text{master budget}\\ \text{average CM}\end{matrix} - \begin{matrix}\text{flexible budget}\\ \text{average CM}\end{matrix}\right) \times \begin{matrix}\text{flexible budget}\\ \text{units}\end{matrix}$$
$$= (\$6.00 - \$5.42857) \times 2{,}100$$
$$= \$1{,}200 \text{ U}$$

These variances indicate that the firm's primary problem is a shortfall in unit sales. Thus management may wish to consider enhancing promotional efforts to generate more customers. To a lesser extent, the mix variance indicates that the firm is selling a smaller proportion of the high-margin products. Thus management may also wish to remind salespeople to steer customers to the higher-margin products.

Figure 19-1 graphs the sales quantity and sales mix variances for this two-product example. The sales mix variance is seen to be the increased contribution margin that could be earned if the firm were able to slide down the line of sales combinations resulting in sales of 2,100 total units to the point where it intersects the line representing sales in the ratio of 2 units of A for each unit of B. The sales quantity variance is the change in contribution margin earned if the firm increases total sales from 2,100 units to 3,000 units while remaining on the line representing sales of 2 units of A for every unit of B.

The sales quantity and sales mix variance calculations generalize to any number of products. Keep in mind that these variances explain only the difference between master budget and flexible budget net income. In

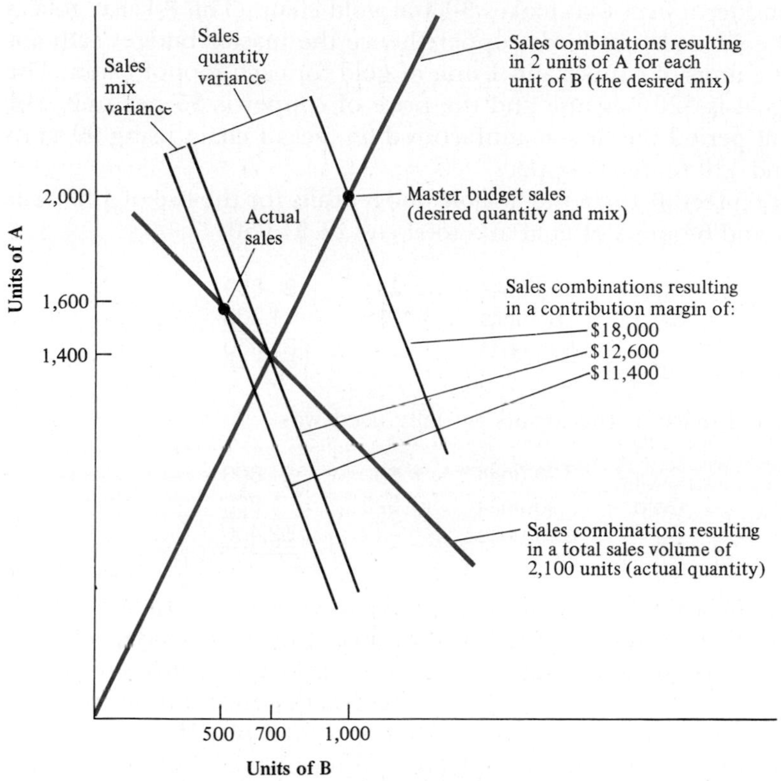


**FIGURE 19-1 Sales mix and quantity variances.** The intersection point of the two colored lines represents the actual sales quantity at the desired mix of products.

addition to these variances, we still have to calculate selling price variances and cost variances to reconcile actual net income with flexible budget net income.

### Production Mix and Yield Variances

When a firm uses several inputs to produce its products and the inputs are in part substitutable for each other (e.g., varying the amounts of gold and copper in making jewelry), management generally would like to ensure that inputs are used in proper proportions. In this case we can calculate the **production mix variance** (also called the **input mix variance, input substitution variance**, or **blend variance**), which will identify the cost of substituting one material for another. The calculation of the substitution variance parallels that of the sales mix variance. Let us demonstrate the calculation through an example.

Consider a firm that makes 8-karat gold chain. The 8-karat gold is one-third gold and two-thirds copper; hence the master budget calls for the use of 2 units of copper and 1 unit of gold for each foot of chain. The price of gold is \$20 per unit and the price of copper is \$5 per unit. For the current period the firm manufactured 65 feet of chain using 90 units of gold and 120 units of copper.

For 65 feet of chain the flexible budget calls for the use of 130 units of copper and 65 units of gold at a total cost of \$1,950.

| | | | |
|---|---|---|---|
| Copper: | 130 units | @ \$5 | \$ 650 |
| Gold: | 65 units | @ \$20 | 1,300 |
| | 195 units | | \$1,950 |

The standard price of the inputs actually used was

| | | | |
|---|---|---|---|
| Copper: | 120 units | @ \$5 | \$ 600 |
| Gold: | 90 units | @ \$20 | 1,800 |
| | 210 units | | \$2,400 |

If we used the approach taken in the previous chapter the total materials quantity variance would be \$450 unfavorable. But in this case, not only did we use more materials than necessary, we also apparently substituted gold for copper. We can estimate the effect of this substitution by calculating the production mix variance. That is, a total of 210 units of gold and copper were used. Had the budgeted proportions of 2 units of copper for each unit of gold been maintained, the firm would have used 140 units of copper and 70 units of gold for a total cost of \$2,100.

| | | | |
|---|---|---|---|
| Copper: | 140 units | @ \$5 | \$ 700 |
| Gold: | 70 units | @ \$20 | 1,400 |
| | 210 units | | \$2,100 |

The \$300 U difference between the \$2,100 cost of using 210 units in the proper proportions and the \$2,400 cost for using 210 units in the actual proportions is the production mix variance. It reflects the additional cost incurred because we substituted gold for copper. The \$150 U difference between the \$2,100 budgeted for using a total of 210 units of input and the \$1,950 standard cost allowed for the output actually achieved represents a **production yield variance**. The yield variance reflects the extra cost incurred because more inputs were used than were called for in the flexible budget.

Figure 19-2 graphically represents the yield and mix variances for the example. As the graph indicates, the mix variance represents the change in costs from sliding down the input combinations line totaling 210 units to the intersection with the line of all combinations representing two units

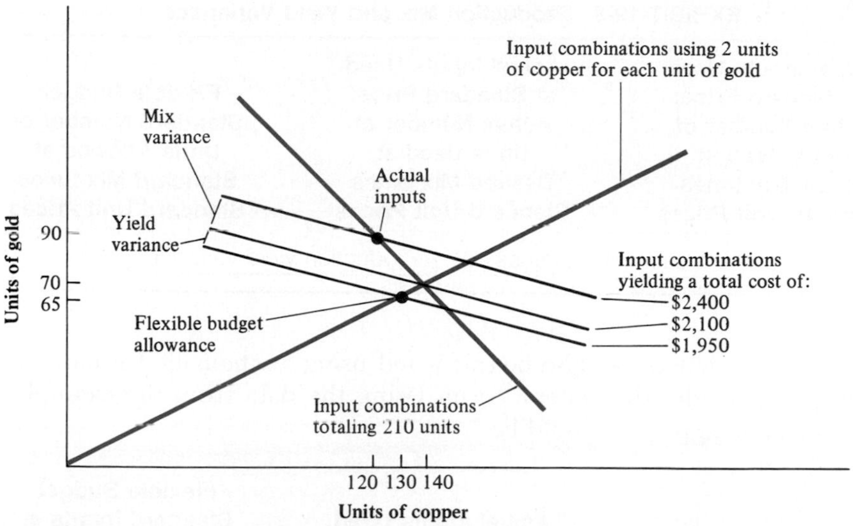


**FIGURE 19-2 Production yield and mix variances.**

of copper for each unit of gold. The yield variance, in turn, is the change in cost if the total amount of resources used had been reduced along the 2-for-1 proportions line to the point representing the inputs needed for the outputs achieved.

As with the sales mix and quantity variances, the production yield and mix variances can also be calculated by formulas. The yield variance is calculated by multiplying the flexible budget average cost of materials by the difference between the total materials allowed in the flexible budget and the total materials actually used. The production mix variance is found by multiplying the total quantity of materials used by the difference between the average standard cost of the materials in the flexible budget and the average standard cost for the materials actually used.

For the example, the flexible budget allowed 195 units of materials costing $1,950, for an average price of $10. The standard cost of the 210 units actually used was $2,400, for an average standard price of $11.42857. Using the formula approach the yield and mix variances are as follows:

$$\text{production yield variance} = \left(\text{total materials allowed} - \text{total materials used}\right) \times \text{flexible budget average price}$$

$$= (195 - 210) \times \$10$$

$$= \$150\ \text{U}$$

$$\text{production mix variance} = \left(\text{flexible budget average price} - \text{actual average standard price}\right) \times \text{total materials used}$$

$$= (\$10.00 - \$11.42857) \times 210$$

$$= \$300\ \text{U}$$

**EXHIBIT 19-5 Production Mix and Yield Variances**

| Actual Inputs Used at Standard Price: Actual Number of Units Used at Actual Mix times Standard Unit Prices | Actual Inputs Used at Standard Price: Actual Number of Units Used at Desired Mix times Standard Unit Prices | Flexible Budget: Standard Number of Units Allowed at Standard Mix times Standard Unit Prices |
|---|---|---|
| Production mix variance | Production yield variance | |

The variances can also be calculated using a schematic format. Exhibit 19-5 provides the general form. Using the data from the example, the schematic approach would be

| Actual Inputs Used at Standard Price and Actual Mix | Actual Inputs Used at Standard Price and Desired Mix | Flexible Budget Standard Inputs at Standard Price and Desired Mix |
|---|---|---|
| $2,400 | $2,100 | $1,950 |
| $300 U | $150 U | |
| Production mix variance | Production yield variance | |

Again, the more detailed variances allow management to pinpoint better the necessary corrective actions that should be taken. The production mix variance indicates that more care should be taken by those persons responsible for blending the copper and gold. They are currently using more gold than called for by the standard. The yield variance is suggestive of excess waste. Thus the persons fabricating the chain should also exercise greater care. These variances explain the difference between the flexible budget and the actual inputs used at standard cost. The materials price variances would still be calculated as in Chapter 18 by comparing the actual inputs used at standard cost to the actual cost of the materials used. Although we have limited our discussion of the yield and mix variances to materials, similar calculations can be made for labor if a firm uses several classes of labor.

## SUMMARY

In addition to the variances for materials, labor, and overhead in production, management can expect to incur variances in other costs and revenues. The objective in calculating variances for these other possible deviations is still the same. We wish to try to pinpoint responsibility for each major source of deviations from plans. The specific variances calculated by a firm will depend on the factors in the environment that can cause variances. Further, the names for the variances used by a firm are frequently a matter of industry convention.

The sale of multiple products and the use of multiple inputs give rise to additional sources of variances. Sales of various products may not be made in the proportions anticipated by management, and inputs may have been substituted for one another. The effect on net income from these changes is captured by the sales mix and the production mix variances.

## DEMONSTRATION PROBLEM

Dempsey Industries produces three products: A, B, and C. The master budget called for the sale of 10,000 units of A at $12, 6,000 units of B at $15, and 8,000 units of C at $9. In addition, the standard variable cost for each product was $7 for A, $9 for B, and $6 for C. In fact, the firm actually produced and sold 11,000 units of A at $11.50, 5,000 units of B at $15.10, and 9,000 units of C at $8.80.

The firm uses two inputs to produce each of the products, X and Y. The standard price per unit of material X is $2 and a unit of Y is $1. The materials budgeted to be used for each product were

| | Materials | |
|---|---|---|
| Product | X (units) | Y (units) |
| A | 2 | 3 |
| B | 4 | 1 |
| C | 1 | 4 |

The firm actually used 54,000 units of X at a cost of $109,620 and 72,000 units of Y at a cost of $73,000.

**Required**

Determine the mix, quantity, and price variances for sales, as well as the yield, mix, and price variances for materials.

**Solution**

The master budget called for the sale of 24,000 units with a total contribution margin of $110,000.

| Product | Unit Sales | Contribution Margin per Unit | Total |
|---|---|---|---|
| A | 10,000 | $5 | $ 50,000 |
| B | 6,000 | 6 | 36,000 |
| C | 8,000 | 3 | 24,000 |
| | 24,000 | | $110,000 |

The average contribution margin per unit anticipated was therefore $4.58333.

The flexible budget is prepared using the actual sales at budgeted costs and selling prices. The flexible budget reflects sales of 25,000 units with a total contribution margin of $112,000, for an average contribution margin of $4.48 per unit.

| Product | Sales | Contribution Margin per Unit | Total |
|---|---|---|---|
| A | 11,000 | $5 | $ 55,000 |
| B | 5,000 | 6 | 30,000 |
| C | 9,000 | 3 | 27,000 |
| | 25,000 | | $112,000 |

Using the formula approach, the sales quantity and mix variances are

$$\text{quantity variance} = \left(\begin{array}{c}\text{master}\\ \text{budget units}\end{array} - \begin{array}{c}\text{flexible}\\ \text{budget units}\end{array}\right) \times \begin{array}{c}\text{master budget}\\ \text{average CM}\end{array}$$

$$= (24{,}000 - 25{,}000) \times \$4.58333$$

$$= \$4{,}583.33\ \text{F}$$

$$\text{mix variance} = \left(\begin{array}{c}\text{master budget}\\ \text{average CM}\end{array} - \begin{array}{c}\text{flexible budget}\\ \text{average CM}\end{array}\right) \times \begin{array}{c}\text{flexible budget}\\ \text{units}\end{array}$$

$$= (\$4.58333 - \$4.48) \times 25{,}000$$

$$= \$2{,}583.33\ \text{U}$$

The sales price variance to record the fact that the firm did not sell its products at budgeted prices is $6,800 unfavorable.

| Product | Budgeted Price | Actual Price | Difference | Units Sold | Selling Price Variance |
|---|---|---|---|---|---|
| A | $12 | $11.50 | $(0.50) | 11,000 | $(5,500) |
| B | 15 | 15.10 | 0.10 | 5,000 | 500 |
| C | 9 | 8.80 | (0.20) | 9,000 | (1,800) |
| Total | | | | | $(6,800) |

The flexible budget would call for the use of 51,000 units of X and 74,000 units of Y for the actual output. At standard prices the average cost for materials would be $176,000 ÷ 125,000 = $1.408 per unit.

| Product | Units of X | Units of Y | Total |
|---|---|---|---|
| A | 11,000 × 2 = 22,000 | 11,000 × 3 = 33,000 | 55,000 |
| B | 5,000 × 4 = 20,000 | 5,000 × 1 = 5,000 | 25,000 |
| C | 9,000 × 1 = 9,000 | 9,000 × 4 = 36,000 | 45,000 |
| | 51,000 | 74,000 | 125,000 |
| Standard price per unit | × $2 | × $1 | × $1.408 |
| Total standard cost | $102,000 | $74,000 | $176,000 |

At standard prices for the actual materials used, the firm incurred an average cost of $180,000 ÷ 126,000 = $1.42857 per unit.

| Material | Actual Use | Standard Price | Total |
|---|---|---|---|
| X | 54,000 | $2 | $108,000 |
| Y | 72,000 | 1 | 72,000 |
| Total | 126,000 | | $180,000 |

Using the formula approach, the production yield and mix variances are

$$\begin{aligned}\text{yield variance} &= \left(\begin{matrix}\text{flexible budget}\\ \text{allowance}\end{matrix} - \begin{matrix}\text{actual units}\\ \text{used}\end{matrix}\right) \times \begin{matrix}\text{flexible budget}\\ \text{average price}\end{matrix}\\ &= (125{,}000 - 126{,}000) \times \$1.408\\ &= \$1{,}408 \text{ U}\end{aligned}$$

$$\begin{aligned}\text{mix variance} &= \left(\begin{matrix}\text{flexible budget}\\ \text{average price}\end{matrix} - \begin{matrix}\text{actual average}\\ \text{standard price}\end{matrix}\right) \times \begin{matrix}\text{actual units}\\ \text{used}\end{matrix}\\ &= (\$1.408 - \$1.42857) \times 126{,}000\\ &= \$2{,}592 \text{ U}\end{aligned}$$

The materials price variance that adjusts for the difference between the standard cost of materials used and the actual cost of materials used is

| Product | Actual Inputs Used at Standard Price | Actual Cost | Cost Variance |
|---|---|---|---|
| X | $108,000 | $109,620 | $1,620 U |
| Y | 72,000 | 73,000 | 1,000 U |
| Total | $180,000 | $182,620 | $2,620 U |

Exhibit 19-6 summarizes the variances in schematic form, as well as reconciling the master budget with the actual contribution margin earned.

**EXHIBIT 19-6 Sales and Production Variances for the Demonstration Problem**

| | Actual | Inputs Used at Standard Actual Mix | Inputs Used at Standard Desired Mix | Flexible Budget Actual Sales Mix | Flexible Budget Desired Sales Mix | Master Budget Desired Sales Mix |
|---|---|---|---|---|---|---|
| Sales | $281,200 | | | $288,000 | $293,750.00 | $282,000 |
| | | $6,800 U Marketing price variance | | | | |
| Material costs | $182,620 | $180,000 | $177,408[a] | $176,000 | $179,166.67[a] | $172,000 |
| | $2,620 U Price | $2,592 U Mix | $1,408 U Yield | | | |
| Contribution margin | $ 98,580 | | | $112,000 | $114,583.33 | $110,000 |
| | | | | $2,583.33 U Sales mix | $4,583.33 F Sales quantity | |

**Reconciliation**

| | | |
|---|---|---|
| Master budget contribution margin | | $110,000 |
| Marketing variances | | |
| Sales quantity variance | $ 4,583.33 | |
| Sales mix variance | (2,583.33) | |
| Selling price variance | (6,800.00) | (4,800) |
| Production variances | | |
| Production yield variance | $(1,408) | |
| Materials mix variance | (2,592) | |
| Materials price variance | (2,620) | (6,620) |
| Actual contribution margin | | $ 98,580 |

[a] Questions 19-8 and 19-9 at the end of the chapter ask you to derive these numbers.

## KEY TERMS AND CONCEPTS

[ Sales quantity variance
Contribution margin variance
Activity variance
Sales volume variance
Output adjustment variance ]
Marketing quantity variance
Production quantity variance
Marketing price variance
Output adjustment cost variance
Sales mix variance
[ Production mix variance
Input mix variance
Input substitution variance
Blend variance ]
Production yield variance

[ Bracketed terms are equivalent in meaning.

## FURTHER READING


Chen, Rosita S. "The Learning Curve Approach to Labor Cost Variance Analysis," *Cost and Management* (July–August 1982), p. 23.

Drake, Louis S. "Effect of Product Mix Changes on Profit Variance," *NAA Bulletin* (October 1961), p. 61.

Gillespie, Jackson F. "An Application of Learning Curves to Standard Costing," *Management Accounting* (September 1981), p. 63.

Horngren, Charles T. "A Contribution Margin Approach to the Analysis of Capacity Utilization," *The Accounting Review* (April 1967), p. 254.

Kapoor, M. Rai. "Contribution Margin Ratio Variance Analysis: A New Management Tool for Profitability Improvement," *Cost and Management* (September–October 1983), p. 29.

Kraft, Kyle K. "Measuring Productivity Efficiency," *Management Accounting* (June 1983), p. 40.

Largay, James A., Philip D. York, and Willis R. Greer, Jr. "Opportunity Cost Variances," *Cost and Management* (November–December 1982), p. 35.

Malcolm, Robert E. "A Note on the Effect of Product Aggregation in Determining Sales Variances," *The Accounting Review* (January 1978), p. 162.

Peles, Yoram C. "A Note on Yield Variance and Mix Variance," *The Accounting Review* (April 1986), p. 325.

Shank, John K., and Neil C. Churchill. "Variance Analysis: A Management-Oriented Approach," *The Accounting Review* (October 1977), p. 950.

Toole, Howard R. "The Learning Curve Model—Its Use and Implications," *Cost and Management* (March–April 1980), p. 36.

Wolk, Harry I., and A. Douglas Hillman. "Materials Mix and Yield Variances: A Suggested Improvement," *The Accounting Review* (July 1972), p. 549.


## QUESTIONS AND EXERCISES

**19-1** What is the sales quantity variance?

**19-2** What is the relationship between the marketing quantity variance, the production quantity variance, and the sales quantity variance?

**19-3** In a process cost environment an unfavorable production quantity variance usually occurs in a period in which there is a large favorable marketing quantity variance. Explain why.

**19-4** Why should variances be calculated for selling and administrative costs?

**19-5** Does the discussion on the effect of variance analysis of a change in inventory levels in this chapter presume the firm uses direct costing or absorption costing? Why?

**19-6** What causes a sales mix variance and what would cause a production mix variance?

**19-7** A side of beef weighs approximately 300 to 360 pounds, and approximately 60% of this finds its way to the meat counter. What types of variances would be associated with the beef?

**19-8** Refer to Exhibit 19-6. In the column "inputs used at standard desired mix," for the row "material costs," appears the number $177,408. How was that number calculated?

**19-9** Refer to Exhibit 19-6. In the column "flexible budget desired sales mix," for the row "material costs," appears the number $179,166.67. How was that number calculated?

**19-10** A process that is supposed to result in 85% usable output actually produces 89%. What type of variance does this describe?

**19-11** A firm planned on selling 400 units at $200 each with total costs expected to be $8,000 plus $50 per unit. It actually sold 410 units at $190 each, with costs totaling $7,800 plus $50 per unit. What is the sales quantity variance?

**19-12** The firm's master budget calls for the production and sale of 5,000 units of product X at a contribution margin of $400 each. During the period, the sales department obtained orders amounting to 5,600 units and production was sufficient to fill 90% of the orders. Determine (a) the marketing quantity variance and (b) the production quantity variance.

**19-13** A law firm budgeted 800 billable hours for the month at an average contribution margin of $30 per hour. The actual results were 820 billable hours at an average billing rate of $1 an hour less than that budgeted. Determine the marketing (a) quantity variance and (b) price variance.

**19-14** A firm projects selling 4,000 units of product A, which has a contribution margin of $10 per unit, and 6,000 units of product B, having a $12-per-unit contribution margin. It actually sells 5,000 of each at the anticipated prices. What are the variances for (a) sales quantity and (b) sales mix?

**19-15** A local CPA firm anticipates 200 hours of billings for the next quarter. Tax work makes up 60% of the total and advisory services make up 40%. Tax work is billed at $50 per hour and advisory services at $40 per hour. Variable costs are $10 per hour for both types of work. During the quarter, 180 hours were billed, and the work was evenly divided between tax and advice. What are the variances for (a) sales quantity and (b) sales mix?

**19-16** A consulting firm has just completed an engagement. Its planned and actual results are as follows:

| Employee Class | Hourly Pay | Planned Hours | Actual Hours |
|---|---|---|---|
| Juniors | $10 | 100 | 110 |
| Seniors | 15 | 20 | 20 |
| Managers | 20 | 10 | 5 |
| Partners | 25 | 5 | 10 |
| Totals | | 135 | 145 |

The firm bills clients $50 per hour, regardless of which class of employee is on the job. What are the variances for (a) sales quantity and (b) sales mix?

**19-17** Newcastle Distillers, located in Scotland, is not actually a distillery. Instead, the firm blends various scotch whiskies, which it purchases, to yield its product. The firm has established the following specifications per batch.

| | |
|---|---|
| Material A (20 units @ £3) | £ 60 |
| Material B (40 units @ £4) | 160 |
| Material C (10 units @ £6) | 60 |
| Total materials cost per batch | £280 |

During the period, 100 batches were produced, requiring an average of 18 units of A, 44 units of B, and 11 units of C each. Determine (a) the production mix variance and (b) the yield variance.

**19-18** The following data represent the expected and actual results for the week.

| | Expected | | | Actual | | |
|---|---|---|---|---|---|---|
| Ingredient X | 100 | @ $6 | $ 600 | 110 | @ $6 | $ 660 |
| Ingredient Y | 200 | @ $5 | 1,000 | 180 | @ $5 | 900 |
| Total | 300 | | $1,600 | 290 | | $1,560 |
| Units produced | | | ÷ 50 | | | ÷ 50 |
| Unit cost | | | $32.00 | | | $31.20 |

What are the (a) mix and (b) yield variances for materials?

## PROBLEMS AND CASES

**19-19 Variances: Working backward from partial information** (SMA adapted).
King Corporation manufactures a special type of metal alloy. Budgeted sales were 10,000 kilograms at $50 per kilogram. Standard variable production and selling costs were $30 per kilogram. Fixed costs were budgeted at $50,000.

Actual fixed costs were $50,000, but the market price realized was $55 per kilogram due to an international shortage. Operating income was below the master budget figure amount by $50,000. Revenue volume variance (this is defined as the actual quantity sold less the budgeted quantity, both at budgeted price) was $100,000 unfavorable. The price variance for variable inputs was $60,000 unfavorable.

**Required**

**a.** Prepare the master budget income statement.
**b.** Prepare the actual cost income statement.
**c.** Reconcile the two income statements by calculating appropriate variances.

**19-20 Marketing profit center and variances** (SMA adapted).
The management of the Douglas Corporation has decided to treat the marketing division of the company as a profit center. The controller realizes that if the marketing division is treated as a profit center, a method of monitoring its performance must be established.

After considerable discussion the corporation decided that the calculation of revenue variances will provide the necessary information to evaluate the performance of the marketing division.

The following information has been gathered for the first 6 months of operations.

1. The master budget projected sales of 200,000 units with revenue of $3,000,000 in the first 6 months.
2. The marketing and accounting departments agree that the standard variable marketing cost is $1.50 per unit.
3. Actual sales price averaged $14.90 per unit.
4. Actual units sold was 205,000 units.
5. Actual variable marketing costs were $300,000.

**Required**
Calculate all appropriate variances in as much detail as the data allow.

**19-21 Marketing and production variances.**
A firm's master budget revealed the following.

| | |
|---|---|
| Sales (50,000 @ $20) | $1,000,000 |
| Direct materials | 250,000 |
| Direct labor | 200,000 |
| Variable overhead | 150,000 |
| Fixed overhead | 300,000 |
| Net income | $ 100,000 |

Orders were received for 44,000 units at a price of $19.75 each. During the period, 45,400 units were produced and sold (that is, 1,400 units from back orders of last period were filled in the current period), yielding the following actual cost income statement.

| | |
|---|---|
| Sales (45,400 @ $19.75) | $896,650 |
| Direct materials | 225,000 |
| Direct labor | 182,000 |
| Variable overhead | 138,000 |
| Fixed overhead | 298,000 |
| Net income | $ 53,650 |

**Required**
Determine the marketing and production quantity variances and the marketing price variance.

**19-22 Sales price, mix, and quantity variances.**
Hamburger Haven's income forecast for 19X7 was $39,000. This budget assumed that the firm would sell one soft drink and one order of french fries for every two hamburgers sold. Management's estimate of the master budget for 19X7 was as follows:

| | Hamburgers | Soft Drinks | Fries | Total |
|---|---|---|---|---|
| Sales (100,000 burgers) | $100,000 | $35,000 | $35,000 | $170,000 |
| Variable costs | 70,000 | 3,500 | 17,500 | 91,000 |
| Contribution margin | $ 30,000 | $31,500 | $17,500 | $ 79,000 |
| Fixed costs | | | | 40,000 |
| Net income | | | | $ 39,000 |

Actual sales for 19X7 turned out to be

| | | |
|---|---|---|
| Hamburgers | 105,000 @ $0.95 | $ 99,750 |
| Soft drinks | 45,000 @ $0.75 | 33,750 |
| Fries | 51,000 @ $0.70 | 35,700 |
| Total sales | | $169,200 |

**Required**
Determine sales price, mix, and quantity variances.

**19-23 Sales mix variances, with graphical solution.**
Alice Machine Ribbons expected to sell one typewriter correction ribbon for each two typewriter ribbons sold. Planned sales and variable costs for 19X6 were as follows:

| | Typewriter | Correction | Total |
|---|---|---|---|
| Sales (100,000 typewriter ribbons) | $300,000 | $150,000 | $450,000 |
| Variable costs | 175,000 | 50,000 | 225,000 |
| Contribution margin | $125,000 | $100,000 | $225,000 |

During 19X6 a competitor came out with an improved correction ribbon at a lower price. Management reacted by dropping its selling price of the correction ribbon, but results were disappointing. Actual sales were

| | |
|---|---|
| Typewriter ribbons (95,000 @ $3.30) | $313,500 |
| Correction ribbons (40,000 @ $2.50) | 100,000 |
| Total sales | $413,500 |

**Required**
**a.** Determine sales price, quantity, and mix variances.
**b.** Graph the quantity and mix variances.

**19-24 Sales quantity, mix, and price variances.**
Metropolitan Motors is an auto retailer. Salespeople have the authority to negotiate with customers for price, but are given target profits. The firm classifies the cars it sells into one of three broad groups: economy, family, or luxury. Target sales and average expected contribution margins per unit for March were budgeted as follows:

| Class | Unit Sales | Average CM |
|---|---|---|
| Economy | 10 | $ 400 |
| Family | 20 | $ 800 |
| Luxury | 5 | $1,300 |

During March the auto manufacturer ran a special promotion to relieve itself of an overstock of economy cars. The manufacturer offered to pay directly to the salespeople a bonus of $75 for each economy car sold. Actual sales and total contribution margin earned by Metropolitan Motors for March turned out to be

| Class | Unit Sales | Total CM Earned |
|---|---|---|
| Economy | 25 | $5,625 |
| Family | 10 | $7,500 |
| Luxury | 3 | $4,200 |

Assume that any changes in the contribution margin are due to deviations from plan in the selling prices negotiated for the cars (all costs met budget).

**Required**

**a.** Determine the sales quantity, mix, and price variances.

**b.** Should the management of Metropolitan Motors be pleased or upset with the manufacturer for running the special promotion? Why?

**19-25 Reconciling budgeted and actual income.**

The Norman Clay Cosmetics Corporation specializes in producing a facial preparation that removes excess oils from the skin. The firm's detailed master budget for the year was as follows:

| | |
|---|---|
| Sales (25,000 units @ $8) | $200,000 |
| Cost of goods sold | |
| Direct materials (12,500 lb @ $0.05) | 625 |
| Direct labor (6,250 hr @ $5) | 31,250 |
| Variable overhead (6,250 hr @ $2.20) | 13,750 |
| Fixed overhead | 15,000 |
| Gross margin | $139,375 |
| Variable selling costs | 75,000 |
| Fixed administration costs | 50,000 |
| Net income | $ 14,375 |

During the year orders were received for 23,000 units of product, but the firm was able to produce and sell only 22,000 units, for gross revenue of $173,800. The firm used 11,200 pounds of materials at a cost of $504. It also used 5,400 hours of labor costing $28,080, and variable overhead amounted to $12,150. Fixed overhead costs totaled $15,500, variable selling costs were $67,000, and fixed administrative costs were $49,700. The firm recognizes marketing price variances in the period that units are delivered to customers.

**Required**

Determine actual cost net income. Reconcile actual and master budget net income by calculating all appropriate variances.

**19-26 Reconciling master budget and actual performance.**

Morgan Enterprises prepared the following master budget for the first quarter of the year.

| | |
|---|---|
| Sales (12,000 units @ $25) | $300,000 |
| Materials (3 lb per unit @ $0.80) | 28,800 |
| Labor (2 hr per unit @ $5) | 120,000 |
| Total overhead | 100,000 |
| Budgeted net income | $ 51,200 |

Variable overhead is budgeted at $1.25 per direct labor hour.

Morgan's actual net income for the first quarter turned out to be somewhat less. The actual cost income statement was as follows:

| | |
|---|---|
| Sales (11,100 units @ $25) | $277,500 |
| Materials (34,000 lb) | 27,880 |
| Labor (22,400 hr) | 110,880 |
| Variable overhead | 29,120 |
| Fixed overhead | 72,000 |
| Actual net income | $ 37,620 |

**Required**
Reconcile the actual net income to master budget income by calculating all the appropriate price and quantity variances.

**19-27 A comprehensive variance problem.**
The president of Lawrence Motors, Inc., is upset. The year's budget projected that the firm would earn $2,499,900. The recently audited financial statements show an actual loss of $2,440,000. The president wants to know what happened.

As a long-time employee of Lawrence Motors, you are aware that the firm manufactures taxicabs to order (the firm does not carry a finished goods inventory). Late last year the firm occupied its new facilities, which were designed to have the capacity to produce 100,000 taxis per year. This is larger than is currently necessary, but management thought it would be cheaper to build the excess capacity then, rather than have to add facilities later.

The master budget for this year called for the production of 65,000 taxis at a cost of $227 million. This assumes materials costs of $1,800 per unit, labor of $900 per unit, variable overhead of $200 per unit, and $600 for fixed costs per unit. Fixed costs were budgeted at $9 million for advertising, $11 million for administration, and $19 million for depreciation, etc. on its facilities.

Revenues for the year were expected to be $229,999,900, or about $3,538.46 per taxi.

During the year, orders were received to produce 68,000 taxis, but trouble with the new facilities limited production to 63,000 units.

An annotated income statement for the year shows the following:

| | |
|---|---|
| Revenues[a] | $221,760,000 |
| Materials[b] | 112,000,000 |
| Labor[c] | 60,000,000 |
| Variable overhead[d] | 13,000,000 |
| Advertising | 9,000,000 |
| Administration | 10,200,000 |
| Capacity costs | 20,000,000 |
| Net income | $ (2,440,000) |

[a]Competition forced a price out.

[b]The direct materials price variance was $2 million favorable.

[c]The direct labor usage variance was $3 million unfavorable.

[d]The variable overhead efficiency (usage) variance was $50,000 unfavorable.

**Required**

**a.** Carefully explain the difference between budgeted and actual income. Attribute the responsibility for the differences by calculating all variances that can be determined.

**b.** Answer the president's question: What is the idle capacity, which we planned when we built the building, costing us?

**19-28 Reconciling the master budget with actual performance.**

Dexter's master budget called for the production and sale of 35,000 units of product. Sales orders were received for 36,200 units, but only 34,600 units were produced and delivered. The firm's actual cost income statement for the period shows

| | |
|---|---|
| Sales | $1,017,240 |
| Raw materials (104,000 lb) | 244,400 |
| Direct labor (51,000 hr) | 242,250 |
| Variable overhead | 147,900 |
| Fixed overhead | 160,000 |
| Gross margin | $ 222,690 |
| Selling and administration | 143,690 |
| Net income | $ 79,000 |

The master budget had called for 3 pounds of materials at $2.50 per pound for each unit of output. Similarly each unit was expected to require 1.5 direct labor hours at $4.50 per hour. Variable overhead was expected to cost $2.80 for each direct labor hour, and fixed overhead was budgeted at $3.00 per direct labor hour. Selling and administrative costs are considered fixed and were budgeted at $140,000. The firm had anticipated a selling price of $29.95 for each unit.

**Required**

**a.** Determine master budget net income.

**b.** Reconcile master budget net income to actual cost net income by calculating all variances.

**19-29 Variances with changing inventories.**

The standard variable cost for a unit of Atlas Industry's product is

| | |
|---|---|
| Materials (3 grams @ $8) | $24 |
| Labor ($\frac{1}{2}$ hour @ $6) | 3 |
| Overhead ($\frac{1}{2}$ hour @ $4) | 2 |
| Total | $29 |

In addition, annual fixed overhead costs are budgeted at $200,000. The firm's 19X2 master budget (its first year of operations) called for the production of 25,000 units and sales of 20,000 units. Actual operations for 19X2 were exactly as planned.

For 19X3, the master budget called for the sale of 22,000 units at $50 each and the production of 20,000 units. During 19X3, sales orders were received for 19,600 units, but only 19,000 units were actually delivered (and booked as sales). There were no production cost variances, and actual unit sales prices averaged $50 during 19X3. The firm produced 20,000 units in 19X3.

**Required**

Reconcile master budget and actual net income for 19X3. (Inventories are carried at FIFO standard absorption cost.)

process or job can be done either of 3 ways

...apsule Comparison of Six Alternative Product-Costing Systems

chap 14 chap 18

WORK-IN-PROCESS INVENTORY "T" Account

process job costing

| | | ACTUAL COSTING | NORMAL COSTING | STANDARD COSTING |
|---|---|---|---|---|
| (1) (2) | DIRECT MATERIALS AND DIRECT LABOR | Actual inputs × Actual prices | Actual inputs × Actual prices | Standard inputs allowed for actual output achieved × Standard prices |
| (1) (2) | VARIABLE FACTORY OVERHEAD | Actual inputs × Actual overhead rates | Actual inputs × Budgeted overhead rates | Standard inputs allowed for actual output achieved × Budgeted overhead rates |
| (1) | FIXED FACTORY OVERHEAD | Actual inputs × Actual overhead rates | Actual inputs × Budgeted overhead rates | Standard inputs allowed for actual output achieved × Budgeted overhead rates |

(1) *Absorption Costing—Includes All Boxes*

(2) *Variable (Direct) Costing—Excludes Bottom Boxes Representing Fixed Factory Overhead*

**19-30 Variances with changing inventory.**
Haborad's per-unit standard costs have remained unchanged for several months. The standard calls for the following.

| | |
|---|---|
| Materials (3 lb @ $6) | $18 |
| Labor (2 hr @ $8) | 16 |
| Variable overhead (2 hr @ $3) | 6 |
| Fixed overhead (2 hr @ $4) | 8 |
| Total | $48 |

The standard cost is based on Haborad's normal monthly volume of 5,000 units. Haborad began the current month with 300 units in finished goods inventory. The firm expected to produce 5,000 units and sell 4,500 units in the current month but actually produced 5,200 units and sold 4,850 units. The planned selling price of $60 per unit was maintained. The actual costs incurred were

| | |
|---|---|
| Materials (15,500 lb) | $ 93,000 |
| Labor (10,400 hr) | 82,680 |
| Variable overhead | 31,200 |
| Fixed overhead | 40,700 |
| Total | $247,580 |

All variances, including the volume variance, are closed to Cost of Goods Sold each month.

**Required**

**a.** Prepare the master budget income statement for the month.
**b.** Prepare the flexible budget income statement for the month.
**c.** What is the actual net income for the month? (Ending inventory is valued at standard cost.)
**d.** Reconcile master budget income, from (a), and actual income, from (c), by calculating the necessary variances and adjustments.

**19-31 Variances with exchange rate fluctuations.**
Headquarters' management is upset with the results reported from its Greek subsidiary. At the beginning of the year the Greek manager and central headquarters had agreed on a budget for the unit in Greece. Sales were budgeted at 200 million drachmas and net income at 30 million drachmas. At the beginning of the year, the exchange rate between the drachma and the dollar was expected to average 130 drachmas = $1 for the year. Therefore, earnings in dollars were projected to be $230,769.

The year-end report shows that the subsidiary had actual sales of 225 million drachmas and actual net income of 33 million drachmas. However, the exchange rate during the year actually averaged 160 drachmas = $1, so earnings in dollars were only $206,250.

The Greek manager was pleased with the results, but headquarters officials were not. The manager pointed out that the unit exceeded both the sales and income targets set in drachmas and said, "Exchange rate fluctuations are beyond my control." The executive vice-president responded, "Our stockholders aren't interested in earnings in drachma or your problems with exchange rates. They want earnings in dollars." The marketing vice-president also noted that with a weaker drachma the subsidiary should have been able to increase its export sales substantially. "You agreed at the beginning of the year that every 10% increase in the exchange rate from 130 should lead to a 6% increase in reported earnings in terms of drachmas. While you may not be able to control exchange rates, you should be able to react to them."

**Required**

Evaluate the performance of the manager of the Greek subsidiary. *Note:* This problem is quite different from the discussion in the chapter, yet the concepts are the same. To evaluate controllable performance, determine a flexible budget income figure in dollars that the manager should have achieved given the actual environment.

19-32 **Materials mix and yield variances** (SMA).

The Fido Company manufactures a popular brand of dog food. The dog food is mixed in 450-kilogram batches. The standard input for material per batch is as follows:

| | Kilograms | Standard Price per Kilogram |
|---|---|---|
| Cereal | 200 | $0.15 |
| Horse meat | 150 | 0.40 |
| Fish parts | 100 | 0.36 |
| Input | 450 | |
| Output | 400 | |

The dog food is packed in cans weighing 5 kilograms. During the month of September, 11,200 cans were produced. The following materials were used during September.

| | Kilograms |
|---|---|
| Cereal | 29,200 |
| Horse meat | 19,800 |
| Fish parts | 14,300 |
| Total input | 63,300 |

Purchases for September were as follows:

| | Kilograms | Total Cost |
|---|---|---|
| Cereal | 30,200 | $ 4,500 |
| Horse meat | 19,500 | 7,950 |
| Fish parts | 14,600 | 5,190 |
| Total | 64,300 | $17,640 |

Fido Company uses a standard cost system and calculates materials price variances at the time of purchase.

**Required**

**a.** Compute the materials mix variance for the month.
**b.** Compute the materials yield variance for the month.

19-33 **Materials price, mix, and yield variances** (CMA adapted).

The LAR Chemical Company manufactures a wide variety of chemical compounds and liquids for industrial uses. The standard mix for producing a single batch of 500 gallons of one liquid is as follows:

| Liquid Chemical | Quantity (gallons) | Cost (per gallon) | Total Cost |
|---|---|---|---|
| Maxan | 100 | $2.00 | $200 |
| Salex | 300 | 0.75 | 225 |
| Cralyn | 225 | 1.00 | 225 |
| Total | 625 | | $650 |

There is a 20% loss in liquid volume during processing due to evaporation. The finished liquid is put into 10-gallon bottles for sale. Thus, the standard materials cost for a 10-gallon bottle is $13.00.

The actual quantities of raw materials and the respective cost of the materials placed in production during November were as follows:

| Liquid Chemical | Quantity (in gallons) | Total Cost |
|---|---|---|
| Maxan | 8,480 | $17,384 |
| Salex | 25,200 | 17,640 |
| Cralyn | 18,540 | 16,686 |
| Total | 52,220 | $51,710 |

During November, 4,000 bottles (40,000 gallons) were produced.

**Required**

**a.** Calculate the total raw material variance for the liquid product for the month of November and then further analyze the total variance into
 **1.** A materials price variance.
 **2.** A materials mix variance.
 **3.** A materials yield variance.

**b.** Explain how LAR Chemical Co. could use each of the three materials variances—price, mix, and yield—to help control the cost of manufacturing this liquid compound.

**19-34 Material yield variance** (CMA).

Steel Slitting Company divides 24-inch widths of rolled sheet steel into 2-inch and 4-inch widths. The 24-inch widths are delivered to Steel Slitting Company by its customers, and the new widths are picked up by the customers after slitting. The cut widths plus scrap loss (caused by starting and ending rolls of steel or jams on the slitters) cannot cost the customers more than acquiring the correct widths direct from steel mills. Therefore, Steel Slitting Company uses tight standard costs to stay competitive.

If bought directly from steel mills, steel would cost customers the following.

| Size (inches) | Gage | Cost per Ton |
|---|---|---|
| 24 | 14 | $125 |
| 24 | 12 | 120 |
| 2 | 14 | 136 |
| 2 | 12 | 130 |
| 4 | 12 | 130 |

Steel Slitting Company's price for slitting a ton of input steel from customers is as follows:

| Size (inches) | Gage | Customer Price per Ton Slit |
|---|---|---|
| 2 | 14 | $8.00 |
| 2 | 12 | 7.00 |
| 4 | 12 | 6.00 |

Standard and actual slitting costs per input ton for October are as follows:

| | 2-Inch Width | | 4-Inch Width | |
|---|---|---|---|---|
| | Standard Cost per Ton[a] | Actual Cost per Ton | Standard Cost per Ton[a] | Actual Cost per Ton |
| Direct labor | $3.00 | $3.10 | $2.50 | $2.60 |
| Variable overhead | 2.80 | 3.00 | 2.00 | 2.10 |
| Nonvariable overhead | 1.00 | 1.00 | 1.00 | 1.00 |
| | $6.80 | $7.10 | $5.50 | $5.70 |
| Customer scrap loss[b] | 1% | 2% | 1% | 3% |

[a]Standard cost per ton is based on width of strips regardless of gage.
[b]Percent of input tons (absorbed by customers).

Budgeted and actual sales for the month of October are as follows:

| Size | Gage | Budgeted Input Tons | Actual Input Tons |
|---|---|---|---|
| 2 | 14 | 500 | 300 |
| 2 | 12 | 400 | 400 |
| 4 | 12 | 100 | 300 |

**Required**

**a.** Steel Slitting Company does not own the material or absorb any yield loss. Can a material yield variance be calculated? If so, how would you calculate it? Would such a calculation be useful to Steel Slitting management? Explain.

**b.** Could the company's customers have done better if they had purchased steel strips directly from steel mills? Explain your answer with appropriate numbers.

**19-35 Labor quantity, mix, and rate variances for chartered accountants.** Anderson and Firth, Chartered Accountants, agreed to review the payment system for a province's social assistance fund. The contract set the billing rate at $40 per hour. In making the bid for the contract, the partners of the firm estimated that the following personnel would be used at the indicated cost per hour.

| Personnel | Hours | Cost per Hour |
|---|---|---|
| Staff | 4,200 | $13 |
| Seniors | 1,100 | 19 |
| Managers | 400 | 27 |
| Partners | 100 | 45 |

During the time that this study was being done, one of the firm's major industrial clients became involved in a significant lawsuit. This client required considerable accounting help in preparing a defense. This, in turn, created a severe scheduling problem for the firm and led to the need to pay the staff accountants overtime. When the study for the province was completed, the following hours and average hourly costs were accumulated for the contract.

| Personnel | Hours | Cost per Hour |
|---|---|---|
| Staff | 3,900 | $15 |
| Seniors | 1,200 | 19 |
| Managers | 500 | 27 |
| Partners | 110 | 45 |

**Required**

**a.** Determine the labor quantity, mix, and rate variances for this contract.

**b.** The industrial client has agreed to reimburse the accounting firm for the difference between the budgeted cost for the provincial contract and the actual costs incurred. What will be the amount of this bill? Will this recoup the accounting firm's entire loss?

**19-36 Direct labour rate, mix, and yield variances** (SMA).

Monson Company manufactures a special assembly which requires three different types of labour inputs: $E_1$, $E_2$, and $E_3$. The standard inputs of labour for the assembly units are: 2 hours of $E_1$, 3 hours of $E_2$, and 5 hours of $E_3$. Standard wage rates per hour are $10, $12, and $8 for $E_1$, $E_2$, and $E_3$, respectively.

In the month of February, 500 assembly units were produced. Recorded inputs of $E_1$, $E_2$, and $E_3$ were 900 hours, 1,800 hours, and 2,100 hours, respectively. Wage rates for $E_1$ and $E_2$ remained at standard, but $E_3$, being in short supply, was paid $8.50 per hour.

**Required**

Determine the following variances, if applicable:

**a.** Labour wage rate variance

**b.** Labour mix variance

**c.** Labour yield variance

**19-37 Labor rate, mix, and usage variances** (CMA adapted).

Landeau Manufacturing Company has a process cost accounting system. An analysis that compares the actual results with both a monthly plan and a flexible budget is prepared monthly. The standard direct labor rates used in the flexible budget are established each year at the time the annual plan is formulated and held constant for the entire year.

The standard direct labor rates in effect for the fiscal year ending June 30, 19X8, and the standard hours allowed for the output for the month of April are shown in the following schedule.

| | Standard Direct Labor Rate per Hour | Standard Direct Labor Hours Allowed for Output |
|---|---|---|
| Class III labor | $8.00 | 500 |
| Class II labor | 7.00 | 500 |
| Class I labor | 5.00 | 500 |

The wage rate for each labor class increased on January 1, 19X8, under the terms of a new union contract negotiated in December 19X7. The standard wage rates were not revised to reflect the new contract.

The actual direct labor hours worked and the actual direct labor rates per hour experienced for the month of April were as follows:

| | Actual Direct Labor Rate per Hour | Actual Direct Labor Hours |
|---|---|---|
| Class III labor | $8.50 | 550 |
| Class II labor | 7.50 | 650 |
| Class I labor | 5.40 | 375 |

**Required**

**a.** Calculate the dollar amount of the total direct labor variance for the month of April for the Landeau Manufacturing Company and analyze the total variance into the following components.
   **1.** Direct labor rate variance
   **2.** Direct labor mix variance
   **3.** Direct labor performance (efficiency) variance

**b.** Discuss the advantages and disadvantages of a standard cost system in which the standard direct labor rates per hour are not changed during the year to reflect such events as a new labor contract.

**19-38 Direct cost variances: Price, quantity, mix, and yield** (SMA).
The Cameron Company produces complex electronic equipment. The production process is performed by a team of employees in different wage scales. The standard cost to produce one unit of equipment is

**STANDARD COST**

| | | | |
|---|---|---|---|
| **Direct labour** | | | |
| **Wage Scale** | **Hours** | **Standard Rate** | |
| $A_2$ | 10 | $ 8 | $ 80 |
| $B_3$ | 15 | 12 | 180 |
| $C_4$ | 5 | 18 | 90 |
| | 30 | | $350 |
| **Direct materials** | | | |
| 1 kit | | | 175 |
| Total standard cost | | | $525 |

During the month, labour charges to production included 9,100 hours of $A_2$, at a total cost of $73,150; 13,150 hours of $B_3$, at a total cost of $156,485; and 4,325 hours of $C_4$, at a total cost of $78,715. There were 918 kits of electronic parts (actual cost $161,320) used during the month. Production for the month consisted of 900 units of the equipment.

**Required**

**a.** Calculate direct materials variances in as much detail as the data permit.
**b.** Calculate labour rate variances in as much detail as the data permit.
**c.** Compute the labour mix variance for the month.
**d.** Compute the labour yield variance for the month.

**19-39 Joint product variances.**

Ibex, Inc., is a producer of a variety of meat products. It uses raw material X to produce products A, B, and C, which sell for $12, $10, and $5 per pound, respectively. A 100-pound quantity of raw material X costs $600 and is expected to yield 50 pounds of A, 30 pounds of B, and 20 pounds of C.

**Required**

**a.** During the past month, 10,000 pounds of raw material X were put into process at a cost of $61,000, and resulted in 4,900 pounds of product A, 3,100 pounds of product B, and 2,000 pounds of product C. Do you consider the month's performance to be satisfactory? Briefly, why or why not?
**b.** Ibex is considering the use of a higher-quality raw material, costing $620 per hundred pounds, in its production process. Such a change would result in an output of 65 pounds of A, 25 pounds of B, and 10 pounds of C per 100 pounds of input. Would you advise the company to use the higher-quality material? Briefly, why or why not?
**c.** During the past month 10,000 pounds of the higher-quality material were put into process at a cost of $63,200 and resulted in 7,000 pounds of A, 2,500 pounds of B, and 500 pounds of C. Do you consider this performance to be satisfactory? Briefly explain.

**19-40 Volume, market, and mix variances** (CMA adapted).

The Artco Company makes three grades of indoor-outdoor carpets. The sales volume for the annual budget is determined by estimating the total market volume for indoor-outdoor carpet and then applying the company's prior year market share, adjusted for planned changes due to company programs for the coming year. The volume is apportioned among the three grades based upon the prior year's product mix, again adjusted for planned changes due to company programs for the coming year.

The company budget for 19X3 and the results of operations for 19X3 are as follows:

**BUDGET**

| | Grade 1 | Grade 2 | Grade 3 | Total |
|---|---|---|---|---|
| Sales (rolls) | 1,000 | 1,000 | 2,000 | 4,000 |
| Sales dollars (000s omitted) | $1,000 | $2,000 | $3,000 | $6,000 |
| Variable expense | 700 | 1,600 | 2,300 | 4,600 |
| Contribution margin | $ 300 | $ 400 | $ 700 | $1,400 |
| Traceable fixed expense | 200 | 200 | 300 | 700 |
| Traceable product margin | $ 100 | $ 200 | $ 400 | $ 700 |
| Selling and administration expense | | | | 250 |
| Net income | | | | $ 450 |

**ACTUAL RESULTS**

| | Grade 1 | Grade 2 | Grade 3 | Total |
|---|---|---|---|---|
| Sales (rolls) | 800 | 1,000 | 2,100 | 3,900 |
| Sales dollars (000s omitted) | $810 | $2,000 | $3,000 | $5,810 |
| Variable expenses | 560 | 1,610 | 2,320 | 4,490 |
| Contribution margin | $250 | $ 390 | $ 680 | $1,320 |
| Traceable fixed expenses | 210 | 220 | 315 | 745 |
| Traceable product margin | $ 40 | $ 170 | $ 365 | $ 575 |
| Selling and administration expense | | | | 275 |
| Net income | | | | $ 300 |

Industry volume was estimated at 40,000 rolls for budgeting purposes. Actual industry volume for 19X3 was 38,000 rolls.

**Required**

**a.** Calculate the profit impact of the unit sales volume variance for 19X3 using budgeted variable margins.

**b.** What portion of the variance, if any, can be attributed to the state of the carpet market?

**c.** What is the dollar impact on profits (using budgeted variable margins) of the shift in product mix from the budgeted mix?

**19-41 Sales mix and quantity variances, as well as material variances.** The Software Development Corporation produces computer programs on diskettes for home computers. The automated nature of this type of business means that fixed costs are very high, but variable costs are minimal. The firm is organized along three product lines: games, business programs, and educational programs. The average budgeted selling prices for each are $16 for games, $55 for business programs, and $20 for educational programs. The standard variable cost consists solely of one blank diskette per program at $2 per diskette without regard to the type of program. Fixed costs for the period were budgeted at $535,000. For the current period the firm budgeted sales of 40,000 games, 2,000 business programs, and 10,000 educational programs. Actual results for the period revealed the following.

| | | | |
|---|---|---|---|
| Sales | | | |
| Games | (35,000 units) | $616,000 | |
| Business | ( 4,000 units) | 198,000 | |
| Educational | (11,000 units) | 220,000 | |
| Total Sales | | | $1,034,000 |
| Variable costs | (50,750 diskettes) | | 106,575 |
| Fixed costs | | | 533,500 |
| Net income | | | $ 393,925 |

**Required**

**a.** Reconcile master budget net income to actual net income by calculating the sales mix variance, sales quantity variance, sales price variance, materials price and quantity variance, and the fixed cost budget variance.

**b.** A new marketing manager was hired during the period. The manager changed prices and redirected sales efforts. Should the new manager be praised or reprimanded?

**c.** An analysis reveals that the firm will have to pay $1.80 per disk during the next period. Prepare next period's master budget assuming a standard of one disk per program, total unit sales of 55,000, and the same sales mix and sales prices as experienced this period.

**19-42 Comprehensive: Multiple products—requires prior study of Chapter 13.** The Chemical Reclaiming Company purchases chemical residue at nominal cost and through a proprietary process is able to separate out three chemicals, which can be sold as new products. For every 1,000 pounds of residue processed, the firm expects to obtain 200 pounds of A, which sells for $4 per pound; 500 pounds of B, which sells for $6 per pound; and 300 pounds of C, which sells for $3 per pound.

**Required**

**a.** A recent 1,000-pound batch of residue produced 900 pounds of finished product. Of this output, 30% was A, which sold for $3 per pound; 60% was B, which sold for $7 per pound; and 10% was C, which sold for $3 per pound.
   **1.** What is the total variance from standard?
   **2.** Analyze the total variance in terms of its parts—price, mix and yield. Identify the variance, the amount, and whether F or U.
   **3.** Interpret (explain) what each of the variances means.
   **4.** What is the significance of these variances as generated by the accounting process?

**b.** The Chemical Reclaiming Company has established a standard purchasing cost of $1 per pound for the residue, although actual prices paid depend on market conditions (competitors use the residue to hold down dust on unpaved driveways). The standard cost of processing has been established as $2 per pound of input.

The actual costs of the 1,000-pound batch referred to in part (a) were $1.10 per pound for the residue and $1.95 for processing. Joint costs are allocated in proportion to the planned relative sales values of the finished products. No separable or identifiable costs are associated with products A, B, and C.
   **1.** What is the standard cost per pound for each of the products A, B, and C?
   **2.** What are the cost variances associated with processing the 1,000-pound batch in question?

**c.** The Chemical Reclaiming Company's only variable costs are $1 per pound for the residual material and $2 per pound for processing. Processing involves labor, containers, and labels. There are no fixed costs of production because the only equipment involved is an old cream separator that the owner of CRC found thrown out with a neighbor's trash. Selling and administrative costs are all fixed at $6,000 per month cash.
   **1.** How many tons of raw material must be processed for the owner of the firm to earn $4,000 monthly before income taxes?
   **2.** Given that the standard cost of processing 1 pound of input is $3, should any of the three products that result be dropped rather than sold? Explain.
   **3.** Given the standard cost per pound for each product as developed in part (b), should any of the three products be dropped rather than sold? Explain.
   **4.** If the market for product C should drop permanently to $2 per pound, should product C continue to be sold? Why or why not?

**19-43 Expected variances, labor mix, material quality** (CMA adapted).

The Lenco Company employs a standard cost system as part of its cost control program. The standard cost per unit is established at the beginning of each year. Standards are not revised during the year for any changes in material or labor inputs or in the manufacturing processes. Any revisions in standards are deferred until the beginning of the next fiscal year. However, in order to recognize such changes in the current year, the company includes planned variances in the monthly budgets prepared after such changes have been introduced.

The following labor standard was set for one of Lenco's products effective July 1, 19X1, the beginning of the fiscal year.

| | |
|---|---|
| Class I labor (4 hr @ $6.00) | $24.00 |
| Class II labor (3 hr @ $7.50) | 22.50 |
| Class V labor (1 hr @ $11.50) | 11.50 |
| Standard labor cost per 100 units | $58.00 |

The standard was based upon the quality of material that had been used in prior years and what was expected to be available for the 19X1–X2 fiscal year. The labor activity is performed by a team consisting of four persons with Class I skills, three persons with Class II skills, and one person with Class V skills. This is the most economical combination for the company's processing system.

The manufacturing operations occurred as expected during the first 5 months of the year. The standard costs contributed to effective cost control during this period. However, there were indications that changes in the operations would be required in the last half of the year. The company had received a significant increase in orders for delivery in the spring. There were an inadequate number of skilled workers available to meet the increased production. As a result, the production teams, beginning in January, would be made up of more Class I labor and less Class II labor than the standard required. The teams would consist of six Class I workers, two Class II workers, and one Class V worker. This labor team would be less efficient than the normal team. Since the reorganized teams work more slowly, only 90 units are produced in the same time period that 100 units would normally be produced. No raw materials are expected to be lost as a result of the change in the labor mix. Completed units have never been rejected in the final inspection process as a consequence of faulty work; this is expected to continue.

In addition, Lenco was notified by its material supplier that a lower-quality material would be supplied after January 1. One unit of raw material normally is required for each good unit produced. Lenco and its supplier estimated that 5% of the units manufactured would be rejected upon final inspection because of defective material. Normally, no units are lost due to defective material.

**Required**

**a.** How much of the lower-quality material must be entered into production in order to produce 42,750 units of good production in January with the new labor teams? Show your calculations.

**b.** How many hours of each class of labor will be needed to produce 42,750 good units from the material input? Show your calculations.

**c.** What amount should be included in the January budget for the planned labor variance due to the labor team and material changes? What amount of this planned labor variance can be associated with (1) the material change and (2) the team change? Show your calculations.

# APPENDIX 19A

# VARIANCES FOR COSTS SUBJECT TO A LEARNING EFFECT

In Chapter 3 we indicated that in many repetitive projects labor costs will be subject to a learning effect.[3] That is, as our employees become more familiar with a task, the subsequent times to complete the task can be accurately predicted with an exponential equation. In our accounting for such a project we must be careful to segregate the learning effect before calculating our cost variances.

Consider, for example, a firm that has a contract to construct 50 planes over a 3-year period. The first unit built required 30,000 labor hours to construct, and the standard cost per labor hour is \$7. This project is subject to an 80% learning effect for labor. With these facts, the average number of labor hours to construct all 50 airplanes can be determined from the formula in Appendix 3B as

$$\begin{aligned}\text{average time for 50 units} &= 30{,}000(50)^{-0.3219}\\ &= 8{,}516 \text{ hours}\end{aligned}$$

For purposes of calculating income, firms typically value all production at the average standard cost expected to be incurred over the production run of the project. Restricting our attention solely to labor costs, the standard cost for each plane then is determined by multiplying the average labor time per plane (8,516 hours) by the standard wage rate (\$7) to get an average standard cost of \$59,612.

Now assume that in the first year of the project the firm constructed 15 of the planes using 186,000 labor hours costing \$1,320,600. Were we efficient in the use of labor? The average standard cost for labor for 15

[3]This appendix relies on the material related to learning curves introduced in Appendix 3B. If that material was not studied, this appendix should be skipped.

planes is 15 × $59,612 = $894,180. Our initial reaction might be that we were grossly inefficient in our use of labor. However, this ignores the learning effect. Because of the learning effect we anticipate that early units will use more than the average number of labor hours. So to evaluate performance we must first determine how much labor was actually anticipated for the first 15 units. We can do so by using the learning curve equation to find the average time for the first 15 units as

$$\text{average time for 15 units} = 30{,}000(15)^{-0.3219}$$
$$= 12{,}547 \text{ hours}$$

We then multiply this average time by the 15 planes manufactured to get the total anticipated time for the 15 planes as 12,547 × 15 = 188,205 hours. At $7 per hour we should have anticipated a cost of $1,317,435 for the 15 planes. Now we can analyze performance as

| Actual Costs | Actual Inputs Used at Standard Price | Flexible Budget: Standard Cost, Anticipated Time | Flexible Budget: Standard Cost, Standard Time |
|---|---|---|---|
| $1,320,600 | $1,302,000 | $1,317,435 | $894,180 |
| $18,600 U (Price variance) | $15,435 F (Quantity variance) | $423,255 (Deferred learning costs) | |

The last term, *deferred learning costs,* is the amount of costs above average standard costs, which we anticipated because of the learning effect. Similar to the volume variance, it arises because we apply costs to production at an average rate that differs from the true underlying cost function. Having removed those expected additional costs we can now see that we actually were more efficient in the use of labor than we had anticipated. On the other hand, we paid labor on average $0.10 per hour more than budgeted.

The deferred learning costs are treated differently than are the variances. Variances are usually written off to the income statement, but the deferred learning costs are carried as an asset on the balance sheet. The rationale for deferring these costs to the balance sheet is that we are currently incurring higher-than-average costs but gaining experience that will allow us in the future to incur lower-than-average costs. It is felt that by charging average costs to the income statement we will reflect more accurately the true earning capacity of the firm. The alternative, to charge the income statement in early years for the actual high costs incurred and in later years the actual low costs incurred, would distort the firm's trend of earnings. Such an approach would make it appear that the firm earned little, or even incurred a loss, in early years and made high profits in the later years of the project. By averaging the costs over the entire project we reflect a more stable earnings pattern.

Let us now return to the example concerning the contract for 50 airplanes. Assume that in the second year we produce 13 additional planes (units 16 through 28) using 100,000 labor hours at a total cost of $695,000. Again we start by calculating the anticipated cost to produce those particular 13 units. We first calculate the total anticipated cost for 28 units and then subtract the cost for the first 15 units. The remainder will be the cost for units 16 through 28.[4]

$$\text{average time for 28 units} = 30{,}000(28)^{-0.3219} = 10{,}263 \text{ hours}$$

| | |
|---|---|
| Total cost for 28 units (10,263 × 28 × $7) | $2,011,548 |
| Total cost for first 15 units | 1,317,435 |
| Anticipated cost for units 16–28 | $ 694,113 |

The analysis of actual performance is as follows:

| Actual Costs | Actual Inputs Used at Standard Price | Flexible Budget: Standard Cost, Anticipated Time | Flexible Budget: Standard Cost, Standard Time |
|---|---|---|---|
| $695,000 | $700,000 | $694,113 | $774,956 |
| $5,000 F (Price variance) | $5,887 U (Quantity variance) | $(80,843) (Deferred learning costs) | |

Finally, assume that in year 3 we produce the remaining 22 units of the production run. These units required 138,000 hours, costing $971,520. Skipping the details, the results are as follows:

| Actual Costs | Actual Inputs Used at Standard Price | Flexible Budget: Standard Cost, Anticipated Time | Flexible Budget: Standard Cost, Standard Time |
|---|---|---|---|
| $971,520 | $966,000 | $969,052 | $1,311,464 |
| $5,520 U (Price variance) | $3,052 F (Quantity variance) | $(342,412) (Deferred learning costs) | |

[4]The computer program LEARN on the disk that accompanies this text will perform these calculations.

Assuming that the units are sold in the same year as they are produced, the journal entries for labor costs, the transfer of units to finished goods, and the sale of units are:

| | | |
|---|---|---|
| **Year 1** | | |
| Work-in-Process | 1,320,600 | |
| Accrued Payroll | | 1,320,600 |
| To record actual labor costs. | | |
| Finished Goods | 1,317,435 | |
| Labor Rate Variance | 18,600 | |
| Labor Quantity Variance | | 15,435 |
| Work-in-Process | | 1,320,600 |
| To transfer completed units. | | |
| Cost of Goods Sold | 894,180 | |
| Deferred Learning Costs | 423,255 | |
| Finished Goods | | 1,317,435 |
| To recognize units sold. | | |
| **Year 2** | | |
| Work-in-Process | 695,000 | |
| Accrued Payroll | | 695,000 |
| To record actual labor costs. | | |
| Finished Goods | 694,113 | |
| Labor Quantity Variance | 5,887 | |
| Labor Rate Variance | | 5,000 |
| Work-in-Process | | 695,000 |
| To transfer completed units. | | |
| Cost of Goods Sold | 774,956 | |
| Deferred Learning Costs | | 80,843 |
| Finished Goods | | 694,113 |
| To recognize units sold. | | |
| **Year 3** | | |
| Work-in-Process | 971,520 | |
| Accrued Payroll | | 971,520 |
| To record actual labor costs. | | |
| Finished Goods | 969,052 | |
| Labor Rate Variance | 5,520 | |
| Labor Quantity Variance | | 3,052 |
| Work-in-Process | | 971,520 |
| To transfer completed units. | | |
| Costs of Goods Sold | 1,311,464 | |
| Deferred Learning Costs | | 342,412 |
| Finished Goods | | 969,052 |
| To recognize units sold. | | |

Notice that finished goods are carried at anticipated standard cost for the units completed. The adjustment for deferred learning costs is made at the time the units are sold. Further, the balance in the Deferred Learning Costs account will be zero at the end of the third year.

In this appendix we have ignored differences between the master budget and the flexible budget. If actual sales were not as planned in the master budget, the difference between master budget income and flexible budget income can be reconciled by using the sales quantity variance or the marketing and production quantity variances.

## QUESTIONS AND EXERCISES: APPENDIX 19A

19-44 Abair Construction has a contract to build 16 units of an item for which all costs are subject to an 85% learning effect. The first unit cost $75,000 to construct. During 19X7 the firm built units 5, 6, 7, and 8 at a total cost of $156,740. Prepare the journal entry transferring the units to Finished Goods from Work-in-Process, and from Finished Goods to Cost of Goods Sold. Separate any efficiency variance from deferred learning costs.

19-45 RSM Electronics builds automatic testing equipment for computer hardware. The labor hours required to assemble this sophisticated equipment normally follow an 80% learning curve. It took 10,000 hours to construct the first unit of item J-48. The firm intends to build a total of 16 J-48s. For budgeting purposes RSM establishes the standard cost of each unit of J-48 to be the estimated average cost to build all 16 units. (a) If labor is paid $6 per hour, what is the anticipated deferred learning cost for selling the second unit of J-48? (b) If labor hours worked were as anticipated for the second unit but labor was paid $6.15 per hour, what is the amount of the labor rate variance?

## PROBLEMS AND CASES: APPENDIX 19A

19-46 **Learning curve: Standard cost, variances, and journal entries.**
Crystal Radio Corporation has received a contract to construct 32 radio testing units for the border patrol. It estimates that the cost to manufacture the first unit will be $5,000. All costs are expected to be subject to a 90% learning effect.

**Required**

**a.** Determine the standard cost to produce a testing unit given a production run of 32 units.

**b.** During the first period, CRC produced 4 testing units at an actual cost of $17,000. Prepare the journal entry to transfer these 4 units from Work-in-Process to Finished Goods and the entry to transfer the units from Finished Goods to Cost of Goods Sold.

**19-47 Learning curves and labor variances.**
A firm has been renting industrial robots to produce its products. The firm specializes in building complex equipment to special orders. The firm is considering the use of people instead of robots as labor on a new project.

The project calls for the production of 10 pieces of equipment. If people are used, the first unit will require 1,400 hours of labor. The laborers will be paid $7 per hour and subsequent units will show an 88% learning effect. If the robots are used, the first unit will require 1,150 hours. The robots cost $6 per hour and are incapable of learning.

**Required**

**a.** If the firm uses people, what additional costs or savings will it incur over using the robots?

**b.** Assume the firm hired the laborers. In the current period the firm produced units 3 and 4 in the production run using 1,880 hours of labor at a cost of $12,878. Determine the labor rate and usage variances.

**19-48 Learning curve: Variances and deferred costs.**
Custom Plastics manufactures an elaborate fire extinguisher that sprays a dry flame retardant. These units require considerable labor to assemble. The product is new; up until the beginning of the week only 30 units had been assembled. The firm intended to manufacture another 50 units this week; however, it was actually able to produce and sell 60 units. The first unit required 20 hours of labor time at $6 per hour. The assembly labor is subject to a 90% learning effect. The firm based its standard cost on an assumed production run of 200 units. During the week 545 labor hours were used to produce the 60 units at a total cost of $3,324.50.

**Required**

Determine the labor price and usage variance and the deferred learning curve costs for the week.

**19-49 Master budget: Learning curves, variances, and deferred costs.**
Midwest Trainers, Inc., has a contract to construct 16 aircraft simulators for a large airline. The first unit required 2,000 labor hours to construct. The firm prepared its master budget assuming that labor for subsequent units would be subject to an 88% learning curve and that the standard cost for labor would be $6.25 per hour. For the current period, the firm produced and sold units 3 and 4, using 2,600 labor hours costing $16,640. The master budget for the current period anticipated the production of units 3, 4, and 5.

**Required**

**a.** Determine the labor costs anticipated in the master budget (at standard cost for the production run).

**b.** Reconcile the master budget costs to actual labor costs by calculating appropriate variances and deferred costs.

**19-50 Learning curves: Reconciling budgeted and actual income.**
Mary's Marine began production of a new line of sailboats last year. For the current year, management had budgeted the production of 42 boats. Last year the firm had manufactured 15 boats. The entire production run of this model is anticipated to be 100 units. The standard cost for each sailboat was derived from the following

information. The first boat should have required 8,000 labor hours to complete. Materials for each boat should cost $32,500 and variable overhead should cost $4 per direct labor hour. Fixed overhead costs should be $250,000 per year and are applied to production on the basis of the number of units manufactured (not on the basis of labor hours). Labor costs are budgeted at $7 per hour. Direct labor and variable overhead are subject to a 90% learning effect. Materials and fixed overhead are not subject to a learning effect.

The master budget for the current period got wet one day. The only legible numbers remaining were sales of 42 units @ $95,000 = $3,990,000 and net income of $539,600.

During the year orders for 41 units were received, but only 40 units were produced and sold. An assistant has prepared the following actual cost income statement for the year.

| | |
|---|---|
| Sales (40 units) | $3,780,000 |
| Materials | 1,350,000 |
| Labor (161,000 hours) | 1,143,100 |
| Variable overhead | 668,150 |
| Fixed overhead | 249,000 |
| Net income | $ 369,750 |

Your assistant also tells you that the materials price variances for the year totaled $37,000 unfavorable.

**Required**
Reconcile the actual reported net income with budgeted net income by calculating all variances and any deferred learning curve costs. What net income figure should the firm report for the year?

**19-51 Learning curves: Comprehensive variance calculations.**
Merlock Industries' master budget called for the production of 15 units of product. The firm anticipated using 2 pounds of materials per unit at a cost of $300 per pound. Labor is subject to an 80% learning effect. The first unit of this production run was built last year using 200 labor hours at a cost of $5 per hour. The budgeted labor rate is $5 per hour. The entire production run for this product is expected to be 64 units. Fixed overhead is budgeted to be $4,000 for the period; variable overhead is budgeted at $0.75 per labor hour.

The firm incurred the following actual costs for the 15 units (units 2 through 16) manufactured and sold during the period.

| | |
|---|---|
| Materials (32.5 pounds) | $10,010.00 |
| Labor (1,175 hours) | 6,051.25 |
| Variable overhead | 822.50 |
| Fixed overhead | 3,850.00 |
| Total | $20,733.75 |

**Required**
Determine variances for materials price and quantity, labor rate and usage, variable overhead spending and efficiency, and fixed overhead budget. Also determine the amount of costs which should be deferred due to learning effects.

VARIANCES FOR COSTS SUBJECT TO A LEARNING EFFECT

**19-52 Performance evaluation: Learning curves and variances.**
Horizon Engineering has obtained a contract from the Defense Department to construct eight prototypes of a laser-directed surface-to-air missile. Horizon's bid price was based upon the assumption that material costs per item would follow a 90% learning curve and labor usage would follow a 70% learning curve. Overhead was not expected to be affected by learning. Using these assumptions and the firm's estimate that the first unit built would require 10,000 hours of labor at $6 per hour and materials would cost $40,000, Horizon prepared the following standard costs per item based on a production run of eight missiles.

| | |
|---|---|
| Standard materials cost | $29,160 |
| Standard labor cost | 20,580 |
| Standard overhead cost | 15,000 |

When the first unit was produced, it was discovered that materials costs were $40,000 and overhead costs were $15,000. However, it took 11,000 hours of labor to produce the first unit. It is believed that this was as efficient as this unit could be produced under the circumstances.

After the second unit was built, the following performance report was prepared for the second unit.

| | Actual Cost | Standard Cost | Variance |
|---|---|---|---|
| Materials | $31,000 | $29,160 | $1,840 U |
| Labor | 27,000 | 20,580 | 6,420 U |
| Overhead | 15,000 | 15,000 | — |

**Required**
Prepare a new performance report that more accurately reflects the efficiency with which the second unit was built.

# APPENDIX 19B

# VARIANCES FROM A PERT/COST BUDGET

PERT/Cost is a budgeting technique that balances the costs to complete individual activities in a project with the costs associated with the completion of the project as a whole.[5] The primary information that we need to establish a PERT/Cost budget is the cost of each activity as a function of the activity's completion time. If we have deviations from the budget, we will use this completion-time cost data to provide more informative variances.

A simple example will demonstrate the types of variances that can be calculated. In Figure 19-3 we have a network of four activities. Also included are the data necessary to set up the optimal PERT/Cost budget. Using the least-cost completion time for each activity results in a completion time of 9 days for the project. This implies a project-related cost of $70 for the 1 day in excess of 8 needed for completion. We can, however, shorten the critical path 1–2–4 by shortening activity 2–4 by 1 day for $60. Since this cost is less than the savings in project costs, we would shorten activity 2–4. The resulting budget allows completion in 8 days, wiping out the project-related cost. Since no more savings can accrue from further shortening of activities, we have the optimal PERT/Cost budget:

| Activity | Completion Time | Cost |
|---|---|---|
| 1–2 | 5 days | $250 |
| 1–3 | 3 days | 120 |
| 2–4 | 3 days | 270 |
| 3–4 | 4 days | 300 |

[5]This appendix relies on material covered in Chapter 10. If Chapter 10 was not studied, this appendix should be skipped.

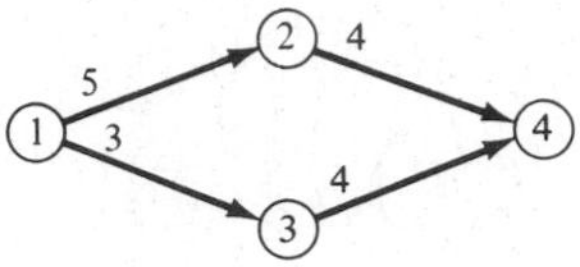


| Activity | Least-Cost Completion Time | Least Cost | Cost to Shorten by One Day | Cost to Lengthen by One Day |
|---|---|---|---|---|
| 1–2 | 5 days | $250 | $75 | $40 |
| 1–3 | 3 | 120 | 50 | 30 |
| 2–4 | 4 | 210 | 60 | 50 |
| 3–4 | 4 | 300 | 90 | 60 |

Project costs are $70 per day for each day in excess of 8 required to complete the project.

**FIGURE 19-3 A simple PERT/Cost example.**

Now let us see what happens if we deviate from the budget. For simplicity we will assume that all activity costs are labor. Of course in a real situation some of the costs for each activity would also be for materials and overhead, but the treatment of these other costs parallels our treatment of labor.

Assume that the $120 budgeted cost to complete activity 1–3 represents the use of 12 labor hours at a standard cost of $10 per hour. However, activity 1–3 was actually completed in 4 days using 16 labor hours costing a total of $156.80. Our initial reaction may be that the supervisor really messed up. Actual costs were $156.80, whereas the budget was only $120. But let us examine the situation more closely. Note that the information in Figure 19-3 indicates that we budgeted a cost of $150 for activity 1–3 if it were to take 4 days (the $120 least cost plus $30 if the activity were lengthened). That is, if we adjust our budget for the actual completion time, the budget allows a cost of $150. This is analogous to a flexible budget, in which we adjust for the number of units produced. But in a PERT/Cost situation the critical element is completion time, so we base our flexible budget on completion time. From the flexible budget figure for actual completion we can then see how the actual results compare to what was expected.

Assume that the $150 budgeted cost for completing activity 1–3 in 4 days represents 15 labor hours at $10 per hour. The analysis of results would be as follows:

| Actual Cost | Actual Inputs Used at Standard Price | Flexible Budget | Original Budget |
|---|---|---|---|
| 16 × $9.80 | 16 × $10 | 15 × $10 | 12 × $10 |
| $156.80 | $160 | $150 | $120 |

| Price variance | Quantity variance | Time variance |
|---|---|---|
| $3.20 F | $10 U | $30 U |

The objective of variance analysis is to pinpoint responsibility for deviations from budget. Here we have the traditional price and quantity variances, which are generally controllable by a production supervisor. In addition, we have the time variance that reflects the increased costs which were incurred due to the delay in the activity. This variance should be the responsibility of the person who caused the delay. The delay may well be due to the project manager for poor scheduling, or it may be due to an uncontrollable factor such as the weather. Whatever the cause, by separating the time variance from the labor price and quantity variances, we get a better measure for responsibility reporting.

Activity 1–3 is not on the critical path. Let us take a look at an additional complication that arises when an activity on the critical path takes longer than budgeted. Assume that the budgeted cost of $250 for activity 1–2 represents 25 labor hours at $10 each, that the cost of $40 to lengthen 1–2 represents the use of an additional 4 hours of labor at $10, and that activity 1–2 is actually completed in 6 days at a cost of $274.05 using 27 labor hours. If completed in 6 days, activity 1–2 should cost $250 + $40 = $290. But notice also that if it takes 6 days to complete activity 1–2, the total *project* completion time is extended to 9 days. This, in turn, means that we will incur the $70 in project costs for exceeding the 8-day completion limit. To reflect responsibility for the additional project cost, it will be included as part of the cost to complete activity 1–2. The variance analysis then becomes

| Actual Cost | Actual Inputs Used at Standard Price | Flexible Budget | Original Budget |
|---|---|---|---|
| 27 × $10.15 + $70 | 27 × $10 + $70 | 29 × $10 + $70 | 25 × $10 |
| $344.05 | $340 | $360 | $250 |

| Price variance | Quantity variance | Time variance |
|---|---|---|
| $4.05 U | $20 F | $110 U |

We have included the extra project cost as part of the flexible budget to reflect that extending the completion time of activity 1–2 causes the additional cost. In this way the $70 shows up as part of the time variance, thus reflecting that the $70 in project costs should be the responsibility of the person, or unit, that delayed the activity.

By the way, if activity 2–4 were now accelerated by another day to bring the project completion time back down to 8 days, we do not change the variance analysis for activity 1–2. Activity 1–2 taken alone would still have forced us to incur the project cost. When activity 2–4 is accelerated, we should then reduce its costs by the $70 project costs saved. This reduction will more than offset the $60 additional costs incurred to speed up the activity and, in effect, give the manager of activity 2–4 credit for having bailed out the project. Part of good responsibility accounting is also giving proper credit to those persons who deserve it.

## QUESTIONS AND EXERCISES: APPENDIX 19B

**19-53** Pitway Construction used PERT/Cost to budget the costs for erecting a hotel. The budgeted cost of installing the roof as a function of time was as follows:

| Time to Completion | Materials Cost | Labor Cost | Equipment Rental | Total |
|---|---|---|---|---|
| 5 days | $20,000 | $16,000 | $5,000 | $41,000 |
| 6 days | 18,000 | 14,000 | 6,000 | 38,000 |
| 7 days | 18,000 | 11,000 | 7,000 | 36,000 |
| 8 days | 18,000 | 11,000 | 8,000 | 37,000 |
| 9 days | 18,000 | 12,000 | 9,000 | 39,000 |

This activity is not on the project's critical path. The roof was actually completed in 8 days. Materials costs were $18,500; labor was $10,800; and equipment rental was $8,000.

Evaluate the performance of the roofing activity. Calculate as many variances as possible.

**19-54** Pat Baty was put in charge of activity 7–8 of a project. This activity was budgeted to cost $8,000 if completed in 7 days, $7,500 if completed in 6 days, and $7,700 if completed in 5 days. After preparing the appropriate PERT/Cost budget, activity 7–8 was budgeted to be completed in 6 days.

This was Pat's first job as a manager. Pat decided to impress the firm's management by completing the activity in just 5 days. The actual cost was $7,650. The firm is subject to a $300 penalty if the project is not completed in its budgeted time.

Evaluate Pat's performance under each of the following independent scenarios.

**a.** Activity 7–8 is not on the critical path.

**b.** Activity 7–8 is on the critical path, and all other activities were completed as scheduled.

**c.** Activity 7–8 is on the critical path and a predecessor activity also on the critical path had taken 1 day longer than it should have.

**d.** Same as (c), except activity 8–9 (also on the critical path) could have been speeded up 1 day at a cost of $125.

## PROBLEMS AND CASES: APPENDIX 19B

**19-55 Variance analysis with PERT/Cost.**

Jerold Industries recently undertook a construction project that had been budgeted using the PERT/Cost technique. Based on the following information, the firm budgeted the project to be completed in 10 days.

| Activity | Least-Cost Time (days) | Least Cost | Cost to Shorten by 1 Day | Fastest Completion Time (days) |
|---|---|---|---|---|
| 1–2 | 3 | $1,800 | $500 | 2 |
| 1–3 | 5 | 2,000 | 800 | 3 |
| 2–4 | 4 | 1,400 | 900 | 2 |
| 3–4 | 6 | 1,200 | 500 | 4 |
| 3–5 | 4 | 1,600 | 600 | 3 |
| 4–6 | 2 | 800 | 700 | 1 |
| 5–6 | 3 | 1,000 | 500 | 2 |

The project requires that a federal inspector be on the site from the start to completion. We are charged $900 per day for the inspector's presence.

**Required**

**a.** Determine the optimal budget for this project.

**b.** Assume that all activities were completed on time except for activity 3–4. Activity 3–4 was an assembly operation. Its costs were solely labor costs. The activity was budgeted to require 240 labor hours. If completed in 6 days, labor was to be paid its normal rate of $5 per hour. If completed in 5 days the average labor rate, including overtime, should have been $7.083. The activity was actually completed in 6 days using 250 labor hours at a total cost of $1,375. Prepare a performance report for the supervisor of activity 3–4.

**19-56 Variance analysis with PERT/Cost.**

Brixton, Inc., undertook a small project that consisted of several interdependent activities. The customer insisted that the project be completed in 54 days. Brixton agreed to a $2,000-per-day penalty for each day in excess of 54 that the project required.

Management sketched the network of activities and indicated the least cost-activity times (above the activity line) and the costs (below the activity line) to shorten each activity by 1 day. The resulting graph was as shown.

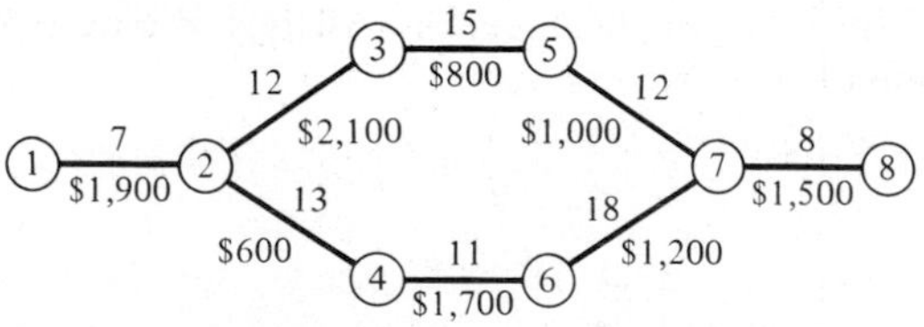


Activity 2–4's fastest completion time was 12 days, whereas activity 6–7 could be speeded up to as few as 14 days. Management's optimal budget therefore was

to complete activity 2–4 in 12 days and 6–7 in 16 days. The total budgeted costs for activity 6–7 (including speed-up costs) were $32,500. Activity 7–8 was budgeted to cost $19,800.

The entire project was on schedule until a problem developed with activity 6–7; it ended up taking 17 days to complete at a total cost of $31,500. Informed of the problem, the manager of activity 7–8 was able to speed up completion of activity 7–8 to finish in 7 days at a total cost of $21,400.

**Required**

Prepare performance reports for the managers of activities 6–7 and 7–8.

**19-57 Performance reports using PERT/Cost: Joint delay.**

The following network describes a small project undertaken by Westwood Industries.

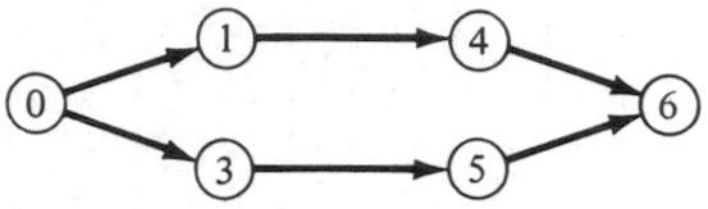


Westwood agreed to a $1,000 penalty if this project was not completed in 15 days. The optimal PERT/Cost budget called for the following completion times for each activity:

| Activity | Time | Activity | Time |
|---|---|---|---|
| 0–1 | 5 days | 0–3 | 2 days |
| 1–4 | 6 days | 3–5 | 7 days |
| 4–6 | 4 days | 5–6 | 6 days |

The budget for activity 4–6 called for the use of 50 labor hours at an average cost of $7.50 if completed in 4 days, and 50 labor hours at an average cost of $7 if finished in 5 days (there would be less overtime). Similarly, activity 5–6 was to use 90 hours of labor at a cost of $7 if completed in 6 days and 100 hours of labor at $6.75 if completed in 7 days.

All went according to plan until day 11 of the project. Both activities 4–6 and 5–6 developed snags. It turned out to take 5 days to complete activity 4–6 using 52 labor hours at an average cost of $7.10. Activity 5–6 was completed in 7 days using 95 labor hours costing $6.80 per hour.

**Required**

**a.** Prepare performance reports for the managers of activities 4–6 and 5–6.

**b.** How would your answer change if only activity 5–6 developed a snag, and upon hearing about the delay, the manager of activity 4–6 intentionally stretched the completion time of that activity?

# CHAPTER 20

# REACTING TO VARIANCES

Now that all the variances that will reconcile master budget net income to actual income have been identified, our next problem is to determine what they mean. In order to interpret the meaning of a variance we must understand the cause of the variance.

The main objective in establishing a standard cost system is to set up an information system that helps us in both planning and control. That is, the standards form the basis for the budgets, and the budgets in turn are used to evaluate alternative courses of action, such as pricing decisions, markets to enter or abandon, size of operations, and so forth. Once an operating strategy has been determined, the budget also becomes a yardstick for measuring performance in reaching budgeted goals. In this context, when we evaluate variances from budget, we want to group variances into three broad categories: (1) those variances that indicate a need to alter our standards, (2) those variances that indicate a need to alter performance, and (3) those variances that should be ignored.

## CAUSES OF VARIANCES

The first category of variances affects our future planning decisions. If, for example, an investigation of the cause of a material price variance reveals that the market price of a particular material has increased significantly beyond the standard cost, we will want to adjust the standard cost. Similarly, the investigation of a materials usage variance might reveal that we incorrectly estimated the amount of materials required per unit of product when we established the standards. Consider, for example, a lathe operation in which 1-inch spools are cut from a 24-inch rod. Quite understandably, a standard might be established that each spool requires 1 inch of rod or, alternatively, that each 24-inch rod will produce 24 spools. But more likely a portion of each rod will be wasted. That is, a portion of each rod is lost in the cutting process and the lathe requires a portion of the rod for gripping it. After taking into account the portions of the rod lost in the machining process, it might be the case that we can only produce 22 spools from each 24-inch rod. In this case the standard quantity of materials per spool should be 24 ÷ 22 or 1.09 inches of rod per spool. Once again, if an investigation of the variance reveals an error in the standard, the proper reaction is to correct the standard. The new standard will then be incorporated into future budgets, which may lead to decisions to change the selling price of the product, scale back the production of the product, or possibly even to abandon the product.

The second category of variances reflects conditions for which the appropriate corrective action is to alter performance. For example, a labor rate variance might arise because a supervisor assigned more skilled laborers to a task than required. A materials price variance may have arisen because we failed to monitor the inventory status of a material, suffered a shortage, and had to special order a shipment from a supplier more expensive than our normal source. Alternatively, we may find upon investigation that there has been an error in record keeping. Labor costs may have been charged to the wrong job or department, or supplies were expensed as purchased instead of as used. In each case, the objective is to call these lapses to the attention of the persons responsible. By doing so, we expect employees to attempt to minimize future deviations from the intended plans.

The last category includes those variances that do not require any corrective action. We know, for example, that standards are point estimates of the *average* range of efficient performance. We are aware that actual efficient performance will sometimes be somewhat higher and sometimes somewhat lower than average. Thus we should expect minor variances from standard. These small anticipated variances do not indicate the need for any managerial response. In fact, if standards are consistently met with no variance, we ought to suspect that someone is manipulating the records. Also included in this last category are variances that are due to causes beyond management control. A flu epidemic that results in heavy absenteeism, and less than normal efficiency from our remaining employees, may well cause a large unfavorable labor efficiency variance. Although the

**EXHIBIT 20-1 Classification and Sources of Variances**

| Management Control | Action to Be taken | Sources of the Variance[a] | Examples of Cause of the Variance |
|---|---|---|---|
| Controllable | Variances signal a need to adjust standards | Prediction error | Prices changed faster than expected. Recession lasted longer than expected. |
| | | Modeling error | Standard does not allow for normal waste. Standard did not allow for equipment set-up time. |
| | Variances signal a need to adjust performance | Implementation error | Supervisor assigned wrong workers to task. Improper supervision led to excess spoilage. |
| | | Measurement error | Employee failed to clock out on job when done. Annual tax payment charged to current expense. |
| Uncontrollable | Variances that should be ignored | Random error | Several employees ill with flu virus. Variance within anticipated error range. |

[a]This classification was developed by Joel Demski, *Information Analysis* (Reading, Mass.: Addison-Wesley, 1972).

result is clearly unfavorable, we would rarely hold anyone responsible for this type of variance.

Exhibit 20-1 summarizes these three broad categories of variances. It reflects our concern with being able to separate **controllable variances**, which signal a need for corrective action, from **uncontrollable variances**, which should be ignored. The controllable variances are further segregated by the type of corrective action needed: adjusting standards or adjusting performance. The third column in Exhibit 20-1 is a further breakdown, which categorizes variances by the type of problem that may lead to the variance. Finally, the fourth column provides several examples of specific causes of each type of variance.

### Management by Exception

Variance reports will be prepared in detail for each operating department. But as we proceed up the organization's hierarchy, the details will be supressed and higher-level managers will receive aggregated reports. This aggregation, in turn, will encourage an approach to supervision called management by exception. Under **management by exception** a manager delegates authority and responsibility to subordinates to carry out delegated tasks. The supervisor then presumes that the lower-level managers can capably handle their duties until evidence to the contrary is provided.

With management by exception, managers do not supervise the details of how tasks are carried out by subordinates. Instead, subordinates are left alone to manage their own affairs. Only if a problem develops that a subordinate does not appear to be able to solve will the supervisor step in to offer assistance and guidance.

In most organizations the use of a management-by-exception strategy is a necessity. As a practical matter, a manager cannot closely supervise the detailed tasks performed by several subordinates. Instead, the manager's supervisory role is generally limited to ensuring that each subordinate is performing assigned tasks consistent with the firm's plans.

## VARIANCE REPORTS

How the aggregation of performance measurement data (variances) assists management by exception can most easily be illustrated by means of an example. We will look at the types of reports prepared by a large wholesale bakery. At the production level it is not unusual to prepare daily reports. In the packaging department, for example, we may prepare a daily report on the number of units of each type of product (bread, dinner rolls, sweet rolls) packaged and the labor hours required. This report will be provided to the departmental supervisor, who can use it to monitor overall labor usage. The packaging department is responsible for seeing that everything baked for a particular day is packaged in time for shipment to the firm's customers (grocery stores). During normal weeks there will be a cycle in the amount of products produced and therefore packaged. Early in the week production will be relatively low, but it will increase substantially on Thursdays and Fridays. In this situation we would expect that early in the week the supervisor would experience unfavorable efficiency variances, which will be offset by favorable variances at the end of the week. Based on production schedules and longer-run budgets, the supervisor is expected to adjust the size of the packaging staff and its mix of full- and part-time employees so that, on the average, the firm's products are packaged with an efficient use of labor.

The daily reports are likely to be rather informal. The supervisor is expected to rely on past experience to determine whether a particular day's report is indicative of a problem. Thus if the supervisor receives a report of a $75 unfavorable labor efficiency variance for a Tuesday, this figure can be compared to previous variances for Tuesdays. If the variance is higher than is typical for a Tuesday, the supervisor can try to be more efficient the rest of the week to make up for this poor performance.

At the end of the week we may prepare a weekly recap of the daily variances. An example of this type of report is given in Exhibit 20-2. The

**EXHIBIT 20-2 Labor Efficiency Variance—Weekly Summary: Packaging Department**

| | Mon. | Tues. | Wed. | Thurs. | Fri. | Total for Week | Total Last Week | Year to Date | Year to Date Last Year |
|---|---|---|---|---|---|---|---|---|---|
| Standard hours | 27 | 24.5 | 31 | 38.5 | 44 | 165 | 165.2 | 1,998 | 1,978 |
| Actual hours | 32 | 32.0 | 32 | 32.0 | 36 | 164 | 164.0 | 1,968 | 1,952 |
| Variance, hours | 5 U | 7.5 U | 1 U | 6.5 F | 8 F | 1 F | 1.2 F | 30 F | 26 F |
| Standard rate | $10 | $10 | $10 | $10 | $10 | $10 | $10 | $ 10 | $ 10 |
| Variance, dollars | $50 U | $75 U | $10 U | $65 F | $80 F | $10 F | $12 F | $ 300 F | $ 260 F |

weekly report compares the current week's performance to the previous week, reports a year-to-date total variance and a comparison to the previous year's total variance at this point. The comparison figures allow the supervisor to put the variance in perspective and to remind the supervisor that our real interest is long-run average performance.

The figures provided in Exhibit 20-2 indicate that the cumulative year-to-date figure is a large (relative to daily variances) favorable variance of $300. In this business there are large increases in production before major holidays. To cover holiday demand the supervisor must borrow workers from other departments and/or hire temporary labor. These laborers are not as efficient as full-time packaging employees, so around holidays we routinely experience unfavorable labor efficiency variances. Since the standards are based on average performance over a year, the standards include an allowance for the expected inefficiency around holidays. Thus at the beginning of each year, when there are few holidays, we expect to build up a favorable cumulative variance, which will be offset later by unfavorable variances when holidays occur.

The packaging department's weekly variance summary will be forwarded to the supervisor's manager, along with weekly summaries for the other departments that report to the same manager. Exhibit 20-3 illustrates the report given to the manager in charge of packaging and distribution. At this level, the manager is concerned only with the total variance for each department for the week and how this performance compares to prior experience. If there seems to be a problem in one of the departments, the manager can review the department's daily reports and discuss the problem with the departmental supervisor.

Exhibit 20-4 presents a similar report to the vice-president in charge of production. Once again we see that only the total variances reflecting each manager's area of responsibility are reported to the vice-president. Finally, Exhibit 20-5 illustrates the report prepared for the firm's president. Note that Exhibits 20-2 through 20-5 have been limited to labor

**EXHIBIT 20-3 Labor Efficiency Variance—Weekly Summary: Packaging and Distribution Manager**

| Department | This Week | Last Week | Year to Date | Year to Date Last Year |
|---|---|---|---|---|
| Packaging | $10 F | $12 F | $300 F | $260 F |
| Shipping | 40 U | 10 U | 100 F | 170 F |
| Delivery | 18 F | 6 U | 20 U | 10 F |
| Totals | $12 U | $ 4 U | $380 F | $440 F |

efficiency variances. In practice, of course, we would be preparing reports for all variances. Also, to allow you to follow the numbers from exhibit to exhibit, we presumed that all reports are prepared weekly. It is more likely that at the vice-presidential and presidential levels the reports are prepared monthly or quarterly.

### Timeliness

At each level of management the expectation is that managers will monitor their own performance and adjust performance as needed, so that when a summary report is prepared for a superior, each manager's overall performance will be approximately at standard. This implies that if our accounting reports are going to be useful to managers, they must be prepared on a timely basis. If a problem develops, we want to inform the manager soon enough that corrective action can be taken to get overall performance in line with budgetary expectations prior to the preparation of a summary report for the manager's superior.

**EXHIBIT 20-4 Labor Efficiency Variance—Weekly Summary: Vice-President, Production**

| Manager | This Week | Last Week | Year to Date | Year to Date Last Year |
|---|---|---|---|---|
| Packaging and distribution | $12 U | $ 4 U | $380 F | $440 F |
| Mixing and baking | 45 F | 15 F | 60 U | 95 U |
| Auxiliary services | 18 U | 10 F | 30 U | 15 U |
| Totals | $15 F | $21 F | $290 F | $330 F |

**EXHIBIT 20-5 Labor Efficiency Variance—Weekly Summary: President**

| Vice-President | This Week | Last Week | Year to Date | Year to Date Last Year |
|---|---|---|---|---|
| Production | $15 F | $21 F | $290 F | $330 F |
| Sales | 40 U | 20 F | 100 U | 50 F |
| Administration | 75 F | 18 F | 50 F | 120 U |
| Totals | $50 F | $59 F | $240 F | $260 F |

### Fairness

Managers must also perceive that our reports are fair if we expect them to adjust their actions based on our accounting reports. For example, if a manager views the method by which we charge for the use of a central computer as unfair, the manager is less likely to control usage variances for computer time. Similarly, if we have a history of errors in preparing reports (miscalculating variances, making arithmetic errors, and so forth), we can expect managers to ignore our reports and not attempt to meet budgetary goals.

### Information Overload

Finally, to be useful, reports must be succinct so that managers can quickly digest important information. Although we have pointed out many advantages of computers for accountants, the ease with which we can now prepare reports tempts us to provide too much data. With computer technology it is quite inexpensive to send a manager not only summary reports on the manager's activities but also the reports given to subordinates and to the subordinates' subordinates. In fact, stories often appear about firms whose accounting systems inundate managers with reams of reports.

The problem of course, is that no one has the time to wade through voluminous reports. A situation called **information overload** occurs, wherein the sheer volume of data makes it difficult for people to comprehend the meaning of information. The important information gets buried in a mountain of trivia. Even if a manager attempts to sort out the relevant from the irrelevant, the important from the unimportant, the task may be so time-consuming that the manager may eventually give up in frustration and ignore all of our reports. Thus in designing our accounting reports, we should keep in mind what information the manager needs to know. We should restrict our accounting reports only to concise, relevant information.

## THE DECISION TO INVESTIGATE A VARIANCE

We indicated that we need to know the causes of variances to interpret and respond to them properly. Left undiscussed was how a manager should decide when to investigate a variance to determine its cause. The approaches to this decision can vary from informal to formal analyses. In some firms, reliance is placed on managers to "know" when an unusual variance should be followed up. In this case we presume that a manager has the experience to recognize developing problems and will act quickly. In these cases our accounting reports may simply report the current and previous-period variances as in Exhibits 20-2 through 20-5.

Another popular approach is to graph variances over time. Graphs such as the one provided in Figure 20-1 provide managers with a visual record of the size of variances that have been experienced in the past. This gives the manager a feel for the size of the normal or random variances that are expected to occur routinely, and thus should make it easier to spot abnormal variances. In addition, the graphical approach may make it easier for managers to see developing trends. For example, in Figure 20-1 the variances for 19X2 seem to be within the size range of variances experienced in 19X1, but the steadily increasing pattern of the variances may nonetheless be indicative of a problem.

The graphical approach is often augmented with predetermined limits which signal that an investigation of a variance should be undertaken when a variance exceeds the set limit. That is, two lines are superimposed on the graph, as in Figure 20-2. In this form the graph is called a **control chart.** Variances that fall within the control limits are ignored (unless a

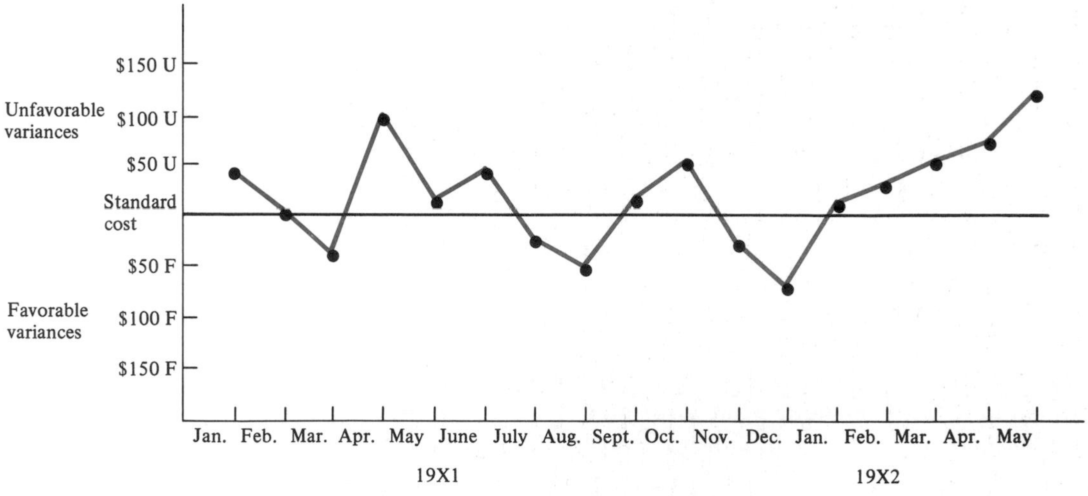


**FIGURE 20-1 Materials usage variance for a machining department.**

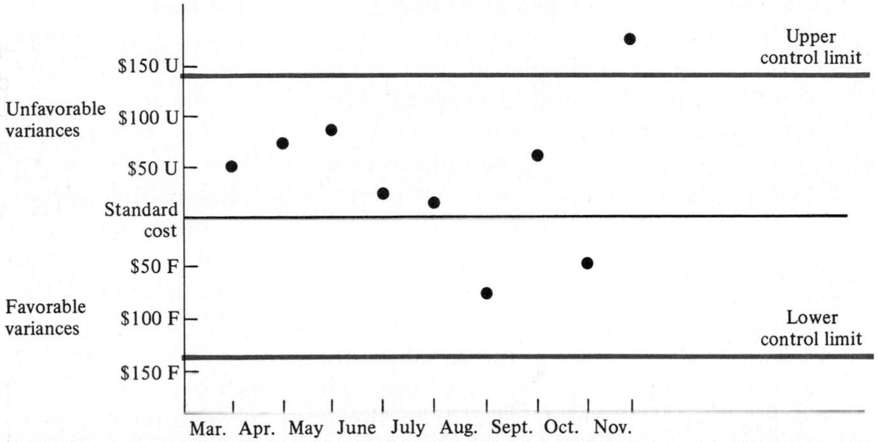


**FIGURE 20-2 A graph of variances with preestablished control limits.**

pattern develops), while variances exceeding the control limits are investigated to determine whether corrective action is required. Thus in Figure 20-2 the variance for November would be investigated because it exceeds the control limit.

### Setting Control Limits

The value of imposing **control limits** on a chart of variances is directly related to the care we exercise in establishing the limits. If the limits are set arbitrarily, we are not guaranteed that we are investigating the right variances. If the limits are set very tight, we will investigate too many variances that in fact do not really require a managerial response. Alternatively, if the limits are too loose, correctable problems may escape our notice. The object is to try to balance the costs incurred in investigating variances with the costs incurred if a correctable problem goes unnoticed. We will look at a formal approach to minimizing the sum of these two costs in the next section, but first we will discuss an approach frequently seen in practice.

### Statistical Control Limits

Production management texts and operations research texts often advocate the use of a control chart for quality control. In this setting, control limits are typically very wide (allowing large deviations before corrective action is taken). For example, a firm may sell large quantities of products, such as integrated circuits, for which it claims a stated maximum rate of defective units. That is, management may guarantee that there will be less than 1% defective units in each batch of integrated circuits sold. Periodically management takes samples of the products and tests them to determine whether they are working properly. Of course, even if the overall rate of defective units in a batch is 1%, we would expect that some samples would reveal more than 1% of the units as defective. If we decide that the batch exceeds the 1% defective rate, we might either discard the batch or inspect all units. Both are expensive alternatives. On the other hand, if we ship the units anyway, and the percentage of defective units is only slightly in excess of 1%, our customers probably will not notice, or, even if they do, they may not care so long as our products are usually within the specified quality tolerance limits. In this situation, the firm can justify very wide control limits because of the relative costs. The costs we incur when we reject a batch are very high relative to the costs of sending too many defective units to a customer. A frequently suggested control limit in this situation is a sample error rate of 3 standard deviations from the stated (1%) error rate. That is, we determine the standard deviation of the possible error rates in a given sample. Then only if a sample shows an error rate that is greater than the stated rate plus 3 times the standard deviation will we throw away or fully inspect a particular batch of circuits.

While the 3-standard-deviation rule makes sense in certain quality control applications, it is not directly applicable to our variance investigation decision, since the costs of not investigating a variance may be quite high relative to the costs of undertaking an investigation. In these cases a much tighter control limit than 3 standard deviations is justified. Unfortunately, the 3-standard-deviation rule seems to have taken on a life of its own. It is frequently cited, even by accountants, as a "practical" rule for deciding when a variance is too big. But the rule is appropriate only when correction costs are very high relative to the costs of not correcting an existing problem. The next section, which examines a more formal approach to the decision of which variances to investigate, clarifies this point.

### Control Limits Based on Relative Costs

The formal approach to analyzing whether a particular variance should be investigated explicitly recognizes the costs incurred in making an investigation, the costs of not correcting a correctable problem, and the probability that a particular variance is indicative of a correctable problem. We begin by considering the actions that are available to management when a variance is reported. We can either investigate the cause of a variance or not investigate the variance. We also know that the variance either arose from a correctable problem or falls into the category of random causes for which no corrective action will be taken. We refer to these as nonrandom and random causes, respectively.

The two management actions and the two causes of variances give us four possible combinations of action and cause, as follows:

1. We can investigate and find a random cause.
2. We can investigate and find a nonrandom cause.
3. We can choose not to investigate and the variance is random.
4. We can choose not to investigate and the variance is nonrandom.

Each of these action-and-cause combinations results in our incurring a different cost. If we investigate and find a random cause, we will have incurred the cost to make an investigation. Let us label the investigation cost $I$. If we investigate and find a nonrandom cause, we will incur both the investigation cost and a cost to correct the cause of the variance (labeled $C$). The total cost of this action-and-cause combination can then be represented as $I + C$.

If we choose not to investigate the cause of a variance and the variance in fact is a random variance, then we do not incur any costs. Finally, if we choose not to investigate, but the variance is really due to a correctable problem, we will incur a loss for failing to correct the problem. For example, if a variance reflects the inefficient use of materials, but we do not investigate the variance, the inefficient use is likely to continue. The cost of the extra materials that could be saved if we knew about the inefficiency is our loss from failure to correct the problem. Let us represent that loss by $L$.

Our decision problem can now be represented in chart form as in Exhibit 20-6. Our problem now is to determine which management action results in the lowest total cost for the firm. Let us assume that we have estimated that it costs $80 to investigate the cause of a variance. Furthermore, the cost to correct the cause of a nonrandom variance is $20, whereas the loss from failure to discover a nonrandom variance is $120. These numbers have been put into a decision table in Exhibit 20-7. Referring to Exhibit 20-7, we can see that if a particular variance is due to a random cause our cheapest action is not to investigate (a zero cost versus a cost of $80). But if the variance is due to a nonrandom cause, we are better off investigating the variance (a cost of $100 versus $120).

**EXHIBIT 20-6 The Variance Investigation Decision Table**

| | Cause | |
|---|---|---|
| Action | Random | Nonrandom |
| Investigate | $I$ | $I + C$ |
| Do not investigate | — | $L$ |

**EXHIBIT 20-7 An Illustrative Decision Table**

| | Cause | |
|---|---|---|
| **Action** | **Random** | **Nonrandom** |
| Investigate | \$80 | \$100 |
| Do not investigate | — | \$120 |

Unfortunately, without investigating we do not know whether a particular variance is due to a random or nonrandom cause. But if we can estimate the probability that a variance is due to a nonrandom cause, we can still solve the problem.

Let us assume that for a particular variance we estimate the probability that it is due to a nonrandom cause as 25%. This, of course, implies that there is a 75% chance that the variance is due to a random cause. We can now calculate the expected costs (the costs weighted by their probabilities) of each management action. For example, if we investigate, there is a 75% chance that we will find the variance to be due to a random cause. Thus there is a 75% chance that we will incur only the \$80 investigation cost. In addition, however, there is a 25% chance that we will find the variance to be nonrandom. In this latter case we incur a total cost of \$100. The expected cost of deciding to investigate the variance is

$$\begin{aligned} E(\text{investigate}) &= 0.75 \times \$80 + 0.25 \times \$100 \\ &= \$85 \end{aligned}$$

If we choose not to investigate, there is still a 75% chance that the variance is random, so in this case we have a 75% chance of not incurring any cost. However, there is also a 25% chance that the variance is nonrandom; hence if we do not investigate, we will incur a loss of \$120. The total expected cost of not investigating is therefore

$$\begin{aligned} E(\text{do not investigate}) &= 0.75 \times \$0 + 0.25 \times \$120 \\ &= \$30 \end{aligned}$$

A comparison of the expected cost of not investigating (\$30) with that of investigating (\$85) indicates that for a variance that has only a 25% chance of being due to a nonrandom cause our best action is not to investigate.

### Indifference Probability

Let us now recast our analysis into general notation. If we let $P_1$ represent the probability that a variance is due to a random cause, and $P_2$ represent the probability that a variance is due to a nonrandom cause, the expected cost calculations can be represented by

$$E(\text{investigate}) = P_1I + P_2(I + C)$$
$$E(\text{do not investigate}) = P_2L$$

We can now use this notation to determine the probability that a variance is due to a nonrandom cause that leaves us indifferent between investigating and not investigating the cause of a variance. We call this the **indifference probability.** Knowing its value will save us a number of computations. That is, if we know the indifference probability, then anytime we get a variance whose probability of being due to a nonrandom cause exceeds the indifference probability, we know we should investigate the cause of the variance. We will not have to calculate the expected cost of each of our actions.

We will be indifferent between investigating and not investigating a variance when the expected cost of the two actions are equal to each other. This indifference can be represented by

$$E(\text{do not investigate}) = E(\text{investigate})$$
$$P_2L = P_1I + P_2(I + C)$$

and because $P_1 + P_2 = 1$, it must be true that $P_1 = 1 - P_2$. Then substituting for $P_1$, we get

$$P_2L = (1 - P_2)I + P_2(I + C)$$
$$P_2L = I - P_2I + P_2I + P_2C$$
$$P_2L = I + P_2C$$
$$P_2(L - C) = I$$
$$P_2 = \frac{I}{L - C}$$

Let us look at how the result can be used with the information from our previous example. In that example we had $L = \$120$, $I = \$80$, and $C = \$20$. Substituting these figures into the equation for the indifference probability yields

$$P_2 = \frac{\$80}{\$120 - \$20}$$
$$= 80\%$$

For this cost structure, the result says that a variance must have a probability of being due to a correctable cause in excess of 80% before an investigation is justified. Thus, if a variance has only a 25% chance of being nonrandom, as in this example, we do not have to calculate the expected cost of investigating and the expected cost of not investigating. Instead we can simply compare the 25% probability with our 80% indifference probability and conclude that an investigation is not warranted.

It may seem strange that in the preceding example we would not investigate variances with a high probability of being due to a nonrandom problem. The cause of this is the very high cost of investigation versus the cost incurred if the problem is not corrected. Thus we might feel that there is a high probability of some minor pilferage of materials leading to a materials quantity variance, but the cost of surveillance to discover whether the minor theft is occurring may be quite high. In this case, on an expected value basis, the cost of finding out the cause of the variance may outweigh the additional costs incurred due to theft. Of course, if the loss incurred is very high relative to the investigation cost, the situation changes, and the indifference probability decreases. For example, consider a firm that uses gold in its manufacturing process. A small quantity variance in the usage of gold could generate a very large loss from failure to discover a correctable cause. If this loss were $1,020, then the critical probability becomes (assuming correction and investigation costs are the same as before)

$$P_2 = \frac{\$80}{\$1{,}020 - \$20}$$
$$= 8\%$$

In this case, variances with only a slight probability of being due to a nonrandom cause are investigated.

### Accounting Data Requirements

We developed the decision rule for investigating variances assuming that certain information was available, but how in fact can we obtain the needed information? The cost information can be obtained by keeping records for a period of time concerning the results of investigation decisions. Thus for all variances investigated during the record-keeping period, we can estimate the cost for each investigator's time, the opportunity costs for possibly disrupting the manufacturing process, and the possible cost due to decreased morale of employees.[1]

[1]This is a particularly difficult number to estimate. There is likely to be some effect because we will be checking up on employees. If the investigation is undertaken in an accusatory manner, the cost could be high; however, if everyone understands we are simply looking for an explanation of a variance, without blame, the cost can be kept low.

Similarly, for those variances found to be due to a correctable cause, we can keep a record of the costs to correct the problem. Again, we need to include the direct expenditures for making the correction and any morale costs. For example, if we find that a variance is due to the inability of a supervisor to oversee the job properly, we may be forced to dismiss the supervisor. The correction costs include not only severance pay and the costs to train a new supervisor, but possibly costs incurred because the former supervisor was well liked. Employees may resent the replacement, venting their feelings with below-average performance or a threat to unionize. Clearly, estimating these costs is extremely difficult.

Finally, the loss that the firm would have incurred had a correctable cause not been corrected must be estimated. Although the extra costs that would have been incurred in a single period might be reasonably estimated, it is often difficult to estimate how long these extra costs would be incurred. Would the next variance report have triggered an investigation if the current variance were overlooked?

The last bit of information needed for the formal decision rule is the estimate of the probability that a particular variance is due to a nonrandom cause. For the model we described, some historical records might suffice.[2] From the records used to develop the cost estimates we will also have available a record of the variances that were investigated and the actual results of the investigations. Assuming that there is a relationship between the size of a variance and the probability that it is due to a nonrandom cause, we could prepare a chart describing the relative frequency of correctable versus noncorrectable causes by size of variance. Records might show, for example, that of all the variances investigated during a period the following results were observed.

| | Cause of the Variance | | | | |
|---|---|---|---|---|---|
| | Random | | Nonrandom | | |
| Size of Variance (percent of standard cost) | Number | % | Number | % | Total Investigations |
| 0%–5% | 18 | 100 | 0 | 0 | 18 |
| 5%–10% | 12 | 75 | 4 | 25 | 16 |
| 10%–15% | 10 | 56 | 8 | 44 | 18 |
| 15%–20% | 9 | 43 | 12 | 57 | 21 |
| 20%–25% | 3 | 33 | 6 | 67 | 9 |
| 25%–100% | 0 | 0 | 2 | 100 | 2 |

[2]The model we have described is very simple. The accounting literature contains many refinements such as different costs for $I$, $C$, and $L$ dependent on the precise cause of the variance, the use of Bayesian statistics to derive the actual value of $P_2$, and models that allow the process to correct itself. However, the model presented incorporates most of the elements accountants must estimate that are common to all the models.

With this information we can use the relative frequency of the number of variances found to be nonrandom for each variance size category as an estimate of the probability that a variance of that size is nonrandom. For example, if the standard cost for an item were $200,000 and a variance of $24,000 were reported (12% of the standard cost), we could estimate from the chart that the probability of the variance being due to a nonrandom cause is 44%.

It should be clear that providing the information required for the investigation decision is quite difficult. However, going through the exercise should nonetheless give management a general approximation of the critical probability of a variance being nonrandom that justifies investigation.

## RESPONSIBILITY VERSUS BLAME

When an investigation reveals that a variance is due to a nonrandom cause, someone is going to be held responsible for the problem. If the variance is due to an error in our standard, either someone made an error in establishing the standard or someone failed to update it when conditions changed. Similarly, if the variance is due to inadequate supervision, the supervisor will be held responsible for the variance. Although lines of responsibility are usually easy to ascertain, we must be careful to realize that responsibility does not equate to blame. For example, if there is excess waste, a supervisor may be held responsible for inadequately explaining the use of a new material to employees. Though responsible for the variance, the supervisor may not be blameworthy if we also discover that several new materials were introduced simultaneously, and the supervisor did as well as could be expected under the circumstances in explaining the use of each to employees.

Even in cases in which the person held responsible for a variance is clearly at fault, we must be careful how we react. People are not perfect; mistakes do occur. In evaluating performance we must be careful to maintain a long-run perspective. Does the employee usually make the right decisions, is performance usually close to standard? If so, occasional lapses can be tolerated. Only when performance is habitually at variance with standard should we consider disciplinary action.

In spite of the preceding paragraph, many managers view our budgets and performance reports as targets that must be rigidly adhered to. Such persons view any deviation from standards as a major problem. In this type of situation we should be aware of some natural responses that are likely to occur, so that abuses can be corrected before they destroy our budgeting and evaluation system.

### Behavioral Responses to Excessive Budgetary Pressure

When excessive pressure is placed on personnel to meet standards, we can anticipate that the standards will be met at least nominally. Unfortunately, the actions that people take to meet the budget may not be in the best interest of the firm. For example, if costs are running ahead of standard on a product, employees might start shorting materials on subsequent products, or performing labor operations in a quicker but haphazard manner. Although cost standards may be met, it may be at the expense of producing an inferior product. Similarly, workers may stockpile favorable variances by not returning excess materials on good days, but instead save them for days when they experience excess materials usage. Labor can similarly be stockpiled by storing completed units produced in excess of standard until they are needed on days in which production quotas are not met. These actions will lead to the firm carrying substantial inventories "off the books" but in which the firm nonetheless may have a significant investment. In addition, increases in productivity are effectively hidden from management by these invisible inventories. As a consequence, the firm's standards (and costs) will become progressively noncompetitive with those of other firms.

**Budgetary slack** is the difference between the actual resources needed to accomplish an objective and the resources budgeted in the standards. Slack can enter the system through means other than those mentioned above. With heavy pressure to meet standards, we can expect people to attempt to influence the setting of the standards to provide a margin of comfort (slack) for meeting the standard. If standards are easily met, we can then anticipate that they will only just be met, with productivity slackening as targets are approached.

In each of these cases, when undue pressure is put on people to meet the budget, "meeting the budget" becomes the goal. But meeting the budget is not the organization's real goal. The actual goal is the production of products in as efficient a way as possible while maintaining a desired quality. The budget and standards are not ends in themselves; rather, they are intended to help us communicate our expectations, coordinate interdependent activities, and diagnose the cause of deviations—both good and bad.

### Necessary Attributes of an Effective Performance Measurement System

Throughout this text we have discussed various attributes that performance measurement systems, such as a standard cost system, should possess. Let us pause here to summarize the major points.

To be effective in influencing performance, budgets and standards must be accepted by employees as representing proper goals. A budget emphasizing cost minimization may be ignored if employees have traditionally been asked to concentrate on quality and there has been no communication on why the goal has been changed. Similarly, if standards have been set so tight that employees believe they are unattainable, the standards are unlikely to be accepted by employees. In both cases better acceptance of the firm's goals and standards may be achieved by consulting with employees when establishing goals and standards.

Performance feedback must be sufficiently rapid that employees can adjust their performance in a timely manner. Rapid feedback should allow employees to take compensatory actions to try to get overall period performance in line with budget. In addition, if there was a specific problem or unusual circumstance that gave rise to a deviation from plans, we want to provide feedback before people forget what the problems or circumstances were. This in turn should help employees associate events with their effect on performance reports.

Employees should be held responsible only for aspects of performance over which they can exercise some control. Inefficiencies in one area should not be passed on to subsequent managers (such as charging higher rates for services when those services have been inefficiently supplied). Similarly, costs that may be charged to a department for product costing purposes (such as fixed overhead) should not be included in performance reports if a manager cannot influence their amount.

Performance feedback should be constructive. We should attempt to identify sources of problems and recommend remedial action so that employees can meet the firm's expectations.

Each of the points just mentioned can be summarized further by stating that performance measurement systems should be perceived as being fair. If a system is viewed as unfair, we cannot expect people to use it as a guide to their actions.

### Dysfunctional Effects of Performance Measurement

In addition to the foregoing attributes of a good performance system, we should also be aware of pervasive problems that affect most systems. Any formal system results in employees putting more effort into those aspects of their jobs that are objectively measured. Unfortunately, we generally cannot include all the attributes of good performance in our performance measures. Thus managers may tend to concentrate on the performance of their own departments without giving much consideration to how their performance is affecting other departments. In competing for resources, managers may concentrate on their own needs without much thought for overall firm needs.

Along the same line, we must be aware that performance measurement tends to lead people to concentrate on short-run objectives. Obviously, promotions and salary increases are likely to depend, at least in part, on current performance. This can lead to attempts to maximize current performance at the expense of future performance. For example, maintenance postponed to keep current costs down may lead to expensive downtime and repairs in the future. This emphasis on the short run is particularly severe in entry level and middle management. At these levels, promotions and transfers are frequent. Thus some managers can focus their attention on short-run returns and be confident that they will be elsewhere by the time any difficulties surface.

We must also be aware that some people may attempt to manipulate the system. Attempts to build slack into any system are nearly universal. It is probably impossible to keep all slack out, but we need to be careful that it does not get so far out of hand as to destroy efforts to improve performance. Similarly, we must be aware that some people may try to manipulate performance measures through falsifying records (hidden inventories or charging costs to a wrong account). This type of behavior can seriously compromise the usefulness of our operating data for projecting future performance and for evaluating the relative profitability of products. To counter this type of activity we should periodically review our internal control systems established to ensure the integrity of our accounting information.

## DISPOSITION OF VARIANCES

Once the cause of a variance has been determined, we are in a position to account for it properly. Our choices are to charge the variance as a period cost (a loss or gain on the income statement), as a product cost (adjust our inventory and cost of goods sold balances), or as a deferred charge (a balance sheet account).

Anticipated variances, such as seasonal variances, which are expected to be offset in the future, should be treated as a deferred charge. For example, in the earlier illustration concerning the packaging department in a bakery, we indicated that the firm generally experienced favorable variances early in the year, offset by unfavorable variances near holidays. In this situation, we should charge the anticipated portion of the monthly or quarterly variances to a deferred charge account in the expectation that they will balance out over the year.

Variances that arise from avoidable causes and variances not expected to be incurred again in the future should be written off as period costs. For example, a materials price variance arising from a purchasing error is not properly part of the product cost but instead should be treated as a loss for the period. Similarly, a favorable efficiency variance arising from unusual efficiency not expected to recur should be treated as a period gain.

Variances that arise because the standards were in error should be treated as product costs. For example, if we erred in our prediction of standard materials prices, the price variance should be treated as a product cost. That is, we want to adjust inventory and cost of goods sold balances to reflect the actual costs of production.

Random variances, as well as those variances that we failed to investigate because we presumed them to be random, present a problem. Arguments can be made that random variances should be deferred, treated as a period cost, or treated as a product cost. If the variances are random, we might argue that they should tend to cancel each other out over time. By deferring them, our income statement will reflect the average costs we expect to incur over the long run. On the other hand, we can argue that random variances, individually, are not expected to recur. Therefore any gains or losses from random effects should be treated as a period cost when incurred. Finally, we might argue that random variances are uncontrollable and reflect actual costs that proved to be necessary to produce the period's products. In the latter case, the variance should be treated as a product cost. Fortunately, random variances are usually immaterial in size. Hence we need not be overly concerned with their proper accounting treatment. As a practical matter, they are usually written off as a current period gain or loss.

## SUMMARY

The variances calculated in previous chapters should lead managers to make one of three responses. The variances should be ignored, the firm's standards should be changed, or efforts should be made to improve performance. The appropriate reaction depends on the underlying cause of the variance.

Whether a variance should be investigated to determine its cause depends on the relative costs and benefits. Formal decision models can help structure the problem and point out the factors to be considered. Unfortunately, the accounting data needed to implement the formal models are often very difficult to obtain.

## DEMONSTRATION PROBLEM

Assume that management estimates the cost to investigate a variance as \$700, the cost to correct the cause of a controllable variance as \$200, and the probability that any variance (regardless of size) is due to a correctable cause as 25%. Assume further that management estimates that the loss due to not discovering a correctable cause of a variance averages 80% of the size of the variance. For example, the loss from failure to discover a correctable $5,000 variance would be $4,000, the loss from a correctable $9,000 variance would be $7,200, and so forth.

**Required**

Determine the minimum size of a variance that justifies investigation.

**Solution**

The formula in the chapter indicates that we are indifferent between investigating a variance and not investigating when the probability of the variance being correctable equals the cost to investigate, divided by the loss from failure to discover a correctable cause reduced by the correction cost. The formula provided is

$$P_2 = \frac{I}{L - C}$$

We can substitute the known values for the probability that a variance is correctable, the investigation cost, and the correction cost into this formula to obtain

$$0.25 = \frac{\$700}{L - \$200}$$

or, rearranging,

$$\begin{aligned} 0.25L - \$50 &= \$700 \\ 0.25L &= \$750 \\ L &= \$3{,}000 \end{aligned}$$

That is, we would investigate a variance when the loss from the failure to discover a correctable problem exceeds $3,000. The problem stated that this loss was estimated to be 80% of the size of the variance, so the following relationship must be true.

$$L = 0.8(\text{size of variance})$$

Substituting the value for the loss that triggers an investigation gives us

$$\begin{aligned} \$3{,}000 &= 0.8(\text{size of variance}) \\ \text{size of variance} &= \$3{,}750 \end{aligned}$$

Given the firm's cost structure, the firm should investigate only variances that exceed $3,750.

## KEY TERMS AND CONCEPTS

Controllable variance
Uncontrollable variance
Management by exception
Information overload
Control chart
Control limits
Indifference probability
Budgetary slack

## FURTHER READING


Brownell, Peter. "The Role of Accounting Data in Performance Evaluation, Budgetary Participation and Organizational Effectiveness," *Journal of Accounting Research* (Spring 1982), p. 12.

Bruns, William J., and John H. Waterhouse. "Budgetary Control and Organization Structure," *Journal of Accounting Research* (Autumn 1975), p. 177.

Buckman, G. A., and Bruce L. Miller. "Optimal Investigation of a Multiple Cost Process System," *Journal of Accounting Research* (Spring 1982), p. 28.

Calvasina, Richard V., and Eugene J. Calvasina. "Standard Costing Games that Managers Play," *Management Accounting* (March 1984), p. 49.

Dittman, David, and Prem Prakash. "Cost Variance Investigation: Markovian Control Versus Optimal Control," *The Accounting Review* (April 1979), p. 358.

Hayes, David C. "The Contingency Theory of Managerial Accounting," *The Accounting Review* (January 1977), p. 22.

Jacobs, Frederic H. "An Evaluation of the Effectiveness of Some Cost Variance Investigation Models," *Journal of Accounting Research* (Spring 1978), p. 190.

Jacobs, Frederic. "When and How to Use Statistical Cost Variance Investigation Techniques," *Cost and Management* (January–February 1983), p. 27.

Kaplan, Robert S. "The Significance and Investigation of Cost Variances: Survey and Extensions," *Journal of Accounting Research* (Autumn 1975), p. 311.

Magee, Robert P. "Cost Control with Imperfect Parameter Knowledge," *The Accounting Review* (January 1977), p. 190.


## QUESTIONS AND EXERCISES

**20-1** "Control presupposes a plan." Discuss briefly.

**20-2** Do cost control and cost reduction mean the same thing?

**20-3** For the quarter, the variances for a particular material indicate an extremely favorable price variance and an extremely unfavorable quantity variance. What might this situation indicate, and who is responsible?

**20-4** A volume variance has arisen because of management's inexperience in budgeting. How should the volume variance be disposed?

**20-5** The price that a firm has been paying for material has been rising about 1% per quarter throughout the year, resulting in substantial unfavorable price variances. How should these variances be handled?

**20-6** A variance has arisen because a department had to resort to a temporary employment agency to obtain workers to complete a task on time. How should this variance be handled?

**20-7** "Nobody says anything when things are going right, but they get on my case when things go wrong." Is this an appropriate case of management by exception?

**20-8** What is the trade-off between timeliness and accuracy where reporting is concerned?

**20-9** Most departments in a firm report minor variances each period, but department 26 consistently meets its budget exactly (all variances are zero). Is the manager of department 26 doing an exceptionally good job?

**20-10** A product passes through several departments. The units transferred out of one department and into another are capable of verification. The firm lets each department manager estimate the degree of completion of the ending inventory in that department. What is wrong with this system?

**20-11** An investigation of several variances revealed a variety of causes. Categorize each of these variances as controllable or uncontrollable, by the type of management action required, and by the source of error, as in Exhibit 20-1.

**a.** Labor efficiency variance; a new employee was unfamiliar with the task.
**b.** Labor efficiency variance; equipment breakdown idled employees.
**c.** Materials usage variance; employee misunderstood instructions and ruined several units of product.
**d.** Materials usage variance; materials were of inferior quality, creating excess waste.
**e.** Overhead spending variance; new equipment was found to be much more economical to run.
**f.** Volume variance; competitor slashed prices and sales orders dropped.
**g.** Overhead spending variance; production scheduling mislaid a big order and hence substantial overtime was incurred to meet promised delivery date.
**h.** Volume variance; excessive absenteeism occurred in a critical production department.
**i.** Materials price variance; an oil embargo caused prices of our petroleum-based raw materials to increase greatly.

**20-12** Upon retirement from government service, Field Marshall Bucharte set up a small munitions factory in Strasbourg, France. The field marshal has asked you for some advice. The firm's records show that materials usage variances greater than 500 francs were investigated 70 times in the past 2 years, and 42 of these investigations revealed that the variance was caused by a correctable problem. If the cost of investigation averages 350 francs, the cost to correct a problem averages 200 francs, and the loss from not discovering a correctable problem is estimated to be 900 francs, should the firm investigate a 700-franc variance? Show why or why not.

**20-13** The cost to investigate the cause of a variance is estimated to be \$800, the cost to correct a problem if it exists is \$300, and the opportunity cost for not discovering a problem if it exists is \$3,500. What is the critical probability that a problem exists that must be surpassed before an investigation is justified?

**20-14** A firm's management estimates that the cost to investigate the cause of a reported variance is \$300, the cost to correct the system if it is not functioning properly is \$800, and the costs of the system continuing to be out of control are \$1,500. Determine the probability that the system is out of control for which management will be indifferent between investigating or not investigating the cause of the variance.

**20-15** Management requires that any variance larger than $500 must be investigated. Historical records show that variances between $500 and $1,000 are due to a correctable cause 70% of the time. If the cost to investigate the cause of a variance is $1,200 and the cost to correct the system when it has failed is $300, what is the minimum opportunity cost for failure to find a correctable problem necessary for management's decision rule to be correct?

**20-16** Mariett is trying to decide whether to investigate the cause of a labor usage variance. The cost to investigate will be $500. If the cause of the variance is anything other than a random occurrence, it is estimated that the cost of correction will be $200. If the probability that the system is out of control is considered to be 0.4, should Mariett investigate? Management estimates it will cost the firm $1,200 if the system is out of control and this is not discovered now.

**20-17** Management is fairly certain of the cost to investigate a variance. The cost is approximately $90. Similarly, management has fairly good records on the cost to correct problems that have been discovered. These costs have averaged $50. Unfortunately, management has been unable to make an accurate determination of the opportunity costs from failure to discover a correctable problem. Various estimates range from $600 to $900. Determine the indifference probability for the investigation decision at both extremes of management's estimates. Should management be very concerned with getting a more accurate estimate?

**20-18** The following weekly labor cost variances were reported for the past quarter. Those with comments on the right were investigated and the comments indicate the findings of the investigation. The other variances were not investigated. From the information given, estimate the probability that a variance greater than $1,000 is due to a correctable problem.

| Week | Variance | Cause |
|---|---|---|
| 1 | $1,200 | Correctable |
| 2 | 1,800 | Correctable |
| 3 | 900 | |
| 4 | 1,500 | Correctable |
| 5 | 2,500 | Correctable |
| 6 | 1,100 | Random |
| 7 | 850 | Correctable |
| 8 | 1,400 | |
| 9 | 1,325 | Random |
| 10 | 1,080 | |
| 11 | 1,700 | Correctable |
| 12 | 860 | Random |
| 13 | 1,250 | Correctable |

**20-19** The chart shown reflects the materials cost variance as a percent of the standard cost allowed in a department for the past several weeks.

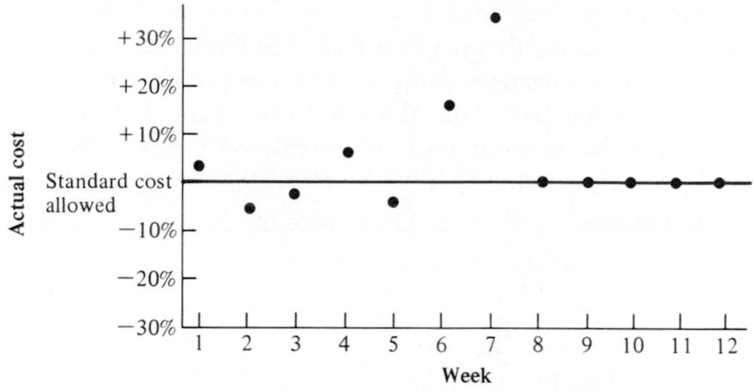


During week 7, management approached the departmental supervisor to ask about the 15% unfavorable materials cost variance incurred in week 6. Unfortunately, the supervisor was upset by the questioning and quit. Another employee took over the position during week 7. In week 8 the new supervisor blamed the very high materials cost variance in week 7 on the previous supervisor.

What do you think of the current supervisor's performance? Would you investigate departmental performance?

**20-20** Management determines that it costs $75 to investigate the cause of a variance. The cost to correct a problem if one exists is $100. Management estimates that the opportunity cost from failure to discover a correctable problem is $200. Management believes that a particular variance reported has a 70% chance of being due to a correctable problem. What is the expected value of the cost of the prediction error if the true value of the opportunity cost for failure to discover a correctable problem is $225?

**20-21** Refer to the demonstration problem at the end of the chapter. Assume that the probability that a variance is due to a correctable cause is 15%. What size variance should now be investigated? Explain why the size has increased or decreased.

## PROBLEMS AND CASES

**20-22** **Cost-benefit analysis of adjustments** (CIA adapted).

The Toys-O Company manufactures a line of plastic science fiction toys. The toys sell for $1 and are very popular. The molding machine is critical to production and must be kept in proper adjustment. By keeping records for recent months, the company has determined that, of the 800 produced daily, the number of toys rejected is equal to 100 divided by the number of adjustments made. Each toy costs $0.70, and the rejected toys are worthless. Each morning the supervisor adjusts the machines before work begins and, after that, takes the responsibility for all adjustments. Each adjustment costs $4, although no product is lost during the operation.

**Required**

Compute the optimal number of adjustments that should be made per day.

**20-23 Cost of investigating variances.**

The management of Advanced Systems Engineering feels that a relationship exists between the size of materials usage variances and the probability that the variance is due to a correctable cause. From past data, the cost accountant developed a regression equation that relates the proportion of correctable variances to the size of the variance. The regression equation, which has an $R^2$ of 0.86, was as follows:

proportion of variances correctable = 0.2 + (0.001 × size of variance in dollars)

Thus a $500 variance is estimated to be correctable 70% of the time.

**Required**

If it costs $49.50 to investigate the cause of a variance, $30 to correct the cause of a variance, and the loss from failure to correct an existing problem is estimated to be $140, what size variances should be investigated?

**20-24 Decision as to whether to investigate a variance.**

From the following record of variances investigated, determine which variances the firm should investigate.

| Variance | Cause | Cost to Investigate | Correction Cost | Opportunity Loss if Not Corrected |
|---|---|---|---|---|
| $1,500 | Random | $175 | $— | $ — |
| 2,000 | Measurement | 190 | 200 | 400 |
| 2,200 | Random | 210 | — | — |
| 2,900 | Model | 225 | 300 | 800 |
| 3,200 | Prediction | 250 | 400 | 900 |
| 3,300 | Random | 225 | — | — |
| 3,800 | Implementation | 375 | 600 | 1,200 |
| 3,950 | Implementation | 350 | 500 | 1,500 |

**Required**

**a.** Should the firm investigate variances in the $1,500-to-$3,000 range? Support your answer.

**b.** Should the firm investigate variances in the $3,000-to-$4,000 range? Support your answer.

**20-25 Investigating labor usage variances.**

The ABC Company reports labor usage variances weekly. A summary of the past 10 reports is as follows:

| Week | Variance | Investigated | Cause | Cost to Correct |
|---|---|---|---|---|
| 1 | $ 200 U | No | | |
| 2 | 1,200 U | Yes | No allowance for set-up | $ 50 |
| 3 | 80 U | No | | |
| 4 | 1,400 F | Yes | Standard time estimate wrong | 100 |
| 5 | 1,900 U | Yes | Machine breakdown, random | — |
| 6 | 90 U | No | | |
| 7 | 100 F | No | | |
| 8 | 1,100 U | No | | |
| 9 | 1,500 U | Yes | Insufficient supervision | 500 |
| 10 | 200 U | No | | |

**Required**

**a.** Although your answer is based on sparse information, estimate the probability that a variance between $1,000 and $2,000 is due to a correctable cause.

**b.** Estimate the expected cost to correct the system if it is "out of control."

**c.** Assume that the cost of investigation is $100 and the expected loss for not discovering the system is out of control is $500. Should variances between $1,000 and $2,000 be investigated?

**20-26 Investigating labor usage variances.**

Irvine Manufacturing uses a standard cost system. In the past, management has reacted to a "large" labor usage variance by calling in the appropriate supervisor and asking for an explanation. Because this demands a substantial amount of the manager's time and the supervisor's time, and because it creates resentment, management has attached a high cost ($1,000) to calling in the supervisor. When the variance has been caused by a controllable factor, the supervisor can correct the problem at an average cost of $300. Management has noted in the past that when a variance is caused by a controllable factor but corrective action is not taken, the cost to the firm of not correcting the problem will turn out to be 5 times the reported variance.

**Required**

**a.** If a labor usage variance of $500 is reported, what is the minimum probability of the process being "out of control" that will justify calling in the supervisor?

**b.** If a labor usage variance of $200 is reported, what is this minimum probability?

**20-27 Determining whether to investigate variances** (SMA).

The standard materials cost for producing a conventional truck at the Fleetliner Company Limited is $28,000. Last week several trucks were produced at an average materials cost of $34,000. U. R. Able, a recent RIA (Registered Industrial Accountant, a Canadian designation) graduate who joined the company as the cost analyst, was asked to decide whether investigation was necessary.

Mr. Able felt that if nothing is done and the process is out of control, the present value of extra costs over the planning horizon is $2,600. The cost to investigate is $380. The cost to correct the process if out of control is $850. He also felt that there is an 80% chance that the process is in control.

**Required**

**a.** Submit computations to show whether the process should be investigated.

**b.** What level of probability that the process is in control would be necessary to make Mr. Able indifferent about investigating the process?

**c.** If the process is out of control, why is the present value of the extra costs incurred substantially less than the current variance between the standard and actual costs of trucks produced?

**20-28 Determining whether to investigate a variance.**

A firm has kept records that establish the probability that a given variance is due to a correctable cause. These probabilities have been categorized by the absolute size of the variance. They are summarized as follows:

| Size of Variance | Probability of Variance Being Due to a Correctable Cause |
|---|---|
| $1–$500 | 0.01 |
| $500–$2,000 | 0.25 |
| $2,000–$4,000 | 0.50 |
| $4,000 or more | 0.70 |

Assume that the expected loss from allowing the system to operate when it is out of control is $5,000, the cost to correct the system when out of control is $1,000, and the cost to investigate is $3,000. Once a correctable problem occurs, it will continue to occur until the process is investigated and corrected.

**Required**

Determine whether or not investigation is the best action in each of the following situations (clearly label the "critical" probability).

**a.** A single variance of $4,500 is observed.

**b.** A variance of $1,000 is observed in the first period, and a variance of $3,000 is observed in the second period.

**c.** A variance of $5,000 is observed in the first period, and a variance of $1,100 is observed in the second period.

**d.** A variance of $3,200 is observed in the first period, a variance of $1,800 is observed in the second period, and a variance of $2,100 is observed in the third period.

**20-29 Comparison of decision rules.**

Management of the Dohlman Companies calculated the standard deviation of direct labor costs at the same time that direct labor standards were established. The standard cost for labor was set at $12 per unit with a standard deviation of $0.50 per unit. Management established a policy of investigating any variance greater than 3 standard deviations from the mean.

Production and labor cost data for the past 6 weeks were

| Week | Units Produced | Actual Labor Cost | Standard Labor Cost | Variance |
|---|---|---|---|---|
| 1 | 2,010 | $25,620 | $24,120 | $1,500 U |
| 2 | 2,150 | 29,800 | 25,800 | 4,000 U |
| 3 | 2,225 | 26,200 | 26,700 | 500 F |
| 4 | 2,380 | 32,160 | 28,560 | 3,600 U |
| 5 | 2,050 | 20,000 | 24,600 | 4,600 F |
| 6 | 2,100 | 27,400 | 25,200 | 2,200 U |

**Required**

**a.** Using management's decision rule, which of these variances would be investigated?

**b.** The cost to investigate a variance is $300, the loss from failure to find a correctable problem is $1,000, and the cost to correct a problem is $100. The probabilities that variances are due to a correctable problem are

| Size of Variance | Probability |
|---|---|
| \$0–\$500 | 0.15 |
| \$500–\$1,000 | 0.25 |
| \$1,000–\$2,000 | 0.35 |
| \$2,000–\$3,000 | 0.45 |
| \$3,000–\$4,000 | 0.55 |
| \$4,000 or more | 0.65 |

Based on this information, which variances should be investigated?

**c.** Which decision rule, (a) or (b), is better, and why?

**20-30 Investigating variance** (SMA).

David Green, foreman of the refining department, has just received a performance report for the department's automated processing machine. The processing machine performs a crucial milling operation on custom units. The performance report shows an above normal rejection rate, which could indicate that a malfunction has occurred in the processing machine. Mr. Green must decide whether or not to order an inspection of the automated processing machine.

Past experience has shown that the cost of an investigation can be described by a uniform probability distribution with a range of \$300 to \$600. The cost of repairs can also be described by a uniform distribution that has a range of \$2,100 to \$2,800.

If the processing machine is malfunctioning and repairs are not made, it will lead to additional costs of \$1,500 per month in the future. Mr. Green is unsure of the ultimate value of the additional costs because the total is affected by the number of months that would elapse until the machine was inspected. The following table provides Mr. Green's estimate of the time until the next inspection would be made.

| Time until Next Inspection (months) | Probability |
|---|---|
| 2 | 0.15 |
| 3 | 0.30 |
| 4 | 0.45 |
| 5 | 0.10 |

Based on past experience and evaluation of the operating results, Mr. Green has estimated that there is a probability of 0.20 that the processing machine is malfunctioning.

**Required**

Should Mr. Green order an investigation? Show supporting calculations.

**20-31 Investigating variances: Costs, losses, probabilities.**

Precision Technologies, Inc., performs extreme tolerance machining mostly for customers in the oil and aircraft industries. PTI uses the very latest computer-controlled cutting tools to produce its products. Nonetheless, because of the high tolerances required, there is a good deal of scrap. The usual causes are failure of the operator to enter the desired dimensions into the computer correctly, worn cutting edges, defects in materials, and other random causes (a heavy truck passing the plant will often cause enough vibration to ruin units in the cutting process). Whatever the cause, excess spoilage shows up as an unfavorable materials usage variance.

Although PTI accepts a wide variety of jobs, a standard job has been defined for planning purposes. The standard order is for 100 pieces of product with materials costing $4.50 per unit, variable operating costs for equipment of $8.00 per unit, and fixed equipment cost budgeted at $12 per unit. Normal spoilage is considered 14.5% (implying that PTI starts production on 117 units to yield, on the average, 100 good units). The unit costs given are prior to the allowance for normal spoilage.

When management decides to investigate unusual material usage variances, an established procedure is followed. First, records kept by the computer of the dimensions entered into it are compared with actual specifications. If there is a discrepancy, it is called to the attention of the operator. It is generally known that excessive errors by an operator will lead to dismissal. This type of investigation typically takes only $\frac{1}{2}$ hour of a manager's time. The average production manager earns $25,000 per year. It is felt that failure to discover specification input errors will lead, on the average, to one additional standard order being spoiled. Although there is some cost associated with pointing out errors to operators, management has not been able to quantify it, so the cost is to be treated as zero.

If specification errors are not found, the cutting machines are disassembled to check cutting edges for excessive wear. This generally requires 3 hours of time from each of two engineers earning $8 per hour. If wear is found, the blades are replaced at a cost of $250. Management estimates that the failure to discover worn blades will result in a 45% spoilage rate on the next six standard jobs, on the average.

If the cutting blades are not worn, the materials variance is assumed to be due to a random cause and further investigation is abandoned. In the past, 50% of the investigations have revealed that excessive usage variances were due to input errors, 40% were due to worn edges, and 10% were considered random.

**Required**

**a.** Determine the cost to investigate a variance, the loss from failure to find the cause, and the cost to correct the cause if it is (1) an input error, (2) a worn blade, and (3) random.

**b.** What is the probability that a variance is due to a correctable cause necessary to justify an investigation?

**20-32 Assigning responsibility for variances.**

A firm's accounting department has just released last month's performance reports, and Bert Smith has been charged with a $20,000 unfavorable price variance on materials acquired last month.

Bert Smith is the purchasing manager for Reliance Manufacturing. Reliance's major product is an automatic-setback thermostat. A critical element in the thermostat is a vacuum tube partially filled with mercury that acts as the on-off switch. Reliance uses approximately 100,000 of these switches per week and normally maintains a 2-week supply on hand. Last month Bert predicted that a teamsters' strike would cut off Reliance's source of supply for the vacuum switches. Accordingly, Bert placed a large special order for the switches. The switches normally cost the firm $0.40 each delivered. In order to ensure a supply of the switches, Bert agreed to pay $0.50 each for 200,000 of the switches, delivered.

In fact, the teamsters did go on strike in the latter part of last month. The strike lasted 3 weeks. Bert has argued that had it not been for his special order, the firm may have had to close the manufacturing operation. This would have cost the firm approximately a half-million dollars.

Alternatively, the firm would have had to go to a great deal of trouble to obtain the switches. While it is not clear that the switches could have been obtained, it is obvious that the cost per unit would have been in excess of a dollar per unit. Bert feels that in light of the circumstances, he should not be charged with the $20,000 unfavorable price variance.

**Required**

**a.** Should Bert be charged with the price variance? Why or why not?

**b.** Would your answer change if the teamsters had not gone on strike as predicted?

**20-33 Disposition of variances.**

Damson Products prepares monthly financial statements. It closes its variance accounts at that time. For the month of May the firm's accounting records revealed the following variances (the comments were supplied by appropriate operating personnel).

| Variance | Amount | Percent of Standard | Comment |
|---|---|---|---|
| Materials price | $ 658 U | 0.04 | Normal fluctuation |
| Materials usage | 12,600 U | 11.36 | $13,000 of materials lost in spring flood |
| Labor rate | 376 F | 0.11 | Normal fluctuation |
| Labor usage | 9,700 U | 9.62 | $9,000 for days plant was closed during flood |
| Variable overhead rate | 507 F | 0.21 | Normal fluctuation |
| Variable overhead quantity | 412 U | 0.18 | Normal fluctuation |
| Fixed overhead spending | 782 F | 0.07 | Normal fluctuation |
| Fixed overhead volume | 22,800 U | 18.29 | $10,200 due to time lost in flood; the rest represents normal decreased spring operations |

The firm uses a fixed overhead rate based on annual operations; however, there is a definite seasonal demand effect, with the spring months being the slow months. In addition, the firm was closed for several days when a nearby stream flooded after heavy rains. The firm does not have flood insurance and the lost material and labor costs were charged to production. At month end the firm has no work in process, the standard cost of finished goods inventory is $34,000, and the standard cost of goods sold is $305,000.

**Required**

**a.** Determine the proper disposition of each variance.

**b.** Prepare journal entries to dispose of the variances.

**c.** What is the cost of finished goods and cost of goods sold after the variance accounts are closed?

**20-34 Disposition of variances.**

The controller's department of Datatech International has completed its analysis of the past year's operating results. The firm manufactures state-of-the-art laser disks for computers. This is a highly automated production process.

During the past year the firm undertook a program to substantially increase its inventory of products. Management is convinced there will soon be a major surge in demand for the disk and wants to assure that sufficient supplies of the disks are available to meet demand. Currently the firm has 350,000 completed disks in finished goods inventory valued at a total standard cost of $2,100,000. The cost of work-in-process inventory at year-end is $90,000, which is approximately the same amount as the previous year.

The plant's cost accountant prepared the following analysis of production costs.

| Item | Actual Cost | Standard Cost | Budget Variance |
|---|---|---|---|
| Materials | $1,560,600 | $1,530,000 | $ 30,600 U |
| Labor | 502,350 | 510,000 | 7,650 F |
| Overhead | 2,142,000 | 3,060,000 | 918,000 F |
| Total | $4,204,950 | $5,100,000 | $895,050 F |

The firm expects variances to fluctuate between ±3% of standards. Hence the materials and labor variances were not investigated. The overhead variance was investigated. An excerpt from the accountant's report follows.

*Overhead is the major cost of producing our products. It is applied to products based on the number of machine hours used. During the year we produced 850,000 disks using 170,000 machine hours. This was consistent with our beginning-of-the-year master plan. However, very early in the year our engineers rearranged the manufacturing operations. This has led to a drastic reduction in the cost of operating our equipment. We did not revise our overhead standard as we were not sure of the amount of savings that we would enjoy. On close analysis of the overhead costs incurred, we believe the actual overhead costs incurred this past year reflect normal efficiency and are indicative of the future costs we will incur. The overhead standard for next year is thus being duly revised.*

Of the 850,000 disks produced during the year, 300,000 were added to finished goods inventory. The average selling price for units sold was $9. The firm uses FIFO costing for inventories. The firm expects to produce 850,000 disks again next year.

**Required**

**a.** What is the current standard cost per disk?

**b.** What should next year's standard cost per disk be?

**c.** Determine the cost of inventories and the firm's reported gross margin after disposal of the manufacturing cost variances.

**20-35 Evaluating a grading scheme.**

Professor E. Z. Grader is very popular; almost all of his students receive A's. This is widely attributed to Professor Grader's superior teaching skills. Grades for this professor's courses are determined as follows:

| | Points |
|---|---|
| Midterm exam | 200 |
| Attendance | 200 |
| Term paper | 200 |
| Final exam | 400 |

A student needs 700 points for an A, 600 points for a B, 500 for a C, and 400 for a D. From the 200 points given for perfect attendance a student loses 5 points for every class missed (there are 40 class meetings); however, attendance is seldom taken.

If the term paper is 20 pages or longer, 200 points are earned; 10 points are lost for each page less than 20 (thus a 12-page paper is worth 120 points).

Professor Grader has given the same midterm exam for the past 20 years. In order to hold down the number of copies in people's files, Professor Grader does not return the exam. Instead the students are simply told the scores received on the exam. A popular business fraternity, however, obtained a copy of the exam in 1982. They have chosen not to share the exam with any person not a member of the fraternity; thus Professor Grader usually observes that grades on this exam are nearly normally distributed.

The final exam is a take-home exam that the students have 2 weeks to complete.

**Required**

Evaluate Professor Grader's grading system as a performance measurement system. Consider the points of view of both the person whose performance is being measured and a person trying to evaluate an individual's performance based upon the grade received in this class.

**20-36 Evaluating a proposal for measuring performance.**

Benerux Industries has been in business for nearly 30 years. The firm's major product is a control unit for elevators. The firm has a reputation for manufacturing a product of exceptional quality. This reputation has allowed the firm to charge a higher price for its unit than its competitors do. The higher price, in turn, has meant that the firm has been comfortably profitable. A major reason for the high quality of the company's product has been a loyal and conscientious work force. Production employees have been with the firm for an average of 18 years.

Recently the firm hired a cost accountant from a local school. After a few months with the firm, the new accountant proposed a performance measurement report consisting of two parts. The first part will report the actual number of units started during each month, the target number of units that should have been started, and a variance. The second part will calculate an actual cost per good unit completed during each month, the target cost per unit, and a variance.

The new accountant provided the following additional information concerning the performance report: The first part of the report concentrates on units started because many units are scrapped in the manufacturing process (to maintain quality). Therefore, the best measure of effort expended is the number of units on which work was begun. The target number of units to be begun in a month is the number of units started in the corresponding month last year plus 5%. In the second part of the report, actual costs per unit will be calculated by dividing total production cost incurred during the month by the number of salable units completed during the month. The target cost per unit is the average cost for manufacturing this kind of product as determined from industry newsletters.

The proposal concluded with the following comments: "This report should be prepared and distributed quarterly. For maximum benefit I suggest that a bonus be awarded whenever units started exceeds target and costs are below target. This system will result in substantially improved profits for the firm. It should be implemented immediately."

**Required**

Evaluate the proposed performance measurement system.

**20-37 Investigation decision and the expected value of perfect information—requires prior study of Appendix 5B** (CMA).

Cilla Company manufactures a line of women's handbags. An operations summary of Cilla's cutting department for May 19X4 included the analysis below.

| | |
|---|---|
| Standard materials cost of production | $314,000 |
| Materials price variance | 0 |
| Unfavorable materials quantity variance | 16,000 |
| Actual materials cost of production | $330,000 |

Donna Cook, cutting department supervisor, gathered the following information for use in deciding whether or not the variance should be investigated.

| | |
|---|---|
| Estimated cost of investigating the variance | $ 4,000 |
| Estimated cost of making the necessary changes if the cutting department is operating improperly | 8,000 |
| Estimated present value of future unfavorable variances that would be saved by making the necessary changes if the cutting department is operating improperly | 40,000 |
| Estimated probability of the cutting department operating properly during the current fiscal year | 90% |

**Required**

**a.** Recommend whether or not Cilla Company should investigate the unfavorable materials quantity variance. Support your recommendation by:
   **1.** Preparing a payoff table for use in making the decision.
   **2.** Computing the expected value of the cost of each possible action.

**b.** Donna Cook is uncertain about the probability estimate for proper operation of the cutting department (i.e., 90%). Determine the probability estimate of the cutting department operating properly that would cause Cilla Company to be indifferent between the two possible actions.

**c.** Assume that a consultant is available to advise Cilla Company and is able to predict accurately the state of the operations in the cutting department. Compute the expected value of the consultant's perfect information.

**20-38 Variances for trash collection: Uses regression—computer recommended.** The City of Noble operates four trash collection routes. The cost of providing this service is a significant amount in the city's budget so the City Council has directed the city manager to monitor the costs closely.

The city manager's staff gathered the following data concerning the cost of operating each route for a 6-month period. Everyone agrees that the routes were operated with normal efficiency during those periods. The staff felt that tons of refuse collected would have been a better measure of activity, but those data are not available. On the other hand, the number of miles put on each truck is readily available and there is likely to be a relationship between the amount of trash picked up and mileage.

| | | Route 1 | Route 2 | Route 3 | Route 4 |
|---|---|---|---|---|---|
| May: | Cost | $8,100 | $6,500 | $6,700 | $5,800 |
| | Mileage | 750 | 1,250 | 1,200 | 2,000 |
| June: | Cost | $7,800 | $7,000 | $6,900 | $6,250 |
| | Mileage | 700 | 1,300 | 1,325 | 2,100 |
| July: | Cost | $7,600 | $7,150 | $7,250 | $6,500 |
| | Mileage | 675 | 1,400 | 1,375 | 2,300 |
| Aug.: | Cost | $8,050 | $7,200 | $7,100 | $6,450 |
| | Mileage | 725 | 1,350 | 1,375 | 2,400 |
| Sept.: | Cost | $8,200 | $6,500 | $6,800 | $6,100 |
| | Mileage | 750 | 1,200 | 1,250 | 2,000 |
| Oct.: | Cost | $8,350 | $6,500 | $6,200 | $5,600 |
| | Mileage | 800 | 1,150 | 1,100 | 1,800 |

Route 1 primarily serves the city's business district, routes 2 and 3 are residential districts within the city limits, and route 4 serves the outlying areas including many rural homes.

For the current month the following operating data were reported.

| | Route 1 | Route 2 | Route 3 | Route 4 |
|---|---|---|---|---|
| Cost | $7,900 | $6,425 | $7,135 | $6,125 |
| Mileage | 700 | 1,200 | 1,300 | 2,000 |

**Required**

**a.** Estimate the cost function for each route using regression. Provide a plausible explanation for why the cost functions differ.

**b.** Prepare a report comparing the current month's costs on each route to the flexible budget amounts derived from the equations developed in part (a).

**c.** The city manager wants any variance that differs from the flexible budget amount by more than two standard errors investigated. Should the costs for any of the routes be investigated?

**20-39 Comprehensive—requires prior study of Chapter 3, Appendix 3A, and Chapters 7, 18, and 19.**

Custom Plastics used regression to estimate the amount of plastic required to make its major product: artificial Christmas trees. The data used in the regression were the weekly output of trees and the total amount of plastic used in each week. From the 25 weeks of data available, the following equation resulted:

$$\text{pounds of plastic used} = 125 \text{ pounds} + 6 \text{ pounds per tree}$$

The fixed usage results because the molds are cleaned every Friday. Approximately 125 pounds of plastic is cleaned out of the molds and discarded.

Next week the firm plans to produce and sell 2,000 trees (it is getting close to Christmas). Wholesalers are expected to pay $13.50 per tree. Each tree is budgeted to require $\frac{1}{2}$ hour of labor time. Labor is budgeted at $7 per hour. There is no variable overhead, but fixed overhead (in addition to the fixed amount of plastic used) is expected to be $2,200 per week. The standard cost for plastic is $0.75 per pound.

**Required**

**a.** Prepare the master budget for next week.

**b.** List three factors that may explain the fact that the $R^2$ from the regression line for materials usage was not as high as management had expected.

**c.** Custom Plastics determines its economic order quantity based on annual averages. Total annual demand for plastic is estimated to be 130,000 pounds. It takes 1 hour of clerical time to prepare an order. The firm rents a truck to pick up each order at a cost of $85. Inventory insurance and taxes amount to $0.10 per pound of plastic for the average number of pounds held in inventory over the year. The firm considers its cost of capital to be 20%. Clerical labor is paid $5 per hour. How many pounds of plastic should be included in each order?

**d.** At the end of the week for which you prepared the master budget, the firm determined that it actually produced and sold 1,800 trees at an average price of $13.35. Labor costs amounted to $6,212.50 for 875 hours. Variable materials costs were $9,086 for the 11,800 pounds of variable materials used. Fixed materials costs were $96.25 and fixed overhead costs amounted to $2,150. Sales orders were received for 1,950 trees, but production was only able to produce the 1,800 trees. Determine actual cost net income for the week and reconcile actual income to master budget income by calculating all appropriate variances.

**e.** At the level of production achieved, the standard error of the estimate for the variable amount of plastic to be used is 500 pounds (this was determined from our regression equation). Remembering that the equation was based on 25 observations, determine the 90% confidence interval for the variable amount of plastic needed to produce the 1,800 trees.

**f.** Management estimates that it costs $90 to investigate the cause of a materials usage variance. If the variance is due to a correctable cause, it requires $120 to correct the problem. On the other hand, the loss from failure to discover a correctable problem is estimated to be $270. Determine the critical probability that a variance is due to a correctable cause above which the firm should investigate the cause of the variance.

**g.** Determine the material usage variance for Custom Plastics for the most recent week in terms of pounds of plastic (actual variable usage versus standard).

**h.** Recall that the standard error of the estimate for the variable amount of plastic used is 500 pounds. Should the material usage variance determined in (g) be investigated? Why?

**i.** Custom Plastics' standard cost system is quite new, but already manufacturing and marketing employees are getting upset with management. Prior to the use of the new performance measurement system, labor-management relations were extremely good. You have been called in as a consultant to identify the source of employee dissatisfaction. Name five possible problem areas with this, or any, performance measurement system that you should consider in your investigation.

# APPENDIX 20

# ADJUSTING STANDARD COSTS TO ACTUAL COSTS

A firm might choose to use standard costing for internal performance reports and control, and yet desire to report actual costs on its external financial statements. In this appendix we examine the necessary calculations and journal entries to adjust standard cost records to yield actual cost financial statements.

For materials we begin by first closing our quantity variances to the inventory and Cost of Goods Sold accounts to restate standard quantities to actual quantities. For example, assume that our standards allow for 5 pounds of materials per unit at a standard price of $3 per pound. During the period we produced 1,000 units of product using 5,500 pounds of materials. There are no units in ending work-in-process, 200 units are in finished goods inventory, and 800 of the units were sold.

Our accounting records prepared on a standard cost basis would carry the completed units at $15 per unit for materials (5 pounds each at $3 per pound). Thus the units in finished goods inventory would be costed at $3,000 for materials and cost of goods sold would include $12,000 for materials. Meanwhile, our materials usage variance would be $1,500 unfavorable (500 excess pounds at $3 per pound). To restate our records to reflect actual usage we can note that actual usage as a percent of standard materials allowed was 5,500 ÷ 5,000 = 110%. Thus multiplying the standard materials allowance in Finished Goods and Cost of Goods Sold by 110% adjusts those accounts to reflect actual materials used, but at standard prices: $3,300 for finished goods and $13,200 for cost of goods sold, an increase of $300 and $1,200, respectively. The journal entry to close the Materials Usage Variance would be

| | | |
|---|---|---|
| Finished Goods Inventory | 300 | |
| Cost of Goods Sold | 1,200 | |
| Raw Materials Usage Variance | | 1,500 |

Once we have adjusted the account balances to reflect actual materials usage, we can make the adjustment to reflect actual materials prices. Now, however, we will also have to consider the raw materials inventory. Assume that we actually purchased 6,200 pounds of materials during the period at a total cost of $21,700 or $3.50 per pound. Our materials price variance would be $3,100 unfavorable. This variance should now be spread over the 700 pounds in raw materials inventory (6,200 pounds purchased less the 5,500 put into process) plus the 5,500 pounds in finished goods and cost of goods sold.

To allocate the price variance we can note that actual materials prices were $3.50 ÷ $3.00 = 116.67% of standard. The materials in raw materials inventory would be carried at a standard cost of $2,100, whereas we previously adjusted the Finished Goods and Cost of Goods Sold accounts to $3,300 and $13,200, respectively, to reflect actual usage in each account. Multiplying each of these balances by 116.67% yields the actual cost balances of $2,450 for Raw Materials, $3,850 for Finished Goods, and $15,400 for Cost of Goods Sold. The entry needed to adjust the balances in these accounts to actual cost would be

| | | |
|---|---|---|
| Raw Materials Inventory | 350 | |
| Finished Goods Inventory | 550 | |
| Cost of Goods Sold | 2,200 | |
| Raw Materials Price Variance | | 3,100 |

The adjustments to restate the accounting records for actual materials usage and prices were complicated by the fact that not all materials were put into production. Some are still in raw materials inventory. This is not a problem with direct labor, so the adjustment to reflect actual labor costs is a bit easier. Assume that the 1,000 units we produced had a standard labor allowance of 2 hours per unit at $6 per hour. Our records indicate that we actually used 2,200 labor hours at a cost of $12,980. Our labor usage variance then is $1,200 unfavorable, and the labor rate variance is $220 favorable.

Because all the labor hours acquired were put into production we do not have to adjust separately for the usage and rate variance. Instead we can simply note that actual labor costs were $12,980 ÷ $12,000 = 108.17% of standard. The finished goods inventory, which contains 200 units of product, would have a $2,400 standard allowance for labor. The 800 units sold would have a $9,600 labor allowance. Multiplying each of these figures by 108.17% will yield actual labor costs of $2,596 and $10,384, respectively. The journal entry to achieve these balances would be

| | | |
|---|---|---|
| Finished Goods Inventory | 196 | |
| Cost of Goods Sold | 784 | |
| Labor Rate Variance | 220 | |
| Labor Usage Variance | | 1,200 |

The adjustment for overhead variances would parallel that required for the labor variances. Since no new issues are involved, we will not go into these variances here. However, the adjustments necessary for overhead will be illustrated in the demonstration problem at the end of the appendix.

## ACTUAL COST ADJUSTMENTS AND INVENTORY FLOW ASSUMPTIONS

In the previous section we acted as if we knew where the units currently produced were (in inventory versus cost of goods sold). Usually we would not know this information and instead would adopt an inventory cost flow assumption: average, FIFO, or LIFO. If we use a FIFO or LIFO cost flow assumption, our calculations to adjust our records to an actual cost basis would have to be preceded by a determination of how many units in each of the inventory accounts represent current period production.

If the firm uses a FIFO flow assumption, it is generally safe to assume that all of the ending inventories were produced or purchased in the current period. However, the LIFO assumption requires more effort. For example, if we begin a period with 400 pounds of material on hand and end the period with 500 pounds, then only 100 pounds of materials would be considered to have been added in the current period. To value the ending raw materials inventory, we would carry forward the beginning of the period cost for the first 400 pounds, assumed to still be on hand, and then add to this figure the current cost for 100 pounds of material.

As the following demonstration problem illustrates, adjusting standard costs to actual costs requires extensive computations. We anticipate that in most cases a cost-benefit analysis would conclude that the effort is not justifiable. However, adjusting standard costs to actual costs is a popular topic on certification exams. Thus you may wish to study the demonstration problem in detail.

## DEMONSTRATION PROBLEM: ADJUSTING STANDARD COSTS TO ACTUAL COSTS

JKL, Inc., began the current period with 3,500 pounds of materials on hand, shown on the balance sheet at $20,650. Beginning work-in-process consisted of 100 units at $2,000, while beginning finished goods inventory consisted of 1,350 units at $26,325.

The firm ended the period with 4,100 pounds of materials in inventory, 200 units of product in process, and 1,500 units in finished goods. During the period 20,000 units were sold.

The firm's master budget for the period called for the production of 24,000 units of product. The budgeted costs were

| | Per Unit | Total |
|---|---|---|
| Materials (2 lb @ $6) | $12.00 | $288,000 |
| Labor ($\frac{1}{2}$ hr @ $7) | 3.50 | 84,000 |
| Variable overhead ($\frac{1}{2}$ hr @ $5) | 2.50 | 60,000 |
| Fixed overhead ($\frac{1}{2}$ hr @ $4) | 2.00 | 48,000 |
| Total | $20.00 | $480,000 |

The standard allowances for resources put into production during the period were 40,500 pounds of materials and 10,100 hours of direct labor. These numbers are based on the following facts. Since 20,000 units were sold, and finished goods inventory increased from 1,350 to 1,500 units, 20,150 units were completed during the period. Our records indicate that all materials were in both beginning and ending work-in-process, so the increase in work-in-process inventory represents 100 equivalent units worth of materials. Hence, in total, 20,250 equivalent units worth of material were put into production. At 2 pounds allowed per unit, this explains the 40,500 pounds standard allowance for materials. The records also indicate that beginning work-in-process had an allowance for 40 standard labor hours while ending work-in-process represents effort for which 65 standard hours were allowed. The total standard allowance for labor then is $\frac{1}{2}$ hour times the 20,150 units completed, less the 40 hours allowed in beginning work-in-process plus the 65 hours in ending work-in-process. That is, $10{,}075 - 40 + 65 = 10{,}100$ standard hours allowed for current production.

Our records also reveal the following variances at the end of the period.

| | |
|---|---|
| Materials price variance | $ 700 F |
| Materials usage variance | 4,800 U |
| Labor rate variance | 650 U |
| Labor usage variance | 325 U |
| Variable overhead spending variance | 160 F |
| Variable overhead efficiency variance | 232 U |
| Fixed overhead spending variance | 525 U |
| Volume variance | 7,600 U |

Only two of these variances were investigated. The materials usage variance was discovered to be largely due to inadequate supervision and instruction. It is estimated that $4,200 of this variance was avoidable. The volume variance was due to an error in predicting the level of demand for our product. We now feel that the actual demand we experienced is an accurate estimate of future demand.

**Required**

Assume the firm wishes to adjust its standard cost records to reflect actual LIFO costs. Prepare the appropriate journal entry.

**Solution**

We start the solution to the problem by tracing the flow of standard costs through our inventory accounts as in Exhibit 20-8. The problem provides the beginning balances in the inventory accounts in both physical unit and dollar terms. The physical unit ending balances and the standard material and labor allowances were also provided. With this information we can fill in all the physical flows in the bottom half of Exhibit 20-8 except for the raw materials taken out of inventory. However, since we know that the standard allowed 40,500 pounds of materials for production and that there was a $4,800 unfavorable usage variance, we know that $4,800 ÷ $6 standard price per pound = 800 pounds more of materials were used than allowed. Therefore, 40,500 + 800 = 41,300 pounds of materials must have been removed from inventory, implying that 41,900 pounds were purchased.

We can trace the dollar flows by noting that all costs would flow into inventories at standard cost. Therefore we can multiply the physical flow of resources by the appropriate standard costs to get the dollar flows. Adding and subtracting the cost flows from the beginning inventory balances gives us the ending balances in inventory as indicated in Exhibit 20-8.

Turning now to the variances, we note that most of the materials usage variance was avoidable and should not be expected to recur again in the future. As such, $4,200 of the variance should be written off as a loss. In contrast, the volume variance was due to a prediction error and, as such, current standard costs

**EXHIBIT 20-8 Inventory Flows for the Demonstration Problem**

**COST FLOWS (STANDARD)**

| Raw Materials | | Work-in-Process[a] | | | Finished Goods | |
|---|---|---|---|---|---|---|
| 20,650 | | | 2,000 | | 26,325 | |
| 251,400 | 247,800 | M | 243,000 | | 403,000 | 400,000 |
| 24,250 | | L | 70,700 | 403,000 | 29,325 | |
| | | VO | 50,500 | | | |
| | | FO | 40,400 | | | |
| | | | 3,600 | | | |

**PHYSICAL FLOWS**

| Raw Materials (units) | | Work-in-Process (units) | | | Finished Goods (units) | |
|---|---|---|---|---|---|---|
| 3,500 lb | | | 100 units | | 1,350 units | |
| 41,900 lb | 41,300 lb | M | 40,500 lb | | 20,150 units | 20,000 units |
| 4,100 lb | | L | 10,100 hr | 20,150 units | 1,500 units | |
| | | VO | 10,100 hr | | | |
| | | FO | 10,100 hr | | | |
| | | | 200 units | | | |

[a]M = materials; L = labor; VO = variable overhead; FO = fixed overhead.

do not reflect the actual costs per unit we expect to incur. Therefore the volume variance should properly be treated as a product cost. Similarly, since the problem asked us to adjust to an actual cost basis, we treat the remaining variances, along with the $600 of the materials usage variance deemed to be random, as product costs.

To convert to a LIFO actual cost system we must estimate the appropriate costs for our ending inventories. With LIFO, the oldest costs will still be in inventory. Because inventories have increased, we bring forward the beginning cost of inventories and add to the beginning cost the current actual cost for the inventory increases experienced during the period.

Let us start with the materials inventory. The actual cost paid for materials purchased during the period can be determined by adjusting the $251,400 standard cost for purchases by the $700 F price variance to get an actual cost of $250,700. Dividing the actual cost by the standard cost reveals that the actual purchase price was 99.722% of standard price.

Raw materials inventory increased from a beginning balance of 3,500 pounds to an ending balance of 4,100 pounds. Under LIFO costing, the 600-pound increase is valued at current costs. The 600 pounds would have a standard cost value of $3,600; multiplying the standard cost by 99.722% gives the actual cost of the

| | | |
|---|---|---|
| Raw materials inventory | | |
| Ending balance before adjustment | | $24,250 |
| Beginning balance | $20,650 | |
| Increase at current actual cost | 3,590 | |
| LIFO actual cost of ending inventory | | 24,240 |
| Decrease in inventory to adjust to actual LIFO cost. | | $ 10 |
| Work-in-process inventory | | |
| Ending balance before adjustment | | $ 3,600 |
| Beginning balance | $ 2,000 | |
| Increase in materials at current cost | 1,200 | |
| Increase in labor at current cost | 177 | |
| Increase in variable overhead at current cost | 125 | |
| Increase in fixed overhead at current cost | 120 | |
| LIFO actual cost of ending inventory | | 3,622 |
| Increase in inventory to adjust to actual LIFO cost. | | $ 22 |
| Finished goods inventory | | |
| Ending balance before adjustment | | $29,325 |
| Beginning balance | $26,325 | |
| Increase in inventory at current cost | 3,067 | |
| LIFO actual cost of ending inventory | | 29,392 |
| Increase in inventory to adjust to actual LIFO cost. | | $ 67 |

inventory increase as \$3,590. Adding the \$3,590 increase to the beginning inventory cost of \$20,650 gives a LIFO ending inventory of \$24,240. Since the current unadjusted balance in raw materials is \$24,250, we need to decrease raw materials by \$10 to get to actual LIFO cost. These calculations are summarized in Exhibit 20-9.

The adjustment of the work-in-process balance to actual LIFO cost is considerably more difficult than the materials inventory account. We have to examine each of the costs (materials, labor, and overhead) separately. We will start with materials.

Exhibit 20-8 indicates that 41,300 pounds of materials left the raw materials inventory. But not all of these costs are to be considered product costs. We said that \$4,200 of the usage variance was controllable and should be written off as a loss. The controllable variance represents \$4,200 ÷ \$6 per pound standard cost = 700 pounds of materials. Hence the materials that will be considered a product cost amount to 41,300 pounds − 700 pounds = 40,600 pounds. Priced at standard cost, these materials are valued at \$243,600. Since actual costs were 99.722% of standard cost, multiplication gives us \$242,923 as the actual cost of materials put into production. Next we can note that the standard cost allowed for materials for the period was \$243,000. Dividing the actual cost of materials put into production by the standard cost allowed gives the adjustment factor. The actual cost for the actual materials used is 99.968% of standard cost.

Work-in-process inventory increased by 100 units during the period. Again, we need to determine the current cost of the inventory additions. The problem states that all materials are in the partially completed units, so the standard cost for the materials in the inventory increase must be 100 × \$12 = \$1,200. Multiplying by the adjustment factor of 99.968% gives the actual cost of the increase, which is also \$1,200 after rounding.

The calculation of the current cost per unit for labor is somewhat easier. The standard cost for labor is \$7 per hour times the 10,100 hours allowed = \$70,700. Adding the \$650 unfavorable rate variance and \$325 unfavorable usage variance gives a total actual labor cost of \$71,675. Division again gives the adjustment factor. The actual cost for labor this period is 101.379% of standard.

Beginning work-in-process was stated to have consisted of 40 standard hours of labor, whereas the ending inventory consisted of 65 standard hours of labor. The inventory increase therefore represents 25 labor hours, which would be carried at standard cost as 25 × \$7 = \$175. Multiplying the standard cost by the 101.379% adjustment factor gives the actual cost for the labor component of the inventory increase as \$177.

Because overhead is applied based on labor, the adjustment to actual variable overhead costs parallels that of labor. The actual variable costs can be determined by adding the \$232 unfavorable efficiency variance and subtracting the \$160 favorable spending variance from the standard variable overhead allowed of \$50,500 to get \$50,572. From this we can determine that actual variable overhead was 100.143% of standard. The standard overhead cost for the 25-hour increase in inventory is 25 hours × \$5 per hour = \$125, so the actual cost must be \$125 × 1.00143, which, after rounding, is still \$125.

Finally, we adjust the work-in-process inventory for actual fixed overhead

**EXHIBIT 20-10 Allocation of Variances to Reflect Actual Costing**

| | Raw Materials Inventory | Work-in-Process Inventory | Finished Goods Inventory | Cost of Goods Sold |
|---|---|---|---|---|
| Materials | $ 10 F | $ 0 | $ 1 F | $ 77 F |
| Labor | — | 2 U | 7 U | 965 U |
| Variable overhead | — | 0 | 1 U | 72 U |
| Fixed overhead | — | 20 U | 60 U | 8,044 U |
| Change in account balance | $ (10) | $22 | $67 | $9,004 |

[a]Volume variance.

costs, which are apparently $48,525 (that is, the $48,000 budgeted fixed costs plus the $525 unfavorable spending variance). Because the volume variance is to be considered a product cost, all fixed overhead costs are assigned to production. The standard fixed overhead applied to production was $4 per hour times 10,100 hours = $40,400. This means that actual fixed overhead is $48,525 ÷ $40,400 = 120.111% of standard. Again, work-in-process increased by 25 hours, which at standard cost would be $100, but at actual cost would be $120.

We can now determine the adjustment necessary to bring the work-in-process account balance to actual LIFO cost. As Exhibit 20-9 indicates, the LIFO ending inventory balance consists of the 100 units of beginning inventory valued at $2,000 plus the current cost of inventory additions. These additions were $1,200 for materials, $177 for labor, $125 for variable overhead, and $120 for fixed overhead. The total actual LIFO cost for inventory should therefore be $3,622. The current unadjusted balance in work-in-process is $3,600, so we need to add $22 to the account to get to actual LIFO cost.

The adjustments to arrive at an actual cost for the current additions to finished goods inventory can use the information we developed in adjusting work-in-process inventory. Exhibit 20-8 indicates that finished goods inventory increased by 150 units during the period. We can now determine the standard costs for these units and multiply by the adjustment factors to get the actual cost of inventory additions, as follows:

| | Standard Cost | Actual Cost as a Percentage of Standard Cost | Actual Cost |
|---|---|---|---|
| Materials (150 × $12) | $1,800 | 99.968% | $1,799 |
| Labor (150 × $3.50) | 525 | 101.379 | 532 |
| Variable overhead (150 × $2.50) | 375 | 100.143 | 376 |
| Fixed overhead (150 × $2) | 300 | 120.111 | 360 |
| Totals | $3,000 | | $3,067 |

| Loss: Excess Materials Usage | Adjusted Account Balance | Price Variance | Quantity Variance | Total | Rounding Error |
|---|---|---|---|---|---|
| $4,188 U | $4,100 U | $700 F | $4,800 U | $4,100 U | $0 |
| — | 974 U | 650 U | 325 U | 975 U | − 1 |
| — | 73 U | 160 F | 232 U | 72 U | + 1 |
| — | 8,124 U | 525 U | 7,600 U[a] | 8,125 U | − 1 |
| $4,188 | | | | Total rounding error | − $1 |

The adjustment needed to bring ending finished goods inventory to actual LIFO cost is presented in Exhibit 20-10.

We can also determine the necessary adjustment to cost of goods sold to get from standard to actual LIFO cost. Since we are using LIFO and since inventories increased, all 20,000 units sold should be at current period actual prices. The actual LIFO cost of goods sold then is

| | Standard Cost | Actual Cost as a Percentage of Standard Cost | Actual Cost |
|---|---|---|---|
| Materials (20,000 × $12) | $240,000 | 99.968% | $239,923 |
| Labor (20,000 × $3.50) | 70,000 | 101.379 | 70,965 |
| Variable overhead (20,000 × $2.50) | 50,000 | 100.143 | 50,072 |
| Fixed overhead (20,000 × $2) | 40,000 | 120.111 | 48,044 |
| Totals | $400,000 | | $409,004 |

Thus we need to add $9,004 to the standard cost of goods sold to get to actual costs. But, as Exhibit 20-10 indicates, there is a $1 rounding error in our calculations, so we also add the rounding error to cost of goods sold.

Finally, we should also adjust the loss from excess materials usage to actual cost. The $4,200 avoidable portion of the variance is currently valued at the standard cost for materials. As we saw earlier, the actual cost for materials was 99.722% of standard; therefore the actual cost of the excess use of materials is $4,188.

We can now close the variance accounts, adjust the statements to an actual LIFO cost basis, and write off the loss from excess usage of materials. The journal entry is

ADJUSTING STANDARD COSTS TO ACTUAL COSTS

| | | |
|---|---|---|
| Cost of Goods Sold | 9,005 | |
| Loss from Excess Materials Usage | 4,188 | |
| Work-in-Process Inventory | 22 | |
| Finished Goods Inventory | 67 | |
| Materials Price Variance | 700 | |
| Variable Overhead Spending Variance | 160 | |
| Materials Usage Variance | | 4,800 |
| Labor Rate Variance | | 650 |
| Labor Usage Variance | | 325 |
| Variable Overhead Efficiency Variance | | 232 |
| Fixed Overhead Spending Variance | | 525 |
| Volume Variance | | 7,600 |
| Raw Materials Inventory | | 10 |

## QUESTIONS AND EXERCISES: APPENDIX 20

**20-40** For each of the following, indicate whether it should be treated as a period cost, a product cost, or neither, and why.

**a.** A direct materials price variance resulting from increased supplier prices
**b.** An unfavorable materials usage variance resulting from use of temporary workers
**c.** A favorable materials usage variance resulting from employing "loose" standards
**d.** A direct labor quantity variance that is highly unfavorable owing to "tight" standards
**e.** A favorable volume variance resulting from a clerical error made when the overhead rate was established
**f.** The cost of an uninsured machine that was destroyed because of inappropriate maintenance procedures
**g.** A volume variance occurring during the firm's "slow season"

**20-41** Determine how you would dispose of each of the following (independent) variances.

**a.** An unfavorable usage variance, which is the natural result of the learning curve effect of producing a new product
**b.** A favorable variance that results from a subcontractor performing work in half the time allowed under PERT/Cost conditions
**c.** An unfavorable usage variance resulting from the substitution of materials of lower quality than given by the standards
**d.** Unfavorable labor and overhead quantity variances caused by a disruption in the power supply
**e.** Unfavorable price variances for fuel owing to an increase in the tax per gallon on diesel fuel
**f.** An unfavorable volume variance resulting from labor receiving three extra paid holidays

## PROBLEMS AND CASES: APPENDIX 20

**20-42 Direct labor variances: No beginning inventories.**
During its first period of operations, Cosard, Inc., had the following direct labor variances.

| | |
|---|---|
| Rate (price) | $40,000 favorable |
| Usage (quantity) | 20,000 unfavorable |

It is thought that the variances are the result of the firm's inexperience in working with standard costs, rather than being related to efficiency. The accounts affected have ending balances as follows:

| | |
|---|---|
| Work-in-Process | $ 60,000 |
| Finished Goods | 110,000 |
| Cost of Goods Sold | 330,000 |

**Required**

**a.** Prorate the variances to the appropriate accounts.
**b.** What are the adjusted balances of these accounts after proration?
**c.** What is the effect of proration versus nonproration on this period's income?

**20-43 Direct materials variances: No beginning inventories.**
Stard, Inc., has employed a standard cost system during its first year of operations. The direct materials price variances totaled $50,000 favorable and usage variances were $150,000 unfavorable. Selected accounts (at standard cost) at the end of the period are as follows:

| | |
|---|---|
| Direct Materials | $ 50,000 |
| Work-in-Process | 100,000 |
| Finished Goods | 150,000 |
| Cost of Goods Sold | 500,000 |

An analysis leads to the conclusion that the variances were the result of inappropriate standards and that they should be treated as product costs.

**Required**

**a.** Prorate the variances to the accounts affected.
**b.** If net income based on standard costs was $200,000 (i.e., before the disposition of variances), what is the net income after the proration?

**20-44 Direct labor variances with beginning inventories.**
Greenlaw, Inc., had a flexible budget variance for the year for direct labor totaling $33 favorable. Management has elected to treat the variance as a product cost. The accounts (at standard cost) affected are as follows:

| | Beginning | Ending |
|---|---|---|
| Work-in-Process[a] | $40 | $ 60 |
| Finished Goods | 80 | 120 |
| Cost of Goods Sold | — | 600 |

[a]The beginning and ending units are essentially complete.

**Required**

**a.** Prorate the variance so as to approximate an actual FIFO cost flow.
**b.** Prorate the variance so as to approximate an actual LIFO cost flow.

**20-45 Direct materials variances with beginning inventories.**
Wright Company manufactures a single product. During the period it experienced a $64,200 unfavorable materials price variance and a $148,000 favorable materials usage variance, both of which are viewed as product costs. The standard costs of materials in various accounts (000s omitted) are as follows:

| | January 1 | December 31 |
|---|---|---|
| Direct Materials | $ 20 | $ 50 |
| Work-in-Process[a] | 30 | 60 |
| Finished Goods | 100 | 80 |
| Cost of Goods Sold | — | 600 |

[a]The beginning and ending units are essentially complete.

**Required**
Prorate the variances so as to approximate a weighted-average cost flow.

**20-46 Proration of variances.**
Miller Industries employs standard costing. During the current period there were no usage variances. The unfavorable price variances that occurred reflect general economic conditions rather than inefficiencies in purchasing.

One unit of material is used to make one unit of finished product. The physical flow for the current period is as follows:

| | Direct Materials | Work-in-Process[a] | Finished Goods |
|---|---|---|---|
| Beginning inventory | 2,000 | 1,000 | 5,000 |
| Increases | 18,000 | 16,000 | 15,000 |
| Total | 20,000 | 17,000 | 20,000 |
| Ending inventory | 4,000 | 2,000 | 6,000 |
| Decreases | 16,000 | 15,000 | 14,000 |

[a]The beginning and ending units are essentially complete.

**Required**
Answer each of the following questions, which are independent of one another.

**a.** To approximate actual FIFO costing, what proportion of the direct materials price variance will be allocated to the ending direct materials inventory?

**b.** To approximate actual weighted-average costing, what proportion of the direct labor price variance will be allocated to the ending work-in-process inventory?

**c.** Of the units completed, some are in finished goods and some have been sold. What proportion of the direct labor price variance allocated to cost of goods manufactured will be assigned to ending finished goods and to cost of goods sold, respectively, to approximate LIFO costing?

**d.** Using Miller's physical data, which method of costing would generate the higher income for the period?

**20-47 Proration of standard cost variances: No work-in-process** (CMA).
Nanron Company has a standard process cost system for all its products. All inventories are carried at standard during the year. The inventories and cost of goods

sold are adjusted for all variances considered material in amount at the end of the fiscal year for financial statement purposes. All products are considered to flow through the manufacturing process to finished goods and ultimate sale in a first-in, first-out pattern.

The standard cost of one of Nanron's products manufactured in the Dixon Plant, unchanged from the prior year, is as follows:

| | |
|---|---|
| Raw materials | $2.00 |
| Direct labor (0.5 hr @ $8) | 4.00 |
| Manufacturing overhead | 3.00 |
| Total standard cost | $9.00 |

There is no work-in-process inventory in this product due to the nature of the product and the manufacturing process.

The following schedule reports the manufacturing and sales activity measured at standard cost for the current fiscal year.

| | Units | Dollars |
|---|---|---|
| Product manufactured | 95,000 | $855,000 |
| Beginning finished goods inventory | 15,000 | 135,000 |
| Goods available for sale | 110,000 | $990,000 |
| Ending finished goods inventory | (19,000) | (171,000) |
| Cost of goods sold | 91,000 | $819,000 |

The manufacturing performance relative to standard costs was not good either this year or last. The balance of the finished goods inventory, $140,800, reported on the balance sheet at the beginning of the year included a $5,800 adjustment for variances from standard cost. The unfavorable standard cost variances for labor for the current fiscal year consisted of a wage rate variance of $32,000 and a labor efficiency variance of 2,500 hours @ $8.00 = $20,000. There were no other variances from standard cost for this year.

**Required**

Assume that the unfavorable labor variances totaling $52,000 are considered material in amount by management and are to be allocated to finished goods inventory and to cost of goods sold. Determine the amount that will be shown on the year-end balance sheet for finished goods inventory and the amount that will be shown for cost of goods sold on the income statement prepared for the fiscal year.

**20-48 Standard direct cost variances** (CPA adapted).

Tolbert Manufacturing Company uses a standard cost system in accounting for the cost of production of product A, its only product. The standard direct costs for the production of 1 unit of product A are as follows:

Direct materials: 10 feet of item 1 at $0.75 per foot and 3 feet of item 2 at $1.00 per foot
Direct labor: 4 hours at $3.50 per hour

There was no inventory on hand at July 1, 19X2. Following is a summary of costs and related data for the production of product A during the year ended June 30, 19X3.

100,000 feet of item 1 were purchased at $0.78 per foot.
30,000 feet of item 2 were purchased at $0.90 per foot.
8,000 units of product A were produced, requiring 78,000 feet of item 1, 26,000 feet of item 2, and 31,000 hours of direct labor at $3.60 per hour.
6,000 units of product A were sold.

At June 30, 19X3, there are 22,000 feet of item 1, 4,000 feet of item 2, and 2,000 completed units of product A on hand. All purchases and transfers are "charged in" at standard.

**Required**

**a.** For the year ended June 30, 19X3, the total debits to the raw materials account for the purchase of item 1 would be
   **1.** $75,000
   **2.** $78,000
   **3.** $58,500
   **4.** $60,000

**b.** For the year ended June 30, 19X3, the total debits to the work-in-process account for direct labor would be
   **1.** $111,600
   **2.** $108,500
   **3.** $112,000
   **4.** $115,100

**c.** Before allocation of standard variances, the balance in the materials usage variance account for item 2 was
   **1.** $1,000 credit
   **2.** $2,600 debit
   **3.** $600 debit
   **4.** $2,000 debit

**d.** If all standard variances are prorated to inventories and cost of goods sold, the amount of materials usage variance for item 2 to be prorated to raw materials inventory would be
   **1.** $0
   **2.** $333 credit
   **3.** $333 debit
   **4.** $500 debit

**e.** If all standard variances are prorated to inventories and cost of goods sold, the amount of materials price variance for item 1 to be prorated to raw materials inventory would be
   **1.** $0
   **2.** $647 debit
   **3.** $600 debit
   **4.** $660 debit

**20-49 Proration of variances.**
Refer to 20-48. For external reporting purposes, Tolbert makes adjustments to its standard costs to approximate actual costs. Prorate all variances so as to make this adjustment.

# COMPREHENSIVE CASE 3

# STANDARD COSTING

Norman Metals was established last year to manufacture two types of valve housings known as alpha and beta. The manufacturing process involves casting the housing and machining smooth the coupling joints. The firm has four manufacturing departments and one overall selling and administration unit. Two of the manufacturing departments, casting and machining, actually work on the products that are manufactured. The other two departments, personnel and maintenance ($SD_1$ and $SD_2$), provide support services.

The firm has completed its first year of operations. During the year, the firm produced 5,000 units of alpha and 8,000 units of beta. Sales, however, totaled only 4,600 units of alpha and 7,300 units of beta. The actual results of operations for Norman Metals for the year are summarized in Exhibit CC3-1. Exhibit CC3-2, in contrast, summarizes the standard cost data and planned level of operations taken from the firm's master budget (developed in Comprehensive Case 1). Our tasks in this case are (1) to illustrate the bookkeeping to record the actual results of operations on a standard cost basis (2) to prepare the actual income statement for the period, and (3) to reconcile the firm's master budget income with its actual net income.

We begin by summarizing the journal entries that would have been made during the period. Norman Metals separates material price variances at the time materials are purchased, so materials are added to inventory at standard price. Norman Metals purchased only the materials actually used (given in Exhibit CC3-1). The entry then is

| | | | |
|---|---|---|---|
| (a) | Raw Materials Inventory | 29,700 | |
| | Materials Price Variance | 1,485 | |
| | Cash | | 31,185 |
| | To record the purchase of materials. | | |
| | Materials Price Variance = ($1.00 − $1.05) | | |
| | × 29,700 lb = $1,485 U | | |

The quantity variance is recognized when we record the usage of materials at standard, as follows:

| | | | |
|---|---|---|---|
| (b) | Work-in-Process: Casting | 30,000 | |
| | Materials Usage Variance | | 300 |
| | Raw Materials Inventory | | 29,700 |
| | To recognize materials put into production. | | |
| | Quantity Variance = (5,000 × \$2 + 8,000 × \$2.50) − \$29,700 = \$300 F | | |

Similarly, both the labor rate and efficiency variances will be recorded when labor is put into work-in-process at standard. That is,

| | | | |
|---|---|---|---|
| ($c_1$) | Work-in-Process: Casting | 37,800.00 | |
| | Labor Rate Variance: Casting | 636.90 | |
| | Labor Efficiency Variance: Casting | 414.00 | |
| | Accrued Payroll | | 38,850.90 |
| | To recognize labor used in production in the casting department. | | |
| | Labor Rate Variance = (\$6.00 − \$6.10) × 6,369 hr = \$636.90 U | | |
| | Labor Efficiency Variance = [(0.3 × 5,000 + 0.6 × 8,000) − 6,369] × \$6.00 = \$414.00 U | | |
| ($c_2$) | Work-in-Process: Machining | 25,200.00 | |
| | Labor Rate Variance: Machining | 424.60 | |
| | Labor Efficiency Variance: Machining | 276.00 | |
| | Accrued Payroll | | 25,900.60 |
| | To recognize direct labor used in the machining department. | | |
| | Labor Rate Variance = (\$6.00 − \$6.10) × 4,246 hr = \$424.60 U | | |
| | Labor Efficiency Variance = [(0.2 × 5,000 + 0.4 × 8,000) − 4,246] × \$6.00 = \$276.00 U | | |

The other actual costs summarized in Exhibit CC3-1 are recorded in entries (d), (e), and (f).

| | | | |
|---|---|---|---|
| (d) | Variable Overhead Control: $SD_1$ | 7,400 | |
| | Variable Overhead Control: $SD_2$ | 9,300 | |
| | Variable Overhead Control: Casting | 18,780 | |
| | Variable Overhead Control: Machining | 12,800 | |
| | Fixed Overhead Control: $SD_1$ | 8,700 | |
| | Fixed Overhead Control: $SD_2$ | 6,100 | |
| | Fixed Overhead Control: Casting | 31,000 | |
| | Fixed Overhead Control: Machining | 4,500 | |
| | Various accounts (Accumulated Depreciation, Cash, Accounts Payable, and others) | | 98,580 |
| | To summarize the various overhead costs incurred. | | |

**EXHIBIT CC3-1 Summary of the Results of Operations**

| | Service Department 1 | Service Department 2 | Casting | Machining | Selling and Administration |
|---|---|---|---|---|---|
| Direct materials | | | | | |
| For alpha, cost | — | — | $10,710 | — | — |
| For alpha, pounds | — | — | 10,200 | — | — |
| For beta, cost | — | — | $20,475 | — | — |
| For beta, pounds | — | — | 19,500 | — | — |
| Direct labor | | | | | |
| For alpha, cost | — | — | $ 9,296.40 | $ 6,197.60 | — |
| For alpha, hours | — | — | 1,524 | 1,016 | — |
| For beta, cost | — | — | $29,554.50 | $19,703 | — |
| For beta, hours | — | — | 4,845 | 3,230 | — |
| Variable overhead costs | $7,400 | $9,300 | $18,780 | $12,800 | — |
| Fixed overhead costs | $8,700 | $6,100 | $31,000 | $ 4,500 | — |
| Sales commissions | — | — | — | — | $31,100 |
| Other selling and administrative costs | — | — | — | — | $35,000 |

| | Alpha | Beta | Total |
|---|---|---|---|
| Actual production, units | 5,000 | 8,000 | |
| Actual sales, units | 4,600 | 7,300 | |
| Actual sales price | × $20 | × $30 | |
| Actual dollar sales | $92,000 | $219,000 | $311,000 |

| | | Debit | Credit |
|---|---|---|---|
| (e) | Sales Commissions | 31,100 | |
| | Cash | | 31,100 |
| | To recognize sales commissions paid. | | |
| (f) | Selling and Administration Expenses | 35,000 | |
| | Various accounts | | 35,000 |
| | To record other costs incurred. | | |

The entries (a) through (f) record the incurrence of cost by the initial responsibility center using the goods or services. Next we take the cost of operating the service departments and allocate these costs to the production departments.

The master budget called for the $SD_1$ variable costs to be assigned to the other departments at a standard rate of $750 per employee, while its fixed costs were to be charged as lump sums of $1,800 to $SD_2$, $2,700 to casting, and $4,500 to machining. The variable costs for $SD_2$ were budgeted at $100 per service call, with fixed costs of $4,200 each charged to casting and machining. During the period there were two employees in $SD_2$, three

**EXHIBIT CC3-2 Summary of Standard Costs and Master Budget Plans**

**MASTER BUDGET PRODUCTION AND SALES PLAN**

| Product | Planned Production | Planned Ending Inventory | Planned Sales | Budgeted Selling Price | Budgeted Sales Dollars |
|---|---|---|---|---|---|
| Alpha | 4,000 | 500 | 3,500 | $18 | $ 63,000 |
| Beta | 10,000 | 1,500 | 8,500 | 31 | 263,500 |
| Total | | | | | $326,500 |

**STANDARD COSTS**

| Standards | Standard Quantity of Inputs per Unit | Standard Price per Unit of Input | Standard Cost per Unit of Output |
|---|---|---|---|
| For alpha (based on 4,000 units) | | | |
| Casting department | | | |
| Direct materials | 2 lb | $1 per lb | $ 2.00 |
| Direct labor | 0.3 hr | $6 per hr | 1.80 |
| Variable overhead | 0.3 hr | $4.30 per hr | 1.29 |
| Fixed overhead | — | $16,000 | 4.00 |
| Total casting department | | | $ 9.09 |
| Machining department | | | |
| Transferred in | 1 unit | $9.09 per unit | $ 9.09 |
| Direct labor | 0.2 hr | $6 per hr | 1.20 |
| Variable overhead | 0.2 hr | $5 per hr | 1.00 |
| Fixed overhead | — | $ 5,000 | 1.25 |
| Total machining department | | | $12.54 |
| For beta (based on 10,000 units) | | | |
| Casting department | | | |
| Direct materials | 2.5 lb | $1 per lb | $ 2.50 |
| Direct labor | 0.6 hr | $6 per hr | 3.60 |
| Variable overhead | 0.6 hr | $4.30 per hr | 2.58 |
| Fixed overhead | — | $24,000 | 2.40 |
| Total casting department | | | $11.08 |
| Machining department | | | |
| Transferred in | 1 unit | $11.08 per unit | $11.08 |
| Direct labor | 0.4 hr | $6 per hr | 2.40 |
| Variable overhead | 0.4 hr | $5 per hr | 2.00 |
| Fixed overhead | — | $ 5,000 | 0.50 |
| Total machining department | | | $15.98 |

**MASTER BUDGET SELLING AND ADMINISTRATIVE EXPENSES**

| | |
|---|---|
| Commissions | $32,650 |
| Other selling and administrative costs | 35,000 |

**EXHIBIT CC3-3 Calculation of Service Department Charges to Other Departments Using the Step Method**

| Service Department | $SD_2$ | Casting | Machining | Total |
|---|---|---|---|---|
| Personnel ($SD_1$) | | | | |
| Variable cost allocation basis (number of employees) | 2 | 3 | 5 | 10 |
| Variable charge ($750 per employee) | $1,500 | $ 2,250 | $3,750 | $ 7,500 |
| Fixed charge (lump sum) | 1,800 | 2,700 | 4,500 | 9,000 |
| Total allocation | $3,300 | $ 4,950 | $8,250 | $16,500 |
| Maintenance ($SD_2$) | | | | |
| Variable cost allocation basis (requests for service) | — | 60 | 40 | 100 |
| Variable charge ($100 per request) | | $ 6,000 | $4,000 | $10,000 |
| Fixed charge (lump sum) | — | 4,200 | 4,200 | 8,400 |
| Total allocation | | $10,200 | $8,200 | $18,400 |

in casting, and five in machining. The casting department made 60 requests for service from $SD_2$ and machining made 40 requests. This information is summarized in Exhibit CC3-3, which also forms the basis for entries (g) and (h).

| | | | |
|---|---|---|---|
| (g) | Variable Overhead Control: $SD_2$ | 1,500 | |
| | Variable Overhead Control: Casting | 2,250 | |
| | Variable Overhead Control: Machining | 3,750 | |
| | Fixed Overhead Control: $SD_2$ | 1,800 | |
| | Fixed Overhead Control: Casting | 2,700 | |
| | Fixed Overhead Control: Machining | 4,500 | |
| | Variable Overhead Applied: $SD_1$ | | 7,500 |
| | Fixed Overhead Applied: $SD_1$ | | 9,000 |
| | To record the application of $SD_1$ costs to the other departments. | | |
| (h) | Variable Overhead Control: Casting | 6,000 | |
| | Variable Overhead Control: Machining | 4,000 | |
| | Fixed Overhead Control: Casting | 4,200 | |
| | Fixed Overhead Control: Machining | 4,200 | |
| | Variable Overhead Applied: $SD_2$ | | 10,000 |
| | Fixed Overhead Applied: $SD_2$ | | 8,400 |
| | To record the application of $SD_2$ costs to the other departments. | | |

Note that these charges for services use standard costs (predetermined rates). Thus the user departments are responsible only for the use of the quantity of services that they have made at the standard rates. If the service departments were unable to provide the services at the standard costs, these deviations will show up later as spending variances for the service departments. The efficiencies or inefficiencies of the service departments will not be passed on to the user departments.

Exhibit CC3-4 provides the documentation for the application of the production departments' overhead to the units produced. The resulting journal entries are

| | | | |
|---|---|---|---|
| (i) | Work-in-Process: Casting | 66,290 | |
| | Variable Overhead Applied: Casting | | 27,090 |
| | Fixed Overhead Applied: Casting | | 39,200 |
| | Work-in-Process: Machining | 31,250 | |
| | Variable Overhead Applied: Machining | | 21,000 |
| | Fixed Overhead Applied: Machining | | 10,250 |
| | To record the application of overhead to production. | | |

**EXHIBIT CC3-4 Determination of Standard Overhead Applied to Production**

| | Alpha | Beta | Total |
|---|---|---|---|
| Casting Department | | | |
| Variable overhead | | | |
| Units produced | 5,000 | 8,000 | |
| Standard hours allowed per unit | 0.3 hr per unit | 0.6 hr per unit | |
| Total standard hours allowed | 1,500 hr | 4,800 hr | |
| Standard variable overhead rate | $4.30 per hr | $4.30 per hr | |
| Variable overhead applied | $6,450 | $20,640 | $27,090 |
| Fixed overhead | | | |
| Units produced | 5,000 | 8,000 | |
| Fixed overhead rate | $4.00 per unit | $2.40 per unit | |
| Fixed overhead applied | $20,000 | $19,200 | $39,200 |
| Machining Department | | | |
| Variable overhead | | | |
| Units produced | 5,000 | 8,000 | |
| Standard hours allowed per unit | 0.2 hr per unit | 0.4 hr per unit | |
| Total standard hours allowed | 1,000 hr | 3,200 hr | |
| Standard variable overhead rate | $5.00 per hr | $5.00 per hr | |
| Variable overhead applied | $5,000 | $16,000 | $21,000 |
| Fixed overhead | | | |
| Units produced | 5,000 | 8,000 | |
| Fixed overhead rate | $1.25 per unit | $0.50 per unit | |
| Fixed overhead applied | $6,250 | $4,000 | $10,250 |

Because all costs were put into work-in-process at standard, we know that completed production is valued at standard cost. Knowing that we completed 5,000 units of alpha and 8,000 units of beta, we can simply multiply the completed units by their standard costs for the casting operation to get the cost of units transferred to the machining department. Using the standard costs of $9.09 and $11.08 as given in Exhibit CC3-2, we get

| | | | |
|---|---|---|---|
| (j) | Work-in-Process: Machining | 134,090 | |
| | Work-in-Process: Casting | | 134,090 |
| | To record the transfer of units to machining. | | |
| | Work-in-Process: Machining = 5,000 × $9.09 + 8,000 × $11.08 – $134,090 | | |

Similarly we can multiply the units completed in the machining department by that department's standard costs of $12.54 and $15.98 to get the cost of goods completed.

| | | | |
|---|---|---|---|
| (k) | Finished Goods Inventory | 190,540 | |
| | Work-in-Process: Machining | | 190,540 |
| | To record the cost of goods completed. | | |
| | Finished Goods Inventory = 5,000 × $12.54 + 8,000 × $15.98 = $190,540 | | |

Notice that the standard cost for the machining department includes the standard costs transferred from the casting department. Therefore the machining department's standard costs are also the total standard manufacturing costs for the products. Thus, the same standard costs are used to record the cost of the 4,600 units of alpha and 7,300 units of beta that were sold.

| | | | |
|---|---|---|---|
| (l) | Cost of Goods Sold | 174,338 | |
| | Finished Goods Inventory | | 174,338 |
| | To record the cost of the units sold. | | |
| | Cost of Goods Sold = 4,600 × $12.54 + 7,300 × $15.98 = $174,338 | | |

We could now close out the overhead control and applied accounts as over- or underapplied overhead. But for those departments for which we have estimated a standard amount of overhead to be incurred per unit of output we can split the differences into spending, efficiency, and volume variances.

For the two service departments we did not budget a relationship between the level of costs incurred, the amount of inputs used, and the amount of services provided. Instead we simply budgeted variable overhead at a cost per unit of service provided. Thus we cannot determine an efficiency variance for the service departments. Similarly, since the fixed costs were simply budgeted as a lump sum charged to the user departments without regard to the amount of service demanded, there will be no volume variance. Hence for the service departments we can only calculate spending variances. These variances will simply be the difference between the overhead costs incurred by the departments and the costs charged to other departments. Exhibit CC3-5 summarizes the previous journal entries that we have made and gives the final balances in the service department accounts, which allows us to prepare the following entries.

| | | | |
|---|---|---|---|
| (m) | Variable Overhead Applied: $SD_1$ | 7,500 | |
| | Variable Overhead Spending Variance: $SD_1$ | | 100 |
| | Variable Overhead Control: $SD_1$ | | 7,400 |
| | Fixed Overhead Applied: $SD_1$ | 9,000 | |
| | Fixed Overhead Spending Variance: $SD_1$ | | 300 |
| | Fixed Overhead Control: $SD_1$ | | 8,700 |
| | Variable Overhead Applied: $SD_2$ | 10,000 | |
| | Variable Overhead Spending Variance: $SD_2$ | 800 | |
| | Variable Overhead Control: $SD_2$ | | 10,800 |
| | Fixed Overhead Applied: $SD_2$ | 8,400 | |
| | Fixed Overhead Spending Variance: $SD_2$ | | 500 |
| | Fixed Overhead Control: $SD_2$ | | 7,900 |
| | To close the service department overhead accounts. | | |

Note that the spending variances allow us to evaluate how well the managers of the service departments were able to control their costs for the services rendered.

In contrast to the situation in the service departments, we did budget the production departments' variable overhead to be a function of the number of direct labor hours used. The number of direct labor hours allowed for production is, in turn, a function of the level of output of the department. Therefore for these departments we can determine both an efficiency and spending variance for variable overhead. In addition, we budgeted a standard fixed overhead rate per unit of product. This standard rate was used to determine the amount of fixed overhead applied to production. To the extent that the number of units actually produced differed from the number anticipated in the master budget, there will be over- or underapplied fixed overhead due to our misestimate of the planned level

**EXHIBIT CC3-5 Balances in the Service Departments' Overhead Accounts before Closing[a]**

| Variable Overhead Control: $SD_1$ | | | Variable Overhead Applied: $SD_1$ | | |
|---|---|---|---|---|---|
| (d) | 7,400 | | | 7,500 | (g) |

| Fixed Overhead Control: $SD_1$ | | | Fixed Overhead Applied: $SD_1$ | | |
|---|---|---|---|---|---|
| (d) | 8,700 | | | 9,000 | (g) |

| Variable Overhead Control: $SD_2$ | | | Variable Overhead Applied: $SD_2$ | | |
|---|---|---|---|---|---|
| (d) | 9,300 | | | 10,000 | (h) |
| (g) | 1,500 | | | | |
| | 10,800 | | | | |

| Fixed Overhead Control: $SD_2$ | | | Fixed Overhead Applied: $SD_2$ | | |
|---|---|---|---|---|---|
| (d) | 6,100 | | | 8,400 | (h) |
| (g) | 1,800 | | | | |
| | 7,900 | | | | |

[a]The letters in parentheses correspond with the journal entries given in the text.

of activity. We separate this latter difference as the volume variance when closing the fixed overhead accounts, leaving a spending variance that reflects the difference between the actual fixed overhead costs incurred and the fixed overhead costs that were budgeted.

To calculate the overhead variances, we will need to know the end of the period balances in each of the overhead applied and control accounts. These balances are given in Exhibit CC3-6. In addition we need to know the actual hours used and the standard hours allowed for production in each department. Although we have already calculated these numbers, they are summarized again in Exhibit CC3-7. Finally, to determine the fixed overhead volume variance we need to know the budgeted amount for fixed overhead for each department. Exhibit CC3-2 indicates that the casting department's total budgeted fixed overhead was $40,000 ($16,000 assigned to alpha and $24,000 to beta); the machining department's fixed overhead was budgeted at $10,000 ($5,000 each for alpha and beta).

We now have all the information required to calculate the overhead variances. For completeness, we will calculate the variances both in schematic form and by the variance formulas. The schematic presentation is

**EXHIBIT CC3-6 The Balances in the Production Departments' Overhead Accounts before Closing[a]**

**Variable Overhead Control: Casting**

| | Debit | Credit |
|---|---|---|
| (d) | 18,780 | |
| (g) | 2,250 | |
| (h) | 6,000 | |
| | 27,030 | |

**Variable Overhead Applied: Casting**

| Debit | Credit | |
|---|---|---|
| | 27,090 | (i) |

**Fixed Overhead Control: Casting**

| | Debit | Credit |
|---|---|---|
| (d) | 31,000 | |
| (g) | 2,700 | |
| (h) | 4,200 | |
| | 37,900 | |

**Fixed Overhead Applied: Casting**

| Debit | Credit | |
|---|---|---|
| | 39,200 | (i) |

**Variable Overhead Control: Machining**

| | Debit | Credit |
|---|---|---|
| (d) | 12,800 | |
| (g) | 3,750 | |
| (h) | 4,000 | |
| | 20,550 | |

**Variable Overhead Applied: Machining**

| Debit | Credit | |
|---|---|---|
| | 21,000 | (i) |

**Fixed Overhead Control: Machining**

| | Debit | Credit |
|---|---|---|
| (d) | 4,500 | |
| (g) | 4,500 | |
| (h) | 4,200 | |
| | 13,200 | |

**Fixed Overhead Applied: Machining**

| Debit | Credit | |
|---|---|---|
| | 10,250 | (i) |

[a]The letters in parentheses correspond with the journal entries given in the text.

given in Exhibit CC3-7, and the formula approach is provided immediately following each journal entry. The journal entries are as follows:

| | | Debit | Credit |
|---|---|---|---|
| (n) | Variable Overhead Applied: Casting | 27,090.00 | |
| | Variable Overhead Efficiency Variance: Casting | 296.70 | |
| | Variable Overhead Spending Variance: Casting | | 356.70 |
| | Variable Overhead Control: Casting | | 27,030.00 |

Efficiency Variance = [(0.3 × 5,000 + 0.6 × 8,000) − 6,369] × \$4.30 = \$296.70 U

Spending Variance = (\$4.30 − \$4.243994) × 6,369 = \$356.70 F

| | Debit | Credit |
|---|---|---|
| Fixed Overhead Applied: Casting | 39,200 | |
| Fixed Overhead Volume Variance: Casting | 800 | |
| Fixed Overhead Spending Variance: Casting | | 2,100 |
| Fixed Overhead Control: Casting | | 37,900 |

Volume Variance[1] = \$4 × (5,000 − 4,000) + \$2.40 × (8,000 − 10,000) = \$800 U

Spending Variance = \$40,000 − \$37,900 = \$2,100 F

[1]Fixed overhead was applied on the basis of units of products manufactured, not the more common direct labor hour basis.

| | | |
|---|---|---|
| Variable Overhead Applied: Machining | 21,000 | |
| Variable Overhead Efficiency Variance: Machining | 230 | |
| Variable Overhead Spending Variance: Machining | | 680 |
| Variable Overhead Control: Machining | | 20,550 |

Efficiency Variance = [(0.2 × 5,000 + 0.4 × 8,000) − 4,246] × $5 = $230 U

Spending Variance = ($5.00 − $4.8398) × 4,246 = $680 F

| | | |
|---|---|---|
| Fixed Overhead Applied: Machining | 10,250 | |
| Fixed Overhead Spending Variance: Machining | 3,200 | |
| Fixed Overhead Volume Variance: Machining | | 250 |
| Fixed Overhead Control: Machining | | 13,200 |

Volume Variance = $1.25 × (5,000 − 4,000) + $0.50 × (8,000 − 10,000) = $250 F

Spending Variance = $10,000 − $13,200 = $3,200 U

To close the production department overhead accounts.

Our last step is to close the variance accounts. They could go to the income statement as separate-line items, be allocated to cost of goods sold and the inventory accounts, or simply closed to cost of goods sold. Management has chosen the latter approach, resulting in the following entry.

| | | | |
|---|---|---|---|
| (o) | Cost of Goods Sold | 3,976.50 | |
| | Materials Usage Variance | 300.00 | |
| | Variable Overhead Spending Variance: $SD_1$ | 100.00 | |
| | Fixed Overhead Spending Variance: $SD_1$ | 300.00 | |
| | Fixed Overhead Spending Variance: $SD_2$ | 500.00 | |
| | Variable Overhead Spending Variance: Casting | 356.70 | |
| | Fixed Overhead Spending Variance: Casting | 2,100.00 | |
| | Variable Overhead Spending Variance: Machining | 680.00 | |
| | Fixed Overhead Volume Variance: Machining | 250.00 | |
| | Materials Price Variance | | 1,485.00 |
| | Labor Rate Variance: Casting | | 636.90 |
| | Labor Efficiency Variance: Casting | | 414.00 |
| | Labor Rate Variance: Machining | | 424.60 |
| | Labor Efficiency Variance: Machining | | 276.00 |
| | Variable Overhead Spending Variance: $SD_2$ | | 800.00 |
| | Variable Overhead Efficiency Variance: Casting | | 296.70 |
| | Fixed Overhead Volume Variance: Casting | | 800.00 |
| | Variable Overhead Efficiency Variance: Machining | | 230.00 |
| | Fixed Overhead Spending Variance: Machining | | 3,200.00 |

To close the variance accounts to cost of goods sold.

Entry (o) completes the recording and disposition of the production variances. In Chapter 19 we also calculated marketing price and quantity variances to reflect that unit sales and selling prices per unit may not have been as budgeted in the master budget. In addition, we also calculated the variances from master budget for selling and administrative expenses. Al-

**EXHIBIT CC3-7 Overhead Variances for the Production Departments**

Standard variable overhead rates (from Exhibit CC3-2)

| | |
|---|---|
| Casting | $4.30 per direct labor hour |
| Machining | $5.00 per direct labor hour |

| | Alpha | Beta | Total |
|---|---|---|---|
| Actual hours used (from Exhibit CC3-1) | | | |
| Casting | 1,524 | 4,845 | 6,369 |
| Machining | 1,016 | 3,230 | 4,246 |
| Standard hours allowed (from Exhibit CC3-4) | | | |
| Casting | 1,500 | 4,800 | 6,300 |
| Machining | 1,000 | 3,200 | 4,200 |

| | | Actual Costs | Inputs at Standard | Flexible Budget |
|---|---|---|---|---|
| Casting: | Variable overhead | (See Exhibit CC3-6) $27,030 | 6,369 × $4.30 $27,386.70 | 6,300 × $4.30 $27,090 |
| | | $356.70 F | | $296.70 U |
| | Fixed overhead | $37,900 | | $40,000 |
| | | | $2,100 F | |

From Exhibit CC3-6 we see that we applied $39,200 of fixed casting overhead to production, so the volume variance is $39,200 − $40,000 = $800 U.

| | | Actual Costs | Inputs at Standard | Flexible Budget |
|---|---|---|---|---|
| Machining: | Variable overhead | (See Exhibit CC3-6) $20,550 | 4,246 × $5.00 $21,230 | 4,200 × $5.00 $21,000 |
| | | $680 F | | $230 U |
| | Fixed overhead | $13,200 | | $10,000 |
| | | | $3,200 U | |

Exhibit CC3-6 shows that we applied $10,250 of fixed machining overhead to production. The volume variance is $10,250 − $10,000 = $250 F.

though these variances are useful for explaining the difference between actual income and master budget income, they are not typically reflected in our formal accounting records. Instead, they are calculated separately, outside of the formal records, as we will do in a moment. For now, let us assume that the firm recorded actual sales and selling and administration expenses. With this assumption we can prepare the firm's actual income statement, given in Exhibit CC3-8.

**EXHIBIT CC3-8 Standard Cost Income Statement**

| | |
|---|---|
| Sales (4,600 × $20 + 7,300 × $30) | $311,000.00 |
| Standard cost of goods sold (4,600 × $12.54 + 7,300 × $15.98) | 174,338.00 |
| Net production cost variance (see closing entry) | 3,976.50 |
| Gross margin | $132,685.50 |
| Sales commissions (Exhibit CC3-1) | 31,100.00 |
| Other selling and administrative costs (Exhibit CC3-1) | 35,000.00 |
| Net income | $ 66,585.50 |

## Reconciliation of Actual Net Income to Master Budget Net Income

Normal Metals' actual income for the period is shown in Exhibit CC3-8 to be $66,585.50. Norman Metals' master budget income was projected to be $79,130 (see Exhibit CC1-9). Let us now reconcile the two income figures to explain what happened. One major source of difference is the production cost variances we just calculated. Part of the remaining difference arises from the fact that the firm failed to sell as many units of the products as anticipated; moreover, the units were not sold at the budgeted selling prices. These differences can be analyzed using either marketing price and quantity variances or sales price, quantity, and mix variances, all of which were discussed in Chapter 19. Because we are dealing with only two products, we calculate the separate price and quantity variance for each product in Exhibit CC3-9.

The price variances are the difference between actual selling prices, given in Exhibit CC3-1, and master budget selling prices (from Exhibit CC3-2) multiplied by the actual number of units sold. In turn the marketing quantity variances are the difference between the number of units actually sold (Exhibit CC3-1) and the master budget number of units we expected to sell (found in Exhibit CC3-2) multiplied by the master budget contribution margins. The calculation of the budgeted contribution margin is included in Exhibit CC3-9. Although there are several ways to determine the budgeted contribution margin, we have chosen to subtract the standard cost less the budgeted fixed cost per unit from its budgeted selling price to get the contribution margin. Note that this yields the alternative approach discussed in Chapter 19 in which the variable selling and administrative costs (sales commissions in this case) are not included in the contribution margin.

The production cost variances were calculated previously. In Exhibit CC3-9 we have combined the separate departmental variances and simply listed the variances by type (materials, labor, and overhead).

**EXHIBIT CC3-9 Reconciliation of Master Budget with Actual Net Income**

| | | |
|---|---|---|
| Master budget net income | | $79,130 |
| Marketing variances[a] | | |
| Alpha price [($20 − $18) × 4,600] | $ 9,200 F | |
| Alpha quantity [(4,600 − 3,500) × $10.71] | 11,781 F | |
| Net for alpha | | 20,981 |
| Beta price [($30 − $31) × 7,300] | $ 7,300 U | |
| Beta quantity [(7,300 − 8,500) × $17.92] | 21,504 U | |
| Net for beta | | (28,804) |
| Production cost variances | | |
| Materials price | $ 1,485 U | |
| Materials usage | 300 F | |
| Net materials variance | | (1,185) |
| Labor rate | $ 1,061.50 U | |
| Labor efficiency | 690 U | |
| Net labor variance | | (1,751.50) |
| Variable overhead spending | $ 336.70 F | |
| Variable overhead efficiency | 526.70 U | |
| Fixed overhead spending | 300 U | |
| Net overhead variance | | (490) |
| Administrative cost variances | | — |
| Sales commission variance | | 1,550 |
| Fixed costs deferred in inventory variance[b] | | (2,845) |
| Actual net income | | $66,585.50 |

[a]Calculation of budgeted contribution margins:

| | Alpha | | Beta | |
|---|---|---|---|---|
| Budgeted selling price | | $18.00 | | $31.00 |
| Budgeted standard cost | $12.54 | | $15.98 | |
| Budgeted fixed cost per unit | (5.25) | 7.29 | (2.90) | 13.08 |
| Budgeted contribution margin | | $10.71 | | $17.92 |

[b]Calculation of variance for fixed costs deferred in ending inventory:

| Product | Master Budget Ending Inventory | Actual Ending Inventory | Fixed Cost per Unit | Anticipated Deferred Fixed Costs | Actual Deferred Fixed Costs | Variance |
|---|---|---|---|---|---|---|
| Alpha | 500 | 400 | $5.25 | $2,625 | $2,100 | $ 525 |
| Beta | 1,500 | 700 | 2.90 | 4,350 | 2,030 | 2,320 |
| Total | | | | $6,975 | $4,130 | $2,845 |

It turns out that Norman Metals' master budget and actual costs for "other selling and administrative expenses" are the same. Hence there is no variance for this item. Sales commissions, however, were budgeted at $32,650 (see Exhibit CC3-2), whereas actual costs were $31,000. This results in the $1,550 favorable sales commission variance listed in Exhibit CC3-9.

The last item listed in the reconciliation needs some explanation. The master budget production plans (summarized in Exhibit CC3-2) anticipated that we would end the period with 500 units of alpha and 1,500 units of beta in ending finished goods inventory. The master budget would therefore have applied fixed overhead to these units. In fact, we ended the period with 400 units of alpha and 700 units of beta in ending inventory. We actually then deferred fixed costs only on these 1,100 units. The remaining fixed costs would have been charged to the income statement. Thus our last item is to reconcile the actual fixed costs deferred in ending inventory with the fixed costs that we anticipated deferring when we prepared the master budget. The calculations are provided in Exhibit CC3-9.

## Evaluation of Results

We can use the global reconciliation of master budget to actual income to gain some insight into how well we have done. A major factor explaining the difference has to do with the marketing variances. Although we were able to sell more alpha and at a higher price than anticipated, this was more than offset by the reduced sales of beta at a reduced selling price. This information should lead management to a discussion with the marketing people to determine whether the projections were wrong, or whether the marketing efforts should be redirected.

It is also disturbing to note that the net outcome of all of the production cost variances is unfavorable. However, we should analyze the detailed variances at the departmental level before taking any action. The sales commission variance is favorable, but a little searching of Exhibits CC3-1 and CC3-2 reveals that the sales commission rate was exactly as budgeted: 10% of sales. Thus this variance is a direct result of the marketing variances and should not be considered favorable in the evaluative sense. Finally, the deferred fixed cost variance results from the failure to produce as many units for inventory as planned. To interpret this variance we would need to know whether we made a conscious decision to reduce inventories (particularly for beta since sales were below expectations) or whether production problems prevented us from achieving our goals.

# CHAPTER 21

# MEASURING SEGMENT PERFORMANCE

The preceding chapters have examined aspects of planning and control for the major revenue-producing activities of a firm. Whether the organization deals in a product or service, we have seen that the basic elements of performance measurement are the same. This chapter briefly examines applications to larger segments of the business. Again, the principles and problems are the same as in revenue-producing activities, although some might argue that implementation is often more difficult.

## SEGMENT PERFORMANCE

As we move up the organization chart, performance measurement becomes more difficult because each successive unit is responsible for a wider range of activities. Using the chart in Figure 21-1 as an example, the lowest **cost centers** are responsible only for providing a product or service of a specified quality at minimal cost. Similarly, revenue centers are charged with generating a target level of sales. But as we proceed up the chart, units become responsible for a wider range of activities. For the firm in Figure 21-1, the various companies, which operate as profit centers, are responsible for both costs and revenues. Further, at the group level, the group president may be held accountable for the amount of investment devoted to the group. At each level we must be careful to define the objective of the responsibility center, and measure performance accordingly.

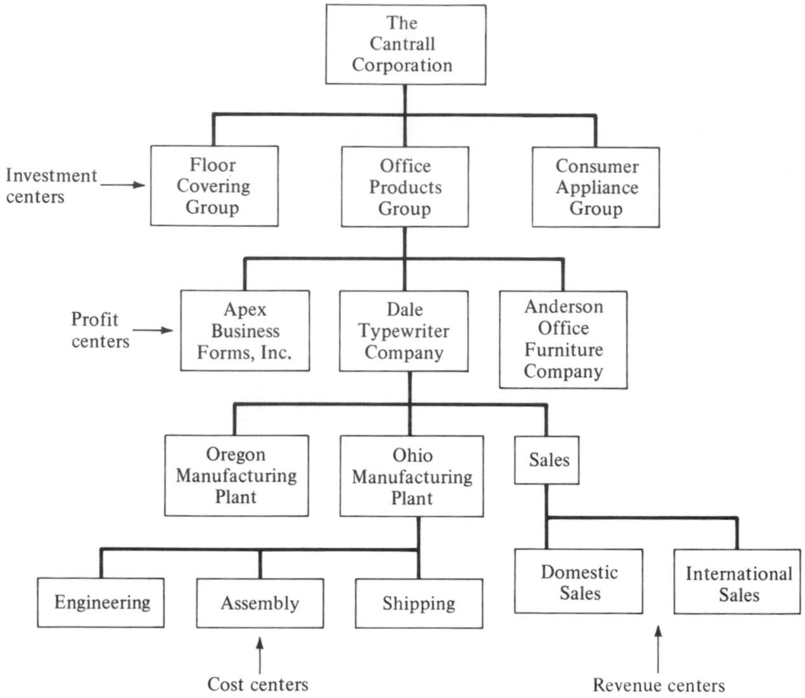


**FIGURE 21-1 Selected responsibility centers for a large firm.**

## Profit Centers

A **profit center** is an organizational subunit that has responsibility for both revenues and expenses. The Dale Typewriter Company in Figure 21-1 appears to be a profit center. A profit center is usually responsible for achieving a desired level of profit. The comprehensive performance reports prepared in Chapter 19 would be useful for the manager of a profit center. The profit center manager can use these reports to pinpoint specific problem areas needing attention. However, reports to higher levels of management, such as the person in charge of the office products group in Figure 21-1, are less detailed. Once again, the reporting objective is to provide managers with an overview of the performance of each of the manager's subordinates. If needed, the manager can request the more detailed performance reports for a particular unit, but we do not routinely inundate managers with excessive information.

The typical performance report, sent to a person with administrative responsibility for several profit centers, consists of actual and budgeted income statements for each profit center. Exhibit 21-1 presents one such report for the Dale Typewriter Company, which is organized on a district

**EXHIBIT 21-1 Profit Center Performance Report**

**DALE TYPEWRITER COMPANY**
**Southern California District Report**

| | San Diego Division | | Long Beach Division | | Northridge Division | | District Total | |
|---|---|---|---|---|---|---|---|---|
| | Actual | Budget | Actual | Budget | Actual | Budget | Actual | Budget |
| Sales | $225 | $230 | $365 | $350 | $195 | $200 | $785 | $780 |
| Cost of goods sold | 125 | 130 | 215 | 210 | 120 | 120 | 460 | 460 |
| Gross margin | $100 | $100 | $150 | $140 | $ 75 | $ 80 | $325 | $320 |
| Sales expenses | 20 | 23 | 35 | 35 | 20 | 20 | 75 | 78 |
| Administration | 35 | 30 | 52 | 50 | 30 | 25 | 117 | 105 |
| Net income | $ 45 | $ 47 | $ 63 | $ 55 | $ 25 | $ 35 | $133 | $137 |

basis. This report allows the district manager to determine whether any division needs attention and reports the overall performance for the district. However this report may not accurately reflect the controllable performance of each division. That is, the income statements for each division may include costs that are not controllable by the division managers. Such costs as district administration costs and an allocation of corporate overhead costs may be charged to each division when calculating net income for external reporting, and yet the divisional manager may have no control over the level of the costs assigned to the division.

Exhibit 21-2 presents a report that more accurately reflects the controllable performance of each division. It highlights several performance measures, each reflecting a different degree of controllability by division and district managers. The first measure is each division's contribution margin. This is the measure over which a division manager should be able to exert the most control. The divisional contribution margin is generally the best measure of the manager's short-run performance. From the contribution margin we subtract the fixed costs directly traceable to each division to yield the **segment margin.** Although the divisional manager may exert a long-run influence on fixed costs, these costs frequently cannot be adjusted in response to short-run fluctuations in environmental conditions. The segment margin is a useful measure of the economic viability of a division in the intermediate term. In the short run we may continue operating a division that earns a positive contribution margin, but a negative segment margin suggests that the division's fixed costs, and most likely capacity, should be reduced.

From the segment margin we subtract the costs incurred to operate the district. These may include district administration costs, district advertising costs, and so forth. The total district margin is most useful as a

**EXHIBIT 21-2 Profit Center Performance Report**

**DALE TYPEWRITER COMPANY**
**Southern California District Report**

| | San Diego Division | | Long Beach Division | | Northridge Division | | District Total | |
|---|---|---|---|---|---|---|---|---|
| | Actual | Budget | Actual | Budget | Actual | Budget | Actual | Budget |
| Sales | $225 | $230 | $365 | $350 | $195 | $200 | $785 | $780 |
| Variable manufacturing costs[a] | 80 | 88 | 143 | 140 | 75 | 80 | 298 | 308 |
| Variable sales and administration[a] | 22 | 23 | 37 | 35 | 19 | 21 | 78 | 79 |
| Contribution margin | $123 | $119 | $185 | $175 | $101 | $ 99 | $409 | $393 |
| Fixed manufacturing costs[a] | 42 | 40 | 60 | 58 | 42 | 40 | 144 | 138 |
| Fixed selling and administration[a] | 12 | 9 | 40 | 45 | 15 | 16 | 67 | 70 |
| Segment margin | $ 69 | $ 70 | $ 85 | $ 72 | $ 44 | $ 43 | $198 | $185 |
| Allocated district costs[b] | 16 | 18 | 11 | 12 | 13 | 5 | 40 | 35 |
| District margin | $ 53 | $ 52 | $ 74 | $ 60 | $ 31 | $ 38 | $158 | $150 |
| Allocated corporate costs | 8 | 5 | 11 | 5 | 6 | 3 | 25 | 13 |
| Net income | $ 45 | $ 47 | $ 63 | $ 55 | $ 25 | $ 35 | $133 | $137 |

[a]Includes only those costs directly traceable to each division.
[b]Includes only those costs directly traceable to the district.

measure of the viability of the entire district. It reflects the contribution that the district is making to corporate overhead and profits. The divisional district margins are generally not good short-run performance measures of the divisional managers because district costs are seldom controllable by the divisional managers. Nonetheless, the divisional district margin may be a useful indication to the district managers of which divisions should be encouraged to try harder to increase district profitability.

Finally, from the district margin we subtract the corporate overhead costs to yield net income. Although these costs are seldom under the control of either the district or divisional managers, the final net income figure is still an indication of the long-term viability of the subunits. If most subunits are able to show a positive net income, then a reported loss for one unit may be an indication that management should divert future resources away from the losing operation into more profitable units.

Although the various performance measures we have provided in Exhibit 21-2 are useful attention-directing devices to alert management to potential problem areas, even this performance report must be used with caution. If we discontinue a particular division, we should not presume that the firm's overall net income will change by the amount of net income reported for that division. The reason this conclusion does not follow is that many of the numbers reported in each division's income statement may be allocated fixed costs. These fixed costs, in turn, may not decrease if a particular division is discontinued. In addition, even though fixed costs might change if a division were discontinued, the amount of costs allocated to a division may be unrelated to the costs that could be avoided if it were discontinued. As we saw in Chapter 13, joint costs are frequently allocated using some easily available basis (such as relative net sales) rather than by a basis that reflects cause-and-effect relationships.

When arbitrary bases for allocating common costs are used, the subunit income figures may be misleading, possibly resulting in hasty and poor decisions. Consider the example in Exhibit 21-3, in which common costs are allocated on a total sales basis. From the information in Part A,

**EXHIBIT 21-3 Potential Effect from Using Net Income as the Basis for Discontinuing a Segment**

| | Profit Center 1 | Profit Center 2 | Profit Center 3 | Total |
|---|---|---|---|---|
| Part A | | | | |
| Sales | $3,000,000 | $2,000,000 | $1,000,000 | $6,000,000 |
| Variable costs | 2,000,000 | 1,400,000 | 600,000 | 4,000,000 |
| Contribution margin | $1,000,000 | $ 600,000 | $ 400,000 | $2,000,000 |
| Separable fixed costs | 800,000 | 250,000 | 100,000 | 1,150,000 |
| Segment margin | $ 200,000 | $ 350,000 | $ 300,000 | $ 850,000 |
| Joint costs[a] | 300,000 | 200,000 | 100,000 | 600,000 |
| Net income | $ (100,000) | $ 150,000 | $ 200,000 | $ 250,000 |
| Part B | | | | |
| Sales | | $2,000,000 | $1,000,000 | $3,000,000 |
| Variable costs | | 1,400,000 | 600,000 | 2,000,000 |
| Contribution margin | | $ 600,000 | $ 400,000 | $1,000,000 |
| Separable fixed costs | | 250,000 | 100,000 | 350,000 |
| Segment margin | | $ 350,000 | $ 300,000 | $ 650,000 |
| Joint costs[b] | | 400,000 | 200,000 | 600,000 |
| Net income | | $ (50,000) | $ 100,000 | $ 50,000 |
| Part C | | | | |
| Sales | | | $1,000,000 | $1,000,000 |
| Variable costs | | | 600,000 | 600,000 |
| Contribution margin | | | $ 400,000 | $ 400,000 |
| Separable fixed costs | | | 100,000 | 100,000 |
| Segment margin | | | $ 300,000 | $ 300,000 |
| Joint costs[c] | | | 600,000 | 600,000 |
| Net income | | | $ (300,000) | $ (300,000) |

[a] $600,000 joint costs allocated on the basis of total sales.

[b] $600,000 joint costs allocated on the basis of sales; Profit Center 1 discontinued.

[c] $600,000 charged to only remaining profit center, since Profit Centers 1 and 2 have been discontinued.

it is quite possible that management might decide to discontinue Profit Center 1, resulting in the situation in Part B. From the report in Part B, management may choose to drop Profit Center 2, which yields the situation in Part C. As can be seen in the illustration, the firm's overall net income would drop from a gain of $250,000 to a loss of $300,000 if such a policy of discontinuing segments were followed. This problem of using arbitrarily allocated joint costs at the segment level, is, of course, precisely the same problem we examined in Chapter 13 at the individual product level.

Although we have made a distinction between controllable and uncontrollable factors for measuring management versus segment performance, many firms do not maintain this distinction. Recent studies in agency theory[1] provide some theoretical support for this position. That is, it has been shown that in some contexts basing managerial rewards (bonuses) on a performance measure that contains some elements uncontrollable by the manager (such as the district margin or even divisional net income) may have a positive overall effect. The manager may well exert more effort on controllable factors to bring total performance up to standard when there is an unfavorable change in an uncontrollable factor. If, for example, allocated corporate overhead rates are increased to the San Diego division because of a decline in the volume of operations in the Long Beach division, the San Diego manager may work harder to overcome the effect of the increased allocation. Unfortunately, the long-term effects of such a bonus policy are not yet well understood. Most accountants still prefer to exclude noncontrollable costs when measuring managerial performance.

### Investment Centers

When management of a center has responsibility for the level of investment retained in the segment, the segment is referred to as an **investment center.** When comparing the performance of several investment centers, a comparison of net income will not necessarily reflect which division has been relatively more profitable for the firm as a whole. For in addition to examining profitability, the firm must also consider the relative amount of investment devoted to each segment. Thus an investment center performance measure typically examines **return on investment (ROI);** the earnings per dollar of divisional investment. Hence, in Exhibit 21-4, although division 1 contributes more income to the firm, its return on in-

[1]**Agency theory** addresses the setting of optimal employment contracts between principals and agents (in our terms, superiors and subordinates). It is concerned with balancing the costs of compensation and monitoring costs (auditing) in the face of potentially different attitudes toward risk on the part of the principals and agents. For a good review of this literature, see the article by Baiman listed at the end of the chapter.

**EXHIBIT 21-4 Return-on-Investment Performance Measures**

| | Division 1 | Division 2 | Total |
|---|---|---|---|
| Part A | | | |
| Sales | $3,000,000 | $1,000,000 | $4,000,000 |
| Income | $27,000 | $20,000 | $47,000 |
| Investment | $900,000 | $200,000 | $1,100,000 |
| Return on investment | 3% | 10% | 4.3% |
| | **Savings Account** | **Division 2** | **Total** |
| Part B | | | |
| Income | $45,000 | $20,000 | $65,000 |
| Investment | $900,000 | $200,000 | $1,100,000 |
| Return on investment | 5% | 10% | 5.9% |

vestment is considerably poorer than division 2. In fact, if the firm could sell division 1 for the book value of its investment and put the proceeds into a 5% savings account, the firm would be better off doing so, as Part B of Exhibit 21-4 indicates.

The return-on-investment calculation is often split into two parts: **return on sales** and **investment turnover.**

$$\text{return on investment} = \text{return on sales} \times \text{investment turnover}$$

$$\frac{\text{income}}{\text{investment}} = \frac{\text{income}}{\text{sales}} \times \frac{\text{sales}}{\text{investment}}$$

The first figure on the right-hand side of the equals sign gives an indication of the income per dollar of sales. A very low figure for return on sales may indicate that the firm should try to increase sales prices, decrease costs, or increase the margin per sales dollar in some other way. The investment turnover, especially if compared to similar divisions or to outside firms, indicates whether the firm is effectively using its investment to generate sales. For example, a very low turnover ratio may indicate that we are carrying far too much inventory for the sales level generated or that our sales effort should be increased.

### Problems with Return on Investment

Although the return-on-investment figure is a popular performance measure for investment centers, there are some significant problems associated with its use. In a multidivisional firm, rates of return are likely to be used to compare the relative performance of divisions. But to do so we must be careful to ensure that the performance measures themselves are comparable. If the divisions are in a wide variety of types of business, it would not be surprising that they use different accounting principles in determining net income. Thus, the definition of the terms making up the ratios themselves would not be strictly comparable. Second, some allowance for risk should be taken into consideration in comparing divisional rates of return. For example, a relatively low but consistent return from an established division in a mature industry may be quite satisfactory. However, the erratic returns to a division in a rapidly changing, high-technology industry may require a very high average return to justify the risks associated with being in the industry.

The use of return on investment for performance measurement can also lead to suboptimization. In this context, **suboptimization** refers to actions taken by a division that are in the division's best interest but are not congruent with the goals of the overall firm. For example, assume that one division has been very successful and is currently earning a 30% rate of return. The use of return on investment as a performance measure will discourage this division from accepting any new investment proposal whose return is less than 30%. This will be true even if the firm as a whole considers investments yielding a 20% return as worthwhile. For the acceptance of an investment earning less than a 30% return will lower the successful division's measure of performance. Consider the case in which the division is earning $30,000 on a $100,000 investment. If the division undertakes an investment of $50,000 that will earn $12,500, or 25%, the division's performance measure will fall from 30% to

$$\frac{\$30,000 + \$12,500}{\$100,000 + \$50,000} = 28\tfrac{1}{3}\%$$

But if the overall firm, including this division, were earning $200,000 on a total investment of $1,000,000, acceptance of the new project would increase the firm's return on investment from 20% to

$$\frac{\$200,000 + \$12,500}{\$1,000,000 + \$50,000} = 20.2\%$$

Of course, just the opposite may occur for a division earning less than the firm's average rate of return. A division with a low rate of return may be encouraged to make investments that raise the division's return on investment and yet be below the returns available elsewhere in the company. In this case the firm's management would probably prefer to transfer the available investment funds to another division.

### Residual Income

The suboptimization problem can be avoided and differential risk easily incorporated in an alternative performance measure called residual income. **Residual income** is a performance measure that reports divisional income after a charge for the use of capital. That is, if a division earns $30,000 on a $100,000 investment and if the firm desires a minimum return on investment of 20%, then residual income would be calculated as follows:

| | |
|---|---|
| Divisional net income | $30,000 |
| Charge for capital (20% × $100,000) | 20,000 |
| Residual income | $10,000 |

The residual income after the charge for capital becomes the division's measure of performance. Note that unlike the return-on-investment measure, a division will improve its residual income performance measure whenever it undertakes an investment project whose return exceeds the specified charge for capital.

Using the data from our previous example, if this division undertakes a $50,000 investment earning a 25% return, its residual income will rise as follows:

| | |
|---|---|
| Divisional net income ($30,000 + $12,500) | $42,500 |
| Charge for capital [20% × ($100,000 + $50,000)] | 30,000 |
| Residual income | $12,500 |

Thus the use of residual income as a performance measure encourages highly profitable divisions to undertake projects with a return higher than its charge for capital, even if the return is lower than the division's current average return on investment. Further, unlike return on investment, weak divisions cannot improve their performance measure, as measured by residual income, by undertaking investments that have a return less than the charge for capital.

Note also that it is a simple matter to incorporate different industry risks into the residual income performance measure. All we need do is adjust the required percentage charge for capital for each division depending on risk. Divisions in high-technology, high-risk fields would have to bear a higher capital charge, whereas divisions in stable markets would bear a lower charge for capital. In this way, residual income can become a risk-adjusted measure of performance.

## DEFINITION OF INVESTMENT

Both the residual income and return-on-investment calculations require us to define and measure investment. The definitional question involves identifying the investment for which we want to hold a divisional manager responsible. That is, the firm provides assets to the manager, but the manager may or may not have the authority to increase or decrease these assets by incurring and repaying debt or returning capital to the parent firm. Depending on the authority granted to managers, three major definitions of investment are commonly seen in practice:[2]

1. Stockholders' equity (net assets)
2. Stockholders' equity plus long-term debt (often noted as total assets less current liabilities)
3. Total equity (total assets)

The first definition is appropriate if the division manager has nearly complete control over all financing and investment decisions. In this case, the firm has invested only the assets represented by total stockholders' equity (original investment plus the earnings that central management has allowed to be retained in the division). The division manager is responsible for maximizing the return on the equity provided by the parent. The manager can choose to incur short- and long-term debt if the manager believes that this will increase the divisional return.

In many cases, however, divisional managers do not have control over the incurrence of long-term debt. These financing decisions are often made at the parent level because the incurrence of substantial debt by any subsidiary may affect the ability of the parent company to acquire debt. In these cases, the total assets contributed by the parent includes both the stockholders' equity and the long-term debt, which, in effect, is provided by the parent. The divisional manager is responsible in this situation for maximizing the return on both sources of assets.

[2]Note that a firm might calculate two return-on-investment figures: one based on the assets under the control of a manager to measure the performance of the manager and another based on the resources committed to the segment to measure the contribution of the segment to the overall firm. The discussion in the next several paragraphs relates to the measures used for managerial performance. These measures are the ones most likely to lead managers to make operating changes.

In the last case, some firms also view current liabilities as a contribution by the parent company. Frequently, working capital management is a centralized corporate function. To the extent that a subsidiary incurs short-term debt, the parent firm must adjust its cash or liability position. In effect, then, the corporate headquarters is supplying the divisional working capital. In this last approach, a divisional manager is held responsible for earning a return on all the assets held at the disposal of the division.

### Idle Assets: An Exception

Each of the foregoing definitions is frequently adjusted to remove certain idle assets from the investment base. In many large firms the divisions are not allowed to immediately dispose of assets that the division no longer wants to retain. Instead, to avoid transaction costs, idle equipment must be listed on an excess equipment list, which is circulated to all other divisions. If another division wishes to acquire the asset, it typically can acquire the asset for its book value.[3]

Typically, divisions must keep idle equipment for one year from the date at which it is made available on an excess equipment list. Since divisional managers do not have control over immediate disposition of this equipment, it is removed from the investment base to recognize that the manager should not be held responsible for making a return on an asset that the manager would prefer to dispose of.

### Measurement of Investment

The measurement of the dollar value of a division's investment also creates problems. Some measures encourage suboptimal divisional asset replacement and retirement decisions and also make it difficult to interpret the performance measures. Two measurement approaches are in widespread use: valuing assets at net book value (original cost less accumulated depreciation) and valuing investment at gross book value (original cost with no adjustment for depreciation).

### Net Book Value

The use of net book value tends to encourage managers to keep equipment beyond its useful economic life and to delay the replacement of assets. In

[3]It is felt that, on the average, a transfer at book value will provide the disposing division with a higher price than it would have received from selling the equipment to an outsider. Similarly, even with transportation charges, the book value is likely to be less than the amount for which the acquiring division could have purchased the equipment from an outside party. The difference between the outside purchase price and the potential outside selling price is referred to as a transaction cost.

the single-asset case, consider an asset whose net book value is $1,000, but whose market value is $2,000. If the asset currently contributes $225 per year to divisional income, then the return on net-book-value investment is 22.5%. If the firm's desired return is 20%, then this asset is contributing to an above-average return on investment and would show a positive residual income (using a 20% capital charge based on the net book value of $1,000). But if the asset can be sold for $2,000 and if we can earn 20% on new investments, we could receive $400 in income by selling the asset and reinvesting the proceeds. The "real" return on investment for this asset worth $2,000 is currently only $225 ÷ $2,000 = 11.25%, which is below the required return.

The use of net book value also results in a tendency for a division's return on investment (ROI) or residual income (RI) to show an increasing trend over time, even if divisional performance is static. This effect results because of the periodic reduction of the investment base due to depreciation. Consider a single-asset division that purchases $100,000 worth of equipment that generates predepreciation earnings of $25,000 over its 10-year life. Assuming no change in operations, no change in the amount of fixed assets held, and that all earnings are paid out in dividends, the performance reports over the 10-year life would be as shown in Exhibit 21-5. Note that we used straight-line depreciation in Exhibit 21-5. Had we used an accelerated method, the trend would be even more pronounced.

**Exhibit 21-5 Return on Investment and Residual Income over Time with Net Book Value as the Investment Base**

| Year | Beginning-of-the-Year Net Book Value | Earnings before Depreciation | Depreciation | Net Earnings | ROI[a] | RI[b] |
|---|---|---|---|---|---|---|
| 1 | $100,000 | $25,000 | $10,000 | $15,000 | 15.0% | $(5,000) |
| 2 | 90,000 | 25,000 | 10,000 | 15,000 | 16.7 | (3,000) |
| 3 | 80,000 | 25,000 | 10,000 | 15,000 | 18.8 | (1,000) |
| 4 | 70,000 | 25,000 | 10,000 | 15,000 | 21.4 | 1,000 |
| 5 | 60,000 | 25,000 | 10,000 | 15,000 | 25.0 | 3,000 |
| 6 | 50,000 | 25,000 | 10,000 | 15,000 | 30.0 | 5,000 |
| 7 | 40,000 | 25,000 | 10,000 | 15,000 | 37.5 | 7,000 |
| 8 | 30,000 | 25,000 | 10,000 | 15,000 | 50.0 | 9,000 |
| 9 | 20,000 | 25,000 | 10,000 | 15,000 | 75.0 | 11,000 |
| 10 | 10,000 | 25,000 | 10,000 | 15,000 | 150.0 | 13,000 |

[a]Calculated on beginning-of-the-year investment. An average investment figure for the year is more common but does not change the trend we are demonstrating.

[b]We assume a 20% charge for capital based on beginning-of-the-year investment.

### Gross Book Value

Measuring investment at gross book value (no allowance for accumulated depreciation) obviously avoids the problem of an increasing performance measure due solely to the decline in net book value. However, it too may motivate managers to make inappropriate asset retention decisions. Whereas the net book value approach tended to encourage managers to hold onto assets too long, the gross book value method motivates managers to dispose of assets too quickly. Assume that we have an asset that is several years old. Its original cost was $10,000, its current market value is $4,000, and it yields annual earnings of $1,000. The return on gross investment for this asset is only 10%. If the firm's desired return is 20%, and if the division's average rate of return is greater than 20%, this asset will reduce the division's reported ROI and reduce reported RI. Hence divisional managers can increase their performance measure by disposing of this asset. But if we calculate the return on investment based on the asset's market value (its opportunity cost), we see that the asset is actually earning a 25% return, which is higher than the desired return.

In both discussions of the alternative measurement bases, we have argued that managers may be led to inappropriate decisions relative to the decisions that would be made based upon the market value of the assets. This should obviously lead to the question: Why not use the market value? The problem is that the market value of assets does not routinely appear in our records (the movement among financial accountants to abandon historical cost accounting for current cost accounting may change this in the future). To date it has not seemed practical (in a cost-benefit sense) to estimate market values solely for divisional performance measurement.

Although divisional performance measures are imperfect, they are quite popular, with ROI based on net book values being the most popular. Return on investment does give a rough approximation of the relative performance of divisions. The illustrations we used to demonstrate potential problems with return on investment are rather extreme examples. They do not reflect the typical case. Apparently many firms believe that for a quick approximation of financial performance, return on investment is a reasonable attention-directing device. Nonetheless, we should be aware of its limitations to avoid overreliance on a fallible yardstick. We should also be aware that ROI measures only financial performance. It does not measure whether management has maintained good public relations, kept employee morale high, or met other important, but nonfinancial, firm goals.

## TRANSFER PRICING

When one profit center in a firm sells a product or service to another profit center in the firm, the selling price is referred to as a **transfer price.** A transfer price differs from a service department cost allocation (see Chapter 12) in only minor theoretical aspects. However, the effects on managerial motivation and behavior generated by transfer prices are often more visible because of the large dollar volume of transactions involved.

In the service department cost allocation situation we are generally interested in two objectives: product costing and choosing the correct level of services to be provided. That is, prices are set for services in order to include service department costs as part of the cost of the firm's finished products. In addition, if prices are set in advance, users can react to the price and choose the level of services desired. Eventually, the capacity to provide services should be adjusted to the level of demand that results in fully utilized capacity when services are priced at average cost.

With service centers, both the service center manager and the manager of the user department have consistent goals. Each manager's performance is measured according to his or her ability to provide services or products at a minimum cost. The provider of the service wishes to keep the cost of services low so that other departments will continue to use the internal service (as opposed to going outside for a service). Low selling prices provide job security and the opportunity for growth for the service center. Similarly, since service department costs become part of the costs for users, the users also would like service department costs to be minimized. In this case the performance measures for both managers are congruent. That is, both managers are motivated by their performance measures to try to minimize the cost of the services provided.

When providers and users of products and services are profit centers, the performance measurement system leads to a conflict of goals. The supplying center is motivated to transfer goods at as high a price as it can

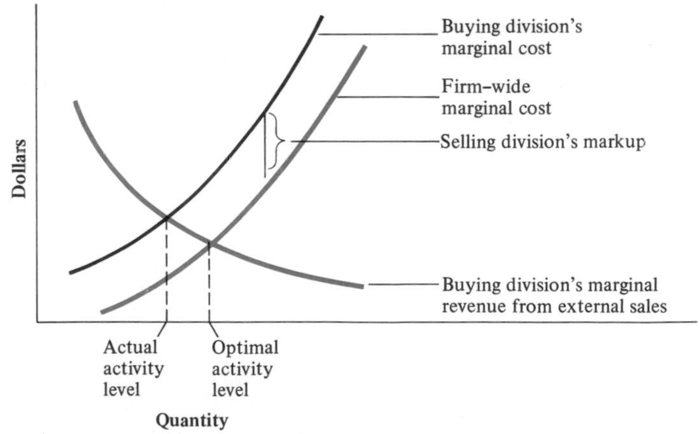


**FIGURE 21-2 Effect of including a profit in the selling division's transfer price.**

get to increase its measure of profits. But the transfer price becomes a cost to the user, so the user still wishes to have transfer prices minimized.

In the profit center setting, not only is there a conflict in the performance measures of the two centers involved in a transfer, there is also a conflict between the performance measurement system and the desire to optimize the level of operations for the firm as a whole. Transfer prices consistent with measuring a division's performance by the profit it earns leads the firm to produce goods in less than optimal quantities. That is, in theory, the division making internal purchases produces and sells its products in a quantity that results in marginal revenue equaling marginal cost. But if the price of transferred goods includes a profit for the selling division, then the buying division's marginal cost is higher than the overall firm's true marginal cost. The result is that the buying division will produce and sell fewer units of product than if the production and sales decision were made on a firm-wide basis. This effect is illustrated in Figure 21-2.

The effect illustrated in Figure 21-2 is easily demonstrated in a special-order situation. Assume division A is producing 100,000 portable radios per year, resulting in the following income.

| | |
|---|---|
| Sales (100,000 × $30) | $3,000,000 |
| Variable costs (100,000 × $15) | 1,500,000 |
| Fixed costs | 900,000 |
| Net income | $ 600,000 |

Division B produces an inexpensive cassette recorder. Its current operations are summarized as follows:

| | |
|---|---|
| Sales (200,000 × $40) | $8,000,000 |
| Variable costs (200,000 × $25) | 5,000,000 |
| Fixed costs | 2,000,000 |
| Net income | $1,000,000 |

Now assume that division B is approached by a distributor of novelty products, who would like to purchase a combination cassette recorder and radio. The buyer is willing to purchase 10,000 such units for $47. Management of division B has determined that the radio produced by division A can easily be incorporated into B's cassette recorder at no additional cost other than the cost of acquiring the radios. Should division B accept the order?

Division B's relevant costs for this decision are its variable costs of $25 to produce the recorder plus the cost of the radio. If division A transfers the radios at their regular selling price of $30, division B's variable costs will be $25 + $30 = $55. Because the variable costs exceed the $47 selling price, the order would be refused. Note that in this case the order would be refused even if division A transferred the radios at "cost" (full cost) of ($1,500,000 + $900,000)/100,000 = $24 per unit. For even then division B's variable costs would be $25 + $24 = $49, which is higher than the offered price of $47. But, from the overall firm's point of view the order should be accepted because the total variable cost to produce the order is division A's cost of $15 plus division B's cost of $25 for a total of only $40. The firm would thus earn a positive contribution margin of $7 per unit on this order.

To avoid the suboptimization problem just described, we might consider setting transfer prices at marginal cost. This approach works if the selling division produces only products or services to be transferred to other divisions, in which case it ought to be evaluated as a cost center rather than as a profit center. But if the selling division also makes substantial external sales, it *is* a profit center. If the selling division is required to transfer products to other divisions at cost, then the division's profits are not an all-inclusive measure of performance. The likely result is that the management of the selling division will not place a very high priority on production of goods to be transferred. Rather, management would probably concentrate its efforts on the goods to be sold externally, adding to the division's profits and its performance measure.

The conflict between the resource allocation decision (how many units of product to produce) and the desire to measure performance using profits is fundamental. When interdivisional transfers take place, a single transfer price is incapable of simultaneously satisfying both objectives. For firms that choose to use a single transfer price, the objective when selecting the transfer price is to minimize the sum of the costs arising from the use of an inappropriate performance measure and the costs from making suboptimal resource transfers.

The transfer price that minimizes the suboptimization costs for a firm must be tailored to each firm. The choice of the best transfer price depends on such factors as: (1) the dollar volume of transfers (are they significant or immaterial), (2) whether there are compelling reasons for insisting that some products be produced internally and transferred (the need to control quality, to provide product availability, or to protect trade secrets), and (3) whether there are alternative sources and outlets for the transferred products. Although we cannot describe an appropriate transfer price for every firm, let us look at some general tendencies for three situations:

1. A competitive external market exists for the transferred products.
2. Transferred products are unique (there is no competitive market), and the order is of a nonrecurring nature.
3. Transferred products are unique, but a long-term commitment to production is required.

### Where a Competitive Market Exists

Earlier we noted that if the supplier of a transferred product can also sell the product externally, the supplier is motivated to concentrate on external sales if no profit is made on internal sales. To encourage the seller to cooperate with the internal buyer, it becomes necessary to compensate the seller for its opportunity costs. That is, the transfer price must be set high enough that the seller's management is motivated to give equal priority to the transferred goods as to external sales. But this does not mean that internal parties must pay the going market rate. The seller should be willing to make internal sales at the market price less any cost savings that the seller experiences in making internal sales. For example, the seller probably will not pay sales commissions on internal sales, nor should there be any risk of bad debts. Reducing the selling price by these cost savings should still maintain the same contribution margin on internal sales as on external sales. At the same time, passing on these cost savings to the buyer somewhat reduces the suboptimal production effect on the overall firm. An example will clarify these points.

Consider again the special order for a combination radio cassette recorder in our previous example. Assume now that division A is operating at full capacity and that the external buyer is willing to pay \$54 for the combined product.

Because division A is operating at full capacity, its total opportunity cost to supply the radio to division B is its variable cost plus the opportunity cost of the forgone sales to regular customers. In the current case the total cost per unit to division A would be its selling price of \$30. That is, if a unit is transferred to division B, division A loses \$15 of contribution margin on the forgone sale to a regular customer and incurs the \$15 variable cost. With division A's transfer price set at \$30, the variable cost to division B to produce the combined product is \$25 + \$30 = \$55, so the \$54 offer would be refused. For the facts as stated, this is also an optimal action from the overall firm's point of view.

Now assume that division A pays its salespeople a 10% commission. This commission is included in the \$15 variable cost for division A. Also assume that commissions are not paid for interdivisional sales. Now, even if division A is at capacity, the analysis changes. The forgone contribution margin for an internal transfer is still \$15, but the variable cost incurred by division A for an internal transfer now drops to \$12 (i.e., the variable cost as originally given less the 10% of \$30, or \$3, commission not paid on internal transfers). Thus division A's total opportunity cost for an internal transfer is \$15 + \$12 = \$27. At a \$27 transfer price division B's total variable cost for a unit is \$25 + \$27 = \$52. In these circumstances, division B would accept the \$54 order. The overall firm and division B will be better off, and division A will earn its normal profit.

### Forced Transfers

When a competitive market exists for transferred products, the possibility exists that internal parties will choose to deal with outsiders rather than make internal transfers. When this occurs, upper-level management often considers forcing profit centers to buy and sell internally. Unfortunately, compelling profit centers to deal internally creates problems.

Profit centers are presumably established to decentralize decision making. The rationale typically is that managers closer to the operating environment have a better feel for the local market. They can receive and evaluate information about local conditions faster and more effectively than central management. By centralizing the decision on transfers, central management is impeding the local manager's flexibility in reacting to changing conditions.

In addition, there are some perverse motivational reactions to forced transfers. If users must buy internally, the supplier becomes a monopoly. Although the supplier may be forced to sell at adjusted market prices (instead of monopoly prices), we should still expect that the locked-in customer will not get as good service as an external customer. For example, one of the authors is affiliated with a university in which the motor pool is a monopoly. Employees must use a university vehicle for local travel. Mileage for using a private vehicle will not be reimbursed unless a motor pool vehicle is unavailable. The motor pool is operated as a profit center, with rental rates—equal to market rates for equivalent cars—charged to an employee's department. Although market prices are set, the motor pool is able to pass costs on to users. It imposes rigid requirements as to advance reservations for cars and restricted times at which vehicles may be picked up and returned. Moreover, the user does not have a choice as to the type of vehicle rented (i.e., compact versus full size; full-size cars are always rented first because they have a higher rental charge) and, in general, motor pool employees are at best civil to users and often surly. Because of the monopoly position of the motor pool, users have no effective means of forcing competitive service.

On the other side, if sellers are forced to supply transferred goods to buyers, buyers can frequently transfer costs to the seller. That is, the buyer may transfer its inventory holding costs to the supplier by placing frequent small orders. Similarly, the buyer may be less than cooperative in projecting future orders and meeting required delivery schedules.

Because of the problems created by forced transfers, many firms allow profit centers to choose whether to deal internally or externally. If there are cost advantages from dealing internally, these should be reflected in the transfer price, and both parties should benefit from internal transfers. On the other hand, many organizations feel that the benefits from requiring transfers to be made internally justifies the cost of the side effects from forcing internal transfers.

### Unique Product, Nonrecurring Order

A general market price will not exist for unique products. But the objective in setting the transfer price is still to encourage both internal parties to participate in the internal transfer. One approach is to have the buyer solicit bids for producing the product and then have the seller accept or reject the order at the lowest bid. However, external suppliers would soon learn that there is no point in devoting a lot of resources to preparing bids if the probability of winning the bid is remote. A second approach is to have the seller prepare a bid using its established pricing formula, which takes into consideration the opportunity cost of capacity. As with any customer, these initial prices are then subject to negotiation (usually dependent on how busy the selling division is). Although mutually agreed-upon negotiated prices should keep both parties happy, there is no guarantee that negotiations will result in a price acceptable to both parties.

### Unique Product, Long-Run Commitment

A more troublesome situation occurs when there is a long-run commitment to supply a buying division. In these cases, the seller's normal pricing formula may not lead to an appropriate initial price from which to begin negotiations. Instead of looking at the opportunity cost of using existing capacity, the seller may need to consider pricing to cover the cost of expanding capacity. This type of situation rarely exists with an external customer, so the seller is not likely to have any guidance in establishing a representative market price. To the extent that labor and equipment are solely dedicated to the particular product, the opportunity cost for using this equipment elsewhere may be very low (or even zero). In these cases, it is common to use a "cost-plus" transfer price. That is, the goods are transferred at the seller's cost plus a "normal" profit margin. The normal profit margin is usually the subject of negotiation between the buyer and the seller.

If cost is used as the starting point for establishing a transfer price, we must decide whether actual costs or standard costs are the appropriate base. As with service department allocations, if actual costs are used, then any inefficiencies of the selling division will be passed on to the buyer. To avoid this problem, standard costs are the preferred basis for transfers.

Finally, the divisions must agree on what costs are to be included in the cost of the product. Should cost be restricted to only direct costs, or should a portion of the seller's indirect costs also be included? As we saw in Chapters 11 to 13, if indirect costs are included, the allocation procedure used can substantially affect the cost of the product. Thus in these situations it is also wise for the parties to agree on the allocation procedures to be used.

### Other Transfer Pricing Objectives

The transfer pricing problem is further complicated for firms operating in several states or multinationally. In these situations, central management may want to impose transfer prices on its divisions to meet firm-wide objectives unrelated to divisional profitability. For example, transfer prices can serve to move reported income from one division to another. Consider a simple example in which division A sells 1,000 units of product costing $15 to produce to division B, which sells the products to outsiders for $25. Assume that each division is located in a separate tax jurisdiction (different state or different country). Further, assume that division A faces a 10% income tax rate and division B must pay a 20% tax rate. In Exhibit 21-6 we illustrate the effect of three different transfer prices on the firm's overall tax liability. Of course, we have picked extreme transfer prices in Exhibit 21-6, which one taxing jurisdiction or the other would likely disallow. Even within the constraints imposed by taxing authorities, however, there still exists some room to manipulate transfer prices to minimize taxes.

A second motivation for central management to impose a transfer price is to increase the competitive position of a division. Assume that division B is in a new foreign market in which central management wishes to capture a significant portion of the market. By setting a very low transfer price, the foreign division will be able to sell its products at a very low price and still report a profit in its performance report. In effect, the producing division may be subsidizing the low prices of the foreign division (by earning less than its normal profit on the goods central management forces it to sell to the foreign division). Again, although many countries have laws to protect their domestic firms from this type of competition, there is usually enough leeway to allow firms at least partially to subsidize foreign operations in this manner.

Multinational firms can also use transfer prices as a means to get cash out of countries that restrict the flow of currency. Many countries have strict limits on the amounts of dividends that foreign subsidiaries can repatriate to the parent company. Usually, however, the restrictions on payments for purchases of goods and materials are much more relaxed. By charging an artificially high transfer price on goods sold to subsidiaries in these countries, the firm can effectively move the profits and the cash to a country that does not have currency restrictions. Again, the degree to which this can be done is restricted by the host government's ability to identify and prohibit "unfair" transfer prices.

Whenever central management imposes a transfer price to meet a corporate-wide objective, we must be very careful in interpreting the measures of divisional performance. To the extent that the imposed transfer price differs from the price that would have been charged had the manager been able to negotiate a transfer price, the division's reported

**EXHIBIT 21-6 The Effect of Transfer Prices on the Tax Liability of a Firm Operating in Several Tax Jurisdictions**

**TRANSFER PRICE $15 PER UNIT**

| | Division A | Division B | Total[a] |
|---|---|---|---|
| Sales | $15,000 | $25,000 | $25,000 |
| Cost of goods sold | 15,000 | 15,000 | 15,000 |
| Income before tax | $ — | $10,000 | $10,000 |
| Tax rate | 10% | 20% | NA |
| Tax | — | 2,000 | 2,000 |
| Net income | $ — | $ 8,000 | $ 8,000 |

**TRANSFER PRICE $20 PER UNIT**

| | Division A | Division B | Total[a] |
|---|---|---|---|
| Sales | $20,000 | $25,000 | $25,000 |
| Cost of goods sold | 15,000 | 20,000 | 15,000 |
| Income before tax | $ 5,000 | $ 5,000 | $10,000 |
| Tax rate | 10% | 20% | NA |
| Tax | 500 | 1,000 | 1,500 |
| Net income | $ 4,500 | $ 4,000 | $ 8,500 |

**TRANSFER PRICE $25 PER UNIT**

| | Division A | Division B | Total[a] |
|---|---|---|---|
| Sales | $25,000 | $25,000 | $25,000 |
| Cost of goods sold | 15,000 | 25,000 | 15,000 |
| Income before tax | $10,000 | $ — | $10,000 |
| Tax rate | 10% | 20% | NA |
| Tax | 1,000 | — | 1,000 |
| Net income | $ 9,000 | $ — | $ 9,000 |

[a]Interdivisional sales have been eliminated in the consolidation.

income is distorted. Further, since the manager was not allowed the authority to make the pricing decision, we cannot hold the manager responsible for the profitability on that portion of the division's activity. On the other hand, we do want to motivate the manager to provide the goods and services in a timely manner at an efficient cost. For this portion of the division's activity we may wish to evaluate peformance by examining actual and budgeted costs and by the division's ability to meet shipping schedules.

Another alternative is to keep two sets of records for divisional performance based on two different sets of transfer prices. One set might be used for preparation of external financial statements, tax returns, and for replying to governmental requests for information. A second set might be prepared for internal use to evaluate divisional performance. However, if taxing officials or government regulators were to discover the second set of records, we suspect that words like deceit, fraud, exploitation, and so forth would soon be aired (possibly in the news media). Thus such a compromise approach to measure performance is politically impractical in most cases.

## SUMMARY

Measuring the performance of responsibility centers that engage in many dissimilar activities is far more difficult than for a center performing a single activity. Nonetheless, performance measures are needed to direct managerial attention to potential problem areas. Although the existing performance measures are flawed, their widespread use suggests that, when used with care, they provide valuable information.

The existence of internal transfers of goods and services between profit centers further aggravates the problem with existing performance measures. The two objectives of maximizing the utilization of resources and measuring individual segment net income seem incompatible. To date, efforts at establishing transfer prices have been directed toward minimizing the combined cost of inaccurate performance measures and suboptimal production decisions.

## DEMONSTRATION PROBLEM

Baxter Industries is a large, diversified holding company.[4] Its operations are organized into eight separate corporations, all wholly owned by Baxter Industries. Two of the corporations report to the group director of personal products, and another two corporations constitute the food processing group. Each corporation, in turn, has several operating divisions. Figure 21-3 is a partial organization chart highlighting the structure of two of the corporations, Baxter Pharmaceuticals, Inc., and Carrie's Frozen Pizza, Inc. This case involves the Albany Division of Baxter Pharmaceuticals and the Albany Division of Carrie's Frozen Pizza.

Baxter Pharmaceuticals has a very large plant in Albany, so large that management constructed its own power-generating facilities. When Carrie's Frozen Pizza decided to construct a plant in the Northeast, a major factor in choosing to locate in Albany was the availability of a parcel of land adjacent to the pharmaceuticals plant. It was determined that the Baxter Pharmaceuticals plant could

[4]This case is based on an actual situation with which the author was involved. Names and locations have been changed to disguise the identity of the firm.

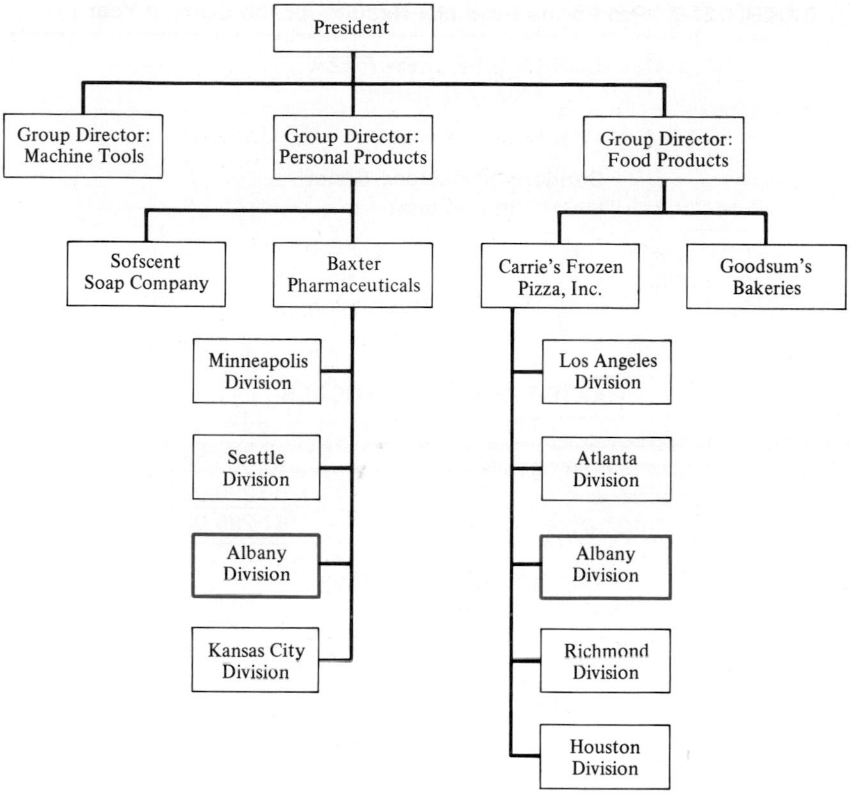


**FIGURE 21-3 Partial organization chart for Baxter Industries, Inc.**

easily provide the pizza division with all of its power requirements at a substantial savings to the firm.

For several years all went well. Baxter measured the use of power by both divisions, determined the average cost to produce the power and charged the pizza division 110% of the cost to provide it with power. Exhibit 21-7 presents managements' estimate of each division's net income for the current year, the calculation of the charge for power costs, and the anticipated end-of-the-year balance sheets for each division.

Last summer a state auditor informed management of the Baxter Pharmaceuticals plant that they must pay sales tax on the sales of power to Carrie's. Management was unsuccessful in arguing that the power was simply an internal transfer. "Because two separate legal entities are involved," the auditor countered, "a sales transaction has occurred. State law is very clear in this situation. Thus, beginning next year, you must pay a 5% sales tax on the price you charge Carrie's Frozen Pizza, Inc., for its power consumption."

Management of the pharmaceuticals plant has also been considering replacing a major portion of the power-generating facilities. The facilities that would

**EXHIBIT 21-7 Pro Forma Financial Results for the Current Year**

**CARRIE'S FROZEN PIZZA**
**Albany Division**

Net income before income tax: $750,000

**Condensed Balance Sheet**
**(in millions)**

| | | | |
|---|---|---|---|
| Current assets | $3.7 | Current liabilities | $2.1 |
| Fixed assets | 4.4 | Long-term debt | 2.5 |
| Total | $8.1 | Owners' equity | 3.5 |
| | | Total | $8.1 |

**BAXTER PHARMACEUTICALS**
**Albany Division**

| | |
|---|---|
| Net income from operations | $1,000,000 |
| Miscellaneous income: Power sales[a] | 220,000 |
| Net income before income tax | $1,220,000 |

**Condensed Balance Sheet**
**(in millions)**

| | | | |
|---|---|---|---|
| Current assets | $ 4.1 | Current liabilities | $ 1.9 |
| Fixed assets | 6.8 | Long-term debt | 1.3 |
| Total | $10.9 | Owners' equity | 7.7 |
| | | Total | $10.9 |

[a]Calculation of power sales:

| | |
|---|---|
| Total power generating costs | $800,000 |
| Proportion of power used by Carrie's | 25% |
| Cost to supply power to Carrie's | $200,000 |
| Profit factor (at 10%) | 20,000 |
| Transfer price for power supplied | $220,000 |

be replaced were acquired 7 years ago for $1 million. They have been depreciated $100,000 per year. Thus the net book value will be $300,000 at year-end, which is approximately what the net proceeds from sale of the equipment will be. The new facilities would require an outlay of $1,500,000. The division has the available cash. The facilities can be installed and ready for use by the beginning of next year and would be depreciated at a rate of $150,000 per year. The new, more efficient facilities will save approximately $200,000 per year in variable power-generating costs.

Except for the possible replacement of part of the power facilities and the imposition of the sales tax, next year's operations in both divisions are expected to be roughly the same as this year. Carrie's Frozen Pizza will again use approximately 25% of the power generated by the Baxter plant.

The central management of Baxter Industries calculates two performance measures for each profit center. The first measure is return on investment with investment measured as the book value of all assets employed by a center. This measure is used as an indication of the division manager's performance in utilizing divisional assets. The second measure is a residual income measure with investment defined as the total stockholders' equity for each center. This second measure is used as a measure of the underlying profitability of each division. In both cases, the performance measures are based on investment as measured by end-of-the-year balances. The firm's charge for capital when calculating residual income is 15%.

**Required**

For each of the following situations assume that divisional net income is reflected in the balance sheet by an increase in total assets and an increase in divisional owners' equity.

**a.** Estimate each division's and each manager's measure of performance for the current year from the pro forma financial statements given in Exhibit 21-7.

**b.** Assuming that there are no changes in the power facilities, or in the way the transfer price is calculated, determine the performance measures for next year, when Baxter will have to pay sales tax on power sales.

**c.** Assume that Baxter Pharmaceuticals replaces the power facilities and uses the same procedure for calculating the power transfer price. Calculate next year's expected performance measures.

**d.** Assume that Baxter Pharmaceuticals replaces the power facilities, but decides to charge Carrie's a nominal $1 for power sales (thus avoiding the sales tax). Calculate each set of performance measures.

**e.** What should the manager of Baxter Pharmaceuticals' Albany Division do?

**Solution**

**a.** The current year's performance measures would be

| | Return on Investment | Residual Income |
|---|---|---|
| Carrie's Frozen Pizza | $\frac{\$750}{\$8,100} = 9.26\%$ | $750,000 − 0.15 × $3,500,000 = $225,000 |
| Baxter Pharmaceuticals | $\frac{\$1,220}{\$10,900} = 11.19\%$ | $1,220,000 − 0.15 × $7,700,000 = $65,000 |

**b.** The charge for power would be the same to Carrie's Frozen Pizza. Its net income therefore would remain unchanged at $750,000. However, the end-of-the-year total assets and total owners' equity would each increase by $750,000. Similarly, the Baxter plant's net income would be the same as the current year except for the added sales tax. The sales tax would be 5% of $220,000 or $11,000. Thus its projected earnings would be $1,209,000. In addition, total assets and total owners' equity for Baxter Pharmaceuticals would increase by $1,209,000 by year-end. The performance measures for next year would be

| | Return on Investment | Residual Income |
|---|---|---|
| Carrie's Frozen Pizza | $\frac{\$750}{\$8,850} = 8.47\%$ | \$750,000 − 0.15 × \$4,250,000 = \$112,500 |
| Baxter Pharmaceuticals | $\frac{\$1,209}{\$12,109} = 9.98\%$ | \$1,209,000 − 0.15 × \$8,909,000 = \$(127,350) |

In each case the performance measures have decreased because net income has stayed static or declined, whereas investment increased by the amounts of earnings.

**c.** The new charge for power given the equipment replacement would be

| | |
|---|---|
| Current cost to produce power | \$800,000 |
| Added depreciation (\$150,000 − \$100,000) | 50,000 |
| Reduced variable costs | (200,000) |
| Net cost to produce power | \$650,000 |
| Carrie's percentage of usage | 25% |
| Cost to provide power to Carrie's | \$162,500 |
| Profit factor (at 10%) | 16,250 |
| Transfer price for power supplied | \$178,750 |

Carrie's Frozen Pizza's net income would increase then by \$220,000 − \$178,750 = \$41,250 to \$791,250. Again, year-end total assets and owners' equity would also increase by \$791,250.

The effect on Baxter Pharmaceuticals' net income is more complex. Its net income would rise by \$150,000 because of the reduced costs to provide power (\$800,000 versus \$650,000), but fall by its reduced sales of power to the pizza division. The reduced sales can be calculated as follows:

| | |
|---|---|
| Net power sales, as is (\$220,000 − 0.05 × \$220,000) | \$209,000 |
| Net power sales, proposed (\$178,750 − 0.05 × \$178,750) | 169,812 |
| Reduced power sales revenue | \$ 39,188 |

Thus Baxter Pharmaceuticals' new net income would be \$1,209,000 + \$150,000 − \$39,188 = \$1,319,812. To calculate performance measures we must once again increase total assets and owners' equity by the planned increase in earnings. The new performance measures are estimated to be as follows:

| | Return on Investment | Residual Income |
|---|---|---|
| Carrie's Frozen Pizza | $\frac{\$791,250}{\$8,891,250} = 8.90\%$ | \$791,250 − 0.15 × \$4,291,250 = \$147,562 |
| Baxter Pharmaceuticals | $\frac{\$1,319,812}{\$12,219,812} = 10.80\%$ | \$1,319,812 − 0.15 × \$9,019,812 = \$(33,160) |

**d.** If the power is supplied to Carrie's free (we can safely ignore the $1 transfer price), the net income for Carrie's will rise by $220,000 over its current level to $970,000. Meanwhile, Baxter Pharmaceuticals' net income will be

| | |
|---|---|
| Current net income | $1,220,000 |
| Reduced costs from new equipment | 150,000 |
| Lost power sales | (220,000) |
| Projected net income | $1,150,000 |

Proceeding as before, our performance measures would be

| | Return on Investment | Residual Income |
|---|---|---|
| Carrie's Frozen Pizza | $\frac{\$970,000}{\$9,070,000} = 10.69\%$ | $970,000 − 0.15 × $4,470,000 = $299,500 |
| Baxter Pharmaceuticals | $\frac{\$1,150,000}{\$12,050,000} = 9.54\%$ | $1,150,000 − 0.15 × $8,850,000 = $(177,500) |

**e.** Based purely on the performance measures, calculated in (b), (c), and (d), the manager of Baxter Pharmaceuticals' Albany Division should select the option in (c). That is, the manager will maximize both the personal and divisional performance measures by acquiring the new facilities, continuing to charge Carrie's the cost plus transfer price, and paying the sales tax. But, the action that is best for the firm is an option that was not considered in the foregoing: Keep the current facilities and reduce the transfer price to $1 per year. An analysis of the new project, using techniques such as those discussed in Chapters 8 and 9, would reveal that the operating savings from the new power-generating equipment do not justify the investment. Assuming that the firm has investment opportunities that return 15%, the firm's capital charge, the firm is better off investing in something other than the power equipment. Similarly, Baxter Industries as a whole is better off with a nominal transfer price for the power to avoid the sales tax. However, let us examine the effect on the performance measures if the power is given away.

Carrie's Frozen Pizza's net income would increase to $970,000, but Baxter Pharmaceuticals' net income would decrease to $1,000,000. Next year's pro forma performance measures would be as follows:

| | Return on Investment | Residual Income |
|---|---|---|
| Carrie's Frozen Pizza | $\frac{\$970,000}{\$9,070,000} = 10.69\%$ | $970,000 − 0.15 × $4,470,000 = $299,500 |
| Baxter Pharmaceuticals | $\frac{\$1,000,000}{\$11,900,000} = 8.40\%$ | $1,000,000 − 0.15 × $8,700,000 = $(305,000) |

The option that is best for Baxter Industries shows the worst results for Baxter Pharmaceuticals.

Earlier we mentioned that this problem was abstracted from a real case. You may be interested to know the actual outcome. The pharmaceuticals plant did not buy the new equipment but continued to charge the transfer price at 110% of cost. The manager indicated that if both plants reported to the same corporate officer, the transfer price might have been lowered. For in that case, the corporate officer could easily see the overall effect of reducing the transfer price on the total profits of the plants under the officer's control. But since the two divisions were in separate corporations reporting to different superiors, the pharmaceutical manager did not believe that the pharmaceutical plant's performance measures would be properly interpreted by upper management if the transfer price were lowered. In this case the manager felt that the $11,000 sales tax was a small price to pay for $209,000 of "profit."

## KEY TERMS AND CONCEPTS

Cost center
Profit center
Segment margin
Agency theory
Investment center
Return on investment (ROI)
Return on sales
Investment turnover
Suboptimization
Residual income
Transfer price

## FURTHER READING


Baiman, Stanley. "Agency Research in Managerial Accounting: A Survey," *Journal of Accounting Literature* (Spring 1982), p. 154.

Baxendale, Sidney J. "Evaluating Managers of Investment Centres," *Cost and Management* (January–February 1984), p. 30.

Benke, Ralph L., Jr., and James Don Edwards. *Transfer Pricing: Techniques and Uses* (New York: National Association of Accountants, 1980).

Brouwer, Curt. "Measuring the Division Manager's Performance," *Management Accounting* (December 1984), p. 30.

Casey, Michael P. "International Transfer Pricing," *Management Accounting* (October 1985), p. 31.

Coburn, David L., Joseph K. Ellis, and Duane R. Milano. "Dilemmas in MNC Transfer Pricing," *Management Accounting* (November 1981), p. 53.

Cowen, Scott S., Laurence C. Phillips, and Linda Stillabower. "Multinational Transfer Pricing," *Management Accounting* (January 1979), p. 17.

Grabski, Severin V. "Transfer Pricing in Complex Organizations: A Review and Integration of Recent Empirical and Analytical Research," *Journal of Accounting Literature* (Spring 1985), p. 33.

Hartman, Bart P. "The Management Accountant's Role in Deleting a Product Line," *Management Accounting* (August 1983), p. 63.
Hirst, Mark K. "Accounting Information and the Evaluation of Subordinate Performance: A Situational Approach," *The Accounting Review* (October 1981), p. 771.
Louderback, Joseph G., and Louis P. Ramsay. "Segment Evaluation Using ROI and RI," *Cost and Management* (January–February 1985), p. 32.
Mays, Robert L., Jr. "Divisional Performance Measurement and Transfer Prices," *Management Accounting* (April 1982), p. 20.
Merville, Larry J., and J. William Petty. "Transfer Pricing for the Multinational Firm," *The Accounting Review* (October 1978), p. 935.
Watson, David J. H., and John V. Baumler. "Transfer Pricing: A Behavioral Context," *The Accounting Review* (July 1975), p. 466.

## QUESTIONS AND EXERCISES

**21-1** Define residual income.

**21-2** Identify the three types of responsibility centers and state, in general terms, the objectives of each.

**21-3** What are the similarities and differences among cost, profit, and investment centers?

**21-4** Cost allocations represent an application of transfer pricing. Cite at least three examples from previous chapters that illustrate this concept.

**21-5** An integrated oil company finds that exploration, recovery, refining, and wholesaling are all profitable divisions but that retailing is not. Should it get out of retailing?

**21-6** What are the financial accounting implications of transfer pricing?

**21-7** A firm's plant in Tennessee manufactures a product, which in turn is shipped to a branch in the Pacific Northwest for sale. Does it make any difference which branch (each is a profit center) is charged for the cost of transportation?

**21-8** A university's budget provides each department with an amount for repair and maintenance. R&M charges each department $40 per hour for such work. R&M has told the Department of Accounting that it will take 3 hours to install a trophy case. The department does not write a check to R&M; instead, the "funds" are merely transferred from one account to another. The departmental secretary has a friend who will do the installation work for $50. Should the friend be given the work?

**21-9** Division A makes high-quality roller bearings to customer specifications. The division typically operates at 80% of capacity; it sells 75% of its output to external customers and 25% to division B. Because the plant is operating at less than full capacity, central management has set the transfer price at division A's standard variable cost. Although division A operates at an average of 80% of capacity, demand for its product is erratic. What problems will this impose on division B?

**21-10** MNC, a multinational corporation, has an assembly plant in the upper Midwest. All components to be assembled are shipped to the plant from other MNC subsidiaries. After assembly, the product is shipped to MNC selling divisions. The plant has a strong, entrenched union representing its workers. MNC uses the plant to evaluate managerial talent, and periodically (more than once a year) a new manager is installed. The sole financial statement used to evaluate the plant manager is the statement of cost of goods manufactured, which is constructed so as to show the volume variance on the bottom line. It is the bottom line that is used to evaluate the manager. What is the implied objective for a new manager?

**21-11** A division of a conglomerate reports sales of $900, variable expenses of $400, traceable fixed expenses of $250, allocated regional expenses of $100, and allocated corporate expenses of $50. Prepare a performance report similar to Exhibit 21-2.

**21-12** Baker, Inc., has two territories, East and West, and each has two regions, North and South. Corporate expenses are allocated to territories on the basis of sales, and territory expenses are allocated to regions on the basis of regional income. Data for the current quarter follow.

| | Sales | Expenses |
|---|---|---|
| East-North | $300 | $200 |
| East-South | 200 | 125 |
| West-North | 200 | 100 |
| West-South | 400 | 250 |
| East | — | 75 |
| West | — | 150 |
| Baker | — | 100 |

Prepare a segment income statement using a format similar to Exhibit 21-2.

**21-13** A branch reports income of $180. Its balance sheet shows the following:

| | Beginning | Ending |
|---|---|---|
| Total liabilities | $600 | $700 |
| Stockholders' equity | 400 | 500 |

What is return on investment if investment is defined as (a) beginning assets, (b) average assets, and (c) average stockholders' equity?

**21-14** (CPA). The following selected data pertain to Beck Company's Beam Division for 19X4:

| | |
|---|---|
| Sales | $1,000,000 |
| Variable costs | 600,000 |
| Traceable fixed costs | 100,000 |
| Average invested capital | 200,000 |
| Imputed interest rate | 15% |

Determine (a) the residual income and (b) the return on investment.

**21-15** A segment reports income of $40,000, residual income of −$10,000, and average investment for the period of $400,000. What is the minimum return being required by management?

**21-16** A division has income after taxes of $50,000, based on sales of $600,000. Total assets employed were $200,000 at the beginning of the year and $250,000 at the end of the year. The firm defines divisional investment as the average total assets available to a division during a year. Determine (a) the return on sales, (b) the asset turnover rate, (c) the return on investment, (d) the relationship among them, and (e) residual income if the division requires a 20% return.

**21-17** For each of the following, determine the unknowns indicated by letters (a) through (i).

| | Case A | Case B | Case C |
|---|---|---|---|
| Income | 10 | d | g |
| Investment | a | e | 300 |
| Sales | b | 500 | h |
| Return on investment | 20% | f | 25% |
| Return on sales | c | 10% | 15% |
| Investment turnover | 3 | 2 | i |

**21-18** Two divisions of Interspatial, Ltd., report summary results as follows:

| | Pluto | Mars |
|---|---|---|
| Sales | $500 | $800 |
| Net income | 100 | 150 |
| Average investment | 200 | 400 |

For each division, determine (a) return on sales, (b) investment turnover, (c) return on investment, and (d) residual income if the cost of capital is 20%.

**21-19** Nexa's division A produces a product that can be sold for $200 or transferred to division B to be incorporated into its product. Division B can buy the part from another supplier at $180. Data on a per-unit basis follow:

| | Division A | Division B |
|---|---|---|
| Selling price | $200 | $600 |
| Variable cost | 100 | 200[a] |
| Fixed cost[b] | 90 | 150 |

[a]Excluding the cost of the component provided by division A or the outside supplier.

[b]All sunk costs.

What is the minimum price to be charged to division B if division A is operating (a) at capacity and (b) below capacity?

**21-20** An international corporation makes a product in one country for $1,000 and sells it in another for $2,000. Income taxes are 30% in the first country and 20% in the second. Both countries disallow losses for tax purposes, and neither recognizes taxes paid to the other country as deductible. What should the transfer price be if the objective is to minimize taxes (i.e., maximize cash flow)?

**21-21** The Hydra Company transfers 60% of the output of its Tucson division to its Tempe division at average full cost. The remaining 2,000 units are sold to others at cost plus 20%. The costs in the Tucson division amount to $100 per unit plus $120,000 per period. The purchasing agent for the Tempe division can purchase the unit from a foreign supplier at 75% of the cost charged by Hydra's Tucson division. Should Tempe be permitted to use the foreign supplier?

**21-22** Division A has been selling a subassembly to division B at $3,000 each and to outsiders for $3,500 each. Division A plans to increase the price to outsiders to $4,200 and to increase the price to division B by a proportionate amount. The cost per unit of producing the subassembly is $900 variable and $1,500 fixed. If division B purchases the part outside the firm, division A's facilities will be idle to this extent; however, 50% of the fixed cost of producing will be eliminated (all of this is out-of-pocket). What is the most that division B should be permitted to pay for the part if it is not purchased from division A?

**21-23** All of the product of a firm's casting division is transferred to the finishing division at $500, which is 25% over cost. Casting's costs are 70% variable. What would the transfer price be if it were based on variable cost alone?

**21-24** All of division A's production is transferred to division B at 110% of cost. Division B adds an amount of cost to the product equal to the transfer price of the product and sells it for 150% of total cost. Division A's cost is $1,000. (a) What does the final product sell for? (b) Prepare income statements for each division and the overall firm if 10 units are transferred and sold externally.

**21-25** A firm has three subsidiaries: $S_1$, $S_2$, and $S_3$. $S_1$ sells all of its output to $S_2$, which in turn sells all of its output to $S_3$. The output of $S_3$ is sold in the market at competitive prices. Income statements for the past quarter are as follows:

| | $S_1$ | $S_2$ | $S_3$ |
|---|---|---|---|
| Sales | $200 | $500 | $800 |
| Cost of sales | | | |
| Transfer price | — | 200 | 500 |
| Costs added by subsidiary | 125 | 100 | 200 |
| Gross profit | $ 75 | $200 | $100 |
| Corporate expenses[a] | 40 | 100 | 160 |
| Net income | $ 35 | $100 | $ (60) |

[a]Allocated as a percentage of sales.

(a) What is net income to the firm? (b) What will net income for each subsidiary be if $S_1$ and $S_2$ raise their selling prices 10%? (c) What will net income to the firm be if $S_1$ and $S_2$ raise their selling prices 10%?

## PROBLEMS AND CASES

**21-26 Return on investment and components** (CICA adapted).

T Limited consists of five operating divisions located throughout Canada and a central corporate office. Each operating division produces and markets its own line of products and sells the product lines of other divisions within its region of the country. Each division prepares its own financial statements, and its manager is evaluated on the basis of the rate that the division has earned on its investment. The division's investment figure used in the calculation has, since the system was started, included all the assets controlled by each divisional manager.

Until last year the investment figure of each division did not include two classes of assets: headquarters' assets and the research department's assets. The associated headquarters and research expenses were not included in the calculation of return on investment. The headquarters facilities were rented. Until recently the research assets also had been small, but by the spring of 19X5 they had grown to just over 10% of the company's total assets. It was expected that more funds would be invested in research facilities in the near future.

In late 19X5, the president of T Limited suggested that all the company's assets be distributed in some way to all the operating divisions. The intent is to make the reported return on investment by the divisions more realistic and to indicate how well the company was doing as a whole.

**Required**

**a.** Outline the arguments for and against using return on investment to measure divisional peformance.

**b.** Evaluate the suggestion made by the president of T Limited.

**21-27 Return on investment and residual income.**

Hewett manufactures integrated chips for several markets. The firm is organized into three independent operating divisions: consumer electronics, industrial products, and defense components. Recent operating results for each division (000s omitted) were as follows:

| | Consumer | Industrial | Defense | Total |
|---|---|---|---|---|
| Sales | $23,600 | $12,400 | $31,500 | $ 67,500 |
| Variable costs | 8,100 | 4,700 | 16,200 | 29,000 |
| Fixed costs | 9,800 | 9,100 | 8,200 | 27,100 |
| Net income | $ 5,700 | $ (1,400) | $ 7,100 | $ 11,400 |
| Total assets | $28,500 | $21,000 | $59,200 | $108,700 |

The corporate research and development department has come up with a new product that could be sold only to foreign sources. The firm does not have an international division, so one of the current divisions will be given the responsibility for handling the new product. The new product will require an investment in assets of $12,000. Sales are projected at $9,000, variable costs will be $2,500, and fixed costs will be $4,700.

**Required**

**a.** If divisional performance is measured by comparing each division's return on assets to that division's previous return on assets, which divisions would want and which would not want the new product?

**b.** If the firm measures performance by computing residual income and charges the consumer division 14% for the use of assets, the industrial division 18%, and the defense division 14%, which divisions would want and which would not want the new product?

**21-28 Return on investment—requires study of Chapter 8** (SMA).

The Alpha Corporation has several product divisions and treats each division as an investment centre. Alpha evaluates the performance of each division using the ROI technique. Alpha considers a 10% ROI to be the minimum acceptable before tax rate of return for a division. Division managers are expected to exceed the 10% required rate of return and are paid a bonus based on the rate of return achieved by their division.

In order to ensure consistency, the company has set rules for the calculation of net income and investment. Net income is defined as income after deduction of depreciation on assets (calculated on a straight-line basis) and deduction of interest on loans undertaken by the division. Investment is defined as net total assets (after deducting accumulated depreciation) less current liabilities.

Division A is one of the most profitable divisions. For the coming year, division A budgets net income of $64.4 million based on an investment of $280 million (before considering any new projects). The research department of division A has developed a potential new product that will generate net cash inflows of $8 million per year in each of the next 5 years. The product will require an investment of $28 million in new facilities that will be worn out at the end of the 5 years.

**Required**

**a.** Using discounted cash flow analysis, determine whether division A should adopt the new product. Show calculations.

**b.** Given the bonus system of Alpha Corporation, will the manager of division A be motivated to adopt the new product? Show calculations to support your answer.

**c.** Briefly discuss *three* limitations of the ROI technique that Alpha uses to evaluate the performance of investment centres.

**21-29 Job order costing for internal uses** (CMA).

The Stevenson Works is a medium-sized manufacturing plant in a capital-intensive industry. The corporation's profitability is very low at the moment. As a result, investment funds are limited and hiring is restricted. These consequences of the corporation's problems have placed a strain on the plant's repair and maintenance program. The result has been a reduction in work efficiency and cost control effectiveness in the repair and maintenance area.

The assistant controller proposes the installation of a maintenance work order system to overcome these problems. This system would require a work order to be prepared for each repair request and for each regular maintenance activity. The maintenance superintendent would record the estimated time to complete a job and send one copy of the work order to the department in which the work was to be done. The work order would also serve as a cost sheet for a job. The actual cost of the parts and supplies used on the job as well as the actual labor costs incurred in completing the job would be recorded directly on the work order. A copy of the completed work order with the actual costs would be the basis of the charge to the department in which the repair or maintenance activity occurred.

The maintenance superintendent opposes the program on the grounds that the added paperwork would be costly and nonproductive. The superintendent states that the departmental clerk who now schedules repair and maintenance activities is doing a good job without all the extra forms the new system would require. The real problem, in the superintendent's opinion, is that that department is understaffed.

**Required**

**a.** Discuss how such a maintenance work order system would aid in cost control.

**b.** Explain how a maintenance work order system might assist the maintenance superintendent in getting authorization to hire more mechanics.

**21-30 Internal cost center versus outside agency** (CMA).

The promotion department of the Doxolby Company is responsible for the design and development of all promotional materials for the corporation. This includes all promotional campaigns and related literature, pamphlets, and brochures. Top management is reviewing the effectiveness of the promotion department to determine whether the department's activities could be managed better and more economically by an outside promotion agency. As a part of this review, top management has asked for a summary of the promotion department's costs for the most recent year. The following cost summary was supplied.

**DOXOLBY COMPANY**
**Promotion Department**
**Costs for the Year Ended November 30, 19X0**

| | |
|---|---|
| Direct department costs | $257,500 |
| Charges from other departments | 44,700 |
| Allocated share of general administration overhead | 22,250 |
| Total costs | $324,450 |

The direct department costs consist of those costs that can be traced directly to the activities of the promotion department, such as staff and clerical salaries including related employee benefits, supplies, and so on. The charges from other departments represent the costs of services that are provided by other departments of Doxolby at the request of the promotion department. The company has developed a charging system for such interdepartmental uses of services. For instance, the "in-house" printing department charges the promotion department for the promotional literature printed. All such services provided to the promotion department by other departments of Doxolby are included in "charges from other departments." General administrative overhead is comprised of such costs as top management salaries and benefits, depreciation, heat, insurance, property taxes, and so on. These costs are allocated to all departments in proportion to the number of employees in each department.

**Required**

Discuss the usefulness of the cost figures as presented for the promotion department of Doxolby as a basis for a comparison with a bid from an outside agency to provide the same type of activities as Doxolby's own promotion department.

**21-31 Segment analysis: Products and markets** (CMA adapted).

The Justa Corporation produces and sells three products: A, B, and C. The three products are sold in a national market and in an overseas market. At the end of the first quarter of the current year, the following income statement has been prepared.

| | Total | National | Overseas |
|---|---|---|---|
| Sales | $1,300,000 | $1,000,000 | $300,000 |
| Cost of goods sold | 1,010,000 | 775,000 | 235,000 |
| Gross margin | $ 290,000 | $ 225,000 | $ 65,000 |
| Selling expenses | $ 105,000 | $ 60,000 | $ 45,000 |
| Administrative expenses | 52,000 | 40,000 | 12,000 |
| | $ 157,000 | $ 100,000 | $ 57,000 |
| Net income | $ 133,000 | $ 125,000 | $ 8,000 |

Management has expressed special concern with the overseas market because of the extremely poor return on sales. This market was entered a year ago because of excess capacity. It was originally believed that the return on sales would improve with time, but after a year no noticeable improvement can be seen from the results as reported in the foregoing quarterly statement.

In an attempt to decide whether to eliminate the overseas market, the following information has been gathered.

| | Products | | |
|---|---|---|---|
| | A | B | C |
| Sales | $500,000 | $400,000 | $400,000 |
| Variable manufacturing expenses as a percentage of sales | 60% | 70% | 60% |
| Variable selling expenses as a percentage of sales | 3% | 2% | 2% |

The sales by markets are as follows:

| Product | National | Overseas |
|---|---|---|
| A | $400,000 | $100,000 |
| B | 300,000 | 100,000 |
| C | 300,000 | 100,000 |

All administrative expenses and fixed manufacturing expenses are common to the three products and the two markets and are fixed for the period. Remaining selling expenses are fixed for the period and separable by market. All fixed expenses are based upon a prorated yearly amount.

**Required**

**a.** Prepare a performance report showing contribution margins by products and market margins.

**b.** Assuming that there are no alternative uses for the Justa Corporation's present capacity, would you recommend dropping the overseas market? Why or why not?

**c.** It is believed that a new product can be ready for sale next year if the Justa Corporation decides to go ahead with continued research. It can be produced by converting equipment currently used in the production of C. This conversion will increase fixed costs by $10,000 per quarter. What must be the minimum contribution margin per quarter for the new product to make the changeover financially feasible?

**21-32 Segment analysis: Discontinuance of a product line** (CMA adapted).
The Scio Division of Georgetown, Inc., manufactures and sells four related product lines. Each product is produced at one or more of the three manufacturing plants

**PRODUCT LINE PROFITABILITY—19X7**
**(000s omitted)**

| | Football Equipment | Baseball Equipment | Hockey Equipment | Miscellaneous Sports Items | Total |
|---|---|---|---|---|---|
| Sales | $2,200 | $1,000 | $1,500 | $500 | $5,200 |
| Cost of goods sold | | | | | |
| Material | $ 400 | $ 175 | $ 300 | $ 90 | $ 965 |
| Labor and variable overhead | 800 | 400 | 600 | 60 | 1,860 |
| Fixed overhead | 350 | 275 | 100 | 50 | 775 |
| Total | $1,550 | $ 850 | $1,000 | $200 | $3,600 |
| Gross profit | $ 650 | $ 150 | $ 500 | $300 | $1,600 |
| Selling expense | | | | | |
| Variable | $ 440 | $ 200 | $ 300 | $100 | $1,040 |
| Fixed | 100 | 50 | 100 | 50 | 300 |
| Corporate administration expenses | 48 | 24 | 36 | 12 | 120 |
| Total | $ 588 | $ 274 | $ 436 | $162 | $1,460 |
| Contribution to corporation | $ 62 | $ (124) | $ 64 | $138 | $ 140 |

**EVANSTON PLANT COSTS—19X7**
**(000s omitted)**

| | Football Equipment | Baseball Equipment | Miscellaneous Sports Items | Total |
|---|---|---|---|---|
| Material | $100 | $175 | $ 90 | $ 365 |
| Labor | $100 | $200 | $ 30 | $ 330 |
| Variable overhead | | | | |
| Supplies | $ 85 | $ 60 | $ 12 | $ 157 |
| Power | 50 | 110 | 7 | 167 |
| Other | 15 | 30 | 11 | 56 |
| Subtotal | $150 | $200 | $ 30 | $ 380 |
| Fixed overhead | | | | |
| Supervision[a] | $ 25 | $ 30 | $ 21 | $ 76 |
| Depreciation[b] | 40 | 115 | 14 | 169 |
| Plant rentals[c] | 35 | 105 | 10 | 150 |
| Other[d] | 20 | 25 | 5 | 50 |
| Subtotal | $120 | $275 | $ 50 | $ 445 |
| Total costs | $470 | $850 | $200 | $1,520 |

[a]The supervision costs represent salary and benefit costs of the supervisors in charge of each product line.

[b]Depreciation cost for machinery and equipment is charged to the product line on which the machinery is used.

[c]The plant is leased. The lease rentals are charged to the product lines on the basis of square feet occupied.

[d]Other fixed overhead costs are the cost of plant administration and are allocated arbitrarily by management decision.

of the division. The first of the tables on page 1021 is a product line profitability statement for the year ended December 31, 19X7, which shows a loss for the baseball equipment line. A similar loss is projected for 19X8.

The baseball equipment is manufactured in the Evanston plant. Some football equipment and all miscellaneous sports items also are processed through this plant. A few of the miscellaneous items are manufactured, and the remainder are purchased for resale. Items purchased for resale are recorded as materials in the records. A separate production line is used to manufacture the items in each product line.

The second table is a schedule of the costs incurred at the Evanston plant in 19X7. Inventories at the end of the year were substantially identical to those at the beginning of the year.

The management of Georgetown, Inc., has requested a profitability study of the baseball equipment line to determine whether the line should be discontinued. The marketing department of the Scio division and the accounting department at the plant have developed the following additional data to be used in the study.

1. If the baseball equipment line is discontinued, the company will lose approximately 10% of its sales in each of the other lines.
2. The equipment now used in the manufacture of baseball equipment is quite specialized. It has a current salvage value of $105,000 and a remaining useful life of 5 years. This equipment cannot be used elsewhere in the company.
3. The plant space now occupied by the baseball equipment line could be closed off from the rest of the plant and subleased for $175,000 per year.
4. If the line is discontinued, the supervisor of the baseball equipment line will be released. In keeping with company policy, he would receive severance pay of $5,000.
5. The company has been able to invest excess funds at 10% per annum.

**Required**

**a.** Should Georgetown, Inc., discontinue the baseball equipment line? Support your answer with appropriate calculations and qualitative arguments.

**b.** A member of the board of directors of Georgetown, Inc., has inquired whether the information regarding the discontinuance of product lines should be included in the financial statements on a regular monthly basis for all product lines. Explain to the board member why this information should or should not be included in the regular monthly financial statements distributed to the board and detail the reasons for your response.

**21-33 Determination of appropriate type of responsibility center** (CMA).
The ATCO Company purchased the Dexter Company 3 years ago. Prior to the acquisition Dexter manufactured and sold plastic products to a wide variety of customers. Dexter has since become a division of ATCO and now manufactures only plastic components for products made by ATCO's Macon division. Macon sells its products to hardware wholesalers.

ATCO's corporate management gives the Dexter division management a considerable amount of authority in running the division's operations. However, corporate management retains authority for decisions regarding capital investments, price setting of all products, and the quantity of each product to be produced by the Dexter division.

ATCO has a formal performance evaluation program for the management of all of its divisions. The performance evaluation program relies heavily on each division's return on investment. The accompanying income statement of Dexter division provides the basis for the evaluation of Dexter's divisional management.

The financial statements for the divisions are prepared by the corporate accounting staff. The corporate general services costs are allocated on the basis of sales dollars, and the computer department's actual costs are apportioned among the divisions on the basis of use. The net division investment includes division fixed assets at net book value (cost less depreciation), division inventory, and corporate working capital apportioned to the divisions on the basis of sales dollars.

**DEXTER DIVISION OF ATCO COMPANY**
**Income Statement**
**For the Year Ended October 31, 19X0**
**(000s omitted)**

| | | |
|---|---|---|
| Sales | | $4,000 |
| Costs and expenses | | |
| Product costs | | |
| Direct materials | $ 500 | |
| Direct labor | 1,100 | |
| Factory overhead | 1,300 | |
| Total | $2,900 | |
| Less: Increase in inventory | 350 | $2,550 |
| Engineering and research | | 120 |
| Shipping and receiving | | 240 |
| Division administration | | |
| Manager's office | $ 210 | |
| Cost accounting | 40 | |
| Personnel | 82 | 332 |
| Corporate costs | | |
| Computer | $ 48 | |
| General services | 230 | 278 |
| Total costs and expenses | | $3,520 |
| Divisional operating income | | $ 480 |
| Net plant investment | | $1,600 |
| Return on investment | | 30% |

**Required**

**a.** Discuss the financial reporting and performance evaluation program of ATCO Company as it relates to the responsibilities of the Dexter division.

**b.** Based upon your response to (a), recommend appropriate revisions of the financial information and reports used to evaluate the performance of Dexter's divisional management. If revisions are not necessary, explain why they are not needed.

**21-34 Cost analysis for segments** (CMA).
Scent Company sells men's toiletries to retail stores throughout the United States. For planning and control purposes, Scent Company is organized into 12 geographic regions, with two to six territories within each region. One salesperson is assigned to each territory and has exclusive rights to all sales made in that territory. Merchandise is shipped from the manufacturing plant to the 12 regional warehouses, and the sales in each territory are shipped from the regional warehouse. National headquarters allocates a specific amount at the beginning of the year for regional advertising.

The net sales for the Scent Company for the year ended September 30 totaled $10 million. Costs incurred by national headquarters for national administration, advertising, and warehousing are summarized as follows:

| | |
|---|---|
| National administration | $250,000 |
| National advertising | 125,000 |
| National warehousing | 175,000 |
| Total | $550,000 |

The results of operations for the South Atlantic region for the year ended September 30 are as follows:

**SCENT COMPANY**
**Statement of Operations for South Atlantic Region**
**For the Year Ended September 30**

| | | |
|---|---|---|
| Net sales | | $900,000 |
| Costs and expenses | | |
| Advertising fees | $ 54,700 | |
| Bad debt expense | 3,600 | |
| Cost of sales | 460,000 | |
| Freight-out | 22,600 | |
| Insurance | 10,000 | |
| Salaries and employee benefits | 81,600 | |
| Sales commissions | 36,000 | |
| Supplies | 12,000 | |
| Travel and entertainment | 14,100 | |
| Wages and employee benefits | 36,000 | |
| Warehouse depreciation | 8,000 | |
| Warehouse operating costs | 15,000 | |
| Total costs and expenses | | 753,600 |
| Territory contribution | | $146,400 |

The South Atlantic region consists of two territories: Green and Purple. The salaries and employee benefits consist of the following items:

| | |
|---|---|
| Regional vice-president | $24,000 |
| Regional marketing manager | 15,000 |
| Regional warehouse manager | 13,400 |
| Sales representatives (one for each territory, with all receiving the same salary base) | 15,600 |
| Employee benefits (20%) | 13,600 |
| Total | $81,600 |

The salespeople receive a base salary plus a 4% commission on all items sold in their territory. Bad debt expense has averaged 0.4% of net sales in the past. Travel and entertainment costs are those incurred by the salespeople calling upon their customers. Freight-out is a function of the quantity of goods shipped and the distance shipped. Of the insurance expense, 30% is spent for protection of the inventory while it is in the regional warehouse and the remainder is incurred for the protection of the warehouse. Supplies are used in the warehouse for packing the merchandise that is shipped. Wages relate to the hourly-paid employees who fill orders in the warehouse. The Warehouse Operating Costs account contains such costs as heat, electricity, and maintenance.

The following cost analyses and statistics by territory for the current year are representative of past experience and are representative of expected future operations.

| | Green | Purple | Total |
|---|---|---|---|
| Sales | $300,000 | $600,000 | $900,000 |
| Cost of sales | $184,000 | $276,000 | $460,000 |
| Advertising fees | $ 21,800 | $ 32,900 | $ 54,700 |
| Travel and entertainment | $ 6,300 | $ 7,800 | $ 14,100 |
| Freight-out | $ 9,000 | $ 13,600 | $ 22,600 |
| Units sold | 150,000 | 350,000 | 500,000 |
| Pounds shipped | 210,000 | 390,000 | 600,000 |
| Miles traveled (salespeople) | 21,600 | 38,400 | 60,000 |

**Required**

**a.** Top management of Scent Company wants the regional vice-presidents to present their operating data in a more meaningful manner. Therefore, management has requested that the regions separate their operating costs into the fixed and variable components of order getting, order filling, and administration. The data are to be presented in the following format.

| | Territory costs | | | |
|---|---|---|---|---|
| | Green | Purple | Regional Costs | Total Costs |
| Order getting | | | | |
| Order filling | | | | |
| Administration | | | | |

Using management's suggested format, prepare a schedule that presents the costs for the region by territory with the costs separated into variable and fixed categories by order-getting, order-filling, and administrative functions.

**b.** Suppose that top management of Scent Company is considering splitting the Purple territory into two separate territories (Red and Blue). From the data that have been presented, identify what data would be relevant to this decision (either for or against) and indicate what other data you would collect to aid top management in its decision.

**c.** If Scent Company keeps its records in accordance with the classification required in (a), can standards and flexible budgets be employed by the company in planning and controlling marketing costs? Give reasons for your answer.

21-35 **Segment performance: Not-for-profit cost center** (CMA adapted). Regional University is a state-supported university with an enrollment of 5,000 full-time students and a faculty of 350. State appropriations are the sole source of operating funds since all tuition and fees collected from students are required to be remitted to the state treasurer. The 19X6 operating appropriation was $12.5 million, which represents an average cost of $2,500 per student.

The basic "product" of the university is the granting of degrees to students who complete degree requirements in a particular program. The departments granting degrees are somewhat analogous to production departments, and the various support departments (i.e., facilities services, academic support services, and administrative services) are similar to overhead departments in a manufacturing environment.

The administration has implemented a model used by a nearby university to analyze operating costs. The university's central administration believes that the new cost model will provide information that will be helpful in assessing the effectiveness of internal resource utilization, in assisting budget preparation and the related budget justification before the legislature, and in providing data for examining options for allocating funds based upon current program costs and projected university enrollments. The cost model is designed to provide information about the traceable direct costs incurred by academic departments and the allocated support costs charged to each academic department. The sum of the traceable direct and allocated support costs are considered the total costs of an academic department. Various cost measures are calculated for each academic department and for the student degree programs (majors) offered by each department.

The accompanying tables show data for the Electrical Engineering Department of Regional University's College of Engineering and have been prepared according to the new cost model. These are examples of data that are prepared for all academic departments and degree programs in the university. The following definitions for student activity measures assist in the interpretation of the cost data:

1. Student credit hour (SCH). The standard measure of instructional activity, which is the equivalent of one student enrolled in an academic course for which one credit hour is granted; for example, a 3-credit-hour course with 20 students equals 60 SCH of instructional activity.
2. Full-time student. A student enrolled for 30 credit hours in an academic year.
3. Equivalent full-time students. The number of credit hours taken by students divided by 30 credit hours.

The first table presents the total instructional costs (traceable direct and allocated support) and the instructional costs per SCH taught by the Electrical Engineering Department. The second table presents the traceable direct and total costs of the electrical engineering degree program, the cost per SCH taken, and the cost per student major.

**Required**

**a.** As shown in the first table, the total traceable direct costs per SCH taught in the Electrical Engineering Department is $83.50. Is this an approximation of the variable costs per SCH taught in that department? Explain your answer.

**b.** As shown in the second table, the annual traceable direct cost per student ma-

**REGIONAL UNIVERSITY—COLLEGE OF ENGINEERING**
**Instructional Costs for the Electrical Engineering Department**
**For the 19X6–X7 Academic Year**

| | Total Cost (000s omitted) | Cost per SCH Taught[a] |
|---|---|---|
| Traceable direct costs | | |
| Salaries and benefits | $ 600 | $ 73.20 |
| Travel expenses | 25 | 3.00 |
| Printing and advertising | 3 | 0.40 |
| Supplies | 29 | 3.50 |
| Equipment | 16 | 1.90 |
| Rentals | 12 | 1.50 |
| Total direct costs | $ 685 | $ 83.50 |
| Allocated support costs | | |
| Facilities services (utilities, building and grounds, and so on)[b] | $ 180 | $ 22.00 |
| Academic support services (library, computer, and so on)[c] | 206 | 25.10 |
| Administrative services (admissions, placement, and so on)[c] | 103 | 12.60 |
| Office of engineering dean[c] | 15 | 1.80 |
| Total allocated support costs | $ 504 | $ 61.50 |
| Total department instructional costs | $1,189 | $145.00 |

[a]8,200 student credit hours (SCH) were taught in the Electrical Engineering Department.

[b]Cost allocated on the basis of square feet occupied.

[c]Cost allocated on the basis of the number of student majors.

**REGIONAL UNIVERSITY—COLLEGE OF ENGINEERING**
**Program Costs of Students Majoring in Electrical Engineering**
**For the 19X6–X7 Academic Year**

| | Traceable Direct Costs[a] | | Total Costs[a] | |
|---|---|---|---|---|
| Department providing instruction | | | | |
| Chemical | ($92.90 × 200) | $ 18,580 | ($169.60 × 200) | $ 33,920 |
| Civil | ($69.80 × 100) | 6,980 | ($147.30 × 100) | 14,730 |
| Electrical | ($83.50 × 6,500) | 542,750 | ($145.00 × 6,500) | 942,500 |
| Mechanical | ($74.80 × 1,150) | 86,020 | ($126.50 × 1,150) | 145,475 |
| All nonengineering[b] | | 112,500 | | 202,500 |
| Costs associated with students enrolled as electrical engineering majors | | $766,830 | | $1,339,125 |
| Electrical engineering degree program costs per SCH taken[c] | | $ 49.60 | | $ 86.70 |
| Electrical engineering degree program costs per student major[d] | | $ 1,489 | | $ 2,600 |

[a]The costs of each academic department used by students majoring in electrical engineering are determined by multiplying the cost per SCH taught in that department by the number of SCH taken by students enrolled in the electrical engineering degree program from that department.

[b]Students majoring in electrical engineering were enrolled in 7,500 SCH from various nonengineering departments. Each nonengineering department has its own traceable direct and total cost per SCH and the cost to the electrical engineering program is charged according to these rates. However, the detail of these charges has been omitted from this schedule.

[c]A total of 15,450 SCH were taken by students in the electrical engineering degree program.

[d]The electrical engineering degree program has 515 full-time equivalent student majors.

joring in electrical engineering is $1,489. Is this an approximation of the annual variable cost per student major in electrical engineering? Explain your answer.

**c.** The allocated support costs per SCH taught are $61.50 for the Electrical Engineering Department and $169.90 − $92.90 = $76.70 for the Chemical Engineering Department. Does this mean that more support costs were allocated to the Chemical Engineering Department? Explain your answer.

**d.** Should traceable direct and total department instructional cost per SCH taught (see first table) be used by the Electrical Engineering Department in preparing its budget for presentation to the university administration? Explain your answer.

**e.** The cost model as employed by Regional University generates data regarding the traceable direct and total program costs in terms of dollars, SCH taken, and student majors for degree programs (the second table is an example of these cost measures for the electrical engineering degree program). If this data were available for all academic departments, could Regional University use the data (1) to measure the cost effectiveness of programs offered by departments, and (2) to justify different tuition rates for different degree programs? Explain your answer in each case.

**21-36 Transfer pricing: Basic** (CIA).
A large, diversified corporation operates its divisions on a decentralized basis. Division A makes product X which can be sold either to division B or to outside customers. At current levels of production, the variable cost of making product X is $1.50 per unit, the fixed cost is $0.30, and the market price is $2.75 per unit.

Division B processes product X into product Y. The additional variable cost for producing product Y is $1.00 per unit. Top management is developing a corporate transfer pricing policy. The following bases for setting transfer prices are being reviewed: (1) full cost, (2) variable cost, and (3) market price.

**Required**

**a.** In order to avoid waste and maximize efficiency up to the transfer point, which of the transfer price bases being reviewed should be used, and why?

**b.** Which of the transfer price bases in the short run would tend to encourage the best utilization of the corporation's productive capacity? Why would this not be true in the long run?

**c.** Identify two possible advantages that division B might expect if it purchased product X from division A at the current market price.

**d.** What possible disadvantage might accrue to division A if it was committed to sell all of its production of X to division B at the current market price?

**21-37 External sales versus transfer** (CPA).
Ajax division of Carlyle Corporation produces electric motors, 20% of which are sold to the Bradley division of Carlyle and the remainder to outside customers. Carlyle treats its divisions as profit centers and allows division managers to choose their sources of sale and supply. Corporate policy requires that all interdivisional sales and purchases be recorded at variable cost as a transfer price. Ajax division's estimated sales and standard cost data for the year ending December 31, 19X2, based on its full capacity of 100,000 units, are as follows:

| | Bradley | Outsiders |
|---|---|---|
| Sales | \$ 900,000 | \$ 8,000,000 |
| Variable costs | (900,000) | (3,600,000) |
| Fixed costs | (300,000) | (1,200,000) |
| Gross margin | \$(300,000) | \$ 3,200,000 |
| Unit sales | 20,000 | 80,000 |

Ajax has an opportunity to sell the above 20,000 units to an outside customer at a price of \$75 per unit on a continuing basis. Bradley can purchase its requirements from an outside supplier at a price of \$85 per unit.

**Required**

Assuming that Ajax division desires to maximize its gross margin, should Ajax take on the new customer and drop its sales to Bradley for 19X2, and why?

21-38 **Transfer pricing with demand functions** (SMA).

The Anne Company manufactures special-purpose valves. The company is organized into two divisions, tubing and assembly. The tubing division makes a specialized pipe that is incorporated in the valves produced by the assembly division. A competitive market exists for the specialized pipe and the tubing division could sell all of its production in this intermediate market at a price of \$50 per unit of pipe.

The market in which the assembly division sells its output is not perfectly competitive. The division faces the following demand function.

$$P = \$90 - \$0.025Q$$

where $P$ = price of a valve
$Q$ = quantity of valves demanded per month

This demand function corresponds to a revenue function $R$ of:

$$R = PQ$$
$$= \$90Q - \$0.025Q^2$$

where revenue = price × quantity

The tubing division has a capacity of 1,000 units of pipe per month. When operating at capacity, the standard full cost of production in the tubing division is \$40 per unit, and the standard variable cost is \$30 per unit.

The assembly division has determined that its cost of production function (excluding the transfer price of specialized pipe) is

$$C = \$10Q + \$0.015Q^2$$

where $C$ = cost of producing $Q$ units
$Q$ = quantity of valves produced

At present, transfers between divisions are made at standard full cost. The tubing division is required to satisfy internal demand before it can make external sales.

**Required**

**a.** Under the present transfer pricing policy, how many units will the assembly division demand from the tubing division? (*Hint:* Calculate marginal cost and marginal revenue.)

**b.** In order to maximize profits for the company as a whole, how many units should be transferred and what would be the appropriate transfer price? What will be the resulting profit for the company? Show supporting calculations.

**c.** Briefly explain the transfer pricing policy that the company should be using.

**21-39 Transfer pricing** (SMA).

The Caplow Company is a multidivisional company, and its managers have been delegated full profit responsibility and complete autonomy to accept or reject transfers from other divisions. Division A produces a subassembly with a ready competitive market. This subassembly is currently used by division B for a final product that is sold outside at $1,200. Division A charges division B market price for the subassembly, which is $700 per unit. Variable costs are $520 and $600 for divisions A and B, respectively.

The manager of division B feels that division A should transfer the subassembly at a lower price than market because at this price division B is unable to make a profit.

**Required**

**a.** Compute division B's profit contribution if transfers are made at the market price, and also the total contribution to profit for the company.

**b.** Assume that division A can sell all its production in the open market. Should division A transfer goods to division B? If so, at what price?

**c.** Assume that division A can sell in the open market only 500 units at $700 per unit out of the 1,000 units that it can produce every month and that a 20% reduction in price is necessary to sell full capacity. Should transfers be made? If so, how many units should it transfer and at what price? Submit a schedule showing comparisons of contribution margins under three different alternatives to support your decision.

**21-40 Transfer pricing** (SMA).

The Westville Company manufactures a soft drink. The company is organized into two divisions, glass and filling. The glass division makes bottles and sells them to the filling division. Each division manager receives a bonus based on the division's net income.

In the market, bottle producers are charging as follows:

| Number of Cases per Month | Total Charge | Average Price per Case |
|---|---|---|
| 11,000 | $135,300 | $12.30 |
| 12,000 | 144,000 | 12.00 |
| 13,000 | 152,750 | 11.75 |
| 14,000 | 158,900 | 11.35 |
| 15,000 | 165,000 | 11.00 |

The costs per case in the glass division are as follows:

| Volume per Month | Glass Division Cost per Case |
|---|---|
| 11,000 | $10.71 |
| 12,000 | 10.52 |
| 13,000 | 10.35 |
| 14,000 | 10.18 |

The filling division's costs (excluding bottle purchases) and selling prices are as follows:

| Volume per Month | Selling Price | Cost per Case |
|---|---|---|
| 11,000 | $38.00 | $24.32 |
| 12,000 | 37.55 | 24.09 |
| 13,000 | 37.20 | 23.91 |
| 14,000 | 36.80 | 23.76 |
| 15,000 | 36.20 | 23.57 |

The current capacities of the divisions are 15,000 cases per month for the filling division and 14,000 cases per month for the glass division.

**Required**

**a.** If market prices are used as transfer prices, what is the most profitable volume for each division and for the company as a whole? Show calculations to support your answer. Assume that transfers and sales are made in units of 1,000 and that the glass division is unable to sell its production in the outside market.

**b.** Under what conditions should market prices *not* be used in determining transfer prices?

**21-41 Transfer pricing: Comprehensive analysis** (CICA adapted).
The executives of World Accord, a multinational corporation, are concerned over the lacklustre performance of Kingcraft, one of World's divisions. The executives rely almost exclusively upon periodic "corporate accounting analysis" of divisional performance, which highlights sales, profits, and investment performance.

Kingcraft manufactures navigational devices in the price-sensitive marine industry. The uniquely designed devices are considered to be of superior quality, giving Kingcraft a competitive edge in the marketplace. In part, the marketing success of the navigational device is due to the specially built electronic rangefinder component supplied to Kingcraft by a sister division known as Tectron.

The per-unit selling price and standard manufacturing cost of the navigational device are set out as follows:

| | |
|---|---|
| Selling price | $2,600 |
| Standard manufacturing cost: | |
| Direct materials, direct labour and variable overhead, including $900 for the electronic rangefinder component | $1,660 |
| Fixed manufacturing overhead | 390 |
| Total standard manufacturing cost | $2,050 |

Fixed manufacturing overhead is allocated on the basis of direct labour hours. The latter is used as a measure of Kingcraft's plant capacity. Each navigational device requires 26 standard labour hours to produce. Over the past year, Kingcraft has been operating at a level of 70% of its practical capacity.

Tug McPhail, the general manager of Kingcraft, was formerly head of Tectron. While with the sister division he had a reputation for "getting the job done" and had enjoyed substantial profit-sharing bonuses. Profit-sharing bonuses are based on the excess of divisional pretax profit (less corporate service costs) over a specified base. Due to the modest growth in profits of Kingcraft, Tug's bonuses have been dramatically reduced since leaving Tectron. Tug's frustrations were compounded because of serious quality control problems at Kingcraft. The rejection rate for imperfect navigational devices has increased. This increased rejection rate is, in some cases, due to faulty electronic rangefinder components. The costs of the rework programs for repairs of faulty electronic rangefinders are costs that must be absorbed by Kingcraft.

Albert Syms, formerly assistant general manager of Kingcraft, is the present general manager of Tectron. His move to Tectron 2 years ago coincided with the appointment of Tug McPhail as head of Kingcraft as a result of the sudden death of the previous general manager. Albert considered his "promotion" a lateral move; however, he decided to make the best of the situation. Since Albert joined Tectron, the division's earnings have increased at a rate of approximately 15% per year. Consequently, Albert has been receiving considerable incentive bonuses.

Sales by Tectron to Kingcraft are significant, though not considered essential to its survival. Gross profit margin as a percentage of costs by product line in Tectron vary only to a minor degree and have remained relatively unchanged for several years. Sales to Kingcraft in recent years have shown only modest increases when compared to the growth in sales by Tectron to its other major customers.

A corporate accounting analysis of World Accord's most recent 5-year performance, together with that of two of its divisions, Kingcraft and Tectron, is shown in the accompanying table. Profits are stated on a pretax basis, with divisional profits reported "after allocation of corporate service costs." Annual corporate service costs to the division amount to 10% of the net book value of divisional investment. A significant portion of the divisional investment is in fixed assets, which are depreciated on a straight-line basis at rates averaging 12% per annum. Investment is reported at net book value as of the end of each accounting period.

**FIVE-YEAR PERFORMANCE ANALYSIS**
**(000s omitted)**

| | World Accord | | | Kingcraft | | | Tectron | | |
|---|---|---|---|---|---|---|---|---|---|
| Year | Investment | Profit[a] | Sales | Investment | Profit[a] | Sales | Investment | Profit[a] | Sales |
| 19X9 | $11,000 | $1,800 | $15,600 | $2,200 | $270 | $2,600 | $800 | $145 | $1,750 |
| 19X8 | 9,800 | 1,675 | 14,300 | 2,050 | 260 | 2,500 | 850 | 126 | 1,600 |
| 19X7 | 9,400 | 1,500 | 13,900 | 1,800 | 255 | 2,550 | 900 | 110 | 1,450 |
| 19X6 | 8,900 | 1,375 | 12,900 | 1,850 | 255 | 2,450 | 850 | 90 | 1,300 |
| 19X5 | 8,300 | 1,275 | 12,000 | 1,750 | 260 | 2,350 | 750 | 80 | 1,200 |

[a]Profits are stated on a pretax basis with divisional profits reported after allocation of corporate service costs.

The transfer prices for goods and services exchanged between divisions are based on the actual full cost of the selling division (including a provision for corporate service costs and divisional administrative costs) plus a "reasonable profit margin." World Accord requires its divisions "to deal internally" to protect industrial secrets.

In an effort to improve profit and investment performance, the president of World Accord is considering combining the two divisions. The president requested that Tug McPhail and Albert Syms present their points of view on this matter. In brief, Syms had reacted positively, stating, "The benefits to be gained from combining the divisions would be to improve administration, enhance quality control, and reduce costly and redundant divisional overheads." On the other hand, McPhail was not receptive to the proposal. He felt that combining the divisions would be "demotivational, reduce divisional effectiveness, and would result in the long term in a reduction of existing levels of profitability." Further, he believed that "quality control is an issue that should be addressed separately."

Subsequently, the president of World Accord discussed the problems of the two divisions with a member of his executive staff, John Marks, a chartered accountant. The president had asked John to prepare a report in which he will evaluate the divisional performance, review the transfer price system, and comment on the corporate reporting system. In this report, he should also consider the potential long-term impact of the proposed combination or other possible alternative solutions.

**Required**
Assume the role of John Marks, chartered accountant, and prepare the requested report for the president of World Accord.

**21-42 Divisional performance: Profit centers and transfer pricing** (CMA).
A. R. Oma, Inc., manufactures a line of men's colognes and after-shave lotions. The manufacturing process is basically a series of mixing operations, with the addition of certain aromatic and coloring ingredients; the finished product is packaged in a company-produced glass bottle and packed in cases containing six bottles.

A. R. Oma feels that the sale of its product is heavily influenced by the appearance and appeal of the bottle and has therefore devoted considerable managerial effort to the bottle production process. This has resulted in the development of certain unique bottle production processes in which management takes considerable pride.

The two areas (i.e., perfume production and bottle manufacture) have evolved over the years in an almost independent manner; in fact, a rivalry has developed between management personnel as to "which division is the more important" to the company. This attitude is probably intensified because the bottle manufacturing plant was purchased intact 10 years ago and no real interchange of management personnel or ideas (except at the top corporate level) has taken place.

Since the acquisition, all bottle production has been absorbed by the perfume manufacturing plant. Each area is considered a separate profit center and evaluated as such. As the new corporate controller you are responsible for the definition of a proper transfer value to use in crediting the bottle production profit center and in debiting the packaging profit center.

At your request, the bottle division's general manager has asked certain other bottle manufacturers to quote a price for the quantity and sizes demanded by the perfume division. These competitive prices are as follows:

| Volume (equivalent cases)[a] | Total Price | Price per Case |
|---|---|---|
| 2,000,000 | $ 4,000,000 | $2.00 |
| 4,000,000 | 7,000,000 | 1.75 |
| 6,000,000 | 10,000,000 | 1.67 |

[a]An "equivalent case" represents 6 bottles.

A cost analysis of the internal bottle plant indicates that they can produce bottles at the following costs.

| Volume (equivalent cases) | Total Price | Cost per Case[a] |
|---|---|---|
| 2,000,000 | $3,200,000 | $1.60 |
| 4,000,000 | 5,200,000 | 1.30 |
| 6,000,000 | 7,200,000 | 1.20 |

[a]The cost analysts point out that these costs represent fixed costs of $1,200,000 and variable costs of $1.00 per equivalent case.

These figures have given rise to considerable corporate discussion as to the proper value to use in the transfer of bottles to the perfume division. This interest is heightened because a significant portion of a division manager's income is an incentive bonus based on profit center results.

The perfume production division has the following costs in addition to the bottle costs.

| Volume (cases) | Total Cost | Cost per Case |
|---|---|---|
| 2,000,000 | $16,400,000 | $8.20 |
| 4,000,000 | 32,400,000 | 8.10 |
| 6,000,000 | 48,400,000 | 8.07 |

After considerable analysis, the marketing research department has furnished you with the following price-demand relationship for the finished product.

| Sales Volume (cases) | Total Sales Revenue | Sales Price per Case |
|---|---|---|
| 2,000,000 | $25,000,000 | $12.50 |
| 4,000,000 | 45,600,000 | 11.40 |
| 6,000,000 | 63,900,000 | 10.65 |

**Required**

**a.** The A. R. Oma Company has used market price transfer prices in the past. Using the current market prices and costs, and assuming a volume of 6,000,000 cases, calculate the income for (1) the bottle division, (2) the perfume division, and (3) the corporation.

**b.** Is this production and sales level the most profitable volume for (1) the bottle division, (2) the perfume division, and (3) the corporation? Explain your answer.

c. The company uses the profit center concept for divisional operation. (1) Define a "profit center." (2) What conditions should exist for a profit center to be established? (3) Should the two divisions of the A. R. Oma Company be organized as profit centers?

21-43 **Divisional performance: Relevant costing and transfer pricing** (CMA adapted). National Industries is a diversified corporation with separate and distinct operating divisions. Each division's performance is evaluated on the basis of total dollar profits and return on division investment.

The WindAir division manufactures and sells air conditioners. The coming year's budgeted income statement, based upon a sales volume of 15,000 units, is as follows:

**WINDAIR DIVISION**
**Budgeted Income Statement**
**For the Fiscal Year**

| | Per Unit | Total (000s omitted) |
|---|---|---|
| Sales revenue | $400 | $6,000 |
| Manufacturing costs | | |
| Compressor | $ 70 | $1,050 |
| Other raw materials | 37 | 555 |
| Direct labor | 30 | 450 |
| Variable overhead | 45 | 675 |
| Fixed overhead | 32 | 480 |
| Total manufacturing costs | $214 | $3,210 |
| Gross margin | $186 | $2,790 |
| Operating expenses | | |
| Variable selling | $ 18 | $ 270 |
| Fixed selling | 19 | 285 |
| Fixed administration | 38 | 570 |
| Total operating expenses | $ 75 | $1,125 |
| Net income before taxes | $111 | $1,665 |

WindAir's manager believes that sales can be increased if the unit selling price of the air conditioners is reduced. A market research study conducted by an independent firm at the request of the manager indicates that a 5% reduction in the selling price ($20) would increase sales volume 16%, or 2,400 units. WindAir has sufficient production capacity to manage this increased volume with no increase in fixed costs.

At the present time WindAir uses a compressor in its units that it purchases from an outside supplier at a cost of $70 per compressor. The manager of WindAir has approached the manager of National Industries' Compressor division regarding the sale of a compressor unit to WindAir. The Compressor division currently manufactures and sells exclusively to outside firms a unit that is similar to the compressor used by WindAir. The specifications of the WindAir compressor are slightly different and would reduce the Compressor division's raw materials cost by $1.50 per unit. In addition, the Compressor division would not incur any variable selling costs for the units sold to WindAir. The manager of WindAir wants all of the compressors it uses to come from one supplier and has offered to pay $50 for each compressor unit.

The Compressor division has the capacity to produce 75,000 units. The coming year's budgeted income statement for the Compressor division, which follows, is based on a sales volume of 64,000 units without considering WindAir's proposal.

**COMPRESSOR DIVISION**
**Budgeted Income Statement**
**For the Fiscal Year**

| | Per Unit | Total (000s omitted) |
|---|---|---|
| Sales revenue | $100 | $6,400 |
| Manufacturing costs | | |
| Raw materials | $ 12 | $ 768 |
| Direct labor | 8 | 512 |
| Variable overhead | 10 | 640 |
| Fixed overhead | 11 | 704 |
| Total manufacturing costs | $ 41 | $2,624 |
| Gross margin | $ 59 | $3,776 |
| Operating expenses | | |
| Variable selling | $ 6 | $ 384 |
| Fixed selling | 4 | 256 |
| Fixed administration | 7 | 448 |
| Total operating expenses | $ 17 | $1,088 |
| Net income before taxes | $ 42 | $2,688 |

**Required**

**a.** Should WindAir division institute the 5% price reduction on its air conditioners even if it cannot acquire the compressors internally for $50 each? Support your conclusion with appropriate calculations.

**b.** Without prejudice to your answer to (a), assume that WindAir needs 17,400 units. Should the Compressor division be willing to supply the compressor units for $50 each? Support your conclusions with appropriate calculations.

**c.** Without prejudice to your answer to (a), assume that WindAir needs 17,400 units. Would it be in the best interest of National Industries for the Compressor division to supply the compressor units at $50 each to the WindAir division? Support your conclusions with appropriate calculations.

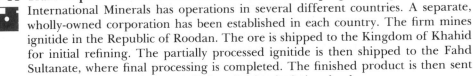

**21-44 Transfer prices in a multinational firm—uses linear programming.** International Minerals has operations in several different countries. A separate, wholly-owned corporation has been established in each country. The firm mines ignitide in the Republic of Roodan. The ore is shipped to the Kingdom of Khahid for initial refining. The partially processed ignitide is then shipped to the Fahd Sultanate, where final processing is completed. The finished product is then sent to International Mineral's marketing division in Switzerland.

The current world market price for refined ignitide is $600 per kilogram. By royal decree, all sales of international firms operating in the Fahd Sultanate must be at prevailing world market prices. The sultan imposes a 30% tax on all corporate profits, but there are no currency restrictions.

The Kingdom of Khahid does not have an income tax, but does impose a 5% value-added tax (a tax of 5% is levied on the difference between a firm's sales and its cost of raw materials). In addition, the kingdom has tight currency controls. Only 25% of a firm's profits may be sent out of the country. The remainder must be reinvested or consumed in the kingdom. There is virtually no problem in obtaining government approval for expenditures for purchases of raw materials. International Minerals has no plans in the foreseeable future for expanding its investment within the kingdom.

The government of Roodan imposes a 3% sales tax and a 15% severance tax. (The tax is 15% of the value of the minerals mined, with the value determined by subtracting labor and depreciation costs from sales and presuming that the difference is the value of the minerals mined. Note that taxes are not subtracted.) There are no currency restrictions in Roodan.

Typical annual operating data for each division are as follows:

| | |
|---|---|
| Roodan division | |
| Sales 200,000 kg of ore @ ? | ? |
| Labor costs | $ 6,800,000 |
| Equipment depreciation | 4,100,000 |
| Taxes | ? |
| Net income | ? |
| Khahid division | |
| Sales 100,000 kg partially refined ore @ ? | ? |
| Purchases 200,000 kg ore | ? |
| Labor costs | 2,600,000 |
| Equipment depreciation | 3,200,000 |
| Taxes | ? |
| Net income | ? |
| Fahd division | |
| Sales 80,000 kg @ $600 | 48,000,000 |
| Purchases 100,000 kg partially refined ore @ ? | ? |
| Labor costs | 3,500,000 |
| Equipment depreciation | 1,000,000 |
| Taxes | ? |
| Net income | ? |

**Required**

Determine what the transfer prices for interdivisional sales should be to minimize taxes. Management has determined that each division must show a minimum net income of $1 million before taxes to avoid the risk of audit or legal complications with the host governments. Use of the computer program LINPRO is recommended.

# PART FIVE

## GOVERNMENT REGULATIONS

# CHAPTER 22

# COST ACCOUNTING FOR GOVERNMENT CONTRACTS

In the late 1960s Congress became concerned that the existence of a wide variety of cost accounting procedures made it difficult for the government to compare bids from contractors for government work. Congress was particularly concerned with cost accounting techniques for defense contracts. These contracts often involve huge dollar amounts for costs, and it was estimated that two-thirds of these contracts were priced to the government on a cost-plus basis. A **cost-plus contract** is one in which a "fair" profit is added either as a fixed fee or as a percentage of total costs incurred for the contract. Cost-plus contracts are typically used when a contract calls for the development of new technology and neither side can accurately predict the cost of developing the technology. Thus not only did divergent practices make it difficult to compare competing bids, but the final price charged to the government by different contractors might vary considerably due to the practices used to accumulate actual costs for the contract.

To promote consistency in cost accounting practices and to try to ensure that the actual costs charged to government contracts fairly reflected the costs incurred to complete those contracts, Congress established the **Cost Accounting Standards Board** (CASB) in August 1970. Funding for the board was authorized and the board began to function in January 1971. Approximately 10 years later, Congress determined that the Cost Accounting Standards Board had accomplished its mission. Funding was discontinued as of October 1, 1980, and the board ceased to exist as of that date. The continuing responsibilities, providing interpretations and assuring contractor compliance, are now handled by the **General Accounting Office** (GAO).

## COST ACCOUNTING STANDARDS

During its existence the board promulgated 20 standards. These **cost accounting standards** can be classified into three groups, as follows:

1. Standards dealing with pervasive matters
2. Standards addressing treatment of specific costs
3. Standards dealing with the allocation of indirect costs

The 20 standards, the dates on which they became effective, and the category to which they belong are listed in Exhibit 22-1.

### General Applicability of CASB Standards

Initially the cost accounting standards applied to all negotiated defense contracts in excess of $100,000. In 1972, coverage of the standards was extended to virtually all government (not just defense) contracts in excess of $100,000. In 1974, firms that have never received a contract for more than $500,000 were excluded from coverage. This effectively eliminates the need for many small firms to comply with the standards but still requires firms that do a large amount of contracting with the government to meet the standards for any contract in excess of $100,000. A further limitation to the standards was made for very large firms for which government contracts were a small portion of their business. Firms for which government contracts amount to less than 10% of the firm's sales *and* the contracts total less than $10 million only have to comply with *Standards 401* and *402*. In effect this allows large firms to continue to use their existing cost accounting system as long as government contracts are a small proportion of their business. Other exemptions exclude foreign governments and foreign businesses from total compliance. In addition, educational institutions (primarily universities) that are subject to other existing regulations are exempt. Finally, since the standards apply only to **negotiated contracts** (basically unique products or services), the standards do not apply to products or services offered at catalog or market prices to the general public. Thus a $20 million contract for newsprint to be sold to the Government Printing Office would not subject the selling firm to the standards so long as the price charged is the same price the firm offers, for the quantities involved, to any purchaser. Even with these exemptions,

**EXHIBIT 22-1 The CASB's Cost Accounting Standards**

| Group[a] | Number | Title | Effective Date |
|---|---|---|---|
| P | 400 | Definitions | 9/1/72 |
| P | 401 | Consistency in Estimating, Accumulating, and Reporting Costs | 7/1/72 |
| P | 402 | Consistency in Allocating Costs Incurred for the Same Purpose | 7/1/72 |
| A | 403 | Allocation of Home Office Expenses to Segments | 9/30/73 |
| S | 404 | Capitalization of Tangible Assets | 7/1/73 |
| P | 405 | Accounting for Unallowable Costs | 4/1/74 |
| P | 406 | Cost Accounting Period | 7/1/74 |
| S | 407 | Use of Standard Costs for Direct Material and Direct Labor | 10/1/74 |
| S | 408 | Accounting for Costs of Compensated Personal Absence | 7/1/75 |
| S | 409 | Depreciation of Tangible Capital Assets | 7/1/75 |
| A | 410 | Allocation of Business Unit General and Administrative Expenses to Final Cost Objectives | 10/1/76 |
| S | 411 | Accounting for Acquisition Costs of Material | 1/1/76 |
| S | 412 | Composition and Measurement of Pension Cost | 1/1/76 |
| S | 413 | Adjustment and Allocation of Pension Cost | 3/10/78 |
| S | 414 | Cost of Money as an Element of the Cost of Facilities Capital | 10/1/76 |
| S | 415 | Accounting for the Cost of Deferred Compensation | 7/10/77 |
| S | 416 | Accounting for Insurance Costs | 7/10/79 |
| S | 417 | Cost of Money as an Element of the Cost of Capital Assets Under Construction | 12/15/80 |
| A | 418 | Allocation of Direct and Indirect Costs | 9/20/80 |
| A | 420 | Accounting for Independent Research and Development Costs and Bid and Proposal Costs | 3/15/80 |

[a]P indicates a pervasive standard; S indicates a standard dealing with a specific cost; and A indicates a standard dealing with the allocation of indirect costs.

a sizable proportion of American business and a tremendous dollar value of business is covered by cost accounting standards. Figure 22-1 summarizes the applicability of the cost accounting standards to private-sector firms.

## SPECIFIC STANDARDS

In the remainder of this chapter we summarize the major impact of each of the standards. In general, all of the standards impose specific record-

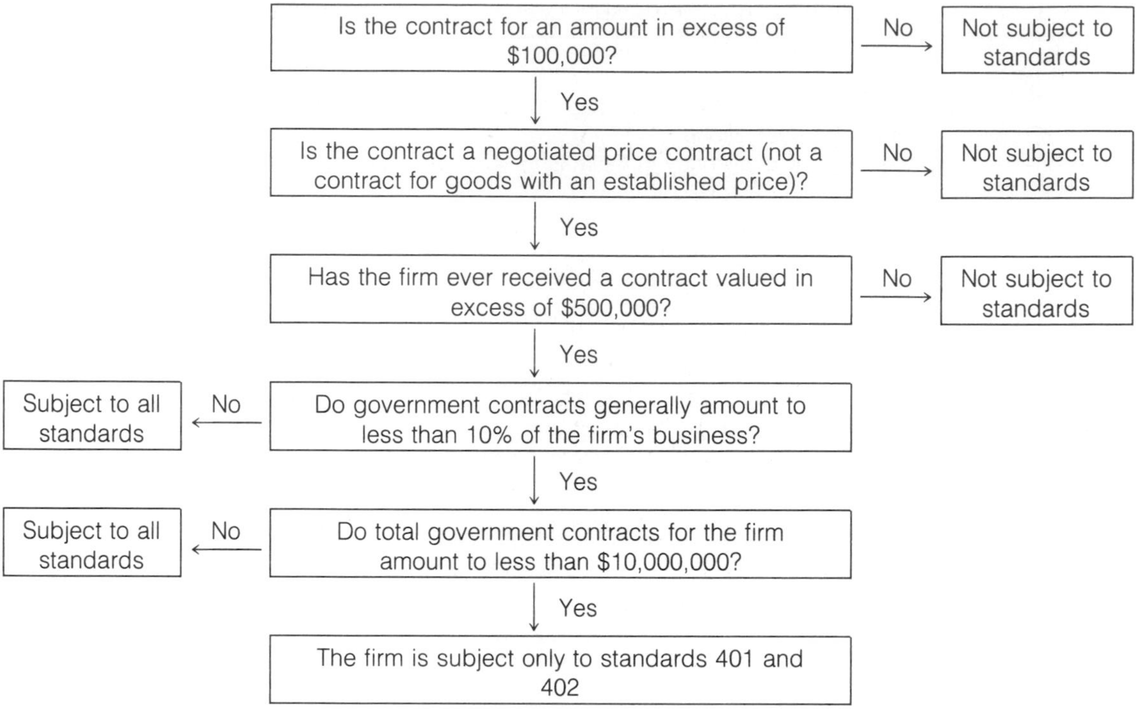


**FIGURE 22-1 Applicability of cost accounting standards for firms in the private sector.**

keeping requirements and require that the firm maintain written statements concerning the firm's cost accounting policies. These general requirements will not be repeated for each standard. In addition, some of the standards have minor exceptions to general rules. Our purpose is to provide an introduction to the standards, not a complete specification of all details. Hence what follows should not be applied to a real situation without first reading the appropriate standard carefully to note any special exceptions or requirements that might apply to a particular firm. Finally, we should note that the CASB standards, unlike the FASB standards, are a matter of law. Thus legal processes can be brought to bear to force compliance with the cost accounting standards.

### Standards Dealing with Pervasive Matters

*Standard 400* defines a large number of cost accounting terms. However, the definitions are not substantially different from those already given in this text, so we will not cover this standard further.

*Standard 401* requires firms to use the same level of detail and the same procedures in preparing a bid on a proposed contract as they use in recording actual costs. This requirement serves two purposes. It makes the auditing of contracts easier because the same level of detail and procedures will be found in the firm's records as in the proposal. Second, it prevents a firm from using an overall average rate for types of costs for which the firm has more detailed records. Thus if a firm's engineering department keeps records of how much time its skilled engineers, earning $20 per hour, spend on a project and also keeps records of the amount of time its engineering staff, earning $10 an hour, spends on projects, the firm must charge contracts for the actual amount of time spent by each group of engineers at their actual rates. The firm cannot use an average rate. That is, if a government contract used 400 hours of skilled engineering time and 900 hours of general engineering time, the contract must be charged as follows:

| | |
|---|---|
| Skilled engineering (400 × $20) | $ 8,000 |
| General engineering (900 × $10) | 9,000 |
| Total | $17,000 |

The firm cannot bill using an average cost of $15 as

| | |
|---|---|
| Total engineering (1,300 × $15) | $19,500 |

*Standard 402* was enacted to prevent the double counting of costs both as direct costs and as overhead (indirect cost) items. Every *type* of cost must be designated either as a direct cost (charged directly to a contract) or an indirect cost (charged through an overhead rate). For example, if a firm routinely charges all administrative travel to overhead, the firm cannot charge administrative travel costs directly to a government contract even if that travel is related to the government contract. For if we charged the contract with both travel costs related solely to the contract plus an overhead charge for travel, the contract would be incurring more than its share of costs. The standard does allow a firm to charge travel costs directly to contracts, but only if all similar travel costs are traced directly to the contracts that gave rise to the travel.

The standard does allow for the possibility that costs may seem very similar and yet be incurred for different purposes. In these cases some of the costs can be treated as direct costs and others as indirect costs. For example, consider a firm that employs a security force (guards at the factory entrance and night watchmen). If these security guards are treated as an overhead item, and if the receipt of a new government contract causes us to hire another guard for routine patrol (the guards need to patrol a larger area), then the cost of the new guard must be included as an overhead item. If, however, the new contract involves classified equipment, and the firm hires a guard specifically to keep unauthorized persons from gaining access to the equipment, the cost of the guard can be charged directly to the contract. The key difference is that the guard is performing different duties than the existing security force. The guard has been acquired solely for the purpose of the contract, and the contract also benefits from the general protection afforded by the regular security group.

The next pervasive standard, *Standard 405,* requires firms to note explicitly any costs the firm incurs that are unallowable as part of the cost of the contract. That is, laws, or conditions of the contract, may forbid the firm from charging certain types of expenses to government contracts (costs of lobbying, pollution fines, or whatever). Nonetheless, good accounting practice requires that these **unallowable costs** be accumulated in a manner that permits effective management control. The standard requires proper accounting for the costs, but records must be maintained that allow these costs to be easily subtracted from the total costs accumulated for a government contract.

A controversial aspect of this standard is that if indirect costs are allocated on the basis of an unallowable cost, then the indirect costs so assigned also become unallowable. For example, assume that a firm's costs for the administration of its corporate legal department are \$500,000 and that these costs are allocated to contracts based on the legal costs incurred directly for each contract. If total direct legal costs of \$1 million were incurred, the administrative costs would be allocated to contracts at the rate of \$0.50 per dollar of direct legal costs. If a particular government contract incurred \$100,000 of allowable direct legal costs and \$40,000 of unallowable direct legal costs, the amount of indirect legal costs that we would normally associate with the contract is $\$0.50 \times \$100{,}000 = \$50{,}000$ plus $\$0.50 \times \$40{,}000 = \$20{,}000$. However, since the \$40,000 of legal costs are unallowable, the allocation of \$20,000 of indirect costs based on this \$40,000 is also unallowable. The total direct and indirect legal costs which can be billed to this contract is thus restricted to $\$100{,}000 + \$50{,}000 = \$150{,}000$. Even though all the administrative costs would normally be allowable, the fact that they are allocated on a base that includes unallowed costs makes a portion of those costs unallowable. The rationale, of course, is that allocations are supposed to represent cause-and-effect relationships. The implication is that the unallowed legal costs caused the firm to incur additional administrative costs and thus these costs take on the character of the disallowed costs. Exhibit 22-2 illustrates an acceptable approach for accounting for unallowable costs.

*Standard 406,* the last of the pervasive standards, requires the firm to use its fiscal year as the basis for establishing its cost accounting period. Thus overhead costs should be accumulated for the fiscal year and be allocated on the basis of an activity measure for the same year. For ex-

**EXHIBIT 22-2 Reporting of Unallowable Costs per Cost Accounting Standard 405**

| | Costs Traced to Contracts | |
|---|---|---|
| | **Government Contract** | **All Other Contracts** |
| Allowable costs except legal costs | $650,000 | $3,000,000 |
| Allowable legal costs | 100,000 | 860,000 |
| Unallowable legal costs | 40,000 | N/A |

Assume that administrative costs for the corporate legal department are $500,000 and are allocated to contracts on the basis of the legal costs traced directly to each contract. Then the appropriate allocation charge is

$$\frac{\text{administrative costs}}{\text{total traceable legal costs}} = \frac{\$500{,}000}{\$100{,}000 + \$40{,}000 + \$860{,}000} = \begin{array}{c}\$0.50 \text{ per dollar}\\ \text{of traceable costs}\end{array}$$

The costs accumulated for the government contract should be reported as follows:

**CONTRACT XXX**

| | |
|---|---|
| List of allowable costs | $650,000 |
| Legal costs: Direct, allowable | 100,000 |
| Legal administrative costs: Allocated | 50,000 |
| Legal costs: Direct, unallowable | 40,000 |
| Legal administrative costs: Allocated | 20,000 |
| Total contract costs | $860,000 |
| Less unallowable costs | 60,000 |
| Total allowable contract costs | $800,000 |

ample, if we have a contract on which we work only from June through August, overhead costs must still be allocated on the basis of an annualized measure. We cannot separately determine overhead for just those 3 months and charge on an activity measure related only to those 3 months. The standard does provide an exception for overhead functions that exist for only a portion of a year. That is, if a firm acquires a computer in July, then the costs of operating the computer need only be allocated over the activity from July through December. Provision is also made for firms that change their fiscal year.

### Standards Addressing the Treatment of Specific Costs

There are 11 standards specifying the proper means of treatment for specific types of costs. For the most part, they simply prescribe the treatment described in intermediate financial accounting texts. In the summaries that follow we limit our discussion to only those requirements that are different from normal treatment.

**EXHIBIT 22-3 Examples of the Application of Standard 404 to the Expense-or-Capitalize Decision**

| Cost of Asset | Useful Life | Decision[a] |
|---|---|---|
| $ 600 | 14 months | May be expensed |
| 800 | 36 months | May be expensed |
| 20,000 | 24 months | May be expensed |
| 4,000 | 30 months | Must be capitalized |

[a]This presumes that the firm adopts the Cost Accounting Standards Board's criteria. If the firm has a more restrictive policy (lower dollar limit or shorter useful life), it must follow its own policy.

*Standard 404* requires that firms capitalize all costs, including allocated overhead, necessary to get a long-lived asset ready for its intended use. The standard does allow firms to expense any item whose cost is less than $1,000 or whose useful life is 2 years or less. The "$1,000-or-2-year" rule is, in effect, the board's materiality limit for capital assets. The application of this rule is illustrated in Exhibit 22-3.

*Standard 407* permits the use of standard costing. As we would expect, variances that are material in amount must be allocated to cost objectives on the basis of the standard costs assigned to those cost objects. Immaterial variances must be assigned to overhead (not charged off as an expense, as we have done in this text). If raw materials price variances are calculated at the time of the purchase of materials instead of use, then a portion of the price variance must be allocated to the raw materials inventory.

*Standard 408* requires firms to accrue the cost of vacation, sick leave, holiday and other costs for paid absence from work. These costs must then be allocated to all cost objects on an accrual basis. Basically this standard prevents firms from charging paid leave costs to expense on a cash basis; that is, if most people take vacations in July, you cannot charge these costs to contracts worked on in July, but rather must spread the costs over all contracts worked on during the year.

*Standard 409* allows contractors to use any depreciation method acceptable for financial reporting and acceptable to the IRS. The standard does impose some costly requirements for firms to justify their selection of the useful life of an asset based on the firm's own past history. That is, firms must be able to provide evidence to support their selection of the useful (or economic) life of an asset. The standard also requires that material gains or losses on the disposition of an asset must be allocated to the cost objects that were charged with depreciation from that asset in the period of disposition. This prevents firms from overdepreciating an asset to raise contract costs and then selling the asset for a gain and recognizing the gain as a nonoperating item in the income statement without restating the costs of the affected contracts. However, because the gain is spread only over the contracts worked on during the year of disposition, some potential for manipulation still exists.

*Standard 411* permits firms to use FIFO, LIFO, moving average, weighted average, or a standard cost method for valuing materials inventory. However, the firm must use the same method for similar categories of materials. In addition, if LIFO is used, it must be on the specific identification basis. That is, LIFO adjustments based on estimates of the change in prices over a period are not allowed (e.g., the dollar value LIFO method is not allowed). The standard also requires that supplies expense be adjusted if the firm ends a period with a material amount of supplies on hand.

*Standard 412* prescribes the appropriate treatment of pension costs. The standard basically follows Accounting Principles Board *Opinion 8*. If a firm has a pension plan that provides for a specific contribution by the firm to the plan, the contribution is the appropriate expense, provided that there is an actual contribution made, or that the firm can be legally forced to make a contribution.

If a firm has a plan that specifies the size of the pension that employees will receive (defines benefits, not contributions), then the cost for a period is to be determined using an actuarial basis. The cost includes the actuarial value of the liability incurred during the period, can include a portion of the firm's unfunded actuarial liability (amortized over a period of at least 10 years but less than 30 years), and must be adjusted for any actuarial gains and losses for the period.

*Standard 413* also deals with pension costs. This standard provides that actuarial gains and losses must be spread only over the future. Further, the allocation of pension costs to business segments must be made on a basis that reflects the factors that gave rise to the pension cost; that is, they should be allocated on the basis of total wages for a segment if the pension cost is a function of wages or on the basis of number of employees if every employee gets the same pension. If a particular business segment's pension costs are materially different from those of the rest of the firm (due to much higher benefits, lower retirement ages, or whatever), then the pension costs of that segment must be independently calculated. Thus the flight testing department of an aircraft manufacturer may need to calculate its pension costs separately. The reason is that employees in this department are likely to retire at a much younger age than the plant-wide average and also receive much higher salaries.

*Standard 414* involves a major departure from traditional accounting practice. It allows contractors to charge an **imputed interest** cost for the use of capital as a cost of completing a contract. The standard allows a firm to multiply the average book value of its capital assets devoted to a

**EXHIBIT 22-4 Calculation of the Imputed Interest on Facilities Devoted to a Contract**

| Date | Cost of Facilities Devoted to the Contract | Accumulated Depreciation for Facilities Devoted to the Contract | Net Book Value of Facilities | Market Value of Facilities[a] | Allowable Interest Rate[b] |
|---|---|---|---|---|---|
| January 1, 19X0 | $1,400,000 | $220,000 | $1,180,000 | $1,500,000 | 12% |
| July 1, 19X0 | 1,400,000 | 250,000 | 1,150,000 | 1,600,000 | 14 |
| January 1, 19X1 | 1,900,000 | 292,000 | 1,608,000 | 2,000,000 | 13 |
| July 1, 19X1 | 2,300,000 | 342,000 | 1,958,000 | 2,200,000 | 11 |
| January 1, 19X2 | 2,300,000 | 392,000 | 1,908,000 | 2,100,000 | 10 |

| | |
|---|---|
| Actual costs incurred for the contract | $22,412,000 |
| Imputed interest allowed as of January 1, 19X2 | |
| January 1, 19X0 to July 1, 19X0 [($1,180,000 + $1,150,000) ÷ 2] × 0.12 × $\frac{1}{2}$ | 69,900 |
| July 1, 19X0 to January 1, 19X1 [($1,150,000 + $1,608,000) ÷ 2] × 0.14 × $\frac{1}{2}$ | 96,530 |
| January 1, 19X1 to July 1, 19X1 [($1,608,000 + $1,958,000) ÷ 2] × 0.13 × $\frac{1}{2}$ | 115,895 |
| July 1, 19X1 to January 1, 19X2 [($1,958,000 + $1,908,000) ÷ 2] × 0.11 × $\frac{1}{2}$ | 106,315 |
| Total allowable contract costs | $22,800,640 |

[a]The market value numbers are irrelevant. The calculations are based on net book values.

[b]The allowable interest rate is provided by the secretary of the Treasury. The rates quoted are annual rates, so they must be multiplied by $\frac{1}{2}$ to adjust them to semiannual rates.

project by an interest rate, called the **contract renegotiation rate,** supplied by the U.S. secretary of the Treasury. The resulting figure can then be treated as the firm's cost for tying up money in the facilities. Although the CASB recognized that firms previously were being compensated for this cost of capital through profit rates higher than will be experienced when these costs are explicitly included in the contract, the board felt that such explicit recognition should lead to more equitable profit rates across contracts. Exhibit 22-4 illustrates the application of *Standard 414*. Exhibit 22-5 gives the allowable interest rates for the past several years. More recent rates can be found in the Federal Register.

*Standard 415* allows firms to accrue the cost of deferred compensation (long-term bonuses, stock option plans, and so forth). Prior to the standard these costs were recognized only when paid. Now if the firm can accurately measure the liability, is legally committed to the payment to a known person, and any conditional events (employee must still be with the firm at time of award or similar conditions) are reasonably certain, then the firm can recognize the present value of the future payments as a cost in the period in which the benefit is earned.

*Standard 416* defines insurance cost as the estimated average loss that will be incurred during a particular length of time plus the costs to administer an insurance program. This definition precludes from insur-

**EXHIBIT 22-5 Allowable Interest Rates for Imputed Interest**

| Year | 1/1 to 6/30 | 7/1 to 12/31 |
|---|---|---|
| 1972 | 6.75 | 6.875 |
| 1973 | 7.125 | 7.75 |
| 1974 | 7.875 | 9.125 |
| 1975 | 8.875 | 8.875 |
| 1976 | 8.75 | 8.5 |
| 1977 | 7.75 | 7.875 |
| 1978 | 8.25 | 9.0 |
| 1979 | 9.875 | 10.25 |
| 1980 | 12.25 | 10.5 |
| 1981 | 14.625 | 14.875 |
| 1982 | 14.75 | 15.5 |
| 1983 | 11.25 | 11.5 |
| 1984 | 12.375 | 14.375 |
| 1985 | 12.125 | 10.375 |

ance cost any payments made to an insurer that will be refunded to the contractor. At the same time, the definition provides the basis for self-insuring firms to estimate the amount of allowable insurance costs. The computation of insurance expense is illustrated in Exhibit 22-6.

**EXHIBIT 22-6 Determining the Cost of Insurance**

**a.** A firm self-insures. The firm has determined that "insurable" losses over the past 10 years have averaged 0.1% of the gross book value of assets. One employee is assigned full-time to oversee the accounting for losses, loss prevention, and so forth at an annual cost of $28,000. The gross book value of assets at the beginning of the year was $36,800,000 and at the end $39,300,000. Actual losses during the year amounted to $4,200. The allowable insurance expense is

| | |
|---|---|
| 0.001($36,800,000 + $39,300,000) ÷ 2 | $38,050 |
| Plus administrative costs | 28,000 |
| Total allowable insurance expense | $66,050 |

**b.** A firm uses an outside insurance company to provide insurance protection. The firm pays premiums of $100,000 per year. After 5 years of continuous coverage, the insurance company will return $35,000 of each of the annual premiums plus interest. The allowable insurance expense is

| | |
|---|---|
| Actual premium paid | $100,000 |
| Less refundable deposit | 35,000 |
| Total allowable insurance expense | $ 65,000 |

*Standard 417* extends Standard 414 to allow firms to impute an interest cost as part of the cost to build capital assets. That is, while a firm is constructing an asset, the firm has money tied up in the asset. One of the costs that the board allows as necessary to get the asset ready for its intended use is an imputed cost for tying up those funds.

The interest cost that may be capitalized during an accounting period is found by multiplying an interest rate provided by the secretary of the Treasury times the average investment in the construction project over the period (or a weighted-average investment if costs were not incurred uniformly during the period). However, imputed interest is allowable only while the asset is under active construction. If the firm suspends construction for a period, interest is not allowable during that period. The allowable interest rates are the same as those given in Exhibit 22-5.

### Standards Dealing with the Allocation of Indirect Costs

The board promulgated four standards with respect to the proper allocation of indirect costs (overhead) to cost objects. As we have seen in this text (Chapters 11 through 13), cost allocation is a difficult problem, one in which techniques need to be adapted to particular circumstances. Hence it is not suprising that in this area the Cost Accounting Standards Board stresses objectives more than solutions, and preferences rather than specific requirements. In each case the board indicates that allocations should attempt to measure cause-ànd-effect relationships. This can best be met, in the board's opinion, by a hierarchy of allocation bases.

The first choice is a basis that reflects the amount of inputs used to provide a service to cost objects.

The second choice is a base that reflects the amount of service provided to each cost object.

The third choice is a measure that reflects the related activity of the cost object receiving services.

The last choice is to use an arbitrary measure of the activity of the cost object receiving services.

*Standard 403* deals with the allocation of **home office expenses** (e.g., corporate headquarters expenses) to the subunits of the firm. The standard requires that these centrally provided costs should be separated to the extent possible into the types of services being provided. That is, we should try to accumulate computer service costs, internal auditing costs, legal costs, and so forth into separate **cost pools.** Then each cost pool should be allocated to the business units of the firm on the basis of the inputs used to provide those services to each unit. Taking this approach, we might allocate computer services to subunits on the basis of the hours of CPU time devoted to each unit, internal audit costs on the number of hours auditors devoted to each unit, and so forth. If the amounts of inputs used to provide a service cannot be measured, then the costs to provide a service should be allocated on the basis of a measure of the service provided to each subunit. Thus a legal department's costs might be allocated on the basis of the number of legal cases handled for each subunit if a measure of the amount of time devoted to each unit is not available. If neither of the foregoing measures is available, the firm can allocate the cost to provide a service to subunits based on a reasonable measure of the activity of the units receiving services. A personnel department's costs might be allocated to subunits based on the number of employees in each subunit, for example.

After the costs to provide identifiable services are allocated as just described, any remaining (residual) home office expenses (such as general administrative expenses) should be allocated to segments on an overall measure of the activity of each segment. However, if the costs are large (the standard supplies a sliding scale), then these costs must be allocated by the following formula:

$$\text{segment's share of residual costs} = \frac{1}{3}\left(\frac{\text{segment's sales}}{\text{total sales}} + \frac{\text{segment's book value of capital assets}}{\text{total book value of capital assets}} + \frac{\text{segment's payroll}}{\text{total payroll}}\right) \times \text{residual costs to be allocated}$$

*Standard 410* is quite similar to 403. It requires that a subunit's general and administrative expenses should be allocated to the activities within the unit (for example, products or contracts) in a manner similar to home office expenses. Once again, the costs of identifiable services (computer services, a personnel office, and so forth) should be allocated on a basis that reflects the cause for the incurrence of costs. The remaining general and administrative expenses (including any home office residual G&A costs allocated to the unit) are to be accumulated in an account and allocated to the unit's activities in proportion to the other total costs incurred for those activities. The choice of whether to use total costs, direct costs, labor costs, or some other subset of costs as the allocation basis is to be made so as to approximate the total effort required for each activity. If, for example, two production departments make a similar product, but one department makes the product out of steel and the other department makes the product out of titanium (a very expensive metal), we should probably exclude materials cost from the allocation base.

A unit's general and administrative costs are to be allocated only to final cost objects (not, for example, to service departments) and are to be allocated last. That is, since we are going to use the cost of each activity as the allocation base, all other costs should be allocated first so that we will have the total of the other costs in the basis. Finally, note that the choice of *cost* as a basis precludes the use of allocating costs in proportion to the sales for each activity.

The CASB originally proposed four standards dealing with the accounting for indirect costs. The four proposals were subsequently reduced to three, and finally issued as a single standard, *Standard 418*.[1] This standard requires the firm to charge actual direct costs to every cost object (unless the firm uses standard costing, as prescribed in Standard 407). Indirect costs may be assigned using predetermined rates for each type of cost pool, with variances that are material allocated back to the cost objects at the end of the period. The standard requires firms to set up separate cost pools (separate overhead accounts) for each group of similar costs—that is, those that can be allocated on the same basis because they result from a similar cause-and-effect relationship.

The board again expresses a preference hierarchy for allocating indirect costs: (1) based on resource consumption to provide services, (2) based on a measure for the services provided, and (3) based on a measure of the benefits received by a cost object. However, if a cost pool reflects basic management activities (versus providing an identifiable service), the pool can be allocated on the basis of a measure of the activities being managed, such as direct labor hours or machine hours.

When cost pools reflect activities that provide service to each other (this is the service department allocation problem of Chapter 12), the firm may use the simultaneous-equations allocation method or the step method for allocating costs between the pools and to final cost objects. Further, the firm can use any other method that provides a final allocation that does not materially differ from these two methods. Originally, the board had expressed a strong preference for the simultaneous-equations method, but contractors apparently complained that they did not have the facilities to implement it. Thus, the step method is included as an acceptable procedure.

*Standard 420* deals with the proper treatment of the costs to prepare bids for competitive contracts, the cost to prepare proposals for work that might lead to contracts, and the costs for a firm's own research and development activities not related to specific contracts. The costs involved in these kinds of activities can be huge. The CASB reported that in 1978 the government reimbursed 90 of the larger defense contractors $1.2 billion for these types of costs.

[1]This, by the way, explains why there is no standard numbered 419. Standard 418 is a combination of proposed standards originally numbered as 417, 418, and 419. When they were collapsed into the single standard numbered 418, the standard proposed as Standard *421* was renumbered and became the current Standard 417. However, Standard 420 had already been issued before the change, so it was not renumbered.

The standard requires that firms accumulate the costs of each separate project. The board does allow firms to accumulate immaterial bid and proposal costs as if they were one project, and immaterial research and development costs can be combined as a different project. The costs of a project include all direct costs for the project and allocated overhead costs with the exception of general and administrative expenses. The board felt that bid, proposal, and research and development (R&D) costs are general and administrative costs and should, in effect, be included with G&A expenses. An exception is made for a business unit that is a free-standing research center. If a segment prepares bids and proposals, and if it provides R&D for other segments of the business, then it is in the business of selling these services. The cost of the services should include all costs to provide the services, including allocated G&A expenses. Thus G&A expenses can be included in this situation as long as the work on these projects is solely for the benefit of segments other than the segment doing the work.

Bid and proposal costs are to be expensed in the period incurred; R&D costs are to be expensed in the period incurred unless applicable laws, regulations, or the contracting agency allows deferral. Once the costs of each project have been accumulated, they are to be allocated to segments and final contracts in the same manner as the firm allocates G&A expenses. That is, any projects that can be charged directly based on a cause-and-effect relationship should be charged directly. On the other hand, the costs of all other projects should be allocated in the manner provided in *Standard 403* for residual G&A expenses (on a basis that measures the activity of each unit in the firm).

## SUMMARY

The cost accounting standards are a matter of law. Firms whose contracts come under the jurisdictional limits defined by the board are compelled to comply with the standards. Fortunately, in most cases, the standards require good cost accounting practices that firms should be implementing in any case. However, some of the record-keeping requirements of the standards are onerous.

## DEMONSTRATION PROBLEM

Transportation Systems, Inc., has a contract, expected to generate revenue of $13 million per year, to provide air transportation to the employees of the Federal

Agency to Fight Waste and Mismanagement in Government (FAFWMG). The firm provides "on-call" charter flights to or from any airport in North America. Many of the continent's major corporations are also clients of Transportation Systems, Inc.

The firm uses job costing. It calculates the direct costs for every flight (labor and fuel are the most important costs). General and administrative costs are applied to jobs in proportion to total direct costs. For the current month, G&A costs totaled $250,000, including a $110,000 monthly premium for liability insurance. The $110,000 represents the "full" premium paid to the insurance company for the month. At the end of the year the insurance company rebates a portion of the premium based on the firm's loss rate. For the past several years, 40% of the premiums have been rebated.

For the current month, the total direct costs of all flights provided to the firm's customers amounted to $2 million. Of this total, $900,000 was charged to flights provided to FAFWMG. Included in the $900,000 was $50,000 in special entertainment costs. On two flights during the month, FAFWMG transported several senators across the country. The $50,000 was spent for fine champagne, gourmet foods, a small orchestra, and a singer. Such lavish entertaining is strictly forbidden by government regulations, but the management of Transportation Systems, Inc., thought it a good idea to make a favorable impression on the senators.

**Required**

**a.** Under what circumstances would Transportation Systems, Inc., be exempt from the cost accounting standards?

**b.** Assuming that this is a negotiated contract that allows a 20% markup over cost for profit, prepare a cost and billing report for the month's services provided to FAFWMG.

**Solution**

**a.** Because the contract is worth more than $10 million, the firm would be subject to the cost accounting standards unless:

1. The firm is an educational institution (unlikely).
2. The firm is a foreign firm or a foreign government (again, unlikely).
3. The firm is charging the government agency on the same basis and at the same rate as it charges any customer of similar size. That is, this is not a negotiated contract, but rather the agency is paying a competitive market rate (this is possible for the situation described).

**b.** Since this is a cost-plus contract, we must first prepare a summary of allowable costs and then add the agreed markup to get the total amount to be billed. From the description given in the problem, it appears that the $50,000 in entertainment costs is not an allowable cost. Hence, according to CASB Standard 405, these costs must be clearly segregated from the direct costs charged to the jobs. It also appears that insurance costs must be adjusted down to the actual expected net premium to comply with Standard 416. The expected refund of 40% of $110,000 = $44,000 reduces the G&A expenses to $206,000. Following the firm's established and acceptable policy of allocating G&A costs in proportion to direct costs, the firm will charge each job with $206,000 ÷ $2,000,000 = $0.103 per dollar of direct costs to cover G&A costs.

With this information available, we can now prepare the cost and billing report for FAFWMG:

| | |
|---|---|
| Total direct costs | $ 900,000 |
| Allocated G&A (0.103 × $900,000) | 92,700 |
| Total costs | $ 992,700 |
| Less: | |
| Unallowable entertainment costs | 50,000 |
| Allocated G&A on unallowed costs | 5,150 |
| Total allowable costs | $ 937,550 |
| Markup 20% | 187,510 |
| Amount due from FAFWMG | $1,125,060 |

Note that, as required by Standard 405, not only are the unallowed costs subtracted from the costs charged to FAFWMG, but also an allowance for the allocated G&A costs must be subtracted as well.

## KEY TERMS AND CONCEPTS

Cost-plus contract
Cost Accounting Standards Board
General Accounting Office
Cost accounting standards
Negotiated contract
Unallowable costs
Imputed interest
Contract renegotiation rate
Home office expenses
Cost pools

## FURTHER READING

Anderson, Henry R. "The G&A Overhead Pool: Accounting Tool or Cop Out?" *Management Accounting* (October 1977), p. 37.

Brackney, William O., and Henry R. Anderson. "Regulation of Cost Accounting: The Answer or the Abyss?" *Management Accounting* (October 1981), p. 24.

Bryant, Keith, Jr., and Carolyn V. Phillips. "Interest on Equity Capital and CASB Standard 414," *Management Accounting* (August 1978), p. 38.

Fuller, K. John. "Impact of CASB Standards," *The CPA Journal* (January 1976), p. 19.

Mansour, Fathi A., and James H. Sellers. "Comparing Cost Accounting Standards with Existing Accounting Standards," *Management Accounting* (April 1978), p. 37.

Reeve, John T. "Could Your Company Pass a Government Contract Inspection?" *Management Accounting* (March 1981), p. 52.

## QUESTIONS AND EXERCISES

**22-1** Why are a contractor's costs of concern to the government?

**22-2** From the point of view of the government, what is the basic purpose of cost accounting standards?

**22-3** What is the similarity between transfer pricing and cost accounting standard objectives?

**22-4** Ignoring the possibility that the cost accounting standards are regulatory nuisances requiring excess paperwork, what benefits might a contractor obtain as a result?

**22-5** Several firms are bidding on a contract to do windows for the government. One firm bids $12 million and, if it gets the bid, this will constitute 60% of the firm's business. Do the cost accounting standards apply?

**22-6** Sutton Research maintains a large fleet of automobiles to be used by the firm's employees. To minimize bookkeeping costs, the firm charges a flat rate of $20 to a contract for each day a car is used by an employee working on a contract. If the use of the car is not easily traceable to a specific contract, no charge is made. At the end of the year, the difference between the total cost to operate the automobile fleet and the total car costs charged to contracts is closed to corporate overhead. Is Sutton's practice consistent with cost accounting standards?

**22-7** Which of the following expenditures for capital assets could be expensed under the provisions of *Standard 404*?

| Item | Cost | Useful Life |
|---|---|---|
| 1 | $5,000 | 2 years |
| 2 | 800 | 10 years |
| 3 | 800 | 1 year |
| 4 | 4,000 | 3 years |
| 5 | 1,200 | 1 year |

**22-8** The Halsey Companies treat warehousing costs as overhead. These costs include depreciation on the warehouse, materials handling costs, security costs, taxes, and so forth. Recently the firm received a military contract. The project requires the firm to keep some radioactive materials on hand for use on the project. The firm constructed a concrete vault in one corner of the warehouse to store these materials. The vault cost $200,000 to construct and will last for at least 20 years. Management has segregated the cost of the vault from other warehousing costs, intends to depreciate the cost of the vault over 2 years (the life of the contract), and intends to charge this depreciation directly to the military contract. Will the cost accounting standards permit management's intended action?

**22-9** The Dennison Corporation determines its overhead application rate by estimating annual overhead costs and annual direct labor hours to be used. Dividing the first of these numbers by the second gives the firm's overhead application rate per direct labor hour. Each quarter, when financial statements are prepared, any over- or underapplied overhead is charged to contracts on the basis of the direct labor hours incurred on each. Is this practice consistent with cost accounting standards?

**22-10** Red Village Security provides two types of services. Its night watchman service provides a relatively limited service. The employees in this area (mostly retired persons working part-time) only patrol a client's facilities and report suspicious activity. These people are not armed and are not expected to take any overt action to prevent a loss. The second service provided by the firm is a guard service. These employees are all full-time employees, are armed while on the job, and are expected to intervene and prevent any losses on the client's premises.

The firm contributes 20% of an employee's wages in excess of $8,000 per year to a fully funded pension plan managed by a large insurance company. Pension costs averaged only 5% of total wages because of the $8,000 floor that must be reached before an employee gets pension benefits.

If the firm gets a negotiated cost-plus contract to provide night watchman service to a government agency, can it charge 105% of labor cost as the total of labor and pension costs? (Assume that the firm is subject to cost accounting standards.)

**22-11** Venus Munitions has numerous contracts to supply various armaments to the military. The firm's operations are scattered throughout the world. The firm self-insures because no insurance company is willing to insure the firm at what management considers a reasonable fee.

The firm's experience is that accidents on the average result in the loss of 1% of the firm's assets each year. However, the losses tend to be very large in some years and very small in other years. To provide available funds for large losses, the firm invests cash in a special fund each year. The annual investment amount is currently 1.5% of the firm's total average assets for the year.

The costs to administer the self-insurance program amount to $125,000 per year. In a year in which total assets average $1 billion, and a building with a book value of $1 million and a replacement cost of $1.4 million was destroyed by an explosion, what is the amount of insurance expense that the cost accounting standards would allow?

**22-12** Determine for the following situations whether the contracting firms will be subject to all of the CASB cost accounting standards, just to Standards 401 and 402, or are exempt from the standards. Firms A through D have not had previous government contracts. (a) Firm A has annual sales of $40 million and receives a negotiated government contract for $600,000. (b) Firm B has total sales of $100 million and receives a negotiated government contract for $2 million. (c) Firm C has total sales of $20 million and receives a negotiated government contract for $350,000. (d) Firm D has total sales of $3 million and receives a contract to supply $600,000 of plain bond paper at the firm's normal catalog price. (e) Firm E has total sales of $8 million. Last year it received its first government contract for $400,000. This year firm E received another contract for $300,000. (f) Firm F has total sales of $15 million. Last year it received a contract for $750,000. This year it received another contract for $200,000. (g) Firm G had total sales of $15 million last year and $20 million this year. Last year it received a contract for $3 million and this year another contract for $275,000. (h) Firm H has annual sales of $500 million and receives a contract for $20 million.

**22-13** Refer to the demonstration problem at the end of the chapter. Assume that $2,000 of the special entertainment costs are allowable costs. Prepare a new cost and billing report.

## PROBLEMS AND CASES

**22-14 Dispute over direct-indirect cost identification.**
TTC, a trucking company, does a substantial amount of government work. During the period in question, TTC recorded direct costs of $3,400,000 on government contracts and $7,500,000 on civilian contracts. In addition, overhead (a homogeneous pool) was $6,783,000. It is allocated to contracts in proportion to direct costs.

However, government auditors are disputing a $900,000 item that TTC identified as a direct cost, allocating $400,000 to government contracts and $500,000 to civilian contracts. These costs were incurred to make TTC's operations more efficient and effective. The government auditors maintain that these costs should be part of the overhead pool rather than direct costs.

**Required**

**a.** Using TTC's approach, what are the total costs to be allocated to government and civilian work, respectively?

**b.** Using the government's approach, what are the total costs to be allocated to each category, respectively?

**c.** Which CASB standard(s), if any, would be likely to resolve the dispute?

**22-15 Misapplication of CASB requirements.**
Midwest Educational Services is a testing service, which provides psychological testing, employment screening tests, advancement tests, and so on, for a wide variety of clients. Each contract received is considered a cost object. MES charges each contract for the time spent by one of its educational psychologists in developing the tests (the only item considered to be direct labor) and the actual cost for printing the number of tests required. All other costs incurred by the firm—secretarial, management, costs of grading and administering the tests, and so forth—are billed through an overhead rate based on direct labor cost.

Last year MES incurred overhead costs of $3 million, of which $2 million was primarily related to the administration and grading of tests. For the current year the firm estimated that it would charge $1.5 million of costs as direct labor. Accordingly, the overhead rate for the current year was set at $2 per direct labor dollar.

In June the firm undertook a large testing program for the government. The firm had to hire a secretary to handle correspondence and other matters directly related to this contract. The secretary was released when the contract was completed. MES billed the government as follows:

| | |
|---|---|
| Professional time (educational psychologist) | $ 25,000 |
| Secretarial support | 1,500 |
| Printing | 10,000 |
| Overhead ($25,000 direct labor @ $2) | 50,000 |
| Total cost | $ 86,500 |
| Profit (20% of cost) | 17,300 |
| Total due | $103,800 |

**Required**
Assuming that MES is subject to CASB regulations, what standards have been violated?

**22-16 Violation of CASB standards and recalculation of costs.**
Trenco, Inc., allocates plant utility costs on the basis of the direct labor hours incurred by each cost object. In 19X0 the firm's total utility costs were $200,000 and 500,000 direct labor hours were used. In 19X1 the firm's total utility costs were $210,000 and the firm used 475,000 direct labor hours.

From November 1, 19X0, through March 31, 19X1, the firm worked on a large government contract. Management determined that the total utility costs incurred for that 5-month period were $110,000. Total direct labor hours used during this period were 250,000, of which 100,000 were used on the government contract. Accordingly, the firm allocated $44,000 of utility costs to the contract.

**Required**
**a.** Explain how Trenco allocated its utility costs to the government contract. What cost accounting standard was violated?
**b.** Assuming that 40,000 of the direct labor hours incurred for the government contract were used in 19X0, with the remaining 60,000 hours used in 19X1, determine the proper allocation of utility costs to the government contract.

**22-17 CASB standards and nonallowable costs.**
Anpax Industries worked on two government contracts subject to cost accounting standards plus a number of nongovernment contracts. The firm uses two overhead cost pools for assigning indirect costs to contracts. The first pool accumulates the cost of using machinery and facilities. Its costs are allocated to contracts based on the number of machine hours used for each contract. The second cost pool accumulates all indirect labor and material costs plus factory administration costs. These costs are allocated to contracts based on the direct labor hours incurred for each contract.

Total costs accumulated for facilities usage this year amounted to $3.6 million. This amount included $800,000 to rearrange factory equipment. Total costs for the indirect and administrative cost pool amounted to $5.4 million.

The machine hours and direct labor hours used for each contract were as follows:

| | Government Contract 1 | Government Contract 2 | All Other Contracts |
|---|---|---|---|
| Machine hours | 40,000 | 70,000 | 350,000 |
| Direct labor hours | 25,000 | 60,000 | 200,000 |

The government contracting officer overseeing these contracts has determined that 5,000 of the direct labor hours incurred for rework on contract 2 are unallowable costs. Direct labor costs average $16 per hour. The officer also has ruled that the machinery rearrangement costs are unallowable.

**Required**

Determine the total labor and overhead costs to be charged to each of the government contracts. (*Note:* Unallowable costs are supposed to be charged to the contracts; these are then subtracted from the total cost of each contract.)

**22-18 Violation of CASB standards and recalculation of contract costs.**

Specialty Casting molds various products to order. The firm has two departments: engineering, consisting of a group of graduate engineers earning, on the average, $12 per hour; and production, which uses unskilled labor earning, on the average, $4 per hour. The engineering department designs the needed molds, and the production department actually manufactures the product.

The firm purchased a molding machine 3 years ago for $1 million. The machine was estimated to be useful for 2 million castings. Therefore, the firm chose to depreciate the machine at the rate of $0.50 per casting. At the beginning of the current year the machine had a book value of $200,000.

The firm uses only one raw material, steel, in its casting production. The firm uses a standard cost system. In the current year the firm's standard cost for steel was $0.08 per pound. The firm also uses a standard cost of $5.33 per hour for all labor.

The firm's operations for the year have been summarized by type of contract as follows:

| | Government Contracts | | All Other Contracts | | Total |
|---|---|---|---|---|---|
| Direct labor: Engineering | 2,000 hr | $ 10,666.67 | 18,000 hr | $ 96,000.00 | $106,666.67 |
| Direct labor: Production | 50,000 hr | 266,666.66 | 50,000 hr | 266,666.67 | 533,333.33 |
| Direct labor variance | | — | | — | — |
| Direct materials | 600,000 lb | 48,000.00 | 400,000 lb | 32,000.00 | 80,000.00 |
| Material price variance ($0.02 per lb F) | | — | | — | (20,000.00) |
| Depreciation | 240,000 units | 120,000.00 | 160,000 units | 80,000.00 | 200,000.00 |
| Gain on sale of machine | | — | | — | (50,000.00) |
| Total costs | | $445,333.33 | | $474,666.67 | $850,000.00 |

**Required**

**a.** Assuming that Specialty Casting is subject to CASB regulations, what standards have been violated?

**b.** Compute contract costs consistent with CASB regulations.

**22-19 CASB requirements and segment income.**

DarTang Industries has its corporate headquarters in Vail, Colorado. The firm has four plants: one in Cleveland (C), one in Newark (N), another in Gary (G), and the fourth in Baltimore (B). The Baltimore plant does a great deal of work for the government, enough to subject the firm to CASB regulations. Corporate headquarters houses all the major corporate executives and provides computer services, internal auditing services, and payroll services. The costs for maintaining the corporate offices by function this year were

| | |
|---|---|
| General and administrative costs | $ 4,000,000 |
| Computer services | 3,500,000 |
| Internal auditing | 1,500,000 |
| Payroll services | 2,000,000 |
| Total corporate headquarter costs | $11,000,000 |

Miscellaneous data related to the operating plants are as follows (000s have been omitted for all dollar figures):

| | Plant | | | | |
|---|---|---|---|---|---|
| | C | N | G | B | Total |
| Sales | $20,000 | $10,000 | $35,000 | $25,000 | $90,000 |
| Income before HQ costs | $ 6,000 | $ 2,000 | $ 5,000 | $ 7,000 | $20,000 |
| HQ costs | ? | ? | ? | ? | $11,000 |
| Net income | ? | ? | ? | ? | $ 9,000 |
| Total labor costs | $ 3,000 | $ 1,000 | $ 2,000 | $ 4,000 | $10,000 |
| Labor turnover | 2% | 5% | 3% | 1% | 2.2% |
| Number of employees | 250 | 75 | 200 | 300 | 825 |
| Computer time used (hours) | 1,500 | 250 | 750 | 3,500 | 6,000 |
| Pages of computer reports | 4,500 | 3,350 | 3,750 | 6,500 | 18,100 |
| Number of auditor hours worked | 20,000 | 10,000 | 30,000 | 40,000 | 100,000 |
| Dollar value of audit adjustments | $250 | $25 | $300 | $100 | $675 |
| Book value of fixed assets and inventory | $10,000 | $ 5,000 | $20,000 | $10,000 | $45,000 |

**Required**

Determine each plant's net income assuming that all costs are "large" in relation to appropriate standards. Reference the appropriate CASB standard.

**22-20 Applicability of CASB Standard 410** (CMA adapted).

The Anderson Company, a moderate-size manufacturing firm, was awarded a negotiated defense contract of $4 million on May 1, 19X8. The company has never been subject to CASB cost accounting standards because it had no defense contracts prior to the $4 million award. Management wishes to continue with the company's present cost accounting practices but is not sure that these practices are in compliance with the CASB standards. The accounting department has been asked to review its cost accounting practices for compliance with these standards.

The Huron Division, which will perform the contract, is one of four segments of the Anderson Company. The review disclosed that the Huron Division includes selling costs as part of its general and administrative expenses. In negotiating the contract the division had used a cost of sales base for allocating general and administrative expenses.

**Required**

**a.** The applicable CASB standard to which Anderson Company must comply in this situation is Standard 410, "Allocation of Business Unit General and Administrative Expenses to Final Cost Objectives." Are selling expenses considered G&A expenses under the provisions of this standard? Explain your answer.

**b.** Did the Huron Division of Anderson Company comply with the provisions of Standard 410 when it used a cost of sales base for allocating G&A expenses? Explain why or why not.

**22-21 Identifying and applying appropriate cost accounting standards.**
Geotech constructed a large piece of special testing equipment for itself. It began work on the equipment on July 1, 19X1, and completed the work on March 31, 19X2. The out-of-pocket cost of construction-in-process for this equipment was $1,200,000 as of December 31, 19X1. Costs were incurred relatively uniformly over this period of time. At completion, the total out-of-pocket costs incurred for the construction of the equipment amounted to $2,300,000. This equipment was used on a nongovernment contract for the remainder of 19X2. A full year's straight-line depreciation (based on a 10-year life and no salvage value) was taken on the equipment. On January 1, 19X3, the equipment was transferred for use exclusively on a government contract. The contract was completed on July 1, 19X3.

The secretary of the Treasury allowed the following annual interest rates for imputed interest for the periods indicated:

| From | To | Rate |
|---|---|---|
| 7/1/X1 | 12/31/X1 | 10.5% |
| 1/1/X2 | 6/30/X2 | 9.8 |
| 7/1/X2 | 12/31/X2 | 8.8 |
| 1/1/X3 | 6/30/X3 | 9.5 |
| 7/1/X3 | 12/31/X3 | 10.2 |

**Required**

**a.** Calculate the total capitalized cost of the equipment allowable by cost accounting standards as of 3/31/X2.

**b.** Determine the amount of costs chargeable to the government contract in 19X3.

**22-22 CASB standards: Capitalization** (CMA adapted).
The Howard Machine Company manufactures small and large milling machines. Selling prices of these machines range from $35,000 to $200,000. During the 5-month period from August 1, 19X4, through December 31, 19X4, the company manufactured a milling machine for its own use. The machine was built as part of the regular production activities. The project required a large amount of time from planning and supervisory personnel, as well as that of some of the company's officers, because it was a more sophisticated type of machine than their regular production models.

Throughout the 5-month period all costs directly associated with the construction of the machine were charged to a special account, the Asset Construction account. An analysis of the charges to this account as of December 31, 19X4, is as follows:

**ASSET CONSTRUCTION ACCOUNT**

| Item Description | | Costs |
|---|---|---|
| Raw materials costs | | |
| Iron castings | | |
| Main housing (3 sections) | $37,480 | |
| Movable heads (2 heads @ $3,900) | 7,800 | |
| Machine bed | 4,760 | |
| Table (2 sections @ $5,500) | 11,000 | $ 61,040 |
| Other raw materials | | |
| Electronic components and wiring | $28,000 | |
| Worm screws and housing | 8,600 | |
| Cutter housings | 2,700 | |
| Conveyer system | 8,400 | |
| Other parts | 2,500 | 50,200 |
| Direct labor costs | | |
| Layout (90 hr @ $5) | $ 450 | |
| Electricians (380 hr @ $9) | 3,420 | |
| Machining (1,100 hr @ $8) | 8,800 | |
| Heat treatment (100 hr @ $7.50) | 750 | |
| Assembly (450 hr @ $7) | 3,150 | |
| Testing (180 hr @ $8) | 1,400 | 18,010 |
| Other direct charges | | |
| Repairs and maintenance during testing period | $ 1,340 | |
| Interest expense from 8/1/X4 to 12/31/X4 on funds borrowed for construction purposes | 4,260 | |
| Additional labor to assist during machine testing period (180 hours @ $5) | 900 | 6,500 |
| Balance: December 31, 19X4 | | $135,750 |

Factory overhead is allocated to normal production as a percentage of direct labor dollars as follows:

| | Factory Overhead Rates (applied as a percentage of direct labor dollars) | | |
|---|---|---|---|
| **Departments** | **Variable** | **Fixed** | **Total** |
| Layout and electricians | 50% | 20% | 70% |
| Machining,[a] heat treatment, and assembly | 50 | 50 | 100 |

[a]All testing is conducted by employees in the machining department.

A flat rate of 40% of direct labor dollars is used to allocate general and administrative overhead.

During the machine testing period a cutter head malfunctioned and did extensive damage to the machine table and one cutter housing. This damage was not anticipated and was the result of an error in the assembly operation. Although no additional raw materials were needed to make the machine operational after the accident, the following labor for rework was required:

| | Direct Labor Hours |
|---|---|
| Electricians | 80 |
| Machining | 200 |
| Assembly | 100 |
| Testing (conducted by machining department) | 20 |

All of these labor charges have been included in the Asset Construction account. In addition, the repairs and maintenance charges of $1,340 included in the account were incurred as a result of the malfunction.

**Required**

**a.** What criteria will be used to determine whether the Howard Machine Company must comply with the cost accounting standards issued by the CASB?

**b.** Assume that Howard Machine Company must comply with the standards issued by the CASB and, as a result, must follow the capitalization requirements promulgated by the CASB (as specified in Standards 404 and 417). What amount would be capitalized under these requirements?

**22-23 Application of CASB standards to several contracts.**
Eastern Seaboard Research, Inc., constructs extremely detailed models of experimental aircraft. These models are used for a variety of wind tunnel and crash tests. Eastern is a wholly-owned subsidiary of U.S. Research Companies, Inc. During 1983 the firm incurred the following general and administrative costs:

| | |
|---|---|
| Administrative salaries | $ 580,000 |
| General accounting | 215,000 |
| Computer center | 650,000 |
| Administrative office occupancy costs | 425,000 |
| Eastern's share of residual G&A costs from U.S. Research | 180,000 |
| Total Eastern G&A costs | $2,050,000 |

During the year the firm worked on contracts for five organizations: Mitsubishi (M), Boeing (B), Rockwell International (RI), McDonnell-Douglas (MD), and NASA. The Mitsubishi and Boeing contracts were for their commercial aircraft; the remaining contracts are related to government projects and are subject to the CASB standards.

Eastern prepared the income statements below for internal use. The cost figures are intended to be used for the determination of the final sales prices for the government-related contracts.

**EASTERN RESEARCH, INC.**
**Income by Contract**

| | M | B | RI | MD | NASA | Total |
|---|---|---|---|---|---|---|
| Anticipated sales value | $600,000 | $1,100,000 | $1,600,000 | $800,000 | $900,000 | $5,000,000 |
| Direct materials costs | 60,000 | 85,000 | 115,000 | 55,000 | 70,000 | 385,000 |
| Direct labor costs | 175,000 | 210,000 | 280,000 | 165,000 | 200,000 | 1,030,000 |
| Factory overhead | 90,000 | 125,000 | 150,000 | 75,000 | 110,000 | 550,000 |
| G&A expenses | 246,000 | 451,000 | 656,000 | 328,000 | 369,000 | 2,050,000 |
| Total costs | $571,000 | $ 871,000 | $1,201,000 | $623,000 | $749,000 | $4,015,000 |
| Net income | $ 29,000 | $ 229,000 | $ 399,000 | $177,000 | $151,000 | $ 985,000 |

**Required**

Assume you are a government auditor. Refigure the total cost of each contract consistent with the cost accounting standards. In your investigation you have noted that the firm's computer was used 30% of the time for general accounting purposes and the remainder of the time for engineering work for each of the contracts. A log of computer usage shows that 300 hours were used on the Mitsubishi contract, 200 hours for the McDonnell-Douglas contract, and 900 hours for the NASA contract. Eastern allocates its general and administrative costs on the basis of the anticipated revenue from each contract.

# APPENDIX

# COMPUTER PROGRAMS

Computer programs that will solve some of the more difficult, and realistic, problems in the text are available on disks compatible with the IBM PC or the Apple II family of computers. Copies of the disks are provided free to instructors and may be duplicated by students using this text.

The programs that are on the disk, a brief description of the program, and the chapter number where the program could first be used are provided below.

| Program Name | Description/Chapter Reference |
|---|---|
| CGMAS | Prepares a statement of cost of goods manufactured and sold and allows "what if" type changes. This very simple program is useful for introducing the use of computers to someone with no prior computer experience. *Chapter 2* |
| REGR | Linear regression with goodness-of-fit measures. *Appendix 3A* |
| MULTREG | Multiple regression allowing up to 50 variables. *Appendix 3A* |
| LEARN | Determines the requirements to complete a specific unit, or set of units, for a product subject to a learning effect. *Appendix 3B* |

| Program Name | Description/Chapter Reference |
|---|---|
| LRNFIT | Fits a curve to data where the requirement to complete the first unit is unknown, the data to be supplied are the total requirements needed for several production lots. Some of the requirements may be subject to a learning effect, and some requirements may be fixed per period. *Appendix 3B* |
| DCVPSIM | Simulation of net income using cost-volume-profit analysis, discrete probability distributions, and dependency between selling prices and sales volume. *Appendix 4A* |
| CCVPSIM | Simulation of net income using cost-volume-profit analysis, and any combination of three continuous probability distributions for the variables. *Appendix 4A* |
| LINPRO | Solves linear-programming problems and provides a complete sensitivity analysis. *Appendix 5A* |
| NPV | Determines the net present value and the present value index for an investment. *Chapter 8* |
| PYMTSCH | Prepares a loan amortization schedule. *Chapter 8* |
| IRR | Determines the internal rate of return for a set of uneven cash flows. *Chapter 8* |
| PVACRS | Determines the present value of the tax shield for an asset subject to ACRS. *Chapter 9* |
| OPSTPAL | Determines the order in which service department costs should be allocated when using the step method if one wishes to minimize or maximize the costs to be assigned to a specific end user. *Chapter 12* |
| MATALLOC | Provides the simultaneous allocation of service department costs using either the gross or net method. *Appendix 12A* |
| PAY | Prepares departmental summaries, employee reports, cost distributions, and journal entries for payroll. *Appendix 14A* |
| PROCESS | Solves process costing problems and allows for rework, spoilage, and salvage values. *Chapter 15 (Chapter 16 for rework and spoilage)* |

# GLOSSARY

**ABC inventory system** An approch to inventory control that categorizes inventory items into three groups based on their dollar volume significance. Inventory levels of large dollar volume items (the A items) are closely controlled while the immaterial items (the C items) are usually purchased in standard lot sizes.

**Abnormal rework** The cost of rework above or below the amount considered normal. Although it should be considered a loss or gain, it is usually treated as a period expense.

**Abnormal spoilage** The cost of spoiled production above or below that amount considered normal. It should be treated as a loss or gain, but it is frequently treated as a period expense.

**Absorption costing** An accounting system that treats fixed manufacturing costs as part of the cost to produce finished goods.

**Absorption rate** Another term for fixed overhead application rate.

**Accelerated cost recovery system** A mandated "depreciation" method for tax purposes for all depreciable assets acquired in 1981 or thereafter.

**Accounting rate of return** Another term for the average rate of return.

**ACRS** Abbreviation for accelerated cost recovery system.

**Activity variance** An infrequently used term for the sales quantity variance.

**Actual cost system** An accounting system that determines the actual cost to provide goods or services. The determination of unit costs must await the end of an accounting period when actual costs and production are known.

**Administrative costs** The costs associated with managing an entity as opposed to the provision of goods and services.

**Agency theory** A theory concerned with optimal contracting between principals and agents, including the selection of reward criteria and reporting systems.

**Allocation** The process of assigning a single cost to more than one cost object.

**Allocation basis** The unit of measure used to assign joint or common costs to cost objects.

**Alternative cost allocation** An allocation scheme that allocates the savings arising from making a joint purchase to the affected cost objects in proportion to the cost object's next best alternative means for acquiring the product or service.

**Amortization schedule** A table showing the periodic principal balance and interest payments over the life of a loan.

**Annuity** A stream of equal payments occurring at regular intervals.

**Application rate** Another term for overhead application rate.

**Applied overhead** The amount of overhead assigned to production during a period.

**Attainable standards** Another term for normal efficiency standards.

**Autocorrelation** Another term for serial correlation.

**Average rate of return** Average annual net income from an investment divided by the average investment.

**Back order** A memo sales order prepared by a vendor for products that customers have ordered but the vendor cannot immediately deliver.

**Bailout factor** The number of periods required until the cash flow from an investment plus its ending salvage value add up to the total cost of the investment.

**Bill of materials** A complete listing of every assembly, subassembly, and part required to manufacture a product.

**Binding constraint** In linear programming, a constraint that actually limits the solution. Only binding constraints have positive shadow prices for the associated slack variables.

**Blend variance** Another term for the production mix variance.

**BOM** Abbreviation for bill of materials.

**Breakeven point** The quantity of units that must be sold for a firm to earn a net income of zero.

**Budget** A formal plan of the objectives, costs, and revenues that a responsibility center is expected to achieve in a subsequent period.

**Budget variance** The difference between the costs allowed in a flexible budget and the actual costs incurred.

**Budgetary slack** The difference between the amount of resources actually needed to accomplish an objective efficiently and the amount of resources included in the budget to meet the objective.

**Burden rate** Another term for the overhead rate.

**By-products** One or more of the products that are acquired in a joint process and are considered immaterial in relation to an entity's main products.

**Capacity variance** Another term for the volume variance.

**Capital budgeting** Planning for the acquisition of long-lived assets.

**Carrying cost** The cost, including the cost of capital, to hold an asset for a period of time.

**CASB** Abbreviation for the Cost Accounting Standards Board.

**Certified management accountant** One who has passed the CMA exam and met the other requirements to hold a CMA certificate.

**Certified public accountant** See CPA.

**Clearing account** A temporary account to which one department makes all debits and another department makes all credits. A nonzero balance in a clearing account quickly signals the existence of an error or the need for an adjusting journal entry.

**Clock card** An individual record by employee of the hours worked.

**CMA** A designation indicating that a person has earned a certificate in management accounting, from the Institute of Management Accounting, which requires the demonstration of professional competence and educational attainment in the field of management accounting.

**Coefficient of determination** $R^2$, the proportion of the variance in a set of data explained by a fitted equation.

**Committed fixed costs** Those fixed costs necessary to maintain a firm's capacity to operate.

**Common costs** Costs to acquire two or more resources only indirectly related to a firm's final product or service. Hence common costs are usually fixed costs relative to output.

**Confidence interval** A range of values calculated statistically that will have a specified probability of including the true value of an estimated parameter.

**Constraint** In linear programming, an equation representing a limitation that places bounds on the space of feasible solutions.

**Contract renegotiation rate** The formal name for the interest rate determined by the secretary of the Treasury for use in imputing interest under CASB Standards 414 and 417.

**Contribution margin** In unit terms, the selling price per unit less the variable cost per unit. In total, a firm's total sales less total variable costs.

**Contribution margin percent** Contribution margin divided by sales.

**Contribution margin ratio** Another term for contribution margin percent.
**Contribution margin variance** Another term for the sales quantity variance.
**Control chart** A graphical presentation of performance, with preestablished limits that trigger an investigation of performance.
**Control limits** The boundaries on a control chart that indicate the size of variances to be investigated.
**Controllable cost** Defined in relation to a specific responsibility center. Those costs that can be influenced by the manager of the responsibility center.
**Controllable variance** A variance that signals the need for corrective action.
**Controller (also Comptroller)** An organization's chief accountant.
**Conversion costs** The sum of direct labor and overhead costs.
**Cost** The value of assets given up, or to be given up, to acquire other assets.
**Cost accounting** The system of techniques and estimation procedures used to determine the cost of products or services provided by an entity. It is a subset of the management accounting system.
**Cost Accounting Standards Board** A government agency, in existence from January 1971 to October 1980, which promulgated cost accounting standards that must be followed by most companies involved in large negotiated contracts with the government.
**Cost allocation** See allocation.
**Cost apportionment** Another term for cost allocation.
**Cost behavior income statement** An income statement that categorizes expenses by whether they are fixed or variable in relation to sales. Also called a direct costing income statement.
**Cost-benefit analysis** The process of comparing the dollar value of the benefits achieved by an action to the dollar value of the costs necessary to accomplish the action in order to determine whether the action should be undertaken.
**Cost center** A responsibility center for which the person in charge has authority only to affect the level of costs incurred to reach the center's objectives.
**Cost function** An equation that describes the level of costs to be incurred as a function of activity level.
**Cost object** Any function, process, organizational unit, or item for which a measurement of cost is desired.
**Cost of capacity** The cost, usually an opportunity cost, for devoting the use of capacity to a particular activity.
**Cost of capital** The cost to obtain funds for investment.
**Cost of a prediction error** The opportunity cost incurred for having selected an inappropriate course of action based upon a prediction that proves to be incorrect.
**Cost-plus contract** A contract that promises to reimburse the contractor for all reasonable costs plus an agreed-upon percentage for profit.
**Cost pool** A group of indirect costs that are allocated to cost objects using the same allocation basis.
**Cost-volume-profit equation** An equation that projects net income in terms of the behavior of a firm's costs relative to sales volume.
**Cost-volume-profit graph** A graph depicting total sales and total costs as a function of unit sales.
**CPA** A certified public accountant, one who has passed the CPA examination and has met state requirements to receive the CPA certificate.
**Critical path** The sequence of activities through a network that determines the minimum time necessary to complete the entire project.
**Cross allocation method** Another term for the simultaneous-equations allocation method.
**CVP** Abbreviation for cost-volume-profit.

**DCF** Abbreviation for discounted cash flow.
**Decentralization** A management approach in which decision-making authority is delegated to the lowest possible responsibility center.
**Decision table** A summary of the interaction of the possible actions that can be undertaken, the true states of nature, the payoffs for each combination, and the probabilities attached to each state of nature.
**Deferred learning costs** The difference between the budgeted cost to produce a particular unit

of product subject to a learning effect and the average budgeted cost for all units in the production program.

**Denominator level** The level of activity called for in the master budget that becomes the basis for the calculation of the fixed overhead application rate.

**Denominator variance** Another term for volume variance.

**Dependent variable** The variable whose behavior is to be explained by an equation involving one or more independent variables. The variable represented by $y$ in the equation $y = a + bx$.

**Depreciation tax shield** The amount of cash inflows from an investment not subject to income tax because of the deductibility of depreciation for tax purposes.

**Differential revenues and costs** Those revenues and costs that change between alternative courses of action being considered.

**Direct allocation method for service department costs** A procedure that ignores the service that service departments provide to other service departments. Service department costs are assigned directly to production or administrative departments.

**Direct cost** A cost that is easily traced to a cost object.

**Direct costing** An accounting system that treats direct materials, direct labor, and variable overhead costs as costs necessary to produce finished goods, but treats fixed manufacturing costs as a period cost.

**Direct labor** The cost of labor services easily traced to a cost object.

**Direct materials** The cost of materials easily traced to a cost object.

**Discretionary costs** Costs usually fixed, for which the level of spending is established by management fiat at the beginning of a period.

**Dual allocation method** Another term for the simultaneous-equations allocation method.

**Dual price** Another term for shadow price.

**Dummy activity** In a network, an activity that indicates a necessary dependency between other activities, but does not itself represent any real action.

**Economic order quantity** The order size for an inventoriable item that minimizes the sum of the cost to place orders and the carrying cost of inventory.

**Effective unit of production** Another term for equivalent unit of production.

**Effectiveness** Achievement of an objective.

**Efficiency** The use of the minimum necessary resources to achieve a level of effectiveness.

**Efficiency variance** Another term for the quantity variance; usually used in the context of overhead costs but sometimes also used in relation to labor costs.

**EOQ** Abbreviation for economic order quantity.

**Equivalent unit of production** The amount of production effort that, if concentrated on a single unit, would result in a completed unit.

**Excess materials requisition slip** A form issued to alert management that a job is using more than the budgeted amount of materials at the time the materials are released to production personnel.

**Expansion path** A presumed ordering of the sequence in which cost objects join a coalition to acquire products or services jointly.

**Expected value** The weighted-average mean of a probabilistic event. The sum of the possible outcomes multiplied by their associated probabilities.

**Expected value of perfect information** The benefit from receiving every possible correct prediction of a variable weighted by the probability that the variable takes on each such value. It is the maximum amount one should be willing to pay for information if one is risk neutral.

**Expenses** The cost of assets given up to generate revenues.

**Factory burden** A synonym for overhead.

**Favorable variance** A variance with a credit balance. It increases reported earnings when closed to the income statement. However, a favorable variance is not necessarily "good." An analysis of the cause of a variance is required before one can label variances as good or bad.

**Feasible solutions** In linear programming, the set of all possible solutions that meet the limitations established by the constraints.

**FIFO** An acronym for first-in, first-out. An inventory cost flow assumption under which the first units of inventory acquired or produced are assumed to be the first units used or sold.

**Finished goods** The inventory of completed goods awaiting sale.

**Finished goods stock cards** A subsidiary ledger indicating the quantities and unit costs of finished goods on hand.

**Fixed costs** Those costs that in the short run and in a firm's relevant range will not change as activity level changes.

**Fixed overhead application rate** The rate determined at the beginning of the accounting period for charging fixed overhead to production during the period.

**Fixed overhead applied account** An account that accumulates all the fixed overhead charges applied to production during a period.

**Fixed overhead control account** The general ledger summary account for recording all fixed overhead costs incurred and accrued during a period.

**Flexible budget** A budget indicating the costs that should have been incurred given the level of effectiveness achieved. The flexible budget is the benchmark used to measure efficiency.

**Full costing** Another term for absorption costing.

**Functional classification income statement** An income statement that categorizes expenses by how resources were used to generate revenues.

**Gantt chart** A chart showing the specific time periods in which the activities that comprise a project are budgeted to be undertaken and completed.

**General Accounting Office** Congress's financial watchdog, which now has responsibility for enforcing the CASB's cost accounting standards.

**Goal congruence** The compatibility of goals between subunits and the overall organization.

**Gross book value** The original cost of assets, with no allowance for accumulated depreciation.

**Half-year convention** When calculating depreciation or cost recovery, the half-year convention treats all acquisitions and retirements of assets as though the transactions had occurred exactly at midyear.

**High-low method** A cost estimation procedure requiring only two data points.

**Home office expense** The cost of maintaining a central administrative unit.

**Homogeneous cost pool** A collection of indirect costs that can reasonably be allocated to cost objects using the same allocation base.

**Ideal standard** A standard based on the assumption of optimal performance with no allowance for anticipated inefficiencies.

**Identity matrix** A matrix conventionally labeled **I,** consisting of ones on the main diagonal and zeros elsewhere. Any matrix multiplied by an identity matrix results in the original matrix.

**Idle capacity** The difference between practical capacity and the capacity actually being used. Idle capacity may be intentionally constructed to provide for future expansion or may have resulted because demand for the firm's products decreased.

**Imputed interest** An estimate of the cost of capital tied up in a project or investment.

**Incremental cost** The additional costs caused by the addition of an activity or the increase in an activity.

**Independent variable** A variable that explains changes in the dependent variable. The causal variable in a cause and effect relationship. The variable represented by $x$ in the equation $y = a + bx$.

**Indifference probability** In the variance investigation decision context, the probability of a variance being due to a controllable or uncontrollable cause that results in management being indifferent between investigating or not investigating the variance.

**Indirect costs** Costs that are not easily traced to a cost object.

**Indirect labor** Labor whose costs are considered overhead.

**Information overload** A condition that results when a person is faced with more information than can be assimilated, and therefore much of the information is lost or ignored.

**Input mix variance** Another term for the production mix variance.

**Input substitution variance** A variance that results because the actual mix of inputs used differed from the budgeted mix of inputs.

**Interest** The cost incurred for the use of capital.

**Internal rate of return** The interest rate earned by a specific investment.

**Inventoriable costs** Costs considered necessary to acquire or manufacture a firm's product or service. These costs include both fixed and variable product costs if absorption costing is used, but only variable costs if an entity uses direct costing.

**Inventory status record** A card or file containing information on the amount of an inventory item on hand, committed to use, and available for use. It also provides lead time information, optimal lot size (if appropriate), preferred supplier, and price information.

**Inverse of a matrix** A matrix that when multiplied by a matrix of interest yields an identity matrix. For example, the inverse of a matrix called **D** would be represented by the notation $\mathbf{D}^{-1}$, and the following relationship would be true: $\mathbf{D} \times \mathbf{D}^{-1} = \mathbf{I}$.

**Investment** An outlay of resources in the present with the intent of generating resource inflows in the future.

**Investment center** An organizational subunit whose management is responsible for revenues, costs, and the level of investment retained in the subunit.

**Investment tax credit** A direct reduction in otherwise payable income taxes that is allowed when investment is made in depreciable property. It is calculated as a percentage of the amount of the investment, with the percentage dependent on the life of the investment.

**Investment turnover** A unit's net sales divided by the investment devoted to the unit.

**IRR** Abbreviation for internal rate of return.

**Job cost sheet** An accounting form used to accumulate the cost of a particular job.

**Job costing** An accounting system that determines the cost of each specific order on which a firm works.

**Joint costs** Costs to acquire two or more resources directly related to the provision of a firm's product or services. Relative to total output, joint costs tend to be variable costs.

**Joint products** Two or more products resulting from a single process.

**Just-in-time system** A production scheduling system devoted to eliminating inventories. The timing of production, delivery of products, and receipt of materials are closely coordinated to assure that products are used or shipped immediately, without storage.

**Lead time** The amount of time that elapses between the placement of an order for inventory and its delivery.

**Learning curve** An exponential equation that in many applications has been found to be an accurate representation of the average amount of time it takes to produce products as workers become more familiar with the production process.

**Least cost activity time** The amount of time required to complete a project if each activity's costs are minimized.

**Least cost project time** The amount of time required to complete a project that minimizes the sum of activity costs and project costs.

**Least-squares analysis** Another term for regression.

**LIFO** An acronym for last-in, first-out. An inventory cost flow assumption under which the most recently acquired or produced units of inventory are assumed to be the first units used or sold.

**Linear normal loss integral** The expected value of a loss function that is linear in relation to a variable whose actual value is represented by a normal distribution.

**Linear programming** A mathematical technique for optimizing a linear objective function subject to linear constraints.

**Linear regression** A mathematical technique that fits a linear equation to a set of data by minimizing the sum of the squared deviations of the data points from the equation.

**Loss** The cost of assets given up for nothing in return.

**Managed costs** Another term for discretionary costs.

**Management accounting** The internal accounting system designed to provide managers with financial operating information to assist in the achievement of the entity's goals.

**Management by exception** A management approach that allows subordinates to manage assigned activities without interference from a superior unless actual performance deviates significantly from planned performance.

**Management by objectives** A management approach in which a superior and subordinate agree on the goals that the subordinate will attempt to achieve in a period. Performance is then measured relative to the preestablished objectives.

**Managerial accounting system** The formal system designed to accumulate and report relevant information that will assist managers to meet an organization's goals.

**Manufacturing costs** Costs considered necessary for a firm's manufacturing activities; includes material, labor, and overhead costs.

**Margin of safety** The difference in terms of unit sales between anticipated unit sales and the unit sales required for breakeven.

**Marginal cost** The change in total cost resulting from a one-unit change in activity level.

**Marginal revenue** The change in total revenues resulting from a one-unit change in units sold.

**Marketing price variance** The difference between the budgeted selling price per unit and the actual selling price per unit multiplied by the actual number of units sold.

**Marketing quantity variance** The difference between the number of units for which sales orders were received and the number of units anticipated in the master budget to be sold multiplied by the budgeted contribution margin per unit.

**Master budget** The budget prepared prior to the beginning of the period outlining the costs and revenues that a firm expects to experience in the ensuing period for its expected level of activity.

**Materials acquisition budget** A projection of the amount and timing of materials required in a period.

**Materials requirements planning system** A computerized inventory control system that monitors inventory status, outstanding purchase orders, and current production in relation to an overall production master plan.

**Methods time measurement** A detailed engineering approach to calculating the standard labor time required to perform an operation.

**Mix variance** See sales mix variance or production mix variance.

**Mixed cost** A cost with both a fixed and a variable component.

**MRP** Abbreviation for materials requirements planning.

**Multiple regression** A mathematical technique for fitting an equation involving several explanatory (independent) variables to a set of data by minimizing the squared deviations of the data from the equation.

**National Association of Accountants** An organization of persons interested in the practice and development of management accounting. The Association's Institute of Management Accounting is responsible for awarding the CMA certificate.

**Natural classification income statement** An income statement that categorizes expenses by the type of resources acquired.

**Negotiated contract** A contract in which the parties bargain such terms as price and product specifications, in contrast to a contract to deliver routine products at prices available to all customers.

**Net book value** The original cost of an asset less accumulated depreciation.

**Net present value** The present value of future benefits from an investment less the present value of the cost of the investment.

**Net realizable value** The eventual selling price of a product or service less any direct costs necessary to make them salable.

**Network** A graphic representation of the temporal relationship of interrelated activities.

**Nonlinear regression** A mathematical technique that fits a curve of a known form to a set of data by minimizing the sum of the squared deviations of the data points from the equation.

**Nonmanufacturing costs** Costs that are not directly traceable to production activities. They generally consist of selling, administrative, and financing costs.

**Normal activity** The average level of activity for a firm over the intermediate time horizon (usually 3 to 5 years).

**Normal cost system** A system that charges actual materials and labor costs to production but applies overhead on the basis of a predetermined overhead rate.

**Normal efficiency standard** A standard that reflects the performance that can be expected to be achieved under usual operating conditions.

**Normal rework** The cost of rework that is considered unavoidable in a production process and is thus considered a product cost.

**Normal spoilage** The amount of spoilage considered unavoidable in a production process and thus included as a product cost.

**NPV** An abbreviation for net present value.

**Objective function** An equation that represents the goal to be optimized in a linear-programming problem.

**Opportunity cost** The benefits forgone by not choosing an alternative course of action.

**Optimal solution** The solution that maximizes or minimizes an objective function subject to constraints.

**Organization chart** A graphic depiction of the lines of responsibility and authority for an organization.

**Output adjustment cost variance** An infrequently used term that explains the difference between variable costs called for in the master budget versus the flexible budget.

**Output adjustment variance** An infrequently used term for the sales quantity variance.

**Overapplied overhead** The amount of overhead costs applied to production in excess of the actual overhead costs incurred.

**Overhead** All product costs except for costs identified as direct materials and direct labor.

**Overhead rate** The amount of overhead assigned to a unit of product or service; usually determined in relation to some common resource input measure such as labor or materials.

**Overtime** Hours worked in excess of 40 hours a week. Typically, overtime hours are paid at the rate of 150% of the regular wage rate. The amount above the regular rate is referred to as the overtime premium.

**Participative budgeting** An approach to preparing budgets in which operating personnel are asked to help in setting budgetary goals and quotas.

**Path** A sequence of activities in a network leading from the beginning of a project to the project's completion.

**Payback period** The number of periods required for the cash inflows from an investment to sum to the total cost of the investment.

**Payback reciprocal** One divided by the payback period; under certain restrictive circumstances, a rough approximation of the internal rate of return.

**Period costs** Costs for assets that are assumed to be used in the period acquired; they are presumed not to have future benefits.

**PERT/Cost** A technique for minimizing the total cost to complete a project consisting of several interrelated activities.

**Practical capacity** The level of capacity reasonably feasible given a firm's physical plant.

**Predetermined overhead rate** An estimated overhead rate established at the beginning of a period for applying overhead to products during the period.

**Present value** The amount of cash received today that is equivalent to receiving a specific amount of cash at a specified future date given a specific interest rate.

**Present value index** The present value of future benefits from an investment divided by the present value of the cost of the investment.

**Present value of an amount** The funds that must be invested at the present time, earning a specified interest rate, to accumulate to a desired amount at a specified time.

**Present value of an annuity** The funds that must be invested in the present, at a specified interest rate, in order to generate a series of equal periodic payments for a specified period of time.

**Present value ratio** Another term for present value index.

**Price variance** The difference between the actual resources used at standard prices and the actual costs incurred. Alternatively, it is the difference between the standard price per unit of resource and the actual price paid per unit of resource multiplied by the actual number of units acquired.

**Prime costs** The sum of direct materials and direct labor costs.

**Principal** The amount of funds borrowed, excluding interest.

**Process costing** An accounting system that determines the average cost for all units of product or service worked on during a particular period of time.

**Processing costs** The sum of direct labor and overhead costs.

**Product costs** Costs necessary for the manufacture of products.

**Production budget** A projection of the amount and timing of products that will need to be produced in a period.

**Production department** An organizational unit that works directly on providing an entity's final goods or services.

**Production mix variance** A variance that results because the actual mix of inputs used in the production process differs from the budgeted mix of inputs.

**Production quantity variance** The difference between the number of units produced and the number of units for which sales orders were received multiplied by the budgeted contribution margin per unit.

**Production yield variance** The difference between the number of units of inputs allowed for production in the flexible budget and the actual number of units of inputs used multiplied by the average cost of inputs called for in the flexible budget.

**Profit center** A responsibility center whose manager has the authority to affect both the costs incurred and the revenues generated by the center.

**Profit graph** A graph relating net income to the volume of sales.

**Profit/volume chart** Another term for profit graph.

**Profit/volume ratio** Another term for contribution margin percent.

**Profitability index** The present value of the cash flows from an investment divided by the present value of the cost of the investment.

**Pro forma financial statement** A budgeted or projected financial statement.

**Quantity variance** The difference between the standard cost allowed in the flexible budget and the inputs actually used, both at standard prices. It is the difference between the resources that should have been used and the resources actually used, both valued at standard cost.

**Rate variance** Another term for price variance; usually used in relation to labor costs.

**Raw materials** The inventory of materials used as inputs to the production process.

**Reciprocal allocation method** Another term for the simultaneous-equations allocation method.

**Recovery property** Depreciable property that qualifies for accelerated cost recovery under the U.S. Tax Code.

**Regression** A mathematical technique that fits an equation to a set of data points by minimizing the sum of the squared deviations of the data points from the equation.

**Relevant costs** All costs that will change between the alternative courses of action being considered.

**Relevant range** The range of activity in which a firm reasonably expects to operate during the next period and the range over which costs are identified as fixed or variable.

**Reorder point** An inventory level that automatically triggers the placement of an order for more goods when stock on hand falls to that level.

**Residual income** A performance measure for an investment center calculated by subtracting a charge for the use of the investment devoted to the center from the center's net income.

**Responsibility accounting** An accounting system that segregates an organization's activities into separately identifiable tasks over which individuals have authority. Performance reports are routinely prepared indicating the degree to which each responsible person has been able to accomplish the task assigned to the individual.

**Responsibility center** An activity, task, or collection of activities controlled by a single individual.

**Return on investment** The income earned by an organizational unit divided by the investment devoted to the unit. Several different definitions of investment devoted to a unit are used in practice.

**Return on sales** A unit's net income divided by net sales.

**Rework** The amount of effort, above and beyond the normal effort to produce a product, that is necessary to repair or adjust defects in units produced.

**RI** Abbreviation for residual income.

**Robinson-Patman Act** A law that prevents a firm from selling its products to competing customers at different prices unless the difference can be justified by different costs.

**ROI** Abbreviation for return on investment.

***R*-square** Another term for coefficient of determination.

**Safety stock** An amount of inventory kept on hand, over and above that thought necessary to cover normal demand, or unusual variations in demand.

**Sales budget** The projected unit and dollar sales for a period.

**Sales mix variance** The difference between the average contribution margin per unit anticipated in the master budget and the average budgeted contribution margin for the units sold as reflected in the flexible budget multiplied by the total number of units sold.

**Sales quantity variance** The difference between total master budget unit sales and flexible budget unit sales multiplied by the average budgeted contribution margin per unit anticipated in the master budget.

**Sales volume variance** Another term for the sales quantity variance.

**Segment** A subunit of an organization, such as a profit center or a sales territory.

**Segment margin** An organizational subunit's total contribution margin earned less any fixed costs directly traceable to the segment.

**Semifixed cost** Another term for step cost.

**Semivariable cost** Another term for mixed cost.

**Sensitivity analysis** An analysis of the effect on a solution to a model of small changes in the model parameters.

**Separable costs** Costs that are capable of being traced on a cause-and-effect basis to a particular cost object.

**Separate processing costs** Costs incurred after the split-off point in a joint process that are traceable to the individual products or services.

**Sequential allocation** Another term for the step allocation method.

**Serial correlation** A functional relationship between ordered data points.

**Service center (or department)** A responsibility center whose objective is to provide internal services to other organizational subunits.

**Set-up time** The time necessary to get a piece of equipment ready to produce a product. It includes the time to install guides or patterns and the time to set tolerances.

**Shadow price** A figure derived from a linear-programming solution that gives the marginal value for acquiring additional resources (the shadow price of a slack variable) or the marginal opportunity cost for including a variable in the solution that was not called for in the optimal solution (the shadow price of a real variable).

**Shapley value allocation** An allocation scheme derived from work done by Lloyd Shapley that allocates costs based on the average incremental cost assigned to a cost object over all possible expansion paths.

**Simplex method** A mathematical procedure for solving linear-programming problems.

**Simulation** A procedure for estimating the distribution of outcomes from a probabilistic process by modeling the process and then recording the outcomes from many trials. For each trial, parameter values are stochastically chosen in a manner consistent with each parameter's probability distribution.

**Simultaneous-equations allocation method** The procedure that allocates service department costs to all users of the service by setting up and solving a set of simultaneous equations.

**Slack time** In a network, the amount of time by which an activity's completion can be delayed without affecting the completion of the project.

**Slack variable** Variables added to the constraints of a linear-programming problem to convert the constraints to equations.

**Spending variance** Another term for the price variance; usually used in relation to overhead costs.

**Split-off point** The point in a joint production process at which the individual products or services become separately identifiable.

**Standard cost** The budgeted cost per unit of product or service for a period.

**Standard cost allowed** The budgeted costs that should have been incurred for the actual number of units of product or service produced in a period.

**Standard cost earned** Another term for standard cost allowed.

**Standard costing** A cost accounting system that keeps inventory records based on the standard costs allowed for production and calculates and reports any variances between the actual costs incurred and the standard costs.

**Standard error of regression parameters** A statistical measure of the amount of variation that is inherent in the estimate of the parameter.

**Standard error of the estimate** A statistical measure of the amount of variation we should expect around the best estimate of a prediction from an equation derived using regression.

**Standard price** The budgeted cost to acquire a unit of resource.

**Standard quantity** The budgeted number of units of resources to be used to produce a unit of product or service.

**Standard quantity allowed** The budgeted number of units of resources that should have been used for the actual number of units of product or service produced in a period.

**Static budget** A budget prepared for one level of activity; frequently used as a synonym for master budget.

**Step cost** A cost that remains constant for a small range of activity and then jumps to a new level, where it stays constant over a small range of activity.

**Step-down method** Another term for the step method of allocation for service department costs.

**Step method of allocation** A service department allocation procedure that allocates a service department's cost only to other service departments whose costs have not yet been allocated.

**Stock-out cost** The actual or opportunity cost incurred by a firm if its inventory level of a particular product falls to zero.

**Suboptimization** A condition that occurs when actions that are in the best interest of a subunit (because of the manner in which performance is measured) are not in the best interest of the overall organization.

**Sunk cost** A cost that has been incurred and cannot be altered by the alternative actions being considered.

**Tag system** An inventory control system in which a tag is attached to a unit to signal that, when the tagged unit is used, an order should be placed for additional units.

**Tax shield** See depreciation tax shield.

**Technical coefficients** In a linear-programming problem, the parameters representing the amount of scarce resources required by a variable.

**Time-adjusted rate of return** Another term for the internal rate of return.

**Transaction costs** The costs incurred to engage in a transaction; including such items as commissions, brokerage fees, sales taxes, and legal expenses.

**Transfer price** The price at which goods and services are exchanged within an organization.

**Transferred-in costs** The production costs that are accumulated for a product in one department and are transferred to another department when the goods are forwarded to that subsequent department.

**Transpose of a matrix** The matrix that results from making the rows of an original matrix into columns.

**Two-bin system** An inventory control system in which units are placed in two separate containers. When the first container is emptied, an order for additional units should be placed.

**Two-step direct allocation method** A service department allocation procedure in which a service department's direct costs are allocated to every user of the service. Any interservice department costs allocated to a service department are then reallocated using the direct method to production and administration departments.

**Unadjusted rate of return** Another term for average rate of return.

**Unallowable cost** A cost item that is not subject to reimbursement in a government contract.

**Uncontrollable variance** A variance resulting from a random cause for which no corrective action can or should be undertaken.

**Underapplied overhead** The amount by which actual overhead costs incurred exceeds the overhead charged to production.

**Unfavorable variance** A variance with a debit balance. It decreases reported income when closed to the income statement. However, an unfavorable variance is not necessarily "bad." An analysis of the cause of a variance is required before one can label a variance good or bad.

**Usage variance** Another term for the quantity variance; generally used in relation to material costs.

**Variable budget** Another term for flexible budget.

**Variable cost** A cost that in the firm's relevant range will vary directly with changes in output. The cost per unit for variable costs will stay constant in the firm's relevant range.

**Variable costing** Another term for direct costing.

**Variable overhead applied account** An account that accumulates all the variable overhead charges that have been applied to production in a period.

**Variable overhead control account** The general ledger summary account for recording all variable overhead costs incurred and accrued during a period.

**Variable overhead rate** A rate, usually based on machine or labor hours, that assigns the cost of variable overhead items to the products or services produced.

**Variable profit** Another term for contribution margin.

**Variances** In the cost accounting context, variances are deviations of actual results from budgeted results. In a statistical context, a variance is a measure of dispersion in a distribution.

**Vector** A matrix consisting of either one row or one column.

**Volume variance** The difference between the master budget fixed overhead and the fixed overhead applied to production.

**Weighted average** In inventory costing a system that calculates the average cost of initial inventory on hand plus any units acquired or produced, weighted by the number of units in each category. The cost of ending inventory and the cost of goods sold are then determined by multiplying the number of units in each category by the weighted-average cost per unit.

**Work-in-process** The inventory of products still in the production process. The account used to accumulate production costs.

**Work sampling** A technique using a large number of random observations for determining the tasks performed, and the time required per task, by personnel. A technique that is particularly useful for setting time standards in service settings.

**Yield variance** See production yield variance.

**Zero-based budgeting** A budgetary approach in which all resources committed to a responsibility center must be justified and listed in terms of priorities and expected results.

**Zero-defect policy** A management attitude that all products produced should be free of defects. Any defects discovered are examined to determine the cause, and the source of the cause is eliminated. In such a system the cost of any rework or spoilage is treated as a loss.

**Zero-stock system** Another term for a just-in-time system.

# INDEX